2006 TAX FACTS AT-A-GLANCE

General Income Tax

Tax Rates

Ordinary Income Top Rate	35%
Regular Capital Gain Top Rate	15%

Standard Deduction

Joint Returns and Surviving Spouse	$10,300
Heads of Households	$7,550
Single Individuals	$5,150
Married Filing Separate	$5,150
Dependent	$850, or $300 plus earned income, if greater
Aged and Blind - Unmarried and not Surviving Spouse	$1,250 each
Aged and Blind - Other	$1,000 each

Overall Limitation on Itemized Deductions

Married Filing Separate	$72,250
Other	$150,500

Personal Exemption ($3,300) Phaseout

Joint Returns and Surviving Spouse	$225,750 - $348,250
Heads of Households	$188,150 - $310,650
Single Individuals	$150,500 - $273,000
Married Filing Separate	$112,875 - $174,125

Kiddie Tax

Amount	$850
Alternative Minimum Tax Exemption	$6,050 plus earned income

Child Tax Credit

Amount	$1,000
Refundable Limit	$11,300

Hope Scholarship Credit

100% Amount	$1,100
50% Amount	$1,100

Hope and Lifetime Learning Credit Phaseout

Joint return	$90,000
Other	$45,000

U.S. Savings Bond Income Exclusion for Qualified Higher Education Expenses Phaseout

Joint return	$94,700 - $124,700
Other	$63,100 - $78,100

Copyright© 2006, The National Underwriter Company

Eligible Long-Term Care

Attained Age in Year	Limitation on Premiums
40 or Less	$280
41 to 50	$530
51 to 60	$1,060
61 to 70	$2,830
More than 70	$3,530
Per Diem Limitation For LTC Benefits	$250

Health/Archer Medical Savings Accounts

Coverage	Minimum Deductible	Maximum Deduction	Out-of-Pocket
Self-only	$1,050/$1800	$2,700/$2,700	$5,250/$3,650
Family	$2,100/$3,650	$5,450/$5,450	$10,500/$6,650

Employee Benefit Limits

Defined Benefit Plans	$175,000
Defined Contribution Plans	$44,000 or 100% of pay
Elective Deferral Limit for 401(k) Plans, SAR-SEPs, and TSAs	$15,000
Catch-up for 401(k) Plans, SAR-SEPs, and TSAs	$5,000
Elective Deferral Limit for SIMPLE IRAs and SIMPLE 401(k) Plans	$10,000
Catch-up for SIMPLE IRAs and SIMPLE 401(k) Plans	$2,500
Elective Deferral Limit for 457 Plans	$15,000
Minimum Compensation Amount for SEPs	$450
Maximum Compensation for VEBAs, SEPs, TSAs, Qualified Plans	$220,000
Highly Compensated Employee Definition Limit	$100,000
ESOP Payout Limits	$175,000, $885,000
Contribution Limit for Traditional & Roth IRAs	$4,000
Catch-up for Traditional & Roth IRAs	$1,000
PBGC maximum monthly guaranteed benefit at age 65	$3,971.59

Estate Planning Amounts

Top Gift and Estate (and GST) Tax Rate	46%
Gift (and GST) Tax Annual Exclusion	$12,000
Annual Exclusion: Non-U.S. Spouse	$120,000
Gift Tax Unified Credit (shelters)	$345,800 ($1,000,000)
Estate Tax Unified Credit (shelters)	$780,800 ($2,000,000)
State Death Tax	Deduction
Estate Tax Deferral: Closely Held Business	$552,000
Special Use Valuation Limitation	$900,000
Qualified Conservation Easement Exclusion	$500,000
GST Exemption	$2,000,000

Social Security Amounts

OASDI - Earnings Base	$94,200
Rate	6.20%
Employer and Employee - Max Tax (each)	$5,840.40
Self-Employed - Max Tax	$11,680.80
HI (Medicare) Rate	1.45%
Cost of Living Benefit Increase	4.1%
Quarter of Coverage Earnings	$970
Earnings Test - Under NRA (normal retirement age) All of 2006	$12,480
Reach NRA During 2006	$33,240

1-800-543-0874
www.NationalUnderwriterStore.com

The National Underwriter Company
A Unit of Highline Media
The Leader in Insurance and Financial Services Information

Order from the complete line of 2006

TAX FACTS

Quantity discount and corporate prices are available. For information, call

800-543-0874

4 WAYS TO ORDER

CALL 800-543-0874

CLICK www.NationalUnderwriterStore.com

MAIL TO: The National Underwriter Co.
Orders Department BB
P.O. Box 14448
Cincinnati, OH 45250-9786

FAX your order form to 800-874-1916
(Please include your return fax number)

SALES TAX

Sales tax is required for residents of the following states:

CA, CT, DC, FL, GA, IL, KS, KY, NJ, NY, OH, PA, WA

SHIPPING AND HANDLING

Order		Total	S&H
$0	to	$39.99	$6.50
$40.00	to	$64.99	$8.50
$65.00	to	$109.99	$11.50
$110.00	to	$154.99	$13.50
$155.00	to	$199.99	$15.50
$200.00	to	$249.99	$17.50

*MAKE CHECKS PAYABLE TO
The National Underwriter Company

**CVV INFORMATION

For Visa/MC, the three-digit CVV# is usually printed on the back of the card.

For AmEx, the four-digit CVV# is usually on the front of the card.

PAYMENT INFORMATION & GUARANTEE

Shipping and handling rates for the continental U.S. only. If your order exceeds total amount listed in chart or for overseas rates, call 800-543-0874. Any discounts do not apply to shipping and handling. Unconditional 30 day guarantee. Product(s) damaged in shipping will be replaced at no cost to you. Claims must be made within 30 days from the invoice date. Prices, information and availability subject to change.

QTY.	TITLES	BOOK	POWER COMBO	ONLINE
	2006 Tax Facts on Insurance & Employee Benefits	☐ $42.95	☐ $59.95	☐ $999.00
	2006 Tax Facts on Investments	☐ $42.95		
	Tax Facts Combo (both titles)		☐ $119.90	
	2006 Field Guide to Estate Planning	☐ $42.95	☐ $59.95	☐ $70.00
	2006 Field Guide to Financial Planning	☐ $42.95	☐ $59.95	☐ $70.00
	2006 ERISA Facts	☐ $42.95		
	2006 Benefits Facts	☐ $56.95		
	2006 Social Security/Medicare Kit	☐ $39.95		
	2006 Social Security Manual	☐ $24.95		
	2006 All About Medicare	☐ $18.50		

✓ Check box to enroll in our Automatic Renewal Program

Name _____ Title _____

Company _____

Street Address _____

City _____ State _____ Zip _____

Business Phone (___) _____ Fax (___) _____

E-mail _____ ☐ May we contact you via e-mail?

Method of Payment | ☐ Charge to my (circle one): MC Visa AmEx ☐ Check enclosed*

Card # _____ CVV#** _____ Exp. Date _____

Signature _____

Your Business Line (please check one)
☐ Life & Health
☐ Property & Casualty
☐ Multi-Lines
☐ Other

Your Business Type (please check one)
☐ Agency/Brokerage
☐ Financial Planner/Advisor/Registered Rep
☐ Home Office
☐ Risk Management
☐ Other

Your Job Function (please check one)
☐ Owner/Principal/GA
☐ Agent/Broker
☐ Financial Advisor
☐ Adjuster/Claims
☐ Other

BB-TFA2006

Did You Know You Could Save 20% On Your Order?

Sign Up Today for The Automatic Renewal Program and SAVE 20%. All of the Tax Facts Annuals titles, except for online formats, are eligible for automatic renewal.

BEST PRICE: Save 20% off the single copy list price every year you are enrolled.

HASSLE FREE: Receive your chosen references every year along with your invoice.

CREDIBILITY: Consistently offer your clients the most authoritative timely information available.

FIRST TO KNOW: Get exclusive access to updates and supplements

The National Underwriter Co.
Orders Department BB
P.O. Box 14448
Cincinnati, OH 45250-0448

Postage Required
Post Office will not deliver without proper postage.

2006 TAX FACTS
On Insurance & Employee Benefits

- Life and Health Insurance
- Annuities
- Employee Plans
- Estate Planning & Trusts
- Business Continuation

Deborah A. Miner, J.D., CLU, ChFC, Editorial Director
April K. Caudill, J.D., CLU, ChFC, Managing Editor
William J. Wagner, J.D., LL.M., CLU, Associate Editor
Joseph F. Stenken, J.D., CLU, ChFC, Assistant Editor
Sonya E. King, J.D., LL.M., Assistant Editor
John H. Fenton, J.D., M.S.B.A., Staff Writer
Connie L. Jump, Supervisor, Editorial Services
Patti O'Leary, Editorial Assistant

The A Unit of Highline Media
National Underwriter Company
The Leader in Insurance and Financial Services Information

P.O. Box 14367 · Cincinnati, Ohio 45250-0367
1-800-543-0874 · www.NationalUnderwriterStore.com

2006 Edition

Tax Facts on Insurance and Employee Benefits (formerly *Tax Facts 1*) is published annually by the Professional Publishing Division of The National Underwriter Company. This edition reflects selected pertinent legislation, regulations, rulings and court decisions as of December 1, 2005. References, at the end of answers, to *ASRS* are to the *Advanced Sales Reference Service*, edited monthly, also published by The National Underwriter Company. For the latest developments throughout the year, check out www.TaxFactsOnline.com.

This publication is designed to provide accurate and authoritative information in regard to the subject matter covered. It is sold with the understanding that the publisher is not engaged in rendering legal, accounting or other professional service. If legal advice or other expert assistance is required, the services of a competent professional person should be sought. —From a Declaration of Principles jointly adopted by a Committee of the American Bar Association and a Committee of Publishers and Associations.

Circular 230 Notice – The content in this publication is not intended or written to be used, and it cannot be used, for the purposes of avoiding U.S. tax penalties.

ISBN 0-87218-678-4
ISSN 0496-9685

Copyright© 1951, 1952, 1954, 1955, 1956, 1957, 1958, 1959, 1960, 1961, 1962, 1963, 1964, 1965, 1966, 1967, 1968, 1969, 1970, 1971, 1972, 1973, 1974, 1975, 1976, 1977, 1978, 1979, 1980, 1981, 1982, 1983, 1984, 1985, 1986, 1987, 1988, 1989, 1990, 1991, 1992, 1993, 1994, 1995, 1996, 1997, 1998, 1999, 2000, 2001, 2002, 2003, 2004, 2005, 2006

The National Underwriter Company
P.O. Box 14367, Cincinnati, Ohio 45250-0367

All rights reserved.
No part of this publication may be reproduced, stored in a retrieval system, or transmitted, in any form or by any means, electronic, mechanical, photocopying, recording, or otherwise, without prior written permission of the publisher.

Printed in U.S.A.

TABLE OF CONTENTS

Page

What's New for 2006 xi
How To Locate New Information xi
How To Keep Up With 2006 Developments xi
How To Use The Guidex xi
About the Citations xi
Planning Point Contributors xiii
Abbreviations xv
EGTRRA 2001 Sunset Provision xvi
Tax Facts Navigators xvii

                                                                                       Q   Q   Q

PART I: FEDERAL INCOME TAX 1-507

Annuities 1-44
   General Rules 1-2
   Amounts Not Received As An Annuity 3-6
      Generally 3-4
      Dividends 5-6
   Amounts Received as an Annuity: Fixed Annuities 7-20
      Basic Rule 7-10
      Life Annuity: Single 11
      Life Annuity: Temporary 12
      Life Annuity: Joint and Survivor 13-17
      Life Annuity: Refund Beneficiary 18
      Fixed Period or Fixed Amount Installments 19
      Annuity Reduced by Partial Withdrawal 20
   Annuity Rules: Variable Annuities 21-25
   Loss 26-27
   Disposition 28-35
      Sale or Purchase of a Contract 28-29
      Policy Exchanges 30
      Gift of an Annuity or Endowment Contract 31-32
      Surrender, Redemption, or Maturity 33-35
   Death 36-37
   Divorce 38
   Charitable Gifts 39
   Withholding 40
   Private Annuity 41-42
   Charitable Gift Annuity 43-44
Business Continuation: Business Life Insurance 45-98
   Premiums 45-60
      General Rules 45-46
      Corporations and Stockholders: Deductibility 47-49
      Corporations and Stockholders: Includable in Income 50-53
      Corporations and Stockholders: Section 162 Bonus Plan 54
      S Corporations 55
      Partnerships and Partners 56-57
      Sole Proprietorships 58-59
      Deduction of Premiums Denied for Reasons Other
        Than Section 264(a)(1) 60

	Q	Q	Q

Annuities and Living Proceeds Received by a Corporation..................................61
Death Proceeds of Business Life Insurance 62-76
   General Rule..62
   Proceeds Taxable Because of Transfer for Value 63-72
   Proceeds Taxable as Dividends or Compensation.........................73
   Proceeds Taxable Because of Lack of Insurable Interest................74
   Proceeds as Restitution of Embezzled Funds 75
   S Corporations 76
Transfer of Policy...77-79
Stock Purchase Agreement...80-88
   Cross Purchase Agreement Between
      Individual Stockholders.......................................80-81
   Stock Redemption...82-88
Accumulated Earnings Tax...89
S Corporations 90-91
Sale or Liquidation of Partnership Interest 92-94
Alternative Minimum Tax..95
Disability Income and Overhead Expenses 96-98
Cafeteria Plans 99-107
   In General 99-106
   Flexible Spending Arrangement... 107
Compensation 108-109
Deferred Compensation 110-131
   Funded Deferred Compensation (Annuities and Trusts) 110-113
   Unfunded Deferred Compensation 114-131
      General Rules 114
      Private Plans 115-122
      Section 457 Plans (Government and
         Tax-Exempt Employers) 123-126
      Plans for State Judges 127
      Excess Benefit Plans 128
      Employee Stock Options............................... 129-131
Educational Benefit Trusts 132
Dependent Care Assistance Programs 133
Employee Death Benefits 134-137
   $5,000 Exclusion 134
   Contractual Death Benefits.......................................135-136
   Voluntary Death Benefits 137
Group Life Insurance 138-153
   Group Term Life Insurance..138-148
      In General 138-145
      Group Carve-Out Plan 146
      Permanent Benefits.. 147-148
   Retired Lives Reserves.. 149
   Group Permanent Insurance 150-151
   Death Benefits... 152
   Group Survivor Income Benefit 153
Health Insurance 154-209
   Personal Health Insurance..154-157
   Employer-Provided Health Insurance........................158-194
      Overview 158
      Employee's Income Taxation 159-164
      Stockholder-Employees, Self-Employed Individuals 165-166

		Q	Q	Q

Employer's Deduction	167
Health Reimbursement Arrangements	168
Withholding	169
Social Security	170
Information Return	171
COBRA Continuation Coverage Requirements	172-185
Portability, Access, and Renewability Rules	186-191
Health Benefits Under A Qualified Plan	192
Disability Income Coverage	193-194
Health and Medical Savings Accounts	195-208
General	195-197
Contributions	198-200
Distributions and Transfers	201-204
Death	205
Social Security	206
Withholding and Reporting	207-208
Archer Medical Savings Accounts	209

Individual Retirement Plans **210-243**

In General	210-216
Eligibility	217-226
Distributions	227-237
Taxation	227-230
Premature Distributions	231-232
Required Minimum Distributions	233-237
Filing Requirements	238
Employer-Sponsored IRAs	239
Simplified Employee Pension (SEP)	240-241
Simple IRA	242-243

Life Insurance **244-310**

Premiums	244-246
Cash Value Increases	247-248
Living Proceeds	249-270
Basic Rules	249-250
Interest-Only Option	251
Dividends	252-258
Policy Loans	259-260
Disposition: Sale or Purchase of a Contract	261-262
Disposition: Policy Exchanges	263
Disposition: Surrender, Redemption, or Maturity	264-266
Accelerated Death Benefit	267
Viatical Settlement	268
Withholding	269
Loss	270
Death Proceeds	271-279
General Rules	271-274
Interest Option	275
Life Income and Installment Options	276
Transferred Policy	277-279
Divorce	280-281
Charitable Gifts	282-285
Single Premium Whole Life Insurance Policy	286
Creditor Insurance	287-294
Premiums	287-291

v

	Q	Q	Q

Bad Debt Deduction 292
Proceeds... 293-294
Government Life Insurance 295
Collection of Delinquent Income Taxes from Life Insurance 296-297
Disability Provisions under Life Policies 298-301
Policies Insuring More Than One Life 302
Value of Unmatured Policy.. 303
Life Insurance Trusts.. 304-310
Long-Term Care Insurance 311-320
   Qualified Long-Term Care Insurance Contract 311-318
      Generally 311-313
      Premiums.. 314-317
      Taxation of Benefits..318
   Non-Qualified Long-Term Care Insurance Contract... 319
   Reporting Requirements 320
Pension And Profit Sharing: Qualification.. 321-361
   Overview 321-322
   Exclusive Benefit Rule... 323
   Minimum Participation and Coverage 324-325
   Nondiscrimination..326-331
   Section 415 Limits 332
   Vesting..333-334
   Automatic Survivor Benefits 335-337
   Required Minimum Distributions...338-347
   Alienation of Benefits..348-349
   Top-Heavy Plan Requirements 350-352
   Miscellaneous Qualification Rules.. 353
   Employees and Employers 354-360
   Retroactive Disqualification 361
Pension And Profit Sharing: Employer Deduction.. 362-367
   Overview 362
   Contributions of Property 363
   Deduction of Employer Contributions..364-367
Pension And Profit Sharing: Plan Types And Features 368-419
   Overview 368
   Insurance Benefits 369-370
   Defined Benefit Plans...371-375
   Defined Contribution Plans 376-380
   Pensions..381-390
      Minimum Funding Standard... 385-390
   Profit Sharing Plans 391-393
   401(k) Plans 394-406
   412(i) Plans 407-408
   Stock Bonus and Employee Stock Ownership Plans 409-416
   S Corporation Plans 417
   Keogh Plans 418-419
Pension And Profit Sharing: Taxation Of Distributions 420-443
   Plan Loans 420-422
   Income Taxation of Participants and Beneficiaries 423-439
      Contributions to a Plan 423
      Cost of Life Insurance Protection Taxable to Employee 424-425
      Overview: Distributions 426
      Preretirement Distributions.. 427-428

Q	Q	Q

    Postretirement Distributions 429
    Lump Sum Distributions 430
    Distribution of Annuity or Life Insurance Contract 431
    Distribution of Employer Securities..432
    Annuity Payments 433-435
    Disability Benefits 436
    Death Benefits... 437-439
  Withholding On Benefits... 440
  Taxation of Trust Funds... 441
  Reversions.. 442
  Prohibited Transactions 443
Rollover **444-456**
Split Dollar Plan.. **457-462**
Tax Sheltered Annuities For Employees Of Section 501(C)(3)
  Organizations And Public Schools **463-493**
  Plan Requirements 466-468
  Contributions 469-477
    Limits 469-474
    Excess Contributions...475
    Post-Retirement Employer Contributions 476
    Roth 403(b) 477
  Changing Issuers 478
  Amounts Received Under the Plan 479-484
    Incidental Life Insurance Protection 481
    Dividends 482
    Loans 483-484
  Distributions.. 485-491
    Premature Distributions 485
    Required Distributions 486-489
    Taxation of Benefits.. 490-491
  Social Security and Withholding Taxes.. 492
  Excise Taxes.. 493
Welfare Benefit Funds.. **494-507**
  General.. 494-503
    Postretirement Medical and Life Insurance Benefits........... 499-500
    Excise Tax on "Disqualified Benefits" 501-503
  Voluntary Employees' Beneficiary Associations (501(c)(9) Trusts)............. 504-507

PART II: FEDERAL ESTATE TAX 600-688

Annuities And Living Proceeds... **600-608**
Life Insurance In Business **609-615**
  Insurance on Key Persons, Partners, Stockholders....................... 609-613
  Partnership Income Continuation... 614
  Split Dollar Insurance Plan 615
Charitable Gifts... **616**
Collection Of Estate Taxes From Beneficiary..**617**
Community (Marital) Property **618-622**
Creditor Insurance **623-624**
Death Proceeds Of Life Insurance **625-637**
  Proceeds Receivable by or for the Benefit of Insured's Estate..................... 627-629
  Proceeds Receivable by Beneficiaries Other than Insured's Estate 630-637
Dividends..**638-639**

| | | | Q | Q | Q |

Divorce 640
Double Indemnity..641
Gifts Within Three Years Of Death 642-643
Government Life Insurance..644
Group Life Insurance..645
Health Insurance 646-647
Individual Retirement Plans.. 648-649
Life Insurance Trusts 650-658
Loans On Life Insurance..659
Marital Deduction 660-670
Multiple-Life Life Insurance 671
Nonqualified Employee Annuity...672
Pension And Profit Sharing Plans (Qualified).. 673-675
Policyholder Other Than Insured 676
Settlement Options--Beneficiary's Estate 677-683
Survivor Income Benefit 684-685
Tax Sheltered Annuities 686
Valuation 687-688

PART III: FEDERAL GIFT TAX 700-744

Annuities... 701-705
Business Life Insurance..706
Charitable Gifts..707
Collection Of Gift Tax 708
Community Property 709-710
Death-Benefit-Only Plans 711
Gift Tax Annual Exclusion 712-717
Gifts Within Three Years Of Death 718
Life Insurance Trusts 719-728
Loans 729
Marital Deduction 730-731
Multiple-Life Life Insurance 732
Premiums 733-734
Proceeds 735
Qualified Plans, Tax Sheltered Annuities And Individual Retirement Plans........... 736-739
Settlement Options--Primary Beneficiary...740
Split Dollar..741
Split-Gift 742
Survivor Income Benefit Plans 743
Valuation 744

PART IV: GENERATION-SKIPPING TRANSFER TAX 750-752

PART IV: FEDERAL TAX—GENERAL 800-956

Federal Income Tax 800-844
   Individuals 800-837
      Filing Requirements 800-801
      Gross Income 802-812
      Adjusted Gross Income 813-816
      Taxable Income--Calculation of Tax 817-818
      Exemptions... 819-820

		Q	Q	Q

    Deductions 821-827
    Rates 828-831
    Credits 832-835
    Social Security Taxes 836-837
Corporations 838-840
Limited Liability Companies 841
Partnerships 842
Trusts And Estates 843-844

Federal Estate Tax 850-871
    Filing and Payment 851
    Calculation of Tax 852
    Gross Estate 853-860
    Exclusion 861
    Valuation 862
    Deductions 863-866
    Credits 867-871

Federal Gift Tax 900-922
    Filing and Payment 901
    Calculation of Tax 902
    Gifts 903-908
        Split-gifts 907
        Disclaimers 908
    Valuation 909-916
        Chapter 14 Special Valuation Rules 912-916
    Exclusions 917-919
    Deductions 920-921
    Unified Credit 922

Generation-Skipping Transfer Tax 950-956

Annuity Tables .... Appendix A
Tax Tables .... Appendix B
One Year Term Rates .... Appendix C
Valuation Tables .... Appendix D
Indexed Employee Benefit Limits .... Appendix E
RMD Tables .... Appendix F
Table I (Group Term Life Insurance Cost) .... Q 142
Table of 2005 Legislation, Regulations and Rulings .... Page 963
Table of Cases .... Page 965
Table of IRC Sections Cited .... Page 981
Guidex .... Page 1007

What's New for 2006?

For 2006, we have added TAX FACTS NAVIGATORS, which were designed to help you identify and locate all the issues related to selected topics. See pages xvii to xxv. The navigators are also cross referenced throughout *Tax Facts*. Also, we are continuing the use of PLANNING POINTS in this edition. Planning points offer practical guidance from leading practitioners or from the *Tax Facts* Editors. We want to thank those practitioners who contributed this year (please see the list of contributors beginning on page xiii). We would also like to encourage other practitioners to submit planning points to be considered for inclusion in future editions of TAX FACTS.

How To Locate New Information

Use the Table of Legislation, Regulations and Rulings and the Table of Cases in the back of the book to find the questions and answers affected by new laws enacted, regulations and rulings issued, and cases decided during the past year.

How To Keep Up With 2006 Developments

The authors and editors of TAX FACTS provide a monthly newsletter (in print and PDF) covering the latest developments (legislation, regulations, rulings, court cases) affecting the subject matter covered in this book. This newsletter, *TaxFacts News*, is cross-referenced to TAX FACTS Q numbers, enabling readers to make marginal notations at appropriate places. (Subscribers to the ADVANCED SALES REFERENCE SERVICE automatically receive *TaxFacts News*.) In addition, *Tax Facts Online* (including both titles – *Tax Facts on Insurance and Employee Benefits* and *Tax Facts on Investments*) is updated continuously, see www.TaxFactsOnline.com.

How To Use The Guidex

The Guidex is a subject matter index adapted to help you locate specific tax information quickly. See, for example, the main entry "second-to-die life insurance." The presence of numbers in all three columns tells you there is information about federal income, estate and gift taxation relating to second-to-die life insurance. The numbers in each case refer to question (Q) numbers, not to page numbers.

About The Citations

Many sources are cited as authority for statements in this book. Knowing something about some of these sources helps one evaluate the significance of a statement. The *Internal Revenue Code* and *valid uncodified tax legislation* are law. *Final Treasury regulations* state the interpretation the IRS will use in enforcing the law and have the effect of law if they are not inconsistent with the statutes. *Temporary regulations* are strong authority. Proposed regulations are generally considered to be the partisan opinions of the IRS and not to bind the IRS or anyone else. Revenue Rulings state the interpretation the IRS will use in applying the law to a particular set of facts. They can be revoked without prior notice but generally revocation is not retroactive. The weight given to *Revenue Rulings* by courts varies. While it is not clear, it seems that *Notices* and *Announcements* bind the IRS to the same extent *Revenue Rulings* do. *Letter Rulings* (including *TAMs*) and *Special Rulings* are only uncertain indications of one line of reasoning at IRS. IRS is not bound to follow them with respect to third parties or future events in a continuing transaction. *Letter Rulings* are not precedent, but courts have considered them in reaching decisions. The IRS believes that *GCMs* cannot be used as precedent. *IRs* and *TIRs* are intended to state an official IRS position. All courts and the IRS follow *Supreme Court decisions*. District courts within a circuit must follow a decision of a court of appeals if the *Tax Court's* decision in a particular case would be appealable to that circuit. Neither the IRS nor any court other than the issuing court is bound to follow a *district court, Tax Court,* or *Court of Federal Claims* decision, although federal courts are strongly influenced by decisions of other federal courts. Tax Court Summary Opinions are issued in matters involving $50,000 or less and have no precedential value, but may indicate the line of reasoning the Tax Court would follow in a particular situation.

As with any generalized treatment, this discussion omits a variety of nuances. Keep in mind that whether and to what extent one may rely on a particular source as "authority" depends in part on the purpose for which the source is to be used. For example, a source may not be authoritative enough to require a favorable determination of tax liability but it may be sufficiently authoritative to avoid application of the penalty for substantial understatement of income.

TAX FACTS ON INVESTMENTS (FORMERLY TAX FACTS 2)

Tax Facts on Investments answers tax questions on investments in stocks, bonds, mutual funds, and tax shelters. The 2006 edition of *Tax Facts on Investments* will be available in February. Forms in the back of this book may be used for ordering or order online at www.NationalUnderwriterStore.com.

Planning Point Contributors

William H. Alley, CLU, ChFC, RHU, LUTCF, MSFS, AEP, CLTC, is Principal and CEO of Alley Financial Group, LLC in Lexington, Kentucky. Bill entered the life insurance business in 1960, having graduated from Columbia Military Academy and attended the University of Kentucky. Bill has developed a successful practice in the areas of retirement and succession planning, estate analysis, financial planning, and business insurance. Bill is a past president of the Lexington and Kentucky Life Underwriters Association, past president of the Lexington Chapter of the Society of Financial Service Professionals, a past trustee of the National Association of Insurance and Financial Advisors and a twenty-five year member of the Million Dollar Round Table. He is also a past National Director for the Society of Financial Service Professionals. Bill is a frequent speaker on insurance and financial planning as well as the author of numerous articles on insurance and financial matters.

Ward B. Anderson, CLU, ChFC, is president of Compensation Planning & Administration Systems, Inc., an employee benefit consulting firm involved in the design, installation and funding of tax qualified retirement plans, selective executive benefit plans and group life, health and disability plans. Ward is currently national President of the Society of Financial Service Professionals. He has been a frequent speaker to legal, accounting and financial planning groups on the topics of estate planning, uses of life insurance, employee benefit planning, taxation of employee benefit plans and planning for retirement plan distributions. Ward attended the University of Kansas and the University of Kansas School of Law.

Lawrence Brody, J.D., LL.M, is a partner in Bryan Cave LLP, a national and international law firm, and a member of the firm's Private Client Group. He is an adjunct professor at Washington University School of Law and a visiting adjunct professor at the University of Miami School of Law. Mr. Brody focuses his practice on estate planning for high net worth individuals and the use of life insurance in estate and non-qualified deferred compensation planning. He is the author of two BNA Tax Management Portfolios and two books for the National Underwriter Company, and is a frequent lecturer at national conferences on estate and insurance planning. Mr. Brody received the designation of Accredited Estate Planner by the National Association of Estate Planners and Councils, and was awarded its Distinguished Accredited Estate Planner designation in 2004.

Fred Burkey, CLU, APA, is an Advanced Sales Consultant with The Union Central Life Insurance Company. He joined Union Central in 1981 after 9 years of insurance sales in the greater Cincinnati area. He has served in agent support departments including pension sales, agency development, and individual annuity sales. Fred is a member of the National Association for Variable Annuities, the Society of Financial Service Professionals, and the National Institute of Pension Administrators.

Donald F. Cady, J.D., LL.M., CLU, is the author of *Field Guide to Estate Planning, Business Planning, & Employee Benefits*, and *Field Guide to Financial Planning*. He is a graduate of St. Lawrence University with a B.A. in Economics, where he received the Wall Street Journal Award for excellence in that subject. He received his J.D. degree from Columbia University School of Law, holds the degree of LL.M. (Taxation) from Emory University School of Law, and is a member of the New York Bar. For twenty years, Don was with the Aetna Life Insurance & Annuity Company in various advanced underwriting positions. Don is a frequent speaker on the subjects of estate planning, business planning and employee benefits for business and professional organizations.

Natalie B. Choate, Esq., is an estate planning attorney with the firm of Bingham McCutchen, LLP, in Boston. A Regent of the American College of Trust & Estate Counsel, she is the author of two books, *Life and Death Planning for Retirement Benefits* and *The QPRT Manual*, and is a frequent lecturer on estate planning topics. She is listed in *The Best Lawyers in America*.

Robert S. Keebler, CPA, MST, is a partner with Virchow, Krause & Company, LLP and chair of the Virchow, Krause Estate and Financial Planning Group. His practice includes family wealth transfer and preservation planning, charitable giving, retirement distribution planning, taxation of securities and investments, and estate administration. Mr. Keebler is nationally recognized as an expert in retirement planning and works collaboratively with other experts on academic reviews and papers, and client matters. He is also a frequent speaker for legal, accounting, insurance and financial planning groups throughout the United States at seminars and conferences on advanced IRA distribution strategies, estate planning and trust administration topics.

Stephan R. Leimberg is CEO of LISI, Leimberg Information Services, Inc., a provider of e-mail/internet news and commentary for professionals on recent cases, rulings, and legislation. He is also CEO of Leimberg & LeClair, Inc., an estate and financial planning software company, and President of Leimberg Associates, Inc., a publishing and software company in Bryn Mawr, Pennsylvania. Leimberg is the author of the acclaimed *Tools and Techniques* series, with titles on estate planning, employee benefits, financial planning, charitable planning, life insurance planning, income tax planning, investment planning, and practice management. Leimberg is a nationally known speaker and an award-winning author.

John L. Olsen, CLU, ChFC, AEP is an estate and financial planner practicing in St. Louis County, Missouri, and principal of Olsen Financial Group. In addition to providing financial, estate, and insurance planning services for clients, John consults with advisors on advanced cases and financial planning software. He is a member of the St. Louis Estate Planning Council and serves on the Board of Directors of the St. Louis Chapter of the Society of Financial Service Professionals and the National Association of Insurance and Financial Advisors, as well as on the Continuing Legal Education Advisory Board of the American Academy of Estate Planning Attorneys.

Martin A. Silfen, Esq., is an attorney and author with 25 years of practice in the areas of retirement planning and estate planning. Mr. Silfen was senior partner in the law firm of Silfen, Segal, Fryer & Shuster, P.C. in Atlanta. He is currently Senior Vice President of Brown Brothers Harriman Trust Company, New York, New York. Mr. Silfen is a nationally recognized expert in retirement tax planning, having authored *The Retirement Plan Distribution Advisor* and served as Retirement Planning columnist for *Personal Financial Planning*. He has also authored several articles for *Estate Planning*.

Abbreviations

Acq. (Nonacq.)	Commissioner's acquiescence (nonacquiescence) in decision
AFTR	American Federal Tax Reports (Prentice-Hall, early decisions)
AFTR2d	American Federal Tax Reports (Prentice-Hall, second series)
AJCA 2004	American Jobs Creation Act of 2004
ASRS	Advanced Sales Reference Service (National Underwriter Co.)
BTA	Board of Tax Appeals decisions (now Tax Court)
BTA Memo	Board of Tax Appeals memorandum decisions
CA or — Cir.	United States Court of Appeals
CB	Cumulative Bulletin of Internal Revenue Service
CCA	Chief Counsel Advice
COBRA	Consolidated Omnibus Budget Reconciliation Act of 1985
Cl. Ct.	U.S. Claims Court (designated U.S. Court of Federal Claims in 1992)
CRTRA 2000	Community Renewal Tax Relief Act of 2000
Ct. Cl.	Court of Claims (designated U.S. Claims Court in 1982)
DOL Adv. Op.	Department of Labor Advisory Opinion
EGTRRA 2001	Economic Growth and Tax Relief Reconciliation Act of 2001
ERISA	Employee Retirement Income Security Act of 1974
ERTA	Economic Recovery Tax Act of 1981
Fed.	Federal Reporter (early decisions)
Fed. Cl.	U.S. Court of Federal Claims
Fed. Reg.	Federal Register
F.2d	Federal Reporter, second series (later decisions of U.S. Court of Appeals to Mid-1993)
F.3rd	Federal Reporter, third series (decisions of U.S. Court of Appeals since Mid-1993)
F. Supp.	Federal Supplement (decisions of U.S. District Courts)
FSA	Field Service Advice
GCM	General Counsel Memorandum (IRS)
HIPAA '96	Health Insurance Portability and Accountability Act
IR	Internal Revenue News Release
IRB	Internal Revenue Bulletin of Internal Revenue Service
IRC	Internal Revenue Code
IRS	Internal Revenue Service
IRSRRA '98	IRS Restructuring and Reform Act of 1998
IT	Income Tax Ruling Series (IRS)
ITCA	Installment Tax Correction Act of 2000
JCWAA	Job Creation and Worker Assistance Act of 2002
JGTRRA 2003	Jobs and Growth Tax Relief Reconciliation Act of 2003
KETRA 2005	Katrina Emergency Tax Relief Act of 2005
Let. Rul.	Letter Ruling (issued by IRS)
OBRA	Omnibus Budget Reconciliation Act of (year of enactment)
P.L.	Public Law
P&PS Rept.	Pension and Profit Sharing Report (Prentice-Hall)
PBGC	Pension Benefit Guaranty Corporation
PFEA 2004	Pension Funding Equity Act of 2004
PTE	Prohibited Transaction Exemption
Prop. Reg.	Proposed Regulation
REA '84	Retirement Equity Act of 1984
Rev. Proc.	Revenue Procedure (issued by IRS)
Rev. Rul.	Revenue Ruling (issued by IRS)
SBJPA '96	Small Business Job Protection Act of 1996

SCA	IRS Service Center Advice
TAM	Technical Advice Memorandum (IRS)
TAMRA '88	Technical and Miscellaneous Revenue Act of 1988
TC	Tax Court (official reports)
TC Memo	Tax Court memorandum decisions (official reports)
TC Summary Opinion	Tax Court Summary Opinion
TD	Treasury Decision
TEFRA	Tax Equity and Fiscal Responsibility Act of 1982
TIR	Technical Information Release (from the IRS)
TRA	Tax Reform Act of (year of enactment)
TRA '97	Taxpayer Relief Act of 1997
URAA '94	Uruguay Round Agreements Act of 1994
US	United States Supreme Court decisions
USERRA '94	Uniformed Services Employment and Reemployment Rights Act of 1994
USTC	United States Tax Cases (Commerce Clearing House)
VTTRA 2001	Victims of Terrorism Tax Relief Act of 2001
WFTRA 2004	Working Families Tax Relief Act of 2004

SUNSET PROVISION

All provisions of, and amendments made by, the Economic Growth and Tax Relief Reconciliation Act of 2001 (EGTRRA 2001) are scheduled to sunset, or expire for taxable, plan, or limitation years beginning after December 31, 2010. With respect to the estate, gift, and generation-skipping provisions of the Act, the amendments are scheduled to expire for estates of decedents dying, gifts made, or generation-skipping transfers after December 31, 2010. The Internal Revenue Code of 1986 and the Employee Retirement Income Security Act of 1974 will apply to such years, and to estates, gifts, and transfers after December 31, 2010, as if the provisions of, and amendments made by, EGTRAA 2001 had never been enacted.

Tax Facts Navigators

BUY-SELL NAVIGATOR

- Whether or not premiums paid by a business for the benefit of the business will be deductible. [Q 45]

- Will death proceeds paid to a business be free of federal income tax, whether the business is a corporation, partnership, or to an individual as a sole proprietorship? [Q 62]

- What constitutes a transfer for value? [Q 64]

- How will a closely held business will be valued for estate tax purposes? [Q 613]

- Will death proceeds of life insurance owned by, and whose death proceeds are payable to, a corporation or partnership be included in the insured's taxable estate? [Q 611, Q 612]

- How is the payment of a life insurance premium by an S corporation treated? [Q 55]

- How will the receipt of death proceeds by an S corporation be treated? [Q 76]

- How will a redemption of stock by an S corporation be treated? [Q 91]

- What is a Section 303 redemption? [Q 85]

- How is life insurance treated for purposes of the AMT? [Q 95]

- What are the family attribution rules and how do they affect buy-sell agreements? [Q 82, Q 83, Q 84]

- Will income retained for the purchase of life insurance cause an accumulated earnings tax problem for the corporation? [Q 89]

EXECUTIVE COMPENSATION NAVIGATOR

Design Issues

- What is reasonable compensation for an executive? What happens if compensation is "unreasonable"? [Q 108].

- Executives often have "Golden Parachutes" that provide generous severance packages in the event of a change in corporate control. If these payments are "excessive," they are subject to special penalties. [Q 109].

- Traditional deferred compensation agreements may be funded, with money secured in an annuity or trust ([Q 110]) or may be unfunded, with money subject to the general creditors of the employer ([Q 114]).

- Stock options ([Q 129]) and restricted stock ([Q 130]]) are common means of compensating executives.

- The American Jobs Creation Act of 2004 imposed new requirements (IRC Section 409A) on deferred compensation arrangements. [Q 115] and [Q 118].

Distribution and Taxation Issues

- Employers generally may deduct deferred compensation payments in the year employees includes the payments in income. [Q 110] and [Q 114].

- Deferred compensation is generally taxable unless subject to a "substantial risk of forfeiture." [Q 112]. Employees are taxed on deferred compensation when they receive the "economic benefit." [Q 116].

- Stock options that meet statutory requirements receive favorable tax treatment. [Q 129].

- Arrangements that violate the requirements of IRC Section 409A incur retroactive taxation, a 20% penalty tax, and inflated interest penalties. [Q115] and [Q 118].

INDIVIDUAL RETIREMENT PLAN NAVIGATOR

Plan Options

- Individuals may contribute up to $4,000 per year (2006) to a traditional IRA ([Q 220])) or a Roth IRA ([Q 221]). Catch-up contributions of $1,000 (2006) for individuals age 50 and over are also permitted. See, generally, [Q 210].

- A self-employed individual may contribute up to 25% of self-employment income, up to $44,000 (2006) to a SEP-IRA. A small employer with a SEP-IRA must also make required contributions on behalf of covered employees. [Q 240].

- A SIMPLE IRA allows salary deferrals for self-employed individuals and small employers of up to $10,000 (2006). Employers must also generally make required matching contributions. Catch-up contributions of $2,500 (2006) for individuals age 50 and over are also permitted. [Q 242].

- A Solo 401(k) plan is 401(k) plan covering only one individual. 401(k) plans permit salary deferral of up to $15,000 (2006). Catch-up contributions of $5,000 (2006) for individuals age 50 and over are also permitted. [Q 398].

Distribution and Taxation Issues

- Contributions to a traditional IRA may be deductible up to the annual contribution limit, depending on an individual's income and "active participation" ([Q 224]) in an employer retirement plan. [Q 220].

- Contributions to a Roth IRA are not tax deductible, but qualifying distributions from a Roth IRA are not subject to federal income tax. [Q 221] and [Q 228].

- Contributions to a SEP-IRA ([Q 240]), a SIMPLE IRA ([Q 243]), or a Solo 401(k) ([Q 398]) are generally tax deductible to the employer making the contribution and are not includible in the employee's income. Salary deferrals under a SIMPLE IRA ([Q 243]) or a Solo 401(k) ([Q 398]) are subject to federal Social Security and unemployment taxes.

- Distributions from a traditional IRA ([Q 227]), a SEP-IRA ([Q 240]), a SIMPLE IRA ([Q 242]), or a Solo 401(k) ([Q 398]) are generally taxable as ordinary income to the recipient.

INTRAFAMILY AND BUSINESS TRANSFER NAVIGATOR

Installment Sales

- How can an installment sale be used to defer the payment of income taxes? [Q 806]

Private Annuity

- How can a private annuity be used to defer the payment of income taxes? [Q 41]

- How is a private annuity taxed to the person making payments? [Q 42]

- How should a private annuity be structured to avoid a taxable gift? [Q 705]

- How can a private annuity be used to remove property from the taxable estate? [Q 608]

Interest-Free and Below Market Rate Loans

- What are the income tax consequences of such loans? [Q 805]

- Are taxable gifts made of foregone interest? [Q 904]

Business Continuation (Buy-Sell)

- Are premiums paid for life insurance used to fund a buy-sell deductible? [Q 45, Q 47, Q 49, Q 56, Q 59]

- Does the payment of premiums result in taxable income to anybody? [Q 46, Q 50, Q 51, Q 52, Q 53]

- Can proceeds of life insurance used to fund a buy-sell be received income tax-free? [Q 62]

- What if there is a transfer for value? [Q 63, Q 64]

- What are the income tax implications of a cross-purchase agreement? [Q 80, Q 81]

- Of an entity agreement? [Q 82]

- What effect does a buy-sell agreement have on gift tax value? [Q 706]

- How can a buy-sell be used to fix estate tax value? [Q 613, Q 915]

Section 303 Stock Redemption

- How can Section 303 stock be used to help solve liquidity problems at death? [Q 85]

Choice of Entities

- How is a partnership taxed? [Q 842]

- An LLC? [Q 841]

- A personal service corporation? [Q 840]

- An S corporation? [Q 839]

- A corporation? [Q 838]

Valuation of Business Interests

- How is a closely-held business valued for estate tax purposes? Are discounts available? [Q 613]

- What special valuation rules apply to transfers of interests in partnerships and corporations? [Q 913, Q 916]

401(k) NAVIGATOR

Design Issues

- 401(k) plans are a type of defined contribution plan that provides for elective deferral contributions by employees. For a brief overview, see [Q 394].

- The amount an employee can defer in any year is subject to a dollar limit, explained in [Q 396]. Catch-up contributions by employees age 50 and over are also allowed; see [Q 397].

- After-tax deferrals are permitted if the plan offers a "qualified Roth contribution program"; see [Q 401] for the applicable requirements.

- Like all qualified plans, 401(k) plans are subject to the qualification requirements (explained at [Q 322] to [Q 360]). In addition, special nondiscrimination and qualification requirements apply (see [Q 395] and [Q 404] to [Q 405]).

- Safe harbor 401(k) plans ([Q 399]) and SIMPLE 401(k) plans ([Q 400]) do not have to perform certain nondiscrimination tests.

- The Internal Revenue Code does not provide any separate requirements for solo 401(k) plans, but many one-employee small businesses find them beneficial; see [Q 398].

Distribution and Taxation Issues

- Special distribution restrictions apply to 401(k) plans, explained at Q 402]; however, 401(k) plans may offer hardship distributions ([Q 403]) and plan loans ([Q 420] to [Q 422]) if specific requirements are met.

- Often when a 401(k) plan fails the special nondiscrimination requirements for 401(k) plans, it makes corrective distributions to one or more highly compensated employees, as explained at [Q 406].

- Participants who invest 401(k) plan proceeds in employer stock may benefit from net unrealized appreciation treatment upon distribution; see [Q 432].

- The tax treatment of preretirement distributions is explained at [Q 427] to [Q 428]. Post retirement distributions are explained beginning at [Q 429].

- The minimum distribution requirements and penalty are explained at [Q 339] to [Q 347].

412(i) PLAN NAVIGATOR

Design Issues

- An IRC Section 412(i) plan is a defined benefit pension plan that is funded by life insurance, annuity contracts, or some combination of the two. [Q 407] provides a brief overview.

- The amount of life insurance that can be provided in a qualified plan is subject to limits, explained in [Q 369]. Note that in 2004 guidance, the IRS categorized certain plans that provide excessive coverage as "listed transactions," meaning that special penalties and disclosure requirements may be applied.

- If the plan meets the special IRC Section 412(i) requirements, it will be exempt from the minimum funding requirements explained in [Q 408]. If these requirements are not satisfied, the plan will be subject to the minimum funding standard explained in [Q 385].

- Like all qualified plans, an IRC Section 412(i) plan must satisfy the qualification requirements (explained at [Q 322] to [Q 360]). In addition, special requirements that are specific to defined benefit plans ([Q 371] to [Q 373]) and pensions ([Q 381] and [Q 384]) apply.

Taxation and Distribution Issues

- Since an IRC Section 412(i) plan is a type of defined benefit plan, the employer is subject to the deduction limit for pensions, explained at [Q 383]. If the employer sponsors more than one plan, it is subject to the limits explained in [Q 366].

- Employee participants are taxed on the cost of current life insurance protection in a 412(i) plan. The method of calculating these costs is explained in [Q 424] and [Q 425].

- Distributions of life insurance contracts from 412(i) plans are subject to the valuation requirements explained in [Q 431].

- The income tax treatment of annuity payouts after retirement is explained at [Q 433] to [Q 435].

- The minimum distribution requirements and penalty are explained at [Q 339] to [Q 347].

LIFE INSURANCE TRUST NAVIGATOR

Income Tax

- Are life insurance proceeds taxable? To the trust? To trust beneficiaries? [Q 310]

- Who is taxed on trust income? The grantor? The trust? Trust beneficiaries? [Q 308]

- What are the general rules for the income taxation of trusts? [Q 843]

Gift Tax

- Can transfers to trust qualify for the gift tax annual exclusion? [Q 724]

- What about annual exclusions for minor beneficiaries? [Q 725]

- Should Crummey withdrawal powers be used for the annual exclusion? [Q 726]

- What is the effect of a beneficiary exercising or not exercising a withdrawal power? [Q 727]

- Can transfers to trust qualify for the gift tax marital deduction? [Q 722]

Generation-Skipping Transfer Tax

- Is the trust generation-skipping? [Q 950]

- When do transfers to trust qualify for the GST annual exclusion? [Q 751]

- How can GST exemption be leveraged with life insurance? [Q 752]

Estate Tax

- How can an irrevocable life insurance trust be used to exclude life insurance proceeds from an insured's estate? [Q 651]

- Under what circumstances are life insurance proceeds includable in an insured's estate? [Q 626]

- Are proceeds payable to insured's estate?

- Does insured have incidents of ownership? [Q 731]

- Does insured have incidents of ownership when insured is the trustee or can remove a trustee? [Q 632]

- Was a life insurance policy transferred to the trust within three years of death? [Q 718]

- What is the effect of a beneficiary exercising or not exercising a withdrawal power? [Q 653]

- Can life insurance proceeds payable to the trust be used to pay insured's estate debts and death taxes? [Q 654]

REQUIRED MINIMUM DISTRIBUTION NAVIGATOR

- The minimum distribution requirements apply to all individual retirement accounts and individual retirement annuities (IRAs – see [Q 233] to [Q 237]), qualified plans ([Q 338] to [Q 346]) and 403(b) tax sheltered annuities ([Q 486] to [Q 489]).

- The penalty for failure to make minimum distributions is 50%, and is imposed on the individual, not the plan. See [Q 233] (IRAs), [Q 339] and [Q 347] (qualified plans) and [Q 486] (tax sheltered annuities).

Lifetime Requirements

- The requirements for lifetime distributions from individual accounts are explained at [Q 234] (IRAs), [Q 341] (qualified plans) and [Q 487] (tax sheltered annuities). Participants with older accumulations (pre-1987) in tax sheltered annuities may be able to delay distributions to age 75 for such amounts (see [Q 486] and [Q 488]).

- An individual's "required beginning date" is generally April 1 of the year after the individual reaches age 70½ (see [Q 234]. For qualified plans (see [Q 340]) and tax sheltered annuities (see [Q 486)], the date may be later.

- A "uniform lifetime table" is used to determine the minimum distribution amount for most purposes. This table appears at [Q 234], [Q 341], and [Q 487].

- To apply the minimum distribution requirements to a qualified plan interest for which there is a qualified domestic relations order (QDRO) in effect, see [Q 345].

- Individuals receiving an annuity payout from a qualified plan are subject to the requirements explained at [Q 342]. Such an individual's required beginning date is determined as explained in [Q 340]. An "incidental benefit rule" applies to qualified plans ([Q 346]) and tax sheltered annuities ([Q 488]).

- The minimum distribution requirements do not apply to Roth IRAs during the owner's lifetime (see [Q 234]); however they do apply after death (see below).

- Required minimum distributions may not be rolled over (see [Q 445], [Q 451], and [Q 452]).

After Death Requirements

- The requirements for after-death distributions are explained at [Q 235] (IRAs), [Q 343] (qualified plans) and [Q 489] (tax sheltered annuities).

- The payout requirements after death depend on the identity and status of the designated beneficiary; see [Q 236] (IRAs), [Q 344] (qualified plans) and [Q 489] (tax sheltered annuities).

- For a trust beneficiary to meet the definition of "designated beneficiary," the trust must satisfy special "see-through trust" requirements explained in [Q 344].

- Special rules apply to surviving spouses; see [Q 235] (IRAs), [Q 343] (qualified plans) and [Q 489] (tax sheltered annuities).

S CORPORATION NAVIGATOR

- In general, how is an S corporation treated for income tax purposes? [Q 839]

- What special rules are there for qualified plans of S corporations? [Q 417]

- How is health insurance coverage for S corporation shareholders treated? [Q 166]

- How are redemption payments of an S corporation taxed? [Q 91]

- What are the income tax consequences of an S corporation paying life insurance premiums? [Q 55]

- How are death proceeds received by an S corporation treated for income tax purposes? [Q 76]

- How is gain realized on the sale of a life insurance policy by an S corporation? [Q 90]

PART I

FEDERAL INCOME TAX

on

INSURANCE AND EMPLOYEE BENEFITS

ANNUITIES

GENERAL RULES

1. What general rules govern the income taxation of payments received under annuity contracts?

The rules in IRC Section 72 govern the income taxation of all amounts received under annuity contracts. IRC Section 72 also covers the tax treatment of policy dividends and forms of premium returns. Except in the case of certain annuity contracts held by nonnatural persons (see Q 2), income credited on a deferred annuity contract is not currently includable in income.

Payments to which IRC Section 72 applies are of three classes: (1) "amounts not received as an annuity;" (2) payments of interest only; and (3) annuities.

The term *annuity* includes all periodic payments resulting from the systematic liquidation of a principal sum. Thus, the term *annuity* refers not only to payments for a life or lives, but also to installment payments that do not involve life contingency; for example, payments under a "fixed period" or "fixed amount" settlement option. Treas. Regs. §1.72-1(b), §1.72-2(b). Annuity payments are taxed under the *annuity rules* in IRC Section 72. These rules determine what portion of each payment is excludable from gross income as a return of the purchaser's investment, and what portion is taxed as interest earned on the investment. The annuity rules, then, apply in taxing life income and other types of installment payments received under immediate and deferred annuity contracts. (See Q 7 to Q 19.) IRC Sec. 72(a); Treas. Reg. §1.72-1.

Payments consisting of interest only, not part of the systematic liquidation of a principal sum, are not *annuity* payments; hence they are not taxed under the annuity rules. Periodic payments on a principal amount that will be returned intact upon demand are interest payments. Rev. Rul. 75-255, 1975-2 CB 22.

All amounts taxable under IRC Section 72 other than annuities and payments of interest are classed as *amounts not received as an annuity*. These include: policy dividends; lump sum cash settlements of cash surrender values; cash withdrawals and amounts received on partial surrender; death benefits under annuity contracts; and a guaranteed refund under a refund life annuity settlement. Treas. Reg. §1.72-11. "Amounts not received as an annuity" are taxable under general rules discussed in Q 3 and Q 4. The taxation of distributions from life insurance policies is discussed in Q 249 and Q 250.

2006 Tax Facts on Insurance & Employee Benefits 1

IRC Section 72 also places a penalty on "premature distributions" (see Q 4) and, for contracts issued after January 18, 1985, imposes post-death distribution requirements (see Q 37).

The income tax treatment of life insurance *death proceeds* is governed by IRC Section 101, not by IRC Section 72. Consequently, the annuity rules in IRC Section 72 do not apply to life income or other installment payments under optional settlements of death proceeds. However, the rules for taxing such payments are similar to the IRC Section 72 annuity rules. See Q 271 to Q 279.

Employee annuities, under both qualified and nonqualified plans, and periodic payments from qualified pension and profit sharing trusts are taxable under IRC Section 72, but because a number of special rules apply to these payments, they are treated separately. (See Q 110 to Q 113, Q 426 to Q 441, Q 490.) *ASRS, Sec. 52, ¶300.1.*

2. How are annuity contracts held by corporations and other non-natural persons taxed?

Except as noted below, to the extent that contributions are made after February 28, 1986 to a deferred annuity contract held by a corporation or another entity that is not a natural person, the contract is not treated for tax purposes as an annuity contract.

Income on the contract is treated as ordinary income received or accrued by the owner during the taxable year. IRC Sec. 72(u). "Income on the contract" is the *excess of* (1) the sum of the net surrender value of the contract at the end of the taxable year and any amounts distributed under the contract during the taxable year and any prior taxable year *over* (2) the sum of the net premiums (amount of premiums paid under the contract reduced by any policyholder dividends) under the contract for the taxable year and prior taxable years and any amounts includable in gross income for prior taxable years under this requirement. IRC Sec. 72(u)(2).

This rule does not apply to any annuity contract that (1) is acquired by the estate of a decedent by reason of the death of the decedent; (2) is held under a qualified pension, profit sharing, or stock bonus plan, as an IRC Section 403(b) tax sheltered annuity, or under an individual retirement plan; (3) is purchased by an employer upon the termination of a qualified pension, profit sharing, or stock bonus plan or tax sheltered annuity program and held by the employer until all amounts under the contract are distributed to the employee for whom the contract was purchased or to his beneficiary; (4) is an immediate annuity (i.e., an annuity that is purchased with a single premium or annuity consideration, the annuity starting date of that is no later than one year from the date of purchase, and which provides for a series of substantially equal periodic payments to be made no less frequently than annually during the annuity period); or (5) is a qualified funding asset (as defined in IRC Section 130(d) but without regard to whether there is a qualified assignment). IRC Sec. 72(u)(3). A *qualified funding asset* is any annuity contract issued by a licensed insurance company that is purchased and held to fund periodic payments for damages, by suit or agreement, on account of personal physical injury or sickness. IRC Sec. 130.

An annuity contract held by a trust or other entity as agent for a natural person is considered held by a natural person. IRC Sec. 72(u)(1). According to the conference report, if a nonnatural person is the nominal owner of an annuity contract but the

ANNUITIES

beneficial owner is a natural person, the annuity contract will be treated as though held by a natural person. H.R. Conf. Rep. No. 99-841 (TRA '86) *reprinted in* 1986-3 CB Vol. 4 401. Also, an annuity owned by a grantor trust will be considered to be owned by the grantor of the trust. See Q 844.

According to the IRS, a trust that owned an annuity contract which was to be distributed, prior to its annuity starting date, to the trust's beneficiary, a natural person, was considered to hold the annuity contract as an agent for a natural person. Let. Ruls. 9204014, 9204010. Where the trustee of an irrevocable trust purchased three single premium deferred annuities, naming the trust as owner and beneficiary of the contracts and a different trust beneficiary as the annuitant of each contract, the nonnatural person rule was not applicable. The terms of the trust provided that the trustee would terminate the trust and distribute an annuity to each trust beneficiary after a certain period of time. Let. Rul. 199905015. Additionally, the Service concluded that the nonnatural person rule does not apply to a trust which had invested trust assets in a single premium deferred variable annuity where the same individual was the sole annuitant under the contract and the sole life beneficiary of the trust. Let. Rul. 9752035.

Where a trustee's duties were limited to purchasing an annuity as directed by an individual and holding legal title to the annuity for his sole benefit and the trustee was not able to exercise any rights under the annuity contract unless directed to do so by the individual, the Service concluded that the trustee was acting as an agent for a natural person. Let. Rul. 9639057. Further, where the trustee of an irrevocable trust purchased an annuity and had the power to select an annuity settlement option or terminate the annuity contract, the annuity was still considered to be owned by a natural person. Let. Rul. 199933033.

An employee-grantor secular trust that held a variable annuity was also considered to hold the contract for a natural person. Let. Rul. 9316018. In a fact situation involving a master trust receiving after-tax participant contributions, the Service concluded that the trustee was acting as an agent for the participant where the trustee's duties were limited to receiving contributions, forwarding the contributions to an insurance company to be paid into a particular group annuity contract, and holding legal title to the contract for the participant's sole benefit. The Service noted that the trustee would be unable to exercise any rights under the annuity contract unless directed by the participant. Let. Rul. 9810015.

A group annuity contract held by a trust for the purpose of providing retirement benefits to a group of natural persons through a plan that was not a qualified retirement plan was considered by the Service to be owned by a natural person. Let. Rul. 200018046.

Further, a bank holding an annuity contract used to fund a pre-need funeral arrangement as trustee was considered to hold the annuity contract as an agent for a natural person. Let. Rul. 9120024. However, a charitable remainder unitrust was not considered to hold an annuity contract as an agent for a natural person and, thus, was required to include income on any annuity contracts in ordinary income each year. Let. Rul. 9009047.

These requirements apply "to contributions to annuity contracts after February 28, 1986." TRA '86 Sec. 1135(b). It is clear that if all contributions to the contract are made after February 28, 1986 the requirements apply to the contract. It seems clear enough that if no contributions are made after February 28, 1986 to an annuity contract, a contract held by a nonnatural person is treated for tax purposes as an annuity contract and is taxed under the annuity rules. See Q 1. However, if contributions have been made both before March 1, 1986 and after February 28, 1986 to contracts held by nonnatural persons, it is not clear whether the income on the contract is allocated to different portions of the contract and whether the portion of the contract allocable to contributions before March 1, 1986 may continue to be treated as an annuity contract for income tax purposes. The Code makes no specific provision for separate treatment of contributions to the same contract made before March 1, 1986 and those made after February 28, 1986. *ASRS, Sec. 52, ¶300.1(f)*.

Amounts Not Received As An Annuity

Generally

3. What is the basic rule for taxing dividends, cash withdrawals and other amounts received under annuity contracts before the annuity starting date?

Dividends, Cash Withdrawals, Loans, Partial Surrender

Policy dividends (unless retained by the insurer as premiums or other consideration), cash withdrawals, amounts received as loans and the value of any part of an annuity contract pledged or assigned, and amounts received on partial surrender under *annuity* contracts entered into *after* August 13, 1982 are taxable as income to the extent that the cash value of the contract immediately before the payment exceeds the investment in the contract. IRC Sec. 72(e).

To the extent the amount received is greater than the excess of cash surrender value over investment in the contract, the amount will be treated as a tax-free return of investment. In effect, these amounts are treated as distributions of interest first and only second as recovery of cost. (In addition, taxable amounts may be subject to a 10% penalty tax unless paid after age 59½ or disability—see Q 4.)

Cash value is determined without regard to any surrender charge. IRC Sec. 72(e)(3). Investment in the contract is, under the general rule, reduced by previously received excludable amounts; however, investment in the contract is increased by loans treated as distributions to the extent the amount is includable in income, but not reduced to the extent it is excludable. IRC Sec. 72(e)(4).

Amounts received that are allocable to an investment made after August 13, 1982 in an annuity contract entered into before August 14, 1982 are treated as received under a contract entered into after August 13, 1982 and are subject to the above "interest first" rule. IRC Sec. 72(e)(5). If an annuity contract has income allocable to earnings on pre-August 14, 1982 and post-August 13, 1982 investments, the amount received is allocable first to investments made prior to August 14, 1982, then to income accumulated with respect to such investments (under the "cost recovery" rule, see next paragraph), then to income accumulated with respect to investments made after August 13, 1982 and finally to investments made after August 13, 1982 (under the "interest-first" rule). Rev. Rul. 85-159, 1985-2 CB 29.

ANNUITIES

Policy dividends, cash withdrawals and amounts received on partial surrender under annuity contracts entered into *before* August 14, 1982 (and allocable to investment in the contract made before August 14, 1982) are taxed under the "cost recovery rule." Under the cost recovery rule, the taxpayer may receive all such amounts tax-free until he has received tax-free amounts equal to his pre-August 14, 1982 investment in the contract; the amounts are taxable only after such basis has been fully recovered. IRC Sec. 72(e)(5).

Where, as part of the purchase of a variable annuity, a taxpayer entered into an investment advisory agreement which stated that the company issuing the annuity would be solely liable for payment of a fee to an investment adviser who would manage the taxpayer's funds in the variable accounts, the fee was considered to be an amount not received as an annuity and, thus, includable in the taxpayer's income to the extent allocable to the income on the contract. Let. Rul. 9342053.

Special rules applicable to amounts received under pension, profit sharing or stock bonus plans, under annuities purchased by any such plan or under IRC Section 403(b) tax sheltered annuities are discussed in Q 433 to Q 435, and Q 490. The rules applicable to loans under qualified plans and under tax sheltered annuity (IRC Section 403(b)) contracts are discussed in Q 420 and Q 483 respectively.

Transfers Without Adequate Consideration

An individual who transfers any annuity contract issued after April 22, 1987, for less than full and adequate consideration will be treated as having received an "amount not received as an annuity" unless the transfer is between spouses or incident to a divorce under the IRC Section 1041 nonrecognition rule (see Q 280). The amount the transferor will be deemed to have received is the *excess* of the cash surrender value of the contract at the time of the transfer *over* the investment in the contract at that time. The transferee's investment in the contract will include the amount, if any, included in income by the transferor. IRC Sec. 72(e)(4)(C).

Other Amounts

The purpose behind the "interest first" rule applicable to investment in contracts after August 13, 1982, is to limit the tax advantages of deferred annuity contracts to long term investment goals, such as income security, and to prevent the use of tax deferred inside build-up as a method of sheltering income on freely withdrawable short term investments.

Consistent with this purpose, other amounts, which are neither interest payments nor annuities, received under annuity contracts, regardless of when entered into, are not treated first as interest distributions but are taxed under the cost recovery rule. These amounts include lump sum settlements on complete surrender (see Q 33), annuity contract death benefits (see Q 36), and amounts received in full discharge of the obligation under the contract that are in the nature of a refund of consideration, such as a guaranteed refund under a refund life annuity settlement (see Q 18). IRC Sec. 72(e)(5).

Multiple Contracts

All annuity contracts entered into after October 21, 1988 that are issued by the same company to the same policyholder during any calendar year will be treated as one annuity contract for purposes of determining under the above rules the amount of any distribution that is includable in income. IRC Sec. 72(e)(11). An annuity that is received as part of an IRC Section 1035 exchange that was undertaken as part of a troubled insurer's rehabilitation process under Revenue Ruling 92-43 (see Q 30) is considered to have been entered into for purposes of the multiple contract rule on the date that the new contract is issued. The newly-received contract is not "grandfathered" back to the issue date of the original annuity for this purpose. Let. Rul. 9442030.

This aggregation rule does not apply to distributions received under qualified pension or profit sharing plans, from an IRC Section 403(b) contract, or from an IRA. IRC Sec. 72(e)(11)(A). The Conference Report on OBRA '89 also states the aggregation rule does not apply to immediate annuities.

If the contract is owned by a corporation or other nonnatural person, see also Q 2.

For amounts received under life insurance or endowment contracts, see Q 249. For distributions received under life insurance policies that are classified as modified endowment contracts, see Q 250.

Effect of Tax Free Exchange

In order to give effect to the grandfathering of pre-August 14, 1982 annuity contracts, a replacement contract obtained in a tax free exchange of annuity contracts (see Q 30) succeeds to the status of the surrendered contract, for purposes of determining when amounts are to be considered invested and for computing the taxability of any withdrawals. Rev. Rul. 85-159, 1985-2 CB 29, Let. Rul. 9442030. Investment in the replacement contract is considered made on, before or after August 13, 1982 to the same extent the investment was made on, before or after August 13, 1982 in the replaced contract. *ASRS, Sec. 52, ¶300.1.*

4. What penalties apply to "premature" distributions under annuity contracts?

In order to discourage the use of annuity contracts as short term tax sheltered investments, a 10% tax is imposed on certain "premature" payments under annuity contracts. IRC Sec. 72(q). The tax applies to any payment received to the extent the payment is includable in income, except it does not apply to any of the following distributions:

(1) any payment made on or after the date on which the taxpayer becomes age 59½;

(2) any payment attributable to the taxpayer's becoming disabled;

(3) any payment allocable to investment in the contract before August 14, 1982, including earnings on pre-August 14, 1982 investment (Rev. Rul. 85-159, 1985-2 CB 29. See also H.R. Conf. Rep. 97-760 (TEFRA '82) *reprinted in* 1982-2 CB 685-686);

(4) any payment made from a qualified pension, profit sharing or stock bonus plan, or under a contract purchased by such a plan, or under an IRC Section 403(b) tax sheltered annuity, or from an individual retirement account or annuity, or from a contract provided life insurance company employees under certain retirement plans (but such payments are subject to similar premature distribution limitations and penalties–see: Q 231, IRA; Q 428, pension, profit sharing, stock bonus; Q 485, tax sheltered annuity);

ANNUITIES   Q 4

(5) any payment made on or after the death of the holder (or the primary annuitant in the case where the holder is a nonnatural person);

(6) any payment made under an immediate annuity contract; (An immediate annuity contract is one that is purchased with a single premium or annuity consideration, the annuity starting date of which is no later than one year from the date of purchase, and that provides for a series of substantially equal periodic payments to be made no less frequently than annually during the annuity period. IRC Sec. 72(u)(4); See Let. Rul. 200036021. Where a deferred annuity contract was exchanged for an immediate annuity contract, the purchase date of the new contract for purposes of the 10% penalty tax was considered to be the date upon which the deferred annuity was purchased. Thus, payments from the replacement contract did not fall within the immediate annuity exception to the penalty tax. Rev. Rul. 92-95, 1992-2 CB 43.);

(7) any payment made from an annuity purchased by an employer upon the termination of a qualified plan and held by the employer until the employee's separation from service;

(8) any payment under a qualified funding asset (i.e., any annuity contract issued by a licensed insurance company that is purchased as a result of a liability to make periodic payments for damages, by suit or agreement, on account of personal physical injury or sickness); or

(9) any payment that is part of a series of substantially equal periodic payments made (not less frequently than annually) for the life or life expectancy of the taxpayer or the joint lives or joint life expectancies of the taxpayer and his designated beneficiary. Payments excepted from the 10% penalty by reason of this exception may be subject to recapture if the series of payments is modified (other than by reason of death or disability) (a) prior to the taxpayer's reaching age 59½, or (b) before the end of a five-year period beginning on the date of the first payment even if the taxpayer has reached age 59½. According to the report of the Conference Committee (TRA '86), the modification that triggers recapture is a change to a method of distribution which would not qualify for the exemption. The tax on the amount recaptured is imposed in the first taxable year of the modification and is equal to the tax (as determined under regulations) that would have been imposed (plus interest) had the exception not applied. H.R. Conf. Rep. No. 99-841 (TRA '86) *reprinted in* 1986-3 CB Vol. 4 403. The Service announced that the three methods used to avoid the 10% penalty when making substantially equal periodic payments from a qualified retirement plan (see Q 232) may also be used to qualify as substantially equal periodic payments from a nonqualified annuity. The "one time election" to change methods may also be used by owners of nonqualified annuities. Finally, there will be no penalty if an individual depletes an account by using one of the approved methods. Notice 2004-15, 2004-9 IRB 526.

Planning Point: From a practical standpoint, it would appear imprudent for an individual younger than age 45 to attempt to qualify for this exception. A period longer than 15 years may afford too much time in which a "material change" could occur. Also, the taxpayer might forget the importance of continuing to satisfy the conditions for this exception to the penalty tax. *Fred Burkey, CLU, APA, The Union Central Life Insurance Company.*

Apparently, if the annuity contract was issued between August 13, 1982, and January 19, 1985, a distribution of income allocable to any investment made 10 or more years before the distribution is not subject to the penalty. For this purpose, amounts includable in income are allocated to the earliest investment in the contract to which amounts were not previously fully allocated. Sec. 72(q)(1) prior to amendment by DEFRA 1984, Sec. 222(a). To facilitate accounting, investments are considered made on January 1 of the year in which they are invested. DEFRA 1984, Sec. 222(c).

There is also a 10% penalty tax on certain premature distributions from life insurance policies classified as modified endowment contracts. See Q 250.

The tax on premature distributions is not taken into consideration for purposes of determining the nonrefundable personal credits, general business credit, or foreign tax credit. See Q 832. *ASRS, Sec. 52, ¶300.1(e).*

Dividends

5. Are the dividends payable on an annuity contract taxable income?

How dividends under annuity contracts are taxed depends on when the contract was purchased. If the annuity contract was purchased *after* August 13, 1982, dividends received before the annuity starting date are taxable to the extent the cash value of the contract (determined without regard to any surrender charge) immediately before the dividend is received exceeds the investment in the contract at the same time. Any excess is treated as a tax-free recovery of investment. If the annuity contract was purchased *before* August 14, 1982 and no additional investment was made in the contract after August 13, 1982, the dividends will be taxed like dividends received under life insurance contracts (generally tax-free until basis has been recovered; see Q 252). IRC Sec. 72(e).

Dividends retained by the insurer as a premium or other consideration for the contract are not included in income. IRC Sec. 72(e)(4)(B). Dividends left with the insurer to accumulate at interest would not be considered retained as premium or consideration.

If any investment has been made after August 13, 1982 in an annuity contract entered into before August 14, 1982, dividends allocable to that investment are includable as dividends on a contract entered into after August 13, 1982. IRC Sec. 72(e)(5). Dividends received under an annuity contract with income allocable to earnings on pre-August 14, 1982 and post-August 13, 1982 investments are allocable first to investments made prior to August 14, 1982, then to income accumulated with respect to such pre-August 14, 1982 investments, then to income accumulated with respect to investments made after August 13, 1982 and finally to investments made after August 13, 1982. Rev. Rul. 85-159, 1985-2 CB 29.

Dividends received after the annuity starting date (see Q 10) are included in gross income regardless of when the contract was entered into or when any investment was made. IRC Sec. 72(e)(2)(A).

A special exception applies to annuity contracts purchased by a qualified pension, profit-sharing or stock bonus plan, an individual retirement account or annuity, or a special plan of a life insurance company for its employees, or purchased as an IRC Section 403(b) tax sheltered annuity. (See Q 427.)

See Q 4 for possible penalty tax on taxable dividends allocable to investment in the contract after August 13, 1982. *ASRS, Sec. 52, ¶200.1.*

ANNUITIES

Q 7

6. What is the tax treatment of dividends where annuity values are paid in installments or as a life income?

Only dividends that were *excludable* from gross income are subtracted from gross premiums to determine the net premium cost used in determining the investment in the contract for purposes of the exclusion ratio. If any excludable accumulated dividends are applied to increase the size of the income payments, they are not subtracted from gross premium but are included in investment in the contract. Any accumulated dividends and interest previously includable in income applied to increase the size of income payments are added to gross premium to determine the investment in the contract. *ASRS, Sec. 52, ¶200.4.*

AMOUNTS RECEIVED AS AN ANNUITY: FIXED ANNUITIES

Basic Rule

7. What is the basic rule for taxing annuity payments?

The basic rule is designed to return the purchaser's investment in equal tax-free amounts over the payment period, and to tax the balance of the amounts received. Each payment, therefore, is part nontaxable return of cost and part taxable income. Any excess interest (dividends) added to the guaranteed payments is reportable as income for the year received.

An *exclusion ratio* (which may be expressed as a fraction or as a percentage) must be determined for the contract. This exclusion ratio is applied to each annuity payment to find the portion of the payment that is excludable from gross income; the balance of the guaranteed annuity payment is includable in gross income for the year received. IRC Sec. 72(b)(1).

The exclusion ratio of an individual whose annuity starting date (see Q 10) is *after December 31, 1986*, applies to payments received until the payment in which the investment in the contract is fully recovered. In that payment, the amount excludable is limited to the balance of the unrecovered investment. Payments received thereafter are fully includable in income. IRC Sec. 72(b)(2). The exclusion ratio as originally determined at an annuity starting date *before January 1, 1987* applies to all payments received throughout the entire payment period, even if the annuitant has recovered his investment. Thus, it is possible for a long-lived annuitant to receive tax-free amounts which in the aggregate exceed his investment in the contract.

The exclusion ratio for a particular contract is the ratio that the total *investment in the contract* (see Q 8) bears to the total *expected return* (see Q 9) under the contract. By dividing the investment in the contract by the expected return, the exclusion ratio can be expressed as a percentage (which the regulations indicate should be rounded to the nearest tenth of a percent). Treas. Reg. §1.72-4(a)(2). For example, assuming that the investment in the contract is $12,650 and expected return is $16,000, the exclusion ratio is $12,650/$16,000, or 79.1% (79.06 rounded to the nearest tenth of a percent). If the monthly payment is $100, the portion to be excluded from gross income is $79.10 (79.1% of $100), and the balance of the payment is included in the gross income. If 12 such monthly payments are received during the taxable year, the total amount to be excluded for the year is $949.20 (12 × $79.10), and the amount to be included is $250.80 ($1,200 − $949.20). Excess interest, if any, must also be included.

2006 Tax Facts on Insurance & Employee Benefits

If the investment in the contract equals or exceeds the expected return, the full amount of each payment is received tax-free. Treas. Reg. §1.72-4(d)(2). However, if the annuity starting date is after December 31, 1986, the excludable amount is limited to the investment in the contract; thereafter, any payments are fully includable in income. IRC Sec. 72(b)(2).

There are a few circumstances that may require the computation of a new exclusion ratio for the contract (see "Withdrawals," Q 20; "Variable annuities," Q 24; and "Sale of contract," Q 29).

For application of the basic annuity rule to various types of fixed annuity payments, see Q 11 to Q 19; for variable annuity payments, see Q 21 to Q 24. If an annuity contract is owned by a nonnatural person, see Q 2. *ASRS, Sec. 52, ¶310.*

8. How do you determine the investment in the contract for purposes of the annuity rules?

Generally speaking, the *investment in the contract* is the gross premium cost or other consideration paid for the contract reduced by amounts previously received under the contract to the extent they were excludable from income. IRC Sec. 72(c).

Premium Cost

Unless the contract has been purchased from a previous owner, the "investment in the contract" is normally premium cost. It is not equal to the policy's cash value. *Stoddard v. Comm.*, TC Memo 1993-400. To arrive at the premium cost, adjustments must usually be made to gross premium cost.

Extra premiums paid for supplementary benefits such as double indemnity, waiver of premiums, and disability income, must be excluded from premium cost. Rev. Rul. 55-349, 1955-1 CB 232; *Est. of Wong Wing Non v. Comm.*, 18 TC 205 (1952). (But see *Moseley v. Comm.*, 72 TC 183 (1979), where life insurance policy premium payments paid into a special reserve account were added to the aggregate premiums for purposes of calculating taxable income when a lifetime distribution was made.) Further, it might seem that premiums waived on account of disability should be treated as part of the premium cost. However, in the only case on the subject, a case dealing with the computation of gain on a matured endowment, the court held that waived premiums could not be included in the taxpayer's cost basis. The court refused to accept the view of the taxpayer that the waived premiums had been constructively received as a tax-free disability benefit and then applied to the payment of premiums. Instead, the court treated as the tax-free disability benefit a portion of the proceeds—the difference between the amount of premiums actually paid and the face amount of the endowment. *Est. of Wong Wing Non*, supra.

Investment in the contract is increased by any amount of a policy loan that was includable in income as an amount received under the contract. IRC Sec. 72(e)(4). See Q 3. Any unrepaid policy loans must be subtracted from gross premiums in determining the investment in the contract for purposes of the exclusion ratio. Treas. Reg. §1.72-6.

If premiums were deposited in advance and discounted, only the amount actually paid is includable in premium cost. However, any increment in the advance premium

ANNUITIES

Q 8

deposit fund that has been reported as taxable income may be added to the discounted premiums in determining cost. Rev. Rul. 65-199, 1965-2 CB 20.

Where the contract is a cash value policy that has provided life insurance protection, premium cost includes the portion of the premiums that has been paid for pure insurance protection (see Q 264).

Where money has been borrowed to pay premiums, interest paid on the loan cannot be included in the cost of the contract. *Chapin v. McGowan*, 271 F.2d 856 (2d Cir. 1959).

In the case of a participating contract, dividends must be taken into account as follows:

If dividends have been received in cash or used to reduce premiums, the aggregate amount of such dividends received or credited before the annuity payments commenced must be subtracted from gross premiums to the extent the dividends were excludable from gross income (see Q 3, Q 249). Also, any dividends that have been applied against principal or interest on policy loans must be subtracted but only to the extent they were excludable from gross income. Treas. Reg. §1.72-6. (Excludable dividends are considered as a partial refund of premiums and therefore as a reduction in the cost of the contract.)

But if excludable dividends have been left on deposit with the insurance company to accumulate at interest, and the dividends and interest are used to produce larger annuity payments, such dividends are not subtracted from gross premiums (they are part of the cost of the larger payments). In this situation, *gross* premiums plus accumulated interest constitute the cost of the contract. (The interest is included as additional cost since it has already been taxed to the policyholder as it was credited from year to year—see "Dividends.") Likewise, any terminal dividend that is applied to increase the annuity payments should not be subtracted from gross premium cost.

Similarly, where dividends have been applied to purchase paid-up additional insurance, and the annuity payments include income from the paid-up additions, *gross* premiums are used as the cost of the contract. (In effect, the dividends constitute the cost of the income from the paid-up additions.)

Cost Other Than Premium Cost

However, the *investment in the contract* is not always premium cost. For example, it is the maturity value or cash surrender value of the contract if such value has been constructively received by the policyholder (see Q 34, Q 265). If the contract has been purchased from a previous owner, the investment in the contract is the consideration paid by the purchaser (see Q 29, Q 262). Also, special rules apply in computing the investment in the contract with respect to employee annuities—that is, annuities on which an employer has paid all or part of the premiums (see Q 113, Q 435, Q 490).

Adjustment for Refund or Period-Certain Guarantee

If the annuity is a life annuity with a refund or period-certain guarantee, a special adjustment must be made to the investment in the contract (whether premium cost or other cost). The value of the refund or period-certain guarantee (as determined by

2006 Tax Facts on Insurance & Employee Benefits

use of a prescribed annuity table, Table III or Table VII, or a formula, depending on when the investment in the contract was made, see Appendix A) must be subtracted from the investment in the contract. It is this *adjusted* investment in the contract that is used in the exclusion ratio (see Q 11, Q 14). IRC Sec. 72(c)(2); Treas. Reg. §1.72-7. *ASRS, Sec. 52, ¶310.2.*

9. How do you compute expected return under the annuity rules?

Generally speaking, expected return is the total amount that the annuitant (or annuitants) can expect to receive under the contract.

If payments are for a fixed period or a fixed amount with no life expectancy involved, expected return is the sum of the guaranteed payments (see Q 19). IRC Sec. 72(c)(3)(B); Treas. Reg. §1.72-5(c).

If payments are to continue for a life or lives, expected return is arrived at by multiplying the sum of one year's annuity payments by the life expectancy of the measuring life or lives. The life expectancy multiple or multiples must be taken from the Annuity Tables prescribed by the IRS. IRC Sec. 72(c)(3). (See Appendix A for IRS Annuity Tables.)

Generally, gender-based Tables I - IV are to be used if the investment in the contract does not include a post-June 30, 1986 investment. Unisex Tables V - VIII are to be used if the investment in the contract includes a post-June 30, 1986 investment. However, transitional rules permit an irrevocable election to use the unisex tables even where there is no post-June 1986 investment and, if investment in the contract includes both a pre-July 1986 investment and a post-June 1986 investment, an election may be made in some situations to make separate computations with respect to each portion of the aggregate investment in the contract using with respect to each portion the tables applicable to it. Treas. Reg. §1.72-9. See Appendix A for details.

The life expectancy for a single life is found in Table I or in Table V, whichever is applicable. See Q 11. The life expectancy multiples for joint and survivor annuities are taken from Tables II and IIA or Tables VI and VIA, whichever are applicable. See Q 13 to Q 16. Treas. Regs. §§1.72-5(a), 1.72-5(b).

The Annuity Tables are entered with the age of the measuring life as of his or her birthday nearest the *annuity starting date* (see Q 10). The multiples in the Annuity Tables are based on monthly payments. Consequently, where the annuity payments are to be received quarterly, semi-annually or annually, the multiples from Tables I, II, and IIA or, as applicable, Tables V, VI, and VIA must be adjusted. This adjustment is made by use of the Frequency of Payment Adjustment Table (Appendix A). No adjustment is required if the payments are monthly. *ASRS, Sec. 52, ¶310.3.*

10. What is the annuity starting date?

The exclusion ratio for taxing annuity payments under a particular contract is determined as of the annuity starting date. This is the "first day of the first period for which an amount is received as an annuity." IRC Sec. 72(c)(4); Treas. Reg. §1.72-4(b). For example, suppose that a person purchases an immediate annuity on July 1 providing for monthly payments beginning August 1. His annuity starting date is July 1 (the first

ANNUITIES

Q 11

payment is for the one-month period beginning July 1st). Payments under settlement options usually commence immediately rather than at the end of the month or other payment period; hence the annuity starting date is the date of the first payment. *ASRS*, Sec. 52, ¶310.1.

Life Annuity: Single

11. How do you compute the excludable portion of payments under a single life annuity?

Following are the steps to be taken in applying the basic annuity rule:

(1) Determine the *investment in the contract* (see Q 8).

(2) Find the life expectancy multiple in Table I or V, whichever is applicable for a person of annuitant's age (and sex, if applicable). (See Appendix A). Multiply the sum of one year's guaranteed annuity payments by the applicable Table I or Table V multiple. This is the *expected return* under the contract.

(3) Divide the *investment in the contract* by the *expected return* under the contract, carrying the quotient to 3 decimal places. This is the exclusion ratio expressed as a percentage (exclusion percentage).

(4) Apply the exclusion percentage to the annuity payment. The result is the portion of the payment that is excludable from gross income. The balance of the payment must be included in gross income. If the annuity starting date is after December 31, 1986, the exclusion percentage applies to payments received only until the investment in the contract is recovered. However, if the annuity starting date was before January 1, 1987, the same exclusion percentage will apply to all payments received throughout the annuitant's lifetime. IRC Sec. 72(b)(2).

Example 1. On October 1, 2005, Mr. Brown purchased an immediate nonrefund annuity that will pay him $125 a month ($1,500 a year) for life, beginning November 1, 2005. He paid $16,000 for the contract. Mr. Brown's age on his birthday nearest the annuity starting date (October 1st) was 68. According to Table V (which he uses because his investment in the contract is post-June 1986), his life expectancy is 17.6 years. Consequently, the expected return under the contract is $26,400 (12 × $125 × 17.6). And the exclusion percentage for the annuity payments is 60.6% ($16,000 ÷ $26,400). Since Mr. Brown received 2 monthly payments in 2005 (a total of $250), he will exclude $151.50 (60.6% of $250) from his gross income for 2005, and he must include $98.50 ($250 - $151.50). Mr. Brown will exclude the amounts so determined for 17.6 years. In 2005, he could exclude $151.50; each year thereafter through 2022, he could exclude $909, for a total exclusion of $15,604.50 ($151.50 excluded in 2005 and $15,453 excluded over the next 17 years). In 2023, he could exclude only $395.50 ($16,000 - $15,604.50). In 2023, he would include in his income $1,104.50 ($1,500 - $395.50) and $1,500 in 2024 and in each year thereafter.

Example 2. If Mr. Brown purchased the contract illustrated above on October 1, 1986 (so that it had an annuity starting date before January 1, 1987), he would exclude $151.50 (60.6% of $250) from his 1986 gross income and would include $98.50 ($250 - $151.50). For each succeeding tax year in which he receives 12 monthly payments (even if he outlives his life expectancy of 17.6 years), he will exclude $909 (60.6% of $1,500), and he will include $591 ($1,500 - $909).

Refund or Period-Certain Guarantee

The computation above is for a straight life annuity (without refund or period-certain guarantee). The exclusion ratio for a single life refund or period-certain guarantee

2006 Tax Facts on Insurance & Employee Benefits

Q 11   FEDERAL INCOME TAX

is determined in the same way, but the *investment in the contract* must first be adjusted by subtracting the value of the refund or period-certain guarantee. The value of the refund or period-certain guarantee is computed by the following steps.

(1) Determine the *duration of the guaranteed amount* (number of years necessary for the total guaranteed return to be fully paid). In the case of a period-certain life annuity, the duration of the guaranteed amount, in years, is known (e.g., 10, 15, or 20 "years certain"). To find the duration of the guaranteed amount, in years, for a cash or installment refund life annuity, divide the total guaranteed amount by the amount of one year's annuity payments, and round the quotient to the nearest whole number of years.

(2) Find the factor in Table III or VII (whichever is applicable, depending on when the investment is made in the contract) under the whole number of years (as determined above) and the age and (if applicable) the sex of the annuitant (see Appendix A). This Table III or Table VII factor is the *percentage value* of the refund or period-certain guarantee.

(3) Apply the applicable Table III or Table VII percentage to the SMALLER of (a) the *investment in the contract*, or (b) the *total guaranteed return* under the contract. The result is the *present value* of the refund or period-certain guarantee.

(4) Subtract the present value of the refund or period-certain guarantee from the *investment in the contract*. The remainder is the *adjusted* investment in the contract to be used in the exclusion ratio. Treas. Reg. §1.72-7(b).

Example 3. On January 1, 2005, a husband, age 65, purchased for $21,053 an immediate installment refund annuity which pays $100 a month for life. The contract provides that in the event the husband does not live long enough to recover the full purchase price, payments will be made to his wife until the total payments under the contract equal the purchase price. The investment in the contract is adjusted for the purpose of determining the exclusion ratio as follows:

Unadjusted investment in the contract	$ 21,053
Amount to be received annually	$ 1,200
Duration of guaranteed amount ($21,053 ÷ $1,200)	17.5 yrs.
Rounded to nearest whole number of years	18
Percentage value of guaranteed refund (Table VII for age 65 and 18 years)	15%
Value of refund feature rounded to nearest dollar (15% of $21,053)	$ 3,158
Adjusted investment in the contract ($21,053 - $3,158)	$ 17,895

Example 4. Assume the contract in Example 3 was purchased as a deferred annuity and the pre-July 1986 investment in the contract is $10,000 and the post-June 1986 investment in the contract is $11,053. If the annuitant elects (as explained in Appendix A) to compute a separate exclusion percentage for the pre-July 1986 and the post-June 1986 amounts, separate computations must be performed to determine the adjusted investment in the contract. The pre-July 1986 investment in the contract and the post-June 1986 investment in the contract are adjusted for the purpose of determining the exclusion ratios in the following manner:

Pre-July 1986 adjustment:

Unadjusted investment in the contract	$10,000
Allocable part of amount to be received annually (($10,000 ÷ $21,053) x $1,200)	$ 570
Duration of guaranteed amount ($10,000 ÷ $570)	17.5 yrs.
Rounded to nearest whole number of years	18
Percentage in Table III for age 65 and 18 years	30%
Present value of refund feature rounded to nearest dollar (30% of $10,000)	$ 3,000
Adjusted pre-July 1986 investment in the contract ($10,000 - $3,000)	$ 7,000

2006 Tax Facts on Insurance & Employee Benefits

ANNUITIES   Q 11

Post-June 1986 adjustment:	
Unadjusted investment in the contract	$11,053
Allocable part of amount to be received annually	
(($11,053 ÷ $21,053) x $1,200)	$ 630
Duration of guaranteed amount ($11,053 ÷ $630)	17.5 yrs.
Rounded to nearest whole number of years	18
Percentage in Table VII for age 65 and 18 years	15%
Present value of refund feature rounded to nearest dollar (15% of $11,053)	$ 1,658
Adjusted post-June 1986 investment in the contract ($11,053 - $1,658)	$ 9,395

Once the investment in the contract has been adjusted by subtracting the value of the refund or period-certain guarantee, an exclusion ratio is determined in the same way as for a straight life annuity. Expected return is computed; then the *adjusted* investment in the contract is divided by expected return. Taking the two examples above, the exclusion ratio for each contract is determined as follows.

Example (3) above.

Investment in the contract (adjusted for refund guarantee)	$17,895
One year's guaranteed annuity payments (12 x $100)	$ 1,200
Life expectancy from Table V, age 65	20 yrs.
Expected return (20 x $1,200)	$24,000
Exclusion ratio ($17,895 ÷ $24,000)	74.6%
Amount excludable from gross income each year in which 12 payments are received (74.6% of $1,200)*	$895.20
Amount includable in gross income ($1,200 - $895.20)*	$304.80

* Since the annuity starting date is after December 31, 1986, the total amount excludable is limited to the investment in the contract; after that has been recovered, the remaining amounts received are includable in income. However, if the annuity has a refund or guarantee feature, the value of the refund or guarantee feature is not subtracted when calculating the unrecovered investment. IRC Sec. 72(b)(4).

Example (4) above.

Pre-July 1986 investment in the contract (adjusted for period certain guarantee)	$ 7,000
One year's guaranteed annuity payments (12 x $100)	$ 1,200
Life expectancy from Table I, male age 65	15 yrs.
Expected return (15 x $1,200)	$18,000
Exclusion ratio ($7,000 ÷ $18,000)	38.9%
Post-June 1986 investment in the contract (adjusted for period certain guarantee)	$ 9,395
One year's guaranteed annuity payments (12 x $100)	$ 1,200
Life expectancy from Table V, age 65	20 yrs.
Expected return (20 x $1,200)	$24,000
Exclusion ratio ($9,395 ÷ $24,000)	39.1%
Sum of pre-July and post-June 1986 ratios	78%
Amount excludable from gross income each year in which twelve payments are received (78% of $1,200)*	$ 936
Amount includable in gross income ($1,200 - 936)*	$ 264

* Since the annuity starting date is after December 31, 1986, the total amount excludable is limited to the investment in the contract; after that has been recovered, the remaining amounts received are includable in income.

ASRS, Sec. 52, ¶320.2.

2006 Tax Facts on Insurance & Employee Benefits

Life Annuity: Temporary

12. How is a temporary life annuity taxed?

A temporary life annuity is one that provides for fixed payments until the death of the annuitant or until the expiration of a specified number of years, whichever occurs earlier. The basic annuity rule (Q 7) applies. That is, the investment in the contract is divided by the expected return under the contract to find the portion of each payment that can be excluded from gross income (the exclusion ratio). However, expected return is determined by multiplying one year's annuity payments by the multiple in Table IV or Table VIII (whichever is applicable, as explained in Appendix A) of the IRS Annuity Tables for the annuitant's age (as of the annuity starting date) and sex (if applicable) and the whole number of years in the specified period. Treas. Reg. §1.72-5(a)(3). Tables IV and VIII are not included in this book but can be found in §1.72-9 of the Treasury Regulations.

A penalty tax may be imposed on payments received under the contract unless one of the exceptions listed in Q 4 is met. *ASRS, Sec. 52, ¶320.3.*

Life Annuity: Joint and Survivor

13. How do you find the excludable portion of payments under a joint and survivor annuity that continues the same income to the survivor as is payable while both annuitants are alive?

The basic annuity rule (Q 7) applies: the *investment in the contract* is divided by the expected return under the contract to find the portion of each payment that can be excluded from gross income (the exclusion ratio). But *expected return* must be computed by using a life expectancy multiple from Table II or Table VI of the IRS Annuity Tables (see Appendix A). With respect to an annuity with a starting date after December 31, 1986, the exclusion ratio applies to payments received until the investment in the contract is recovered. However, if the annuity starting date was before January 1, 1987, the exclusion ratio as originally computed applies to all payments received under the contract: to those received by the survivor as well as to those received while both annuitants are alive. IRC Sec. 72(b)(2). The steps in the computation of the exclusion ratio are as follows:

(1) Determine the *investment in the contract* (see Q 8).

(2) Find the joint and survivor life expectancy multiple in Table II or Table VI (depending on when the investment in the contract was made—see Appendix A) under the sexes (if applicable) and ages of the annuitants. Multiply one year's guaranteed annuity payments by the applicable Table II or Table VI multiple. This is the *expected return* under the contract.

(3) Divide the *investment in the contract* by the *expected return*, carrying the quotient to three decimal places. This is the *exclusion ratio* expressed as a percentage (the exclusion percentage).

(4) Apply the exclusion percentage to the annuity payment. The result is the portion of the payment that is excludable from gross income. The balance of the payment must be included in gross income.

ANNUITIES

Q 14

Example. After June 30, 1986, Mr. and Mrs. Black purchase an immediate joint and survivor annuity. The annuity will provide payments of $100 a month while both are alive and until the death of the survivor. Mr. Black's age on his birthday nearest the annuity starting date is 65; Mrs. Black's, 63. The single premium is $22,000.

Investment in the contract	$22,000
One year's annuity payments (12 x $100)	$ 1,200
Joint and survivor life expectancy multiple from Table VI (ages 65, 63)	26
Expected return (26 x $1,200)	$31,200
Exclusion ratio ($22,000 ÷ $31,200)	70.5%
Amount excludable from gross income each year in which 12 payments are received (70.5% of $1,200)*	$ 846
Amount includable in gross income each year ($1,200 - $846)*	$ 354

* If the annuity starting date is after December 31, 1986, the total amount excludable is limited to the investment in the contract; after that has been recovered, the remaining amounts received are includable in income.

ASRS, Sec. 52, ¶320.6.

14. How do you find the excludable portion of payments under a level payment joint and survivor annuity with refund or period certain guarantee?

The exclusion ratio is determined as in Q 13, except that the *investment in the contract* must first be adjusted by subtracting the value of the refund or period certain guarantee. This value is determined by the following steps.

Investment in the Contract Before July 1986

If Table II is used to determine the expected return for pre-July 1986 investment, the following method is used to determine the adjustment to the investment in the contract. Treas. Reg. §1.72-7(c)(2). If Table VI is used to determine expected return for pre-July 1986 investment, investment in the contract is adjusted using the formula for post-July 1986 investment (see subhead below). Treas. Reg. §1.72-7(c)(1).

(1) Determine the *duration of the guaranteed amount* (the number of years necessary for the guaranteed amount to be fully paid). In the case of a period certain and life annuity, this is the number of years in the guaranteed period (e.g., 10, 15, or 20 "years certain"). To find the duration of the guaranteed amount, in years, for a cash or installment refund annuity, divide the total amount guaranteed under the contract by the amount of one year's annuity payments. Round the quotient to the nearest whole number of years.

(2) If the annuitants are not of the same sex, substitute for the female a male five years younger (or for the male, a female five years older). Then find the refund percentage factors in Table III under the whole number of years, as determined in (1), and the age of each annuitant of the same sex. (For Table III factors, see Appendix A). Add these two Table III factors.

(3) Using ages of the same sex, as adjusted in (2), add to the age of the older annuitant the number of years indicated in the table below opposite the number of years by which the ages differ.

2006 Tax Facts on Insurance & Employee Benefits

Q 14   FEDERAL INCOME TAX

Number of years difference in age (two male annuitants or two female annuitants)	older age in years
0 to 1, inclusive	9
2 to 3, inclusive	8
4 to 5, inclusive	7
6 to 8, inclusive	6
9 to 11, inclusive	5
12 to 15, inclusive	4
16 to 20, inclusive	3
21 to 27, inclusive	2
28 to 42, inclusive	1
Over 42	0

(4) Find the refund percentage factor in Table III under the whole number of years as determined in (1) and the age of the older annuitant as adjusted in (3).

(5) Subtract the Table III factor found in (4) from the sum of the Table III factors found in (2). The balance, if any, is the percentage value of the refund or period certain guarantee. If there is no balance, no adjustment in the *investment in the contract* need be made for the value of the refund or period certain guarantee. If there is a balance, continue as follows:

(6) Apply the percentage value of the refund or period certain guarantee as determined in (5) to the SMALLER of: (a) the investment in the contract (see Q 8), or (b) the total guaranteed return under the contract. The result is the dollar value of the refund or period certain guarantee.

(7) Subtract the dollar value of the refund or period certain guarantee from the investment in the contract. The remainder is the *adjusted* investment in the contract to be used in determining the exclusion ratio.

Example. Mr. and Mrs. Green purchase an immediate joint and survivor annuity that will pay $200 a month for 10 years certain and as long thereafter as either is alive. Mr. Green is 70 years old as of his birthday nearest the annuity starting date. Mrs. Green is 65. The single premium is $35,000. The total guaranteed amount is $24,000.

Investment in the contract (unadjusted)	$35,000
Percentage factor from Table III for male, age 70, and 10-year guarantee	21%
Percentage factor from Table III for male, age 60, and 10-year guarantee	11%
Sum of percentage refund factors	32%
Difference in years of age between two males, age 70 and 60	10
Addition in years to older age (Table above)	5
Percentage refund factor from Table III for male, age 75 and 10-year guarantee	29%
Difference between percentages	3%
Dollar value of period certain guarantee (3% of $24,000)	720
Adjusted investment in the contract	$34,280
Table II multiple for male, age 70, and female, age 65	20.7
Expected return (20.7 x $2,400)	$49,680
Exclusion ratio ($34,280 ÷ $49,680)	69%
Excludable from gross income each year (69% of $2,400)*	$ 1,656
Includible in gross income each year ($2,400 - $1,656)*	$ 744

* If the annuity starting date is after December 31, 1986, the total amount excludable is limited to the investment in the contract; after that has been recovered, the remaining amounts received are includable in income. However, if the annuity has a refund or guarantee feature, the value of the refund or guarantee feature is not subtracted when calculating the unrecovered investment. IRC Sec. 72(b)(4).

2006 Tax Facts on Insurance & Employee Benefits

ANNUITIES

Q 15

Investment in the Contract After June 1986

Where investment in the contract has been made after June 30, 1986, the regulations provide a complex formula for determining the percentage factor that was developed for pre-July 1986 investment using the first five steps above. That percentage factor is then applied as explained in steps 6 and 7 above. Treas. Reg. §1.72-7(c)(1)(i). The IRS will determine the amount of the adjustment on request. Treas. Reg. §1.72-7(c)(4). *ASRS, Sec. 52, ¶320.7.*

15. How do you compute the tax exempt portion of payments under a joint and survivor annuity where the size of the payments will increase or decrease after the first death?

Some joint and survivor annuities provide that the size of the annuity payment will decrease after the first death–regardless of which annuitant dies first (e.g., joint and ½ or joint and 2/3 survivor annuity). Sometimes, but rarely, the joint and survivor annuity will provide for increased payments after the first death. The exclusion ratio is determined in the usual way, by dividing the investment in the contract by the expected return under the contract (see Q 7). However, expected return must be computed in the following manner. Treas. Reg. §1.72-5(b)(5).

(1) Find the joint and survivor multiple in Table II or Table VI (depending on when the investment in the contract was made, as explained in Appendix A) under both annuitants' ages and, if applicable, appropriate sexes. (For Table II or Table VI factor, see Appendix A.) Multiply the amount of one year's annuity payments *to the survivor* by this Table II or Table VI multiple.

(2) Find the joint life multiple in Table IIA or Table VIA (depending on when the investment in the contract was made) under both annuitants' ages and, if applicable, appropriate sexes. (For Table IIA or VIA factor, see Appendix A.) Determine the *difference* between the amount of one year's annuity payments before the first death and the amount of one year's annuity payments after the first death. Multiply this difference in amount by the multiple from Table IIA or VIA, whichever is applicable.

(3) If payments are to be *smaller* after the first death, expected return is the *sum* of (1) and (2). If payments are to be *larger* after the first death, expected return is the *difference* between (1) and (2).

After computing expected return, determine the exclusion ratio under the basic annuity rule: divide the investment in the contract (see Q 8) by the expected return under the contract (as computed above). This same exclusion ratio is applied to payments received before the first death and to payments received by the survivor. However, with respect to an annuity having a starting date after December 31, 1986, the exclusion ratio is applied to payments only until the investment in the contract is recovered. IRC Sec. 72(b)(2).

Example 1. After July 30, 1986, Mr. and Mrs. Brown buy an immediate joint and survivor annuity which will provide monthly payments of $117 ($1,404 a year) for as long as both live, and monthly payments of $78 ($936 a year) to the survivor. As of the annuity starting date he is 65 years old; she is 63. The expected return is computed as follows.

2006 Tax Facts on Insurance & Employee Benefits

Joint and survivor multiple from Table VI (ages 65,63)	26	
Portion of expected return (26 x $936)		$24,336.00
Joint life multiple from Table VIA (ages 65, 63)	15.6	
Difference between annual annuity payment before the first death and annual annuity payment to the survivor ($1,404 - $936)	$468	
Portion of expected return (15.6 x $468)		$ 7,300.80
Expected return		$31,636.80

Assuming that Mr. Brown paid $22,000 for the contract, the exclusion ratio is 69.5% ($22,000 ÷ $31,636.80). During their joint lives the portion of each monthly payment to be excluded from gross income is $81.31 (69.5% of $117), or $975.72 a year. The portion to be included is $35.69 ($117 - $81.31), or $428.28 a year. After the first death, the portion of each monthly payment to be excluded from gross income will be $54.21 (69.5% of $78), or $650.52 a year. And $23.79 of each payment ($78 - $54.21), or $285.48 a year, will be included. If the annuity starting date is after December 31, 1986, the total amount excludable is limited to the investment in the contract. Thus, if Mr. Brown lives for 23 years, he may exclude $81.31 from each payment for 22 years ((12 × 22) × $81.31 = $21,465.84). In the 23rd year he may exclude $534.16 ($22,000 - $21,465.84) or $81.31 from each of the first six payments, but only $46.30 from the seventh. The balance is entirely includable in his income, and on his death, his widow must include the full amount of each payment in income.

Example 2. Assume that in the example above, there is a pre-July 1986 investment in the contract of $12,000 and a post-June 1986 investment in the contract of $10,000. Mr. Brown elects to calculate the exclusion percentage for each portion. The pre-July exclusion ratio would be 44.6% ($12,000 ÷ $26,910–the expected return on the contract determined by using Tables II and IIA and the age and sex of both annuitants). The post-June 1986 exclusion ratio is $10,000 ÷ $31,636.80 or 31.6%. The amount excludable from each monthly payment while both are alive would be $89.15 (44.6% of $117 plus 31.6% of $117) and the remaining $27.85 would be included in gross income. If the annuity starting date is after December 31, 1986, the total amount excludable is limited to the investment in the contract.

ASRS, Sec. 52, ¶320.8.

16. How is the tax exempt portion of payments determined for a joint and survivor annuity where the size of the payments will be reduced only if a specified annuitant dies first?

For example, the settlement may provide payments of a stipulated amount for so long as the husband lives, but payments of a reduced amount to his wife if she survives him. But if she dies first, payments to the husband will remain the same. The exclusion ratio for such an annuity is determined in the usual way, by dividing the *investment in the contract* by the *expected return* under the contract (see Q 7). However, expected return must be computed in the following manner (Treas. Reg. §1.72-5(b)(2)).

(1) Find the joint and survivor multiple in Table II or VI (whichever is applicable, depending on when the investment in the contract was made, as explained in Appendix A) under the ages and (if applicable) sexes of the annuitants. Then find the single life expectancy multiple in Table I or V, whichever is applicable, under the age and (if applicable) the sex of the first (specified) annuitant. (See Appendix A for Annuity Tables.) Subtract the applicable Table I or Table V multiple from the applicable Table II or Table VI multiple, and multiply the amount payable annually to the second annuitant (the reduced payment) by the *difference* between the multiples.

(2) Multiply the amount payable annually to the *first* annuitant by the Table I or Table V multiple (whichever is applicable).

(3) Add the results of (1) and (2). This is the *expected return* under the contract.

ANNUITIES Q 17

Then proceed in the usual manner: divide the investment in the contract (see Q 8) by the expected return under the contract (as computed above).

Example. After June 30, 1986, a husband and wife purchase a joint and survivor annuity providing payments of $100 a month for his life and, after his death, payments to her of $50 a month for the remainder of her life. As of the annuity starting date he is 70 years old and she is 67.

Multiple from Table VI (ages 70, 67)	22
Multiple from Table V (age 70)	16
Difference (multiple applicable to second annuitant)	6
Portion of expected return, second annuitant (6 x $600)	$ 3,600
Portion of expected return, first annuitant (16 x $1,200)	19,200
Expected return under the contract	$22,800

Assuming that the investment in the contract is $14,310, the exclusion ratio is 62.8% ($14,310 ÷ $22,800). While the husband lives, $62.80 of each monthly payment (62.8% of $100) is excluded from gross income, and the remaining $37.20 of each payment must be included in gross income. After the husband's death, the surviving wife will exclude $31.40 of each payment (62.8% of $50), and the remaining $18.60 of each payment will be includable in her gross income. If the annuity starting date is after December 31, 1986, the total amount excludable is limited to the investment in the contract. Thus, if the husband lives 15 years and receives 180 payments, the unrecovered investment in the contract at his death is $3,006 ($14,310 - (180 × $62.80)). The surviving wife can exclude $31.40 for 95 payments, and $23 from the 96th payment ($3,006 - (95 × 31.40) = $23). She may exclude nothing thereafter.

ASRS, Sec. 52, ¶320.9.

17. What are the income tax consequences to the surviving annuitant under a joint and survivor annuity?

The survivor continues to exclude from gross income the same percentage of each payment that was excludable before the first annuitant's death. With respect to annuities having a starting date after December 31, 1986, the total exclusion by the first annuitant and the survivor may not exceed the investment in the contract. See Q 13 to Q 16.

In addition, if the value of the survivor annuity was subject to estate tax, the survivor may be entitled to an income tax deduction for part of the tax paid. IRC Sec. 691(d). The deduction in most cases will be small. In a general way, it is computed as follows: The portion of the guaranteed annual payment that will be excluded from the survivor's gross income (under the exclusion ratio) is multiplied by the survivor's life expectancy at date of first annuitant's death. The result is subtracted from the estate tax value of the survivor's annuity. The total income tax deduction allowable is the tax attributable to the *remainder* of the value of the survivor's annuity. This total deduction is prorated over the survivor's life expectancy as of the date of the first annuitant's death, and a prorated amount is deductible from the survivor's gross income each year. But no further deduction is allowable after the end of the survivor's life expectancy. The foregoing treatment applies only where the primary annuitant died after 1953. Treas. Reg. §1.691(d)-1.

Planning Point: Joint ownership of non-qualified annuities creates more problems than it solves - including forced distribution at EITHER owner's death. Avoid joint ownership whenever possible. *John L. Olsen, CLU, ChFC, AEP, Olsen Financial Group.*

ASRS, Sec. 52, ¶330.1.

2006 Tax Facts on Insurance & Employee Benefits

Life Annuity: Refund Beneficiary

18. If the annuitant dies before receiving the full amount guaranteed under a refund or period certain life annuity, is the balance of the guaranteed amount taxable income to the refund beneficiary?

The beneficiary will have no taxable income unless the total amount the beneficiary receives when added to amounts that were received tax free by the annuitant (the excludable portion of the annuity payments) exceeds the investment in the contract. In other words, all amounts received by the beneficiary are exempt from tax until the investment in the contract has been recovered tax free; thereafter, receipts (if any) are taxable income. For purposes of calculating the unrecovered investment in the contract, the value of the refund or guarantee feature is not subtracted. IRC Sec. 72(b)(4).

The amount received by the beneficiary is considered paid in full discharge of the obligation under the contract in the nature of a refund of consideration and therefore comes under the cost recovery rule regardless of when the contract was entered into or when investments were made in the contract. IRC Sec. 72(e)(5); Treas. Regs. §§1.72-11(a), 1.72-11(c). This rule applies whether the refund is received in one sum or in installments.

However, if the refund or commuted value of remaining installments certain is applied anew under an annuity option for the beneficiary, the payments will be taxed under the annuity rules. A new exclusion ratio will be determined for the beneficiary. IRC Sec. 72(e)(5)(E); Treas. Regs. §§1.72-11(c), 1.72-11(e).

If the refund beneficiary of an annuitant whose annuity starting date is after July 1, 1986 does not recover the balance of the investment in the contract that was not recovered by the annuitant, he may take a deduction for the unrecovered balance. IRC Sec. 72(b)(3). See Q 27.

Any payment made on or after the death of an annuity holder is not subject to the 10% premature distribution tax. See Q 4. *ASRS, Sec. 52, ¶320.14.*

Fixed Period or Fixed Amount Installments

19. How is the excludable portion of an annuity payment under a fixed period or fixed amount option computed?

The basic annuity rule (Q 7) applies: divide the *investment in the contract* (Q 8) by the *expected return* under the contract to determine the exclusion ratio for the payments. Apply this ratio to each payment to find the portion that is excludable from gross income. The balance of the payment is includable in gross income.

If payments are for a fixed number of years (without regard to life expectancy), *expected return* is the guaranteed amount receivable each year multiplied by the fixed number of years. Treas. Reg. §1.72-5(c).

If payments are for a fixed amount (without regard to life expectancy) *expected return* is the total guaranteed return. Additional payments made after the guaranteed period (due to excess interest) are fully taxable. Treas. Reg. §1.72-5(d).

ANNUITIES   Q 20

To compute the excludable portion of each payment by a short method, divide the investment in the contract by the number of guaranteed payments. The result will never vary more than slightly from the exact computation.

> *Example 1.* The owner of a maturing $25,000 endowment elects to receive the proceeds in equal annual payments of $2,785 for a fixed 10-year period. Assuming that his investment in the contract is $22,500, he may exclude $2,250 ($22,500 ÷ 10) from gross income each year. He must include the balance of amounts received during the year in gross income.

> *Example 2.* The owner of a maturing $25,000 endowment elects to take the proceeds in monthly payments of $200. The company's rate book shows that payments of $200 are guaranteed for 144 months. Assuming that his investment in the contract is $22,500, he can exclude $156.25 ($22,500 ÷ 144) of each payment from gross income, and must include $43.75 ($200 - $156.25). Thus, for a full 12 months' payments, he excludes $1,875 (12 × $156.25) and includes $525 ($2,400 - $1,875). Additional payments received after the 144 month period are fully taxable.

If the payee dies before the guaranteed period expires, his beneficiary will exclude the same portion of each payment as originally computed. Treas. Reg. §1.72-11(c)(2), Ex. 4.

A penalty tax may be imposed on any payments received under the contract unless one of the exceptions listed in Q 4 is met. *ASRS, Sec. 52, ¶ 320.11, 320.12.*

Annuity Reduced by Partial Withdrawal

20. What are the income tax results when an annuitant makes a partial lump sum withdrawal and takes a reduced annuity for the same term or the same payments for a different term?

Reduced annuity for same term. The nontaxable portion of the lump sum withdrawn is an amount that bears the same ratio to the unrecovered investment in the contract as the *reduction* in the annuity payment bears to the original payment. The original exclusion ratio will apply to the reduced payments; that is, the same percentage of each payment will be excludable from gross income. Treas. Reg. §1.72-11(f).

> *Example.* Mr. Gray pays $20,000 for a life annuity paying him $100 a month. At the annuity starting date his life expectancy is 20 years. His total expected return is therefore $24,000 (20 × $1,200), and the exclusion ratio for the payment is 5/6 ($20,000/$24,000). He receives annuity payments for five years (a total of $6,000) and excludes a total of $5,000 ($1,000 a year) from gross income. At the beginning of the next year, Mr. Gray agrees with the insurer to take a reduced annuity of $75 a month and a lump sum cash payment of $4,000. He will continue to exclude 5/6 of each annuity payment from gross income; that is, $62.50 (5/6 of $75). Of the lump sum, he will include $250 in gross income and exclude $3,750, determined as follows:

Investment in the contract..	$20,000
Less amounts previously excluded	5,000
Unrecovered investment	$15,000
Ratio of reduction in payment to original payment ($25/$100)	¼
Lump sum received...	$ 4,000
Less ¼ of unrecovered investment (¼ of $15,000)...	3,750
Portion of lump sum taxable..	$ 250

Same payments for different term. If the annuity contract was purchased before August 14, 1982 (and no additional investment was made after August 13, 1982 in the contract), the lump sum withdrawn is excludable from gross income as "an amount not received as an annuity" that is received before the annuity starting date. Thus, the lump sum is subtracted from the unrecovered premium cost, and the balance used as the investment in the contract. A new exclusion ratio must be computed for the annuity payments. Treas. Reg. §1.72-11(e).

However, if the lump sum withdrawn is allocable to investment in an annuity contract made after August 13, 1982, it would appear there may be a taxable withdrawal of interest if the cash surrender value of the contract exceeds investment in the contract (see Q 3, Q 4) and a new exclusion ratio must be computed, using an investment in the contract reduced by any amount of the lump sum excludable as a return of investment. *ASRS, Sec. 52, ¶330.2.*

ANNUITY RULES: VARIABLE ANNUITIES

21. Is the purchaser of a deferred variable annuity taxed on any income during the accumulation period?

An annuity owner who is a natural person will pay no income tax until he either surrenders the annuity for cash or starts to receive an income under the contract. Amounts received "not as an annuity" prior to the annuity starting date are subject to the rules discussed in Q 3, Q 4.

However, a variable annuity contract will not be treated as an annuity and taxed as explained in this and the following questions (Q 22 to Q 24) *unless* the underlying investments of the segregated asset account are "adequately diversified," according to regulations prescribed by the IRS. IRC Sec. 817(h); Treas. Reg. §1.817-5. See Q 25.

If the owner of the contract is a person other than a natural person (a corporation, for example) see Q 2.

22. How are the payments under a variable annuity taxed?

Both fixed dollar and variable annuity payments are subject to the same basic tax rule: a fixed portion of each annuity payment is excludable from gross income as a tax-free recovery of the purchaser's investment, and the balance is taxable as ordinary income. In the case of a variable annuity however, the excludable portion is not determined by calculating an "exclusion ratio" as it is for a fixed dollar annuity (see Q 7). Since the expected return under a variable annuity is unknown, it is considered to be equal to the investment in the contract. Thus, the excludable portion is determined by dividing the investment in the contract (adjusted for any period-certain or refund guarantee) by the number of years over which it is anticipated the annuity will be paid. Treas. Reg. §1.72-2(b)(3).

If payments are to be made for a fixed number of years without regard to life expectancy, the divisor is the fixed number of years. If payments are to be made for a single life, the divisor is the appropriate life expectancy multiple from Table I or Table V, whichever is applicable (depending on when the investment in the contract was made, as explained in Appendix A) of the IRS annuity tables (Appendix A). If payments are to be made on a joint and survivor basis, based on the same number of units throughout both lifetimes, the divisor is the appropriate joint and survivor multiple from Table II or Table VI, whichever is applicable (depending on when the investment in the contract is made—see Appendix A). (The regulations explain the method for computing the exclusion where the number of units is to be reduced after the first

ANNUITIES   Q 23

death.) The life expectancy multiple need not be adjusted if payments are monthly. But if they are to be made less frequently (annually, semi-annually, quarterly), the multiple must be adjusted (see Frequency of Payment Adjustment Table, Appendix A). Treas. Regs. §§1.72-2(b)(3), 1.72-4(d).

The amount so determined may be excluded from gross income each year for as long as the payments are received if the annuity starting date is before January 1, 1987 (even after the annuitant has outlived his life expectancy and recovered his cost tax-free). In the case of an annuity starting date after 1986, the amount determined may be excluded from gross income only until the investment in the contract is recovered. IRC Sec. 72(b)(2).

Where payments are received for only part of a year (as for the first year if monthly payments commence after January), the exclusion is a pro-rata share of a year's exclusion. Treas. Reg. §1.72-2(b)(3).

If the annuity settlement provides a period-certain or refund guarantee, the investment in the contract must be adjusted before being prorated over the payment period (see Q 23). *ASRS, Sec. 52, ¶320.13.*

23. How is the value of a refund or period-certain guarantee determined under a variable annuity contract?

If the variable annuity settlement provides a refund or period-certain guarantee, the investment in the contract must be reduced by the value of the guarantee before being prorated for the yearly exclusion. Treas. Reg. §1.72-7(d). The value of such a guarantee in connection with a single life annuity is determined as follows:

Find the refund percentage factor in Table III or Table VII (whichever is applicable, depending on the date the investment in the contract was made, as explained in Appendix A) under the age and (if applicable) sex of the annuitant and the number of years in the guaranteed period (see Tables in Appendix A). Where the settlement provides that proceeds from a given number of units will be paid for a period-certain and life thereafter, we already have the number of years in the guaranteed period (e.g., 10, 15, 20 "years certain"). But if the settlement specifies a guaranteed amount, we divide this guaranteed amount by an amount determined by placing payments received during the first taxable year (to the extent that such payments reduce the guaranteed amount) on an annual basis. (Thus, if monthly payments begin in August, the total amount received in the first taxable year is divided by 5, then multiplied by 12.) The quotient is rounded to the nearest whole number of years, and is used in entering Table III or Table VII, as applicable. The appropriate Table III or Table VII multiple is applied to whichever is *smaller*: (a) the investment in the contract, or (b) the product of the payments received in the first taxable year, placed on an annual basis, multiplied by the number of years for which payment of the proceeds of a unit or units is guaranteed. The following illustration is taken from the regulations (Treas. Reg. §1.72-7(d)(2)):

> *Example*: Mr. Brown, a 50-year-old male, purchases for $25,000, a contract which provides for variable monthly payments to be paid to him for his life. The contract also provides that if he should die before receiving payments for 15 years, payments shall continue according to the original formula to his estate or beneficiary until payments have been made for that period. Beginning with the month of September, Mr. Brown receives payments which total $450 for the first taxable year of receipt. This amount, placed on an annual basis, is $1,350 ($450 divided by 4 or $112.50; $112.50 multiplied by 12, or $1,350).

If there is no post-June 1986 investment in the contract, the guaranteed amount is considered to be $20,250 ($1,350 × 15), and the multiple from Table III (for male 50, 15 guaranteed years), nine percent, applied to $20,250 (since this amount is less than the investment in the contract), results in a refund adjustment of $1,822.50. The latter amount, subtracted from the investment in the contract of $25,000, results in an adjusted investment in the contract of $23,177.50. If Mr. Brown dies before receiving payments for 15 years and the remaining payments are made to Mr. Green, his beneficiary, Mr. Green shall exclude the entire amount of such payments from his gross income until the amounts so received by Mr. Green, together with the amounts received by Mr. Brown and excludable from Mr. Brown's gross income, equal or exceed $25,000. Any excess and any payments thereafter received by Mr. Green shall be fully includable in gross income.

Assume the total investment in the contract was made after June 30, 1986. The applicable multiple found in Table VII is three percent. When this is applied to the guaranteed amount of $20,250, it results in a refund adjustment of $607.50. The adjusted investment in the contract is $24,392.50 ($25,000 - $607.50).

ASRS, Sec. 52, ¶320.13.

24. If payments from a variable annuity drop below the excludable amount for any year, is the balance of the exclusion lost?

No. If the amount received in any taxable year is less than the excludable amount as originally determined, the annuitant may elect to redetermine the excludable amount in a succeeding taxable year in which he receives another payment. The aggregate loss in exclusions for the prior year (or years) is divided by the number of years remaining in the fixed period or, in the case of a life annuity, by the annuitant's life expectancy computed as of the first day of the first period for which an amount is received as an annuity in the taxable year of election. The amount so determined is added to the originally determined excludable amount. Treas. Reg. §1.72-4(d)(3).

Example 1: Mr. Brown is a male 65 years old as of his birthday nearest July 1, 1985, the annuity starting date of a contract he purchased for $21,000. There is no investment in the contract after June 30, 1986. The contract provides variable monthly payments for Mr. Brown's life. Since Mr. Brown's life expectancy is 15 years (Table I), he may exclude $1,400 of the annuity payments from his gross income each year ($21,000 ÷ 15). Assume that in each year before 1988, he receives more than $1,400; but in 1988, he receives only $800–$600 less than his allowable exclusion. He may elect, in his return for 1989, to recompute his annual exclusion. Mr. Brown's age, as of his birthday nearest the first period for which he receives an annuity payment in 1989 (the year of election) is 69, and the life expectancy for that age is 12.6. Thus, he may add $47.61 to his previous annual exclusion, and exclude $1,447.61 in 1989 and subsequent years. This additional exclusion is obtained by dividing $600 (the difference between the amount he received in 1988 and his allowable exclusion for that year) by 12.6.

Example 2: Mr. Green purchases a variable annuity contract which provides payments for life. The annuity starting date is June 30, 2004, when Mr. Green is 64 years old. Mr. Green receives a payment of $1,000 on June 30, 2005, but receives no other payment until June 30, 2007. Mr. Green's total investment in the contract is $25,000. Mr. Green's pre-July 1986 investment in the contract is $12,000. Mr. Green may redetermine his excludable amount as above, using the Table V life expectancy. If, instead, he elects to make separate computations for his pre-July 1986 investment and his post June-1986 investment (see Appendix A), his additional excludable amount is determined as follows.

Pre-July 1986 investment in the contract allocable to taxable years 2004 and 2005 ($12,000 ÷ 15.1 [multiple from Table I for a male age 64] = $794.70; $794.40 x 2 years = $1,589.40)	$1,589.40
Less: portion of total payments allocable to pre-July 1986 investment in the contract actually received as an annuity in 2004 and 2005 ($12,000/$25,000 x $1,000)	480.00
Difference	$1,109.40

ANNUITIES

Q 25

Post-June 1986 investment in the contract allocable to taxable years 2004 and
2005 ($13,000 ÷ 20.3 [multiple from Table V for male age 64] = $640.39;
$640.39 x 2 years = $1,280.78.. $1,280.78
Less portion of total payments allocable to post-July 1986 investment in the contract
actually received as an annuity in 2004 and 2005 ($13,000/$25,000 x $1,000) 520.00
Difference... $ 760.78

Because the applicable portions of the total payment received in 2005 under the contract ($480 allocable to the pre-July 1986 investment in the contract and $520 allocable to the post-June 1986 investment in the contract) do not exceed the portion of the corresponding investment in the contract allocable to the year ($794.70 pre-July 1986 and $640.39 post-June 1986) the entire amount of each applicable portion is excludable from gross income and Mr. Green may redetermine his excludable amounts as follows:

Divide the amount by which the portion of total payment actually received allocable to
pre-July 1986 investment in the contract is less than the pre-July 1986 investment in
the contract allocable to 2004 and 2005 ($1,109.40) by the life expectancy under
Table I for Mr. Green, age 66 (14.4 - .5 [frequency multiple]; $1,109.40 ÷ 13.9) .... $ 79.81
Add the amount originally determined with respect to pre-July 1986 investment
in the contract.. 794.70
Amount excludable with respect to pre-July 1986 investment.......................... $874.51

Divide the amount by which the portion of total payment actually received allocable
to post-June 1986 investment in the contract is less than the post-June 1986
investment in the contract allocable to 2004 and 2005 ($760.78) by the life expectancy
under Table V for Mr. Green, age 66 (19.2 - .5 [frequency multiple];
$760.78 ÷ 18.7)... $ 40.68
Add the amount originally determined with respect to post-June 1986 investment
in the contract.. 640.39
Amount excludable with respect to post-June 1986 investment.................... $681.07

ASRS, Sec. 52, ¶320.13.

25. What is a "wraparound" or "investment" annuity? How is the owner taxed prior to the annuity starting date?

"Investment annuity" and "wraparound annuity" are terms for arrangements under which an insurance company agrees to provide an annuity funded by investment assets placed by or for the policyholder with a custodian or by investment solely in specifically identified assets, such as XY Mutual Fund, held in a segregated account of the insurer. The IRS has ruled that under these arrangements sufficient control over the investment assets is retained by the policyholder so that income on the assets prior to the annuity starting date is currently taxable to the policyholder rather than to the insurance company. *Christoffersen v. U.S.*, 84-2 USTC ¶9990 (8th Cir. 1984), *rev'g* 84-1 USTC ¶9216 (N.D. Iowa 1984), *cert. denied*, 473 U.S. 905 (1985); Rev. Rul. 81-225, 1981-2 CB 12 (as clarified by Rev. Rul. 82-55, 1982-1 CB 12); Rev. Rul. 80-274, 1980-2 CB 27; Rev. Rul. 77-85, 1977-1 CB 12.

However, in some instances the policyholder's degree of control over the investment decisions has been insufficient, so that the IRS considered the insurance company, rather than the policyholder, the owner of the contracts. Rev. Rul. 82-54 1982-1 CB 11; Let. Ruls. 9839034, 9433030.

If an owner of a variable annuity does not have control of the investments of a sub-account within a variable annuity, the owner will be entitled to tax deferral on the growth of the annuity. Rev. Rul. 2003-91, 2003-33 CB 347.

2006 Tax Facts on Insurance & Employee Benefits

The Service has ruled on whether the "hedge funds" within the sub-accounts of variable annuities and variable life insurance contracts will be treated as owned by the insurance company or the contract owner. Generally, if the hedge funds are available to the general public, the sub-account will be treated as owned by the contract owner and therefore not entitled to tax deferral. However, if the hedge funds are available only through an investment in the variable annuity, tax deferral is available. Rev. Rul. 2003-92, 2003-33 CB 350.

The Service has also ruled that the contract owner of a variable annuity can invest in sub-accounts that invest in mutual funds that are available only through the purchase of variable contracts without losing the variable annuity's tax deferral. Rev. Rul. 2005-7, 2005-6 IRB 464.

With the exception of certain contracts grandfathered under Revenue Rulings 77-85 and 81-225, the underlying investments of the segregated asset accounts of variable contracts must meet diversification requirements set forth in regulations. IRC Sec. 817(h); Treas. Reg. §1.817-5. *ASRS, Sec. 52, ¶320.13.*

Loss

26. Does the surrender or sale of an annuity contract ever result in a deductible loss?

A loss deduction can be claimed only if the loss is incurred in connection with the taxpayer's trade or business or in a transaction entered into for profit. IRC Sec. 165. Generally, the purchase of a personal *annuity* contract is considered a transaction entered into for profit. Consequently, if a taxpayer sustains a loss upon surrender of a refund annuity contract, he may claim a deduction for the loss, regardless of whether he purchased the contract in connection with his trade or business or as a personal investment. The amount of the loss is determined by subtracting the cash surrender value from the taxpayer's "basis" for the contract. His "basis" is gross premium cost less all amounts previously received tax free under the contract (e.g., any excludable dividends (see Q 3) and the excludable portion of any prior annuity payments). The loss is ordinary loss, not capital loss. Rev. Rul. 61-201, 1961-2 CB 46; *Cohan v. Comm.*, 39 F.2d 540 (2nd Cir. 1930), aff'g 11 BTA 743. But if the taxpayer purchased the contract for purely personal reasons, and not for profit, no loss deduction will be allowed. For example, in one case, the taxpayer purchased annuities on the lives of relatives, giving the relatives ownership of the contracts. Later he acquired the contracts by gift and surrendered them at a loss. The court disallowed a loss deduction on the ground that the contracts were not bought for profit but to provide financial security for the relatives. *Early v. Atkinson*, 175 F.2d 118 (4th Cir. 1949).

Where a loss from an annuity is actually taken by the taxpayer on Form 1040 has generated a great deal of discussion. Some say that the loss should be treated as a miscellaneous itemized deduction that is not subject to the 2% floor on miscellaneous itemized deductions. Others, say it is a miscellaneous itemized deduction subject to the 2% floor. And finally, others take a more aggressive approach and say that the loss can be taken on the front of the Form 1040 on the line labeled "Other gains or (losses)."

Note that in the 2004 edition of IRS Publication 575 (Pension and Annuity Income), the IRS says that a loss under a variable annuity is treated as a miscellaneous itemized deduction subject to the 2% floor. IRS Pub. 575, p. 19. *ASRS, Sec. 52, ¶330.4.*

27. Is a deductible loss sustained under a straight life annuity if the annuitant dies before payments received equal the annuitant's cost?

If the annuitant's annuity starting date is after July 1, 1986, a deduction may be taken on the individual's final income tax return for the unrecovered investment in the contract. IRC Sec. 72(b)(3)(A). Similarly, a refund beneficiary may deduct any unrecovered investment in the contract in excess of the excludable refund. IRC Sec. 72(b)(3)(B). For purposes of determining if the individual has a net operating loss, the deduction is treated as if it were attributable to a trade or business. IRC Sec. 72(b)(3)(C).

If an annuitant's annuity starting date was before July 2, 1986, there is no deductible loss since the annuitant has received all that the contract called for. *Industrial Trust Co. v. Broderick*, 94 F.2d 927 (1st Cir. 1938); Rev. Rul. 72-193, 1972-1 CB 58; see also *Est. of Lambert v. Comm.*, 40 BTA 802 (1939). The result is the same for one who purchases an annuity on the life of another person who dies prematurely. *Helvering v. Louis*, 77 F.2d 386 (D.C. App. Ct., 1935). For example, no loss deduction was allowed where a husband purchased a single premium nonrefundable annuity on the life of his wife, and his wife died before his cost had been recovered. Deduction was disallowed on the ground that the transaction was not entered into for profit. *White v. U.S.*, 19 AFTR 2d 658 (N.D. Tex. 1966). *ASRS, Sec. 52, ¶330.9.*

DISPOSITION

Sale or Purchase of a Contract

28. If the owner of an annuity contract sells the contract, what are the income tax consequences to the seller?

Gain is taxed to the seller as ordinary income—not as capital gain. Thus, where deferred annuities were sold shortly before maturity, the gain was held to be ordinary income. *First Nat'l Bank of Kansas City v. Comm.*, 309 F.2d 587 (8th Cir. 1962) aff'g *Katz v. Comm.*, TC Memo 1961-270; *Roff v. Comm.*, 304 F.2d 450 (3rd Cir. 1962) aff'g 36 TC 818; *Arnfeld v. U.S.*, 163 F. Supp. 865 (Ct. Cl. 1958), cert. denied 359 U.S. 943. According to the decided cases, the amount of taxable gain is determined in the same way as upon surrender of a contract (see Q 33). In other words, gain is determined by subtracting net premium cost (gross premiums less dividends to the extent excludable from income) from the sale price.

However, where an annuity contract is sold after maturity, the cost basis of the contract (for purpose of computing the seller's gain) must be reduced by the aggregate excludable portions of the annuity payments that have been received. But the adjusted cost basis cannot be reduced below zero (for example, where the annuitant has outlived his life expectancy and was able to exclude amounts in excess of his net premium cost). Treas. Reg. §1.1021-1. The taxable gain, that is, cannot be greater than the sale price. Where an *annuity* contract is sold for less than its cost basis, apparently the seller realizes an ordinary loss. (See Q 26.)

If the contract sold is subject to a nonrecourse loan, the transferor's obligation under the loan is discharged and the amount of the loan is considered an amount received on the transfer. Treas. Reg. §1.1001-2(a). *ASRS, Sec. 52, ¶330.15.*

29. How is the purchaser of an annuity contract taxed?

If the purchaser receives lifetime proceeds under the contract, he is taxed in the same way as an original owner would be taxed, but with the following differences. His cost basis is the consideration he paid for the contract, plus any premiums he paid after the purchase, and less any excludable dividends and unrepaid excludable loans received by him after the purchase. If the contract is purchased after payments commence under a life income or installment option, a new exclusion ratio must be determined, based on the purchaser's cost and expected return computed as of the purchaser's annuity starting date. The purchaser's annuity starting date is the beginning of the first period for which the purchaser receives an annuity payment under the contract (see Q 7 to Q 9). Treas. Regs. §§1.72-4(b)(2), 1.72-10(a). If the purchaser of an annuity is a corporation, or other nonnatural person, see Q 2.

Policy Exchanges

30. Does tax liability arise when a policyholder exchanges one annuity contract for another?

The Code provides that the following are *nontaxable* exchanges: (1) the exchange of a life insurance policy for another life insurance policy or for an endowment or annuity contract; (2) the exchange of an endowment contract for an annuity contract, or for an endowment contract under which payments will begin no later than payments would have begun under the contract exchanged; (3) the exchange of an annuity contract for another annuity contract. IRC Sec. 1035(a). These rules do not apply to any exchange having the effect of transferring property to any non-United States person. IRC Sec. 1035(c).

If an annuity is exchanged for another annuity, the contracts must be payable to the same person or persons. Otherwise, the exchange does not qualify as a tax free exchange under IRC Section 1035(a). Treas. Reg. §1.1035-1. The Code defines an annuity for this purpose as a contract with an insurance company that may be payable during the life of the annuitant only in installments. IRC Sec. 1035(b)(2). Despite the singular reference in IRC Section 1035(a)(3) to "an annuity contract for an annuity contract," the Service concluded that nonrecognition treatment under IRC Section 1035 was appropriate where one single premium annuity was exchanged for two annuity contracts, one a single premium contract and the other a flexible premium contract, and all three contracts were issued by the same insurance company. Let. Rul. 9644016. In another private letter ruling, the Service concluded that one annuity could properly be exchanged under IRC Section 1035 for two annuities, issued by either the same or a different insurance company. Let. Rul. 199937042.

Further, the exchange of two life insurance policies for a single annuity contract has also been considered a proper IRC Section 1035 exchange. Let. Rul. 9708016. See also Let. Rul. 9820018. The exchange of one annuity for a second annuity with a term life insurance rider attached was afforded income tax-free treatment under IRC Section 1035. Let. Rul. 200022003. A proper IRC Section 1035 exchange also occurred where an annuity holder transferred directly a portion of the funds in one annuity to a second

ANNUITIES

Q 30

newly-issued annuity. *Conway v. Comm.*, 111 TC 350 (1998), *acq.* 1999-2 CB xvi. An assignment of an annuity contract for consolidation with a pre-existing annuity contract is a tax-free exchange under section 1035, even though the two annuities were issued by different insurance companies. Rev. Rul. 2002-75, 2002-2 CB 812.

The exchange of a life insurance policy, endowment contract, or fixed annuity contract for a variable annuity contract with the same company or a different company qualifies as a tax free exchange under IRC Section 1035(a). Rev. Rul. 72-358, 1972-2 CB 473; Rev. Rul. 68-235, 1968-1 CB 360. (Although the exchange of a variable annuity for a fixed annuity is not specifically addressed in these rulings, there does not appear to be any evidence that would prohibit such an exchange from qualifying for IRC Section 1035 treatment.) Additionally, the exchange of an annuity contract issued by a domestic insurer for an annuity contract issued by a foreign insurer was considered a permissible IRC Section 1035 exchange. Let. Rul. 9319024.

The Definition of "Exchange"

The distinction between an "exchange" and a surrender and purchase is not always clear. Where an annuity contract of one insurer was assigned, prior to maturity, to another insurer for a new contract of the second insurer, the transaction was considered an "exchange." Rev. Rul. 72-358, 1972-2 CB 473. The "exchange" of an annuity contract received as part of a distribution from a terminated profit-sharing plan for another annuity with similar restrictions as to transferability, spousal consent, minimum distribution, and the incidental benefit rule was granted IRC Section 1035 treatment. Let. Rul. 9233054. Further, the surrender of a non-assignable annuity contract distributed by a pension trust and immediate endorsement of the check by the annuitant to the new insurer in a single integrated transaction under a binding exchange agreement with the new insurer has been privately ruled by IRS an "exchange." Let. Ruls. 8526038, 8501012, 8344029, and 8343010. On the other hand, where the contract is assignable, IRS has required a direct transfer of funds between insurance companies. See Let. Rul. 8741052. Compare Let. Ruls. 8515063 and 8310033. However, the Tax Court allowed an exchange where the taxpayer surrendered an annuity contract for cash and then purchased another annuity contract. *Greene v. Comm.*, 85 TC 1024 (1985), *acq.* 1986-2 CB 1. The exchange of nontransferable tax sheltered (IRC Section 403(b)) annuity contracts is discussed in Q 478.

The IRS has also ruled privately that a valid exchange did not occur where the taxpayer surrendered one life insurance policy and then placed the funds in a second policy purchased one month earlier. Let. Rul. 8810010. In another instance, the Service viewed several transactions as "steps" in one integrated exchange. The taxpayer purchased an annuity contract then later withdrew an amount equal to his basis from the contract, placing the funds in a single premium life insurance policy. Next, he exchanged the annuity for another annuity, treating this part of the transaction as a tax-free exchange under IRC Section 1035. The IRS disagreed, characterizing the events as a single exchange, with the value of the life insurance policy received as taxable boot. TAM 8905004. See also Let. Rul. 9141025.

As discussed above, the Tax Court, in *Conway v. Commissioner*, 111 TC 350 (1998), *acq.* 1999-2 CB xvi, held that a 1035 exchange occurred when the taxpayer transferred a portion of the funds from one annuity to a second newly-issued annuity. The Service later ruled that the proper way to allocate investment in the contract when one

2006 Tax Facts on Insurance & Employee Benefits

annuity is "split up" into two annuities is on a pro rata basis based on the cash surrender value of the annuity before and after the partial exchange. For example, if 60% of an annuity's cash surrender value is transferred to a new annuity, the investment in the contract of the "new" annuity will be 60% of the investment in the contract of the "old" annuity, and the investment in the contract of the "old" annuity will be 40% of what it was before the partial exchange. Rev. Rul. 2003-76, 2003-33 CB 355. The Service has also said that it is considering issuing regulations to prevent abuse when one annuity is split into two annuities using Section 1035. The Service also issued interim guidance until these regulations are finalized. The Service will conclude that a split of an annuity and then a subsequent surrender or distribution from the second annuity will be considered one transaction if the distribution or surrender is completed within 24 months of the exchange. The taxpayer will be able to overcome the presumption that the transaction was entered into for an improper tax avoidance purpose by demonstrating that circumstances required a surrender or distribution. Notice 2003-51, 2003-33 CB 361.

Planning Point: Although the rules under Code section 1035 now cover a broader array of annuity exchanges, funds in nonqualified annuities are not freely movable. For example, the IRS does not provide guidance on the transfer of a portion of the funds in one annuity to a second existing annuity. It is not certain that such a transaction is covered under Section 1035 and therefore this type of transaction may not receive tax-free treatment. *Fred Burkey, CLU, APA, The Union Central Life Insurance Company.*

Exchanges Where the Insurer is Under Rehabilitation

The Service will allow a valid exchange where funds come into the contract or policy in a series of transactions if the insurer issuing the contract or policy to be exchanged is subject to a "rehabilitation, conservatorship, or similar state proceeding." Rev. Rul. 92-43, 1992-1 CB 288.

Funds may be transferred in this "serial" manner if: (1) the old policy or contract is issued by an insurer subject to a "rehabilitation, conservatorship, insolvency, or similar state proceeding" at the time of the cash distribution; (2) the policyowner withdraws the full amount of the cash distribution to which he is entitled under the terms of the state proceeding; (3) the exchange would otherwise qualify for IRC Section 1035 treatment; and (4) the policyowner transfers the funds received from the old contract to a single new contract issued by another insurer not later than 60 days after receipt. If the amount transferred is not the full amount to which the policyowner is ultimately entitled, the policyowner must assign his right to any subsequent distributions to the issuer of the new contract for investment in that contract. Rev. Proc. 92-44, 1992-1 CB 875, as modified by Rev. Proc. 92-44A, 1992-1 CB 876; Let. Rul. 9335054. If a nonqualified annuity contract is exchanged under IRC Section 1035 within the scope of Revenue Ruling 92-43 (i.e., as part of a rehabilitation proceeding), the annuity received will retain the attributes of the annuity for which it was exchanged for purposes of determining when amounts are to be considered invested and for computing the taxability of any withdrawals (see Q 3). Let. Rul. 9442030.

Recognition of Gain

If no cash or other non-like kind property is received in connection with an exchange, any gain will not be recognized. But the cost basis of the new policy will be the same as the cost basis of the old policy (plus any premiums paid and less any excludable dividends received after the exchange).

If cash or other non-like kind property is received in connection with any of the above exchanges, any gain will be recognized to the extent of the cash or other property received. Treas. Reg. §1.1031(b)-1(a). The amount of any policy loan that the other party to the exchange takes property subject to or assumes (reduced by any loan taken subject to or assumed by the first party) is treated as money received on the exchange. Treas. Reg. §1.1031(b)-1(c).

Taxable Exchanges

All other kinds of exchanges are taxable. For example, if a policyholder exchanges an endowment or annuity contract for a whole life policy, gain will be fully taxable to him in the year of exchange. The gain is ordinary income—not capital gain. Treas. Reg. §1.1035-1; Rev. Rul. 54-264, 1954-2 CB 57; *Barrett v. Comm.*, 16 AFTR2d 5380 (1st Cir. 1965) *aff'g* 42 TC 993. Apparently the government's position (that these exchanges are taxable) is based on the fact that life insurance death proceeds are exempt from income tax. Consequently, the government views any exchange that increases the possibility of eliminating the tax by extending the period of life insurance protection, or by providing life insurance protection where none existed as a method of tax avoidance.

The amount of taxable gain is determined by subtracting (1) net premium cost (gross premiums less any excludable dividends) from (2) the value of the new policy plus any cash or the fair market value of any other property received in the exchange. The value of the new policy, for this purpose, is not cash surrender value but fair market value. Thus, if the new policy is single-premium or paid-up, its value is replacement cost (the price that a person of the same age and sex as the insured would have to pay for a similar policy with the same company on the date of exchange). *Parsons v. Comm.*, 16 TC 256 (1951); *Barrett*, supra; Rev. Rul. 54-264, supra. If the new policy is premium-paying, apparently its value is its interpolated terminal reserve plus any unearned premium as of the date of exchange (see Q 303). See Rev. Rul. 59-195, 1959-1 CB 18.

An exchange where both contracts or policies are issued by the same insurer (i.e., an "in-house" exchange) is not subject to the reporting requirements for IRC Section 1035 exchanges (see IRC Section 6047(d)) provided that the exchange does not result in a designated distribution and the insurer's records are sufficient to determine the policyholder's basis. Rev. Proc. 92-26, 1992-1 CB 744.

The effect of a tax free exchange of annuity contracts on taxation of amounts received under the replacing contract is discussed in Q 3 and Q 37. *ASRS, Sec. 52, ¶330.11.*

Gift of an Annuity or Endowment Contract

31. Can the owner of an annuity contract avoid income and penalty taxes by assigning the right to receive the payments to another individual while retaining ownership of the contract?

No. It is a basic tax principle that fruit is attributed to the tree on which it grows. Without the transfer of the underlying contract, a gift or gratuitous assignment of income will not shift the taxability of the income away from the owner of the contract.

Q 32 FEDERAL INCOME TAX

This applies to income accumulated on the contract before the assignment as well as any accruing after. See *Helvering v. Eubank*, 311 U.S. 112 (1940); *Lucas v. Earl*, 281 U.S. 111 (1930); *Van Brunt v. Comm.*, 11 BTA 406 (1928). Thus, withdrawals and annuity payments are taxable to the owner, even if paid to a third party. It would apparently follow that any liability for a premature distribution penalty would be the owner's and would be based on the owner's age, death or disability. Where the owner makes a gift of the underlying contract, see Q 32. *ASRS, Sec. 52, ¶330.10.*

32. What are the income tax results when an unmatured annuity or endowment contract is transferred as a gift?

An individual who transfers an annuity contract issued after April 22, 1987, for less than full and adequate consideration is treated as having received as "an amount not received as annuity" (see Q 3) an amount equal to the excess of the cash surrender value of the contract at the time of transfer over the investment in the contract at that time. Thus, the individual realizes in the year of the transfer any gain on the contract allocable to investment in the contract after August 13, 1982. IRC Sec. 72(e)(4)(C). The IRS has ruled privately that the distribution of an annuity contract by a trust to a trust beneficiary will not be treated as an assignment for less than full and adequate consideration since, for purposes of this rule, the trust is not considered to be an individual. Let. Ruls. 9204010, 9204014. This rule does not apply to transfers between spouses (or between former spouses incident to a divorce and pursuant to an instrument executed or modified after July 18, 1984), except that it does apply to a gift of a contract in trust for such a spouse to the extent that gain must be recognized because of any loan to which the contract is subject. See Q 280.

If the cash surrender value of an annuity contract issued prior to April 23, 1987 at the time of gift exceeds the donor's cost basis, and the donee subsequently surrenders the contract, the donor must report as taxable income the "gain" existing at the time of gift. In other words, the donor is taxed on the difference between the premiums he has paid (less any excludable dividends he has received) and the cash surrender value of the contract at the time of gift. The balance of the gain, if any, is taxed to the donee. The proper year for the donor to include the gain in his gross income is the year in which the contract is surrendered by the donee. Rev. Rul. 69-102, 1969-1 CB 32.

Annuity payments under a contract that has been transferred as a gift are taxed under the annuity rules (see Q 7 to Q 24). With respect to gifts of annuities issued after April 22, 1987, the amount of gain, if any, that is included in the transferor's income as a result of the transfer will increase the transferee's investment in the contract. IRC Sec. 72(e)(4)(C)(iii). If the contract was issued before April 23, 1987, all premiums paid and excludable dividends received by both donor and donee prior to the commencement of the annuity payments are taken into account in determining the investment in the contract. The annuity starting date and expected return are determined as though no transfer has taken place. Treas. Reg. §1.72-10(b). However, the IRS has not ruled on whether, if the contract was transferred when the cash surrender value exceeded the donor's cost basis, the donor must include any portion of the payments in his gross income or how such portion would be determined.

Where a gift is conditioned on payment by the donee of the donor's gift tax liability, the Supreme Court has ruled that income is realized by the donor to the extent the gift tax exceeds the donor's basis in the property. *Diedrich v. Comm.*, 82-1 USTC

¶9419 (1982). The gain is included in the donor's income for the year in which the gift tax is paid by the donee. *Weeden v. Comm.*, 82-2 USTC ¶9556 (9th Cir. 1982). However, payment of federal or state gift tax by the donee (or agreement to pay such tax) does not result in income to the donor in the case of net gifts made before March 4, 1981. TRA '84, Sec. 1026.

If the contract transferred is subject to a nonrecourse loan, the transferor's obligation under the loan is discharged and the amount of the loan is treated as an amount received with the result that gain is recognized to the extent the loan exceeds the adjusted basis. Treas. Reg. §1.1001-2(a); Let. Rul. 8951056. See Q 64 with regard to any transfer for value aspect.

If the gift is to a corporation or other nonnatural person, see Q 2. *ASRS, Sec. 52,* ¶ *330.10, 1000.7.*

Surrender, Redemption, or Maturity

33. What are the income tax results when the owner of an annuity contract takes the lifetime maturity proceeds or cash surrender value in a one sum cash payment?

Amounts received on complete surrender, redemption or maturity are taxed under the cost recovery rule (see Q 3, Q 249). If the maturity proceeds or cash surrender value exceeds the cost of the contract, the excess is taxable income in the year of maturity or surrender even if proceeds are not received until a later tax year. *Kappel v. U.S.*, 34 AFTR 2d 74-5025 (W.D. Pa. 1974). (For computation of "cost," see Q 8.) The gain is ordinary income, not capital gain. IRC Sec. 72(e); Treas. Reg. §1.72-11(d); *Bodine v. Comm.*, 103 F.2d 982 (3rd Cir. 1939); *Cobbs v. Comm.*, 39 BTA 642 (1939).

The Internal Revenue Code provides that aggregate premiums are the cost basis for computing *gain* upon the lifetime maturity or surrender of an annuity contract (see Q 8). IRC Sec. 72(e)(6). *ASRS, Sec. 52,* ¶*330.3.*

34. If a policyholder elects to receive endowment maturity proceeds or cash surrender values under a life income or installment option, is the gain on the policy taxable to him in the year of maturity or surrender?

Ordinarily, a cash basis taxpayer is treated as having *constructively received* an amount of cash when it first becomes available to him without substantial limitations or restrictions. He must report this amount as taxable income even though he has not actually received it. Treas. Reg. §1.451-2.

When an endowment contract matures, or any type of contract is surrendered, generally a lump sum payment becomes available to the policyholder unless, *before* the maturity or surrender date, he has elected to postpone receipt of the proceeds under a settlement option. However, such a lump sum will not be considered constructively received in the year of maturity or surrender if, within 60 days after the lump sum becomes available and before receiving any payment in cash, the policyholder exercises an option or agrees with the insurer to take the proceeds as an annuity. IRC Sec. 72(h); Treas. Reg. §1.72-12. The 60-day extension is allowed only for the election of a life income or other installment-type settlement (those considered "annuities" under the income tax law, see Q 1). It does not apply to an election to leave the proceeds on deposit at interest—such an election must be made *before* maturity or surrender to avoid constructive receipt (see Q 251).

If there is a gain on the contract but the proceeds are not constructively received, the policyholder is not taxed on the gain in the year of maturity or surrender. For the purpose of taxing the annuity payments, however, his investment in the contract (cost) is premium cost—not the maturity or cash surrender value. In effect, then, the policyholder's taxable gain will be spread ratably over the payment period.

If there is a gain on the contract and the proceeds are constructively received (as where the election is made after the 60-day period), the full gain is taxable to the policyholder in the year of constructive receipt as if he had actually received a one-sum cash payment (see Q 264). For the purpose of taxing the annuity payments, his investment in the contract (cost) would then be, not premium cost, but the entire lump sum applied under the settlement option. Although the larger cost would result in a larger excludable portion for the annuity payments, usually it is advisable for the policyholder to avoid being taxed on the entire gain in one year.

Even where the cash surrender value is less than net premium cost, it appears that net premiums may be used as "cost" in determining the exclusion ratio for the annuity payments—provided the cash surrender value is not constructively received in the year of surrender. IRC Sec. 72(c)(1); Treas. Reg. §1.72-6(a)(1). *ASRS, Sec. 52, ¶330.5.*

35. Is the full gain on a deferred annuity or retirement income contract taxable in the year the contract matures?

If the contract provides for automatic settlement under an annuity option, the lump sum proceeds are not constructively received in the year of maturity (see Q 34). IRC Sec. 72(h); Treas. Reg. §1.72-12. The annuity payments (whether life income or installment) are taxed under the regular annuity rules (see Q 7 to Q 24). In computing the exclusion ratio for the payments, the amount to be used as the *investment in the contract* is premium cost—not the maturity value (see Q 8). Of course, if the contract owner takes a one-sum settlement at maturity, he must include the gain in gross income for the year in which he receives the payment (see Q 33). For election to leave life insurance proceeds on deposit at interest, see Q 251.

In the case of a retirement income contract that is subject to the IRC Section 7702 definition of a life insurance contract (see Q 273) *and* that is an insurance contract under state law but does not meet one of the two alternative tests provided in IRC Section 7702, income on the contract will be taxed as it accrues (see Q 247) and, apparently, any such unrecovered amounts previously includable in income will increase the investment in the contract.

See Q 2 if the deferred annuity contract is owned by a person other than a natural person, such as a corporation. *ASRS, Sec. 52, ¶330.6.*

DEATH

36. If the annuitant dies before his deferred annuity matures, is the amount payable at his death subject to income tax?

ANNUITIES

Q 36

Yes. Generally, an annuity contract provides that if the annuitant dies before the annuity starting date, the beneficiary will be paid as a death benefit the amount of premium paid or the accumulation value of the contract. The gain, if any, is taxable as ordinary income to the beneficiary. The death benefit under an annuity contract does not qualify for tax exemption under IRC Section 101(a) *as life insurance* proceeds payable by reason of insured's death. Gain is measured by subtracting (1) total gross premiums from (2) the death benefit plus aggregate dividends and any other amounts that have been received under the contract which were excludable from gross income (see Q 3). IRC Sec. 72(e)(5)(E); Treas. Reg. §1.72-11(c); Rev. Rul. 55-313, 1955-1 CB 219. See *Malesa v. Comm.*, TC Memo 1996-396. In addition, the death benefit paid upon the death of the owner/annuitant is income in respect of a decedent (IRD) to the extent that the death benefit amount exceeds the basis in the annuity contract, and may be eligible for a special income tax deduction for the estate tax attributable to the IRD (see Q 827). Rev. Rul. 2005-30, 2005-20 IRB 1015.

Planning Point: The owner of a non-qualified annuity should generally be named as the annuitant. Where the owner and annuitant are two different individuals, problems can result - especially if the annuity is annuitant-driven. (All annuities issued since 1986 are "owner driven;" the death benefit is triggered by death of the owner. Some are also annuitant-driven; the death benefit is triggered by death of the annuitant). If the owner and annuitant are the same person, the type does not matter; if they are not, it does. *John L. Olsen, CLU, ChFC, AEP, Olsen Financial Group.*

However, the beneficiary will not be taxed on the gain in the year of death if he or she elects, within 60 days after the death benefit is payable, to apply the death benefit under a life income or installment option (see Q 34). IRC Sec. 72(h). The periodic payments will then be taxable to the beneficiary under the regular annuity rules (see Q 7 to Q 19). The exclusion ratio for the contract will be based on the decedent's investment in the contract and the beneficiary's expected return. Treas. Regs. §§1.72-11(a), 1.72-11(e).

The same rules apply to variable annuity contracts purchased after October 20, 1979 and to contributions made after October 20, 1979 to variable annuities issued prior to this date. Rev. Rul. 79-335, 1979-2 CB 292. However, if the owner of a variable annuity contract acquired prior to October 21, 1979 (including any contributions applied to such an annuity contract pursuant to a binding commitment entered into before that date) dies prior to the annuity starting date, the contract acquires a new cost basis. The basis of the contract in the hands of the beneficiary will be the value of the contract at the date of the decedent's death (or the alternate valuation date). If that basis equals the amount received by the beneficiary there will be no income taxable gain and the appreciation in the value of the contract while owned by the decedent will escape income tax entirely. Rev. Rul. 79-335, 1979-2 CB 292. But where a variable annuity contract purchased before October 21, 1979 had been exchanged for another variable annuity contract under IRC Section 1035 after October 20, 1979 and the annuity owner died prior to the annuity starting date, the beneficiary was not entitled to a step-up in basis. TAM 9346002; Let. Rul. 9245035.

Normally the death benefit is payable at death. If it is not payable until a later time and the annuitant was also the owner of the annuity contract, see Q 37. *ASRS, Sec. 52, ¶330.8.*

37. What distributions are required when the owner of an annuity contract dies before the entire interest in the contract has been distributed?

A contract issued after January 18, 1985, will not be treated as an annuity contract and taxed under IRC Section 72 unless it provides that if any *owner* dies (1) on or after the annuity starting date and before the entire interest in the contract has been distributed, the remaining portion will be distributed at least as rapidly as under the method of distribution being used as of the date of the owner's death and (2) before the annuity starting date, the entire interest in the contract will be distributed within 5 years after the owner's death. IRC Sec. 72(s)(1). In the case of joint owners of a contract issued after April 22, 1987, these distribution requirements are applied at the first death. TRA '86, Sec. 1826.

Planning Point: Avoid naming a client's revocable living trust (or any trust, as a general rule) as the beneficiary of a non-qualified annuity if any stretch out of taxation of the gain is desired. A surviving spouse of the holder can annuitize over his/her lifetime or treat the annuity as his/her own; if that same spouse is the trustee of the decedent's trust, both opportunities are probably unavailable. *John L. Olsen, CLU, ChFC, AEP, Olsen Financial Group.*

For purposes of meeting these requirements, if any portion of the owner's interest is to be distributed to a designated beneficiary over the life of such beneficiary (or over a period not extending beyond the life expectancy of the beneficiary) and such distribution begins within one year after the owner's death, that portion will be treated as distributed on the day such distribution begins.

> *Example*: A (age 50) buys an annuity contract and is the owner. He names his son (age 25) as the annuitant, with annuity payments to begin when his son becomes age 45. The father dies at age 58 and the son (now age 33) becomes the new owner of the contract. Under the provisions, there must be a distribution of the entire interest in the contract within five years of the father's death or there must be annuitization of the contract within one year of such date. (Example taken from the General Explanation of the Deficit Reduction Act of 1984 at p. 660.)

If the designated beneficiary (that is, the person who becomes the new owner) is the surviving spouse of the owner, then the distribution requirements are applied by treating the spouse as the owner. IRC Sec. 72(s)(3).

Amounts distributed under these requirements are taxed under the general rules applicable to amounts distributed under annuity contracts. These rules are intended to prevent protracted deferral of tax on the gain in the contract through successive ownership of the contract.

Where the owner of a contract issued after April 22, 1987, is a corporation or other nonnatural person, the primary annuitant will be treated as the owner of the contract. *Primary annuitant* means the individual whose life is of primary importance in affecting the timing or amount of the payout under the contract (e.g., the measuring life). IRC Sec. 72(s)(6). For purposes of the distribution requirements, a change in the primary annuitant of such a contract will be treated as the death of the owner. IRC Sec. 72(s)(7). Where the owner is a corporation or other nonnatural person, see also Q 2.

These requirements do not apply to annuities purchased to fund periodic payment of damages on account of personal injuries or sickness. IRC Sec. 72(s)(5)(D).

While these requirements do not apply with respect to qualified pension, profit sharing and stock bonus plans, IRC Section 403(b) tax sheltered annuities, and individual retirement annuities, similar distribution requirements do apply (see Q 235, Q 343, Q 489).

Effect of Exchange

According to the report of the conference committee (TRA '84), an annuity contract issued after January 18, 1985, in exchange for one issued earlier will be considered a new contract and subject to the distribution requirements. H.R. Conf. Rep. No. 98-861 (TRA '84) *reprinted in* 1984-3 CB Vol. 2 331-332. *ASRS, Sec. 52, ¶300.1(g)*.

DIVORCE

38. If an individual purchases an annuity contract to meet alimony payments, how are the payments taxed to the recipient? What are the tax results to the purchaser?

If incident to a divorce, an annuity contract payable to the former spouse is transferred or assigned to the former spouse after July 18, 1984 (unless the transfer is pursuant to an instrument in effect on or before such date), legislative history states that he "will be entitled to the usual annuity treatment, including recovery of the transferor's investment in the contract ... notwithstanding that the annuity payments ... qualify as alimony ...." General Explanation of the Deficit Reduction Act of 1984, at p. 711. (If both spouses elected, the same treatment applied to a transfer made after December 31, 1983, and on or before July 18, 1984.)

There is nothing in the Code that directly supports this resolution of the conflict between the rules that "[g]ross income includes amounts received as alimony ..." (IRC Sec. 71(a)) and that amounts received as an annuity under an annuity contract are taxable under rules that permit tax free recovery of cost over the payment period (IRC Sec. 72). If the recipient of the annuity contract is permitted to recover the purchaser's "investment in the contract," there should be no deduction allowed for the alimony by the purchaser. There is no gain taxable to the purchaser on the transfer. IRC Sec. 1041.

With respect to annuity contracts transferred before July 19, 1984 or pursuant to instruments in effect before July 19, 1984 (unless the election referred to above applies), payments under the contract to a recipient spouse in discharge of the payor spouse's alimony obligations are fully taxable to the recipient and he cannot recover the payor's investment in the contract tax free. IRC Sec. 72(k), as then in effect; Treas. Reg. §1.72-14(b); Treas. Reg. §1.71-1(c)(2). The payor spouse cannot take an income tax deduction for the payments even though they are taxable to the recipient spouse. IRC Sec. 71(d), as then in effect; IRC Sec. 215, as then in effect. Where there is no transfer, but the payor spouse purchases an annuity, retaining ownership of the contract and receiving the payments himself, he can recover his investment under the annuity rule. If he then makes periodic alimony payments directly to his former spouse, he can deduct the payments. IRC Sec. 72; IRC Sec. 215. The recipient spouse, of course, would include the full amount of the alimony payments in gross income. IRC Sec. 71. *ASRS, Sec. 52, ¶900.2*.

CHARITABLE GIFTS

39. May a charitable contribution deduction be taken for the gift of a maturing annuity or endowment contract?

Yes, subject to the limits on deductions for gifts to charities (see Q 824).

If a policyholder gives an annuity contract that was issued after April 22, 1987, whether in the year it matures or in a year prior to maturity, he is treated as if he received at that time the excess of the cash surrender value at the time of the transfer over his investment in the contract. IRC Sec. 72(e)(4)(C). Thus, he must recognize in the year of the gift his gain on the contract. Consequently, his charitable gift need not be reduced by the amount of ordinary gain he would realize on a sale at the time of the gift. Treas. Reg. §1.170A-4(a).

If a policyholder gives a maturing annuity contract that was issued prior to April 23, 1987 or gives any endowment contract to a charity in the year it matures he must include in gross income the excess of the maturity value over his basis. *Friedman v. Comm.*, 15 AFTR 2d 1174 (6th Cir. 1965); Rev. Rul. 69-102, 1969-1 CB 32. However, he may take a deduction for the full maturity value (within the limits discussed in Q 824). Treas. Reg. §1.170A-4(a). Where an endowment contract (or annuity contract issued before April 23, 1987) is contributed in years before the year the contract matures, Revenue Ruling 69-102 (above) holds that the donor must include in his income in the year the contract is surrendered or matures the excess of the cash surrender value at the time of the gift over the donor's basis; however, the Code limits his deduction to his cost basis. IRC Sec. 170(e)(1)(A). (The ruling concerned a gift in the year immediately before the contract matured but may not be limited to that year.) This ruling, if accepted at face value, means the donor must include in income amounts given to the charity that are not deductible.

Planning Point: A potential tax trap exists where an annuity issued before April 23, 1987 is given to a charity near the end of the donor's tax year. If the charity surrenders the annuity after the end of the donor's tax year, the donor may not deduct the value of the gift, only the donor's investment in the contract. What's more, the donor will incur income taxation to the extent of the donor's gain in the contract in the year in which the charity takes distributions from or surrenders the annuity. *Fred Burkey, CLU, APA, The Union Central Life Insurance Company.*

For a gift to a charity in connection with purchase of an annuity from the charitable organization, see Q 43. *ASRS, Sec. 52, ¶1000.*

WITHHOLDING

40. Are amounts received under commercial annuity contracts subject to withholding?

Yes; however, the payee generally may elect not to have anything withheld. Only the amount it is reasonable to believe is includable in income is subject to withholding. Amounts are to be withheld from periodic payments at the same rate as wages. Payments are periodic, even if they are variable, if they are payable over a period of more than a

ANNUITIES

Q 41

year. If payments are not periodic, 10% of the includable amount is withheld. Payments made to the beneficiary of a deceased payee are subject to withholding under the same rules. IRC Secs. 3405(a), 3405(b); Temp. Treas. Reg. §35.3405-1T (A-9, A-10, A-12, A-17, F-19 through 24).

An election out of withholding will be ineffective, generally, if a payee does not furnish his taxpayer identification number (TIN, usually his social security number) to the payor or furnishes an incorrect TIN to the payor and the payor is so notified by the IRS. IRC Sec. 3405(e)(12).

Payments under qualified pension, profit sharing and stock bonus plans are discussed in Q 440; payments under IRC Section 403(b) tax sheltered annuities are discussed in Q 490 and Q 491; private annuities are discussed in Q 41. *ASRS, Sec. 53, ¶20.13(a)*.

PRIVATE ANNUITY

41. How are payments received under a private annuity taxed?

A private annuity is an unsecured promise of one person (the obligor) to make fixed payments to another person (the annuitant) for life in return for the transfer of property from the annuitant to the obligor. According to a general counsel memorandum, an unsecured promise to make fixed payments until a stated monetary amount is reached or until the annuitant's death, whichever occurs first, will be treated as a private annuity (instead of an installment sale with a contingent price) if the stated monetary amount would not be received by the annuitant before the expiration of his life expectancy (as determined under the appropriate annuity table and as determined at the time of the agreement—see Appendix A). GCM 39503 (5-7-86). A private annuity is to be distinguished from a commercial annuity issued by a life insurance company, and from an annuity payable by an organization (e.g., a charity) that issues annuities "from time to time." For treatment of the latter see Q 43 and Q 44. The typical private annuity involves the transfer of appreciated property (usually a capital asset) from parents or grandparents to one or more children or grandchildren.

The basic rules for taxing the payments received by the annuitant under a private life annuity are set forth in Revenue Ruling 69-74, 1969-1 CB 43. According to this ruling, the payments must be divided into three elements: (1) a "recovery of basis" element; (2) a "gain element" eligible for capital gain treatment for the period of the annuitant's life expectancy, but taxable as ordinary income thereafter; and (3) an "annuity element" that is taxable as ordinary income.

(1) The portion of each payment that is to be excluded from gross income as a recovery of basis is determined by applying the basic annuity rule (see Q 7). Thus, an exclusion percentage is obtained by dividing the *investment in the contract* by the *expected return* under the contract. The *investment in the contract* in a private annuity situation is the adjusted basis (see Q 816) of the property transferred. However, if the adjusted basis of the property transferred is greater than the present value of the annuity, the annuitant's investment in the contract for purposes of IRC Section 72(b) is the present value of the annuity on the date of the exchange. *LaFargue v. Comm.*, 86-2 USTC ¶9715 (9th Cir. 1986), aff'g TC Memo 1985-90; *Benson v. Comm.*, 80 TC 789 (1983). *Expected return* and *annuity starting date* are the same as explained in Q 9 and Q 10. Thus, *expected return* is obtained by multiplying one year's annuity payments by

2006 Tax Facts on Insurance & Employee Benefits

the appropriate multiple from Table I or Table V of the income tax Annuity Tables (see Appendix A), whichever is applicable depending on when the investment in the contract is made, as explained in Appendix A.

If the annuity starting date is before January 1, 1987, the amount determined above to be excludable from income as a recovery of basis is excluded from all payments received, even if the annuitant outlives his life expectancy. However, if the annuity starting date is after December 31, 1986, then the exclusion percentage is applied only to payments received until the investment in the contract is recovered. Thereafter, the portion excludable under the percentage is included as ordinary income. IRC Sec. 72(b)(2).

(2) The capital gain portion, if any, is determined by dividing the gain by the life expectancy of the annuitant. Gain is the excess of *present value* of the annuity (it may not be the same as fair market value of the property) over the adjusted basis of the property. The present value of the annuity is obtained from the Estate and Gift Tax Valuation Tables (see Q 910). The life expectancy of the annuitant is obtained from Table I or Table V of the income tax Annuity Tables, whichever is applicable depending on when the investment in the contract is made (Appendix A). This portion is reportable as capital gain for the period of the annuitant's life expectancy, and thereafter as ordinary income. Recovery of capital gain may not be deferred until the entire investment in the contract has been recovered. *Garvey, Inc. v. U.S.*, 83-1 USTC ¶9163 (U.S. Cl. Ct. 1983), aff'd. 84-1 USTC ¶9214 (Fed. Cir. 1984), *cert. denied*.

(3) The remaining portion of each payment is ordinary income.

If the *fair market value of the property* transferred exceeds the *present value of the annuity* (as determined from the applicable Estate and Gift Tax Valuation Tables), the difference is treated as a gift to the obligor (see Q 705). *Benson v. Comm.*, supra; *LaFargue v. Comm.*, supra.

Example. Mrs. White is a widow, age 66, with two adult children. She owns a rental property with an adjusted basis of $30,000 and a fair market value of $135,000. On January 1, she transfers this building to her children in exchange for their unsecured promise to pay her $1000 a month ($12,000 a year) for life beginning January 31.

Assume that the valuation table interest rate for January is 5.0%; therefore, the present value of the annuity equals $126,078: $12,000 × 10.2733 (annuity factor) × 1.0227 (annuity adjustment factor). (For an explanation of the valuation table factors, see Appendix D and Example 2 thereunder.) The fair market value of the property exceeds the present value of the annuity by $8,922: $135,000 - $126,078. This is a gift by Mrs. White to her children and subject to gift tax. Mrs. White's life expectancy (Table V in Appendix A) is 19.2 years.

(1) Mrs. White will exclude from gross income as a recovery of basis $130, or 13% of each payment (until she recovers $30,000, since her annuity starting date is after December 31, 1986). The 13% exclusion percentage is obtained by dividing $30,000 (investment in the contract) by $230,400 (expected return: 19.2 × $12,000). (See Q 11.)

(2) She will report $417 of each payment as capital gain for 19.2 years. This portion is obtained by dividing her gain of $96,078 (excess of present value of annuity [$126,078] over adjusted basis of the property [$30,000]) by 19.2, her life expectancy ($96,078 ÷ 19.2 = $5,004 a year or $417 a month). After 19.2 years, she will report this $417 as ordinary income.

(3) She will report the balance of each payment, or $453 ($1,000 - ($130 + $417)) as ordinary income. (Since her annuity starting date is after December 31, 1986, she will also report as ordinary income the portion of each payment no longer excludable as recovery of capital after her investment in the contract has been recovered.)

According to the Tax Court, Revenue Ruling 69-74 is not applicable if the promise to pay the annuity is secured; securing the promise will cause the entire capital gain on the transfer of the property to be taxable to the annuitant in the year of transfer and the investment in the contract would be the present value of the annuity, but not more than the fair market value of the property transferred. *Est. of Bell v. Comm.*, 60 TC 469 (1973); *212 Corp. v. Comm.*, 70 TC 788 (1978). In a private letter ruling a private annuity arrangement was still taxed as such despite the presence of a cost-of-living adjustment applicable to the monthly annuity payments and a minimum payment provision which stated that if the annuitant had not received a specified dollar amount prior to her death, the remaining amount would be paid to her estate. The annuitant also had the option to accelerate the payments and receive a lump sum amount equal to the minimum payment amount less annuity payments previously received. Let. Rul. 9009064.

When a private annuity became worthless the determination that the loss was a capital loss not an ordinary loss was upheld in *McIngvale v. Comm.*, 936 F.2d 833 (5th Cir. 1991) aff'g TC Memo 1990-340.

Whether a transfer to a trust will be treated as a sale in exchange for a private annuity or a transfer in trust with a right to income retained depends on the circumstances in the case. However, properly done, a transfer to a trust will be treated as a private annuity transaction. See *Est. of Fabric v. Comm.*, 83 TC 932 (1984); *Stern v. Comm.*, 84-2 USTC ¶9949 (9th Cir. 1984); *LaFargue v. Comm.*, 50 AFTR 2d 82-5944 (9th Cir. 1982) (followed by the Tax Court in *Benson v. Comm.*, above, because an appeal would go to the ninth circuit). Purported transfers in trust were held sham transactions in *Horstmier v. Comm.*, TC Memo 1983-409.

Amounts received under a private annuity contract are not subject to withholding because such amounts are not paid under a "commercial annuity," that is, one issued by a licensed insurance company.

For estate tax implications of a private annuity, see Q 608.

ASRS, Sec. 52, ¶340.

42. What are the tax consequences to the obligor in a private annuity transaction?

The annuity payments made by the obligor are treated as capital expenditures for the acquisition of the property. No interest deduction is allowed with respect to the payments. *Garvey, Inc. v. U.S.*, 83-1 USTC ¶9163 (U.S. Cl. Ct. 1983), *aff'd* 84-1 USTC ¶9214 (Fed Cir.), *cert. den.* 469 U.S. 823 (1984); *Bell v. Comm.*, 76 TC 232 (1981). However, depreciation deductions may be taken if the property is depreciable. The initial basis for depreciation is the present value of the annuity (as determined by the appropriate Estate and Gift Tax Valuation Tables, see Q 910). When actual payments exceed the initial basis, the basis for depreciation is the actual payments made less prior depreciation. Rev. Rul. 55-119, 1955-1 CB 352.

When payments exceed the initial basis, loss is not deductible until the property is sold. *Perkins v. U.S.*, 83-1 USTC ¶9250 (9th Cir. 1983). If the property is sold after the annuitant's death, the obligor's basis for determining gain or loss is the total of annuity payments made less depreciation taken, if any.

If the property is sold before the annuitant's death, the obligor's basis for *gain* is the total payments actually made plus the actuarial value, as of the date of sale, of payments to be made in the future. The obligor's basis for *loss* is the total amount of payments made as of the date of sale. If the selling price is less than the basis for gain but more than the basis for loss, the obligor realizes neither gain nor loss. Adjustment for annuity payments made after the sale may be made by deducting loss or by reporting additional gain. Rev. Rul. 55-119, supra. *ASRS, Sec. 52, ¶340.*

CHARITABLE GIFT ANNUITY

43. How are payments received under a charitable gift annuity agreement taxed?

A charitable gift annuity agreement is a contractual obligation undertaken by a charity to pay an annuity to an individual in return for an amount transferred by the individual, notwithstanding the fact that the payments might exceed the amount transferred. The contractual obligation is backed by the charity's assets. The typical charitable gift annuity, like the private annuity, can involve the transfer of appreciated property.

The tax consequences of a charitable gift annuity involve (1) an immediate charitable gift, deductible within the limits of IRC Section 170 (see Q 824), (2) income tax on a portion of the annuity payments, and (3) a recovery of principal element, which will be made up of part taxable gain and part excludable adjusted basis if appreciated property is transferred for the annuity. See Treas. Reg. §1.1011-2(c) Ex. 8.

(1) A charitable contribution is made in the amount by which cash or the fair market value of property transferred to the charity exceeds the present value of the annuity. The American Council on Gift Annuities, a voluntary group sponsored by charitable organizations, recommends uniform annuity rates based on the annuitant's age at the date of the gift. See Table on Uniform Gift Annuity Rates in Appendix A. The uniform annuity rate is applied to the transfer and determines the amount of the annuity paid to the annuitant each year. The present value of a charitable gift annuity issued is determined under Estate and Gift Tax Valuation Tables (see Q 910).

(2) When the annuitant receives annuity payments, a percentage of each payment reflects a return of principal. This percentage (the "exclusion ratio") is determined by the basic annuity rule, that is, by dividing the *investment in the contract* by the *expected return*. The *investment in the contract* in the charitable annuity situation is the lesser of the present value of the annuity or the fair market value of the property transferred to the charity. The *expected return* is the annual annuity amount multiplied by the years of life expectancy of the donor at the time of the gift (using the applicable income tax Annuity Tables in Appendix A). If the annuity starting date is after December 31, 1986, the return of principal portion is excludable only until the investment in the contract is fully recovered. Thereafter, that portion is included in income as ordinary income. IRC Sec. 72(b)(2).

If, however, the donor has transferred appreciated property to the charity, he has a gain (either capital gain or ordinary gain depending on the property) to the extent the fair market value of the property exceeds his adjusted basis. In this situation, the bargain sale rules apply. Under these rules, proportionate portions of the donor's basis are considered part of the charitable gift and part of the investment in the annuity contract.

Thus, his return of principal element of each payment consists of two segments: one represents return of gain which is taxed as capital or ordinary gain; the other represents return of his adjusted basis and is excluded from his income. The portion of the gain that is taxed is the percentage that the investment in the contract bears to the total amount transferred. As long as the annuity is nonassignable, the donor may take the gain into income ratably over his life expectancy. After all the gain is reported, that portion of his annuity payment is excluded from income as well as the return of basis portion, if his annuity starting date was before January 1, 1987. However, if his annuity starting date is after December 31, 1986, the Code provides that amounts are not excludable after the investment in the contract has been recovered. Thus, it appears that once the annuitant has outlived his life expectancy, and recovered his investment in the contract, the entire payment is included in income as ordinary income.

If the donor dies before all of the gain is reported (and he is the sole annuitant), no further gain is reported. If the annuity starting date is after July 1, 1986, the Code provides that if annuity payments cease by reason of the death of the sole annuitant before the investment in the contract has been recovered, the unrecovered investment in the contract may be deducted. IRC Sec. 72(b)(3). See Q 27. Because the unrecovered investment in the contract where appreciated property has been given for the annuity includes the unrecognized gain portion, it is likely the deduction will be limited to the unrecovered basis.

(3) The portion of each payment in excess of the return of principal element is ordinary income.

Example. Ed White is a widower, age 70. He owns securities with an adjusted basis of $6,000 and a fair market value of $10,000. On January 1 he transfers the securities to ABC Charity in exchange for a life annuity, payable in semiannual installments. For purposes of this example, assume that the uniform annuity rate (recommended by the American Council on Gift Annuities as shown in Appendix A) is 6.5%, and thus the annuity payment is $650 per year.

(1) According to the applicable Estate and Gift Tax Valuation Tables (see Q 910), the present value of the annuity for Mr. White is $6,011 (9.1350 [annuity factor] × 1.0123 [annuity adjustment factor for semiannual payments] × $650 [the donor's annual annuity]). (Mr. White elected to use an interest rate for a month as explained in Q 910 with an interest rate that is assumed to be 5.0% for purposes of this example; Appendix D explains the derivation of Valuation Table factors from the interest rate.) The difference between the $10,000 fair market value of the property and the $6,011 value of the annuity, or $3,989, is the charitable contribution portion of the transfer. According to Table V (Appendix A), Mr. White has a life expectancy of 16 years which is adjusted to 15.8 (16 - .2) to reflect the frequency of payments (adjustment factor for semiannual payments with 6 months from the annuity starting date to the first payment date is -.2, see introduction to Appendix A).

(2) Of each $325 semiannual payment, 58.5%, or $190 represents return of principal. This percentage is found by dividing $6,011 (the value of the annuity, or investment in the contract) by $10,270 (the expected return: $650 × 15.8). Of this principal amount, $76 is gain ([$6,011 - ($6,000 × ($6,011 ÷ $10,000)] ÷ [15.8 × 2]). Mr. White must report the $76 as capital gain until all his gain is recognized, or until he dies, if that is earlier. Mr. White will exclude the balance of the principal, $114 ($190 - $76), as return of adjusted basis.

(3) The balance of each annuity payment, $135, is the amount that Mr. White must report as ordinary income ($325 - $190). After all the gain and investment in the contract has been recovered (approximately 15.8 years), each payment is fully taxable as ordinary income.

The gift portion of the transfer qualifies for a gift tax charitable deduction (see Q 921). With respect to estate taxes, a donor who designates an annuity only for himself will not have any amount relative to the gift annuity transfer included in his gross estate. See Rev. Rul. 80-281, 1980-2 CB 282; Let. Rul. 8045010. Also, see IRC Sec. 2522(a) and IRC Sec. 2503(a). *ASRS, Sec. 52, ¶350.*

44. What are the tax consequences to the obligor in a charitable annuity transaction?

Property transferred in return for a charitable gift annuity could fall into the general definition of "debt financed property" found in IRC Section 514(b)(1) since the charity acquires the gift subject to the promise to pay the donor an annuity. However, in a private letter ruling, the Service has held that issuing a charitable gift annuity will not result in income from an unrelated trade or business nor will income earned by the charitable organization from investing the charitable gift annuity funds be considered unrelated debt-financed income. Let. Rul. 200449033. See also Let. Rul. 9743054.

A charity's obligation to pay an annuity will be exempt from the debt financed property rules of IRC Section 514 if the following conditions are met: the annuity must be the sole consideration paid for the property transferred; the present value of the annuity must be less than 90% of the value of the property received in exchange; it must be payable over the lives of one or two annuitants; the contract must not guarantee a minimum number of payments or specify a maximum number of payments; and the contract must not provide for adjustments to the amount of annuity paid based on income earned by the transferred property or any other property. IRC Sec. 514(c)(5).

Issuing charitable gift annuities does not affect the tax exempt status of the organization if the annuity meets the requirements above and a portion of the amount transferred in return for the annuity is allowable as a charitable deduction. IRC Sec. 501(m). *ASRS, Sec. 52, ¶350.*

BUSINESS CONTINUATION: BUSINESS LIFE INSURANCE

PREMIUMS

General Rules

45. Are premiums paid on business life insurance deductible as business expenses?

As a general rule, life insurance premiums are not deductible if the premium payer has any interest in the policy or proceeds.

IRC Section 264(a)(1) expressly provides that no deduction shall be allowed for premiums paid on any life insurance policy (or endowment or annuity contract) if the taxpayer is directly or indirectly a beneficiary under the policy or contract. Where IRC Section 264(a)(1) applies, the premiums are not deductible even though they would otherwise be deductible as ordinary and necessary business expenses. Treas. Reg. §1.264-1(a). The rule under IRC Section 264(a)(1) is an "all or nothing" rule: even though the premium payer has a right to receive only a portion of the proceeds, the entire premium is nondeductible. The deduction cannot be divided; it must be either allowed or disallowed in total. Rev. Rul. 66-203, 1966-2 CB 104. Also, the rule under IRC Section 264(a)(1) applies regardless of the form of insurance; it makes no difference whether the premiums are paid on term, ordinary life, or endowment policies.

Deduction of the premium is clearly prohibited under IRC Section 264(a)(1) where the taxpayer (premium payer) is designated as beneficiary in the policy. For example, premiums paid on key person insurance, where the employer is normally both owner and beneficiary of the policy, are clearly nondeductible by reason of IRC Section 264(a)(1). But the deduction is likewise denied, under IRC Section 264(a)(1), where the taxpayer (premium payer) is only indirectly a beneficiary under the policy. Thus, the deduction is denied where the taxpayer, even though not the named beneficiary, has some beneficial interest in the policy—such as the right to change the beneficiary, to make loans, to surrender the policy for cash, or to draw against proceeds held in trust for the insured's wife. Rev. Rul. 70-148, 1970-1 CB 60; Rev. Rul. 66-203, supra; *Wilcox Invest. Co. v. Comm.*, 3 TC 458 (1944); see *Brock v. Comm.*, TC Memo 1982-335; *Omaha Elevator Co. v. Comm.*, 6 BTA 817 (1927).

An employer *can*, however, deduct premiums paid on insurance covering the life of an employee if: (1) the employer is not directly or indirectly a beneficiary under the policy, and (2) the premiums represent additional reasonable compensation for services rendered by the employee. Thus, if the employer has no ownership rights or beneficial interest in the policy, and the proceeds are payable to the employee's estate or personal beneficiary, the premiums ordinarily are deductible by the employer as additional *compensation* to the employee. IRC Sec. 162(a); Treas. Reg. §1.162-7; *Brown Agency, Inc. v. Comm.* 21 BTA 1111 (1931), acq. XI-1 CB 9; *Berizzi Bros. Co. v. Comm.*, 16 BTA 1307 (1929), acq. XI-1 CB 6; *Peerless Pacific Co. v. Comm.*, 10 BTA 103 (1928). The deduction will not be denied merely because the employer may derive some benefit indirectly from the increased efficiency of the employee. Treas. Reg. §1.264-1(b). *ASRS, Sec. 53, ¶¶14.1, 14.2.*

46. Are premiums paid on business life insurance taxable income to the insured?

Generally speaking, the premiums are not taxable to the insured if the insurance is purchased for the benefit of the business and the insured has no interest in the policy. Thus, premiums paid on key person life insurance—where the employer is both owner and beneficiary of the policy—are not taxable to the insured employee. *Casale v. Comm.*, 247 F.2d 440 (2d Cir. 1957); *U.S. v. Leuschner*, 11 AFTR 2d 782 (S.D. Cal. 1962); *Lacey v. Comm.*, 41 TC 329 (1963), acq. 1964-2 CB 6; Rev. Rul. 59-184, 1959-1 CB 65. However, if life insurance premiums are paid by an employer on a policy insuring the life of an employee and the proceeds of such insurance are payable to the beneficiary of the employee, there is generally some taxable income to the employee (see Q 52 to Q 53). But there are exceptions to this general rule in the case of group life insurance (see Q 142) and qualified pension and profit sharing plans (see Q 424). *ASRS, Sec. 53, ¶¶15.1, 15.2.*

Corporations and Stockholders: Deductibility

47. Can a corporation deduct the premiums it pays on a policy insuring the life of an employee or stockholder?

Not if the corporation is either directly or indirectly a beneficiary under the policy (see Q 45). IRC Sec. 264(a)(1). This is true even if the corporation has only a partial beneficial interest in the policy. *National Indus. Investors, Inc. v. Comm.*, TC Memo 1996-151. A corporation cannot deduct the premiums it pays on key person insurance, or on a policy insuring the life of a stockholder purchased to fund the corporation's redemption of the insured's stock. Normally, in these instances, the corporation is both owner and beneficiary of the policy, so a deduction is not allowed by reason of IRC Section 264(a)(1). But even though the corporation may have no right to the cash value of the policy, and no right to name or change the beneficiary, the corporation cannot deduct the premiums if the policy proceeds are to be used in payment for stock that is to be surrendered to the corporation. In this case, the deduction is not allowed because the premium payments are not ordinary and necessary business expenses, but capital expenditures (payments for the acquisition of a corporate asset—treasury stock). Rev. Rul. 70-117, 1970-1 CB 30.

On the other hand, if the corporation purchases life insurance for an employee, and the corporation has no ownership rights or beneficial interest in the policy, the premiums are ordinarily deductible as additional compensation for the employee's services. IRC Sec. 162(a).

In order to be deductible, however, the premium payments must constitute reasonable compensation. Treas. Reg. §1.162-7. The question of whether compensation is "reasonable" can arise in the case of a stockholder-employee of a close corporation. If the total amount paid to and on behalf of the stockholder-employee is an unreasonable return for his services, the IRS may treat the premium payments as a distribution of profits (dividends) rather than as compensation. This may also be the result where there is no evidence (such as board of directors' minutes) to show that the premium payments were intended as compensation. *Boecking v. Comm.*, TC Memo 1993-497; *Est. of Worster v. Comm.*, TC Memo 1984-123; *Champion Trophy Mfg. Corp. v. Comm.*, TC Memo 1972-250; *C. F. Smith Co. v. Comm.*, TC Memo 1954-86; *Hubert Trans-*

BUSINESS CONTINUATION: BUSINESS LIFE INSURANCE   Q 50

fer & Storage Co. v. Comm., TC Memo 1948; *Semon Bache & Co. v. Comm.*, 22 BTA 200 (1931), aff'd 53 F.2d 1084 (2d Cir. 1931); *Arthur R. Womrath, Inc. v. Comm.*, 22 BTA 335 (1931); *L. Hyman & Co. v. Comm.*, 21 BTA 159 (1930); *Charlton & Co. v. Comm.*, 6 BTA 946 (1927);. The deduction will certainly be disallowed where the surrounding circumstances affirmatively show that the premiums were not paid as compensation. In *Atlas Heating & Ventilating Co. v. Comm.*, 18 BTA 389 (1929), for example, the evidence showed that the premiums were actually paid to fund a stock purchase agreement between the individual stockholders; consequently, they were not compensation, but dividends. The policies were owned by the stockholder-employees and the proceeds were payable to their personal beneficiaries. But each insured had agreed that, upon his death, an amount of stock, equal in value to the proceeds received by his beneficiary, would be turned in to the corporation and then distributed pro rata to the surviving stockholders.

In the case of an S corporation, see Q 55. *ASRS, Sec. 53, ¶14.5.*

48. If a stockholder pays premiums on insurance on the life of one of the corporation's officers and the corporation is beneficiary of the proceeds, may the stockholder deduct his premium payments as business expenses?

No, the premium payments are not related to the taxpayer's trade or business. The business of the corporation is not the stockholder's business. *Cappon v. Comm.*, 28 BTA 357 (1933). *ASRS, Sec. 53, ¶14.5.*

49. If a stockholder purchases insurance on the life of another stockholder to fund his obligations under a cross purchase plan, can he deduct the premiums he pays on the policy?

No, the premium payments are in the nature of capital expenditures (that is, amounts paid to acquire a capital asset). See Rev. Rul. 70-117, 1970-1 CB 30; *Whitaker v. Comm.*, 34 TC 106 (1960). *ASRS, Sec. 53, ¶14.5.*

Corporations and Stockholders: Includable in Income

50. Where a key person life insurance policy is owned by and payable to the employer corporation, are premiums paid by the corporation taxable to the key person?

No. *Casale v. Comm.*, 247 F.2d 440 (2d Cir. 1957); Rev. Rul. 59-184, 1959-1 CB 65. In *Casale*, the insured was president of the corporation and owned 98% of its stock. The corporation was both owner and beneficiary of a retirement income contract on the president's life which the corporation had purchased to hedge its obligation to the insured under a deferred compensation agreement. The Tax Court held that the premiums paid by the corporation were taxable income to the insured. But the Tax Court was reversed on the grounds that the corporation's separate entity could not be ignored, and that the insured had received no current economic benefit which would constitute taxable income. The Internal Revenue Service has agreed to follow the Second Circuit's decision as precedent in dealing with similar cases (Rev. Rul. 59-184, supra). See also: *U.S. v. Leuschner*, 11 AFTR 2d 782 (S.D. Cal. 1962); *Lacey v. Comm.*, 41 TC 329 (1963), acq., 1964-2 CB 6.

However, see *Goldsmith v. U.S.*, 78-1 USTC ¶9312 (Ct. Cl. 1978), Q 116. *ASRS, Sec. 53, ¶15.1.*

51. Are premiums paid by a corporation on life insurance to fund a stock redemption agreement taxable to the insured stockholder?

No, the premiums do not constitute income to the stockholder, even though the stockholder has the right to designate the beneficiary, provided the beneficiary's right to receive the proceeds is conditioned upon the transfer of stock to the corporation. *Sanders v. Fox*, 253 F.2d 855 (10th Cir. 1958); *Prunier v. Comm.*, 248 F.2d 818 (1st Cir. 1957); Rev. Rul. 59-184, 1959-1 CB 65. Likewise, the premiums are not taxable income to the insured stockholder when a trustee is named beneficiary, provided the trustee is obligated to use the proceeds to purchase insured's stock for the corporation. Rev. Rul. 70-117, 1970-1 CB 30. *ASRS, Sec. 53, ¶15.*

52. Are life insurance premiums paid by a corporate employer taxable income to the insured employee if the proceeds are payable to the employee's estate or personal beneficiary?

Policy Owned by Employee

Yes. Treas. Reg. §1.61-2(d)(2)(ii)(A); *Canaday v. Guitteau*, 86 F.2d 303 (6th Cir. 1936); *Yuengling v. Comm.*, 69 F.2d 971 (3rd Cir. 1934); *Lee v. U.S.*, 219 F. Supp. 225 (W.D.S.C. 1963); *Pettit v. Comm.*, TC Memo 1960-130; *Jameson v. Comm.*, TC Memo 1942; *Danforth v. Comm.*, 18 BTA 1221 (1930); *Adams v. Comm.*, 18 BTA 381 (1929). If dividends are applied to reduce current premiums, only the net premium is taxable income to the employee. *Weeks v. Comm.*, 16 TC 248 (1951); *Sturgis v. Comm.*, TC Memo 1951.

As a rule, the premium payments are considered additional compensation to the employee and therefore deductible by the employer. But if the employer is a close corporation and the employee a stockholder, the Internal Revenue Service may contend they are dividends taxable to the insured but not deductible by the corporation (see Q 47; in the case of an S corporation, see also Q 55). Even where the insured employee (and owner of the corporation) was not the owner of the policy but his son or wife was owner and beneficiary, the payment of premiums on the insurance was considered an economic benefit to the employee and as such includable in his gross income. *Brock v. Comm.*, TC Memo 1982-335; *Champion Trophy Mfg. Corp. v. Comm.*, TC Memo 1972-250; see IRC Sec. 301(c).

Where a stockholder-employee contends that premiums paid by the corporation on his personal insurance were merely loans, the premiums will be taxed to him as dividends unless he can produce evidence to show that he intended to reimburse the corporation for its outlays. *Schwartz v. Comm.*, TC Memo 1963-340; *Jameson v. Comm.*, TC Memo 1942.

Policy Owned by Corporation

Unless the insured is a stockholder and the insurance is to be used to fund an agreement for the purchase of his stock (see Q 51), the tax results of such an arrangement are uncertain. The regulations state: "Generally, life insurance premiums paid by an employer on the life of his employee where the proceeds of such insurance are payable to the beneficiary of such employee are part of the gross income of the employee." Treas. Reg. §1.61-2(d)(2)(ii)(A). This suggests that the entire premium is taxable to the employee. In one case, where the employee's beneficiary was named *irrevocably*, the full premiums were taxed to the employee even though the corporation owned the policy. *Comm. v. Bonwit*, 87 F.2d 764 (2nd Cir. 1937), reversing 33 BTA 507. However, where the corporation owned the policy designating the insured employee's family as beneficiary and could change the beneficiary, premium payments were not income to the employee. *Rodebaugh v. Comm.*, TC Memo 1974-36, aff'd, 75-2 USTC ¶9526 (6th Cir. 1975), but this point was not appealed. The Tax Court there suggested that the P.S. 58 costs might be taxable to the employee each year his family is beneficiary. (After 2001, P.S. 58 rates may generally not be used, but Table 2001 may be used; see Q 459.) *ASRS, Sec. 53, ¶¶15.2, 15.3.*

53. If a corporation pays life insurance premiums on policies owned by stockholders, and the policies are used to fund a cross purchase agreement, are the premium payments taxable income to the stockholders?

Yes, they are considered distributions of dividends to the stockholders who own the policies. *Doran v. Comm.*, 246 F.2d 934 (9th Cir. 1957); Rev. Rul. 59-184, 1959-1 CB 65. In the case of an S corporation, see Q 55. *ASRS, Sec. 53, ¶15.3.*

Corporations and Stockholders: Section 162 Bonus Plan

54. What is a "Section 162 bonus plan"? What are the income tax consequences to the employee and the employer?

An "IRC Section 162 bonus plan" or an "executive bonus plan" is a nonqualified employee benefit arrangement in which an employer pays a compensation bonus to a selected employee, who then uses the bonus payment to pay the premiums on a life insurance policy insuring his life. The policy is owned personally by the employee.

Generally, the compensation bonus is deductible to the corporate employer if the employee's total compensation is a reasonable amount. IRC Sec. 162(a)(1), Treas. Reg. §1.162-9. Whether used to pay the policy premiums or not (see Q 52), the compensation bonus is includable in gross income to the employee. IRC Sec. 61(a). At death, the policy death proceeds are received by the employee's beneficiary income tax-free. IRC Sec. 101(a)(1). See Q 271. Any policy withdrawals, surrenders or loans made by the employee are taxed as they would be if the employee had purchased the policy without the benefit of the bonus arrangement. See Q 249, Q 250, Q 260. *ASRS, Sec. 63, ¶170.*

S Corporations

55. When an S corporation pays the premium on a life insurance policy insuring a shareholder or employee, what are the tax consequences?

Generally, an S corporation does not pay taxes; instead, items of income, deduction, loss and credit are passed through to the shareholders who report their pro rata shares on their individual returns. Payment of premiums by an S corporation should be characterized as a nondeductible expense, as deductible compensation, or as a nondeductible distribution of profits under the same general rules applicable to regular (C) corporations (see Q 47 to Q 53). However, the resulting tax treatment of the shareholders would, in some instances, differ.

2006 Tax Facts on Insurance & Employee Benefits

Where the payment is a nondeductible expense, as it would be if the corporation were both owner and beneficiary of a key person policy, each shareholder reduces his basis in his shares by his proportionate part of the nondeductible expense. IRC Sec. 1367(a)(2)(D).

If the particular premium payments are considered compensation (for example, the employee owns the policy or has a beneficial interest in it—see Q 52 to Q 53), the amount of compensation would be deductible in determining the corporation's income or loss which is reported pro rata by each shareholder. The amount of the compensation would then be included in income by the insured employee. IRC Secs. 1363, 1366.

If the premium payment is considered a distribution with respect to stock to an individual shareholder (Q 52, Q 53) the tax treatment would depend on whether or not the corporation has accumulated earnings and profits. If the corporation has no accumulated earnings and profits, the payment is treated first as a return of investment and then as capital gain. If the corporation has accumulated earnings and profits, part of the distribution might be treated as a dividend. IRC Sec. 1368. An S corporation may have accumulated earnings and profits from years when it was a C corporation or as the result of a corporate acquisition. How S corporation distributions are taxed is explained in Q 839. *ASRS, Sec. 43, ¶20.10.*

Partnerships and Partners

56. Are premiums paid by a partnership, or by a partner, for insurance on the life of a copartner, deductible?

No, regardless of who is named beneficiary of the proceeds. Premiums paid for any life insurance, or endowment or annuity contract, are not deductible if the taxpayer is directly or indirectly a beneficiary under the policy or contract. IRC Sec. 264(a)(1). Whether the insurance is purchased as a key person policy or to finance the purchase of insured's partnership interest, the premium paying partner will benefit from the policy. Treas. Reg. §1.264-1; *Yarnall v. Comm.*, 9 TC 616 (1947), aff'd 170 F.2d 272 (3rd Cir. 1948); *McKay v. Comm.*, 10 BTA 949 (1928). However, for insurance purchased by a partnership on the life of an employee who is not a partner, see Q 45 and Q 46. *ASRS, Sec. 53, ¶14.4.*

57. Are premiums paid by a partner for insurance on his own life deductible by him if the proceeds are payable to the partnership or to a copartner?

No. Premiums paid on any life insurance policy, or endowment or annuity contract, are not deductible if the taxpayer is directly or indirectly a beneficiary under the policy or contract. IRC Sec. 264(a)(1). Whether the policy is purchased as key person insurance, or to finance the purchase of an insured's partnership interest, the insured's estate (and, therefore, the insured) will benefit from the policy. *Keefe v. Comm.*, 15 TC 947 (1950); *Nussbaum v. Comm.*, 19 BTA 868 (1930). If a partner takes out insurance on his own life and irrevocably designates his copartner as beneficiary in order to induce the copartner to leave his investment in the firm, the insured partner is indirectly a beneficiary under the policy. Treas. Reg. §1.264-1(b). *ASRS, Sec. 53, ¶14.4.*

BUSINESS CONTINUATION: BUSINESS LIFE INSURANCE   Q 60

Sole Proprietorships

58. If a sole proprietor uses business funds to purchase insurance on his own life, are the premium payments deductible as a business expense?

No, regardless of who is beneficiary under the policy. The premium payments are nondeductible personal expenses, because a sole proprietor and his business are considered one and the same for tax purposes. IRC Sec. 262(a); Treas. Reg. §1.262-1(b)(1). For insurance purchased by a sole proprietor on the life of an employee, see Q 45 and Q 46. *ASRS, Sec. 53, ¶14.3.*

59. If an employee of a sole proprietor purchases insurance on the life of the sole proprietor, are the premiums deductible by the employee?

No. The premiums are nondeductible because they are either personal expenses or expenses allocable to tax-exempt income (the death proceeds). IRC Secs. 262(a), 265(a)(1); see *Whitaker v. Comm.*, 34 TC 106 (1960). *ASRS, Sec. 53, ¶14.2.*

Deduction of Premiums Denied for Reasons Other Than Section 264(a)(1)

60. If a taxpayer, in the course of his business, purchases a policy on the life of a person who is not his employee may he deduct the premiums?

In most instances, the disallowance of a deduction for business life insurance premiums will be by reason of IRC Section 264(a)(1). Nevertheless, the deduction will ordinarily be barred on other grounds if the taxpayer (premium payer) has an interest in the policy. Thus, the deduction may be denied for any of the following reasons: the premiums are not ordinary and necessary business expenses within the meaning of IRC Section 162(a); the premiums are expenses incurred to obtain tax-exempt income (the death proceeds) and consequently are nondeductible under IRC Section 265(a)(1); the premiums constitute capital expenditures. The cases and rulings below illustrate denial of the deduction for reasons other than IRC Section 264(a)(1):

> A corporation paid premiums on insurance on the lives of two stockholders to fund an entity purchase agreement. The proceeds were payable to the trustee who was to administer the plan. In holding that the premiums were nondeductible, the IRS did not rely on IRC Section 264, but held that payment of the premiums was a capital expenditure for acquisition of the stock. Rev. Rul. 70-117, 1970-1 CB 30.

> Premiums paid by a manager of persons in the entertainment field on an insurance policy covering the life of one of the entertainers are not deductible where the manager is the beneficiary under the policy. The premiums are not ordinary and necessary business expenses within the meaning of IRC Section 162. Rev. Rul. 55-714, 1955-2 CB 51.

> Premiums paid on insurance covering the lives of individuals acting as taxpayer's sales agents are not deductible where the taxpayer is the beneficiary. The premiums are in the nature of a capital investment, and are not ordinary and necessary business expenses. *Merrimac Hat Corp. v. Comm.*, 29 BTA 690 (1934).

> Under a conditional sales contract for the sale of a sole proprietorship, the purchaser was required to carry insurance on the life of the seller. The purchaser, who was the beneficiary, agreed to use the proceeds to pay the balance of the purchase price in event of the seller's death. It was held that the premiums were not deductible because they were in the nature of a capital investment. *Whitaker v. Comm.*, 34 TC 106 (1960).

Taxpayer purchased the contingent remaindermen's interests in a trust. He also purchased insurance on the lives of the remaindermen to protect his investment in the event the remaindermen failed to survive the life tenant. Taxpayer claimed a deduction for his premium payments. The Tax Court held that the premiums were not deductible expenses; they were expenses incurred for obtaining tax-exempt income and consequently were nondeductible by reason of the predecessor to IRC Section 265(a)(1). *Jones v. Comm.*, 25 TC 4 (1955), aff'd, 231 F.2d 655 (3rd Cir. 1956).

ASRS, Sec. 53, ¶14.6.

ANNUITIES AND LIVING PROCEEDS RECEIVED BY A CORPORATION

61. How is a corporation taxed on payments under an annuity contract or on living proceeds from an endowment or life insurance contract?

Generally, with respect to living proceeds from endowment and life insurance contracts, the same rules apply that are applicable to personal insurance and endowment contracts (see "Living Proceeds," Q 249 to Q 270). See IRC Sec. 11(a).

However, to the extent that contributions are made after February 28, 1986 to a deferred annuity contract held by a corporation or other entity that is not a natural person, the contract is not treated for tax purposes as an annuity contract. Income on the contract is treated as ordinary income received or accrued by the owner during the taxable year. IRC Sec. 72(u). Thus, if payments received in a year plus amounts received in prior years plus the net surrender value at the end of the year, if any, exceed premiums paid in the year and in prior years plus amounts included in income in prior years, the excess amount is includable in income. The rule and exceptions are discussed in Q 2. To the extent an annuity contract is not subject to this rule, payments received under the contract will be subject to the rules applicable to personal annuity contracts. *ASRS, Sec. 52, ¶300.1(f); Sec. 53, ¶16.6.*

DEATH PROCEEDS OF BUSINESS LIFE INSURANCE

General Rule

62. Are the death proceeds of business life insurance exempt from income tax?

Under the rules applicable to life insurance contracts generally, the entire lump sum payable at insured's death is exempt from regularly calculated income tax whether the beneficiary is an individual, a corporation, a partnership, a trust, or the insured's estate. IRC Sec. 101(a); Treas. Reg. §1.101-1(a); *U.S. v. Supplee-Biddle Hardware Co.*, 265 U.S. 189 (1924). See Q 271, Q 273. If the proceeds are paid out under a life income or other installment option, the amount payable at death may be prorated and recovered from the payments in equal tax free amounts over the payment period; but the interest element is taxable (see Q 276). Proceeds received by a partnership or by an S corporation retain their tax-exempt character when passed on to the individual partners or shareholders. But proceeds received tax free by a regular (C) corporation are, when paid out, usually taxable to the recipients as compensation or dividends (see Q 55, Q 73).

However, death proceeds are not always wholly tax-exempt. For example, the Code expressly provides that the proceeds are taxable, under some circumstances, where the policy has previously been sold or otherwise transferred for a valuable consideration (Q

BUSINESS CONTINUATION: BUSINESS LIFE INSURANCE Q 63

63 to Q 72). The Code also provides a special rule for proceeds payable under a qualified pension or profit sharing plan–only the amount in excess of the cash surrender value is tax-exempt under IRC Section 101(a)–(see Q 437 to Q 439). The same rule applies to proceeds received under a tax sheltered annuity (see Q 491) and proceeds received under individual retirement endowment contracts (see Q 229). There are other instances, too, where the exemption is not available because the proceeds are not considered to be received as "life insurance" proceeds. Included here are proceeds that are taxable as dividends or compensation (Q 73), proceeds taxable because of lack of insurable interest (Q 74), proceeds taxable as a return of embezzled funds (Q 75), and proceeds of creditor insurance (Q 293, Q 294).

Even though proceeds are tax-exempt, it has been ruled, they can reduce an otherwise deductible capital loss. Where liquidation of a business after a partner's death resulted in a loss but life insurance on that partner had been purchased by the other partner for the express purpose of protecting his capital investment in the business, the court ruled that because the loss was compensated for by insurance it was not deductible. IRC Section 165(a) provides that "[t]here shall be allowed as a deduction any loss sustained during the taxable year and not compensated for by insurance or otherwise." *Johnson v. Comm.*, 66 TC 897 (1976), aff'd, 78-1 USTC ¶9367 (4th Cir. 1978).

For the treatment of proceeds under the alternative minimum tax, see Q 95. *ASRS, Sec. 53, ¶16.*

Proceeds Taxable Because of Transfer for Value

63. Will the sale or other transfer for value of an existing life insurance policy or any interest in a policy cause loss of income tax exemption for the death proceeds?

Yes, as a general rule. IRC Section 101(a)(2) provides that if a policy, or any interest in a policy, is transferred for a valuable consideration, the death proceeds will generally be exempt only to the extent of the consideration paid by the transferee and net premiums, if any, paid by the transferee after the transfer. Also, any interest paid or accrued by the transferee on indebtedness with respect to the policy is added to the exempt amount if the interest is not deductible under IRC Section 264(a)(4). IRC Sec. 101(a)(2). This provision regarding interest paid or accrued applies to contracts issued after June 8, 1997 in taxable years ending after this date. Further, for purposes of this provision any material increase in the death benefit or other material change in the contract shall be treated as a new contract with certain limited exceptions. TRA '97, Sec. 1084(d).

The balance of the death proceeds is taxable as ordinary income. This is the so-called "transfer for value rule." But if the sale or other transfer for value comes within any of the following exceptions to the transfer for value rule, the exemption is available despite the sale or other transfer for value:

(1) If the sale or other transfer for value is to the insured himself (see Q 65). IRC Sec. 101(a)(2)(B).

(2) If the sale or other transfer for value is to a partner of the insured, to a partnership in which the insured is a partner, or to a corporation in which the insured is an officer or shareholder (see Q 67 to Q 72). IRC Sec. 101(a)(2)(B). Members of a limited

2006 Tax Facts on Insurance & Employee Benefits

liability company (LLC) taxed as a partnership are considered to be "partners" for this purpose. Let. Rul. 9625013.

(3) If the basis for determining gain or loss in the hands of the transferee is determined in whole or in part by reference to the basis of the transferor; for example, where a policy is transferred from one corporation to another in a tax free reorganization (see Q 72), where the policy is transferred between spouses (see Q 279) or where a policy is acquired in part by gift. IRC Sec. 101(a)(2)(A); Rev. Rul. 69-187, 1969-1 CB 45; Let. Rul. 8951056. See Q 64. *ASRS, Sec. 52, ¶520.3; Sec. 53, ¶16.2.*

64. What constitutes a "transfer for value" of a life insurance policy or an interest in a policy?

Any transfer for a valuable consideration of a right to receive all or part of the proceeds of a life insurance policy is a transfer for value. The transfer for value rule extends far beyond outright sales of policies. The naming of a beneficiary in exchange for any kind of valuable consideration would constitute a transfer for value of an interest in the policy. Even the creation by separate contract of a right to receive all or part of the proceeds would constitute a transfer for value. On the other hand, a mere pledging or assignment of a policy as collateral security is not a "transfer for value." Treas. Reg. §1.101-1(b)(4). The transfer of a policy by a corporation to a stockholder as a distribution in liquidation is a transfer for value. *Lambeth v. Comm.*, 38 BTA 351 (1938). A transfer for value can occur even though the policy transferred has no cash surrender value. *James F. Waters, Inc. v. Comm.*, 160 F.2d 596 (9th Cir. 1947). And a transfer will be considered a "transfer for value" even though no purchase price is paid for the policy or interest in the policy, provided the transferor receives some other valuable consideration. *Monroe v. Patterson*, 8 AFTR 2d 5142 (N.D. Ala. 1961).

In the *Monroe* case two policies were purchased on the life of an officer-stockholder, one by the insured and the other by the corporation. Subsequently, the insured entered into an agreement with two employees for the purchase of his stock at his death. The policies were transferred to a trustee for use in partially financing the agreement and the employees took over the payment of premiums. Upon the insured's death, the proceeds were applied to the purchase of his stock. The court held that the employees were transferees for value even though they had paid no purchase price for the policies. Their agreement to make the premium payments and to purchase the stock constituted a valuable consideration. Consequently the employees were taxed on the difference between the premiums they had paid and the proceeds applied toward their purchase of the insured's stock. *Monroe v. Patterson*, supra.

Where two shareholders assigned to each other existing policies (having no cash values) on their own lives to fund a cross-purchase agreement, there was found a transfer for value. Let. Rul. 7734048. Similarly, where a partnership named two partners as cross-beneficiaries on policies owned by the partnership, a transfer for value had taken place. Let. Rul. 9012063.

However, if the transferor receives no valuable consideration whatsoever, there is no "transfer for value." *Haverty Realty & Investment Co. v. Comm.*, 3 TC 161 (1944).

Because a transfer of a policy subject to a nonrecourse loan discharges the transferor of his obligation under the loan, he is treated as receiving an amount equal to

BUSINESS CONTINUATION: BUSINESS LIFE INSURANCE   Q 66

the discharged obligation. Treas. Reg. §1.1001-2(a). Thus, there may be a transfer for value when a life insurance contract is transferred which is subject to a policy loan. Nonetheless, where the value of the policy exceeded the outstanding loan, the transfer was ruled in part a gift and within one of the exceptions to the transfer for value rule because the basis of the policy in the hands of the transferee was determinable in part by reference to the basis of the policy in the hands of the transferor (see Q 63, #3). Rev. Rul. 69-187, 1969-1 CB 45. In Letter Ruling 8951056, the "gratuitous" transfer of a policy subject to a nonrecourse loan was held a part gift, part sale. Because the transferor's basis was greater than the amount of the loan, the basis of the policy in the hands of the transferee was the basis in the hands of the transferor at the time of transfer and thus the transfer fell within the same exception to the transfer for value rule. But see Let. Rul. 8628007.

The transfer of a policy to a grantor trust treated as owned by the transferor was determined not a transfer for value where the insureds, terms, conditions, benefits and beneficial interests (other than naming the trustee as beneficiary and nominal owner) did not change. Let. Rul. 9041052. The replacement of a jointly owned policy with two separately owned policies was determined not a transfer for value. Let. Rul. 9852041. For transfer to a grantor trust owned by the insured, see Q 65. Transfers of policies to a qualified retirement plan are discussed in Q 437. *ASRS, Sec. 52, ¶520.3, Sec. 53, ¶16.2.*

65. Can an existing life insurance policy be sold to the insured himself without loss of income tax exemption for the death proceeds?

Yes, sale to the insured himself is an exception to the transfer for value rule (see Q 63). IRC Sec. 101(a)(2)(B). For example, if a corporation purchases a policy insuring a key person and later sells it to the insured, the proceeds will be received wholly tax-exempt by the beneficiary despite the sale to the insured. See Let. Rul. 8906034. Moreover, a transfer to a trust which is treated as owned wholly or in part by the insured comes within the exception as a transfer to the insured, but only to the extent the insured is treated as owner. *Swanson v. Comm.*, 75-2 USTC ¶9528 (8th Cir. 1975). (An individual is treated as owner of a trust where he retains control over property he has transferred to the trust, so that the income on that property is taxable to him under IRC Sections 671-679. See Q 844.)

Where a policy is transferred more than once, but the last transfer, or the last transfer for value, is to the insured himself, the proceeds will be wholly tax-exempt regardless of any previous sale or other transfer for value. Treas. Reg. §1.101-1(b)(3)(ii). But if the insured transfers the policy for a valuable consideration, and the transfer does not come within any of the exceptions to the transfer for value rule, the proceeds will again lose their tax-exempt status. *ASRS, Sec. 53, ¶16.2.*

66. If an employer or employer's qualified plan sells or distributes a policy on an employee's life to the insured's spouse, or to another member of insured's family, will the transfer cause loss of tax exemption for the death proceeds?

Generally, yes, unless the transferee is a bona fide business partner of the insured. Such a transfer does not come within any of the exceptions to the transfer for value rule (see Q 63). If a sale is involved, the death proceeds will be taxable to the extent that they exceed the consideration paid by the purchaser plus net premiums, if any, paid after the

2006 Tax Facts on Insurance & Employee Benefits

sale. (Also, any interest paid or accrued by the transferee on policy indebtedness may be added to the exempt amount under certain circumstances. See Q 63.)

But even if the spouse or family member pays nothing for the policy, the transfer may be considered a transfer for value on the ground that the employee's past or promised future services constituted a valuable consideration for the transfer. The proceeds then would probably be taxable to the extent that they exceed the value of the contract at the time of transfer plus any subsequent premium payments and certain policy indebtedness. A transfer to the insured, followed by a gift from the insured to his spouse or family member (see Q 64) or a sale to his spouse after July 18, 1984 (see Q 279) would avoid taxation of the proceeds under the transfer for value rule. A federal appeals court refused to treat a direct transfer by an employer to the wife of an insured employee for a consideration as two transfers merged into one: a transfer to the insured employee and then a gift from him to his wife. *Est. of Rath v. U.S.*, 79-2 USTC ¶9654 (6th Cir. 1979). *ASRS, Sec. 53, ¶16.2.*

67. If a policyholder sells his life insurance policy to a corporation, will the sale result in a loss of the tax exemption for the death proceeds?

Not if the *insured* is an officer or shareholder of the corporation. IRC Section 101(a)(2)(B) provides that the transfer for value rule does not apply if the transfer is "to a corporation in which the insured is a shareholder or officer." (See Q 63.) Moreover, where a policy is transferred more than once, but the last transfer is to a corporation in which the insured is an officer or shareholder, the proceeds will be wholly tax-exempt regardless of any previous sale or other transfer for value. Treas. Reg. §1.101-1(b)(3)(ii).

However, the proceeds will lose their income tax-exempt status by sale to the corporation if the insured is merely a non-stockholder, non-officer employee or director since such a sale does not come within the exceptions to the transfer for value rule (see Q 63). Also, it is doubtful whether a person who is only nominally an officer, with no real executive authority or duties, would be considered an "officer." See Rev. Rul. 80-314, 1980-2 CB 152. The regulations do not define the term "officer" for this purpose. It should be noted that the important relationship is that between the *insured* and the corporation. In other words, even though the policyholder is not the insured, the exception will apply provided the insured is an officer or shareholder in the corporation to which the policy is transferred.

Where the employer purchases a policy from an employee for contribution to a qualified plan, see Q 437. *ASRS, Sec. 53, ¶16.2.*

68. If a corporation sells or distributes a life insurance policy to a stockholder who is not the insured, will the transfer cause a loss of the tax exemption for the death proceeds?

The transfer of a policy *to* a corporation in which the *insured* is a shareholder can be made without loss of the tax exemption, even where the transferor is not the insured (see Q 67). IRC Sec. 101(a)(2)(B). However, the exception does not apply to a transfer in the reverse direction. (See also Q 69.) *ASRS, Sec. 53, ¶16.2.*

69. Does a transfer for value problem arise when an insurance-funded stock redemption plan is changed to a cross-purchase plan, or vice versa?

BUSINESS CONTINUATION: BUSINESS LIFE INSURANCE   Q 70

If the corporation sells a policy on stockholder A's life to stockholder B, the proceeds will lose their tax-exempt status (see Q 68). Even if the corporation does not sell the policies, but merely distributes them to the stockholders, there will be a transfer for value. Valuable consideration may be found, for example, in relieving the corporation of its obligation to continue premium payments and its obligation to redeem the stock, or in satisfying the corporation's dividend obligation to its stockholders. See *Lambeth v. Comm.*, 38 BTA 351 (1938); *Monroe v. Patterson*, 8 AFTR 2d 5142 (N.D. Ala. 1961). The danger cannot be averted by a transfer to the insured and a subsequent transfer by the insured to another stockholder (see Q 70). However, a transfer by a corporation to a shareholder was ruled within an exception where the stockholders were also partners in a bona fide (although unrelated) partnership. Let. Rul. 9347016, Let. Rul. 9045004. Similarly, the transfer of a reverse split dollar policy from a corporation to two shareholders who were also partners of the insured for the purpose of funding a cross purchase agreement fell within the partner exception to the transfer for value rule. Let. Rul. 9701026. Further, the transfer of policies insuring shareholders/partners from a corporation to a partnership established specifically to receive and manage the policies was considered within the partnership exception to the transfer for value rule. Let. Rul. 9309021.

On the other hand, a change from a cross-purchase plan (between individual stockholders) to a stock redemption plan can be accomplished without violating the transfer for value rule. In each instance, a stockholder will be transferring a policy he owns on another stockholder's life to a corporation in which the insured is a shareholder. Such a transfer qualifies as one of the exceptions to the transfer for value rule (see Q 67). IRC Sec. 101(a)(2)(B). *ASRS, Sec. 53, ¶16.2.*

70. Will the transfer of a life insurance policy by one stockholder to another, or by a stockholder's estate to a surviving stockholder, cause loss of tax exemption for the proceeds?

Yes, unless the person to whom the policy is transferred is the insured himself (see Q 65), or unless the stockholders are also partners in a bona fide partnership (see Q 71). The exceptions to the transfer for value rule do not include transfers between individual stockholders (see Q 68). IRC Sec. 101(a)(2). This is important to note in connection with an insurance funded buy-sell agreement on the cross-purchase plan where the plan involves more than two stockholders. After the first death, a survivor may wish to purchase a policy on the life of another survivor from the deceased's estate. Such a purchase would disqualify the death proceeds for income tax exemption. Or, suppose the parties to a stock redemption plan wish to change to a cross-purchase plan and the corporation sells or distributes the policies to the insureds themselves. If the insureds then sell the policies to each other, or exchange policies, the proceeds will lose their tax-exempt status. Even if no money is involved in the transaction, a valuable consideration can be found in the reciprocal transfers. (See Q 64.)

To avoid transfer for value problems, some planners recommend that a policy owned by a shareholder on his own life be transferred to the corporation of which he is a shareholder. Subsequent to the transfer, the corporation enters into an endorsement split dollar agreement with an employee who desires to purchase the shares upon the shareholder's death. *ASRS, Sec. 53, ¶16.2.*

2006 Tax Facts on Insurance & Employee Benefits

71. Will transfers of life insurance policies between partners, or between partners and the partnership, or to a partner of the insured, or to a partnership in which insured is a partner result in a loss of the income tax exemption for the death proceeds?

No. The transfer for value rule does not apply where the policy is transferred to a partner of the insured or to a partnership in which the insured is a partner. IRC Sec. 101(a)(2)(B). However, the partnership must actually operate as one, and not exist in form only. *Swanson v. Comm.*, 75-2 USTC ¶9528 (8th Cir. 1975), aff'g TC Memo 1974-61. But see Let. Rul. 9309021. A partner can sell a policy on his life to the partnership or to another partner. A retiring partner can sell to an incoming partner the policy he owns on another partner's life. Or, a partnership can sell a policy to the insured partner or to a copartner of the insured. Also, where a partnership owns a key person policy on the life of a non-partner, there is no transfer for value when a new partner enters or an existing partner leaves the partnership, provided the partnership is not terminated by such an action. Let. Rul. 9410039. However, sale of a policy to a member of insured's family who is not a partner would disqualify the proceeds for exemption. Where there is an insurance-funded buy-sell agreement between more than two partners, and a partner dies, a surviving partner may buy policies on the lives of other surviving partners from the deceased's estate without loss of tax exemption for the death proceeds. See Let. Rul. 9727024.

The Service has ruled privately that members of a limited liability company (LLC), which was classified as a partnership for federal tax purposes, would be considered "partners" for purposes of the transfer for value rule. Let. Rul. 9625013.

A transfer for value by a corporation to a partnership in which an insured shareholder is a partner comes within the exception. Let. Rul. 9042023. Similarly, a transfer to shareholders who are partners, even though in an unrelated partnership, falls within the exception. Let. Rul. 9347016, Let. Rul. 9045004. Further, the Service has ruled privately that the transfer of policies insuring shareholders/partners from a corporation to a partnership established specifically to receive and manage the policies comes within the exception. Let. Rul. 9309021. A sale of policies by an insured's grantor trust (see Q 844) to a limited partnership where the insured was a limited partner was ruled within the exemption. Let. Rul. 9843024. However, the Service has indicated that it will not issue rulings concerning whether or not the exception applies to a transfer of a life insurance policy to an unincorporated organization where substantially all of the organization's assets consist or will consist of life insurance policies on the lives of its members. Rev. Proc. 2005-3, 2005-1 IRB 118.

If a policy is transferred more than once, and the last transfer, or the last transfer for value, is to a partner of the insured, or to a partnership in which the insured is a partner, the proceeds will be entirely tax-exempt regardless of any previous transfer for value. Treas. Reg. §1.101-1(b)(3)(ii). *ASRS, Sec. 53, ¶16.2.*

72. If a life insurance policy is transferred to a corporation in a tax free organization or reorganization, will the transfer cause a loss of the tax exemption for the proceeds?

Not if the insured is an officer or shareholder in the corporation to which the policy is transferred (see Q 67).

BUSINESS CONTINUATION: BUSINESS LIFE INSURANCE   Q 73

Moreover, even where the insured is not an officer or shareholder of the transferee corporation, the proceeds will not lose their tax-exempt status if the policy is transferred as part of a general tax free transfer. For example, a transfer of property in organizing a corporation is tax free if immediately after the transfer the persons who exchanged property for stock own at least 80% of the voting stock and 80% of all other classes of stock in the corporation. Such a transfer usually takes place, for example, when an unincorporated business is incorporated. IRC Secs. 351(a), 368(c). Other examples of tax free transfers would include tax free reorganizations. Tax free reorganizations include, for example, statutory mergers and consolidations, and the transfers of substantially all the property of one corporation solely in exchange for the voting stock of another corporation. IRC Sec. 368. Where an asset changes hands in a tax free transfer, the tax basis of the asset does not change. IRC Sec. 358. Consequently, such a transfer comes within the exception to the transfer for value rule set forth in IRC Section 101(a)(2)(A). (See Q 63.)

However, if the proceeds would not have been exempt had the policy been retained by the transferor, the tax free transfer will not cause them to become tax-exempt unless the insured is an officer or shareholder of the transferee corporation. Treas. Reg. §1.101-1(b)(3).

If a corporation purchases the assets of another corporation (not a tax free reorganization), and those assets include a life insurance policy, the sale will cause loss of exemption for the proceeds unless the insured is an officer or shareholder of the purchasing corporation (see Q 67). IRC Sec. 101(a)(2)(B); *Spokane Dry Goods Co. v. Comm.*, TC Memo 1943. *ASRS, Sec. 53, ¶16.2.*

Proceeds Taxable as Dividends or Compensation

73. Under what circumstances are the death proceeds of life insurance taxable as dividends or compensation?

Proceeds that have been received tax free by a C corporation lose their tax exempt character as life insurance proceeds on distribution to employees or shareholders. Consequently, where a corporation is both owner and beneficiary of a policy, the proceeds will generally be tax free to the corporation; but if the corporation distributes the proceeds to its shareholders, the shareholders will be treated as having received a taxable dividend. *Cummings v. Comm.*, 73 F.2d 477 (1st Cir. 1934); *May v. Comm.*, 20 BTA 282 (1930); *Webster v. Comm.*, BTA Memo 1935; Rev. Rul. 71-79, 1971-1 CB 112. Or, if the insured is an employee and the proceeds are received by the corporation and then paid to the employee's widow or other personal beneficiary under the terms of an employment contract, they may be treated as taxable compensation for his past services. *Essenfeld v. Comm.*, 11 AFTR 2d 303 (2d Cir. 1962).

On the other hand, if the corporation has no ownership rights in the policy and is not the beneficiary, the proceeds should be received tax free by the beneficiary as life insurance proceeds. See Q 271, Q 273. IRC Sec. 101(a). Where a corporation paid the premiums on a policy that was held by a trustee for the benefit of certain shareholders and the corporation had no ownership rights in the policy, the court held the proceeds received by the shareholders were tax exempt life insurance proceeds. *Doran v. Comm.*, 246 F.2d 934 (9th Cir. 1957). The IRS has indicated, however, that the *premiums* when paid by the corporation may, in some circumstances, be taxed to the shareholders as dividends. See Rev. Rul. 59-184, 1959-1 CB 65. See also Q 52.

However, where the corporation owns the policy and is not the beneficiary, it appears that the proceeds are taxable as dividends (and possibly as compensation). Where the proceeds of a policy were payable to a trustee for the benefit of shareholders but the corporation had substantial ownership rights in the policy, the court conceded that the proceeds were life insurance proceeds but said that they were also in the nature of dividends and, under such circumstances, the dividend provisions of the tax law would prevail. *Golden v. Comm.*, 113 F.2d 590 (3rd Cir. 1940). The U.S. Court of Appeals for the Sixth Circuit, however, reached an opposite conclusion in the *Ducros* case. There, the policy was owned by the corporation and individual stockholders were named as revocable beneficiaries in the policy. The court held that the proceeds, received by the shareholders directly from the insurance company, were life insurance proceeds and, therefore, tax exempt. *Ducros v. Comm.*, 272 F.2d 49 (6th Cir. 1959). The IRS has announced its refusal to follow the *Ducros* decision as precedent in disposing of similar cases. Rev. Rul. 61-134, 1961-2 CB 250. Revenue Ruling 61-134 states that: "It is the position of the Service that life insurance proceeds paid to stockholders of a corporation are taxable as dividends in cases where the corporation uses its earnings to pay the insurance premiums and has all incidents of ownership including the right to name itself beneficiary, even though the corporation does not name itself beneficiary and, therefore, is not entitled to and does not in fact receive the proceeds." The same principle should apply if the proceeds of a corporate owned policy are payable directly to an insured employee's beneficiary; but the proceeds would ordinarily be taxable compensation rather than dividends. Nonetheless, a Technical Advice Memorandum has held that proceeds of a corporate owned and paid for life insurance policy naming as revocable beneficiary the wife of the insured-stockholder were not dividends (because she was not a stockholder and the estate-stockholder was not a beneficiary) and were not income in respect of a decedent, but life insurance death proceeds tax free under IRC Section 101(a). TAM 8144001.

Assuming, but not deciding on, the validity of Estate Tax Regulation Section 20.2042-1(c)(6) (see Q 610), the Tax Court has held that where a corporation owned insurance on the life of a controlling stockholder, and where the beneficiary named by the corporation was the insured's wife, who owned stock in the corporation, the death proceeds were not taxable to the beneficiary as a dividend but were excludable from her income as proceeds of life insurance under IRC Section 101(a)(1). *Est. of Horne v. Comm.*, 64 TC 1020 (1975), acq. in result, 1980-1 CB 1.

In the case of an S corporation, each shareholder increases his basis in his stock by his share of the tax-free death proceeds received by the corporation. Thereafter, any distribution of the proceeds should be determined to be compensation or a distribution with respect to stock as if it were a regular C corporation. A distribution with respect to stock is taxed as explained in Q 839.

Where insurance is used to fund a stock redemption agreement, see Q 88. *ASRS, Sec. 53, ¶¶16.3, 16.3(a)*.

Proceeds Taxable Because of Lack of Insurable Interest

74. If a corporation takes out a life insurance policy on a person in whose life the corporation has no insurable interest, will the death proceeds be exempt from income tax?

BUSINESS CONTINUATION: BUSINESS LIFE INSURANCE — Q 77

There is danger that the proceeds may be considered taxable income from a wagering contract instead of tax-exempt life insurance proceeds. *Atlantic Oil Co. v. Patterson*, 13 AFTR 2d 1267 (5th Cir. 1964); see also *U.S. v. Supplee-Biddle Hardware Co.*, 265 U.S. 189 (1924). However, if there is an insurable interest when the policy is taken out, the contract generally will not be considered a wagering contract, even if an insurable interest is not present at death. *Ducros v. Comm.*, 272 F.2d 49 (6th Cir. 1959). Insurable interest is determined by the laws of the various states. Consequently, if there is insurable interest under the applicable state law, the death proceeds should qualify as "life insurance" proceeds under section 101(a) of the Internal Revenue Code. See *ASRS, Sec. 12, ¶20*, for discussion of insurable interest and summary of state laws. See *ASRS, Sec. 53, ¶16.4* for taxation of proceeds.

Proceeds as Restitution of Embezzled Funds

75. Where a life insurance policy is assigned to an employer in restitution of funds embezzled by the insured, are the proceeds tax-exempt to the employer?

No; the employer does not receive the proceeds as life insurance payable by reason of insured's death but as a restitution of embezzled funds. Consequently, the income tax exclusion under IRC Section 101(a) does not apply. If the employer has claimed a loss deduction, he must report the proceeds as a recovery of a previously deducted embezzlement loss. *Tennessee Foundry & Mach. Co. v. Comm.*, 22 AFTR 2d 5285 (6th Cir. 1968). *ASRS, Sec. 53, ¶16.5.*

S Corporations

76. How are the death proceeds of a life insurance policy purchased by an S corporation taxed?

Where an S corporation is the beneficiary of a policy, and death proceeds are received as tax-exempt income, each stockholder's pro rata share of the proceeds is tax-exempt to him and the basis of his stock is increased by his share of the tax-exempt proceeds. IRC Secs. 1366(a)(1)(A), 1367(a)(1)(A). An S corporation's delay in receiving death proceeds that will be used to purchase a deceased shareholder's shares will still result in an increase in the basis of all the shareholder's shares, not just the shares of the surviving shareholders. Let. Rul. 200409010.

If the corporation is neither owner nor beneficiary, proceeds of a policy paid for by the corporation should be tax free to the beneficiary as life insurance proceeds. If the corporation owns the policy but is not the beneficiary, the characterization of the proceeds is not entirely clear. See Q 73. However, if they are treated as a distribution of profits (dividends in the case of a regular C corporation), they would be taxed as return of basis, capital gain and/or dividends, as explained in Q 839. If the proceeds paid to the beneficiary of a policy owned by the corporation are treated as corporate distributions, they should also be treated as tax free proceeds to the corporation which increase each shareholder's basis pro rata. *ASRS, Sec. 43, ¶20.10.*

Transfer of Policy

77. If an employer that owns a policy on the life of an employee sells the policy to the employee for its cash surrender value, can the sale result in taxable income to the employee? To the employer?

2006 Tax Facts on Insurance & Employee Benefits

Transfers of property after June 30, 1969 in connection with the performance of services are governed by IRC Section 83. Effective for transfers after February 12, 2004, regulations under IRC Section 83 provide that: "In the case of a transfer of a life insurance contract, retirement income contract, endowment contract, or other contract providing life insurance protection, or any undivided interest therein, the policy cash value and all other rights under such contract (including any supplemental agreements thereto and whether or not guaranteed), other than current life insurance protection, are treated as property..." However, for policies that are part of split dollar arrangements that are NOT subject to the split dollar regulations (see Q 459), only the cash surrender value will be considered "property." Treas. Reg. §1.83-3(e). Therefore, if the policy's actual value was more than the cash surrender value, then the sale may result in taxable income to the employee.

Under prior regulations where only the cash surrender value was considered property, the IRS concluded that where full ownership of a life insurance policy was transferred from an employer corporation to a key person, IRC Section 83 required that the employee include the policy's cash surrender value (less any payments he made for the policy) in income. Let. Rul. 8905010.

If a policy is sold by an employer for its cash surrender value, which is less than the total premiums paid, the employer can exclude from gross income the amount received from the sale of the insurance policy to the employee. Rev. Rul. 70-38, 1970-1 CB 11. However, no loss deduction is allowable when total premiums paid exceed the sale price (see Q 270). *ASRS, Sec. 53, ¶18.1.*

78. If an employee or stockholder sells his life insurance policy to the corporation for its cash surrender value, does he realize a taxable gain?

Yes, if the cash surrender value is greater than his net premium cost. The gain is ordinary income; not capital gain. *Gallun v. Comm.*, 13 AFTR 2d 660 (7th Cir. 1964). Normally, there is no deductible loss where a policy is sold for its cash surrender value. (See Q 270.) If the policy sold is subject to a nonrecourse loan, the amount realized on the sale includes the amount of the loan. Treas. Reg. §1.1001-2(a). See Q 64. *ASRS, Sec. 53, ¶18.4.*

79. If a corporation transfers a life insurance policy to an employee or stockholder without consideration, what are the income tax results?

The entire value of the policy is taxable to the employee or stockholder as compensation or as a dividend (distribution with respect to stock; in the case of an S corporation, see Q 839). (For value of unmatured policy, see Q 303.) Where the transferee is a stockholder-employee, the circumstances of the distribution will determine whether it is compensation or dividend. The case of *Thornley v. Comm.*, 41 TC 145 (1963), dealt with insurance on the lives of two stockholders; the policies had been purchased by the corporation to fund a stock redemption agreement. The agreement provided that upon the first death, policies on the survivor's life were to be distributed to him without cost. The Tax Court held that the value of the unmatured policies was taxable as a dividend to the survivor in the year his associate died. In another Tax Court case, the value of a life insurance policy constituted long-term capital gain to an officer-stockholder who received the policy in exchange for his stock in the corporation. *Parsons v. Comm.*, 54 TC 54 (1970). But, in a similar case, capital gains treatment was denied where there was no proof that the policy was received as part of the redemption price of the stock. *Wilkin v. Comm.*, TC Memo 1969-130.

However, if the employee's rights are subject to a substantial risk of forfeiture (see Q 112), the value is not taxable until his rights become substantially vested. The net premium cost of life insurance protection is taxable to him during the period the contract remains substantially nonvested. Treas. Reg. §1.83-1(a)(2).

If the employee takes the policy subject to a nonrecourse loan, he has given consideration to the extent of the loan amount. See Q 64. *ASRS, Sec. 53, ¶¶18.2, 18.3.*

STOCK PURCHASE AGREEMENT

Cross Purchase Agreement Between Individual Stockholders

80. Will the sale of a deceased's stock under a cross-purchase insurance-funded buy-sell agreement result in income tax liability to deceased's estate?

Normally, there will be no taxable gain to the deceased's estate if the stock is sold to surviving individual shareholders under a standard buy-sell agreement. At the stockholder's death, his stock receives a new tax basis equal to its fair market value at the time of death (or alternate valuation date)—see Q 816. As the sale price under a properly designed buy-sell agreement is usually accepted as the fair market value of the stock, the basis and sale price will normally be the same (see Q 613). Consequently, there should be no capital gain. Because individuals, rather than the corporation, purchase the stock, the payment cannot be regarded as a dividend (see Q 82). *ASRS, Sec. 43, ¶40.8, Sec. 53 ¶20.8(a).*

81. What are the income tax effects of funding a stock purchase agreement with life insurance?

Premiums

Regardless of whether the stockholder pays the premiums on a policy on the life of another stockholder or on a policy on his own life to fund the agreement, he cannot deduct his premium payments (see Q 49). IRC Secs. 262, 265(a)(1).

If the stockholders attempt to use company-paid group term life insurance to fund their buy-sell agreement, the company may be denied a deduction for its premium payments. The Internal Revenue Service has held, in a private ruling, that the premium payments under these circumstances are not related to the corporation's trade or business. Letter Ruling to Century Planning Corp., dated 6-28-62, signed by Arthur Singer, Acting Director, Tax Ruling Division (reproduced in ASRS, Sec. 43, at ¶40.8(g)(1)). Moreover, if the stockholders reciprocally name each other as beneficiaries of their insurance or reciprocally agree to apply the proceeds to the purchase of their stock, the proceeds may be taxable under the transfer for value rule (see Q 64).

The premiums paid by his associate stockholders are not taxable income to the insured. But if the *corporation* pays the premiums on insurance to fund a buy-sell agreement between the individual stockholders, the premium payments will be taxable dividends to the stockholders (see Q 53). *Doran v. Comm.*, 246 F.2d 934 (9th Cir. 1957);

Paramount-Richards Theatres, Inc. v. Comm., 153 F.2d 602 (5th Cir. 1946); see also Rev. Rul. 59-184, 1959-1 CB 65. (If an S corporation pays the premiums, see Q 55.)

Death Proceeds

The death proceeds are received free of income tax by the surviving stockholders (see Q 62). IRC Sec. 101(a). Each survivor applies the tax free proceeds he receives to purchase stock from the deceased's estate.

Cost Basis

The amount the survivor pays the estate for the stock becomes his cost basis in the stock. This cost basis will be used to calculate his gain or loss should he dispose of the stock during his lifetime. If, however, the survivor holds the stock until his own death, the stock will receive a stepped-up basis. See Q 816.

Ordinarily, the agreement gives each survivor a right to purchase from the deceased's estate the unmatured policy on his own life. If the agreement calls for transfer of the policy without cost to the insured, it would seem that his cost basis for the stock should be reduced by the value of the policy. But the Sixth Circuit Court of Appeals has held otherwise. *Storey v. U.S.*, 10 AFTR 2d 5301 (6th Cir. 1962).

After the first death, continued use of the policies to fund the buy-sell agreement between the survivors will bring adverse tax results under the transfer for value rule (see Q 70). *ASRS, Sec. 40, ¶70, Sec. 53, ¶¶15, 16*.

Planning Point: In comparison to a stock redemption agreement, use of a cross purchase agreement between stockholders provides flexibility to convert to a stock redemption agreement using the same life insurance policies (Q 69), provides the surviving stockholders with an increased cost basis (Q 80), avoids increasing the estate tax value of the decedents estate (Q 81), avoids application of the family attribution rules (Q 82), and does not expose the death benefits to the alternative minimum tax (Q 95). With multiple stockholders, the number of policies required to fund the cross purchase agreement can be reduced by using a "trusteed cross purchase agreement" and having the trustee, as an escrow agent, own a life insurance policy on each stockholder. *Donald F. Cady, J.D., LL.M., CLU.*

Stock Redemption

82. If a corporation redeems all of its stock owned by a deceased stockholder's estate, will the amount paid by the corporation be taxed as a dividend distribution to the estate?

As a general rule, any payment by a corporation (other than an S corporation) to a shareholder will be treated as a dividend rather than a capital transaction (sale or exchange), even if the payment is made to redeem stock. IRC Sec. 301(a); Rev. Rul. 55-515, 1955-2 CB 222. If a payment is treated as a dividend, the entire amount paid to an individual will generally be taxed at 15% (see Q 815 for the treatment of dividends), with no deduction for basis, and earnings and profit of the corporation will be reduced by the amount of money or other property distributed by the corporation. IRC Secs. 312(a), 316(a). However, there are several exceptions, discussed below, to the general rule that allow a payment to be treated as a sale or exchange. If a payment is characterized as a sale or exchange, it will be taxed as a capital gain. (For details, see Q 815.)

BUSINESS CONTINUATION: BUSINESS LIFE INSURANCE Q 82

In the context of closely held corporations, the characterization of a stock redemption is important for at least two additional reasons: (1) If a redemption is treated as a sale or exchange, the basis of the shares, if any, retained by the seller is unaffected by the transaction. If the redemption is treated as a dividend, the basis of the shares redeemed is added to the basis of the shares retained. Treas. Reg. §1.302-2(c). (2) If a redemption is treated as a sale or exchange, the part of the distribution properly chargeable to earnings and profits is an amount not in excess of the ratable share of earnings and profits of the corporation attributable to the redeemed stock. IRC Sec. 312(n)(7). If the redemption is treated as a dividend, earnings and profits of the corporation are reduced by the amount of money or other property distributed by the corporation. IRC Secs. 312(a), 316(a).

One of the exceptions to dividend treatment mentioned above is contained in IRC Section 302(b)(3). IRC Section 302(b)(3) provides that if the corporation redeems all of a shareholder's remaining shares (so that the shareholder's interest in the corporation is terminated), the amount paid by the corporation will be treated, not as a dividend, but as payment in exchange for the stock. In other words, the redemption will be treated as a capital transaction (see Q 86). *Zenz v. Quinlivan*, 213 F.2d 914 (6th Cir. 1954); Rev. Ruls. 55-745, 1955-2 CB 223, 77-293, 1977-2 CB 91, and 77-455, 1977-2 CB 93.

There will be no taxable dividend, then, if the corporation redeems *all* of its stock "owned by" the estate. But in determining what stock is owned by the estate, the "constructive ownership" (or "attribution-of-ownership") rules, contained in IRC Section 318, must be applied. Consequently, in order to achieve non-dividend treatment under IRC Section 302(b)(3), the corporation must redeem not only all of its shares *actually* owned by the estate, but also all of its shares *constructively* owned by the estate. One of these constructive ownership rules provides that shares owned by a beneficiary of an estate are considered owned by the estate. IRC Sec. 318(a)(3). For example, assume that decedent owned 250 shares of Corporation X's stock, so that his estate now actually owns 250 shares. Assume further that a beneficiary of decedent's estate owns 50 shares. Because the estate constructively owns the beneficiary's 50 shares, the estate is deemed to own a total of 300 shares. Redemption of the 250 shares actually owned, therefore, will not effect a redemption of all the stock owned by the estate. Furthermore, stock owned by a close family member of a beneficiary of the estate may be attributed to the estate beneficiary (because of the *family* constructive ownership rules), and through the estate beneficiary to the estate. IRC Sec. 318(a)(5)(A). An estate beneficiary would be considered to own, by way of the family attribution rules, shares owned by his spouse, his children, his grandchildren and his parents. IRC Sec. 318(a)(1).

It has been held that where, because of hostility among family members, a redeeming shareholder is prevented from exercising control over the stock he would be deemed to own constructively under the attribution rules, the attribution rules will not be applied to him. *Robin Haft Trust v. Comm.*, 75-1 USTC ¶9209 (1st Cir. 1975), vacating and remanding 61 TC 398. On the other hand, the IRS has indicated it will not follow the *Haft Trust* decision, and has ruled that the existence of family hostility will not affect its application of the attribution rules. However, if certain conditions are met, the IRS will not apply the ruling to taxpayers who have acted in reliance on the IRS's previously announced position on this issue. Rev. Rul. 80-26, 1980-1 CB 66. The Fifth Circuit has also taken the position that the existence of family hostility does not prevent application of the attribution rules, thus creating disagreement between the two circuit courts ruling on the question. *David Metzger Trust v. Comm.*, 82-2 USTC ¶9718 (5th

2006 Tax Facts on Insurance & Employee Benefits

Cir. 1982), aff'g 76 TC 42 (1981), cert. den. 463 U.S. 1207 (1983). The Tax Court has consistently held that hostility within the family does not affect application of the attribution rules. *Robin Haft Trust v. Comm.*, above; *David Metzger Trust v. Comm.*, above; *Cerone v. Comm.*, 87 TC 1 (1986).

The constructive ownership rules are complicated and their application requires expert legal advice. In general, it may be said that danger of dividend tax treatment exists in every case involving a family-owned corporation. There are, however, means available in some cases to avoid the harsh operation of the rules, for which see Q 83 and Q 84. For information about a *partial* redemption that will escape dividend tax treatment even in a family-owned corporation, see Q 85. *ASRS, Sec. 43, ¶40.8.*

83. How can the attribution of stock ownership among family members be avoided?

In attempting to qualify under the complete redemption rules (Q 82), the adverse effect of the *family* attribution rules (i.e., the rules that attribute stock ownership between family members, as distinct from other attribution rules which attribute stock ownership from or to estates, trusts or business entities) may ordinarily be overcome (i.e., waived) if the shareholder from whom the stock is redeemed: (a) retains no interest in the corporation (except as a creditor) immediately after redemption; (b) does not acquire any such interest (other than stock acquired by bequest or inheritance) within 10 years after the date of the redemption; and (c) files an agreement (called a waiver agreement) to notify the IRS of the redeeming shareholder's acquisition of a forbidden interest within the 10-year period. IRC Sec. 302(c)(2)(A). (As for what constitutes a forbidden retained interest, see the following cases and rulings: *Lynch v. Comm.*, 86-2 USTC ¶9731 (9th Cir. 1986); *Cerone v. Comm.*, 87 TC 1 (1986); *Seda v. Comm.*, 82 TC 484 (1984); *Est. of Lennard*, 61 TC 554 (1974), acq. in result, 1974-2 CB 3; Rev. Rul. 70-104, 1970-1 CB 66; Rev. Rul. 71-426, 1971-2 CB 173; Rev. Rul. 71-562, 1971-2 CB 173; Rev. Rul. 84-135, 1984-2 CB 80.)

With regard to distributions after August 31, 1982, an entity, such as a trust or estate, terminating its interest may waive the family attribution rules as long as the related party (the beneficiary, stockholder, or partner through whom ownership of the stock is attributed to the entity) joins in the waiver. The language of the Code prohibits waiver of entity attribution. IRC Sec. 302(c)(2)(C).

The family attribution rules will not be waived: (1) if any portion of the redeemed stock was acquired, directly or indirectly, by the redeeming shareholder within 10 years before the redemption from any member of his family named in the family attribution rules; or (2) if any member of the redeeming shareholder's family named in the family attribution rules owns (at the time of the redemption) stock in the corporation and such person acquired any stock in the corporation from the redeeming shareholder within 10 years before the redemption, unless the stock so acquired is redeemed in the same transaction. However, the foregoing limitation does not apply if the acquisition (as in (1)) or the disposition (as in (2)) by the redeeming shareholder did not have as one of its principal purposes the avoidance of federal income tax. IRC Sec. 302(c)(2)(B). One ruling illustrates the application of this "limitation on the limitation." A son and his father's estate owned all the outstanding stock of X corporation. The son's mother was the sole beneficiary of the estate. The son was active in the business, his mother was not. After the executor distributed the stock to the mother, X corporation redeemed all the

BUSINESS CONTINUATION: BUSINESS LIFE INSURANCE   Q 85

mother's stock so that the son could have complete ownership of X corporation. The mother's waiver agreement was effective to prevent the attribution to her of her son's stock, even though she had acquired the redeemed stock indirectly from her husband within 10 years of the redemption, because her acquisition of the stock did not have as one of its principal purposes the avoidance of federal income tax. Rev. Rul. 79-67, 1979-1 CB 128. *ASRS, Sec. 43, ¶40.8(b)(1).*

84. Can an executor avoid the attribution of stock ownership from an estate beneficiary to the estate by distributing the beneficiary's legacy before the redemption of the estate-held stock occurs?

As a relief provision, the regulations state that: "A person shall no longer be considered a beneficiary of an estate when all the property to which he is entitled has been received by him, when he no longer has a claim against the estate arising out of having been a beneficiary, and when there is only a remote possibility that it will be necessary for the estate to seek the return of property or to seek payment from him by contribution or otherwise to satisfy claims against the estate or expenses of administration." Treas. Reg. §1.318-3(a). Thus, the estate-beneficiary constructive ownership rules can be avoided, in some instances, by distributing the beneficiary-shareholder's legacy to him before the redemption takes place. Many states have apportionment laws calling for allocation of estate taxes among estate beneficiaries in all cases where the decedent did not direct otherwise by will. If distribution of a legacy to the beneficiary-shareholder in such a state is made before payment of estate taxes or without deduction for the beneficiary's share of the taxes, the shareholder will still be considered a beneficiary of the estate within the meaning of the regulation even after the distribution. *Est. of Webber v. U.S.*, 22 AFTR 2d 5911 (6th Cir. 1968).

Moreover, even if the shareholder's legacy has been distributed to him and he no longer has any claim against the estate, or the estate against him, if a member of his family is still a beneficiary of the estate, his shares may be attributed to the estate through the family member. IRC Sec. 318(a)(5)(A).

The relief provision under Treasury Regulation Section 1.318-3(a) is not available if a residuary legatee of the estate owns stock—because a residuary legatee's interest in the estate does not cease until the estate is closed. Rev. Rul. 60-18, 1960-1 CB 145.

Moreover, if a trust is a beneficiary of the estate and a surviving shareholder is a beneficiary of the trust, the surviving shareholder's stock will be attributed to the trust, and through the trust to the estate. Rev. Rul. 67-24, 1967-1 CB 75; Rev. Rul. 71-261, 1971-1 CB 108. *ASRS, Sec. 43, ¶40.8(b)(1).*

85. What is a "Section 303 stock redemption"?

It is a redemption of stock under the provisions of IRC Section 303. Estates comprised largely of close corporation stock generally have a liquidity problem. Congress enacted IRC Section 303 expressly to aid estates in solving this problem, and to protect small businesses from forced liquidations or mergers due to the heavy impact of death taxes. (However, in the proper circumstances, stock of a public corporation may also be redeemed under IRC Section 303.) Within the limits of IRC Section 303, surplus can be withdrawn from the corporation free of income tax.

2006 Tax Facts on Insurance & Employee Benefits

IRC Section 303 provides that, under stipulated conditions, a corporation can redeem part of a deceased stockholder's shares without the redemption being treated as a dividend. Instead, the redemption price will be treated as payment in exchange for the stock (a capital transaction). See Q 86. An IRC Section 303 redemption can safely be used in connection with the stock of a family-owned corporation because the constructive ownership rules are not applied in an IRC Section 303 redemption (see Q 82). IRC Secs. 318(a), 318(b).

The stock of any corporation (including an S corporation) may qualify for an IRC Section 303 redemption. Also, any *class* of stock may be redeemed under IRC Section 303. Thus, a nonvoting stock (common or preferred), issued as a stock dividend, or issued in a lifetime or postdeath recapitalization, can qualify for the redemption. Treas. Reg. §1.303-2(d). Where a corporation issued nonvoting shares immediately prior to and as a part of the same transaction as the redemption, a valid IRC Section 303 redemption was made. Rev. Rul. 87-132, 1987-2 CB 82. "IRC Section 306 stock" is preferred stock distributed to shareholders as a stock dividend, the sale or redemption of which may subject the proceeds to income tax treatment as dividend income because of special rules contained in IRC Section 306. However, a distribution in redemption of IRC Section 306 stock will qualify under IRC Section 303 to the extent the conditions of IRC Section 303 are met. Treas. Reg. §1.303-2(d).

The following conditions must be met if the stock redemption is to qualify under IRC Section 303 for nondividend treatment:

(1) The stock that is to be redeemed must be includable in the decedent's gross estate for federal estate tax purposes.

(2) The value (for federal estate tax purposes) of all the stock of the redeeming corporation which is includable in decedent's gross estate must comprise more than 35% of the value of decedent's *adjusted gross estate*. IRC Sec. 303(b)(2)(A). (The "adjusted gross estate" for this purpose is the gross estate (see Q 853) less deductions for estate expenses, indebtedness and taxes (IRC Sec. 2053) and for unreimbursed casualty and theft losses (IRC Sec. 2054)–see Q 863.) The total value of all classes of stock includable in the gross estate is taken into account to determine whether this 35% test is met, regardless of which class of stock is to be redeemed. Treas. Reg. §1.303-2(c)(1).

IRC Section 303(b) provides that a corporate distribution in redemption of stock will qualify as an IRC Section 303 redemption if all the stock of the corporation *which is included in determining the value of the gross estate* exceeds 35% of the adjusted gross estate. While most gifts made by a donor within three years of his death are not brought back into his gross estate under the bringback rule of IRC Section 2035, certain kinds of gifts are. These are described in Q 860 in the second paragraph, the "first kind of exception" gifts. Gifts of corporation stock which fall within this classification are part of the gross estate for purposes of computing the 35% requirement (or the 20% requirement, below) and the corporation's redemption of this stock will qualify as a sale or exchange if all the other requirements of IRC Section 303 are satisfied. IRC Section 2035(c)(1)(A) states generally that the three-year bringback rule will apply *for the purposes of IRC Section 303(b)*. The Treasury and the IRS interpret the foregoing as follows: If the decedent makes a gift (of any kind of property) within three years of his death, the value of the property given will be included in the decedent's gross estate for purposes of determining whether the value of the corporation stock in question exceeds

BUSINESS CONTINUATION: BUSINESS LIFE INSURANCE   Q 85

35% of the value of the gross estate, *but* a distribution in redemption of that stock will not qualify as an IRC Section 303 redemption unless the stock redeemed is actually a part of the decedent's gross estate. Rev. Rul. 84-76, 1984-1 CB 91.

The stock of two or more corporations will be treated as that of a single corporation provided 20% or more of the value of all of the outstanding stock of each corporation is includable in decedent's gross estate. IRC Sec. 303(b)(2)(B). Only stock directly owned is taken into account in determining whether the 20% test has been met (constructive ownership rules do not apply even when they would benefit the taxpayer). *Est. of Byrd v. Comm.*, 21 AFTR 2d 313 (5th Cir. 1967). But stock which, at decedent's death, represents the surviving spouse's interest in property held by the decedent and the surviving spouse as community property or as joint tenants, tenants by the entirety, or tenants in common is considered to be includable in decedent's gross estate for the purpose of meeting the 20% requirement. IRC Sec. 303(b)(2)(B). The 20% test is not an elective provision; that is, if a distribution in redemption of stock qualifies under IRC Section 303 only by reason of the application of the 20% test and also qualifies for sale treatment under another section of the Code, the executor may not elect to have only the latter section of the Code apply and thus retain undiminished the IRC Section 303 limits for later use; all distributions which qualify under IRC Section 303 are treated as IRC Section 303 redemptions in the order they are made. Treas. Reg. §1.303-2(g); Rev. Rul. 79-401, 1979-2 CB 128.

(3) The dollar amount that can be paid out by the corporation under protection of IRC Section 303 is limited to an amount equal to the sum of: (a) all estate taxes (the generation-skipping transfer tax imposed by reason of the decedent's death is for this purpose considered an estate tax) and inheritance taxes (federal and state) attributable to decedent's death (plus interest, if any, collected on these taxes), and (b) funeral and administration expenses allowable as deductions to the estate under IRC Section 2053. IRC Secs. 303(a), 303(d).

(4) The stock must be redeemed not later than (a) three years and 90 days after the estate tax return is filed (estate tax returns must be filed within nine months after death), (b) 60 days after a Tax Court decision on an estate tax deficiency becomes final, or (c) if an extension of time for payment of the tax is elected under IRC Section 6166 (see Q 851), the time determined under the applicable section for payment of the installments. However, for any redemption made more than four years after decedent's death, capital gains treatment is available only for a distribution in an amount which is the lesser of: (1) the amount of the qualifying death taxes and funeral and administration expenses which are unpaid immediately before the distribution, or (2) the aggregate of these amounts which are paid within one year after the distribution. IRC Secs. 303(b)(1), 303(b)(4).

(5) The shareholder from whom the stock is redeemed must be one whose interest is reduced directly (or through a binding obligation to contribute) by payment of qualifying death taxes and funeral and administration expenses, and the redemption will qualify for capital gains treatment only to the extent of such reduction. IRC Sec. 303(b)(3). That is, "...the party whose shares are redeemed [must actually have] a liability for estate taxes, state death taxes, or funeral and administration expenses in an amount at least equal to the amount of the redemption." H.R. Rep. No. 94-1380 at 35 (Estate and Gift Tax Reform Act of 1976), *reprinted in* 1976-3 CB (Vol. 3) 735 at 769. *ASRS, Sec. 43, ¶40.8(c)*.

86. Does the redemption under an insurance-funded stock redemption agreement result in capital gain to the deceased stockholder's estate?

Normally, the estate realizes no capital gain as a result of the redemption. Where the redemption is a capital transaction (see Q 82 to Q 85), the estate has no tax liability unless the price paid by the corporation exceeds the tax basis of the stock redeemed. When a stockholder dies, his stock receives a new basis equal to its fair market value at date of death (or alternate valuation date). IRC Sec. 1014. As the sale price under a proper stock redemption agreement is generally accepted as the fair market value of the shares (see Q 613), sale price should equal the estate's basis and no gain or loss should be realized by the estate. *ASRS, Sec. 43, ¶40.8(d)(5).*

87. If a close corporation redeems stock from a decedent's estate, is the amount paid for the stock taxable as a constructive dividend to the surviving stockholder or stockholders?

A surviving stockholder will not be treated as having received a constructive dividend merely because the percentage of his interest in the corporation is increased by the redemption. *Holsey v. Comm.*, 258 F.2d 865 (3rd Cir. 1958); Rev. Rul. 58-614, 1958-2 CB 920. The redemption may result in a constructive dividend to a survivor if he had an obligation to purchase the stock (e.g., under a cross purchase agreement), and redemption by the corporation satisfies his personal obligation. *Smith v. Comm.*, 70 TC 651 (1978). However, the survivor does not realize taxable income from the redemption unless his obligation to purchase the stock was primary and unconditional. Thus, there is no constructive dividend if the survivor has assigned his obligation to the corporation before the conditions for performance of his contract arose, or if the buyout contract contained a provision permitting the stockholder to call upon the corporation to buy the stock, or if the survivor could have elected not to buy the stock. *Pulliam v. Comm.*, TC Memo 1984-470; Rev. Rul. 69-608, 1969-2 CB 42; see also *Bunney v. Comm.*, TC Memo 1988-112. *ASRS, Sec. 43, ¶40.8(d)(4).*

88. What are the income tax results of funding a stock redemption agreement with life insurance?

Premiums

The IRS does not consider premiums paid by a corporation under a stock redemption agreement to be ordinary and necessary business expenses. Furthermore, regardless of who is named beneficiary in the policy (the corporation, a trust, or the insured's spouse or estate), the corporation is either directly or indirectly a beneficiary under the policy since the proceeds will be used to discharge its obligation to redeem the stock. Consequently, the corporation cannot deduct its premium payments. IRC Secs. 162(a), 264(a)(1); Rev. Rul. 70-117, 1970-1 CB 30. (See Q 47.) But also, regardless of who is beneficiary, the premium payments are not taxable income to the stockholders if the corporation owns the policy and the right of the beneficiary to receive the proceeds is conditioned upon the transfer of stock to the corporation (see Q 51).

Death Proceeds

The death proceeds are ordinarily received tax free. IRC Sec. 101(a). However, the death proceeds may be subject to tax under the corporate alternative minimum tax. IRC Sec. 56. See Q 95.

Cost Basis

Because the proceeds become part of the general assets of the corporation, the value of the stock owned by each surviving stockholder will be increased by a share (proportionate to his stock interest) of the difference between the death proceeds and the cash surrender value prior to death. But the cost basis of the survivor's stock will not be increased. Consequently, the increase in value due to the insurance may result in some additional gain if the survivor sells his stock during his lifetime. (Compare with result under stock purchase plan–Q 81.) If he holds his stock until death, the stock will receive a new tax basis equal to its fair market value at the time of his death (see Q 816), thus eliminating this effect.

In the case of an S corporation, each shareholder's basis *is* increased by his share of the tax-free death proceeds when they are received by the corporation–see Q 839.

The corporation has no income tax basis problem; even if the redeemed stock is carried as treasury stock and is subsequently resold, the corporation realizes no gain regardless of basis. IRC Sec. 1032(a); Treas. Reg. §1.1032-1(a).

Effect on Corporate Earnings and Profits

Revenue Ruling 54-230, 1954-1 CB 114, states that earnings and profits will be increased by the excess of the insurance proceeds over the aggregate premiums paid (apparently on the assumption that no part of the *premiums* have been deducted from earnings and profits). For taxable years beginning after July 18, 1984, if a corporation distributes amounts in a redemption under IRC Sections 302(a) or 303, the part of the distribution properly chargeable to earnings and profits is an amount not in excess of the ratable share of the earnings and profits of the corporation accumulated after February 28, 1913 attributable to the stock redeemed. IRC Sec. 312(n)(7). The Conference Committee (TRA '84) indicates that priorities between different classes of stock may be taken into account in allocating earnings between classes and that redemption of preferred stock which is not convertible or participating to any significant extent in corporate growth should be charged to the capital account only. H.R. Conf. Rep. No. 98-861 (TRA '84) *reprinted in* 1984-3 CB (vol. 2) 94.

See also "Accumulated Earnings Tax," Q 89. *ASRS, Sec. 43, ¶40.8(a).*

ACCUMULATED EARNINGS TAX

89. Is it likely that the accumulated earnings tax will be imposed because of the use of corporate earnings to purchase business life insurance?

This penalty tax is imposed when a corporation, in order to prevent profits from being taxed to its shareholders, retains earnings not needed in the business. IRC Sec. 531. In computing the amount of income subject to the tax, a credit is allowed for accumulations to meet reasonable current and anticipated business needs. (Note that JGTRRA 2003 reduced the accumulated earnings tax rate to 15%. See Q 838.) Consequently, the tax should not be imposed upon income retained for the purchase of life insurance if the insurance serves a valid business need and is generally related to that need. See *General Smelting Co. v. Comm.*, 4 TC 313 (1944); *Reynard Corp. v. Comm.*, 37 BTA 552 (1938).

The purchase of life insurance to compensate the corporation for loss of a key person's service through early death is a reasonable business need, and earnings used for such purpose are therefore not subject to the penalty tax. *Harry A. Koch Co. v. Vinal*, 13 AFTR 2d 1241 (D. Neb. 1964); *Vuono-Lione, Inc. v. Comm.*, TC Memo 1965-96; see also *Emeloid Co. v. Comm.*, 189 F.2d 230 (3rd Cir. 1951); *Bradford-Robinson Printing Co. v. Comm.*, 1 AFTR 2d 1278 (D. Colo. 1957). Although *Emeloid Co.* is not an accumulated earnings tax case, it is excellent authority for the proposition that key person life insurance is a reasonable business need. Likewise, an accumulation of earnings to meet the corporation's obligations incurred under a deferred compensation agreement should be considered a reasonable business need. *John P. Scripps Newspapers v. Comm.*, 44 TC 453 (1965); *Okla. Press Pub. Co. v. U.S.*, 27 AFTR 2d 71-656 (10th Cir. 1971), on remand, 28 AFTR 2d 71-5722 (E.D. Okla. 1971); see Treas. Reg. §1.537-2(b)(3). In *Novelart Mfg. Co. v. Comm.*, 52 TC 794 (1969), aff'd, 26 AFTR 2d 70-5837 (6th Cir. 1970), premiums for key person life insurance were included in the taxable base upon which the accumulated earnings tax is imposed. However, the taxpayer failed to argue that because key person life insurance is a reasonable business need, the premiums should be included in the calculation of the accumulated earnings credit. Instead, the taxpayer argued only that the amounts paid out for life insurance premiums no longer were available for distribution and should not be included in the measure of the tax because the tax is imposed on what is accumulated rather than on what is distributed. The argument was dismissed as inconsistent with the rules in the Code for calculating the tax. It has also been held that the cash surrender value of key person life insurance is not considered a liquid asset, along with cash and marketable securities, in determining whether further accumulations to finance plans for business expansion are necessary. *Motor Fuel Carriers, Inc. v. Comm.*, 77-2 USTC ¶9661 (5th Cir. 1977). See also *A.T. Williams Oil Co. v. Comm.*, TC Memo 1981-461.

Under certain circumstances, for example, to promote corporate harmony, efficiency of management or to enable a corporation to continue its accustomed practices or policies, an accumulation of earnings to fund a stock redemption may constitute an accumulation for a "reasonable need of the business." *Mountain State Steel Foundries, Inc. v. Comm.*, 6 AFTR 2d 5910 (4th Cir. 1960); *Oman Construction Co. v. Comm.*, TC Memo 1965-325; *Dill Mfg. Co. v. Comm.*, 39 BTA 1023 (1939); *Gazette Publishing Co. v. Self*, 103 F. Supp. 779 (E.D. Ark. 1952). But see also *John B. Lambert & Assoc. v. U.S.*, 76-1 USTC ¶9466 (Ct. Cl. 1976). Although the following cases do not deal with the accumulated earnings tax, they contain persuasive statements concerning the business need for life insurance to fund close corporation stock redemptions. *Emeloid Co. v. Comm.*, supra; *Sanders v. Fox*, 253 F.2d 855 (10th Cir. 1958); *Prunier v. Comm.*, 248 F.2d 818 (1st Cir. 1957).

Several cases (not involving life insurance) have held that an accumulation of income for the purpose of effecting an IRC Section 303 redemption (a redemption of stock to pay death taxes and administration and funeral expenses–see Q 85) serves the purpose of the individual stockholder rather than the purpose of the corporation. The effect of these cases is limited by IRC Section 537, which provides that the term "reasonable needs of the business" includes the IRC Section 303 redemption needs of the business. However, the Code language is not clear on the extent to which accumulations in years prior to the stockholder's death are to have protection from the tax. The Code limits the amount of tax sheltered accumulation in the year of the stockholder's death or in a subsequent year, but as to accumulations in earlier years says only that the tax is to be applied without regard to the fact (if such is the case) that distributions in an IRC Section 303 redemption were subsequently made. The regulations say that the reasonableness of accumulations in years prior to a year in which the shareholder dies is to be determined solely upon the facts and circumstances existing at the times the accumulations occur. Treas. Reg. §1.537-1(e)(3).

In the case of a professional corporation (see Q 838), a stock redemption following a shareholder's death is usually *not* made under IRC Section 303 but is a *complete redemption* of all the shareholder's stock under IRC Section 302 (see Q 82). The requirement of many state laws that the corporation must purchase the stock of a deceased or disqualified professional would appear to establish a valid business purpose for accumulations to fund such redemptions. Consequently, an accumulation under these circumstances, particularly if funded by life insurance, should be immune from imposition of the accumulated earnings tax. *ASRS, Sec. 43, ¶20.6.*

S CORPORATIONS

90. How is gain realized by an S corporation on sale, surrender, or redemption of a life insurance or endowment policy taxed?

Each stockholder's pro rata share of any gain received by an S corporation, such as on endowment maturity or the sale or surrender of a life insurance policy, will be included in his gross income and will increase his basis in his stock. IRC Secs. 1366(a)(1), 1367(a)(1)(A). *ASRS, Sec. 43, ¶¶20.10, 40.8(h).*

91. If an S corporation redeems the stock of a shareholder, how are the redemption payments taxed?

If an S corporation has no accumulated earnings and profits (accumulated when it was a C corporation or as a result of a corporate acquisition), a redemption of stock will be treated as a capital transaction—that is, it will be tax free to the extent of the shareholder's basis and any excess will be capital gain. IRC Sec. 1368(b).

However, if an S corporation has accumulated earnings and profits, part of the payment by the corporation could be treated as a dividend. See Q 839 for an explanation of the taxation of distributions. The exceptions to dividend treatment under IRC Sections 302(a) and 303(a) are available to S corporations. See Q 82 to Q 85. *ASRS, Sec. 43, ¶¶20.10, 40.8(h).*

SALE OR LIQUIDATION OF PARTNERSHIP INTEREST

92. What are the income tax results when a deceased partner's interest is sold or liquidated under a business purchase agreement?

The term "liquidation" refers to the termination of a partner's entire interest by means of a distribution or series of distributions by the partnership (entity plan). IRC Sec. 761(d). The term "sale" refers to the purchase of the deceased's partnership interest by the surviving partner or partners individually (cross-purchase plan). See IRC Sec. 741.

Liquidation

The portion of the partnership's payment which is allocable to the deceased partner's interest in partnership property (if capital is not a material income-producing factor for the partnership and the deceased partner was a general partner, then payments for an interest in partnership property will not include unrealized receivables or goodwill, unless the partnership agreement provides for payments for goodwill) is treated as payment for the purchase of a capital asset. IRC Sec. 736(b). However, the estate or other successor in interest should realize no gain or loss if the partnership has elected to adjust the basis of the partnership property to reflect the new basis of the deceased's partnership interest because such basis will be determined under the "stepped-up" basis rules. (See Q 816). See IRC Secs. 734, 743, 754. Generally, the valuation placed by the partners upon a partner's interest in partnership property in an arm's length agreement will be regarded as correct. Treas. Reg. §1.736-1(b)(1).

The amount of any money or the fair market value of any property received by a partner in exchange for all or a part of his interest in the partnership attributable to unrealized receivables of the partnership or inventory items of the partnership is considered an amount realized from the sale or exchange of property other than a capital asset. IRC Sec. 751(a). Amounts realized from the sale of property other than a capital asset are generally treated as ordinary income.

Generally, the basis of such items may also be adjusted if the partnership elects. Payments for the deceased's interest in partnership property are not deductible by the partnership; but they increase pro rata the basis for each remaining partner's partnership interest.

Under a liquidation agreement, the partners may elect to treat amounts paid for goodwill as either the purchase price for a capital asset or as ordinary income. However, for partners retiring or dying on or after January 5, 1993 or for payments made under a written contract that was binding as of January 4, 1993, an additional requirement applies to the election to treat goodwill as ordinary income. This treatment may be elected only if capital is not a material income-producing factor in the partnership and the retiring or deceased partner was a general partner. IRC Sec. 736(b)(3). Where the agreement provides that part of the purchase price is for goodwill, the amount allocable to goodwill will also be treated as having been paid for the deceased's interest in partnership property (see above). The regulations state that the payment for goodwill (to be treated as a capital transaction) must be "reasonable"; however, the value placed on goodwill by the partners in an arm's length agreement (whether specific in amount or determined by formula) will generally be regarded as the correct value. Treas. Reg. §1.736-1(b)(3). If the material income-producing factor/general partner requirement mentioned above is met and the agreement makes no provision for goodwill, or stipulates that payment for goodwill is to be treated as income, the amount paid for goodwill is taxable as ordinary income to the estate or other recipient. If treated as ordinary income, it is deductible by the partnership. IRC Sec. 736(b)(2); *Foxman v. Comm.*, 16 AFTR 2d 5931 (3rd Cir. 1965); *Umstead v. U.S.*, 13 AFTR 2d 592 (4th Cir. 1964); *Smith v. Comm.*, 37 TC 1033, aff'd, 11 AFTR 2d 508 (10th Cir. 1962); *Pickett v. Comm.*, TC Memo 1965-196. Election to treat payment for goodwill as a capital investment or ordinary income may be made in either the original articles of partnership or in a subsequent business purchase agreement. *Jackson Investment Co. v. Comm.*, 15 AFTR 2d 1125 (9th Cir. 1965). The IRS has ruled that determination as to whether a professional practice has saleable goodwill will be made on the basis of all the facts in the particular case, and not on the basis of whether the business is dependent solely upon the personal characteristics of the owner. Rev. Rul. 64-235, 1964-2 CB 18, as modified by Rev. Rul. 70-45, 1970-1 CB 17. See also *Butler v.*

BUSINESS CONTINUATION: BUSINESS LIFE INSURANCE   Q 92

Comm., 46 TC 280 (1966); *Phillips v. Comm.*, 40 TC 157 (1963); *Wheeling v. Comm.*, TC Memo 1964-128.

The portion of the partnership payment which is allocable to the deceased's interest in unrealized receivables or inventory items of the partnership is ordinary income to the estate or other recipient. IRC Sec. 751(a). Unrealized receivables include such items as accounts receivable not previously includable in the taxable income of the partners, and the depreciation which is treated as ordinary income, under IRC Sections 1245 and 1250, upon sale of depreciable property. IRC Sec. 751. In determining the value of unrealized receivables, full account will be taken of the estimated cost of completing performance of the contract and of the time between the sale and time of payment. Treas. Reg. §1.751-1(c)(3). Payments for unrealized receivables are deductible by the partnership. IRC Sec. 736(a); Treas. Reg. §1.736-1(a)(4).

Any additional amounts paid by the partnership are treated as ordinary income. (See Q 93.)

Ordinary income payments in a liquidation of a deceased partner's interest are "income in respect of a decedent." IRC Sec. 753. Consequently, the recipient of the income is entitled to an income tax deduction for any portion of the federal death taxes (including the generation-skipping transfer tax imposed on a taxable termination or a direct skip occurring as a result of decedent's death) paid by decedent's estate which is attributable to the value of such income. IRC Sec. 691(c). (See Q 827.)

A partnership, even a two person partnership, will not be considered to have terminated so long as liquidation payments under IRC Section 736 are being made. Treas. Reg. §1.708-1(b)(1)(i); Treas. Reg. §1.736-1(a)(6); *Haines v. U.S.*, 76-1 USTC ¶9222 (D.N.J. 1976).

Sale

Where the deceased partner's interest is sold to the surviving partner or partners as individuals, the income tax results with respect to the purchase of the deceased's interest in partnership property are essentially the same as in a liquidation (see above). This portion of the purchase is considered a capital transaction for purposes of determining gain or loss to the deceased's estate (see Q 816). The survivors' interests in partnership property receive an increase in basis for this portion of their payment. IRC Sec. 742. A slight difference in tax law exists, however, between a liquidation and a sale, with respect to payment for goodwill. In a sale, payments for goodwill must be treated as part of the capital transaction; the partners do not have an option to treat such payments as ordinary income. *Karan v. Comm.*, 12 AFTR 2d 5032 (7th Cir. 1963). Payments for unrealized receivables, as in a liquidation, are taxable as ordinary income to the deceased's estate or other recipient. Unrealized receivables are generally "income in respect of a decedent," and therefore do not receive a new basis because of the death of the partner, even though an election to adjust basis is in effect. *Woodhall v. Comm.*, 29 AFTR 2d 72-394 (9th Cir. 1972); *George Edward Quick Trust v. Comm.*, 27 AFTR 2d 71-1581 (8th Cir. 1971). The survivors cannot deduct their payments for unrealized receivables. But they can elect, on behalf of the partnership, to adjust the basis of the partnership assets. By such an election, the partnership's basis for its unrealized receivables (usually zero) is stepped-up for the benefit of each purchasing partner to reflect the amount he paid for his share of the receivables. Thus, when the receivables are collected by

2006 Tax Facts on Insurance & Employee Benefits

the partnership, each partner's share will result in ordinary income only to the extent that it exceeds the price he paid for his interest in the receivables. IRC Secs. 754, 743. *ASRS, Sec. 42, ¶40.6*.

93. What are the income tax results of a partnership income continuation plan?

The partnership can agree to make payments (other than payments in liquidation of his partnership interest) to a retiring partner or to the estate or beneficiary of a deceased partner. The payments may be either (1) periodic guaranteed amounts, or (2) a share of future profits. In either case, the payments will be taxed as ordinary income to the payee. Rev. Rul. 71-507, 1971-2 CB 331. Payments of a guaranteed amount will be deductible by the partnership. Treas. Reg. §1.736-1(a)(4). Similarly, payments representing a share of profits will reduce the remaining or surviving partners' share of distributable taxable income. IRC Sec. 736(a). This tax treatment applies only to payments made by the partnership as an entity, and not to payments made by individual remaining or surviving partners. However, a partnership, even a two person partnership, will not be considered as having terminated so long as these payments are being made. Treas. Reg. §1.736-1(a)(6). *ASRS, Sec. 42, ¶40.6(d)(2)*.

94. What is the tax treatment of life insurance purchased to fund a partnership business purchase agreement?

The premiums are not deductible whether paid by the individual partners or by the partnership (see Q 56). IRC Sec. 264(a)(1). The death proceeds, whether received by the partners or the partnership, are exempt from income tax (see Q 62). IRC Sec. 101(a). The basis to the partners of their partnership interests is increased by the proceeds received by the partnership. IRC Sec. 705(a)(1)(B). Likewise, under a cross-purchase plan, each partner's basis for his partnership interest will be increased by the amount he pays for his share of the deceased partner's interest. IRC Sec. 1012. Policies can be freely sold or exchanged between the partners, or between the partners and the partnership, without fear of adverse tax consequences from the transfer for value rule (see Q 71). (Even though the proceeds are made payable directly to the insured's personal beneficiary the survivor may be able to include the proceeds in his cost basis if there is a legally binding agreement between the partners to apply the proceeds to the purchase of the business interest. See *Mushro v. Comm.*, 50 TC 43 (1968), nonacq. 1970-2 CB xxii. But see *Legallet v. Comm.*, 41 BTA 294 (1940).) *ASRS, Sec. 42, ¶40.6(d)*.

ALTERNATIVE MINIMUM TAX

95. How is corporate owned life insurance treated for purposes of the corporate alternative minimum tax?

Unless it qualifies for the small corporation exemption, a corporation may be subject to the corporate alternative minimum tax (AMT). How this fairly complicated tax is calculated is discussed generally in Q 838. One component of the corporate AMT, known as the adjusted current earnings (ACE) adjustment, has a potential effect on corporate owned life insurance policies.

A C corporation must adjust its reported income to reflect its adjusted current earnings (ACE) (or, before 1990, its book income). Inside buildup and payment of death

BUSINESS CONTINUATION: BUSINESS LIFE INSURANCE Q 95

proceeds of corporate owned life insurance will affect the ACE adjustment. They will not necessarily subject the corporation to the AMT because life insurance is only one of many factors which determine whether the corporation must pay the AMT.

Seventy-five percent of the amount by which a C corporation's ACE exceeds its alternative minimum taxable income (AMTI) (determined without regard to ACE or the AMT net operating loss) is added to AMTI. On the other hand, 75% of the amount by which a C corporation's AMTI (determined without regard to ACE or the AMT net operating loss) exceeds its ACE is subtracted from AMTI to the extent that aggregate increases in AMTI based on ACE in prior years exceed aggregate decreases in AMTI based on ACE in prior years. IRC Sec. 56(g).

Regulations offer the guidelines set forth below with respect to the effect of corporate owned life insurance contracts on ACE. Treas. Reg. §1.56(g)-1(c)(5).

Inside buildup. Income on the contract with respect to a tax year is included in ACE for the year, except the tax year in which the insured dies or the contract is completely surrendered for its entire net surrender value. The income is calculated from the beginning of the tax year to the date of any distribution, from immediately after any distribution to the date of the next distribution, and from the last distribution in the tax year through the end of the tax year.

Solely for purposes of computing ACE, basis in the contract is increased for positive income on the contract included in ACE. The income on the contract for ACE is: (a) the contract's net surrender value at the end of the period plus any distributions during the period that are not taxed because they represent return of basis in the contract for purposes of ACE, minus (b) the net surrender value at the end of the preceding period plus any premiums paid during the period.

Distributions. A distribution (whether a partial withdrawal or an amount received on complete surrender) is included in ACE (under the rules of IRC Section 72(e), explained in Q 249) taking into account the taxpayer's basis for purposes of computing ACE. (Its basis is its basis for ACE as of the end of the immediately preceding period plus premiums paid before the distribution.) The basis in the contract for purposes of ACE is reduced by the amount not included in ACE because it represents recovery of ACE basis. If the ACE basis in the contract exceeds the death benefit received, the resulting loss may be deducted from ACE.

Death benefits. Death benefits are excluded from gross income under IRC Section 101. The excess of the contractual death benefit over the taxpayer's basis for purposes of ACE at the time of death is included in ACE. Any outstanding policy loan treated as discharged or forgiven upon death of the insured is included in the amount of the death benefit.

Term life insurance without net surrender value. ACE is reduced by premiums paid to the extent allocable to coverage provided during the year; premiums not so allocable must be included in basis. The *death benefit* is included in ACE as explained in the previous paragraph.

Policies involving divided ownership. The above requirements apply to the separate ownership interests as though each interest were a separate contract.

Example. Brown Corporation has a policy with a net surrender value of $14,774 as of the end of 2005. The policy had a surrender value of $11,231 at the end of 2004 and a basis of $9,821 ($8,800 aggregate premiums paid plus $1,021 included in ACE as inside buildup in 2004). Brown Corporation paid a premium of $2,200 in 2005. The corporation must include in ACE for 2005 $1,343 ($14,774 - [$11,231 + $2,200]). The basis in the contract for purposes of ACE is increased by $1,343 of income on the contract included in ACE for 2005 and the $2,200 premium paid in 2005 ($13,364).

Assume instead that, in 2005, Mrs. Brown, the insured, dies after the $2,200 premium was paid. Brown Corporation received the $100,000 death benefit. No amount of inside buildup is included in income; instead, the corporation must include in ACE the excess of the death benefit over the basis for ACE, $87,979 ($100,000-[$9,821 + $2,200]).

Assume that Mrs. Brown did not die in 2005. Brown Corporation paid a premium of $2,200 in 2006 and received a distribution of $16,200 on February 1, 2006 leaving a net surrender value of $915. On March 1, 2006 Brown Corporation pays an additional premium of $5,000. The net surrender value of the contract at the end of 2006 is $6,417. Brown Corporation must include $636 of the distribution in income: $16,200 (distribution) - $15,564 (basis for ACE as of the time of the distribution).

The income on the contract includable in ACE for 2006 is determined separately for the period before the distribution and the period after it. There is no income on the contract for the period beginning January 1, 2006 and ending at the time of the distribution on February 1, 2006: [$915 (net surrender value at the end of the period) + $15,564 (distribution of basis)] - [$14,774 (net surrender value at the end of 2005) + $2,200 (premiums paid during the period)] = ($495). Because the net result is negative, no income is included for this period. Income on the contract for the period beginning immediately after the distribution through the end of the taxable year is $502: $6,417 (net surrender value at the end of 2005) - [$915 (net surrender value at the end of the preceding period) + $5,000 (premiums paid during the period)]. At the end of 2006, Brown Corporation's basis in the contract for ACE is $5,502: $502 (income on the contract) + $5,000 (premium) + $0 (the basis at the end of the previous period). Brown Corporation includes in ACE in 2006 a total of $1,138 ($502 income on the contract) + $636 (income from distribution). See Treas. Reg. §1.56(g)-1(c)(5)(vii).

ASRS, Sec. 43, ¶20.4; Sec. 53, ¶17.

DISABILITY INCOME AND OVERHEAD EXPENSES

96. If a corporation buys disability insurance on a key person under which benefits are paid to the corporation, what are the tax results?

The corporation cannot deduct the premiums it pays, but can exclude the insurance benefits from its gross income. Rev. Rul. 66-262, 1966-2 CB 105. The disability income, regardless of amount, is wholly tax-exempt to the corporation under IRC Section 104(a)(3). Rev. Rul. 66-262, supra; *Castner Garage, Ltd. v. Comm.*, 43 BTA 1 (1940), acq. Since the disability income is tax-exempt, deduction for the premiums is disallowable under IRC Section 265(a)(1), on the ground that the premiums are expenses paid to acquire tax-exempt income. *Rugby Prod. Ltd. v. Comm.*, 100 TC 531 (1993); Rev. Rul. 66-262, supra. An accidental death benefit may be tax-exempt to the corporation under IRC Section 101(a) as death proceeds of life insurance. See Q 271. Premiums paid for tax-exempt accidental death coverage are nondeductible under IRC Section 264(a)(1). See Q 45. Rev. Rul. 66-262, supra. *ASRS, Sec. 67, ¶130.*

97. Are premiums paid for "overhead expense" insurance deductible as a business expense?

The IRS has ruled that premiums paid on an overhead expense disability policy, a special type of contract that reimburses professionals or owner-operators for overhead expenses actually incurred during periods of disability, are deductible as a business expense and the proceeds are taxable. Rev. Rul. 55-264, 1955-1 CB 11. However, the ruling relates to self-employed individuals.

Premiums paid on standard personal disability insurance are not deductible as a business expense, but the proceeds are tax-exempt as compensation for personal injuries or sickness. See Q 193. Rev. Rul. 55-331, 1955-1 CB 271; Rev. Rul. 70-394, 1970-2 CB 34. This is so even though the taxpayer intends to use the benefits to pay his overhead expenses during periods of disability. Rev. Rul. 58-480, 1958-2 CB 62; *Blaess v. Comm.*, 28 TC 710 (1957); *Andrews v. Comm.*, TC Memo 1970-32. *ASRS, Sec. 67, ¶120.5.*

98. If disability insurance is purchased on the lives of business owners to fund a disability buy-out, what are the tax results?

Whether the purchaser, policyowner, beneficiary, and premium payor is the business entity (entity purchase agreement) or the business owners (cross purchase agreement), the premiums are nondeductible and the proceeds are exempt from regularly calculated income tax. IRC Secs. 104(a)(3), 265(a)(1); Rev. Rul. 66-262, 1966-2 CB 105. See Q 96.

Where the buy-out occurs between a corporation and a disabled shareholder, if the transaction qualifies as a complete redemption of all the shareholder's shares, the redemption will be treated as a capital transaction (see Q 82) (i.e., the transaction will be considered the sale of a capital asset and the selling shareholder's gain or loss will be measured and taxed as explained in Q 815 and Q 816). A disability buy-out between shareholders is also a capital transaction, taxed accordingly. IRC Secs. 61(a)(3), 1001, 1011, 1221, and 1222.

Where the buy-out occurs between a partnership and a disabled partner, resulting in a termination of the disabled partner's interest, the transaction is taxed under the rules applying to a *liquidation* of a partner's interest. See Q 92. Where the buy-out occurs between partners, the transaction is taxed under the rules applying to a *sale* of a partner's interest. See Q 92.

When the disabled business owner realizes gain on the sale of his business interest, the amount of the gain is includable in his gross income in the taxable year in which the gain is actually or constructively received. Treas. Reg. §1.451-1(a). If the sale qualifies as an installment sale, a proportionate part of the gain is reportable in each taxable year installment payments are received. See Q 806.

CAFETERIA PLANS

In General

99. What is a cafeteria plan?

A cafeteria plan (or "flexible benefit plan") is a written plan in which all participants are employees who may choose among two or more benefits consisting of cash and "qualified benefits." IRC Sec. 125(d)(1). With certain limited exceptions, a cafeteria plan cannot provide for deferred compensation. See Q 100. IRC Sec. 125(d)(2). Some cafeteria plans provide for salary reduction contributions by the employee and others provide benefits in addition to salary. In either case, the effect is to permit participants to purchase certain benefits with pre-tax dollars.

A plan may provide for automatic enrollment whereby an employee's salary is reduced to pay for "qualified benefits" unless the employee affirmatively elects cash. Rev. Rul. 2002-27, 2002-1 CB 925.

The written plan document must contain: (1) a description of the benefits, including periods of coverage; (2) rules regarding eligibility for participation; (3) procedures governing elections; (4) the manner in which employer contributions are to be made, such as by salary reduction or nonelective employer contributions; (5) the plan year; and (6) the maximum amount of employer contributions to the plan. This amount must include the maximum amount of elective, or salary reduction, contributions available to any employee stated as either a maximum dollar amount or maximum percentage of compensation or the method for determining the maximum amount or percentage. Prop. Treas. Regs. §§1.125-1, A-3, 1.125-2, A-3.

The plan document need not be self-contained, but may incorporate by reference separate written plans. Prop. Treas. Reg. §1.125-1, A-3.

Former employees may be participants (although the plan may not be established predominantly for their benefit), but self-employed individuals may not. Prop. Treas. Reg. §1.125-1, A-4. For years beginning after 1985, a full-time life insurance salesperson who is treated as an employee for social security purposes will also be considered an employee for cafeteria plan purposes. IRC Sec. 7701(a)(20). *ASRS, Sec. 58A, ¶130.1.*

100. What benefits may be offered under a cafeteria plan?

Participants in a cafeteria plan may choose among two or more benefits consisting of cash and qualified benefits. IRC Sec. 125(d)(1)(B). A cash benefit includes not only cash, but a benefit which may be purchased with after-tax dollars, or the value of which is generally treated as taxable compensation to the employee (provided the benefit does not defer receipt of compensation). Prop. Treas. Reg. §1.125-2, A-4(b).

A qualified benefit is a benefit that is not includable in the gross income of the employee because of an express statutory exclusion, and that does not defer receipt of compensation. However, contributions to Archer Medical Savings Accounts (see Q 209), qualified scholarships, educational assistance programs, or excludable fringe benefits are not qualified benefits. No product that is advertised, marketed, or offered as long-term care insurance is a qualified benefit. IRC Sec. 125(f).

CAFETERIA PLANS   Q 100

With respect to insurance type benefits, such as those provided under accident and health plans and group term life insurance plans, the benefit is the coverage under the plan. Accident and health benefits are qualified benefits to the extent that coverage is excludable under IRC Section 106. Prop. Treas. Reg. §1.125-2, A-4(a)(2)(i). Accidental death coverage offered in a cafeteria plan under an individual accident insurance policy is excludable from the employee's income under IRC Section 106. Let. Ruls. 8801015, 8922048. A cafeteria plan can offer group term life insurance coverage on employees participating in the plan. Coverage that is includable in income only because it exceeds the $50,000 excludable limit under IRC Section 79 may also be offered in a cafeteria plan. Prop. Treas. Reg. §1.125-2, A-4(a)(2)(ii). The application of IRC Section 79 to group term life insurance and IRC Section 106 to accident or health benefits is explained in Q 138 to Q 143 and Q 159. Accident and health coverage, group term life insurance coverage, and benefits under a dependent care assistance program remain "qualified" even if they must be included in income because a nondiscrimination requirement has been violated (e.g., IRC Sec. 129(d)). See Q 133. Prop. Treas. Reg. §1.125-2, A-4(a)(2)(iii). Health coverage and dependent care assistance under flexible spending arrangements are qualified benefits if they meet the requirements explained in Q 107.

Generally, a cafeteria plan cannot provide for deferred compensation, permit participants to carry over unused benefits or contributions from one plan year to another, or permit participants to purchase a benefit that will be provided in a subsequent plan year. However, a cafeteria plan may permit a participant in a profit sharing, stock bonus, or rural cooperative plan that has a qualified cash or deferred arrangement to elect to have the employer contribute on his behalf to the plan. See Q 395. IRC Sec. 125(d)(2). After-tax employee contributions to a qualified plan subject to IRC Section 401(m) (see Q 405) are permissible under a cafeteria plan, even if matching contributions are made by the employer. Prop. Treas. Reg. §1.125-2, A-4(c).

A flexible spending arrangement (FSA) may allow a grace period of no more than 2½ months following the end of the plan year for participants to incur and submit expenses for reimbursement. Notice 2005-42, 2005-23 IRB 1204. See Q 107.

A cafeteria plan may also permit a participant to elect to have the employer contribute to a Health Savings Account (HSA) on his behalf. See Q 195. IRC Sec. 125(d)(2)(D). Unused balances in HSAs funded through a cafeteria plan may be carried over from one plan year to another.

Under the general rule, life, health, disability, or long-term care insurance with an investment feature, such as whole life insurance, or an arrangement which reimburses premium payments for other accident or health coverage extending beyond the end of the plan year cannot be purchased. Prop. Treas. Regs. §§1.125-1, A-7, 1.125-2, A-5(a). However, supplemental health insurance policies which provide coverage for cancer and other specific diseases do not result in the deferral of compensation and are properly considered accident and health benefits under IRC Section 106. TAM 199936046.

A cafeteria plan maintained by an educational organization described in IRC Section 170(b)(1)(A)(ii) (i.e., one with a regular curriculum and an on-site faculty and student body) can allow participants to elect postretirement term life insurance coverage. The postretirement life insurance coverage must be fully paid up upon retirement and must not have a cash surrender value at any time. Postretirement life insurance coverage meeting these conditions will be treated as group term life insurance under IRC Section 79. IRC Sec. 125(d)(2)(C).

2006 Tax Facts on Insurance & Employee Benefits

In order to provide tax favored benefits to highly compensated employees and "key employees," a cafeteria plan must meet certain nondiscrimination requirements and avoid concentration of benefits in key employees. See Q 102. *ASRS, Sec. 58A, ¶130.2.*

101. What are the income tax benefits of a cafeteria plan?

As a general rule, a participant in a cafeteria plan (as defined in Q 99), is not treated as being in constructive receipt of taxable income solely because he has the opportunity, before a cash benefit becomes available, to elect among cash and "qualified" benefits (generally, nontaxable benefits, but as defined in Q 100). IRC Sec. 125; Prop. Treas. Reg. §1.125-2, A-2.

However, in order to avoid taxation, a participant must elect the qualified benefits before the cash benefit becomes currently available. That is, the election must be made before the specified period for which the benefit will be provided begins–generally, the plan year. Prop. Treas. Reg. §1.125-1, A-15.

For the income tax effect of a discriminatory plan on highly compensated individuals, see Q 102. *ASRS, Sec. 58A, ¶130.3.*

102. What nondiscrimination requirements apply to cafeteria plans?

If the plan discriminates in favor of highly compensated individuals as to eligibility to participate or in favor of highly compensated participants as to contributions or benefits, highly compensated participants will be considered in constructive receipt of the available cash benefit. IRC Sec. 125(b)(1). The "highly compensated" are officers, shareholders owning more than 5% of the voting power or value of all classes of stock, those who are highly compensated, and a spouse or dependent of any of them. IRC Sec. 125(e).

Participation will be nondiscriminatory if: (1) it benefits a classification of employees found by the Secretary of Treasury not to discriminate in favor of employees who are officers, shareholders or highly compensated; (2) no more than three years of employment are required for participation and the employment requirement for each employee is the same; and (3) eligible employees begin participation by the first day of the first plan year after the employment requirement is satisfied. IRC Sec. 125(g)(3).

A plan will not be discriminatory as to benefits if total benefits or nontaxable benefits attributable to highly compensated employees, measured as a percentage of compensation, are not significantly greater (or are lower) than total benefits or nontaxable benefits attributable to other employees (measured on the same basis), provided the plan is not otherwise discriminatory. H. Rep. No. 95-1445 (Revenue Act of 1978) *reprinted in* 1978-3 CB 238; Sen. Rep. No. 95-1263 (Revenue Act of 1978) *reprinted in* 1978-3 CB 373.

If a cafeteria plan offers health benefits, the plan is not discriminatory as to contributions and benefits if: (1) contributions for each participant include an amount that either (a) is equal to 100% of the cost of the health benefit coverage under the plan of the majority of the highly compensated participants who are similarly situated (e.g., same family size), or (b) is equal to or exceeds 75% of the cost of the most expensive health benefit coverage elected by any similarly situated participant; and (2) contribu-

CAFETERIA PLANS

tions or benefits in excess of (1) above bear a uniform relationship to compensation. IRC Sec. 125(g)(2).

A plan is considered to satisfy all discrimination tests if it is maintained under a collective bargaining agreement between employee representatives and one or more employers. IRC Sec. 125(g)(1).

In addition, a "key employee" (as defined for purposes of the top-heavy rules, see Q 357) will be considered in constructive receipt of the available cash benefit option in any plan year in which nontaxable benefits provided under the plan to key employees exceed 25% of the aggregate of such benefits provided all employees under the plan. For this purpose, excess group term life insurance coverage that is includable in income is not considered a nontaxable benefit. IRC Sec. 125(b)(2).

Employees of (1) a controlled group of corporations; (2) employers under common control; or (3) members of an "affiliated service group" are treated as employed by a single employer. IRC Sec. 125(g)(4). See Q 360 for definition of "affiliated service group."

Amounts that the employer contributes to a cafeteria plan pursuant to a salary reduction agreement will be treated as employer contributions to the extent that the agreement relates to compensation that has not been actually or constructively received by the employee as of the date of the agreement and subsequently does not become currently available to the employee. Prop. Treas. Reg. §1.125-1, A-6. *ASRS, Sec. 58A, ¶130.4.*

103. When can benefit elections under a cafeteria plan be changed?

A cafeteria plan may permit an employee to revoke an election during a period of coverage and to make a new election relating to a qualified benefits plan only in certain instances. Treas. Reg. §1.125-4(a).

In General

A cafeteria plan may permit an employee to revoke an election for coverage under a group health plan during a period of coverage and make a new election that corresponds with the special enrollment rights of IRC Section 9801(f). (This IRC Section deals generally with special enrollment periods for persons losing other group health plan coverage and dependent beneficiaries.) Treas. Reg. §1.125-4(b).

Certain changes are permitted in regards to a judgment, decree, or order resulting from a divorce, legal separation, annulment, or change in legal custody (including a qualified medical child support order) that requires accident or health coverage for an employee's child or for a foster child who is a dependent of the employee. A cafeteria plan may change the employee's election to provide coverage for the child if an order requires coverage for the child under the employer's plan. Also, the plan may permit the employee to make an election change to cancel coverage for the child if an order requires the spouse, former spouse, or other individual to provide coverage for the child *and* that coverage is actually provided. Treas. Reg. §1.125-4(d).

Additionally, if an employee, spouse, or dependent who is enrolled in the employer's accident or health plan becomes entitled to coverage under Part A or Part B of Medicare or Medicaid, the plan may permit the employee to make a prospective election change to reduce or cancel coverage of that employee, spouse, or dependent under the accident or health plan. If an employee, spouse, or dependent who has been entitled to such Medicare or Medicaid coverage loses eligibility for the coverage, the plan may allow the employee to make a prospective election to commence or increase coverage of that employee, spouse, or dependent under the accident or health plan. Treas. Reg. §1.125-4(e).

An employee taking a leave under the Family and Medical Leave Act (FMLA) may revoke an existing election of accident or health plan coverage and make such election as provided for under the FMLA for the remaining portion of the period of coverage. Treas. Reg. §1.125-4(g). See Q 104.

Regarding contributions under a qualified cash or deferred arrangement, the regulations state that these provisions do not apply to elective contributions under such an arrangement, within the meaning of IRC Section 401(k), or employee contributions subject to IRC Section 401(m). Therefore, a cafeteria plan may allow an employee to modify or revoke elections as provided by these IRC Sections and their regulations. Treas. Reg. §1.125-4(h).

Change in Status

A plan may permit an employee to revoke an election during a period of coverage with respect to a qualified benefits plan and make a new election for the remaining portion of the period if a change in status (as defined below) occurs and the election change meets the consistency rule (as explained below). Treas. Reg. §1.125-4(c)(1). For this purpose, change in status events are:

(1) events that change an employee's legal marital status, including marriage, death of a spouse, divorce, legal separation, and annulment;

(2) events that change an employee's number of dependents such as birth, death, adoption, and placement for adoption;

(3) events that change the employment status of the employee, the employee's spouse, or the employee's dependent, such as a termination or commencement of employment, a strike or lockout, a commencement of or return from an unpaid leave of absence, and a change in work site. (If the eligibility conditions of the cafeteria plan or other employee benefit plan of the employer of the employee, spouse, or dependent depend on the employment status of that individual and there is a change in that individual's employment status, so that the individual becomes or ceases to be eligible under the plan, then the change is a change in employment.);

(4) events that cause an employee's dependent to satisfy or cease to satisfy eligibility requirements for coverage due to reaching a certain age, student status, or any other similar provision;

(5) a change in the place of residence of the employee, spouse, or dependent; and

(6) for purposes of adoption assistance provided through a cafeteria plan, the commencement or termination of an adoption proceeding.

Treas. Reg. §1.125-4(c)(2).

CAFETERIA PLANS Q 103

Consistency Rule

The consistency rule states that an election change is not properly made with respect to accident or health coverage or group term life insurance unless it is on account of or corresponds with a change in status that affects eligibility for coverage under an employer's plan.

For example, if a dependent dies or otherwise ceases to satisfy the eligibility requirements for coverage, the employee's election to cancel health insurance coverage for any other dependent, for the employee, or the employee's spouse does not correspond to the change in status.

There is an exception to the consistency rule for COBRA coverage. If the employee, spouse, or dependent becomes eligible for COBRA continuation coverage (see Q 173) under the employer's group health plan, a cafeteria plan may allow the employee to elect to increase payments under the cafeteria plan to pay for the COBRA coverage.

With respect to group term life insurance and disability coverage, an election under a cafeteria plan to increase or decrease coverage in response to any of the above listed changes in status is deemed to correspond to that change in status. Treas. Reg. §1.125-4(c)(3).

An election change satisfies the consistency rule with respect to other qualified benefits if it is on account of and corresponds with a change in status that affects eligibility for coverage under an employer's plan. An election change also satisfies the consistency rule if it is on account of and corresponds with a change in status that affects dependent care expenses, as set forth in IRC Section 129 (see Q 133), or adoption assistance expenses, as described in IRC Section 137. Regulations provide examples of the application of the consistency rule. Treas. Reg. §1.125-4(c)(3).

Significant Cost or Coverage Changes

The rules regarding election changes due to a significant cost or coverage change apply to all types of qualified benefits offered under a cafeteria plan, but not to health flexible spending arrangements (FSAs). Treas. Reg. §1.125-4(f)(1).

A plan may automatically make a prospective change in an employee's salary reduction amount if the cost of a qualified benefits plan increases or decreases during a period of coverage. Treas. Reg. §1.125-4(f)(2)(i). If the cost of a benefit package option *significantly* increases during a period of coverage, the cafeteria plan may allow employees to either increase their salary reduction amounts or revoke their elections for this benefit and elect another benefit package option that offers similar coverage on a prospective basis. Treas. Reg. §1.125-4(f)(2)(ii). If the cost of a qualified benefits plan significantly decreases during the year, the cafeteria plan may allow all employees, even those who have previously not participated in the plan, to elect to participate in the plan for the option with such decrease in cost. Treas. Reg. §1.125-4(f)(2)(ii). Also, a cost change applies in the case of dependent care assistance only if the cost change is imposed by a dependent care provider who is not a relative of the employee, as defined in IRC Section 152. Treas. Reg. §1.125-4(f)(2)(iv).

If an employee has a significant curtailment of coverage under a plan during a period of coverage that is a "loss of coverage," the cafeteria plan may permit the employee to revoke his election under the plan and elect to receive, on a prospective basis,

2006 Tax Facts on Insurance & Employee Benefits

coverage under another option providing similar coverage. The employee may drop the coverage if no similar option is available. A "loss of coverage" means a complete loss of coverage under the benefit package option or other coverage option (e.g., the elimination of an option, an HMO ceasing to be available in the area, or losing all coverage under the option by reason of an overall lifetime or annual limitation). Treas. Reg. § 1.125-4(f)(3)(ii).

If an employee has a significant curtailment of coverage under a plan during a period of coverage that is not a "loss of coverage" (e.g., significant increase in the deductible, the co-pay, or the out-of-pocket expense), the cafeteria plan may permit the employee to revoke his election under the plan and elect to receive, on a prospective basis, coverage under another option providing similar coverage. Treas. Reg. §1.125-4(f)(3)(i).

If a plan adds a new benefit package option or improves an existing benefit package option or other coverage option during a period of coverage, the cafeteria plan may allow eligible employees (whether or not they have previously made an election under the cafeteria plan) to revoke their election and to make an election on a prospective basis for coverage under the new or improved option. Treas. Reg. §1.125-4(f)(3)(iii).

A cafeteria plan may allow an employee to make a prospective election change that corresponds to a change made under another employer plan (including a plan of the same employer or of another employer) or to add coverage under a cafeteria plan for the employee, spouse, or dependent if the employee, spouse, or dependent loses coverage under any group health plan sponsored by a governmental or educational institution. See Treas. Regs. §§1.125-4(f)(4), 1.125-4(f)(5).

Applicability Dates

In general, these regulations addressing election changes are applicable for cafeteria plan years beginning on or after January 1, 2001. The regulations specifically addressing election changes as a result of cost or coverage changes are applicable for cafeteria plan years beginning on or after January 1, 2002. Likewise, the requirement that coverage must indeed be provided for a child by the spouse, former spouse or other individual pursuant to a judgment, decree or order before a cafeteria plan may permit the employee to make an election change to cancel coverage for the child is subject to the later applicability date. Treas. Reg. §1.125-4(j). *ASRS, Sec. 58A, ¶130.3.*

104. How are cafeteria plan benefits affected by the Family and Medical Leave Act?

The interaction between IRC Section 125 and the Family and Medical Leave Act of 1993 (FMLA) was first addressed in proposed regulations published in 1995. Final regulations were published in October 2001, and are applicable for plan years beginning on or after January 1, 2002.

Under the 1995 proposed regulations, employers had to permit employees on FMLA leave to revoke an existing election of group health plan coverage (including a flexible spending arrangement, see Q 107) under a cafeteria plan for the remainder of the coverage period. Prop. Treas. Reg. §1.125-3, A-1. Under the 2001 final regulations, employers may require employees to continue coverage if the employer pays the employee's portion of the coverage cost. Treas. Reg. §1.125-3, A-1.

CAFETERIA PLANS   Q 104

Employees on FMLA leave are generally entitled to revoke or change elections in the same manner as the employees not on FMLA leave. Upon returning from the FMLA leave, the employee is entitled to be reinstated in the plan if the employee's coverage terminated during the leave, either by revocation or nonpayment of premiums. Treas. Reg. §1.125-3, A-1.

Health FSAs

A health flexible spending arrangement (health FSA, see Q 107) is subject to the same general rules as a traditional cafeteria plan, as discussed above.

The employee must be permitted to reinstate his coverage under the plan following the FMLA leave, as if he had not taken the leave. The employer may require that employees be reinstated following an FMLA leave if it also requires reinstatement for employees returning from non-FMLA leave. Treas. Reg. §1.125-3, A-6(a)(2).

For so long as the employee's coverage under the health FSA is continued (whether voluntarily or involuntarily), the entire amount of his health FSA, less any previous reimbursements, must be available for reimbursement of his health expenses. Treas. Reg. §1.125-3, A-6(b)(1). If the employee's coverage is terminated at any time during FMLA leave, he may not be reimbursed for expenses incurred while coverage was terminated. Treas. Reg. §1.125-3, A-6(b)(2)(i).

Payment Options

In general, whatever payment options are available to employees on non-FMLA leave must also be made available to employees on FMLA leave. Treas. Reg. §1.125-3, A-3(b). *Employers* must continue to contribute the same share of the premium cost that they were paying prior to the FMLA leave. Treas. Reg. §1.125-3, A-2. *Employees* who choose to continue health coverage during an FMLA leave must pay the same portion of the cost of such coverage that they paid while actively at work. Treas. Reg. §1.125-3, A-2. Employers may choose to waive this requirement, provided that they do so on a nondiscriminatory basis.

A cafeteria plan may generally offer employees on *unpaid* FMLA leave up to three options for paying for their health coverage under a cafeteria plan or health FSA. Treas. Reg. §1.125-3, A-3(a). These rules do not apply where paid leave is substituted for unpaid FMLA leave, in which case the employer must offer the payment method normally available during other types of paid leave. Treas. Reg. §1.125-3, A-4.

Any of the three payment options discussed below may generally be made on a pre-tax salary reduction basis, to the extent that the employee on FMLA leave has any taxable compensation (including the cash value of unused sick days or vacation days). A restriction applies when an employee's FMLA leave spans two plan years. In such a case, the plan may not operate in a manner that would allow employees on FMLA leave to defer compensation from one plan year to a subsequent plan year. Treas. Reg. §1.125-3, A-5. Any of the three payment options may also be made on an after-tax basis.

"Pre-pay" Option. Under this option, the employer allows the employee to pay the amounts due for the FMLA leave period prior to the commencement of FMLA leave. Treas. Reg. §1.125-3(a)(1)(i). Under no circumstances may the pre-pay option be the only option offered to employees on FMLA leave. The employer may offer the pre-pay

option to employees on FMLA leave even if such option is not offered to employees on other types of unpaid leave. Treas. Reg. §1.125-3, A-3(b)(1).

"Pay-as-you-go" Option. Under this option, employees pay their portion of the health care costs according to a payment schedule. This schedule may be (1) the same as the schedule that would be in effect if they were not on FMLA leave; (2) the same schedule upon which COBRA payments would be made (see Q 180); (3) the same schedule as applies to other employees on other, unpaid non-FMLA leave; or (4) any other schedule that (a) the employee and the employer voluntarily agree upon, and (b) is not inconsistent with the regulations. Treas. Reg. §1.125-3, A-3(a)(2)(i). The employer may not offer employees on FMLA leave only the pre-pay option and the catch-up option if the pay-as-you-go option is offered to employees on unpaid non-FMLA leave. Treas. Reg. §1.125-3, A-3(b)(3).

"Catch-up" Option. Under this option, an employer continues providing coverage during FMLA leave. Treas. Reg. §1.125-3, A-3(a)(3)(i). The catch-up option may be the sole option offered by the employer only if it is the sole option offered to employees on unpaid non-FMLA leave. Treas. Reg. §1.125-3, A-3(b)(2).

In general, the employer and the employee must agree in advance that (1) coverage will continue during the FMLA leave; (2) the employer assumes responsibility for the payment of employee's portion of the health care costs during the FMLA leave; and (3) the employee will repay such amounts when he returns from FMLA leave.

Employer's Right of Recoupment. An employer is not required to continue the coverage of an employee on FMLA leave who fails to make the required premium payments when due. But if the employer *does* continue coverage, the employer is entitled to recoup the missed payments under the "catch-up" option, without the employee's prior agreement. Treas. Regs. §§1.125-3, A-3(a)(2)(iii), 1.125-3, A-3(a)(3)(ii).

Health FSAs. Health FSAs are generally subject to the same payment rules as traditional cafeteria plans. Treas. Reg. §1.125-3, A-6(a)(1). The regulations do not make clear whether the employer's right of recoupment, discussed above, applies to health FSAs. If so, it would appear to represent a significant departure from the general risk-shifting rule applicable to health FSAs. See Q 107.

Non-Health Benefits

Under both the proposed and final regulations, employers are not required to continue an employees' non-health benefits provided under a cafeteria plan (e.g., life insurance) during an FMLA leave. Rather, whether an employee is entitled to the continuation of non-health benefits must be decided under the employer's policy applicable to employees on non-FMLA leave. Treas. Reg. §1.125-3, A-7. *ASRS, Sec. 58A, ¶130.2.*

105. Are amounts received under a cafeteria plan subject to social security and federal unemployment taxes?

Amounts received by participants, or their beneficiaries, under a cafeteria plan are not treated as wages. Thus, these amounts are not subject to tax under the Federal Insurance Contributions Act (FICA) or under the Federal Unemployment Tax Act (FUTA) if such payments would not be treated as wages without regard to the plan and it is

CAFETERIA PLANS   Q 107

reasonable to believe that IRC Section 125 would not treat any wages as constructively received. IRC Secs. 3121(a)(5), 3306(b)(5). *ASRS, Sec. 58A, ¶130.3*.

106. Must an employer sponsoring a cafeteria plan file an information return for the plan with the IRS?

Under IRC Section 6039D, an employer sponsoring a cafeteria plan must file an information return with the IRS. This return must indicate the number of the employer's employees, the number of employees eligible to participate in the plan, the number of employees actually participating in the plan, the cost of the plan, the identity of the employer and the type of business in which it is engaged, and the number of its highly compensated employees in the above categories.

Currently, however, the IRS has suspended the operation of these reporting requirements with respect to cafeteria plans. Notice 2002-24, 2002-1 CB 785; Notice 90-24, 1990-1 CB 335. This suspension is in effect for plan years beginning prior to the issuance of further guidance from the IRS. *ASRS, Sec. 58A, ¶130.5*.

FLEXIBLE SPENDING ARRANGEMENT

107. What is a flexible spending arrangement?

A flexible spending arrangement (FSA) is a program under IRC Section 125, by which specified, incurred expenses may be reimbursed. This benefit may be provided as a stand-alone plan or as part of a traditional cafeteria plan. The most common types are health FSAs and dependent care assistance FSAs.

In order for the coverage provided through an FSA to qualify for the exclusion from income under IRC Section 105 and IRC Section 106 (health FSAs) (see Q 159, Q 160) or IRC Section 129 (dependent care FSAs) (see Q 133), the FSA must meet the following requirements.

Health FSAs

Although health coverage under an FSA need not be provided under commercial insurance, it must demonstrate the risk shifting and risk distribution characteristics of insurance. Reimbursements under a health FSA must be paid specifically to reimburse medical expenses that have been incurred previously. A health FSA cannot operate so as to provide coverage only for periods during which the participants expect to incur medical expenses, if such period is shorter than a plan year. Prop. Treas. Reg. §1.125-2, A-7(a). In addition, the maximum amount of reimbursement must be available at all times throughout the period of coverage (properly reduced for prior reimbursements for the same period of coverage), without regard to the extent to which the participant has paid the required premiums for the coverage period, and without a premium payment schedule based on the rate or amount of covered claims incurred in the coverage period. Prop. Treas. Reg. §1.125-2, A-7(b)(2).

The period of coverage must be 12 months, or in the case of a short first plan year, the entire first year (or the short plan year where the plan year is changed). Election changes may not be permitted to increase or decrease coverage during a coverage year, but prospective changes may be allowed consistent with certain changes in family status.

2006 Tax Facts on Insurance & Employee Benefits

See Q 103. The plan may permit the period of coverage to be terminated if the employee fails to pay premiums, provided that the terms of the plan prohibit the employee from making a new election during the remaining period of coverage. The plan may permit revocation of existing elections by an employee who terminated service. Prop. Treas. Reg. §1.125-2, A-7(b)(3).

A plan may provide a grace period of no more than 2½ months following the end of the plan year for participants to incur and submit expenses for reimbursement. Notice 2005-42, 2005-23 IRB 1204. The grace period must apply to all participants in the plan. Plans may adopt a grace period for the current plan year by amending the plan document before the end of the current plan year.

The plan may reimburse medical expenses of the kind described under IRC Section 213(d) (see Q 826), but may not reimburse for premiums paid for other health plan coverage. Prop. Treas. Reg. §1.125-2, A-7(b)(4). The plan may reimburse for non-prescription over-the-counter drugs. Rev. Rul. 2003-102, 2003-36 IRB 559. Employer-provided coverage for qualified long-term care services provided through an FSA is included in the employee's gross income. IRC Sec. 106(c)(1).

The medical expenses must be for medical care provided during the period of coverage with substantiation that the expense claimed has been incurred and is not reimbursable under other health coverage. Prop. Treas. Regs. §§1.125-2, A-7(b)(5), 1.125-2, A-7(b)(6); Rev. Proc. 2003-43, 2003-21 IRB 935. See *Grande v. Allison Engine Co.*, 2000 U.S Dist. LEXIS 12220 (S.D. Ind. 2000). The IRS has approved the use of employer-issued debit and credit cards to pay for medical expenses as incurred, provided that the employer has in place sufficient procedures to substantiate the payments. Rev. Proc. 2003-43, 2003-21 IRB 935.

Dependent Care Assistance FSAs

Substantially the same rules apply to dependent care FSAs as to health FSAs except that the maximum amount of reimbursement need not be available throughout the period of coverage. A plan may limit a participant's reimbursement to amounts actually contributed to the plan and still available in the participant's account. Prop. Treas. Reg. §1.125-2, A-7(b)(8). Contributions to a dependent care FSA may not exceed $5,000 during a taxable year. IRC Sec. 129(a)(2)(A).

Like a health FSA, a dependent care FSA may permit a grace period of no more than 2½ months following the end of the plan year for participants to incur and submit expenses for reimbursement. Notice 2005-42, 2005-23 IRB 1204.

Plan Experience and Coverage

Any experience gain or income of an FSA may be (1) used to reduce premiums for the following year; or (2) returned to the premium payors as dividends or premium refunds on a reasonable basis, but in no case based on their individual claims experience. Prop. Treas. Reg. §1.125-2, A-7(b)(7).

The maximum amount of reimbursement for a period of coverage under an FSA may not be substantially in excess of the total "premium" for the coverage. The maximum amount of reimbursement is not considered to be substantially in excess of the total premium if the maximum amount is less than 500% of the premium. This definition is applicable to plan years beginning after December 31, 1989. Prop. Treas. Reg. §1.125-2, A-7.

Informal IRS Guidance on FSAs. In August of 2001, the IRS provided informal, *non-binding* guidance regarding FSAs. In a departure from previous informal guidance, the IRS informally indicated that orthodontia expenses should be treated differently from other medical expenses. Under this reasoning, if orthodontia expenses are paid in a lump sum when treatment commences, rather than over the course of treatment, they could be reimbursed under an FSA when paid. Finally, the IRS informally clarified that there is no *de minimis* claim amount that need not be substantiated; employers and plan administrators may not disregard the substantiation requirements for small claims. *ASRS, Sec. 58A, ¶130.2.*

COMPENSATION

108. What are the limitations on an employer's deduction for compensation paid to an employee?

Generally

An employer may deduct all ordinary and necessary business expenses including "a reasonable allowance for salaries or other compensation for personal services actually rendered." IRC Sec. 162(a)(1). "Reasonable" compensation is defined as "such amount as would ordinarily be paid for like services by like enterprises under like circumstances." Treas. Reg. §1.162-7(b)(3). Similarly, a salary that exceeds what is customarily paid for such services is considered unreasonable or excessive. Items other than wages may be considered in determining whether compensation is excessive. For example, the amount of loans forgiven on key person insurance policies for two top executives when the policies were transferred to them was used in determining whether their compensation was unreasonable. *Avis Indus. Corp. v. Comm.*, TC Memo 1995-434. Compensation is generally the total amount of compensation paid to an employee, rather than that paid to all employees as a group. *L. Schepp Co.*, 25 BTA 419 (1932).

If the IRS finds compensation to be unreasonable, it may reclassify it as a dividend, if paid to an employee-shareholder. See Treas. Reg. §1.162-7(b)(1). *Botany Worsted Mills v. U.S.*, 278 U.S. 282 (1929); *Alexander Shokai, Inc. v. Comm.*, TC Memo 1992-41, aff'd, 94-2 USTC ¶50,460 (9th Cir. 1994); *Bruno v. Comm.*, TC Memo 1990-109. The fact that the corporation had never declared a dividend was a factor in determining whether amounts paid to an individual who was president, director, and sole shareholder were actually disguised dividends. *Eberl's Claim Serv., Inc. v. Comm.*, 87 AFTR2d 897 (10th Cir. 2001). Bonuses that are disproportionately high in relation to salaries may actually be dividends in disguise, especially if the employee receiving the "bonus" is the company's sole or majority shareholder. *Rapco, Inc. v. Comm.*, 96-1 USTC ¶50,297 (2nd Cir. 1996); *Labelgraphics, Inc. v. Comm.*, TC Memo 1998-343, aff'd 2000-2 USTC ¶50,648 (9th Cir. 2000). But see *Exacto Spring Corp. v. Comm.*, 99-2 USTC ¶50,964 (7th Cir. 1999).

Compensation in Excess of $1,000,000

There is also an upper limitation on the amount that a corporation may deduct for compensation paid to certain executives. IRC Sec. 162(m). No deduction is permitted for "applicable employee remuneration" in excess of $1,000,000 paid to any "covered employee" by any "publicly-held corporation." IRC Sec. 162(m)(1).

Covered Employee. A "covered employee" is the corporation's chief executive officer or any other employee who is one of the corporation's four highest compensated officers. IRC Sec. 162(m)(3). This determination is made under the executive compensation disclosure rules of the Securities Exchange Act of 1934. Treas. Reg. §1.162-27(c)(2)(ii).

Publicly-held Corporation. A "publicly-held corporation" is any corporation that issues a class of common equity securities and is required to be registered under Section 12 of the Securities Exchange Act of 1934. The determination is made on the last day of the corporation's taxable year. Treas. Reg. §1.162-27(c)(1)(i).

Applicable employee remuneration. "Applicable employee remuneration" is the aggregate amount of remuneration paid to the employee for services performed (whether or not during the taxable year) that would be deductible if not for this limitation. IRC Sec. 162(m)(4). Not included are amounts not considered to be wages for FICA under IRC Sections 3121(a)(5)(A) through 3121(a)(5)(D), including payments to or from any qualified plan, SEP, or IRC Section 403(b) tax sheltered annuity. Treas. Reg. §1.162-27(c)(3)(ii)(A). Pension plan payments received by a CEO who retired and then returned to work within the same tax year were not considered applicable employee remuneration. Let. Rul. 9745002. Also excluded are: (1) any benefit provided to an employee that is reasonably believed to be excludable from his gross income; and (2) salary reduction contributions described in IRC Section 3121(v)(1) (see Q 423). Treas. Reg. §1.162-27(c)(3)(ii)(B).

Specifically excluded from the definition of applicable employee remuneration are commission payments, which are generally defined as any remuneration paid on a commission basis solely due to income generated directly by the employee's performance. IRC Sec. 162(m)(4)(B). Certain other performance-based compensation (e.g., stock options and stock appreciation rights) payable solely upon the attainment of at least one performance goal is also excluded, but only if: (1) the goals are set by a compensation committee of the corporation's board of directors, made up solely of at least two outside directors; (2) the terms under which the compensation will be paid are disclosed to the corporation's shareholders and approved by a majority vote prior to the time of payment; and (3) the compensation committee certifies that the performance goals have been attained before payment is made. IRC Sec. 162(m)(4)(C).

Amounts paid under a binding contract (1) in effect on February 17, 1993; and (2) not modified before the remuneration is paid are also excluded. IRC Sec. 162(m)(4)(D); Treas. Reg. §1.162-27(h)(1)(iii). If a contract entered into on or before February 17, 1993, is renewed after this date, it becomes subject to the deduction limitation. Treas. Reg. §1.162-27(h)(1)(i). The IRS has concluded that a proposed supplemental executive retirement plan (SERP–see Q 114), affecting employees subject to pre-1993 employment contracts, did not provide for increased compensation or the payment of additional compensation under substantially the same elements and conditions covered under the employment agreements and thus was not considered a material modification of those agreements pursuant to Treasury Regulation §1.162-27(h)(1)(iii)(c). Let. Rul. 9619046. *ASRS, Sec. 63, ¶160.*

109. What are "excess parachute payments" and how are they taxed?

Generally

Agreements providing a generous package of severance and benefits to top executives and key personnel in the event of a takeover or merger are commonly referred to as "golden parachutes." "Excess parachute payments," as defined in IRC Section 280G are subject to two tax sanctions: (1) no employer deduction is allowed, and (2) the recipient is subject to a 20% penalty tax. IRC Sec. 4999.

A "parachute payment" is defined in the Code as any payment in the nature of compensation to a disqualified individual which is (1) contingent on a change in the ownership or effective control of the corporation or a substantial portion of its assets *and* the present value of the payments contingent on such change *equals or exceeds* three times the individual's average annual compensation from the corporation in the five taxable years ending before the date of the change, *or* (2) pursuant to an agreement which violates any generally enforced securities laws or regulations. IRC Sec. 280G(b)(2). The present value of the payments contingent on the change in ownership or control is to be determined as of the date of the change, using a discount rate equal to 120% of the applicable federal rate. A transfer of property will be treated as a payment and taken into account at its fair market value.

A "disqualified individual" is (1) any employee, independent contractor, or other person specified in the regulations who performs personal services for a corporation and (2) is an officer, shareholder, or highly compensated individual of such corporation. For this purpose, "highly compensated individual" only includes an individual who is a member of the group consisting of the highest paid 1% of the employees of the corporation or, if less, the highest paid 250 employees of the corporation.

Generally, a payment will not be considered contingent if it is substantially certain at the time of the change that the payment would have been made whether or not the change occurred. However, if a payment is made under a contract entered into or amended within one year of a change in ownership or control, it is presumed to be a parachute payment, unless it can be shown "by clear and convincing evidence" that the payment was not contingent upon the change in ownership or control. IRC Sec. 280G(b)(2)(C).

The term "parachute payment" does not include: (1) any payment to a disqualified individual with respect to a "small business corporation" as defined in IRC Section 1361(b) (which does not have more than 1 class of stock and not more than 100 stockholders, all of whom are generally individuals but none of whom are nonresident aliens); (2) any payment to a disqualified individual with respect to a corporation if, immediately before the change, no stock was readily tradable on an established securities market or otherwise and shareholder approval of the payment was obtained after adequate and informed disclosure by a vote of persons, who immediately before the change, owned more than 75 percent of the voting power of all outstanding stock of the corporation; and (3) any payment to or from a qualified pension, profit sharing, or stock bonus plan, or a tax sheltered annuity plan; or a simplified employee pension plan. IRC Secs. 280G(b)(5) and (6). IRC Section 280G applies to agreements entered into or amended after June 14, 1984. Treas. Reg. §1.280G-1, Q&A 47

Calculating the "Excess Amount"

The amount of a parachute payment which is nondeductible and subject to the excise tax (i.e., the "excess parachute payment") is the amount of the payment *in excess* of that portion of the base amount allocable to that payment.

The "base amount" is the average of the individual's annual compensation paid by the corporation undergoing the change in ownership and includable in the gross income of the individual in the most recent five taxable years ending before the date on which the change in ownership or control occurs. If the individual has been employed by the corporation for less than five years, then his base amount is figured using the annual compensation for the years actually employed. Compensation of individuals employed for a portion of a taxable year should be annualized (i.e., $30,000 in compensation for four months of employment with the corporation would be $90,000 on an annual basis).

To determine the "excess parachute payment," the base amount is multiplied by the ratio of the present value of the parachute payment to the present value of all parachute payments expected; the result is then subtracted from the amount of the parachute payment.

$$\text{excess parachute payment} = \text{parachute payment} - \frac{\text{present value of the parachute payment}}{\text{present value of all parachute payments expected}} \times \text{base amount}$$

The present value is to be determined at the time the contingency occurs, using a discount rate of 120% of the applicable federal rate.

Any amount the taxpayer can prove is "reasonable compensation" will not be treated as a parachute payment. IRC Sec. 280G(b)(4); Treas. Reg. §1.280G-1, Q&A 40-44. See Q 108 for a general discussion on standards for "reasonable compensation." *ASRS, Sec. 63, ¶140.*

DEFERRED COMPENSATION

FUNDED DEFERRED COMPENSATION (ANNUITIES AND TRUSTS)

110. Is an employee taxed on premiums paid by his employer under a nonqualified annuity plan, or on contributions to a non-exempt employee's trust? How is the employer taxed?

Employee Taxation

As a general rule, the employee is currently taxed on a contribution to a trust or a premium paid for an annuity contract (paid after August 1, 1969) to the extent that his interest is substantially vested when the payment is made. An interest is substantially vested if it is (1) transferable or (2) not subject to a substantial risk of forfeiture. An interest is transferable if it can be transferred free of a substantial risk of forfeiture. See Q 112. See IRC Secs. 402(b)(1), 403(c), 83(a); Treas. Regs. §§1.402(b)-1(a)(1), 1.403(c)-1(a), 1.83-1(a)(1), 1.83-3(b), 1.83-3(d).

DEFERRED COMPENSATION   Q 110

A partner is immediately taxable on his distributive share of contributions made to a trust in which the partnership has a substantially vested interest, even if the partner's right is not substantially vested. *U.S. v. Basye*, 410 U.S. 441 (1973).

If the employee's rights change from substantially nonvested to substantially vested, the value of his interest in the trust or the value of the annuity contract on the date of change (to the extent such value is attributable to post-August 1, 1969 contributions) must be included in his gross income for the taxable year in which the change occurs. The value on the date of change probably also constitutes "wages" for the purposes of withholding, see Temp. Treas. Reg. §35.3405-1T, A-18, and Let. Rul. 9417013, and for the purposes of FICA and FUTA, see Q 122. The value of an annuity contract is its cash surrender value. See IRC Secs. 402(b)(1), 403(c), 83(a); Treas. Regs. §§1.402(b)-1(b), 1.403(c)-1(b).

If only part of an employee's interest in a trust or an annuity contract changes from substantially nonvested to substantially vested during any taxable year, then only that corresponding part is includable in gross income for the year. Treas. Regs. §§1.402(b)-1(b)(4), 1.403(c)-1(b)(3).

An employee is not taxed on the value of a vested interest in a trust attributable to contributions made while the trust was exempt under IRC Section 501(a). Treas. Reg. §1.402(b)-1(b)(1).

Special rules apply to trusts that lose their tax qualification because of a failure to satisfy the applicable minimum participation or minimum coverage tests. See IRC Sec. 402(b)(4). The IRS has taken the controversial position that these special rules apply to non-exempt trusts that were never intended to be tax qualified. As a result, the IRS would tax highly compensated employees (HCEs—see Q 356) participating in trust-funded nonqualified plans that fail the minimum participation or minimum coverage tests applicable to qualified plans (see Q 326 through Q 328), which most nonqualified plans will fail, under a special rule. See Q 111.

There is no tax liability when an employee's rights in the value of a trust or annuity (attributable to contributions or premiums paid on or before August 1, 1969) change from forfeitable to nonforfeitable. Prior to August 1, 1969, an employee was not taxed when payments were made to a nonqualified trust or as premiums to a nonqualified annuity plan if his rights at the time were forfeitable. See IRC Secs. 402(b) and 403(b) prior to amendment by P.L. 91-172 (TRA '69). Thus, the employee did not incur tax liability when his forfeitable rights later became nonforfeitable. This old law still applies to trust and annuity values attributable to payments made on or before August 1, 1969. Treas. Regs. §§1.402(b)-1(d), 1.403(c)-1(d).

Where an employer amended its unfunded nonqualified deferred compensation plan to provide those participants in pay status with a choice between a lump sum payment of the present value of their future benefits or an annuity contract securing their rights to the remaining payments under the plan with a corresponding tax gross-up payment from the employer, any participant who chose the annuity contract would include in gross income the purchase price for such participant's benefits under the contract and the tax gross-up payment in the year paid (or made available, if earlier). Let. Rul. 9713006.

For taxation of annuity payments to an employee, see Q 113.

2006 Tax Facts on Insurance & Employee Benefits

Employer Taxation

The employer, whether a cash or accrual basis taxpayer, can take a deduction for a contribution or premium paid in the year in which an amount attributable thereto is includable in the employee's gross income. IRC Sec. 404(a)(5); Treas. Regs. §§1.404(a)-1(c), 1.404(a)-12(b)(1). This deduction cannot be more than the amount of the contribution; it cannot include any earnings on the contribution before they are included in the employee's income. See Treas. Reg. §1.404(a)-12(b)(1). It seems reasonable to conclude that, if an employee includes only part of a contribution or premium in income in a given tax year, then the employer can deduct that part of the contribution or premium in that tax year. See *Harwood Assoc., Inc. v. Comm.*, 63 TC 255 (1974); *Wellons v. Comm.*, TC Memo 1992-704, at n.2, *aff'd on other grounds*, 31 F.3d 569, 94-2 USTC ¶50,402 (7th Cir. 1994). If more than one employee participates in a funded deferred compensation plan, the deduction will be allowed only if separate accounts are maintained for each employee. IRC Sec. 404(a)(5); Treas. Reg. §1.404(a)-12(b)(3); *Wigutow v. Comm.*, TC Memo 1983-620. However, the employer is not allowed a deduction at any time for contributions made or premiums paid on or before August 1, 1969, if the employee's rights were forfeitable at the time. Treas. Reg. §1.404(a)-12(c). Contributions or premiums paid or accrued on behalf of an independent contractor may be deducted only in the year in which amounts attributable thereto are includable in the independent contractor's gross income. IRC Sec. 404(d); Rev. Rul. 88-68, 1988-2 CB 117; see Temp. Treas. Reg. §1.404(d)1T.

With respect to contributions made after February 28, 1986, to annuity contracts held by a corporation, partnership, or trust (i.e., a nonnatural person), the "income on the contract" for the tax year of the policyholder is generally treated as ordinary income received or accrued by the contract owner during such taxable year. IRC Sec. 72(u). See Q 2. See also H.R. Rep. 99-426 (TRA '86), *reprinted in* 1986-3 CB (vol. 2) 703, 704; the General Explanation of TRA '86, at 658.

Also, corporate ownership of life insurance may result in exposure to the corporate alternative minimum tax. See Q 95.

The IRS has taken the position that a nonexempt employee's trust funded deferred compensation cannot be considered an employer-grantor trust. As a result, the employer will not be taxed on the trust's income, but it also cannot claim the trust's deductions and credits. See, e.g., Let. Rul. 9302017. Proposed regulations have affirmed the position of the IRS. Prop. Treas. Reg. §1.671-1(g). See Q 111.

Funded deferred compensation may take the form of either a salary continuation or pure deferred compensation plan. See Q 114.

The fact that a trust to fund a previously unfunded deferred compensation agreement was established as part of a nontaxable (IRC Section 337) corporate liquidation did not alter its treatment as an employee trust. *Teget v. U.S.*, 552 F.2d 236, 77-1 USTC ¶9315 (8th Cir. 1977).

A nonqualified deferred compensation plan funded by a trust or annuity (other than an "excess benefit plan," see Q 128) must provide for minimum vesting generally comparable to that required in qualified retirement plans. See ERISA Sec. 201; Q 333. However, government plans and many church plans are exempt from ERISA.

DEFERRED COMPENSATION   Q 111

The above rules do not apply to nonqualified annuities purchased by tax-exempt organizations and public schools (see Q 463 to Q 493) or to individual retirement accounts and annuities (see Q 210 to Q 238).

IRC Section 404(a)(11)

Generally, if vacation pay is paid to an employee within 2½ months after the end of the applicable tax year, it is deductible for the tax year in which it is earned (vested), and is not treated as deferred compensation. Temp. Treas. Reg. §1.404(b)-1T, A-2. Employers may not deduct accrued vacation or severance pay unless it is actually received by employees. IRC Sec. 404(a)(11).

Actual receipt is defined only by what it is not: (1) a note or letter evidencing the employer's indebtedness (whether or not guaranteed by an instrument or third party); (2) a promise to provide future service or property (whether or not evidenced by written agreement); (3) an amount transferred by a loan, refundable deposit, or contingent payment; or (4) amounts set aside in a trust for an employee. See IRSRRA '98, Sec. 7001, H.R. Conf. Rep. No. 105-599.

The IRS provided settlement options for taxpayers who had accelerated the deduction of accrued employee benefits (primarily vacation pay, disability pay, and sick pay) secured by a letter of credit, bond, or similar financial instrument, in reliance upon *Schmidt Baking Co., Inc.v. Comm.*, 107 TC 271 (1996) (employer allowed to deduct accrued vacation liabilities because it had obtained an irrevocable letter of credit guaranteeing such obligation within 2½ months of the year of deduction), which Section 404(a)(11) expressly overturned for years ending after July 22, 1998. See Rev. Proc. 99-26, 1999-1 CB 1244. The IRS has also published guidance explaining the automatic accounting method change necessary to comply with IRC Section 404(a)(11). See Notice 99-16, 1999-1 CB 501. *ASRS, Sec. 64, ¶¶430-430.5.*

111. What is a "secular trust" and how is it taxed?

A secular trust is an irrevocable trust established to formally fund and secure nonqualified deferred compensation benefits, so called to distinguish it from a rabbi trust. See Q 118. Funds placed in a secular trust are not subject to the claims of the employer's creditors. Thus, unlike a rabbi trust, a secular trust *can* protect its participants against both the employer's future *unwillingness* to pay promised benefits and the employer's future *inability* to pay promised benefits.

Secular trusts are not as popular as rabbi trusts, in part because of questions surrounding their taxation.

Taxation of Employee

The IRS believes that IRC Section 402(b)(1) through IRC Section 402(b)(4) govern the taxation of employee-participants in an *employer-funded* secular trust. See Let. Ruls. 9502030, 9302017, 9212024, 9212019, 9207010, 9206009. Under the general timing rule of IRC Section 402(b)(1), contributions to a secular trust are immediately included in the income of the employee to the extent that they are substantially vested. Treas. Reg. §1.402(b)-1(a)(1). Further, in any tax year in which any part of an employee's interest in the trust changes from substantially nonvested to substantially vested, the employee will be required to include that portion in income as of the date of the change. See IRC Sec. 402(b)(1); Treas. Regs. §§1.402(b)-1(b)(1), 1.402(b)-1(b)(4).

2006 Tax Facts on Insurance & Employee Benefits

An interest is substantially vested if it is (1) transferable or (2) not subject to a substantial risk of forfeiture. See Q 112. See Treas. Regs. §§1.402(b)-1(a)(1), 1.83-3(b).

With respect to the taxation of distributions from an employer-funded secular trust, the IRS has previously indicated that the rules of IRC Section 72 (except IRC Section 72(e)(5)) apply. See, generally, Q 113. Under this approach, distributions would be taxable except to the extent that they represent amounts previously taxed. See Let. Ruls. 9302017, 9212024, 9212019. Consequently, it would seem that a highly compensated employee who has been taxed on his entire "vested accrued benefit" would not be taxed again upon receipt of a lump sum distribution.

The IRS has questioned the applicability of IRC Section 72 to distributions from employer-funded secular trusts to highly compensated employees (HCEs)—as defined in IRC Section 414(q), see Q 356—participating in plans that fail the minimum participation or the minimum coverage tests applicable to *qualified* retirement plans (which most nonqualified plans will fail), adopting the controversial position that a special rule under IRC Section 402(b)(4) should be applied to tax HCEs each year on their "vested accrued benefit" in the trust (minus amounts previously taxed). Thus, HCEs will be taxed on vested contributions *and* on vested earnings on those contributions. See Let. Ruls. 9502030, 9417013, 9302017, 9212024, 9212019, 9207010. Apparently, the IRS would tax HCEs on their vested earnings even where they consist of unrealized appreciation of capital assets or nominally tax-free or tax deferred income (e.g., from municipal bonds or life insurance). Further, the IRS believes that any right to receive trust payments in compensation for these taxes will also be taxable as part of the vested accrued benefit. See Let. Ruls. 9302017, 9212019.

The IRS believes that as long as a failure to satisfy the minimum participation test or the minimum coverage test is not the only feature of the plan that keeps the secular trust from being treated as a tax-qualified trust (and it generally will not be), then any participants who are not highly compensated will be taxed under the general rules of IRC Section 402(b)(1), described above. See, e.g., Let. Rul. 9206009.

The 10% penalty for certain premature annuity distributions under IRC Section 72(q) may apply to distributions from employer-funded secular trusts if the deferred compensation plan behind the trust is considered to be an annuity (i.e., if it provides for the payment of benefits in a series of periodic payments over a fixed period of time, or over a lifetime). See Let. Ruls. 9502030, 9212024, 9212019.

Employee-funded secular trusts (where the employee establishes the trust, but the employer administers it and contributes to it) are analyzed differently. The employee generally has a choice between receiving cash (or its equivalent; e.g., an immediately surrenderable annuity or life insurance policy) currently or a cash contribution to the trust. Sometimes the employee has the choice between withdrawing contributions from the trust or leaving them in. In these situations, the IRS has generally ruled that the employee constructively received the employer-contributed cash and then assigned it to the trust. Thus, the IRS has generally held the employee to be currently taxable on employer contributions to the trust. See Let. Ruls. 9548015, 9548014, 9437011, 9337016, 9328007, 9322011, 9316018, 9316008, 9235044, 9031031, 8843021, 8841023. See also Let. Rul. 9450004 (employee who could keep or contribute cash to trust was currently taxable on amounts contributed, although keeping cash would jeopardize future contributions and benefits).

DEFERRED COMPENSATION   Q 111

An employee who establishes and is considered to be the owner of an employee-funded secular trust under the grantor-trust rules should not have to include the income on annuity contracts held by the trust in income each year. See Let. Ruls. 9322011, 9316018. See Q 2.

Employer's Deduction

It is the position of the IRS that an employer can take a deduction for a contribution to an *employer-funded* secular trust in the year in which it is includable in employee income. See Let. Ruls. 9502030, 9417013, 9302017, 9212024, 9212019. But the rules of IRC Section 404(a)(5) limit the employer's deduction to the amount of the contribution; it can never include "earnings" on that amount between contribution and inclusion in the employee's income. See Treas. Reg. §1.404(a)-12(b)(1); Let. Ruls. 9502030, 9417013, 9302017, 9212024, 9212019.

An employer cannot increase its "contributions" and thus its deductions by drafting the trust agreement to require that: (1) the trust distribute its earnings to the employer; and (2) that the trustee retain those earnings as "re-contributions" to the trust. The IRS has indicated that it will not recognize such deemed distributions and re-contributions. See Let. Rul. 9302017.

If a secular trust covers more than one employee, the employer will be able to take a deduction for contributions only if the trust maintains separate accounts for the various employees. See Let. Ruls. 9502030, 9302017, 9212024, 9212019, 9207010, 9206009. According to the IRS, the separate account rule is satisfied only if the trust document requires that the income earned on participants' accounts be allocated to their accounts. See Treas. Reg. §1.404(a)-12(b)(3); Let. Ruls. 9207010, 9206009.

The IRS has also granted employers immediate deductions for trust contributions where participants could choose between receiving current compensation outright or having it contributed to a trust, and where trust participants could choose between withdrawing contributions from the trust or leaving them in the trust. The IRS regarded these situations as *employee-funded* trusts and gave the employers deductions for the payment of compensation. See Let. Ruls. 9548015, 9548014, 9437011, 9337016, 9328007, 9322011, 9316018, 9316008, 9235044, 9031031, 8843021, 8841023. See also Let. Rul. 9450004 (employer allowed immediate deduction where employee could keep or contribute cash to employee-funded trust).

Taxation of Trust

The IRS believes that a secular trust can never be an employer-grantor trust. Thus, an employer-funded secular trust is a separate, taxable entity. Unless secular trust earnings are distributable or are distributed annually, the trust will be taxed on those earnings. See Let. Ruls. 9502030, 9417013, 9302017, 9212024, 9212019, 9207010, 9206009.

Proposed regulations have affirmed this position. Prop. Treas. Reg. §1.671-1(g) (employer not treated as an owner of any portion of a domestic, nonexempt employees' trust under IRC Section 402(b) if part of a deferred compensation plan, regardless of whether the employer has power of interest described in IRC Section 673 through IRC Section 677).

Because the IRS would generally tax HCEs each year on vested trust earnings (and would generally tax other employees on at least some trust earnings when a substantially

2006 Tax Facts on Insurance & Employee Benefits

nonvested interest becomes substantially vested), double taxation of trust earnings is a very real possibility. Funding secular trusts with life insurance may eliminate this by eliminating taxation of the trust. The IRS has not considered the use of life insurance in secular trusts, but under generally applicable tax rules, the inside build-up (or "earnings") on life insurance should not be taxed to the trust while it holds the policies. However, the use of life insurance probably will not save employees from taxation on trust earnings.

It is also possible to avoid trust (and therefore double) taxation by using *employee-funded secular trusts*. Employee-funded trusts are generally treated as employee-grantor trusts, because the trust income is generally held solely for the employee's benefit. As a result, the trust income is generally taxed to the employee only. See Let. Ruls. 9548015, 9548014, 9450004, 9437011, 9337016, 9328007, 9322011, 9316018, 9316008, 9235044, 9212024, 8843021, 8841023. Compare Let. Rul. 9620005 (group of secular trusts, each with a separate employee grantor, pooled investment resources together to form a master trust, will be taxed as a partnership, thereby avoiding double taxation applicable to corporations).

ERISA Implications

Use of a secular trust (at least a trust other than an employee-grantor trust) will probably cause a deferred compensation plan subject to ERISA to be funded for ERISA purposes. See, e.g., *Dependahl v. Falstaff Brewing Corp.*, 653 F.2d 1208 (8th Cir. 1981) (plan is funded when employee can look to property separate from employer's ordinary assets for satisfaction of benefit obligations), *aff'g in part* 491 F. Supp. 1188 (E.D. Mo. 1980), *cert. denied*, 454 U.S. 968 (1981) and 454 U.S. 1084 (1981). Funded plans are generally required to meet ERISA's Title I requirements. ***ASRS, Sec. 64, ¶¶310-350, 430.5.***

112. What is meant by "a substantial risk of forfeiture"?

A person's rights in property are subject to a substantial risk of forfeiture if: (1) his full enjoyment of the property is conditioned upon the future performance (or refraining from performance) of substantial services by any individual, or the occurrence of a condition related to a purpose of the transfer; and (2) the possibility of forfeiture if the condition is not satisfied is substantial. IRC Sec. 83(c)(1); Treas. Reg. §1.83-3(c)(1). Whether a risk of forfeiture is substantial depends upon the facts and circumstances. Treas. Reg. §1.83-3(c)(1).

Because the inquiry is so fact-based, there is little definitive guidance as to the sorts of services that will be considered substantial. However, the regularity of performance and the time spent in performing the required services tend to indicate whether they are substantial. Treas. Reg. §1.83-3(c)(2). Furthermore, it is not clear how far into the future an arrangement must require substantial services in order to require adequate "future performance." See, generally, Treas. Reg. §1.83-3(c)(4). Nonetheless, the regulations' examples describe arrangements requiring employees to work for periods as short as one and two years as imposing substantial risks of forfeiture. See Treas. Reg. §1.83-3(c)(4), Ex. 1 and Ex. 3.

For examples of service requirements that have constituted a substantial risk of forfeiture in the context of IRC Section 457(f) plans (Q 126), see generally Let. Ruls. 9642046, 9642038, 9628020, 9628011, 9627007, 9623027, 9549009, 9444028, 9215019, 9030025.

DEFERRED COMPENSATION   Q 112

Some things are clear. Requiring that property be returned if the employee is discharged for cause or for committing a crime will not create a substantial risk of forfeiture. Treas. Reg. §1.83-3(c)(2). The IRS has indicated that benefits would be taxable once a participant has met age and service requirements under an IRC Section 457 plan (see Q 124), although the benefits remained forfeitable if participants were fired for cause, and noted that forfeiture upon termination for cause was not sufficient to constitute a substantial risk of forfeiture under Treas. Reg. §1.83-3(c)(2). TAM 199902032. See also *Burnetta v. Comm.*, 68 TC 387 (1977) (crime–decided before adoption of regulation), *acq.*, 1978-2 CB 1.

A covenant not to compete will not ordinarily result in a substantial risk of forfeiture, unless the particular facts and circumstances indicate otherwise. Treas. Reg. §1.83-3(c)(2); see also Let. Ruls. 9548015, 9548014.

Similarly, the requirement that a retiring employee render consulting services upon the request of his former employer does not result in a substantial risk of forfeiture, unless the employee is, in fact, expected to perform substantial consulting services. Treas. Reg. §1.83-3(c)(2). See also *Richardson v. Comm.*, 64 TC 621 (1975) (decided before regulation).

Imposing a sufficient condition on the full enjoyment of the property is not in itself enough to create a substantial risk of forfeiture; the possibility of forfeiture if the condition is not satisfied must be substantial. This possibility may be substantial even if there are circumstances under which failure to satisfy the condition will not result in forfeiture of the property. For example, the possibility of forfeiture is substantial where an employee would generally lose his deferred compensation upon termination of employment before completing the required services, but would not forfeit those benefits if his early termination were due to death or permanent disability. See Rev. Rul. 75-448, 1975-2 CB 55. The possibility that a forfeiture might not be enforced in the event of normal or early retirement before the satisfaction of the condition might not undermine the substantial risk of forfeiture. See Let. Rul. 9431021; but compare Let. Rul. 9215019 (where employer could accelerate vesting of employee's benefits under an IRC Section 457 plan anytime on or after three years of service under the plan, employee's benefits would not appear to be subject to a substantial risk of forfeiture after three years; existence of such risk is a question of fact).

Special scrutiny will be applied in determining whether the risk of forfeiture is substantial concerning a property transfer from a corporation to a controlling shareholder-employee. In such situations, a restriction that would otherwise be considered to impose a substantial risk of forfeiture will be considered to impose such a risk only if the chance that the corporation will enforce the restriction is substantial. See Treas. Reg. §1.83-3(c)(3). Compare *Ludden v. Comm.*, 68 TC 826 (1977) (possibility of forfeiture did not amount to a substantial risk of forfeiture because there was too little chance that the shareholder-employees would cause themselves to be fired), *aff'd on other grounds*, 620 F.2d 700, 45 AFTR 2d 80-1068 (9th Cir. 1980).

It is not clear whether one can effectively extend a substantial risk of forfeiture. One letter ruling has concluded that as long as the future services required of the employee were and would continue to be substantial, an agreement between the employer and the employee postponing the vesting date of restricted stock would not in itself trigger taxation of the stock. Let. Rul. 9431021. However, the ruling has generated controversy, particularly with respect to efforts to extend its reasoning to ineligible IRC Section 457(f) plans (see Q 126). *ASRS, Sec. 64, ¶430.2(b)*.

113. How is an employee taxed on the payments he receives from a nonqualified annuity or nonexempt trust?

Annuity payments are taxable to the employee under the general rules in IRC Section 72 relating to the taxation of annuities. IRC Sec. 403(c). See Q 7 (payments in annuitization phase), Q 3 (payments in accumulation phase). The employee's investment in the contract, for purposes of figuring the exclusion ratio, consists of all amounts attributable to employer contributions that were taxed to the employee and premiums paid by the employee (if any). Investment in the contract includes the value of the annuity taxed to the employee when his interest changed from nonvested to vested. Let. Rul. 7728042.

Payments under a nonexempt trust are also generally taxed under the rules relating to annuities, except that distributions of trust income before the annuity starting date are subject to inclusion in income under the generally applicable "interest first" rule without regard to the "cost recovery" rule retained (for certain cases) by IRC Section 72(e)(5). IRC Sec. 402(b)(2). See Q 7, Q 3. Furthermore, a distribution from the trust before the "annuity starting date" for the periodic payments will be treated as distributed in the following order: (1) income earned on employee contributions made after August 1, 1969; (2) other amounts attributable to employee contributions; (3) amounts attributable to employer contributions (made after August 1, 1969 and not previously includable in employee's gross income); (4) amounts attributable to employer contributions made on or before August 1, 1969; (5) the remaining interest in the trust attributable to employer contributions. Treas. Reg. §1.402(b)-1(c)(2). However, the IRS has privately questioned whether the annuity rules of IRC Section 72 are applicable to distributions to highly compensated employees from an employer-funded nonexempt trust under a plan that fails the minimum participation or the minimum coverage tests applicable to qualified plans (see Q 324, Q 325); the taxation of such distributions is unclear. See Let. Ruls. 9502030, 9417013; see also Q 111.

If the distribution consists of an annuity contract, the entire value of the annuity, less the investment in the contract, is included in gross income. Treas. Reg. §1.402(b)-1(c)(1).

For applications of FICA and FUTA to deferred compensation payments, see Q 122. *ASRS, Sec. 64, ¶430.3*.

UNFUNDED DEFERRED COMPENSATION

General Rules

114. What are the tax benefits of a deferred compensation agreement with an employer?

A properly planned deferred compensation agreement postpones payment for currently rendered services until a future date, with the effect of postponing the taxation of such compensation until it is received. Under a typical deferred compensation agreement, an employer promises to pay an employee fixed or variable amounts for life or

DEFERRED COMPENSATION   Q 115

for a guaranteed number of years. When the deferred amount is received, the employee may be in a lower income tax bracket. See Q 121. Additionally, many employers use this type of plan to provide benefits in excess of the limitations placed on qualified plan benefits. For example, a "SERP" (Supplemental Executive Retirement Plan) is a type of plan for a selected group of executives that generally provides extra retirement benefits. An "excess benefit plan" is a special kind of supplemental plan. See Q 128.

Commentators divide nonqualified deferred compensation plans into two broad categories: pure deferred compensation plans and salary continuation plans. Both unfunded and funded deferred compensation plans may be divided into these categories. See Q 110. However, because the taxation of the two types of plans is similar, the difference is mostly theoretical. In this text, the term "deferred compensation" should be understood to refer to both pure deferred compensation plans and salary continuation plans.

A "pure deferred compensation plan" involves an agreement between the employer and employee, whereby the employee defers receipt of some portion of present compensation (or a raise or bonus, or a portion thereof) in exchange for the employer's promise to pay a deferred benefit in the future. Some commentators refer to this as an "in lieu of" plan.

A "salary continuation plan" is a benefit provided by the employer in addition to all other forms of compensation—the employer promises to pay a deferred benefit, but there is no corresponding reduction in the employee's present compensation, raise, or bonus.

See Q 115 for a discussion of general principles of law applicable to private deferred compensation agreements. See Q 123 and Q 124 for an explanation of special requirements that apply to deferred compensation agreements with state and local governments and their agencies and with organizations exempt from tax under IRC Section 501. See Q 127 for deferred compensation plans covering state judges. *ASRS, Sec. 64, ¶¶110-130.*

Private Plans

115. What requirements must be met by a private deferred compensation plan?

In General

A private deferred compensation plan is a plan entered into with any employer other than: (1) a state; (2) a political subdivision of a state (e.g., a local government); (3) an agency or instrumentality of (1) or (2); or (4) an organization exempt from tax under IRC Section 501.

For the rules concerning nonqualified deferred compensation plans sponsored by government or tax-exempt employers, see Q 123 through Q 126.

Although private deferred compensation agreements are most frequently entered into with employees of corporations, they may also be entered into with employees of other business organizations and with independent contractors. See, e.g., Rev. Rul. 60-31, 1960-1 CB 174, as modified by Rev. Rul. 70-435, 1970-2 CB 100; Rev. Rul. 69-474, 1969-2 CB 105; *Robinson v. Comm.*, 44 TC 20 (1965), *acq.*, 1970-2 CB xxi,

1976-2 CB 2 (correction); Let. Ruls. 9546008, 9540003, 9422025, 9245015, 9122019, 9052016. For example, a director's fees can be deferred through an unfunded deferred compensation agreement with the corporation. Rev. Rul. 71-419, 1971-2 CB 220; Let. Ruls. 9546008, 9525031, 9505012, 9420009, 8903088, 8637085, 8541043. But if an employer or service recipient transfers its payment obligation to a third party, efforts to defer payments from the third party may not be effective. See Rev. Rul. 69-50, 1969-1 CB 140, as amplified in Rev. Rul. 77-420, 1977-2 CB 172 (deferral of physicians' payments from Blue Shield type organization ineffective); TAM 9336001 (deferral of plaintiffs' attorney's fees under structured settlement with defendants' liability insurers ineffective); contra *Childs v. Comm.*, 103 TC 634 (1994), *aff'd*, 89 F.3d 856 (11th Cir. 1996) (deferral of plaintiffs' attorneys' fees under structured settlement with defendant's liability insurers effective).

General Rules

The employer may pay deferred amounts as additional compensation, or employees may voluntarily agree to reduce current salary. See Rev. Rul. 69-650, 1969-2 CB 106.

The plan must provide that participants have the status of general unsecured creditors of the employer and that the plan constitutes a mere promise by the employer to pay benefits in the future.

The plan must also state that it is the intention of the parties that it be unfunded for tax and ERISA purposes.

The plan must define the time and method for paying deferred compensation for each event (e.g., retirement) that would entitle a participant to a distribution of benefits.

If the plan refers to a trust or other informal funding mechanism, additional rules must be satisfied. See Q 117 and Q 118.

Statutory Requirements

Distributions

In the American Jobs Creation Act of 2004, Congress imposed additional requirements to avoid constructive receipt. Under new IRC Section 409A, a participant may only receive a distribution of previously deferred compensation upon the occurrence of one of six events:

- separation from service;
- the date the participant becomes disabled;
- death;
- a fixed time (or pursuant to a fixed scheduled) specified in the plan at the date of the deferral;
- a change in the ownership or effective control of the corporation or assets of the corporation, to the extent provided in regulations; or
- the occurrence of an unforeseeable emergency.

DEFERRED COMPENSATION   Q 115

IRC Sec. 409A(a)(2)(A) ; Prop. Treas. Reg. § 1.409A-3. In addition, key employees (as defined in IRC Section 416(i)) of publicly traded corporations may not take distributions until six months after separation from service (or, if earlier, the date of death of the employee). IRC Sec. 409A(a)(2)(B)(i).

Under proposed regulations, a change in ownership occurs when an individual or persons acting as a group acquires more than 50 percent of the total fair market value or total voting power of the corporation. Prop. Treas. Reg. § 1.409A-3(g)(5)(v). Ownership under these rules is subject to attribution under IRC Section 318(a). Prop. Treas. Reg. § 1.409A-3(g)(5)(iii). A change in effective control occurs when an individual or persons acting as a group acquires 35 percent or more of the total voting power of the stock of the corporation within a 12-month period or where there is an adversarial change in a majority of the membership of the board of directors within a 12-month period. Prop. Treas. Reg. § 1.409A-3(g)(5)(vi). A change in the ownership of a substantial portion of the assets of the corporation occurs when an individual or persons acting as a group acquires assets equal to or greater than 40 percent of the total gross fair market value of the corporation. Prop. Treas. Reg. § 1.409A-3(g)(5)(vii).

Within the meaning of IRC Section 409A(a)(2)(A), "unforeseeable emergency" means "a severe financial hardship to the participant resulting from an illness or accident of the participant, the participant's spouse, or a dependent (as defined in section 152(a)) of the participant, loss of the participant's property due to casualty, or other similar extraordinary and unforeseeable circumstances arising as a result of events beyond the control of the participant." Prop. Treas. Reg. § 1.409A-3(g)(3).

Deferral Elections

IRC Section 409A also imposes requirements for participants making elections to defer compensation. Participants now must generally make deferral elections prior to the end of the preceding taxable year. IRC Sec. 409A(a)(4)(B)(i). In the first year in which a participant becomes eligible to participate in a plan, however, the participant may make an election within 30 days after the date of eligibility, but only with respect to services to be performed subsequent to the election. IRC Sec. 409A(a)(4)(B)(ii); Prop. Treas. Reg. § 1.409A-2. In the case of any performance-based compensation covering a period of at least 12 months, a participant must make an election no later than 6 months before the end of the covered period. IRC Sec. 409A(a)(4)(B)(iii); Prop. Treas. Reg. § 1.409A-2(a)(7).

Changes in Time or Form of Payment

A separate set of new election rules allows participants to elect to delay distributions or change the form of distributions from a plan as long as the plan requires the new election to be made at least 12 months in advance. IRC Sec. 409A(a)(4)(C)(i); Prop. Treas. Reg. § 1.409A-2(b). In addition any election to delay a distribution must delay the distribution at least five years from the date of the new election (unless made on account of disability, death, or an unforeseeable emergency). IRC Sec. 409A(a)(4)(C)(ii). An election related to a scheduled series of distributions made pursuant to a fixed schedule must be made at least 12 months in advance of the first such scheduled payment. IRC Sec. 409A(a)(4)(C)(iii).

Proposed regulations generally provide that each separately identified amount to which an employee is entitled to receive on a determinable date is a separate payment. Prop. Treas. Reg. § 1.409A-2(b)(2). A series of installment payments under a single plan will generally be treated as a single payment; however, a plan may specify that a series of installment payments is to be treated as a series of separate payments. Prop. Treas. Reg. § 1.409A-2(b)(2)(iii).

Acceleration of Payments

Proposed regulations define other circumstances under which a plan may permit the acceleration of payments:

1. to comply with a domestic relations order,

2. to comply with a conflict-of-interest divestiture requirement (see IRC Section 1043),

3. to pay income taxes due upon a vesting event under a plan subject to IRC Section 457(f),

4. to pay the FICA or other employment taxes imposed on compensation deferred under the plan,

5. to pay any amount included in income under IRC Section 409A, or

7. to terminate a participant's interest in a plan

   a. after separation from service where the payment is not greater than $10,000,

   b. where all arrangements of the same type are terminated,

   c. in the 12 months following a change in control event, or

   d. upon a corporate dissolution or bankruptcy, or

8. to terminate a deferral election following an unforeseeable emergency.

Prop. Treas. Reg. § 1.409A-2(h).

Short-Term Deferrals

Under proposed regulations, a deferral of compensation does not occur when amounts are paid within 2½ months after the end of the year in which the employee obtains a legally-binding right to the amounts. Under this rule, many multi-year bonus arrangements that require payments promptly after the amounts vest will not be subject to IRC Section 409A. Prop. Treas. Reg. § 1.409A-1(b)(4).

Independent Contractors

Under proposed regulations, IRC Section 409A does not generally apply to amounts deferred under an arrangement between a service recipient and an unrelated independent contractor, if, during the contractor's taxable year in which the amount is deferred, the contractor provides significant services to each of two or more service recipients that are unrelated, both to each other and to the independent contractor. Prop. Treas. Reg. § 1.409A-1(f)(3). A safe harbor rule provides that an independent contractor will be treated as providing significant services to more than one service recipient where not more than 70% of the total revenue of the trade or business is derived from any particular service recipient (or group of related service recipients). Prop. Treas. Reg. § 1.409A-1(f)(3)(iii).

DEFERRED COMPENSATION   Q 115

Penalties

IRC Section 409A also includes substantial penalties for failing to meet the statutory requirements when deferring compensation. Any violation of the above requirements results in retroactive constructive receipt, with the deferred compensation being taxable to the participant as of the time of the intended deferral. IRC Sec. 409A(a)(1)(A)(i). In addition to the normal income tax on the compensation, the participant must pay an additional 20% tax, as well as interest at a rate 1% higher than the normal underpayment rate. IRC Sec. 409A(a)(1)(B).

Effective Dates

The requirements of IRC Section 409A generally apply to amounts deferred after December 31, 2004. The requirements also apply to amounts deferred prior to January 1, 2005 if the plan under which the deferral is made is materially modified after October 3, 2004. There is an exception for material modifications made pursuant to IRS guidance. Proposed regulations under IRC Section 409A are to be effective January 1, 2007. Prop. Treas. Reg. §§ 1.409A-1 through 1.409A-6.

A plan is materially modified if a new benefit or right is added or if a benefit or right existing as of October 3, 2004 is materially enhanced and such addition or enhancement affects amounts earned and vested before January 1, 2005. The reduction of an existing benefit is not a material modification. Prop. Treas. Reg. § 1.409A-6(a)(4).

Planning Point: Employers should use great care in making any modifications to existing deferred compensation arrangements in order to avoid unexpected application of IRC Section 409A. According to proposed regulations, a material modification may be a formal plan amendment or may occur simply by virtue of an employer's exercise of discretion in the plan participant's favor.

Constructive Receipt

Tax deferment will not be achieved if, prior to the *actual receipt* of payments, the employee is in *constructive receipt* of the income under the agreement. Income is constructively received if the employee can draw upon it at any time. However, income is not constructively received if the employee's control of its receipt is subject to substantial limitations or restrictions. Some agreements contain contingencies that may cause the employee to forfeit future payments. So long as the employee's rights are forfeitable, there can be no constructive receipt. See Treas. Regs. §§1.451-1, 1.451-2. However, the IRS has ruled that the employee will not be in constructive receipt of income even though his rights are *nonforfeitable* if: (1) the agreement is entered into before the compensation is earned; and (2) the employer's promise to pay is not secured in any way. Rev. Rul. 60-31, 1960-1 CB 174, as modified by Rev. Rul. 70-435, 1970-2 CB 100. See also *Comm. v. Olmsted Inc. Life Agency*, 304 F.2d 16 (8th Cir. 1962); *Comm. v. Oates*, 207 F.2d 711 (7th Cir. 1953); *Robinson v. Comm.*, 44 TC 20 (1965), *acq.*, 1970-2 CB xxi, 1976-2 CB 2 (correction); *Basila v. Comm.*, 36 TC 111 (1961), *acq.*, 1962-1 CB 3; *Gann v. Comm.*, 31 TC 211 (1958), *acq.*, 1960-1 CB 4; *Veit v. Comm.*, 8 TC 809 (1947), *acq.*, 1947-2 CB 4.

The American Jobs Creation Act of 2004 created new requirements for elections to defer compensation. IRC Sec. 409A(a)(4). For prior deferrals not subject to IRC Section 409A, there was some conflict between the IRS and the courts with respect to the consequences of an election to defer compensation *after* the earning period commences.

2006 Tax Facts on Insurance & Employee Benefits   109

Q 115   FEDERAL INCOME TAX

The IRS seems to believe that a deferral election after the earning period commences will results in constructive receipt of the deferred amounts, even if made before the deferred amounts are payable. For example, in TAM 8632003, the IRS found constructive receipt where a participant in a shadow stock plan elected, just prior to surrendering his shares, to take the value of his shares in 10 installment payments rather than in one lump sum. The IRS refused to permit further deferral of amounts already earned and determinable, believing that the fact that the benefits were not yet payable at the time of the election was an insufficient restriction on the availability of the money. See also Let. Rul. 9336001 (election to defer must be made before earning compensation to avoid constructive receipt). See also the discussion of Rev. Proc. 71-19, 1971-1 CB 698, as amplified by Rev. Proc. 92-65, 1992-2 CB 428, in "IRS Rulings," below. But see Let. Rul. 9506008 (plan allowing elections to defer bonus payments on or before May 31st of the year for which the deferral is to be effective did not cause constructive receipt; no express consideration of effect of election provision); see also Let. Rul. 9525031 (contributions to rabbi trust do not result in income to participants or beneficiaries until benefits are paid or made available in context of plan allowing election to further defer compensation through choice of payout method *after* termination of services; no express consideration of effect of election provision).

Courts have looked more favorably upon elections to defer compensation after the earning period commences but before the compensation was payable. For example, the Tax Court considered the same plan addressed in TAM 8632003, above, and reaffirmed its position that an election to further defer compensation not yet due under the original deferred compensation agreement does not necessarily result in constructive receipt. See *Martin v. Comm.*, 96 TC 814 (1991). See also *Childs v. Comm.*, 103 TC 634 (1994), *aff'd*, 89 F.3d 856 (11th Cir. 1996); *Oates v. Comm.*, 18 TC 570 (1952), *aff'd*, 207 F.2d 711 (7th Cir. 1953), *acq.*, 1960-1 CB 5; *Veit v. Comm.*, 8 TCM 919 (1949); *Veit v. Comm.*, 8 TC 809 (1947), *acq.*, 1947-2 CB 4. While the IRS did acquiesce in *Oates* and in the first *Veit* case, it tried to distinguish those cases and the second *Veit* case in TAM 8632003, above. Specifically, the court ruled that participants in a shadow stock plan who chose, *after* earning their deferred benefits but *before* those benefits were payable, to extend the deferral of their benefits by taking them in 10 installment payments, rather than in one lump sum, did not constructively receive all of their benefits when they received their first installment. In reaching its decision, the court considered several factors, noting that they were not the only factors it could have considered, and that any one of the factors, by itself, might not have been sufficient to support the decision. The court considered the most significant factor to be that the participants never had unrestricted rights to a lump sum payment of benefits, because access to their benefits was conditioned upon their cashing in their shares and giving up future participation in the plan. The *Martin* case is enigmatic, though, and commentators have suggested that it should not be relied upon too heavily. See 18 Pens. Rep. (BNA) 1664 (1991).

A provision in an unfunded deferred compensation plan permitting hardship withdrawals upon unforeseeable emergency will not necessarily result in constructive receipt. See, e.g., Rev. Proc. 92-65, Sec. 3.01(c), 1992-2 CB 428, amplifying Rev. Proc. 71-19, 1971-1 CB 698; Let. Ruls. 9546008, 9505012, 9332038. Such a provision is most likely to avoid IRS challenge if it defines "unforeseeable emergency" as an unanticipated event beyond the participant's (or beneficiary's) control, which would cause severe financial hardship if early withdrawal were not permitted. Language similar to that in Treas. Regs. §§1.457-2(h)(4) and 1.457-2(h)(5) may be used. The plan should provide that any withdrawal will be limited to the amount necessary to meet the emergency. See Rev. Proc.

DEFERRED COMPENSATION   Q 115

92-65, Sec. 3.01(c), above. However, while an appropriate hardship withdrawal provision should not trigger constructive receipt *before* a qualifying emergency is at hand, such a provision may trigger constructive receipt *when* a qualifying emergency arises. Let. Rul. 9501032; but see Let. Rul. 9546008 (no constructive receipt of deferred compensation until deferred amounts are distributed on account of unforeseeable emergency).

Employees who were permitted to transfer assets from rabbi trusts to segregated bank accounts under their control or to employee-funded secular trusts but declined to do so were in constructive receipt of the amounts that could have been transferred. Let. Rul. 9337016.

A parent corporation's guarantee of its subsidiary's deferred compensation obligations may not put the employees in constructive receipt of income. Let. Ruls. 8906022, 8741078.

Special concerns are present if compensation is deferred for a controlling shareholder. If a controlling shareholder can (through his control of the corporation) effectively remove any restrictions on his immediate receipt of the money, the IRS may argue that he is in constructive receipt, because nothing really stands between him and the money. See, e.g., TAM 8828004. It is hard to eliminate these concerns in advance, because the IRS will not issue advance rulings on the tax consequences of a controlling shareholder-employee's participation in a nonqualified deferred compensation plan. See Rev. Proc. 2003-3, Sec. 3.01(34), 2003-1 IRB 113, 116. However, the courts may be less willing to impose constructive receipt in such situations. See, e.g., *Carnahan v. Comm.*, TC Memo 1994-163 (controlling shareholder's power to withdraw corporate funds is not sufficient to cause constructive receipt), *aff'd without opinion*, 95-2 USTC ¶50,592 (D.C. Cir. 1995); cf. *Casale v. Comm.*, 247 F.2d 440, 57-2 USTC ¶9920 (2d. Cir. 1957) (controlling shareholder did not receive constructive dividends when corporation paid premiums on a policy insuring shareholder's life and backing corporation's nonqualified deferred compensation obligations; the IRS has stated that it will follow this decision, Rev. Rul. 59-184, 1959-1 CB 65); *Commerce Union Bank v. U.S.*, 76-2 USTC ¶13,157 (M.D. Tenn. 1976) (controlling shareholder's power to compel immediate payout of qualified plan interest did not cause constructive receipt for estate tax purposes); *First Trust Co. of St. Paul v. U.S.*, 321 F. Supp. 1025, 71-1 USTC ¶12,729 (D. Minn. 1970) (same). But see *Congleton v. Comm.*, TC Memo 1979-130 (controlling shareholder established restrictions on payment of his salary, and thus he could ignore them).

If a nonqualified deferred compensation plan is subject to registration as a security with the Securities and Exchange Commission (SEC), failure to register the plan may have tax implications. A participant in such a plan may be able to rescind the deferral of his compensation. Such a right to rescind could cause the participant to be in constructive receipt of the deferred amounts. Currently, though, the IRS has *not* resolved the nature and extent of any tax implications arising from a failure to register a plan with the SEC. Further complicating matters, the SEC has *not* formally clarified which nonqualified plans are subject to the registration requirement.

IRS Rulings

The IRS has refused to issue advance rulings concerning the tax consequences of an unfunded arrangement if the arrangement fails to meet the following requirements. Some the requirements parallel those in IRC Section 409A, discussed above.

2006 Tax Facts on Insurance & Employee Benefits

Any initial election to defer compensation generally must be made before the beginning of the period of service for which the compensation is payable, regardless of the existence of forfeiture provisions. But see Let. Rul. 9506008 (advance ruling on tax consequences of plan even though plan allowed elections to defer bonus payments on or before May 31 of the compensation year with respect to which the deferral was to be effective; no express consideration of effect of election provision). If any election other than the initial election to defer compensation can be made after the beginning of the period of service, the plan must set forth substantial forfeiture provisions that must remain in effect throughout the entire period of the deferral. But see Let. Rul. 9525031 (advance ruling on tax consequences of rabbi trust arrangement even though plan allowed election to further defer compensation through choice of payout method *after* termination of services and ruling disclosed no substantial forfeiture provisions; no express consideration of effect of election provision). The plan must define the time and method for paying deferred compensation for each event (such as retirement) entitling a participant to benefits. The plan may specify the date of payment or provide that payments will begin within 30 days after a triggering event. If the plan provides for the early payment of benefits in the case of an "unforeseeable emergency," "unforeseeable emergency" must be defined as an unanticipated emergency caused by an event beyond the control of the participant or beneficiary that would cause severe financial hardship if early withdrawal were not permitted. The plan must also provide that any early withdrawal will be limited to the amount necessary to meet the emergency. Language similar to that in Treasury Regulations §§1.457-2(h)(4) and 1.457-2(h)(5) may be used. The plan must provide that participants have the status of general unsecured creditors of the employer and that the plan constitutes a mere promise by the employer to pay benefits in the future. The plan must also state that it is the intention of the parties that it be unfunded for tax and ERISA purposes. The plan must provide that a participant's rights to benefits cannot be anticipated, alienated, sold, transferred, assigned, pledged, encumbered, attached, or garnished by the participant's or the participant's beneficiary's creditors. Rev. Proc. 2003-3, Sec. 3.01(35), 2003-1 IRB 113, 116; Rev. Proc. 71-19, 1971-1 CB 698, as amplified by Rev. Proc. 92-65, 1992-2 CB 428.

The IRS will decline to issue an advance ruling with respect to the taxation of an independent contractor unless such contractor is identified. Rev. Proc. 2003-3, Sec. 3.01(36), 2003-1 IRB 113, 116. The IRS will not issue advance rulings on the tax consequences of a deferred compensation arrangement with respect to a controlling shareholder-employee eligible to participate in the arrangement. Rev. Proc. 2003-3, Sec. 3.01(34), 2003-1 IRB 113, 116.

The IRS has declined to issue a private ruling where the employer retained the right to pay deferred compensation benefits in either a lump sum or periodic payments, noting that exercise of the employer's discretion in a manner consistent with the employee's wishes would raise an issue of constructive receipt. Let. Rul. 8830069.

Transfer to Qualified Plan

A private letter ruling has held that employees who elect to cancel their interests in an unfunded nonqualified deferred compensation plan in exchange for substitute interests in a qualified plan would be taxable on the present value of their accrued benefits in the qualified plan upon the funding of those new interests, and would have to include the value of future benefits attributable to future compensation when the cash (that otherwise would have been received under the nonqualified plan) would have been includable. Let. Rul. 9436051.

DEFERRED COMPENSATION

ERISA Requirements

Deferred compensation plans may be required to meet various requirements under ERISA, including funding and vesting requirements. See, generally, ERISA, Titles I and IV. However, certain plans, including "top hat" plans (see below), "excess benefit" plans (see Q 128), and plans that provide payments to a retired partner or a deceased partner's successor in interest under IRC Section 736 are exempt from some or all of these ERISA requirements. See ERISA Secs. 4(b), 201, 301, 401, 4021.

"Top Hat" Plans

A "top hat" plan is an unfunded plan maintained primarily to provide deferred compensation for a select group of management or highly compensated employees. ERISA Sec. 201(2).

The determination of whether a plan is offered to a "select group" is a facts and circumstance determination. See, e.g., *Demery v. Extebank*, 216 F.3d 283 (2d Cir. 2000) ("select group" requirement was met where plan was offered to 15.34% of employees, since they were all either management or highly compensated employees). Where all management employees were eligible for a plan, it was held not to meet the select group requirement. *Carrabba v. Randalls Food Mkts, Inc.*, 252 F.3d 721 (5th Cir. 2001), *cert. denied*, 26 EBC 2920 (US Sup. Ct. 2001).

Top hat plans are subject to a different standard of review from other ERISA plans, because they are exempt from most of ERISA's substantive rules. They are subject to a *de novo* review unless the plan documents expressly grant deference to the plan administrator, rather than the standard of *Firestone v. Bruch*, 489 U.S. 101 (1989), under which plan administrator's decisions are given deference unless found to be arbitrary and capricious. *Goldstein v. Johnson & Johnson*, 251 F.3d. 433 (3d Cir. 2001).

Where a Supplemental Executive Retirement Plan (SERP) (see Q 114) was found to be a top hat plan rather than an excess benefit plan (see Q 128), claim could not be brought in state court, but was subject to ERISA preemption. *Garratt v. Knowles*, 245 F.3d 941 (7th Cir. 2001).

A top hat plan may be used as a temporary holding device for 401(k) elective deferrals (see Q 119). Let. Rul. 2001116406. *ASRS, Sec. 64, ¶¶310-360, 420, 440, 480.3*.

116. What is meant by the "economic benefit" theory?

Under the economic benefit theory, an employee is taxed when he receives something other than cash that has a determinable, present economic value. The danger, in the deferred compensation context, is that an arrangement for providing future benefits will be considered to provide the employee with a current economic benefit capable of valuation. Current taxation arises when assets are unconditionally and irrevocably paid into a fund or trust to be used for the employee's sole benefit. See, e.g., *Sproull v. Comm.*, 16 TC 244 (1951), *aff'd per curiam*, 194 F.2d 541 (6th Cir. 1952); Rev. Rul. 60-31, sit. 4, 1960-1 CB 174.

The employer *can* establish a reserve for satisfying its future deferred compensation obligations while preserving the "unfunded and unsecured" nature of its promise, provided that the reserve is wholly owned by the employer and remains subject to the claims of its general creditors: "A mere promise to pay, not represented by notes or secured in any way, is not regarded as a receipt of income." Rev. Rul. 60-31, 1960-1 CB 174, 177. See *Minor v. U.S.*, 772 F.2d 1472, 85-2 USTC ¶9717 (9th Cir. 1985) (unfunded plans do not confer a present, taxable economic benefit). Cf. Treas. Reg. §1.83-3(e) (an unfunded and unsecured promise of future payment is not taxable under IRC Section 83, which codifies the economic benefit theory).

It has generally been accepted that deferred compensation benefits can be backed by life insurance or annuities without creating a currently taxable economic benefit. See, e.g., *Casale v. Comm.*, 247 F.2d 440 (2d Cir. 1957) (the Service has said it will follow this decision–Rev. Rul. 59-184, 1959-1 CB 65); Rev. Rul. 72-25, 1972-1 CB 127; Rev. Rul. 68-99, 1968-1 CB 193; TAM 8828004; Rev. Rul. 60-31, 1960-1 CB 174 (where deferred amounts were payable upon death or disability, amounts received in cash or cash equivalent–economic benefit–must be included in income, while mere unsecured promise to pay not receipt of income). See also *Minor v. U.S.*, above; *Centre v. Comm.*, 55 TC 16 (1970).

In the *Goldsmith* case (*Goldsmith v. U.S.*, 586 F.2d 810, 78-2 USTC ¶9804 (Ct. Cl. 1978)), however, the court found that the promises of pre-retirement death and disability benefits provided the employee with a current economic benefit–current life insurance and disability insurance protection–even though the corporation was owner and beneficiary of the policy, which was subject to the claims of its general creditors. The court did not find constructive receipt of the promised future payments, but ruled that the portion of the premium attributable to life, accidental death, and disability benefits was taxable to the employee. The *Goldsmith* case appears to be anomalous–since it was decided, the IRS has not treated pre-retirement death or disability benefits as creating a currently taxable economic benefit. See, e.g., Let. Ruls. 9517019, 9510009, 9505012, 9504006, 9427018, 9403016, 9347012, 9323025, 9309017, 9142020, 8103089, 7940017. Compare this treatment with that intended by Congress under IRC Section 457 deferred compensation plans. See Q 125. *ASRS, Sec. 64, ¶410.3.*

117. What is the impact of the use of an informal funding or other security device in connection with a private deferred compensation plan?

A deferred compensation plan cannot be formally funded (that is, the employee cannot be given an interest in any trust or escrowed fund or in any asset, such as an annuity or life insurance contract) without adverse tax consequences. See Q 110 to Q 113. But the agreement can be informally funded without jeopardizing tax deferral. For example, an employer can set aside assets in a "rabbi" trust (Q 118) to provide funds for payment of deferred compensation obligations, as long as the employees have no interest in those assets and they remain the employer's property, subject to the claims of the employer's general creditors. See, e.g., *Minor v. U.S.*, 772 F.2d 1472, 85-2 USTC ¶9717 (9th Cir. 1985); see also *McAllister v. Resolution Trust Corp.*, 201 F.3d 570 (5th Cir. 2000); *Goodman v. Resolution Trust Corp.*, 7 F.3d 1123 (4th Cir. 1993) (both underscoring that beneficiaries of rabbi trusts take the risk of trust assets being subject to the claims of the employer's general creditors for the benefit of favorable tax treatment). Rabbi trusts are very popular devices for informally funding deferred compensation. See Q 118.

The IRS has not considered a plan that sets aside assets in an escrow account to be "formally funded" if the assets are subject to the claims of the employer's general creditors. See Let. Ruls. 8901041, 8509023.

DEFERRED COMPENSATION   Q 117

It has been generally accepted for some time that an employer may informally fund its obligation by setting aside a fund composed of life insurance contracts, annuities, mutual funds, securities, etc., without adverse tax consequences to the employee, so long as the fund remains the unrestricted asset of the employer and the employee has no interest in it. See, e.g., Rev. Rul. 72-25, 1972-1 CB 127 (annuity contract); Rev. Rul. 68-99, 1968-1 CB 193 (life insurance). Thus, a deferred compensation plan should not be regarded as "funded" for tax purposes merely because the employer purchases a life insurance policy or an annuity contract to ensure that funds will be available when needed. The Tax Court stretched these rules a bit in ruling that payment obligations to attorneys under a structured settlement were unfunded, even though the attorneys were annuitants under the annuities financing the obligations. See *Childs v. Comm.*, 103 TC 634 (1994), *aff'd*, 89 F.3d 856 (11th Cir. 1996).

Securing or distributing deferred compensation upon the employer's falling net worth or other financial events unacceptably secures the payment of the promised benefits. IRC Sec. 409A(b)(2). This includes hybrid rabbi/secular trust arrangements that distribute assets from nominal rabbi trusts to secular trusts on the occurrence of triggering events indicating the employer's financial difficulty. Under any such arrangement, otherwise deferred compensation is immediately taxable and subject to a 20% additional tax. Interest on the underpayment of taxes is due at the normal underpayment rate plus 1%. IRC Sec. 409A(b)(4).

Setting aside assets in an offshore trust to directly or indirectly fund deferred compensation also unacceptably secures the payment of the promised benefits. IRC Sec. 409A(b)(1). Under any such arrangement, the otherwise deferred compensation is immediately taxable and subject to a 20% additional tax. Interest on the underpayment of taxes is due at the normal underpayment rate plus 1%. IRC Sec. 409A(b)(4).

One court has ruled that a death benefit only plan backed by corporate-owned life insurance is "funded" for ERISA purposes. See *Dependahl v. Falstaff Brewing Corp.*, 491 F. Supp. 1188 (E.D. Mo. 1980), *aff'd in part*, 653 F.2d 1208 (8th Cir. 1981), *cert. denied*, 454 U.S. 968 (1981) and 454 U.S. 1084 (1981). The decision has been criticized, but the result, if ever accepted by other courts, could have far reaching tax implications. If a plan is "funded" for ERISA purposes, it is generally required to satisfy ERISA's exclusive purpose rule and meet certain minimum vesting and funding standards. Once these requirements are met, the plan may no longer be considered "informally funded" for tax purposes, and adverse tax consequences may follow. In 1987, the same court that decided *Dependahl* concluded that a nonqualified deferred compensation plan informally funded with life insurance was not funded for ERISA purposes, and thus was not subject to minimum vesting and funding standards. See *Belsky v. First Nat'l Life Ins. Co.*, 818 F.2d 661 (8th Cir. 1987). The court distinguished this case from *Dependahl*, in part, by noting that the *Belsky* agreement stated specifically that the employee's only right against the employer was that of an unsecured creditor. For courts finding plans backed by life insurance or annuities to be unfunded, see *Reliable Home Health Care Inc. v. Union Central Ins. Co.*, 295 F.3d 505 (5th Cir. 2002); *Miller v. Heller*, 915 F. Supp. 651 (S.D.N.Y. 1996); *The Northwestern Mut. Ins. Co. v. Resolution Trust Corp.*, 848 F. Supp. 1515 (N.D. Ala. 1994); *Darden v. Nationwide Mut. Life Ins. Co.*, 717 F. Supp. 388 (E.D.N.C. 1989), *aff'd*, 922 F.2d 203 (4th Cir.), *cert. denied*, 502 U.S. 906 (1991); *Belka v. Rowe Furniture Corp.*, 571 F. Supp. 1249 (D. Md. 1983).

The DOL has issued various advisory opinions permitting the use of an employer-owned asset to finance different types of plans while the plans maintained their "unfunded" status under ERISA. See DOL Adv. 92-22A (cash value element of split dollar life insurance policy under death benefit plan is not a plan asset); DOL Adv. Op. 92-02A (stop-loss insurance policy backing medical expense plan obligations is not plan asset of death benefit plan); DOL Adv. Op. 81-11A (corporate-owned life insurance is not plan asset of death benefit plan). The DOL has stated that plan assets include any property, tangible or intangible, in which the plan has a beneficial ownership interest. DOL Adv. Op. 94-31A. According to footnote three in Advisory Opinion 94-31A, the "beneficial ownership interest" analysis is not relevant in the context of excess benefit and top hat plans. But see *Miller v. Heller*, 915 F. Supp. 651 (S.D.N.Y. 1996) (in holding that a deferred compensation plan is an unfunded top hat plan, the court interpreted footnote three in Advisory Opinion 94-31A to mean that the DOL's *entire* analysis for determining whether assets are plan assets is not relevant to the issue of whether the plan is funded). The DOL reasoned that its position was supported by the special nature of these plans, the participating employees' ability to affect or substantially influence the design and operation of the plan, and the rulings of the IRS surrounding the tax consequences of using rabbi trusts with these plans. What sort of plan asset analysis is relevant in that context is not clear, although the DOL does have a working premise that rabbi trusts meeting with IRS approval will not cause excess benefit or top hat plans to be funded for ERISA purposes. See, e.g., DOL Adv. Op. 92-13A. See also DOL Adv. Op. 90-14A (great deference is given to the position of the IRS regarding deferred compensation plans when determining, for ERISA purposes, whether a top hat plan is funded).

An insurance policy used to informally fund a plan should be held by the employer and not distributed to the employee at any time; otherwise, the employee will be taxed on the value of the contract when he receives it. *Centre v. Comm.*, 55 TC 16 (1970); *Morse v. Comm.*, 17 TC 1244 (1952), *aff'd*, 202 F.2d 69 (2nd Cir. 1953). See Treas. Reg. §1.83-3(e). See also Q 79. The employer cannot deduct its premium payments. IRC Sec. 264(a)(1). But the employer receives the death proceeds tax free. However, proceeds paid to a corporation may be, in part at least, includable in the corporation's income for alternative minimum tax purposes. IRC Secs. 56-59. See Q 95. For tax results on surrender of the policy, see Q 264, Q 265. For accumulated earnings tax, see Q 89.

An employee is not taxable on the premiums paid by the employer or on any portion of the value of the policy or annuity, *provided* that the employer applies for, owns, is beneficiary of, and pays for the policy or annuity contract and uses it merely as a reserve for the employer's obligations under the deferred compensation agreement. *Casale v. Comm.*, 247 F.2d 440 (2nd Cir. 1957) (the IRS has said it will follow this decision, Rev. Rul. 59-184, 1959-1 CB 65); Rev. Rul. 72-25, 1972-1 CB 127; Rev. Rul. 68-99, 1968-1 CB 193; Let. Ruls. 8607032, 8607031; TAM 8828004. See also Let. Rul. 9122019. But see *Goldsmith v. U.S.*, 586 F.2d 810, 78-2 USTC ¶9804 (Ct. Cl. 1978), discussed in Q 116. Where the employee receives basic life insurance protection and a vested right in the annual increase in the cash surrender value of the policy, the premiums will be taxable to the employee. *Frost v. Comm.*, 52 TC 89 (1969).

With respect to contributions made after February 28, 1986, to annuity contracts held by a corporation, partnership, or trust (i.e., a nonnatural person), "the income on the contract" for the tax year of the policyholder is generally treated as ordinary income received or accrued by the contract owner during such taxable year. IRC Sec. 72(u). See Q 2. Also, corporate ownership of life insurance may result in exposure to the corporate alternative minimum tax. See Q 95.

DEFERRED COMPENSATION Q 117

The IRS has privately ruled that an employee's purchase of a surety bond (with no reimbursement from his employer) as protection against nonpayment of unfunded deferred compensation benefits would not, by itself, cause deferred amounts to be includable in income prior to receipt. See Let. Rul. 8406012. However, the IRS also warned that an *employer*-paid surety bond would cause current taxation. A later letter ruling has blurred somewhat the line between employee-provided and employer-provided surety bonds—the IRS has hinted, without clearly distinguishing between employee-paid and employer-paid surety bonds, that the use of a surety bond to protect deferred compensation could cause the promise to be secured, resulting in taxation under IRC Section 83 when the deferred compensation is substantially vested (that is, either not subject to a substantial risk of forfeiture or transferable to a third party free of such a risk). Let. Rul. 9241006. Whether the IRS meant to question both employer-provided and employee-provided surety bonds is not clear.

The IRS has privately ruled that an employee can buy indemnification insurance to protect his deferred benefits without causing immediate taxation. This result holds even if the employer reimburses the employee for the premium payments, as long as the employer has no other involvement in the arrangement (the employee's premium payments must be treated as nondeductible personal expenses, and any premium reimbursements must be included in the employee's income). See Let. Rul. 9344038. The ERISA consequences of such an arrangement are not clear.

On occasion, third-party guarantees of benefit promises have received favorable treatment. For example, a parent corporation's guarantee of its subsidiary's deferred compensation obligations did not accelerate the taxation of the benefits. See Let. Ruls. 8906022, 8741078. See also *Berry v. U.S.*, 593 F. Supp. 80 (M.D.N.C. 1984), *aff'd per curiam*, 760 F.2d 85 (4th Cir. 1985) (a guarantee does not make a promise secured, because the guarantee is itself a mere promise to pay); *Childs v. Comm.*, 103 TC 634 (1994) (same), *aff'd*, 89 F.3d 856 (11th Cir. 1996). But see TAM 9336001 (the conclusion that plaintiffs' promise to pay their attorney was funded and secured and subject to IRC Section 83 where they irrevocably ordered defendants' insurers to pay the plaintiffs' attorney his fees out of plaintiffs' recovery and defendants' insurers paid the attorney by purchasing annuities for him was "strengthened" by the fact that a defendant and the defendants' insurers guaranteed to make the annuity payments, should the annuity issuer default); Let. Rul. 8406012 (the current value of protection provided by an employer-paid surety bond or other guarantee arrangement constitutes a taxable economic benefit); cf. Let. Rul. 9331006 (protecting deferred compensation benefits by giving employees certificates of participation secured by irrevocable standby letters of credit secured promise and triggered application of IRC Section 83); Let. Rul. 9443006 (employer's purchase of irrevocable standby letter of credit beyond the reach of its general creditors to back its promise to pay accrued vacation benefits secured promise and triggered taxation under IRC Section 83).

There is some controversy between the IRS and the Tax Court over whether a promise to pay will be "funded" for tax purposes if the obligation is transferred to a third party. The IRS is likely to think that the employer's promise is funded, even if the third party pays the transferred obligations out of general revenues or sets aside a fund that remains its general asset and to which the employee has no special claim. See Rev. Rul. 69-50, 1969-1 CB 140, as amplified in Rev. Rul. 77-420, 1977-2 CB 172; TAM 9336001. The Tax Court does not seem to think that the transfer will automatically result in funding; rather, the Tax Court is more likely to examine whether any property is specially set aside by the new obligor for the employee. See *Childs v. Comm.*, 103 TC 634 (1994), *aff'd*, 89 F.3d 856 (11th Cir. 1996). *ASRS, Sec. 64,* ¶*420.5*.

118. What is a "rabbi" trust and what are the income tax consequences of using such a trust to provide nonqualified deferred compensation benefits to employees?

A rabbi trust is a vehicle for accumulating assets to support unfunded deferred compensation obligations. Established by the employer with an independent trustee, a rabbi trust is designed to (1) provide employees with some assurance that their promised benefits will be paid while (2) preserving the tax deferral that is at the heart of unfunded deferred compensation plans. To accomplish these ends, a rabbi trust is generally irrevocable. But—and this is the key characteristic of a rabbi trust—a rabbi trust provides that its assets remain subject to the claims of the employer's general creditors in the event of the employer's insolvency or bankruptcy. See *McAllister v. Resolution Trust Corp.*, 201 F.3d 570 (5th Cir. 2000); *Goodman v. Resolution Trust Corp.*, 7 F.3d 1123 (4th Cir. 1993) (both underscoring that beneficiaries of rabbi trusts take the risk of trust assets being subject to the claims of the employer's general creditors for the benefit of favorable tax treatment). These trusts are called "rabbi" trusts because the first such trust approved by the IRS was set up for a rabbi. See Let. Rul. 8113017.

Securing or distributing deferred compensation upon the employer's falling net worth or other financial events unacceptably secures the payment of the promised benefits. IRC Sec. 409A(b)(2). This includes hybrid rabbi/secular trust arrangements that distribute assets from nominal rabbi trusts to secular trusts on the occurrence of triggering events indicating the employer's financial difficulty. Under any such arrangement, otherwise deferred compensation is immediately taxable and subject to a 20% additional tax. Interest on the underpayment of taxes is due at the normal underpayment rate plus 1%. IRC Sec. 409A(b)(4).

Setting aside assets in an offshore trust to directly or indirectly fund deferred compensation also unacceptably secures the payment of the promised benefits. IRC Sec. 409A(b)(1), as added by the American Jobs Creation Act of 2004. Under any such arrangement, the otherwise deferred compensation is immediately taxable and subject to a 20% additional tax. Interest on the underpayment of taxes is due at the normal underpayment rate plus 1%. IRC Sec. 409A(b)(4).

Planning Point: The American Jobs Creation Act of 2004 has called into question many prior decisions and rulings in the deferred compensation arena. Employers and employees should exercise caution in structuring deferred compensation plans, especially using rabbi trusts and other informal funding mechanisms.

The combination of security, albeit imperfect—a rabbi trust can protect an employee against the employer's future *unwillingness* to pay promised benefits, but it cannot protect an employee against the employer's future *inability* to pay—and tax deferral offered by a rabbi trust has made them very popular. In fact, the rabbi trust is so popular that the IRS has released a model rabbi trust instrument to aid taxpayers and to expedite the processing of requests for advance rulings on these arrangements. See Rev. Proc. 92-64, 1992-2 CB 422. The IRS model trust is intended to serve as a safe harbor for employers. Used properly, the model trust will not, by itself, cause employees to be in constructive receipt of income or to incur an economic benefit. Of

DEFERRED COMPENSATION   Q 118

course, whether an unfunded deferred compensation plan using the model rabbi trust effectively defers taxation will depend upon whether the underlying plan effectively defers compensation. The IRS will continue to issue advance rulings on the tax treatment of: (1) unfunded deferred compensation plans that do not use a trust; and (2) unfunded deferred compensation plans that use the model trust. But the IRS will no longer, except in rare and unusual circumstances, issue advance rulings on unfunded deferred compensation arrangements that use a trust other than the model trust. See Rev. Proc. 92-64, 1992-2 CB 422, 423, Sec. 3.

The model trust language contains all provisions necessary for operation of the trust except provisions describing the trustee's investment powers. The parties involved must provide language describing the investment powers of the trustee, and those powers must include some investment discretion. Proper use of the model trust requires that its language be adopted verbatim, except where substitute language is expressly permitted. Although it is somewhat puzzling in light of the claim by the IRS that it will not rule on plans that do not use the model trust, the employer may add additional text to the model trust language, as long as such text is "not inconsistent with" the model trust language. See Rev. Proc. 92-64, 1992-2 CB 422, 423, Secs. 4.01 and 5.01.

The rights of plan participants to trust assets must be merely the rights of unsecured creditors. Participants' rights cannot be alienable or assignable. The assets of the trust must remain subject to the claims of the employer's general creditors in the event of insolvency or bankruptcy. See sections 1(d) and 13(b) of the model trust, at 1992-2 CB 424 and 427; but see *Goodman v. Resolution Trust Corp.*, 7 F.3d 1123 (4th Cir. 1993) (assets in a rabbi trust must be subject to the claims of creditors at all times).

In at least one older letter ruling, the IRS found that the use of a third-party guarantee as an additional security measure did not undermine the tax-effectiveness of a rabbi trust. See Let. Rul. 8906022 (employer established a rabbi trust and its corporate parent also guaranteed the obligations).

The board of directors and the highest ranking officer of the employer must be required to notify the trustee of the employer's insolvency or bankruptcy, and the trustee must be required to cease benefit payments upon the company's insolvency or bankruptcy. See section 3(b)(1) of the model trust, at 1992-2 CB 425.

If the model trust is used properly, it should not cause a plan to lose its status as "unfunded." In other words, contributions to a rabbi trust should not cause immediate taxation to employees; employees should not have income until the deferred benefits are received or otherwise made available. See, e.g., Rev. Proc. 92-64, Sec. 3, 1992-2 CB 422, 423; Let. Ruls. 9732008, 9723013, 9601036, 9548015, 9542032, 9536027, 9443016, 9442012, 9442004. Contributions to a rabbi trust for the benefit of a corporation's directors have been treated similarly. See, e.g., Let. Ruls. 9525031, 9505012, 9452035, 9301012, 9144019, 9117032, 9115054. Relatedly, contributions to a rabbi trust should not be considered "wages" subject to income tax withholding until benefits are actually or constructively received. See Let. Rul. 9525031.

A proper rabbi trust should *not* be considered an IRC Section 402(b) nonexempt employees' trust. Contributions to a proper rabbi trust should *not* be subject to IRC Section 83. See, e.g., Let. Ruls. 9732006, 9548015, 9542032, 9536027, 9443016, 9442012, 9442004.

2006 Tax Facts on Insurance & Employee Benefits

The employer should receive no deduction for amounts contributed to the trust, but should receive a deduction when benefit payments are includable in the employee's income. See Q 120. In pre-model trust days, the employer was generally considered the owner of the trust under IRC Section 677, and was required to include the income, deductions, and credits generated by the trust in computing the employer's taxable income. See, e.g., Let. Ruls. 9314005, 9242007, 9214035.

The IRS will generally issue advance rulings on the grantor trust status of trusts following the model trust. Rev. Proc. 92-64, Sec. 3, 1992-2 CB 422, 423. Such model trust rulings seem entirely consistent with past rulings. See, e.g., Let. Ruls. 9542032, 9536027, 9443016, 9442012, 9442004. In pre-model trust rulings, the IRS generally conditioned favorable tax treatment upon the satisfaction of two additional requirements: (1) that creation of the trust did not cause the plan to be other than unfunded for ERISA purposes; and (2) that trust provisions requiring that the trust's assets be available to satisfy the claims of general creditors in the event of insolvency or bankruptcy were enforceable under state and federal law. See, e.g., Let. Ruls. 9314005, 9242007, 9214035, 8634031. The same conditions have been imposed in model trust rulings. See, e.g., Let. Ruls. 9548015, 9517019, 9504006, 9443016, 9442012, 9442004; see also Rev. Proc. 92-64, Sec. 4.02, 1992-2 CB 422, 423; sections 1(d), 1(c) and 3(b) of the model trust, at 1992-2 CB 424, 425.

The concern of the IRS with respect to the ERISA issue seems to be that if the use of a rabbi trust causes the underlying plan to be other than unfunded for ERISA purposes, then the plan would generally be subject to Title I of ERISA, and the application of Title I provisions, such as the exclusive purpose rule and the vesting and funding requirements, would cause the plan to be funded for tax purposes and require the accelerated taxation of contributions to the rabbi trust. The DOL's position seems to be that at least rabbi trusts maintained in connection with excess benefit or top hat plans will not cause the underlying plans to be funded for ERISA purposes. See DOL Adv. Op. 94-31A, fn.3; DOL Adv. Op. 92-13A. At least one court has noted that the use of a rabbi trust will not cause a top hat plan to lose its ERISA exemption as long as: (1) the trust assets remain subject to the claims of the employer's creditors in the event of insolvency; and (2) the participants' interests are inalienable and unassignable. See *Nagy v. Riblet Prod. Corp.*, 13 EBC 1743 (N.D. Ind. 1990), *amended on other grounds and reconsideration denied*, 1991 U.S. Dist. Lexis 11739 (N.D. Ind. 1991). Nonetheless, rulings on plans using the model trust are supposed to state that the IRS expresses no opinion on the ERISA consequences of using a rabbi trust. See Rev. Proc. 92-64, Sec. 3, 1992-2 CB 422, 423.

In past private letter rulings, the IRS has allowed the use of a rabbi trust in conjunction with a deferred compensation plan that permits hardship withdrawals, ruling that the hardship withdrawal provision will not cause amounts deferred to be taxable before they are paid or made available. In these letter rulings, "hardship" is generally defined as an unforeseeable financial emergency caused by events beyond the participant's control. The amount that can be withdrawn is generally limited to that amount needed to satisfy the emergency need. See, e.g., Let. Ruls. 9242007, 9121069; see also Let. Ruls. 9306022, 9122034. IRS guidelines for giving advanced rulings on unfunded deferred compensation plans expressly permit the use of certain hardship withdrawal provisions. See Rev. Proc. 92-65, Sec. 3.01(c), 1992-2 CB 428. See Q 115. Thus, it would seem that a rabbi trust conforming to the model trust could be used in conjunction with a deferred compensation plan permitting an acceptable hardship withdrawal.

DEFERRED COMPENSATION Q 118

See Let. Rul. 9505012 (provision permitting hardship withdrawals upon unforeseeable financial emergency beyond participant's control in plan informally funded by a presumably model trust does not cause deferred amounts to be taxable before paid or made available); see also, e.g., Let. Rul. 9542032 (model trust used in conjunction with plan permitting hardship withdrawals, but no clear ruling on tax consequences of hardship withdrawal provision); Let. Rul. 9517019 (same); cf. Let. Rul. 9332038 (hardship withdrawal provision in plan informally funded by a trust using model trust language but not conforming to model trust format does not cause deferred amounts to be taxable before paid or made available). While an appropriate hardship withdrawal provision should not trigger taxation before deferred amounts are paid or made available, such a provision may trigger constructive receipt *at the time when a qualifying emergency arises*. See Let. Rul. 9501032; but see Let. Rul. 9546008 (in the context of a plan permitting distributions in event of unforeseeable emergency, holding no constructive receipt of deferred compensation before deferred amounts are paid out).

The trustee may be given the power to invest in the employer's securities. If the trustee is given that power, the trust must: (1) be revocable; or (2) include a provision that the employer can substitute assets of equal value for any assets held by the trust. See IRS model Trust, section 5(a), Rev. Proc. 92-64, 1992-2 CB 425. Where presumably model trusts separately serving a parent and affiliates could invest in the parent's stock, it was ruled that: (1) dividends paid on the parent's stock held by the parent's trusts would not be includable in the parent's income in the year paid; (2) no gain or loss would be recognized by the parent upon transfer of its stock from its trusts to its participants or their beneficiaries; and (3) no gain or loss would be recognized by the affiliates upon the direct transfer of the parent's stock to the affiliates' participants or their beneficiaries if that stock was transferred directly by the parent to the participants or beneficiaries and neither the affiliates nor their trusts were the legal or beneficial owners of parent's stock. Let. Rul. 9505012. Regulations under IRC Section 1032 (see Q 88) generally permit nonrecognition treatment for transfers of stock from an issuing corporation to an acquiring corporation, if the acquiring corporation immediately disposes of such stock. A transfer of a parent corporation's stock to a rabbi trust for the benefit of a subsidiary's employee would not qualify for this nonrecognition treatment, because the stock is not immediately distributed to the participant. The IRS has announced that nonrecognition treatment is available for such transfers, albeit under a different theory. The IRS will treat the parent corporation, rather than the subsidiary corporation, as the grantor and owner of the rabbi trust, so long as the trust provides that: (1) stock not transferred to the subsidiary's employees reverts to the parent; and (2) the parent's creditors can reach the stock. Notice 2000-56, 2000-43 IRB 393. The IRS has indicated that it will rule on model rabbi trusts that have been modified to comply with this notice.

The trust must provide that, if life insurance is held by the trust, the trustee will have no power to: (1) name any entity other than the trust as beneficiary; (2) assign the policy to any entity other than a successor trustee; or (3) to loan to any entity the proceeds of any borrowing against the policy (but an optional provision permits the loan of such borrowings to the employer). See IRS model Trust, sections 8(e) and 8(f), Rev. Proc. 92-64, 1992-2 CB 426.

Taxpayers that adopt the model trust and wish to obtain an advance ruling on the underlying deferred compensation plan must not only follow the standard guidelines for obtaining a ruling on an unfunded deferred compensation plan (see Q 115) but must also follow other guidelines unique to plans using a trust. First, the plan must provide that the trust and any assets held by it will conform to the terms of the model trust. Second, taxpayers must generally include a representation that the *plan* is not inconsistent with the terms of the trust with the letter ruling request. Third, the language of the trust must generally conform with the model text, and taxpayers must generally include a representation that the *trust* conforms to the model trust language (including the order in which the provisions appear) and that the trust does not contain any inconsistent language (in substituted portions or elsewhere) that conflicts with the model trust language. Provisions may be renumbered if appropriate, any bracketed model trust language may be omitted, and blanks may be filled in. Fourth, the request for a letter ruling generally must include a copy of the trust document on which all substituted or added language is clearly marked and on which the required investment authority text is indicated. Fifth, the request for a ruling must generally contain a representation that the trust is a valid trust under state law, and that all of the material terms and provisions of the trust, including the creditors' rights clause, are enforceable under the appropriate state laws. Finally, the trustee must generally be an independent third party that may be granted corporate trustee powers under state law, such as a bank trust department or a similar party. See Rev. Proc. 2003-3, Secs. 3.01(35), 4.01(33), 2003-1 IRB 113; Rev. Proc. 92-64, Secs. 3 and 4, 1992-2 CB 422, 423.

The IRS has issued several private letter rulings addressing the deductibility of interest paid on life insurance policy loans after the policies are transferred to a rabbi trust. See Q 260. *ASRS, Sec. 64, ¶¶310.2(b), 420.5(c).*

119. Can a private nonqualified deferred compensation plan serve as a temporary holding device for 401(k) elective deferrals?

Yes, according to a 1995 private letter ruling approving a particular nonqualified/ 401(k) "wrap-around" or "pour-over" plan. See Let. Rul. 9530038. Since that time, more rulings approving the use of wrap around plans have been issued. Let. Ruls. 200116046, 200012083, 199924067, 9752018, 9752017. Note that wrap-around plans have been primarily used to maximize elective deferrals under both an IRC Section 401(k) plan and a nonqualified plan. Thus, such an arrangement may be unnecessary due to the manner in which the actual deferral percentage test for 401(k) plans is now administered (see Q 404). Some plans will elect to use the *current year testing method*, however, and for these plans a wrap-around plan will continue to provide planning opportunities.

In addition, under proposed regulations, a wrap-around plan will not violate IRC Section 409A if it meets certain requirements. Prop. Treas. Reg. § 1.409A-3(h)(3). In particular, such a linkage may not result in a decrease in deferrals in the nonqualified arrangement in excess of the deferral limits under IRC Section 402(g). Prop. Treas. Reg. § 1.409A-3(h)(3)(iii).

Background. An employer seeking to maximize highly compensated employees' (HCEs) elective deferrals to its 401(k) plan established an unfunded, nonqualified salary reduction plan to temporarily hold elective deferrals until the maximum amount of 401(k) elective deferrals could be determined. Employees could defer compensation into the proposed nonqualified plan by entering into salary reduction agreements by December 31st of the prior year. These employees would then receive "matching" contributions under the nonqualified plan equal to their matching contributions under the 401(k) plan. The employer would determine the maximum amount of elective con-

DEFERRED COMPENSATION

Q 120

tributions that the HCEs could make to the 401(k) plan for the current year as soon as practicable each year, but no later than January 31st of the next year. The lesser of the maximum allowable amount or the amount actually deferred under the nonqualified plan would be distributed in cash to the HCEs by March 15th of the following year *unless they irrevocably elected to have such amounts contributed as elective deferrals to the 401(k) plan at the same time they elected to defer compensation into the nonqualified plan.* Where such election was made, the "elective deferrals" and the appropriate "matching" contributions made under the nonqualified plan would be contributed directly to the 401(k) plan. However, earnings under the nonqualified plan would not be contributed to the 401(k) plan. Presumably, any balance in the nonqualified plan would remain in the nonqualified plan.

Ruling. The IRS ruled that amounts initially held in the nonqualified plan would be treated as made to the 401(k) plan in the year of deferral under the nonqualified plan, and would be excluded from income under IRC Section 402(e)(3). Amounts distributed to an employee that he did not elect to contribute to the 401(k) plan would be taxable in the year the compensation was earned.

Apparently, the key to the success of this arrangement was the requirement that the election to transfer amounts to the 401(k) plan had to be made *at the same time as the election to initially defer compensation into the nonqualified plan, before the beginning of the year in which the compensation was earned.* The IRS had earlier approved, and then revoked its approval, of a similar arrangement where the election to transfer amounts to a 401(k) plan could be made *after the initial election to defer compensation into the nonqualified plan and after the close of the year in which the amounts were earned.* See Let. Ruls. 9423034 and 9414051, revoking Let. Rul. 9317037. Apparently, the IRS was concerned that this latter arrangement raised the specter of constructive receipt. See Q 115.

Another private letter ruling approved a similar arrangement utilizing a rabbi trust (see Q 118) in connection with the nonqualified plan. See Let. Rul. 9752018.

One ruling (involving a top hat plan, see Q 115) specifically indicated that amounts must be transferred from the nonqualified plan to the 401(k) plan no later than March 15th. Let. Rul. 200116046.

In general, a 401(k) plan will be disqualified if *any* employer-provided benefit (other than matching contributions) is contingent upon the employee's elective deferrals under the 401(k) plan. See Q 395. But the 401(k) regulations provide that participation in a nonqualified deferred compensation plan is treated as contingent only to the extent that the employee may receive additional deferred compensation under the nonqualified deferred compensation plan based upon whether he makes elective deferrals under the 401(k) plan. These regulations explicitly state that a provision under a nonqualified deferred compensation plan requiring an employee to have made the maximum permissible elective deferral under the 401(k) plan is not treated as contingent. See, e.g., Let. Rul. 199902002 (deferrals under a nonqualified plan permitting deferral up to 15% of compensation if participants have made maximum allowable 401(k) elective deferrals were not impermissibly conditioned upon elective deferrals).

120. When are deferred amounts deductible by the employer?

Generally, the employer can take a deduction for deferred compensation only when it is includable in the employee's income, regardless of whether the employer is on a cash or accrual basis of accounting. IRC Sec. 404(a)(5); Treas. Regs. §§1.404(a)-1(c), 1.404(a)-12(b)(2). See also *Lundy Packing Co. v. U.S.*, 302 F. Supp. 182 (E.D.N.C. 1969), *aff'd per curiam*, 421 F.2d 850 (4th Cir. 1970); *Springfield Prod., Inc. v. Comm.*, TC Memo 1979-23. Likewise, deduction of amounts deferred for an independent contractor can be taken only when they are includable in the independent contractor's gross income. IRC Sec. 404(d).

The IRS confirmed that payments made under an executive compensation plan within 2½ months of the end of the year in which employees vest do not constitute deferred compensation, and thus may be deducted in the year in which employees vest, rather than the year in which the employees actually receive the payments. Let. Rul. 199923045. See also the discussion under the heading "Employer Taxation" in Q 110.

Previously, there was some controversy over the proper timing of an accrual basis employer's deduction for amounts credited as "interest" to employee accounts under a nonqualified deferred compensation plan. The weight of authority currently holds that IRC Section 404(a)(5) governs the deduction for such amounts, which must be postponed until such amounts are includable in employee income. Amounts representing "interest" cannot be currently deducted by an accrual basis employer under IRC Section 163. *Albertson's, Inc. v. Comm.*, 42 F.3d 537 (9th Cir. 1994), *vacating in part* 12 F.3d 1529 (9th Cir. 1993), *aff'g in part* 95 TC 415 (1990) (divided court), *en banc reh'g denied*, (9th Cir. 1995), *cert. denied*, 516 U.S. 807 (1995); Notice 94-38, 1994-1 CB 350; Let. Rul. 9201019; TAM 8619006.

To be deductible, deferred compensation payments must represent reasonable compensation for the employee's services when added to current compensation. What is reasonable is a question of fact in each case. One of the factors considered in determining the reasonableness of compensation is whether amounts paid are intended to compensate for past, under-compensated services. See, e.g., Treas. Reg. §1.404(a)-1(b); *Lucas v. Ox Fibre Brush Co.*, 281 U.S. 115 (1930); *Avis Ind. Corp. and Subsidiaries. v. Comm.*, TC Memo 1995-434; *Acme Constr. Co., Inc. v. Comm.*, TC Memo 1995-6; *Comtec Sys., Inc. v. Comm.*, TC Memo 1995-4; *Modernage Developers, Inc. v. Comm.*, TC Memo 1993-591, *aff'd without opinion*, 95-1 USTC ¶50,196 (2d Cir. 1995). Thus, deferred compensation for past services may be deductible, even if the total of such compensation and other compensation for the current year is in excess of reasonable compensation for services performed in the current year, *as long as* that total, plus all compensation paid to the employee in prior years, is reasonable for all of the services performed through the current year. See Treas. Reg. §1.404(a)-1(b); compare *Acme Constr.*, above, (reasonableness of compensation in year at issue demonstrated, in part, by fact that the compensation included catch-up pay for earlier, under-compensated years); *Comtec Sys.*, above, (same).

Little difficulty with reasonableness of compensation should be encountered with respect to non-shareholder or minority shareholder employees. A finding of unreasonableness in the case of a controlling shareholder is more likely. See, e.g., *Nelson Bros., Inc. v. Comm.*, TC Memo 1992-726 (benefits paid to surviving spouse of controlling shareholder of a closely held corporation were not reasonable compensation where (1) the controlling shareholder had not been under-compensated in previous years; (2) the controlling shareholder's compensation exceeded the amounts paid by comparable companies; (3) the payments were not part of a pattern of benefits provided to employees; and (4) there was an absence of dividends). Deferred compensation payments were held

DEFERRED COMPENSATION   Q 122

to be reasonable where the controlling shareholder was inadequately paid during his life and the surviving spouse, to whom payments were made, did not inherit controlling stock ownership. *Andrews Distrib. Co., Inc. v. Comm.*, TC Memo 1972-146. See also *Yeomans Distrib. Co. v. U.S.*, 85-1 USTC ¶9260 (C.D. Ill. 1985).

Publicly-held corporations generally are not permitted to deduct compensation in excess of $1 million per tax year to certain top-level employees. See IRC Sec. 162(m). See Q 108.

Golden parachute rules may limit the amount of the deduction for deferred compensation payments contingent upon a change in ownership or control of a corporation or made under an agreement that violates a generally enforced securities law or regulation. See Q 109. See IRC Sec. 280G. *ASRS, Sec. 64, ¶420.7, Sec. 63, ¶¶140, 160.1.*

121. How are deferred compensation payments taxed when they are received by the employee or beneficiary?

When payments are actually or constructively received, they are taxed as ordinary income. Deferred compensation payments are "wages" subject to regular income tax withholding (and not the special withholding rules that apply to pensions, etc.) when actually or constructively received. See IRC Sec. 3401(a), as added by the American Jobs Creation Act of 2004; Rev. Rul. 82-176, 1982-2 CB 223; Rev. Rul. 77-25, 1977-1 CB 301; Temp. Treas. Reg. §35.3405-1T, A-18; cf. Let. Rul. 9525031 (contributions to rabbi trust were not subject to income tax withholding because they were not the actual or constructive payment of wages).

Deferred compensation that is subject to constructive receipt and taxation under IRC Section 409A is subject to a 20% additional tax. See Q 115 and Q 117. Interest on the underpayment of taxes retroactively imposed is due at the normal underpayment rate plus 1%. IRC Sec. 409A(b)(4).

Where an unfunded plan paid deferred compensation benefits in the form of a commercial single premium annuity at the termination of employment, a private ruling concluded that the value of the contract would be includable in the recipient's income at the time of distribution, in accordance with the rules of IRC Section 83. Let. Rul. 9521029.

Payments made to a beneficiary are "income in respect of a decedent," and, as such, are taxed as they would have been to the employee. It is not clear whether the same withholding rules apply. For treatment of death benefits under deferred compensation agreements, see Q 135.

Benefits assigned by an employee to an ex-spouse in a divorce agreement will be taxed to the employee, rather than to the ex-spouse. There is no framework for the assignment of nonqualified deferred compensation—other than eligible Section 457 plans (see Q 124)—similar to the framework for the assignment of qualified plan benefits through a qualified domestic relations order (QDRO). See Let. Rul. 9340032. *ASRS, Sec. 64, ¶420.6.*

122. Are contributions to and postretirement payments from a deferred compensation plan subject to FICA and FUTA taxes?

2006 Tax Facts on Insurance & Employee Benefits

Q 122 FEDERAL INCOME TAX

There are two timing rules for the treatment of deferred compensation amounts under the Federal Insurance Contributions Act (FICA) and the Federal Unemployment Tax Act (FUTA)–the "general timing rule" and the "special timing rule." The general timing rule provides that amounts taxable as wages are generally taxed when paid or "constructively received" (see Q 115). The special timing rule applies to amounts deferred by an employee under a traditional deferred compensation plan of an employer covered by FICA. The special timing rule applies to salary reduction plans and supplemental plans, funded plans and unfunded plans, private plans and (eligible or ineligible) IRC Section 457 plans. It does not apply to "excess (golden) parachute payments."

An employee's "amount deferred" is considered to be "wages" for FICA purposes at the *later of* the date when: (1) the services are performed; or (2) the employee's rights to such amount are no longer subject to a "substantial risk of forfeiture" (see Q 112). See IRC Secs. 3121(v)(2)(A), 3121(v)(2)(C); Treas. Reg. §1.3121(v)(2)(a)(2); *Buffalo Bills, Inc. v. U.S.*, 31 Fed. Cl. 794 (1994), *appeal dismissed without opinion*, 56 F.3d 84, 1995 U.S. App. Lexis 27184 (Fed. Cir. 1995); *Hoerl & Assoc., P.C. v. U.S.*, 996 F.2d 226 (10th Cir. 1993), *aff'g in part, rev'g in part, and remanding* 785 F. Supp. 1430 (D. Colo. 1992); Let. Ruls. 9443006 (fn. 1), 9442012, 9417013; 9347006, 9024069 *as revised by* Let. Rul. 9025067; TAMs 9051003, 9050006.

Similar rules apply for FUTA (federal unemployment tax) purposes, although the taxable wage base for FUTA purposes is smaller ($7,000). See IRC Secs. 3306(r)(2), 3306(b)(1).

Where an amount deferred cannot be readily calculated by the last day of the year, employers may choose between two alternative methods: the *estimated method* and the *lag method*.

Under the estimated method, the employer treats a reasonably estimated amount as wages paid on the last day of the calendar year. If the employer underestimates, it may treat the shortfall as wages in the first year or in the first quarter of the next year (the second year). If the employer overestimates, it may claim a refund or credit.

Under the lag method, the employer may calculate the end-of-year amount deferred on any date in the first quarter of the next calendar year. The amount deferred will be treated as wages paid and received on that date, and the amount deferred that would otherwise have been taken into account on the last day of the year must be increased by income through the date on which the amount is taken into account. Treas. Regs. §§31.3121(v)(2)-1(f), 31.3306(r)(2)-1(a).

Plans Excluded

The following plans and benefits are not considered deferred compensation for FICA and FUTA purposes:

(1) Stock options, stock appreciation rights, and other stock value rights, but not phantom stock plans or other arrangements under which an employee is awarded the right to receive a fixed payment equal to the value of a specified number of shares of employer stock;

(2) Some restricted property received in connection with the performance of services;

DEFERRED COMPENSATION   Q 122

    (3)   Compensatory time, disability pay, severance pay, and death benefits;

    (4)   Certain benefits provided in connection with impending termination, including window benefits;

    (5)   Excess (golden) parachute payments;

    (6)   Benefits established 12 months before an employee's termination, if there was an indication that benefits were provided in contemplation of termination;

    (7)   Benefits established after termination of employment; and

    (8)   Compensation paid for current services.

Treas. Regs. §§31.3121(v)(2)-1(b)(4), 31.3306(r)(2)-1(a).

Account Balance Plan versus Nonaccount Balance Plan

The manner of determining the amount deferred for a given period depends upon whether the deferred compensation plan is an account balance plan or a nonaccount balance plan.

Account Balance Plan

A plan is an *account balance plan* only if, under its terms: (1) a principal amount is credited to an employee's individual account; (2) the income attributable to each principal amount is credited or debited to the individual account; and (3) the benefits payable to the employee are based solely on the balance credited to his individual account. Treas. Regs. §§31.3121(v)(2)-1(c)(1), 31.3306(r)(2)-1(a); see also Let. Rul. 9417013 (amounts deferred in defined-contribution-type plan with delayed vesting are amounts attributable to employer contributions when they vest).

If the plan is an *account balance plan*, the amount deferred for a period equals the principal amount credited to the employee's account for the period, increased or decreased by any income or loss attributable thereto through the date when the principal amount must be taken into account as wages for FICA and FUTA purposes.

The regulations explain that "income attributable to the amount taken into account" means any amount that, under the terms of the plan, is credited on behalf of an employee and attributable to an amount previously taken into account, but only if the income is based on a rate of return that does not exceed either (1) the actual rate of return on a predetermined actual investment; or (2) a reasonable rate of interest, if no predetermined actual investment has been specified.

Nonaccount Balance Plan

If the plan is a *nonaccount balance plan*, the amount deferred for a given period equals the present value of the additional future payment or payments to which the employee has obtained a legally binding right under the plan during that period. The present value must be determined as of the date when the amount deferred must be taken into account as wages, using actuarial assumptions and methods that are reasonable as of that date. Treas. Regs. §§31.3121(v)(2)-1(c)(2), 31.3306(r)(2)-1(a).

2006 Tax Facts on Insurance & Employee Benefits

With respect to these defined-benefit-type plans, the IRS has ruled privately that when a deferred compensation plan promises to pay a fixed amount in the future, the "amount deferred" is the present value of the expected benefits at the time when the benefits are considered wages for FICA purposes. The discount (that is, the income attributable to the amount deferred) is not treated as wages in that or any later year. TAMs 9051003, 9050006. Thus, if the deferred compensation payments under such a plan vest (become non-forfeitable) upon retirement, then the present value of the expected payments will be treated as wages for FICA purposes in the year of retirement.

An employer may treat a portion of a nonaccount balance plan as a separate account balance plan if that portion satisfies the definition of an account balance plan and the amount payable under that portion is determined independently of the amount payable under the other portion of the plan. Treas. Regs. §§31.3121(v)(2)-1(c)(1)(iii)(B), 31.3306(r)(2)-1(a).

The "income attributable to the amount taken into account" means the increase, due solely to the passage of time, in the present value of the future payments to which the employee has obtained a legally binding right, the present value of which constituted the amount taken into account, but only if determined using reasonable actuarial methods. Treas. Regs. §§31.3121(v)(2)-1(d)(2), 31.3306(r)(2)-1(a).

The final regulations provide that an amount deferred under a nonaccount balance plan need not be taken into account as wages under the special timing rule until the earliest date on which the amount deferred is reasonably ascertainable.

An amount deferred is reasonably ascertainable when there are no actuarial (or other assumptions) needed to determine the amount deferred other than interest, mortality, or cost-of-living assumptions. Treas. Regs. §§31.3121(v)(2)-1(e)(4)(i), 31.3306(r)(2)-1(a). For example, the IRS ruled that a participant's benefits under an IRC Section 457 plan (see Q 124) would not be subject to FICA tax simply because the plan's age and service requirements had been met, because benefits were not 'reasonably ascertainable' at that time. Similarly, the benefits would not be subject to income tax withholding at that time, because they are not treated as constructively received until actually received for income tax withholding. TAM 199902032.

No amount deferred under a deferred compensation plan may be taken into account as FICA or FUTA wages before the plan is established. Treas. Regs. §§31.3121(v)(2)-1(e)(1), 31.3306(r)(2)-1(a).

Nonduplication Rule

A nonduplication rule designed to prevent double taxation provides that once an amount is treated as wages, it (and any income attributable to it) will not be treated as wages for FICA or FUTA purposes in any later year. IRC Secs. 3121(v)(2)(B), 3306(r)(2)(B). A deferred amount is treated as taken into account for FICA and FUTA purposes when it is included in computing the amount of wages, but only to the extent that any additional tax for the year resulting from the inclusion is actually paid before the expiration of the period of limitation for the year. A failure to so take a deferred amount into account subjects it (and any income attributable thereto) to inclusion when actually or constructively paid. Treas. Regs. §§31.3121(v)(2)-1(a)(2)(iii), 31.3306(r)(2)-1(a).

DEFERRED COMPENSATION

Q 123

Self-Employed Individuals and Corporate Directors

Self-employed individuals pay social security taxes through self-employment (SECA) taxes rather than FICA taxes. Deferred compensation of self-employed individuals is usually counted for SECA tax purposes when it is includable in income for income tax purposes. See IRC Sec. 1402(a); Treas. Reg. §1.1402(a)-1(c). So, deferred compensation of self-employed individuals is generally counted for SECA purposes when paid, or, if earlier, when it is constructively received (see, e.g., Let. Ruls. 9609011, 9540003).

Likewise, corporate directors who defer their fees generally count those fees for SECA purposes when paid or constructively received. See Q 115. IRC Secs. 1402(a), 9022(b), 5123(a); Treas. Reg. §1.1402(a)-1(c); Let. Rul. 8819012.

For a discussion of the SECA taxation of deferred commission payments to self-employed life insurance agents, see Q 803.

Earnings Base Subject to Tax

OASDI Portion

The wage base for the old age, survivors, and disability insurance (OASDI) portion of the FICA tax and the taxable earnings base for the OASDI portion of the SECA tax are both $94,200 for 2006. The amount was $90,000 for 2005.

Medicare Hospital Insurance Portion

There is no taxable wage base cap for the Medicare hospital insurance portion of the FICA tax, so all deferred compensation counted as wages for FICA purposes is subject to at least the hospital portion of the FICA tax. IRC Sec. 3121(a)(1). Nor is there an earnings base cap for the hospital insurance portion of the SECA tax. IRC Sec. 1402(b)(1). *ASRS, Sec. 64, ¶470.1.*

Section 457 Plans (Government and Tax-Exempt Employers)

123. Are the tax benefits of a nonqualified deferred compensation plan available through an agreement with a state or local government or other tax-exempt employer?

Yes. Receipt and taxation of compensation for services performed for a state or local government may be deferred under an IRC Section 457 plan. For this purpose, a state or local government includes a state, a political subdivision of a state, or any agency or instrumentality of either of them. A plan of a tax-exempt rural electric cooperative and its tax-exempt affiliates is included under these same rules. Deferred compensation plans covering state judges may not be governed under these rules. See Q 127. While the Code does not appear to provide for tax-exempt employers and governmental entities to maintain SIMPLE IRA plans (see Q 242), the IRS has stated that they may do so. Notice 97-6, 1997-1 CB 353. See also *General Explanation of Tax Legislation Enacted in the 104th Congress* (JCT-12-96), n. 130, p. 140 (the 1996 Blue Book) (SIMPLE IRA plans of tax-exempt employers and governmental entities are not subject to the limits of IRC Section 457).

IRC Section 457 also generally applies to deferred compensation agreements entered into with nongovernmental organizations exempt from tax under IRC Section 501 (for the most part, nonprofit organizations serving some public or charitable purpose).

2006 Tax Facts on Insurance & Employee Benefits

Amounts deferred under agreements with such tax-exempt organizations (other than tax-exempt rural electric cooperatives) in taxable years prior to December 31, 1986 do not fall within the rules applicable to IRC Section 457 plans (see "Grandfather Rule," below).

Neither a church (as defined in IRC Section 3121(w)(3)(A)), nor a church-controlled organization (as defined in IRC Section 3121(w)(3)(B)), nor the Federal government or any agency or instrumentality thereof is an eligible employer for purposes of IRC Section 457. IRC Sec. 457(e)(13); Treas. Reg. §1.457-2(e).

In Notice 2005-58, 2005-33 IRB 295, the IRS reversed a decision from a 2004 private letter ruling (Let. Rul. 2004-30013) that a federally chartered credit union was not an eligible employer under IRC Section 457 because it was a federal instrumentality under IRC Section 501(c)(1). Pending the release of further guidance, a federal credit union that has consistently claimed the status of a non-governmental tax-exempt organization for employee benefit plan purposes may establish and maintain an "eligible" plan under IRC Section 457.

An "eligible" IRC Section 457 plan is one that meets the annual deferral limits and other requirements of IRC Section 457. See Q 124. See Treas. Reg. §1.457-2(f). Plans that do not meet these limits are referred to as "ineligible" plans. See Q 126. See Treas. Reg. §1.457-2(h).

Plans Not Subject to IRC Section 457

In general, bona fide vacation leave, sick leave, compensatory time, severance pay, disability pay, and death benefit plans are not considered to be plans providing for the deferral of compensation and, thus, are not subject to IRC Section 457. IRC Sec. 457(e)(11). The IRS has issued interim guidance for certain broad-based, nonelective severance pay plans of a state or local government in existence before 1999 with respect to the timing of reporting payments. See Ann. 2000-1, 2000-2 IRB 294.

Length of service awards accruing to bona fide volunteers (or their beneficiaries) due to "qualified services" after December 31, 1996 are also excluded from coverage. IRC Sec. 457(e)(11)(A)(ii). "Qualified services," for this purpose, means fire fighting and prevention services, emergency medical services, and ambulance services. IRC Sec. 457(e)(11)(C). This exclusion does not apply when the accrued aggregate amount of the award in any year of service exceeds $3,000. IRC Sec. 457(e)(11)(B).

IRC Section 457 also does not apply to nonelective deferred compensation attributable to services not performed as an employee. Deferred compensation is treated as nonelective for this purpose if all individuals with the same relationship to the employer are covered under the same plan, with no individual variations or options under the plan. IRC Sec. 457(e)(12).

Grandfather Rule

Amounts deferred under plans of nongovernmental tax-exempt organizations for taxable years beginning after December 31, 1986 are not subject to IRC Section 457 if made pursuant to an agreement that (1) was in writing on August 16, 1986; and (2) provides for yearly deferrals of a fixed amount or an amount determined by a fixed formula. TRA '86, Sec. 1107(c)(3)(B). This grandfather provision is available

DEFERRED COMPENSATION   Q 124

only to those individuals covered under the plan on August 16, 1986. TAMRA '88, Sec. 1011(e)(6).

Any modification to the written plan that directly or indirectly alters the fixed amount or the fixed formula will subject the plan to the limitations of IRC Section 457. Notice 87-13, 1987-1 CB 432. However, apparently, modifications that reduce benefits will not. See TAMRA '88, Sec. 6064(d)(3); Let. Ruls. 9538021, 9334021, 9250008.

Where promised retirement benefits provided (as a matter of practice) solely through a grandfathered nonqualified plan were offset by benefits from a qualified plan without altering the fixed formula determining the total of promised benefits, the grandfathered status of the nonqualified plan was not affected. Let. Rul. 9549003. Likewise, an amendment to allow for the diversification into different mutual funds for the deemed investment of a participant's account and not limiting such participant to his original mutual fund investment options was found not to modify the basic formula and not to affect the grandfather status of the plan. Let. Rul. 9721012.

Where, in the context of a parent-subsidiary structure established before August 16, 1986, a participant in the subsidiary's plan became an employee of the parent and was paid by the parent but retained his positions and responsibilities with, but not his compensation from, the subsidiary, a proposal to amend the subsidiary's plan to cover the participant's employment with the parent was found not to modify the plan's fixed formula and not to affect the grandfathered status of the plan. Let. Rul. 9548006.

The IRS has indicated that amendments providing for selection of investment alternatives and an election to receive an annual cash payment did not adversely affect the plan's grandfathered status under the Tax Reform Act of 1986. Let. Rul. 9822038. *ASRS, Sec. 64, ¶ 420.2(b)(1), 420.2(b)(6).*

124. What requirements must an IRC Section 457 plan meet?

A deferred compensation plan under IRC Section 457 must meet certain requirements, set forth below. There is no prohibition against discrimination among these requirements. An IRC Section 457 plan that is not administered in accordance with these requirements will be treated as "ineligible," see Q 126. IRC Sec. 457(b)(6). Plans paying solely length of service awards to bona fide volunteers or their beneficiaries on account of such volunteers' qualified services are exempt from these requirements. IRC Sec. 457(e)(11)(A)(ii).

It should be noted that the Economic Growth and Tax Relief Reconciliation Act of 2001 (EGTRRA 2001) made many changes in the rules applicable to IRC Section 457 plans. In addition, final regulations were issued in 2003 and are generally effective for taxable years beginning after December 31, 2001. Treas. Reg. §1.457-12.

Permissible Participants

Only individuals may participate, but they may be either employees or independent contractors. Partnerships and corporations cannot be participants. Sen. Rep. 95-1263 (Revenue Act of 1978), *reprinted in* 1978-3 CB (vol.1) 364.) Where local government employees were hired by a water company as part of privatization, they could no longer participate in the local government's IRC Section 457 plan. IRS Information Letter 2000-0300.

2006 Tax Facts on Insurance & Employee Benefits

It should be noted that nongovernmental tax-exempt employers must structure their plans to take advantage of an ERISA exemption—for example, by allowing only a select group of management or highly compensated employees to participate. Otherwise, the plan would be subject to the exclusive purpose and funding requirements of Title I of ERISA, and a nongovernmental tax-exempt IRC Section 457 plan cannot, by definition, meet those requirements. See Let. Rul. 8950056.

Timing of Deferred Compensation Agreement

Generally, compensation may be deferred for any calendar month, but only if a deferral agreement has been entered into *before* the beginning of that month. IRC Sec. 457(b)(4). However, an IRC Section 457 plan may permit a newly hired employee to enter into an agreement before his first day of employment, under which deferrals will be made for the first month in which he is employed. Nonelective employer contributions are treated as being made under an agreement entered into before the first day of the calendar month. Treas. Reg. §1.457-4(b).

An IRC Section 457 plan may permit deferrals pursuant to an automatic election, under which a fixed percentage of an employee's compensation is deferred unless he affirmatively elects to receive it in cash. Rev. Rul. 2000-33, 2000-2 CB 142.

Availability of Amounts Payable

An IRC Section 457 plan generally cannot provide that amounts will be made available before (1) the calendar year in which the participant attains age 70½; (2) the date when the participant has a severance from employment (see below); or (3) the date when the participant is faced with "an unforeseeable emergency" (see below). IRC Sec. 457(d)(1)(A).

A participant in an eligible nongovernmental, tax-exempt IRC Section 457 plan may make a one-time election, *after* amounts are available and *before* commencement of distributions, to defer commencement of distributions. IRC Sec. 457(e)(9)(B). See Q 126.

The premature distribution penalty applicable to qualified retirement plans generally does not apply to distributions from an IRC Section 457 plan, except to the extent that the distribution is attributable to rollovers from a qualified retirement plan or IRC Section 403(b) plan, for which IRC Section 457 plans are required to separately account (see discussion under "Rollovers," below). IRC Sec. 72(t)(9).

Severance from Employment

A severance from employment occurs when a participant ceases to be employed by the employer sponsoring the plan. IRC Sec. 457(d)(1)(A)(ii); Treas. Reg. §1.457-6(b). An employee will not experience a severance from employment merely because any portion of his benefit is transferred (other than by a rollover or elective transfer) from his former employer's plan to the plan of his new employer. EGTRRA 2001 Conf. Rep., *reprinted in* the General Explanation of EGTRRA 2001, p. 161.

Under the regulations, an independent contractor is considered to have separated from service upon an expiration of all contracts under which services are performed, if such expiration is considered a good faith and complete termination of the contractual relationship. Good faith is lacking where a renewal of the contractual relationship or the independent contractor becoming an employee is anticipated. Treas. Reg. §1.457-6(b)(2).

DEFERRED COMPENSATION

Q 124

Unforeseeable Emergency

An unforeseeable emergency must be defined in the plan as a severe financial hardship of participants or beneficiaries resulting from illnesses or accidents of the participants or beneficiaries or of their spouses or dependents, the loss of the participants' or beneficiaries' property due to casualty, or other similar extraordinary and unforeseeable circumstances arising as a result of events beyond their control. Examples in the regulations include the imminent foreclosure of or eviction from a primary residence or the need to pay for medical or funeral expenses. Treas. Reg. §1.457-6(c)(2)(i). Whether an event is an unforeseeable emergency will depend upon the relevant facts and circumstances of each case. However, a distribution on account of an unforeseeable emergency may not be made where the emergency may be relieved through reimbursement or compensation from insurance or otherwise, by liquidation of a participant's assets if liquidation in itself would not cause severe financial hardship, or cessation of deferrals under the plan. Treas. Reg. §1.457-6(c)(2)(ii). In addition, the distribution must be limited to the amount reasonably necessary to satisfy the emergency need (including amounts necessary to pay taxes or penalties reasonably expected to result from the distribution). Treas. Reg. §1.457-6(c)(2)(iii).

Distributions made at any time on or after August 25, 2005 and before January 1, 2007 by an individual whose principal place of abode on August 28, 2005 was located in the Hurricane Katrina disaster area and who sustained an economic loss by reason of Hurricane Katrina are treated as permissible distributions under IRC Section 457(d)(1)(A). Total distributions under this provision may not exceed $100,000. Section 101, KETRA 2005.

A court *did* find a severe financial hardship where the participant's spouse gave birth to a severely ill child and had to cease working in order to care for such child. *Sanchez v. City of Hartford*, 89 F. Supp. 2d 210 (D. Ct. 2000).

Loans

Any amount received as a loan from an eligible nongovernmental IRC Section 457 plan is treated as a distribution in violation of the distribution requirements. Treas. Reg. §1.457-6(f)(1). However, a facts and circumstances standard is applied to amounts received as loans from an eligible governmental IRC Section 457 plan to determine whether the loan is bona fide and for the exclusive purpose of benefitting participants and beneficiaries. Factors considered include whether the loan has a fixed repayment schedule, a reasonable rate of interest, and repayment safeguards. Treas. Reg. §1.457-6(f)(2). Such loans are taxed under the rules of IRC Section 72(p) – see Q 420. Treas. Reg. §1.457-7(b)(3).

Domestic Relations Orders

The qualified domestic relations order (QDRO) rules applicable to qualified plans (see Q 349) also apply to eligible IRC Section 457 plans, so that the IRC Section 457(d) distribution rules are not violated if an eligible IRC Section 457 plan makes a distribution to an alternate payee pursuant to a QDRO. IRC Secs. 414(p)(10), 414(p)(11).

Required Minimum Distributions

For distributions *after December 31, 2001*, an eligible IRC Section 457 plan is generally subject only to the same required minimum distribution rules as apply to qualified retirement plans. IRC Sec. 457(d)(2). These rules generally require a plan to begin distribution of an employee's interest no later than his required beginning date.

2006 Tax Facts on Insurance & Employee Benefits

See IRC Sec. 401(a)(9)(A). For a detailed discussion of the rules that apply to qualified retirement plans, see Q 339 through Q 346.

"Required beginning date" generally means April 1 of the calendar year following the *later* of (1) the year in which the employee attains age 70½; or (2) the year in which he retires. IRC Sec. 401(a)(9)(C). A special rule applies to a "5% owner" (as defined in IRC Section 416–see Q 357), for whom required beginning date means April 1 of the calendar year following the year in which he attains age 70½. IRC Sec. 401(a)(9)(C)(ii)(I). Although this rule technically applies only to IRC Section 457 plans maintained by tax-exempt employers (not to governmental or church plans), as a practical matter, tax-exempt employers are as unlikely as governments and churches to have 5% owners. An IRC Section 457 plan may provide that the required beginning date for *all employees* is April 1 of the calendar year following the calendar year in which the employee attains age 70½. Treas. Reg. §1.401(a)(9)-2, A-2(e).

Penalty. An excise tax of 50% of the amount by which the required minimum distribution for the year exceeds the amount actually distributed is imposed on the payee. IRC Sec. 4974; see also Q 347.

Treatment of Plan Assets

Governmental plans. An eligible IRC Section 457 plan of a governmental employer must hold all plan assets and income thereon in a trust, custodial account, or annuity contract for the exclusive benefit of participants and their beneficiaries. This account is exempt from tax under IRC Section 501(a). IRC Sec. 457(g); Treas. Reg. §1.457-8(a).

Nongovernmental tax-exempt plans. An IRC Section 457 plan of a nongovernmental tax-exempt employer must provide that amounts deferred, all property purchased with those amounts, and the income thereon remain the property of the employer sponsoring the plan, and subject to the claims of its general creditors. IRC Sec. 457(b)(6); Treas. Reg. §1.457-8(b). The participants may not have a secured interest in property held under such an IRC Section 457 plan. A rabbi trust (see Q 118) may be established without causing such an IRC Section 457 plan to violate this requirement. See, e.g., Let. Ruls. 9517026, 9436015.

Deferral Limits

An IRC Section 457 plan must provide that the annual deferral amount may not exceed the lesser of (1) 100% of includable compensation; or (2) the applicable dollar limit. The dollar limit is $15,000 in 2006. The limit was $14,000 in 2005. After 2006, cost-of-living adjustments will be made in $500 increments. IRC Sec. 457(b)(2). "Annual deferral" is defined to include not only elective salary deferral contributions, but also non-elective employer contributions. Treas. Reg. §1.457-2(b). The annual deferral amount does not include any rollover amounts received by the plan on behalf of the participant. Treas. Reg. §1.457-4(c)(1)(iii).

Any amount deferred in excess of the IRC Section 457 plan's deferral limits is considered an excess deferral. Likewise, where an individual participates in more than one IRC Section 457 plan, amounts deferred not in excess of the applicable plan's deferral limits, but that nevertheless exceed the individual participant's deferral limit are also considered excess deferrals. Treas. Regs. §§1.457-4(e)(1), 1.457-5. Amounts that exceed a governmental IRC Section 457 plan's deferral limits must be distributed to the

DEFERRED COMPENSATION   Q 124

participant, along with allocable net income, as soon as administratively practicable after the plan determines that the amount constitutes an excess deferral. Treas. Reg. §1.457-4(e)(2). If a nongovernmental tax-exempt IRC Section 457 plan's deferral limits are exceeded, the plan will be treated as an ineligible plan. Treas. Reg. §1.457-4(e)(3). For these purposes, all plans in which the individual participates as a result of his relationship with a single employer are treated as a single plan. Treas. Regs. §§1.457-4(e)(2), 1.457-4(e)(3). Where excess deferrals have arisen out of a failure to satisfy the individual deferral limitation, an IRC Section 457 plan may provide that the excess deferral will be distributed as soon as administratively practicable after the plan determines that the amount constitutes an excess deferral. If the IRC Section 457 plan does not distribute the excess deferral, it will not lose its status as an eligible plan, but the participant must include the excess amount in income for the later of: (1) the taxable year in which it was deferred; or (2) the first taxable year in which there is no longer a substantial risk of forfeiture. Treas. Reg. §1.457-4(e)(4).

The contribution limits under IRC Section 457 are not coordinated with the IRC Section 402(g) limits on elective deferrals under IRC Section 401(k) plans and IRC Section 403(b) plans. IRC Sec. 457(c).

> *Example.* In 2006, an employee works for a not-for-profit organization sponsoring an IRC Section 457 plan, and "moonlights" as a sales representative for a business sponsoring a 401(k) plan. The employee can defer up to $15,000 under the IRC Section 457 plan *and* up to $15,000 under the 401(k) plan (prior to 2002, the employee was limited to the maximum deferral amount under the IRC Section 457 plan).

These limitations do not apply to qualified governmental excess benefit arrangements under IRC Section 415(m)(3). IRC Sec. 457(e)(14).

Some employers have avoided the deferral limitations by deliberately failing to satisfy the trust requirements under IRC Section 457(g)—so that the IRS would rule the plan to be an *ineligible* plan (see Q 126)—while maintaining a substantial risk of forfeiture (Q 112) in order to avoid current taxation. See, e.g., Let. Rul. 9823014.

Compensation. "Includable compensation" has the meaning given to "participant's compensation" by IRC Section 415(c)(3). See Q 331. IRC Sec. 457(e)(5). Includable compensation is determined without regard to community property laws. IRC Sec. 457(e)(7). Compensation is taken into account at its present value in the plan year in which it is deferred (or, if the compensation deferred is subject to a substantial risk of forfeiture, at its present value in the plan year in which such risk is first eliminated). IRC Sec. 457(e)(6).

"Catch-up" Provisions

IRC Section 457 Catch-up Rules. An eligible IRC Section 457 plan can provide for catch-up contributions in one or more of a participant's last three taxable years ending before he attains normal retirement age under the plan. For those years, in addition to the normal limits, a participant may defer a catch-up amount equal to the portions of normal deferral limits unused in prior taxable years for which the participant was eligible to participate in the plan. IRC Sec. 457(b)(3); Treas. Reg. §1.457-4(c)(3). During those years, the limit on deferrals is increased to the lesser of (1) twice the amount of the regularly applicable dollar limit (2 × $15,000 in 2006); or (2) the underutilized limitation. Treas. Reg. §1.457-4(c)(3)(i). Note that the Section 457 catch-up rules cannot be used for the year in which the participant attains Normal Retirement Age. See, e.g., Treas. Reg. §1.457-4(c)(3)(D)(vi), Ex. 3. The underutilized limitation is the sum of: (1) the otherwise applicable limit for the year; plus (2) the amount by which the applicable limit in preceding years exceeded the participant's actual deferral for those years. Treas. Reg. §1.457-4(c)(3)(ii). For purposes of determining the underutilized limitation for pre-2002 years, participants remain subject to the rules in effect for those prior years (e.g., includable compensation is reduced by all pre-tax contributions and the previous coordination rules apply.). See Treas. Regs. §1.457-4(c)(3)(iii), 1.457-4(c)(iv). A participant cannot elect to have the IRC Section 457 catch-up rules apply more than once, even if he failed to use it in all three years before he reached retirement age, and even if he rejoined the plan or participated in another plan after retirement.

For purposes of the IRC Section 457 catch-up rules, the IRC Section 457 plan must generally specify the plan's normal retirement age. Under the regulations, an IRC Section 457 plan may define normal retirement age as any age on or after the earlier of: (1) age 65; or (2) the age when participants may retire and receive immediate retirement benefits (without actuarial or other reduction) under the basic defined benefit plan of the government or tax-exempt entity, but in any event, no later than age 70½. A special rule provides that IRC Section 457 plans may permit participants to designate a normal retirement age within these ages instead of designating a normal retirement age. A participant may not have more than one normal retirement age under different plans sponsored by the employer sponsoring the IRC Section 457 plan for purposes of the IRC Section 457 catch-up rules. Treas. Reg. §1.457-4(c)(3)(v)(A). (Plans that include among their participants qualified police or firefighters may designate an earlier normal retirement age for such qualified police and firefighters, see Treas. Reg. §1.457-4(c)(3)(v)(B).)

Age 50 Catch-up Rules. An additional catch-up rule applies for eligible IRC Section 457 plans of governmental employers. IRC Sec. 414(v)(6)(A)(iii); Treas. Reg. §1.414(v)-1(a)(1). Additional contributions are allowed for participants who have attained age 50 by the end of the taxable year. IRC Sec. 414(v)(5). (See also Q 397.) All eligible IRC Section 457 governmental plans of an employer are treated as a single plan. IRC Sec. 414(v)(2)(D). The additional amount is the lesser of (1) the applicable dollar amount; or (2) the participant's compensation, reduced by the amount of any other elective deferrals that the participant made for that year. Treas. Reg. §1.457-4(c)(2)(i).

The applicable dollar amount for eligible IRC Section 457 governmental plans is $5,000 in 2006. The applicable dollar amount was $4,000 for 2005. The $5,000 limit will be indexed for inflation for years beginning after 2006. IRC Sec. 457(e)(15); Treas. Reg. §1.457-4(c)(2)(i). An individual participating in more than one plan is subject to one annual dollar limit for all catch-up contributions during the taxable year. Treas. Reg. §1.414(v)-1(f)(1). Catch-up contributions by participants age 50 or over, made under the provisions of IRC Section 414(v), are not subject to any otherwise-applicable limitation of IRC Section 457(b)(2) (determined without regard to IRC Section 457(b)(3)). IRC Sec. 414(v)(3)(A). See Q 397 for additional details on the requirements for the new catch-up contributions.

During the last three years before a participant reaches Normal Retirement Age, the age 50 catch-up rules do not apply if a higher catch-up amount would be permitted under the IRC Section 457 catch-up rules referenced above. Thus, an individual who is eligible for additional deferrals under both the age 50 catch-up and the IRC Section

DEFERRED COMPENSATION

Q 124

457 catch-up rules is entitled to the greater of (1) the applicable dollar limit in effect for the plan year plus the age 50 catch-up contribution amount, disregarding the IRC Section 457 catch-up rules; or (2) the applicable dollar limit in effect for the plan year plus the contribution amount under the IRC Section 457 catch-up rules, disregarding the age 50 catch-up rules. Treas. Reg. §1.457-4(c)(2)(ii).

Small Distributions and Transfers

If a participant's total distribution is $5,000 or less, the participant may elect to receive such amount (or the IRC Section 457 plan may provide for an involuntary cashout of such amount) if (1) no amount has been deferred by the participant during the 2-year period ending on the date of distribution; and (2) there has been no prior distribution under this provision. IRC Sec. 457(e)(9); Notice 98-8, 1998-4 IRB 6.

Participants are permitted to make tax-free transfers between eligible IRC Section 457 plans as long as the amounts transferred are not actually or constructively received prior to the transfer. See IRC Sec. 457(e)(10); Let. Ruls. 199923010, 8946019, 8906066. However, according to the regulations, plan-to-plan transfers must meet certain requirements and are permitted only from one governmental plan to another, or from one nongovernmental tax-exempt plan to another, not between a governmental plan and a nongovernmental tax-exempt plan. In addition, no direct transfer may be made from a governmental plan to a qualified retirement plan except in the context of a service credit purchase, discussed below. A tax-exempt plan may not directly transfer assets to a qualified retirement plan, and a qualified retirement plan may not directly transfer assets to either a governmental plan or a nongovernmental tax-exempt plan. Treas. Reg. §1.457-10(b)(1).

Employees that deferred amounts to an IRC Section 457 plan in which they were ineligible to participate cannot transfer such amounts, under IRC Section 457(e)(10), to an IRC Section 457 plan in which they *are* eligible to participate. Let. Rul. 9540057.

Rollovers

Distributions may be rolled over to and from eligible IRC Section 457 plans of governmental employers under rules similar to those for qualified retirement plans and TSAs. IRC Sec. 457(d)(1)(C); Treas. Reg. §1.457-7(b)(2). If an eligible IRC Section 457 plan of a governmental employer receives a rollover from a qualified retirement plan or a TSA, it must separately account for such rollover amounts thereafter. IRC Secs. 402(c)(8)(B), 403(b)(8)(A)(ii).

The following rules applicable to rollovers from qualified retirement plans (see Q 445) are also applicable to rollovers to and from eligible IRC Section 457 plans of governmental employers: (1) maximum amount of rollover; (2) 60-day limitation; (3) definition of eligible rollover distribution; (4) sales of distributed property; (5) frozen deposits; and (6) surviving spouse rollovers. IRC Sec. 457(e)(16). The direct rollover rules, automatic rollover option, and withholding rules applicable to qualified retirement plans (see Q 447) also apply. IRC Secs. 457(d)(1)(C), 3401(a)(12)(E).

Transfers between eligible IRC Section 457 plans remain the only option for eligible IRC Section 457 plans of *nongovernmental tax-exempt organizations*. IRC Sec. 457(d)(1)(C).

2006 Tax Facts on Insurance & Employee Benefits

Service Credit Purchase

In many states, participants may use "permissive service credits" to increase their retirement benefits under the state's defined benefit retirement plan(s). For this purpose, permissive service credit means credit for a period of service that a plan recognizes only if the employee contributes an amount, determined by the plan, that does not exceed the amount necessary to fund the benefit attributable to such period of service. Such contributions must be voluntary and made in addition to regular employee contributions, and are generally subject to the limits of IRC Section 415. EGTRRA 2001 Conf. Rep., *reprinted in* the General Explanation of EGTRRA 2001, pp. 161, 162.

Participants may exclude from income amounts directly transferred (i.e., from trustee to trustee) from an IRC Section 457 plan of a governmental employer to a governmental defined benefit plan in order to purchase permissive service credits. Likewise, a participant may use such directly transferred amounts to repay contributions or earnings that were previously refunded because of a forfeiture of service credit, under either the transferee plan or another IRC Section 457 plan maintained by a governmental employer in the same state. IRC Sec. 457(e)(17).

IRS Rulings

The IRS will issue advance rulings on the tax consequences of unfunded deferred compensation plans only if certain conditions are met (see the discussion under "IRS Rulings" in Q 115); it is not clear whether or to what extent these conditions apply to IRC Section 457 plans. It is clear, though, that the IRS will not issue an advance ruling on the tax consequences of an IRC Section 457 plan to independent contractors, unless all such independent contractors are identified. Rev. Proc. 2003-3, Sec. 3.01(36), 2003-1 CB 113, 116.

For the taxation of amounts deferred under an IRC Section 457 plan, see Q 126. *ASRS, Sec. 64, ¶420.2(b).*

125. Is the cost of current life insurance protection under an IRC Section 457 plan taxable to participants? Are death benefits under an IRC Section 457 plan excludable from gross income?

If life insurance is purchased with amounts deferred under an IRC Section 457 plan, the cost of current life insurance protection is not taxed to the participant, as long as the employer (1) retains all the incidents of ownership in the policy; (2) is the sole beneficiary under the policy; and (3) is under no obligation to transfer the policy or pass through the proceeds of the policy. See Sen. Rep. 95-1263 (Revenue Act of 1978), *reprinted in* 1978-3 CB (vol. 1) 364; H. Rep. 95-1445 (Revenue Act of 1978), *reprinted in* 1978-3 CB (vol. 1) 227; Treas. Reg. §1.457-8(b)(1). See Q 123.

If an IRC Section 457 plan provides a death benefit, any such death benefit will not qualify for exclusion from gross income as life insurance proceeds under IRC Section 101(a). Treas. Reg. §1.457-10(d). Instead it is to be treated under the deferred compensation rules. Let. Rul. 9008043. *ASRS, Sec. 64, ¶420.2(b).*

126. How are the participants in an eligible IRC Section 457 plan taxed? In an ineligible plan?

Eligible Governmental IRC Section 457 Plan

Amounts deferred under an eligible governmental IRC Section 457 plan, and any income attributable to such amounts, are includable in the participant's gross income for the taxable year in which they are paid to the participant (or beneficiary). IRC Sec. 457(a)(1)(A); Treas. Reg. §1.457-7(b)(1).

Unless a taxpayer elects otherwise, any amount of a qualified Hurricane Katrina distribution required to be included in gross income shall be so included ratably over the 3-year taxable period beginning with such year. Qualified Hurricane Katrina distributions are distributions not exceeding $100,000 in the aggregate from qualified retirement plans, individual retirement plans, tax sheltered annuities under IRC Section 403(b), or eligible governmental plans under IRC Section 457 made at any time on or after August 25, 2005 and before January 1, 2007 by an individual whose principal place of abode on August 28, 2005 was located in the Hurricane Katrina disaster area and who sustained an economic loss by reason of Hurricane Katrina. Section 101(e), KETRA 2005.

Eligible Nongovernmental Tax-Exempt IRC Section 457 Plan

Distributions of amounts deferred under eligible IRC Section 457 plans sponsored by nongovernmental tax-exempt organizations are includable in the participant's gross income for the taxable year in which they are made available to the participant (or beneficiary), without regard to whether they have actually been distributed. IRC Sec. 457(a)(1)(B); Treas. Reg. §1.457-7(c)(1). Such amounts are not considered to be available simply because the participant or beneficiary is permitted to direct the investment of amounts deferred under the plan. Treas. Reg. §1.457-7(c)(1).

Amounts are generally considered made available and, hence, includable in income as of the earliest date on which the plan permits distributions to be made on or after severance of employment, but not later than the date on which the required minimum distribution rules of IRC Section 401(a)(9) would require commencement of distributions. Treas. Reg. §1.457-7(c)(2)(i). Plans may provide a period during which participants are permitted to elect to defer the payment of all or a portion of amounts deferred until a fixed or determinable date in the future. This election period must expire before the first time when any amounts deferred are considered made available to the participant. Treas. Reg. §1.457-7(c)(2)(ii)(A). If the participant fails to make this election, the amounts deferred would generally be includable in income when made available as discussed above. Plans may, however, provide for a "default payment schedule" to be used if no election is made, in which case amounts deferred are includable in income for the year in which such amounts are first made available under the default payment schedule. Treas. Reg. §1.457-7(c)(2)(ii)(B). In addition, a plan may provide for a second, one-time election to further defer payment of amounts deferred beyond the initial distribution deferral. Participants may not, however, elect to accelerate commencement of such distributions. Amounts deferred are not treated as available merely because the participant may elect this second deferral. Participants may be permitted to make this second deferral election even if they (1) have previously received a distribution on account of an unforeseeable emergency; (2) have previously received a cash-out distribution of an amount of $5,000 or less; (3) have previously made (or revoked) other elections regarding deferral or mode of payment; or (4) are subject to a default payment schedule deferring the commencement of benefit distribution. Treas. Reg. §1.457-7(c)(2)(iii).

A plan may provide participants with an opportunity to elect among methods of payment, provided such election is made before the amounts deferred are to be distributed according to the participant's (or beneficiary's) initial or additional distribution deferral election. If the participant does not make an election regarding the mode of payment, the amounts deferred are included in his gross income when they become available pursuant to either his initial or additional election, unless such amounts are subject to, and includable in income according to, a default payment schedule. Treas. Reg. §1.457-7(c)(2)(iv).

In addition, amounts are not considered made available to a participant or beneficiary solely because a participant or beneficiary may elect to receive a distribution (1) on account of an unforeseeable emergency; or (2) or a cash-out distribution of $5,000 or less. Treas. Regs. §§1.457-7(c)(2)(i)(A), 1.457-7(c)(2)(i)(B).

The use of a rabbi trust in connection with an eligible nongovernmental tax-exempt IRC Section 457 plan should not affect the tax treatment of participants or their beneficiaries. See, e.g., Let. Ruls. 9517026, 9436015.

Ineligible IRC Section 457 Plan

As a general rule, compensation deferred under an *ineligible* IRC Section 457 plan is includable in gross income in the first taxable year during which it is not subject to a "substantial risk of forfeiture." See Q 112. IRC Sec. 457(f)(1)(A); Treas. Reg. §1.457-11(a)(1). Where no substantial risk of forfeiture exists in the initial year of deferral, all compensation deferred under the plan must be included in the participant's gross income for that year.

A participant's right to deferred compensation under an ineligible IRC Section 457 plan is subject to a substantial risk of forfeiture if it is conditioned on the future performance of substantial services by any individual. IRC Sec. 457(f)(3)(B); Treas. Reg. §1.83-3(c). Distributions from an ineligible plan are taxed according to the annuity rules. IRC Sec. 457(f)(1)(B); Treas. Reg. §1.457-11(a)(4). Property (including an insurance contract or annuity) distributed from an ineligible plan is includable in gross income at its fair market value. H. Rep. 95-1445 (Revenue Act of 1978), *reprinted in* 1978-3 CB (vol. 1) 227; Sen. Rep. 95-1263 (Revenue Act of 1978), *reprinted in* 1978-3 CB (vol. 1) 364. Once the annuity contract has been distributed, payments or withdrawals from that contract may be subject to the "interest first" rule. See Q 3, Q 249.

Prior to the issuance of regulations, it was not entirely clear when earnings on compensation deferred under an ineligible plan would be includable in gross income. The regulations provide that if amounts deferred are subject to a substantial risk of forfeiture, then the amount includable in gross income for the first taxable year in which there is no substantial risk of forfeiture includes earnings up to the date of the lapse. Treas. Reg. §1.457-11(a)(2). Earnings accruing after the date of the lapse are not includable in gross income until paid or otherwise made available, provided that the participant's (or beneficiary's) interest in any assets of the employer is not senior to that of the employer's general creditors. Treas. Reg. §1.457-11(a)(3).

These rules pertaining to the tax treatment of ineligible IRC Section 457 plans do not extend to (1) any plan qualified under IRC Section 401, IRC Section 403, or IRC Section 415(m); (2) that portion of any plan which consists of a nonexempt trust to which IRC Section 402(b) applies; and (3) any transfer of property to which IRC

DEFERRED COMPENSATION
Q 126

Section 83 applies. IRC Sec. 457(f)(2); Treas. Reg. §1.457-11(b). lations clarify that these provisions do not apply if the IRC Section 83 transfer occurs before the lapse of a substantial risk of forfeiture applicable to amounts deferred under an ineligible plan. If, on the other hand, the IRC Section 83 transfer occurs after the lapse of a substantial risk of forfeiture, the provisions do apply. If such property is includable in income under IRC Section 457(f) upon the lapse of a substantial risk of forfeiture, then when the property is later made available to the participant, the amount includable is the excess of the value of the property when made available, over the amount previously included in income upon the lapse. Treas. Reg. §1.457-11(d)(1). This section does not apply to an option that (1) has no readily ascertainable fair market value (as defined in IRC Section 83(e)(3)); and (2) was granted on or before May 8, 2002. Treas. Reg. §1.457-12.

If a plan ceases to be an eligible governmental plan, amounts subsequently deferred by participants will be includable in income when deferred, or, if later, when the amounts deferred cease to be subject to a substantial risk of forfeiture. Amounts deferred before the date on which the plan ceases to be an eligible governmental plan, and any earnings thereon, will be treated as if the plan continues to be an eligible governmental plan and, thus, will not be includable in income until paid to the participant or beneficiary. Treas. Reg. §1.457-9.

Rulings on Ineligible Plans

The creation of a rabbi trust in connection with an ineligible 457 plan does not affect the tax treatment of amounts deferred thereunder. See, e.g., Let. Ruls. 200009051, 9713014, 9701024, 9444028, 9430013, 9422038.

The right to designate "deemed" investments in an ineligible 457 plan will not result in current taxation under the constructive receipt doctrine (see Q 115), the economic benefit doctrine (see Q 116), or on account of a transfer of property under IRC Section 83. Let. Ruls. 9815039, 9805030.

An IRC Section 457 plan established to provide additional benefits for an employee on an extended leave of absence was an ineligible plan, because it was unfunded and no trust was established (as would otherwise be required by IRC Section 457(g)), and because a settlement agreement called for deferrals in excess of the IRC Section 457(b) maximum amount. The IRS found that a plan provision requiring service of the participant (then age 44) until age 50 was a substantial risk of forfeiture. Let. Rul. 9835017.

Reporting and Withholding

Annual Reporting. Deferrals under an eligible IRC Section 457 plan (and earnings thereon) are not subject to withholding when deferred, but they must be reported annually on the participant's Form W-2 (according to the Form W-2 instructions). Notice 2000-38, 2000-33 IRB 174.

Income Tax Withholding. Payments from 457 plans are wages subject to regular income tax withholding, not under the withholding rules that apply to pensions. Rev. Rul. 82-46, 1982-1 CB 158; Temp. Treas. Reg. §35.3405-1, A-23.

Employers are generally liable for withholding from 457 plan distributions. If a trustee (or custodian or insurance carrier treated as a trustee) of a governmental plan makes distributions from such plan's trust or custodial account, then that person is responsible for withholding income tax and reporting the distributions. Notice 2000-38, 2000-33 IRB 174.

FICA and FUTA. Amounts deferred under both eligible and ineligible 457 plans are generally subject to social security taxes under the Federal Insurance Contributions Act (FICA) and federal unemployment taxes under the Federal Unemployment Tax Act (FUTA) at the *later of* (1) the date when the services are performed; or (2) the date when the employee's right to such amounts is no longer subject to a substantial risk of forfeiture (see Q 112). See IRC Secs. 3121(a)(5), 3121(v)(2), 3306(b)(5), 3306(r)(2). See also Let. Rul. 9024069, as modified by Let. Rul. 9025067; compare SSA Inf. Rel. No. 112 (Dec. 1993). For more detail on the application of FICA and FUTA taxes to deferred compensation, see Q 122.

Service performed in the employ of a state or political subdivision thereof is exempt from FUTA, and may also be exempt from FICA. IRC Secs. 3306(c)(7), 3121(b)(7).

Length of service awards from an eligible employer accruing to bona fide volunteers (or their beneficiaries) due to "qualified services" after December 31, 1996, which are exempted from the IRC Section 457 plan requirements (see Q 123, Q 124) and maintained by an eligible employer are not considered "wages" for FICA purposes. IRC Sec. 3121(a)(5)(I). *ASRS, Sec. 64, ¶420.2(b)*.

Plans for State Judges

127. What rules apply to nonqualified deferred compensation plans covering state judges?

A nonqualified deferred compensation plan covering state judges is taxed under the rules applicable to funded and unfunded nonqualified deferred compensation plans if: (1) the plan has been continuously in existence since December 31, 1978; (2) the plan requires all eligible judges to participate and contribute the same fixed percentage of their basic or regular compensation; (3) the plan provides no judge with an option as to contributions or benefits, which, if exercised, would affect the amount of his includable compensation; (4) retirement benefits under the plan are a percentage of the compensation of judges holding similar positions in the state; and (5) benefits paid to any participant in any year do not exceed the limitation of IRC Section 415(b) (see Q 332). Rev. Act of 1978, Sec. 131 (as amended by TEFRA, Sec. 252). See *Foil v. Comm.*, 91-1 USTC ¶50,016 (5th Cir. 1990); *Yegan v. Comm.*, TC Memo 1989-291; *Mettler v. Comm.*, TC Memo 1989-301; *Stewart v. Comm.*, TC Memo 1989-365. *ASRS, Sec. 64, ¶420.2(c)*.

Excess Benefit Plans

128. What is an excess benefit plan? How is it taxed?

ERISA Section 3(36) defines an "excess benefit" plan as a nonqualified plan maintained by an employer solely for the purpose of providing benefits for certain employees in excess of the limitations on contributions and benefits imposed by IRC Section 415 (see Q 332). ERISA Section 3(36) has never been amended to include the limitations on compensation imposed by IRC Section 401(a)(17) ($220,000 in 2006). If an excess benefit plan cannot restore these benefits, its usefulness is limited. One case seems to indicate that an excess benefit plan *can* replace benefits limited by IRC Section 401(a)(17), provided that the plan was never amended to take the 401(a)(17)

DEFERRED COMPENSATION   Q 129

limits into account. *Gamble v. Group Hospitalization*, 38 F.3d 126 (4th Cir. 1994). On the other hand, a Supplemental Executive Retirement Plan (SERP) (see Q 114) intended as an excess benefit plan was held to be a top hat plan (see Q 115) because it was not specifically limited to restoring benefits lost under IRC Section 415. *Garratt v. Knowles*, 245 F.3d 941 (7th Cir. 2001).

An excess benefit plan can be funded or unfunded. If it is *unfunded*, an excess benefit plan need not comply with any of ERISA's requirements. Even if it is *funded*, an excess benefit plan is exempt from ERISA's minimum participation, vesting, funding, and plan termination insurance provisions. ERISA Secs. 4(b)(5), 201(7), 301(a)(9), 4021(b)(8).

In contrast to the special treatment afforded by ERISA, excess benefit plans remain subject to the tax rules applicable to deferred compensation plans. See, generally, Q 110. The employer's deduction is deferred until amounts are includable in the employee's gross income, and the employee is generally taxed upon payments when they are received. See Q 110, Q 120.

"Qualified governmental excess benefit arrangements" are excess benefit plans maintained by state and local governmental employers. The requirements for such plans are set forth in IRC Section 415(m) (see, e.g., Let. Rul. 199923056). For a discussion of the interaction between IRC Section 415(m) and IRC Section 457, see Q 124. *ASRS, Sec. 64, ¶310.*

Employee Stock Options

129. What are employee stock options and how are they taxed?

An employee stock option gives an employee the right to buy a certain number of shares in the employer's corporation at a fixed price within a specified period of time. The price at which the option is offered is called the "grant" price and is usually at or below the stock's current market value. It is assumed that the stock will increase in value, allowing the employee to profit by the difference. Should the stock price decrease below the grant price, the option is "underwater" and the employee simply does not "exercise" the option to purchase the stock; he is not at risk for out-of-pocket losses.

There are two principal kinds of stock option programs, each with unique rules and tax consequences: "qualified" or "incentive stock options" (ISOs), sometimes also referred to as "statutory stock options," and non-qualified stock options (NQSOs), sometimes also referred to as "nonstatutory stock options." Some executive plans, however, use performance-based options, which provide that the option holder will not realize any value from the option unless specified conditions are met, such as the share price exceeding a certain value above the grant price, or the company outperforming the industry. Performance-based plans can require special plan accounting.

ISOs

For a stock option to qualify as an ISO (and thus receive special tax treatment under IRC Section 421(a)), it must meet the requirements of IRC Section 422 when granted and at all times from the grant until its exercise. The key requirements are that an ISO have an exercise price not less than the fair market value of the stock at the time of the grant, expire within no more than 10 years, and be generally nontransferable and exercisable only by the grantee. IRC Sec. 422; Treas. Reg. §1.422-2.

2006 Tax Facts on Insurance & Employee Benefits

Tax Implications for Employee

An employee receiving an ISO realizes no income upon its receipt or exercise. See IRC Sec. 422(a) (incorporating by reference the nonrecognition provisions of IRC Sec. 421(a)(1)). Instead, the employee is taxed when he disposes of the stock acquired with the ISO.

Disposition generally means any sale, exchange, gift, or transfer of legal title of stock. It does not include a transfer from a decedent to his estate, a transfer by a bequest or inheritance, or any transfer of ISO stock between spouses or incident to a divorce. IRC Secs. 424(c)(1), 424(c)(4).

The tax treatment of the disposition of ISO stock depends upon whether it was disposed of within the statutory holding period for ISO stock. The ISO statutory holding period is the later of two years from the date of the grant or one year from the date when the shares were transferred to the employee upon exercise. IRC Sec. 422(a)(1).

If the employee disposes of the stock within the holding period, he first recognizes ordinary income, measured by the difference between the option price and the fair market value of the stock at the time of exercise, and second, capital gain measured by the difference between the fair market value of the stock at exercise and the proceeds of the sale. IRC Secs. 421(b), 422(c)(2). When an employee disposes of ISO stock after the holding period, all of the gain is capital gain, measured by the difference between the option price and the sale proceeds. IRC Sec. 1001(a).

Although the exercise of an ISO does not result in an immediate taxable event, any deferred gain is includable as an adjustment in calculating the Alternative Minimum Tax (AMT). See Q 829.

Tax Implications For Employer

An employer granting an ISO is not entitled to a deduction with respect to the option upon its grant or its exercise. IRC Sec. 421(a)(2). The amount received by the employer as the exercise price will be considered the amount received by the employer for the transfer of the ISO stock. IRC Sec. 421(a)(3). If the employee disposes of the stock prior to the end of the requisite holding period, the employer may generally take a deduction for the amount that the employee recognized as ordinary income in the same year in which the employee recognizes the income. IRC Sec. 421(b).

Reporting and Withholding

The employer has no obligation to pay FICA or FUTA taxes, or to withhold federal income taxes when an option is granted. Pending further guidance from the IRS, employers are also not obligated to pay or withhold FICA and FUTA taxes upon the exercise of ISOs. Notice 2002-47, 2002-28 IRB 97. The IRS has announced that any rule imposing FICA or FUTA upon the exercise of ISOs will not take effect before January 1st following the second anniversary of the announcement.

NQSOs

An NQSO is generally an option to purchase employer stock that does not satisfy the legal requirements of an ISO.

Tax Implications for Employee

The tax implications of an NQSO are governed by IRC Section 83. Generally, an employee is not taxed on an NQSO at grant unless it has a readily ascertainable

DEFERRED COMPENSATION

Q 129

fair market value and is not subject to a substantial risk of forfeiture. IRC Secs. 83(a), 83(e)(3). Options generally do not have a readily ascertainable fair market value unless they are publicly traded. Treas. Reg. §1.83-7(b)(1). If an NQSO does not have a readily ascertainable fair market value at grant, it is taxed at the time of exercise. Treas. Reg. §1.83-7(a). If an NQSO with a readily ascertainable fair market value is subject to a substantial risk of forfeiture, it is taxed when the risk of forfeiture lapses. IRC Sec. 83(a)(1). When taxed, the employee will recognize the excess of the market value of shares receivable over the grant price as ordinary income subject to FICA, FUTA, and federal income tax. IRC Sec. 83(a).

Within 30 days of the grant of an NQSO subject to a substantial risk of forfeiture, an employee may elect under IRC Section 83(b) to be taxed currently on the fair market value of the option. Any appreciation after the election is taxable as a capital gain. If the NQSO is ultimately forfeited, no deduction is allowed for that forfeiture. IRC Sec. 83(b)(1).

Tax Implications for Employer

The employer has a corresponding deduction (in the same amount and at the same time) as the ordinary income recognized by the employee. IRC Sec. 83(h). In general, compensation paid in the form of stock options normally triggers the receipt of wages for the purpose of employment tax and withholding provisions in the amount of the income generated under IRC Section 83(a) (see Rev. Rul. 79-305, 1979-2 CB 550; Rev. Rul. 78-185, 1978-1 CB 304).

Deferred Compensation

NQSOs exercisable at less than the fair market value at the date of grant will be subject to the rules governing deferred compensation plans under IRC Section 409A. See Q 115. Where the exercise price can never be less than the fair market value of the underlying stock at the date of grant, and where there is no other feature for the deferral of compensation, a stock option will not constitute deferred compensation subject to IRC Section 409A. Prop. Treas. Reg. §1.409A-1(b)(5). The proposed regulations also allow plans to substitute non-discounted stock options and stock appreciation rights for discounted options and rights until December 31, 2006.

Under a prior ruling, stock options could be "converted" to a deferred compensation plan free of tax under limited circumstances. Where employees could choose to retain or surrender both ISOs and NQSOs in exchange for an initial deferral amount under a nonqualified deferred compensation plan, the IRS indicated that neither the opportunity to surrender the options, nor their actual surrender, would create taxable income for participants under either the constructive receipt or economic benefit doctrines. Let. Rul. 199901006. For a discussion of the theories of constructive receipt and economic benefit, see Q 115 and Q 116, respectively.

Reporting and Withholding

The employer has no obligation to pay employment taxes or to withhold federal income taxes upon the grant of NQSOs. Upon exercise, the employer must treat the excess of the market value of shares received over the grant price as wages subject to FICA, FUTA, and federal income tax withholding in the pay period in which the income arises. The employer has no obligation to withhold or pay federal income or employment taxes upon the sale of shares purchased by option.

2006 Tax Facts on Insurance & Employee Benefits

Employers are to use code "V" in box 12 on Form W-2 to identify the amount of compensation to be included in an employee's wages in connection with the exercise of an employer-provided NQSO. Completion of code V is addressed in the instructions for Forms W-2 and W-3. Employers must report the excess of the fair market value of the stock received upon exercise of the option over the amount paid for that stock on Form W-2 in boxes 1, 3 (up to the social security wage base), 5, and 12 (using code V) when an employee (or former employee) exercises his options. Ann. 2000-97, 2000-48 IRB 557; Ann. 2001-7, 2001-3 IRB 357.

Department of Labor Issues

Generally speaking, an ISO is not subject to ERISA's reporting requirements and a summary plan description need not be distributed to participants. The employer must, however, furnish a statement to the employee on or before January 31st of the year following the year in which he exercises the ISO, stating details about the options granted. IRC Sec. 6039(a).

130. What is restricted stock?

A restricted stock award is an outright grant of shares by a company to an individual, usually an employee, without any payment by the recipient (or for only a nominal payment). Generally, the shares of stock are subject to a contractual provision under which the granting company has the right (but not the obligation) to repurchase or reacquire the shares from the recipient upon the occurrence of a specified event (e.g., termination of employment). This right of repurchase or reacquisition expires after a specified period of time, either all at once or in increments (for example, a grant of 1000 shares with 200 shares vesting annually over a 5-year period). The expiration of this right is referred to as "vesting." During the period that the shares of stock may be repurchased or reacquired, the recipient is prohibited from selling (or otherwise transferring) the shares. This is why the shares are called "restricted stock." *Executive Compensation: A Guide for Investors*, U.S. Securities and Exchange Commission, at http:www.sec.gov/investor/pubs/execompo0803.htm. Although the passage of time typically serves as the primary restriction for such stock, vesting may depend on restrictions other than time (e.g., satisfying corporate performance goals, such as reaching a specified level of profitability.)

For the tax treatment of restricted stock (including the taxability of dividends on restricted stock), see Q 131.

131. How is restricted stock taxed? How are dividends on restricted stock taxed?

The tax implications of restricted stock are governed by IRC Section 83. In general, restricted stock does not constitute taxable income to the employee at the time it is granted (unless it is "substantially vested," see below, upon grant). An employee who receives restricted stock must include the fair market value of that stock in his income in the year the stock becomes "substantially vested" (see below); the amount the employee paid for the restricted stock, if any, must be subtracted from this amount. Restricted stock becomes *substantially vested* in the year in which (1) the stock becomes transferable, *or* (2) the stock is no longer subject to a substantial risk of forfeiture. IRC Sec. 83(a).

Within 30 days of receiving the restricted stock, an employee may *elect* under IRC Section 83(b) to be taxed on the fair market value of the stock *currently* rather than the year the stock becomes substantially vested. Any appreciation after the election is taxable as a capital gain. However, if the restricted stock is ultimately forfeited, no deduction is allowed for that forfeiture. IRC Sec. 83(b).

The employer has a corresponding deduction, in the same amount and at the same time, as the ordinary income recognized by the employee. IRC Sec. 83(h). In general, compensation paid in the form of restricted stock normally triggers the receipt of wages for the purpose of employment tax and withholding provisions in the amount of the income generated under IRC Section 83(a). See Rev. Rul. 79-305, 1979-2 CB 350.

Dividends received on restricted stock are extra compensation to the employee. The employer includes these payments on the employee's Form W-2. With respect to dividends received on restricted stock that the employee choses to include in his income in the year transferred, such dividends are treated the same as any other dividends. The employee should receive a Form 1099-DIV showing these dividends. These dividends should not be included in the employee's wages on his income tax return; instead, the employee should report them as dividends.

EDUCATIONAL BENEFIT TRUSTS

132. How are the benefits paid under an educational benefit trust taxed? When may an employer deduct contributions?

An educational benefit trust is a plan to defray the educational expenses of employees' children. Where employer contributions to an educational benefit trust are related to an employee's service, they are taxed as compensation to the employee when they are either: (1) paid to or for the benefit of the children; or (2) no longer subject to a substantial risk of forfeiture. *Grant-Jacoby, Inc. v. Comm.*, 73 TC 700 (1980); *Armantrout v. Comm.*, 67 TC 996 (1977), *aff'd*, 570 F.2d 210 (7th Cir. 1978); Treas. Reg. §1.83-3(c)(4), Ex. 2; Rev. Rul. 75-448, 1975-2 CB 55; TAM 8535002. See also *Wheeler v. U.S.*, 768 F.2d 1333 (Fed. Cir. 1985), *cert. denied*, 474 U.S. 1081; *Citrus Orthopedic Medical Group, Inc. v. Comm.*, 72 TC 461 (1979).

Amounts paid to children of stockholder-employees are treated as compensation, not dividends, where the plan is adopted for business reasons – to attract and retain employees. *Grant-Jacoby, Inc. v. Comm.*, above.

Where a bona fide debtor-creditor relationship is not intended, amounts are treated as compensation even though called "loans." *Saunders v. Comm.*, TC Memo 1982-655, *aff'd*, 720 F.2d 871, 83-2 USTC ¶88,609 (5th Cir. 1983) (overly generous loan forgiveness provisions in plan indicated true loan not intended). See Let. Rul. 8137001.

If an educational benefit trust is considered a welfare benefit fund, it is subject to IRC Section 419, under which the employer's deduction is effectively deferred until benefits are includable in employees' income. IRC Sections 419 and 419A generally apply to post-1985 contributions. Prior to that time, there was some controversy regarding the timing of the employer's deduction. For years, the position of the IRS was that benefits provided under an educational benefit trust related to the employee's service constituted a deferral of compensation and, therefore, the employer's deductions should be taken when the benefits are paid out under IRC Section 404(a)(5). See *Grant-Jacoby, Inc. v. Comm.*, 73 TC 700 (1980); *Citrus Orthopedic Medical Group, Inc. v. Comm.*, 72

TC 461 (1979); Rev. Rul. 75-448, 1975-2 CB 55. The IRS has since privately ruled that an educational benefit trust was a "welfare benefit fund," and that the deduction of contributions was controlled by IRC Section 419. Let. Rul. 8737022.

Educational benefit trusts cannot take advantage of the (limited) immediate deductions for advance funding under the general rule of IRC Section 419, because they do not have "qualified asset accounts." IRC Sec. 419A(a). Thus, the employer's deduction is generally limited to the amount includable in income by employees that year, minus the trust's after-tax income.

The general rule of IRC Section 419(b), which limits the deduction of welfare benefit fund contributions to the fund's "qualified cost," does not apply to contributions to a collectively bargained welfare benefit fund. The IRS has ruled that such contributions could be deducted in the year contributed, provided that they constitute ordinary and necessary expenses. See Let. Rul. 9510048. This ruling is questionable, however, because it is based on a temporary regulation (published before the current statutory text), which provides more generous treatment for collectively bargained funds than the current statute.

For a more detailed treatment of welfare benefit funds, see Q 495 and Q 496.

DEPENDENT CARE ASSISTANCE PROGRAMS

133. What are the income tax consequences of an employer-sponsored dependent care assistance program?

Plan Requirements

A dependent care assistance program (DCAP) is a separate written plan of an employer for the exclusive benefit of providing employees with payment for or the provision of services, which, if paid for by the employee, would be considered employment-related expenses under IRC Section 21(b)(2). IRC Secs. 129(d)(1), 129(e)(1). Generally, employment-related expenses are amounts incurred to permit the taxpayer to be gainfully employed while he has one or more dependents under age 13 (for whom he is entitled to a personal exemption deduction under IRC Section 151(c)), or a dependent or spouse who cannot care for themselves. The expenses may be for household services or for the care of such dependents. IRC Sec. 21(b)(2). The plan is not required to be funded. IRC Sec. 129(d)(5).

Non-highly compensated employees may exclude from income a limited amount for services paid or incurred by the employer under such a program provided during a taxable year. IRC Sec. 129(d)(1). In order for highly compensated employees to enjoy the same income tax exclusion, the program must meet the following additional requirements:

(1) plan contributions or benefits must not discriminate in favor of highly compensated employees (as defined in IRC Section 414(q) – see Q 356) or their dependents;

(2) the program must benefit employees in a classification that does not discriminate in favor of highly compensated employees or their dependents;

DEPENDENT CARE ASSISTANCE PROGRAMS   Q 133

(3) no more than 25% of the amounts paid by the employer for dependent care assistance may be provided for the class of shareholders and owners each of whom owns more than 5% of the stock or of the capital or profits interest in the employer (certain attribution rules under IRC Section 1563 apply);

(4) reasonable notification of the availability and terms of the program must be provided to eligible employees;

(5) the plan must provide each employee, on or before January 31st, with a written statement of the expenses or amounts paid by the employer in providing such employee with dependent care assistance during the previous calendar year; *and*

(6) the average benefits provided to non-highly compensated employees under all plans of the employer must equal at least 55% of the average benefits provided to the highly compensated employees under all plans of the employer. IRC Sec. 129(d).

If benefits are provided through a salary reduction agreement, the plan may disregard any employee with compensation less than $25,000 for purposes of the 55% test. IRC Sec. 129(d)(8)(B). For this purpose, compensation is defined in IRC Section 414(q)(4), but regulations may permit an employer to elect to determine compensation on any other nondiscriminatory basis. IRC Sec. 129(d)(8)(B).

For purposes of the eligibility and benefits requirements (items (2) and (6) above), the employer may exclude from consideration: (1) employees who have not attained age 21 and completed one year of service (provided all such employees are excluded); and (2) employees covered by a collective bargaining agreement (provided there is evidence of good faith bargaining regarding dependent care assistance). IRC Sec. 129(d)(9).

A program will not fail to meet the requirements above, other than the 25% test applicable to more-than-5% shareholders, or the 55% test applicable to benefits, merely because of the utilization rates for different types of assistance available under the program. The 55% test may be applied on a separate line of business basis. See IRC Sec. 414(r).

Amount Excludable

The employee may exclude up to $5,000 paid or incurred by the employer for dependent care assistance provided during a tax year. IRC Sec. 129(a). In the case of a married individual filing separately, the excludable amount is limited to $2,500. Furthermore, the amount excluded cannot exceed the earned income of an unmarried employee or the lesser of the earned income of a married employee or the earned income of the employee's spouse. IRC Sec. 129(b).

An employee cannot exclude from gross income any amount paid to an individual with respect to whom the employee or the employee's spouse is entitled to take a personal exemption deduction under IRC Section 151(c) (see Q 819) or who is a child of the employee under 19 years of age at the close of the taxable year. IRC Sec. 129(c).

2006 Tax Facts on Insurance & Employee Benefits

With respect to on-site facilities, the amount of dependent care assistance excluded is based on utilization by a dependent and the value of the services provided with respect to that dependent. IRC Sec. 129(e)(8).

Grace period. An employer may – at the employer's option – amend its plan document to include a grace period, which must not extend beyond the fifteenth day of the third calendar month after the end of the immediately preceding plan year to which it relates (i.e., the "2½ month rule"). If a plan document is amended to include a grace period, a participant who has unused benefits or contributions relating to a particular qualified benefit from the immediately preceding plan year, and who incurs expenses for that same qualified benefit during the grace period, may be paid or reimbursed for those expenses from the unused benefits or contributions as if the expenses had been incurred in the immediately preceding plan year. The effect of the grace period is that the participant may have as long as 14 months and 15 days (i.e., the 12 months in the current plan year plus the grace period) to use the benefits or contributions for a plan year before those amounts are "forfeited" under the "use-it-or-lose-it" rule. Notice 2005-42, 2005-23 IRB 1204.

Coordination with Dependent Care Credit

The amount of employment-related expenses available in calculating the dependent care credit of IRC Section 21 is reduced by the amount excludable from gross income under IRC Section 129. IRC Sec. 21(c).

Employer's Deduction

Generally, the employer's expenses incurred in providing benefits under a dependent care assistance program are deductible to the employer as ordinary and necessary business expenses under IRC Section 162.

Sole Proprietors and Partners

An individual who owns the entire interest in an unincorporated trade or business is treated as his own employer. A partnership is treated as the employer of each partner who is an employee under the plan. IRC Sec. 129(e)(4). A self-employed individual (within the meaning of 401(c)(1)) is considered an employee. IRC Sec. 129(e)(3).

Reporting Requirements

The employee cannot exclude from gross income any amount paid or incurred by the employer for dependent care assistance unless the name, address, and taxpayer identification number of the person (name and address in the case of a tax-exempt 501(c)(3) organization) providing the services are included on the return. However, if this information was not provided, but the taxpayer exercised due diligence in attempting to do so, the amount shall not be included in the employee's gross income. IRC Sec. 129(e)(9).

IRC Section 6039D generally requires an employer maintaining a dependent care assistance plan to file an information return with the IRS, which indicates: (1) the number of its employees; (2) the number of employees eligible to participate in the plan; (3) the number of employees participating in the plan, (4) the number of highly compensated employees (HCEs) of the employer; (5) the number of HCEs eligible to participate in the plan; (6) the number of HCEs actually participating in the plan; (7)

the cost of the plan; (8) the identity of the employer; and (9) the type of business in which it is engaged. However, for plan years beginning prior to the issuance of further guidance from the IRS, these reporting requirements are suspended for dependent care assistance plans. Notice 2002-24, 2002-16 IRB 785; Notice 90-24, 1990-1 CB 335. *ASRS, Sec. 58A, ¶160.*

EMPLOYEE DEATH BENEFITS

$5,000 EXCLUSION

134. What is the "$5,000 employee death benefit exclusion"?

Before its repeal, IRC Section 101(b) provided that up to $5,000, paid by or on behalf of an employer as a death benefit to an employee's estate or beneficiary, was free of income tax. However, this $5,000 employee death benefit exclusion was repealed and, thus, is not available for decedents dying after August 20, 1996. IRC Sec. 101(b) prior to repeal by SBJPA '96, Sec. 1402(a). *ASRS, Sec. 53, ¶20.4(g).*

CONTRACTUAL DEATH BENEFITS

135. If an employer is under contract to pay a death benefit to an employee's surviving spouse, is the benefit taxable income to the surviving spouse?

Death benefits payable under contract, or pursuant to an established plan of the employer, are taxable income. *Flarsheim v. U.S.*, 156 F.2d 105 (8th Cir. 1946); *Est. of Davis v. Comm.*, TC Memo 1952; *Varnedoe v. Allen*, 158 F.2d 467 (5th Cir. 1946); *Simpson v. U.S.*, 261 F.2d 497 (7th Cir. 1958); *Waters v. Comm.*, TC Memo 1963-252; *Robinson v. Comm.*, 42 TC 403 (1964); IT 3972, 1949-2 CB 15. Employee death benefits that are payable by reason of the death of certain terrorist attack victims are excludable from gross income. IRC Sec. 101(i).

Frequently, death benefits are funded by insurance on the life of the employee, with the insurance owned by and payable to the employer. But the fact that the death payments come from proceeds received tax-free by the employer does not cause them to be tax-exempt to the employee's surviving spouse. The surviving spouse receives them as compensation payments from the employer and not as life insurance proceeds. *Essenfeld v. Comm.*, 311 F.2d 208 (2nd Cir. 1962). (For tax effects of insurance funding, see Q 45, Q 46, and Q 62.) Employee death benefits rarely qualify as life insurance benefits wholly excludable under IRC Section 101(a). See *Edgar v. Comm.*, TC Memo 1979-524. See also Q 271, Q 273, Q 153.

Contractual death benefits are "income in respect of a decedent." *Est. of Wright v. Comm.*, 336 F.2d 121 (2nd Cir. 1964); *Essenfeld v. Comm.*, supra; *Est. of Bausch v. Comm.*, 186 F.2d 313 (2nd Cir. 1951); *Est. of O'Daniel v. Comm.*, 173 F.2d 966 (2nd Cir. 1949). Consequently, where an estate tax has been paid, the recipient of the death payments is entitled to an income tax deduction for that portion of the estate tax attributable to the value of the payments. See Q 827. *ASRS, Sec. 53, ¶20.4(g).*

136. Is a contractual death benefit payable to a surviving spouse deductible by the employer?

2006 Tax Facts on Insurance & Employee Benefits

The employer can deduct the death payments provided they represent reasonable additional compensation for the employee's services. *Southern Fruit Distributors v. U.S.*, 32 AFTR 2d 73-5598 (M.D. Fla. 1973). See Q 108. However, payments can be deducted only in the year they are includable in the employee's income, regardless of the accounting method used by the employer. IRC Sec. 404(a)(5); Rev. Rul. 55-212, 1955-1 CB 299; *Seavey & Flarsheim Brokerage Co. v. Comm.*, 41 BTA 198 (1940); *Bleichroeder Bing & Co. v. Comm.*, TC Memo 1953; *H.T. Cushman Mfg. Co. v. Comm.*, TC Memo 1943.

Usually questions as to whether the death payments constitute compensation for the employee's services and, if so, whether the compensation is reasonable, will arise only in connection with payments for stockholder-employees of a close corporation. In the following cases it was held that the payments—even though made under contract—were not compensation but rather, payments under a plan to provide financial security for the families of the stockholder-employees. Hence, the deductions were disallowed. *Willmark Serv. Sys., Inc. v. Comm.*, TC Memo 1965-294, aff'd 368 F.2d 359 (2d Cir. 1966); *Wallace v. Comm.*, TC Memo 1967-11; *M.S.D. Inc. v. U.S.*, 77-1 USTC ¶9366 (N.D. Ohio 1977), aff'd 79-2 USTC ¶9712 (6th Cir. 1979). On the other hand, payments were held reasonable and for a substantial business purpose in *M. Buten and Sons, Inc. v. Comm.*, TC Memo 1972-44.

An employer who prefunds benefits will be subject to limits discussed in Q 496 and Q 497. However, if the benefit is considered deferred compensation, the deduction is subject to the rules in Q 110 or Q 120. *ASRS, Sec. 53, ¶20.4(g)*.

Voluntary Death Benefits

137. If an employer voluntarily pays a death benefit to an employee's surviving spouse, is the benefit taxable income to the surviving spouse? Is it deductible by the employer?

The IRS has taken the position that voluntary death benefits are not gifts but compensation and are taxable income. Rev. Rul. 62-102, 1962-2 CB 37, Let. Rul. 8919021. The courts, following the rules laid down by the U.S. Supreme Court in *Comm. v. Duberstein*, 363 U.S. 278 (1960), have divided on the question of whether these payments are tax-free gifts or taxable compensation. Each case has been decided on its facts. See *Sweeney v. Comm.*, TC Memo 1987-550. However, payments made after December 31, 1986 by an employer "to, or for the benefit of" an employee are not excludable as gifts. IRC Sec. 102(c). Thus, a death benefit paid by an employer after December 31, 1986, would appear to be a payment for the benefit of an employee and, if so, would not be excludable as a gift. Employee death benefits that are payable by reason of the death of certain terrorist attack victims are excludable from gross income. IRC Sec. 101(i).

To be deductible by the employer, a voluntary death benefit must qualify as an ordinary and necessary business expense. IRC Sec. 404(a)(5); Treas. Reg. §1.404(a)-12. The payments will be deductible, therefore, if the circumstances show that they are additional reasonable compensation for the employee's services, or otherwise qualify as ordinary and necessary business expense. *Rubber Assoc., Inc. v. Comm.*, 335 F.2d 75 (6th Cir. 1964); *J. Aron & Co. v. Comm.*, TC Memo 1963-164; *Oppenheimer Casting Co. v. Comm.*, TC Memo 1963-216; *The John B. Canepa Co. v. Comm.*, TC Memo 1963-337; *Maltzman v. Comm.*, TC Memo 1964-136; *Weyenberg Shoe Mfg. Co. v. Comm.*, TC

Memo 1964-322; *Associated Ark. Newspapers Inc. v. Johnson*, 18 AFTR 2d 5894 (E.D. Ark. 1966); *Fifth Ave. Coach Lines, Inc. v. Comm.*, 31 TC 1080 (1959).

The deduction will be denied if the facts indicate that the payment was purely a gift or was made for the personal satisfaction of the directors. *Graybar Elect. Co., Inc. v. Comm.*, 267 F.2d 403 (2nd Cir. 1959); *Interstate Drop Forge Co. v. Comm.*, 326 F.2d 743 (7th Cir. 1964); *Loewy Drug Co. v. Comm.*, 356 F.2d 928 (4th Cir. 1965); *Vesuvius Crucible Co. v. Comm.*, 356 F.2d 948 (3rd Cir. 1965); *Montgomery Eng'g Co. v. Comm.*, 344 F.2d 996 (3rd Cir. 1965); *Greentree's Inc. v. U.S.* 16 AFTR 2d 5368 (E.D. Va. 1965); *Fouke Fur Co. v. Comm.*, 261 F. Supp. 367 (E.D. Mo. 1966).

Where the widow is a controlling stockholder, the payments may very likely be treated as constructive dividends. In such a case, the entire death benefit would be taxable to her and not deductible by the corporation. *Lengsfield v. Comm.*, 241 F.2d 508 (5th Cir. 1957); *Schner-Block Co., Inc. v. Comm.*, 329 F.2d 875 (2nd Cir. 1964), aff'g TC Memo 1963-166; *Barbourville Brick Co. v. Comm.*, 37 TC 7 (1961); *Nickerson Lumber Co. v. U.S.*, 214 F. Supp. 87 (D. Mass. 1963); *Bacon v. Comm.*, 12 AFTR 2d 6076 (E.D. Ky. 1963). Even where the widow does not own a controlling interest, the payments may be treated as dividends, if the corporation is owned by a closely knit family group. *Jordanos, Inc. v. Comm.*, 395 F.2d 829 (9th Cir. 1968). However, the payments will not be treated as dividends merely because the employee was a minority stockholder. Nor will they be treated as dividends in all cases where the widow is a substantial, but not controlling, stockholder. *Ft. Orange Paper Co. v. Comm.*, TC Memo 1960-170; *Plastic Binding Corp. v. Comm.*, TC Memo 1967-147; see also *John C. Nordt Co. v. Comm.*, 46 TC 431 (1966). *ASRS, Sec. 53, ¶20.4(g).*

GROUP LIFE INSURANCE

Group Term Life Insurance

In General

138. What are the tax benefits of employer provided group term life insurance?

An employer may provide employees with up to $50,000 of group term life insurance protection each year without cost to employees. Generally, the taxable value of group term insurance in excess of the exclusion amount is determined under a table (Table I) provided by the Service. See Q 142. However, the exclusion is not available unless the insurance provided under the plan satisfies the definition of "group term life insurance." See Q 139, Q 140. If the term insurance provided does not meet the definition of group term life insurance, the employer's premium cost is includable in the employee's income.

If the plan provides group term life insurance that is discriminatory, the exclusion is not available to key employees. See Q 143. The taxable cost to the key employee of the entire amount of insurance under such a discriminatory plan is the higher of the actual cost or the cost under Table I.

Generally, the premium paid by the employer is deductible. Group term life insurance may be provided under term policies or under policies providing a permanent benefit.

See Q 147. An employer may also provide permanent life insurance to employees on a group basis. See Q 150, Q 151.

The death benefit of group life insurance, whether term or permanent, is generally excludable from the beneficiary's income. See Q 152.

139. What is group term life insurance?

Unless life insurance provided by an employer meets the following requirements, it is not group term life insurance qualifying for special tax exclusion by employees. Treas. Reg. §1.79-1(a). The life insurance must meet four conditions:

(1) It must *provide a general death benefit*, excludable from gross income under IRC Section 101(a). Under the regulations, travel insurance and accident and health insurance (including amounts payable under a double indemnity clause rider) do not provide a general death benefit. Treas. Reg. §1.79-1(f)(3). Employer contributions for such benefits are contributions to a health plan under IRC Section 106 instead of section 79 (see Q 159).

(2) It must be *provided to a group of employees* as compensation for personal services performed as an employee. A group of employees is all employees of an employer, or fewer than all if membership in the group is determined solely on the basis of age, marital status, or factors related to employment such as membership in a union, duties performed, compensation received and length of service. The purchase of something other than group term life insurance generally is not a factor related to employment. (For example, credit life insurance provided to all employees who purchase automobiles is not provided to a group within the definition, because membership is not determined solely on the basis of age, marital status or factors related to employment.) However, participation in an employer's pension, profit sharing or accident and health plan is considered a factor related to employment, even if employee contributions are required. Ownership of stock in the employer corporation is not a factor related to employment. However, participation in an employer's stock bonus plan may be a factor related to employment. A group of employees may include stockholder-employees (except more-than-2% shareholders in an S corporation). Treas. Reg. §1.79-0. If the group of employees consists of fewer than 10 employees, see Q 140.

A person is an employee if his relationship to the person for whom services are performed is that of employer-employee, or if he formerly performed services as an employee (except to the extent he currently performs services as an independent contractor). Treas. Reg. §1.79-0. Insurance on the life of a self-employed person, whether he is the employer or someone who performs services for the employer as an independent contractor, is not excludable. Thus, insurance for a partner or sole proprietor is not excludable even though he is included in the coverage for his employees. S corporation employees who own more than 2% of the outstanding stock or more than 2% of the total voting power of the corporation are treated like partners; therefore, insurance is not excludable to the extent it covers such stockholders. IRC Sec. 1372. Other S corporation employees may take the exclusion. Insurance provided for an individual in his capacity as a corporate owner or as a director does not qualify for the exclusion. *Whipple Chrysler-Plymouth v. Comm.*, TC Memo 1972-55; *Enright v. Comm.*, 56 TC 1261 (1971). Insurance for a commission salesperson is not excludable unless an employer-employee relationship exists between the salesperson

GROUP LIFE INSURANCE   Q 139

and the company that pays the premiums. Rev. Rul. 56-400, 1956-2 CB 116; see also IRC Sec. 3508. However, full-time life insurance salespersons who are classified as employees for social security purposes are considered employees for group term. IRC Sec. 7701(a)(20); Treas. Reg. §1.79-0.

(3) The insurance must be *provided under a policy carried directly or indirectly by the employer*. A policy meets this requirement if the employer pays any part of the cost (directly or through another person) or arranges for payment by employees and charges at least one employee less than his Table I cost and at least one other employee more than his Table I cost. The policy can be a master policy or a group of individual policies.

Regulations define the term "policy" as including all obligations of an insurer that are offered or are available to a group of employees because of the employment relationship, even if they are in separate documents. Treas. Reg. §1.79-0. However, an employer may elect to treat obligations not providing permanent benefits as separate policies if the premiums are "properly allocated." The employer also may elect to treat an obligation providing permanent insurance as a separate policy if (1) the employee buys the policy directly from the insurer and pays the full cost; (2) the employer's part in the sale is limited to selection of the insurer, the type of coverage, and certain sales assistance, such as providing employee lists to the insurer, permitting use of the employer's premises for solicitation, and collecting premiums through payroll deduction; (3) the obligation is sold on the same terms and in substantial amounts to individuals who do not purchase, and whose employers do not purchase, any other obligations from the insurer; and (4) no employer-provided benefit is conditioned on purchase of the obligation. Treas. Reg. §1.79-0.

Supplemental group term life insurance paid for entirely by employees was not considered group term life insurance under IRC Section 79 where the supplemental policy and the basic group term life insurance paid for by the employer were not considered the same policy because they were provided by unrelated insurers. Let. Rul. 8518037. See also Let. Rul. 8820022. Where employee-paid supplemental group term life insurance was purchased from the same insurer providing basic employer-paid group term life insurance, the supplemental and basic coverages were treated as one policy under IRC Section 79. However, because premiums were allocated properly, the employer could elect to treat the coverage as three separate policies, (basic coverage, supplemental smoker coverage, and supplemental nonsmoker coverage) for purposes of deciding whether the policies were carried directly or indirectly by the employer. Thus, the employees had no imputed income from the supplemental coverage. Let. Ruls. 9227019, 9149033. See also Let. Rul. 200033011.

In another private ruling, supplemental life insurance coverage offered by a VEBA was considered part of the employer's policy issued by the same insurer, but the employer could elect to treat it as a separate policy because there were no permanent benefits and the premiums were properly allocated between the VEBA's supplementary coverage and the employer's coverage. The coverage under the VEBA's policy was not provided directly or indirectly by the employer because the employer was not paying any part of the coverage and because all rates charged the participants were less than the Table I rates. Let. Rul. 8906023. In a similar situation, a supplemental employee group term life insurance program provided through a VEBA was not treated as a policy carried directly or indirectly by the employer. Thus, assuming that the employer elected to treat its basic life insurance program and its supplemental group term insurance as separate policies,

2006 Tax Facts on Insurance & Employee Benefits

Q 140 FEDERAL INCOME TAX

under IRC Section 79(a) no income was imputed to the employees who purchased the supplemental coverage. Let. Ruls. 9611058, 9549029.

(4) The amount of insurance provided each employee must be *computed under a formula that precludes individual selection* of such amounts. The formula must be based on factors such as age, years of service, compensation or position. This requirement may be satisfied even if the amount of insurance provided is determined under alternative schedules based on the amount each employee elects to contribute. However, the amount of insurance under each schedule must be computed under a formula that precludes individual selection.

Where one factor (percentage of compensation) of a two factor formula covered all employees but one, and the other factor (position) applied to only one position held by only one individual, the president, the Tax Court held the formula did not preclude individual selection of jumbo coverage for the president. *Towne v. Comm.*, 78 TC 791 (1982). See also *Whitcomb v. Comm.*, 84-1 USTC ¶9472 (1st Cir. 1984). On the other hand, a formula based on positions that included several individuals in each category was held to preclude individual selection. *N.W.D. Investment Co. v. Comm.*, TC Memo 1982-564. Where the amount of an employee's insurance protection under the group program is reduced by the amount of his death benefit under the employer's pension plan, the group protection is not group term life insurance because the formula for determining the amount is based on a factor other than (and not comparable to) age, years of service, compensation or position. Let. Rul. 8342008. A provision in a group term life insurance plan that offered employees the option to reduce their coverage by certain amounts (but not below $50,000) was found not to preclude individual selection of the insurance amounts. Let. Ruls. 9701027, 9319026.

Instead of a lump sum settlement of death benefits, an employer may select payment of equal installments over a fixed period of time without affecting the plan's status as group term life insurance. Rev. Rul. 77-163, 1977-1 CB 18.

Federal group term life insurance covering federal civilian employees qualifies as group term life insurance. Rev. Rul. 55-357, 1955-1 CB 13.

If the insurer providing group term life insurance also makes available a permanent benefit to members of the group because of the employment relationship, see Q 147.

Term life insurance to be provided after retirement that is offered by certain educational institutions under a cafeteria plan is treated as group term life insurance. IRC Sec. 125(d)(2)(C). See Q 99.

If employer-provided term life insurance does not qualify as group term insurance, the premium paid by the employer is includable in the employee's income. Treas. Reg. §1.61-2(d)(2)(ii)(A); Let. Rul. 8636018. *ASRS, Sec. 66, ¶310.2*.

140. Is term insurance provided to a group of fewer than 10 employees "group term insurance"?

GROUP LIFE INSURANCE   Q 140

Yes. As a general rule, life insurance provided to a group cannot qualify as group term life insurance for income tax purposes unless, at some time during the calendar year, it is provided to at least 10 full-time employees who are members of the group of employees of the employer.

However, insurance for fewer than 10 employees may also qualify as group term life insurance if: (1) it is provided for all full-time employees; and (2) the amount of protection is computed either as a uniform percentage of compensation or on the basis of coverage brackets established by the insurer under which no bracket exceeds 2½ times the next lower bracket and the lowest bracket is at least 10% of the highest bracket; eligibility and amount of coverage may be based on evidence of insurability but determined solely on the basis of a medical questionnaire completed by the employee and not requiring a physical examination (Treas. Reg. §1.79-1(c)); additional voluntary medical information may not be made the basis of a premium rate determination (Rev. Rul. 75-528, 1975-2 CB 35).

For the purposes of determining how many, and if all eligible, are included in the group, employees who elect not to receive insurance are considered included even if they would have to contribute toward the cost of term insurance. But, if the employee must contribute to the cost of benefits other than term insurance (such as permanent benefits) in order to get term insurance, he is not counted in determining if term life insurance is provided to 10 or more employees if he declined the term insurance. Treas. Reg. §1.79-1(c)(5).

While bona fide brackets that are temporarily empty probably do not disqualify a plan, a bracket not used since a plan's inception the previous year was disregarded, with the result that protection provided in the bracket immediately above was more than 2½ times that provided in the bracket immediately below. Rev. Rul. 80-220, 1980-2 CB 35.

If evidence of insurability is not a factor, then insurance not meeting the above requirements, which provides protection for fewer than 10 full-time employees, may nevertheless qualify if: (1) it is provided under a common plan to the employees of two or more unrelated employers; (2) insurance is restricted to, but *mandatory* for, *all employees* of an employer who belong to or are represented by a particular organization that carries on substantial activities other than obtaining insurance (such as a union).

Insurance for fewer than 10 full-time employees will not be disqualified merely because, under the terms of the policy, no insurance is provided for those employed less than six months or who are part-time employees (that is, whose customary employment is not more than 20 hours per week or five months in any calendar year), or those who are age 65 or older. Treas. Reg. §1.79-1(c)(4).

For purposes of determining how many employees are provided insurance, all life insurance provided under policies carried by the employer is taken into account even if the policies are with different insurers. Treas. Reg. §1.79-1(c). This gives support to the concept that supplemental coverage for fewer than 10 may be "superimposed" on an existing group term life insurance program covering more than 10 employees without taking into consideration the special requirements for groups of fewer than 10. See also Rev. Rul. 70-162, 1970-1 CB 21. *ASRS, Sec. 66, ¶310.2(b).*

2006 Tax Facts on Insurance & Employee Benefits

141. Are the premiums paid for group term life insurance deductible business expenses?

Yes, the premiums paid by an employer for group term insurance on the lives of employees are deductible. IRC Sec. 162(a); see Rev. Rul. 56-400, 1956-2 CB 116. This is so even if the plan discriminates in favor of key employees (see Q 143).

A corporation may deduct the premiums it pays for coverage on the lives of commission salespersons irrespective of whether an employer-employee relationship exists between the salesperson and the corporation. Rev. Rul. 56-400, above. No deduction will be allowed for the cost of coverage on the life of an employee, if the employer is directly or indirectly a beneficiary under the policy. IRC Sec. 264(a). If the group term proceeds are to be used to fund a buy-sell agreement between stockholders of the corporation, the IRS may deny the corporation a business expense deduction for its premium payments (see Q 81). Contributions will not be deductible unless, when considered with all the employee's other compensation, they are reasonable (see Q 108).

However, current deduction of contributions to a "welfare benefit fund" to provide group life insurance to employees is strictly limited. Contributions to such a fund to provide life insurance benefits to employees are subject to the requirements discussed in Q 496. See Q 494 for what is considered a "welfare benefit fund." *ASRS, Sec. 66, ¶310.5.*

142. Is the cost of group term life insurance coverage, provided by an employer, taxable income to an insured employee?

Generally, the cost of up to $50,000 of group term life insurance coverage is tax exempt. The cost of coverage in excess of $50,000 is taxable to the employee. An employee who is working for more than one employer must combine all group term coverage, and is entitled to exclude the cost for no more than $50,000. If the employee contributes toward the cost of the insurance, all of his contribution (for coverage up to $50,000 and for excess coverage) is allocable to coverage in excess of $50,000. In other words, he may subtract his full contribution from the amount that would otherwise be taxable to him. IRC Sec. 79. However, the employee cannot carry over from year to year any unused portion of his contributions.

The cost of coverage in excess of $50,000 (the amount that is taxable to the employee) is to be calculated on a monthly basis. The steps are as follows: (1) find the total amount of group term life insurance coverage for the employee in each calendar month of his taxable year (if a change occurs during any month, take the average at the beginning and end of the month); (2) subtract $50,000 from each month's coverage; (3) to the balance, if any, for each month, apply the appropriate rate from the following tables of monthly premium rates; (4) from the sum of the monthly costs, subtract total employee contributions for the year, if any. Treas. Reg. §1.79-3. The cost is determined on the basis of the life insurance protection provided to the employee during his tax year, without regard to when the premiums are paid by the employer.

To compute the cost of excess group term life insurance coverage, the rates in the table immediately below should be used. Treas. Reg. §1.79-3(d)(2).

GROUP LIFE INSURANCE   Q 142

Uniform Premiums for $1,000 of Group Term Life Insurance Protection*
Rates Applicable to Cost of Group-Term Life Insurance
Provided After June 30, 1999

5-Year Age Bracket	Cost per $1,000 of Protection for One-Month Period
Under 25	$0.05
25 to 29	.06
30 to 34	.08
35 to 39	.09
40 to 44	.10
45 to 49	.15
50 to 54	.23
55 to 59	.43
60 to 64	.66
65 to 69	$1.27
70 and above	2.06

*In using the above table, the age of the employee is his attained age on the last day of his taxable year.

The regulations take into account the definition of group term life insurance under state law. The exemption is not available for amounts of insurance in excess of the maximum amount that can be provided by a single contract of group term life insurance under applicable state law–regardless of the general $50,000 allowance. "Applicable state law" means the state whose laws govern the terms and conditions of the policy. Rev. Rul. 69-423, 1969-2 CB 12. The employee will be taxed on the actual premium for any coverage exceeding the state maximum. Treas. Reg. §1.79-1(e).

The fact that an employer purchases group term life insurance coverage for its employees from a wholly-owned subsidiary insurance company does not preclude the employees from excluding an amount equal to the cost of $50,000 of coverage from income. Rev. Rul. 92-93, 1992-2 CB 45.

Group term coverage on the lives of an employee's spouse and dependents is not included in the exemption. However, the cost of such coverage will be income-tax free if the face amount does not exceed $2,000. Notice 89-110, 1989-2 CB 447. In determining whether coverage in excess of $2,000 is excludable from income as a de minimis fringe benefit, only the excess of the cost over the amount paid by the employee on an after tax basis for the coverage is taken into consideration.

Where dependent group term life insurance was available to employees through a voluntary employees' beneficiary association (VEBA) and the employer's only role in the arrangement was to provide administrative services as an independent contractor, the life insurance coverage was not a fringe benefit subject to taxation under Treasury Regulation Section 1.61-21 or 1.61-2(d)(2)(ii)(b). Thus, no amount was includable in income to the employees. Let. Ruls. 9549029, 9151033. Where an employer's group term life insurance plan permits employees to extend group life benefits to domestic partners and their dependents, the cost of such group term coverage is not excludable from income under either IRC Section 79 or IRC Section 132(a)(4). Rather, the Table I cost of the coverage is includable in the employee's gross income under IRC Section 61. Let. Rul. 9717018.

2006 Tax Facts on Insurance & Employee Benefits

Q 143 FEDERAL INCOME TAX

Additional Exclusion

There are certain exceptions to the $50,000 ceiling on tax exempt coverage. The cost of group term life insurance, even for amounts over $50,000, is tax exempt:

(1) to a former employee who (a) has terminated his employment with the employer (as an employee) and has become permanently disabled; or (b) terminated his employment on or before January 1, 1984 and was covered by the plan (or a predecessor plan) when he retired if the plan was in existence on January 1, 1984 or the plan is a comparable successor to such a plan; or (c) who has terminated his employment (as an employee) after January 1, 1984 having attained age 55 on or before January 1, 1984 and having been employed by the employer at any time during 1983 if the plan was in existence on January 1, 1984 or the plan is a comparable successor to such a plan (unless the individual retires under the plan after 1986 and the plan is discriminatory after that date not taking into account insurance provided employees who retired before January 1, 1987); (2) if a charitable organization is designated as beneficiary (such a designation may be made with respect to all or any portion of the proceeds–but no charitable contributions deduction is allowable for such a designation); or (3) if the employer is beneficiary (unless the employer is required to pay the proceeds over to the employee's estate or beneficiary). IRC Sec. 79(b); Treas. Reg. §1.79-2; TRA '84 Sec. 223(d), as amended by TRA '86, Sec. 1827(b)(1); Temp. Treas. Reg. §1.79-4T, A-1. See also Let. Rul. 9149010.

Generally, any contribution toward group term life insurance (but not toward permanent benefits) made by the employee during the taxable year reduces, dollar for dollar, the amount that would otherwise be included in his gross income for term insurance. No reduction is permitted, however, for a prepayment made by the employee for coverage after retirement, or for payments allocable to insurance the cost of which is not taxed because of one of the foregoing exceptions. Treas. Regs. §§1.79-2(a)(2), 1.79-3(g)(2).

The exemption of the cost of up to $50,000 of group term life is not available with respect to group term insurance purchased under a qualified employees' trust or annuity plan; the provisions of IRC Section 72(m)(3) and Treasury Regulation Section 1.72-16 apply to the cost of such protection purchased under qualified plans, and no part of such cost is excludable from the employee's gross income (see Q 424). IRC Sec. 79(b)(3); Treas. Reg. §1.79-2(d).

Premiums for supplemental insurance in excess of maximum coverage of $50,000 provided by an employer under a group term insurance plan are not taxable to the insured employee when paid by a family member to whom the employee has assigned the insurance. Rev. Rul. 71-587, 1971-2 CB 89. But if the cost of the coverage in excess of $50,000 is shared by the employer and the assignee, the employer's portion of such cost is includable in the insured employee's gross income. Rev. Rul. 73-174, 1973-1 CB 43.

The exemption for the first $50,000 is not available to "key employees" if the plan discriminates in their favor. See Q 143. *ASRS, Sec. 66, ¶¶310.1(a)-(d), 310.4*.

143. Must group term life insurance provide nondiscriminatory benefits? How is group term life insurance taxed if the plan is discriminatory?

If the plan covers any "key employees" (defined below) and the plan discriminates in favor of them either as to eligibility to participate or with respect to the kind or amount of benefits, the key employees may not exclude the cost of the first $50,000 of coverage. A key employee in a discriminatory plan must include the higher of the actual cost or the specified uniform premium Table I cost (see Q 142). Employees who are not key employees may exclude the cost of $50,000 of coverage even if the plan is discriminatory. IRC Sec. 79(d).

A "key employee" is essentially the same as a key employee in a top heavy plan (see Q 357). IRC Sec. 79(d)(6). He is an employee who, at any time during the employer's tax year was: (1) an officer of the employer having annual compensation greater than $140,000 (in 2006)–not more than the greater of three individuals or 10% of the employees need be considered officers, but in any event no more than 50 individuals; (2) a more-than-5%-owner of the employer; or (3) a more-than-1%-owner (determined without considering those employees who are not counted in testing for discriminatory eligibility) having an annual compensation from the employer of more than $150,000. IRC Sec. 416(i).

The term key employee also includes any former employee who was a key employee when he retired or separated from service. IRC Sec. 79(d)(6). For purposes of determining corporate ownership, the attribution rules of IRC Section 318 apply. Rules similar to the attribution rules apply to determine noncorporate ownership. (In calculating attribution from a corporation, a 5% ownership test will apply rather than a 50% test.) In determining the percentages of ownership, only the particular employer is considered; other members of a controlled group of corporations or businesses under common control and other members of an affiliated service group are not aggregated. However, they are aggregated for purposes of determining the employee's compensation and in testing for discrimination. IRC Sec. 414(t); see also Temp. Treas. Reg. §1.79-4T, A-5.

A plan is considered discriminatory in favor of key employees with respect to *eligibility to participate* unless: (1) it benefits at least 70% of all employees; (2) at least 85% of the participants are not key employees; (3) the plan benefits a class of employees found by the Secretary not to be discriminatory; or (4) if the plan is part of a cafeteria plan, the requirements for cafeteria plans are met (see Q 99). IRC Sec. 79(d)(3)(A). Employees with less than three years of service, part time and seasonal employees, employees excluded from the plan who are covered by a collective bargaining agreement (if group term life insurance was the subject of good faith bargaining), and certain nonresident aliens do not need to be counted. IRC Sec. 79(d)(3)(B).

Benefits will be considered discriminatory unless all benefits available to key employee participants are available to all other participants. IRC Sec. 79(d)(4). Benefits will not be discriminatory merely because the amount of insurance bears a uniform relationship to the total compensation of the employees, or to their basic or regular rate of compensation. IRC Sec. 79(d)(5).

All policies providing group term life insurance to a key employee or key employees carried directly or indirectly by an employer will be considered a single plan for purposes of determining whether an employer's group term insurance plan is discriminatory. An employer may treat two or more policies that do not provide group term life insurance to a common key employee as constituting a single plan. Temp. Treas. Reg. §1.79-4T, A-5.

Exemption for Church Plans

Church plans for church employees are exempt from the nondiscrimination requirements. A church plan is generally one established by a church or convention or association of churches tax-exempt under IRC Section 501(c)(3). A church employee includes a minister, or an employee of an organization that is tax exempt under IRC Section 501(c)(3), but does not include an employee of an educational organization above the secondary level (other than a school for religious training) or an employee of certain hospital or medical research organizations. IRC Sec. 79(d)(7). *ASRS, Sec. 66, ¶310.1(b).*

144. Is the cost of employer-provided group term life insurance subject to social security tax?

The cost of group term life insurance that is includable in the gross income of the employee is considered "wages" subject to social security tax. IRC Sec. 3121(a)(2). See Q 836. This provision applies generally to group term life insurance coverage in effect after December 31, 1987, but does not apply to coverage of former employees who separated from service before January 1, 1989 to the extent the cost is not for any period the employee was employed by the employer after separation.

The general rule is that the employee may exclude the cost of the first $50,000 of employer-provided group term life insurance from income. See Q 142. Therefore, generally, only the cost of coverage in excess of $50,000 will be subject to the social security tax.

The employer is required to report amounts includable in the wages of current employees for purposes of the social security tax on the employees' W-2. Generally, the employer may treat the wages as though paid on any basis so long as they are treated as paid at least once each year. Notice 88-82, 1988-2 CB 398.

The social security tax must be paid by the employee if the payment for the group term life insurance is considered wages and is for periods during which there is no longer an employment relationship between the employer and the employee. The employer is required to state the portion of an employee's wages that consist of payments for group term life insurance and the amount of the social security tax separately. IRC Sec. 3102(d). *ASRS, Sec. 66, ¶350.*

145. What information returns must an employer who maintains a group term life insurance plan file with regard to the plan?

The cost of excess group term life insurance is not subject to withholding, but an employer who provides excess coverage must file an information return for each calendar year, and must provide statements to the employees receiving such excess coverage. Each employer reports as if it were the only employer carrying group term insurance on the employee. IRC Sec. 6052(a).

An employer who maintains a group term life insurance plan is required to file an information return with the Service indicating the number of its employees, the number of employees eligible to participate in the plan, the number of employees participating in the plan, the cost of the plan, and identifying the employer and the type of business in which it is engaged. The employer must also report on the return the number of highly compensated employees of the employer, the number of highly compensated employees eligible to participate in the plan and the number of such employees actually participating in the plan. IRC Sec. 6039D. However, for plan years beginning prior to the issuance of further guidance from the IRS, group term life insurance plans are not required to meet the reporting requirements of Code section 6039D. Notice 90-24 1990-1 CB 335. *ASRS, Sec. 66, ¶310.7.*

Group Carve-Out Plan

146. If an employer provides life insurance under a group term life insurance policy, what are the advantages of a group carve-out plan to the employees and the employer?

Under a group carve-out plan an employer removes or "carves-out" one or more highly-compensated employees from the life insurance coverage provided by a group term life insurance policy under IRC Section 79. The "carved-out" employees are provided life insurance coverage through individual policies. Low term insurance rates on individual policies and lower minimum premiums on permanent policies contribute to the popularity of this type of plan. Also, the portability of the individual policies makes this arrangement attractive to the highly-compensated executives who are typically selected to participate.

Early in the development of the group carve-out plan, employees were provided coverage with individual policies that were still a part of the group insurance "plan" (see Q 139). Currently, the purchase and ownership of the individual life insurance policies is often structured in one of several ways including a split dollar arrangement (see Q 457), an IRC Section 162 bonus plan (see Q 54), or a death benefit only arrangement (see Q 685).

Under a group carve-out plan, the income tax consequences to both the employer and the "carved-out" employees are the same as if the alternative method of providing life insurance coverage existed independently of the group term plan. However, in a possible exception to this general rule, the IRS concluded that a split dollar arrangement entered into as part of a group carve-out plan should be taxed as group term life insurance. Thus, the economic benefit taxed to an employee was measured by the Table I rates (see Q 142) rather than the insurer's substitute rates that were used with the split dollar arrangement (see Q 458). TAM 200002047.

In deciding whether to adopt a carve-out arrangement, the fact that the individual policy arrangements mentioned above generally do not afford the employer a deduction for the policy premiums must be considered. The premiums for group term life insurance are generally deductible to the employer (see Q 141). *ASRS, Sec. 66, ¶340.*

Permanent Benefits

147. May any part of the benefit under a policy be treated as group term life insurance if the policy also provides permanent benefits? If so, what part?

A policy that provides a permanent benefit may be treated in part as group term life insurance if (1) the policy or the employer designates in writing the part of the death benefit provided each employee that is group term life insurance; and (2) the part of the death benefit designated as group term for any policy year is at least the difference between the total death benefit under the policy and the employee's "deemed death benefit" at the end of the policy year. ("Deemed death benefit" is defined below). Treas. Reg. §1.79-1(b).

A permanent benefit is an "economic value extending beyond one policy year ... that is provided under a life insurance policy." Treas. Reg. §1.79-0. For example, paid-up or cash surrender values are permanent benefits. However, the following features are not permanent benefits: (1) a right to convert (or continue) life insurance after group life insurance coverage terminates; (2) any other feature that provides no economic benefit to the employee other than current insurance protection; (3) a feature providing term life insurance at a level premium for a period of five years or less.

To determine whether a policy provides a permanent benefit, it is necessary to determine what is "a policy." Under the broad definition of a policy provided in the regulations (see Q 139), if permanent benefits are provided by reason of the employment relationship under unrelated plans, to members of a group provided group term life insurance issued by the same insurer (or an affiliate), they would appear to be permanent benefits under the same "policy" that provides group term life insurance.

If "a policy" providing group life insurance provides permanent benefits, the cost of the permanent benefits, reduced by amounts paid for them by the employee (but not by amounts paid for group term life insurance), is included in the employee's income according to a formula. The formula for determining the annual cost of the permanent benefit is: $X(DDB2 - DDB1)$. $DDB2$ is the employee's deemed death benefit at the end of the policy year; $DDB1$ is the employee's deemed death benefit at the end of the preceding policy year; and X is the premium for one dollar of paid-up whole life insurance at the employee's attained age at the beginning of the policy year. Treas. Reg. §1.79-1(d)(2).

The deemed death benefit at the end of a policy year is equal to R/Y where R is the net level premium reserve at the end of that policy year for all benefits provided to the employee by the policy, or if greater, the cash value at the end of the policy year; and Y is the premium for one dollar of paid-up whole life insurance at the employee's age at the end of the policy year. Treas. Reg. §1.79-1(d)(3).

The net level premium reserve (R) and the net single premiums (X or Y) in the formulas must be based on the 1958 CSO Mortality Table and 4% interest. Treas. Reg. §1.79-1(d)(4).

If the policy year and the employee's tax year are not the same, the cost of the permanent benefits is allocated between the employee's tax years. The cost allocated to the tax year in which the policy year begins is determined by multiplying the cost of the permanent benefit for the policy year (using the formula for determining cost) by the fraction of the annual premium paid during the employee's tax year. The balance of the cost, if any, is allocated to the next employee tax year. Each tax year the employee totals the costs of permanent benefits allocated to that year. *ASRS, Sec. 66, ¶310.3.*

148. How are dividends paid an employee under a policy that provides both permanent benefits and group term life insurance taxed?

If the employee pays nothing toward the cost of permanent benefits, all dividends under the policy that are actually or constructively received by the employee are includable in his income. Treas. Reg. §1.79-1(d)(5).

GROUP LIFE INSURANCE   Q 149

If the employee pays a part or all of the cost of the permanent benefits, the amount of dividends includable by the employee is determined under this formula: (D + C) - (PI + DI + AP) where D equals the total dividends received by the employee in his current and all preceding taxable years; C equals the total cost of permanent benefits for his current and all preceding tax years, using the formula in Q 147; PI equals the total premium included in the employee's income under the formula of Q 147 for the current and all preceding tax years of the employee; DI equals the total amount of dividends included in the employee's income under the formula in this answer for all preceding tax years of the employee; and AP equals the total amount paid for the permanent benefits by the employee in the current and all preceding tax years of the employee. Treas. Reg. §1.79-1(d)(5). It appears that an employee who pays no more than allocated cost will be taxed under the formula on the amount of dividends he receives. *ASRS, Sec. 66, ¶310.3(e)*.

RETIRED LIVES RESERVES

149. What is a retired lives reserve? Is the employee taxed on employer contributions to such a reserve? May the employer deduct contributions to the reserve?

A retired lives reserve is a fund for continuing group term life insurance on retired employees. Employer contributions to the reserve should not be taxable to a current employee if he has no present interest in the fund—that is, if he is not in actual or constructive receipt of any part of the fund or of a current economic benefit. When an employee retires, the present value of any future group term life insurance coverage that may become nonforfeitable upon retirement (or the value of the amount set aside by an employer to fund such coverage) will not be taxed to the employee immediately upon retirement. The includable cost of group term insurance will be included in the income of a retired employee under IRC Section 79 for the year in which the coverage is received, regardless of whether the coverage vests upon retirement. IRC Sec. 83(e)(5).

Contributions to a retired lives reserve to fund postretirement life insurance benefits over the working lives of covered employees may be subject to the limitations on deduction of contributions to welfare benefit funds discussed in Q 496. Temporary regulations provide that certain retired lives reserves maintained by an insurance company are "funds." Temp. Treas. Reg. §1.419-1T, A-3(c); Ann. 86-45, 1986-15 IRB 52. See Q 494. Contributions to a fund to provide postretirement life insurance for a "key employee" must be accounted for separately. See Q 499.

A letter ruling concluded there was no income to an employer arising out of: (1) the employer's assignment to an IRC Section 501(c)(9) trust (a voluntary employees' beneficiary association) of all its rights in an insurance policy under which the insurer maintained a retired lives reserve, (2) an agreement by the trustee with the insurance company that amounts credited to the reserve would be invested (under the general direction of the trustee) in a separate account of the insurer or used to purchase annuity contracts, and (3) payments to the trustee under the annuity contracts to be used to provide group term life insurance for retired employees. The conclusion reached in the ruling was based on the fact that at the time of the transfer the employer had no right to recover the reserve as long as any active or retired employee remained alive and the possibility of reversion was unrealistic because of the large number of employees. Let. Rul. 8741021. See also Let. Rul. 9542022. See Q 501.

If the plan provides life insurance benefits exclusively for retirees, legislative history states the plan would be a deferred compensation plan. H.R. Conf. Rep. No. 98-861 (TRA '84) *reprinted in* 1984-3 CB 411. The employer's deduction would be limited under IRC Section 404(a)(5) to the amount includable in the employee's income, and allowed only if separate accounts are maintained for each covered employee. *ASRS, Sec. 66, ¶310.6.*

GROUP PERMANENT INSURANCE

150. Is the cost of group permanent life insurance paid by an employer taxable income to the insured employee?

Where a group life insurance policy provides permanent benefits but does not meet the requirements necessary for any part of the benefit to be treated as group term life insurance (see Q 147), the employee will be taxed as follows: Generally premiums paid by an employer for insurance on the life of an employee are includable in the insured employee's gross income if the proceeds of the insurance are payable to the beneficiary of the employee. Treas. Reg. §1.61-2(d)(2)(ii). For the tax treatment of the cost of group permanent insurance under a qualified plan, see Q 424. *ASRS, Sec. 66, ¶320.*

151. Are the premiums that an employer pays on group permanent life insurance for its employees deductible by the employer?

Yes, if each employee's right to the insurance on his life is nonforfeitable when the premiums are paid. However, if the employee has only a *forfeitable* right to the insurance, the employer cannot deduct the premium payments.

If the employee's rights change from forfeitable to nonforfeitable, the employer may deduct the fair market value of the policy in the employer's taxable year in which (or with which) ends the employee's tax year in which the employee's rights become nonforfeitable, and the fair market value of the policy is includable in the employee's gross income. IRC Sec. 83(h); Treas. Reg. §1.83-6(a)(1). (See Q 303 for the fair market value of a life insurance contract.) Generally, the employee will be deemed to have included the amount as compensation in gross income if the employer satisfies the reporting requirements of IRC Section 6041 or IRC Section 6041A. Treas. Reg. §1.83-6(a)(2). Premiums paid after the employee's rights become nonforfeitable are deductible when the premiums are paid. *ASRS, Sec. 66, ¶320.2.*

DEATH BENEFITS

152. Are the death proceeds payable under group life insurance exempt from income tax?

Yes, the death proceeds received by individuals are wholly tax exempt whether received from group permanent or group term insurance. IRC Sec. 101(a); Treas. Reg. §1.101-1. Where group term life insurance coverage is provided to the domestic partners of employees by an employer, death proceeds paid upon the death of a domestic partner are excluded from income under IRC Section 101. Let. Rul. 9717018. Generally, the same rules as are applicable to proceeds under individual policies apply (Q 271 to Q 276). Special rules apply if the insurance is payable under a qualified pension or profit sharing plan (see Q 437, Q 438). *ASRS, Sec. 66, ¶330.*

Group Survivor Income Benefit

153. What is group survivor income benefit insurance?

A group term product that provides for a death benefit only if there is a survivor who qualifies for benefits under the plan (a lump sum payment of the commuted value of benefits is not available) may be called a "reversionary annuity" or "life insurance." However, regardless of the name, a plan that shifts the risk of loss resulting from premature death from the individual or the family to a large group contains an essential ingredient of insurance. *Helvering v. LeGierse*, 312 U.S. 531 (1941).

An individual "survivorship annuity" has been characterized as life insurance in *Cowles v. U.S.*, 59 F. Supp. 633 (S.D.N.Y. 1945), *rev'd* 152 F.2d 212 (2nd Cir. 1945). See also *Est. of Lumpkin v. Comm.*, 31 AFTR 2d 73-1381 (5th Cir. 1973), and *Est. of Connelly v. U.S.*, 77-1 USTC ¶13,179 (3rd Cir. 1977). Benefits under a self-insured state program were held life insurance proceeds in *Ross v. Odom*, 22 AFTR 2d 5624 (5th Cir. 1968). See also Let. Ruls. 199921036, 9840040.

On the other hand, another self-insured state program was held not to be insurance because of lack of actuarial soundness and because of lack of a definite death benefit payable upon death, as there was no death benefit if there was no surviving spouse. The court reasoned that absent a definite benefit payable in any event upon the employee's death there was no risk-shifting. *Davis v. U.S.*, 27 AFTR 2d 71-844 (S.D. W. Va. 1971). See also *Barnes v. U.S.*, 86-2 USTC ¶9692 (7th Cir. 1986), cert. denied, 480 U.S. 945 (1987). Following the reasoning of the *Barnes* case, the Service concluded that a program that paid a monthly benefit to only certain survivors upon an employee's death did not exhibit the risk-shifting characteristic of life insurance. Thus, the death benefit was not eligible for tax-free treatment under IRC Section 101(a), but was taxed as an employee death benefit. TAM 9117005.

Generally, policies issued after December 31, 1984, will be life insurance contracts if they meet the definition discussed in Q 273.

If these products are held to be life insurance, they will be taxed as group term life insurance, if they meet the requirements in Q 139. See Q 685 and Q 645.

If they are annuities, the tax consequences would be as explained in Q 110 to Q 113 and Q 685. *ASRS, Sec. 66, ¶¶510-540.*

HEALTH INSURANCE

Personal Health Insurance

154. Are premiums paid for personal health insurance deductible as medical expenses?

Premiums paid for *medical care* insurance (hospital, surgical, and medical expense reimbursement coverage) are deductible as a medical expense to the extent that, when added to all other unreimbursed medical expenses, the total exceeds 7.5% of the taxpayer's adjusted gross income. See Q 826. No deduction may be taken for medical care premiums or any other medical expenses unless the taxpayer itemizes his deductions. IRC Sec. 213(a). The limitation on itemized deductions for certain high-income individuals is not applicable to medical expenses deductible under IRC Section 213. IRC Sec. 68(c). See Q 821.

Only premiums for medical care insurance are deductible as a medical expense. Premiums for non-medical benefits, such as disability income (see Q 193), accidental death and dismemberment, and waiver of premium under a life insurance policy, are not deductible. IRC Sec. 213(d)(1). Generally, amounts paid for any qualified long-term care insurance contract or for qualified long-term care services are included in the definition of "medical care" and, thus, are eligible for income tax deduction, subject to certain limitations. IRC Sec. 213(d)(1). See Q 314.

Compulsory contributions to a state disability benefits fund are not deductible as medical expenses, but are deductible as taxes. *McGowan v. Comm.*, 67 TC 599 (1976); *Trujillo v. Comm.*, 68 TC 670 (1977). However, employee contributions to an alternative employer plan providing disability benefits required by state law are nondeductible personal expenses. Rev. Rul. 81-192 (N.Y.), 1981-2 CB 50; Rev. Rul. 81-193 (N.J.), 1981-2 CB 52; Rev. Rul. 81-194 (Cal.), 1981-2 CB 54.

If a policy provides both medical and non-medical benefits, a deduction will be allowed for the medical portion of the premium only if the medical charge is reasonable in relation to the total premium, and is stated separately in either the policy or in a statement furnished by the insurance company. IRC Sec. 213(d)(6). Similarly, since the deduction is limited to the expenses of the taxpayer, his spouse, and his dependents, where the premium provides medical care for others, too, (as in automobile insurance) and the portion applicable to the taxpayer, his spouse, and his dependents is not separately stated, no deduction is allowed. Rev. Rul. 73-483, 1973-2 CB 75.

If a policy provides only indemnity for hospital and surgical expenses, the premiums qualify as medical care premiums even though the benefits are stated amounts that will be paid without regard to the actual amount of expense incurred. Rev. Rul. 58-602, 1958-2 CB 109, modified by Rev. Rul. 68-212, 1968-1 CB 91. (See Q 156.) But premiums paid for a hospital insurance policy that provides a stated payment for each week the insured is hospitalized (not to exceed a specified number of weeks), regardless of whether the insured receives other payments for reimbursement, do not qualify as medical care premiums, and hence are not deductible. Rev. Rul. 68-451, 1968-2 CB 111. Premiums paid for critical illness insurance would appear not to be deductible because the benefit is payable regardless of any actual medical expenses incurred or reimbursement received. See Treas. Reg. §1.213-1(e)(4). A deduction will

HEALTH INSURANCE   Q 155

also be denied for employees' contributions to a plan which provides that employees absent from work because of sickness are to be paid a percentage of wages earned on that day by co-employees. Rev. Rul. 73-347, 1973-2 CB 25.

Premiums paid for a policy that provides reimbursement for the cost of prescription drugs are deductible as medical care insurance premiums. Rev. Rul. 68-433, 1968-2 CB 104.

Medicare premiums, paid by persons age 65 or older, under the supplementary medical insurance or prescription drug programs, are deductible as medical care insurance premiums. But taxes paid by employees and self-employed persons for basic hospital insurance under Medicare are not deductible. IRC Sec. 213(d)(1)(D); Rev. Rul. 66-216, 1966-2 CB 100.

Premiums prepaid by a taxpayer before he is 65 for insurance covering medical care for himself, his spouse, and dependents after he is 65 are deductible when paid, provided they are payable on a level-premium basis for 10 years or more or until age 65 (but in no case for fewer than five years). IRC Sec. 213(d)(7).

Payments made to an institution for the provision of lifetime care are deductible under IRC Section 213(a) in the year paid to the extent that the payments are properly allocable to medical care, even if the care is to be provided in the future or possibly not provided at all. Rev. Rul. 76-481, 1976-2 CB 82; Rev. Rul. 75-303, 1975-2 CB 87; Rev. Rul. 75-302, 1975-2 CB 86. However, the IRS has stated that these rulings should not be interpreted to permit a current deduction of payments for future medical care (including medical insurance) provided beyond the current tax year in situations where future lifetime care is not of the type associated with these rulings. Rev. Rul. 93-72, 1993-2 CB 77. *ASRS, Sec. 53, ¶20.5(i); Sec. 67, ¶210.*

155. Are the benefits received under a personal health insurance policy taxable income?

No. As a rule, all types of benefits from personal health insurance are entirely exempt from income tax. This includes disability income (see Q 193), dismemberment and sight loss benefits, critical illness benefits, and hospital, surgical, and other medical expense reimbursement. There is no limit on the amount of benefits, including the amount of disability income, that can be received tax free under personally paid health insurance (or under an arrangement having the effect of accident or health insurance). IRC Sec. 104(a)(3); Rev. Rul. 55-331, 1955-1 CB 271, modified by Rev. Rul. 68-212, 1968-1 CB 91; Rev. Rul. 70-394, 1970-2 CB 34. However, at least one court has held that the IRC Section 104(a)(3) exclusion is not available where the taxpayer's claims for insurance benefits were not made in good faith and were not based on a true illness or injury. *Dodge v. Comm.*, 93-1 USTC ¶50,021 (8th Cir. 1992).

The accidental death benefit under a health insurance policy may be tax-exempt to the beneficiary as death proceeds of life insurance. See Q 273. IRC Sec. 101(a); Treas. Reg. §1.101-1(a). Disability benefits received for loss of income or earning capacity under "no fault" insurance are excludable from gross income. Rev. Rul. 73-155, 1973-1 CB 50. See also Let. Rul. 7751104, allowing the exclusion to an insured to whom policies were transferred by a professional service corporation in which he was the sole stockholder.

Health insurance benefits are tax-exempt not only if received by the insured, but also if received by a person having an insurable interest in the insured. See IRC Sec. 104; *Castner Garage, Ltd. v. Comm.*, 43 BTA 1 (1940), acq.

However, medical expense reimbursement benefits must be taken into account in computing a taxpayer's medical expense deduction. Since only *unreimbursed* expenses are deductible, the total amount of medical expenses paid during the taxable year must be reduced by the total amount of reimbursements received in the taxable year. Rev. Rul. 56-18, 1956-1 CB 135. Likewise, if medical expenses are deducted in the year they are paid, and then reimbursed in a later year, the taxpayer (or his estate, where the deduction is taken on the decedent's final return but later reimbursed to his estate) must include the reimbursement–to the extent of the prior year's deduction–in gross income for the later year. Treas. Regs. §§1.104-1, 1.213-1(g); Rev. Rul. 78-292, 1978-2 CB 233. Where the value of a decedent's right to the reimbursement proceeds, which is income in respect of a decedent (see Rev. Rul. 78-292, above), is included in his estate (see Q 647), an income tax deduction is available for the portion of estate tax attributable to such value. See Q 827. Disability income is not treated as reimbursement for medical expenses, and, therefore, does not offset such expenses. *Deming v. Comm.*, 9 TC 388 (1947), acq. 1948-1 CB 1.

> *Example:* Mr. Jones, whose adjusted gross income for 2005 was $25,000, paid $3,000 in medical expenses during that year. On his 2005 return, he took a medical expense deduction of $1,125 [$3,000 - $1,875 (7.5% of his adjusted gross income)]. In 2006, Mr. Jones receives the following benefits from his health insurance: disability income, $1,200; reimbursement for 2005 doctor and hospital bills, $400. He must report $400 as taxable income on his 2006 return. Had Mr. Jones received the reimbursement in 2005, his medical expense deduction for that year would have been limited to $725 ($3,000 - $400 [reimbursement] - $1,875 [7.5% of adjusted gross income]). But he would have received the entire amount of insurance benefits, including the medical expense reimbursement, tax free.

ASRS, Sec. 67, ¶220.

156. If the benefits received for specific medical expenses exceed those expenses, must the excess be treated as reimbursement for other medical expenses?

Yes. In computing net unreimbursed expenses for the medical expense deduction (see Q 826), total medical expense benefits received during the taxable year (whether received by the taxpayer or the provider of the service) must be subtracted from total medical expenses paid. Rev. Rul. 56-18, 1956-1 CB 135. If reimbursements for the year equal or exceed medical expenses for the year, the taxpayer is not entitled to a medical expense deduction. However, any excess reimbursement need not be included in the taxpayer's gross income unless the reimbursements are partially attributable to the contributions of the taxpayer's employer. Rev. Rul. 69-154, 1969-1 CB 46. *ASRS, Sec. 53, ¶20.5(i).*

157. If an annuity is used to fund a judgment on or settlement of a claim for damages on account of personal injuries or sickness, how are the damage payments taxed?

Other than punitive damages, any damages received on account of personal physical injuries or physical sickness are not includable in gross income. This is true whether the damages are received by suit or agreement or as a lump sum or periodic payments.

IRC Sec. 104(a)(2). Further, for this purpose, emotional distress is not treated as a physical injury or physical sickness. However, this rule regarding emotional distress does not apply to any damages that do not exceed the amount paid for medical care (as described generally in IRC Section 213) attributable to emotional distress. IRC Sec. 104(a). The phrase "other than punitive damages" does not apply to punitive damages awarded in a wrongful death action with respect to which applicable state law, as in effect on September 13, 1995, provides that only punitive damages may be awarded in such an action. IRC Sec. 104(c).

If a lump sum payment representing the present value of future damages is invested for the benefit of a claimant who has actual or constructive receipt or the economic benefit of the lump sum, only the amount of the lump sum payment is treated as received as damages and excludable. None of the income from investment of the payment is excludable. Rev. Rul. 65-29, 1965-1 CB 59; Rev. Rul. 76-133, 1976-1 CB 34.

However, where damages are to be paid periodically and the person injured has no right to the discounted present value of the payments or any control over investment of the present value, the entire amount of each periodic payment is excludable, including earnings on the fund. Thus, where a single premium annuity is purchased by the person obligated to make the damage payments to provide him with a source of funds, and the person receiving payments has no interest in the contract and can rely only on the general credit of the payor, the entire amount of each periodic payment is excludable. Rev. Rul. 79-220, 1979-2 CB 74; Let. Rul. 8321017.

EMPLOYER-PROVIDED HEALTH INSURANCE

Overview

158. What requirements apply to employer-provided health plans?

The value of employer-provided coverage under accident or health insurance is generally not taxable income to covered employees. See Q 159, Q 160, Q 161. Special tax rules apply to accident or health benefits provided by a closely held C corporation to its stockholder-employees (Q 165) and to health coverage for partners, sole proprietors, and S corporation shareholders (Q 166). Domestic partnership benefits are also subject to special tax rules. See Q 164.

Self-funded health plans are subject to nondiscrimination rules. See Q 162. No nondiscrimination rules apply to plans providing health coverage through a policy of accident and health insurance.

Health plans sponsored by certain employers (see Q 174) are subject to the COBRA Continuation Coverage rules. See Q 173 to Q 185. Certain group health plans are subject to portability, access, and renewability requirements. See Q 186 to Q 191.

Employee's Income Taxation

159. Is the value of employer-provided coverage under accident or health insurance taxable income to the employee?

Generally, no. This includes medical expense and dismemberment and sight loss coverage for the employee, his spouse, and dependents, and coverage providing for disability income for the employee. See Q 194. There is no specific limit on the amount of employer-provided coverage that may be excluded from the employee's gross income. The coverage is tax-exempt to the employee whether it is provided under a group or individual insurance policy. IRC Sec. 106(a). See also Treas. Reg. §1.106-1; Rev. Rul. 58-90, 1958-1 CB 88; Rev. Rul. 56-632, 1956-1 CB 101. (Coverage under an uninsured plan is explained in Q 161.) Likewise, the value of critical illness coverage is not taxable income to the employee. Apparently accidental death coverage is also excludable from the employee's gross income under IRC Section 106(a). See Treas. Reg. §1.106-1; Treas. Reg. §1.79-1(f)(3); Let. Ruls. 8801015, 8922048. The value of consumer medical cards purchased by a partnership for its employees was excludable from the employees' income under IRC Section 106(a). Let. Rul. 9814023.

Where the employer applies salary reduction amounts to the payment of health insurance premiums for employees, the salary reduction amounts are excludable from gross income under IRC Section 106. Rev. Rul. 2002-03, 2002-1 CB 316. If an employee pays the premiums on his personally-owned medical expense insurance and is reimbursed by his employer, the reimbursement is likewise excludable from the employee's gross income under IRC Section 106. See Rev. Rul. 61-146, 1961-2 CB 25; see *Larkin v. Comm.*, 48 TC 629 (1967), Footnote #3; Let. Rul. 9840044. However, where the employer simply pays the employee or retiree a sum that may be used to pay the premium but is not required to be so used, the sum is taxable to the employee. Rev. Rul. 75-241, 1975-1 CB 316, Let. Rul. 9022060. See also Let. Rul. 9104050.

According to the IRS, where an employee is offered a choice between a lower salary and employer-paid health insurance or a higher salary and no health insurance, he must include the full amount of the higher salary in income regardless of his choice. An employee selecting the health insurance option is considered to have received the higher salary and, in turn, paid a portion of the salary equal to the health insurance premium to the insurance company. Let. Rul. 9406002. See also Let. Rul. 9513027. However, a federal district court faced with a similar fact situation has ruled that for employees who accept the employer-paid health insurance coverage, the difference between the higher salary and the lower one is not subject to FICA and FUTA taxes or to income tax withholding. *Express Oil Change, Inc. v. U.S.*, 78 AFTR2d ¶96-5476 (N.D. Ala. 1996), *aff'd* 83 AFTR2d ¶99-302 (11th Cir. 1998).

Where a taxpayer's contribution to a fund providing retiree health benefits is deducted from his after-tax salary, it is considered an employee contribution and is includable in the taxpayer's income under IRC Section 61. In contrast, where the employer increases or "grosses up" the taxpayer's salary and then deducts the fund contribution from the taxpayer's after-tax salary, the contribution is considered to be an employer contribution, which is excludable from the gross income of the taxpayer under IRC Section 106. Let. Rul. 9625012. A return of premium rider on a health insurance policy was ruled a benefit in addition to accident and health benefits and the premium paid by the employer was not excludable by the employee. Let. Rul. 8804010.

Employer-provided accident and health coverage for an employee and his spouse and dependents, both before and after retirement, and also for his surviving spouse and dependents after his death, does not have to be included in gross income by the active or retired employee or, after his death, by his survivors. Rev. Rul. 82-196, 1982-2 CB 53; GCM 38917 (11-17-82).

If an employer's accident and health plan continues to provide coverage, pursuant to a collective bargaining agreement, for an employee who is laid off, the value of the coverage is excluded from the gross income of the laid-off employee. See Rev. Rul. 85-121, 1985-2 CB 57. Terminated employees who receive medical coverage under a medical plan that is part of the (former) employer's severance plan are considered to be employees for purposes of IRC Sections 105 and 106. Thus, the employer's contributions toward medical care for the employees are excludable from income under IRC Section 106. Let. Rul. 9612008. Otherwise, the exclusion is available only to active employees. Full-time life insurance salespersons are considered employees if they are employees for social security purposes. IRC Sec. 7701(a)(20). But coverage for other commission salespersons is taxable income to the salespersons, unless an employer-employee relationship exists. Rev. Rul. 56-400, 1956-2 CB 116; see also IRC Sec. 3508. In the case of shareholder-employees owning more than 2% of the stock of an S corporation, see Q 166.

Generally, discrimination does not affect exclusion of the value of the coverage. Even if a self-insured medical expense reimbursement plan discriminates in favor of highly compensated employees, the value of coverage is not taxable; only the reimbursements are affected. See Q 162. *ASRS, Sec. 67, ¶320.1.*

160. Are payments received by employees under employer-provided accident or health insurance taxable income?

Hospital, Surgical, and Medical Expense

Amounts received by an employee under employer-provided accident or health insurance (group or individual) that reimburse the employee for hospital, surgical, and other medical expenses incurred for care of the employee, his spouse, and dependents are generally tax-exempt without limit. Nonetheless, benefits must be included in gross income to the extent that they reimburse the employee for any expenses that he deducted in a prior year. Moreover, if reimbursements exceed actual expenses, the excess must be included in gross income to the extent that it is attributable to employer contributions. IRC Sec. 105(b); Treas. Reg. §1.105-2; Rev. Rul. 69-154, 1969-1 CB 46.

Where an employer "reimburses" employees for salary reduction contributions applied to the payment of health insurance premiums, such amounts are not excludable under IRC Section 105(b) because there are no employee-paid premiums to reimburse. Rev. Rul. 2002-3, 2002-1 CB 316. Likewise, where the employer applies salary reduction contributions to the payment of health insurance premiums and then pays the amount of the salary reduction to employees regardless of whether the employee incurs expenses for medical care, these so-called "advance reimbursements" or "loans" are not excludable from gross income under IRC Section 105(b) and are subject to FICA and FUTA taxes. Rev. Rul. 2002-80, 2002-2 CB 925.

Sight Loss and Dismemberment

Payments (not related to absence from work) for the permanent loss, or loss of use, of a member or function of the body, or permanent disfigurement of the employee, his spouse, or a dependent are excluded from income, if the amounts paid are computed with reference to the nature of the injury. IRC Sec. 105(c). A lump-sum payment for incurable cancer (under a group life-and-disability policy) qualified for tax exemption under this provision. Rev. Rul. 63-181, 1963-2 CB 74. Benefits determined by the length of service rather than the type and severity of the injury did not qualify for the exemption. *Beisler v. Comm.*, 814 F.2d 1304 (9th Cir. 1987); *West v. Comm.*, TC Memo 1992-617. (See also *Rosen v. U.S.*, 829 F.2d 506 (4th Cir. 1987).) Benefits determined as a percentage of the disabled employee's salary rather than the nature of his injury were not excludable from income. *Colton v. Comm.*, TC Memo 1995-275; *Webster v. Comm.*, 94-2 USTC ¶50,586 (M.D. Tenn. 1994). An employee who has permanently lost a bodily member or function but is working and drawing a salary cannot exclude a portion of that salary as payment for loss of the member or function if that portion was not computed with reference to the loss. *Laverty v. Comm.*, 61 TC 160 (1973) *aff'd* 75-2 USTC ¶9712 (9th Cir. 1975).

Critical Illness Benefits

Amounts received by an employee under employer-provided critical illness policies, where the value of the coverage was not includable in the employee's gross income, are includable in the employee's gross income. The exclusion from gross income under IRC Section 105(b) applies only to amounts paid specifically to reimburse medical care expenses. Since critical illness insurance policies pay a benefit irrespective of whether any medical expenses are incurred, such amounts are not excludable under IRC Section 105(b). See Treas. Regs. §§1.105-2, 1.213-1(e).

Wage Continuation and Disability Income

Generally, "sick pay," wage continuation payments, and disability income payments, both preretirement and postretirement, are fully includable in gross income and taxable to the employee. See Let. Ruls. 9103043, 9036049. See Q 194.

Accidental Death Benefit

Accidental death benefits under an employer's plan are received income tax free by the employee's beneficiary under IRC Section 101(a) as life insurance proceeds payable by reason of the insured's death. Treas. Reg. §1.101-1(a). Death benefits payable under life insurance contracts issued after December 31, 1984, are excludable only if the contract meets the statutory definition of a life insurance contract in IRC Section 7702. See Q 273.

Survivors Benefits

Benefits paid to a surviving spouse and dependents under an employer accident and health plan, which provided coverage for an employee and his spouse and dependents both before and after retirement and to his surviving spouse and dependents after his death, are excludable to the extent that they would be if paid to the employee. Rev. Rul. 82-196, 1982-2 CB 53; GCM 38917 (11-17-82). *ASRS, Sec. 67, ¶320.5*.

161. Are benefits provided under an employer's noninsured accident and health plan excludable from the employee's income?

To be tax-exempt on the same basis as insured plans (see Q 159, Q 160), uninsured benefits must be received under an accident and health plan for employees. IRC Sec. 105(e). While there must be a *plan* for uninsured payments, the plan need not follow a particular legal form; thus, a provision for disability pay in an employment contract has been held to satisfy the condition. *Andress v. U.S.*, 198 F. Supp. 371 (N.D. Ohio, 1961). It is not necessary for tax purposes that the plan be in writing or that the employee's rights to benefits under the plan be enforceable. For example, an employer's custom or policy of continuing wages during disability, known to the employees generally, has been held to constitute a plan. *Niekamp v. U.S.*, 240 F. Supp. 195 (E.D. Mo. 1965); *Pickle*, TC Memo 1971-304. However, if the employee's rights are not enforceable, he must, on the date he became sick or injured, have been covered by a plan (or a program, policy, or custom having the effect of a plan), and notice or knowledge of such plan must have been readily available to him. Treas. Reg. §1.105-5(a). In order for there to be a plan, the employer must commit to certain rules and regulations governing payment, and these rules must be made known to employees as a definite policy before accident or sickness arises; *ad hoc* payments at the complete discretion of the employer do not qualify as a plan. *Est. of Kaufman*, 35 TC 663 (1961), *aff'd* 300 F.2d 128 (6th Cir. 1962); *Lang*, 41 TC 352 (1963); *Levine*, 50 TC 422 (1968); *Est. of Chism*, TC Memo 1962-6, *aff'd* 322 F.2d 956 (9th Cir. 1963); *Burr*, TC Memo 1966-112; *Frazier v. Comm.*, TC Memo 1994-358; *Harris*, 77-1 USTC ¶9414 (E.D. Va. 1977).

The plan must be *for employees*. A plan may cover one or more employees, and there may be different plans for different employees or classes of employees. Treas. Reg. §1.105-5(a); *Andress v. U.S.*, above. But a plan that is found to cover individuals in a capacity other than their employee status, even though they are employees, is not a plan for employees (see Q 165). Self-employed individuals and certain shareholders owning more than 2% of the stock of an S corporation are not treated as employees for the purpose of determining the excludability of employer-provided accident and health benefits. IRC Sec. 105(g); Treas. Reg. §1.105-5(b). See Q 166.

In addition, uninsured medical expense reimbursement plans for employees must meet nondiscrimination requirements in order for medical expense reimbursements to be tax free to highly compensated employees. See Q 162. *ASRS, Sec. 67, ¶320.6.*

162. What nondiscrimination requirements apply to employer provided health benefits?

Insured Plans

Other than the rules concerning discrimination based on health status under HIPAA '96—which apply generally to both insured and uninsured plans (see Q 186, Q 188)—a plan that provides health benefits through an accident or health insurance policy need not meet the nondiscrimination requirements of IRC Section 105(h) (discussed below) in order for covered employees to enjoy the tax benefits described in Q 160.

An accident or health insurance policy may be an individual or a group policy issued by a licensed insurance company, or "an arrangement in the nature of a prepaid health care plan" regulated under federal or state law (e.g., an HMO). However, unless the policy involves shifting of risk to an unrelated third party, the plan will be considered "self-insured." A plan is not considered self-insured merely because prior claims experience is one factor in determining the premium (see, for example, Let. Rul. 8235047). Furthermore, a policy of a captive insurance company is not considered self-insurance if, for the plan year, premiums paid to the captive insurer by unrelated companies are at least one-half of the total premiums received and the policy is similar to those sold to unrelated companies. Treas. Reg. §1.105-11(b). Likewise, a plan that reimburses employees for premiums paid under an insured plan does not have to satisfy nondiscrimination requirements.

Self-insured Plans

Nondiscrimination requirements *do* apply to self-insured health benefits. Generally, benefits under a self-insured plan are excludable from the employee's gross income. See Q 161. However, if a self-insured medical expense reimbursement plan or the self-insured part of a partly-insured medical expense reimbursement plan discriminates in favor of "highly compensated individuals," certain amounts paid to "highly compensated individuals" are taxable to them.

A self-insured plan is one in which reimbursement of medical expenses is not provided under a policy of accident and health insurance. IRC Sec. 105(h)(6). According to regulations, a plan underwritten by a cost-plus policy or a policy that, in effect, merely provides administrative or bookkeeping services is considered self-insured. Treas. Reg. §1.105-11(b).

A medical expense reimbursement plan cannot be implemented retroactively. To allow this would render meaningless the nondiscrimination requirements of IRC Section 105 (discussed below). *Wollenburg v. U.S.*, 75 F. Supp. 2d 1032 (DC Neb. 1999); *American Family Mut. Ins. Co. v. U.S.*, 815 F. Supp. 1206 (WD Wisc. 1992). See also Rev. Rul. 2002-58, 2002-38 IRB 541.

A self-insured plan may not discriminate in favor of "highly compensated individuals" (as described below), either with respect to eligibility to participate or benefits.

Eligibility. A plan discriminates as to *eligibility to participate* unless the plan benefits:

(1) 70% or more of all employees, or 80% or more of all the employees who are eligible to benefit under the plan if 70% or more of all employees are eligible to benefit under the plan; or

(2) such employees as qualify under a classification set up by the employer and found by IRS not to be discriminatory in favor of highly compensated individuals. IRC Sec. 105(h)(3)(A).

Excludable Employees. For purposes of these eligibility requirements, the employer may exclude from consideration those employees who: (1) have not completed three years of service at the beginning of the plan year (years of service during which an individual was ineligible under (2), (3), (4) or (5) must be counted for this purpose); (2) have not attained age 25 at the beginning of the plan year; (3) are part-time or seasonal employees (described below); (4) are covered by a collective bargaining agreement (if health benefits were the subject of good faith bargaining); and (5) are nonresident aliens with no U.S.-source earned income. IRC Sec. 105(h)(3)(B).

Part-time and Seasonal Workers. Employees customarily employed for fewer than 35 hours per week are considered part-time, and employees customarily employed for fewer than nine months per year are considered seasonal, if similarly situated employees of the employer (or in the same industry or location) are employed for substantially more hours or months, as applicable. Treas. Reg. §1.105-11(c). Employees customarily employed for fewer than 25 hours per week or seven months per year are considered part-time or seasonal under a safe harbor rule. Treas. Reg. §1.105-11(c)(2).

HEALTH INSURANCE   Q 163

Benefits. A plan discriminates as to *benefits* "unless all benefits provided for participants who are highly compensated individuals are provided for all other participants." IRC Sec. 105(h)(4). Benefits are not available to all participants if some participants become eligible immediately and others after a waiting period. Let. Ruls. 8411050, 8336065. Benefits available to dependents of highly compensated employees must be equally available to dependents of all other participating employees. The test is applied to benefits *subject* to reimbursement, rather than to the actual benefit payments or claims. Any maximum limit on the amount of reimbursement must be uniform for all participants and for all dependents, regardless of years of service or age. Further, the plan will be considered discriminatory if (1) the type or amount of benefits subject to reimbursement is offered in proportion to compensation; and (2) highly compensated employees are covered by the plan. A plan will not be considered discriminatory in operation merely because highly compensated participants *utilize* a broad range of plan benefits to a greater extent than do other participants. Treas. Reg. §1.105-11(c)(3).

An employer's plan will not violate the nondiscrimination rules merely because benefits under the plan are offset by benefits paid under a self-insured or insured plan of the employer or of another employer, or by benefits paid under Medicare or other federal or state law. A self-insured plan may take into account benefits provided under another plan only to the extent that the benefit is the same under both plans. Treas. Reg. §1.105-11(c)(1). Benefits provided to a retired employee who was highly compensated must be the same as benefits provided to all other retired participants.

For purposes of applying the nondiscrimination rules, all employees of a controlled group of corporations, of employers under common control, and of members of an affiliated service group (see Q 359, Q 360) are treated as employed by a single employer. IRC Sec. 105(h).

Highly Compensated Individual. An employee is a "highly compensated individual" if he falls into any *one* of the following three classifications:

(1) one of the five highest paid officers;

(2) a shareholder who owns—either actually or constructively through application of the attribution rules (see Q 83)—more than 10% in value of the employer's stock; or

(3) among the highest paid 25% (rounded to the nearest higher whole number) of all employees (other than excludable employees (described above) who are not participants, and not including retired participants). IRC Sec. 105(h)(5). Fiscal year plans may determine compensation on the basis of the calendar year ending in the plan year.

A participant's status as officer or stockholder with respect to a particular benefit is determined at the time when the benefit is provided. Treas. Reg. §1.105-11(d). *ASRS*, Sec. 67, ¶320.4.

163. How are amounts paid by an employer to highly compensated employees under a discriminatory self-insured medical expense reimbursement plan taxed?

The amount paid under a discriminatory self-insured medical expense reimbursement plan to a highly compensated individual that is taxable is the *excess reimbursement.* IRC Sec. 105(h)(1). Two situations produce an excess reimbursement:

2006 Tax Facts on Insurance & Employee Benefits

(1) In the case of a *benefit* available to a highly compensated individual but not to all other participants (or which otherwise discriminates in favor of highly compensated individuals), the total amount reimbursed under the plan to the employee with respect to such benefit is an excess reimbursement.

(2) In the case of benefits available to all other participants (and not otherwise discriminatory) where the plan discriminates as to *participation*, excess reimbursement is determined by multiplying the total amount reimbursed to the highly compensated individual *for the plan year* by a fraction. The numerator is the total amount reimbursed to all participants who are highly compensated individuals under the plan for the plan year; the denominator is the total amount reimbursed to all employees under the plan for such plan year. In determining the fraction, no account is taken of any reimbursement attributable to a benefit not available to all other participants. IRC Sec. 105(h)(7).

Multiple plans may be designated as a single plan for purposes of satisfying nondiscrimination requirements. An employee who elects to participate in an optional HMO offered by the plan is considered benefited by the plan only if the employer's contributions with respect to the employee are at least equal to what would have been made to the self-insured plan, and the HMO is designated, with the self-insured plan, as a single plan. (The regulations do not suggest how to determine "contributions" to a self-insured plan.)

Unless the plan provides otherwise, reimbursements will be attributed to the plan year in which payment is made; thus, they will be taxed in the individual's tax year in which the plan year ends.

Amounts reimbursed for medical diagnostic procedures for employees (not dependents) performed at a facility that provides only medical services are not considered a part of the plan and do not come within these rules requiring nondiscriminatory treatment. Treas. Reg. §1.105-11(g).

Contributory Plan

Reimbursements attributable to employee contributions are received tax free, subject to inclusion if the expense was previously deducted (see Q 160). Amounts attributable to employer contributions are determined in the ratio that employer contributions bear to total contributions for the calendar years immediately preceding the year of receipt (up to three years; if the plan has been in effect for less than a year, over that period.) Treas. Reg. §1.105-11(i).

Withholding

The employer does not have to withhold income tax on an amount paid for any medical care reimbursement made to or for the benefit of an employee under a self-insured medical reimbursement plan (within the meaning of IRC Section 105(h)(6)). IRC Sec. 3401(a)(20).

164. What are "domestic partnership" benefits, and how are they taxed?

Domestic partner benefits are benefits that an employer voluntarily offers to an employee's unmarried partner. An employee's domestic partner may be of the same sex or the opposite sex. The employer decides the plan's definition of domestic partner.

HEALTH INSURANCE

Q 165

Employers may offer a range of domestic partnership benefits, such as family, bereavement, sick leave, and relocation benefits. In general, however, most people mean employer-provided health insurance coverage when they speak of domestic partnership benefits.

An employee is taxed on the value of employer-provided health benefits for his or her domestic partner, unless the domestic partner qualifies as the employee's dependent under IRC Section 151. The tax is determined by assessing the fair market value of the coverage provided to the domestic partner. This amount is then reported on the employee's W-2 form and is subjected to Social Security (FICA) and federal income tax withholding taxes.

Any amount received by the domestic partner as payment or reimbursement of plan benefits will not be included in the income of the employee or the domestic partner to the extent that (1) the coverage provided to the domestic partner was paid for by the employee's plan contributions; or (2) the fair market value of the coverage was included in the employee's income under IRC Section 104(a)(3). Let. Ruls. 9850011, 9717018, 9603011. See also Let. Ruls. 9109060, 9034048. See also Field Service Advice 199911012.

Coverage of domestic partners (whether or not they qualify as dependents) under an employer-provided health plan will not otherwise affect the ability of employees to exclude amounts paid, directly or indirectly, by the plan to reimburse employees for expenses incurred for medical care of the employees, their spouses, and dependents.

Cafeteria Plans and Flexible Spending Accounts. Contributions used to provide coverage for a non-dependent domestic partner are treated as taxable income. Benefits under flexible spending accounts may not be provided to such a domestic partner, because such accounts can include only nontaxable income. See Q 99.

COBRA. A domestic partner may not make an independent election for COBRA coverage. A domestic partner may be part of an employee's election. See Q 173 through Q 185.

HIPAA. Domestic partners that are not dependents are not covered by HIPAA. However, employers providing health insurance to domestic partners may voluntarily include them in HIPAA certification procedures. See Q 186.

Stockholder-Employees, Self-Employed Individuals

165. How are accident or health benefits taxed if they are provided by a closely held C corporation to its stockholder-employees only?

In order to provide tax free coverage and benefits, an employer's accident or health plan must be *for employees.* IRC Sec. 105(e). The IRS can challenge tax benefits claimed under a plan that covers only stockholder-employees on the ground that the plan is not for employees. The underlying problem is in establishing that the stockholder-employees are covered *as employees* rather than as stockholders. If this cannot be established, then premiums or benefits are likely to be treated as dividends–premiums nondeductible by the corporation and premiums or benefits includable in the gross incomes of the covered stockholder-employees. *Larkin v. Comm.*, 48 TC 629 (1967), *aff'd* 394 F.2d 494 (1st Cir. 1968); *Levine v. Comm.*, 50 TC 422 (1968); *Smithback v. Comm.*, TC Memo 1969-136; *Est. of Leidy v. Comm.*, 77-1 USTC ¶9144 (4th Cir. 1977).

2006 Tax Facts on Insurance & Employee Benefits

Courts have taken the position that the tax benefits of employer-provided health insurance are available in a plan that covers only stockholder-employees *if* the plan covers a class of employees that can be rationally segregated from the other employees, if any, on a criterion other than their being stockholders. *Bogene, Inc. v. Comm.*, TC Memo 1968-147; *Smith v. Comm.*, TC Memo 1970-243; *Seidel v. Comm.*, TC Memo 1971-238; *Epstein v. Comm.*, TC Memo 1972-53; *American Foundry v. Comm.*, 76-1 USTC ¶9401 (9th Cir. 1976); *Charlie Sturgill Motor Co. v. Comm.*, TC Memo 1973-281; *Oleander Co., Inc. v. U.S.*, 82-1 USTC ¶9395 (E.D.N.C. 1981); *Giberson v. Comm.*, TC Memo 1982-338; *Est. of Leidy*, above; *Wigutow v. Comm.*, TC Memo 1983-620.

Bogene, *Smith*, *Seidel*, and *Epstein* were decided in favor of the taxpayers; the plans in all of them covered only the active and compensated officers of the corporation, who were also stockholders. In *Smith* and *Seidel*, the officer-shareholders were also the only employees, but in *Bogene* and *Epstein*, there were other employees who were not shareholders and who were not covered. The plan in *American Foundry* covered only two of five active officers of a family corporation and was held not to be a plan for employees. The plan in *Sturgill* covered four officer-stockholders of a family corporation, but two of the four were not active or compensated as officer-employees and the plan was held not to be one for employees. The plan in *Leidy* covered only the president (sole stockholder) and the vice president, who was no longer active in the company. In *American Foundry* and in *Sturgill*, the courts allowed the corporation to deduct reimbursement payments to the active officers as reasonable compensation, even though the payments were not excludable by the shareholder-employees under IRC Section 105.

In the case of an S corporation, see Q 166. *ASRS, Sec. 67, ¶120.1.*

166. How is health insurance coverage for partners, sole proprietors, and S corporation shareholders taxed?

Partners and Sole Proprietors

Generally, partners and sole proprietors are self-employed individuals, not employees, and the rules for personal health insurance usually apply (see Q 154, Q 155). However, partners and sole proprietors can deduct 100% of amounts paid during a taxable year for insurance that provides medical care for the individual, his spouse, and dependents during the tax year. IRC Sec. 162(l). Additionally, certain premiums paid for long-term care insurance are eligible for this deduction. IRC Secs. 162(l)(2)(C), 213(d)(1). See Q 315.

The deduction is not available to a partner or sole proprietor for any calendar month in which he is eligible to participate in any subsidized health plan maintained by any employer of the self-employed individual or his spouse. IRC Sec. 162(l). This rule is applied separately to plans that include coverage for qualified long-term care services or are qualified long-term care insurance contracts (see Q 311), and plans that do not include such coverage and are not such contracts. IRC Sec. 162(l)(2)(B).

The deduction is allowable in calculating adjusted gross income and is limited to the self-employed individual's earned income for the tax year that is derived from the trade or business with respect to which the plan providing medical care coverage is established. (Earned income is, in general, net earnings from self-employment with respect to a trade or business in which the personal services of the taxpayer are a material income producing factor. See also Q 358 if contributions are made to a qualified retirement plan.)

HEALTH INSURANCE
Q 166

Any amounts paid for such insurance may not be taken into account in computing the amount of any medical expense deduction under IRC Section 213. IRC Sec. 162(l)(3). Any amount paid for such insurance may not be taken into account in computing net-earnings from self-employment for the purpose of determining the tax on self-employment income. IRC Sec. 162(l)(4).

If a partnership pays accident and health insurance premiums for services rendered by the partners in their capacity as partners and without regard to partnership income, the premium payments are considered to be "guaranteed" payments under IRC Section 707(c). Thus, the premiums are deductible by the partnership under IRC Section 162 (subject to IRC Section 263) and includable in the partners' income under IRC Section 61. The partner may not exclude the premium payments from income under IRC Section 106, but may deduct the payments to the extent allowable under IRC Section 162(l), as discussed above. Rev. Rul. 91-26, 1991-1 CB 184.

Reasoning that consumer medical cards that provide discounts on certain medical services and items are not an insurance product, the IRS concluded that the cost of such cards purchased for partners is not deductible by the partners under either IRC Section 162(l) or IRC Section 213. Let. Rul. 9814023.

Regarding the income tax consequences of a self-funded medical reimbursement plan set up by a partnership, the IRS concluded that payments from the plan made to partners and their dependents are excludable from the partners' income and premiums paid by the partners for coverage under the self-funded plan are deductible, subject to the limitations of IRC Section 162(l). Let. Rul. 200007025.

There is no limit, however, on the amount of *benefits* a partner or sole proprietor can receive tax free. Rev. Rul. 56-326, 1956-2 CB 100; Rev. Rul. 58-90, 1958-1 CB 88. But for tax treatment of business overhead disability insurance, see Q 97.

IRS rulings have indicated that coverage purchased by a sole proprietor or partnership for non-owner-employees, including the owner's spouse, are generally subject to the same rules that apply in any other employer-employee situation. Rev. Rul. 71-588, 1971-2 CB 91; TAM 9409006. See Q 159 through Q 167. In 2001, the IRS issued settlement guidelines that address whether a self-employed individual ("employer-spouse") may hire his spouse as an employee ("employee-spouse") and provide family health benefits to the employee-spouse, who then elects family coverage including the employer-spouse. Essentially, the IRS position is that if the employee-spouse is a bona fide employee, the employer-spouse may deduct the cost of the coverage, and the value of the coverage is also excludable from the employee-spouse's gross income. IRS agents are to use the settlement guidelines to closely scrutinize whether an employee-spouse qualifies as a bona fide employee—merely calling a spouse an employee is insufficient. Part-time employment does not negate employee status, but nominal or insignificant services that have no economic substance or independent significance will be challenged. IRS Settlement Guidelines, 2001 TNT 222-25 (Nov. 16, 2001); see also *Poyda v. Comm.*, TC Summary Opinion 2001-91.

S Corporation Shareholder-Employees

A shareholder-employee who owns more than 2% (attribution rules apply) of the outstanding stock or voting power of an S corporation will be treated like a partner, not an employee. IRC Sec. 1372. Thus, accident and health insurance premium payments for more-than-2% shareholders paid in consideration for services rendered are treated like guaranteed payments made to partners. Therefore, the S corporation can deduct the premiums under IRC Section 162 and the shareholder-employee must include the premium payments in income under IRC Section 61 and cannot exclude them under IRC Section 106. The shareholder-employee may then deduct the cost of the premiums to the extent permitted by IRC Section 162(l), as discussed above. Rev. Rul. 91-26, 1991-1 CB 184.

With respect to coverage purchased by an S corporation for employees not owning any stock and for shareholder-employees owning 2% or less of the outstanding stock or voting power, the same rules apply as in any other employer-employee situation. See Q 159, Q 210, Q 211, Q 212, Q 213. *ASRS, Sec. 67, ¶¶120.2, 120.3.*

Employer's Deduction

167. May an employer deduct the cost of premiums paid for accident and health insurance for employees as a business expense?

As a general rule, an employer can deduct all premiums paid for health insurance for one or more employees as a business expense. This includes premiums for medical expense insurance and dismemberment and sight loss coverage for the employee, his spouse, and dependents, disability income for the employee (see Q 194), and accidental death coverage. For deductibility of long-term care insurance premiums, see Q 317.

The premiums are deductible by the employer whether the coverage is provided under a group policy or under individual policies. However, the deduction for health insurance is allowable only if the benefits are payable to employees or their beneficiaries; it is not allowable if the benefits are payable to the employer. Treas. Reg. §1.162-10(a); Rev. Rul. 58-90, 1958-1 CB 88; Rev. Rul. 56-632, 1956-2 CB 101; Rev. Rul. 210, 1953-2 CB 114. But, where the spouse of the employer is a bona fide employee and the employer is covered as a family member, the premium is deductible. Rev. Rul. 71-588, 1971-2 CB 91; TAM 9409006. A corporation can deduct the premiums it pays on group hospitalization coverage for commission salespersons, regardless of whether they are employees. Rev. Rul. 56-400, 1956-2 CB 116. The premiums must qualify as additional reasonable compensation to the insured. *Ernest Holdeman & Collet, Inc. v. Comm.*, TC Memo 1960-10. See Rev. Rul. 58-90, supra.

If the payment is considered made to a "fund" that is part of an employer plan to provide the benefit, the deduction for amounts paid or accrued may be limited as explained in Q 494.

An accrual basis employer that provides medical benefits to employees directly (instead of through insurance or an intermediary fund) may not deduct amounts estimated to be necessary to pay for medical care provided in the year, but for which claims have not been filed with the employer by the end of the year, if filing a claim is necessary to establish the employer's liability for payment. *U.S. v. General Dynamics Corp.*, 481 U.S. 239 (1987).

In the case of a plan covering stockholder-employees only, see Q 165; in case of an S corporation, partnership, or sole proprietor employer, see Q 166.

Where health benefits are provided through a fund, see Q 494. *ASRS, Sec. 67, ¶330.*

Health Reimbursement Arrangements

168. What is a Health Reimbursement Arrangement (HRA) and how is it taxed?

According to IRS guidance, an HRA is an arrangement that: (1) is solely employer-funded, not paid for directly or indirectly by salary reduction contributions under a cafeteria plan; and (2) reimburses employees for substantiated medical care expenses (see Q 826) incurred by the employee and the employee's spouse and dependents—as defined in IRC Section 152 (see Q 820)—up to a maximum dollar amount per coverage period. The IRS has approved the use of employer-issued debit and credit cards to pay for medical expenses as incurred, provided that the employer has in place sufficient procedures to substantiate the payments. Rev. Proc. 2003-43, 2003-21 IRB 935. Unused amounts in an individual's account must be carried forward to increase the maximum reimbursement amount in subsequent coverage periods. Notice 2002-45, 2002-2 CB 93; Rev. Rul. 2002-41, 2002-2 CB 75. HRAs are not available for self-employed individuals.

Employer-provided coverage and medical care reimbursement amounts under an HRA are excludable from the employee's gross income under IRC Section 106 and IRC Section 105(b), assuming all requirements for HRAs are met. Notice 2002-45, above; Rev. Rul. 2002-41, above.

According to Notice 2002-45, an HRA may not offer cash-outs at any time, even upon termination of service or retirement; however, it may continue to reimburse former employees for medical care expenses after such events, even if the employee does not elect COBRA continuation coverage. An HRA is a group health plan and, thus, subject to the COBRA continuation coverage requirements. See Q 173 through Q 185.

HRAs may not be used to reimburse expenses incurred before the HRA was in existence, nor expenses that are deductible under Section 213 for a prior taxable year. However, an unreimbursed claim incurred in one coverage period may be reimbursed in a later coverage period, so long as the individual was covered under the HRA when the claim was incurred. Notice 2002-45, above.

An employee may not be reimbursed for the same medical care expense by both an HRA and an IRC Section 125 health FSA. Technically, ordering rules from the IRS specify that the HRA benefits must be exhausted before FSA reimbursements may be made. However, an HRA can be drafted to specify that coverage under the HRA is available only after expenses exceeding the dollar amount of the IRC Section 125 FSA have been paid. Thus, an employee could exhaust his FSA coverage (which is not allowed to be carried over) before tapping into his HRA coverage (which can be carried over). Notice 2002-45, above.

The notice makes it clear that employer contributions to an HRA may not be attributable in any way to salary reductions. Thus, the HRA cannot be offered under a cafeteria plan, but it can be offered in conjunction with a cafeteria plan. Where the HRA is offered in conjunction with another accident or health plan funded pursuant to salary reductions, then a "facts and circumstances" test is used to determine if the salary reductions are attributable to the HRA. If the salary reduction amount for a coverage period to fund the non-HRA accident or health plan exceeds the actual cost of the non-specified accident or health plan coverage, the salary reduction will be attributed to the HRA. An example of the application of this rule can be found in Rev. Rul. 2002-41, above.

Since an HRA may not be paid for through salary reduction, the following restrictions on health FSAs are not applicable to HRAs: (1) the ban against a benefit that defers compensation by permitting employees to carry over unused elective contributions or plan benefits from one plan year to another plan year; (2) the requirement that the maximum amount of reimbursement must be available at all times during the coverage period; (3) the mandatory twelve-month period of coverage; and (4) the limitation that medical expenses reimbursed must be incurred during the period of coverage. Notice 2002-45, above. Future guidance will modify proposed regulations under IRC Section 125 to clarify that HRAs are not subject to the regulations applicable to health FSAs that are provided pursuant to a salary reduction election under a cafeteria plan.

Withholding

169. Are wage continuation payments under an accident and health plan subject to withholding?

Employers (or former employers) must withhold tax from payments made to an employee for a period of absence from work due to injury or sickness. If the employer has shifted the insurance risk to an insurer or trust, no income tax need be withheld from wage continuation payments that an insurance company or a separate trust makes on behalf of an employer. Treas. Reg. §31.3401(a)-1(b)(8); Rev. Rul. 77-89, 1977-1 CB 300. However, amounts paid (under a plan to which the employer is a party) as sick pay during a temporary absence may be withheld by a third party payor at the employee's request. IRC Sec. 3402(o); Treas. Reg. §31.3402(o)-3. (Amounts paid by a third party are wages subject to mandatory withholding if the insurance risk is not shifted by such an arrangement, because the third party is acting as the employer's agent if the employer reimburses the insurance company or trust on a cost plus fee basis. Treas. Reg. §31.3401(a)-1(b)(8).) *ASRS, Sec. 53, ¶¶20.4(i), 20.4(j); Sec. 67, ¶320.4.*

Social Security

170. Is employer-provided "sick pay" subject to social security and federal unemployment tax?

Preretirement wage continuation payments by an employer or an insurance company to an employee because of his sickness or disability are subject to social security tax (FICA) and federal unemployment tax (FUTA) for the first six calendar months after the last month in which the employee worked for the employer. After six months, they are exempt from social security and federal unemployment tax. IRC Secs. 3121(a)(4), 3306(b)(4). The portion of payments from a contributory plan attributable to employee contributions is generally not subject to social security tax. See IRC Sec. 6051(f)(2)(B); Treas. Reg. §31.6051-3(b)(4). It would seem the same exemption for employee contributions would apply with respect to federal unemployment tax. *ASRS, Sec. 67, ¶320.5.*

Information Return

171. Must an employer who maintains an accident or health plan file an information return with respect to the plan?

A plan that covers fewer than 100 employees on the first day of the plan year and is unfunded, fully insured, or a combination of unfunded and fully insured is exempt from the requirement to file an annual report (Form 5500 series) with the IRS. All other plans must file a Form 5500. *Instructions to Form 5500, Annual Return/Report of Employee Benefit Plan, p.3.*

IRC Section 6039D requires an employer maintaining *any* accident or health plan to file an annual information return with the IRS for years beginning after December 31, 1988. However, until the issuance of further guidance, the IRS has indefinitely suspended the reporting requirements of IRC Section 6039D. Notice 90-24, 1990-1 CB 335.

If in effect, IRC Section 6039D would require the following information to be reported: the number of employer's (1) employees; (2) employees eligible to participate in the plan; (3) employees participating in the plan; (4) highly compensated employees (HCEs); (5) HCEs eligible to participate in the plan; and (6) HCEs actually participating in the plan. The return must also report (1) the cost of the plan; (2) the identity of the employer; and (3) the type of business in which the employer is engaged. IRC Sec. 6039D. *ASRS, Sec. 67, ¶350.*

172. What notice must an employer who maintains an accident or health plan provide to Medicare-eligible individuals?

COBRA Continuation Coverage Requirements

Employers and plan sponsors who offer prescription drug coverage to individuals eligible for Medicare Part D must advise those individuals whether the offered coverage is "creditable." Under the Medicare Prescription Drug, Improvement, and Modernization Act of 2003 (MMA), eligible individuals who do not enroll in Part D when first available, but who enroll later, have to pay higher premiums permanently, unless they have creditable prescription drug coverage.

To determine that coverage is creditable, a sponsor need only determine that total expected paid claims for Medicare beneficiaries under the sponsor's plan will be at least equal to the total expected paid claims for the same beneficiaries under the defined standard prescription drug coverage under Part D. The determination of creditable coverage status for disclosure purposes does not require attestation by a qualified actuary (unless the employer or union is applying for the retiree drug subsidy available under the MMA).

To assist sponsors in making the determination that coverage is creditable, the Center for Medicare & Medicaid Studies (CMS) issued guidance with example "safe harbor" benefit designs. A plan design will automatically be deemed creditable if it includes

1. coverage for brand and generic prescriptions;

2. reasonable access to retail providers and, optionally, for mail order coverage;

3. benefits payments designed to pay on average at least 60% of participants' prescription drug expenses; and

4. at least one of the following:

    a. an annual prescription drug benefit maximum of at least $25,000,

b. an actuarial expectation that the plan will pay benefits of at least $2,000 per Medicare-eligible individual in 2006, or

   c. for plans that cover both medical expenses and prescription drugs, an annual deductible of no more than $250, an annual benefit maximum of at least $25,000, and a lifetime maximum of at least $1,000,000.

Under the CMS guidance, once a sponsor determines whether coverage is creditable, the sponsor must provide notice to all Part D-eligible individuals covered by or applying for the plan, including Part D-eligible dependents. In lieu of determining who is Part D eligible, an employer sponsor may provide notice to all active employees, along with an explanation of why the notice is being provided.

The required notice to beneficiaries must, at a minimum,

1. contain a statement that the employer has determined that the coverage is creditable (or not creditable),

2. explain the meaning of creditable coverage,

3. explain why creditable coverage is important, and caution that higher Part D premiums could result if there is a break in creditable coverage of 63 days or more before enrolling in a Part D plan, and

4. if coverage is not creditable, explain that an individual may only enroll in Part D from November 15, 2005 through May 15, 2006 and at other specified times thereafter.

The CMS guidance includes model initial notices that a sponsor may choose to use. Sponsors were required to provide initial notices to beneficiaries by November 15, 2005. Sponsors must also disclose to CMS whether the coverage is creditable. CMS will outline the requirements for this disclosure in future guidance. 42 CFR § 423.56. *ASRS, Sec. 15, ¶100.*

173. What coverage continuation or "COBRA" requirements must certain group health plans meet?

Any insured or self-funded group health plan maintained by an employer to provide health care, directly or otherwise, to the employer's employees, former employees, or their families must generally offer COBRA continuation coverage. IRC Sec. 4980B(g)(2); Treas. Reg. §54.4980B-2, A-1. Certain plans are exempt from the COBRA continuation coverage rules. See Q 174. Insured plans are not only those providing coverage under group policies, but include any arrangement to provide health care to two or more employees under individual policies. Treas. Reg. §54.4980B-2, A-1.

Generally, COBRA does not require plan sponsors to offer continuation coverage for disability income coverage. *Austell v. Raymond James & Assoc., Inc.*, 80 AFTR2d ¶97-5160 (4th Cir. 1997). For contracts issued after 1996, the COBRA requirements do not apply to plans under which substantially all of the coverage is for qualified long-term care services. IRC Sec. 4980B(g)(2). A plan may use any reasonable method to determine whether substantially all of the coverage under the plan is for qualified long-term care

HEALTH INSURANCE   Q 173

services. Treas. Reg. §54.4980B-2, A-1(e). Additionally, amounts contributed by an employer to an Archer MSA (Medical Savings Account—see Q 209) are not considered part of a group health plan subject to the COBRA continuation requirements. Treas. Reg. §54.4980B-2, A-1(f).

Employer-sponsored health care plans subject to the COBRA requirements must provide that if, as a result of a *qualifying event*, any *qualified beneficiary* would lose coverage under the plan, the qualified beneficiary must be entitled to elect, within the *election period*, *continuation coverage* under the plan. IRC Sec. 4980B(f)(1); Treas. Reg. §54.4980B-1, A-1.

Further, generally, a group health plan will not meet the COBRA requirements unless the plan's coverage of the cost of pediatric vaccines is not reduced below the coverage provided by the plan as of May 1, 1993. IRC Sec. 4980B(f)(1).

Continuation Coverage Defined

COBRA continuation coverage must consist of coverage identical to that provided under the plan to similarly situated beneficiaries with respect to whom a qualifying event has not occurred. Any modification of coverage for similarly situated beneficiaries must also apply in the same manner for all COBRA qualified beneficiaries. IRC Sec. 4980B(f)(2). A case brought under the COBRA provisions of ERISA held that an employer did not meet its obligation to offer continuation coverage where the only health plan available to a qualified beneficiary (following the insolvency of a self-insured multiemployer trust under which she had originally elected COBRA coverage) was a geographically-restrictive HMO which did not provide service in the area of her residence. *Coble v. Bonita House, Inc.*, 789 F. Supp. 320 (N. D. Cal. 1992).

Qualified beneficiaries electing COBRA coverage are generally subject to the same deductibles as similarly situated non-COBRA beneficiaries. Treas. Reg. §54.4980B-5, A-2. Amounts accumulated toward deductibles, plan benefits, and plan cost limits prior to a qualifying event are carried over into the COBRA continuation coverage period. Treas. Regs. §§54.4980B-5, A-2, 54.4980B-5, A-3.

Generally, a qualified beneficiary electing COBRA continuation coverage need not be given the opportunity to change coverage from the type he was receiving prior to the qualifying event, even where the coverage is of lesser or no value to the qualified beneficiary, except in two situations. First, if a qualified beneficiary was participating in a region-specific plan that does not provide services in the region to which he is relocating, the qualified beneficiary must be able, within a reasonable period after requesting other coverage, to elect the alternative coverage that the employer or employee organization makes available to active employees. However, an employer or employee organization is not required to make any other coverage available to a relocating qualified beneficiary if the only coverage that the employer makes available to active employees is not available in the area where the qualified beneficiary is relocating. Second, if the employer or employee organization makes an open enrollment period available to similarly situated active employees, the same open enrollment period rights must be offered to each qualified beneficiary receiving COBRA coverage. Treas. Reg. §54.4980B-5, A-4.

Effective Dates of COBRA Requirements and Regulations

Generally, the COBRA continuation coverage requirements are in effect for plan years beginning on or after July 1, 1986, with slightly later dates applicable to group health plans maintained pursuant to collective bargaining agreements. COBRA, Sec. 1001(e). In 1999, the IRS issued proposed and final COBRA regulations, which were in effect with respect to qualifying events occurring in plan years beginning on or after January 1, 2000. In January of 2001, the IRS issued final regulations supplementing the 1999 final regulations and adopting the proposed regulations with modifications. In general, these 2001 regulations apply with respect to qualifying events occurring on or after January 1, 2002. 66 Fed. Reg. 1843 (1-10-01). In 2003, the Department of Labor issued proposed regulations updating the various notice and disclosure requirements under COBRA (see Q 183). The regulations were effective in their final form for plan years beginning in 2004. 29 CFR Part 2590, 68 Fed. Reg. 31831 (05-28-03). *ASRS, Sec. 67, ¶¶410, 420.3, 430.5.*

174. Are all employers subject to the COBRA continuation coverage requirements?

No. Church plans (as defined in IRC Section 414(e)), governmental plans (as defined in IRC Section 414(d)), and "small-employer plans" are not subject to the COBRA continuation coverage requirements. IRC Sec. 4980B(d).

A small-employer plan is defined as a group health plan maintained by an employer that normally employed fewer than 20 employees during the preceding calendar year on a typical business day. IRC Sec. 4980B(d). Under final regulations, an employer is considered to have employed fewer than 20 employees during a calendar year if it had fewer than 20 employees on at least 50% of its typical business days during that year. Treas. Reg. §54.4980B-2, A-5. Only common law employees are taken into account for purposes of the small-employer exception. Self-employed individuals, independent contractors, and directors are not counted. Treas. Reg. §54.4980B-2, A-5. In the case of a multiemployer plan, a small-employer plan is a group health plan under which each of the employers contributing to the plan for a calendar year normally employed fewer than 20 employees during the preceding calendar year. Treas. Reg. §54.4980B-2, A-5. *ASRS, Sec. 67, ¶420.2.*

175. What is a qualifying event for purposes of the COBRA continuation coverage requirements?

A qualifying event is any of the following events that, but for the required COBRA continuation coverage, would result in the loss of coverage of (1) a covered employee; or (2) the spouse or dependent child of a covered employee under the plan:

1. death of a covered employee;

2. voluntary or involuntary termination—for reasons other than the covered employee's gross misconduct (see Q 176)—or reduction in hours of the covered employee's employment;

3. divorce or legal separation of the covered employee;

4. the covered employee becoming entitled to Medicare benefits;

5. a dependent child ceasing to be a dependent child for purposes of the plan;

6. a proceeding under the bankruptcy provisions of the U.S. Code with respect to the employer from whose employment the covered employee retired at any time.

IRC Sec. 4980B(f)(3); Treas. Reg. §54.4980B-4, A-1.

The taking of a leave under the Family and Medical Leave Act of 1993 (FMLA) is not a qualifying event. However, a qualifying event does occur when an employee is covered under the employer's group health plan the day before an FMLA leave, the employee does not come back to work at the end of the leave, and the employee would lose coverage under the plan (other than under the COBRA continuation coverage) before the end of what would be the maximum coverage period. The same is true for a spouse or dependent child of the employee. Treas. Reg. §54.4980B-10, A-1. The date that such a qualifying event occurs is the last day of the employee's FMLA leave, and the period of maximum coverage is measured from this day. Treas. Reg. §54.4980B-10, A-2.

However, if an employer eliminates coverage for a class of employees to which the employee on FMLA leave would otherwise have belonged on or before the last day of the employee's FMLA leave, there is no qualifying event. Treas. Reg. §54.4980B-10, A-1. A qualifying event can occur even if an employee does not pay his share of the premiums for coverage under the group health plan during an FMLA leave, or even if the employee declined coverage during the FMLA leave. Treas. Reg. §54.4980B-10, A-3; Notice 94-103, 1994-2 CB 569. Further, COBRA continuation coverage may not be conditioned upon the employee reimbursing the employer for premiums paid by the employer for group health plan coverage during an FMLA leave taken by the employee. Treas. Reg. §54.4980B-10, A-5.

There is no qualifying event where, following a termination of employment, a loss of coverage does not occur until after the end of what would have been the maximum period of COBRA continuation coverage. *Williams v. Teamsters Local Union No. 727*, Case No. 03 C 2122 (N.D. Ill., 10-22-03).

The call to active military duty of reserve personnel has been characterized as a qualifying event by the IRS. Although not specifically stated, presumably the event is a reduction in hours. Notice 90-58, 1990-2 CB 345. *ASRS, Sec. 67, ¶430.1.*

176. What is meant by the term "gross misconduct"?

If a covered employee's employment is terminated for "gross misconduct," no COBRA continuation coverage is available to him or to his qualified beneficiaries. IRC Sec. 4980B(f)(3)(B); ERISA Sec. 603(2). If the employer fails to notify the employee at the time of his termination that it is on account of gross misconduct, its ability to deny COBRA coverage may be undermined. See, e.g., *Mlsna v. Unitel Com., Inc.*, 91 F.3d 876 (7th Cir. 1996).

The fact that the employer has grounds to terminate an employee for gross misconduct does not support a denial of COBRA coverage if the employee voluntarily resigns in order to avoid being fired. And an allegation of gross misconduct after a voluntary termination cannot be used to evade liability where the employer has not properly processed a COBRA election and the carrier refuses to extend coverage.

Conery v. Bath Assoc., 803 F. Supp. 1388 (N.D. Ind. 1992). The Seventh Circuit Court of Appeals decided that it is not sufficient that the employer believed, in good faith, that the employee had engaged in gross misconduct. The district court had held that the proper test is not whether an employee actually engaged in gross misconduct, but whether the employer believed in good faith that she had. The appeals court held that COBRA requires more than a good faith belief by the employer, and that the employee should have been given the chance to demonstrate that the employer was mistaken, and thus obtain her COBRA rights. *Kariotis v. Navistar Int'l Transp. Corp.*, 131 F.3d 672 (7th Cir. 1997).

An insurance carrier is bound by the employer's determination, and cannot decline COBRA coverage merely because the employer might have been entitled to terminate the employee on grounds of gross misconduct. *Conery v. Bath Assoc.*, 803 F. Supp. 1388 (N.D. Ind. 1992).

Case Law Examples

Gross misconduct is not defined in the statute or in the regulations. The IRS has announced that it will not issue rulings on whether an action constitutes gross misconduct for COBRA purposes. Rev. Proc. 92-3, 1992-1 CB 561. For these reasons, the concept of gross misconduct has developed through case law. Mere incompetence is not gross misconduct. *Mlsna v. Unitel Com., Inc.*, 91 F.3d 876 (7th Cir. 1996). One court has held that breach of a company confidence did not constitute "gross misconduct." *Paris v. F. Korbel & Bros., Inc.*, 751 F. Supp. 834 (N.D. Cal. 1990). An employee did not engage in gross misconduct by falsifying mileage reports, failing to attend mandatory meetings, and receiving an unsolicited offer of employment. *Cabral v. The Olsten Corp.*, 843 F. Supp. 701 (M.D. Fla. 1994).

Under a state law definition of gross misconduct, an employee who admitted stealing the employer's merchandise was considered to have been terminated for gross misconduct and, thus, was not entitled to COBRA continuation coverage. *Burke v. American Stores Employee Benefit Plan*, 818 F. Supp. 1131 (N.D. Ill. 1993). "Cash handling irregularities, invoice irregularities, and the failure to improve the performance of one of defendant's stores" was held to be gross misconduct. *Avina v. Texas Pig Stands, Inc.*, 1991 U.S. Dist. LEXIS 13957 (W.D. Tex. 1991).

In a case where the court concluded that Congress left the definition of gross misconduct up to the individual employer, two employees who had been terminated for refusing to comply with the directions of a supervisor were considered to have been terminated for gross misconduct. *Bryant v. Food Lion, Inc.*, 100 F. Supp.2d 346 (D. S.C. 2000).

A bank employee who cashed a fellow employee's check knowing there were insufficient funds to satisfy it, and held the check in her cash drawer until the check could be covered was held to have been terminated for gross misconduct. *Moffitt v. Blue Cross & Blue Shield Miss.*, 722 F. Supp. 1391 (N.D. Miss. 1989). A bank employee's violation of the employer's corporate credit card policy and blatant misrepresentation concerning a small loan application to a federal agency constituted gross misconduct. *Johnson v. Shawmut Nat'l Corp.*, 1994 U.S. Dist. LEXIS 19437 (D. Mass, 1994).

In some cases, the conduct was egregious. One court held that a security guard who "deserted his post...and was found asleep at his residence" and falsified records, creating a

HEALTH INSURANCE   Q 177

fictional guard in order to collect another paycheck, was terminated for gross misconduct. *Adkins v. United Int'l Investigative Servs, Inc.*, 1992 U.S. Dist. LEXIS 4719 (N.D. Calif. 1992). Throwing an apple at a co-worker and uttering racial slurs was found to be gross misconduct. *Nakisa v. Continental Airlines*, 26 EBC 1568 (S.D. Texas 2001).

Misconduct need not take place on the job to constitute gross misconduct. Off-duty behavior may also eliminate an employee's right to elect COBRA coverage. Gross misconduct was found where an employee assaulted a subordinate (with whom he was having a romantic relationship) while away from the workplace. *Zickafoose v. UB Servs., Inc.*, 23 F. Supp.2d 652 (S.D.W.V. 1998). Having an accident while driving a company vehicle under the influence of alcohol and on company business constituted gross misconduct, even though a misdemeanor offense under state law. *Collins v. Aggreko, Inc.*, 884 F. Supp. 450 (D. Utah 1995). *ASRS, Sec. 67, ¶430.1.*

177. How long must COBRA continuation coverage be provided?

COBRA continuation coverage must be provided from the date of the qualifying event until the earliest date when any one of the following events occurs:

1. The passage of the maximum required period of coverage.

2. The date on which the employer ceases to provide any group health plan to any employee.

3. The date on which coverage ceases under the plan by reason of a failure to make timely payment of the applicable premium (see Q 180).

4. The date on which the qualified beneficiary *first becomes*, after the date of the election, covered (as an employee, or otherwise) under any other plan providing health care (see below) that does not contain any exclusion or limitation with respect to any pre-existing condition of such beneficiary (other than such an exclusion or limitation which does not apply to, or is satisfied by, such beneficiary by reason of the portability, access, and renewability requirements for group health plans found in the Code as well as in similar sections of ERISA and the Public Health Service Act–see Q 186 through Q 191).

5. The date on which the qualified beneficiary (other than a retired covered employee or a spouse, surviving spouse, or dependent child of the covered employee) first becomes, after the date of the election, entitled to Medicare benefits (see below).

6. In the case of a qualified beneficiary who is disabled at any time during the first 60 days of continuation coverage, the month that begins more than 30 days after the date when the Social Security Administration has made a final determination (under title II or XVI of the Social Security Act) that he is no longer disabled.

IRC Sec. 4980B(f)(2)(B).

Becomes Covered. Applying a strict reading of IRC Section 4980B(f)(2)(B), the Supreme Court found that an employee whose employment has been terminated is

2006 Tax Facts on Insurance & Employee Benefits

eligible to elect COBRA continuation coverage under his former employer's group health plan despite the fact that he also had coverage under another plan offered by his spouse's employer at the time his employment was terminated. In effect, the Court concluded that an employee with coverage under another plan *at the time of termination of employment* does not fall within the requirement that, "the qualified beneficiary first becomes, after the date of the election,..." covered under any another medical care plan. *Geissal v. Moore Medical Corp.*, 524 U.S. 74 (1998); 118 S. Ct. 1869 (1998); Treas. Reg. §54.4980B-7, A-2. See also Ann. 98-22, 1998-12 IRB 33.

A plan of the federal government is not considered another plan providing health care for this purpose, because the federal government is not an employer under IRC Section 5000(d). Thus, eligibility for a federal government group health plan will not terminate COBRA continuation coverage. Notice 90-58, 1990-2 CB 345. See also *McGee v. Funderburg*, 17 F.3d 1122 (8th Cir. 1994).

Medicare. Being entitled to Medicare benefits is defined not as mere eligibility for benefits, but as actual enrollment in either Part A or Part B of Medicare. Treas. Reg. §54.4980B-7, A-3. However, entitlement to Medicare benefits will not terminate the obligation to provide continuation coverage to qualified beneficiaries entitled to continuation coverage by virtue of a proceeding in a case under the bankruptcy provisions of the U.S. Code.

Maximum Required Period of Coverage

The general maximum required period of coverage is 36 months from the date of the qualifying event. IRC Sec. 4980B(f)(2)(B)(i)(IV). There are, however, significant exceptions.

Termination or Reduction of Hours. When the qualifying event is the termination—other than by reason of the covered employee's gross misconduct (see Q 176)—or the reduction in hours of the covered employee's employment, the maximum required period of coverage is generally 18 months from the date of the termination or reduction. IRC Sec. 4980B(f)(2)(B)(i)(I). However, if another qualifying event (other than a proceeding in a case under the bankruptcy provisions of the U.S. Code) occurs during the 18-month period following the termination or reduction of hours, the maximum required period is extended to 36 months from the date of the termination or reduction. IRC Sec. 4980B(f)(2)(B)(i)(II).

Disability. In the case of a qualified beneficiary who is determined, under title II or title XVI of the Social Security Act, to have been disabled any time during the first 60 days of continuation coverage, any reference to 18 months dealing with termination of employment, a reduction in hours, or with multiple qualifying events is deemed to be a reference to 29 months with respect to all qualified beneficiaries. This extension applies only if the qualified beneficiary has provided the plan administrator with appropriate notice of the determination of disability within 60 days of the determination, and provides the plan administrator with notice within 30 days of the date of any final determination that the qualified beneficiary is no longer disabled. IRC Sec. 4980B(f)(2)(B)(i).

Regulations clarify that this extension of coverage to 29 months due to disability is available if three conditions are satisfied: (1) a termination or reduction of hours of a covered employee's employment occurs; (2) an individual (whether or not the covered

HEALTH INSURANCE

Q 178

employee) who is a qualified beneficiary in connection with the qualifying event described in (1) is determined to have been disabled at any time during the first 60 days of COBRA coverage; and (3) any of the qualified beneficiaries affected by the qualifying event described in (1) provides notice to the plan administrator of the disability determination on a date that is both within 60 days after the date when the determination is issued and before the end of the original 18-month period. This extension due to disability applies independently to each qualified beneficiary, whether or not he is disabled. Treas. Reg. §54.4980B-7, A-5.

Medicare Entitlement. In the case of a termination—other than by gross misconduct (see Q 176)—or a reduction in hours that occurs fewer than 18 months after the date when the covered employee became entitled to Medicare benefits, the period of coverage for qualified beneficiaries other than the covered employee shall not terminate before the close of the 36-month period beginning on the date when the covered employee became so entitled. IRC Sec. 4980B(f)(2)(B)(i)(V).

Employer's Bankruptcy. The bankruptcy of an employer is the only qualifying event that can result in a maximum required period of coverage of more than 36 months. Treas. Reg. §54.4980B-7, A-6. Where the qualifying event is a proceeding in a case under the bankruptcy provisions of the U.S. Code and the covered employee is alive when the bankruptcy proceedings commence, the maximum required period extends until the death of the covered employee, or, in the case of the surviving spouse or dependent children of the covered employee, until 36 months after the covered employee's date of death. When the covered employee dies before the bankruptcy proceedings commence and his surviving spouse is, as a surviving spouse, a beneficiary under the plan on the day before bankruptcy proceedings commence, the maximum required period extends until the surviving spouse's date of death. IRC Sec. 4980B(f)(2)(B)(i)(III).

Conversion Option. A qualified beneficiary must be given the option to convert the insurance coverage during the 180 day period ending on the expiration of the COBRA continuation coverage period if such a conversion option is otherwise generally available to similarly situated non-COBRA beneficiaries. IRC Sec. 4980B(f)(2)(E); Treas. Reg. §54.4980B-7, A-8. *ASRS, Sec. 67, ¶440.*

178. Who is a qualified beneficiary for purposes of the COBRA continuation coverage requirements?

Generally, with respect to a covered employee under a group health plan, a qualified beneficiary is any other individual who, on the day prior to that covered employee's qualifying event, is a covered employee's spouse or dependent child. A child born to or placed for adoption with the covered employee during the period of continuation coverage is included in the definition of qualified beneficiary. IRC Sec. 4980B(g)(1)(A); Treas. Reg. §54.4980B-3, A-1.

If the qualifying event is a proceeding in a case under the bankruptcy provisions of the U.S. Code, a qualified beneficiary is any covered employee who retired on or before the date of substantial elimination of coverage and individuals who, on the day before the bankruptcy proceedings commence, were covered under the plan as the covered employee's spouse (or surviving spouse) or dependent children. IRC Sec. 4980B(g)(1)(D); Treas. Reg. §54.4980B-3, A-1.

Where the qualifying event is a change in the employment status of the covered employee, the qualified beneficiaries are the covered employee and his spouse and dependent children covered under the plan on the day before the qualifying event. IRC Sec. 4980B(g)(1).

If the qualifying event is the covered employee's death, divorce, or legal separation, or his entitlement to Medicare, the qualified beneficiaries are the covered employee's spouse and dependent children who were covered under the plan the day before the qualifying event. IRC Sec. 4980B(g).

If the qualifying event is the loss of a covered child's dependent status, then that dependent child is the only qualified beneficiary.

The term qualified beneficiary does not include an individual who is covered under the group health plan due to another individual's election of COBRA continuation coverage and not by a prior qualifying event. This means that an individual who marries a qualified beneficiary other than the covered employee on or after the date of the qualifying event does not become a qualified beneficiary in his or her own right by reason of the marriage. Likewise, a child born to or placed for adoption with such a qualified beneficiary does not become a qualified beneficiary. Such new family members do not become qualified beneficiaries themselves, even if they become covered under the group health plan. Treas. Reg. §54.4980B-3, A-1.

A person whose status as a covered employee is attributable to a time when the person was a nonresident alien who received no earned income from the person's employer that constituted income from sources within the United States is not a qualified beneficiary. IRC Sec. 4980B(g)(1)(C).

An individual who does not elect COBRA continuation coverage ceases to be a qualified beneficiary at the end of the election period. Treas. Reg. §54.4980B-3, A-1. *ASRS, Sec. 67, ¶430.3.*

179. Who is a covered employee for purposes of the COBRA continuation coverage requirements?

A covered employee is any individual who is or was provided coverage under a group health plan by virtue of the individual's performance of services for one or more persons maintaining the plan (including as an employee defined in IRC Section 401(c)(1)) or because of membership in an employee organization that maintains the plan. In addition, the following persons are employees if their relationship to the employer maintaining the plan makes them eligible to be covered under the plan: (1) self-employed individuals; (2) independent contractors (and their agents and independent contractors); and (3) corporate directors. IRC Sec. 4980B(f)(7); Treas. Reg. §54.4980B-3, A-2.

A person eligible for coverage but not actually covered is not a covered employee.

Final COBRA regulations introduce the term "similarly situated nonCOBRA beneficiaries," which is defined as the group of covered employees, their spouses, or dependent children receiving coverage under the employer's (employee organization's) group health plan for a reason other than the rights provided under the COBRA requirements and who are most similarly situated to the situation of the qualified beneficiary

HEALTH INSURANCE

just before the qualifying event, based on all the facts and circumstances. Treas. Reg. §54.4980B-3, A-3. *ASRS, Sec. 67, ¶430.2.*

180. Who must pay the cost of COBRA continuation coverage and how is the cost calculated?

The plan may require the qualified beneficiary to pay a premium for continuation coverage. Generally, the premium cannot exceed a percentage of the "applicable premium."

The applicable premium is the plan's cost for similarly situated beneficiaries with respect to whom a qualifying event has not occurred. The applicable premium for each determination period must be fixed by the plan before the determination period begins. A determination period is defined as any 12-month period selected by the plan, provided that it is applied consistently from one year to the next. Since the determination period is a single period for any benefit package, each qualified beneficiary will not have a separate determination period. Treas. Reg. §54.4980B-8, A-2(a).

The percentage of the applicable premium that may be charged is generally 102%. IRC Sec. 4980B(f)(2)(C); Treas. Reg. §54.4980B-8, A-1. However, in the case of a disabled qualified beneficiary, the premium may be as much as 150% of the applicable premium for any month after the 18th month of continuation coverage. IRC Sec. 4980B(f)(2)(C). A plan may require payment equal to 150% of the applicable premium if a disabled qualified beneficiary experiences a second qualifying event during the disability extension (after the-18th-month) period. The 150% amount may be charged until the end of the 36-month maximum period of coverage (i.e., from the beginning of the 19th month through the end of the 36th month). Treas. Reg. §54.4980B-8, A-1(b). A plan that does so will not fail to comply with the nondiscrimination requirements of IRC Section 9802(b). See Q 188. Treas. Reg. §54.4980B-8, A-1(c).

Coverage may not be conditioned upon evidence of insurability, and cannot be contingent upon the employee's reimbursement of his employer for group health plan premiums paid during a leave taken under the Family and Medical Leave Act of 1993. IRC Sec. 4980B(f)(2)(D); Treas. Reg. §54.4980B-10, A-5; Notice 94-103, 1994-2 CB 569.

During a determination period, the plan may increase the cost of the COBRA coverage only if: (1) the plan has previously charged less than the maximum amount permitted and even after the increase the maximum amount will not be exceeded; or (2) a qualified beneficiary changes his coverage. If a plan allows similarly situated active employees to change their coverage, each qualified beneficiary must be given the same opportunity. Treas. Reg. §54.4980B-8, A-2(b).

The qualified beneficiary must be permitted to make premium payments on at least a monthly basis. Treas. Reg. §54.4980B-8, A-3. Any person or entity may make the required payment for COBRA continuation coverage on behalf of a qualified beneficiary. Treas. Reg. §54.4980B-8, A-5.

COBRA premiums must be paid in a timely fashion, which is defined as 45 days after the date of election for the period between the qualifying event and the election, and 30 days after the first date of the period for all other periods. Treas. Reg. §54.4980B-8, A-5. An employer may retroactively terminate COBRA continuation coverage if the initial premium is not timely paid. The employer is not required to "set off" the premium amount against the amount of a claim incurred during the 60-day election period but before the election was made. See, e.g., *Goletto v. W. H. Braum Inc.*, 25 EBC 1974 (10th Cir. 2001).

A plan must treat a timely payment that is not significantly less than the required amount as full payment, unless the plan notifies the qualified beneficiary of the amount of the deficiency and grants a reasonable period for payment. A reasonable period of time for this purpose is 30 days after the date when the notice is provided. An amount will be considered as "not significantly less" if the shortfall is no greater than the lesser of $50 or 10% of the amount the required amount. Treas. Reg. §54.4980B-8, A-5(b).

Revenue Ruling 96-8 provides some guidance in the area of determining COBRA costs. Rev. Rul. 96-8, 1996-1 CB 286.

In response to Hurricane Katrina, the Department of Labor and the IRS issued a notice waiving certain deadlines under COBRA for employers and employees in the declared disaster area, including the deadline for paying COBRA premiums. Under this notice, plans and participants must disregard the period between August 29, 2005 and February 28, 2006 in calculating any deadlines under COBRA. 70 Fed. Reg. 59620 (Oct. 12, 2005).

Health Coverage Tax Credit

Under the Trade Act of 2002, certain eligible individuals are entitled to receive a refundable, advanceable tax credit (see Q 832) equal to 65 percent of the cost of certain types of health coverage, including COBRA continuation coverage. See Q 181. IRC Secs. 35, 7527. *ASRS, Sec. 67, ¶460.*

181. What is the Health Coverage Tax Credit?

Under the Trade Act of 2002, certain eligible individuals are entitled to receive a refundable tax credit (see Q 832) equal to 65 percent of the cost of certain types of health coverage, including COBRA continuation coverage. IRC Sec. 35. Eligible individuals are (1) those displaced workers qualifying for assistance under the Trade Adjustment Assistance program and (2) individuals age 55 or older receiving a benefit from the Pension Benefit Guarantee Corporation. IRC Sec. 35(c).

The Trade Act of 2002 also made the tax credit advanceable, and, under the "Health Coverage Tax Credit" (HCTC) program established by the Treasury Department, eligible individuals receive a "qualified health insurance costs credit eligibility certificate." IRC Sec. 7527. These individuals can pay 35 percent of a required premium to providers along with the certificate, and the government will pay the remaining 65 percent of the premium. Providers are required to file a prescribed information return identifying the individuals receiving subsidized coverage and the amount and timing of the payments. IRC Sec. 6050T. Providers must provide each covered individual a statement with the information reported for that individual. IRC Sec. 6050T(c). The HCTC program was effective August 1, 2003. *ASRS, Sec. 67, ¶450.*

182. When must an election to receive COBRA continuation coverage be made?

HEALTH INSURANCE   Q 182

The period during which a qualified beneficiary may elect continuation coverage runs from the date when the qualified beneficiary's coverage terminates under the plan by reason of a qualifying event until 60 days after the later of (1) the date when the coverage terminates; or (2) the date when notice is provided by the plan administrator to any qualified beneficiary of the right to continued coverage. IRC Sec. 4980B(f)(5).

A COBRA continuation coverage election is considered to be made on the date it is sent to the plan administrator. Treas. Reg. §54.4980B-6, A-1. If the election is made at any time during this period, the continuation coverage is provided from the date when coverage is lost. IRC Sec. 4980B(f)(5); Treas. Reg. §54.4980B-6, A-3.

Where a former employee became incapacitated 10 days after resigning without making a continuation coverage election, the 60-day election period was "tolled." Thus, a continuation coverage election made by the former employee's temporary administrator approximately 70 days after the resignation was found to be timely. *Branch v. G. Bernd Co.*, 955 F.2d 1574 (11th Cir. 1992).

Each qualified beneficiary must be offered the opportunity to make an independent election to receive COBRA continuation coverage. If a qualified beneficiary who is either a covered employee or his spouse makes an election which does not specify for whom the election is being made, regulations provide that the election will be deemed to include an election for all other qualified beneficiaries. IRC Sec. 4980B(f)(5)(B); Treas. Reg. §54.4980B-6, A-6.

If the qualified beneficiary waives his or her right to COBRA coverage but subsequently revokes the waiver prior to the end of the election period, the employer must provide the qualified beneficiary with prospective coverage, but not for the period between the waiver and the revocation. A waiver or revocation of a waiver is considered to have been made on the date it is sent. Treas. Reg. §54.4980B-6, A-4.

An employer must not withhold any compensation or other benefits to which a qualified beneficiary is entitled in order to coerce the qualified beneficiary into a decision concerning COBRA continuation coverage. Treas. Reg. §54.4980B-6, A-5.

In response to Hurricane Katrina, the Department of Labor and the IRS issued a notice waiving certain deadlines under COBRA for employers and employees in the declared disaster area, including the deadline for electing COBRA continuation coverage. Under this notice, plans and participants must disregard the period between August 29, 2005 and February 28, 2006 in calculating any deadlines under COBRA. 70 Fed. Reg. 59620 (Oct. 12, 2005).

Second COBRA Election Period

The Trade Act of 2002 added a second 60-day COBRA election period for individuals eligible under the Trade Adjustment Assistance program (TAA) if the individuals did not elect COBRA coverage during their initial election period. IRC Sec. 4980B(f)(5)(C). The second election period begins on the first day of the month in which an individual becomes TAA eligible, but no election can be made more than six months after the initial TAA-related loss of coverage. IRC Sec. 4980B(f)(5)(C)(i). Any election during the second election period is retroactive to the first day of the second election period. IRC Sec. 4980B(f)(5)(C)(ii). *ASRS, Sec. 67, ¶450.*

183. What notice of COBRA continuation coverage is required?

Employer's Initial Notice. The plan must provide written notice of their COBRA continuation coverage rights to each covered employee and spouse at the commencement of their coverage under the plan. IRC Section 4980B(f)(6)(A).

Notice to Plan Administrator. The employer must notify the plan administrator within 30 days of the date when any of the following qualifying events occur: (1) the death of a covered employee; (2) the termination (or reduction in hours) of employment of a covered employee; (3) the covered employee's becoming entitled to Medicare benefits; or (4) a proceeding in a case under the bankruptcy provisions of the U.S. Code. IRC Section 4980B(f)(6)(B).

Notice to Employer. A covered employee (or his spouse) must notify the employer of a divorce or legal separation within 60 days. IRC Sec. 4980B(f)(6)(C). At least one court has permitted the covered employee to terminate coverage for his soon to be ex-spouse, and denied the spouse the COBRA coverage she sought upon learning that her coverage had been terminated, because neither she nor the covered employee had provided timely notice of the divorce to the employer. See *Johnson v. Northwest Airlines, Inc.*, 2001 U.S. Dist. LEXIS 2160 (N.D. CA. 2001). But where the covered employee told the plan administrator that he had divorced his spouse *before* directing that her coverage be terminated, the notice requirement was satisfied and the spouse had to be notified of her right to elect COBRA continuation coverage. *Phillips v. Saratoga Harness Racing Inc.*, 240 F.3d 174 (2d Cir. 2001). See also Rev. Rul 2002-88, 2002-52 IRB 995.

An individual who ceases to be a dependent child is required to notify the employer of this occurrence within 60 days. IRC Sec. 4980B(f)(6)(C).

Notice to Qualified Beneficiary. Within 14 days of receiving notice from the employer, the plan administrator must notify any qualified beneficiary with respect to the qualifying event. IRC Sec. 4980B(f)(6)(D). However, if coverage is continued at the employer's expense after the qualifying event, this notice may be delayed until coverage is actually lost. *Wilcock v. National Distributors, Inc.*, 2001 U.S. Dist. LEXIS 11413 (D. Maine 2001). This notice requirement will be deemed satisfied if the notice is sent to the qualified beneficiary's last known address by first class mail, unless the plan administrator has reason to know that this method of delivery has failed. See *Wooderson v. American Airlines Inc.*, 2001 U.S. Dist. LEXIS 3721 (N.D. Texas 2001).

Notice of Disability. Additionally, each qualified beneficiary determined under title II or XVI of the Social Security Act to have been disabled at any time during the first 60 days of continuation coverage must notify the plan administrator of such determination within 60 days after the date of that determination and must notify the plan administrator of any final determination that the qualified beneficiary is no longer disabled within 30 days of the date of that determination. IRC Sec. 4980B(f)(6)(C).

Statute of Limitations. Because neither the COBRA statute nor ERISA contains a statute of limitations for making a claim that the employer did not timely provide notice, courts may look to state statutes of limitations. See *Mattson v. Farrell Distributing Corp.*, 163 F. Supp.2d 411 (D. Vt. 2001).

Exhaustion of Administrative Remedies. While covered employees and qualified beneficiaries must generally exhaust their administrative remedies under the plan before bringing suit, in the case of a failure to provide the COBRA election notice, such exhaustion of remedies is not required. *Thompson v. Origin Tech. in Business, Inc.*, 2001 U.S. Dist. LEXIS 12609 (N.D. Texas 2001).

ERISA and PHSA. COBRA continuation coverage is not only a tax requirement. There are similar requirements under ERISA and the Public Health Service Act (PHSA) with other sanctions. The Department of Labor issued proposed regulations in 2003 updating the various notices and disclosures required under COBRA. 29 CFR Part 2590, 68 Fed. Reg. 31831 (5-28-03). The new regulations, which are proposed to be effective in their final form for plan years beginning in 2004, provide rules that "set minimum standards for the timing and content of the notices required under [COBRA] and establish standards for administering the notice process." *ASRS, Sec. 67, ¶470.*

184. Which entity is responsible for providing COBRA continuation coverage following a business reorganization?

Generally, the parties to a business reorganization transaction are free to allocate the responsibility for providing COBRA continuation coverage by contract even if the contract assigns the COBRA responsibility to a party other than the party to which it would be assigned under the final regulations. However, if the assigned party defaults on its responsibility to provide COBRA coverage and the other party would have had the responsibility under the final regulations, the responsibility will return to this other party. Treas. Reg. §54.4980B-9, A-7.

For both sales of stock and sales of substantial assets, final regulations provide that the seller retains the obligation to provide COBRA continuation coverage to existing qualified beneficiaries, provided that the seller continues to maintain a group health plan. Treas. Reg. §54.4980B-9, A-8(a). In the event of a stock sale where the seller ceases to provide any group health plan to any employee in connection with the sale and is therefore not responsible for providing COBRA continuation coverage, final regulations provide that the buyer is responsible for providing COBRA continuation coverage to existing qualified beneficiaries. Treas. Reg. §54.4980B-9, A-8(b)(1). In the event of an asset sale where the seller ceases to provide any group health plan and the buyer continues the business operations associated with the assets purchased without interruption, the buyer is considered to be a successor employer to the seller. As a successor employer, the buyer is obligated to offer COBRA continuation coverage. Final regulations provide examples as to which party has the obligation to offer COBRA continuation coverage with respect to both asset sales and stock sales. Treas. Reg. §54.4980B-9, A-8(c)(1).

Multiemployer Plans. It is not considered a COBRA qualifying event if an employer stops making contributions to a multiemployer plan. Further, when an employer stops making contributions to a multiemployer group health plan, the plan continues to be obligated to make COBRA continuation coverage available to qualified beneficiaries associated with the employer. However, once the employer provides group health insurance to a significant number of employees who were formerly covered under the multiemployer plan (or starts contributing to another multiemployer plan), the employer's plan (or the new multiemployer plan) must assume the COBRA obligation. Treas. Reg. §54.4980B-9, A-10. *ASRS, Sec. 67, ¶420.5.*

185. What is the effect of noncompliance with the COBRA continuation coverage requirements?

Statutory Penalties

The penalty for failure to make continuation coverage available is an excise tax of $100 per day during the noncompliance period with respect to each qualified beneficiary (limited to $200 per day in the case of more than one qualified beneficiary in the same family.) Attorney's fees may also be available. Where a covered employee's wife and children were not participants on the date of the qualifying event, the award was limited to penalties and attorney's fees based on the covered employee only. *Wright v. Hanna Steel Corp.*, 270 F.3d 1336 (11th Cir. 2001).

The noncompliance period begins on the date when the failure first begins and continues until (1) the failure is corrected; or (2) the date that is six months after the last date on which the employer could have been required to provide continuation coverage to the beneficiary. IRC Sec. 4980B(b).

However, no tax is imposed for the period during which it is shown that none of the persons liable for the tax knew (or, by exercising reasonable diligence, would have known) that the failure existed. Generally, too, there is no tax if the failure was due to reasonable cause, not willful neglect, and is corrected within the first 30 days of the noncompliance period. IRC Sec. 4980B(c).

Normally, the employer is liable for the tax, except in the case of a multiemployer plan, where the excise tax is imposed directly on the plan. IRC Sec. 4980B(e); Treas. Reg. §54.4980B-2, A-10. In addition, a person responsible for administering the plan (or providing benefits under it pursuant to a written agreement) is liable if that person causes the failure by failing to perform one or more of its responsibilities. A person may also be liable if he fails to comply, within 45 days, with a written request of the employer, the plan administrator, or, in limited situations, a qualified beneficiary, to provide the benefits that the person provides to similarly situated active employees. IRC Sec. 4980B(e). See *Paris v. Korbel*, 751 F. Supp. 834 (N.D. Cal. 1990). Further, this excise tax may be imposed on a third party, such as an insurer or third party administrator, if the third party assumes certain responsibilities. See Treas. Reg. §54.4980B-2, A-10.

In the case of single employer plans, the maximum excise tax for failures due to reasonable cause, not willful neglect, is 10% of the aggregate amount paid by the employer during the preceding tax year for medical care coverage, or, if less, $500,000. The maximum excise tax in the case of a person other than the employer is limited to $2,000,000 with respect to all plans.

In the case of a failure due to reasonable cause, the Secretary of the Treasury may waive part or all of the tax to the extent it is excessive relative to the failure involved. The determination of the excessiveness of the excise tax is to be made based on the seriousness of the failure, not on a particular taxpayer's ability to pay the tax. IRC Sec. 4980B(c)(5).

Failure to make continuation coverage available will be treated as corrected if it is retroactively undone to the extent possible, and the qualified beneficiary is placed in as good a financial position as he would have been in had the failure not occurred and had the beneficiary elected the most favorable coverage in light of the expenses he incurred since the failure first occurred. IRC Sec. 4980B(g)(4).

Other Remedies

In addition to the excise taxes discussed above, other civil remedies are available under ERISA. ERISA Sec. 502. Employees or other qualified beneficiaries can bring civil actions to obtain "other equitable relief" (e.g., injunction and restitution) and to recover additional penalties of up to $100 per day for failure to provide required notices or to furnish requested information. ERISA Secs. 502(a)(1), 502(a)(3). Compensatory damages are not available. See *Geissal v. Moore Med. Corp.*, 158 F. Supp.2d 976 (E.D. Mo. 2001). *ASRS, Sec. 67, ¶480*.

Portability, Access, and Renewability Rules

186. What portability, access, and renewability requirements must be satisfied by group health plans?

Group health plans must comply with certain requirements concerning limitations on pre-existing condition exclusions (Q 187), discrimination based on health status (see Q 188), and guaranteed renewability in multiemployer plans (Q 189).

A "group health plan" is defined as "a plan (including a self-insured plan) of, or contributed to by, an employer (including a self-employed person) or employee organization to provide health care (directly or otherwise) to the employees, former employees, the employer, others associated or formerly associated with the employer in a business relationship, or their families." IRC Sec. 5000(b)(1).

These requirements do not apply to plans with fewer than two participants. Nor do they apply to plans providing only accident or disability income insurance coverage, or issued as a supplement to liability insurance, worker's compensation, automobile medical payment insurance, or credit-only insurance. Also excluded is coverage for on-site medical clinics, and other similar insurance coverage under which benefits for medical care are incidental to other insurance benefits. The requirements are not applicable to plans providing limited dental or vision benefits, benefits for long-term care, nursing home care, home health care, or community-based care, if such coverage is offered separately. Plans providing coverage only for a specific disease or illness and hospital indemnity insurance, if offered as an independent non-coordinated benefit, are not subject to these rules. Nor do these requirements apply to government plans (as defined in IRC Section 414(d)) or Medicare supplemental health insurance, if offered as a separate insurance policy or certificate. IRC Secs. 9831, 9832(c).

Penalties for noncompliance are imposed by IRC Section 4980D. See Q 191.

Mental Health Parity. For plan years beginning on or after January 1, 1998, group health plans are required to provide "parity" between mental health benefits and medical and surgical benefits. ERISA Sec. 712. The mental health parity provision originally expired September 30, 2001, but was later renewed effective January 10, 2002. The mental health parity provision has been renewed again, with the latest renewal expiring on December 31, 2005. ERISA Sec. 712(f). For this purpose, mental health benefits are defined as benefits with respect to mental health services, as defined by the plan, but not including benefits for treatment of substance abuse or chemical dependency. ERISA Sec. 712(e)(4). *ASRS, Sec. 67, ¶360*.

187. What are the rules concerning pre-existing condition exclusions under HIPAA '96?

The Health Insurance Portability and Accountability Act of 1996 (HIPAA '96) defines a pre-existing condition exclusion as "a limitation or exclusion of benefits relating to a condition based on the fact that the condition was present before the date of enrollment for such coverage, whether or not any medical advice, diagnosis, care or treatment was recommended or received before such date." IRC Sec. 9801(b)(1)(A).

A group health plan may impose a pre-existing condition exclusion on a participant or a beneficiary only if: (1) the exclusion relates to a physical or mental condition, regardless of cause, for which medical advice, diagnosis, care, or treatment was either recommended or received within the six months prior to the enrollment date (the 6-month look-back rule); (2) the exclusion extends for no more than 12 months after the enrollment date or 18 months for a late enrollee (the look-forward rule); and (3) the exclusion period is reduced by the length of the aggregate of the periods of creditable coverage applicable to the participant or beneficiary as of the enrollment date. IRC Sec. 9801(a).

Generally, the 6-month period under item (1) above begins on the 6-month anniversary date preceding the enrollment date. Regulations provide examples of how this period is determined. See Temp. Treas. Reg. §54.9801-3T(a)(1)(i).

The 12-month period (18-month period for late enrollees) under item (2) above is determined by looking to the anniversary of the enrollment date. Thus, if the enrollment date was August 1, 2001, the 12-month period after the enrollment date began on August 1, 2001 and would run through July 31, 2002. Temp. Treas. Reg. §54.9801-3T(a)(1)(ii).

"Creditable coverage" under item (3) above is coverage of an individual under many types of health plans, including a group health plan, health insurance coverage, Part A or Part B of Medicare, a state health benefits risk pool, and a public health plan. IRC Sec. 9801(c)(1). An individual will not receive credit for prior coverage if there was a break in coverage. For this purpose, a break in coverage is a period of at least 63 days, occurring before the enrollment date, during which the individual was not covered under any creditable coverage. IRC Sec. 9801(c)(2)(A). Generally, a waiting period for coverage under a group health plan is not counted for this purpose. IRC Sec. 9801(c)(2)(B). Regulations provide guidance on how to determine an individual's creditable coverage by using the standard method or, for certain categories of benefits, by using an alternative method. See Temp. Treas. Reg. §54.9801-4T.

Generally, a group health plan must provide certificates of creditable coverage. Temp. Treas. Reg. §54.9801-5T(a)(1). An entity required to provide a certificate may meet its obligation if another party provides a certificate that includes information about an individual's creditable coverage and waiting period. Temp. Treas. Reg. §54.9801-5T(a)(1).

A certificate of creditable coverage must be provided to participants or dependents who are or were covered under a group health plan upon the occurrence of any one of several events. A certificate must be issued automatically to COBRA qualified beneficiaries (see Q 178) upon the occurrence of a qualified event (see Q 175). A certificate

HEALTH INSURANCE   Q 188

must also be provided automatically to any qualified beneficiary who would lose coverage under the plan in the absence of COBRA continuation coverage (or alternative coverage elected instead of COBRA coverage). A certificate must be issued automatically to other individuals when coverage ceases. The employer must automatically provide a certificate to individuals who are not qualified beneficiaries entitled to elect COBRA when they cease to be covered under the plan, and to COBRA qualified beneficiaries when COBRA continuation coverage ceases. The automatic certificate must be provided to such individuals when their coverage under the plan ceases, even if they have already received a certificate upon the COBRA qualified event. Temp. Treas. Reg. §54.9801-5T(a)(2). Further, a certificate of creditable coverage must also be provided automatically if a request for one is made by or on behalf of an individual within 24 months of the time coverage ends. Temp. Treas. Reg. §54.9801-5T(a)(2).

HIPAA '96 also prohibits a group health plan from imposing a pre-existing condition exclusion on a newborn who is covered under creditable coverage on the last day of a 30-day period beginning with the date of birth. IRC Sec. 9801(d)(1). Neither can a group health plan impose a pre-existing condition exclusion on an adopted child under the age of 18 who is covered under creditable coverage on the last day of a 30-day period beginning on the date of adoption. IRC Sec. 9801(d)(2).

Finally, HIPAA '96 prohibits a group health plan from imposing a pre-existing condition exclusion relating to pregnancy. IRC Sec. 9801(d)(3).

In response to Hurricane Katrina, the Department of Labor and the IRS issued a notice waiving certain deadlines under HIPAA for employers and employees in the declared disaster area. Under this notice, plans and participants must disregard the period between August 29, 2005 and February 28, 2006 in calculating any deadlines under HIPAA. 70 Fed. Reg. 59620 (Oct. 12, 2005).

188. What are the rules concerning discrimination based on health status under HIPAA '96?

The Health Insurance Portability and Accountability Act of 1996 (HIPAA '96) prohibits a group health plan from establishing rules for eligibility or continued eligibility under the plan based on certain factors. These factors may be in relation to either the individual or his dependents.

The prohibited factors include health status, medical conditions (including both physical and mental illness), claims experience, receipt of health care, medical history, genetic information, evidence of insurability, and disability. IRC Sec. 9802(a)(1). Evidence of insurability includes participation in motorcycling, snowmobiling, all-terrain vehicle riding, horseback riding, skiing, and similar activities, and conditions arising from domestic violence. Temp. Treas. Reg. §54.9802-1T(a)(2). A plan need not provide coverage for any particular benefit to any group of similarly situated individuals. Treas. Reg. §54.9802-1(b)(2).

A group health plan may not require an individual to pay a premium greater than the premium for a similarly situated participant or beneficiary based on any of the factors listed above, as a condition of either enrollment or continued enrollment. IRC Sec. 9802(b)(1). According to the regulations, this rule does not restrict the amount that an issuer may charge an employer for coverage, or prevent the plan from providing premium discounts or other financial incentives for employees who participate in a wellness plan. Treas. Reg. §54.9802-1(c).

A church plan (as defined in IRC Section 414(e)) does not fail to meet these requirements solely because the plan requires evidence of good health for coverage of: (1) any employee, in the case of an employer with 10 or fewer employees; (2) any self-employed individual; or (3) any individual who enrolls in the plan after the first 90 days of initial eligibility. This exception is applicable for a given plan year only if the plan included these provisions on July 15, 1997, and at all times thereafter before the beginning of such year. IRC Sec. 9802(c).

189. What is the Guaranteed Renewability requirement?

A group health plan that is a multiemployer plan or a multiple employer welfare arrangement cannot deny an employer continued access to the same or different coverage under the plan except in the case of: (1) nonpayment of contributions; (2) fraud or other intentional misrepresentation by the employer; (3) noncompliance with material plan provisions; (4) the plan no longer offers coverage in a geographic area; (5) a network plan where there is no longer an individual enrolled through the employer who lives or works in the service area of the network plan; and (6) failure to meet the terms of a collective bargaining agreement. IRC Sec. 9803(a).

190. What rules apply to group health plan benefits provided to newborns and mothers?

A group health plan providing hospital stay benefits for either a mother or a newborn in connection with childbirth may not limit such stay to less than 48 hours for a normal delivery or 96 hours for delivery by caesarean section. IRC Sec. 9811(a)(1).

Group health plans are also prohibited from taking certain other actions that would have the effect of limiting benefits in connection with mothers, newborns, and childbirth. IRC Sec. 9811(b). See Temp. Treas. Reg. §54.9811-1T.

191. What penalties applies to a group health plan's failure to meet the portability, access, and renewability requirements?

An excise tax is imposed on the employer sponsoring any group health plan that fails to meet the portability, access, and renewability requirements. The amount of the tax is $100 for each individual to whom the failure relates, for each day in the noncompliance period. IRC Secs. 4980D(a), 4980D(b). The noncompliance period begins on the date when a failure first occurs, and ends on the date when it is corrected. IRC Sec. 4980D(b)(2). A failure is considered corrected if it is retroactively undone and the person to whom the failure relates has been placed in as good a financial position as he would have been in if the failure had not occurred. IRC Sec. 4980D(f)(3).

Although the employer sponsoring the plan is generally liable for the tax, in the case of a multiemployer plan, the plan is liable. Additionally, in the case of a failure that relates to guaranteed renewability (Q 189) with respect to a multiple employer welfare arrangement, the plan is liable. IRC Sec. 4980D(e).

A special rule applies in the case of one or more failures relating to an individual that are not corrected before a notice of examination of income tax liability is sent to

HEALTH INSURANCE

the employer, and which either occurred or continued during the examination period. In such a case, the amount of the tax shall not be less than the lesser of: (1) $2,500; or (2) the amount of tax that normally would be imposed, without regard to IRC Sections 4980D(c)(1) and 4980D(c)(2). Where violations are more than *de minimis*, $15,000 is substituted for $2,500. IRC Sec. 4980D(b)(3)(B). The provisions regarding income tax liability examinations do not apply to church plans (as defined in IRC Section 414(e)). IRC Sec. 4980D(b)(3)(C).

The $100 per day tax is not imposed if the person who would otherwise be liable for the tax can demonstrate that he did not know about the failure, and would not have known about the failure through the exercise of reasonable diligence. IRC Sec. 4980D(c)(1). Further, no tax is imposed if the failure was due to reasonable cause, not willful neglect, and is corrected within 30 days after the person who would be liable for the tax first knew or, by exercising reasonable diligence, would have known about the failure. For church plans, the failure must be corrected before the close of the correction period, as determined under the rules of IRC Section 414(e)(4)(C). IRC Sec. 4980D(c)(2).

There are other limits on the tax that may be applied in the case of unintentional failures. For failures with respect to single employer plans, the tax shall not exceed the lesser of: (1) 10% of the aggregate amount paid by the employer during the preceding taxable year for group health plans; or (2) $500,000. IRC Sec. 4980D(c)(3)(A). For failures with respect to a specified multiple employer health plan, the tax shall not exceed the lesser of: (1) 10% of the amount paid by the plan trust to provide medical care directly or through insurance, reimbursement, or otherwise; or (2) $500,000. IRC Sec. 4980D(c)(3)(B). A specified multiple employer health plan is defined as a group health plan that is any multiemployer plan or any multiple employer welfare arrangement as defined in Section 3(40) of ERISA. IRC Sec. 4980D(f)(2). IRC Section 4980D(c)(4) provides that a portion or all of the tax imposed may be waived if it is excessive in relation to the failure involved and is due to reasonable cause.

In the case of a small employer providing health coverage solely through a health insurance contract, no tax is imposed for any failure (other than a failure attributable to IRC Section 9811–see Q 190) arising "solely because of the health insurance coverage offered by such insurer." IRC Sec. 4980D(d)(1). For this purpose, a small employer is one that employed (1) an average of at least two but not more than 50 employees on business days during the preceding calendar year; and (2) at least two employees on the first day of the plan year. If an employer was not in existence during the preceding year, this determination is based on the average number of employees that it is reasonably expected that the employer will employ on business days in the current calendar year. IRC Sec. 4980D(d)(2). *ASRS, Sec. 67, ¶360.*

Health Benefits Under A Qualified Plan

192. Can health benefits be provided for employees under qualified pension and profit sharing plans?

A qualified profit sharing plan may, within limits, provide health insurance benefits for its employee-participants. See Q 369. A qualified pension plan may provide disability pensions, but will not qualify if it provides regular health insurance benefits for active employees. A qualified pension plan may, however, provide health insurance benefits for retired employees. See Q 369. For tax consequences to the employee, see Q 423 and Q 436. *ASRS, Sec. 53, ¶20.4(j); Sec. 59.*

Disability Income Coverage

193. How is personal disability income coverage taxed?

Deduction

Premiums for non-medical benefits such as personal disability income covereage are not deductible. IRC Sec. 213(d)(1). Only premiums for medical care insurance are deductible as a medical expense. See Q 154.

Taxation of Benefits

As a rule, benefits from personal disability income coverage are entirely exempt from income tax. There is no limit on the amount of benefits, including the amount of disability income, that can be received tax free under personally paid disability income coverage. IRC Sec. 104(a)(3); Rev. Rul. 55-331, 1955-1 CB 271, modified by Rev. Rul. 68-212, 1968-1 CB 91; Rev. Rul. 70-394, 1970-2 CB 34.

If benefits are received under a plan to which both an employer and the employee have contributed, the portion of the disability income attributable to the employee's contributions is tax-free. Treas. Reg. §1.105-1(c). See Q 194.

194. How is employer-provided disability income coverage taxed?

Deduction

As a general rule, an employer can deduct all premiums paid for disability income coverage, as with all premiums paid for health insurance (see Q 167), for one or more employees as a business expense.

The premiums are deductible by the employer whether the coverage is provided under a group policy or under individual policies. However, the deduction is allowable only if the benefits are payable to employees or their beneficiaries; it is not allowable if the benefits are payable to the employer. Treas. Reg. §1.162-10(a); Rev. Rul. 58-90, 1958-1 CB 88; Rev. Rul. 56-632, 1956-2 CB 101; Rev. Rul. 210, 1953-2 CB 114.

The deduction of premiums paid for a disability income policy insuring an employee-shareholder was prohibited where the corporation was the premium payor, owner, and beneficiary of the policy. The Tax Court held that IRC Section 265(a) prevented the deduction since the premiums were funds expended to produce tax-exempt income. (The court stated that the disability income policy benefits, had any been paid, would have been tax-exempt under IRC Section 104(a)(3).) *Rugby Prod. Ltd. v. Comm.*, 100 TC 531 (1993). See Rev. Rul. 66-262, 1966-2 CB 105.

Taxation of Benefits

Generally, "sick pay," wage continuation payments, and disability income payments, both preretirement and postretirement, are fully includable in gross income and taxable to the employee. See Let. Ruls. 9103043, 9036049. Specifically, long-term disability income payments received under a policy paid for by the employer were

HEALTH INSURANCE   Q 195

fully includable in income to the taxpayer. *Cash v. Comm.*, TC Memo 1994-166; *Rabideau v. Comm.*, TC Memo 1997-230. See also *Pearson v. Comm.*, TC Memo 2000-160; *Crandall v. Comm.*, TC Memo 1996-463. A disabled former employee could not exclude from income a lump sum payment received from the insurance company that provided his employer-paid long-term disability coverage. The lump sum nature of the settlement did not change the nature of the payment into something other than payment received under accident or health insurance. *Kees v. Comm.*, TC Memo 1999-41.

If benefits are received under a plan to which the employee has contributed, the portion of the disability income attributable to the employee's contributions is tax-free. Treas. Reg. §1.105-1(c). Under an individual policy, the employee's contributions for the current policy year are taken into consideration. With a group policy, the employee's contributions for the last three years, if known, are considered. Treas. Reg. §1.105-1(d).

An employer may allow employees to elect on an annual basis whether to have the premiums for a group disability income policy included in their income for that year. An employee who elects to have premiums included in his income will not be taxed on benefits received during a period of disability beginning in that tax year. Rev. Rul. 2004-55, 2004-26 IRB 1081. An employee's election will be effective for each tax year, without regard to employer and employee contributions for prior years.

Where an employee/owner reimbursed his corporation for payment of premiums on a disability income policy, the benefit payments that he received while disabled were excludable from income under IRC Section 104(a)(3). *Bouquett v. Comm.*, TC Memo 1994-212. Where an employer initially paid disability income insurance premiums but, prior to a second period of benefit payments, the employee took responsibility for paying the premiums personally, the benefits paid from the disability income policy during the second benefit-paying period were not includable in the employee's income. Let. Rul. 9741035. See also Let. Rul. 200019005.

Premiums paid by a former employee under an earlier long-term disability plan were not considered paid toward a later plan from which the employee received benefit payments. Thus, the disability benefits were includable in income. *Chernik v. Comm.*, TC Memo 1999-313. If the employer merely withholds employee contributions and makes none himself, the payments are excludable. Rev. Rul. 73-347, 1973-2 CB 25. A tax credit for disability retirement income is available to some taxpayers. See Q 833. *ASRS, Sec. 67, ¶320.5.*

HEALTH AND MEDICAL SAVINGS ACCOUNTS

General

195. What is a Health Savings Account (HSA) and how can one be established?

An HSA is a trust created exclusively for the purpose of paying the qualified medical expenses of the account holder. IRC Sec. 223(d)(1). An account beneficiary is the individual on whose behalf the HSA was established. IRC Sec. 223(d)(3).

An HSA must be created by a written governing instrument, which states that: (1) no contribution will be accepted unless it is in cash (except in the case of a rollover contribution (see Q 203)); (2) no contribution will be accepted to the extent that such contribution, when added to previous contributions to the trust for the calendar year, exceeds the contribution limit for the calendar year; (3) the trustee is a bank, an insurance company, or another person who satisfies the Secretary's requirements; (4) no part of the trust assets will be invested in life insurance contracts; (5) the trust assets will not be commingled with other property (with certain limited exceptions); and (6) the interest of an individual in the balance of his account is nonforfeitable. IRC Sec. 223(d)(1).

HSAs are available to any employer or individual for an account beneficiary who has high deductible health insurance coverage. See Q 197. An eligible individual or an employer may establish an HSA with a qualified HSA custodian or trustee. No permission or authorization is needed from the IRS to set up an HSA. As mentioned above, any insurance company or bank can act as a trustee. Additionally, any person already approved by the IRS to act as an individual retirement arrangement (IRA) trustee or custodian is automatically approved to act in the same capacity for HSAs. Notice 2004-50, 2004-33 IRB 196, A-72; Notice 2004-2, 2004-2 IRB 269, A-9, A-10.

While an HSA is similar to an IRA in some respects, a taxpayer cannot use an IRA as an HSA, nor can he combine an IRA with an HSA. See Notice 2004-2, above.

Generally, contributions to an HSA may be made either (1) by the individual, (2) by his employer, (3) or both. If made by the individual taxpayer, the HSA contributions are deductible from income. IRC Sec. 223(a). If made by an employer, HSA contributions are excluded from the employee's income. See IRC Sec. 106(d)(1). The HSA itself is exempt from income tax. IRC Sec. 223(e)(1). Contributions may be made through a cafeteria plan under IRC Section 125. See Q 99. IRC Sec. 125(d)(2)(D).

Distributions from HSAs are not includable in gross income if they are used exclusively to pay qualified medical expenses. IRC Sec. 223(f)(1). Distributions used for other purposes are includable in gross income and may be subject to a penalty, with some exceptions. IRC Secs. 223(f)(2), 223(f)(4). See Q 202.

An employer's contributions to an HSA are not considered part of a group health plan subject to the COBRA continuation coverage requirements. See Q 173. See IRC Secs. 106(b)(5), 106(d)(2). Therefore, a plan is not required to make COBRA continuation coverage available with respect to an HSA. See Treas. Reg. §54.4980B-2, A-1 regarding Archer MSAs. *ASRS, Sec. 67, ¶610.*

196. Who is an "eligible individual" for purposes of a Health Savings Account (HSA)?

For purposes of an HSA, an "eligible individual" is an individual, who (1) for any month, is covered under a high deductible health plan as of the first day of that month; and (2) is *not* also covered under any non-high deductible health plan providing coverage for any benefit covered under the high deductible health plan. IRC Sec. 223(c)(1)(A).

An individual enrolled in Medicare Part A or Part B may not contribute to an HSA. IRC Sec. 223(b)(7). Mere eligibility for Medicare, however, does not preclude HSA contributions. Notice 2004-50, 2004-33 IRB 196, A-3.

HEALTH INSURANCE
Q 197

An individual may not contribute to an HSA for a given month if he has received medical benefits through the Department of Veterans Affairs within the previous three months. Mere eligibility for VA medical benefits will not disqualify an otherwise eligible individual from making HSA contributions. Notice 2004-50, 2004-33 IRB 196, A-5.

A separate prescription drug plan that provides any benefits before the required high deductible is satisfied will normally prevent a beneficiary from qualifying as an eligible individual. Rev. Rul. 2004-38, 2004-15 IRB 717. For calendars years 2004 and 2005 only, the IRS has provided transition relief such that an individual will not fail to be an eligible individual solely by virtue of coverage by a separate prescription drug plan. Rev. Proc. 2004-22, 2004-15 IRB 727.

An individual will not fail to be an eligible individual solely because the individual is covered under an Employee Assistance Program, disease management program, or wellness program, if the program does not provide significant benefits in the nature of medical care or treatment. Notice 2004-50, 2004-33 IRB 196, A-10.

Certain types of insurance are not taken into account in determining whether an individual is eligible for an HSA. Specifically, insurance for a specific disease or illness, hospitalization insurance paying a fixed daily amount, and insurance providing coverage that relates to certain liabilities are disregarded. IRC Sec. 223(c)(3). In addition, coverage provided (by insurance or otherwise) for accidents, disability, dental care, vision care, or long-term care will not adversely impact HSA or Archer MSA eligibility. IRC Sec. 223(c)(1)(B). *ASRS, Sec. 67, ¶620.*

197. What is a "high deductible health plan" for purposes of a Health Saving Account (HSA)?

For HSAs, in the case of self-only coverage, a high deductible health plan is defined as a health plan with an annual deductible of not less than $1,050 in 2006 ($1,000 in 2005) and required annual out-of-pocket expenses of not more than $5,250 in 2006 ($5,100 in 2005). IRC Sec. 223(c)(2)(A); Rev. Proc. 2005-70, 2005-47 IRB 979.

In the case of family coverage, a high deductible health plan is a health plan with an annual deductible of not less than $2,100 in 2006 ($2,000 in 2005) and required annual out-of-pocket expenses of not more than $10,500 in 2006 ($10,200 in 2005). IRC Sec. 223(c)(2)(A); Rev. Proc. 2005-70, 2005-47 IRB 979. For this purpose, family coverage is defined as any coverage other than self-only coverage. IRC Sec. 223(c)(5).

The deductible limits for high deductible health plans are based on a 12-month period. If a plan deductible may be satisfied over a period longer than 12 months, the minimum annual deductible under IRC Section 223(c)(2)(A) must be increased on a pro-rata basis to take into account the longer period. Notice 2004-50, 2004-33 IRB 196, A-24.

A high deductible health plan may impose a reasonable lifetime limit on benefits provide under the plan, as long as the lifetime limit on benefits is not designed to circumvent the maximum annual out-of-pocket limitation. Notice 2004-50, 2004-33 IRB 196, A-14. A plan with no limitation on out-of-pocket expenses, either by design or by its express terms, does not qualify as a high deductible health plan. Notice 2004-50, 2004-33 IRB 196, A-17.

A high deductible health plan may provide coverage for preventive care without application of the annual deductible. IRC Sec. 223(c)(2)(C). The IRS has provided guidance and safe harbor guidelines on what constitutes preventive care. Notice 2004-23, 2004-15 IRB 725; Notice 2004-50, 2004-33 IRB 196. Under the safe harbor, preventive care includes, but is not limited to, periodic check-ups, routine prenatal and well-child care, immunizations, tobacco cessation programs, obesity weight-loss programs, and various health screening services. Preventive care may include drugs or medications taken to prevent the occurrence or reoccurrence of a disease which is not currently present. Notice 2004-50, 2004-33 IRB 196, A-27.

In addition, for months before January 1, 2006, a health plan will not fail to qualify as a high deductible health plan solely because it complies with state health insurance laws that mandate coverage without regard to a deductible or before the high deductible is satisfied. Notice 2004-43, 2004-27 IRB 10. This transition relief only applies to disqualifying benefits mandated by state laws that were in effect on January 1, 2004. This relief extends to non-calendar year health plans with benefit periods of 12 months or less that begin before January 1, 2006. Notice 2005-83, 2005-49 IRB 1075.

General

Out-of-pocket expenses include deductibles, co-payments, and other amounts that the participant must pay for covered benefits. Premiums, however, are not considered out-of-pocket expenses. Notice 2004-2, 2004-2 IRB 269, A-3; Notice 96-53, 1996-2 CB 219, A-4.

The annual deductible amounts and the out-of-pocket expense amounts stated above are adjusted for the cost of living. Any increases are made in multiples of $50. IRC Sec. 223(g). *ASRS, Sec. 67, ¶620.*

Contributions

198. What are the limits on amounts contributed to a Health Savings Account (HSA)?

An eligible individual may deduct the aggregate amount paid in cash into an HSA during the taxable year, subject to a limitation in 2006 of $2,700 ($2,650 for 2005) for self-only coverage and $5,450 ($5,250 for 2006) for individuals with family coverage. IRC Secs. 223(a), 223(b)(2); Rev. Proc. 2005-70, 2005-47 IRB 979.

The determination between self-only and family coverage is made as of the first day of the month. The limitation is calculated on a monthly basis and the allowable deduction for a taxable year cannot exceed the sum of the monthly limitations for the months during which the individual was an eligible individual (see Q 196). IRC Sec. 223(b)(1). For example, a person with self-only coverage under a high deductible health plan with an annual deductible of $3,000, would be limited to an annual contribution equal to $2,700, and a monthly contribution limit of $225 ($2,700 divided by 12). However, if the person was an eligible individual for only the first eight months of the year, the contribution limit for the year would be $1,800 (eight months multiplied by the monthly limit of $225). Although the annual contribution level is determined for each month, the annual contribution can be made in a single payment, if desired. IRC Sec. 223(b); Notice 2004-2, 2004-2 IRB 269, A-12.

HEALTH INSURANCE   Q 199

Individuals who attain age 55 before the close of the taxable year are eligible for an additional contribution amount over and above that calculated under IRC Section 223(b)(1) and IRC Section 223(b)(2). IRC Sec. 223(b)(3). The additional contribution amount is $700 for 2006 ($600 for 2005) and increases $100 per year until it reaches $1,000 for 2009 and later years. IRC Sec. 223(b)(3).

For married individuals, if either spouse has family coverage, then both spouses are treated as having only such family coverage, and the deduction limitation is divided equally between them, unless they agree on a different division. IRC Sec. 223(b)(5). If two spouses both have family coverage under different plans, both spouses are treated as having only the family coverage with the lowest deductible. IRC Sec. 223(b)(5).

An HSA may be offered in conjunction with a cafeteria plan (see Q 99). Both a high deductible health plan and an HSA are qualified benefits under a cafeteria plan. IRC Sec. 125(d)(2)(D).

Employer contributions to an HSA are treated as employer-provided coverage for medical expenses to the extent that the contributions do not exceed the applicable amount of allowable HSA contributions. IRC Sec. 106(d)(1).

Further, an employee will not be required to include any amount in income simply because he may choose between employer contributions to an HSA and employer contributions to another health plan. IRC Secs. 106(b)(2), 106(d)(2).

An employer can generally deduct amounts paid to accident and health plans for employees as a business expense. See Q 167.

An individual may not deduct any amount paid into his HSA which amount is excludable from gross income under IRC Section 106(d). IRC Sec. 223(b)(4).

No deduction is allowed for any amount contributed to an HSA with respect to any individual for whom another taxpayer may take a deduction under IRC Section 151 (deductions for personal exemptions) for the taxable year. IRC Sec. 223(b)(6). *ASRS, Sec. 67, ¶640.*

199. Must an employer offering Health Savings Accounts (HSAs) to its employees contribute the same amount for each employee?

An employer offering HSAs to its employees must make "comparable" contributions to the HSAs for all comparable participating employees for each coverage period during the calendar year. IRC Secs. 4980E, 4980G. IRC Section 4980G incorporates the comparability rules of IRC Section 4980E by reference. Prop. Treas. Reg. § 54.4980G-1, A-1.

Comparable contributions are defined as contributions that are either (1) the same amount; or (2) the same percentage of the annual deductible limit under the high deductible health plan. IRC Sec. 4980E(d); Prop. Treas. Reg. § 54.4980G-4, A-1.

Comparable participating employees are all employees who (1) in the same category of employee and (2) have the same category of coverage. Category of employee refers to full-time employees, part-time employees, and former employers. Prop. Treas. Reg.

§ 54.4980G-3, A-4. Category of coverage refers to self-only and family type coverages. IRC Sec. 4980E(d)(3); Prop. Treas. Reg. § 54.4980G-1, A-2.

If an employer fails to meet the comparability requirements, a penalty tax is imposed, equal to 35% of the aggregate amount contributed by the employer to the HSAs of the employees for their taxable years ending with or within the calendar year. IRC Secs. 4980E(a), 4980E(b); Prop. Treas. Reg. § 54.4980G-1, A-4. See Notice 2004-50, 2004-33 IRB 196, A-46.

Employer contributions made to HSAs through a cafeteria plan, including "matching contributions," are not subject to the comparability rules, but are subject to the IRC Section 125 nondiscrimination rules. Notice 2004-50, 2004-33 IRB 196, A-47; IRC Sec. 125 (b), (c), and (g); Prop. Treas. Reg. § 1.125-1, A-19. *ASRS, Sec. 67, ¶640.*

200. What is the penalty for making excess contributions to a Health Savings Account (HSA)? May excess contributions be withdrawn or reduced?

If an HSA receives any excess contributions for a taxable year, distributions from the HSA are not includable in income to the extent that the distributions do not exceed the aggregate excess contributions to all HSAs of the individual for the taxable year if: (1) the distribution is received by the individual on or before the last day for filing the individual's income tax return for the year (including extensions); and (2) the distribution is accompanied by the amount of net income attributable to the excess contribution. Any net income must be included in the individual's gross income for the taxable year in which it is received. IRC Sec. 223(f)(3)(A).

Excess contributions to an HSA are subject to a 6% tax. However, the tax may not exceed 6% of the value of the account, determined at the close of the taxable year. IRC Sec. 4973(a).

Excess contributions are defined, for this purpose, as the sum of: (1) the aggregate amount contributed for the taxable year to the accounts, excluding rollover contributions, which is neither excludable from gross income under IRC Section 106(b) nor allowable as a deduction under IRC Section 223; and (2) this amount for the preceding taxable year reduced by the sum of (a) the distributions from the accounts that were included in gross income under IRC Section 223(f)(2), and (b) the excess of the maximum amount allowable as a deduction under IRC Section 223(b)(1), for the taxable year over the amount contributed for the taxable year. IRC Secs. 4973(g).

For this purposes, any excess contributions distributed from an HSA are treated as amounts not contributed. IRC Secs. 4973(g). *ASRS, Sec. 67, ¶640.*

Distributions and Transfers

201. How are funds accumulated in a Health Savings Account (HSA) taxed prior to distribution?

An HSA is generally exempt from income tax unless it ceases to be an HSA. IRC Sec. 223(e)(1).

# HEALTH INSURANCE	Q 203

In addition, rules similar to those applicable to individual retirement arrangements (IRAs) regarding the loss of income tax exemption for an account where an employee engages in a prohibited transaction (see IRC Sec. 408(e)(2)) and those regarding the effect of pledging an account as security (see IRC Sec. 408(e)(4)) apply to HSAs. Any amounts treated as distributed under such rules will be treated as not used to pay qualified medical expenses. IRC Sec. 223(e)(2). See Q 214. *ASRS, Sec. 67, ¶610.*

202. How are amounts distributed from a Health Savings Account (HSA) taxed?

A distribution from an HSA used exclusively to pay the qualified medical expenses of any account holder is not includable in gross income. IRC Sec. 223(f)(1). In contrast, any distribution from an HSA that is not used exclusively to pay the qualified medical expenses of the account holder must be included in the account holder's gross income. IRC Sec. 223(f)(2).

In addition, any distribution that is includable in income because it was not used to pay qualified medical expenses is also subject to a penalty tax. IRC Sec. 223(f)(4)(A). The penalty tax is 10% of includable income for a distribution from an HSA. IRC Sec. 223(f)(4)(A). Includable distributions received after an HSA holder becomes disabled (within the meaning of IRC Section 72(m)(7)), dies, or reaches the age of Medicare eligibility are not subject to the penalty tax. IRC Sec. 223(f)(4)(B), 223(f)(4)(C).

"Qualified medical expenses" are amounts paid by the account holder for medical care (as defined in IRC Section 213(d), see Q 826) for the individual, his spouse, and any dependent to the extent that the expenses are not compensated by insurance or otherwise. IRC Sec. 223(d)(2). With several exceptions, the payment of insurance premiums is not a qualified medical expense. The exceptions include (1) any expense for coverage under a health plan during a period of COBRA continuation coverage; (2) a qualified long-term care insurance contract (as defined under IRC Section 7702B(b), see Q 311), or (3) a health plan paid for during a period in which the individual is receiving unemployment compensation. IRC Sec. 223(d)(2).

An account holder may pay qualified long-term care insurance premiums with distributions from an HSA, even if contributions to the HSA were made by salary-reduction through an IRC Section 125 cafeteria plan. The amount of the qualified long-term care insurance premiums that constitute qualified medical expenses, however, are limited to the age-based limits found in IRC Section 213(d)(10), as adjusted annually. Notice 2004-50, 2004-33 IRB 196, A-40.

An HSA account holder may make tax free distributions to reimburse "qualified medical expenses" from prior tax years, as long as the expenses were incurred after the HSA was established. There is no time limit on when a distribution must occur. Notice 2004-50, 2004-33 IRB 196, A-39.

It is not an HSA trustee or custodian nor an employer who must determine whether a distribution is used for medical expenses. Rather, this responsibility falls to individual account holders. Notice 2004-2, 2004-2 IRB 269, A-29, A-30. *ASRS, Sec. 67, ¶650.*

203. Can funds in one Health Savings Account (HSA) be transferred to another HSA?

2006 Tax Facts on Insurance & Employee Benefits	213

Funds may be transferred (or rolled over) from one HSA to another or from an Archer MSA (see Q 209) to an HSA, provided that the account holder effects the transfer within 60 days of receiving the distribution. IRC Sec. 220(f)(5)(A), 223(f)(5)(A).

An HSA rollover may take place only once a year. This year is not a calendar year, but a rolling 12-month period ending on the day when the account holder receives the distribution to be rolled over. IRC Secs. 220(f)(5)(B), 223(f)(5)(B).

Transfers of HSA amounts directly from one HSA trustee to another HSA trustee (a trustee-to-trustee transfer) are not subject to the limitations under IRC Section 223(f)(5). There is no limit on the number of trustee-to-trustee transfers allowed during a year. Notice 2004-50, 2004-33 IRB 196, A-56. *ASRS, Sec. 67, ¶660.*

204. Can an individual's interest in a Health Savings Account (HSA) be transferred as part of a divorce or separation?

An individual's interest in an HSA may be transferred without income taxation from one spouse to another (or from a spouse to a former spouse) if the transfer is made under a divorce or separation instrument described in IRC Section 71(b)(2)(A). Following such a transfer, the interest in the HSA is treated as the interest of the transferee spouse. IRC Sec. 223(f)(7). *ASRS, Sec. 67, ¶660.*

Death

205. What happens to a Health Savings Account (HSA) upon the death of the account holder? Can a surviving spouse continue the account?

The disposition of an HSA at the death of the account holder depends upon who is the "designated beneficiary." If the account holder's surviving spouse is the designated beneficiary, then, when the account holder dies, the surviving spouse is treated as the account holder. IRC Sec. 223(f)(8)(A).

If the account holder's estate is the designated beneficiary, the fair market value of the assets in the HSA must be included for the estate's last taxable year. IRC Sec. 223(f)(8)(B)(i)(II). A deduction is allowed to any person (other than the decedent or the decedent's spouse) under IRC Section 691(c) with respect to amounts included in gross income by such person. IRC Sec. 223(f)(8)(B)(ii)(II).

If anyone other than a surviving spouse or the account holder's estate is the designated beneficiary, the account ceases to be an HSA as of the date of the account holder's death, and the fair market value of the assets in the account must be included in such designated beneficiary's gross income for the year. IRC Sec. 223(f)(8)(B)(i). The amount that must be included in gross income is reduced by the amount of qualified medical expenses that were incurred by the decedent account holder before his death and paid by the designated beneficiary within one year after the date of death. IRC Sec. 223(f)(8)(B)(ii)(I). *ASRS, Sec. 67, ¶670.*

Social Security

206. Are amounts contributed to a Health Savings Account (HSA) subject to social security taxes?

HEALTH INSURANCE

The definition of "wages" for purposes of the federal unemployment tax (FUTA) does not include any payment made to or for the benefit of an employee if it is reasonable to believe that the employee will be able to exclude the payment from income under IRC Section 106(d), which deals with contributions to HSAs. IRC Sec. 3306(b)(18). Unfortunately, a similar change was not made to IRC Section 3121(a) with regard to FICA. However, the IRS has stated that employer contributions to an HSA are not subject to employment taxes such as FICA *and* FUTA. Notice 2004-2, 2004-2 IRB 269, A-19. A similar statement has been made by the joint committee on taxation. See General Explanation of Tax Legislation Enacted in the 104th Congress (JCT-12-96), n. 1642, p. 324. *ASRS, Sec. 67, ¶650.*

Withholding and Reporting

207. Are employer contributions to a Health Savings Account (HSA) on behalf of an employee subject to withholding?

HSA contributions made to or for the benefit of an employee, which it is reasonable to believe will be excludable from the employee's income under IRC Section 106(d), dealing with contributions to HSAs, are not subject to income tax withholding. IRC Sec. 3401(a)(22); Notice 2004-2, 2004-2 IRB 269, A-19. *ASRS, Sec. 67, ¶650.*

208. What tax reporting requirements apply to a Health Savings Account (HSA)?

Each year, employers must report on the Form W-2 to each employee the amount contributed to an HSA for the employee or the employee's spouse. The report must be received by January 31 of the following year. IRC Sec. 6051(a); Notice 2004-2, 2004-2 IRB 269, A-34. *ASRS, Sec. 67, ¶680.*

ARCHER MEDICAL SAVINGS ACCOUNTS

209. What is an Archer Medical Savings Account (MSA) and how is it taxed?

An Archer MSA is a trust created exclusively for the purpose of paying the qualified medical expenses of the account holder. IRC Sec. 220(d)(1). An account holder is the individual on whose behalf the Archer MSA was established. IRC Sec. 220(d)(3).

Archer MSAs are still available (see Pilot Cutoff below) to small business employees and self-employed individuals with high deductible health insurance coverage. Any insurance company or bank can act as a trustee. Additionally, any person already approved by the IRS to act as an individual retirement arrangement (IRA) trustee or custodian is automatically approved to act in the same capacity for Archer MSAs. Notice 96-53, 1996-2 CB 219, A-9, A-10.

Contributions

Generally, contributions to an Archer MSA may be made either (1) by the individual or (2) by his small employer, but not by both. Notice 96-53, 1996-2 CB 219, A-12. If made by the individual taxpayer, the Archer MSA contributions are deductible from income. IRC Sec. 220(a). If made by a small employer, Archer MSA contributions are excluded from the employee's income. See IRC Sec. 106(b)(1). The Archer MSA itself is exempt from income tax. IRC Sec. 220(e)(1).

Distributions

Distributions from Archer MSAs are not includable in gross income if they are used exclusively to pay qualified medical expenses. IRC Sec. 220(f)(1). Distributions used for other purposes *are* includable in gross income and may be subject to a 15% penalty tax, with some exceptions. IRC Secs. 220(f)(2), 220(f)(4).

High Deductible Health Plan

For Archer MSAs, in the case of self-only coverage, a high deductible health plan is defined as a health plan with an annual deductible of not less than $1,800 ($1,750 for 2005) and not more than $2,700 ($2,650 for 2005), and required annual out-of-pocket expenses of not more than $3,650 ($3,500 for 2005). IRC Sec. 220(c)(2)(A). Rev. Proc. 2005-70, 2005-47 IRB 979.

In the case of family coverage, a high deductible health plan is a health plan with an annual deductible of not less than $3,650 ($3,500 for 2005) and not more than $5,450 ($5,250 for 2005) and required annual out-of-pocket expenses of not more than $6,650 ($6,450 for 2005). IRC Sec. 220(c)(2)(A); Rev. Proc. 2005-70, 2005-47 IRB 979. For this purpose, family coverage is defined as any coverage other than self-only coverage. IRC Sec. 220(c)(5).

Deduction

An eligible individual may deduct the aggregate amount paid in cash into the Archer MSA during the taxable year, subject to a limitation of 65% of the annual deductible for individuals with self-only coverage and 75% of the annual deductible for individuals with family coverage. IRC Secs. 220(a), 220(b)(2).

For married individuals, if either spouse has family coverage, then both spouses are treated as having only such family coverage, and the deduction limitation is divided equally between them, unless they agree on a different division. IRC Sec. 220(b)(3). If two spouses both have family coverage under different plans, both spouses are treated as having only the family coverage with the lowest deductible. IRC Sec. 220(b)(3).

An Archer MSA deduction cannot exceed an employee's compensation attributable to employment with the small employer offering the high deductible health plan. Similarly, the Archer MSA deduction cannot exceed a self-employed individual's earned income derived from the trade or business with respect to which the high deductible plan is established. IRC Sec. 220(b)(4).

Excess Contributions

Excess contributions to an HSA or an Archer MSA are subject to a 6% tax. However, the tax may not exceed 6% of the value of the account, determined at the close of the taxable year. IRC Sec. 4973(a) as amended by the Medicare Act of 2003.

Pilot Cutoff

Archer MSAs were initially available on a pilot basis. The cut-off year for new accounts under the Archer MSA pilot program was originally 2003, but was extended to the end of 2005. IRC Sec. 220(i)(2). See also Ann. 2002-90, 2002-40 IRB 684.

No individual is treated as an eligible individual for any taxable year beginning after the cut-off year unless: (a) the individual was an active Archer MSA participant for any taxable year ending on or before the close of the cut-off year; or (2) the individual first became an active Archer MSA participant for a taxable year ending after the cut-off year by reason of coverage under a high deductible health plan of an Archer MSA-participating employer. IRC Sec. 220(i)(1). *ASRS, Sec. 67, ¶610, 630.*

INDIVIDUAL RETIREMENT PLANS

IN GENERAL

210. What is an individual retirement plan?

A traditional individual retirement plan is a personal retirement savings program toward which eligible individuals may contribute both deductible and nondeductible payments with the benefit of *tax-deferred* build up of income. A Roth individual retirement plan is a personal retirement savings program toward which eligible individuals may contribute only nondeductible payments with the potential benefit of *tax-free* build up of income. See Q 228. A Roth individual retirement plan must clearly be designated as such at the time of establishment, and that designation cannot later be changed—the recharacterization of a Roth IRA will require the execution of new documents (see Q 222). IRC Sec. 408A(b); Treas. Reg. §1.408A-2, A-2. With respect to both traditional and Roth individual retirement plans, some individuals may also contribute to such plans for their spouses. See Q 218.

There are two kinds of traditional and Roth individual retirement plans. They are: individual retirement accounts and individual retirement annuities.

Individual Retirement Account

This is a written trust or custodial account. IRC Secs. 408(a), 408(h), 408A(a). Contributions to it must be in cash and may not exceed the maximum annual contribution limit for the tax year—except for rollover contributions (see Q 444), for contributions to a SIMPLE IRA (see Q 242), and for employer contributions to simplified employee pensions (see Q 240). IRC Sec. 408(a)(1). See Q 220, Q 221. (A wire order from a broker to a custodian will constitute a "cash contribution" on the date payment and registration instructions are received by the broker, providing an agency arrangement recognized by and binding under state law exists between the broker and the custodian. Let. Ruls. 9034068, 8837034.) The trustee or custodian must be a bank, a federally insured credit union, a building and loan association or other person who satisfies requirements of the Internal Revenue Service. IRC Secs. 408(a)(2), 408(n). A trustee acceptable to the Service cannot be an individual, but can be a corporation or partnership which demonstrates that it has fiduciary ability (including continuity of life, established location, fiduciary experience and fiduciary and financial responsibility), capacity to account for the interests of a large number of individuals, fitness to handle retirement funds, ability to administer fiduciary powers (including maintenance of a separate trust division), and adequate net worth (at least $250,000 initially). Treas. Regs. §§1.408-2(b)(2), 1.408-2(e).

The interest of the individual in the balance of his individual retirement account must be nonforfeitable, and the assets must not be commingled with other property except in a common trust fund or common investment fund. In such a trust, they may be pooled with trust funds of regular qualified plans. IRC Secs. 408(a)(4), 408(a)(5), 408(e)(6); Rev. Rul. 81-100, 1981-1 CB 326; see also *Nichola v. Comm.*, TC Memo 1992-105. No part of the trust funds may be invested in life insurance. IRC Sec. 408(a)(3). An account generally may not invest in collectibles. See Q 214. An account may invest in annuity contracts that provide, in the case of death prior to the time distributions commence, for a payment equal to the sum of the premiums paid, or, if greater, the cash

INDIVIDUAL RETIREMENT PLANS   Q 210

value of the contract. Treas. Reg. §1.408-2(b)(3). An account may not use any part of
its assets to purchase an endowment contract issued after November 6, 1978. Treas.
Regs. §§1.408-4(f), 1.408-3(e)(1)(ix). With respect to traditional individual retirement
accounts, distribution of the individual's interest must begin by April 1 of the year
after the year in which he reaches age 70½ and must be made over a limited period. In
addition, distributions must comply with the incidental death benefit requirements of
IRC Section 401(a). See Q 234. IRC Secs. 408(a)(6), 408A(c)(5). With respect to both
traditional and Roth accounts, required minimum distribution requirements must be
met upon death of the owner. See Q 235. IRC Secs. 408(a)(6), 408A(c)(5).

Individual Retirement Annuity

This may be an annuity or an endowment contract issued by an insurance company.
IRC Secs. 408(b), 408A(a). (But an endowment contract *issued* after November 6, 1978
will not qualify. Treas. Reg. §1.408-3(e)(1)(ix).) The contract must be nontransferable.
A contract will be considered transferable if it can be used as security for any loan other
than a loan from the issuer in an amount not greater than the cash value of the contract.
Even so, a policy loan would cause the contract to cease to be an individual retirement
annuity or endowment contract as of the first day of the owner's tax year in which the
loan was made. IRC Sec. 408(e)(3); Treas. Reg. §1.408-3(c). See Q 214. Contracts
issued after November 6, 1978 may not have fixed premiums. IRC Sec. 408(b)(2)(A).
The annual premium on behalf of any individual may not exceed the maximum annual contribution limit for the tax year—except in the case of a SIMPLE IRA (see
Q 242) or a simplified employee pension (see Q 240). IRC Sec. 408(b)(2)(B). See Q 220,
Q 221. Any refund of premium must be applied to the payment of future premiums or
the purchase of additional benefits before the close of the calendar year of the refund.
IRC Sec. 408(b)(2)(C). The interest of the owner must be nonforfeitable. IRC Sec.
408(b)(4). With respect to traditional individual retirement annuities, distribution must
begin by April 1 of the year after the year in which the owner reaches age 70½ and the
period over which distribution may be made is limited. In addition, distributions must
comply with the incidental death benefit requirements of IRC Section 401(a). See
Q 234. IRC Secs. 408(b)(3), 408A(c)(5). With respect to both traditional and Roth
annuities, required minimum distribution requirements must be met upon death of the
owner. See Q 235. IRC Secs. 408(a)(6), 408A(c)(5).

The Service has privately ruled that a contract that includes a substantial element of
life insurance will not qualify as an individual retirement annuity. Let. Rul. 8439026.

Proposed regulations state that in order for a flexible premium annuity to qualify
as an individual retirement annuity, the contract must provide that (1) at no time after
the initial premium has been paid will a specified renewal premium be required; (2)
the contract may be continued as a paid-up annuity under its nonforfeiture provision if
premium payments cease altogether; and (3) if the contract is continued on a paid-up
basis, it may be reinstated at any date prior to its maturity date by a payment of premium
to the insurer. (Two exceptions allow the insurer to set a minimum premium (not in
excess of $50) and to terminate certain contracts where premiums have not been paid
for an extended period and the paid-up benefit would be less than $20 a month.) A
flexible premium contract will not be considered to have fixed premiums merely because
a maximum annual premium is set, an annual charge is placed against the policy value,
or because the contract requires a level annual premium for supplementary benefits
(such as a waiver of premium feature). Prop. Treas. Reg. §1.408-3(f).

A participation certificate in a group annuity contract meeting the above requirements will be considered an individual retirement annuity if there is a separate accounting for the benefit allocable to each participant-owner and the group contract is for the exclusive benefit of the participant-owners and their beneficiaries. Treas. Reg. §1.408-3(a).

A "wraparound annuity" contract entered into on or before September 25, 1981 as an individual retirement annuity will continue to be treated for tax purposes as an individual retirement annuity provided no contributions are made on behalf of any individual who was not included under the contract on that date. "Wraparound annuity," as used here, refers to an insurance company contract containing typical deferred annuity provisions, but which also promises to allocate net premiums to an account invested in shares of a specific mutual fund that is available to the general public without purchase of the annuity contract. Rev. Rul. 81-225, 1981-2 CB 12, as clarified by Rev. Rul. 82-55, 1982-1 CB 12. Effective November 16, 1999, annuity contracts in which the premiums are invested at the direction of the IRA owners in "publicly available securities" (i.e., mutual funds that are available for public purchase) will be treated as an individual retirement annuity contract if no additional federal income tax liability would have been incurred if the owner had instead contributed such amount into an individual retirement account where the funds were commingled in a common investment fund. Rev. Proc. 99-44, 1999-48 IRB 598, modifying Rev. Rul. 81-225, 1981-2 CB 12.

Retirement Bonds

Prior to TRA '84, the Code provided for the issuance of *retirement bonds*. IRC Sec. 409, as in effect prior to repeal by TRA '84. These were issued by the U.S. government, with interest to be paid on redemption. Sales of these bonds were suspended as of April 30, 1982. Treasury Release (4-27-82). Subsequently, the Treasury Department announced that *existing* bonds could be redeemed by their holders at any time without being subject to a premature distribution penalty. See Q 231. Treasury Announcement (7-26-84). Also, existing bonds can be rolled over into other individual retirement plans, under rules applicable to rollovers from individual retirement plans. See Q 452. IRC Sec. 409(b)(3)(C), prior to repeal. *ASRS, Sec. 62, ¶310.*

211. What is a "deemed IRA"?

For plan years beginning after December 31, 2002, a qualified plan, IRC Section 403(b) tax sheltered annuity plan, or eligible IRC Section 457 governmental plan may allow employees to make voluntary employee contributions to a separate account or annuity established under the plan. If such account or annuity meets the rules for traditional IRAs under IRC Section 408 or for Roth IRAs under IRC Section 408A, then such account or annuity will be "deemed" an IRA and not a qualified employer plan. A voluntary employee contribution is any non-mandatory contribution that the individual designates as such. Such "deemed IRAs" will not be subject to the IRC rules governing the employer plan; however, they will be subject to the exclusive benefit and fiduciary rules of ERISA to the extent they otherwise apply to the employer plan. IRC Sec. 408(q). See Rev. Proc. 2003-13, 2003-4 IRB 1.

Under final regulations, deemed IRAs and the plan under which they are adopted are generally treated as separate entities, with each subject to the rules generally applicable to that type of entity. Treas. Reg. §1.408(q)-1. The regulations further provide that the "availability of a deemed IRA is not a benefit, right or feature of the qualified

INDIVIDUAL RETIREMENT PLANS   Q 212

employer plan," meaning that eligibility for and contributions to deemed IRAs are not subject to the general nondiscrimination requirements applicable to qualified plans. Treas. Reg. §1.408(q)-1(f)(6).

The regulations provide three exceptions to treating a qualified plan and deemed IRAs as separate entities. First, the qualified plan documents must contain the deemed IRA provisions and be in effect at the time the deemed IRA contributions are accepted. Plans offering deemed IRAs have until the plan year beginning in 2004 to have such provisions in writing. Treas. Reg. §1.408(q)-1(d)(1).

Second, deemed IRA and qualified plan assets may be commingled. The prohibition against commingling in IRC Section 408(a)(5) (see Q 210) does not apply to deemed IRA and qualified plan assets. Deemed IRA and qualified plan assets may still not be further commingled with non-plan assets. Treas. Reg. §1.408(q)-1(d)(2).

Third, if deemed IRA and qualified plan assets are commingled in a single trust, the failure of any of the deemed IRAs maintained by a plan to meet the requirements of IRC Section 408 (traditional IRAs) or IRC Section 408A (Roth IRAs) can disqualify the qualified plan, requiring correction through the Employee Plans Compliance Resolution System or another administrative procedure. See Q 322. Likewise, the disqualification of the plan can cause the individual accounts to be no longer deemed IRAs. Treas. Reg. §1.408(q)-1(g).

If deemed IRA and qualified plan assets are maintained in separate trusts, a qualified plan will not be disqualified solely because of the failure of any of the deemed IRAs to meet the requirements of IRC Section 408 (traditional IRAs) or IRC Section 408A (Roth IRAs). Likewise, if separate trusts are maintained, individual accounts will not fail to be deemed IRAs solely because of the disqualification of the plan. Treas. Reg. §1.408(q)-1(g).

212. What information must be provided to a buyer of an IRA?

A "disclosure statement" and a copy of the governing instrument must be furnished to the individual at least seven days before the plan is purchased or established, whichever is earlier, or as late as the time it is purchased or established, whichever is earlier, if the individual is permitted to revoke the plan within at least seven days. An individual revoking his plan is entitled to return of the full amount he paid without adjustment for sales commission, administrative expenses, or fluctuation in market value. Treas. Reg. §1.408-6(d)(4). If the governing instrument is amended after the IRA is no longer subject to revocation, a copy of the amendment (and possibly a "disclosure statement") must be furnished to the individual not later than the 30th day after the later of the date the amendment is adopted or becomes effective. See Treas. Reg. §1.408-6(d)(4)(ii)(C).

The regulations also provide that, if values under an individual retirement arrangement are guaranteed or can be projected, the trustee or issuer must in certain instances disclose to an IRA purchaser the amounts guaranteed or projected to be withdrawable. Basically, these regulations provide that the trustee must show the owner the amount he could receive if he closed his account and paid any surrender charges or penalties, at the end of each of the first five years after the initial contribution, and at ages 60, 65 and 70. Treas. Reg. §1.408-6(d)(4)(v). In making the disclosure, the trustee must show the amount guaranteed (or projected) to be withdrawable, *after reduction for all charges or penalties that may be applied.* The disclosures required for values at the owner's ages 60, 65 and 70 must be based on the actual age of the individual at the time of the disclosure. If a guaranteed rate is actually lower than the rate currently being paid on an account, the disclosure statement may use the higher rate, but must clearly indicate that the guaranteed rate is lower. Rev. Rul. 86-78, 1986-1 CB 208.

For the reporting requirements imposed on IRA trustees with respect to required minimum distributions, see Q 237. *ASRS, Sec. 62, ¶340.*

213. What is the saver's credit and who can claim it?

Certain lower-income taxpayers may claim a temporary, nonrefundable credit for "qualified retirement savings contributions" in taxable years beginning after 2001 and before 2007. IRC Sec. 25B. "Qualified retirement savings contributions" include contributions to Roth or traditional IRAs, as well as elective deferrals to a 401(k) plan (see Q 394), an IRC Section 403(b) tax sheltered annuity (see Q 465), an eligible IRC Section 457 governmental plan (see Q 124), a SIMPLE IRA (see Q 242), and a salary reduction SEP (see Q 241). Voluntary after-tax contributions to a qualified plan or 403(b) tax sheltered annuity are also eligible for the credit. IRC Sec. 25B(d)(1); Ann. 2001-106, 2001-44 IRB 416, A-5. The fact that contributions are made pursuant to a negative election (i.e., automatic enrollment) will not preclude a participant from claiming the saver's credit. See Ann. 2001-106, above. Contributions made to an IRA that are withdrawn, together with the net income attributable to such contribution, on or before the due date (including extensions of time) for filing the federal income tax return of the contributing individual are not considered eligible contributions. See Ann. 2001-106, above, A-5.

However, in order to prevent "churning" (simply switching existing retirement funds from one account to another to qualify for the credit), the total of qualified retirement savings contributions is reduced by certain distributions received by the taxpayer during the prior two taxable years and the current taxable year for which the credit is claimed, including the period up to the due date (plus extensions) for filing the federal income tax return for the current taxable year. Distributions received by the taxpayer's spouse during the same time period are also counted if the taxpayer and spouse filed jointly both for the year during which a distribution was made and the year for which the credit is taken. Corrective distributions of excess contributions and excess aggregate contributions (see Q 406), excess deferrals (see Q 396), dividends paid on employer securities under Section 404(k) (see Q 415), and loans treated as distributions (see Q 420) are not taken into account. IRC Sec. 25B(d)(2); Ann. 2001-106, above, A-4.

The credit is allowed against the sum of the regular tax and the alternative minimum tax (minus certain other credits) and is allowed in addition to any other deduction or exclusion that would otherwise apply. IRC Sec. 25B(g); Ann. 2001-106, above, A-7 and A-8.

To be eligible to claim the credit, the taxpayer must be at least 18 as of the end of the tax year and must not be claimed as a dependent by someone else or be a full-time student. Full-time students include any individual who is enrolled in school during some part of each of five months during the year and is enrolled for the number of hours or courses the school considers to be full-time. IRC Sec. 25B(c); Ann. 2001-106, above, A-2.

INDIVIDUAL RETIREMENT PLANS   Q 214

The amount of the credit is limited to an "applicable percentage" of IRA contributions and elective deferrals up to $2,000. The "applicable percentages" are as follows:

ADJUSTED GROSS INCOME

| Joint return | | Head of a household | | All other cases | | Applicable |
Over	Not over	Over	Not over	Over	Not over	percentage
0	$30,000	0	$22,500	0	$15,000	50%
30,000	32,500	22,500	24,375	15,000	16,250	20%
32,500	50,000	24,375	37,500	16,250	25,000	10%
50,000		37,500		25,000		0%

For this purpose, *adjusted gross income* is calculated without regard to the exclusions for income derived from certain foreign sources or sources within United States possessions. IRC Sec. 25B(e).

For married taxpayers filing jointly, contributions by or for either or both spouses, up to $2,000 per year for each spouse, may give rise to the saver's credit. Ann. 2001-106, above, A-9. *ASRS, Sec. 62, ¶415.*

214. When are funds accumulated in an IRA taxed?

Generally, funds accumulated in a traditional IRA are not taxable until they are actually distributed (see Q 227) and funds accumulated in a Roth IRA may or may not be taxable upon actual distribution (see Q 228). However, special rules may treat funds accumulated in an IRA as a "deemed distribution" and, thus, includable in income under the rules discussed in Q 227 for traditional IRAs and in Q 228 for Roth IRAs.

A distribution of a nontransferable, nonforfeitable annuity contract that provides for payments to begin by age 70½ and not to extend beyond certain limits is not taxable, but payments made under such an annuity would be includable in income under the appropriate rules.

A contribution (excess or otherwise) may be distributed income tax free under the rules discussed in Q 226 (provided, in the case of a traditional IRA, no deduction was allowed for the contribution). If net income allocable to the contribution is distributed before the due date for filing the tax return for the year in which the contribution was made, it must be included in income for the tax year for which the contribution was made even if the distribution was actually made after the end of that year. See IRC Sec. 408(d)(4); Treas. Reg. §1.408-4(c). With respect to distributions of excess contributions after this deadline, the net income amount is included in income in the year distributed. Any net income amount may also be subject to penalty tax as a premature distribution.

An individual may transfer, without tax, his IRA to his spouse or former spouse under a divorce or separate maintenance decree or a written instrument incident to the divorce. The IRA is then maintained for the benefit of the former spouse. IRC Sec. 408(d)(6). However, any other assignment of an IRA is a deemed distribution of the amount assigned. Treas. Reg. §1.408-4(a)(2). Where an individual rolled over his interest in a tax sheltered annuity pursuant to a QDRO (see Q 349) to an IRA, the subsequent transfer of the IRA to the individual's spouse was considered a "transfer incident to a divorce" and, thus, nontaxable to either spouse. Let. Rul. 8916083. A taxpayer was liable for taxes on a distribution from his IRA that he subsequently

2006 Tax Facts on Insurance & Employee Benefits

Q 214   FEDERAL INCOME TAX

turned over to his ex-wife in satisfaction of a family court order because it was not a "transfer incident to divorce" and the family court order was not a QDRO because it did not specifically require the transfer of assets to come from the IRA. *Czepiel v. Comm.*, TC Memo 1999-289. A transfer of funds between the IRAs of a husband and wife that does not come within the divorce exception is a deemed distribution in spite of provisions in the Code which provide that no gain is recognized on transfers between spouses. See Let. Ruls. 9422060, 8820086. The transfer of a portion of a husband's IRA to his wife to be placed in an IRA for her benefit that was the result of a private written agreement between the two which was not considered incident to a divorce was not eligible for nontaxable treatment under IRC Section 408(d)(6). Let. Rul. 9344027. Where a taxpayer received a full distribution from his IRA and endorsed the distribution check over to his soon-to-be-ex-wife, the husband was determined to have failed to satisfy the requirements for a non-taxable transfer incident to divorce and was liable for taxation on the entire proceeds of the IRA distribution. *Jones v. Comm.*, TC Memo 2000-219.

Where two traditional IRAs were classified as community property, the distributions of the deceased spouse's community interest in the IRAs to relatives other than her surviving husband were taxable only to those recipients and not to the husband. State community property laws, although disregarded for some purposes (see Q 217, Q 218), are not preempted by IRC Section 408(g). See Let. Rul. 8040101. In a case of first impression, the Tax Court has ruled that the recognition of community property interests in IRAs would conflict with existing federal tax rules. IRC Section 408(g) requires application without regard to community property laws. By reason of IRC Section 408(g), the former spouse is not treated as a distributee on any portion of the IRA distribution for purposes of federal income tax rules despite her community property interest in the assets. Therefore, a distribution from an IRA to a former spouse is taxable to the account holder unless it is executed pursuant to decree of divorce, or other written maintenance decree under IRC Section 408(d)(6). *Bunney v. Comm.*, 114 TC No. 17 (2000). Where the taxpayers requested that an IRA be reclassified under state marital property law from individual property to marital property, no distribution under IRC Section 408(d)(1) was deemed to have occurred. Let. Ruls. 199937055, 9419036. The involuntary garnishment of a husband's IRA and resulting transfer of such funds to the former spouse to satisfy arrearages in child support payments was a deemed distribution to the husband because it discharged a legal obligation owed by the husband. *Vorwald v. Comm.*, TC Memo 1997-15.

Where a taxpayer transferred funds from a single IRA into two newly-created IRAs, the direct trustee-to-trustee transfers were not considered distributions under IRC Section 408(d)(1). Let. Rul. 9438019. See also Rev. Rul. 78-406, 1978-2 CB 157; Let. Rul. 9433032. The division of a decedent's IRA into separate subaccounts does not result in current taxation of the IRA beneficiaries. Let. Rul. 200008044.

If any assets of an individual retirement account are used to purchase collectibles (works of art, gems, antiques, metals, etc.), the amount so used will be treated as distributed from the account (and may also be subject to penalty as a premature distribution). However, a plan may invest in certain gold or silver coins issued by the United States, any coins issued under the laws of a state, and certain platinum coins. IRC Sec. 408(m). A plan may buy gold, silver, platinum, and palladium bullion of a fineness sufficient for the commodities market, but only if the bullion remains in the physical possession of the IRA trustee. IRC Sec. 408(m); Let. Rul. 200217059.

INDIVIDUAL RETIREMENT PLANS   Q 214

If any part of an individual retirement account is used by the individual as security for a loan, that portion is deemed distributed on the first day of the tax year in which the loan was made. IRC Sec. 408(e)(4); Treas. Reg. §1.408-4(d)(2); Let. Ruls. 8335117, 8019103, 8011116. However, amounts rolled over into an IRA from a qualified plan by one of the twenty-five highest paid employees may be pledged as security for repayments that may have to be made to the plan in the event of an early plan termination. See, e.g., Let. Ruls. 8845060, 8803087, 8751049. See also Treas. Reg. §1.401-4(c). (A less-than-60-day interest-free loan from an IRA is possible under the rollover rules. See Q 454. See Let. Rul. 9010007.)

If the owner of an individual retirement annuity borrows money under or by use of the contract in any tax year, including a policy loan, the annuity ceases to qualify as an individual retirement annuity as of the first day of the tax year and the fair market value of the contract would be deemed distributed on that day. See IRC Sec. 408(e)(3). See also *Griswold v. Comm.*, 85 TC 869 (1985).

If an individual engages in a prohibited transaction during a year, his individual retirement account ceases to qualify as such as of the first day of that tax year. (But he is not liable for a prohibited transaction tax. IRC Sec. 4975(c)(3).) The fair market value of *all* the assets in the account is deemed distributed on that day. See Treas. Reg. §1.408-1(c)(2). If the account is maintained by an employer, only the separate account of the individual involved is disqualified and deemed distributed. IRC Sec. 408(e)(2). The transfer to an individual retirement account of a personal note received in a terminating distribution from a qualified plan and the holding of that note is a prohibited transaction. TAM 8849001. The use of IRA funds to invest in a personal retirement residence of the taxpayer is considered a prohibited transaction under IRC Section 4975(c)(1)(D) and, thus, treated as a distribution. *Harris v. Comm.*, TC Memo 1994-22.

Whether a purchase of life insurance in conjunction with an individual retirement plan but with non-plan funds constitutes a prohibited transaction apparently depends on the circumstances. IRS has held that the purchase of insurance on the depositor's life *by the trustee* of the account with non-plan funds amounted to an indirect prohibited transaction by the depositor. Let. Rul. 8245075. However, IRS has also ruled that the solicitation by an association of individuals who maintain individual retirement plans with the association for enrollment in a group life plan did not result in a prohibited transaction where premiums would be paid by the individuals and not out of plan funds. Let. Rul. 8338141.

Institutions may offer limited financial incentives to IRA and Keogh holders without running afoul of the prohibited transaction rules provided certain conditions are met. Generally, the value of the incentive must not exceed $10 for deposits of less than $5,000 and $20 for deposits of $5,000 or more. These requirements are also applicable to SEPs that allow participants to transfer their SEP balances to IRAs sponsored by other financial institutions. PTE 93-1, 58 Fed. Reg. 3567, 1-11-93; PTE 93-33, 58 Fed. Reg. 31053, 5-28-93, as amended at 59 Fed. Reg. 22686, 5-2-94. On October 21, 1998 the Department of Labor proposed an amendment to PTE 93-33 that would expand the coverage of this exemption to include Education IRAs and SIMPLE IRAs. If adopted, the proposed amendment will be retroactively effective to January 1, 1998. 63 Fed. Reg. 56231, 10-21-98.

A distribution of any amount may be received free of federal income tax to the extent the amount is contributed within 60 days to another plan under the rollover rules. See Q 452.

For the penalty tax imposed on accumulated amounts not distributed in accordance with the required minimum distribution rules, see Q 233. *ASRS, Sec. 62, ¶¶420.1(c), 420.1(d)*.

215. How are the earnings on an IRA taxed?

An IRA offers tax free build up on contributions. The earnings on a traditional IRA are tax deferred to the owner; that is, they are not taxed until the owner begins receiving distributions. See Q 227. The earnings on a Roth IRA may or may not be taxed upon distribution. See Q 228. However, like a trust that is part of a qualified plan, an individual retirement account is subject to taxes for its unrelated business income. See Q 441, Q 498.

Tax deferral is lost if an individual engages in a prohibited transaction or borrows under or by use of an individual retirement annuity. The loss occurs as of the first day of the tax year in which the prohibited transaction or borrowing occurred. IRC Sec. 408(e); Treas. Reg. §1.408-1. In the case of an account established by an employer or association of employees, only the separate account of the individual loses its deferred status. *ASRS, Sec. 62, ¶110*.

216. Are IRAs subject to attachment?

ERISA provides that benefits under "pension plans" must not be assigned or alienated. ERISA Sec. 206(d)(1). This provision has been construed as protecting pension benefits from claims of creditors. However, ERISA defines a "pension plan" as a plan established or maintained by an employer to provide retirement income to employees. An individual retirement plan is generally not maintained by an employer and, thus, is not protected under federal law by the anti-alienation clause of ERISA. *Patterson v. Shumate*, 504 U.S. 753 (1992).

The Bankruptcy Abuse Prevention and Consumer Protection Act of 2005 provides exemptions for a debtor's interest in qualified retirement plans, SEP IRAs, SIMPLE IRAs, and traditional and Roth IRAs. 11 U.S.C. § 522(b)(2)(C). These exemptions are available whether or not the debtor otherwise elects state or federal exemptions. The new bankruptcy provisions were effective October 17, 2005.

The exemption for contributory (non-rollover) traditional and Roth IRAs is limited to $1 million in the aggregate, unless the bankruptcy court determines that "the interests of justice so require." 11 U.S.C. § 522(n). The exemption for IRA balances rolled over from other retirement accounts with an unlimited exemption is unlimited.

Planning Point: Although assets rolled over from non-IRA retirement accounts—and future earnings on those assets—do not lose their unlimited exemption by virtue of the rollover, taxpayers with significant IRA balances are advised to keep their contributory and rollover IRA accounts segregated. Otherwise, to the extent that rollover IRA assets are commingled with contributory IRA assets, it may be difficult to calculate the value of the assets attributable to the rollover.

INDIVIDUAL RETIREMENT PLANS   Q 218

Under prior law, the United States Supreme Court held that the federal bankruptcy exemption did protect traditional IRAs. Rousey v. Jacoway, 544 U.S. ___ (2005).

Outside the bankrupcty context, the Seventh Circuit has ruled that because ERISA's anti-alienation provisions do not apply to assets contained in IRAs such assets may be seized under criminal forfeiture proceedings brought by the federal government. Infelise v. U.S., 159 F.3d 300 (7th Cir. 1998). The Tenth Circuit Court has held that an IRA trustee was not in breach of its' fiduciary duty to an IRA account holder when the trustee responded to an IRS service of notice of levy for delinquent taxes owed by the account holder by turning over to the IRS assets held in the account. Kane v. Capital Guardian Trust Co., 98-2 USTC (10th Cir. 1998).

ELIGIBILITY

217. What individuals may establish an individual retirement plan?

Virtually any individual who wishes to do so may establish his own traditional individual retirement plan. However, in order to deduct contributions to such a plan once it is established and avoid tax penalties for excess contributions, an individual (1) must have compensation (either earned income of an employee or self-employed person, or alimony), and (2) must not have attained age 70½ during the taxable year for which the contribution is made. IRC Sec. 219. If an individual is an "active participant" (see Q 224), his deduction may be limited. See Q 220. Any individual who can make a rollover contribution (see Q 444) may establish an individual retirement plan (or more than one plan) to receive it. Special Ruling 9-28-76. See Q 446 to Q 454.

In order to establish a Roth individual retirement plan, an individual (1) must have compensation (either earned income of an employee or self-employed person, or alimony), and (2) must *not* have adjusted gross income (a) of $160,000 or above in the case of a taxpayer filing a joint return, (b) of $110,000 or above in the case of a taxpayer filing a single or head-of-household return, or (c) of $10,000 or above in the case of a married individual filing separately. IRC Secs. 219, 408A. An individual who satisfies these requirements may establish and contribute to a Roth IRA even if he has attained age 70½. IRC Sec. 408A(c)(4).

As to what constitutes "compensation," see Q 223. An estate may not make a contribution on behalf of the decedent. Let. Rul. 8439066. *ASRS, Sec. 62, ¶410.1(a)*.

218. May a person contribute to an individual retirement plan for his spouse?

A married individual may make contributions to a traditional individual retirement plan for a non-working spouse if (1) the non-working spouse and working spouse file a joint return for the taxable year and (2) the amount of compensation (if any) includable in the non-working spouse's gross income for the taxable year is less than the compensation includable in the working spouse's gross income for the taxable year. IRC Sec. 219(c)(2). The deductibility of such contributions depends upon whether the non-working spouse or working spouse is an "active participant" (see Q 224) and upon the married couple's adjusted gross income. See Q 220. IRC Sec. 219(g). Community property laws are disregarded for purposes of this deduction. IRC Sec. 219(f)(2).

2006 Tax Facts on Insurance & Employee Benefits

A married individual may make contributions to a Roth individual retirement plan (Roth IRA) for a non-working spouse if (a) statements (1) and (2) above apply, *and* (b) the adjusted gross income of the married couple is less than $160,000. See Q 221. IRC Secs. 219(c)(2), 408A(c)(3). As to what constitutes "compensation" for these purposes, see Q 223. (The joint return rule implicitly requires that, except where one or both have died, the contributing individual and his spouse have identical taxable years. IRC Sec. 6013.)

An eligible individual may make contributions to a spousal plan even if he does not own or contribute to an individual retirement plan for himself. However, where plans are maintained for both the contributing individual and his spouse, the plans may be separate plans, or they may be sub-accounts of a single plan; a jointly-owned plan is not permitted. Nonetheless, each spouse may have a right of survivorship with respect to the sub-account of the other spouse. See General Explanation of the Tax Reform Act of 1976 *reprinted in* 1976-3 CB 442.

If the earner spouse dies during the taxable year, the surviving spouse may contribute to the spousal IRA if a joint return is filed for the year. No amount may be contributed to the IRA of the deceased spouse. Let. Rul. 8527083.

The contributing individual must have been married to his spouse as of the last day of their tax year. An individual legally separated under a decree of divorce or separate maintenance is not married for these purposes. IRC Sec. 6013(d)(2). *ASRS, Sec. 62, ¶410.1(a)*.

219. When must contributions to IRAs be made?

A contribution made on account of the tax year of the contributing individual may be deducted in that year. Contributions to existing or new plans may be made and new plans may be established as late as the time when the individual's tax return for the year is due (excluding extensions) and, with respect to traditional IRAs, nonetheless be deducted in that tax year if the contribution is made on account of that year. This applies both to contributions to individual plans and contributions to spousal plans. IRC Secs. 219(f)(3), 408A(c)(7). A postmark is evidence of the timeliness of the contribution. Let. Ruls. 8633080, 8611090, 8536085. *ASRS, Sec. 62, ¶¶410.1(a), 410.2(a)*.

220. How much may an individual contribute to a traditional individual retirement plan? How much may he deduct?

Contributions to traditional IRAs are limited at two levels. First, there is a limit on the amount of contributions that may be deducted for income tax purposes. Second, there is a limit with respect to the amount of total contributions that can be made, deductible and nondeductible. Contributions to an individual retirement plan are not subject to the general limits on contributions and benefits of IRC Section 415. See Q 332. (See Q 240 for the effect of IRC Section 415 on simplified employee pensions.) The source of the funds contributed to an IRA is not determinative as to eligibility or deductibility so long as the contributing individual has includable compensation at least equal to the amount of the contribution. See Let. Rul. 8326163.

Deductible Contributions

If an eligible individual contributes on his own behalf to a traditional IRA, he generally may deduct amounts contributed in cash up to the lesser of the "deductible

INDIVIDUAL RETIREMENT PLANS   Q 220

amount" for the taxable year or 100% of *compensation* includable in his gross income for such year. IRC Sec. 219(b)(1). The "deductible amount" is $4,000 for taxable years beginning in 2005 through 2007, and $5,000 for 2008. (It was $3,000 for 2002 through 2004.) IRC Sec. 219(b)(5)(a). The $5,000 amount will be indexed for inflation in increments of $500 for taxable years beginning in 2009 and 2010. IRC Sec. 219(b)(5)(C). The "deductible amount" for taxable years beginning in 2006 through 2010 is increased by $1,000 for individuals who have attained age 50 before the close of the tax year. This catch-up amount was $500 for taxable years beginning in 2002 through 2005. IRC Sec. 219(b)(5)(B). See Q 397. (Employer contributions to a simplified employee pension and any amounts contributed to a SIMPLE IRA are not subject to this limitation.) IRC Sec. 219(b). The overall maximum contribution limit is also equal to the "deductible amount." IRC Sec. 408(a)(1). Contributions made to Roth IRAs for the taxable year reduce both deductible and overall contribution limits (see Q 221). As to what constitutes "compensation," see Q 223.

The actual maximum deduction allowed to an individual for a cash contribution to a traditional IRA *for a non-working spouse* for a taxable year is the lesser of (1) the "deductible amount" or (2) 100% of the non-working spouse's includable compensation, plus 100% of the working spouse's includable compensation minus (a) the amount of any IRA deduction taken by the working spouse for the year, and (b) the amount of any contribution made to a Roth IRA by the working spouse. IRC Sec. 219(c)(1). Likewise, contributions to Roth IRAs for a non-working spouse reduce this limit (see Q 221). While a husband and wife who file jointly and are both under age 50 are permitted a maximum deduction of up to $8,000 in 2005 through 2007 ($4,000 for each spouse), the deduction for each spouse is computed separately.

The deduction for contributions made to individual and spousal plans may be reduced or eliminated if the individual or his spouse is an "active participant" (see Q 224). The amount of the reduction is the amount that bears the same ratio to the overall limit as the taxpayer's *adjusted gross income* (AGI) in excess of an "applicable dollar amount" bears to $10,000 ($20,000 in the case of a joint return for taxable years beginning after 2006). IRC Sec. 219(g)(2). Thus, the amount of the reduction is calculated as follows:

$$\text{"deductible amount"} \times \frac{\text{AGI} - \text{"applicable dollar amount"}}{\$10,000}$$

In the case of a taxpayer who is an active participant and files a single or head-of-household return, the "applicable dollar amount" is $50,000 for taxable years beginning in 2005 and thereafter. IRC Sec. 219(g)(3)(B)(ii).

In the case of married taxpayers who file a joint return and both spouses are active participants *or* only one is an active participant, the "applicable dollar amount" for the spouses who are active participants is:

For taxable years beginning in:	The "applicable dollar amount" is:
2006	$75,000
2007 and thereafter	$80,000

IRC Sec. 219(g)(3)(B)(i). The applicable dollar limit was $70,000 for 2005.

2006 Tax Facts on Insurance & Employee Benefits

In the case of married taxpayers who file a joint return and only one is an active participant, the "applicable dollar amount" for the non-active participant spouse is $150,000. The denominator in the fraction remains at $10,000 (it does not increase to $20,000 in 2007). IRC Sec. 219(g)(7).

In the case of a married individual filing a separate return where either spouse is an active participant, the "applicable dollar amount" is $0. IRC Sec. 219(g)(3)(B)(iii).

Thus, for taxable years beginning in 2005, the IRA deduction limit is $0 for (1) individuals who are active participants and file a single or head-of-household return with AGI of $60,000 and above, (2) married individuals who are active participants and file a joint return with AGI of $80,000 and above, (3) married individuals whose spouses are active participants but they are not and file a joint return with AGI of $160,000 and above, and (4) married individuals who are active participants *or* their spouses are active participants and file separately with AGI of $10,000 and above. The amount of the reduction is rounded to the next lowest multiple of $10. IRC Sec. 219(g)(2)(C). Unless the individual's deduction limit is reduced to zero, the Code permits a minimum deduction of $200. IRC Sec. 219(g)(2)(B).

For this purpose, AGI is calculated without regard to the exclusions for foreign earned income, qualified adoption expenses paid by the employer and interest on qualified United States savings bonds used to pay higher education expenses, and social security benefits includable in gross income under IRC Section 86 (see Q 807) and losses or gains on passive investments under IRC Section 469 are taken into account. Also for this purpose, contributions to a traditional IRA are not deducted in determining AGI. IRC Sec. 219(g)(3)(A); See Treas. Reg. §1.408A-3, A-5.

The deduction is taken from gross income so that an individual who does not itemize his deductions may take advantage of the retirement savings deduction. IRC Sec. 62(a)(7). No deduction may be taken for a contribution *on behalf of* an individual who has attained age 70½ before the end of the tax year. IRC Sec. 219(d)(1). An individual over age 70½ may take a deduction for a contribution made on behalf of a spouse who is under age 70½. An excess contribution made in one year can be deducted in a subsequent year to the extent the excess is absorbed in the later year. See Q 226.

The cost of a disability waiver of premium feature in an individual retirement annuity is deductible under IRC Section 219, but where an individual contributes to an annuity for the benefit of himself and his non-employed spouse, the waiver of premium feature may only be allocated to the working spouse's interest. Let. Rul. 7851087.

No deduction is allowed for contributions to an IRA if the individual for whose benefit the IRA is maintained acquired that IRA by reason of the death of another individual after 1983. This, however, does not apply where the acquiring individual is the surviving spouse of the deceased individual. IRC Secs. 219(d)(4), 408(d)(3)(C)(ii).

For the limits on contributions to Roth IRAs, see Q 221. For the limits on contributions to simplified employee pensions, see Q 240. For the limits on contributions to a SIMPLE IRA, see Q 242.

Nondeductible Contributions

The Code permits nondeductible IRA contributions to be made to a traditional IRA. The limit on nondeductible contributions is equal to the *excess of* the "deductible amount,"

INDIVIDUAL RETIREMENT PLANS

Q 221

discussed above, *over* the actual maximum deduction. IRC Sec. 408(o). Contributions made to Roth IRAs for the taxable year reduce this limit. See Q 221. This limit is not reduced because an individual's AGI exceeds certain limits (in contrast, see Q 221 with respect to contributions to Roth IRAs). A taxpayer may elect to treat contributions that would otherwise be deductible as nondeductible. Nondeductible contributions must be reported on the individual's tax return and penalties apply if the required form is not filed or the amount of such contributions is overstated. See Q 238.

Endowment Contracts

Endowment contracts issued after November 6, 1978 do not qualify as individual retirement annuities; therefore, contributions to such contracts are not deductible. See Treas. Regs. §§1.408-4(f), 1.408-3(e)(1)(ix). Furthermore, in the case of contributions to an endowment contract individual retirement annuity issued before November 7, 1978, no deduction is allowed for contributions that are allocable to the purchase of life insurance protection. The amount allocable to life insurance protection is determined by multiplying the death benefit payable during the tax year less the cash value at the end of the year by the net premium cost. (See Q 434 for purposes of valuing the economic benefit of current life insurance protection.) The nondeductible amount may be contributed to another funding medium and a deduction taken so that the maximum deduction may be used, but it may not be used to pay the premium for an annuity if the total premium on behalf of any one individual would then exceed the maximum annual contribution limit. *ASRS, Sec. 62, ¶410.2.*

221. How much may an individual contribute to a Roth IRA?

An eligible individual may contribute cash to a Roth IRA on his own behalf up to the *lesser of* the maximum annual contribution limit (equal to the "deductible amount" under IRC Section 219(b)(5)(A)) or 100% of *compensation* includable in his gross income for the taxable year *reduced by* any contributions made to traditional IRAs for the taxable year on his own behalf. IRC Sec. 408A(c)(2). The maximum annual contribution limit is $4,000 for taxable years beginning in 2005 through 2007, and $5,000 for 2008. (The contribution limit was $3,000 for 2002 through 2004.) See IRC Sec. 219(b)(5)(A). The $5,000 amount will be indexed for inflation in increments of $500 for taxable years beginning in 2009 and 2010. See IRC Sec. 219(b)(5)(C). The maximum annual contribution limit for taxable years beginning in 2006 through 2010 is increased by $1,000 for individuals who have attained age 50 before the close of the tax year. This catch-up amount was $500 for taxable years beginning in 2002 through 2005. IRC Sec. 219(b)(5)(B). See Q 397. SEPs and SIMPLE IRAs may not be designated as Roth IRAs and contributions to a SEP or SIMPLE IRA will not affect the amount that an individual can contribute to a Roth IRA. IRC Sec. 408A(f). Qualified rollover contributions (see Q 222) do not count towards this limit. IRC Sec. 408A(c)(6). As to what constitutes "compensation," see Q 223. Roth IRA contributions are not deductible and can be made even after the individual turns age 70½. IRC Secs. 408A(c)(1), 408A(c)(4).

An individual may contribute cash to a Roth IRA *for a non-working spouse* for a taxable year up to the maximum deductible limit (disregarding active participant restrictions) permitted with respect to traditional IRAs for such non-working spouse (see Q 220), reduced by any such contributions made to traditional IRAs for the taxable year on behalf of the non-working spouse. See IRC Secs. 408A(c)(2), 219(b)(1), 219(c).

2006 Tax Facts on Insurance & Employee Benefits

Thus, a married couple (both spouses under age 50) may be permitted a maximum contribution of up to $8,000 for 2005 through 2007 ($4,000 for each spouse).

The maximum contribution permitted to an individual Roth IRA or a spousal Roth IRA is reduced or eliminated for certain high-income taxpayers. The amount of the reduction is the amount that bears the same ratio to the overall limit as the taxpayer's *adjusted gross income* (AGI) in excess of an "applicable dollar amount" bears to $15,000 ($10,000 in the case of a joint return). IRC Sec. 408A(c)(3). Thus, the amount of the reduction is calculated as follows:

$$\text{maximum contribution} \times \frac{\text{AGI - "applicable dollar amount"}}{\$15,000 \ (\$10,000 \text{ if a joint return})}$$

The "applicable dollar amount" is (1) $95,000 in the case of an individual filing a single return, (2) $150,000 in the case of a married couple filing a joint return, and (3) $0 in the case of a married person filing separately. Thus, the Roth IRA contribution limit is $0 for (1) individuals filing a single return with AGI of $110,000 and above, (2) married couples filing a joint return with AGI of $160,000 and above, and (3) a married individual filing separately with AGI of $10,000 and above. The amount of the reduction is rounded to the next lowest multiple of $10. Unless the individual's contribution limit is reduced to zero, the Code permits a minimum contribution of $200. IRC Sec. 408A(c)(3)(A).

For this purpose, AGI is calculated without regard to the exclusions for foreign earned income, qualified adoption expenses paid by the employer and interest on qualified United States savings bonds used to pay higher education expenses. Social Security benefits includable in gross income under IRC Section 86 (see Q 807) and losses or gains on passive investments under IRC Section 469 are taken into account. Also for this purpose, deductible contributions to a traditional IRA plan are not taken into account in determining AGI; amounts included in gross income as a result of a rollover or conversion from a traditional IRA to a Roth IRA are not taken into account for purposes of determining the maximum contribution limit for a Roth IRA. *ASRS, Sec. 62, ¶410.3.*

222. Can an individual roll over or convert a traditional IRA into a Roth IRA?

Yes. A "qualified rollover contribution" may be made from a traditional IRA to a Roth IRA if the taxpayer has adjusted gross income (AGI) of $100,000 or less for the taxable year of the distribution to which the rollover relates and the taxpayer is not a married individual filing a separate return. IRC Secs. 408A(c)(3)(B), 408A(e). Amounts that are held in a SEP or a SIMPLE IRA (which have been held in the account for two or more years) may also be converted to a Roth IRA. Treas. Reg. §1.408A-4, A-4. The taxpayer must include in income the amount of the distribution from the traditional IRA, SEP or SIMPLE IRA that would be includable if the distribution were not rolled over. IRC Secs. 408A(d)(3)(A)(i), 408A(d)(3)(C). (See Q 227 for taxation of amounts distributed from such IRAs.) Thus, if only deductible contributions were made to the traditional IRA, the entire amount of the distribution would be includable in income in the year rolled over or converted. (Special rules applied for conversions made before January 1, 1999.) While the 10% premature distribution penalty (see Q 231) does not apply at the time of the conversion of a traditional IRA to a Roth IRA, it does apply to any converted amounts distributed during the 5-year period beginning with the year of the conversion. IRC Sec. 408A(d)(3)(F).

INDIVIDUAL RETIREMENT PLANS

Q 222

Non-rollover contributions made to a traditional IRA for a taxable year (and any earnings allocable thereto) may be transferred to a Roth IRA on or before the due date (excluding extensions of time) for filing the federal income tax return of the contributing individual and no such amount will be includable in income, providing no deduction was allowed with respect to such contributions. IRC Sec. 408(d)(3)(D). Such contributions would be subject to the maximum annual contribution limits. See Q 221.

For these purposes, a "qualified rollover contribution" is any rollover contribution to a Roth IRA from a traditional IRA that meets the requirements of IRC Section 408(d)(3). See Q 452. However, a rollover or conversion of a traditional IRA to a Roth IRA does not count toward the one IRA-to-IRA rollover in a year's time limit. See Q 452. IRC Sec. 408A(e). The taxpayer's AGI is calculated without regard to the exclusions for foreign earned income, qualified adoption expenses paid by the employer and interest on qualified United States savings bonds used to pay higher education expenses. Social security benefits includable in gross income under IRC Section 86 (see Q 807) and losses or gains on passive investments under IRC Section 469 are taken into account. Also, deductible contributions to a traditional IRA are not taken into account in determining AGI. Amounts included in gross income as a result of the rollover or conversion from a traditional IRA to a Roth IRA are not taken into account. IRC Sec. 408A(c)(3)(C)(i). For tax years beginning in 2005, the definition of AGI has been modified to exclude minimum required distributions to IRA owners aged 70½ or older, solely for purposes of determining eligibility to convert a regular IRA to a Roth IRA. IRC Sec. 408A(c)(3)(C)(i).

Qualified rollover contributions do not count toward the annual maximum contribution limit applicable to Roth IRAs. See Q 221. IRC Sec. 408A(c)(6)(B).

Recharacterizations

Generally, if a taxpayer has rolled over funds from a traditional IRA to a Roth IRA during the taxable year, and later discovers his AGI is in excess of $100,000 (or for any other reason wants the transaction undone), the taxpayer has until the due date for filing his return (including extensions) to correct such a conversion without penalty, to the extent all earnings and income allocable to the conversion are also transferred back to the original IRA, and no deduction was allowed with respect to the original conversion. IRC Sec. 408A(d)(6). This "recharacterization" in the form of a trustee-to-trustee transfer results in the recharacterized contribution being treated as a contribution made to the transferee IRA, instead of to the transferor IRA. See Treas. Reg. §1.408A-5. A taxpayer can apply to the IRS for relief from the time limit for making a recharacterization. See Let. Ruls. 200234073, 200213030.

For purposes of a recharacterized contribution, the net income attributable to a contribution made to an IRA is determined by allocating to the contribution a pro-rata portion of the earnings or losses accrued by the IRA during the period the IRA held the contribution. This allows the taxpayer to claim any net income that is a negative amount. Prop. Treas. Reg. §1.408A-5; Notice 2000-39, 2000-30 IRB 132.

A time restriction is placed on reconversions (i.e., converting to a Roth IRA a second time after recharacterizing a first conversion). For recharacterizations occurring after 1999, a person can reconvert back to a Roth IRA but only after the later of (1) the beginning of the next year, or (2) 30 days after the recharacterization. Treas. Reg. §1.408A-5, A-9.

2006 Tax Facts on Insurance & Employee Benefits

Reconversions and recharacterizations occurring after December 31, 2000 must be reported on Form 1099-R and Form 5498. This rule applies to recharacterizations and reconversions of amounts contributed prior to January 1, 2001, whether or not the account holder is using the same trustee. This new reporting method eliminates the alternative reporting methods applicable for 1998 and 1999. The new reporting method requires prior year recharacterizations to be reported under separate codes. All recharacterized contributions received by an IRA in the same year are permitted to be totalled and reported on a single Form 5498. Notice 2000-30, 2000-25 IRB 1266. *ASRS, Sec. 62, ¶410.4.*

223. What is "compensation" for purposes of IRA eligibility rules and deduction limits?

For purposes of the eligibility rules and deduction limits applicable to IRAs, "compensation" means wages, salary, professional fees, or other amounts derived from, or received for, personal services actually rendered. "Compensation" also includes alimony paid under a divorce or separation agreement that is includable in the income of the recipient under IRC Section 71. IRC Secs. 219(f)(1), 408A(a); Treas. Reg. §1.408A-3, A-4. See Q 808. In the case of a self-employed individual, "compensation" includes earned income from personal services, but in computing the maximum IRA or SEP contribution, such income must be reduced by any qualified retirement plan contributions made by such individual on his own behalf. Earned income not subject to self-employment tax because of an individual's religious beliefs is "compensation." IRC Sec. 219(f)(1). An individual whose income for the tax year consists solely of interest, dividend and pension income has no "compensation" and cannot deduct any portion of a traditional IRA contribution. *King v. Comm.*, TC Memo 1996-231.

"Compensation" does not include any amount received as deferred compensation, nor any social security or railroad retirement benefits required to be included in gross income. See Q 807. IRC Secs. 86(f)(3), 219(f)(1); Treas. Reg. §1.219-1(c)(1). Payments made to employees terminated because of a restructuring of the company are deferred compensation and may not be used as a basis for IRA contributions. Let. Ruls. 8534106, 8519051. Also, amounts received from an employer as deferred incentive awards, whether in the form of cash, stock options, or stock appreciation rights, are not "compensation." Let. Rul. 8304088. However, incentive pay awarded in one year for services performed in that year but paid in the following year is considered "compensation" in that second year. Let. Rul. 8707051.

The IRS has ruled that disability income payments, whether made under public or private plans, do not constitute "compensation." See Let. Ruls. 8331069, 8325080, 8014110. Also, unemployment benefits do not constitute "compensation" because they are paid due to an inability to earn wages and not for personal services actually rendered. *Russell v. Comm.*, TC Memo 1996-278. Additionally, the Service has issued a compensation "safe harbor." The amount properly shown in the box for "wages, tips, other compensation," less any amount properly shown in the box for "nonqualified plans," on Form W-2 is considered compensation for purposes of calculating an individual's IRA contribution. See Rev. Proc. 91-18, 1991-1 CB 522.

Amounts paid by a husband to his wife to manage their jointly-owned investment property may not be treated by the wife, on a joint return, as compensation for purposes of an IRA contribution. Let. Rul. 8535001. Likewise, wages paid to a wife

INDIVIDUAL RETIREMENT PLANS   Q 224

by her spouse and deposited in their joint account are not considered as compensation because deposit in a joint account does not constitute actual payment of wages to the wife. Let. Rul. 8707004. However, payment in hogs rather than cash by a husband to his wife for her services in running their farm was considered to be compensation for purposes of making an IRA contribution. TAM 9202003.

A self-employed individual who shows a net loss for the tax year cannot take any IRA deduction. *Est. of Hall v. Comm.*, TC Memo 1979-342. But a salaried employee who is also self-employed is to disregard net losses from self-employment when computing his maximum deduction. Rev. Rul. 79-286, 1979-2 CB 121. *ASRS, Sec. 62, ¶410.1(b)*.

224. Who is an "active participant" for purposes of IRA eligibility rules and deduction limits?

If an individual is an "active participant" in a qualified corporate or Keogh pension, profit sharing, stock bonus, or annuity plan, in a simplified employee pension, in a 403(b) tax sheltered annuity, SIMPLE IRA, or in a government plan, his deduction limit for contributions to a traditional IRA may be reduced or eliminated. See Q 220. The limitation applies if the individual or his spouse was an active participant for any part of the plan year that ended with or within the taxable year. IRC Sec. 219(g)(1); see *Wartes v. Comm.*, TC Memo 1993-84.

Participation in Social Security, Railroad Retirement (tier I or II) or in an eligible IRC Section 457 deferred compensation plan (see Q 123) is not taken into consideration. IRC Sec. 219(g)(5); Notice 87-16, 1987-1 CB 446, A-7. Federal judges are treated as active participants. OBRA '87, Sec. 10103. Active participants include any individual who is an active participant in a plan established for employees by the United States, a State or political subdivision thereof, or by an agency or instrumentality of any of the foregoing. IRC Sec. 291(g)(5)(A)(iii). A district court judge in the state of Nebraska who participated in the Nebraska Retirement Fund for Judges was found to be an employee of the state (not an officer of the state) and, thus, he was an active participant. *Fuhrman v. Comm.*, TC Memo 1997-34. Full-time active duty officers in the United States Air Force were found to be active participants. See *Morales-Caban v. Comm.*, TC Memo 1993-466. However, certain members of the armed forces reserves and certain volunteer firemen covered under government plans are not considered active participants. IRC Sec. 219(g)(6). A teacher employed by a municipal school district in Michigan was found to be an active participant in the employment-based, qualified retirement plan provided by the state based upon his being an employee of a state or political subdivision through his employment in the school district. *Neumeister v. Comm.*, TC Memo 2000-41. Active participant status for a tax year must be reported by the employer on the employee's Form W-2.

Active participant status is determined without regard to whether such individual's rights under the plan, trust, or contract are nonforfeitable. IRC Sec. 219(g)(5), flush language; see *Nicolai v. Comm.*, TC Memo 1997-108; *Wartes v. Comm.*, TC Memo 1993-84. Active participant status is further determined under the rules provided in Notice 87-16, 1987-1 CB 446, and Treasury Regulation Section 1.219-2 (active participant rules in effect prior to the Economic Recovery Tax Act of 1981).

In the case of a *defined benefit plan*, an individual who is not excluded under the eligibility provisions of the plan for the plan year ending with or within the individual's

2006 Tax Facts on Insurance & Employee Benefits

taxable year is an active participant in the plan, regardless of whether such individual has elected to decline participation in the plan, has failed to make a mandatory contribution specified under the plan, or has failed to perform the minimum service required to accrue a benefit under the plan. Notice 87-16, above, A-15; Treas. Reg. §1.219-2(b)(1); see *Nicolai v. Comm.*, TC Memo 1997-108. An individual in a plan under which accruals for *all* have ceased is *not* an active participant. (But where benefits may vary with future compensation, all accruals are not considered to have ceased.) Notice 87-16, above, A-16; Treas. Reg. §1.219-2(b)(3); Let. Rul. 8948008.

In the case of a *profit sharing* or *stock bonus plan*, an individual is an active participant if any employer contribution is deemed added or any forfeiture is allocated to the individual's account during the individual's taxable year. Treas. Reg. §1.219-2(d)(1); see *Tolley v. Comm.*, 1997-244. A contribution is treated as made to an individual's account on the later of the date the contribution is made or allocated. Treas. Reg. §1.219-2(d)(1). However, if the right to an allocation is conditioned on the performance of a specified number of hours (or on the employment of the participant on a specified day) and the individual does not meet the condition for a particular year, he is not an active participant with respect to the taxable year within which such plan year ends. Notice 87-16, above, A-20; Let. Rul. 8919064. Where contributions to a plan are purely discretionary and no amount attributable to forfeitures or contributions has been allocated to an individual's account by the last day of the plan year, such individual is not an active participant for the taxable year in which such plan year ends. But, if the employer contributes an amount after the end of the plan year for that prior plan year, the individual is generally an active participant for the taxable year in which the contribution is made. Notice 87-16, above; Let. Rul. 9008056.

An individual is an active participant in a *money purchase pension plan* if any contribution or forfeiture is required to be allocated to his account for the plan year ending with or within his taxable year, even if he was not employed at any time during the taxable year. Treas. Reg. §1.219-2(c).

An individual is an active participant for any taxable year in which he makes a voluntary or mandatory contribution. Treas. Reg. §1.219-2(e); see *Felber v. Comm.*, TC Memo 1992-418; *Wade v. Comm.*, TC Memo 2001-114. He is not treated as an active participant if only earnings (rather than contributions or forfeitures) are allocated to his account. Notice 87-16, above, A-16, A-19.

An individual is not considered an active participant in a plan integrated with social security if his compensation is less than the minimum needed to accrue a benefit or to be eligible for an allocation in the plan. Notice 87-16, above, A-9.

There is no *de minimis* rule for active participant status (i.e., if an individual has only $1 allocated to his account during the year, he is still an active participant). Active participant status is determined without regard to whether the individual is vested in any portion of his benefit. *ASRS, Sec. 62, ¶410.2(b)*.

225. Are fees or commissions paid in connection with an IRA deductible? Is interest paid on amounts borrowed to fund an IRA deductible?

The Service has ruled that the payment of administrative or trustee fees incurred in connection with an individual retirement account may be claimed as an itemized

INDIVIDUAL RETIREMENT PLANS

Q 226

miscellaneous deduction (i.e., for the production or collection of income) if such fees are *separately billed and paid*. Rev. Rul. 84-146, 1984-2 CB 61; Let. Ruls. 9005010, 8951010. Furthermore, if separately billed and paid, the payment of such fees does not constitute a contribution to the individual retirement account and thus will not be an excess contribution or reduce the amount that may be contributed to the account or, in the case of a traditional IRA, deducted. See Q 220. See Let. Ruls. 8432109, 8329058, 8329055, 8329049. Deduction of administrative fees is subject to the 2% floor on itemized miscellaneous deductions (see Q 814).

Sales commissions on individual retirement annuities that are billed directly by an insurance agent to the client and paid separately by the client are not separately deductible, but are subject to the overall limits on contributions and deductions. Let. Rul. 8747072. Likewise, broker's commissions incurred in connection with the purchase of securities on behalf of an IRA are not separately deductible, but are subject to the overall limits. Rev. Rul. 86-142, 1986-2 CB 60; Let. Rul. 8711095. An annual maintenance fee charged for self-directed brokerage accounts that did not vary with the number of transactions, the number of securities involved or the dollar amount and that was paid to the trustee, not the broker, was not treated as a commission but was separately deductible as an administrative fee. Let. Rul. 8835062. Likewise, brokerage account "wrap fees," which were based on a percentage of assets under management, but which did not vary based on the number of trades in the account, were not treated as a commission and were separately deductible as an administrative fee. Let. Rul. 200507021.

The Service has held that the payment of fees associated with flexible premium variable annuity contracts that are paid directly from subaccounts within the contract would not be considered a distribution from the contract. The Service ruled that assessing expenses against the contract is unrelated to whether or not the participant is currently entitled to benefits under the contract. Therefore, such payments are an expense of the contract and not a distribution. Let. Rul. 9845003.

The Service has ruled that since interest paid on amounts borrowed to fund an IRA is not allocable to tax-exempt income (see Q 215), the deduction of such interest is not subject to the general prohibition against deducting interest incurred or carried to purchase tax-exempts. Let. Rul. 8527082. See IRC Secs. 163(a), 265. However, because such interest is "on amounts borrowed to buy or carry property held for investment," it would seem that it should be classified as "investment interest expense" and the deduction limited. See Q 823. *ASRS, Sec. 62, ¶410.1(d)*.

226. What is the penalty for making excessive contributions to an IRA? Under what circumstances may contributions be withdrawn or reduced?

If contributions are made in excess of the maximum contribution limit for traditional IRAs (see Q 220) or for Roth IRAs (see Q 221), the contributing individual is liable for a nondeductible excise tax of 6% of the amount of the excess (not to exceed 6% of the value of the account or annuity, determined as of the close of the tax year). IRC Sec. 4973(a). A contribution by a person ineligible to make the contribution is an excess contribution even if it is made through inadvertence. *Orzechowski v. Comm.*, 69 TC 750 (1978), *aff'd* 79-1 USTC ¶9220 (2nd Cir. 1979); *Tallon v. Comm.*, TC Memo 1979-423; *Johnson v. Comm.*, 74 TC 1057 (1980). In the case of an endowment contract described in IRC Section 408(b), the tax does not apply to amounts allocable

Q 226

to life, health, accident, or other insurance. IRC Sec. 4973(a). It also does not apply to premiums waived under a disability waiver of premium feature in an individual retirement annuity. See Let. Rul. 7851087. Nor does it apply to "rollover" contributions to a traditional IRA or "qualified rollover contributions" to a Roth IRA. IRC Secs. 4973(b)(1)(A), 4973(f)(1)(A). However, it does apply if the "rollover" contribution does not qualify for rollover. The Tax Court did not accept the argument that an IRA created in a failed rollover attempt is not a valid IRA and, thus, the 6% penalty should not apply. *Martin v. Comm.*, TC Memo 1993-399; *Michel v. Comm.*, TC Memo 1989-670. Likewise, a failed Roth IRA conversation that is not recharacterized, is subject to the 6% penalty. SCA 200148051.

The IRS has ruled that earnings credited to an IRA that are attributable to a non-IRA companion account maintained at the same financial institution (a "super IRA") are treated as contributions to the IRA; when coupled with a cash contribution, these amounts may be an excess contribution subject to the penalty tax. Rev. Rul. 85-62, 1985-1 CB 153. However, an interest bonus credited to an individual retirement account is not included in the calculation of an excess contribution. Let. Rul. 8722068.

Any contribution (excess or otherwise) may be withdrawn, together with the net income attributable to such contribution, on or before the due date (including extensions of time) for filing the federal income tax return of the contributing individual and the amount will be treated as if never contributed, regardless of the size of the contribution. IRC Secs. 4973(b), 408(d)(4). Thus, such a distribution is not included in gross income and is not subject to the 10% premature distribution excise tax. Such a distribution of an excess contribution is also not subject to the 6% excess contribution excise tax. The accompanying distribution of the net income is includable in income and is subject to penalty as a premature distribution. IRC Sec. 408(d)(4), flush language. See Q 227, Q 231. Net income attributable to a contribution is determined by allocating to the contribution a pro-rata portion of the earnings or losses accrued by the IRA during the period the IRA held the contribution. Net income may be a negative amount. Prop. Treas. Reg. §1.408-11; Notice 2000-39, 2000-30 IRB 132.

Relief may be granted for failure to meet the above deadline if the taxpayer has taken all necessary and reasonable steps, such as properly notifying the financial institution, in order to comply with the law. *Childs v. Comm.*, TC Memo 1996-267; *Thompson v. Comm.*, TC Memo 1996-266. Excess amounts that are not withdrawn by this method are subject to the 6% excise tax in the year of contribution and are carried over and taxed each year until the year the excess is reduced.

By contributing less than the maximum limit in a year, an excess contribution in a previous year may be absorbed up to the unused maximum limit for the year. IRC Secs. 4973(b)(2), 4973(f)(2). With respect to traditional IRAs, both the amount contributed and the amount of excess absorbed may be deductible subject to the active participant rules (see Q 220) and no taxable income or premature distribution tax is involved. (However, the deduction must be reduced if the excess was improperly deducted in a year closed to IRS challenge.) IRC Sec. 219(f)(6); Prop. Treas. Reg. §1.219-1(e).

Where all or a portion of the excess is attributable to an excess "rollover" contribution that resulted from the individual's reliance on erroneous information supplied by the plan, trust or institution making the distribution, distribution of the portion of the excess attributable to the erroneous information is not included in income and is not subject to the 10% premature distribution tax. IRC Sec. 408(d)(5)(B). It is not necessary

INDIVIDUAL RETIREMENT PLANS

Q 227

to withdraw earnings on the excess; however, any earnings withdrawn would be taxable income and subject to the 10% tax if premature.

The excess may also be reduced by a distribution includable in income. Such a distribution is subject to the 10% excise tax if it is a premature distribution, as well as income tax. Where a taxpayer amended his tax return to include an excess contribution in income in the year contributed, the Tax Court ruled that the distribution of the excess in a later year was includable under the rules of IRC Section 72 and that the excess contribution included in income in the prior year constituted an "investment in the contract" and as such was not taxable a second time upon the actual distribution of such excess. *Campbell v. Comm.*, 108 TC 54 (1997).

There is no 6% excess contributions excise tax on the amount of the reduction in the year of withdrawal.

For purposes of the excess contribution rules, if an excess contribution is invested in a time deposit (such as a CD) that is subject to an early withdrawal penalty of the trustee, the amount reportable as an excess contribution upon distribution of the excess is the total amount actually distributed from the plan *after* the imposition of the early withdrawal penalty. Let. Ruls. 8643070, 8642061.

A decline in asset value does not remove an excess contribution. H. R. Conf. Rep. 93-1280 (ERISA '74) *reprinted in* 1974-3 CB 501-502. *ASRS, Sec. 62, ¶410.5.*

DISTRIBUTIONS

Taxation

227. How are amounts distributed from a traditional IRA taxed?

Distributions from a traditional IRA are generally taxed under IRC Section 72 (relating to the taxation of annuities). IRC Sec. 408(d)(1). Under these rules, a portion of the distribution may be excludable from income. The amount excludable from the taxpayer's income for a year is that amount of the distribution that bears the same ratio to the amount received as the taxpayer's investment in the contract (i.e., nondeductible contributions) bears to the expected return under the contract. (In no case, however, will the total amount excluded exceed the unrecovered investment in the contract. IRC Sec. 72(b).) For these purposes, all traditional IRAs are treated as one contract, all distributions during the year are treated as one distribution, and the value of the contract, income on the contract, and investment in the contract are computed as of the close of the calendar year with or within which the taxable year begins. IRC Sec. 408(d)(2). Thus, the nontaxable portion of a distribution (whether from a traditional individual retirement annuity or account) is equal to the following:

$$\frac{\text{Unrecovered Nondeductible Contributions}}{\text{Total IRA Account Balance + Distribution amount + Outstanding Rollovers}} \times \text{Distribution Amount}$$

The *total IRA account balance* is the balance in *all* traditional IRAs owned by the taxpayer, as of December 31 of the year of the distribution. To this amount is added the

2006 Tax Facts on Insurance & Employee Benefits

239

amount of any distributions made (i.e., the amounts for which the nontaxable portion is being computed) and any outstanding rollover amounts (i.e., any amounts distributed by a traditional IRA within 60 days of the end of the year, which have not yet been rolled over into another plan, but which is rolled over in the following year). (If it is not rolled over, the amount is not treated as an outstanding rollover.) Notice 87-16, 1987-1 CB 446.

Nondeductible contributions will not be excluded from gross income as investment in the contract where the taxpayer is unable to document the nontaxable basis through the filing of Form 8606, Nondeductible IRAs (Contributions, Distributions and Basis) for the year in which such nondeductible contributions were made and the year in which they were distributed. *Alpern v. Comm.*, TC Memo 2000-246. See Q 238.

If the owner dies prior to recovering his full investment in the contract, the unrecovered portion is allowed as a deduction on his final year's tax return. IRC Sec. 72(b)(3). Also, an individual may now recognize a loss on a traditional IRA, but only when all amounts have been distributed and the total distributed is less than the individual's unrecovered basis. Notice 87-16, above, A-6.

Despite the pro-rata rule applicable generally to distributions from a traditional IRA, distributions after 2001 that are rolled over to a qualified plan, an IRC Section 403(b) tax sheltered annuity, or an eligible IRC Section 457 governmental plan are treated as coming first from all non-after-tax contributions and earnings in all of the IRAs of the owner. IRC Sec. 408(d)(3)(H). Because after-tax contributions cannot be rolled over to eligible retirement plans other than another IRA (see Q 446, Q 452), this ordering rule effectively allows the owner to roll over the maximum amount permitted. Appropriate adjustments must be made in applying IRC Section 72 to other IRA distributions in the same taxable year and subsequent years. IRC Sec. 408(d)(3)(H)(ii)(III).

The fact that IRA funds were distributed by the financial institution's receiver following insolvency proceedings did not change the nature of the distribution. The taxpayers were taxed on the distribution since a timely rollover was not made. *Aronson v. Comm.*, 89 TC 283 (1992). Likewise, the transfer of IRA funds by the financial institution into a "trust account" was a taxable distribution to the taxpayer even though the taxpayer had intended to transfer the IRA funds to another IRA and had named the account a "trust IRA"; the money was, in fact, transferred into a trust account and not an IRA. Let. Rul. 199901029. In addition, a failed Roth IRA conversion that is not recharacterized is treated as a distribution from a traditional IRA and taxed accordingly. SGA 200148051.

Taxpayers who were defrauded of their account balances by their investment advisor, who convinced them to make IRA rollover investments that he subsequently embezzled, were liable for taxes on the amount of assets stolen because the account holders failed to take the necessary steps required to properly set-up IRA rollover accounts. FSA 199933038.

Unless a taxpayer elects otherwise, any amount of a qualified Hurricane Katrina distribution required to be included in gross income shall be so included ratably over the 3-year taxable period beginning with such year. Qualified Hurricane Katrina distributions are distributions not exceeding $100,000 in the aggregate from qualified retirement plans, individual retirement plans, tax sheltered annuities under IRC Section 403(b),

INDIVIDUAL RETIREMENT PLANS

Q 228

or eligible governmental plans under IRC Section 457 made at any time on or after August 25, 2005 and before January 1, 2007 by an individual whose principal place of abode on August 28, 2005 was located in the Hurricane Katrina disaster area and who sustained an economic loss by reason of Hurricane Katrina. Notice 2005-92, 2005-51 IRB___; Sec. 101(e), KETRA 2005.

If a qualified Hurricane Katrina distribution is an eligible rollover distribution (see Q 452), it may be recontributed to an eligible rollover plan no later than 3 years from the day after such distribution was received. See Q 454. Notice 2005-92, 2005-51 IRB ___; Sec. 101(e), KETRA 2005.

Certain premature distributions are subject to an additional tax. See Q 231. As to what constitutes a "deemed distribution" from a traditional IRA, see Q 214. For the estate tax marital deduction implications of distributions from a traditional IRA, see Q 649. *ASRS, Sec. 62, ¶420.1(a).*

228. How are amounts distributed from a Roth IRA taxed?

Where a Roth IRA contains both contributions and conversion amounts, there are ordering rules that apply in determining which amounts are withdrawn. In applying the ordering rules, traditional IRAs are not aggregated with Roth IRAs. All Roth IRAs are aggregated with each other. Regular Roth IRA contributions are deemed to be withdrawn first, then converted amounts (in order if there has been more than one conversion). Withdrawals of converted amounts are treated first as coming from converted amounts that were includable in income. The ordering rules continue to treat earnings as being withdrawn after contributions. IRC Sec. 408A(d)(4); Treas. Reg. §1.408A-6, A-8.

"Qualified distributions" from a Roth IRA are not includable in gross income. IRC Sec. 408A(d)(1). Thus, earnings are tax-free, not tax deferred as with traditional IRAs. A "qualified distribution" is any distribution made after the five-taxable year period beginning with the first taxable year for which the individual made a contribution to a Roth IRA (or such individual's spouse made a contribution to a Roth IRA) established for such individual *and* such distribution meets one of the following requirements:

(1) it is made on or after the date on which the individual attains age 59½;

(2) it is made to a beneficiary (or to the estate of the individual) on or after the death of the individual;

(3) it is attributable to the individual's being disabled (within the meaning of IRC Section 72(m)(7)); or

(4) it is a "qualified first-time homebuyer distribution" (see below).

IRC Secs. 408A(d)(2).

A "qualified first-time homebuyer distribution" is defined as any payment or distribution that is used within 120 days after the day it was received by the individual to pay the qualified acquisition costs of a principal residence of a first-time homebuyer. IRC Sec. 72(t)(8)(A). The aggregate amount of payments or distributions received by

2006 Tax Facts on Insurance & Employee Benefits

an individual from all Roth and traditional IRAs that may be treated as qualified first-time homebuyer distributions is limited to a lifetime maximum of $10,000. IRC Sec. 72(t)(8)(B). The first-time homebuyer may be the individual, his spouse, any child, grandchild, or ancestor of the individual or his spouse. A first-time homebuyer is further defined as an individual (and, if married, such individual's spouse) who has had no present ownership interest in a principal residence during the two-year period ending on the date of acquisition of the residence for which the distribution is being made. IRC Sec. 72(t)(8)(D)(i). The date of acquisition is the date on which a binding contract to acquire the residence is entered into or the date construction or reconstruction of the residence begins. IRC Sec. 72(t)(8)(d)(iii). Qualified acquisition costs are defined as the costs of acquiring, constructing or reconstructing a residence, including reasonable settlement, financing, or other closing costs. IRC Sec. 72(t)(8)(C).

In calculating the five-taxable-year period, it is important to remember that contributions to Roth IRAs, as with traditional IRAs, may be made as late as the due date for filing the individual's tax return for the year (without extensions). See Q 219. Thus, if a contribution is made to a Roth IRA between January 1, 2003 and April 15, 2003 for the 2002 taxable year, the five-taxable-year holding period begins to run in 2002.

For purposes of determining whether a distribution from a Roth IRA that is allocable to a "qualified rollover contribution" (see Q 222) from a traditional IRA is a "qualified distribution," the five-taxable-year period begins with the taxable year for which the conversion applies. A subsequent conversion will not start the running of a new five-taxable year period. IRC Sec. 408A(d)(2)(B).

The five-taxable-year period for determining a "qualified distribution" is not recalculated upon the death of the Roth IRA owner; the five-taxable-year period of the beneficiary includes the period the Roth IRA was held by the decedent. Treas. Reg. §1.408A-6, A-7.

Any nonqualified distribution will be includable in income, but only to the extent that the distribution, along with all previous distributions from the Roth IRA, exceeds the aggregate amount of contributions to the Roth IRA. See IRC Sec. 408A(d)(1). For this purposes, all Roth IRAs are aggregated. To the extent such distributions are taxable, the 10% premature distribution penalty may apply. See Q 231. However, distributions allocable to "qualified rollover contributions" (see Q 222) will be subject to the premature distribution penalty regardless of whether the distribution is taxable if the distribution is made within the five-year period beginning with the tax year in which the contribution was made. IRC Sec. 408A(d)(3)(F); Treas. Reg. §1.408A-6, A-5. Distributions of excess contributions and earnings upon these contributions are not qualified distributions. IRC Sec. 408A(d)(2)(C).

A transfer of a Roth IRA by gift would constitute an assignment of the Roth IRA, with the effect that the assets of the Roth IRA would be deemed to be distributed to the Roth IRA owner and, accordingly, treated as no longer held in a Roth IRA. Treas. Reg. §1.408A-6, A-19.

Unless a taxpayer elects otherwise, any amount of a qualified Hurricane Katrina distribution required to be included in gross income shall be so included ratably over the 3-year taxable period beginning with such year. Qualified Hurricane Katrina distributions are distributions not exceeding $100,000 in the aggregate from qualified retirement

INDIVIDUAL RETIREMENT PLANS   Q 230

plans, individual retirement plans, tax sheltered annuities under IRC Section 403(b), or eligible governmental plans under IRC Section 457 made at any time on or after August 25, 2005 and before January 1, 2007 by an individual whose principal place of abode on August 28, 2005 was located in the Hurricane Katrina disaster area and who sustained an economic loss by reason of Hurricane Katrina. See Notice 2005-92, 2005-51 IRB ___. Section 101(e), KETRA 2005.

If a qualified Hurricane Katrina distribution is an eligible rollover distribution (see Q 452), it may be recontributed to an eligible rollover plan no later than 3 years from the day after such distribution was received. See Q 454. Notice 2005-92, 2005-51 IRB ___; Sec. 101(e), KETRA 2005.

For the estate tax marital deduction implications of distributions from a Roth IRA, see Q 649. *ASRS, Sec. 62, ¶420.1(b)*.

229. Are the death proceeds of an individual retirement endowment contract taxable?

If no nondeductible contributions (see Q 220) have been made by the taxpayer to any traditional individual retirement plan, the portion of the death benefit of an endowment contract equal to the cash value immediately before death is included in gross income as a federal income taxable distribution. The balance is federal income tax free as proceeds of life insurance under IRC Section 101(a). If the death benefit is paid in installments, the amount representing life insurance proceeds is prorated and recovered tax free under IRC Section 101(d). Treas. Reg. §1.408-3(e)(2).

If nondeductible contributions to any such individual retirement plan have been made, it would seem that a portion of the cash value of the contract should be treated as a recovery of basis and, as such, nontaxable. See Q 227.

230. Are amounts received from IRAs subject to withholding?

Taxable distributions from traditional IRAs are subject to income tax withholding: if the distribution is in the form of an annuity or similar payments, amounts are withheld as though each distribution were a payment of wages pursuant to the recipient's Form W-4; in the case of any other kind of distribution, a flat 10% is withheld. IRC Sec. 3405(e)(1)(A); Temp. Treas. Reg. §35.3405-1. Even though distributions from a traditional IRA may be partly nontaxable because of nondeductible contributions, the payor is to treat any amount withdrawn as includable in income. IRC Sec. 3405(e)(1)(B). A recipient generally can elect not to have the tax withheld. IRC Secs. 3405(a)(2), 3405(b)(2).

Planning Point: A recipient of a taxable IRA distribution should project his income tax liability for the year and pay in an appropriate amount of estimated tax payments to avoid penalties for under-withholding. 10% or even 20% withholding is generally insufficient to cover federal income tax liability. Taxpayers should similarly project their state and local tax liabilities as well. *Martin Silfen, J.D., Brown Brothers, Harriman Trust Co., LLC.*

Distributions from Roth IRAs are subject to income tax withholding, but only to the extent that it is reasonable to believe the amount withdrawn would be includable in income. IRC Sec. 3405(e)(1)(B). *ASRS, Sec. 62, ¶420.5*.

2006 Tax Facts on Insurance & Employee Benefits

Premature Distributions

231. What penalties apply to premature distributions from an IRA?

Except as noted below, amounts distributed from a traditional IRA or a Roth IRA to the individual for whom the plan is maintained before such individual reaches age 59½ are premature distributions. To the extent such distributions are taxable, they are subject to an additional tax equal to 10% of the amount of the distribution that is includable in gross income in the tax year. IRC Sec. 72(t). The tax is increased to 25% in the case of distributions from SIMPLE IRAs (see Q 242) during the first two years of participation. IRC Sec. 72(t)(6).

The 10% penalty tax does not apply to distributions:

(1) made to a beneficiary, or the individual's estate, on or after the death of the individual. IRC Sec. 72(t)(2)(A)(i).

(2) attributable to the individual's disability. IRC Sec. 72(t)(2)(A)(ii).

(3) made for medical care, but only to the extent allowable as a medical expense deduction for amounts paid during the taxable year for medical care (determined without regard to whether the individual itemizes). IRC Secs. 72(t)(2)(B), 72(t)(3)(A). Thus, only amounts in excess of 7.5% of the individual's adjusted gross income escape the 10% penalty.

Planning Point: If an IRA owner pays health insurance premiums in a year of unemployment, and he expects to need an IRA distribution within the next few years at a time when he does not anticipate that any other exception will apply, he should consider taking an IRA distribution in the year of unemployment, in order to avoid a future penalty tax on that amount. *Martin Silfen, J.D., Brown Brothers, Harriman Trust Co., LLC.*

(4) made by unemployed individuals for the payment of health insurance premiums. The 7.5% floor, described above, does not have to be met if the individual has received unemployment compensation for at least 12 weeks and the withdrawal is made in either the year such unemployment compensation was received or the year immediately following the year in which the unemployment compensation was received. This exception also applies to self-employed individuals whose sole reason for not receiving unemployment compensation is that they were self-employed. The exception ceases to apply once the individual has been reemployed for a period of 60 days. IRC Sec. 72(t)(2)(D).

Planning Point: If an IRA owner has higher education expenses in a year and he expects to need an IRA distribution within the next few years at a time when he does not anticipate that any other exception will apply, he should consider taking an IRA distribution in the year of the higher education expenses, in order to avoid a future penalty tax on that amount. *Martin Silfen, J.D., Brown Brothers, Harriman Trust Co., LLC.*

(5) made to pay "qualified higher education expenses" during the taxable year for the taxpayer, the taxpayer's spouse and the child or grandchild of the taxpayer or the taxpayer's spouse. IRC Sec. 72(t)(2)(E). "Qualified higher education expenses" means tuition, fees, books, supplies, and equipment required for the enrollment or attendance of the student at any "eligible educational institution" and, for tax years beginning after 2001, includes expenses for special needs services in the case of a

INDIVIDUAL RETIREMENT PLANS   Q 231

special needs beneficiary (see Q 810) that are incurred in connection with such enrollment or attendance. Room and board (up to a certain amount) is also included if the student is enrolled at least half-time. IRC Secs. 72(t)(7), 529(e)(3). "Qualified higher education expenses" must be incurred for the taxable year of the distribution. *Lodder-Beckert v. Comm.*, T.C. Memo 2005-162 (2005). These expenses must be reduced by any scholarships received by the individual, any educational assistance provided to the individual, or any payment for such expenses (other than a gift, devise, bequest or inheritance) that is excludable from gross income. IRC Sec. 72(t)(7)(B). An "eligible educational institution" is any college, university, vocational school or other postsecondary educational institution described in section 481 of the Higher Education Act of 1965. See IRC Sec. 529(e)(5). Thus, virtually all accredited public, nonprofit and proprietary postsecondary institutions are considered eligible educational institutions. Notice 97-60, 1997-2 CB 310, at 14 (Sec. 3, A16). This exception to the 10% penalty is not available if the withdrawal qualifies for one of the other exceptions provided under IRC Section 72(t)(2) (other than the following exception for "qualified first-time homebuyers"). IRC Sec. 72(t)(2)(E).

(6) that are "qualified first-time homebuyer distributions." See Q 228. This exception to the 10% penalty is not available if the withdrawal qualifies for one of the other exceptions provided under IRC Section 72(t)(2). IRC Sec. 72(t)(2)(F). Taxpayers who took such a distribution after February 28, 2005 and before August 29, 2005 in order to purchase or build a home within the Hurricane Katrina disaster area, but who were unable to do so, may during the period from August 25, 2005 to February 28, 2006 roll the distribution back into an IRA if no home was in fact purchased or constructed. Amounts repaid under this provision will be treated as a timely trustee to trustee transfer of an eligible rollover distribution. See Q 454. Notice 2005-92, 2005-51 IRB ___; Sec. 102, KETRA 2005.

(7) that are part of a series of substantially equal periodic payments made (at least annually) for the life or life expectancy of the individual or the joint lives or joint life expectancy of the individual and his designated beneficiary. See Q 232 for details.

(8) made at any time on or after August 25, 2005 and before January 1, 2007 by an individual whose principal place of abode on August 28, 2005 was located in the Hurricane Katrina disaster area and who sustained an economic loss by reason of Hurricane Katrina. Total distributions under this provision may not exceed $100,000. Notice 2005-92, 2005-51 IRB ___; Sec. 101, KETRA 2005.

The penalty tax has been held not to apply to compulsory distributions where the IRS levied upon a taxpayer's IRA and where the federal government seized a taxpayer's IRA as part of a plea agreement. *Larotonda v. Comm.*, 89 TC 287 (1987); *Murillo v. Comm.*, TC Memo 1998-13, affd. 166 F.3d 1201 (2nd Cir. 1998). Where, however, a taxpayer himself withdrew from his IRA to satisfy a court order to pay alimony and child support, the penalty tax did apply. *Baas v. Comm.*, TC Memo 2002-130. See also *Czepiel v. Comm.*, TC Memo 1999-289, affd. by order (1st Cir. 2000).

No premature distribution occurs where accumulation units in an individual retirement annuity are surrendered to purchase a disability waiver of premium feature. See Let. Rul. 7851087. Ineligibility to set up an individual retirement plan does not prevent imposition of this penalty. *Orzechowski v. Comm.*, 69 TC 750 (1978), *aff'd* 79-1 USTC ¶7220 (2nd Cir. 1979). The fact that an IRA distribution was mandated by the insolvency of the financial institution issuing the IRA did not prevent the application of the 10% penalty tax when the funds were received and not rolled over. *Aronson v. Comm.*, 89 TC 283 (1992).

The amount reportable as a premature distribution from a time deposit (such as a CD) which is subject to an early withdrawal penalty of the trustee is the *net* amount of the distribution, after deduction of any early withdrawal penalty imposed by the trustee. Let. Ruls. 8643070, 8642061.

It appears that amounts includable in income as a result of a prohibited transaction, or as a result of borrowing on an annuity contract, or using an account as security for a loan would be subject to the 10% penalty. *ASRS, Sec. 62, ¶420.2.*

232. How are substantially equal periodic payments from an IRA calculated for purposes of Section 72(t)?

The Internal Revenue Code states that the 10% premature distribution tax (see Q 231) will not apply to distributions that are part of a series of *substantially equal periodic payments* made at least annually, for the life or life expectancy of the individual or the joint lives or joint life expectancy of the individual and his designated beneficiary. IRC Sec. 72(t)(2)(A)(iv).

The IRS has approved three methods, explained below, under which payments will be considered to be "substantially equal periodic payments." These methods were first explained in 1989 guidance, then modified in 2002. Rev. Rul. 2002-62, 2002-2 CB 710, modifying Notice 89-25, 1989-1 CB 662, A-12. Regardless of which method is used, the series of payments must continue for the longer of five years or until the individual reaches age 59½. Ordinarily, a "modification" (see below) that occurs before this duration requirement is met will result in the penalty and interest being imposed on the entire series of payments, in the year the modification occurs. IRC Sec. 72(t)(4). However, a "one time election" (see below) to change methods is permitted if certain requirements are met. Rev. Rul. 2002-62, above. A change in the payment series as a result of disability or death also does not trigger the penalty. IRC Sec. 72(t)(4).

The three approved methods are as follows:

Required minimum distribution (RMD) method. This method requires use of a calculation that would be acceptable for purposes of calculating the required minimum distributions under IRC Section 401(a)(9). Consequently, the account balance, the life expectancy and the resulting annual payments are redetermined each year. Such annual fluctuations will not be considered modifications. Rev. Rul. 2002-62, above, Sec. 2.01(a). Under this method, the same life expectancy table used for the first distribution year must be used for each following year. Rev. Rul. 2002-62, above, Sec. 2.02(a).

Fixed amortization method. Under this method, the annual payment is determined by amortizing the individual's account balance in level amounts over a specified number of years determined using the chosen life expectancy and interest rate as explained below. Rev. Rul. 2002-62, above, Sec. 2.01(b). The account balance, life expectancy and resulting annual payment are determined once for the first distribution year, and the annual payment is the same amount in each year thereafter. Rev. Rul. 2002-62, above, Sec. 2.01(b). However, the ability to recalculate the amount of the payment each year

INDIVIDUAL RETIREMENT PLANS   Q 232

by using the taxpayer's life expectancy with the amortization method was approved in Let. Rul. 200432021.

Fixed annuitization method: Under this method, the annual payment is determined by dividing the individual's account balance by an annuity factor that is the present value of an annuity of $1 per year beginning at the individual's age attained in the first distribution year and continuing for the life of the individual (or the joint lives of the individual and a beneficiary). The annuity factor is derived using the mortality table provided in the 2002 IRS guidance, and an interest rate chosen as explained below. The account balance, annuity factor, interest rate and resulting annual payment are all determined once for the first distribution year, and the annual payment is the same amount each year thereafter. Rev. Rul. 2002-62, above, Sec. 2.01(c). However, the ability to recalculate the amount of the payment each year by using the taxpayer's life expectancy with the annuitization method was approved in Let. Rul. 200432023.

Life expectancy tables: There are three life expectancy table options in the 2002 guidance, all taken from the 2002 RMD regulations (see Treas. Reg. §1.401(a)(9)-9): the single life expectancy table, the joint and last survivor life expectancy table, and the uniform lifetime table. (Since the uniform lifetime table in the RMD regulations begins at age 70, the Service included an expanded version covering a broader range of ages.) See Rev. Rul. 2002-62, above, Sec. 2.02(a). All three tables are reproduced at Appendix F.

Interest rates: An interest rate must be used that does not exceed 120% of the federal mid-term rate (determined in accordance with Section 1274(d)) for *either* of the two months immediately preceding the month in which the distribution begins. Rev. Rul. 2002-62, above, Sec. 2.02(c).

Multiple accounts. In earlier private rulings decided under pre-2002 guidance, the IRS stated that individual retirement plans did not have to be aggregated for purposes of calculating a series of substantially equal periodic payments. See Let. Ruls. 200309028, 9050030. If a taxpayer owns more than one IRA, any combination of the IRAs may be taken into account in determining the distributions by aggregating the account balances of those IRAs. However, a portion of one or more of the IRAs may not be excluded in order to limit the periodic payment to a predetermined amount. Let. Rul. 9705033.

Planning Point: The ability to split up or aggregate IRAs in advance of commencing the payout makes the calculation extremely flexible. Furthermore, creating separate accounts is a good way to avoid tying up any more IRA funds than is absolutely necessary to support the needed payout.

If an individual with more than one IRA does choose to base a series of substantially equal periodic payments on the total of all his IRAs, the annual distribution may be received from any or all of the accounts. See Let. Rul. 9705033.

Modification Defined

Except in the event of death or disability, a change in payouts after the series has begun will generally constitute a "modification" and, thus, trigger the penalty. IRC Sec. 72(t)(4). The IRS has stated under the 1989 guidance that a change that does not alter the annual payout (such as a change from quarterly to monthly payments) is not a modification for this purpose. Let. Rul. 8919052. The receipt of a qualified Hurricane Katrina distribution (see Q 227) will not be treated as a change in a series of substantially equal periodic payments. Notice 2005-92, 2005-51 IRB ___, Sec. 4H.

One-time change to RMD method. The Service has stated that an individual who begins distributions using either the amortization method or the annuitization method may, in any subsequent year, switch to the RMD method to determine the payment for the year of the switch and all subsequent years. Regardless of when the payments began, a taxpayer making such a change will not be treated as having made a "modification" within the meaning of the Code. Rev. Rul. 2002-62, above, Sec. 2.03(b).

Planning Point: This ability to switch to the RMD method makes the amortization and annuity methods more attractive, particularly for a participant who has a short-term need for larger distributions which he expects will diminish in a few years. *Martin Silfen, J.D., Brown Brothers, Harriman Trust Co., LLC.*

A modification to the series of payments generally will occur if the taxpayer makes (1) any addition to the account balance (other than gains or losses), (2) any nontaxable transfer of a portion of the account balance to another retirement plan, or (3) a rollover of the amount received, resulting in such amount not being taxable. Rev. Rul. 2002-62, above, Sec. 2.02(e). However, a taxpayer who made the one-time RMD method change late in 2002 was permitted to roll over amounts in excess of the RMD amount back to the IRA in early 2003 even though the 60-day limit (see Q 454) had elapsed. Let. Rul. 200419031.

The commencement of another series of substantially equal periodic payments (i.e., from a different IRA) does not constitute a modification of an existing payout, and the IRS has stated privately that nothing in the IRC or regulations prevents a subsequent payout series. See Let. Rul. 200033048.

Special Rules

The 2002 guidance took effect for any series of payments that began on or after January 1, 2003. The penalty under Section 72(t) will not be applied if, as a result of applying an acceptable method of determining substantially equal periodic payments, an individual depletes his or her account and is unable to complete the payouts for the required duration period under Section 72(t)(4). Rev. Rul. 2002-62, above, Secs. 2.03(a) and 3. *ASRS, Sec. 62, ¶420.2.*

Required Minimum Distributions

233. What are the minimum distribution requirements for individual retirement plans? What is the effect of failure to meet the requirements?

Amounts accumulated in a traditional individual retirement account or annuity (IRA) must be distributed in compliance with the minimum distribution requirements set forth in the Code and explained in final regulations. IRC Secs. 408(a)(6), 408(b)(3), 401(a)(9). Roth IRAs are not subject to the lifetime minimum distribution requirements, but are subject to the after-death distribution requirements explained in Q 235. For the calculation of lifetime distributions, see Q 234; for after-death distributions, see Q 235. Reporting requirements pertaining to IRA required minimum distributions are explained in Q 237.

INDIVIDUAL RETIREMENT PLANS   Q 233

Under final regulations released in April, 2002, traditional IRAs, SEP IRAs and SIMPLE IRAs are generally subject to the minimum distribution requirements that apply to qualified plans. Treas. Reg. §1.408-8, A-1, A-2. (See Q 339 to Q 346.) The required beginning date for lifetime distributions from IRAs is April 1 of the calendar year following the calendar year in which the individual attains age 70½. Treas. Reg. §1.408-8, A-3; see Q 234. An individual reaches age 70½ on the date that is six calendar months after his 70th birthday. Treas. Reg. §1.401(a)(9)-2, A-3.

More than one IRA. If an individual owns more than one IRA, the required minimum distribution must be calculated separately for each IRA, but the total may then be taken from any one or more of the IRAs. However, this rule allows aggregation only of amounts that an individual is required to take as the IRA owner, or a separate aggregation of amounts in IRAs that an individual is required to take as the beneficiary of a decedent. Amounts taken as an IRA owner may not be aggregated with amounts taken as a beneficiary, for purposes of meeting the minimum distribution requirements. Similarly, distributions from Roth IRAs and 403(b) contracts or annuities may not be aggregated with traditional IRA distributions to meet the distribution requirements for either type of account. Treas. Reg. §1.408-8, A-9.

Rollovers and Transfers. Amounts distributed during a calendar year in which a minimum distribution is required are treated as required minimum distributions to the extent that the total required distribution for the year for that IRA has not yet been satisfied. Consequently, such a distribution is not eligible for rollover. Treas. Reg. §1.408-8, A-4. However, the minimum distribution requirement may be satisfied by a distribution from another IRA owned by the same individual. Treas. Reg. §1.408-8, A-9. In the event of a transfer from one IRA to another, the transferor IRA must distribute in the year of transfer any amount required under these rules, determined without regard to the transfer. Treas. Reg. §1.408-8, A-8. The transfer amount itself will not be treated as a distribution for required distribution purposes. See Treas. Reg. §1.401(a)(9)-7, A-3.

Penalty. A penalty tax is imposed on the payee if the amount distributed under an IRA for a calendar year is less than the required minimum distribution for the year. The penalty is equal to 50% of the amount by which the distribution made in the calendar year falls short of the required amount. The tax is imposed on the payee. IRC Sec. 4974(a); Treas. Reg. §54.4974-1. Generally, the penalty will be imposed in the calendar year in which the amount was required to be distributed. But if the distribution was required by April 1, the penalty will be imposed for the calendar year in which the minimum distribution was required, even though the required distribution was for the preceding year. Treas. Regs. §§54.4974-2, A-1, 54.4974-2, A-6.

The penalty tax may be waived if the payee establishes to the satisfaction of the IRS that the shortfall was due to reasonable error and that reasonable steps are being taken to remedy the shortfall. IRC Sec. 4974; Treas. Reg. §54.4974-2, A-7(a).

The minimum distribution requirements will not be treated as violated and, thus, the 50% excise tax will not apply where a shortfall occurs because assets are invested in a contract issued by an insurance company in state insurer delinquency proceedings. See Treas. Reg. §1.401(a)(9)-8, A-8. *ASRS, Sec. 62, ¶420.3.*

234. How are the minimum distribution requirements met during an IRA owner's lifetime?

Under final regulations issued in April, 2002, distributions from a traditional individual retirement account or annuity (IRA) must begin by April 1 of the year after the year in which the owner reaches age 70½, whether or not the owner has retired. Treas. Reg. §1.408-8, A-3. (IRA owners working beyond age 70½ are not permitted to delay distributions until after retirement.) No minimum distribution is required during life from a Roth IRA. Unless the owner's entire interest is distributed on or before his required beginning date, distributions of the balance must begin by that date and must, at a minimum, be distributed over the time period set forth in the final regulations, as explained below.

Uniform Lifetime Table. Under the final regulations, required minimum distributions from an individual retirement arrangement during the owner's lifetime are calculated by dividing the owner's account balance by the applicable distribution period determined from the following table:

Uniform Lifetime Table

Age of Employee	Distribution Period	Age of Employee	Distribution Period	Age of Employee	Distribution Period
70	27.4	86	14.1	101	5.9
71	26.5	87	13.4	102	5.5
72	25.6	88	12.7	103	5.2
73	24.7	89	12.0	104	4.9
74	23.8	90	11.4	105	4.5
75	22.9	91	10.8	106	4.2
76	22.0	92	10.2	107	3.9
77	21.2	93	9.6	108	3.7
78	20.3	94	9.1	109	3.4
79	19.5	95	8.6	110	3.1
80	18.7	96	8.1	111	2.9
81	17.9	97	7.6	112	2.6
82	17.1	98	7.1	113	2.4
83	16.3	99	6.7	114	2.1
84	15.5	100	6.3	115	1.9
85	14.8				

Treas. Reg. §1.401(a)(9)-9, A-2. The amount of an individual's lifetime required distribution is calculated without regard to the beneficiary's age, except in the case of a spouse beneficiary who is more than 10 years younger than the owner. See Treas. Reg. §1.401(a)(9)-5, A-4.

The distribution required by April 1 is actually the distribution required for the year in which the owner attains age 70½. Distributions for each calendar year after the year the owner becomes age 70½ (including the year of his required beginning date) must be made by December 31 of that year. Treas. Reg. §1.401(a)(9)-5, A-1(b).

For purposes of calculating minimum distributions from an IRA for a distribution calendar year, the account balance is determined as of December 31 of the immediately preceding calendar year (i.e., the valuation calendar year). Treas. Reg. §1.408-8, A-6. Under earlier regulations, for purposes of calculating the required distribution for the calendar year that includes an owner's required beginning date, the account balance as of

INDIVIDUAL RETIREMENT PLANS   Q 235

December 31 of the preceding calendar year was reduced by any distributions received from January 1 through March 31 of that year. The 2002 final regulations eliminated this provision, in an effort to simplify the required minimum distribution calculation. Treas. Reg. §1.408-8, A-6.

> *Example*: Mr. Gephart is an IRA owner born on July 9, 1934. He reached age 70 on July 9, 2004, and age 70½ on January 9, 2005 (i.e., six months after his 70th birthday). Consequently, Mr. Gephart's required beginning date is April 1, 2006. Assume that as of December 31, 2004, the value of Mr. Gephart's IRA was $265,000. Since Mr. Gephart's age *in 2005* (the year for which his first distribution will be made) is 71, the applicable distribution period from the table above is 26.5 years. Thus, the required distribution for calendar year 2005 is $10,000 ($265,000 ÷ 26.5). Assume that Mr. Gephart receives this amount shortly before his required beginning date of April 1, 2006.
>
> Assume that the value of Mr. Gephart's account balance as of December 31, 2005 is $256,000. This account balance is *not* reduced by the distribution received in early 2006. As a result, Mr. Gephart's required minimum distribution *for* 2006, which is due by December 31, 2006, is $10,000 ($256,000 ÷ 25.6). Also, receiving a distribution of more than the required minimum will not reduce the amount Mr. Gephart is required to take in a subsequent year. Treas. Regs. §§1.408-8, A-6, 1.401(a)(9)-5, A-3.

Spouse beneficiary. If the IRA owner's spouse is the only beneficiary of the owner's entire interest at all times during the distribution year, the owner may receive distributions over the longer of the distribution period determined from the table above, or the joint and survivor life expectancy of the owner and spouse. Treas. Reg. §1.401(a)(9)-5, A-4(b). The joint and survivor life expectancy will provide a longer payout period only if the spouse is more than 10 years younger than the IRA owner. For details on the definition of "designated beneficiary" see Q 236.

Distributions as annuity payments. IRA required minimum distributions that are made as annuity payments are calculated in the same manner under the final regulations as required minimum distributions from defined benefit plans. See Treas. Regs. §§1.408-8, A-1, 1.401(a)(9)-6; see Q 342. The IRS provided interim relief from these requirements by stating that minimum distributions under an annuity contract will be deemed under the final regulations to satisfy the requirements of the regulations in their temporary form. See Rev. Proc. 2003-10, 2003-2 IRB 259; Notice 2003-2, 2003-1 CB 257. *ASRS Sec. 62, ¶420.3(a).*

235. How are the minimum distribution requirements met after the death of an IRA owner?

The minimum distribution requirements that apply after the death of a traditional or Roth IRA owner depend on whether he died before or after his required beginning date. Generally, distributions are treated as having begun in accordance with the minimum distribution requirements under IRC Section 401(a)(9)(A)(ii). However, if distributions *irrevocably* (except for acceleration) began prior to the required beginning date in the form of an annuity that meets the minimum distribution rules, the annuity starting date will be treated as the required beginning date for purposes of calculating lifetime and after death minimum distribution requirements. Treas. Reg. §1.401(a)(9)-6, A-10; Treas. Reg. §1.408-8, A-1. Final regulations explaining the minimum distribution requirements were published in April 2002. See TD 8987, 67 Fed. Reg. 18988 (4-17-02). (The regulations governing annuity payouts were finalized in 2004.)

Death Before Required Beginning Date

If an IRA owner dies *before* his required beginning date, distributions must be made under one of two methods:

2006 Tax Facts on Insurance & Employee Benefits

(1) *Life expectancy rule:* if any portion of the interest is payable to, or for the benefit of, a designated beneficiary, that portion must be distributed over the life (or life expectancy) of the designated beneficiary (see Q 236), beginning within one year of the owner's death. IRC Sec. 401(a)(9)(B)(iii), Treas. Reg. §1.401(a)(9)-3, A-1(a). To the extent that the interest is payable to a nonspouse beneficiary, distributions must begin by the end of the calendar year immediately following the calendar year in which the IRA owner died. Treas. Reg. §1.401(a)(9)-3, A-3. The nonspouse beneficiary's life expectancy for this purpose is measured as of his birthday in the year following the year of the owner's death. In subsequent years, this amount is reduced by one for each calendar year that has elapsed since the year of the owner's death. See Treas. Reg. §1.401(a)(9)-5, A-5(c)(1). For the treatment of multiple beneficiaries, see Q 236.

A surviving spouse who is the sole designated beneficiary of the IRA generally may elect to treat the IRA as his or her own (see "Surviving Spouse's Election" below). Unless this election is made, distributions to a surviving spouse beneficiary must begin by the later of (i) the end of the calendar year immediately following the calendar year in which the owner died, or (ii) the end of the calendar year in which the owner would have reached age 70½. See IRC Sec. 401(a)(9)(B)(iv); Treas. Reg. §1.401(a)(9)-3, A-3. The payout period is the surviving spouse's life expectancy, based on his or her attained age in each calendar year for which a minimum distribution is required. Treas. Reg. §1.401(a)(9)-5, A-5(c)(2). After the surviving spouse dies, the payout period is his or her remaining life expectancy, based on the age of the spouse in the calendar year of death, reduced by one for each calendar year that elapses thereafter. Treas. Reg. §1.401(a)(9)-5, A-5(c)(2).

(2) *Five year rule*: the entire interest must be distributed within five years after the death of the IRA owner (regardless of who or what entity receives the distribution). IRC Sec. 401(a)(9)(B)(ii), Treas. Reg. §1.401(a)(9)-3, A-1(a). In order to satisfy this rule, the entire interest must be distributed by the end of the calendar year that contains the fifth anniversary of the date of the IRA owner's death. Treas. Reg. §1.401(a)(9)-3, A-2.

The 2002 final regulations set forth tables containing single and joint and survivor life expectancies for calculating required minimum distributions, as well as a "Uniform Lifetime Table" for determining the appropriate distribution periods. See Treas. Reg. §1.401(a)(9)-9. See Appendix F for details.

Death on or After Required Beginning Date

If the owner of an IRA dies *on or after* the date distributions have begun (i.e., generally his required beginning date), but before his entire interest in the IRA has been distributed, the Code states that the entire remaining balance must generally be distributed at least as rapidly as under the method of distribution in effect as of the owner's date of death. See IRC Sec. 401(a)(9)(B)(i).

Under the final regulations, if the IRA owner does not have a designated beneficiary as of the date on which the designated beneficiary is determined (i.e., September 30 of the year after death, see Q 236), his interest is distributed over his remaining life expectancy, using the age of the owner in the calendar year of his death, reduced by one for each calendar year that elapses thereafter. See Treas. Reg. §1.401(a)(9)-5, A-5(c)(3).

If the owner *does* have a designated beneficiary as of the determination date (see Q 236), the beneficiary's interest is distributed over the longer of (i) the beneficiary's life expectancy, calculated as described above at "Life Expectancy Rule" (i.e., under

INDIVIDUAL RETIREMENT PLANS   Q 236

Treas. Reg. §1.401(a)(9)-5, A-5(c)(1) or (2)) or (ii) the remaining life expectancy of the owner, determined using the age of the owner in the calendar year of his death, reduced by one for each calendar year that elapses thereafter (i.e., under Treas. Reg. §1.401(a)(9)-5, A-5(c)(3)). Treas. Reg. §1.401(a)(9)-5, A-5(a)(1). For the treatment of multiple beneficiaries and separate accounts, see Q 236.

Surviving Spouse's Election

A surviving spouse of an IRA owner who is the sole beneficiary of an IRA and who has an unlimited right to make withdrawals from the IRA may elect to treat the entire account as his or her own IRA. This election can be made at any time after the IRA owner's death. Treas. Reg. §1.408-8, A-5(a).

Any minimum distribution that was required to be made to the deceased owner, but had not been made to him before his death must be made to the surviving spouse in the year of the death, but in all other respects, required distributions after the owner's death are determined as if the surviving spouse were the owner. Treas. Reg. §1.408-8, A-5(a).

The surviving spouse will be *deemed* to have made the election to treat the IRA as his or her own if: (1) any required amounts in the account have not been distributed under the requirements for after-death required minimum distributions, or (2) any additional amounts are contributed to the account, or to an account or annuity to which the surviving spouse has rolled over the amounts. Treas. Reg. §1.408-8, A-5(b).

The result of a surviving spouse making the election to treat an IRA as his or her own is that the surviving spouse will then be considered the IRA owner for all other purposes under the Code (for example, for purposes of the 10% penalty on premature distributions). Treas. Reg. §1.408-8, A-5(c).

Death of surviving spouse beneficiary. In the event that a surviving spouse beneficiary dies after the IRA owner, but before distributions to the spouse have begun, the 5-year rule and the life expectancy rule described above will be applied as though the surviving spouse were the IRA owner. See IRC Sec. 401(a)(9)(B)(iv)(II); Treas. Reg. §1.401(a)(9)-4, A-4(b); see Let. Rul. 200436017. As a result, the distribution period is determined by the life expectancy of the surviving spouse's designated beneficiary, determined as of September 30 of the year after the surviving spouse's death. Treas. Reg. §1.401(a)(9)-4, A-4(b). However, this provision does not allow a new spouse of the deceased IRA owner's surviving spouse to delay distributions under the surviving spouse rules of IRC Section 401(a)(9)(B)(iv). Treas. Reg. §1.401(a)(9)-3, A-5.

Stretch IRA. The term "stretch IRA" does not appear in the Internal Revenue Code, but simply describes, in popular usage, the practice of IRA distribution planning that successfully permits the beneficiaries (e.g., surviving spouse and child of the owner) to receive distributions over their individual life expectancies under the foregoing rules, and satisfy the requirements for separate accounts (see Q 236). *ASRS, Sec. 62, ¶¶420.3(b), 420.3(c).*

236. Who is a "designated beneficiary" for purposes of required minimum distributions from an IRA? What are the rules for multiple beneficiaries and separate accounts?

A designated beneficiary is an individual (or a trust meeting certain requirements, see Q 344) designated as a beneficiary, either by the terms of the IRA document or

2006 Tax Facts on Insurance & Employee Benefits

by an affirmative election by the IRA owner, or the surviving spouse. See Treas. Reg. §1.401(a)(9)-4, A-1. For lifetime distributions, the identity and age of the designated beneficiary do not affect the IRA owner's distributions unless the designated beneficiary is a spouse more than 10 years younger than the owner.

The designated beneficiary need not be specified by name in order to be a designated beneficiary so long as he is identifiable under the terms of the IRA, as of the determination date. Treas. Reg. §1.401(a)(9)-4, A-1. For special rules governing contingent and successor beneficiaries, see Q 344.

Determination date. For purposes of after-death minimum distribution requirements, the final regulations require that a beneficiary determination be made as of *September 30* of the year after the year of the IRA owner's death. Treas. Reg. §1.401(a)(9)-4, A-4(a). This date is designed to provide ample time following the determination to calculate and make the required distribution prior to the December 31 deadline. See TD 8987, 67 Fed. Reg. 18988 (4-17-02). (Exceptions to the September 30 deadline may apply if the account is payable as an annuity, or if a surviving spouse beneficiary dies after the IRA owner but before distributions have begun.) Consequently, an individual who was a beneficiary as of the date of the owner's death, but is not a beneficiary as of September 30 of the following year (e.g., because he disclaims entitlement to the benefit or because he receives the entire benefit to which he is entitled before that date) is not taken into account for purposes of determining the distribution period for required minimum distributions after the owner's death. Treas. Reg. §1.401(a)(9)-4, A-4(a). A disclaiming beneficiary's receipt (prior to disclaiming the benefit) of a required distribution in the year after death will not result in the beneficiary being treated as a designated beneficiary for subsequent years. Rev. Rul. 2005-36, 2005-26 IRB 1368.

No beneficiary. If the beneficiary is not an individual or a permitted trust, the IRA owner will be treated as having no beneficiary. An IRA owner's estate may not be a designated beneficiary. Treas. Reg. §1.401(a)(9)-4, A-3.

Trust as beneficiary. As a general rule, only an individual (not an estate or a trust) may be a designated beneficiary for required minimum distribution purposes. However, if the special requirements for a "see-through" trust are met (see Q 344), the beneficiaries of a trust may be treated as if they had been designated as the beneficiaries of the IRA for required minimum distribution purposes (but not for purposes of "separate account treatment," see below).

Multiple Beneficiaries and Separate Accounts

If more than one beneficiary is designated as of the date on which the determination is made, the final regulations provide that the beneficiary with the shortest life expectancy (i.e., generally the oldest) will be the designated beneficiary for purposes of determining the distribution period. Treas. Reg. §1.401(a)(9)-5, A-7(a).

As an exception to the "oldest beneficiary" rule, the final regulations provide that if an individual account (including an IRA, see Treas. Reg. §1.408-8, A-1(a)) is divided into *separate accounts* (as defined below) with different beneficiaries, the separate accounts do not have to be aggregated for purposes of determining the required minimum distributions for years subsequent to the calendar year in which the separate accounts were established (or date of death, if later). Treas. Reg. §1.401(a)(9)-8, A-2(a)(2). (In 2004 this rule was modified to permit separate account treatment for *the year following the year of death*, provided the separate accounts are actually established by the end of the calendar year following death. See TD 9130, 2004-26 IRB 1082.)

For purposes of Section 401(a)(9), "separate accounts" are defined as portions of an employee's benefit [or IRA] representing the separate interests of the employee's beneficiaries under the plan as of his date of death. The separate accounting *must allocate* all post-death investment gains and losses, contributions, and forfeitures for the period prior to the establishment of the separate accounts on a pro rata basis in a reasonable and consistent manner among the accounts. Once the separate accounts are actually established, the separate accounting can provide for separate investments in each account, with gains and losses attributable to such investments allocable only to that account. A separate accounting must also allocate any post-death distribution to the separate account of the beneficiary receiving it. Treas. Reg. §1.401(a)(9)-8, A-3.

Planning Point: When leaving an IRA to multiple beneficiaries, an owner may leave a fixed dollar ("pecuniary") amount to one or more or them, with a "residual" gift to one or more other beneficiaries, or use "fractional"-type gifts for all beneficiaries. Though both methods are legal and acceptable, fractional gifts are usually preferable, for two reasons.

First, if the owner uses a pecuniary gift (such as "pay $10,000 to Beneficiary A and the balance of the account to Beneficiary B"), the IRA provider may not know whether to give the "pecuniary" beneficiary just the flat dollar amount or to give him the dollar amount plus or minus gains or losses that accrue after the date of death. The IRA provider's documents and policies should spell this out, but many do not.

Second, if the gift is truly a flat dollar amount, not adjusted for gains or losses occurring after the date of death, then that gift cannot qualify under the regulations as a "separate account" (see above) for minimum distribution purposes. Thus, the beneficiary of the flat dollar gift and the beneficiaries of the "residuary" gift will be considered beneficiaries of the same account. This means that, unless the pecuniary beneficiary's share is distributed (or disclaimed) in full prior to September 30 of the year after the year of death, the residuary share beneficiaries will not be able to use the life expectancy payout method if the pecuniary beneficiary is a charity (a nonindividual). *Natalie B. Choate, Esq., Bingham McCutchen.*

Separate accounts using individual life expectancies. The regulations state that when separate accounts are established with different beneficiaries, the "applicable distribution period" is determined for each separate account disregarding the other beneficiaries *only* if the separate account is established no later than December 31 of the year following the decedent's death. Treas. Reg. §1.401(a)(9)-8, A-2(a)(2). If this deadline is not met, separate accounts can be established at any time, according to the Preamble to the final regulations, but the distribution period in effect prior to the separation of the accounts (generally the life expectancy of the oldest beneficiary) will continue to be applied. See TD 8987, 67 Fed. Reg. 18988 (4-17-02).

The regulations state that if a trust is the beneficiary of an employee's plan interest, separate account treatment is not available to the beneficiaries of the trust. Treas. Reg. §1.401(a)(9)-4, A-5(c). The IRS has determined repeatedly that the establishment of separate shares did not entitle multiple beneficiaries of the same trust to use their own life expectancies as the distribution period. See Let. Ruls. 200307095, 200444033, 200528031. However, the Service has privately ruled that where separate individual trusts were named as beneficiaries, the ability of each beneficiary to use his or her life expectancy was preserved even though the trusts were governed by a single "master trust." See Let. Rul. 200537044.

Separate accounts using oldest beneficiary's life expectancy. If the foregoing requirements are not met (i.e., if separate accounts are not established by the deadline or to the extent the IRA proceeds were payable to one trust benefiting more than one individual), the IRA may, nonetheless, be segregated into separate accounts, but the "applicable distribution period" will be the life expectancy of the beneficiary with the shortest life expectancy. See Treas. Reg. §1.401(a)(9)-8, A-2(a)(2). The fact that the trust meets the requirements for a "see-through trust" (see Q 344) does not change this result. See Let. Rul. 200317044.

The IRS has repeatedly applied this rule where IRA proceeds were left to a single trust benefiting more than one child of the IRA owner. See Let. Ruls. 200317041, 200349009, 200410019. Trust terms ordering the subdivision of the account (i.e., creating separate IRAs titled in the name of the decedent for the benefit of the individual account beneficiaries) do not alter this result. See Let. Ruls. 200317043, 200432027. Where the trust established by the decedent to receive IRA proceeds included provisions or a subtrust benefiting the surviving spouse, the surviving spouse's life expectancy was found to be controlling. See Let. Ruls. 200410019, 200438044. Finally, where a father had failed to designated an IRA beneficiary, making his estate, which was left to his three children, the beneficiary, the decedent's remaining life expectancy was controlling; still a subdivision of the IRA was permitted. Let. Rul. 200343030.

For details regarding contingent and successor beneficiaries, as well as other special rules, see Q 344. *ASRS, Sec. 62, ¶¶420.3(b), 420.3(c).*

237. What reporting requirements are imposed on IRA trustees with respect to required minimum distributions?

Reporting requirements for IRA trustees (including issuers and custodians of individual retirement accounts and individual retirement annuities) were first published in the 2001 proposed regulations, but specific guidance was not issued until the 2002 final regulations were published. See TD 8987, 67 Fed. Reg. 18988 (4-17-02); Notice 2002-27, 2002-1 CB 814.

Two reporting requirements are imposed on IRA trustees by Notice 2002-27: one to the IRA owner, and one to the IRS. For IRA owners, the notice states that "If a minimum distribution is required with respect to an IRA for a calendar year and the IRA owner is alive at the beginning of the year, the trustee that held the IRA as of December 31 of the prior year must provide a statement to the IRA owner by January 31 of the calendar year...." The statement must satisfy one of the following alternatives:

(1) it must inform the IRA owner of the *amount* of the required minimum distribution and the *date* by which it is required; or

(2) it must inform the IRA owner that a minimum distribution is required with respect to the IRA, and offer to calculate the amount of the distribution upon request by the owner.

INDIVIDUAL RETIREMENT PLANS   Q 239

The Service has clarified that a trustee may use either of these two alternatives, or may use one alternative for some IRA owners and the other for other IRA owners. Notice 2003-3, 2003-1 CB 258, clarifying Notice 2002-27, above.

The reporting requirements apply only to lifetime distributions, which generally use the "Uniform Lifetime Table" set forth in Q 234. The IRA owner is presumed *not* to have a spouse more than ten years younger than the owner. See Notice 2002-27, above.

No reporting is required for after death distributions, or for 403(b) tax sheltered annuity distributions. *ASRS, Sec. 62, ¶420.3(d).*

FILING REQUIREMENTS

238. What IRS filing requirements must be met by an individual retirement plan participant?

An individual who establishes an individual retirement plan does not need to file a Form 5329 for any year in which there is no plan activity other than making contributions (other than rollover contributions) and permissible distributions. He does need to file the return if there is a tax due because of a premature distribution (Q 231), excess contribution (Q 226), or excess accumulation (Q 233). IRC Secs. 6058(d), 6058(e).

Nondeductible Contributions

If an individual makes a nondeductible contribution to a traditional IRA for any year, he must report on Form 8606: (a) the amount of the nondeductible contributions for the taxable year; (b) the amount of distributions from individual retirement plans for the taxable year; (c) the excess of the aggregate amount of nondeductible contributions for all preceding years over the aggregate amount of distributions that were excludable from income for such taxable years; (d) the aggregate balance of all individual retirement plans as of the close of the year in which the taxable year begins; and (e) any other information as prescribed by the Secretary of the Treasury. IRC Sec. 408(o). Failure to file Form 8606 will result in a $50 penalty unless it is shown that such failure was due to reasonable cause. IRC Sec. 6693(b)(2). Failure of a taxpayer to file Form 8606 resulted in his failure to appropriately document his basis in the IRA and in such contributions being taxed a second time upon distribution. *Alpern v. Comm.*, TC Memo 2000-246. See Q 227. Overstatement of a nondeductible contribution is subject to a penalty tax of $100 per occurrence. IRC Sec. 6693(b)(1). *ASRS, Sec. 62, ¶610.*

EMPLOYER-SPONSORED IRAS

239. May an employer contribute to an IRA on behalf of an employee? May an employer or union establish an individual retirement account for its employees or members?

Yes. An employer may contribute to a traditional or Roth IRA on behalf of any eligible employee (or his eligible spouse as described in Q 218). However, any contribution made by the employer must be included in the employee's gross income as compensation for the year for which the contribution was made. IRC Sec. 219(f)(5); see Prop. Treas. Reg. §1.219(a)-2(c)(4). The employer's contribution is treated as though made by the employee and subject to the maximum contribution limits applicable to individual retirement plans (see Q 220, Q 221). If the contribution is made to a traditional IRA and the employee is eligible, the employee may take a deduction subject to the limits in Q 220. The employer deducts the contribution as salary or other compensation and not as a contribution to a retirement plan. IRC Sec. 162; Treas. Reg. §1.219-1(c)(4). Because amounts contributed by an employer are compensation to the employee, they are subject to FICA (social security tax), FUTA (federal unemployment tax), and income tax withholding. H. R. Conf. Rep. 93-1280 (ERISA '74) *reprinted in* 1974-3 CB 500; H. Rep. 93-807, *reprinted in* 1974-3 Supp. CB 367; IRC Sec. 3401(a)(12)(C).

A trust that will be treated as an individual retirement account may be set up by an employer or association of employees for the benefit of employees, members, or employees of members (or the eligible spouses of any of the foregoing) *if* the trust meets all the requirements of an individual retirement account (see Q 210) *and* there is a separate accounting maintained for each employee, member or spouse. A contribution made by an employer to such trust on behalf of an employee will be treated as a contribution to an individual retirement plan. The assets of an employer or association trust may be held in a common fund for the account of all individuals who have an interest in the trust. Such trust may include amounts held for former employees or members and employees temporarily on leave. To qualify as an "association of employees" there must initially have been some nexus between the employees (e.g., common employer, common industry, etc.). An association may include members who are self-employed. IRC Sec. 408(c); Treas. Reg. §1.408-2(c).

Employer contributions to an individual retirement plan (or employer or association trust that is treated as an individual retirement account) are not required to meet any nondiscrimination rules. However, an employer generally cannot satisfy the coverage requirement for a qualified plan by contributing to an individual retirement account (including an employer or association trust treated as an individual retirement account) or individual retirement annuity on behalf of employees not covered under the qualified plan. H. R. Conf. Rep. 93-1280 (ERISA '74) *reprinted in* 1974-3 CB 499.

The use of a payroll deduction program to fund employee IRAs will not subject the employer to Title I of ERISA (reporting and disclosure, participation and vesting, etc.) where employer involvement is limited. Labor. Reg. §2510.3-2(d); see IB 99-1, 64 Fed. Reg. 32999 (6-18-99).

An employer may also establish "deemed IRAs" for employees under a qualified plan. See Q 211. An employer may contribute amounts higher than the usual individual retirement plan limits by establishing a simplified employee pension program (see Q 240) or a SIMPLE IRA (see Q 242). *ASRS, Sec. 62, ¶410.1(c).*

SIMPLIFIED EMPLOYEE PENSION (SEP)

240. What is a simplified employee pension?

A simplified employee pension (SEP) is a traditional individual retirement account or individual retirement annuity (IRA–see Q 210) that may accept an expanded rate of contributions from one or more employers. IRC Sec. 408(k). It is owned by the employee, who may be self-employed.

In order for an IRA to be a SEP, certain requirements must be satisfied:

INDIVIDUAL RETIREMENT PLANS   Q 240

(1) The employer must contribute to the SEP of each employee (including certain "leased" employees – see Q 355) who is at least 21 years old, has performed services for the employer during the year for which the contribution is made (including any such employee who, because of death or termination of employment, is no longer employed on the date contributions are actually made), *and* for at least three of the immediately preceding five years has received at least $450 in compensation (in 2006) from the employer for the year. IRC Sec. 408(k)(2)(C). (See Appendix E for earlier years.) The employer may not require that an employee be employed as of a particular date in the year. Prop. Treas. Reg. §1.408-7(d)(3). Employees covered by a collective bargaining agreement may be excluded from participation if retirement benefits have been the subject of good faith bargaining. Similarly, nonresident aliens may be excluded if they received no income from the employer that is considered to be from U.S. sources. IRC Sec. 408(k)(2).

(2) Employer contributions must not discriminate in favor of any highly compensated employee. See Q 356. Employees who are excluded from participation as nonresident aliens, or because they are covered by a collective bargaining agreement, are not considered for purposes of determining whether there is discrimination. IRC Sec. 408(k)(3).

Unless employer contributions bear a uniform relationship to total compensation (or earned income in the case of self-employed individuals) they will be discriminatory. However, compensation or earned income in excess of $220,000 (in 2006) is not to be taken into account. IRC Sec. 408(k)(3)(C). This compensation limit is indexed for inflation in increments of $5,000. (See Appendix E for the indexed amounts for earlier years.) IRC Secs. 408(k)(8), 401(a)(17). Presumably, a constant percentage of compensation would meet the nondiscrimination requirement. A rate of contribution that decreases as compensation increases will be considered uniform. Prop. Treas. Reg. §1.408-8(c). The IRS has informally approved a method of contribution that in effect required that an identical dollar amount be contributed on behalf of all participants. See Let. Rul. 8824019.

SEPs can be integrated under the rules applicable to qualified plans. See Q 330. IRC Sec. 408(k)(3)(D); TAMRA '88, Sec. 1011(f)(7).

(3) Employer contributions must be determined under a definite written allocation formula that specifies the manner in which the allocation is computed and what requirements an employee must satisfy to share in the allocation. However, the employer may vary the allocation formula from year to year so long as there is a timely amendment to the plan that indicates the new formula. Prop. Treas. Reg. §1.408-7(e). No minimum funding standards are imposed.

(4) The employer contribution may not be conditioned on the employee's keeping any part of it in the pension and the employer may not prohibit withdrawals from the plan. IRC Sec. 408(k)(4).

(5) If the SEP is top-heavy (see Q 351), it is subject to the minimum contribution rules applicable to such plans. See Q 352B. IRC Secs. 408(k)(1)(B), 416(c)(2). Employer contributions to a SEP may be taken into account in determining whether qualified plans of the employer are top-heavy. See Q 351.

Should an eligible employee or former employee not have an IRA on the date contributions are made, the employer is required to establish one on the employee's behalf. See Prop. Treas. Reg. §1.408-7(d)(2). A SEP plan need not be established until the contribution is made for the year (i.e., it may be established after the end of the year–see "Employer's Deduction," below).

A controlled group of corporations or employers under common control or employers composing an "affiliated service group" (see Q 359, Q 360) are treated as a single employer. Thus, if contributions are made to SEPs for employees in one business, they may have to be made for employees of another business if the two are under common control or constitute an affiliated service group. IRC Secs. 414(b), 414(c), 414(m); Let. Rul. 8041045.

SEPs are treated as defined contribution plans for purposes of the overall limits on employer contributions (see Q 332). IRC Sec. 415(a)(2)(C). For plan years beginning in 2006, the annual additions limit is the lesser of $44,000 or 100% of compensation. IRC Sec. 415(c)(2). Any contribution *by an employer* to a SEP must be aggregated with all other employer contributions by that employer to defined contribution plans for purposes of the Section 415(c) limit on annual additions. For purposes of the foregoing rules, the definition of compensation set forth in Section 414(s) applies (see Q 331). IRC Sec. 408(k)(7)(B). Catch-up contributions, which are available in plans that provide for elective deferral contributions (see, e.g., Q 241, Q 242, Q 394), are not available in SEPs.

Treatment of Contributions

An employee may treat his SEP account as a traditional IRA and make deductible or nondeductible contributions to it under the rules described in Q 217 to Q 233.

Exclusion. Contributions made by an employer on behalf of an employee to a SEP are excludable from the employee's income to the extent that they do not exceed *the lesser of* 25% of compensation from the employer (determined without regard to that employer's contribution to the SEP) or $44,000. IRC Secs. 402(h)(2), 415(c)(1)(A). Consequently, taking into account the $220,000 limit on compensation, the Code would effectively limit SEP contributions to $44,000 for 2005 ($44,000 is less than ($220,000 × 25%). However, as a result of an apparent oversight by Congress, compensation, for this purpose only, is *includable* compensation (i.e., not including elective deferrals). See IRC Sec. 402(h)(2)(A).

If an individual is employed by more than one employer (other than employers who are under common control or compose a controlled or affiliated service group) during the tax year, the 25% limit is applied separately to each employer. See IRC Sec. 219(b)(2). Under proposed regulations, contributions by (and compensation received from) employers who are under common control or who are members of a controlled group must be aggregated for purposes of this limit. See Prop. Treas. Reg. §1.219-3(c). It would seem that the IRS may also require such aggregation where the employers are members of an affiliated service group.

If an individual is self-employed with respect to more than one trade or business, the maximum contribution will be the lesser of the amount determined by applying the limit separately to each trade or business *or* the amount determined by applying the limit as if the trades or businesses constituted one employer. See Prop. Treas. Reg. §1.219-

INDIVIDUAL RETIREMENT PLANS   Q 241

3(c)(2). In an integrated plan, the 415 dollar limit must be reduced in the case of a highly compensated employee (as defined in Q 356). IRC Sec. 402(h)(2)(B). Contributions are not subject to income tax withholding, FICA or FUTA. IRC Secs. 3401(a)(12)(C), 3121(a)(5)(C), 3306(b)(5)(C). See also Rev. Rul. 65-209, 1965-2 CB 414.

The Employer's Deduction

Employer contributions for a calendar year are deductible, under IRC Section 404, for the tax year in which the calendar year ends. An employer may elect to use its taxable year instead of the calendar year for purposes of determining contributions to a SEP. IRC Sec. 404(h)(1)(A). Employer contributions made on account of a calendar year or an employer's taxable year may be made as late as the due date (plus extensions) of the employer's tax return for such year and be treated as if contributed on the last day of that year. IRC Sec. 404(h)(1)(B). The due date for C corporations is 2½ months following the close of such year and for self-employed individuals is 3½ months following the close of such year. IRC Secs. 6012(a), 6072.

The maximum employer deduction amount is 25% of compensation for the calendar year (or, if applicable, the taxable year). IRC Sec. 404(h)(1)(C). (For years before 2002, the maximum was 15%.) "Compensation," for this purpose, *includes* elective deferrals and certain other contributions made on a pre-tax basis. See IRC Sec. 404(a)(12), 404(n).

Contributions in excess of the 25% deductible limit may be carried over and deducted in succeeding years. See IRC Sec. 404(h)(1)(C). However, the employer is subject to an excise tax on nondeductible contributions–see Q 367. If the employer also contributes to a qualified profit sharing or stock bonus plan, the 25% deductible limit for that plan is reduced by the amount of the allowable deduction for contributions to the SEPs with respect to participants in the stock bonus or profit sharing plan. IRC Sec. 404(h)(2). If the employer also contributes to any other type of qualified plan, the SEP is treated as a separate profit sharing or stock bonus plan for purposes of applying the combination deduction limit of IRC Section 404(a)(7) (see Q 366). IRC Sec. 404(h)(3). *ASRS, Sec. 62, ¶720.*

241. What is a SAR-SEP? What requirements must be met if a simplified employee pension is offered on a cash or deferred basis?

A SAR-SEP is a simplified employee pension that is offered on a salary reduction (i.e., cash or deferred) basis. In other words, the plan permits individual employees to elect to have contributions made to the SEP or to receive the contribution in cash. Such a SEP must otherwise meet the requirements in Q 240, as well as those explained below, *and* the plan had to be established before 1997. No new SAR-SEPs are permitted after 1996, but those in effect prior to 1997 may continue to operate, receive contributions, and add new employees. See IRC Sec. 408(k)(6)(H). For an explanation of SIMPLE IRAs, which offer a salary deferral feature, see Q 242.

A SAR-SEP may be maintained by an employer who had 25 or fewer employees who were eligible to participate in the plan at any time during the prior taxable year. The amount that an employee chooses to defer and contribute to the SEP is referred to as an elective deferral. Elective deferrals are subject to the same $15,000 cap (in 2006) as elective deferrals to IRC Section 401(k) plans. IRC Sec. 402(g)(1). (See Q 396 for the definition of "elective deferral" and rules for participants in more than one plan; see Appendix E for the indexed amounts in earlier years.) Such deferrals are also subject

2006 Tax Facts on Insurance & Employee Benefits

to FICA and FUTA withholding. IRC Secs. 3121(a)(5)(C), 3306(b)(5)(C). Certain lower income taxpayers may be eligible to claim the saver's credit for elective deferrals to a SAR-SEP. See Q 213.

In addition to the elective deferrals described above, a SAR-SEP may permit additional elective deferrals by individuals age 50 or over, referred to as "catch-up contributions." See IRC Secs. 414(v)(1), 414(v)(6)(A)(iv). The dollar limit on catch-up contributions to a SAR-SEP is $5,000 in 2006. IRC Sec. 414(v)(2)(B)(i). For details on the requirements for catch-up contributions, see Q 397.

Employee Exclusion. Contributions made by an employer on behalf of an employee to a SAR-SEP are excludable from the employee's income to the extent that they do not exceed the lesser of 25% of "compensation" from the employer, or $44,000 (in 2006, as indexed). IRC Secs. 402(h)(2)(A), 415(c)(1)(A). However, as a result of an apparent oversight by Congress, *compensation*, for this purpose only, is *includable* compensation (i.e., not including elective deferrals). See IRC Sec. 402(h)(2)(A).

The election to defer salary into a SAR-SEP account is available only if (1) at least 50% of the employees of the employer eligible to participate elect to have amounts contributed to the SEP, and (2) the deferral percentage for each highly compensated eligible employee does not exceed the average deferral percentage for all other nonhighly compensated eligible employees by more than 125%. IRC Sec. 408(k)(6). Catch-up contributions are not taken into account for this purpose. IRC Sec. 414(v)(3)(A). Compensation or earned income in excess of $220,000 (in 2006, as indexed) is not to be taken into account in determining an employee's deferral percentage. IRC Sec. 408(k)(6)(D). This amount is indexed for inflation in increments of $5,000. (See Appendix E for the amounts in earlier years.)

A SEP will not be treated as failing to meet the deferral percentage requirement if, before the end of the following plan year, any excess contribution (i.e., in excess of 125%), plus any income attributable to such, is distributed, or treated as distributed and then contributed by the employee to the plan. IRC Secs. 408(k)(6)(C), 401(k)(8). (Such a recharacterization of contributions is not permitted in the absence of regulations. General Explanation of TRA '86, p. 639.) However, unless the excess is distributed within 2½ months after the end of the plan year, the employer will be subject to a 10% excise tax. IRC Sec. 4979. Any excess amounts so distributed are generally treated as received by the recipient in the taxable year for which the original contribution was made; however, if total excess contributions distributed to a recipient under the plan for a plan year are less than $100, the distributions will be treated as received in the taxable year of distribution. IRC Sec. 4979(f)(2).

Since an employer may not force an employee to take a distribution of excess deferrals because the contributions are held in an individual retirement plan controlled by the employee, the Secretary of Treasury has the authority to prescribe necessary rules to insure that excess contributions are distributed, including reporting requirements and the requirement that contributions may not be withdrawn until a determination is made that the deferral percentage test has been satisfied. IRC Sec. 408(k)(6)(F). Any distribution or transfer before such a determination has been made will be subject to ordinary income tax as well as to the premature distribution penalty, regardless of whether the penalty tax would otherwise apply. IRC Sec. 408(d)(7).

INDIVIDUAL RETIREMENT PLANS

A plan will not be treated as violating any applicable limit of Section 408(k) merely on account of the making of (or right to make) catch-up contributions by participants age 50 or over, under the provisions of IRC Section 414(v), so long as a universal availability requirement is met. IRC Sec. 414(v)(3)(B). In addition, catch-up contributions are not taken into account for purposes of the employer deduction limitation explained in Q 240. IRC Sec. 414(v)(3)(A). See Q 397 for details on the requirements for catch-up contributions.

State or local governments and other tax-exempt organizations may not offer cash or deferred SEPs. IRC Sec. 408(k)(6)(E). *ASRS, Sec. 62, ¶720.2.*

SIMPLE IRA

242. What is a SIMPLE IRA plan?

A SIMPLE (which stands for Savings Incentive Match Plan for Employees) IRA plan is a simplified, tax-favored retirement plan for small employers that provides for elective contributions by employees and meets certain vesting, participation and administrative requirements described below. IRC Sec. 408(p)(1); Notice 98-4, 1998-1 CB 269; General Explanation of Tax Legislation Enacted in the 104th Congress (JCT-12-96), p. 140 (the 1996 Blue Book).

A SIMPLE IRA plan may permit contributions only under a *qualified salary reduction arrangement* (however, catch-up contributions—see below—will not violate this requirement). A qualified salary reduction arrangement is defined as a written arrangement of an "eligible employer" (defined below) under which: (i) employees eligible to participate may elect to receive payments in cash or contribute them to a SIMPLE IRA, (ii) the amount to which such an election applies must be expressed as a percentage of compensation and may not exceed $10,000 per year (in 2006); however, the amount of the contribution may also be expressed as a dollar amount, (iii) the employer must make matching contributions or nonelective contributions to the account according to one of the formulas described below, and (iv) no contributions other than those described in (i) and (iii) may be made to the account. IRC Sec. 408(p)(2); Notice 98-4, above. Certain lower income taxpayers may be eligible to claim the saver's credit for elective deferrals to a SIMPLE IRA. See Q 213.

Elective Deferral and Catch-up Contributions

The $10,000 elective deferral amount for 2006 is indexed for inflation. IRC Secs. 408(p)(2)(A)(ii), 408(p)(2)(E). A SIMPLE IRA plan may also permit catch-up contributions by participants who reach age 50 (or over) by the end of the plan year. See IRC Sec. 414(v). The limit on catch-up contributions to SIMPLE IRAs is the lesser of (a) a specified dollar limit, or (b) the excess (if any) of the participant's compensation over any other elective deferrals for the year made without regard to the catch-up limits. IRC Sec. 414(v)(2)(A). The dollar limit is $2,500 in 2006. IRC Sec. 414(v)(2)(B)(ii).

A SIMPLE IRA will not be treated as violating any of the applicable limitations of Section 408(p) merely on account of the making of (or right to make) catch-up contributions, provided a universal availability requirement is met. IRC Sec. 414(v)(3); see Prop. Treas. Reg. §1.414(v)-1(d). See Q 397 for details on the requirements for catch-up contributions.

Elective contribution amounts made under the salary reduction portion (i.e., those subject to the $10,000 limit) of a SIMPLE IRA plan are counted in the overall limit ($15,000 in 2006) on elective deferrals by any individual. IRC Sec. 402(g)(3)(D). See Q 396 for the definition of "elective deferral." Thus, for example, an individual under age 50 who defers the maximum of $10,000 to a SIMPLE IRA of one employer and participates in a 401(k) plan of another employer would be limited to an elective deferral of $5,000 in 2006 ($15,000 - $10,000) to the 401(k) plan. See IRC Sec. 402(g)(3). Catch-up contributions are not subject to the limits of IRC Section 402(g) and do not reduce an individual's otherwise applicable deferral limit under any other plan. IRC Sec. 414(v)(3)(A).

Employer Contributions

The requirements for the employer's matching contributions or nonelective contributions are as follows:

Matching formula: Under this formula, the employer is generally required to match employee elective contributions dollar-for-dollar up to an amount not exceeding 3% of the employee's compensation. IRC Sec. 408(p)(2)(A)(iii). (Matching of catch-up contributions is not required. See REG-142499-01, 66 Fed. Reg. 53555 (10-23-01).) A special rule permits the employer to elect a lower percentage matching contribution for all eligible employees (not less than 1% of each employee's compensation). To get the lower percentage, the employer has to notify the employees of the election within a reasonable period of time before the 60-day election period for electing to participate in the plan. Also, the employer may not use the lower percentage if the election would result in the percentage being lower than 3% in more than two out of the five years ending with the current year. If the employer (or a predecessor employer) has maintained the plan for less than five years, the employer will be treated as if the percentage was 3% in the prior years during which the arrangement was not in effect. IRC Sec. 408(p)(2)(C)(ii). Also, if the employer made nonelective contributions for a year (instead of matching contributions) under the formula described below, it will be treated as having a percentage of 3% in that year. Notice 98-4, above.

The compensation limit under IRC Section 401(a)(17) does not apply for purposes of the matching formula; thus, the 3% match could reach the maximum of $10,000 (in 2006) for an employee with compensation of $333,333 in a year. See Notice 98-4, above; IRC Sec. 401(a)(17).

A matching contribution made to a SIMPLE IRA on behalf of a self-employed individual is not treated as an elective employer contribution for purposes of the limit on such contributions. IRC Sec. 408(p)(9). The purpose of this provision is to treat self-employed individuals in the same manner as employees for purposes of the limit on elective contributions.

Nonelective contribution formula: Instead of making matching contributions, an employer can elect to make a nonelective contribution of 2% of compensation on behalf of each eligible employee with at least $5,000 in compensation from the employer for the year. If the employer makes this election, it must notify the employees within a reasonable time before the 60-day election period for electing to participate in the plan. IRC Sec. 408(p)(2)(B). The compensation limit under IRC Section 401(a)(17) does apply for purposes of this formula; thus, the maximum amount that could be contributed in

INDIVIDUAL RETIREMENT PLANS — Q 242

nonelective contributions for an employee would be $4,400 (i.e., 2% of $220,000 (in 2006)). See IRC Sec. 408(p)(2)(B)(ii).

A SIMPLE IRA is not subject to the nondiscrimination or top-heavy rules, and the reporting requirements it must meet are simplified. See IRC Secs. 408(p)(1), 416(g)(4), 408(l)(2).

Definitions

An arrangement will not be treated as a *qualified salary reduction arrangement* if the employer, or a predecessor employer, maintained another qualified plan (including a 403(a) annuity, a 403(b) tax sheltered annuity, a SEP, or a governmental plan other than an IRC Section 457 plan) under which contributions were made or benefits accrued for service during any year in which the SIMPLE IRA plan was in effect. However, if only employees *other than* those covered under a collectively bargained agreement are eligible to participate in the SIMPLE IRA plan, this rule will be applied without regard to a collectively bargained plan. IRC Sec. 408(p)(2)(D). Also, for purposes of this rule, transfers, rollovers or forfeitures are disregarded except to the extent that forfeitures replace otherwise required contributions. Notice 98-4, above.

Only an *eligible employer* may adopt a SIMPLE IRA plan. An "eligible employer" is defined as an employer who employed no more than 100 employees earning at least $5,000 from the employer during the preceding year. IRC Sec. 408(p)(2)(C)(i). For purposes of this limitation, *all* employees employed at any time during the calendar year are taken into account, even those who are excludable or are ineligible to participate. Furthermore, certain self-employed individuals who receive earned income from the employer during the year must be counted for purposes of the 100-employee limitation. Notice 98-4, above. The 1996 Blue Book describes the exclusive plan requirement described in the preceding paragraph as part of the definition of an "eligible employer." 1996 Blue Book, p. 140. An employer who maintains a plan in which only collectively bargained employees may participate is not precluded from offering a SIMPLE IRA to its noncollectively bargained employees. IRC Sec. 408(p)(2)(D)(i).

Generally, an eligible employer who ceases to be eligible after having established and maintained a SIMPLE IRA plan for at least one year will, nonetheless, continue to be treated as eligible for the following two years. IRC Sec. 408(p)(2)(C)(i)(II). However, special rules apply where a failure to remain eligible (or to meet any other requirement of IRC Section 408(p)) was due to an acquisition, disposition or similar transaction involving another eligible employer. See IRC Sec. 408(p)(10).

Compensation, for purposes of most of the SIMPLE IRA provisions, includes wages (as defined for income tax withholding purposes), elective contributions made under a SIMPLE IRA plan, and elective deferrals, including compensation deferred under an IRC Section 457 plan. IRC Sec. 408(p)(6)(A). A self-employed individual who is treated as an employee may be a participant in a SIMPLE IRA plan; for this purpose, "compensation" means net earnings from self-employment, prior to subtracting the SIMPLE IRA plan contribution. IRC Sec. 408(p)(6)(A)(ii). An employee's elective deferrals under a 401(k) plan, a SAR-SEP, and a 403(b) annuity contract are also included in the meaning of compensation for purposes of the 100-employee limitation (i.e., the $5,000 threshold) and the eligibility requirements. Notice 98-4, above.

2006 Tax Facts on Insurance & Employee Benefits

Special Rules

Contributions under a SIMPLE IRA plan may be made only to a SIMPLE IRA, and a SIMPLE IRA may receive only contributions under a SIMPLE IRA plan and rollovers or transfers from another SIMPLE IRA account. Notice 98-4, above, A-2. All contributions to a SIMPLE IRA account must be fully vested and may not be subject to any prohibition on withdrawals, nor conditioned on their retention in the account. IRC Secs. 408(p)(3), 408(k)(4). However, the premature distribution penalty for withdrawals is increased to 25% during the first two years of participation (see Q 243). IRC Sec. 72(t)(6).

The *participation* requirements for SIMPLE IRAs state that all nonexcludable employees who received at least $5,000 in compensation from the employer during any two preceding years and are reasonably expected to receive at least $5,000 in compensation during the year must be eligible to make the cash or deferred election (if the matching formula is used) or to receive nonelective contributions (if the nonelective formula is used). IRC Sec. 408(p)(4)(A). Of course, employers are free to impose less restrictive eligibility requirements, such as a $3,000 compensation threshold, but they may not impose more restrictive ones. Notice 98-4, above. The $5,000 threshold compensation amount is not scheduled to be indexed for inflation. Nonresident aliens who received no U.S. income and employees subject to a collective bargaining agreement generally are excludable employees for purposes of the participation requirement. IRC Sec. 408(p)(4)(B). An employee who participates in another plan of a different employer may participate in a SIMPLE IRA plan, but will be subject to the aggregate limit of $15,000 (in 2006) on elective deferrals. An employer who establishes a SIMPLE IRA plan is not responsible for monitoring compliance with this limitation. Notice 98-4, above.

Tax-exempt employers and governmental entities are permitted to maintain SIMPLE IRA plans. Excludable contributions may be made to the SIMPLE IRA of employees of tax-exempt employers and governmental entities on the same basis as contributions may be made to employees of other eligible employers. Notice 98-4, above. Related employers (i.e., controlled groups, partnerships or sole proprietorships under common control, and affiliated service groups) must be treated as a single employer for purposes of the SIMPLE IRA rules, and leased employees will be treated as employed by the employer. Consequently, all employees (and leased employees) of an employer who satisfy the eligibility requirements (see below) must be permitted to participate in the SIMPLE IRA of a related employer. Notice 98-4, above.

The administrative requirements for SIMPLE IRA plans state that an employer must make elective employer contributions (elective deferrals) within 30 days after the last day of the month with respect to which the contributions are to be made, and that matching and nonelective contributions must be made no later than the filing date for the return for the taxable year (including extensions). IRC Secs. 408(p)(5)(A), 404(m)(2)(B).

Planning Point: While the IRS requires elective employer contributions within 30 days after the month with respect to which the contributions are made, the Department of Labor requires that employee deferrals be made *as soon as practicable* after the deferral, but in no event later than 15 days after the deferral was made. *Ward Anderson, CLU, ChFC, Anderson Edelman.*

INDIVIDUAL RETIREMENT PLANS   Q 243

Employees must have the right to terminate participation at any time during the year; however, the plan may preclude the employee from resuming participation thereafter until the beginning of the next year. IRC Sec. 408(p)(5)(B). The 1996 Blue Book adds that a plan may (but is not required to) permit an individual to make other changes to his salary reduction election during the year (e.g., such as reducing the contribution amount). 1996 Blue Book, p. 141.

Generally, each employee must have 60 days before the first day of any year, (and 60 days before the first day the employee is eligible to participate) to elect whether to participate in the plan, or to modify his deferral amount. IRC Sec. 408(p)(5)(C). A SIMPLE IRA plan must be maintained on a calendar year basis. See Notice 98-4, above. The IRS apparently has adopted a requirement that a plan be adopted not later than October 1 of the year for which the plan is established, but states that the October 1 requirement "does not apply to a new employer that comes into existence after October 1 of the year the SIMPLE IRA Plan is established if the employer establishes the SIMPLE IRA Plan as soon as administratively feasible after the employer comes into existence." See Notice 98-4, above, at K-1. See Q 243 regarding the tax treatment of SIMPLE IRA plan contributions, distributions and rollovers. See Q 400 regarding SIMPLE 401(k) plans. *ASRS, Sec. 62, ¶750.*

243. How are SIMPLE IRA plan contributions taxed?

There are four possible types of contributions to a SIMPLE IRA plan: salary reduction contributions, catch-up contributions, matching contributions, and nonelective contributions. See IRC Secs. 408(p)(2), 414(v). Catch-up contributions are additional elective deferrals (not subject to the $10,000 ceiling in 2006) for individuals age 50 or over. See Q 242, Q 397.) All SIMPLE IRA contributions are excludable from the employee's income, provided they meet certain design requirements set forth in the Code. See IRC Secs. 402(k), 402(h)(1), 402(e)(3); see IRC Sec. 414(v); Notice 98-4, 1998-1 CB 25. Moreover, certain lower income taxpayers may be eligible to claim the saver's credit for salary reduction contributions to a SIMPLE IRA. See Q 213.

Contributions to a SIMPLE IRA are not subject to *income tax* withholding; however, salary reduction contributions are included in wages for purposes of Social Security tax, and federal unemployment tax (i.e., FICA and FUTA). Consequently, salary deferrals are subject to FICA and FUTA withholding. (It appears that "salary deferrals," for this purpose, would include catch-up contributions. See IRC Secs. 414(v)(1), 414(v)(6)(B).) In contrast, matching contributions and nonelective contributions are excluded from wages for purposes of Social Security tax, and federal unemployment tax; thus, they are not subject to FICA or FUTA withholding. See IRC Secs. 3121(a), 3306(a), 3401(a)(12); Notice 98-4, above.

Employer contributions to a SIMPLE IRA are generally deductible by the employer. IRC Sec. 404(m)(1). Matching and nonelective contributions can be made after the close of the tax year to which they are attributable, provided they are made before the due date for filing the return for the taxable year (including extensions). IRC Sec. 404(m)(2)(B). Contributions to a SIMPLE IRA are not subject to the annual dollar limit for traditional or Roth IRAs. IRC Sec. 408(p)(8). Nondeductible contributions are subject to a 10% penalty. IRC Sec. 4972(d)(1)(A)(iv).

SIMPLE IRA accounts themselves are not subject to tax. The taxation of distributions from a SIMPLE IRA are the same as under a traditional IRA; thus, contributions generally are not taxable until withdrawn. IRC Secs. 402(k), 402(h)(3); General Explanation of Tax Legislation Enacted in the 104th Congress (JCT-12-96), p. 141 (the 1996 Blue Book). However, the premature distribution penalty (see Q 231) is increased to 25% during the first two years of participation in a SIMPLE IRA; after the 2-year period has elapsed, the penalty is 10%. IRC Sec. 72(t)(6).

Rollovers (see Q 452) may be made from one SIMPLE IRA to another SIMPLE IRA at any time, but a rollover from a SIMPLE IRA to a traditional IRA is permitted only in the case of distributions to which the 25% early distribution penalty does not apply. IRC Sec. 408(d)(3)(G). During the 2-year period that the 25% penalty is imposed, such a transfer would be treated as a distribution from the SIMPLE IRA and a contribution to the other IRA that does not qualify as a rollover contribution. Notice 98-4, above. To the extent that an employee is no longer participating in a SIMPLE IRA plan and two years have expired since the employee first participated in the plan, the employee may treat the SIMPLE IRA account as a traditional IRA. 1996 Blue Book, p. 141. *ASRS, Sec. 62, ¶760.*

LIFE INSURANCE

PREMIUMS

244. Are premiums paid on personal life insurance deductible for income tax purposes?

No; they are a personal expense and hence not deductible. IRC Sec. 262(a). The regulations specifically provide that "[p]remiums paid for life insurance by the insured are not deductible." Treas. Reg. §1.262-1(b)(1). It is immaterial whether the premiums are paid by the insured or by some other person. For example, premiums paid by an individual for insurance on the life of his spouse are nondeductible personal expenses of the individual. The premiums are not deductible regardless of whether the insurance is government life insurance or regular commercial life insurance. *Kutz v. Comm.*, 5 BTA 239 (1926). Although life insurance premiums, as such, are not deductible, they may be deductible as charitable contributions (see Q 282 to Q 285), or as payment of alimony (see Q 281). Likewise, payments for a personal annuity contract are ordinarily not deductible. *ASRS, Sec. 52, ¶100.1.*

245. If a taxpayer borrows funds to purchase or carry a life insurance, endowment or annuity contract, can he deduct the interest paid on the loan?

Single Premium Contract

Interest paid or accrued on indebtedness incurred to purchase or continue in effect a single premium life insurance, endowment or annuity contract purchased after March 1, 1954 is not deductible. IRC Sec. 264(a)(2). For this purpose, a single premium contract is defined as one on which substantially all the premiums are paid within four years from date of purchase, or on which an amount is deposited with the insurer for payment of a substantial number of future premiums. IRC Sec. 264(c). Payment in the first four years of 73% of total annual premiums for a limited-pay policy was held not to constitute payment of "substantially all" of the premiums. *Dudderar v. Comm.*, 44 TC 632 (1965), acq. 1966-2 CB 4. And payment of eight annual premiums in the first four years on a whole life policy was held to be neither "substantially all" nor a "substantial number" of the premiums. *Campbell v. Cen-Tex, Inc.*, 19 AFTR 2d 1330 (5th Cir. 1967). See, also, *Woodson-Tenent Labs, Inc. v. U.S.*, 29 AFTR 2d 72-531 (6th Cir. 1972).

Where a single premium annuity is used as collateral to either obtain or continue a mortgage, the Service has found that IRC Section 264(a)(2) disallows the allocable amount of mortgage interest to the extent that the mortgage is collateralized by the annuity. However, this result does not hold where a taxpayer's use of available cash to purchase an annuity results in a larger home mortgage or where a taxpayer does not surrender an annuity even though cash obtained from the surrender would make it possible to reduce the amount of the mortgage. Rev. Rul. 95-53, 1995-2 CB 30. A general counsel memorandum has concluded that borrowing against the cash value of a single premium life insurance policy is equivalent to using the policy as collateral. GCM 39534 (7-17-86).

In restating the rule concerning single premium contracts, the conference committee report (TRA '86) states that "no inference is intended that universal life insurance policies are always treated as single premium contracts." H.R. Conf. Rep. No. 99-841 (TRA '86) *reprinted in* 1986-3 CB 341. See also General Explanation of the Tax Reform Act of 1986 at pp. 579, 580. It is still unclear whether the four exceptions applicable to contracts other than single premium contracts, discussed below, can be used in the case of universal life contracts.

Other than Single Premium Contract

Deduction is denied under IRC Section 264(a)(3) for interest on indebtedness incurred or continued to purchase or carry a life insurance, endowment, or annuity contract (which is not a single premium contract) if it is purchased pursuant to a plan of purchase that contemplates the systematic direct or indirect borrowing of part or all of the increases in the cash value of such contract (either from the insurer or otherwise).

There are four exceptions to this disallowance rule. IRC Sec. 264(d). However, with respect to interest paid or accrued on policies or contracts covering an individual who is a "key person" the deduction may be limited as explained in Q 260, even if one of the four exceptions to this disallowance rule is met. In addition, the interest deduction may be denied as explained in Q 823.

The four exceptions are:

(1) *The seven-year exception.* Where no part of four of the annual premiums due during the seven-year period, beginning with the date of payment for the first premium on the contract, is paid by means of indebtedness, the deduction will not be disallowed under this rule. If there is a substantial increase in the premiums, a new seven-year period for the contract commences on the date the first increased premium is paid. However, a new seven-year period does not begin upon transfer of the policy, whether for value or by gift. Rev. Rul. 71-309, 1971-2 CB 168, See also Let. Rul. 9033023. Modification of a life insurance policy after December 31, 1990, necessitated by the insurer's financial insolvency will not cause a new seven-year period to commence. Rev. Proc. 92-57, 1992-2 CB 410; Let. Rul. 9239026. See also Let. Rul. 9305013. The addition to a policy of a provision that interest on policy loans is now payable in arrears rather than in advance will not cause a new seven-year period to begin. Let. Rul. 9737007. A systematic plan of purchase will be presumed where there is borrowing in connection with more than 3 of the annual premiums due during the seven-year period, but will not be presumed earlier. Treas. Reg. §1.264-4(c). Once the taxpayer has used borrowed funds to pay the first four premiums, he cannot undo the effect of his action by repaying the policy loan. Rev. Rul. 72-609, 1972-2 CB 199. If in any year during the seven-year period, the taxpayer borrows more than an amount necessary to pay one annual premium, the excess will be considered to have been borrowed to pay premiums that have been paid in prior years with non-borrowed funds (beginning with the first prior year and working backwards). For example, suppose that a taxpayer, in Year 1, purchased a $100,000 policy and the annual premium is $2,200. He paid the first four premiums without borrowing. In Year 5, he borrows $10,000 with respect to the policy. The borrowing will be attributed first to paying the premium for the current year, Year 5, and then attributable to paying the premium for Years 4, 3, 2 and 1 (in part). If borrowing in any year exceeds the premium for the current year *and* premiums paid in prior years without borrowing, the excess will be attributed to premiums (if any) paid in advance for future years. However, once the seven-year exception has been satisfied, and the seven-year period has expired, there would appear to be no limit under this exception

to the amount that might be borrowed (from the policy or otherwise) to pay premiums on the policy. (But if a substantial number of premiums are *prepaid,* the policy might be considered a single-premium policy—see first paragraph above.) Thus, 3 of the first seven annual premiums may be borrowed, and the interest deduction would not be disallowed by reason of this rule, provided the balance of premiums during the seven-year period is paid with non-borrowed funds. But if the seven-year exception is not met, and the taxpayer cannot rebut the presumption of a systematic plan of borrowing, the interest deduction will be disallowed under this rule for all future years and for all prior years not closed by the statute of limitations. Assuming, of course, that none of the other exceptions to this rule applies. Treas. Reg. §1.264-4(d)(1).

(2) *$100-a-year exception.* Regardless of whether there is a systematic plan of borrowing, the interest deduction will not be disallowed under this rule for any taxable year in which the interest (in connection with such plans) does not exceed $100. But where such interest exceeds $100, the entire amount of interest (not just the amount in excess of $100) is nondeductible under IRC Section 264(a)(3). Treas. Reg. §1.264-4(d)(2).

(3) *Unforeseen event exception.* If the indebtedness is incurred because of an unforeseen substantial loss of income or unforeseen substantial increase in the taxpayer's financial obligations, the deduction will not be disallowed under this rule even though the loan is used to pay premiums on the contract. An event is not "unforeseen," however, if at the time the contract was purchased it could have been foreseen. Treas. Reg. §1.264-4(d)(3).

(4) *Trade or business exception.* If the indebtedness is incurred in connection with the taxpayer's trade or business, the interest deduction will not be denied under IRC Section 264(a)(3). Thus, if an insurance policy is pledged as part of the collateral for a loan, the interest deductions will come within this exception if the taxpayer can show that the amounts borrowed were actually used to finance the expansion of inventory or other similar business needs. The Service has ruled privately that a company that borrowed against key person life insurance policies to take advantage of their lower interest rate and generally improve its financial position by reducing its overall debt was considered to have incurred the policy loan interest in connection with its trade or business. Let. Rul. 9138049. But borrowing to finance business life insurance (such as key person, split dollar or stock purchase plans) is not considered to be incurred in connection with the borrower's trade or business. Treas. Reg. §1.264-4(d)(4); *American Body & Equipment Co. v. U.S.,* 75-1 USTC ¶9403 (5th Cir. 1975). Systematic borrowing to finance a life insurance policy, the net death proceeds of which and the amounts borrowed in excess of premiums, are used to fund employee retirement benefits is not debt incurred in connection with the employer's trade or business. Rev. Rul. 81-255, 1981-2 CB 79.

The interest deduction will not be disallowed *under IRC Section 264(a)(3)* if any one of these exceptions applies. For example, even though the purchase of business life insurance does not come within the trade or business exception, the interest deduction may be allowed if the borrowing comes within the four-out-of-seven exception provided no other IRC Section operates to disallow or limit the interest deduction (see Q 260 and Q 823).

A plan was held to involve systematic borrowing that contemplated purchase of mutual fund shares and a policy of whole life insurance by insured's use of the shares as security for notes executed each year in the amount of the cumulative premium and accrued interest. Rev. Rul. 74-500, 1974-2 CB 91. Where there is a systematic plan of borrowing, the borrowing will be treated as a plan for borrowing the increases in cash value of the policy, regardless of whether the borrowing is direct or indirect. That is, whether the borrowing is from the insurer, a bank or some other person. Moreover, such a plan need not involve a pledge of the contract, but may contemplate unsecured borrowing or the use of other property. Treas. Reg. §1.264-4(c)(2). Where there is a systematic plan, and none of the exceptions applies, deduction will be disallowed for interest on the entire amount borrowed, not just for interest on borrowing equal to the increases in the cash value. Treas. Reg. §1.264-4(b).

The general disallowance rule applies only with respect to contracts purchased after August 6, 1963. However, the regulations state that this date relates to the date of purchase by the taxpayer, whether purchase is from the insurer or from a previous policyowner. Where a policy issued in 1959 was to be exchanged the purchase date of the new policy was considered the date upon which the exchange was made, with the taxpayer losing the benefit of a policy issued prior to August 6, 1963. GCM 39728 (4-29-88).

These disallowance rules cannot be avoided by having one spouse use funds borrowed by the other. Where a husband borrowed money and transferred it to his wife who used it to buy tax-exempt securities, the interest deduction was denied on the basis that the transfer of the borrowed funds was without economic substance because the purpose of the husband's borrowing was to enable the wife to buy tax-exempt securities. Rev. Rul. 79-272, 1979-2 CB 124. *ASRS, Sec. 52, ¶¶700.3-700.7.*

246. Is the interest increment earned on prepaid life insurance premiums taxable income?

Yes. Any increment in the value of prepaid life insurance or annuity premiums or premium deposit funds will constitute taxable income in the year it is applied to the payment of a premium or is made available for withdrawal, whichever occurs first. Rev. Rul. 65-199, 1965-2 CB 20. The interest treated as taxable income will, however, be included in the cost basis of the contract. Thus, for the purposes of IRC Section 72, the cost of the contract would be the amount of premiums paid other than by discount, plus the amount of discounted funds and any increments on such funds that were subject to income taxation. The rule taxing interest increments has no applicability, however, to single premium policies. A later ruling explains in detail how the interest will be taxed. Rev. Rul. 66-120, 1966-1 CB 14. *ASRS, Sec. 52, ¶100.2.*

CASH VALUE INCREASES

247. Are the annual increases in the cash surrender value of a life insurance policy taxable income to the policyholder?

In a case involving a cash basis taxpayer, the Tax Court held that the cash values were not constructively received by the taxpayer where he could not reach them without surrendering the policy. The necessity of surrendering the policy constituted a substantial "limitation or restriction" on their receipt. *Cohen v. Comm.*, 39 TC 1055 (1963), *acq.* 1964-1 CB 4. Likewise, the Tax Court has held that the cash surrender values of paid-up additions are not constructively received by the policyholder. *Nesbitt v. Comm.*, 43 TC 629 (1965). Similarly, it would appear that the same "limitation or restriction" would prevent accrual for an accrual basis taxpayer, since income does not accrue until

LIFE INSURANCE

Q 249

"all the events have occurred which fix the right to receive the income." Treas. Reg. §1.446-1(c)(1)(ii). The same rule applies whether the policy is a single premium policy or a periodic premium policy.

Tax on the "inside buildup" of cash surrender values is generally not deferred in the case of contracts issued after December 31, 1984 that do not meet the statutory definition of a "life insurance contract" (see Q 273). IRC Sec. 7702(g). In such cases, the *excess* of the sum of (1) the increase in net surrender value (cash surrender value less any surrender charges) during the taxable year and (2) the cost of life insurance protection for the year *over* premiums paid under the contract during the year is taxable to the policyholder as ordinary income. IRC Sec. 7702(g)(1)(B). "Premiums paid" generally means those paid under the contract less amounts received but excludable from income under IRC Section 72(e) (e.g., dividends). IRC Sec. 7702(f)(1). The cost of the life insurance protection is the lesser of the cost of individual insurance on the life of the insured determined on the basis of uniform premiums or the mortality charge, if any, stated in the contract. IRC Sec. 7702(g)(1)(D). If the contract originally meets the statutory definition and then ceases to do so, income on the contract for all prior years is included in gross income in the year it ceases to meet the definition. IRC Sec. 7702(g)(1)(C).

If a variable insurance contract is an insurance contract under applicable state law and would otherwise meet the definitional requirements of IRC Section 7702, the annual increases in cash surrender value may nevertheless be taxed under the rules in the above paragraph if the underlying segregated asset account is not adequately diversified (see Q 25).

If a policy does not meet the IRC Section 7702(a) definition of a life insurance contract, the income on the contract for the year is considered a nonperiodic distribution and is subject to certain reporting and withholding requirements. The same is true for a variable life insurance contract that does not meet the diversification requirements of regulations under IRC Section 817(h). Rev. Rul. 91-17 1991-1 CB 190.

The "inside buildup" of cash surrender values of corporate owned life insurance is generally included in the calculation of the alternative minimum tax. See Q 95. *ASRS, Sec. 52, ¶330.14.*

248. Is the owner of a limited-pay life insurance policy liable for any tax when the policy becomes paid-up?

No. Taxable income is not realized unless the policy is sold or surrendered. *ASRS, Sec. 52, ¶330.13.*

LIVING PROCEEDS

Basic Rules

249. What are the rules for taxing living proceeds received under life insurance policies and endowment contracts?

The rules in IRC Section 72 govern the income taxation of amounts received as *living proceeds* from life insurance policies and endowment contracts. (Living proceeds

2006 Tax Facts on Insurance & Employee Benefits

273

are, generally, proceeds received during the insured's lifetime.) IRC Section 72 also covers the tax treatment of policy dividends and forms of premium returns.

Payments to which IRC Section 72 applies are of three classes: (1) "amounts not received as an annuity"; (2) payments of interest only; and (3) annuities.

Where living proceeds are held by an insurer under an agreement to pay interest, the interest payments are taxable in full. (See Q 251.) IRC Sec. 72(j); Treas. Reg. §1.72-14(a). Periodic payments on a principal amount that will be returned intact upon demand are interest payments. Rev. Rul. 75-255, 1975-2 CB 22.

All amounts taxable under IRC Section 72 other than annuities and payments of interest are classed as *amounts not received as an annuity*. These include: policy dividends; lump sum cash settlements of cash surrender values and endowment maturity proceeds; and cash withdrawals and amounts received on partial surrender. Treas. Reg. §1.72-11.

The income tax treatment of life insurance *death proceeds* is governed by IRC Section 101, not by IRC Section 72. Consequently, the annuity rules in IRC Section 72 do not apply to life income or other installment payments under optional settlements of death proceeds. However, the rules for taxing such payments are similar to the IRC Section 72 annuity rules. See Q 271 to Q 279.

Living proceeds received under life insurance contracts and endowment policies are taxed according to the same rules, whether they are single premium or periodic premium policies. Except for interest and annuity settlements, they are taxed under the "cost recovery rule" no matter when the contract was entered into or when premiums were paid. In other words, such amounts are included in gross income only to the extent they exceed the investment in the contract (as reduced by any prior excludable distributions under the contract). However, living proceeds or distributions received from a life insurance policy that has failed the seven pay test of IRC Section 7702A(b) and, thus, is classified as a modified endowment contract are taxed under different rules. See Q 250.

Planning Point. Assuming no policy loans, dividends, or prior cash value surrenders, a life insurance contract can be surrendered with no taxable gain, provided the aggregate premiums are equal to or exceed the cash values (Q 264). Assume after 15 years the aggregate premiums of a universal life policy are equal to the cash values, the policy is surrendered, and nothing is included in gross income. Over the life of this contract *untaxed* interest earnings have been used to pay the mortality charges (i.e., the amount-at-risk element of the contract). In contrast, if term insurance had been originally purchased, premiums would have come from after-tax income. *Donald F. Cady, J.D., LL.M, CLU.*

Further, cash distributions received as a result of certain changes in the benefits of a contract may not be taxed under the cost recovery rule, but under the "interest-first" rule. Any change in the benefits under a life insurance contract or in other terms of the contract (other than automatic increases such as change due to the growth of the cash surrender value, payment of guideline premiums, or changes initiated by the company) that was not reflected in any earlier determination or adjustment will require a redetermination as to whether the definitional guidelines of IRC Section 7702 are still satisfied (see Q 273). IRC Sec. 7702(f)(7)(A). (However, a modification made to a life insurance contract after December 31, 1990, that is necessitated by the insurer's financial insolvency will not cause retesting under IRC Section 7702(f)(7)(B)-(E). Rev. Proc. 92-57, 1992-2 CB 410; Let. Rul. 9239026. See also Let. Rul. 9305013.) If such a change occurs during the 15-year period beginning on the issue date of the policy *and* reduces the benefits under the contract, then any cash distribution made to the policyholder as a result of such change will be taxed as ordinary income to the extent there is income on the contract; however, the amount to be included will be limited to the applicable recapture ceiling. IRC Sec. 7702(f)(7)(B).

If the change occurs during the five-year period beginning on the issue date of a policy which originally qualified under IRC Section 7702 by satisfying the cash value accumulation test (i.e., a traditional life policy), the recapture ceiling is the *excess of* the cash surrender value of the contract immediately before the reduction *over* the net single premium immediately after the reduction. If the change occurs during the five-year period beginning on the issue date of a policy which originally qualified under IRC Section 7702 by satisfying the guideline premium/cash value corridor tests (i.e., a universal life policy), the recapture ceiling is the greater of (1) the *excess of* the aggregate premiums paid under the contract immediately before the reduction *over* the guideline premium limitation for the contract, taking into account the proper adjustment for the change in benefits; or (2) the *excess of* the cash surrender value of the contract immediately before the reduction *over* the cash value corridor immediately after the reduction. IRC Sec. 7702(f)(7)(C).

If the change occurs after the five-year period and during the 15-year period beginning on the date of issue of the policy, the recapture ceiling is the *excess of* the cash surrender value of the contract immediately before the reduction *over* the cash value corridor immediately after the reduction. IRC Sec. 7702(f)(7)(D).

Distributions made in anticipation of a reduction in benefits under the contract will be treated as resulting from a change in the contract. Any distribution that reduces the cash surrender value of a contract and that is made within two years before a reduction in benefits under such contract will be treated as made in anticipation of a reduction. IRC Sec. 7702(f)(7)(E).

The Service has provided examples of how these rules work. Rev. Rul. 2003-95, 2003-33 IRB 358.

Policy loans under life insurance policies and endowment contracts are not treated as distributions. See Q 259. However, the treatment differs for loans made from life insurance policies classified as modified endowment contracts (see Q 250). IRC Secs. 72(e)(5)(A)(i), 7702(f)(7)(B)(iii).

If a loan is still outstanding when a policy is surrendered or allowed to lapse, the borrowed amount becomes taxable at that time to the extent the cash value exceeds the owner's basis in the contract, as if the borrowed amount was actually received at the time of surrender or lapse and used to pay off the loan. (If a policy loan is outstanding at the time of an IRC Section 1035 tax-free exchange, the amount of the *net* reduction in the taxpayer's outstanding loan will be considered as "boot" (see Q 263) and taxable as ordinary income at that time to the extent there is income on the contract.) If a loan is outstanding at the time of death, the distribution of the face amount of the policy will be reduced by the amount of the outstanding loan. Proceeds received on account of the death of the insured are generally tax-free (see Q 271). However, the benefit of tax-free death proceeds in excess of cost may be lost in the case of a policy transferred for value (see Q 63 to Q 72).

Policies not meeting the definition of a "life insurance contract" are taxed under rules discussed in Q 247. *ASRS, Sec. 52, ¶300.1(h)*.

250. How are distributions from a life insurance policy that is classified as a modified endowment contract (MEC) taxed?

A modified endowment contract is one that meets the requirements of IRC Section 7702 (see Q 273), was entered into on or after June 21, 1988, and fails to meet the seven pay test. IRC Sec. 7702A(a)(1). A contract that is received in exchange for a contract meeting this definition is also a modified endowment contract. IRC Sec. 7702A(a)(2). Distributions from modified endowment contracts are subject to taxation rules that differ from the rules governing the taxation of distributions from life insurance policies that are not modified endowment contracts. See Q 249.

Seven Pay Test

A life insurance contract will fail the seven pay test if the accumulated amount paid under the contract at any time during the first seven contract years exceeds the sum of the net level premiums that would have been paid on or before such time if the contract provided for paid-up future benefits after the payment of the seven level annual payments. IRC Sec. 7702A(b). Generally, the "amount paid" under the contract is defined as the premiums paid less distributions not including amounts includable in gross income. IRC Sec. 7702A(e)(1). An amount received as a loan or the repayment of a loan does not affect the amount paid under the contract. H. R. Conf. Rep. No. 100-1104 (TAMRA '88) *reprinted in* 1988-3 CB 593. Additionally, amounts paid as premiums during the contract year but returned to the policyholder with interest within 60 days after the end of the contract year will reduce the sum of the premiums paid during the contract year. IRC Sec. 7702A(e)(1)(B). The interest paid on the premiums returned must be included in gross income. IRC Sec. 7702A(e)(1)(C).

Where a whole life insurance policy is coupled with an increasing whole life rider and a term insurance rider and the amount of coverage provided under the term rider increases or decreases solely in relation to the amount of coverage provided by the base policy and whole life rider, the IRS has ruled privately that the policy's "future benefits" for purposes of IRC Section 7702A(b) are equal to the aggregate amount of insurance coverage provided under the base policy, the whole life rider, and the term insurance rider at the time the policy is issued. Let. Rul. 9519023. Where a variable whole life policy is coupled with a 20-year decreasing term rider, the future benefits for purposes of IRC Section 7702A(b) are equal to the coverage under the base policy plus the lowest amount of coverage under the term rider at any time during the first seven contract years. Let. Rul. 9513015.

The seven level premiums are determined when the contact is issued and the first contract year death benefit is deemed to be provided to the contract's maturity, disregarding any scheduled death benefit decrease after the first seven years. IRC Sec. 7702A(c)(1). In one private letter ruling, the death benefit for purposes of applying IRC

LIFE INSURANCE   Q 250

Section 7702A(c)(1)(B) was the policy's "target death benefit," defined as the sum of the base policy death benefit and a rider death benefit. Let. Rul. 9741046.

If there is a reduction in benefits under the contract within the first seven contract years, the seven pay test is applied as if the contract had originally been issued at the reduced benefit level. However, any reduction in benefits due to the nonpayment of premiums is not taken into account if the benefits are reinstated within 90 days after the reduction. IRC Sec. 7702A(c)(2).

In the case of a contract that pays a death benefit only upon the death of one insured that follows or occurs at the same time as the death of another insured, if the death benefit is reduced below the lowest level of death benefit provided during the contract's first seven years, the modified endowment contract rules must be applied as if the contract had originally been issued at that lower benefit level. This rule is effective for contracts entered into on or after September 14, 1989. IRC Sec. 7702A(c)(6).

Distributions

Generally, distributions from modified endowment contracts are taxed differently than distributions from policies that meet the seven pay test. (See Q 249). Distributions, including loans, from a modified endowment contract are taxable as income at the time received to the extent that the cash value of the contract immediately before the payment exceeds the investment in the contract. IRC Sec. 72(e)(10). Basically, this means that distributions from modified endowment contracts are taxed as income first and recovery of basis second. The investment in the contract is increased to the extent that a distribution was includable in the taxpayer's income. A loan that is retained by the insurance company to pay policy premiums is considered an amount received under the contract. H. R. Conf. Rep. No. 100-1104 (TAMRA '88) *reprinted in* 1988-3 CB 592.

Distributions made during the contract year and any subsequent contract year in which the contract fails the seven pay test are taxed as discussed above. In addition, under regulations, distributions in anticipation of a failure of the seven pay test are also taxed as above. A distribution made within two years prior to the failure of the seven pay test is a distribution made in anticipation of a failure. IRC Sec. 7702A(d).

This manner of taxation for distributions does not apply to the assignment or pledge of a modified endowment contract to pay burial or prearranged funeral expenses if the contract's maximum death benefit does not exceed $25,000. IRC Sec. 72(e)(10)(B).

For the purpose of determining the amount includable in gross income, all modified endowment contracts issued by the same company to the same policyholder within any calendar year are treated as one modified endowment contract. This rule does not apply generally to contracts purchased by a trust described in IRC Section 401(a) that is exempt from tax under IRC Section 501(a), purchased as part of an IRC Section 403(a) plan, or described in IRC Section 403(b), or to an individual retirement annuity or an individual retirement account. IRC Sec. 72(e)(11).

Penalty Tax

A 10% penalty tax is imposed on any amount received by a taxpayer under a modified endowment contract that is includable in gross income unless the distribution is

2006 Tax Facts on Insurance & Employee Benefits

made after the taxpayer becomes disabled, attains age 59½ or the distribution is part of a series of substantially equal periodic payments made for the taxpayer's life or life expectancy or the joint lives or joint life expectancies of the taxpayer and his beneficiary. IRC Sec. 72(v).

Effective Date

Subject to the following exceptions, life insurance contracts entered into after June 20, 1988, are subject to the seven pay test. TAMRA '88 Sec. 5012(e)(1). Contracts entered into prior to this date are "grandfathered" for purposes of the seven pay test.

If the death benefit under a grandfathered contract increases by more than $150,000 over the death benefit in effect as of October 20, 1988, the contract becomes subject to the material change rules (discussed below) and may lose its grandfathered status. This rule does not apply if the contract required at least seven annual premiums as of June 21, 1988, and the policyholder continued to make at least seven annual premium payments. TAMRA '88 Sec. 5012(e)(2), as amended by OBRA '89 Sec. 7815(a)(2). In determining whether a material change has occurred, the death benefit payable as of June 20, 1988, rather than the lowest death benefit payable during the first seven years is applicable. H.R. Conf. Rep. No. 100-1104, (TAMRA '88) *reprinted in* 1988-3 CB 595-596.

A policy entered into before June 21, 1988, may lose its grandfathered status and, therefore, be treated as if it were entered into after this date, if (1) the policy death benefit is increased or an additional qualified benefit is purchased after June 20, 1988, and (2) prior to June 21, 1988, the contract owner did not have the right to obtain such an increase or addition without providing additional evidence of insurability. If a term life insurance contract is converted after June 20, 1988, to a policy that is not term insurance, without regard to the right of the owner to such a conversion, the policy will lose its grandfathered status. TAMRA '88 Sec. 5012(e)(3). A policy entered into before June 21, 1988, did not lose its grandfathered status where the insurer changed the policy loan provision to make interest payable in arrears rather than in advance. Let. Ruls. 9714029, 9412023, 9117011. See also Let. Rul. 9150045. The Service has stated that modification of a life insurance contract after December 31, 1990, that is necessitated by the insurer's insolvency will not affect the date on which the contract was issued, entered into, or purchased for purposes of IRC Section 7702. Rev. Proc. 92-57, 1992-2 CB 410; Let. Rul. 9239026. See also Let. Ruls. 199908013, 9305013.

Material Changes to the Contract

If there is a material change in the benefits or terms, the contract will be treated as a new contract entered into on the day the material change was effective and the seven pay test, with appropriate adjustments to reflect the cash surrender value of the contract, must be met again. IRC Sec. 7702A(c)(3)(A). However, modification of a life insurance contract after December 31, 1990, that is necessitated by the insurer's financial insolvency will not cause a new seven year period for purposes of the seven pay test to commence. Rev. Proc. 92-57, 1992-2 CB 410; Let. Ruls. 199908013, 9239026.

For a contract that has been materially changed, the seven pay premium for each of the seven years following the change is reduced by the cash surrender value of the contract as of the effective date of the material change multiplied by a fraction, the numerator of which is the seven pay premium for future benefits under the contract

LIFE INSURANCE   Q 250

and the denominator is the net single premium for future benefits under the contract. H.R. Conf. Rep. No. 100-1104, (TAMRA '88) *reprinted in* 1988-3 CB 595.

A material change is defined as any increase in the death benefit under the contract or any increase in, or addition of, a qualified additional benefit under the contract. IRC Sec. 7702A(c)(3)(B). However, any increase due to the payment of premiums necessary to fund the lowest level of the death benefit and qualified additional benefits payable in the first seven contract years or to the crediting of interest or other earnings, including dividends, is not considered a material change. Additionally, to the extent provided in regulations, any cost-of-living increase funded over the period during which premiums are required to be paid under the contract and based on a broad-based index is not considered a material change. IRC Sec. 7702A(c)(3)(B).

For purposes of IRC Sections 101(f), 7702, and 7702A, a material change to a contract does not occur when a rider that is treated as a qualified long-term care insurance contract under IRC Section 7702B is issued or when any provision required to conform any other long-term care rider to these requirements is added. HIPAA '96, Sec. 321(f)(4). See Q 311.

Dividends

Any dividend of a modified endowment contract that is retained by the insurer to pay either principal or interest on a policy loan is an amount received under the contract. See IRC Sec. 72(e)(1)(B). Any dividend that is retained by the insurer for purposes of purchasing paid-up insurance is not an amount received under the contract. See 72(e)(4)(B); see also H.R. Conf. Rep. No. 100-1104, (TAMRA '88) *reprinted in* 1988-3 CB 592.

Policy Exchanges

The effect of an IRC Section 1035 exchange on the grandfathered status of a policy issued prior to June 21, 1988, and thus not subject to the seven pay test of IRC Section 7702A is not entirely clear. (See H.R. Conf. Rep. No. 100-1104, (TAMRA '88) *reprinted in* 1988-3 CB 596.) In a private ruling, the IRS has taken the position that a life insurance contract received in an IRC Section 1035 exchange for a life insurance contract issued before June 21, 1988, will be considered as issued and entered into on the date that it is received in exchange for the previous contract and, thus, apparently be subject to the seven pay test. Let. Rul. 9044022.

If a modified endowment contract that requires the payment of at least seven annual premiums was entered into after June 20, 1988, but before November 10, 1988, and was then exchanged within the three months following November 10, 1988, for a contract that meets the requirements of the seven pay test, the new contract is not treated as a modified endowment contract if the taxpayer recognized gain, to the extent that there was any, on the exchange. TAMRA '88 Sec. 5012(e)(4).

Procedure to Remedy Failures

Life insurance companies may correct "inadvertent non-egregious" failures to comply with the modified endowment contract rules by submitting a request for relief to the Internal Revenue Service. The request must meet certain requirements and give detailed information about the modified endowment contracts at issue. To obtain relief,

2006 Tax Facts on Insurance & Employee Benefits

a life insurance company must pay an amount calculated individually for each policy and bring the policies into compliance with IRC Section 7702A by, generally, increasing the policy's death benefit or refunding excess premiums and earnings. Not all life insurance policies are eligible for correction under this procedure. Rev. Proc. 2001-42, 2001-2 CB 212. *ASRS, Sec. 52, ¶300.1(i).*

Interest-Only Option

251. What are the tax consequences of leaving life insurance cash surrender values or endowment maturity proceeds with the insurer under the interest-only option?

The interest is fully taxable to the payee as it is received or credited. IRC Sec. 72(j); Treas. Reg. §1.72-14(a).

However, in one case a policyholder agreed with the insurance company before maturity of her endowment to leave the maturity proceeds on deposit and have the interest accumulated for 10 years. The agreement prohibited any withdrawals during the 10-year period. It was held that the interest was not taxable each year as credited, but only after 10 years when it became withdrawable. *Fleming v. Comm.*, 241 F.2d 78 (5th Cir. 1957).

Under some circumstances, election of the interest option will postpone tax on the proceeds. If the option is elected *before* maturity or surrender without reservation of the right to withdraw the proceeds, the proceeds are not constructively received in the year of maturity or surrender. *Frackelton v. Comm.*, 46 BTA 883 (1942), acq.; see *Fleming v. Comm.*, supra. But if right of withdrawal is retained, apparently the IRS considers the proceeds as constructively received when they first become withdrawable. See Treas. Reg. §1.451-2; *Blum v. Higgins*, 150 F.2d 471 (2d Cir. 1945). (It can be argued, however, that the proceeds are not constructively received where the policyholder has a contractual right to change to another option.) If the option is elected on or after the maturity or surrender date, the proceeds are constructively received in the year of maturity or surrender. (The 60-day extension rule, applicable to the election of a life income or installment option, does not apply to an election of the interest option—see Q 265.)

If the proceeds are constructively received, the entire gain on the contract (if any) is taxable in the year of constructive receipt as if the proceeds had been actually received in a one sum settlement (see Q 264). If the proceeds are not constructively received, the gain will be taxable to the person who ultimately receives the proceeds. IRC Secs. 61(a), 691(a). *ASRS, Sec. 52, ¶330.7.*

Dividends

252. Are the dividends payable on a participating life insurance policy taxable income?

As a general rule, all dividends paid or credited before the maturity or surrender of a contract are tax-exempt as return of investment until an amount equal to the policyholder's basis has been recovered. More specifically, when aggregate dividends plus all other amounts that have been received tax-free under the contract exceed aggregate gross premiums, the excess is taxable income. IRC Sec. 72(e)(5); Treas. Reg. §1.72-11(b)(1). (See, however, Q 250.)

LIFE INSURANCE

Q 254

It is immaterial whether the dividends are taken in cash, applied against current premiums, used to purchase paid-up additions, or left with the insurance company to accumulate at interest. Thus, accumulated dividends are not taxable either currently or when withdrawn (but the *interest* on accumulated dividends is taxable—see Q 253) until aggregate dividends plus all other amounts that have been received tax-free under the contract exceed aggregate gross premiums. At that point, the excess is taxable income. IRC Sec. 72(e)(5). It is also immaterial whether the policy is premium-paying or paid-up. However, dividends paid on life insurance policies that are classified as modified endowment contracts under IRC Section 7702A may be taxed differently. See Q 250.

Dividends are considered to be a partial return of basis; hence they reduce the cost basis of the contract. This reduction in cost must be taken into account in computing gain or loss upon the sale, surrender, exchange, or lifetime maturity of a contract (see Q 8). *ASRS, Sec. 52, ¶200.1.*

253. Is the interest earned on life insurance dividend accumulations currently taxable to the policyholder?

Yes, the interest must be included in the policyholder's gross income for the first taxable year during which it can be withdrawn, whether or not it is actually withdrawn. Treas. Reg. §1.451-2. If the interest is credited annually and is subject to withdrawal annually, it constitutes gross income to the policyholder each year as it is credited to his account. But if the interest is withdrawable only on the anniversary date of the policy (or some other specified date), it is gross income to the policyholder for the taxable year in which the anniversary date (or other specified date) falls. Treas. Reg. §1.61-7. The Tax Court has held that the interest can be included in the policyholder's gross income only for the first taxable year in which he either actually or constructively receives it (the first year it is withdrawable)—IRS cannot include the interest in the policyholder's gross income for a later year, even though the interest was not reported in the year it was constructively received. To tax the interest, IRS must reopen the policyholder's return for the prior year. *Cohen v. Comm.*, 39 TC 1055 (1963), acq. 1964-1 CB 4. *ASRS, Sec. 52, ¶200.2.*

254. What is the tax treatment of life insurance dividends where endowment maturity values or cash surrender values are paid in installments or as a life income?

In the case of life insurance cash surrender values and endowment maturity values, total excludable dividends paid or credited before the payments commence are subtracted from gross premiums to determine the net premium cost of the contract. IRC Sec. 72(c)(1). It is this net premium cost that is used in computing the portion of the payment that may be excluded from gross income (the *investment in the contract* for purpose of the exclusion ratio). But if accumulated dividends and interest are applied to increase the size of the income payments, dividends are not subtracted from gross premiums but are included in the *investment in the contract.* That is, gross premiums plus the interest on the accumulated dividends constitute the cost of the increased payments (see Q 8). (For treatment of dividends that are used to purchase paid-up additions, see Q 255). Dividends credited after the installment or life income payments commence (excess interest earnings) must be included in gross income. IRC Sec. 72(e)(2); Treas. Reg. §1.72-11(b). *ASRS, Sec. 52, ¶200.4.*

2006 Tax Facts on Insurance & Employee Benefits

255. What are the tax results when life insurance or endowment dividends are used to purchase paid-up insurance additions?

Normally, no tax liability will arise at any time. Dividends not in excess of investment in the contract are not taxable income (see, however, Q 250 with regard to MECs); the annual increase in the cash values of the paid-up additions is not taxed to the policyholder; and death proceeds are tax-free. IRC Sec. 72(e)(5); *Nesbitt v. Comm.*, 43 TC 629 (1965); IRC Sec. 101(a). In effect, dividends reduce the cost basis of the original amount of insurance and constitute the cost of the paid-up additions. Consequently upon maturity, sale or surrender during the insured's lifetime, gross premiums are used as the cost of the insurance in computing gain upon the entire amount of proceeds, including proceeds from the additions. Likewise, if policy values, including values of the paid-up additions, are paid in installments or as a life income during the insured's lifetime, gross premiums are used as the *investment in the contract* in computing the exclusion ratio for the payments (see Q 8).

The treatment of cash value increases and the death benefit of a contract subject to the definitional requirements of IRC Section 7702 will be different if the contract fails to meet certain requirements. See Q 273. *ASRS, Sec. 52, ¶200.3.*

256. Are dividends that are credited to a paid-up life insurance or endowment policy taxable income?

Regardless of whether the policy is premium paying or paid-up, dividends credited to an unmatured life insurance or endowment contract are taxed as discussed in Q 252.

257. If accumulated or post-mortem life insurance dividends are received by a deceased insured's beneficiary, are they taxable income to the beneficiary?

No. Accumulated dividends are exempt as property received by inheritance. IRC Sec. 102. Terminal and post-mortem dividends are exempt as amounts received under a life insurance contract and paid by reason of the death of the insured. IRC Sec. 101(a)(1). Moreover, it appears that accumulated interest, if constructively received by the policyholder in a prior year, is not taxable to the beneficiary even though the policyholder neglected to report the interest. *Cohen v. Comm.*, 39 TC 1055, (1963) acq. See Q 278. *ASRS, Sec. 52, ¶200.5.*

258. Where life insurance death proceeds are held under a settlement option, are excess interest dividends taxable to the beneficiary?

Yes, unless the proceeds are payable under a life income or installment option and the beneficiary is the surviving spouse of an insured who died before October 23, 1986. A surviving spouse of an insured who died before October 23, 1986 may exclude up to $1,000 annually of the interest (guaranteed and excess) received under an installment or life income option. (See Q 276.) *ASRS, Sec. 52, ¶200.6.*

Policy Loans

259. To what extent are life insurance policy loans taxable?

A loan taken from a life insurance policy that *is not* classified as a modified endowment contract under IRC Section 7702A is not includable in income because it is not treated as a distribution under IRC Section 72. IRC Sec. 72(e)(5).

LIFE INSURANCE   Q 260

In contrast, a loan taken from a life insurance policy that *is* classified as a modified endowment contract is treated as a distribution under IRC Section 72 and is includable in income at the time received to the extent that the cash value of the contract immediately before the distribution exceeds the investment in the contract. IRC Sec. 72(e). See Q 250. Unless the loan is made under certain specific circumstances (see Q 250), a 10% penalty tax is imposed on the amount of the loan that is includable in gross income. IRC Sec. 72(v).

If a loan is still outstanding when a policy is surrendered or allowed to lapse, the borrowed amount becomes taxable at that time to the extent the cash value exceeds the owner's basis in the contract, as if the borrowed amount was actually received at the time of surrender or lapse and used to pay off the loan. See *Atwood v. Comm.*, TC Memo 1999-61. If a loan is outstanding at the time of death, the distribution of the face amount of the policy usually is reduced by the amount of the outstanding loan.

See Q 263 for the treatment of a policy with an outstanding loan at the time of an IRC Section 1035 exchange. For the rules governing the deductibility of policy loan interest, see Q 260, Q 245. *ASRS, Sec. 52, ¶700.1.*

260. Can a life insurance policyowner take an income tax deduction for the interest he pays on a policy loan?

To be deductible, interest paid by a policyowner on a policy loan must meet the rules discussed in this question and, if applicable, the rules discussed in Q 245. However, if the interest is deductible under those rules, the amount of the deduction may be limited depending on whether the interest is classified as personal, trade or business, investment interest, or interest taken into account in computing income or loss from passive activities. See Q 823. Generally, the determination is made by tracing the use to which the loan proceeds are put. See Temp. Treas. Reg. §1.163-8T. Thus, interest on a loan used to pay premiums on personal life insurance may come within an exception explained in Q 245, but the deduction may not be available since personal interest is not deductible (see Q 823). There is little guidance as to whether interest on a loan used to buy life insurance can be considered investment interest. See Q 270. Borrowing to finance business life insurance has generally not been considered incurred in connection with the borrower's trade or business. See Q 245.

General Rule of Nondeductibility for Policy Loan Interest

Generally, no deduction is allowed for any interest paid or accrued on any indebtedness with respect to one or more life insurance policies owned by the taxpayer covering the life of any individual, or any endowment or annuity contracts owned by the taxpayer covering any individual. IRC Sec. 264(a)(4). This provision is effective generally for contracts issued after June 8, 1997, in taxable years ending after this date. For purposes of this effective date, any material increase in the death benefit or other material change in the contract will be treated as a new contract except that, in the case of a master contract, the addition of covered lives shall be treated as a new contract only with respect to the additional covered lives. (See IRC Sec. 264(f)(4)(E) for the definition of "master contract.") TRA '97, Sec. 1084(d), as amended by IRSRRA '98, Sec. 6010(o)(3)(B).

For contracts issued prior to June 9, 1997, the general rule under IRC Section 264(a)(4) states that no deduction is allowed for any interest paid or accrued on any indebtedness with respect to one or more life insurance policies owned by a taxpayer that covered the life of any individual (or any endowment or annuity contracts owned by a taxpayer that cover any individual) who is an officer or employee of, or is financially interested in, any trade or business carried on by the taxpayer. IRC Sec. 264(a)(4), prior to amendment by Sec. 1084(b)(1) of TRA '97.

Prior to 1996 legislation, there was an exception to this general rule for policies with less than $50,000 of indebtedness. However, effective for interest paid or accrued after October 13, 1995, the ability to deduct policy loan interest paid on company-owned life insurance policies with loans of less than $50,000 was eliminated. IRC Sec. 264(a)(4), as amended by HIPAA '96, Sec. 501(a) but before amendment by Sec. 1084 of TRA '97. Certain transition rules apply as discussed below.

Allocation of Interest Expense to Policy Cash Values

No deduction will be allowed for the portion of the taxpayer's interest expense that is allocable to unborrowed policy cash values. IRC Sec. 264(f)(1). This portion that is allocable to unborrowed policy cash values is an amount that bears the same ratio to the interest expense as the taxpayer's average unborrowed policy cash values of life insurance policies and annuity and endowment contracts issued after June 8, 1997 bears to the sum of: (1) in the case of assets of the taxpayer that are life insurance policies or annuity or endowment contracts, the average unborrowed policy cash values; and (2) in the case of assets of the taxpayer that do not fall into this category, the average adjusted bases of such assets. IRC Sec. 264(f)(2).

"Unborrowed policy cash value" is defined as the excess of the cash surrender value of a policy or contract (determined without regard to surrender charges) over the amount of any loan with respect to the policy or contract. For purposes of this provision, if the cash surrender value of a policy determined without reference to any surrender charge does not reasonably approximate its actual value, the amount taken into account is the greater of the amount of the insurance company liability or the insurance company reserve for the policy. IRC Sec. 264(f)(3).

There is an exception to this general rule of nondeductibility of policy loan interest expense that is allocable to unborrowed policy cash values. The exception applies to any policy or contract owned by an entity engaged in a trade or business if the policy or contract covers only one individual who, at the time first covered by the policy or contract, is: (1) a 20% owner of the entity; or (2) an individual (who is not a 20% owner but) who is an officer, director or employee of the trade or business. (A 20% owner is defined in IRC Section 264(e)(4), discussed below.) A policy or contract covering a 20% owner will not fail to come within this exception simply because it covers both the owner and the owner's spouse. IRC Sec. 264(f)(4)(A). Apparently, spouses of officers, directors, or employees who are not also 20% owners cannot be covered and still have the policy or contract qualify for this exception. For purposes of this rule, if coverage for each insured under a master contract (which is not a group life insurance contract) is treated as a separate contract for certain purposes, the coverage for each insured is treated as a separate contract. IRC Sec. 264(f)(4)(E).

This general rule of nondeductibility of policy loan interest expense that is allocable to unborrowed policy cash values does not apply to annuities held by a natural person as provided in IRC Section 72(u) (see Q 2). IRC Sec. 264(f)(4)(B). However, if a trade or business, with the exception of a sole proprietorship, is directly or indirectly a beneficiary under the policy or contract it is not considered to be owned by a natural person. IRC Sec. 264(f)(5)(A).

This provision is effective generally for contracts issued after June 8, 1997, in taxable years ending after this date. For purposes of this effective date, any material increase in the death benefit or other material change in the contract will be treated as a new contract except that, in the case of a master contract, the addition of covered lives shall be treated as a new contract only with respect to the additional covered lives. (See IRC Sec. 264(f)(4)(E) for the definition of "master contract.") TRA '97, Sec. 1084(d) as amended by IRSRRA '98. Sec. 6010(o)(3)(B).

Policy on a Key Person

The general nondeductibility rule does not apply to any interest paid or accrued on any indebtedness with respect to policies or contracts covering an individual who is a "key person" to the extent that the aggregate amount of the indebtedness with respect to policies and contracts covering the individual does not exceed $50,000. IRC Sec. 264(e)(1).

A "key person" is an officer or 20% owner of the taxpayer. The number of persons who may be treated as key persons is limited to the greater of: (1) five individuals; or (2) the lesser of 5% of the total officers and employees or 20 individuals. IRC Sec. 264(e)(3). A 20% owner is defined as any person who owns directly 20% or more of the outstanding stock of the corporation or stock possessing 20% or more of the total combined voting power of all the corporation's stock, if the taxpayer is a corporation. If the taxpayer is not a corporation, a 20% owner is any person who owns 20% or more of the capital or profits interest in the taxpayer. IRC Sec. 264(e)(4).

Generally, all members of a controlled group are treated as a single taxpayer for purposes of determining a 20% owner of a corporation and for applying the $50,000 limitation. This limitation is allocated among the members of a controlled group in a manner prescribed by the Secretary. IRC Sec. 264(e)(5)(A).

Interest in excess of that which would have been determined had the "applicable rate of interest" been used cannot be deducted. IRC Sec. 264(e)(2)(A). The applicable rate of interest for any month is the interest rate described as Moody's Corporate Bond Yield Average – Monthly Average Corporates as published by Moody's Investors Service. IRC Sec. 264(e)(2)(B).

The Code also specifies a manner in which to determine the applicable rate of interest for pre-1986 contracts. For a contract purchased on or before June 20, 1986 with a fixed rate of interest, the applicable rate of interest for any month is the Moody's rate as described above for the month in which the contract was purchased. For a contract purchased on or before June 20, 1986 with a variable rate of interest, the applicable rate of interest for any month in an applicable period is the Moody's rate for the third month preceding the first month in such period. "Applicable period" is the 12-month period beginning on the date the policy is issued unless the taxpayer elects a number of months (not greater than 12) other than such 12-month period to be its applicable period. Such an election, if made, shall apply to the taxpayer's first taxable year ending on or after October 13, 1995 and all subsequent taxable years. IRC Sec. 264(e)(2)(B)(ii).

If any amount was received from a life insurance policy or endowment or annuity contract subject to IRC Section 264(a)(4) upon the complete surrender, redemption or maturity of the policy or contract during calendar years 1996, 1997 or 1998 or in full discharge during these years of the obligation under the policy or contract that was in the nature of a refund of the consideration paid for the policy or contract then the amount is includable in gross income ratably over the four-taxable-year period beginning with the taxable year the amount would have been included in income but for this provision. HIPAA '96, Sec. 501(d)(1).

General Interest Deduction Rules

Interest is deductible by a cash basis taxpayer only to the extent he actually pays it in cash or cash equivalent in the tax year. IRC Sec. 163; Treas. Reg. §1.163-1. Thus, if the interest due on a policy loan is not paid but is merely deducted by the insurer from the principal at the time of making the loan or merely added to the loan principal, it is not currently deductible by a cash basis taxpayer. Rev. Rul. 73-482, 1973-2 CB 44; *Thomason v. Comm.*, 33 BTA 576 (1935); *Prime v. Comm.*, 39 BTA 487 (1939). Likewise, a cash basis taxpayer cannot deduct interest owing on a policy loan that is deducted by the company from the proceeds of a new loan with the balance being remitted to the policyholder. *Keith v. Comm.*, 139 F.2d 596 (2d Cir. 1944). But if interest that has been deducted from or added to the principal amount of the policy loan is later paid, it is deductible by the cash basis taxpayer when paid. Rev. Rul. 73-482, above. See *Cheeseman v. Comm.*, TC Memo 1969-259. Where interest has been added to loan principal, a deduction is allowable when, upon maturity or surrender of the policy or upon the death of the insured, the company deducts the accumulated interest from the proceeds. *Est. of Hooks v. Comm.*, 22 TC 502 (1954), acq. 1955-1 CB 5.

Cash basis taxpayers deduct prepaid interest over the period to which it relates, not in the year it is prepaid. IRC Sec. 461(g). An accrual basis taxpayer can deduct interest in the year it accrues, regardless of whether the interest is actually paid in that year. *Corlett v. Comm.*, TC Memo 1946-046; IRC Sec. 461(h).

Only the person who owns the policy when the interest accrues is entitled to the deduction. A policyowner who takes out a policy loan and later makes an absolute assignment of the policy subject to the loan is not entitled to deduct interest that accrues after the assignment. For example, if a father continues to pay interest on policy loans after giving the policy to his children, he cannot deduct payments of interest accruing after the transfer. *Dean v. Comm.*, 35 TC 1083 (1961). Nor can a husband deduct on a separate return the interest he pays on a policy loan where the policy is owned by his wife. *Colston v. Burnet*, 59 F.2d 867 (DC Cir. 1932); see *Sherman v. Comm.*, 18 TC 746 (1952), nonacq. 1964-2 CB 9. Similarly, a person to whom the policy has been assigned cannot pay and deduct interest that has accrued before the assignment. *Fox v. Comm.*, 43 BTA 895 (1941); see also *Orange Securities Corp. v. Comm.*, 45 BTA 24 (1941).

Where a policyholder makes unspecified installment payments covering both premiums and interest, payments will be applied first toward premiums, and only the balance will be considered deductible interest. *Evans v. Comm.*, TC Memo 1946-102. But payments specified and applied as interest will be treated as such. *Kay v. Comm.*, 44 TC 660 (1965).

IRC Section 265(a)(2) forbids the deduction of interest on loans to purchase or carry tax-exempt investments. Borrowing to enable the insured to buy a key person policy on himself from his employer was held sufficiently unrelated to insured's investment in tax-exempt bonds so that interest on the loan was deductible to the extent that

LIFE INSURANCE   Q 261

the tax-exempt bonds were not used as collateral for the loan. *Levitt v. U.S.*, 517 F.2d 1339 (8th Cir. 1975).

Several cases have disallowed the deduction of interest on loans that were considered "sham" transactions–that is, which offered the taxpayer nothing of economic substance other than a hoped-for deduction. *Knetsch v. U.S.*, 364 U.S. 361 (1960); *Goldman v. U.S.*, 403 F.2d 776 (10th Cir. 1968); *Golsen v. Comm.*, 445 F.2d 985 (10th Cir. 1971); *Salley v. Comm.*, 464 F.2d 479 (5th Cir. 1972); *Winn-Dixie Stores, Inc. v. Comm.*, 2001-2 USTC ¶50,495 (11th Cir. 2001); *IRS v. CM Holdings, Inc.*, 2002-2 USTC ¶50,596 (3rd Cir. 2002); *American Elect. Power Co. v. U.S.*, 2003-1 USTC ¶50,416 (6th Cir. 2003). See also TAM 199901005; TAM 9812005.

Annual loans against cash value to pay current premiums were not considered "sham" in *Coors v. U.S.*, 1978-1 USTC ¶9250 (Ct. Cl. 1978); *Lee v. U.S.*, 1978-1 USTC ¶9252 (Ct. Cl. 1978); and *Golsen v. U.S.*, 46 AFTR 2d 80-5900 (Ct. Cl. 1980). Factors considered important in these cases were: there was no prepayment of interest or premiums; the owner needed liquidity to meet premium payments; death benefits were at all times substantial; policies were standard policies and the loans straightforward, ordinary and available to any policyholder. See also *Salley v. Comm.*, above. The deduction of interest on a policy loan in each of the first three policy years and the subsequent surrender of the policy in the fourth year was not considered a sham where a change in the tax law eliminated the insured's need for the policy death benefit. *Shirar v. Comm.*, TC Memo 1987-492 rev'd, 916 F.2d 1414 (9th Cir. 1990). In a case where the life insurance plan was ruled not a sham, the court found the company had insurable interests on the over 20,000 insureds. *Dow Chemical Co. v. U.S.*, 2003-2 USTC ¶50,681 (E.D. Mich. 2003), *modifying* 2003-1 USTC ¶50,346.

In a case involving corporate owned life insurance policies, the Tax Court held that payments from the corporation to the insurance companies were not "interest" paid on policy loans but were, in fact, constructive dividends to the insured shareholders. The court noted that payment of these amounts by the corporation conferred an economic benefit on the shareholders by increasing both the policy cash values and the death benefits. *Young v. Comm.*, TC Memo 1995-379.

Deduction of interest paid on a policy loan by a grantor trust is discussed in Q 309. See also Q 484. *ASRS, Sec. 52, ¶¶700.1, 700.2, 700.9.*

Disposition: Sale or Purchase of a Contract

261. If the owner of a life insurance or endowment contract sells the contract, what are the income tax consequences to the seller?

Gain up to the amount of the contract's cash surrender value is taxed to the seller as ordinary income. *Gallun v. Comm.*, 327 F.2d 809 (7th Cir. 1964); *Comm. v. Phillips*, 275 F.2d 33 (4th Cir. 1960); *Est. of Crocker v. Comm.*, 37 TC 605 (1962); *Neese v. Comm.*, TC Memo 1964-288; see also *Cohen v. Comm.*, 39 TC 1055 (1963). According to the decided cases, the amount of taxable gain is determined in the same way as upon surrender of a contract (see Q 264). In other words, gain is determined by subtracting net premium cost (gross premiums less dividends to the extent excludable from income) from the sale price. For the treatment of amounts received from a viatical settlement provider, see Q 268. Recent guidance indicates that on a sale of a life insurance policy,

2006 Tax Facts on Insurance & Employee Benefits

the IRS will consider the basis of the contract to be the premiums paid minus the cost of insurance protection. ILM 200504001.

Whether gain in excess of the contract's cash surrender value (such as in a life settlement) is ordinary income or capital gain has not been settled. Some have argued that the entire gain is ordinary income, but others contend that gain in excess of the contract's cash surrender value should receive capital gain treatment. In support of the argument that a portion of a life settlement may be treated as a capital gain, proponents point to a footnote in the *Phillips* case where the IRS conceded that in certain situations the sale of a life insurance contract might result in capital gain treatment. *Comm. v. Phillips*, 275 F.2d 33, fn.3 (4th Cir. 1960). However, in a technical advice memorandum, the Service pointed out that even if a life insurance contract is treated as a capital asset, the entire gain from the sale of a contract should be treated as ordinary income. TAM 200452033.

Normally there will be no loss when a *life insurance* policy is sold for its cash surrender value. (See Q 270.)

If the contract sold is subject to a nonrecourse loan, the transferor's obligation under the loan is discharged and the amount of the loan is considered an amount received on the transfer. Treas. Reg. §1.1001-2(a); Let. Rul. 8951056. *ASRS, Sec. 52, ¶330.15.*

262. How is the purchaser of a life insurance or endowment contract taxed?

If the purchaser receives lifetime proceeds under the contract, he is taxed in the same way as an original owner would be taxed, but with the following differences. His cost basis is the consideration he paid for the contract, plus any premiums he paid after the purchase, and less any excludable dividends and unrepaid excludable loans received by him after the purchase. If the contract is purchased after payments commence under a life income or installment option, a new exclusion ratio must be determined, based on the purchaser's cost and expected return computed as of the purchaser's annuity starting date. The purchaser's annuity starting date is the beginning of the first period for which the purchaser receives an annuity payment under the contract (see Q 7 to Q 9). Treas. Regs. §§1.72-4(b)(2), 1.72-10(a). It should also be noted that the purchase of a life insurance policy will, under some circumstances, result in loss of the income tax exemption for the death proceeds (see Q 63 through Q 72).

Disposition: Policy Exchanges

263. Does tax liability arise when a policyholder exchanges one life insurance contract for another one?

The Code provides that the following are *nontaxable* exchanges: (1) the exchange of a life insurance policy for another life insurance policy or for an endowment or annuity contract; (2) the exchange of an endowment contract for an annuity contract, or for an endowment contract under which payments will begin no later than payments would have begun under the contract exchanged; (3) the exchange of an annuity contract for another annuity contract. IRC Sec. 1035(a). These rules do not apply to any exchange having the effect of transferring property to any non-United States person. IRC Sec. 1035(c).

LIFE INSURANCE

Q 263

If an exchange involves life insurance policies, the policies must be on the life of the same insured. Otherwise, the exchange does not qualify as a tax free exchange under IRC Section 1035(a). Treas. Reg. §1.1035-1.

In a private ruling, the IRS concluded that exchanges involving policies insuring a single life for a policy insuring two lives do not qualify for nonrecognition treatment under IRC Section 1035. The Service reached this outcome in each of the following situations: (1) Spouse A exchanges a policy insuring only his life for a policy which insures the lives of both Spouse A and Spouse B; (2) Spouse A exchanges two life insurance policies, one of which insures Spouse A and the other of which insures Spouse B, for a single second-to-die policy insuring the lives of both Spouse A and Spouse B; (3) Spouse A and Spouse B jointly exchange separate policies each of which insures the life of one spouse for a single jointly-owned second-to-die policy which insures the lives of both Spouse A and Spouse B; (4) A trust owns and exchanges a policy insuring the life of Spouse A for a policy which insures the lives of both Spouse A and Spouse B; (5) A trust owns and exchanges two life insurance policies, one of which insures Spouse A and the other of which insures Spouse B, for a single second-to-die policy insuring the lives of both Spouse A and Spouse B. Let. Rul. 9542037.

However, also in a private ruling, the IRS has sanctioned IRC Section 1035 treatment of the exchange of a joint and last survivor life insurance policy, following the death of one of the insured persons, for a universal variable life insurance policy that insures the survivor. The Service noted that at the time of the exchange, both policies were insuring the same single life and that the new policy would better suit the policyowner's needs since it was less costly. Let. Rul. 9248013. The Service reached the same conclusion in another private ruling in which a second-to-die policy was exchanged after the death of one insured for a policy insuring only the survivor. Let. Rul. 9330040.

The IRS has also ruled privately that the exchange of two individual life insurance policies for two participating interests in a group universal life insurance policy qualifies as a valid IRC Section 1035(a) transfer. Let. Rul. 9017062.

The Service has concluded that the exchange of two nonparticipating flexible premium life insurance policies, each issued by a different life insurance company, for a single nonparticipating flexible premium variable annuity contract, issued by a third life insurance company, is a proper IRC Section 1035 exchange. The Service agreed that the annuity could be initially issued in the amount of the proceeds received from the first policy and then increased in value when the proceeds of the remaining policy arrived. Let. Rul. 9708016. Where a life insurance policy was exchanged for an annuity plus an additional cash payment the Service concluded that the exchange qualified for IRC Section 1035 treatment. The additional cash payment into the newly-issued annuity was needed in order to meet the annuity's minimum premium requirement. Further, noting that administrative delays should not convert a tax-free exchange to a taxable one, the Service concluded that if the two amounts were not received at the same time, the insurance company could issue the annuity in an amount equal to the cash payment and then later increase the value of the annuity when the funds from the life insurance policy were received. Let. Rul. 9820018.

Where a whole life policy with an outstanding loan was exchanged for another whole life policy subject to the same indebtedness, the exchange was treated as an entirely tax-free exchange. Let. Ruls. 8806058 and 8604033. The IRS reached the same conclusion where one policy was exchanged for another subject to the same indebtedness and the taxpayer contemplated making withdrawals or partial surrenders from the policy to reduce the indebtedness. Let. Rul. 8816015. The cost basis of the new contract will be the cost basis of the old, plus the amount of gain recognized and less the amount of cash or other property received (with proper adjustments for premiums paid and dividends received after the exchange). IRC Sec. 1031(d); Treas. Reg. §1.1031(d)-1.

The substitution of one insured for another under an exchange-of-insureds option on a corporate-owned key person policy is treated by the IRS as a sale or other disposition under IRC Section 1001 and not as a tax free exchange under IRC Section 1035(a). Rev. Rul. 90-109, 1990-2 CB 191.

See Q 250 for a discussion of the effect of an IRC Section 1035 exchange on the grandfathered status of a policy issued prior to June 21, 1988 and thus not subject to the seven pay test of IRC Section 7702A.

ASRS, Sec. 52, ¶330.11.

Disposition: Surrender, Redemption, or Maturity

264. What are the income tax results when the owner of a life insurance or endowment contract takes the lifetime maturity proceeds or cash surrender value in a one sum cash payment?

Amounts received on complete surrender, redemption or maturity are taxed under the cost recovery rule (see Q 3, Q 249). If the maturity proceeds or cash surrender value exceeds the cost of the contract, the excess is taxable income in the year of maturity or surrender even if proceeds are not received until a later tax year. See *Kappel v. U.S.*, 34 AFTR 2d 74-5025 (W.D. Pa. 1974). (For computation of "cost," see Q 8.) The gain is ordinary income, not capital gain. IRC Sec. 72(e); Treas. Reg. §1.72-11(d); *Blum v. Higgins*, 150 F.2d 471 (2nd Cir. 1945); *Avery v. Comm.*, 111 F.2d 19 (9th Cir. 1940); *Bodine v. Comm.*, 103 F.2d 982 (3rd Cir. 1939); *Perkins v. Comm.*, 41 BTA 1225 (1940); *Cobbs v. Comm.*, 39 BTA 642 (1939); *Hellman v. Comm.*, 33 BTA 901 (1936).

The Internal Revenue Code provides that aggregate premiums are the cost basis for computing *gain* upon the lifetime maturity or surrender of a life insurance or endowment contract (see Q 8). IRC Sec. 72(e)(6). Consequently, although the portion of the premiums paid for current life insurance protection is generally a nondeductible personal expense, that portion may nevertheless be included in the cost basis of the contract for the purpose of computing gain upon the surrender or lifetime maturity of the policy.

Example. Mr. Green purchases a whole life policy in the face amount of $100,000. He uses dividends to purchase paid-up additions. Over a 20-year period gross premiums amount to $47,180. Of this amount, $13,018 represents the net protection portion of the premiums, and $34,162 the investment portion. At the end of the 20-year period, Mr. Green surrenders his policy for its cash surrender value of $48,258 (cash value of the original $100,000 policy plus cash value of insurance additions). His cost basis for gain is $47,180 (not $47,180 less $13,018). Thus, his taxable gain is $1,078 ($48,258 - $47,180), not $14,096 ($48,258 - $34,162).

But, the Service has ruled privately that, at time of assignment to a viatical settlement company, the basis of a whole life policy was equal to premiums paid less the sum of the cost of insurance protection provided up to the assignment date and any amounts, such

LIFE INSURANCE   Q 267

as dividends, that were received under the contract but not included in gross income. The cost of insurance protection was found to equal the aggregate premiums paid less the cash value of the policy. Let. Rul. 9443020.

For an exception to the general rule that gain on endowment maturities and cash surrenders is taxable income, see Q 295 on government life insurance. *ASRS, Sec. 52, ¶330.3.*

265. If a life insurance policyholder elects to receive endowment maturity proceeds or cash surrender values under a life income or installment option, is the gain on the policy taxable to him in the year of maturity or surrender?

Ordinarily, a cash basis taxpayer is treated as having *constructively received* an amount of cash when it first becomes available to him without substantial limitations or restrictions. He must report this amount as taxable income even though he has not actually received it. Treas. Reg. §1.451-2. When an endowment contract matures, or any type of contract is surrendered, generally a lump sum payment becomes available to the policyholder unless, *before* the maturity or surrender date, he has elected to postpone receipt of the proceeds under a settlement option. However, for an exception to this general rule, see Q 34. *ASRS, Sec. 52, ¶330.5.*

266. Is it possible to postpone tax on the gain at maturity of an endowment contract?

Yes, by electing to have the proceeds paid under an installment or life income option the gain can be spread over a fixed period of years or the payee's lifetime (see Q 265). Or, tax on the gain may be postponed by electing the interest-only option before maturity and retaining no withdrawal rights (see Q 251). Or, apparently the endowment may be exchanged before maturity for a deferred annuity (see Q 30, Q 263). The IRS has ruled that the exchange of an endowment for a variable annuity is a tax-free exchange. Rev. Rul. 72-358, 1972-2 CB 473; Rev. Rul. 68-235, 1968-1 CB 360. Some contracts provide that the owner may elect to continue the contract in force to an optional maturity date. If the contract so provides and the election is made before the original maturity date, the owner should not be in constructive receipt of the gain under the policy before the optional maturity date. However, there are no specific rulings on this.

See also Q 273 with regard to contracts subject to the definitional rules of IRC Section 7702. *ASRS, Sec. 52, ¶330.5.*

Accelerated Death Benefit

267. What is the income tax treatment of an accelerated death benefit payment from a life insurance contract?

Generally, any amount received under a life insurance contract on the life of a terminally ill insured or a chronically ill insured will be treated as an amount paid by reason of the death of the insured. IRC Sec. 101(g)(1). Amounts received under a life insurance contract by reason of the death of the insured are not includable in gross income. IRC Sec. 101(a). See Q 271. Thus, an accelerated death benefit meeting these requirements will generally be received free of income tax.

2006 Tax Facts on Insurance & Employee Benefits

However, amounts paid to a chronically ill individual are subject to the same limitations that apply to long-term care benefits. Generally, this is a limitation of $250 per day in benefits. IRC Secs. 101(g)(3)(D), 7702B(d). See Q 318. More specifically, if the total periodic long-term care payments received from all policies and any periodic payments received that are treated as paid by reason of the death of the insured (under IRC Section 101(g)) exceed a per diem limitation, the excess must be included in income (without regard to IRC Section 72). (If the insured is terminally ill when a payment treated under IRC Section 101(g) is received, the payment is not taken into account for this purpose.) IRC Sec. 7702B(d)(1). The per diem limitation is equal to the excess of the greater of the $250 per day limitation or the costs incurred for qualified long-term care services provided for the insured over the total payments received as reimbursement for qualified long-term care services for the insured. IRC Sec. 7702B(d)(2). The amount of the limitation, $250 per day, applies in 2006 and is adjusted for inflation. IRC Sec. 7702B(d)(4), IRC Sec. 7702B(d)(5). Accelerated death benefits paid to terminally ill individuals are not subject to this limit.

A terminally ill individual is a person who has been certified by a physician as having an illness or physical condition that can reasonably be expected to result in death within 24 months following the certification. IRC Sec. 101(g)(4)(A).

A chronically ill individual is a person who is not terminally ill and who has been certified by a licensed health care practitioner as unable to perform, without substantial assistance, at least two activities of daily living (ADLs) for at least 90 days or a person with a similar level of disability. Further, a person may be considered chronically ill if he requires substantial supervision to protect himself from threats to his health and safety due to a severe cognitive impairment and this condition has been certified by a health care practitioner within the previous 12 months. IRC Secs. 101(g)(4)(B), 7702B(c)(2)(A). See Q 311. The activities of daily living are: (1) eating; (2) toileting; (3) transferring; (4) bathing; (5) dressing; and (6) continence. IRC Sec. 7702B(c)(2)(B).

There are several special rules that apply to chronically ill insureds. Generally, the tax treatment outlined above will not apply to any payment received for any period unless the payment is for costs incurred by the payee (who has not been compensated by insurance or otherwise) for qualified long-term care services provided to the insured for the period. Additionally, the terms of the contract under which the payments are made must comply with: (1) the requirements of IRC Section 7702B(b)(1)(B); (2) the requirements of IRC Sections 7702B(g) and 4980C that the Secretary specifies as applying to such a purchase, assignment, or other arrangement; (3) standards adopted by the National Association of Insurance Commissioners (NAIC) that apply specifically to chronically ill insureds (if such standards are adopted, similar standards under number (2) above cease to apply); and (4) standards adopted by the state in which the policyholder resides (if such standards are adopted, the analogous requirements under number (2) and, subject to IRC Section 4980C(f), standards under number (3) above cease to apply). IRC Sec. 101(g)(3)(B).

"Qualified long-term care services" are defined as "... necessary diagnostic, preventive, therapeutic, curing, treating, mitigating, and rehabilitative services, and maintenance or personal care services, which..." are required by a chronically ill individual and are provided under a plan of care set forth by a licensed health care practitioner. IRC Sec. 101(g)(4)(C); IRC Sec. 7702B(c)(1).

LIFE INSURANCE

Q 268

There is one exception to this general rule of non-includability for accelerated death benefits. The rules outlined above do not apply to any amount paid to any taxpayer other than the insured if the taxpayer has an insurable interest in the life of the insured because the insured is a director, officer, or employee of the taxpayer or if the insured is financially interested in any trade or business of the taxpayer. IRC Sec. 101(g)(5). *ASRS, Sec. 52, ¶¶1300, 1300.1.*

Viatical Settlement

268. What is the income tax treatment of an amount received from a viatical settlement provider?

If any portion of the death benefit under a life insurance contract on the life of a terminally or chronically ill insured is sold or assigned to a viatical settlement provider, the amount paid for the sale or assignment will be treated as an amount paid under the life insurance contract by reason of the insured's death. IRC Sec. 101(g)(2)(A). In other words, such an amount will not be includable in income. See IRC Sec. 101(a). See Q 271.

A viatical settlement provider is defined as "... any person regularly engaged in the trade or business of purchasing, or taking assignments of, life insurance contracts on the lives of insureds..." who are terminally or chronically ill provided that certain licensing and other requirements are met. IRC Sec. 101(g)(2)(B)(i). To be considered a viatical settlement provider a person must be licensed for such purposes in the state in which the insured resides. The Service has provided guidance on when viatical settlement providers will be considered licensed. Rev. Rul. 2002-82, 2002-2 CB 978.

If an insured resides in a state that does not require this type of licensing, the person must meet the standards for either a terminally ill individual or a chronically ill individual, whichever applies to the insured. IRC Sec. 101(g)(2)(B). The requirements applicable to an insured who is a terminally ill individual are met if the person: (1) meets the requirements of sections 8 and 9 of the Viatical Settlements Model Act of the NAIC; and (2) meets the requirements of the Model Regulations of the NAIC in determining amounts paid by such person in connection with such purchases or assignments. IRC Sec. 101(g)(2)(B)(ii). The requirements applicable to an insured who is a chronically ill individual are met if the person: (1) meets requirements similar to the requirements of sections 8 and 9 of the Viatical Settlements Model Act of the NAIC; and (2) meets the standards of the NAIC for evaluating the reasonableness of amounts paid by such person in connection with such purchases or assignments with respect to chronically ill individuals. IRC Sec. 101(g)(2)(B)(iii).

A terminally ill individual is a person who has been certified by a physician as having an illness or physical condition that can reasonably be expected to result in death within 24 months following the certification. IRC Sec. 101(g)(4)(A).

A chronically ill individual is a person who is not terminally ill and who has been certified by a licensed health care practitioner as being unable to perform, without substantial assistance, at least two activities of daily living (ADLs) for at least 90 days or a person with a similar level of disability. Further, a person may be considered chronically ill if he requires substantial supervision to protect himself from threats to his health and safety due to severe cognitive impairment and this condition has been certified by a health care practitioner within the previous 12 months. IRC Secs. 101(g)(4)(B),

7702B(c)(2)(A). See Q 311. The activities of daily living are: (1) eating; (2) toileting; (3) transferring; (4) bathing; (5) dressing; and (6) continence. IRC Sec. 7702B(c)(2)(B).

There are several special rules that apply to chronically ill insureds. Generally, the tax treatment outlined above will not apply to any payment received for any period unless such payment is for costs incurred by the payee (who has not been compensated by insurance or otherwise) for qualified long-term care services provided to the insured for the period. Additionally, the terms of the contract under which such payments are made must comply with: (1) the requirements of IRC Section 7702B(b)(1)(B); (2) the requirements of IRC Sections 7702B(g) and 4980C (see Q 311) that the Secretary specifies as applying to such a purchase, assignment, or other arrangement; (3) standards adopted by the NAIC that apply specifically to chronically ill insureds (if such standards are adopted, similar standards under number (2) above cease to apply); and (4) standards adopted by the state in which the policyholder resides (if such standards are adopted, the analogous requirements under number (2) and, subject to IRC Section 4980C(f), standards under number (3) above cease to apply). IRC Sec. 101(g)(3)(B).

There is one exception to this general rule of non-includability for viatical settlements. The rules outlined above do not apply to any amount paid to any taxpayer other than the insured if the taxpayer has an insurable interest in the life of the insured because the insured is a director, officer or employee of the taxpayer or if the insured is financially interested in any trade or business of the taxpayer. IRC Sec. 101(g)(5). *ASRS, Sec. 52, ¶1300.3.*

Withholding

269. Are amounts received as living proceeds of life insurance and endowment contracts subject to withholding?

Yes; however, the payee generally may elect not to have anything withheld. Only the amount it is reasonable to believe is includable in income is subject to withholding. Amounts are to be withheld from periodic payments at the same rate as wages. Payments are periodic, even if they are variable, if they are payable over a period of more than a year. If payments are not periodic, 10% of the includable amount is withheld. Payments made to the beneficiary of a deceased payee are subject to withholding under the same rules. IRC Secs. 3405(a), 3405(b); Temp. Treas. Reg. §35.3405-1T (A-9, A-10, A-12, A-17, F-19 through 24). An election out of withholding will be ineffective, generally, if a payee does not furnish his taxpayer identification number (TIN, usually his social security number) to the payor or furnishes an incorrect TIN to the payor and the payor is so notified by the IRS. IRC Sec. 3405(e)(12). *ASRS, Sec. 53, ¶20.13(a).*

Loss

270. Does the surrender or sale of a life insurance or endowment contract ever result in a deductible loss?

A loss deduction can be claimed only if the loss is incurred in connection with the taxpayer's trade or business or in a transaction entered into for profit. IRC Sec. 165. If the surrendered contract is a life insurance policy, ordinarily there will be no deductible loss even though the cash surrender value is less than net premium cost. The Code expressly provides that the cost basis of a policy for computing gain is "aggregate premiums paid" (see Q 265). But the Code is silent with respect to cost basis for computing loss. Several

LIFE INSURANCE   Q 271

courts have held, however, that the portion of the premiums paid for life insurance protection cannot be included in the cost basis. They reason that this portion is not recoverable investment, but a nondeductible expense. *London Shoe Co., Inc. v. Comm.*, 80 F.2d 230 (2nd Cir. 1935); *Century Wood Preserving Co. v. Comm.*, 69 F.2d 967 (3rd Cir. 1934); *Keystone Consol. Publishing Co. v. Comm.*, 26 BTA 1210 (1932). There can be no loss, therefore, if the cash surrender value equals the policy reserve. But if the contract is surrendered in a policy year when the reserve exceeds the cash surrender value, the difference *may* be allowable as a loss provided the policy was purchased in connection with the taxpayer's trade or business or in a transaction entered into for profit. See *London Shoe Co., Inc.*, supra. Apparently the Tax Court considers the purchase of a personal cash value policy as a transaction entered into for profit to the extent of the policy's investment feature. *Cohen v. Comm.*, 44 BTA 709 (1941); *Fleming v. Comm.*, TC Memo 1945. But a Texas district court does not consider it a transaction for profit even to this extent. *Arnold v. U.S.*, 180 F. Supp. 746 (N.D. Texas 1959).

A different situation exists where, because of the insurance company's insolvency, the policyowner receives less than the stated cash surrender value. In this case, the difference between the amount received and the stated cash surrender value is a deductible loss. *Cohen*, supra; *Fleming*, supra. *ASRS, Sec. 52, ¶330.4.*

DEATH PROCEEDS

General Rules

271. Are life insurance proceeds payable by reason of the insured's death taxable income to the beneficiary?

No, as a general rule death proceeds are excludable from the beneficiary's gross income. IRC Sec. 101(a)(1). Death proceeds from single premium, periodic premium or flexible premium policies are received income tax free by the beneficiary regardless of whether the beneficiary is an individual, a corporation, a partnership, a trustee, or the insured's estate. Treas. Reg. §1.101-1(a)(1). With some exceptions (as noted below), the exclusion generally applies regardless of who paid the premiums or who owned the policy.

Planning Point: When presenting a Key Person proposal it is important to ask the prospect, "How much additional gross sales would it take to equal the income-tax-free benefits of life insurance?" Also point out that the sales revenue will be needed at a time when the business has lost a person critical to the creation of that revenue. *William H. Alley, CLU, ChFC, MSFS, LUTCF, Alley Financial Group, LLC.*

Proceeds from group life insurance can qualify for the exclusion as well as proceeds from individual policies. Under certain conditions, accelerated death benefits paid prior to the death of a chronically or terminally ill insured may qualify for this exclusion. See Q 267. On the other hand, death benefits under annuity contracts are not proceeds of life insurance within the meaning of IRC Section 101(a)(1).

In order to come within the exclusion, the proceeds must be paid "by reason of the death of the insured." In other words, the exclusion applies only to proceeds that are payable because the insured's death has matured the policy. Where the policy has matured during the insured's lifetime, amounts payable to the beneficiary, even though payable at insured's death, are not "death proceeds." Proceeds paid on a policy covering a missing-in-action member of the uniformed services were excludable, even though no official finding of death had been made by the Defense Department. Rev. Rul. 78-372, 1978-2 CB 93.

If the death proceeds are paid under a life insurance contract (as defined in Q 273), the exclusion extends to the full amount of the policy proceeds. For example, if an insured dies after having paid $6,000 in premiums on a $100,000 policy, the full face amount of $100,000 is excludable from the beneficiary's gross income (not just the $6,000 that represents a return of premiums). The face amount of paid-up additional insurance and the lump sum payable under a double indemnity provision are also excludable under IRC Section 101(a)(1). Where the death proceeds are received in a one-sum cash payment, then, the entire amount received is free of income tax. However, the exclusion does not extend to interest earned on the proceeds after the insured's death. Thus, if the proceeds are held by the insurer at interest, the interest is taxable (see Q 275). If the proceeds are held by the insurer under a life income or other installment option, the tax-exempt proceeds are prorated over the payment period, and the balance of each payment is taxable income (see Q 276).

In the case of a contract issued, generally, after 1984 that is a life insurance contract under applicable law but does not meet the definitional requirements explained in Q 273, only the excess of the death benefit over the net surrender value (cash surrender value less any surrender charges) will be excludable from the income of the beneficiary as a death benefit. IRC Sec. 7702(g)(2). Generally, the exclusion is similarly limited to the amount of the death benefit in excess of the net surrender value in the case of a flexible premium contract that is subject to but fails to meet the guidelines of IRC Section 101(f) (see Q 273). Nevertheless, in either case, a part of the cash surrender value will also be excludable as a recovery of basis to the extent the basis has not been previously recovered; presumably, where a contract subject to the definition of a life insurance contract in IRC Section 7702 fails to meet that definition, or a variable contract is not adequately diversified, unrecovered cash value increases previously includable in income will be recoverable tax free as a part of basis.

In addition, all or part of the proceeds may be taxable income in the following circumstances: in some instances where the policy or an interest in the policy has been transferred for a valuable consideration (see Q 63, Q 277); where the proceeds are received under a qualified pension or profit sharing plan (see Q 437); where the proceeds are received under a tax sheltered annuity for an employee of a tax-exempt organization or public school (see Q 481); where the proceeds are received under an individual retirement endowment contract (see Q 229); where the proceeds are received by a creditor from insurance on the life of the debtor (see Q 293, Q 294); where there is no insurable interest in the life of the insured (see Q 74); where the proceeds are received as corporate dividends or compensation (see Q 73); where the proceeds are received as alimony by a divorced spouse (see Q 280); where the proceeds are received as restitution of embezzled funds (see Q 75); and proceeds received by a corporation may be subject to an alternative minimum tax (see Q 95). *ASRS, Sec. 52, ¶500.*

272. Is the death benefit under the double indemnity clause of a life insurance policy subject to federal income tax?

No, it is generally tax-exempt as proceeds payable by reason of an insured's death. IRC Sec. 101(a); Treas. Reg. §1.101-1(a)(1). If the proceeds are held under a settlement option, the regular rules apply. (See Q 275, Q 276.)

273. What Is a "life insurance contract" for purposes of the death benefit exclusion?

Contracts Issued After 1984

Generally, in order for death proceeds of life insurance contracts (including endowment contracts) issued after December 31, 1984 to be fully excludable from the beneficiary's gross income, the life insurance contract must be a life insurance contract under the applicable state law *and* meet one of two alternative tests: the cash value accumulation test or the guideline premium and corridor test. IRC Sec. 7702(a). Any plan or arrangement provided by a church or a convention or association of churches to its employees or their beneficiaries that provides for the payment of a death benefit is not required to meet the requirement that the arrangement constitute a life insurance contract under applicable law. IRC Sec. 7702(j).

The IRS may waive an insurer's failure to satisfy the requirements of IRC Section 7702(a) if the errors were reasonable and reasonable steps to remedy the errors have been taken. IRC Sec. 7702(f)(8). Where six life insurance policies were temporarily out of compliance with the guideline premium test requirements due to the inadvertence of the insurer's employees during a change in computer systems, the IRS granted such a waiver after the insurer increased the policy death benefits. Let. Rul. 9042039. See also Let. Ruls. 9801042, 9727025, 9621016. Where clerical errors involving lost records, missed testing dates, and the failure to make scheduled premium adjustments combined with the conversion of the insurance company's policy administration system from a manual procedure to a fully computerized one to cause policies to be out of compliance, the Service granted a waiver provided the policies were brought into compliance within 90 days. Let. Rul. 9416017. See also Let. Ruls. 200006030, 199924028, 9834020, 9838014. Where a clerk failed to realize that a certificate holder had paid in additional premiums that put a group universal life certificate out of compliance, the Service granted a waiver provided that the company refund the excess premiums, with interest, or increase the policy death benefit from the time of noncompliance. Let. Rul. 9623068. See also Let. Ruls. 200027030, 9805010, 9601039, 9517042, 9322023, 9146016, 9146011. However, the Service refused to waive an insurer's failure to satisfy these requirements where several policies were discovered to be out of compliance due to the company's use of a software program which contained an "inherent structural flaw." Let. Rul. 9202008.

Modification of a life insurance contract after December 31, 1990, that is necessitated by the insurer's insolvency will not affect the date on which the contract was issued, entered into, or purchased for purposes of IRC Section 7702. Rev. Proc. 92-57, 1992-2 CB 410; Let. Rul. 9239026. See also Let. Rul. 9305013.

The Cash Value Accumulation Test

To satisfy the cash value accumulation test, the cash surrender value of a contract, according to its terms, must not at any time exceed the net single premium that would be necessary at such time to fund future benefits (death benefits, endowment benefits, and charges for certain additional benefits, such as disability waiver) under the contract. IRC Sec. 7702(b). The *cash surrender value* of a contract is its cash value, disregarding any surrender charges, policy loans or reasonable termination benefits. The *net single premium* is determined by using (1) an annual effective interest rate of 4% or the interest rate(s) guaranteed in the contract, whichever is greater; (2) the mortality charges specified in the contract or if not specified, the charges used in figuring the statutory reserves for the contract; and (3) any other charges specified in the contract.

For contracts issued on or after October 21, 1988, the mortality charges used must be reasonable charges that meet requirements, if any, in regulations and that do not exceed the mortality charges specified in the "prevailing commissioners' standard tables" at the time the contract is issued. IRC Sec. 7702(c)(3)(B)(i). (The prevailing commissioners' standard tables are defined in IRC Section 807(d)(5).) The exercise of an option to change a policy's death benefit after October 21, 1988, added to the policy by endorsement prior to this date, did not cause the policy to become subject to the reasonable mortality requirements of IRC Section 7702(c)(3)(B)(i), as amended by TAMRA. Let. Rul. 9853033.

For contracts insuring only one life that are entered into on or after October 21, 1988, proposed regulations provide three safe harbors for meeting the reasonable mortality charge requirement. Prop. Treas. Reg. §1.7702-1. A contract issued before October 21, 1988, having mortality charges that do not differ materially from the charges actually expected to be made will be treated as meeting the reasonable mortality charge requirements. TAMRA '88 Sec. 5011(c). Any other reasonable charges taken into account for purposes of determining the net single premium must be reasonably expected to actually be paid and must be actually specified in the contract. IRC Sec. 7702(c)(3)(B)(ii).

The Guideline Premium and Cash Value Corridor Test

To meet the second alternative test, the contract must first meet certain guideline premium requirements and, second, the contract must fall within the *cash value corridor*. For the contract to meet the guideline premium requirement, the sum of the premiums paid under the contract must not at any time exceed *the greater of* (1) the guideline single premium as of such time or (2) the sum of the guideline level premiums to such date. IRC Sec. 7702(c). *Premiums paid* for purposes of this section means those paid under the contract less excludable amounts received not as an annuity under IRC Section 72(e) (e.g., dividends). IRC Sec. 7702(f)(1). The *guideline single premium* is the premium necessary to fund future benefits under the contract, determined at the time the contract is issued using the same factors as for the net single premium (above), except the annual effective rate of interest is 6% instead of 4%. The *guideline level premium* is the level annual amount payable over a period not ending before the insured becomes 95, computed in the same manner as the single guideline premium, except the annual effective rate remains at four percent. IRC Sec. 7702(c). The Code sets forth certain rules for computing the guideline premiums and benefits and provides special rules that, in limited circumstances, make exceptions for failing to meet the guideline premium requirements or allow premiums paid to be returned at the end of the year to correct such failures. IRC Sec. 7702(f)(1)(B).

A contract falls within the *cash value corridor* if the death benefit payable under the contract at any time is at least equal to an applicable percentage of the cash surrender value (see table below).

LIFE INSURANCE

Q 273

Table

In the case of an insured with an attained age as of the beginning of the contract year of:		The applicable percentage decreases by a ratable portion for each full year:	
More than	But not more than	From	To
0	40	250	250
40	45	250	215
45	50	215	185
50	55	185	150
55	60	150	130
60	65	130	120
65	70	120	115
70	75	115	105
75	90	105	105
90	95	105	100

The determination of whether a variable life insurance contract meets either of the two alternative tests must be made whenever the death benefit under the contract changes, but at least once each 12-month period. A variable life insurance contract will not be treated as a life insurance contract, and taxed accordingly, for any period that the underlying investments of the segregated asset account are not "adequately diversified." IRC Sec. 817(h). See Q 25.

The Service has ruled that sub-accounts within variable life policies that were invested in hedge funds available to the general public would be considered owned by the policy owners, and thus currently taxed on the income. Rev. Rul. 2003-92, 2003-33 IRB 350. Sub-accounts within a variable life contract may invest in mutual funds that are available to the general public. Let. Rul. 200420017.

Contracts Issued Before 1985

Contracts issued after June 30, 1984 that provide an increasing death benefit and have premium funding more rapid than 10-year level premium payments must satisfy the above definition generally applicable to contracts issued after 1984, with certain exceptions. DEFRA Sec. 221(d)(2).

A policy issued before January 1, 1985 that is exchanged for one issued after December 31, 1984 will, according to the General Explanation of the Deficit Reduction Act of 1984, be treated as a contract issued after 1984 and subject to the definitional requirements of IRC Section 7702 discussed above. The General Explanation states that a change in policy terms after December 31, 1984 could be considered an exchange with the effect of bringing the policy under the IRC Section 7702 definitional requirements. Examples of "changes in terms" given are changes in "amount or pattern of death benefit, the premium pattern, the rate or rates guaranteed on issuance of the contract, or mortality and expense charges." General Explanation of the Deficit Reduction Act of 1984 at p. 656. A change in minor administrative provisions or a loan rate change generally would not be considered to result in an exchange, the General Explanation adds. Modification of a life insurance contract after December 31, 1990, that is necessitated by the insurer's insolvency will not affect the date on which the contract was issued, entered into, or purchased for purposes of IRC Section 101(f). Rev. Proc. 92-57, 1992-2 CB 410; Let. Rul. 9239026.

Otherwise, universal life insurance, and any other flexible premium contract, issued before January 1, 1985 will receive the death proceeds exclusion only if (1) the sum of the premiums does not exceed at any time a guideline premium (see below) *and* the death benefit is not less than a certain percentage of the cash value (140% until the start of the policy year the insured attains age 40, thereafter reducing 1% for each year over 40, but not below 105%) *or* (2) the contract provides that the cash value may not at any time exceed the net single premium for the death benefit at that time.

The guideline premium is the greater of (1) the single premium necessary to fund future benefits under the contract based on the maximum mortality rates and other charges fixed in the contract and the minimum interest rate guaranteed in the contract at issue, but at least 6%, or (2) the aggregate level annual amounts payable over the life of the contract (at least 20 years but not extending beyond age 95, if earlier) computed like the single premium guideline using an annual effective rate of 4% instead of 6%. The IRS can allow excessive premiums paid in error to be returned (with interest) within 60 days after the end of the policy year; in such case, the policy will still qualify as life insurance. IRC Sec. 101(f).

The death benefit of a flexible premium contract entered into before January 1, 1983 will be excludable if the contract met the requirements on September 3, 1983. In determining if the level annual premium guideline is met by such a contract, an annual effective interest rate of 3% may be substituted for 4%. TEFRA Sec. 266(c).

For life insurance contracts (other than flexible premium contracts) issued before January 1, 1985, there is no clear definition of "life insurance" for purposes of the tax-free death benefit; however, the death proceeds are not considered proceeds of life insurance unless the contract under which they are paid provided protection against the risk of early death. The IRS has taken the position for income tax purposes, that a contract is a life insurance contract if at any time it contained an element of life insurance risk. See Rev. Rul. 66-322, 1966-2 CB 123. Thus, the Service apparently has not attempted to tax the proceeds of a retirement income contract, even when insured's death has occurred after the cash value has exceeded the face amount but before maturity of the contract. This ruling involved a contract purchased by a qualified retirement plan and IRS could attempt to limit its position to such contracts. See GCM 38934 (12-8-82); GCM 39022 (8-12-83). On the other hand, the Tax Court has held that a retirement income contract is an annuity contract once the element of risk has disappeared. *Evans v. Comm.*, 56 TC 1142 (1971). The Service has also ruled that the exclusion also applies to variable life insurance death benefits that may increase or decrease, but not below a guaranteed minimum amount, on each policy anniversary depending on the investment experience of the separate account of the prior year's net premium. Rev. Rul. 79-87, 1979-1 CB 73. Regulations provide that death benefits having the characteristics of life insurance proceeds payable by death under contracts such as workers compensation and accident and health contracts are excludable under IRC Section 101(a). Treas. Reg. §1.101-1(a)(1). *ASRS, Sec. 52, ¶500.1.*

274. If a life insurance policy is owned by someone other than the insured, how are proceeds taxed under the income tax laws?

In the same manner as if the insured owned the policy. (See Q 249 to Q 270 for an explanation of living proceeds and Q 271 to Q 279 for an explanation of death proceeds.) However, where a person retains all the incidents of ownership in an endowment or annuity contract but designates another to receive the maturity proceeds, the proceeds will be taxed to the owner rather than to the payee (see Q 31). For possible gift tax consequences where a policy is owned by one individual but insures another, see Q 735.

Interest Option

275. If life insurance death proceeds are left on deposit with the insurance company under an interest-only option, is the interest taxable income to the beneficiary?

Yes, all amounts paid or credited to the beneficiary as interest (excess and guaranteed) must be included in the beneficiary's gross income regardless of whether the insured or beneficiary elected the option. IRC Sec. 101(c); Treas. Reg. §1.101-3(a); *U.S. v. Heilbroner*, 100 F.2d 379 (2nd Cir. 1938); *Kinnear v. Comm.*, 20 BTA 718 (1930); *Rivera v. Comm.*, TC Memo 1994-625. The interest is taxable in the first year that it can be withdrawn. If the beneficiary elects an option under which there is no right to withdraw either principal or interest for a specified number of years, the entire amount of accumulated interest is taxable in the year during which it first becomes withdrawable. Treas. Reg. §1.101-4 (g), Ex. 1. But if the beneficiary has a right to withdraw principal, the interest is taxable when credited even though the agreement stipulates that the interest cannot be withdrawn. *Strauss v. Comm.*, 21 TC 104 (1953); see also Rev. Rul. 68-586, 1968-2 CB 195.

The principal amount held by the insurer, representing the value of the proceeds at insured's death, is income-tax free to the recipient when withdrawn (see Q 271).

For tax treatment where proceeds are held for a period under the interest option and subsequently paid under a life income or installment settlement, see Q 276. *ASRS, Sec. 52, ¶510.1.*

Life Income and Installment Options

276. If excludable death proceeds are held by an insurer and paid under a life income or installment option, how are the payments treated for income tax purposes?

The "amount held by the insurer" (usually the one-sum proceeds payable at the insured's death) is prorated over the payment period. (If the settlement arrangement involves a life income with a guaranteed refund, or a guaranteed number of payments, the value of the guarantee must be subtracted from the one-sum proceeds before making the proration.) These prorated amounts determine the portion of each payment that may be treated as a return of principal. Consequently, the beneficiary may exclude this portion of each payment from gross income. IRC Sec. 101(d)(1); Treas. Reg. §1.101-4(a)(1)(i). All amounts received in excess of these prorated amounts are treated as interest, and are taxable as ordinary income to any beneficiary other than the surviving spouse of an insured who died before October 23, 1986. Such a surviving spouse is entitled to exclude up to $1,000 of such interest annually in addition to the prorated amount of principal. IRC Sec. 101(d)(1)(B), prior to repeal by TRA '86, Sec. 1001(a); Treas. Reg. §1.101-4(a)(1)(ii).

Life Income Option

If the installments are payable for the lifetime of the beneficiary, the "amount held by the insurer" is divided by the beneficiary's life expectancy to determine the

Q 276 FEDERAL INCOME TAX

amount that may be excluded from gross income each year as return of principal. In the case of amounts paid with respect to deaths occurring after October 22, 1986, the beneficiary's life expectancy must be determined by use of IRS annuity tables V and VI. IRC Sec. 101(d)(2)(B)(ii); Treas. Reg. §1.101-7. In the case of amounts paid with respect to deaths occurring before October 23, 1986, the beneficiary's life expectancy is taken from the mortality table that the insurer uses in determining the amount of the installments (not from the IRS annuity tables). Treas. Reg. §1.101-4(c). If there is a refund or period-certain guarantee, the amount held by the insurer must be reduced by the present value of the guarantee before prorating for the exclusion. Treas. Reg. §1.101-4(e). The present value of the guarantee is determined by using the insurer's interest rate and the applicable mortality table. The excludable amount, once determined, remains the same even though the beneficiary outlives his or her life expectancy. The balance of the payments is taxable income to any beneficiary other than the surviving spouse of an insured who died before October 23, 1986. The spouse of such an insured may exclude up to $1,000 of interest each year in addition to excluding the prorated amount of principal. If the beneficiary dies before receiving all guaranteed amounts, the secondary beneficiary receives the balance of the guaranteed refund, or guaranteed payments, tax-free. Treas. Reg. §1.101-4(d)(3). However, excess interest allowed by the company in addition to the guaranteed refund would be taxable income to the secondary beneficiary. Treas. Reg. §1.101-4(d)(3) and (g), Ex. 7.

Example. Insured died after October 22, 1986. His widow elects to receive $75,000 of death proceeds under a refund life income option. The company guarantees her payments of $4,000 a year. According to Table V and the interest rate used by the insurer, her life expectancy is 25 years and the present value of the refund guarantee is $13,500. The $75,000 must first be reduced by the value of the refund guarantee ($75,000 - $13,500 = $61,500). This reduced amount, $61,500, is then divided by her life expectancy to find the amount that she may exclude from gross income each year as return of principal. This amount is $2,460 ($61,500 ÷ 25). Her taxable income from the guaranteed payment is $1,540 a year ($4,000 - $2,460). If the widow dies before receiving the full $75,000, the balance of the guaranteed amount will be received tax-free by the secondary beneficiary.

If a joint-and-survivor option is elected, the "amount held by the insurer" is divided by the life expectancy of the beneficiaries as a group to determine the annual exclusion of principal (see above for the appropriate mortality table to be used). The same amount of principal is excludable during the joint lives and the lifetime of the survivor. Treas. Reg. §1.101-4(d)(2) and (g), Ex. 5.

Fixed Period Option

The "amount held by the insurer" is divided by the number of installment payments to be made in the fixed period. The quotient is the portion of each payment that is excludable from the beneficiary's gross income as a return of principal. The balance of each guaranteed payment must generally be included in the beneficiary's gross income. In addition to the prorated amount of principal, the surviving spouse of an insured who died before October 23, 1986 may exclude up to $1,000 of interest each year (guaranteed and excess). Treas. Reg. §1.101-4(a)(2), Ex. 1 and 2. If the primary beneficiary dies before the end of the fixed period, the secondary beneficiary may exclude the same amount of prorated principal from gross income, but all interest (guaranteed and excess) is includable. Treas. Reg. §1.101-4(a)(2), Ex. 3.

Example. Insured died after October 22, 1986. His widow elects to receive $50,000 of proceeds in 10 annual installments of $5,500 each. As a second payment, she receives $5,950 (guaranteed payment plus $450 excess interest). She may exclude $5,000 of the payment as a return of principal ($50,000 ÷ 10). Consequently, she must include in income the balance of the payment ($950).

LIFE INSURANCE   Q 276

Fixed Amount Option

The "amount held by the insurer" is divided by the number of payments required to exhaust principal and guaranteed interest. The quotient is the portion of each payment that is excludable from the beneficiary's gross income as return of principal. The balance of each guaranteed payment must generally be included in the beneficiary's gross income. Treas. Reg. §1.101-4(g), Ex. 2. The surviving spouse of an insured who died before October 23, 1986 may exclude up to $1,000 of interest each year in addition to the prorated amount of principal. Payments extending beyond the guaranteed period (payments comprised entirely of excess interest) are fully taxable. (There is a difference of opinion as to whether the surviving spouse's $1,000 annual interest exclusion, even if otherwise available, can be applied to these additional excess interest payments.) If the primary beneficiary dies before the end of the guaranteed payment period, the secondary beneficiary may exclude the same amount of prorated principal from gross income.

Surviving Spouse's $1,000 Annual Exclusion

In addition to the prorated exclusion of principal (see above), the surviving spouse of an insured *who died prior to October 23, 1986* is entitled to exclude from gross income up to $1,000 of interest (guaranteed and excess) in each taxable year. (The surviving spouse's $1,000 annual exclusion was repealed for surviving spouses of insureds who die after October 22, 1986.) No more than $1,000 of interest may be excluded annually with respect to one insured, regardless of the number of policies. But if the beneficiary is the surviving spouse of more than one insured, he or she is entitled to a $1,000 annual interest exclusion with respect to policies on the life of each insured. IRC Sec. 101(d)(1)(B), prior to repeal by TRA '86, Sec. 1001(a); Treas. Reg. §1.101-4(a)(2), Ex. 2. To qualify for this additional exclusion, the surviving spouse must have been married to the insured when he died. An absolute divorce disqualifies the beneficiary, although a legal separation or an interlocutory decree does not. Treas. Reg. §1.101-4(a)(1)(ii); see *Eccles v. Comm.*, 19 TC 1049 (1953), aff'd 208 F.2d 796 (4th Cir. 1953). The surviving spouse's remarriage does not affect his or her qualification. Rev. Rul. 72-164, 1972-1 CB 28. This $1,000 annual exclusion is available only with respect to the interest element in life income or installment payments; it is not available with respect to interest payments under an interest-only option. In other words, the settlement must provide for a substantial diminution of principal during the period the interest is received. Treas. Reg. §1.101-3(a). It would appear that because payments of proceeds (including interest) from National Service Life Insurance (NSLI) are otherwise exempted from taxation, the receipt of NSLI proceeds under an installment settlement will not reduce the $1,000 annual exclusion (see Q 295).

Change From Interest-Only Option to Life Income or Installment Option

The surviving spouse of an insured who died before October 23, 1986, is not precluded from obtaining the benefits of the $1,000 annual interest exclusion at a later date simply because the surviving spouse originally elected to leave the proceeds with the insurer under the interest-only option. A new election to take the proceeds under a life income or other installment option will entitle the surviving spouse to the annual interest exclusion. Rev. Rul. 65-284, 1965-2 CB 28. During the time the proceeds are held under the interest-only option the interest will be fully taxable to him or her as received (see Q 275). Payments under the life income or installment option will be treated as explained above.

2006 Tax Facts on Insurance & Employee Benefits

Insured Died Before August 17, 1954

In tax years beginning before January 1, 1977, the full installment or life income payment was tax-free to the beneficiary except excess interest, provided the option was elected under a contract right. IRC Sec. 101(f) as in effect prior to January 1, 1977. Effective for tax years beginning on or after January 1, 1977, IRC Section 101(f) was repealed. TRA '76, Sec. 1901(a)(16). As a result, these payments fall within the general rules (above) applicable where the insured died after August 16, 1954. *ASRS, Sec. 52, ¶¶510.2-510.6.*

Transferred Policy

277. If an existing life insurance policy is sold or otherwise transferred for a valuable consideration, are the death proceeds wholly tax-exempt?

As a general rule, death proceeds are wholly exempt from income tax (see Q 271, Q 273). As a basic exception to this rule however, the proceeds are not wholly exempt if the policy, or any interest in the policy, has been transferred, by assignment or otherwise, for a valuable consideration. IRC Sec. 101(a)(2). This exception is known as the "transfer for value rule." Under this rule, the proceeds will be subject to income tax to the extent that they exceed the consideration paid (and premiums subsequently paid) by the person to whom the policy is transferred. Also, for contracts issued after June 8, 1997 (in taxable years ending after this date) any interest paid or accrued by the transferee on indebtedness with respect to the policy is added to the amount exempt from tax after the transfer if the interest is not deductible under IRC Section 264(a)(4). IRC Sec. 101(a)(2).

This unfavorable result is avoided if the transfer for value is "to the insured, to a partner of the insured, or to a partnership in which the insured is a partner, or to a corporation in which the insured is a shareholder or officer." IRC Sec. 101(a)(2)(B). (For application of the transfer for value rule to business insurance, see Q 63 to Q 72.)

However, the unfavorable result is not avoided merely because the person to whom the policy is transferred has an insurable interest in the insured. For example, often an insured will transfer his policy to his son or daughter. If the transfer is a gift, the named beneficiary will receive the proceeds wholly free of income tax. But if the insured receives a valuable consideration for the transfer, the proceeds will be taxable income to the beneficiary (to the extent they exceed the consideration, premiums, and other amounts subsequently paid). Treas. Reg. §1.101-1(b); *Bean v. Comm.* TC Memo 1955-195. The fact that no money was exchanged for the policy does not mean, necessarily, that the transfer was a gift and therefore not subject to the transfer for value rule. For example, where two insured individuals assign policies on their own lives to each other at about the same time, it could be argued that neither transfer was a gift. The transfer of a policy subject to a nonrecourse loan may be a transfer for value. See Q 64. However, where a policy is owned by someone other than the insured, a transfer for value to the insured will not cause loss of tax exemption for the proceeds. Moreover, in the case of successive transfers, the proceeds will be wholly tax-exempt if the final transfer, or the last transfer for value, is to the insured himself or his partner, or a partnership in which the insured is a partner, or a corporation in which the insured is a shareholder or officer. IRC Sec. 101(a)(2)(B); Treas. Reg. §1.101-1(b). See Q 279 for transfer to a spouse (or former spouse, if incident to a divorce). *ASRS, Sec. 52, ¶520.3.*

LIFE INSURANCE

Q 280

278. Are the death proceeds of life insurance wholly tax-exempt if the policy has been transferred as a gift?

Generally, the donee steps into the shoes of the donor. Thus, the entire proceeds are exempt if they would have been exempt had the policy been retained by the donor. But if the donor purchases the policy from another owner, then only the consideration paid by the donor, plus net premiums (and certain other amounts) subsequently paid by donor and donee, is exempt. As an exception to this general rule, however, the proceeds will be wholly tax-exempt—despite any previous transfer for value—if the final transfer is made *to* the insured, a partner of the insured, a partnership in which the insured is a partner, or a corporation in which the insured is an officer or shareholder. Treas. Reg. §1.101-1(b); *Hacker v. Comm.*, 36 BTA 659 (1937). The IRS has ruled that where a life insurance policy that is subject to a policy loan is transferred, there is a transfer for value, but if the transfer is partly a gift it may come within one of the exceptions to the transfer for value rule (see Q 63, #3). Rev. Rul. 69-187, 1969-1 CB 45; Let. Rul. 8951056. *ASRS, Sec. 52, ¶520.4.*

279. Will the transfer of a life insurance policy between spouses result in loss of tax exemption for the death proceeds?

The transfer of a life insurance policy between spouses (or former spouses if incident to a divorce—see Q 280) generally will not result in the loss of exemption for the death proceeds if the transfer occurs after July 18, 1984 (unless the transfer is pursuant to an instrument in effect on or before such date) or after December 31, 1983 and both spouses (or former spouses if incident to a divorce) elect to have the nonrecognition rules of IRC Section 1041 apply.

The transferee is treated as having acquired the policy by gift and the transferor's basis is carried over to the transferee. IRC Sec. 1041. IRC Section 101(a)(2)(A) provides that the transfer for value rule does not apply if the basis of the contract for determining gain or loss in the hands of the transferee is determined by reference to the basis of the contract in the hands of the transferor. However, if a life insurance policy with a loan is transferred in trust and gain is recognized (see Q 280), the basis in the transferee's hands is adjusted to reflect the gain, but the transfer may nonetheless come within an exception to the transfer for value rule (see Q 63 #3).

If the transfer occurs either prior to July 19, 1984 or after July 18, 1984 but pursuant to an instrument in effect before such date *and* no election to have the nonrecognition rules of IRC Section 1041 apply has been made, then the nature of the transfer determines whether the transfer for value rule applies. If the transfer was made pursuant to a property settlement agreement incident to a divorce, then the policy may be considered to have been transferred for value (e.g., in exchange for the release of marital rights). If the transfer between spouses was in the nature of a gift, then no loss of the exemption would result. *ASRS, Sec. 52, ¶900.3.*

DIVORCE

280. If, in connection with a divorce settlement, an individual transfers an existing life insurance policy to or purchases a policy for his former spouse what are the income tax results?

2006 Tax Facts on Insurance & Employee Benefits

305

IRC Section 1041 Transfer of Policy

Generally, no gain is recognized by the transferor if an existing policy is transferred to a spouse, or former spouse incident to a divorce, after July 18, 1984 (unless the transfer is pursuant to an instrument in effect on or before such date or the transfer is, under certain circumstances, in trust).

When no gain is recognized, the transferee will be treated as having acquired the policy by gift and the transferor's cost basis for the policy (net premiums paid) is carried over to the transferee. IRC Sec. 1041. In addition, any such transfer of an existing policy will not cause the proceeds to be includable in the income of the transferee under the transfer for value rule. See Q 279. A transfer is incident to a divorce if the transfer occurs within one year after the date the marriage ceases or is related to the cessation of the marriage. Temp. Treas. Reg. §1.1041-1T, A-6. A transfer of a policy is treated as related to the cessation of the marriage if the transfer is pursuant to a divorce or separation instrument (see Q 808) and the transfer occurs not more than six years after the date on which the marriage ceases. Temp. Treas. Reg. §1.1041-1T, A-7.

However, if property is transferred in trust for the benefit of the spouse, or former spouse, gain will be recognized by the transferor to the extent that the sum of the liabilities assumed, plus the amount of liabilities to which the property is subject, exceeds the total of the adjusted basis of all property transferred. Therefore, where a policy with a loan is transferred in trust, gain will be recognized to the extent the total liabilities of all property transferred to the trust exceed the total basis of all items of property transferred. Where gain is recognized on a transfer in trust, the transferee's basis is adjusted to reflect the amount of gain recognized by the transferor. According to the General Explanation, payments from an insurance trust to which the property is transferred for the benefit of a spouse or former spouse will be taxed to the spouse or former spouse as a beneficiary and not taxed as alimony. General Explanation of the Deficit Reduction Act of 1984, at p. 711.

Both spouses or both former spouses may elect to have these rules apply to all transfers after 1983 and may also elect to have these rules apply to transfers after July 18, 1984 under divorce or separation instruments in effect before July 19, 1984.

Other Transfer of Policy

If an existing policy is transferred before July 19, 1984 or after July 18, 1984 but pursuant to an instrument in effect prior to such date (and no election is made to have the IRC Section 1041 nonrecognition rules apply), then the following rules apply.

If the fair market value of the policy at the time of transfer exceeds the transferor's cost basis for the policy (net premiums paid), the transferor may have some taxable gain. (For fair market value, see Q 303.) In *Comm. v. Davis*, 370 U.S. 65 (1962), the U.S. Supreme Court held that a transfer of property by a husband in exchange for his wife's relinquishment of her marital rights is a taxable exchange, and the value of the marital rights exchanged is equal to the fair market value of the property at time of transfer. The *Davis* rule apparently would apply to such a transfer involving a life insurance policy.

The value of the policy transferred would not be taxable to the transferee and would not be deductible by the transferor. *Ashcraft v. Comm.*, 252 F.2d 200 (7th Cir. 1958), aff'g 28 TC 356 (1957). The same results would follow if a spouse purchased a single

LIFE INSURANCE

Q 281

premium policy for his former spouse pursuant to the divorce settlement. *Morrison v. Comm.*, TC Memo 1956. These values are not taxable to the recipient and deductible by the payor because they represent single sum payments rather than periodic payments of alimony.

Transfer of an existing policy can result in adverse tax consequences to the former spouse. If the policy is assigned to the former spouse, the proceeds are received as life insurance proceeds and not as alimony income. However, it would seem that the former spouse is a purchaser for value and, consequently, the proceeds would be subject to the transfer for value rule (see Q 277, Q 279). See *Comm. v. Davis*, supra. Hence, the profit (the excess of the proceeds over the value of the contract on the date of transfer plus all premiums and certain other amounts paid thereafter) would be taxable to the former spouse as ordinary income. IRC Sec. 101(a)(2).

Policy Owned by Former Spouse

If the policy is not transferred but the former spouse is required, under the divorce decree or agreement, to own and maintain a policy as security for post-death payments, installment payments of the proceeds would be taxable as alimony to the recipient spouse. Payments from an insurance trust that is established to discharge post-death obligations are fully taxable to the recipient spouse. IRC Sec. 71; IRC Sec. 682; Treas. Regs. §§1.71-1(c)(2), 1.101-5. *ASRS, Sec. 52, ¶900.3*.

281. If an individual is required by a court decree or separation agreement to pay premiums on a life insurance policy for his former spouse, are the premiums taxable income to the recipient spouse? Are they deductible by the payor spouse?

Premiums Paid Pursuant to Instruments Executed After 1984

Assuming that all the other alimony requirements are met (see Q 808), premiums paid by the payor spouse for term or whole life insurance on his life pursuant to a divorce or separation instrument executed after December 31, 1984 will qualify as alimony payments on behalf of the recipient spouse to the extent that the recipient spouse is the owner of the policy. Temp. Treas. Reg. §1.71-1T, A-6. Premium payments that qualify as alimony payments are generally deductible by the payor spouse. See IRC Sec. 215.

Premiums Paid Pursuant to Instruments Executed Before 1985

If an existing policy is absolutely assigned to a recipient spouse, or a new policy that gives full ownership rights is purchased for the recipient spouse, the premiums are includable in the recipient spouse's gross income and are deductible by the spouse who assigned or purchased the policy. *See, e.g. Carmichael v. Comm.*, 14 TC 1356 (1950); Rev. Rul. 70-218, 1970-1 CB 19. This is the result even though, under the terms of the decree or agreement, (1) the payor's obligation to pay premiums will cease upon the remarriage of the recipient spouse (*Hyde v. Comm.*, 301 F.2d 279 (2nd Cir. 1962)), or (2) the recipient spouse's rights in the insurance terminate if he does not survive the payor spouse, or (3) the recipient spouse's exercise of ownership rights is subject to the approval of the divorce court (*Stevens v. Comm.*, 439 F.2d 69 (2nd Cir. 1971)).

But if the payor spouse retains ownership rights in the policy, or if the recipient spouse's interest is contingent (as where the policy itself or the right to name the beneficiary will revert to the payor upon the recipient spouse's death or remarriage), the premiums are not taxable to the recipient spouse and are not deductible by the payor. See e.g. *Kiesling v. Comm.*, 349 F.2d 110 (3rd Cir. 1965); *Sperling v. Comm.*, TC Memo 1982-681.

It is not sufficient that the decree or agreement requires that the recipient spouse is to remain primary beneficiary; the payor spouse must give up all ownership and control. Rev. Rul. 57-125, 1957-1 CB 27; *Greenway v. Comm.*, TC Memo 1980-97. However, a voluntary assignment not required by the decree or agreement is not sufficient. *Cole v. U.S.*, 76-1 USTC ¶9256 (E.D. Ill. 1975). Payments are not deductible alimony taxable to a recipient spouse where a policy is assigned to a trust that confers only a lifetime interest and the children are remaindermen. *Kinney v. Comm.*, TC Memo 1958-209. Where the policy is placed in escrow merely as security for the payor's obligation to pay alimony it is clear, under the foregoing rules, that the premiums are not taxable to the recipient nor deductible by the payor. *Ardner v. Comm.*, 191 F.2d 857 (6th Cir. 1957); *Blumenthal v. Comm.*, 183 F.2d 15 (3rd Cir. 1950).

The Tax Court has held that even though a policy is assigned absolutely to the recipient spouse and the payor spouse is required to pay premiums, if the policy is *term* insurance, the premiums are neither includable in the recipient's income nor deductible by the payor. *Brodersen v. Comm.*, 57 TC 412 (1971). The result is the same even where the term policy has a conversion privilege, if the recipient would have to pay the additional premium on conversion. *Wright v. Comm.*, 62 TC 377 (1974), aff'd 76-2 USTC ¶9736 (7th Cir. 1976).

Similarly, a payor spouse's policy loan repayments required by a separation agreement are not taxable to the recipient spouse, nor deductible by the payor, where the payor retains ownership of the policy and the recipient is irrevocable beneficiary only until death or remarriage. *Auerbach v. Comm.*, TC Memo 1975-219.

The payor spouse's deduction, provided by IRC Section 215, is based upon the inclusion of the same item in the recipient's gross income under IRC Section 71 (see Q 808). *Mandel v. Comm.*, 229 F.2d 382 (7th Cir. 1956). *ASRS, Sec. 52, ¶900.4.*

CHARITABLE GIFTS

282. May a charitable contribution deduction be taken for the gift of a life insurance policy or premium? For the gift of a maturing annuity or endowment contract?

Yes, subject to the limits on deductions for gifts to charities (see Q 824).

The amount of any charitable contribution must be reduced by the amount of gain that would have represented ordinary income to the donor had he sold the property at its fair market value. IRC Sec. 170(e)(1)(A). Gain realized from the sale of a life insurance contract is taxed to the seller as ordinary income (see Q 261). Therefore, the deduction for a gift of a life insurance policy to a charity is restricted to the donor's cost basis in the contract when the value of the contract exceeds the premium payments. Thus, if a policyowner assigns the policy itself to a qualified charity, or to a trustee with a charity as irrevocable beneficiary, the amount deductible as a charitable contribution is either the value of the policy or the policyowner's cost basis, whichever is less. See *Behrend v.*

LIFE INSURANCE   Q 283

Comm., 23 BTA 1037 (1931), *acq.* X-2 CB 5; *Tuttle v. U.S.*, 350 F. Supp. 484 (1969). (See Q 303.) However, it is not necessary to reduce the amount of the contribution where, by reason of the transfer, ordinary income is recognized by the donor in the same taxable year in which the contribution is made. Treas. Reg. §1.170A-4(a). Letter Ruling 9110016, which denied a charitable deduction where a policy was assigned to a charity that had no insurable interest under state law, was revoked after the taxpayer decided to not proceed with the transaction. Let. Rul. 9147040.

Premium payments are also deductible charitable contributions if a charitable organization or a trustee of an irrevocable charitable trust owns the policy. *Hunton v. Comm.*, 1 TC 821 (1943); *Behrend v. Comm.*, 23 BTA 1037 (1931); Let. Ruls. 8708083, 8304068. It is not settled whether premium payments made by the donor to the *insurer* to maintain a policy given to the charity, instead of making cash payments directly to the *charity* in the amount of the premiums, are gifts *to* the charity or merely gifts *for the use* of the charity. The difference is important when the donor wishes to take a charitable deduction of more than 30% of his adjusted gross income—see Q 824. Where the policy is merely assigned to a charitable organization as security for a note, the premiums are not deductible even though the note is equal to the face value of the policy and is payable from the proceeds at either insured's death or maturity of the policy. The reason is that the note could be paid off and the policy recovered after the insured has obtained charitable deductions for the premium payments. A corporation, as well as an individual, can take a charitable contribution deduction for payment of premiums on a policy that has been assigned to a charitable organization. Rev. Rul. 58-372, 1958-2 CB 99. *ASRS, Sec. 52, ¶1000.*

283. May a charitable contribution deduction be taken for a gift of an interest in a split dollar arrangement?

Applicable to transfers made after February 8, 1999, no deduction is allowed for a transfer to a charitable organization if in connection with the transfer the charitable organization directly or indirectly pays, or has previously paid, any premium on any "personal benefit contract" with respect to the transferor. Further, no deduction is allowed if there is an understanding or expectation that any person will directly or indirectly pay any premium on a personal benefit contract with respect to the transferor. IRC Sec. 170(f)(10)(A).

A personal benefit contract is any life insurance, annuity, or endowment contract if a direct or indirect beneficiary under the contract is the transferor, a member of the transferor's family or any other person (other than certain charitable organizations) designated by the transferor. IRC Sec. 170(f)(10)(B).

In a case decided under rules in effect before 1999, a charitable deduction was not allowed where the charity provided a receipt stating that the donors received no benefit from their charitable contribution. The court held that in fact the donors were receiving a benefit under the charitable split dollar arrangement. *Addis v. Comm.*, 2004-2 USTC ¶50,291 (9th Cir. 2004).

There are exceptions to the disallowance rule for certain transfers involving charitable gift annuity contracts (see Q 43) and charitable remainder trusts (see Q 825). IRC Secs. 170(f)(10)(D), 170(f)(10)(E). See Q 824 for a general discussion of income tax deductions for charitable giving; see Q 865 for a general discussion of estate tax deductions for charitable giving.

A charitable organization that pays premiums after December 17, 1999, on a life insurance, annuity, or endowment contract in connection with a transfer for which a charitable deduction was not allowable is subject to a penalty tax equal to the amount of premiums paid. IRC Sec. 170(f)(10)(F). The IRS has indicated that other penalties may be imposed on charitable organizations involved in charitable split dollar plans. Notice 99-36, 1999-2 CB 1284.

In a ruling involving a paid-up policy, the IRS took the position that no deduction will be allowed for gifts made after July 31, 1969 involving a split dollar plan in which the donor gives a charity the cash surrender value and a noncharitable beneficiary the balance. A gift of the cash surrender value is considered a gift of less than an entire interest in the property whether the donor retains the right to designate the beneficiary of the risk portion or irrevocably designates the beneficiary prior to making the gift. Rev. Rul. 76-143, 1976-1 CB 63. Two 1969 revenue rulings, which allow a deduction, apply only to gifts made on or before July 31, 1969. Rev. Rul. 69-79, 1969-1 CB 63; Rev. Rul. 69-215, 1969-1 CB 63. *ASRS, Sec. 52, ¶1000.6.*

284. May a charitable contribution deduction be taken for a gift of a life insurance policy if the donor retains a right, shared with the donee charity, to change charitable beneficiaries?

While the Code generally disallows a charitable deduction for gifts of less than the donor's entire interest in property, it does permit limited exceptions to this rule. One of these is a gift of an "undivided interest" in property. This means that the donor may give less than his entire interest and still take a charitable gift deduction if he gives "a fraction or percentage of each and every substantial interest or right" he owns in the property. IRC Sec. 170(f)(3)(B)(ii); Treas. Reg. §1.170A-7(b)(1)(i).

In a letter ruling, the IRS took the position that a gift of a life insurance policy to a charity was deductible even though the donor retained the right, exercisable in conjunction with the donee charity, to change the charitable beneficiaries. The IRS reasoned that by sharing the right to change charitable beneficiaries, the donor had given an undivided interest in the right he retained and thus the gift came within the exception to the rule against deducting partial interest gifts. Let. Rul. 8030043. *ASRS, Sec. 52, ¶1000.6.*

285. May a charitable contribution deduction be taken for a gift of the annuity portion of a split life contract?

The IRS has ruled that a gift to charity of the annuity portion of a split life contract is not deductible because it is a gift of less than the donor's entire interest in property. See IRC Sec. 170(f)(3). The IRS reasoned that the donor, prior to making the gift, exercised the right to purchase the annual term insurance and, thus, he had retained a right in the property. Furthermore, his subsequent annual cash contributions equal to the annuity premiums were treated by IRS as given in exchange for the charity's continued election to allow the donor to renew the term life insurance. Thus, he continued to retain the right to purchase the annual term insurance. Because he retained a right, his gift of the annuity portion was of less than his entire interest in the property. Rev. Rul. 76-1, 1976-1 CB 57. The ruling did not clearly deal with the deduction of the annual cash contributions and some commentators believe they might be deductible. However, the reasoning of the IRS (that the annual contributions were in exchange for the continued

LIFE INSURANCE   Q 287

right to renew the term insurance) suggests that the donor's entire interest in the cash contributions was not given. *ASRS, Sec. 52, ¶1000.6.*

SINGLE PREMIUM WHOLE LIFE INSURANCE POLICY

286. How is a single premium life insurance policy, including a single premium variable life insurance policy, taxed?

For income tax purposes, a single premium life insurance policy is generally treated in the same manner as a multiple-premium life insurance policy. For all life insurance policies that meet the definition of life insurance (see Q 273), cash surrender value increases are generally not taxed until received (see Q 247) and death proceeds are generally received income tax free (see Q 271).

The tax treatment of policy loans depends on whether the policy is treated as a modified endowment contract. Policies entered into on or after June 21, 1988, that do not meet the seven pay test of IRC Section 7702A(b) are classified as modified endowment contracts. Loans from modified endowment contracts are taxable as income at the time received to the extent that the cash value of the contract immediately before the payment exceeds the investment in the contract. IRC Sec. 72(e). These distributions may also be subject to a penalty tax of 10%. IRC Sec. 72(v). See Q 250 for a detailed explanation.

Generally, life insurance policies, including single premium policies, issued prior to June 21, 1988, are grandfathered and not subject to the seven pay test. Loans from these policies will not be treated as taxable income. Loans from policies that are not grandfathered but that meet the requirements of the seven pay test are also not treated as taxable income. (However, any outstanding loan becomes taxable income at the time of policy surrender or lapse to the extent that the loan exceeds the owner's basis in the contract. See Q 249.) If the policy death proceeds are tax free, the amount of the loan is not taxed; it is treated as part of the tax free death proceeds (see Q 273). Note that a grandfathered policy may lose its grandfathered status if it undergoes a material change in its terms or benefits or is exchanged for another life insurance policy under IRC Section 1035. See Q 250.

CREDITOR INSURANCE

Premiums

287. If a debtor pays premiums on a life insurance policy on his life in favor of his creditor, may he take an income tax deduction for his premium payments?

No, regardless of whether he takes out a new policy for the benefit of the creditor or assigns an existing policy to him. The deduction will be denied even though the debtor was required to take out the policy to obtain the loan. If the debt is personal, the premiums are nondeductible personal expenses. IRC Sec. 262. If the debt is a business debt, the deduction is denied under IRC Section 264(a)(1). IRC Section 264(a)(1) provides that no deduction will be allowed for premiums on any life insurance policy, or endowment or annuity contract, if the taxpayer is directly or indirectly a beneficiary under the policy or contract. For this purpose, the insured debtor is at least indirectly a

Q 288 FEDERAL INCOME TAX

beneficiary under the policy since the proceeds may be used to satisfy his debt. *Glassner v. Comm.*, 17 AFTR 2d 651 (3rd Cir.), *cert. denied*, 385 U.S. 819 (1966); *Klein v. Comm.*, 84 F.2d 310 (7th Cir. 1936); *Rieck v. Heiner*, 25 F.2d 453 (3rd Cir. 1928); *O'Donohue v. Comm.*, 33 TC 698 (1960); *Barron v. Comm.*, 14 BTA 1022 (1929); *Lynch v. Comm.*, BTA Memo 1941; *Hanson v. Comm.*, TC Memo 1970-15; Rev. Rul. 68-5, 1968-1 CB 99. IRC Section 264(a)(1) also acts as a bar to a nonbusiness deduction. The deduction was denied for premiums the taxpayer paid on insurance used as collateral for a bank loan to a company in which he was a major stockholder; the premiums were paid to protect his personal securities which were also part of the collateral for the loan. *Carbine v. Comm.*, 85-2 USTC ¶9854 (11th Cir. 1985).

The deduction is disallowed even where the premium payer is merely a guarantor and therefore only secondarily liable for the debt. *Carbine v. Comm.*, supra; *Jefferson v. Helvering*, 121 F.2d 16 (D.C. Cir. 1941); *D'Angelo Assoc., Inc. v. Comm.*, 70 TC 121 (1978), acq. in result, 1979-1 CB 1. *ASRS, Sec. 52*, ¶800.2.

288. Can a creditor deduct premiums he pays on life insurance he purchases on the life of his debtor?

Based on the reasoning of the cases cited in Q 290, it appears unlikely that the creditor can secure a nonbusiness expense deduction. Moreover, where proceeds are receivable as tax-exempt life insurance proceeds, it would appear that deduction of the premiums is prohibited by IRC Section 265(a)(1). (See Q 60.) If the debtor is directly or indirectly a beneficiary under the policy the deduction is prohibited by IRC Section 264(a)(1). (See Q 45.) The IRS has allowed a business expense deduction for premiums paid by a taxpayer in the business of selling property, for 1-year term insurance purchased on the lives of installment purchasers, where no separate charge was made for the insurance, and where the death proceeds (payable to seller) were in the amount of the unpaid balance of the purchase price. Proceeds receivable by the seller were treated as collections on the purchase price, *not* as life insurance proceeds excludable under IRC Section 101(a). Rev. Rul. 70-254, 1970-1 CB 31. *ASRS, Sec. 52,* ¶¶*800.3, 800.4.*

289. If a creditor pays premiums on a life insurance policy held as collateral security for a business debt, can the creditor claim an income tax deduction for the premium payments?

The IRS takes the position that the creditor cannot claim a deduction unless he shows that his right to reimbursement for the premium payment is worthless in the year of payment. Thus, if the creditor has a right to proceed against the debtor for reimbursement, the debtor must be insolvent or the claim must be otherwise uncollectible. If he has a right, express or implied, to reimbursement from the policy, the cash surrender value must be insufficient to cover the balance of the unpaid debt and the premium payment. If he has both rights, both must be worthless. Rev. Rul. 75-46, 1975-1 CB 55. Premiums that are not deductible are treated as additional advances that increase the debt.

The courts, however, have allowed the deduction without regard to the taxpayer's ability to recover the premium out of the cash surrender value of the policies. *Comm. v. Charleston Nat'l Bank*, 20 TC 253 (1953) aff'd 213 F.2d 45 (4th Cir. 1954); *First Nat'l Bank & Trust Co. v. Jones*, 143 F.2d 652 (10th Cir. 1944); *Federal Nat'l Bank v. Comm.*, 16 TC 54 (1951); *Dominion Nat'l Bank v. Comm.*, 26 BTA 421 (1932), acq.

The Service would disallow a deduction for the premium payment if the creditor has taken a bad debt deduction for the debt, and the cash surrender value of the policy is sufficient to provide reimbursement for the premium payment. But in *Charleston Nat'l Bank*, supra, the court held that the premium payment was deductible even though the creditor had taken a bad debt deduction for the debt and the cash surrender value exceeded the current premium and premium payments not deducted in prior years.

The deduction is allowable not as a bad debt but as an ordinary and necessary business expense, incident to the protection of the collateral. *First Nat'l Bank & Trust Co. v. Jones*, supra; *Blumenthal v. Comm.*, TC Memo 1963-269, aff'd 14 AFTR 2d 5094 (4th Cir. 1964); *Lock Moore & Co., Ltd. v. Comm.*, 7 BTA 1008 (1927); *Dominion Nat'l Bank v. Comm.*, supra. See also Rev. Rul. 75-46, above.

If premiums that have been deducted are later recovered from the proceeds, the recovery must be reported as taxable income. But if the premiums have not been deducted, the recovery will be tax free. *St. Louis Refrigerating & Cold Storage Co. v. U.S.*, 162 F.2d 394 (8th Cir. 1947); *First Nat'l Bank v. Comm.*, TC Memo 1943. *ASRS, Sec. 52, ¶¶800.3, 800.4.*

290. If a creditor pays premiums on a life insurance policy securing a non-business debt, can he deduct the premium payments?

The deduction has been denied on the ground that the premium payments are a capital investment rather than expenses incurred "for the production or collection of income, or for the management, conservation and maintenance of property held for the production of income." *U.S. v. Mellinger*, 228 F.2d 688 (5th Cir. 1956); *Est. of Hall v. Comm.*, 17 TC 20 (1951); *Home News Publishing Co. v. Comm.*, TC Memo 1969-167; see also *Blumenthal v. Comm.*, TC Memo 1963-269, aff'd 14 AFTR 2d 5094 (4th Cir. 1964); *Leslie v. Comm.*, 6 TC 488 (1946); *Whitaker v. Comm.*, 34 TC 106 (1960). *ASRS, Sec. 52, ¶800.4.*

291. If a stockholder's personal life insurance is used as collateral security for the corporation's debt, are the premiums deductible?

If the insured stockholder pays the premiums, he is denied a deduction on the ground that the premium payments are not an ordinary and necessary expense of carrying on his (the stockholder's) business. *Morison v. Comm.*, TC Memo 1960-243. If the corporation pays the premiums, they are nondeductible under IRC Section 264(a)(1) because the corporation is indirectly a beneficiary under the policy. See *Peerless Pattern Co. v. Comm.*, 29 BTA 767 (1934); *Hewitt Grain & Provision Co. v. Comm.*, 14 BTA 281 (1928); *Williamson Veneer Co. v. Comm.*, 10 BTA 1259 (1928); *Joy Floral Co. v. Comm.*, 7 BTA 800 (1927); *Favorite Panama Hat Co. v. Comm.*, TC Memo 1943; Rev. Rul. 68-5, 1968-1 CB 99. *ASRS, Sec. 52, ¶800.8.*

Bad Debt Deduction

292. May a creditor take a bad debt deduction for a worthless debt even though he holds, as collateral security, an insurance policy on the life of the debtor?

Yes, provided the cash surrender value of the policy is less than the debt. He may deduct the difference between the cash surrender value and the debt or, if the policy has no cash surrender value, he may deduct the full amount of the worthless debt. He may take the deduction even though he continues to hold the policy, and the face of the policy exceeds the debt. Collateral security need not be liquidated to establish the worthless portion of the debt. *Dominion Nat'l Bank v. Comm.*, 26 BTA 421 (1932), acq.; *Hatboro Nat'l Bank v. Comm.*, 24 TC 786 (1955); *Northern Nat'l Bank v. Comm.*, 16 BTA 608 (1929), acq.; *Hart-Wood Lumber Co. v. Comm.*, 5 BTA 1171 (1927), acq.; *Citizens Trust Co. v. Comm.*, 2 BTA 1239 (1925); see *Ross v. Comm.*, 72 F.2d 122 (7th Cir. 1934). If a deduction was not previously taken, a deduction for the uncollectible balance may be taken in the year the creditor surrenders the policy. *Mattlage v. Comm.*, 3 BTA 242 (1925). However, no bad debt deduction will be allowed at any time for advances that were made when prior loans exceeded the face of the policy and the debtor was insolvent. *Blumenthal v. Comm.*, TC Memo 1963-269, *aff'd* 14 AFTR 2d 5094 (4th Cir. 1964). *ASRS, Sec. 52, ¶800.1.*

Proceeds

293. Are the proceeds received by a creditor from insurance he purchased on the life of his debtor exempt from income tax as life insurance proceeds?

If the creditor has an insurable interest other than as creditor (e.g., debtor is also a key person) and has the unconditional right to retain proceeds unaffected by the size of the debt, the proceeds are received tax free. *Thomsen & Sons, Inc. v. U.S.*, 73-2 USTC ¶9637 (7th Cir. 1973); *Harrison v. Comm.*, 59 TC 578 (1973), acq. 1973-2 CB 2.

In some states, a creditor's insurable interest in his debtor is limited to indemnification of the amount of debt (plus premiums he has paid) as of the insured's death. Any excess the creditor must hold for the debtor's estate. Where this is so it would appear, based on the reasoning of Rev. Rul. 70-254 and the *Landfield* case (see Q 294), that the proceeds would not be considered to have been paid by reason of the insured's death, and therefore would not be exempt as life insurance proceeds under IRC Section 101(a).

However, courts in other states have held that where the creditor initiates the purchase of insurance and pays the premiums, if the amount of the insurance is reasonably proportionate to the amount of the debt and if the debtor consents to the insurance, the creditor's insurable interest, or right of recovery, goes to the full proceeds, not just to the amount of debt, expenses and interest. Thus, even if the debtor has paid the debt before his death, the creditor is entitled to the full proceeds. Under this view, it would appear that the proceeds would be received "by reason of the death of the insured" and should therefore be entitled to the exemption of IRC Section 101(a). If the proceeds are receivable as tax-exempt life insurance proceeds, it would appear that deduction of the premiums would be denied by reason of IRC Section 265(a)(1). IRC Section 265(a)(1) provides that expenses incurred for acquiring tax-exempt income are not deductible. *ASRS, Sec. 52, ¶800.7.*

294. Are life insurance proceeds received by a creditor as collateral assignee or beneficiary "as interest appears" exempt from income tax?

If the creditor is collateral assignee, he receives the proceeds as a recovery on the collateral and not as life insurance proceeds. Treas. Reg. §1.101-1(b)(4). Consequently, if the creditor has not taken a bad debt deduction, the proceeds are received by him tax-free as a return of capital. They are tax-free, that is, to the extent of the unpaid debt and any premiums the creditor has paid but not deducted (see Q 290, Q 291). But if the creditor has received the tax benefit of a bad debt deduction, the proceeds must be reported as taxable income (except to the extent they represent a recovery of premium payments for which no deduction has been taken). If a portion of the proceeds represents interest on the debt, that portion is taxed as ordinary income to the creditor. *St. Louis Refrigerating & Cold Storage Co. v. U.S.*, 162 F.2d 394 (8th Cir. 1947); *First Nat'l Bank v. Comm.*, TC Memo 1943.

If the creditor is named beneficiary "as his interest might appear" on a policy owned by the debtor, the creditor receives the proceeds as payment of the debt and not as life insurance proceeds. Since the creditor must prove the debt to collect the proceeds, the proceeds are received because of the insured's indebtedness rather than "by reason of the death of the insured," and hence are not exempt under IRC Section 101(a). The proceeds therefore constitute taxable income to the creditor to the same extent that direct repayment of the loan would have resulted in income. This is so, regardless of whether the debtor or the creditor has paid the premiums. *Landfield Fin. Co. v. U.S.*, 24 AFTR 2d 69-5744 (7th Cir. 1969); *McCamant v. Comm.*, 32 TC 824 (1959); Rev. Rul. 70-254, 1970-1 CB 31.

A different situation arises if the creditor takes title to the insurance policy and releases the debtor from further obligation. Under these circumstances, the proceeds are received as life insurance proceeds, but a transfer for value has taken place (see Q 63). As a result, the proceeds are taxable income to the creditor to the extent that they exceed the value of the policy at time of transfer and premiums and certain other amounts (see Q 63) paid after the transfer. *Federal Nat'l Bank v. Comm.*, 16 TC 54 (1951). But there should be no tax liability under the transfer for value rule if the creditor is a partner of the insured, a partnership in which the insured is a partner, or a corporation in which the insured is an officer or stockholder. IRC Sec. 101(a)(2)(B). *ASRS, Sec. 52, ¶800.5.*

GOVERNMENT LIFE INSURANCE

295. Are the proceeds of government life insurance exempt from income tax?

Yes. The entire death proceeds are exempt, including the interest element in installment settlements. Likewise, any gain realized on lifetime proceeds from matured endowments or surrender of policies is exempt from income tax. Dividends are also exempt from income tax. 38 U.S.C. §5301(a); Rev. Rul. 71-306, 1971-2 CB 76. The interest on accumulated dividends is not taxable. Rev. Rul. 91-14, 1991-1 CB 18. Accumulated dividends applied to the purchase of additional National Service Life Insurance and the additional paid-up insurance acquired are not subject to federal income tax. Rev. Rul. 72-604, 1972-2 CB 35. *ASRS, Sec. 52, ¶1200.*

COLLECTION OF DELINQUENT INCOME TAXES FROM LIFE INSURANCE

296. Can the federal government reach the cash values of a taxpayer's life insurance for collection of his back income taxes?

Yes. The law is well settled that the state exemption laws cannot immunize the cash values of a taxpayer's life insurance from federal tax collection. Moreover, the government can enforce its tax lien despite a gratuitous assignment of the policy with intent to avoid tax collection. *Knox v. Great West Life Assurance Co.*, 212 F.2d 784 (6th Cir. 1954); *U.S. v. Heffron*, 158 F.2d 657 (9th Cir. 1947).

Under a summary levy procedure, IRS may reach the *loan value* of a policy subject to a tax lien, but the policy may be kept in force. IRC Sec. 6321. The insurance company pays over the present loan value of the policy or, if less, the balance of the tax liability. The company must also pay IRS the amount of any policy loans (other than automatic premium loans) made after the company had notice of the lien. The company is not liable, however, for policy loans made before it had notice of the lien, or for automatic premium loans made after it had notice if the automatic premium loan agreement was entered into before it had notice. IRC Sec. 6323(b)(9).

The statute says the tax levy is satisfied if the insurer pays over "the amount which the person against whom the tax is assessed could have had advanced to him" by the insurer *on the date prescribed in the statute for the satisfaction of the levy* (plus any amounts advanced by the insurer after knowledge of the lien other than under a preexisting automatic premium loan provision in the policy). IRC Sec. 6332(b).

The IRS can reach funds in an annuity contract under the same summary levy procedure mentioned above. IRC Sec. 6321; See *Prudential Ins. Co. v. Allen*, 98-1 USTC ¶50365 (S.D. Ind. 1998). Further, the IRS can reach insurance commission payments with a tax lien also. Where several life insurance agents assigned their commissions to another agent and that agent, in turn, assigned the funds to an irrevocable trust, the IRS was able to reach the commissions to satisfy a tax lien against several of the agents. *American Trust v. American Community Mut. Ins. Co.*, 98-1 USTC ¶50369 (6th Cir. 1998). *ASRS, Sec. 13, ¶100.13(a).*

297. Can the federal government collect the insured's delinquent income taxes from a beneficiary who receives life insurance death proceeds?

The government's tax lien survives the insured's death. Consequently, if a tax lien has attached to the cash surrender value during the insured's life, the taxes can be collected from the proceeds to the extent of the cash surrender value at death. But if life insurance proceeds are exempt from the claims of insured's creditors under applicable *state* law, the insured's unpaid taxes cannot be collected from that portion of the proceeds that exceeds the cash surrender value. *U.S. v. Bess*, 357 U.S. 51 (1958). If the tax assessment was not made until *after* insured's death, the beneficiary is not liable for any of the insured's back taxes provided the proceeds are exempt from claims of insured's creditors under state law. *Comm. v. Stern*, 357 U.S. 39 (1958).

A different situation exists where the beneficiary is a surviving spouse who has filed joint returns with the insured. Where joint returns have been filed, the surviving spouse is generally liable for the back taxes in his or her own right. IRC Sec. 6013(d)(3). Thus, the entire proceeds received by the surviving spouse may be subject to a lien for the unpaid taxes. Where a wife who was the beneficiary of a policy insuring her husband's life had been indicted but not yet convicted of his murder at the time the IRS served a levy on the policy proceeds, the court found that, under applicable state law, the wife had a property interest in the proceeds and thus the insurance company acted properly in paying the proceeds to the IRS in response to the levy. *State Farm v. Howell*, 96-1 USTC ¶50092 (8th Cir. 1996). Where a surviving spouse used the proceeds of a policy

LIFE INSURANCE   Q 301

insuring the deceased spouse to purchase annuities for the benefit of their children, the IRS was able to reach the funds, in payment of the couple's delinquent income taxes, after the annuity purchase. *Flake v. U.S.*, 95-2 USTC ¶50588 (D. Ariz. 1995). Where a wife received two death benefit checks from policies insuring her husband's life, placed the checks in a safe deposit box, and then attempted to renounce her interest in the death proceeds under state law after the IRS seized the checks for payment of taxes, a district court granted the government's motion for summary judgment saying that the wife had accepted the proceeds which were subject to IRS lien. *Federated Life Ins. Co. v. Simmons*, 97-2 USTC ¶50490 (N.D. Ga. 1997). *ASRS, Sec. 13, ¶100.13(b)*.

DISABILITY PROVISIONS UNDER LIFE POLICIES

298. Are premiums paid for disability provisions under a life insurance policy deductible as medical expenses?

No. IRC Sec. 213(d)(1). *ASRS, Sec. 52, ¶600.1.*

299. Is disability income payable under the provisions of a personal life insurance policy exempt from income tax?

Yes, benefits received under a disability rider are tax-exempt as "amounts received through accident or health insurance ... for personal injuries or sickness." There is no limit on the amount of such income that can be received tax-free. IRC Sec. 104(a)(3). Benefits are exempt whether received by the insured, or by a person having an insurable interest in the insured. *Castner Garage, Ltd. v. Comm.*, 43 BTA 1 (1940), acq. *ASRS, Sec. 52, ¶600.2.*

300. Are life insurance premiums that have been waived because of the insured's disability taxable income to the insured?

No. When waived, the premiums should be exempt as "amounts received through accident or health insurance ... for personal injuries or sickness." IRC Sec. 104(a)(3). However, the Tax Court seems to have indicated that they are not constructively received by the insured. Although not directly addressed in the case, apparently the waived premiums would not be taxable to the insured since they were not constructively received by the insured. *Est. of Wong Wing Non v. Comm.*, 18 TC 205 (1952).

Note that since premiums paid for a supplementary benefit such as waiver of premium must be excluded from premium cost (see Q 8), a policy on which premiums have been waived for a period of years may generate a greater amount of taxable income or generate taxable income at an earlier date than a similar policy where the same premiums have been paid by the taxpayer. This would be so because a policy where premiums have been waived would have a lower cost basis than a similar policy where the taxpayer paid the premiums. *ASRS, Sec. 52, ¶600.4.*

301. If a corporation attaches a disability income rider to a key person life insurance policy, what are the tax consequences to the corporation and to the key person?

Where the employee is designated payee of the disability income, results are uncertain. However, it would seem that the disability rider should be treated as accident and health insurance, separable from the life insurance, and that the results would be as follows:

the corporation could deduct, as business expenses, the premiums paid for the disability income coverage (IRC Sec. 162(a)); the premiums would not be taxable to the key person (IRC Sec. 106(a)); and the disability income would be taxable to the key person (IRC Sec. 104(a)(3)). A tax credit may be available to the key person. See Q 833.

If the disability income is payable to the corporation, the corporation cannot deduct the premium payments (IRC Sec. 265(a)(1)), but the disability income is tax-exempt to the corporation. IRC Sec. 104(a)(3); *Castner Garage, Ltd. v. Comm.*, 43 BTA 1 (1940), acq.; *Rugby Prod. Ltd. v. Comm.*, 100 TC 531 (1993); Rev. Rul. 66-262, 1966-2 CB 105. If the corporation uses the disability income to make disability retirement payments to the key person, it would seem that the corporation could deduct the payments as compensation expense. The payments would be taxable to the key person (IRC Sec. 104(a)(3)), but he might be eligible for a tax credit. See Q 833. *ASRS, Sec. 52, ¶600.1.*

POLICIES INSURING MORE THAN ONE LIFE

302. Does the income taxation of a life insurance policy that insures more than one life differ from the taxation of a policy that insures a single life?

Basically, no. A life insurance policy that insures more than one life receives the same income tax treatment as a policy that insures only one life. These multiple-life policies may insure two or more lives. Typically, a "first-to-die" or "joint life" policy pays a death benefit at the death of the first insured person to die while a "second-to-die" or "survivorship" policy does not pay a death benefit until the death of the survivor. Estate planning and business continuation planning are two of the more common uses for these types of policies.

Generally, multiple-life policies are subject to the same definition of life insurance applicable to policies insuring a single life. One exception is that for purposes of calculating the net single premium under IRC Section 7702, multiple-life policies may not take advantage of the three safe harbor tests set forth in proposed regulations for meeting the reasonable mortality charge requirement. Prop. Treas. Reg. §1.7702-1(c). See Q 273.

For multiple-life policies that meet the definition of life insurance, cash surrender value increases are generally not taxed until received (see Q 247) and death proceeds are generally received income tax free (see Q 271). Multiple-life policies are subject to the seven pay test of IRC Section 7702A(b) (see Q 250) in the same manner as single life policies. Distributions from life insurance policies entered into before June 21, 1988, or from policies entered into on or after this date that meet the seven pay test are included in gross income only to the extent they exceed the investment in the contract (see Q 249). Policies entered into on or after June 21, 1988, that do not meet the seven pay test become classified as modified endowment contracts. Distributions, including loans, from modified endowment contracts are subject to taxation rules that are generally less favorable than the rules governing the taxation of distributions from life insurance policies that are not modified endowment contracts (see Q 250).

In a private letter ruling, the IRS has concluded that exchanges involving policies insuring a single life for a policy insuring two lives do not qualify for nonrecognition treatment under IRC Section 1035. The Service reached this outcome in five similar fact patterns (see Q 263). Let. Rul. 9542037. However, also in a private ruling, the Service

LIFE INSURANCE   Q 303

has approved IRC Section 1035 treatment of the exchange of a joint and last survivor life insurance policy, following the death of one of the insured persons, for a universal variable life insurance policy that insures the survivor. Let. Rul. 9248013; see also Let. Rul. 9330040. (See, generally, Q 263).

There has been no formal guidance from the IRS as to which rates should be used to measure economic benefit when a multiple-life policy is used in an arrangement that requires the insured(s) to include the economic benefit of the coverage in income. The most frequently used rates have been those derived from U.S. Life Table 38, which is also used to derive the P.S. 58 rates. However, P.S. 58 rates may generally not be used in arrangements entered into after January 27, 2002, but Table 2001 may be used. According to the Service, taxpayers should make appropriate adjustments to the Table 2001 rates if the life insurance protection covers more than one life. Notice 2002-8, 2002-1 CB 398. Where the policy death benefit is payable at the second death, it is generally believed that following the first death, the Table 2001 rates (or P.S. 58 rates, if appropriate) for single lives should be used to measure the survivor's economic benefit. See Appendix C for P.S. 58 and Table 2001 rates.

For estate taxation of policies insuring more than one life, see Q 671. For gift taxation of these policies, see Q 732.

VALUE OF UNMATURED POLICY

303. How is the value of a life insurance policy determined for income tax purposes?

Transfers of property after June 30, 1969, in connection with the performance of services are governed by IRC Section 83. For transfers before February 13, 2004, Treasury Regulation Section 1.83-3(e) provided that, "In the case of a transfer of a life insurance contract, retirement income contract, endowment contract, or other contract providing life insurance protection, only the cash surrender value of the contract is considered to be property."

However, new regulations have recently been issued under IRC Section 83. These regulations change the definition of what constitutes property with regard to a life insurance contract. The new definition treats as property as generally the policy's fair market value (specifically the policy cash value and all other rights under the contract (including any supplemental agreements to the contract, whether or not they are guaranteed), other than current life insurance protection). However, for transfers of life insurance contracts that are part of split dollar arrangements that are NOT subject to the split dollar regulations (see Q 459), only the cash surrender value of the contract is considered property. Treas. Reg. §1.83-3(e). This new definition is effective for any transfer occurring after February 12, 2004.

The Service has provided a safe harbor on how to determine the fair market value of a life insurance contract. Rev. Proc. 2005-25, 2005-17 IRB 962. The fair market value of a life insurance contract may be the greater of either: (1) the interpolated terminal reserve and any unearned premiums, plus a pro rata portion of a reasonable estimate of dividends expected to be paid for that policy year, or (2) the product of the "PERC amount" (PERC stands for premiums, earnings, and reasonable charges) and the applicable "Average Surrender Factor."

The PERC amount for a life insurance contract that is not a variable contract is the aggregate of: (1) the premiums paid on the policy without a reduction for dividends that offset the premiums, plus (2) dividends that are applied to purchase paid-up insurance, plus (3) any other amounts credited, or otherwise made available, to the policyholder, including interest and similar income items, but not including dividends used to offset premiums and dividends used to purchase paid up insurance, minus (4) reasonable mortality charges and other reasonable charges, but only if those charges are actually charged, and those charges are not expected to be refunded, rebated, or otherwise reversed, minus (5) any distributions (including dividends and dividends held on account), withdrawals, or partial surrenders taken prior to the valuation date.

The PERC amount for a variable life contract is the aggregate of: (1) the premiums paid on the policy without a reduction for dividends that offset the premiums, plus (2) dividends that are applied to increase the value of the contract, including dividends used to purchase paid-up insurance, plus or minus (3) all adjustments that reflect the investment return and the market value of the contract's segregated asset accounts, minus (4) reasonable mortality charges and other reasonable charges, but only if those charges are actually charged on or before the valuation date and those charges are not expected to be refunded, rebated, or otherwise reversed, minus (5) any distributions (including dividends and dividends held on account), withdrawals, or partial surrenders taken prior to the valuation date.

The Average Surrender Factor is 1.0 when valuing life insurance contracts for purposes of the rules regarding group-term life (Section 79), property transferred in connection with the performance of services (Section 83), and certain transfers involving deferred compensation arrangements (Section 402(b)). This is because under these rules no adjustment for potential surrender charges is allowed.

The IRS pointed out that the formulas in its safe harbor rules must be interpreted in a reasonable manner, consistent with the purpose of determining the contract's fair market value. Specifically the rules are not allowed to be interpreted in such a way to understate a contract's fair market value.

For transfers of property before July 1, 1969, the IRS ruled that the value of an unmatured policy is determined for income tax purposes in the same manner as for gift tax purposes (see Q 744). Rev. Rul. 59-195, 1959-1 CB 18. In one case the court accepted the value stipulated by the parties in an arm's length agreement. *Gravois Planing Mill v. Comm.*, 9 AFTR 2d 733 (8th Cir. 1962).

LIFE INSURANCE TRUSTS

304. Under what circumstances will a life insurance trust result in income tax savings for the grantor?

Obviously, no income tax saving can be achieved by the creation of an unfunded life insurance trust. The life insurance policy creates no currently taxable income regardless of whether it is placed in trust. Income tax saving can result only where income-producing property is placed in trust to fund the premium payments, and only if tax liability is shifted from the grantor to a lower bracket taxpayer—that is, to the trust or to a trust beneficiary.

LIFE INSURANCE

Q 305

A funded revocable trust will not result in income tax saving. If the trust is revocable, the income from the funding property will be taxed to the grantor. But even if the trust is irrevocable, there are other conditions that will cause the trust income to be taxed to the grantor.

Generally speaking, trust income is taxable to the grantor: (1) if the grantor or trustee, or both, can revoke the trust without the beneficiary's consent; (2) if the trust income is, or in the discretion of the grantor or a non-adverse party, or both, may be (a) distributed to the grantor or the grantor's spouse, (b) accumulated for future distribution to the grantor or the grantor's spouse (see Q 306), or (c) applied to pay premiums on insurance on the life of the grantor or the grantor's spouse (see Q 305); (3) if the income is or may be used for the support of the grantor's spouse or is actually used for the support of a person whom the grantor is legally obligated to support, or is or may be applied in discharge of any other obligation of the grantor; (4) if the grantor retains certain administrative powers or the power to control beneficial enjoyment of trust principal or income; (5) if, at the inception of the trust, the value of a reversionary interest exceeds 5% of the value of the trust. IRC Secs. 671-677; Rev. Rul. 75-257, 1975-2 CB 251. See Q 910 for the valuation tables required to be used. However, if the income of the trust is payable to a lineal descendant of the grantor and it is provided that the grantor's reversionary interest takes effect only upon the death of the beneficiary before the beneficiary attains age 21, the income of the trust will not be taxed to the grantor even though the value of the grantor's reversionary interest exceeds 5% of the value of the trust. IRC Sec. 673(b). *ASRS, Sec. 52, ¶1100.2, Sec. 53, ¶21.2.*

305. If the income of an irrevocable funded life insurance trust is used to pay premiums on a policy insuring the grantor's life, is the income so used taxable to the grantor?

Yes, unless the policy is irrevocably payable to a charity. IRC Sec. 677(a)(3); *Burnet v. Wells*, 289 U.S. 670 (1933). It is immaterial whether the insurance is taken out by the grantor before the trust is created, or by the trustee after it is created. *Stockstrom v. Comm.*, 3 TC 664 (1944). The rule applies to income used to pay the investment portion of the premium as well as to that used for pure insurance protection. *Heffelfinger v. Comm.*, 87 F.2d 991 (8th Cir. 1937), *cert. denied* 302 U.S. 690 (1937). And it applies to income used for policies dedicated to business uses as well as to those for personal estate planning purposes. *Vreeland v. Comm.*, 16 TC 1041 (1951).

Moreover, trust income is taxable to the grantor if, without the approval or consent of an adverse party, it *may* be used for the payment of premiums on insurance on the grantor's life, even though it is not actually used for this purpose. Thus, where policies on the grantor's life are placed in the trust, trust income is taxable to the grantor to the extent that the trustee has discretionary power to use it for premium payments. *Rieck v. Comm.*, 118 F.2d 110 (3rd Cir. 1941).

But if the policies are owned by the grantor or by someone other than the trust, the statute applies only if the trust income is actually used to pay the premiums, or if the trustee is specifically authorized to use it for this purpose. *Iverson v. Comm.*, 3 TC 756 (1944); *Weil v. Comm.*, 3 TC 579 (1944), acq.

Where the trustee is empowered to purchase insurance on the grantor's life, but does not do so, the grantor is not taxed merely because of the trustee's power; there must be policies existing in the tax year upon which it would have been possible for the trustee to pay premiums. *Rand v. Comm.*, 116 F.2d 929 (8th Cir. 1941) *aff'd* 40 BTA 233 (1939), *cert. denied* 313 U.S. 594 (1941); *Corning v. Comm.*, 104 F.2d 329 (6th Cir. 1939); *Comm. v. Mott*, 85 F.2d 315 (6th Cir. 1936); *Moore v. Comm.*, 39 BTA 808 (1939), acq.; *Weil v. Comm.*, supra. And where a trust beneficiary has voluntarily used income received from the trust to pay premiums on insurance on the grantor's life, the income has not been taxed to the grantor. *Hexter v. Comm.*, 47 BTA 483 (1942), acq.; *Booth v. Comm.*, 3 TC 605 (1944), acq.

Because the law states that the trust income will be taxed to the grantor if it is used to pay the premiums "without the approval or consent of any adverse party,"(IRC Sec. 677(a)) some writers have suggested that it may be possible, in some cases, to use trust income for such premium payments. However, if a beneficiary uses the trust income to pay premiums subject to the grantor's direction or pursuant to an understanding with the grantor, the income will be taxable to the grantor. *Dunning v. Comm.*, 36 BTA 1222 (1937); *Foster v. Comm.*, 8 TC 197 (1947), acq. Thus, where the income of a trust for the benefit of grantor's children is to be used for premium payments on insurance on the grantor's life, the income will be taxable to the grantor even though each beneficiary is to consent in writing (revocable at will) to have his share of the income applied to the payment of premiums. Rev. Rul. 66-313, 1966-2 CB 245. *ASRS, Sec. 52, ¶1100.1.*

306. Can a grantor create an irrevocable funded life insurance trust, carrying insurance on the grantor's spouse, without being taxed on trust income used for premium payments?

No. The grantor is taxed on trust income used for the payment of insurance premiums on the life of the grantor or the *grantor's spouse*. IRC Sec. 677(a)(3). If the insurance is on the life of someone other than the grantor or the grantor's spouse, however, this provision does not apply. For example, a grandmother can fund a trust carrying insurance on the life of her son in favor of her grandchildren without being taxed on the trust income under IRC Section 677(a)(3). *ASRS, Sec. 52, ¶1100.2.*

307. Under what circumstances is life insurance trust income taxable to some person other than the trust, grantor, or income beneficiary?

A person who has exclusive power to vest the corpus or income of a trust in himself (even though the power cannot be exercised in the case of a minor because no guardian has been appointed), or who has released such a power but retained controls similar to those that would subject the grantor to tax, is taxed on the income of the trust (see Q 304). IRC Sec. 678; Rev. Rul. 81-6, 1981-1 CB 385. But if the *grantor* is taxable on the trust income, the other person will not be taxed under this rule, at least with respect to a power to vest income. Where a grantor transfers a business interest to a trust, the trust may, under certain circumstances, be viewed by IRS as a business organization itself. See Rev. Rul. 75-258, 1975-2 CB 503.

308. What income is taxable to a life insurance trust? What income is taxable to trust beneficiaries?

Generally, the trust is taxed on: (1) income that, under the terms of the trust, is accumulated for future distribution to someone other than the grantor, and (2) income that the trustee has discretion to accumulate or distribute, but that is not paid or credited to a beneficiary in the taxable year. IRC Sec. 641; Treas. Reg. §1.641(a)-2. Trust beneficiaries are taxable on income that is distributed to them, or should have been distributed to them, in the taxable year, to the extent that the income does not exceed the trust's "distributable net income" for the year. IRC Secs. 652, 662.

To deter taxpayers from shifting tax liability to a lower bracket beneficiary, trust income taxable to a beneficiary under 14 years of age may be taxed at his parents' marginal tax rate. See Q 818. *ASRS, Sec. 53, ¶21.1.*

309. May the grantor of a life insurance trust take a deduction for interest paid by the trust on a policy loan where the policy is held by the trust?

Apparently, if the grantor is taxed as the owner of the trust, he is allowed an interest deduction to the same extent as any other owner of the policy (see Q 260, Q 245). The Code provides that where the grantor (or any other person) is treated as the owner of any part of a trust, the trust's deductions, as well as income and credits against tax, attributable to that part of the trust will be taken into account in computing that person's taxable income. IRC Sec. 671. A grantor is treated as owner of that part of a trust the income from which may be used in certain ways (see Q 304 to Q 306). Trusts that are treated as owned by the grantor are sometimes referred to as "defective" because the pass-through of trust income is undesirable, as a general rule. However, a "defective" trust may be useful if a deduction can be passed through to the grantor. (Where favorable estate tax results are sought, attention should also be given to the matters discussed in Q 650 to Q 658.)

The Service has ruled privately that where nonadverse trustees had authority to use trust income to pay premiums on policies on the grantor's life (not irrevocably payable for a charitable purpose), or had discretion to pay trust income and/or principal to the grantor's wife, the grantor would be taxed as owner of the trust and could take the trust's deductions. Let. Ruls. 8118051, 8007080, 7909031. *ASRS, Secs. 51, 52, ¶700.1.*

310. Are death proceeds of life insurance taxable income if they are payable to a trust?

No, they are generally tax exempt income to the trustee and to the beneficiary when distributed. See Q 271, Q 273. But where the proceeds are retained by the trust, earnings on the proceeds are taxed in the same manner as other trust income. IRC Sec. 101; Treas. Reg. §1.101-1. The $1,000 annual interest exclusion, available where insurance proceeds are payable to a surviving spouse of an insured who died before October 23, 1986 under a life income or installment option, is not available if the proceeds are payable to a trust (see Q 276). Under some circumstances, proceeds of a policy transferred for value to a trust may not be wholly tax exempt (see Q 63, Q 65).

LONG-TERM CARE INSURANCE

QUALIFIED LONG-TERM CARE INSURANCE CONTRACT

Generally

311. What is a qualified long-term care insurance contract?

Generally

A long-term care insurance policy issued after 1996 meets the definition of a "qualified long-term care insurance contract," under IRC Section 7702B(b), if

Q 311

1. the only insurance protection provided under the contract is coverage of qualified long-term care services (see Q 312);

2. the contract does not pay or reimburse expenses incurred for services that are reimbursable under Title XVIII of the Social Security Act (or would be reimbursable but for the application of a deductible or coinsurance amount);

3. the contract is guaranteed renewable;

4. the contract does not provide for a cash surrender value or other money that can be paid, assigned or pledged as collateral for a loan or borrowed; and

5. all premium refunds and dividends under the contract are to be applied as a reduction in future premiums or to increase future benefits. An exception to this rule is for a refund made on the death of the insured or upon a complete surrender or cancellation of the contract that cannot exceed the aggregate premiums paid. Any refund given upon cancellation or complete surrender of the policy will be includable in income to the extent that any deduction or exclusion was allowable with respect to the premiums. IRC Sec. 7702B(b)(2)(C).

In addition, the contract must satisfy certain consumer protection provisions concerning model regulation and model act provisions, disclosure, and nonforfeitability. See IRC Sec. 7702B(g).

A policy will be considered to meet the disclosure requirements if the issuer of the long-term care insurance policy discloses in the policy and in the required outline of coverage that the policy is intended to be a qualified long-term care insurance contract under IRC Section 7702B(b). IRC Sec. 4980C(d).

The nonforfeiture requirement is met for any level premium contract if the issuer of the contract offers to the policyholder (including any group policyholder) a nonforfeiture provision that

1. is appropriately captioned;

2. provides for a benefit available in the event of a default in the payment of any premiums and the amount of the benefit may be adjusted only as necessary to reflect changes in claims, persistency and interest as reflected in changes in rates for premium paying contracts approved for the same contract form; and

3. provides for at least one of the following: (a) reduced paid-up insurance; (b) extended term insurance; (c) shortened benefit period; or (d) other similar approved offerings. IRC Sec. 7702B(g)(4).

Also, a qualified long-term care insurance contract that is approved must be delivered to the policyholder within 30 days of the approval date. IRC Sec. 4980C(c)(2). Further, if a claim under a qualified long-term care insurance contract is denied, the issuer must provide a written explanation of the reasons for the denial and make available all information relating to the denial within 60 days of a written request from the policyholder. IRC Sec. 4980C(c)(3).

LONG-TERM CARE INSURANCE   Q 311

The penalty for not meeting the disclosure and issuer responsibility requirements is a tax equal to $100 per insured for each day that any of these requirements are not met for each qualified long-term care insurance contract. IRC Sec. 4980C(b)(1). If a failure is due to reasonable cause and not willful neglect, the Secretary may waive part or all of the penalty tax if paying the tax would be excessive in relation to the failure. IRC Sec. 4980C(b)(2).

For the treatment of long-term care insurance contracts issued before 1997, see Q 313.

Life Insurance Policy Providing Long-Term Care Coverage

Any long-term care insurance coverage, qualified or otherwise, that is provided by a rider on or as part of a life insurance contract will be treated as a separate contract. IRC Sec. 7702B(e)(1). Concerning the application of IRC Section 7702, generally, the guideline premium limitation will be increased by the sum of any charges (but not premium payments) against the life insurance contract's cash surrender value (within the meaning of IRC Section 7702(f)(2)(A)) for such coverage made to that date less any such charges which reduce the premiums paid for the contact (within the meaning of IRC Section 7702(f)(1)). IRC Sec. 7702B(e)(2). See Q 273.

Further, there is no deduction permitted under IRC Section 213(a) for charges against the life insurance contract's cash surrender value unless the charges are includable in income as a result of the application of IRC Section 72(e)(10) (which deals with modified endowment contracts) and the rider is a qualified long-term care insurance contract. IRC Sec. 7702B(e)(3).

Cafeteria Plans

Any product that is advertised, marketed or offered as long-term care insurance is not a qualified benefit under a cafeteria plan. IRC Sec. 125(f). See Q 99. However, long-term care insurance premiums may be paid through a Health Savings Account included in a cafeteria plan. See Q 202.

Flexible Spending Arrangements

Employer-provided coverage for qualified long-term care services provided through a flexible spending arrangement (FSA) is includable in the employee's gross income. IRC Sec. 106(c)(1). For purposes of this rule, a flexible spending arrangement is a benefit program that provides employees with coverage under which specified incurred expenses may be reimbursed and the maximum amount of reimbursement that is reasonably available to a participant for such coverage is less than 500% of the value of such coverage. For an insured plan, the maximum amount reasonably available is determined on the basis of the underlying coverage. IRC Sec. 106(c)(2). See Q 99.

COBRA Continuation Coverage Requirements

The COBRA continuation coverage requirements applicable to group health plans will not apply to plans under which substantially all of the coverage is for long-term care services. IRC Sec. 4980B(g)(2). This provision is effective for contracts issued after 1996. HIPAA '96, Sec. 321(f)(1). A plan may use any reasonable method to determine whether substantially all of the coverage under the plan is for qualified long-term care services. Treas. Reg. §54.4980B-2, A-1(e). See Q 173. *ASRS, Sec. 67, ¶750.*

2006 Tax Facts on Insurance & Employee Benefits

312. What are "qualified long-term care services"?

"Qualified long-term care services" are defined as any "necessary diagnostic, preventive, therapeutic, curing, treating, mitigating, and rehabilitative services, and maintenance or personal care services" that are required by a chronically ill individual and are provided under a plan of care set forth by a licensed health care practitioner. IRC Sec. 7702B(c)(1).

A "chronically ill individual" is a person who has been certified by a licensed health care practitioner as being unable to perform, without substantial assistance, at least two activities of daily living (ADLs) for at least 90 days or a person with a similar level of disability (the ADL benefit trigger). (Note that this 90-day requirement does not establish a waiting period before which benefits may be paid or before which services may constitute qualified long-term care services. Notice 97-31, 1997-1 CB 417.) Further, a person may be considered chronically ill if he requires substantial supervision to protect himself from threats to his health and safety due to severe cognitive impairment and this condition has been certified by a licensed health care practitioner within the previous 12 months (the cognitive impairment trigger). IRC Sec. 7702B(c)(2)(A).

The activities of daily living are: (1) eating; (2) toileting; (3) transferring; (4) bathing; (5) dressing; and (6) continence. To be considered a qualified long-term care insurance contract a policy must take into account at least five of these ADLs in determining whether a person is a chronically ill individual under the ADL benefit trigger as defined above. IRC Sec. 7702B(c)(2)(B).

For purposes of the ADL benefit trigger, taxpayers may rely upon certain safe-harbor definitions. First, the term "substantial assistance" is defined to mean "hands-on assistance" and "standby assistance." Further, "hands-on assistance" is the physical assistance of another person without which an individual would not be able to complete an ADL. "Standby assistance" is defined to mean the presence of another individual that is needed to prevent an individual from injury while performing an ADL. Notice 97-31, 1997-1 CB 417.

For purposes of the cognitive impairment benefit trigger, there are several safe-harbor definitions that may be relied upon. A "severe cognitive impairment" is defined as a loss or deterioration in intellectual capacity that is similar to Alzheimer's disease and like forms of irreversible dementia and is measured by clinical evidence and standardized tests that reliably measure impairment in short-term or long-term memory, orientation to people, places or time and deductive or abstract reasoning. Further, "substantial supervision" is defined as continual supervision by another person that is needed to protect the severely cognitively impaired person from threats to his health or safety. Notice 97-31, 1997-1 CB 417.

Another safe harbor provision states that when an insurance company applies the ADL trigger to any post-1996 contracts it may use the same standards that it uses to determine whether an individual is unable to perform an ADL for eligibility purposes for benefit payments under its pre-1997 contracts. Further, in applying the cognitive impairment trigger to post-1996 contracts, an insurance company may use the same standards that it uses to determine whether an individual qualifies for benefits due to cognitive impairment under its pre-1997 contracts. Notice 97-31, 1997-1 CB 417. However, the Service cautions that this safe harbor which permits the use of pre-1997 contract standards is applicable only for purposes of determining whether a person is unable to perform an ADL due to a loss of functional capacity or requires substantial supervision to protect himself due to severe cognitive impairment. The safe harbor does not apply for purposes of the other statutory requirements of IRC Section 7702B(c)(2) such as the requirement that the individual's loss of capacity apply to at least two of five or six ADLs, the certification requirement, or the 90-day requirement. These three requirements must be satisfied before a person can be considered chronically ill under either the ADL trigger or the cognitive impairment trigger regardless of whether the insurance company's pre-1997 contracts impose such requirements. Notice 97-31, 1997-1 CB 417. *ASRS, Sec. 67, ¶750.*

313. How are long-term care contracts issued before 1997 treated?

Any contract issued before January 1, 1997 that met the long-term care insurance requirements of the state in which the contract was situated at the time it was issued will be treated for tax purposes as a qualified long-term care insurance contract and services provided under the contract or reimbursed by the contract will be treated as qualified long-term care services. HIPAA '96 Sec. 321(f)(2). Regulations provide that a pre-1997 long-term care insurance contract is treated as a qualified long-term care insurance contract whether or not the contract satisfies IRC Section 7702B(b). Treas. Reg. §1.7702B-2(b)(1).

A pre-1997 long-term care insurance contract is any insurance contract with an issue date before January 1, 1997, that met the long-term care insurance requirements of the state in which the contract was situated on the issue date. Further, the long-term care requirements of the state are the state laws that are intended to regulate insurance coverage that constitutes long-term care insurance (as defined in the NAIC Long-Term Care Insurance Model Act on August 21, 1996). Treas. Reg. §1.7702B-2(b)(2).

For this purpose, the issue date of a contract is the issue date assigned by the insurance company. However, the issue date cannot be earlier than the date upon which the policyholder submitted the application for coverage. Further, if the period of time between the date the application is submitted and the date upon which coverage becomes effective is substantially longer than under the insurance company's usual business practice the issue date is the date upon which coverage becomes effective, assuming this date is later than the issue date assigned by the company. The "free-look" period is not taken into account in determining the contract's issue date. The issue date of a group contract is the date upon which coverage becomes effective. Treas. Reg. §1.7702B-2(b)(3).

A contract issued in exchange for an existing contract after December 31, 1996, is considered a contract issued after this date and any change (as defined below) in a contract is treated as the issuance of a new contract with an issue date that cannot be earlier than the date that the change takes effect. Further, if a change described in the regulations occurs to some certificates under a group policy but not to others, the insurance coverage under the changed certificates is treated as coverage under a newly-issued (i.e., no longer grandfathered) group contract while the insurance coverage provided under the unchanged certificates continues to be treated as covered under the original (i.e., grandfathered) contract. Treas. Reg. §1.7702B-2(b)(3).

For this purpose, the following changes are treated as the issuance of a new contract: (1) a change in the terms of the contract that alters the amount or timing of an item payable by the policyholder (or certificate holder), the insured, or the insurance company; (2) a substitution of the insured under an individual contract; or (3) a material change in the contractual terms or in the plan under which the contract was issued relating to eligibility for membership in the group covered under a group contract. Treas. Reg. §1.7702B-2(b)(4).

The following items are not treated as the issuance of a new contract: (1) a policyholder's exercise of any right provided under the contract in effect on December 31, 1996, or a right required by applicable state law to be provided to the policyholder; (2) a change in premium payment mode; (3) a class-wide increase or decrease in premiums for a guaranteed renewable or noncancellable policy; (4) a premium reduction due to the purchase of a long-term care insurance contract by a family member of the policyholder; (5) a reduction in coverage requested by the policyholder; (6) a reduction in premiums as a result of extending to a policyholder a discount applicable to similar categories of individuals pursuant to a premium rate structure that was in effect on December 31, 1996, for the issuer's pre-1997 long-term care insurance contracts of the same type; (7) the addition of alternative benefit forms that the policyholder may choose (without a premium increase); (8) the addition of a rider to a pre-1997 long-term care insurance contract if the rider issued separately would be a qualified long-term care insurance contract under IRC Section 7702B and any regulations issued under this section; (9) the deletion of a rider or contract provision that prohibited coordination of benefits with Medicare; (10) the exercise of a continuation or a conversion right that is provided under a pre-1997 group contract and that, in accordance with the terms of the contract as in effect on December 31, 1996, provides for coverage under an individual contract following an individual's ineligibility for continued coverage under the group contract; and (11) the substitution of one insurer for another insurer in an assumption reinsurance transaction. Treas. Reg. §1.7702B-2(b)(4). The regulations provide examples of the correct application of these rules. Treas. Reg. §1.7702B-2(b)(5).

Treasury Regulation §1.7702B-2 is effective January 1, 1999, with respect to pre-1997 contracts. Treas. Reg. §1.7702B-2(c). For purposes of determining whether a change made before January 1, 1999, to a pre-1997 contract should have been treated as the issuance of a new contract, taxpayers may rely on Notice 97-31, 1997-1 CB 417. Further, a change made before January 1, 1999, to a pre-1997 contract will not be treated as the issuance of a new contract if the change would not be so treated under the final regulations. Note that taxpayers may not rely upon Notice 97-31 with respect to changes made after 1998. *ASRS, Sec. 67, ¶760.*

Premiums

314. Are premiums paid for a qualified long-term care insurance contract deductible as medical expenses?

Generally, amounts paid for any qualified long-term care insurance contract or for qualified long-term care services are included in the definition of "medical care" and, thus, are eligible for income tax deduction, subject to certain limitations. IRC Sec. 213(d)(1)(D). Amounts paid for the medical care of a taxpayer, his spouse or dependents are deductible subject to the 7.5% adjusted gross income floor. IRC Sec. 213(a). See Q 826.

However, the deduction for eligible long-term care premiums that are paid during any taxable year for a qualified long-term care insurance contract (as defined in IRC

LONG-TERM CARE INSURANCE   Q 316

Section 7702B(b), see Q 311) is subject to an additional dollar amount limitation that increases with the age of the insured individual. In 2006, for persons age 40 or less the limitation amount is $280 ($270 for 2005). For ages 41 through 50, the limitation amount is $530 ($510 for 2005); for ages 51 through 60, the limitation amount is $1,060 ($1,020 for 2005); for ages 61 through 70, the limitation amount is $2,830 ($2,720 for 2005) and for those over 70, the limitation amount is $3,530 ($3,400 for 2005). The age is the individual's attained age before the close of the taxable year. IRC Sec. 213(d)(10)(A). Rev. Proc. 2005-50, 2005-47 IRB 979. The limitation amounts are indexed annually. IRC Sec. 213(d)(10)(B).

An amount paid for qualified long-term care services (as defined in IRC Section 7702B(c), see Q 311) will not be treated as paid for medical care if the service is provided by the individual's spouse or a relative unless the service is provided by a licensed professional. A "relative" is generally any individual who can be considered a dependent under the Code (see IRC Section 152(a)(1) through (8)). Also, the service may not be provided by a corporation or partnership that is related to the individual (within the meaning of IRC Sections 267(b) or 707(b)). IRC Sec. 213(d)(11). *ASRS, Sec. 67, ¶720.*

315. May a self-employed individual deduct premiums paid for a qualified long-term care insurance contract?

Because amounts paid for qualified long-term care insurance contracts come within the definition of medical care, qualified long-term care insurance premiums are eligible for deduction from income by self-employed persons. IRC Secs. 162(l), 213(d). The amount of eligible qualified long-term care insurance premiums that may be deducted is subject to the dollar amount limitations discussed in Q 314. See IRC Sec. 162(l)(2)(C).

The deduction is not available to a self-employed individual for any calendar month in which he is eligible to participate in any subsidized health plan maintained by any employer of the self-employed individual or his spouse. This rule is applied separately to plans that include coverage for qualified long-term care services or are qualified long-term care insurance contracts (see Q 311) and plans that do not include such coverage and are not such contracts. IRC Sec. 162(l)(2)(B).

Beginning in 2003, 100% of amounts paid during the taxable year for insurance—including long-term care insurance up to the annual limitations (see Q 314)—that provides medical care for the individual, his spouse, and dependents can be deducted by a self-employed individual. IRC Sec. 162(l)(1)(B). Generally, sole proprietors, partners and S corporation shareholders owning more than 2% of the S corporation's shares may take advantage of this deduction. See Q 166. *ASRS, Sec. 67, ¶780.*

316. Are long-term care insurance premiums paid by an employer includable in income to the employees?

Any plan of an employer providing coverage under a qualified long-term care insurance contract is generally treated as an accident and health plan with respect to such coverage. IRC Sec. 7702B(a)(3). Thus, premiums for long-term care insurance coverage paid by an employer are not includable in the gross incomes of employees. See IRC Sec. 106(a); see House Comm. Report on Sec. 321 of HIPAA '96, P.L. 104-191.

317. May an employer deduct as a business expense the premiums paid for a qualified long-term care insurance contract for employees?

An employer plan providing coverage under a qualified long-term care insurance contract is treated as an accident and health insurance plan with respect to this coverage. IRC Sec. 7702B(a)(3). An employer may generally deduct health insurance premiums paid for employees as a business expense. See Q 167. Thus, premiums for a qualified long-term care insurance contract paid by an employer for employees are similarly deductible. *ASRS, Sec. 67, ¶720.*

Taxation of Benefits

318. Are benefits received under a qualified long-term care insurance contract taxable income?

A qualified long-term care insurance contract is treated as an accident and health insurance contract. IRC Sec. 7702B(a)(1). See Q 311. Thus, amounts (other than dividends or premium refunds) received under such a contract are treated as amounts received for personal injuries and sickness and are treated as reimbursement for expenses actually incurred for medical care. IRC Sec. 7702B(a)(2). Amounts received for personal injuries and sickness are generally not includable in gross income. See IRC Secs. 104(a)(3), 105(b). See Q 155.

However, there is a limit on the amount of qualified long-term care benefits that may be excluded from income. Generally, if the total periodic payments received under all qualified long-term care insurance contracts and any periodic payments received as an accelerated death benefit under IRC Section 101(g) (see Q 267) exceed a per diem limitation, the excess must be included in income (without regard to IRC Section 72). If the insured is terminally ill when a payment treated under IRC Section 101(g) is received, the payment is not taken into account for this purpose. IRC Sec. 7702B(d)(1).

The per diem limitation is equal to the excess of the greater of a $250 per day limitation in 2006 or the costs incurred for qualified long-term care services provided for the insured over the total payments received as reimbursement for qualified long-term care services for the insured. IRC Sec. 7702B(d)(2); Rev. Proc. 2005-70, 2005-47 IRB 979. (The per day limitation was $240 in 2005.) This figure is adjusted for inflation annually. IRC Secs. 7702B(d)(4), 7702B(d)(5). *ASRS, Sec. 67, ¶730.*

NON-QUALIFIED LONG-TERM CARE INSURANCE CONTRACT

319. How is a long-term care insurance policy that is not a "qualified long-term care insurance contract" taxed?

Policies that do not meet the definition of a qualified long-term care insurance contract under IRC Section 7702B(b) are generally referred to as "nonqualified" long-term care policies. See Q 311. The Internal Revenue Code does not address the income taxation of premiums paid for or benefits received from these nonqualified policies. Commentators have noted that the fact that Congress enacted favorable income tax treatment specifically for qualified long-term care insurance contracts in IRC Section 7702B can be interpreted as an indication that nonqualified policies will not receive such favorable taxation.

LONG-TERM CARE INSURANCE

When dealing with the "qualified vs. nonqualified" issue, it is important to remember the grandfather provision, which states that any contract issued before January 1, 1997, that met the long-term care insurance requirements of the state in which the contract was sitused at the time it was issued will be treated for tax purposes as a qualified long-term care insurance contract and services provided under the contract or reimbursed by the contract will be treated as qualified long-term care services. HIPAA '96 Sec. 321(f)(2). See also Treas. Reg. §1.7702B-2. See Q 311.

REPORTING REQUIREMENTS

320. What reporting requirements are applicable to long-term care benefits?

Any person paying long-term care benefits must file a return that sets forth: (1) the aggregate amount of long-term care benefits paid by the person to any individual during any calendar year; (2) whether or not such benefits are paid, either fully or partially, on a per diem or other periodic basis without regard to the expenses incurred during the period; (3) the name, address, and taxpayer identification number (TIN) of such individual; and (4) the name, address, and TIN of the chronically ill or terminally ill individual for whom the benefits are paid. IRC Sec. 6050Q(a).

Additionally, any person required to make such a return must provide a written statement to each individual whose name is reported under the above requirement. The statement must show the name, address, and phone number of the information contact of the person making the payments and the aggregate amount of long-term care benefits paid to the individual that is required to be shown on the above-mentioned return. This written statement must reach the individual on or before January 31 of the year following the calendar year for which the return was required. IRC Sec. 6050Q(b). (Although IRC Section 6050Q which contains these reporting requirements does not specify, presumably the term "person" is used to encompass not only individuals but also companies paying long-term care benefits.)

For purposes of these reporting requirements, a "long-term care benefit" is any payment under a product that is advertised, marketed or offered as long-term care insurance and any payment that is excludable from gross income as an accelerated death benefit under IRC Section 101(g). IRC Sec. 6050Q(c). *ASRS, Sec. 67, ¶770.*

PENSION AND PROFIT SHARING: QUALIFICATION

OVERVIEW

321. What are the primary tax advantages of a qualified pension, annuity, profit sharing, or stock bonus plan?

Assuming the qualification requirements set forth in the Internal Revenue Code are met (see below), the following tax advantages are available for qualified plans: (1) The employer can take a current business expense deduction (within limits) for its contributions to the plan even though the employees are not currently taxed on these contributions (see Q 362 to Q 366); (2) An employee pays no tax until benefits are distributed regardless of whether he has a forfeitable or nonforfeitable right to the contributions made on his behalf (see Q 423); (3) Distributions meeting certain requirements may be eligible for rollover or special tax treatment (see Q 427 to Q 432, Q 437, Q 445); (4) Annuity and installment payments are taxable only as received (see Q 433 to Q 436, Q 438); (5) The fund within the plan earns and compounds income on a tax free basis (see Q 441); and (6) Certain small employers (i.e., with fewer than 100 employees earning compensation over $5,000 per year) may be able to claim a business tax credit equal to 50% of qualified startup costs of an eligible employer plan. The maximum credit is $500 per year, which may be taken for up to three years. For details, see IRC Sec. 45E.

The general qualification requirements that apply to all qualified plans are explained at Q 322 to Q 361. Plan-specific qualification requirements and deduction limits applicable to each type of plan are explained at Q 371 to Q 419. Self-employed persons (i.e., sole proprietors and partners—see Q 358) may participate in qualified plans as "employees." For special rules applicable to self-employed individuals, see Q 417 to Q 419. *ASRS, Sec. 59, ¶¶100, 110.*

322. What requirements must be met in order for a plan to be "qualified"?

The basic requirements that a plan must meet in order to gain the special tax advantages of a "qualified plan" are set forth in IRC Section 401(a). A plan that fails to meet these requirements, either on its face or in operation, is technically subject to disqualification; however, most plan qualification failures can be corrected through one of the voluntary correction programs collectively known as the Employee Plans Compliance Resolution System (EPCRS). For details, see Rev. Proc. 2003-44, 2003-1 CB 1051.

To meet the basic qualification requirements of IRC Section 401(a), a plan must:

...be established in the United States by an employer for the benefit of employees or their beneficiaries (see Q 323);

...prohibit the use of plan assets for purposes other than the exclusive benefit of the employees or their beneficiaries until such time as all liabilities to employees and their beneficiaries have been satisfied (see Q 323);

...meet minimum age and service standards (see Q 324), and minimum coverage requirements (see Q 325);

PENSION AND PROFIT SHARING: QUALIFICATION — Q 322

...provide for contributions or benefits that are not discriminatory (see Q 326 to Q 330 in general, and Q 404 to Q 405 with respect to 401(k) plans);

...provide for contributions or benefits that do not exceed the IRC Section 415 limitations (see Q 332, Q 372, and Q 377);

...meet the minimum vesting standards (see Q 333 to Q 334);

...provide for distributions that satisfy both the commencement rules and the minimum distribution requirements (see Q 338 to Q 347);

...provide for automatic survivor benefits under certain circumstances (see Q 335 to Q 337);

...contain provisions that meet the requirements for "top-heavy" plans and provide that such provisions will become effective should the plan become top-heavy (see Q 350 to Q 352);

...prohibit the assignment or alienation of benefits (see Q 348 to Q 349); and

...meet the miscellaneous requirements described in Q 353.

In addition, a plan, and its underlying trust, *custodial account, annuity contract*, or contract (other than a life, health or accident, property, casualty or liability insurance contract) issued by an insurance company, must meet certain other plan-specific qualification requirements, depending on the type of plan being used (e.g., profit sharing, etc.). See Q 368 to Q 418.

Generally, a plan must provide that if the distributee of an eligible rollover elects to have the distribution paid directly to an eligible plan, and specifies the plan, the distribution will be made in the form of a direct rollover, provided the distribution would have been includable in gross income if not rolled over. IRC Sec. 401(a)(31)(A). However, after-tax amounts may be the subject of a direct rollover under certain circumstances, provided they are separately accounted for. See IRC Sec. 401(a)(31)(B). If the distributee does not elect to have the distribution made as a direct rollover, it will be subject to 20% income tax withholding. IRC Sec. 3405(c); Treas. Reg. §1.401(a)(31)-1, A-1(b)(1).

For distributions made after March 27, 2005, a plan must provide that if a distribution in excess of $1,000 and up to $5,000 is made, and the distributee does not elect to roll over or receive the distribution, the plan will transfer the distribution to an IRA established to receive the distribution. IRC Sec. 401(a)(31)(B). This provision was added by EGTRRA 2001, but did not take effect until DOL regulations were finalized. The final regulations (Labor Reg. §2550.404a-2, 69 Fed. Reg. 58018 (9-28-2004)) became effective March 28, 2005; see Q 447 for details. The plan must also notify the distributee in writing of the rollover. IRC Sec. 401(a)(31)(B).

In addition, the plan administrator must provide a written explanation to the distributee of his right to elect a direct rollover, and the withholding consequences of not making the election. IRC Sec. 402(f). An updated safe harbor explanation that meets this requirement was provided in Notice 2002-3, 2002-1 CB 289. See Q 445 for an explanation of the rollover provisions for qualified plans.

2006 Tax Facts on Insurance & Employee Benefits

Q 322

A qualified plan sponsor may elect to maintain *deemed IRAs* for employees who wish to make voluntary traditional or Roth IRA contributions by means of payroll deduction. See IRC Sec. 408(q); Treas. Reg. §1.408(q)-1(a). See Q 211 for details.

The plan must be a definite funded written program and arrangement that is communicated to the employees. Treas. Reg. §1.401-1(a)(2); Rev. Rul. 71-90, 1971-1 CB 115; Rev. Rul. 71-91, 1971-1 CB 116; Let. Rul. 8752001. The plan may be expressed in more than one writing or memorandum, but must embody all essential elements required by IRC Section 401(a) to be a "plan." It cannot be established retroactively. *Engineered Timber Sales, Inc. v. Comm.*, 74 TC 808 (1980), appeal dismissed (5th Cir. 1981); *G&W Leach Co. v. Comm.*, TC Memo 1981-91.

The assets of a custodial account must be held by a bank or other person who demonstrates to the satisfaction of the IRS that the manner in which he will hold the assets will be consistent with the requirements qualified plans must meet. An annuity contract must be nontransferable if issued after 1962. IRC Sec. 401(g); Treas. Reg. §1.401-8(d)(2). The person holding the assets of the account or the contract is treated as the trustee thereof. IRC Sec. 401(f). Thus, it is possible for a nontrusteed profit sharing plan funded solely with annuity contracts to qualify.

A trust must have economic reality. Thus, where trust assets were used as their own by the officers of the contributing corporation who were also the only trustees, beneficiaries and stockholders, the trust was held a nullity for tax purposes. *Lansing v. Comm.*, TC Memo 1976-313. A qualified trust did not exist where participants had the right to hold, acquire and dispose of amounts attributable to their account balances at will. Rev. Rul. 89-52, 1989-1 CB 110. If certain requirements are met, trusts that are part of qualified retirement plans or individual retirement accounts and government retirement plans (whether or not qualified and whether or not the assets of such government plans are held in trust) may pool their assets in a domestic group trust without affecting the qualified status of the individual trusts. IRC Sec. 401(a)(24); Rev. Rul. 81-100, 1981-1 CB 326.

Failure to timely amend a plan to meet newly enacted or modified qualification requirements can result in revocation of a plan's qualified status, even if the plan has been terminated. See *Basch Eng'g, Inc. v. Comm.*, TC Memo 1990-212; *Fazi v. Comm.*, 102 TC 695 (1994). (A terminated plan is subject to the qualification rules until such time as all the assets are distributed in satisfaction of its liabilities.) Courts have permitted amendments made after stipulated deadlines to be given retroactive effect where no circumstances have arisen that call into operation the objectionable provisions of the plan and where the employer exercised reasonable diligence in attempting to obtain a favorable determination. *Bollinger v. Comm.*, 77 TC 1353 (1981); *Oakton Distributors, Inc. v. Comm.*, 73 TC 182 (1979). "Reasonable diligence" was not exercised where application for a determination was not made for over 5½ years after the enactment of TEFRA and over 3½ years after TRA '84 and REA. *Stark Truss Co., Inc. v. Comm.*, TC Memo 1991-329. See also, *Kollipara Rajsheker, M.D., Inc. v. Comm.*, TC Memo 1992-628.

Special rules applicable to collectively bargained plans are found in IRC Section 413. See also, Treas. Reg. §1.413-1. For plans covering self-employed individuals, see also Q 417, Q 418, and Q 358. *ASRS, Sec. 59, ¶400.*

EXCLUSIVE BENEFIT RULE

323. What is the "exclusive benefit rule" of plan qualification?

The plan must be established in the United States by an employer for the exclusive benefit of employees or their beneficiaries. IRC Sec. 401(a).

A plan will not qualify if it includes participants who are not employees of the employer who established and maintains the plan (except in the case of "leased employees"; see Q 355). Rev. Rul. 69-493, 1969-2 CB 88. Generally, an individual is an employee for the purpose of participating in a qualified plan if he is an employee under the "common law" rules (see Q 354); however, under IRC Section 3508 certain real estate agents and direct sellers of consumer products are specifically defined as non-employees. (An individual is an employee under the common law rules if the person or organization for whom he performs services has the right to control and direct his work, not only as to the result to be accomplished, but also as to the details and means by which the result is accomplished. Treas. Reg. §31.3121(d)-1(c)(2); *Packard v. Comm.*, 63 TC 621 (1975).)

Self-employed individuals are eligible to participate in their own qualified plans under the same rules applicable to common law employees, but some special rules apply (see Q 358, Q 418). Generally, participation by independent contractors who are not employees of a corporation in the corporation's plan would be a violation of the exclusive benefit rule; however, the IRS has not been inclined to disqualify plans on this ground alone. See, e.g., *Lozon v. Comm.*, TC Memo 1997-250.

Stockholders, even sole owners of corporations, who are bona fide employees of corporations (including professional corporations and associations and S corporations) are eligible to participate in a qualified plan of the corporation as regular employees, not as self-employed individuals. Treas. Reg. §1.401-1(b)(3); Rev. Rul. 63-108, 1963-1 CB 87; Rev. Rul. 55-81, 1955-1 CB 392; *Thomas Kiddie, M.D., Inc. v. Comm.*, 69 TC 1055 (1978). A full-time life insurance salesperson who is an employee for Social Security purposes can participate in a qualified plan as a regular employee. See IRC Sec. 7701(a)(20). He cannot set up a plan as a self-employed individual. Treas. Reg. §1.401-10(b)(3).

The primary purpose of benefiting employees or their beneficiaries must be maintained with respect to investment of trust funds as well as with respect to other activities of the trust. Rev. Rul. 73-380, 1973-2 CB 124; Rev. Rul. 73-282, 1973-2 CB 123; Rev. Rul. 73-532, 1973-2 CB 128; Rev. Rul. 69-494, 1969-2 CB 88; *Feroleto Steel Co. v. Comm.*, 69 TC 97 (1977); *Bing Management Co., Inc. v. Comm.*, TC Memo 1977-403.

The use of the exclusive benefit rule to disqualify a plan where trust funds have been misappropriated generally occurs only under egregious circumstances. For example, where a plan loaned out almost all of its assets to the company president, without seeking adequate security, a fair return, or prompt repayment, the plan was held not to be operated for the exclusive benefit of the employees and the plan was disqualified. *Winger's Dept. Store, Inc. v. Comm.*, 82 TC 869 (1984). Likewise, where a corporation's sole shareholder/plan trustee caused the plan to make 22 unsecured loans to himself and none of the loans bore a reasonable rate of interest nor were adequately secured, the exclusive benefit rule was violated and the plan disqualified. TAM 9145006; see also TAM 9701001.

However, a loan made by a plan to an employer from excess funds that would have ultimately been returned to the employer did not violate the exclusive benefit requirement (this was despite the imposition of the excise tax on prohibited transactions). See TAM 9430002. The Tax Court has held that even a violation of the prudent investor rule (failure to diversify) did not rise to the level of a violation of the exclusive benefit rule. See *Shedco, Inc v. Comm.*, TC Memo 1998-295.

The IRS has stated that where an ESOP trust contained a provision permitting the trustee to consider nonfinancial, employment-related factors in evaluating tender offers for company stock, the exclusive benefit rule was violated. GCM 39870 (4-17-92).

The garnishment of an individual's plan interest under the Federal Debt Collections Procedures Act (FDCPA) to pay a judgment for restitution or fines will not violate the exclusive benefit rule. Let. Rul. 200426027.

No Reversion to Employer

Under the plan it must be impossible at any time prior to the satisfaction of all liabilities with respect to employees and their beneficiaries for any part of the funds to be used for or diverted to purposes other than for the exclusive benefit of the employees or their beneficiaries. IRC Sec. 401(a)(2).

As a rule, therefore, no sums may be refunded to the employer. However, a plan may provide for the return of a contribution (and any earnings) where (1) the contribution is conditioned on the initial qualification of the plan; (2) the plan receives an adverse determination with respect to its qualification, and (3) the application for determination is made within the time prescribed by law for filing the employer's return for the taxable year in which such plan was adopted or such later date as the Secretary of Treasury may prescribe. Rev. Rul. 91-4, 1991-1 CB 54; see also ERISA Sec. 403(c)(2)(B).

Furthermore, a plan may provide for return to the employer of contributions made by reason of a good faith mistake of fact and of contributions conditioned on deductibility where there has been a good faith mistake in determining deductibility. Earnings attributable to any excess contribution based on a good faith mistake may not be returned to the employer, but losses attributable to such contributions must reduce the amount returned. Rev. Rul. 91-4, above; see also ERISA Secs. 403(c)(2)(A), 403(c)(2)(C).

Employer contributions made to satisfy the quarterly contribution requirements (see Q 375) may revert to the employer if the contribution is conditioned on its deductibility, a requested letter ruling disallows the deduction, and the contribution is returned to the employer within one year from the date of the disallowance of the deduction. Rev. Proc. 90-49, 1990-2 CB 620. Documentation must be provided showing that the contribution was conditioned on deductibility at the time it was made; board resolutions dated after the contribution is made are not sufficient. Let. Ruls. 9021049, 8948056. A letter ruling request may not be needed if the employer contribution is less than $25,000 and certain other requirements are met. See Rev. Proc. 90-49, above, Sec. 4.

Also, if, upon termination of a pension plan (but not a profit sharing plan), all fixed and contingent liabilities to the employees and their beneficiaries have been satisfied, the employer may recover any surplus existing because of actuarial "error." Treas. Reg. §1.401-2(b); Rev. Rul. 70-421, 1970-2 CB 85; Rev. Rul. 71-152, 1971-1 CB 126; Rev. Rul. 73-55, 1973-1 CB 196; Rev. Rul. 71-149, 1971-1 CB 118. However, the plan must

PENSION AND PROFIT SHARING: QUALIFICATION   Q 324

specifically provide for such a reversion. See ERISA Sec. 4044(d)(1). Thus, where a plan had no such provision, the employer was required to distribute surplus assets to the former employees (or their surviving spouses) covered by the plan. *Rinard v. Eastern Co.*, 978 F.2d 265 (6th Cir. 1992), cert. denied, 113 S.Ct. 1843 (1993). Furthermore, the calculation of the employees' share of residual assets must result in an equitable distribution before the surplus assets may revert to the employer. See *Holland v. Amalgamated Sugar Co.*, 787 F. Supp. 996 (D.C. Utah 1992). An excise tax may apply to any employer reversion—see Q 442.

If a pension or annuity plan maintains a separate account that provides for the payment of medical benefits to retired employees, their spouses and their dependents, any amount remaining in such an account following the satisfaction of all liabilities to provide the benefits must be returned to the employer even though liabilities exist with respect to other portions of the plan. IRC Sec. 401(h)(5). *ASRS, Sec. 59, ¶¶490.1, 490.2(a)*.

MINIMUM PARTICIPATION AND COVERAGE

324. What minimum "age and service" requirements apply to qualified plans?

A plan may not require, as a condition of participation in the plan, that an employee complete a period of service extending beyond the later of (a) age 21, or (b) the completion of one year of service *or* the completion of two years of service if the plan provides that after not more than two years of service each participant has a nonforfeitable right to 100% of his accrued benefit. In the case of a plan maintained exclusively for employees of a tax-exempt (under IRC Section 501(a)) educational institution, the minimum age limitation can be 26 instead of 21, but only if the plan provides that each participant having at least one year of service has a nonforfeitable right to 100% of his accrued benefit. IRC Secs. 401(a)(3), 410(a)(1). See Temp. Treas. Reg. §1.410(a)-3T. An additional minimum participation rule (i.e., the 50/40 test) applies to defined benefit plans *only*; see Q 373.) A plan generally may not exclude from participation in the plan employees who are *beyond a specified age*. IRC Sec. 410(a)(2).

A plan must provide that any employee who has satisfied the minimum age and service requirements specified above and who is otherwise entitled to participate in the plan is to commence participation in the plan no later than the *earlier* of (1) the first day of the first plan year beginning after the date on which the employee satisfied such requirements, or (2) the date six months after the date on which he satisfied such requirements, unless the employee was separated from service before the date referred to in (1) or (2), whichever is applicable. (For illustrations, see Rev. Rul. 80-360, 1980-2 CB 142.) IRC Sec. 410(a)(4); Treas. Reg. §1.410(a)-4(b)(1).

In a 2004 memorandum to its staff, the IRS expressed disapproval with plans that attempt to satisfy various Code requirements by limiting participation to highly compensated employees and to rank and file employees with very short periods of service. Such plans may be the subject of adverse rulings, or other action. Memorandum dated October 22, 2004, Carol D. Gold, Director Employee Plans.

The foregoing provisions do not require that the employee be eligible for plan participation merely because he satisfies the specified age and service requirements. Other requirements, not related to age or service, may be imposed by a plan as a condition

2006 Tax Facts on Insurance & Employee Benefits   337

of participation. Treas. Reg. §1.410(a)-3(d). See Q 325. Nevertheless, if the effect of some other plan provision is to impose an additional age or service requirement, that provision will be treated as an age or service requirement even if it does not specifically refer to age or service. Treas. Reg. §1.410(a)-3(e)(1). The IRS has stated that the exclusion of part-time employees from plan participation will violate the participation rules under IRC Section 410(a), even if such an exclusion would otherwise satisfy IRC Section 410(b). IRS Field Directive (November 22, 1994), CCH Pension Plan Guide ¶23,902F; see also TAM 9508003.

The term "year of service" means a 12-month period, measured from the date the employee enters service, during which the employee has worked at least 1,000 hours; special rules apply where there are breaks in service and where there is absence from work due to pregnancy, childbirth, or adoption of a child. IRC Secs. 410(a)(3), 410(a)(5); Treas. Regs. §§1.410(a)-5, 1.410(a)-6. See Temp. Treas. Reg. §1.410(a)-8T, Treas. Reg. §1.410(a)-9. Special rules also apply in the cases of seasonal industries and maritime industries. IRC Secs. 410(a)(3)(B), 410(a)(3)(D); Treas. Reg. §1.410(a)-5. The IRS has stated that the exclusion of part-time employees from plan participation may be considered discriminatory and, in any event, will violate the participation rules under IRC Section 410(a) as described above. IRS Field Directive (November 22, 1994), CCH Pension Plan Guide ¶23,902F.

Past service with former employers may be used for the purpose of determining eligibility to participate in a plan provided (1) the former employers are specified in the plan or trust, (2) all employees having such past service are treated uniformly, and (3) the use of such past service factor does not produce discrimination in favor of the highly compensated employees (see Q 326). See Rev. Rul. 72-5, 1972-1 CB 106. The IRS has also permitted individuals to be credited for services performed as partners or sole proprietors prior to becoming employees in a successor corporation for this purpose. See Let. Rul. 7742003. *ASRS, Sec. 59, ¶410.5.*

325. What is the "minimum coverage" requirement for qualified plans?

A qualified plan must meet the minimum coverage test set forth in IRC Section 410(b) and regulations thereunder. IRC Sec. 401(a)(3). Under these provisions, a plan must satisfy either a *ratio percentage test* or an *average benefit test*. Governmental plans (whether maintained by a state or local government, or the United States government) are exempt from this requirement and the regulations implementing it. See IRC Secs. 410(c)(1)(A), 401(a)(5)(G); Notice 2003-6, 2003-1 CB 298. Section 401(k) plans are subject to certain modifications of the coverage requirements; see Q 395.

A plan will not be treated as violating the coverage requirements of Section 410(b) merely on account of the making of (or right to make) catch-up contributions by participants age 50 or over, under the provisions of IRC Section 414(v), so long as a universal availability requirement is met. IRC Sec. 414(v)(3)(B). See Q 397 for details on the requirements for catch-up contributions.

Ratio Percentage Test

The Code states that a qualified plan must benefit either (a) 70% of all nonhighly compensated employees, (i.e., the percentage test) *or* (b) a percentage of the nonhighly compensated employees that is at least 70% of the percentage of highly compensated

PENSION AND PROFIT SHARING: QUALIFICATION   Q 325

employees benefiting under the plan (i.e., the ratio test). IRC Sec. 410(b)(1). Regulations incorporate these two tests into a *ratio percentage test*, which requires that the plan's ratio percentage for the plan year be at least 70%. Treas. Reg. §1.410(b)-2(b)(2)(i). A plan's ratio percentage is determined by dividing the percentage of the nonhighly compensated employees who benefit under the plan by the percentage of the highly compensated employees who benefit under the plan. Treas. Reg. §1.410(b)-9.

Example: Rayford Steel Company has a profit sharing plan that covers 90 of its 100 nonexcludable highly compensated employees and 130 of its 200 nonexcludable nonhighly compensated employees. The plan's ratio percentage is determined by dividing (a) the percentage of the nonhighly compensated employees who benefit under the plan (130/200, or 65%) by (b) the percentage of the highly compensated employees who benefit under the plan (90/100, or 90%). Rayford Steel's ratio percentage is 65/90, or 72.22%; thus, it passes the ratio percentage test.

Average Benefit Test

A plan that cannot satisfy the ratio percentage test may still pass the coverage requirement by satisfying the average benefit test. The average benefits test has two parts: (a) the "nondiscriminatory classification" test, *and* (b) the "average benefit percentage" test. Both of these requirements must be met for a plan to satisfy the average benefit test. Treas. Reg. §1.410(b)-2(b)(3); see IRC Sec. 410(b)(2).

Nondiscriminatory classification test. In order to pass the nondiscriminatory classification test, the Code states that a plan must benefit "such employees as qualify under a classification set up by the employer and found by the Secretary not to be discriminatory in favor of highly compensated employees." IRC Sec. 410(b)(2)(A)(i). Regulations state that this test has two subparts: (1) the classification of employees must be reasonable; it must reflect a bona fide business classification of employees (Treas. Reg. §1.410(b)-4(b)), *and* (2) the classification must be nondiscriminatory, based on a facts and circumstances test or a safe harbor percentage test as explained below (Treas. Reg. §1.410(b)-4(c)).

To determine whether a classification is nondiscriminatory, the plan's ratio percentage (as defined above) is compared to a table (described below) that is set forth in the regulations. This comparison produces one of three results: (1) if the plan's ratio percentage falls below the unsafe harbor percentage, it is discriminatory; (2) if the plan's ratio percentage falls between the safe harbor and unsafe harbor amounts, it must satisfy a facts and circumstances test; or (3) if the plan's ratio percentage falls at or above the safe harbor amount, the plan is nondiscriminatory. Treas. Reg. §1.410(b)-4(c).

The regulations contain a table setting forth a safe harbor percentage and an unsafe harbor percentage for every nonhighly compensated employee concentration level. See Treas. Reg. §1.410(b)-4(c)(4)(iv). The table begins with a nonhighly compensated employee concentration of zero to 60%, and for that level provides a safe harbor percentage of 50% and an unsafe harbor percentage of 40%. In other words, for an employer with 100 employees, of whom 40 are highly compensated and only 60 are nonhighly compensated, the classification would automatically be nondiscriminatory under the safe harbor if its ratio percentage were 50% or higher.

The safe harbor percentage is reduced by ¾ of a percentage point (but not below 20.75%) for each whole percentage point by which the nonhighly compensated employee concentration percentage exceeds 60%. Thus, for an employer with a nonhighly compensated employee concentration percentage of 99%, the safe harbor percentage would be 20.75%. Treas. Regs. §§1.410(b)-4(c)(2), 1.410(b)-4(c)(4)(i).

2006 Tax Facts on Insurance & Employee Benefits

The unsafe harbor percentage is reduced by ¾ of a percentage point (but not below 20%) for every whole percentage point by which the nonhighly compensated employee concentration percentage exceeds 60%. Treas. Reg. §1.410(b)-4(c)(4)(ii).

Example. Omega Corporation has 200 nonexcludable employees, of whom 120 are nonhighly compensated and 80 are highly compensated employees. Omega maintains a plan that benefits 60 nonhighly compensated employees and 72 highly compensated employees. Thus, the plan's ratio percentage is 55.56% ([60/120]/[72/80] = 50%/90% = 0.5556), which is below the percentage necessary to satisfy the ratio percentage test described above. Omega's nonhighly compensated employee concentration percentage is 60% (120/200); thus, Omega's safe harbor percentage is 50% and its unsafe harbor percentage is 40%. Because the plan's ratio percentage (55.56%) is greater than the safe harbor percentage (50%), the plan's classification satisfies the safe harbor.

Average benefit percentage test. The second part of the average benefit test requires that the average benefit percentage for nonhighly compensated employees be at least 70% of the average benefit percentage for highly compensated employees. IRC Sec. 410(b)(2)(A)(ii); Treas. Reg. §1.410(b)-5(a).

An employee's *benefit percentage* is his employer-provided contributions (including forfeitures and elective deferrals) or benefits under all qualified plans maintained by the employer, expressed as a percentage of his compensation. IRC Sec. 410(b)(2)(C)(i). Employee contributions and benefits attributable to employee contributions are not taken into account in calculating employee benefit percentages. Treas. Reg. §1.410(b)-5(d)(2). Regulations permit benefit percentages to be determined on either a contributions or a benefits basis, but the benefit percentages for any testing period must be determined in the same manner for all plans in the testing group. See Treas. Reg. §1.410(b)-5(d)(5).

The *average benefit percentage* means the average of the benefit percentages calculated separately with regard to each employee in the group. IRC Sec. 410(b)(2)(B). An employer may not disregard any qualified plan in determining benefit percentages, even if the plan satisfies the percentage test or ratio test standing alone; however, an employer who maintains separate lines of business (see below) may test those businesses separately. The benefit percentage for any plan year is computed on the basis of contributions or benefits for that year or, at the election of the employer, any consecutive plan year period (up to three years) ending with the plan year and specified in the election. An election under this provision cannot be revoked or modified without the consent of the Secretary of the Treasury. IRC Sec. 410(b)(2)(C).

A plan maintained by an employer that has no employees other than highly compensated employees for any year or that benefits no highly compensated active employees for any year is treated as meeting the minimum coverage requirements. IRC Sec. 410(b)(6)(F); Treas. Regs. §§1.410(b)-2(b)(5), 1.410(b)-2(b)(6).

Miscellaneous Rules

Separate lines of business. An employer who operates "separate lines of business" may apply the above tests separately with respect to employees in each line of business, so long as any such plan benefits a class of employees that is determined, on a company wide basis, not to be discriminatory in favor of highly compensated employees. IRC Sec. 410(b)(5). A separate line of business exists if the employer, for bona fide business reasons, maintains separate lines of business or operating units. A separate line of business, however, cannot have less than 50 employees (disregarding any employees excluded from the top-paid group when determining which employees are highly compensated—see

PENSION AND PROFIT SHARING: QUALIFICATION Q 325

Q 356). A separate line of business must also either meet a statutory safe harbor (with regard to ratios of highly compensated employees) provided in the Code, meet one of the administrative safe harbors provided in final regulations, or request and receive an individual determination from the IRS that the separate line of business satisfies administrative scrutiny. IRC Sec. 414(r); Treas. Regs. §§1.414(r)-5, 1.414(r)-6.

Former employees. Active and former employees are tested separately for purposes of these rules. Treas. Reg. §1.410(b)-2(a). A plan satisfies the coverage requirement with respect to former employees only if, under all the relevant facts and circumstances, the group of former employees does not discriminate significantly in favor of highly compensated former employees. Treas. Reg. §1.410(b)-2(c)(2).

Excludable employees. Employees who can be excluded from consideration in meeting the coverage tests generally include (1) employees covered by a collective bargaining agreement (provided that retirement benefits were the subject of good faith bargaining between the employee representatives and the employer), and (2) nonresident aliens who receive no U.S. earned income. IRC Sec. 410(b)(3); Treas. Regs. §§1.410(b)-6(d), 1.410(b)-9. Although a plan may permit an otherwise eligible employee to waive his right to participate, such a waiver may, under some circumstances, result in discriminatory coverage. See Rev. Rul. 80-351, 1980-2 CB 152. But see *Olmo v. Comm.*, TC Memo 1979-286. Generally, employees who have not satisfied the plan's minimum age and service requirements may also be excluded from consideration in meeting the above tests, but only if *all* such employees are excluded. IRC Sec. 410(b)(4). However, for purposes of the *average benefit percentage* component, the employer can exclude only those employees who have not satisfied the *lowest* minimum age and service requirements for any plan taken into account. IRC Sec. 410(b)(2)(D).

If a plan applies minimum age and service eligibility conditions that are permissible under IRC Section 410(a)(1) and excludes all employees who do not satisfy those conditions, then all employees who fail to satisfy those requirements are excludable employees with respect to that plan. However, such an employee *may* be treated as an excludable employee if he terminates employment with not more than 500 hours of service. Treas. Reg. §1.410(b)-6(f)(1). An employee is treated as meeting the age and service requirements on the date any employee with the same age and service would be eligible to commence participation in the plan. Treas. Reg. §1.410(b)-6(b)(1).

Employees treated as benefiting. Generally, for purposes of meeting the above tests, an employee "benefits" under a plan for a year only if the employee accrues a benefit or receives an allocation under the plan for that year. However, in the case of a 401(k) plan, any individual who is eligible to make elective deferrals is treated as benefiting under the plan. Treas. Reg. §1.410(b)-3(a). (Of course, for purposes of meeting the average benefit percentage part of the average benefit test, only actual benefits, rather than mere eligibility, are taken into account.) IRC Sec. 410(b)(6)(E). See General Explanation of TRA '86, p. 674. An employee is treated as "benefiting" under a plan for a plan year if the employee satisfies all of the applicable conditions for accruing a benefit for such a year but fails to accrue a benefit solely because of the IRC Section 415 limits or some other uniformly applicable plan benefit limit. Treas. Regs. §§1.410(b)-3(a)(2)(ii), 1.410(b)-3(a)(2)(iii).

Mandatory disaggregation. Some plans or portions of plans must be disaggregated for purposes of meeting the minimum coverage rules. The mandatory disaggregation requirement specifies that certain single plans must be treated as comprising separate plans, each of which is subject to the minimum coverage requirements.

Some of the plans that generally have to be disaggregated for coverage purposes are: (1) the portion of a plan that includes a cash or deferred arrangement subject to IRC Section 401(k) (or matching and employee after-tax contributions subject to IRC Section 401(m)) and the portion that does not; (2) the portion of a plan that is an ESOP and the portion that is a non-ESOP (note that this varies from the proposed disaggregation rules that would apply under proposed regulations for ADP/ACP testing purposes only; see Treas. Reg. §1.401(k)-1(b)(4)(v); see Q 404, Q 405); (3) the portion of a plan that benefits otherwise excludable employees and the portion that does not, (4) a plan that benefits the employees of a separate line of business and any plan maintained by any other line of business if the employer elects to use the separate line of business rules, and (5) the portion of a plan that benefits employees under a collective bargaining arrangement and the portion that benefits nonunion employees. Treas. Reg. §1.410(b)-7(c)(4). For testing the benefits of employees who change from one qualified separate line of business to another, a "reasonable" treatment must be used. Treas. Reg. §1.410(b)-7(c)(4)(i)(D). A multiple employer plan is also treated as comprising separate plans each of which is maintained by a separate employer and must generally satisfy the minimum coverage requirements by reference only to such employer's employees. Treas. Reg. §1.410(b)-7(c)(4)(ii)(C).

Permissive aggregation. For purposes of applying the ratio percentage test and the nondiscriminatory classification test, an employer may elect to designate two or more of its plans as a single plan, but only if the plans have the same plan years. Treas. Regs. §§1.410(b)-7(d)(1), 1.410(b)-7(d)(5). If plans are aggregated under this rule, such plans must be treated as a single plan for all purposes under IRC Sections 410(b) and 401(a)(4). Treas. Reg. §1.410(b)-7(d). (Of course, plans that are required to be disaggregated under the rules described above cannot be aggregated under this rule.) Furthermore, for purposes of applying these tests, the following plans must also be disaggregated: (1) the portion of a plan that is an ESOP and the portion that is a non-ESOP, and (2) the portion of a plan that includes a cash or deferred arrangement subject to IRC Section 401(k) (or matching and employee after-tax contributions subject to IRC Section 401(m)) and the portion that does not. Treas. Regs. §§1.410(b)-7(c), 1.410(b)-7(d)(2).

For purposes of applying the average benefit percentage test, all plans that may be aggregated under the permissive aggregation rules *must* be aggregated and treated as a single plan. In addition, plans (or portions of plans) that are ESOPs or that are subject to IRC Section 401(k) or 401(m) must also be aggregated with all other qualified plans of the employer. IRC Sec. 401(k)(4)(C); Treas. Reg. §1.410(b)-7(e). A special rule in the final regulations permits benefits provided to collectively bargained employees and noncollectively bargained employees to be considered together, for purposes of the average benefit percentage test only, if certain requirements are met. See Treas. Reg. §1.410(b)-5(f).

Snapshot testing. The Code states that a plan will be considered as meeting the minimum coverage requirement during the whole of any taxable year of the plan if on one day in each quarter it satisfied such requirement. IRC Sec. 401(a)(6). However, employers may demonstrate compliance with the coverage requirement using "snapshot" testing on a single day during the plan year, provided that day is representative of the employer's work force and the plan's coverage throughout the plan year. Rev. Proc. 93-42, 1993-2 CB 540.

PENSION AND PROFIT SHARING: QUALIFICATION   Q 325

Corrective amendments. A plan that does not satisfy the minimum coverage requirement during a plan year may be retroactively amended by the fifteenth day of the tenth month after the close of the plan year to satisfy one of the tests. Treas. Regs. §§1.401(a)(4)-11(g)(2), 1.401(a)(4)-11(g)(3)(iv). Any retroactive amendments must separately satisfy the nondiscrimination and minimum coverage requirements, and cannot violate the anti-cutback rule of IRC Section 411(d)(6) (see Q 328, Q 334). Treas. Reg. §1.401(a)(4)-11(g)(3).

Merger or acquisition. The Code provides certain transition relief from the coverage rules in the event of a merger or acquisition. See IRC Sec. 410(b)(6)(C). The IRS has provided guidance for certain changes in plan sponsors' controlled group, offering temporary relief from the coverage requirements, provided that (1) each plan satisfied the coverage requirements prior to the change in the controlled group, and (2) no significant change in the plan or its coverage takes place during the transition period (other than the change resulting from the merger or acquisition itself). For details, see Rev. Rul. 2004-11, 2004-7 IRB 480.

Effect of noncompliance. Special rules apply to a plan that fails to qualify solely because it does not meet one of the coverage tests. In such a case, contributions on behalf of nonhighly compensated employees will not be taxed under the rules for nonqualified plans. (Presumably, all other complications arising from plan disqualification would apply.) Instead, highly compensated employees will be required to include in income the amount of their vested accrued benefits (other than their investment in the contract). IRC Sec. 402(b)(2).

The minimum coverage requirement is generally inapplicable to church plans, and governmental plans are treated as meeting the coverage provisions. See IRC Secs. 410(c)(1)(B), 410(c)(2). The coverage regulations generally apply to tax-exempt organizations; however, noncontributory plans maintained by certain tax-exempt organizations (a society, order or association described in IRC Sections 501(c)(8) or 501(c)(9)) are not subject to the coverage requirements. IRC Sec. 410(c)(1)(D).

Plan for sole shareholder. A corporation may have a qualified plan even though it has only one permanent employee and that employee owns all the stock of the corporation. But if the plan is either designed or operated so that only the shareholder-employee can ever benefit, it will not qualify. Provision must be made for participation of future employees if any are hired. Rev. Rul. 63-108, 1963-1 CB 87; Rev. Rul. 55-81, 1955-1 CB 392. A pension plan will not fail to qualify merely because it is established by a corporation that is operated for the purpose of selling the services, abilities or talents of its only employee who is also its principal or sole shareholder. Rev. Rul. 72-4, 1972-1 CB 105 (Rev. Rul. 55-81 amplified). However, the plan of a corporation's sole shareholder was disqualified for violating the coverage requirement after it was shown that the only two hired personnel of the company, who had been excluded from the plan as independent contractors, were in fact employees. See *Kenney v. Comm.*, TC Memo 1995-431.

As to which individuals must be treated as "employees" and what organizations make up an employer, see Q 354, Q 355, Q 359, and Q 360. *ASRS, Sec. 59, ¶¶410.2, 410.3.*

2006 Tax Facts on Insurance & Employee Benefits

NONDISCRIMINATION

326. What are the requirements a plan must meet to be nondiscriminatory?

There are three basic requirements a plan must meet in order to be considered nondiscriminatory under IRC Section 401(a)(4):

(1) contributions or benefits must not discriminate in favor of "highly compensated employees" (defined in IRC Section 414(q)–see Q 356), as described below;

(2) benefits, rights and features provided under the plan must be made available to employees in a nondiscriminatory manner (see Q 327); and

(3) the effect of plan amendments (including grants of past service credit) and plan terminations must be nondiscriminatory (see Q 328). Treas. Reg. §1.401(a)(4)-1(b)(1).

Employees not included in the plan but who are covered by a collective bargaining agreement can be excluded from consideration in meeting the nondiscrimination requirement if there is evidence that retirement benefits were the subject of good faith bargaining between the employee representatives and the employer; however, if the union employees are covered under the plan, benefits or contributions must be provided for them on a nondiscriminatory basis. Nonresident aliens with no U.S. earned income may also be excluded. IRC Secs. 401(a)(4), 410(b)(3). See, e.g., Let. Rul. 8419001.

State and local governmental plans generally are not subject to the requirements of IRC Section 401(a)(4). See IRC Sec. 401(a)(5)(G); Notice 95-48, 1995-2 CB 332. The IRS has stated that other governmental plans within the meaning of IRC Section 414(d) (i.e., plans established and maintained for its employees by the government of the United States or by any agency or instrumentality of it), will be deemed to satisfy the nondiscrimination requirements under IRC Section 401(a)(4) until the first day of the first plan year beginning after the date final regulations are issued. Notice 2003-6, 2003-1 CB 298. In earlier guidance, the IRS stated that nonelecting church plans are not subject to the requirements of Section 401(a)(4) "until further notice, but in no case earlier than the first plan year on or after January 1, 2003"; however, such plans are subject to a reasonable, good faith standard. Notice 2001-46, 2001-2 CB 122.

The regulations under IRC Section 401(a)(4) provide the *exclusive* rules for determining whether a plan satisfies the nondiscrimination requirements of IRC Section 401(a)(4). Treas. Reg. §1.401(a)(4)-1(a). The requirement that a plan provide nondiscriminatory contributions or benefits is in the alternative; it is not required that both contributions and benefits be nondiscriminatory. A plan may satisfy this requirement on the basis of either contributions or benefits, regardless of whether the plan is a defined benefit plan or a defined contribution plan. The process of testing defined benefit plans on the basis of contributions or defined contribution plans on the basis of benefits is referred to as cross testing (see Q 329).

A plan will not be considered discriminatory merely because contributions or benefits bear a uniform relationship to the employees' compensation. IRC Sec. 401(a)(5)(B). ("Compensation" is defined in Q 331.) A plan will satisfy IRC Section 401(a)(4) only if

PENSION AND PROFIT SHARING: QUALIFICATION — Q 326

it complies both in form and in actual operation with the regulations explained below; in making this determination intent is irrelevant. Treas. Reg. §1.401(a)(4)-1(a).

A plan also will not be treated as discriminatory merely on account of the making of (or right to make) catch-up contributions by participants 50 or over, under the provisions of IRC Section 414(v), so long as a universal availability requirement is met. IRC Sec. 414(v)(3)(B). See Q 397 for details on the requirements for catch-up contributions.

There are two basic options for ascertaining that a plan provides nondiscriminatory contributions or benefits: design the plan to meet one of the safe harbors, or pass the general test on an annual basis. Plans that do not meet the requirements for one of the safe harbors must use the general test. The safe harbor methods are design-based; essentially, they require the plan to have uniformity provisions that reduce the risk of discrimination, so that annual testing is unnecessary. As a result, the safe harbors are simpler and less costly to apply than the general test, which focuses on actual plan results and requires annual review.

Defined contribution safe harbors. The regulations set forth two safe harbor designs for defined contribution plans. Neither of the safe harbors allows the use of permitted disparity. Under the first safe harbor, referred to as a *uniform allocation formula*, a defined contribution plan will be nondiscriminatory if it allocates employer contributions and forfeitures for the year under an allocation formula that allocates to each employee (1) the same percentage of plan year compensation, (2) the same dollar amount, *or* (3) the same dollar amount for each uniform unit of service (not exceeding one week) performed by the employee during the year. Treas. Reg. §1.401(a)(4)-2(b)(2).

The second safe harbor design is referred to as a *uniform points allocation formula*. Such a formula allows a defined contribution plan (other than an ESOP) to be nondiscriminatory even though contributions are weighted for age and/or service, as well as for compensation. See Treas. Reg. §1.401(a)(4)-2(b)(3).

The use of either of these safe harbors is not precluded by a plan that has non-uniform benefits if the sole reason for the nonuniformity is that the plan provides lower benefits to highly compensated employees than to other employees. Treas. Reg. §1.401(a)(4)-2(b)(4)(v).

General test for defined contribution plans. Defined contribution plans (other than plans subject to IRC Section 401(k) or 401(m)) that do not satisfy one of the safe harbors generally will meet the "nondiscrimination in amount" requirement only if each "rate group" satisfies the minimum coverage requirements of IRC Section 410(b). For this purpose, a "rate group" exists for each highly compensated employee in the plan, and consists of the highly compensated employee (HCE) and all other employees in the plan (whether highly compensated or nonhighly compensated) who have an allocation rate greater than or equal to the highly compensated employee's allocation rate. In other words, each employee, regardless of compensation level, is in the rate group for every HCE who has an allocation rate less than or equal to that employee's allocation rate. Treas. Reg. §1.401(a)(4)-2(c)(1).

Defined benefit safe harbors. The final regulations provide a set of uniformity requirements that apply to all of the defined benefit safe harbors. Generally, the plan must provide a uniform normal retirement benefit in the same form for all employees, using a uniform normal retirement age. For purposes of this requirement, Social Security retirement age will be treated as a uniform retirement age. IRC Sec. 401(a)(5)(F). The regulations provide for three safe harbors: one for unit credit plans, one for fractional accrual plans (including flat benefit plans), and one for insurance contract plans. Treas. Reg. §1.401(a)(4)-3(b).

General test for defined benefit plans. Defined benefit plans that do not satisfy any of the safe harbors will satisfy the "nondiscriminatory in amount" requirement only if they satisfy the general test, which requires the calculation of accrual rates and an analysis of their distribution. The general test will be satisfied if each "rate group" satisfies the minimum coverage requirements of IRC Section 410(b). For this purpose, a "rate group" exists for each highly compensated employee in the plan, and consists of the highly compensated employee and all other employees in the plan (whether highly compensated or nonhighly compensated) who have a normal accrual rate greater than or equal to the highly compensated employee's normal accrual rate, *and* who also have a most valuable accrual rate greater than or equal to the highly compensated employee's most valuable accrual rate. In other words, an employee is in the rate group for each highly compensated employee who has a normal accrual rate less than or equal to the employee's normal accrual rate and who also has a most valuable accrual rate less than or equal to the employee's most valuable accrual rate. Treas. Reg. §1.401(a)(4)-3(c)(1).

The regulations provide a facts and circumstances "safety valve" for certain defined benefit plans that would pass the general test if no more than 5% of the highly compensated employees were disregarded. If the IRS determines, on the basis of all the relevant facts and circumstances, that such a plan does not discriminate with respect to the amount of employer-provided benefits, the plan will pass the general test. (For purposes of calculating the 5%, the number of highly compensated employees may be rounded to the nearest whole number.) Treas. Reg. §1.401(a)(4)-3(c)(3).

Target plan benefits. The regulations provide a safe harbor testing method for target benefit plans. Because target benefit plans are defined contribution plans that determine allocations based on a defined benefit funding approach, the safe harbor is included in the rules for cross testing.

Generally, a target benefit plan will be deemed to meet the "nondiscrimination in amount" requirement if: (1) it satisfies uniformity requirements with respect to normal retirement age and allocation formula (Social Security retirement age will be treated as a uniform retirement age–IRC Sec. 401(a)(5)(F)); (2) it provides a stated benefit formula that complies with one of the defined benefit plan safe harbors that uses the fractional accrual rule; (3) employer contributions are determined under an individual level premium funding method specified in the regulations, based on an employee's stated benefit and "theoretical reserve"; (4) employee contributions (if any) are not used to fund the stated benefit; *and* (5) the stated benefit formula satisfies Treas. Reg. §1.401(l)-3, if permitted disparity is taken into account. Treas. Reg. §1.401(a)(4)-8(b)(3).

401(k) plans. Special nondiscrimination tests and design-based safe harbors apply in the case of contributions to 401(k) and 401(m) plans (see Q 404 to Q 406). IRC Secs. 401(k), 401(m); Treas. Reg. §1.401(a)(4)-1(b)(2)(ii)(B).

Short service employees. The IRS released guidance late in 2004 expressing disapproval with plans that attempt to satisfy the nondiscrimination requirements by limiting

PENSION AND PROFIT SHARING: QUALIFICATION — Q 326

participation to highly compensated employees and to rank and file employees with very short periods of service. The Service noted that sponsors of such plans use "plan designs and hiring practices that limit the nonhighly compensated employees who accrue benefits under the plan primarily to employees with very small amounts of compensation" and that most such employees never vest in their benefits. Such plans may be the subject of adverse rulings, or other action. Memorandum dated October 22, 2004, Carol D. Gold, Director Employee Plans.

Aggregation and restructuring. Under certain circumstances, a plan may be aggregated (combined) with other plans or restructured (treated as two or more separate plans) for purposes of meeting the nondiscrimination in amount requirement. Where plans are restructured, each component plan must separately satisfy the nondiscrimination requirements and the coverage requirements (see Q 325). See Treas. Reg. §1.401(a)(4)-9(c).

If two or more plans are permissively aggregated and treated as constituting a single plan for purposes of satisfying the minimum coverage requirements (see Q 325), the aggregated plans must also be treated as a single plan for purposes of meeting the nondiscrimination requirements. Treas. Reg. §1.401(a)(4)-9(a). The regulations include guidelines for determining whether several such plans, when considered as a unit, provide contributions and benefits that discriminate in favor of highly compensated employees. A disability plan that is not a pension, profit sharing, stock bonus or annuity plan may not be aggregated with such plans for this purpose. See Rev. Rul. 81-33, 1981-1 CB 173. Special rules are provided for applying the nondiscrimination requirements to an aggregated plan that includes both a defined benefit plan and a defined contribution plan. See Treas. Reg. §1.401(a)(4)-9(b). Special rules apply where an aggregated plan includes a new comparability plan. See Treas. Reg. §1.401(a)(4)-9(c)(3)(ii), Q 329.

Integrated plans. An integrated defined benefit plan will not be considered discriminatory merely because the plan is integrated with Social Security (i.e., the plan uses the permitted disparity rules). See IRC Sec. 401(a)(5)(D). A number of the safe harbor defined benefit plan designs provided in the nondiscrimination regulations allow permitted disparity to be used; however, a defined contribution plan must pass the general test in order to use permitted disparity. For details on Social Security integration, see Q 330.

Substantiation. Employers may demonstrate compliance with the "nondiscrimination in amount" requirement by using "snapshot" testing on a single day during the plan year, provided that day is representative of the employer's work force and the plan's coverage throughout the plan year. Rev. Proc. 93-42, 1993-2 CB 540.

Past service credits. The effect of plan provisions with respect to grants of past service must be nondiscriminatory. The determination of whether credit for past service causes discrimination is made on a facts and circumstances basis.

A plan provision that credits pre-participation service or imputed service to any highly compensated employee will be considered nondiscriminatory if, based on all the facts and circumstances: (1) the provision applies on the same terms to all similarly-situated nonhighly compensated employees, (2) there is a legitimate business purpose for crediting the service, and (3) the crediting of the service does not discriminate significantly in favor of highly compensated employees. Treas. Reg. §1.401(a)(4)-11(d)(3)(iii). For an explanation of the nondiscrimination requirements for plan amendments granting past service credit, see Q 328.

Twenty-five highest paid HCEs. A plan must provide certain restrictions limiting the benefits that can be paid to the 25 highest paid highly compensated employees. Essentially, this rule places limitations on the availability of a lump sum payment to such employees, unless plan assets exceed a certain percentage of liabilities, or the value of the benefit paid to the restricted employee is negligible, or the value of the benefit does not exceed $5,000. See Treas. Reg. §1.401(a)(4)-5(b)(3); IRC Sec. 411(a)(11)(A); Rev. Rul. 92-76, 1992-2 CB 76. See also, Treas. Regs. §§1.401-4(c)(1), 1.401-4(c)(2), 1.401-4(c)(7). The IRS has determined that this requirement was met where a bond or a letter of credit secured repayment of the restricted amount by a rollover IRA. Let. Ruls. 9631031, 9743051. The termination of escrow arrangements established in connection with these provisions was permitted in private rulings. Let. Ruls. 9417031, 9419040. Guidelines for nondiscriminatory allocation of assets on termination of a defined benefit plan are set forth in Rev. Rul. 80-229, 1980-2 CB 133.

As to what individuals must be treated as "employees" and what organizations make up an employer, see Q 354, Q 355, Q 359, and Q 360. *ASRS, Sec. 59, ¶420.*

327. What are the requirements with respect to nondiscriminatory availability of plan benefits, rights and features?

The benefits, rights, and features provided under a plan (i.e., all optional forms of benefit, ancillary benefits, and other rights and features available to any employee under the plan) must be made available in a nondiscriminatory manner. Benefits, rights and features generally will meet this requirement only if each benefit, right and feature satisfies a "current availability" requirement and an "effective availability" requirement. Treas. Regs. §§1.401(a)(4)-1(b)(3), 1.401(a)(4)-4(a).

Generally, the *current availability* requirement is satisfied if the group of employees to whom the benefit, right or feature is currently available during the plan year satisfies the minimum coverage test (see Q 325) without regard to the average benefit percentage test. Treas. Reg. §1.401(a)(4)-4(b)(1).

Current availability is based on the current facts and circumstances of the employee; the fact that an employee may, in the future, satisfy an eligibility condition does not make the benefit option currently available to that employee. But conditions based on termination of employment, disability, or hardship, or conditions based on age or length of service (other than those that must be satisfied within a specified period of time) may be disregarded in determining current availability. Treas. Reg. §1.401(a)(4)-4(b)(2).

In order to satisfy the *effective availability* requirement, the group of employees to whom a benefit, right or feature is effectively available must not, based on all the facts and circumstances, substantially favor highly compensated employees. Treas. Reg. §1.401(a)(4)-4(c)(1). Thus, for example, a matching contribution that is available only to employees deferring a relatively high percentage of income would fail this requirement if the level of deferral required makes the match effectively unavailable to most nonhighly compensated employees.

A plan that offers *catch-up contributions* will not be treated as violating these requirements merely on account of the making of (or right to make) catch-up contributions by participants 50 or over, under the provisions of IRC Section 414(v), so long as a *universal availability* requirement is met. IRC Sec. 414(v)(3)(B). See Q 397 for details.

PENSION AND PROFIT SHARING: QUALIFICATION Q 328

The IRS has issued guidance under which two optional forms of benefit that differ only with respect to the timing of their commencement generally may be aggregated and treated as a single optional form of benefit solely for purposes of satisfying the nondiscriminatory current and effective availability requirements. See Notice 97-75, 1997-2 CB 337. Thus, for example, a preretirement age 70½ distribution option that is available only to 5% owners (as required under IRC Section 401(a)(9), see Q 340) may be aggregated with another optional form of benefit that differs only in the timing of the commencement of payments, provided certain requirements are met. Notice 97-75, above, A-5.

Generally, the fact that subsidized early retirement benefits and joint and survivor annuities are based on an employee's Social Security retirement age will not result in their being treated as unavailable to employees on the same terms. IRC Sec. 401(a)(5)(F)(ii).

Employers may substantiate compliance with the current availability requirement by using "snapshot" testing on a single day during the plan year, provided that day is representative of the employer's work force and the plan's coverage throughout the plan year. Rev. Proc. 93-42, 1993-2 CB 540. For additional guidelines on substantiating nondiscrimination in the amount of benefits, rights and features, see Rev. Proc. 93-39, 1993-2 CB 513, as modified by Rev. Proc. 94-37, 1994-1 CB 349.

The IRS determined that where a plan, in operation, permitted highly compensated employees to direct their own investments, which resulted in their earning a substantially higher return than that earned on contributions by rank and file employees, the plan violated IRC Section 401(a)(4). The Service commented that even if their investment decisions had resulted in a lower return or a loss, the opportunity for the highly compensated employees to make their own investment decisions would still result in discrimination. TAM 9137001. *ASRS, Sec. 59, ¶420.1(b)*.

328. What are the nondiscrimination requirements a plan must meet with respect to plan amendments and terminations?

The timing of plan amendments must not have the effect of discriminating significantly in favor of highly compensated employees. Treas. Reg. §1.401(a)(4)-1(b)(4). For this purpose, a plan amendment includes the establishment or termination of the plan, as well as any change in the benefits, rights, or features, the benefit formulas, or the allocation formulas under the plan. Treas. Reg. §1.401(a)(4)-5(a).

The regulations provide a facts and circumstances test for determining whether a plan amendment or series of amendments has the effect of discriminating significantly in favor of highly compensated employees, or former highly compensated employees. Treas. Reg. §1.401(a)(4)-5(a)(2).

The timing of a plan amendment that grants past service credit (or increases benefits attributable to years of service for a period in the past) will be deemed to be nondiscriminatory if the following four safe harbor requirements are met: (1) the period for which the credit is granted does not exceed the five years preceding the current year, (2) the past service credit is granted on a reasonably uniform basis to all employees, (3) benefits attributable to the period are determined by applying the current plan formula, *and* (4) the service credited is service (including pre-participation or imputed service)

2006 Tax Facts on Insurance & Employee Benefits

with the employer or a previous employer. Treas. Reg. §1.401(a)(4)-5(a)(3). See Q 326 regarding plan provisions that credit pre-participation service or imputed service to any highly compensated employee.

Guidelines for nondiscriminatory allocation of assets on termination of a defined benefit plan are set forth in Rev. Rul. 80-229, 1980-2 CB 133. *ASRS, Sec. 59, ¶¶420.1(c), 420.1(d)*.

329. What are the requirements for cross tested plans?

Cross testing is the process by which defined contribution plans are tested for nondiscrimination on the basis of benefits and defined benefit plans on the basis of contributions. Since cross testing generally results in higher contribution rates for older employees, such plans are sometimes referred to as "age weighted." (However, age weighting is also available without cross testing, under a uniform points allocation formula safe harbor for defined contribution plans. See Treas. Reg. §1.401(a)(4)-2(b)(3)(i).) The general rules for converting allocations under a defined contribution plan to equivalent benefits and for converting benefits under a defined benefit plan to equivalent allocation rates are explained at Treas. Reg. §1.401(a)(4)-8.

The most common form of cross testing is "new comparability" testing of profit sharing plans. The new comparability feature uses cross testing to show that contributions under the plan provide nondiscriminatory benefits. Cross testing can also involve aggregating a defined benefit plan with a defined contribution plan, and testing the plans together on the basis of the benefits they provide.

Final regulations set forth three testing alternatives under which a cross tested defined contribution plan can satisfy the nondiscrimination in amount requirement, as well as rules for testing the combination of a defined benefit plan and a defined contribution plan on a benefits basis.

(1) Minimum allocation gateway. The minimum allocation gateway test sets forth two standards for new comparability plans. First, if the allocation rate for each nonhighly compensated employee (NHCE) in the plan is at least one-third of the allocation rate of the highly compensated employee (HCE) with the highest allocation rate under the plan, the gateway will be satisfied. In the alternative, if the allocation rate for each NHCE is at least 5% of his compensation (within the meaning of IRC Section 415(c)(3); see Q 331), the gateway will be satisfied. Treas. Reg. §1.401(a)(4)-8(b)(1)(vi)(A). The gateway is deemed satisfied if each NHCE receives an allocation of at least 5% of the NHCE's compensation, based on the plan year compensation. Treas. Reg. §1.401(a)(4)-8(b)(1)(vi)(B).

(2) Broadly available allocation rates. A new comparability plan need not satisfy the minimum allocation gateway if it provides for "broadly available allocation rates." To be broadly available, each allocation rate must be currently available to a group of employees that satisfies IRC Section 410(b), without regard to the average benefit percentage test (see Q 325). Treas. Reg. §1.401(a)(4)-8(b)(1)(iii)(A). Final regulations liberalized this determination somewhat by allowing groups receiving two different allocation rates to be aggregated for purposes of determining whether allocation rates are "broadly available." Thus, for example, a group receiving a 3% allocation rate could be aggregated with a group receiving a 10% allocation rate if each group passes the coverage test (not

PENSION AND PROFIT SHARING: QUALIFICATION   Q 330

counting the average benefit percentage test). Rev. Rul. 2001-30, 2001-1 CB 46. Differences in allocation rates resulting from permitted disparity under the Section 1.401(l) regulations may be disregarded. Treas. Reg. §1.401(a)(4)-8(b)(1)(vii).

For purposes of the "broadly available" test, certain *transition allocations* may be disregarded. See Treas. Reg. §1.401(a)(4)-8(b)(1)(iii)(B).

(3) Age-based allocation rates. A plan that provides for age-based allocation rates will also be excepted from the minimum allocation gateway if it has a "gradual age or service schedule." A plan has a gradual age or service schedule if the allocation formula for all employees under the plan provides for a single schedule of allocation rates that (i) defines a series of bands based solely on age, years of service or points representing the sum of the two, which applies to all employees whose age, years of service or points are within each band, and (ii) the allocation rates under the schedule increase smoothly at regular intervals (as defined in the regulations). Sample schedules of smoothly-increasing allocation schedules, based on the sum of age and service, are included in the final regulations. Treas. Reg. §1.401(a)(4)-8(b)(1)(iv)(A). Certain plans that fail the safe harbor for target benefit plans (see Treas. Reg. §1.401(a)(4)-8(b)(3)) may also satisfy the requirements for age-based allocation rates if the plan's allocation rates are based on a uniform target benefit allocation. See Treas. Reg. §1.401(a)(4)-8(b)(1)(v).

Combination of defined benefit/defined contribution plans. A defined benefit plan, benefitting primarily HCEs, may be aggregated with a defined contribution plan benefitting primarily NHCEs, if a gateway similar to the one described above is met. Treas. Reg. §1.401(a)(4)-9(b)(2)(v)(A) and (D). In the alternative, if the combined plan is "primarily defined benefit in character" or consists of "broadly available separate plans," as defined in regulations, it may be nondiscriminatory without satisfying the gateway. See Treas. Reg. §1.401(a)(4)-9(b)(1)(v)(B) and (C).

The IRS released guidance late in 2004 expressing disapproval with plans that attempt to satisfy the nondiscrimination requirements by limiting participation to highly compensated employees and to rank and file employees with very short periods of service. By way of example, the Service stated that a plan cross tested under the forgoing provisions violates the nondiscrimination requirements of IRC Sec. 401(a)(4) (see Q 326) where: (1) the plan excludes most or all permanent NHCEs, (2) the plan covers a group of NHCEs who were hired temporarily for short periods of time, (3) the plan allocates a higher percentage of compensation to the accounts of the HCEs than to those of the NHCEs covered by the plan, and (4) compensation earned by the NHCEs covered by the plan is significantly less than the compensation earned by the NHCEs not covered by the plan. Memorandum dated October 22, 2004, Carol D. Gold, Director Employee Plans. *ASRS, Sec. 59, ¶420.4.*

330. What is permitted disparity? How does it work?

The permitted disparity (Social Security integration) rules are an exception to the general nondiscrimination requirement, based on the premise that most employers pay Social Security tax, and thus help to fund a greater portion of the replacement income of lower paid workers. The rules under IRC Section 401(l) permit a plan to take this disparity into consideration, so that when retirement benefits under both the plan and Social Security are taken into account, a uniform percentage of compensation is provided to all workers.

An integrated plan will not be considered discriminatory merely because plan contributions or benefits favor the highly compensated employees *if* certain disparity limits are met. IRC Sec. 401(a)(5)(C). If the requirements of IRC Section 401(l) are met, the disparity (or the benefit offset in an offset plan, see below) will be disregarded in determining whether the plan satisfies the nondiscrimination rules in Q 326. Treas. Reg. §1.401(l)-1(a)(1). The regulations under IRC Section 401(l) provide the *exclusive* means for a plan to satisfy IRC Sections 401(l) and 401(a)(5)(C). Treas. Reg. §1.401(l)-1(a)(3).

Disparity is not permitted with respect to: (1) ESOPs, (2) elective contributions under a qualified cash or deferred arrangement, or employee or matching contributions as defined in IRC Sections 401(k) and 401(m) (see Q 395 to Q 403); or (3) certain government plans that are not subject to the Federal Insurance Contributions Act (FICA) or the Railroad Retirement Tax Act. Treas. Reg. §1.401(l)-1(a)(4).

Defined Contribution Plans

A defined contribution plan may provide for disparity in the rates of employer contributions allocated to employees' accounts if it meets all of the following requirements:

1. The plan must be a defined contribution excess plan (i.e., a defined contribution plan under which the rate of allocations above the integration level is greater than the rate of allocations at or below the integration level). Treas. Regs. §§1.401(l)-2(a)(2), 1.401(l)-1(c)(16)(ii).

2. The disparity must not exceed the *maximum excess allowance*. The maximum excess allowance is the lesser of (1) the base contribution percentage, or (2) the greater of (i) 5.7 percentage points, or (ii) the percentage equal to the portion of the rate of Social Security tax (in effect for the year) attributable to old-age insurance. IRC Sec. 401(l)(2). (The IRS will publish the percentage rate of the portion attributable to old-age insurance when it exceeds 5.7%.) Treas. Regs. §§1.401(l)-2(a)(3), 1.401(l)-2(b).

3. The plan must satisfy the overall permitted disparity limits described below. Treas. Regs. §§1.401(l)-2(b)(1), 1.401(l)-5.

4. The disparity for all employees under the plan must be uniform. To be uniform the plan must use the same *base contribution percentage* and *excess contribution percentage* for all employees in the plan. Treas. Regs. §§1.401(l)-2(a)(4), 1.401(l)-2(c). The "excess contribution percentage" is the percentage of an employee's compensation contributed to the plan that is attributable to compensation in excess of the "integration level." The "base contribution percentage" is the percentage of an employee's compensation that is contributed to the plan and that is attributable to compensation *not* in excess of the integration level. IRC Sec. 401(l)(2)(B).

5. The integration level must be equal to the taxable wage base in effect as of the beginning of the plan year, or, if lower, must satisfy one of two alternative tests. Treas. Regs. §§1.401(l)-2(a)(5), 1.401(l)-2(d). The "integration level" is the amount of compensation specified under the plan at or below which the rate of contributions (expressed as a percentage) is less than the rate of contribution above such level. IRC Sec. 401(l)(5)(A).

PENSION AND PROFIT SHARING: QUALIFICATION Q 330

Special rules apply to target benefit plans. See Treas. Reg. §1.401(a)(4)-8(b)(3)(i)(C) and Q 326. Cash balance plans (see Q 374) that meet the safe harbor requirements provided in final regulations under IRC Section 401(a)(4) may satisfy the permitted disparity rules on the basis of the defined contribution plan rules. Treas. Reg. §1.401(a)(4)-8(c)(3)(iii)(B).

Defined Benefit Plans

A defined benefit plan will not be considered discriminatory merely because the plan provides that a participant's retirement benefit may not exceed the excess of (1) the participant's final pay with the employer, over (2) the retirement benefit, under Social Security law, derived from employer contributions attributable to service by the participant with the employer. IRC Sec. 401(a)(5)(D)(i); Treas. Reg. §1.401(a)(5)-1(d)(2). The participant's final pay is the highest compensation paid to the participant (by the employer) for any year that ends during the 5-year period ending with the year in which the participant separated from service. IRC Sec. 401(a)(5)(D)(ii). Compensation in excess of $220,000 (in 2006; see Appendix E for earlier years), may not be taken into account. Treas. Reg. §1.401(a)(5)-1(e)(2); IRC Sec. 401(a)(17).

A defined benefit plan may provide for disparity in the rates of employer-provided benefits if it meets all of the following requirements:

1. The plan must be a defined benefit excess plan or an offset plan. Treas. Reg. §1.401(l)-3(a)(2).

2. The disparity for all employees under the plan must not exceed the *maximum excess allowance* (in the case of an excess plan) or the *maximum offset allowance* (in the case of an offset plan). Treas. Regs. §§1.401(l)-3(a)(3), 1.401(l)-3(b)(1).

The "maximum excess allowance" is the lesser of (i) .75% (subject to reduction as described below) or (ii) the base benefit percentage for the plan year. Treas. Reg. §1.401(l)-3(b)(2). The maximum excess allowance cannot exceed the base benefit percentage. IRC Sec. 401(l)(4)(A).

The "maximum offset allowance" is the lesser of (i) .75% (reduced as described below) or (ii) one-half of the gross benefit percentage, multiplied by a fraction (not to exceed one), of which the numerator is the employee's *average annual compensation*, and the denominator is the employee's *final average compensation* up to the offset level. Treas. Reg. §1.401(l)-3(b)(3). The maximum offset allowance may not exceed 50% of the benefit that would have otherwise accrued. IRC Sec. 401(l)(4)(B). (For plans meeting the maximum offset allowance limitation, the "PIA Offset" safe harbor described below may be available.)

3. The plan must satisfy the overall permitted disparity limits described below. Treas. Reg. §1.401(l)-3(b)(1).

4. The disparity for all employees under the plan must be uniform. To be uniform, an excess plan must use the same base benefit percentage and the same excess benefit percentage for all employees with the same number of years of service. An offset plan is uniform only if it uses the same gross benefit percentage and the same offset percentage for all employees with the same number of years of service. The disparity provided under a plan that determines each employee's accrued benefit under the fractional accrual

method in IRC Section 411(b)(1)(C) is subject to special uniformity requirements. Treas. Regs. §§1.401(l)-3(a)(4), 1.401(l)-3(c)(1).

5. The integration level (under an excess plan) or offset level (under an offset plan) for each participant must be (i) the participant's "covered compensation" (see below), (ii) a uniform percentage (above 100%) of covered compensation, (iii) a uniform dollar amount or (iv) one of two intermediate amounts as specified in the regulations. Treas. Reg. §1.401(l)-3(d). See IRC Sec. 401(l)(5)(A).

The regulations under IRC Sections 401(a)(4) and 401(l) provide a "PIA offset" safe harbor for those defined benefit plans that limit the offset to the maximum offset allowance described above. Under the safe harbor, a defined benefit plan that satisfies any of the existing safe harbors provided in the regulations under IRC Section 401(a)(4) will not fail to be a safe harbor plan merely because it offsets benefits by a percentage of PIA. Treas. Reg. §1.401(l)-3(c)(2)(ix).

Covered compensation means the average of the taxable wage bases for the 35 calendar years ending with the last day of the calendar year an individual attains Social Security retirement age. Treas. Reg. §1.401(l)-1(c)(7)(i). The IRS publishes tables annually for determining employees' covered compensation. See Rev. Rul. 2005-72, 2005-46 IRB 944 for the 2006 covered compensation table.

Average annual compensation is the participant's highest average annual compensation for (i) any period of at least three consecutive years, or (ii) if shorter, the participant's full period of service. IRC Sec. 401(l)(5)(C). Treas. Regs. §§1.401(l)-1(c)(2), 1.401(a)(4)-3(e)(2). *Final annual compensation* is the participant's average annual compensation for the 3-consecutive year period ending with the current year, or, if shorter, the participant's full period of service, but not exceeding the contribution and benefit base in effect for Social Security purposes for the year. IRC Sec. 401(l)(5)(D); Treas. Reg. §1.401(l)-1(c)(17).

Final regulations require certain reductions in the .75% factor if the integration or offset level exceeds covered compensation or if benefits begin at an age other than Social Security retirement age. These reductions may be determined on an individual basis by comparing each employee's final average to the employee's covered compensation. Treas. Regs. §§1.401(l)-3(d)(9), 1.401(l)-3(e). For more specifics on integrating defined benefit plans, see Treas. Reg. §1.401(l)-3.

Overall Permitted Disparity

The Code specifies that in the case of an employee covered by two or more plans of an employer, regulations are to provide rules preventing the multiple use of the disparity otherwise permitted under IRC Section 401(l). Consequently, final regulations provide both an annual overall limit and a cumulative overall limit. Treas. Reg. §1.401(l)-5.

The annual overall permitted disparity limit requires the determination of a fraction based on the disparity provided to an employee for the plan year under each plan. The annual overall limit is met if the sum of those fractions does not exceed one. Treas. Reg. §1.401(l)-5(b)(1).

The cumulative permitted disparity limit is generally satisfied if the total of an employee's annual disparity fractions under all plans for all years of service does not exceed 35. Treas. Regs. §§1.401(l)-5(c)(1)(i), 1.401(l)-5(c)(2). *ASRS, Sec. 59, ¶420.3*.

331. What is "compensation" for purposes of nondiscrimination in a qualified plan?

For purposes of the nondiscrimination rules and any other provision of the Code that specifically refers to IRC Section 414(s), "compensation" is defined in terms of IRC Section 415(c)(3) compensation, but compensation in excess of $220,000 (in 2006) is not taken into account (see Q 353F). IRC Secs. 401(a)(17), 414(s)(1). The limit is indexed for inflation in increments of $5,000. IRC Sec. 401(a)(17); see Treas. Reg. §1.401(a)(17)-1(a). See Appendix E for the indexed amounts for prior years.

Generally, IRC Section 415(c)(3) compensation is the compensation of the participant from the employer for the year. IRC Section 415(c)(3) compensation includes (but is not limited to) wages, salaries, fees for professional services and other amounts received for personal services actually rendered in the course of employment with the employer to the extent that the amounts are includable in income. (See Treas. Reg. §1.415-2(d) for what items of compensation are included in and excluded from IRC Section 415(c)(3) compensation.) IRC Section 415(c)(3) (and hence, IRC Section 414(s)) will automatically be satisfied by the use of wages as defined for income tax withholding purposes, or wages reportable in Box 1 of Form W-2 (which may include certain items that are not "wages" for withholding purposes). Treas. Regs. §§1.414(s)-1(c)(2), 1.415-2(d)(11).

Compensation includes elective deferrals, as well as any amounts contributed or deferred by the employer at the election of the employee that are excluded from income under a cafeteria plan, a qualified transportation fringe benefit plan, or an IRC Section 457 plan. IRC Sec. 415(c)(3)(D). (However, IRC Section 414(s) permits an employer to either exclude or include such deferrals, as described below.)

Employers may demonstrate that a definition of compensation is nondiscriminatory using "snapshot" testing on a single day during the plan year, provided that day is representative of the employer's work force and the plan's coverage throughout the plan year. Rev. Proc. 93-42, 1993-2 CB 540.

A definition of compensation other than IRC Section 415(c)(3) compensation can still satisfy IRC Section 414(s) if it meets the safe harbor definition or meets one of the alternative definitions plus a nondiscrimination test. IRC Sec. 414(s)(3). The safe harbor definition is IRC Section 415(c)(3) compensation, reduced by (1) reimbursements or other expense allowances, (2) fringe benefits (cash and noncash), (3) moving expenses, (4) deferred compensation, and (5) welfare benefits. Treas. Reg. §1.414(s)-1(c)(3). An alternative definition that defines compensation based on the rate of pay of each employee satisfies IRC Section 414(s) if the definition is nondiscriminatory and meets certain other requirements specified in the regulations. Treas. Reg. §1.414(s)-1(e).

Generally, an employer may elect not to treat any of the following items as compensation: (1) elective contributions to a cafeteria plan, a qualified transportation fringe benefit plan, an IRC Section 401(k) arrangement, a cash or deferred SEP, or a tax sheltered annuity; (2) compensation deferred under an IRC Section 457 plan, and (3) employee contributions to a government employer pick-up plan. IRC Sec. 414(s)(2); Treas. Reg. §1.414(s)-1(c)(4).

Any other *reasonable* alternative definition of compensation can satisfy IRC Section 414(s) if it does not, by design, favor highly compensated employees and it meets a nondiscriminatory requirement. An alternative definition of compensation meets the nondiscriminatory requirement if the average percentage of total compensation included under the alternative definition for the employer's highly compensated employees as a group does not exceed by more than a de minimis amount the average percentage of total compensation included under the alternative definition for the employer's other employees as a group. Treas. Reg. §1.414(s)-1(d). Self-employed individuals are subject to special rules for purposes of using an alternative definition. See Treas. Regs. §§1.414(s)-1(d)(3)(iii)(B), 1.414(s)-1(g).

Compensation may have a slightly different definition for other purposes of the Code. *ASRS, Sec. 59, ¶490.4(e).*

SECTION 415 LIMITS

332. What are the Section 415 limits for qualified plans?

IRC Section 415 sets maximum levels for contributions or benefits that a qualified plan may provide. The plan's provisions must preclude the possibility that benefits or contributions will exceed the limitations set forth in IRC Section 415 for any limitation year. See IRC Sec. 401(a)(16); Prop. Treas. Reg. §1.415(a)-1(d).

For limitation years beginning in 2006, the highest *annual benefit* payable under a defined benefit plan (or under all such plans aggregated, if the employer has more than one) must not exceed the lesser of: (a) 100% of the participant's average compensation in his *high three years of service*, or (b) $175,000 (in 2006, as indexed). IRC Sec. 415(b)(1). See Q 372 for details on the application of the 415 limits to defined benefit plans.

The "annual additions" to a participant's account under a defined contribution plan (or all such accounts aggregated, if the employer has more than one defined contribution plan) must not exceed the lesser of: (a) 100% of the participant's compensation, or (b) $44,000 (as indexed for 2006). IRC Sec. 415(c). See Q 377 for details on the application of the 415 limits to defined contribution plans.

Unless the plan provides otherwise, a *limitation year* is the calendar year. Prop. Treas. Reg. §1.415(j)-1(a). Contributions in excess of the Section 415 limits disqualify a plan for the year made and all subsequent years until such excess is corrected. See Prop. Treas. Reg. §1.415(a)-1(a)(3); *Martin Fireproofing Profit Sharing Plan and Trust v. Comm.*, 92 TC 1173 (1989). The proposed regulations referenced throughout this question were issued in May, 2005 and are proposed to be effective for limitation years beginning on or after January 1, 2007. REG-130241-04, 70 Fed. Reg. 31214 (May 31, 2005).

For purposes of the IRC Section 415 limits, a benefit provided to an alternate payee of a participant pursuant to a qualified domestic relations order (QDRO, see Q 349) is treated as if it were provided to the participant. Prop. Treas. Reg. §1.415(a)-1(f)(5).

A controlled group of corporations or a group of trades or businesses under common control (each defined using a 50% rather than 80% test—see Q 359), or all members of an affiliated service group (see Q 360) are considered one employer for purposes of applying the limitations on contributions or benefits. IRC Secs. 415(g), 415(h), 414(m); see Prop. Treas. Reg. §1.415(a)-1(f)(2).

PENSION AND PROFIT SHARING: QUALIFICATION   Q 333

A plan may incorporate the 415 limits by reference, and will not fail to meet the definitely determinable benefit requirement (for defined benefit plans) or the definite predetermined allocation formula requirement (for defined contribution plans), merely because it incorporates the limits of Section 415 by reference. See Prop. Treas. Reg. §1.415(a)-1(d)(3). *ASRS, Sec. 59, ¶470.*

VESTING

333. What are the vesting standards that a qualified plan must meet?

A plan must meet the following minimum standards concerning nonforfeitability of benefits (vesting) (IRC Sec. 401(a)(7); for top heavy vesting, see Q 352):

A. An employee's right to his normal retirement benefit must be nonforfeitable upon the attainment of normal retirement age. IRC Sec. 411(a). "Normal retirement age" is defined in the Code as the earlier of (a) normal retirement age under the plan, or (b) the later of age 65 or the fifth anniversary of the date participation commenced. IRC Sec. 411(a)(8). "Normal retirement benefit" means the employee's *accrued* benefit without regard to whether it is vested; thus, a plan cannot qualify if it provides no retirement benefits for employees with less than five years of vesting service before normal retirement age. See Rev. Rul. 84-69, 1984-1 CB 125. See also *Board of Trustees of N.Y. Hotel Trades Council & Hotel Assoc. of N.Y. City, Inc. Pension Fund v. Comm.*, TC Memo 1981-597, app. dismissed (2nd Cir. 1982); *Trustees of the Taxicab Indus. Pension Fund v. Comm.*, TC Memo 1981-651; *Caterpillar Tractor Co. v. Comm.*, 72 TC 1088 (1979). A plan that provides that an employee's right to his normal retirement benefit becomes nonforfeitable on his *normal retirement date* will fail to meet this requirement if his *normal retirement date*, as defined in the plan, may occur after his "normal retirement age" as defined in IRC Section 411 (e.g., where *normal retirement date* is defined in the plan to be the first day of the calendar month following the employee's 65th birthday). Rev. Rul. 81-211, 1981-2 CB 98.

B. An employee's rights in his accrued benefit derived from his own contributions must be nonforfeitable. IRC Sec. 411(a)(1). Nonetheless, once annuity payments begin, a forfeiture does not arise merely because payments cease on the death of the participant. Treas. Reg. §1.411(a)-4(b)(1)(ii). For rules relating to allocation of accrued benefits between employer and mandatory employee contributions, see Rev. Rul. 76-47, 1976-1 CB 109 and Rev. Rul. 78-202, 1978-1 CB 124, as amplified by Rev. Rul. 89-60, 1989-1 CB 113.

C. If the present value of an employee's vested accrued benefit exceeds $5,000, the benefit may not be immediately distributed without the consent of the participant. IRC Sec. 411(a)(11)(A). In addition, for distributions on or after March 28, 2005, if the present value of a participant's vested accrued benefit exceeds $1,000, absent an election by the participant, distributions must be transferred directly to an IRA. See IRC Sec. 401(a)(31(B); Labor Reg. §2550.404a-2; for details see Q 447.

The present value for this purpose is determined using the interest rate required by IRC Section 417(e)(3). IRC Sec. 411(a)(11)(B); see also Notice 2004-78, 2004-48 IRB 879. For purposes of the $5,000 limit, the vested accrued benefit may be determined without regard to rollover contributions and earnings allocable to them. See IRC Sec. 411(a)(11)(D). The allocation of plan administrative expenses to former (but not current) employees on a pro rata or other reasonable basis does not violate this requirement. See Rev. Rul. 2004-10, 2004-7 IRB 484.

The consent must be made within certain time limits, generally not less than 30 days, nor more than 90 days, before the distribution commences, and may be made only after the participant receives notice of his distribution options, and an explanation of their relative values, as specified in regulations. Generally, the use of certain electronic media for meeting the consent requirement is permitted. See Prop. Treas. Reg. §§1.411(a)-11, 1.401(a)-21.

A participant's consent to a distribution is invalid if, under the plan, a significant detriment is imposed on any participant who does not consent to the distribution. Treas. Reg. §1.411(a)-11(c)(2)(i). The IRS ruled that where a plan provided a broad range of investment alternatives to employee participants, but not to participants who terminated employment prior to normal retirement age, a significant detriment was imposed. Consequently, the consents obtained from participants were invalid and the plan failed to satisfy IRC Section 411(a)(11). Rev. Rul. 96-47, 1996-2 CB 35.

D. If an employee's benefit accruals (or allocations, in the case of a defined contribution plan) cease, or if the rate of an employee's benefit accrual (or rate of allocation) is reduced because of the attainment of any age, the plan will not satisfy the vesting requirements of the Internal Revenue Code. IRC Secs. 411(b)(1)(H), 411(b)(2).

E. An employee must be given nonforfeitable rights to his accrued benefits derived from employer contributions in accordance with *one* of the following vesting schedules:

"Five year cliff vesting." An employee who has at least five years of service must have a nonforfeitable right to 100% of his accrued benefit. IRC Sec. 411(a)(2)(A). See Temp. Treas. Reg. §1.411(a)-3T(b). In the case of matching contributions (as defined in IRC Sec. 401(m)(4)(A)), a *three year* cliff vesting requirement must be satisfied. IRC Sec. 411(a)(12)(A).

"Three to seven year vesting." An employee who has completed at least *three years of service* must have a nonforfeitable right to at least the following percentages of his accrued benefit: 20% after three years of service, 40% after four years of service, 60% after five years of service, 80% after six years of service, and 100% after seven years of service. IRC Sec. 411(a)(2)(B). See Temp. Treas. Reg. §1.411(a)-3T(c). In the case of matching contributions (as defined in IRC Sec. 401(m)(4)(A)), gradual vesting must take place over a *two to six year period* (20% after two years of service, 40% after three years of service, etc.). IRC Sec. 411(a)(12)(B).

Although it is often permissible for a plan to satisfy one of these requirements with regard to one group of employees and the other requirement with regard to another group, a plan must satisfy one of the requirements with regard to all of a particular employee's years of service. Temp. Treas. Reg. §1.411(a)-3T(a)(2).

A right to an accrued benefit is considered to be "nonforfeitable" at a particular time if, at that time and thereafter, it is an unconditional right. Temp. Treas. Reg. §1.411(a)-4T(a).

PENSION AND PROFIT SHARING: QUALIFICATION Q 333

The term "year of service" generally means a 12-month period designated by the plan during which the employee has worked at least 1,000 hours. IRC Sec. 411(a)(5). All years of an employee's service with the employer are taken into account for purposes of computing the nonforfeitable percentages specified above, except those years specifically excluded in IRC Section 411(a). See Treas. Regs. §§1.411(a)-5; 1.411(a)-6.

The term "accrued benefit" means, in the case of a defined benefit plan, the employee's accrued benefit determined under the plan (see Q 373) expressed in the form of an annual benefit commencing at normal retirement age, or, in the case of any other kind of plan, the balance of the employee's account. IRC Sec. 411(a); Treas. Reg. §1.411(a)-7. Generally, the accrued benefit of a participant may not be decreased by an amendment to the plan (see Q 334).

If a plan's vesting schedule is modified by a plan amendment, each participant with at least three years of service must be permitted to elect to have his nonforfeitable percentage computed under the plan without regard to the amendment. IRC Sec. 411(a)(10); Temp. Treas. Reg. §1.411(a)-8T(b). (For this purpose, years of service are calculated without regard to the exceptions set forth in IRC Section 411(a)(4). Temp. Treas. Reg. §1.411(a)-8T(b)(3).)

Courts make a distinction between "vesting" and "nonforfeitability." A participant is *vested* when he has an immediate, fixed right of present or future enjoyment of his accrued benefit. But a plan may provide that a vested benefit will be *forfeited* in whole or in part if, for example, the participant terminates his employment and goes to work for a competitor of the employer or commits a crime against the employer. Rev. Rul. 85-31, 1985-1 CB 153. Thus for example, a participant could be offered immediate 100% vesting of his benefit under a plan, but the benefit could be forfeitable (to the extent the benefit would not be vested under the closest Code and ERISA schedules) if he commits certain forbidden acts.

Cases have held that such forfeiture provisions are enforceable only to the extent that the accrued benefit forfeited by commission of the forbidden act is in excess of the nonforfeitable accrued benefit derived from employer contributions to which the participant was entitled under the nearest equivalent ERISA vesting schedule at the time the forfeiture occurred. *Clark v. Lauren Young Tire Center Profit Sharing Trust*, 816 F.2d 480 (9th Cir. 1987); *Noell v. American Design, Inc.*, 764 F.2d 827 (11th Cir. 1985); *Nedrow v. MacFarlane & Hays Co. Employees' Profit Sharing Plan & Trust*, 476 F. Supp. 934 (E.D. Mich. 1979); *Fremont v. McGraw Edison*, 606 F.2d 752 (7th Cir. 1979); *Hepple v. Roberts & Dybdahl, Inc.*, 622 F.2d 962 (8th Cir. 1980); *Hummell v. S.E. Rykoff & Co.*, 2 EBC 1417 (9th Cir. 1980); *Montgomery v. Lowe*, 507 F. Supp. 618 (S.D. Texas 1981). The temporary regulations generally follow this reasoning. See Temp. Treas. Reg. §1.411(a)-4T.

The vesting rules do not require a plan to provide a preretirement death benefit, aside from the employee's accrued benefit derived from his own contributions. The Code provides, "A right to an accrued benefit derived from employer contributions shall not be treated as forfeitable solely because the plan provides that it is not payable if the participant dies ..." except as required by the survivor annuity provisions. IRC Sec. 411(a)(3)(A). See Q 336. A reversion to the employer of contributions made under a mistake of fact or a mistake as to deductibility is not a forfeiture even if it results in adjustment of an entirely or partially nonforfeitable account, provided the return is limited to an amount that does not reduce a participant's balance below what it would have been had the mistaken amount not been contributed. Rev. Rul. 77-200, 1977-1 CB 98, superseded by Rev. Rul. 91-4, 1991-1 CB 54.

A plan may provide that payment of benefits to a retired employee is suspended for any period during which he resumes active employment with the employer who maintains the plan (or, in the case of a multiemployer plan, in the same industry, the same trade or craft, and the same geographic area covered by the plan as when his benefits commenced) without violating the nonforfeitability rules. IRC Sec. 411(a)(3)(B). However, the provision must be carefully drafted and administered to comply with applicable regulations and rulings. See Labor Reg. §2530.203-3; Rev. Rul. 81-140, 1981-1 CB 180; Notice 82-23, 1982-2 CB 752.

Where there is a pattern of abuse (such as dismissing employees to prevent vesting), a more rapid rate of vesting may be required. ERISA Conf. Comm. Report, 1974-3 CB 437. The determination of whether there is a pattern of abuse depends solely on the facts and circumstances in each case. Prop. Treas. Reg. §1.411(d)-1; IR 80-85.

Full vesting required on plan termination or discontinuance of contributions. The plan *must* provide that upon its termination or partial termination (or, in the case of a profit sharing plan, also upon complete discontinuance of contributions), benefits accrued to the date of termination (or date of discontinuance of contributions) become nonforfeitable to the extent funded at such date. IRC Sec. 411(d)(3); Treas. Reg. §1.411(d)-2. Unless other facts suggest a partial termination, the mere merger or conversion of a money purchase pension plan into a profit sharing plan does not result in a partial termination for this purpose, provided that: (a) all employees who are covered by the money purchase plan remain covered under the continuing profit sharing plan, (b) the money purchase plan assets and liabilities retain their characterization under the profit sharing plan, and (c) the employees vest in the profit sharing plan under the same vesting schedule that existed under the money purchase plan. Rev. Rul. 2002-42, 2002-2 CB 76.

Complete discontinuance of contributions may occur if amounts contributed by the employer are not substantial enough to reflect an intent to continue to maintain the plan. On the other hand, temporary suspension may not ripen into discontinuance. Failure for five years by an employer to make contributions solely because there are no current or accumulated profits does not constitute discontinuance where it is reasonable to expect profits to exist in future years. Rev. Rul. 80-146, 1980-1 CB 90. Whether discontinuance has occurred depends on all the facts and circumstances. Thus, a provision that discontinuance will occur only when the ratio of aggregate contributions to compensation falls below a predetermined figure does not meet this qualification requirement. Rev. Rul. 80-277, 1980-2 CB 153.

Reduction of benefits by offset. The vesting requirements are not violated by a provision requiring pension payments to be reduced, or offset, by amounts received by the pensioner under a state workers' compensation law. Furthermore, state laws prohibiting offset of retirement benefits by workers' compensation benefits are preempted by ERISA. *Alessi v. Raybestos-Manhattan, Inc.*; *Buczynski v. General Motors Corp.*, 47 AFTR 2d 81-1513 (Sup. Ct. 1981). Vesting requirements were not violated where, under a severance pay plan, an employee's severance pay was reduced by the actuarial value, at discharge, of the employee's vested interest in a qualified pension plan. The severance pay plan was not a pension plan under ERISA subject

PENSION AND PROFIT SHARING: QUALIFICATION   Q 334

to vesting standards. *Spitzler v. New York Post Corp.*, 620 F.2d 19 (2nd Cir. 1980). A pension plan whose benefits may be offset by benefits under a profit sharing plan will be considered to satisfy benefit accrual requirements if (1) the accrued benefit determined without regard to the offset satisfies the vesting requirements and (2) the offset is equal to the vested portion of the account balance in the profit sharing plan (or a specified portion of the vested account balance). Rev. Rul. 76-259, 1976-2 CB 111. *ASRS, Sec. 59, ¶460.*

334. What is the anti-cutback rule and what benefits does it protect?

The accrued benefit of a participant generally may not be decreased (directly or indirectly) by an amendment to the plan. IRC Sec. 411(d)(6)(A); ERISA Sec. 204(g). This provision is referred to as the anti-cutback rule. (An exception is provided in certain cases of substantial business hardship; see below.)

Except as otherwise provided below, a plan amendment that has the effect of (1) eliminating or reducing an early retirement benefit or a retirement-type subsidy or (2) eliminating certain optional forms of benefit attributable to service before the amendment, is treated as impermissibly reducing accrued benefits. IRC Sec. 411(d)(6)(B); see Treas. Reg. §1.411(d)-4, A-1(a).

The anti-cutback rule does not prohibit any plan amendment that reduces or eliminates benefits or subsidies that create significant burdens or complexities for the plan and plan participants, unless the amendment adversely affects the rights of any participant in a more than de minimis manner. See IRC Sec. 411(d)(6)(B). However, if a series of plan amendments made at different times have the effect, when taken together, of reducing or eliminating a protected benefit in a more than *de minimis* manner, the amendment will violate IRC Sec. 411(d)(6). See Treas. Reg. §1.411(d)-4, A-2(c).

Employee stock ownership plans (ESOPs, see Q 413) will not be treated as failing to meet the anti-cutback requirement merely on account of modifying distribution options in a nondiscriminatory manner. IRC Sec. 411(d)(6)(C); Treas. Reg. §1.411(d)-4, A-2(d).

Transfers between plans. Generally, benefits that are protected under IRC Section 411(d)(6) may not be eliminated by reason of a transfer, or any transaction amending or having the effect of amending a plan to transfer benefits. However, a defined contribution "transferee" plan (e.g., in a merger, acquisition, consolidation, or similar transaction) will not be treated as failing the anti-cutback rule merely because the transferee plan does not provide some or all of the forms of distribution previously available under a "transferor" plan, if certain requirements are met. IRC Sec. 411(d)(6)(D); see Treas. Reg. §1.411(d)-4, A-3(b).

Elimination of a form of distribution. Generally, except to the extent provided in regulations, a defined contribution plan will not be treated as failing the anti-cutback rule merely because of the elimination of a form of distribution previously available under the plan, provided that, with respect to any participant: (i) a single sum payment is available to the participant at the same time or times as the form of distribution being eliminated, and (ii) the single sum payment is based on the same or greater portion of the participant's account as the form of distribution being eliminated. IRC Sec. 411(d)(6)(E).

Redundancy rule. A plan generally may be amended to eliminate an optional form of benefit with respect to benefits accrued before the amendment date if the optional form of benefit is redundant with a retained optional form of benefit. Treas. Reg. §1.411(d)-3(c)(1)(ii). For this purpose, the regulations identify six basic "families" of optional forms of benefit: (1) the 50% or more joint and contingent family, (2) the below 50% joint and contingent family, (3) the 10 years or less term certain and life annuity family, (4) the greater than 10 years term certain and life annuity family, (5) the 10 years or less level installment family, and (6) the greater than 10 years level installment family. See Treas. Reg. §1.411(d)-3(c)(4). However, the redundancy rule does not apply to certain "core options" (see alternative rule, below) unless the retained optional form of benefit and the eliminated option are identical except for differences described in the proposed regulations. See Treas. Reg. §1.411(d)-3(c)(2)(ii).

Alternative rule. In the alternative, an employer is permitted to eliminate a protected benefit if (a) the amendment does not apply to participants with annuity starting dates less than four years after the date the amendment is adopted and (b) certain "core options" are retained. See Treas. Reg. §1.411(d)-3(d). The "core options" generally mean: (i) a straight life annuity, (ii) a 75% joint and contingent annuity, (iii) a 10-year certain and life annuity, and (iv) the most valuable option for a participant with a short life expectancy. see Treas. Reg. §1.411(d)-3(g)(5).

Benefits Protected

An employee's accrued benefit is the balance of the employee's account held under the plan; however, the IRS has stated that it also includes amounts to which the participant is entitled under the terms of the plan, even where the bookkeeping process of crediting those amounts to the participant's account has not yet occurred. TAM 9735001. Thus, a retroactive amendment to a defined contribution plan's allocation formula after the contribution for the year had been made but before the allocation had taken place was determined to have violated IRC Section 411(d)(6), because it reduced the amounts allocated to some of the participants. See TAM 9735001.

The elimination of a cost-of-living adjustment (COLA) provision through termination of a plan violated the ERISA prohibition against the reduction of accrued benefits. *Hickey v. Chicago Truck Drivers, Helpers and Warehouse Workers Union,* 980 F.2d 1080 (7th Cir. 1992); but see "Benefits Not Protected" below. It has also been held that a company's limitation of a lump sum distribution option, resulting in a decrease in former employees' accrued benefits violated the ERISA provision and IRC Section 411(d)(6). *Auwater v. Donohue Paper Sales Corp. Defined Benefit Pension Plan,* 93-1 USTC ¶50,096 (E.D. NY 1992).

The Supreme Court has determined that the rule prohibiting cutbacks of early retirement benefits or retirement-type subsidies was violated when a company adopted a plan amendment expanding the range of post-retirement employment that would disqualify retired construction workers from receiving pension benefits. *Central Laborers' Pension Fund v. Heinz,* 124 S.Ct. 2230 (2004). However, the IRS has limited the retroactive application of this provision. See Rev. Proc. 2005-23, 2005-18 IRB 991.

A change in actuarial factors may result in a violation of the anti-cutback rule. A cash balance plan (see Q 374) was determined to have violated the rule where its use of a lower interest rate than was guaranteed by the plan resulted in a taxpayer receiving less than the actuarial equivalent of her normal retirement benefit. See *Edsen v. Bank of Boston*, 2002-2 USTC ¶50,738 (2nd Cir. 2000). The IRS has provided guidance as to when a change in actuarial factors will indirectly affect accrued benefits, as well as acceptable methods for preventing a violation of the vesting rules as a result of such a change. See Rev. Rul. 81-12, 1981-1 CB 228.

Benefits Not Protected

In spite of the fact that a cost of living adjustment (COLA) provision may constitute an essential element of an accrued benefit (see *Hickey v. Chicago Truck Drivers, Helpers and Warehouse Workers Union* above), a COLA provision was not an accrued benefit with respect to retirees who retired before the provision was adopted, even though it was made available to them. *Sheet Metal Workers' Nat'l Pension Fund Bd. of Trustees v. Comm.*, 117 TC 220 (2001), *aff'd* 2003-1 USTC ¶50,221 (4th Cir. 2003).

Regulations permit profit sharing or stock bonus plans (as well as cash or deferred arrangements) to be amended to eliminate hardship withdrawal provisions, without violating IRC Section 411(d)(6). Treas. Reg. §1.411(d)-4, A-2(b)(2)(x).

Generally, plan amendments (adopted within the remedial amendment period) necessary to bring the plan into compliance with the Code, or prevent unintended benefit increases as a result of a Code amendment, are afforded relief from IRC Section 411(d)(6). See, e.g., Rev. Proc. 94-13, 1994-1 CB 566 (reduction of compensation limit under IRC Section 401(a)(17)); Notice 99-44, 1999-2 CB 326 (repeal of combined plan limit). Thus, for example, the elimination of the right to receive employer securities from an S corporation ESOP does not violate IRC Section 411(d)(6). See Treas. Reg. §1.411(d)-4, A-2(d), A-11. Nor does the elimination of the right to receive a distribution prior to retirement after age 70½ (see Q 340), if certain conditions are met. See Treas. Reg. §1.411(d)-4, A-10.

The following benefits are not protected under IRC Section 411(d)(6) and may be reduced or otherwise amended: (1) ancillary life insurance protection; (2) accident or health insurance benefits; (3) availability of loans; (4) the right to make after-tax contributions or elective deferrals; and (5) the right to direct investments. Treas. Reg. §1.411(d)-4, A-1(d); see Rev. Rul. 96-47, 1996-2 CB 35. Generally ancillary benefits, other rights or features, and any other benefits not described in section 411(d)(6) are not protected under section 411(d)(6). See Treas. Reg. §1.411(d)-4, A-1(d).

In spite of the protection provided to early retirement benefits, the IRS determined that where an employer offered an early retirement window benefit repeatedly for substantially consecutive, limited periods of time, its failure to offer the benefit permanently did not violate IRC Section 411(d)(6). Rev. Rul. 92-66, 1992-2 CB 92.

Special Rules

Plans subject to the funding standards of ERISA Section 302 (generally, defined benefit plans, money purchase pensions and target benefit plans), must meet a notice requirement if the plan is amended in a manner that significantly reduces the participants' rate of future benefit accruals. ERISA Sec. 204(h).

Under limited circumstances, a retroactive plan amendment reducing benefits may be available in the case of a substantial business hardship where it is determined that a waiver of the minimum funding standard (see Q 389) is unavailable or inadequate.

IRC Sec. 412(c)(8). Among the factors the IRS will consider in determining whether a substantial business hardship exists are whether: (1) the employer is operating at an economic loss; (2) there is substantial unemployment or underemployment in the trade or business and the industry concerned; (3) the sales and profits of the industry are depressed or declining; and (4) it is reasonable to expect that the plan will be continued only if the waiver is granted. IRC Sec. 412(d)(2). The Service permitted such an amendment to a plan whose sponsor was insolvent and expected no additional revenues (however, the plan's only participants and the sponsor's only employees were the five owners of the business). See Let. Rul. 9736044. *ASRS, Sec. 59, ¶450.*

AUTOMATIC SURVIVOR BENEFITS

335. Which types of plans are subject to the automatic survivor benefit requirements?

The automatic survivor benefit requirements (i.e., the requirement that a plan provide the qualified joint and survivor annuity (QJSA) and qualified preretirement survivor annuity (QPSA) forms of benefit – see Q 336) apply to all defined benefit plans and to those defined contribution plans which are subject to the minimum funding standards (e.g., target benefit and money purchase pensions). IRC Sec. 401(a)(11)(B).

The automatic survivor benefit requirements may also apply to any participant under any other defined contribution plans *unless*: (a) the plan provides that in the event of the participant's death, his nonforfeitable accrued benefit will be paid in full to his surviving spouse (or to another designated beneficiary if the spouse consents or if there is no surviving spouse); (b) the participant does not elect payment of benefits in the form of a life annuity; and (c) with respect to such participant, the plan is not a direct or an indirect transferee of a plan to which the automatic survivor annuity requirements apply. IRC Sec. 401(a)(11)(B); Treas. Reg. §1.401(a)-20, A-3.

If the three requirements in the preceding paragraph are met, the automatic survivor benefit requirements will not apply to the portion of benefits accrued under a tax credit ESOP or leveraged ESOP if the participant has the right (1) to demand distribution in the form of employer securities, or (2) to require repurchase by the employer of non-publicly traded securities. IRC Secs. 401(a)(11)(C), 409(h). *ASRS, Sec. 59, ¶460.*

336. What forms of survivor benefits must be provided under a qualified plan?

Plans that are subject to the automatic survivor benefit requirements (see Q 335) must provide that, unless waived by the participant with the consent of his spouse (see Q 337), retirement benefits will be paid in the form of a "qualified joint and survivor annuity." IRC Sec. 401(a)(11); Treas. Reg. §1.401(a)-20. An unmarried participant must be provided with a life annuity, unless he elects another form of benefit. Treas. Reg. §1.401(a)-20, A-25. Furthermore, such plans must provide that if a vested participant dies prior to the *annuity starting date*, leaving a surviving spouse, benefits will be paid in the form of a "qualified preretirement survivor annuity"; however, this also may be waived by the participant with the consent of his spouse (see Q 337). These requirements apply to retirement benefits derived from employer and employee contributions and those attributable to rollover contributions. Treas. Reg. §1.401(a)-20, A-11.

If the present value of the participant's benefit does not exceed $5,000, the plan may provide for a lump sum cash-out of the qualified joint and survivor annuity or a qualified preretirement survivor annuity benefit. However, after the participant's annuity starting date (see below) such a cash-out may be made only if the participant and his spouse (or surviving spouse) consent in writing. IRC Sec. 417(e)(1); Treas. Reg. §1.417(e)-1(b)(2)(i).

The "annuity starting date" is the first day of the first period for which an amount is payable as an annuity (regardless of when or whether payment is actually made) or, in the case of benefits not payable in the form of an annuity, the date on which all events have occurred which entitle the participant to the benefit. IRC Sec. 417(f)(2); Treas. Reg. §1.401(a)-20, A-10(b)(2). This requirement applies only to those benefits in which a participant was vested immediately prior to his death under a defined benefit plan and to all nonforfeitable benefits that are payable under a defined contribution plan. Treas. Reg. §1.401(a)-20, A-12.

Qualified joint and survivor annuity (QJSA) means an annuity: (1) for the life of the participant, with a survivor annuity for the life of his spouse that is not less than one-half (nor greater than 100%) of the amount of the annuity payable during the joint lives of the participant and his spouse, *and* (2) that is the actuarial equivalent of a single annuity for the life of the participant. (Any annuity having the foregoing effect will be treated as a QJSA.) IRC Sec. 417(b). With respect to married participants, the qualified joint and survivor annuity must be at least as valuable as any other optional form of benefit payable under the plan at the same time. If a plan has two joint and survivor annuities that satisfy the QJSA requirements and one has a greater actuarial value than the other, the more valuable one is the QJSA. A plan may designate which joint and survivor annuity is the QJSA if the plan offers two actuarially equivalent joint and survivor annuities that meet the QJSA requirements; however, the plan may allow a participant to elect out of the designated QJSA in favor of the other joint and survivor annuity without spousal consent. Treas. Reg. §1.401(a)-20, A-16.

A plan must permit a participant to receive a distribution under a QJSA when the participant attains the earliest retirement age under the plan. The earliest retirement age is the earlier of (1) the earliest age at which a participant could receive a distribution under the plan or (2) the early retirement age determined under the plan (or, if no early retirement age, the normal retirement age under the plan). Treas. Reg. §1.401(a)-20, A-17.

Qualified preretirement survivor annuity (QPSA) means a survivor annuity for the life of the surviving spouse of the participant under which payments are to begin not later than the month in which the participant would have reached the earliest retirement age provided under the plan, and that meets the following requirements with respect to the amount of the annuity:

(1) In the case of a defined contribution plan, the actuarial equivalent of the survivor annuity must not be less than one-half of the participant's vested account balance as of the date of his death. Treas. Reg. §1.401(a)-20, A-20.

(2) In the case of all other plans, (a) if the participant died *after* the date he attained the earliest retirement age provided under the plan, the payments to the surviving spouse must not be less than the amounts that would have been payable under the survivor

portion of a qualified joint and survivor annuity had the participant retired with an immediate qualified joint and survivor annuity on the day before he died; or (b) if the participant died *on or before* the date he would have reached the earliest retirement age, the payments to the surviving spouse must not be less than the amounts that would have been paid under the survivor portion of a QJSA had the participant separated from service on the earlier of the actual time of separation or death, survived to the earliest retirement age, retired with an immediate qualified joint and survivor annuity at the earliest retirement age, *and* died on the day after he reached the earliest retirement age. IRC Sec. 417(c); Treas. Reg. §1.401(a)-20, A-18. In any case, however, payments to the surviving spouse must not violate the incidental benefit rule (see Q 369). Sen. Fin. Comm. Rep. to P.L. 98-397. See Rev. Rul. 85-15, 1985-1 CB 132.

A defined benefit plan must permit the surviving spouse to receive distributions under the QPSA no later than the month in which the participant would have attained the earliest retirement age. In the case of a defined contribution plan, the spouse must be permitted to elect to begin receiving payments under the QPSA within a reasonable time after the participant's death. Treas. Reg. §1.401(a)-20, A-22.

A plan generally is not required to provide either the QJSA or the QPSA in any case where the participant and his spouse were not married throughout the 1-year period ending on the *earlier of* the participant's annuity starting date (see above) *or* the date of the participant's death. However, if a participant marries within one year before the annuity starting date and he and his spouse were married for at least a 1-year period ending on or before the date of the participant's death, such participant and such spouse are treated as though they had been married throughout the 1-year period ending on the participant's annuity starting date. IRC Sec. 417(d); Treas. Reg. §1.401(a)-20, A-25(b)(2). Special rules may apply where there is a qualified domestic relations order (QDRO) in effect that applies to plan benefits (see Q 349).

Planning Point: Because of the administrative difficulties involved, plan sponsors should consider whether the costs of imposing a one-year of marriage requirement outweigh any potential savings. *Martin Silfen, J.D., Brown Brothers Harriman Trust Co., LLC.*

Written Notice

A plan generally must, within certain specified periods, provide each participant (vested and nonvested, married or unmarried) with a written explanation of the automatic survivor annuity forms of benefit and of the participant's (and his spouse's) rights with respect to waiving such benefits. IRC Sec. 417(a)(3). Proposed regulations would allow plans to provide notices of automatic survivor benefits in electronic form, provided certain requirements are met. See Prop. Treas. Reg. §1.417(a)(3)-1(a)(3); Prop. Treas. Reg. §1.401(a)-21.

The explanation may be provided after the annuity starting date; however, the *applicable election period* (i.e., for waiving the benefit – see Q 337) may not end before the 30th day after the explanation is provided. IRC Sec. 417(a)(7). (Under certain circumstances, a "retroactive annuity starting date" may be permitted; see Treas. Reg. §1.417(e)-1(b)(3)(iv); see Q 337.) The plan may allow the participant (with any applicable spousal consent) to waive the 30-day requirement if the distribution begins more than seven days after the explanation is provided. IRC Sec. 417(a)(7)(B); TD 8796, 1999-1 CB 344. Sample language for the required explanation was provided by the IRS in Notice 97-10, 1997-1 CB 370.

PENSION AND PROFIT SHARING: QUALIFICATION   Q 337

The explanation must include information on the financial effect and relative value comparisons of any optional forms of benefit compared to the value of the QJSA. This may be offered in the form of generally applicable information *or* as information that is specific to the participant to whom it is provided. Details and procedures for making the required disclosures, as well as a sample disclosure, are set forth in final regulations. See Treas. Reg. §1.417(a)(3)-1. The final regulations are effective for certain qualified joint and survivor annuity explanations with annuity starting dates after February 1, 2006; however, for optional forms of benefit subject to the requirements of IRC Section 417(e)(3) (e.g., single sums), the explanation must be provided with respect to annuity starting dates after October 1, 2004. See Prop. Treas. Reg. §1.401(a)-20; REG-152914-04, 2005-9 IRB 650.

A plan that fully subsidizes a qualified survivor annuity is not required to provide an explanation unless it offers participants an election to waive the benefit or designate a beneficiary. IRC Secs. 417(a)(3), 417(a)(5); Treas. Reg. §1.401(a)-20, A-35 to A-37.

Special Rules

The present value of the accrued benefit generally must be determined using the annual interest rate on 30-year Treasury securities for the month before the date of distribution; however, temporary regulations permit the employer to base the determination on a monthly, quarterly or annual interest rate. Also, the rate may be determined using any month during a "stability period" of up to five months, provided the plan specifies which month will be used. In any event, the interest rate must be determined in a consistent manner that is applied uniformly to all plan participants. IRC Sec. 417(e)(3); Treas. Reg. §1.417(e)-1(d)(4).

Corrective distributions of excess contributions and excess aggregate contributions (see Q 406) as well as of excess deferrals (see Q 396) are not subject to the spousal consent rules. Treas. Regs. §§1.401(k)-1(f)(4)(iii); 1.401(m)-1(e)(3)(iii).

Generally, plans that offer plan loans (see Q 420 to Q 422) and are subject to the automatic survivor benefit requirements must provide that no portion of the accrued benefit of the participant may be used as security for any loan unless, at the time the security agreement is entered into, the participant's spouse consents to the use of the accrued benefit as security. IRC Secs. 417(a)(1), 417(a)(4); Treas. Reg. §1.401(a)-20, A-24. If spousal consent is not obtained or is not required at the time benefits are used as security, it is not required at the time of any setoff of the loan against the accrued benefit, even if the participant is married to a different spouse at the time of the setoff. Treas. Reg. §1.401(a)-20, A-24(b).

The automatic survivor benefit rules generally do not apply to a beneficiary who murders his participant spouse. See *Mendez-Bellido v. Board of Trustees of Div. 1181*, 709 F. Supp. 329 (E.D. NY 1989). See also, Let. Ruls. 8908063, 8905058. However, an employee's widow convicted of his murder was held entitled to receive the preretirement annuity where applicable state law made her a constructive trustee of the annuity. *George Pfau's Sons Co. v. Neal*, 1996 Ind. App. Lexis 671 (Ct. App. Ind. 1996). *ASRS, Sec. 59, ¶480.4.*

337. Under what circumstances may survivor benefits required under a qualified plan be waived?

A qualified plan generally must provide that participants may elect (or revoke an election) to waive the qualified joint and survivor annuity (QJSA) and/or the qualified preretirement survivor annuity (QPSA) forms of benefit (see Q 336) at any time during the *applicable election period*. However, the plan must also provide that such an election will not be effective unless (1) the spouse of the participant (if any) consents in writing to the election, (2) the election designates a beneficiary, or a form of benefits, which may not be changed without spousal consent (unless the consent expressly permits future designations by the participant without further spousal consent), and (3) the consent acknowledges the effect of the election and is witnessed by a plan representative or notary public. IRC Sec. 417(a)(2); Treas. Reg. §1.401(a)-20, A-31. The IRS has provided guidance specifying certain information that should be disclosed in spousal consent forms. See Notice 94-23, 1994-1 CB 340.

An election made without the consent of the spouse is effective only if it is established to the satisfaction of a plan representative that there is no spouse, that the spouse cannot be located, or under certain other specified circumstances which prevent securing such consent. See Treas. Reg. §1.401(a)-20, A-27. Any consent by the spouse of a participant, or proof that consent cannot be obtained from such spouse, is effective only with respect to that spouse (except in the case of plan benefits securing a loan–see Q 336). IRC Sec. 417(a)(2); Treas. Reg. §1.401(a)-20, A-29.

Planning Point: An employer should consider writing the plan document to do what superseded state statutes may not do (i.e., state that a participant's designation of his spouse as beneficiary automatically becomes void upon his divorce unless he reaffirms that designation after his divorce). *Martin Silfen, J.D., Brown Brothers Harriman Trust Co., LLC.*

A spousal waiver that had not been properly witnessed or notarized was struck down despite the wife's acknowledgement that she had signed the form, because the waiver did not meet the requirements clearly set forth in the Code and ERISA. See *Lasche v. George W. Lasche Basic Profit Sharing Plan*, 1997 U.S. App. Lexis 9986 (11th Cir. 1997). However, in an earlier district court ruling, the lack of a written, notarized spousal consent did not render the designation of a non-spouse beneficiary completely ineffective; the designation remained effective to the extent the benefits exceeded what was required to be paid to the spouse. *Profit Sharing Plan for Employees of Republic Fin. Services, Inc. v. MBank Dallas, N.A.*, 683 F. Supp. 592 (N.D. Tex. 1988). But see *United Parcel Service, Inc. v. Riley*, 532 N.Y.S.2d 473 (1988).

A prenuptial agreement (or similar contract) entered into prior to marriage is not, by itself, effective to waive a widow's surviving spouse benefits. Treas. Reg. §1.401(a)-20, A-28; *Hurwitz v. Sher*, 982 F.2d 778 (2nd Cir. 1992), cert. denied 113 S.Ct. 2345; *Nellis v. Boeing*, 1992 U.S. Dist. Lexis 8510 (D.C. Kan. 1992). (Both cases were decided under parallel provisions found in ERISA Section 205(c) and IRC Section 417(a).) See also, *Pedro Enter., Inc. v. Perdue*, 998 F.2d 491 (7th Cir. 1993). For a valid waiver to occur, ERISA requires a notarized waiver containing specific language, by a spouse who actually has (by marriage) the statutory benefits being waived. In addition, the spouse executing the waiver must designated an alternative beneficiary. See *Hagwood v. Newton*, 27 EBC 1882 (4th Cir. 2002).

The Court of Appeals for the Eighth Circuit held that neither a prenuptial agreement with a participant's second wife, nor a separation agreement in which his first wife had "relinquished any right, title or interest in and to any ... pension plans" constituted a valid waiver; thus, the court divided the benefit equally between them upon his death.

PENSION AND PROFIT SHARING: QUALIFICATION   Q 337

National Auto. Dealers and Assoc. Retirement Trust v. Arbeitman, 89 F.3d 496 (8th Cir. 1996). However, the Court of Appeals for the Fourth Circuit found that a valid waiver was executed where the separation agreement specified the plan in which the interest was waived, even though the ex-wife was still named as beneficiary. *Estate of Altobelli v. IBM*, 77 F.3d 78 (4th Cir. 1996).

A plan is not required to permit a waiver of the QJSA or QPSA form of benefit if it fully subsidizes the cost of such benefit and does not permit a participant to waive the benefit or designate another beneficiary. (A plan fully subsidizes the cost of a benefit if the failure to waive the benefit would not result in a decrease of any plan benefits to the waiving participant and would not result in increased contributions from that participant.) IRC Sec. 417(a)(5).

Applicable Election Period

With respect to the QJSA form of benefit, the *applicable election period* is the 90-day period ending on the annuity starting date. IRC Sec. 417(a)(6)(A). Generally, the plan may not commence the distribution of any portion of a participant's accrued benefit to which these requirements apply unless the applicable consent requirements are satisfied. Treas. Reg. §1.417(e)-1(b)(1).

Generally, the plan must provide participants with written notice of the QJSA requirement no less than 30 days and no more than 90 days before the annuity starting date. Treas. Reg. §1.417(e)-1(b)(3). However, if the participant, after receiving the written explanation of the QJSA, affirmatively elects a form of distribution (with spousal consent), the plan will not fail to satisfy the requirements of IRC Section 417(a) merely because the annuity starting date is less than 30 days after the written explanation was provided to the participant, provided four requirements are met: (1) the plan administrator must provide information to the participant clearly indicating that the participant has a right to at least 30 days to consider whether to waive the QJSA and consent to another form of distribution; (2) the participant must be permitted to revoke an affirmative distribution election at least until the annuity starting date, or, if later, at any time prior to the expiration of the 7-day period that begins the day the explanation of the QJSA is provided to the participant; (3) the annuity starting date must be after the date the explanation of the QJSA is provided (except as provided in IRC Section 417(a)(7), see Q 336); *and* (4) distribution in accordance with the affirmative election must not begin before the expiration of the 7-day period that begins the day the explanation of the QJSA is provided to the participant. Treas. Reg. §1.417(e)-1(b)(3)(ii).

Prior to the issuance of the regulations under IRC Section 417, a district court sided with the IRS in finding that an election to waive the QJSA made prior to the 90-day period was invalid. *Jacobs v. Reed College TIAA-CREF Retirement Plan*, 1990 U.S. Dist. LEXIS 14614 (D. Ore 1990).

With respect to the QPSA form of benefit, the *applicable election period* begins on the first day of the plan year in which the participant attains age 35 and ends on the date of his death; however, where a participant has separated from service with the employer, such election period with respect to previously accrued benefits may begin no later than the date of separation. IRC Sec. 417(a)(6)(B).

Generally, the applicable election period may not end before the 30th day after the plan provides the explanation required under IRC Section 417(a)(3). See Treas. Reg.

§1.417(e)-1(b)(3)(ii). Under that rule, a plan generally must, within certain specified periods, provide each participant (vested and nonvested, married or unmarried) with a written explanation of the automatic survivor annuity forms of benefit and of the participant's (and his spouse's) rights with respect to waiving the benefits (see Q 336). *ASRS, Sec. 59, ¶480.4.*

REQUIRED MINIMUM DISTRIBUTIONS

338. When is a qualified plan required to offer distributions from a qualified plan? What is a TEFRA 242(b) election?

A plan must meet two separate sets of rules with regard to the commencement of benefits.

First, a plan must provide that, unless a participant elects otherwise, payments of benefits to him begin within 60 days after the close of the latest of: (1) the plan year in which the participant attains the earlier of age 65 or the normal retirement age specified under the plan, (2) the plan year in which the 10th anniversary of the participant's plan participation occurs, or (3) the plan year in which the participant terminates his service with the employer. IRC Sec. 401(a)(14).

Second, a plan must meet the minimum distribution requirements set forth at IRC Section 401(a)(9) and explained at Q 339 to Q 345.

TEFRA Section 242(b)(2) Election

A participant is not subject to the minimum distribution requirements if he designated, *before January 1, 1984,* a method of distribution that would have been permissible under pre-TEFRA law. TEFRA, Sec. 242(b)(2); TRA '84, Sec. 521(d)(3). The final regulations published in April, 2002 stated that the transitional election rule in TEFRA Section 242(b)(2) was preserved, and that a plan will not be disqualified merely because it pays benefits in accordance with such an election. Furthermore, satisfaction of the spousal consent requirements of IRC Section 417 will not be considered a revocation of the pre-1984 designation. Treas. Reg. §1.401(a)(9)-8, A-13.

If an employee elects to transfer an amount for which a Section 242(b)(2) election was made from one plan to another, the transfer will be treated as a distribution and rollover. However, if the transfer is not at the election of the employee (e.g., in the case of a merger, spinoff or consolidation), the election may be preserved if the amount is separately accounted for by the transferee plan. Treas. Reg. §1.401(a)(9)-8, A-14.

The IRS determined that the distribution and rollover of an amount subject to a 242(b)(2) election terminated the distributee's election, but did not result in triggering of "catch-up" required minimum distributions. See Let Rul. 200510035. Where a decedent made a 242(b)(2) election but did not name a beneficiary, the distribution of his plan interest had to be made under IRC Section 401(a)(9). Let. Rul. 9638040. A pre-TEFRA beneficiary designation that set forth a payment method which conflicted with the plan provisions, specified no start date for distributions, and provided for no payments to the participant was ineffective under pre-TEFRA law. Let. Rul. 199908060.

Regulations proposed in 1987 stated that generally, any distribution made to a participant that was not consistent with the participant's Section 242(b)(2) election, as

PENSION AND PROFIT SHARING: QUALIFICATION Q 339

well as any change in a properly executed election (other than a beneficiary change that does not alter the period of distribution) would trigger the revocation of the election, thus necessitating distributions in accordance with the requirements in effect at the time of revocation. See (1987) Prop. Treas. Regs. §§1.401(a)(9)-1, J-1 to J-5; Notice 83-23, 1983-2 CB 418; Let. Ruls. 9430035, 9617048. However, a distribution pursuant to a plan provision permitting a participant to withdraw all or part of his accrued benefit derived from his own contributions did not revoke the employee's Section 242(b)(2) election. Let. Rul. 9310026. A change in the entity maintaining the plan with respect to which the designation was made (e.g., from a corporation to a partnership) did not invalidate an employee's Section 242(b) election. Let. Rul. 8938073. A revocation of a Section 242(b)(2) election by a participant with respect to one plan does not result in revocation for another plan, even if the assets of both plans are held in a commingled trust. Let. Rul. 9013011. *ASRS, Sec. 59, ¶¶480.1, 945.1(a), 945.1(b).*

339. What are the "minimum distribution" requirements for qualified plans?

To be qualified, a plan must set forth the statutory rules of IRC Section 401(a)(9), including the incidental death benefit requirement in IRC Section 401(a)(9)(G). The plan must also provide that distributions will be made in accordance with the minimum distribution requirements set forth in Treasury regulations, as explained below. For an overview, see the Minimum Distribution Navigator on p. xxiii. In addition, the plan must provide that the minimum distribution rules override any distribution options offered under the plan that are inconsistent with these requirements. IRC Sec. 401(a)(9); Treas. Reg. §1.401(a)(9)-1, A-3(a).

The minimum distribution requirements include the rules prescribed by the IRS and Treasury for meeting the Code's requirements. Proposed regulations governing minimum distributions were first issued in 1987, then simplified and reproposed in 2001. Final regulations were issued in April, 2002 governing all issues except annuity distributions from defined benefit plans, which were addressed by temporary and proposed regulations. See TD 8987, 67 Fed. Reg. 18988 (4-17-02). Final regulations governing annuity distributions and related matters were issued in 2004. Treas. Reg. §1.401(a)(9)-6, see Q 342.

The final regulations are generally effective for determining required minimum distributions for calendar years beginning on or after January 1, 2003. Treas. Reg. §1.401(a)(9)-1, A-2(a). Distributions for calendar year 2002 could be calculated under the 2002 regulations, the 2001 regulations or the 1987 regulations. See TD 8987, above. Defined contribution plan amendments were required by the last day of the first year beginning on or after January 1, 2003, and the IRS provided model plan amendments for this purpose. See Rev. Proc. 2002-29, 2002-1 CB 1176.

Unless otherwise noted, the questions that follow explain the rules set forth in the final 2002 regulations. The regulations themselves are complex, and should be reviewed carefully with regard to any specific case. See Q 340 for an explanation of the required beginning date, Q 341 regarding the minimum distribution requirements from individual accounts during the employee's lifetime, Q 342 regarding annuity payouts from defined benefit plans, Q 343 for after-death distribution requirements, Q 344 regarding designated beneficiaries, and Q 345 regarding the effect of a qualified domestic relations order on required distributions.

2006 Tax Facts on Insurance & Employee Benefits

Failure to make minimum distributions. Although a plan that fails in its operation to meet the minimum distribution requirements with respect to all required distributions is technically subject to disqualification, the preamble to the 2001 proposed regulations stated that such failures could be corrected through the Employee Plans Compliance Resolution System (EPCRS–see Rev. Proc. 2003-44, 2003-1 CB 1051.)

Besides the qualification implications, if an amount distributed from a plan is less than the required minimum distribution, an excise tax equal to 50% of the shortfall is generally levied against the individual (not the plan). IRC Sec. 4974; see Q 347. However, the 2002 regulations stated that the tax could be waived if the payee established to the satisfaction of the IRS that the shortfall was due to reasonable error, and that reasonable steps were being taken to remedy the shortfall. Treas. Reg. §54.4974-2, A-7(a). Generally, the excise tax will be waived automatically if the beneficiary is an individual whose minimum distribution amount is determined under the life expectancy rule for after death distributions, and the entire benefit to which that beneficiary is entitled is distributed under the 5-year rule. Treas. Reg. §54.4974-2, A-7(b).

The minimum distribution requirements will not be treated as violated and, thus, the 50% excise tax will not apply where a shortfall occurs because assets are invested in a contract issued by an insurance company in state insurer delinquency proceedings. To the extent that a distribution otherwise required under IRC Section 401(a)(9) is not made during the state insurer delinquency proceedings, this amount and any additional amount accrued during this period will be treated as though it is not vested. Treas. Reg. §1.401(a)(9)-8, A-8. *ASRS, Sec. 59,* ¶945.1(c).

340. What is an individual's "required beginning date" for purposes of required minimum distributions from a qualified plan?

In order to be qualified, a plan must provide that the entire interest of each employee will be distributed not later than his required beginning date, or will be distributed beginning not later than the required beginning date over certain prescribed time periods. See IRC Sec. 401(a)(9)(A).

For purposes of the minimum distribution rules explained in Q 339 to Q 345, and the minimum distribution incidental benefit rule explained in Q 346, the term "required beginning date" means April 1 of the calendar year following the *later* of (a) the year in which the employee attains age 70½, or (b) the year in which the employee (other than a 5% owner) retires from the employer maintaining the plan. IRC Sec. 401(a)(9)(C).

In the case of a 5% owner, "required beginning date" means April 1 of the calendar year following the year in which the employee attains age 70½. IRC Sec. 401(a)(9)(C)(ii)(I). However, the IRS determined that where a 5% owner rolled over his account balance to the plan of another employer in which he was not a 5% owner (after receiving the required distribution for the year in question), he could delay distributions from the new plan until his retirement after age 70½. See Let. Rul. 200453015.

Under final regulations issued in 2002, a plan is *permitted* to provide that the required beginning date for all employees is April 1 of the calendar year following the calendar year in which the employee attains age 70½, regardless of whether the employee is a 5% owner. Treas. Reg. §1.401(a)(9)-2, A-2(e).

PENSION AND PROFIT SHARING: QUALIFICATION Q 341

Annuity payout. If distributions began irrevocably (except for acceleration) prior to the required beginning date in the form of an annuity that meets the minimum distribution rules, the annuity starting date will be treated as the required beginning date for purposes of calculating lifetime and after death minimum distribution requirements. Treas. Reg. §1.401(a)(9)-6, A-10; see Q 342.

An individual reaches age 70½ on the date that is six calendar months after his 70th birthday. For example, if an employee's date of birth was June 30, 1933, he would reach age 70 on June 30, 2003, and he would reach age 70½ on December 30, 2003. Consequently, assuming he is retired or a 5% owner, his required beginning date would be April 1, 2004. However, if the same employee's birthday were July 1, 1933, he would reach age 70½ on January 1, 2004, and his required beginning date would be April 1, 2005. Treas. Reg. §1.401(a)(9)-2, A-3. *ASRS, Sec. 59, ¶945.3(a)*.

341. What are the minimum distribution requirements for individual account plans during the lifetime of the employee?

In order to satisfy IRC Section 401(a)(9)(A), the entire interest of each employee must either be distributed to the employee in its entirety not later than the required beginning date, or must be distributed starting not later than the required beginning date over the life (or life expectancy) of the employee (or the employee and a beneficiary). IRC Sec. 401(a)(9)(A). Final regulations issued in 2002 took effect for calculating distributions required for calendar years beginning on or after January 1, 2003. Treas. Reg. §1.401(a)(9)-1, A-2.

Uniform Lifetime Table. Under the final regulations, required minimum distributions from an individual account under a defined contribution plan during the owner's lifetime are calculated by dividing the employee's account balance by the applicable distribution period determined from the following table:

Uniform Lifetime Table

Age of Employee	Distribution Period	Age of Employee	Distribution Period	Age of Employee	Distribution Period
70	27.4	86	14.1	101	5.9
71	26.5	87	13.4	102	5.5
72	25.6	88	12.7	103	5.2
73	24.7	89	12.0	104	4.9
74	23.8	90	11.4	105	4.5
75	22.9	91	10.8	106	4.2
76	22.0	92	10.2	107	3.9
77	21.2	93	9.6	108	3.7
78	20.3	94	9.1	109	3.4
79	19.5	95	8.6	110	3.1
80	18.7	96	8.1	111	2.9
81	17.9	97	7.6	112	2.6
82	17.1	98	7.1	113	2.4
83	16.3	99	6.7	114	2.1
84	15.5	100	6.3	115	1.9
85	14.8				

Treas. Reg. §1.401(a)(9)-9, A-2. For an example showing the calculation under this rule, see Q 234. An expanded form of this table is shown in Appendix F. The amount of an individual's lifetime required distribution is calculated without regard to the beneficiary's age, except in the case of a spouse beneficiary who is more than 10 years younger than the employee. See Treas. Reg. §1.401(a)(9)-5, A-4.

If the sole designated beneficiary is the employee's spouse, the distribution period during the employee's lifetime is the longer of (a) the uniform lifetime table, above, or (b) the joint and survivor life expectancy of the employee and spouse using their attained ages in the distribution calendar year. Treas. Reg. §1.401(a)(9)-5, A-4(b). The 2002 lifetime table, and the 2002 single life table and joint and survivor life expectancy tables (as provided by Treas. Reg. §1.401(a)(9)-9) are set forth in Appendix F. As a practical matter, the joint and survivor life expectancy table will produce a longer (and thus, lower) payout only if the spouse beneficiary is more than 10 years younger than the employee.

Account balance. For purposes of calculating minimum distributions, the account balance is determined as of the last valuation date in the immediately preceding calendar year (i.e., the valuation calendar year). Treas. Reg. §1.401(a)(9)-5, A-3(a). Under the 2001 (and earlier) proposed regulations, for purposes of calculating the required distribution for the calendar year that included an employee's required beginning date, the account balance as of December 31 of the preceding calendar year was reduced by any distributions received from January 1 through March 31 of that year. The 2002 final regulations eliminated this provision. See Treas. Reg. §1.401(a)(9)-5, A-3(c).

The account balance is increased by the amount of any contributions or forfeitures allocated to the employee's account as of dates in the valuation calendar year after the valuation date. Contributions include contributions made after the close of the valuation calendar year that are allocated as of a date in the valuation calendar year. Treas. Reg. §1.401(a)(9)-5, A-3(b). The account balance is decreased by any distributions made during the valuation calendar year, after the valuation date. Treas. Reg. §1.401(a)(9)-5, A-3(c)(1).

Employee not fully vested. If a portion of an employee's individual account is not vested as of his required beginning date, the benefit used to calculate the required minimum distribution for any year is determined without regard to whether all of the benefit is vested, and distributions will be treated as being paid from the vested portion of the benefit first. If the required minimum distribution amount is greater than the vested benefit, only the vested portion is required to be distributed. Treas. Reg. §1.401(a)(9)-5, A-8. In any event, the required minimum distribution amount will never exceed the entire vested account balance on the date of distribution. Treas. Reg. §1.401(a)(9)-5, A-1(a). The required minimum distribution for subsequent years, however, must be increased by the sum of amounts not distributed in prior calendar years because the employee's vested benefit was less than the required minimum distribution amount. See Treas. Reg. §1.401(a)(9)-5, A-8.

Special rules. Generally, distributions made prior to an individual's required beginning date are not subject to these rules. However, if distributions begin under a distribution option (such as an annuity) that provides for payments after the individual's required beginning date, distributions that will be made under the option on and after such date must satisfy these rules or the entire option fails from the beginning. Treas. Reg. §1.401(a)(9)-2, A-4.

Distributions in excess of the amounts required under these rules do not reduce the amount required in subsequent years. Treas. Reg. §1.401(a)(9)-5, A-2. Rollovers

PENSION AND PROFIT SHARING: QUALIFICATION

Q 342

and transfers among plans during years in which distributions are required under these rules can have a significant effect on the application of the minimum distribution rules. Treas. Reg. §1.401(a)(9)-7. For rules that apply to distributions when a QDRO is in effect, see Q 345. Rules pertaining to separate accounts or segregated shares under a single plan, to employees participating in more than one plan, and other special rules affecting the application of the minimum distribution requirements, are set forth at Treas. Reg. §1.401(a)(9)-8.

The final regulations state that distributions made in accordance with the provisions set forth in Treas. Reg. §1.401(a)(9)-5, as explained above, will satisfy the minimum distribution incidental benefit requirement (see Q 346). Treas. Reg. §1.401(a)(9)-5, A-1(d). *ASRS, Sec. 59, ¶945.3(b).*

342. What are the minimum distribution requirements for annuity payouts from a defined benefit plan?

Final regulations published in June, 2004 set forth requirements that annuity distributions under a defined benefit plan must meet to satisfy IRC Section 401(a)(9)(A). See TD 9130, 2004-26 IRB 1082. The final regulations are widely viewed as taxpayer-friendly, expanding the flexibility permitted for annuity increases and for forms of distributions.

The final regulations retain the general rule that distributions must be paid in periodic payments at least annually, for the employee's life (or the joint lives of an employee and beneficiary), or over a period certain that is not longer than the life expectancy (or joint and survivor life expectancy) of the employee (or the employee and a beneficiary), as set forth in the Code's provisions for lifetime and after death distributions. Treas. Regs. §§1.401(a)(9)-6, A-1(a); 1.401(a)(9)-6, A-3; see IRC Sec. 401(a)(9)(A). The annuity may also be a life annuity (or joint and survivor annuity) with a period certain, so long as the life (or lives) and period certain each meet the foregoing requirements. Treas. Reg. §1.401(a)(9)-6, A-1(b).

Distributions from an annuity contract must commence on or before the employee's required beginning date. The first payment must be the payment that is required for one payment interval. The second payment need not be made until the end of the next payment interval, even if the interval ends in the next calendar year. Treas. Reg. §1.401(a)(9)-6, A-1(c). Examples of payment intervals include monthly, bimonthly, semi-annually and annually. All benefit accruals as of the last day of the first distribution calendar year must be included in the calculation of the amount of the life annuity payments for payment intervals ending on or after the employee's required beginning date. Treas. Reg. §1.401(a)(9)-6, A-1(c)(1).

Period certain limitations. Generally, the period certain for annuity distributions commencing during the life of an employee, with an annuity starting date on or after the required beginning date, may not exceed the amount set forth in the "Uniform Lifetime Table" in Q 341. However, if an employee's spouse is the sole beneficiary as of the annuity starting date, and the annuity provides only a period certain and no life annuity, the period certain may be as long as the joint and survivor life expectancy of the employee and spouse, based on their ages as of their birthdays in the calendar year that contains the annuity starting date. Treas. Reg. §1.401(a)(9)-6, A-3(a).

2006 Tax Facts on Insurance & Employee Benefits

Employee not fully vested. If any portion of the employee's benefit is not fully vested as of his required beginning date, his required minimum distribution will be calculated as though the portion that is not vested has not yet accrued. As additional vesting occurs, such amounts will be treated as additional accruals. Treas. Reg. §1.401(a)(9)-6, A-6. If additional benefits accrue after the participant's required beginning date, such amounts will be treated separately for purposes of the minimum distribution rules. See Treas. Reg. §1.401(a)(9)-6, A-5.

Actuarial increase requirement. If an employee (other than a 5% owner) retires after the calendar year he reaches age 70½, a defined benefit plan must actuarially increase the employee's accrued benefit to take into account any period after age 70½ during which the employee was not receiving benefits under the plan. IRC Sec. 401(a)(9)(C)(ii). Generally, the increase must be provided starting on April 1 of the year after the employee reaches age 70½, and ending on the date when required minimum distributions commence in an amount sufficient to satisfy the Code requirements. Treas. Reg. §1.401(a)(9)-6, A-7(a). This actuarial increase requirement does not apply to: (1) plans that provide the same required beginning date (i.e., April 1 of the year after the employee reaches age 70½), for all employees regardless of whether they are 5% owners, and make distributions accordingly, or (2) governmental or church plans. Treas. Regs. §§1.401(a)(9)-6, A-7(c), 1.401(a)(9)-6, A-7(d).

Nonincreasing annuity requirement. Except as otherwise provided (see below) annuity payments must be nonincreasing, or increase only in accordance with: (1) an annual percentage not exceeding that of an eligible cost-of-living index (e.g., one issued by the Bureau of Labor Statistics, or certain others defined in the regulations) (2) a percentage increase that occurs at specified times (e.g., at specified ages) and does not exceed the cumulative total of annual percentage increases in an eligible cost of living index (see (1)) since the annuity starting date; (3) increases to the extent of the reduction in the amount of the employee's payments to provide for a survivor benefit upon death (if the beneficiary dies or is no longer subject to a QDRO), (4) increases that result from a plan amendment; or (5) increases to allow a beneficiary to convert the survivor portion of a joint and survivor annuity into a single sum distribution upon the employee's death. See Treas. Reg. §1.401(a)(9)-6, A-14(a).

Additional permitted increases for annuity contracts purchased from insurance companies. If the total future expected payments from an annuity purchased from an insurance company exceed the total value being annuitized, payments under the annuity will not fail to satisfy the nonincreasing payment requirement merely because the payments are increased in accordance with one or more of the following: (1) by a constant percentage, applied not less frequently than annually; (2) to provide a final payment upon the employee's death that does not exceed the excess of the total value being annuitized over the total of payments before the death of the employee; (3) as a result of dividend payments or other payments resulting from certain actuarial gains; and (4) an acceleration of payments under the annuity (as defined in the regulations). See Treas. Regs. §§1.401(a)(9)-6, A-14(c), 1.401(a)(9)-6, A-14(e).

Additional permitted increases for annuity payments from a qualified trust. In the case of annuity payments paid under a qualified defined benefit plan (i.e., paid directly from the trust rather than a commercial annuity), payments will not fail to satisfy the nonincreasing payment requirement merely because the payments are increased in accordance with one or more of the following: (1) by a constant percentage, applied not less frequently than

PENSION AND PROFIT SHARING: QUALIFICATION   Q 342

annually, at a rate that is less than 5% per year; (2) to provide a final payment upon the death of the employee that does not exceed the excess of the actuarial present value of the employee's accrued benefit (as defined in the regulations) over the total of payments before the death of the employee; or (3) as a result of dividend payments or other payments resulting from actuarial gain (measured and paid as specified in the regulations). See Treas. Regs. §§1.401(a)(9)-6, A-14(d), 1.401(a)(9)-6, A-14(e).

An annuity contract purchased with the employee's benefit by the plan from an insurance company will not fail to satisfy the rules of Section 401(a)(9) merely because of the purchase, provided the payments meet the foregoing requirements. Treas. Reg. §1.401(a)(9)-6, A-4. If the annuity contract is purchased after the required beginning date, the first payment interval must begin on or before the purchase date, and the payment amount required for one interval must be made no later than the end of that payment interval. Treas. Reg. §1.401(a)(9)-6, A-4.

Changes in form of distribution. In addition to the foregoing permitted increases, the final regulations permit the employee or beneficiary to change the form of distributions in response to various changes in circumstances. The annuity stream must otherwise satisfy the regulations, and certain other requirements must be met (e.g., the new payout must satisfy IRC Sec. 401(a)(9), and the modification must be treated as a new annuity starting date under Sections 415 and 417; see Treas. Reg. §1.401(a)(9)-6, A-13(c)). If these conditions are met, the annuity payment period may be changed and the payments may be modified if: (1) the modification occurs at the time the employee retires, or in connection with a plan termination; (2) the annuity payments prior to modification are annuity payments paid over a period certain without life contingencies; or (3) the employee gets married and the annuity payments after modification are paid under a qualified joint and survivor annuity over the joint lives of the employee and spouse. See Treas. Reg. §1.401(a)(9)-6, A-13(b).

Payments to children. Payments under a defined benefit plan or annuity contract that are made to an employee's surviving child (pursuant to IRC Sec. 401(a)(9)(F)) until the child reaches the age of majority may be treated (for required minimum distribution purposes) as having been paid to the surviving spouse, provided that once the child reaches the age of majority, they are payable to the surviving spouse. For this purpose, a child under age 26 who has not completed "a specified course of education" may be treated as not having reached the age of majority. Furthermore, a child who is disabled may be treated as not having reached the age of majority as long as the child continues to be disabled. The child will not be taken into consideration for purposes of the MDIB requirement (see Q 342) and the increase in payments to the surviving spouse that results when the child recovers or reaches the age of majority will not be considered an increase for purposes of the nonincreasing annuity requirement. Treas. Reg. §1.401(a)(9)-6, A-15.

Special rules. The distribution of an annuity contract is not a distribution for purposes of meeting the required minimum distribution requirements of IRC Section 401(a)(9). Treas. Reg. §1.401(a)(9)-8, A-10. If the employee's entire accrued benefit is paid in the form of a lump sum distribution, the portion that is a required minimum distribution will be determined by treating the distribution either (1) as if it were from an individual account plan (see Q 341), or (2) as if it were an annuity that would satisfy the regulations with an annuity starting date on the first day of the distribution calendar year for which the required minimum distribution is being determined, and one year of annuity payments constitutes the required minimum distribution. See Treas. Reg. §1.401(a)(9)-6, A-1(d).

In the case of an annuity contract under an individual account plan that has not yet been annuitized, the required minimum distribution for the period prior to the date annuity payments commence is determined by treating the value of an employee's entire interest under an annuity contract as an individual account. Thus, the required minimum distribution would be determined under Treas. Reg. §1.401(a)(9)-5 (rules for individual account plans, see Q 341).

The final regulations are retroactively effective for purposes of determining required distributions for calendar years beginning on or after January 1, 2003. See TD 9130, 2004-26 IRB 1082; Treas. Reg. §1.401(a)(9)-6, A-17. However, distributions made from a defined benefit plan or annuity contract for calendar years 2003, 2004 and 2005 did not have to comply entirely with the new regulations, provided they satisfied a reasonable good faith interpretation of IRC Sec. 401(a)(9). Treas. Reg. §1.401(a)(9)-6, A-17.

A grandfather rule for governmental plans states that an annuity distribution option provided under the terms of a governmental plan, as in effect on April 17, 2002, will not fail to satisfy the requirements of Section 401(a)(9) merely because the payments do not satisfy the final regulations. Furthermore, for governmental plans, the reasonable, good faith reliance period extends to the 90th day after the opening of the first legislative session of the legislative body with the authority to amend the plan (if that date is later than December 31, 2005). Treas. Reg. §1.401(a)(9)-6, A-17. *ASRS, Sec. 59, ¶945.5.*

343. How are the minimum distribution requirements met after the death of the employee?

The minimum distribution requirements that apply after the death of an employee depend on whether he died before or after his required beginning date. Generally, for this purpose, distributions are treated as having begun in accordance with the minimum distribution requirements under IRC Section 401(a)(9)(A)(ii), without regard to whether payments have been made before that date. Treas. Reg. §1.401(a)(9)-2, A-6(a). However, if distributions *irrevocably* (except for acceleration) began prior to the required beginning date in the form of an annuity that satisfies the minimum distribution rules (see Q 342), the annuity starting date will be treated as the required beginning date for purposes of calculating lifetime and after death minimum distribution requirements. Treas. Reg. §1.401(a)(9)-6, A-10, A-11. For the definition of required beginning date, see Q 340.

Final regulations explaining the minimum distribution requirements were published in April 2002 and final regulations governing annuity payouts from defined benefit plans were published in 2004; see Q 342.

Death Before Required Beginning Date

If an employee dies *before* his required beginning date, distributions must be made under one of two methods:

(1) *Life expectancy rule:* if any portion of the interest is payable to, or for the benefit of, a designated beneficiary, that portion must be distributed over the life (or life expectancy) of the beneficiary, beginning within one year of the employee's death. IRC Sec. 401(a)(9)(B)(iii); Treas. Reg. §1.401(a)(9)-3, A-1(a).

PENSION AND PROFIT SHARING: QUALIFICATION   Q 343

To the extent that the interest is payable to a *nonspouse beneficiary*, distributions must begin by the end of the calendar year immediately following the calendar year in which the employee died. Treas. Reg. §1.401(a)(9)-3, A-3(a). The nonspouse beneficiary's life expectancy for this purpose is measured as of his birthday in the year following the year of the employee's death. In subsequent years, this amount is reduced by one for each calendar year that has elapsed since the year immediately following the year of the employee's death. See Treas. Reg. §1.401(a)(9)-5, A-5(c)(1).

(2) *Five year rule*: if there is no designated beneficiary, or if the foregoing rule is not satisfied, the entire interest must be distributed within five years after the death of the employee (regardless of who or what entity receives the distribution). IRC Sec. 401(a)(9)(B)(ii), Treas. Reg. §1.401(a)(9)-3, A-1(a). In order to satisfy this rule, the entire interest must be distributed by the end of the calendar year that contains the fifth anniversary of the date of the employee's death. Treas. Reg. §1.401(a)(9)-3, A-2.

Surviving spouse beneficiary. If the sole designated beneficiary is the employee's surviving spouse, distributions must begin by the later of (i) the end of the calendar year immediately following the calendar year in which the employee died, or (ii) the end of the calendar year in which the employee would have reached age 70½. See IRC Sec. 401(a)(9)(B)(iv); Treas. Reg. §1.401(a)(9)-3, A-3(b).

In the event that a surviving spouse beneficiary dies after the employee, but before distributions to the spouse have begun, the 5-year rule and the life expectancy rule for surviving spouses will be applied as though the surviving spouse were the employee. See IRC Sec. 401(a)(9)(B)(iv)(II); Treas. Reg. §1.401(a)(9)-3, A-5. The payout period during the surviving spouse's life is measured by the surviving spouse's life expectancy as of his or her birthday in each distribution calendar year for which a minimum distribution is required after the year of the employee's death. Treas. Reg. §1.401(a)(9)-5, A-5(c)(2). The provision that treats a surviving spouse as though the surviving spouse were the employee (i.e., the surviving spouse rules of IRC Section 401(a)(9)(B)(iv)) will not allow a new spouse of the deceased employee's spouse to continue delaying distributions. Treas. Reg. §1.401(a)(9)-3, A-5.

Life expectancy tables. The 2002 final regulations set forth tables containing single and joint and survivor life expectancies for calculating required minimum distributions, as well as a "Uniform Lifetime Table" for determining the appropriate distribution periods. See Treas. Reg. §1.401(a)(9)-9; see Appendix F.

Plan provisions. Unless a plan adopts a provision specifying otherwise, if distributions to an employee have not begun prior to his death, they must be made automatically either under the life expectancy rule described above, or, if there is no designated beneficiary, under the 5-year rule. Treas. Regs. §§1.401(a)(9)-1, A-3(c), 1.401(a)(9)-3, A-4(a). A plan may adopt a provision specifying that the 5-year rule will apply after the death of an employee, or a provision allowing employees (or beneficiaries) to elect whether the 5-year rule or the life expectancy rule will be applied. Treas. Regs. §§1.401(a)(9)-3, A-4(b), 1.401(a)(9)-3, A-4(c).

Death on or After Required Beginning Date

If the employee dies *on or after* distributions have begun (i.e., generally on or after his required beginning date), but before his entire interest in the plan has been distributed, the Code states that the entire remaining balance must generally be distributed at least as rapidly as under the method of distribution in effect as of the employee's date of death. See IRC Sec. 401(a)(9)(B)(i). Generally, this method of distribution will depend on whether the distribution was in the form of distributions from an individual account under a defined contribution plan, or annuity payments from a defined benefit plan. Treas. Reg. §1.401(a)(9)-2, A-5.

Under the final regulations, a beneficiary determination is made as of *September 30* of the year after the year of the employee's death. Treas. Reg. §1.401(a)(9)-4, A-4(a). If the employee *does not* have a "designated beneficiary" (see Q 344) as of that date, his interest is distributed over his remaining life expectancy, using the age of the employee in the calendar year of his death, reduced by one for each calendar year that elapses thereafter. See Treas. Reg. §1.401(a)(9)-5, A-5(c)(3).

If the employee *does* have a designated beneficiary as of the determination date, the beneficiary's interest is distributed over the longer of (i) the beneficiary's life expectancy, calculated as described above at "Life Expectancy Rule" (i.e., under Treas. Reg. §1.401(a)(9)-5, A-5(c)(1) or (2)) *or* (ii) the remaining life expectancy of the employee, determined using the age of the employee in the calendar year of his death, reduced by one for each calendar year that elapses thereafter (i.e., under Treas. Reg. §1.401(a)(9)-5, A-5(c)(3)). Treas. Reg. §1.401(a)(9)-5, A-5(a)(1). *ASRS, Sec. 59, ¶945.4.*

344. How is the "designated beneficiary" determined for purposes of the minimum distribution requirements? What are the separate account rules?

A "designated beneficiary" means any individual designated as a beneficiary by the employee. IRC Sec. 401(a)(9)(E). However, under final regulations, an individual may be designated as a beneficiary under the plan either by the terms of the plan or, if the plan so provides, by an affirmative election by the employee (or the employee's surviving spouse) specifying the beneficiary. Treas. Reg. §1.401(a)(9)-4, A-1. The fact that an employee's interest under the plan passes to a certain individual under applicable state law, however, does not make that individual a designated beneficiary unless the individual is designated as a beneficiary under the plan. Treas. Reg. §1.401(a)(9)-4, A-1.

Regulations finalized in 2002 took effect January 1, 2003. The regulations governing annuity distributions from defined benefit plans were finalized in 2004. See Q 342. Under the final regulations, a beneficiary designated as such under the plan is an *individual* (or certain trusts, see below) who is entitled to a portion of an employee's benefit, contingent on the employee's death or another specified event. A designated beneficiary need not be specified by name in the plan or by the employee to the plan in order to be a designated beneficiary so long as the individual who is to be the beneficiary is identifiable under the plan as of the date the beneficiary is determined. However, the choice of beneficiary is subject to the Code's provisions for joint and survivor annuities, QDROs, and consent requirements (see Q 336, Q 337, Q 349). Treas. Reg. §1.401(a)(9)-4, A-2. For an explanation of the effect of a QDRO on the minimum distribution requirements, see Q 345.

In order to be a designated beneficiary for purposes, an individual must be a beneficiary on the date of the employee's death. However, the determination of the existence and identity of a designated beneficiary for purposes of minimum distributions is made on September 30 of the calendar year following the year of the employee's death. Treas. Reg. §1.401(a)(9)-4, A-4(a). (Exceptions may apply if the account is payable as an annuity, or if a surviving spouse beneficiary dies after the employee but before distributions have begun.) This is in order that a distribution may be calculated and made by the deadline of December 31 following the year of the employee's death.

Consequently, an individual who was a beneficiary as of the date of the employee's death, but is not a beneficiary as of September 30 of the following year (e.g., because he disclaims entitlement to the benefit or because he receives the entire benefit to which he is entitled before that date) is not taken into account for purposes of determining the distribution period for required minimum distributions after the employee's death. Treas. Reg. §1.401(a)(9)-4, A-4(a). A disclaiming beneficiary's receipt (prior to disclaiming the benefit) of a required distribution in the year after death will not result the beneficiary being treated as a designated beneficiary for subsequent years. Rev. Rul. 2005-36, 2005-26 IRB 1368.

An entity other than an individual or a trust meeting the requirements set forth below may not be a designated beneficiary for required minimum distribution purposes. Thus, for example, the employee's estate may not be a designated beneficiary. Treas. Reg. §1.401(a)(9)-4, A-3.

Multiple beneficiaries. If more than one beneficiary is designated with respect to an employee as of the date on which the designated beneficiary is to be determined, the designated beneficiary with the shortest life expectancy is the measuring life for purposes of determining the distribution period. Treas. Regs. §1.401(a)(9)-5, A-7(a)(1). (Special rules, explained below, apply if the employee's benefit is divided into separate accounts, or segregated shares, and the beneficiaries of each account differ.)

Contingent and successor beneficiaries. If a beneficiary's entitlement to an employee's benefit is contingent on an event other than the employee's death, or the death of another beneficiary, the contingent beneficiary will be considered a designated beneficiary for purposes of determining which designated beneficiary has the shortest life expectancy. Treas. Reg. §1.401(a)(9)-5, A-7(b). The fact that the contingency may be extremely remote (e.g., two children predeceasing a 67-year-old relative) does not appear to affect this outcome. See Let. Rul. 200228025. In contrast, if a "successor beneficiary's" entitlement is contingent on the death of another beneficiary, the successor beneficiary's life expectancy cannot be counted for purposes of determining which designated beneficiary has the shortest life expectancy, unless the other beneficiary dies prior to the date on which the beneficiary is determined. Treas. Reg. §1.401(a)(9)-5, A-7(c)(1).

Separate Account Rules

The final regulations provide that if an employee's benefit is divided into *separate accounts* under a defined contribution plan (or in the case of a defined benefit plan, into segregated shares) and the separate accounts have different beneficiaries, the accounts do not have to be aggregated for purposes of determining the required minimum distributions for years subsequent to the calendar year in which they were established (or date of death, if later). Treas. Reg. §1.401(a)(9)-8, A-2(a)(2). In 2004 this rule was modified to permit separate account treatment for the year following the year of death, provided the separate accounts are actually established by the end of the calendar year following death. See T.D. 9130, 2004-26 IRB 1082.

For purposes of Section 401(a)(9), "separate accounts" are portions of an employee's benefit representing the separate interests of the employee's beneficiaries under the plan as of his date of death. The separate accounting *must* allocate all post-death investment gains and losses, contributions, and forfeitures for the period prior to the establishment of the separate accounts on a pro rata basis in a reasonable and consistent manner among the accounts. Once the separate accounts are actually established, the separate accounting can provide for separate investments in each account, with gains and losses attributable to such investments allocable only to that account. A separate accounting must also allocate any post-death distribution to the separate account of the beneficiary receiving it. Treas. Reg. §1.401(a)(9)-8, A-3.

The "applicable distribution period" is determined for each separate account disregarding the other beneficiaries (i.e., allowing each beneficiary to use his or her own life expectancy) *only* if the separate account is established no later than December 31 of the year following the decedent's death. Treas. Reg. §1.401(a)(9)-8, A-2(a)(2). If this deadline is not met, separate accounts can be established at any time, according to the Preamble to the final regulations, but the distribution period in effect prior to the separation of the accounts (generally the life expectancy of the oldest beneficiary) will continue to be applied. See TD 8987, 67 Fed. Reg. 18988 (4-17-02).

The regulations state that if a trust is the beneficiary of an employee's plan interest, separate account treatment is not available to the beneficiaries of the trust. Treas. Reg. §1.401(a)(9)-4, A-5(c). The IRS has determined repeatedly that the establishment of separate shares did not entitle multiple beneficiaries of the same trust to use their own life expectancies as the distribution period. See, e.g., Let. Ruls. 200307095, 200444033, 200528031. However, the Service has privately ruled that where separate individual trusts were named as beneficiaries, the ability of each beneficiary to use his or her life expectancy was preserved even though the trusts were governed by a single "master trust." See Let. Rul. 200537044.

If the December 31 deadline is missed, or if the plan beneficiary is a trust with multiple beneficiaries, separate accounts may still be established (e.g., for administrative convenience); however, the applicable distribution period will be the shortest life expectancy of the various beneficiaries. See Treas. Reg. §1.401(a)(9)-8, A-2(a)(2). The fact that the trust meets the requirements for a "see-through trust" (see below) does not change this result. See Let. Rul. 200317044.

Trust Beneficiary

As a general rule, only an individual may be a designated beneficiary for required minimum distribution purposes. However, if special requirements are met, the beneficiaries of a trust may be treated as having been designated as beneficiaries of the employee under the plan for required minimum distribution purposes. The 2002 final regulations state that "during any period during which required minimum distributions are being determined by treating the beneficiaries of the trust as designated beneficiaries of the employee" the requirements will be met if: (1) the trust is a valid trust under state law, or would be but for the fact that there is no corpus, (2) the trust is irrevocable or will, by its terms, become irrevocable upon the death of the employee, (3) the beneficiaries of the trust who are beneficiaries with respect to the trust's interest in the employee's benefit are identifiable from the trust instrument, as described below, and (4) the documentation described below has been provided to the plan administrator. Treas. Reg.

§1.401(a)(9)-4, A-5(b). A trust that satisfies these requirements is sometimes referred to as a "see-through trust."

The IRS has privately ruled that a "see-through" trust's provision for payment of expenses such as funeral and burial costs, probate administration expenses and estate costs, whether before or after September 30 of the year after the decedent's death, did not preclude the trust from meeting the foregoing requirements. See Let. Ruls. 200432027, 200432028, 200432029.

Beneficiaries identifiable from trust instrument. A designated beneficiary need not be specified by name in the plan or by the employee to the plan in order to be a designated beneficiary, so long as the individual who is to be the beneficiary is identifiable under the plan as of the date the beneficiary is determined (see above). The members of a class of beneficiaries capable of expansion or contraction will be treated as identifiable if it is possible, as of the date the beneficiary is determined, to identify the class member with the shortest life expectancy. Treas. Reg. §1.401(a)(9)-4, A-1.

Documentation Requirements

Lifetime distributions. To satisfy the documentation requirement for trust beneficiaries to be treated as designated beneficiaries for purposes of lifetime distributions, the employee must meet one of two requirements:

(1) he must provide to the plan administrator a copy of the trust and agree that if the trust instrument is amended at any time in the future, the employee will, within a reasonable time, provide the plan administrator with a copy of any such amendment; *or*

(2) he must provide the plan administrator with a list of all the beneficiaries (including contingent and remainder beneficiaries, as well as a description of the conditions on their entitlement) of the trust. If the spouse is the sole beneficiary, a description of the conditions of the remaindermen beneficiaries' entitlement sufficient to establish that fact must be provided. The employee must certify that to the best of the employee's knowledge, the list is correct and complete, and that the other requirements for the beneficiaries of the trust to be treated as designated beneficiaries have been satisfied. The employee must also agree to provide a copy of the trust instrument upon demand. In any event, if the trust is amended, the employee must provide a copy of any such amendment, or provide a corrected certification to the extent that the amendment changes the information previously certified. Treas. Reg. §1.401(a)(9)-4, A-6.

After-death distributions. To satisfy the documentation requirements for required minimum distributions after the death of the employee (or after the death of the surviving spouse, if he or she dies after the employee but before distributions have begun), the trustee must meet following requirements by *October 31* of the calendar year after the year of the employee's death:

(1) he must (a) provide the plan administrator with a final list of all the beneficiaries (including contingent and remainder beneficiaries, as well as a description of the conditions on their entitlement) as of September 30 of the calendar year following the calendar year of the employee's death; (b) certify that to the best of his knowledge the list is correct and complete and that the trust meets the general requirements listed above for all trust beneficiaries; and (c) agree to provide a copy of the trust instrument to the plan administrator upon demand; *or*

(2) he must provide the plan administrator with a copy of the actual trust document for the trust that is named as a beneficiary of the employee under the plan as of the employee's date of death. Treas. Reg. §1.401(a)(9)-4, A-6(b).

The final regulations add that if the foregoing requirements are met, a plan will not fail to satisfy Section 401(a)(9) merely because the actual terms of the trust instrument are inconsistent with the information in the certifications or trust instruments previously provided. However, this relief applies only if the plan administrator reasonably relied on the information provided, and the required minimum distributions for calendar years after the discrepancy is discovered are determined based on the actual terms of the trust instrument. Treas. Reg. §1.401(a)(9)-4, A-6(c)(1). The actual trust terms will govern for purposes of determining the amount of any excise tax under Section 4974 (see Q 347). Treas. Reg. §1.401(a)(9)-4, A-6(c)(2). *ASRS, Sec. 59, ¶945.2.*

345. Who is the employee's spouse or surviving spouse for purposes of the minimum distribution requirements? What is the effect of a QDRO?

For purposes of the minimum distribution requirements under IRC Section 401(a)(9), unless a qualified domestic relations order is in effect (see below) an individual will be considered a spouse or surviving spouse of an employee if that individual is treated under applicable state law as the spouse or surviving spouse of the employee. For purposes of the life expectancy rule applied after an employee's death, the spouse of the employee is determined as of the employee's date of death. Treas. Reg. §1.401(a)(9)-8, A-5.

If a portion of an employee's benefit is payable to a former spouse pursuant to a qualified domestic relations order (QDRO, see Q 349), the former spouse to whom the benefit is payable will be treated as a spouse (or surviving spouse, as the case may be) of the employee for purposes of the minimum distribution and MDIB requirements. Treas. Reg. §1.401(a)(9)-8, A-6(a).

If the QDRO provides that the employee's benefit is to be divided and a portion is to be allocated to an alternate payee, that portion will be treated as a separate account (or segregated share) for purposes of satisfying the minimum distribution requirements. For example, distributions from the account will generally satisfy IRC Section 401(a)(9) if required minimum distributions begin not later than the employee's required beginning date, using the rules for individual accounts. Treas. Reg. §1.401(a)(9)-8, A-6(b)(1).

A distribution of the separate account allocated to an alternate payee will satisfy the lifetime distribution requirements if the distribution begins no later than the employee's required beginning date (see Q 340), and is made over the life (or life expectancy) of the payee.

Planning Point: Because of these rules, distributions to a child pursuant to a QDRO can be stretched out over a greater period than would otherwise be allowed under the minimum distribution rules. *Martin Silfen, J.D., Brown Brothers Harriman Trust Co., LLC.*

If the alternate payee dies after distributions have begun but before the employee dies, distribution of the remaining portion of the benefit allocated to the alternate payee must be made in accordance with the lifetime distribution rules for individual accounts (Q 341) or annuity payouts (Q 342). Treas. Reg. §1.401(a)(9)-8, A-6(b)(2).

PENSION AND PROFIT SHARING: QUALIFICATION — Q 346

If the QDRO provides that a portion of the employee's benefit is to be paid to an alternate payee, but does not provide for the benefit to be divided, the alternate payee's portion will *not* be treated as a separate account (or segregated share) of the employee. Instead, the alternate payee's portion will be aggregated with any amount distributed to the employee and will be treated, for purposes of meeting the minimum distribution requirement, as if it had been distributed to the employee. Treas. Reg. §1.401(a)(9)-8, A-6(c).

A plan will not fail to satisfy IRC Section 401(a)(9) merely because it fails to distribute a required amount during the period in which the qualified status of a domestic relations order is being determined, provided it does not extend beyond the 18-month period described in the Code and ERISA. Any distributions delayed under this rule will be treated as though they had not been vested at the time distribution was required. Treas. Reg. §1.401(a)(9)-8, A-7. *ASRS, Sec. 59, ¶945.3(d).*

346. What is the "incidental benefit rule" for qualified plans?

The term "incidental benefit rule" or "incidental death benefit rule" is commonly used to refer to two similar, but separate, rules. One limits pre-retirement distributions in the form of nonretirement benefits such as life, accident, or health insurance. (For an explanation of that rule, see Q 369.) The second is a rule codified in the Code and regulations, and more properly referred to as the "minimum distribution incidental benefit (MDIB) rule." The purpose of the MDIB rule is to insure that funds are accumulated under a qualified plan primarily for distribution to the employee participants, and that payments to their beneficiaries are merely "incidental." Cf. Rev. Rul. 56-656, 1956-2 CB 280; Rev. Rul. 60-59, 1960-1 CB 154.

The MDIB requirement applies only during the employee's life. See IRC Sec. 401(a)(9)(G); Treas. Reg. §1.401(a)(9)-2, A-1(b). Under regulations finalized in 2002 and 2004, the MDIB requirement will be met if:

(1) nonannuity distributions are made in accordance with the individual account rules of IRC Section 401(a)(9) (see Q 341), Treas. Reg. §1.401(a)(9)-5, A-1(d);

(2) the employee's benefit is payable in the form of a life annuity for the life of the employee that satisfies the requirements of IRC Section 401(a)(9) (see Q 342), Treas. Reg. §1.401(a)(9)-6, A-2(a); or

(3) the employee's sole beneficiary as of the annuity starting date is the employee's spouse, and the distributions otherwise satisfy IRC Section 401(a)(9). (But payments under the annuity must be nonincreasing, except for the exceptions explained at Q 342.) Treas. Reg. §1.401(a)(9)-6, A-2(b).

The final regulations issued in 2002 (the "2002 regulations") adopted simplified calculation rules first proposed in 2001 for lifetime distributions from individual accounts. The 2002 regulations are generally effective for determining required minimum distributions for calendar years beginning on or after January 1, 2003 (see Treas. Reg. §1.401(a)(9)-1, A-2(a)). In 2004, final regulations were adopted governing certain annuity distributions from defined benefit plans. See TD 9130, 2004-26 IRB 1082; see Q 342 for details.

Q 346 FEDERAL INCOME TAX

The 2002 final regulations also included updated tables that take into account longer life expectancies. Distributions for calendar year 2002 could be calculated under the 2002 regulations, the 2001 regulations or the 1987 regulations. See TD 8987, 67 Fed. Reg. 18988 (4-17-02). Defined contribution plan amendments are required by the last day of the first year beginning on or after January 1, 2003; the IRS has provided model plan amendments for this purpose. See Rev. Proc. 2002-29, 2002-1 CB 1176.

If distributions begin under a particular distribution option that is in the form of a joint and survivor annuity for the joint lives of the employee and a nonspouse beneficiary, the MDIB requirement will not be satisfied as of the date distributions begin unless the distribution option provides that annuity payments to be made to the employee on and after his required beginning date will satisfy the conditions set forth in Treas. Reg. §1.401(a)(9)-6, A-2(c). Under those provisions, the periodic annuity payment payable to the survivor must not at any time on and after the employee's required beginning date exceed the applicable percentage of the annuity payment payable to the employee using the following table:

Excess of Participant's Age over Beneficiary's Age	Applicable Percentage	Excess of Participant's Age over Beneficiary's Age	Applicable Percentage	Excess of Participant's Age over Beneficiary's Age	Applicable Percentage
10 or less	100	22	70	34	57
11	96	23	68	35	56
12	93	24	67	36	56
13	90	25	66	37	55
14	87	26	64	38	55
15	84	27	63	39	54
16	82	28	62	40	54
17	79	29	61	41	53
18	77	30	60	42	53
19	75	31	59	43	53
20	73	32	59	44 and greater	52
21	72	33	58		

Treas. Reg. §1.401(a)(9)-6, A-2(c)(2). The applicable percentage is based on how much older the participant is than the beneficiary as of their attained ages on their birthdays in the first calendar year for which distributions to the participant are required. For example, if the beneficiary is 10 or fewer years younger, the survivor annuity may be 100%. If the age difference is greater than 10 years, the maximum survivor annuity permitted is less than 100%. If there is more than one beneficiary, the age of the youngest beneficiary is used. Treas. Reg. §1.401(a)(9)-6, A-2(c).

If a distribution form includes a life annuity and a period certain, the amount of the annuity payments payable to the beneficiary need not be reduced during the period certain, but in the case of a joint and survivor annuity with a period certain, the amount of the annuity payments payable to the beneficiary must satisfy the foregoing requirements *after* the expiration of the period certain. Treas. Reg. §1.401(a)(9)-6, A-2(d).

Period certain limitations. The period certain for annuity distributions commencing during the life of the employee with an annuity starting date on or after his required beginning date generally may not exceed the applicable distribution period for the employee (see table at Q 341) for the calendar year that contains the annuity starting date. However, if the employee's spouse is his sole beneficiary, and the annuity provides only

PENSION AND PROFIT SHARING: QUALIFICATION   Q 347

a period certain and no life annuity, the period certain may last as long as the joint and survivor life expectancy of the employee and spouse, if that period is longer than the applicable distribution period for the employee. Treas. Reg. §1.401(a)(9)-6, A-3(a). If distributions commence after the death of the employee under the life expectancy rule explained in Q 343, the period certain for any distributions commencing after death cannot exceed the distribution period determined under the life expectancy provisions of Treas. Reg. §1.401(a)(9)-5, A-5(b).

Application of penalty. If the amount required to be distributed under the MDIB requirements exceeds the amount required under the regular minimum distribution rules (see Q 339 to Q 345), the shortfall is subject to a 50% excise tax (levied on the individual, not the plan). See IRC Sec. 4974. For details, see Q 347. *ASRS, Sec. 59, ¶945.5.*

347. How is an individual taxed when a qualified plan distribution fails to meet the minimum distribution requirements?

An excise tax equal to 50% of the amount by which the required distribution exceeds the amount actually distributed is imposed on the recipient. IRC Sec. 4974(a).

The amount that must be distributed from a plan for a calendar year is the *greater of* (1) the amount that must be distributed for that year under the required minimum distribution (RMD) rules (see Q 339 to Q 345); or (2) the amount required to be distributed for that year under the minimum distribution incidental benefit (MDIB) rule (see Q 346).

The excise tax is imposed on the recipient of the distribution for his taxable year beginning with or within the calendar year for which the distribution is required. IRC Sec. 4974; Treas. Reg. §54.4974-2, A-6. For purposes of the excise tax, a distribution for a participant's first distribution year not required until April 1 of the following year (i.e., the required beginning date) is treated as required in the calendar year containing the participant's required beginning date. Treas. Reg. §54.4974-2, A-6. See Q 340.

The excise tax may be waived if the Commissioner is satisfied that (1) the shortfall was due to reasonable error; and (2) reasonable steps are being taken to remedy it. IRC Sec. 4974(d); Treas. Reg. §54.4974-2, A-7. In addition, if an employee dies before his required beginning date, the excise tax will be automatically waived if: (1) the recipient is the sole beneficiary; (2) the RMD amount for a calendar year is determined under the life expectancy rule explained in Q 343; and (3) the entire distribution is completed by the end of the fifth calendar year following the calendar year of employee's date of death. Treas. Reg. §54.4974-2, A-7.

Individual Accounts

If distributions are being made in a form *other than an annuity* (under a contract purchased from a life insurance company or directly from a defined benefit plan), the rules for individual accounts apply and the shortfall is determined by subtracting the actual amount of the distribution from the amount required under the RMD rules or the MDIB rule (whichever is greater). For this purpose, if there is more than one permissible method for determining a required distribution, the default method provided by the regulations is used *unless* the plan provides otherwise. For the permissible and default methods available under various circumstances, see Q 341 to Q 345. Of course, if distributions following the death of the participant are to be made under a method that complies with the 5-year rule (see Q 343), no amounts need be distributed, and thus there can be no excise tax, until the fifth calendar year following the death. In that year, the recipient's entire remaining balance is the minimum required distribution. Treas. Reg. §54.4974-2, A-3(c).

Annuity Distributions

For purposes of the following rules, determinations as to whether there is a designated beneficiary and which designated beneficiary's life expectancy is controlling are made under the rules explained in Q 344. See Treas. Reg. §54.4974-2, A-4(b)(1)(ii).

If distributions are being made under an annuity contract purchased from a life insurance company, or under an annuity option of a defined benefit plan, and that annuity contract or option would meet the requirements of both the RMD rules and the MDIB rule, the shortfall is determined by subtracting the actual amount of distributions for the calendar year from the amount that should have been made for that calendar year under the provisions of the contract or option. Treas. Reg. §54.4974-2, A-4(a).

If the annuity contract or option is an impermissible contract or option (i.e., one that fails to meet either the RMD rules or the MDIB rule), the shortfall is determined by subtracting the actual amount distributed for the calendar year from the minimum distribution determined under the following rules:

(1) In the case of a defined benefit plan, if *distributions commence before the death* of the participant, the minimum distribution is the amount that would have been distributed under the plan's joint and survivor annuity option for the lives of the participant and designated beneficiary, which (a) is permissible under both the RMD rules and the MDIB rule, and (b) provides the greatest level amount payable to the participant on an annual basis. If the plan does not provide such an option, or there is no designated beneficiary, the minimum distribution is the amount that would have been distributed under the plan's life annuity option payable in a level amount for the life of the participant with no survivor benefit. Treas. Reg. §54.4974-2, A-4(b)(1)(i).

(2) In the case of a defined benefit plan, if *distributions commence after the death* of the participant and a designated beneficiary is named under the impermissible annuity option, the minimum distribution is the amount that would have been distributed under the plan's life annuity option payable in a level amount for the life of the beneficiary. If there is no designated beneficiary, no amount need be distributed until the fifth calendar year following the participant's death, at which time the entire interest must be distributed. Treas. Regs. §§54.4974-2, A-4(b)(1)(ii), 54.4974-2, A-4(b)(3).

(3) In the case of a defined contribution plan, if *distributions commence before the death* of the participant, the minimum distribution is the amount that would have been distributed from an annuity contract purchased under the plan's joint and survivor annuity option for the lives of the participant and designated beneficiary, which is both (a) permissible under the RMD rules and the MDIB rule, and (b) provides the greatest level amount payable to the participant on an annual basis. If there is no designated beneficiary, the minimum distribution is the amount that would have been distributed from a contract purchased under the plan's life annuity option providing level payments for the life of the participant with no survivor benefit. Treas. Reg. §54.4974-2, A-4(b)(2).

PENSION AND PROFIT SHARING: QUALIFICATION   Q 348

If the plan does not provide a permissible annuity distribution option, the minimum distribution is the amount that would have been distributed under a theoretical annuity contract purchased with the amount used to purchase the impermissible annuity. If there is a designated beneficiary, this theoretical contract is a joint and survivor annuity, which (a) provides level annual payments, (b) would be permissible under the RMD rules, and (c) provides the maximum survivor benefit permissible under the MDIB rule. If there is no designated beneficiary, the theoretical contract is a life annuity for the life of the participant, which provides level annual payments, and which is permissible under the RMD rules and the MDIB rule. Treas. Reg. §54.4974-2, A-4(b)(2).

(4) In the case of a defined contribution plan, if *distributions commence after the death* of the participant and a designated beneficiary is named under the impermissible annuity option, the minimum distribution is the amount that would have been distributed under a theoretical life annuity for the life of the designated beneficiary, which provides level annual payments, and which would be permissible under the RMD rules. If there is no designated beneficiary, no amount need be distributed until the fifth calendar year following the participant's death, at which time the entire interest must be distributed. Treas. Regs. §§54.4974-2, A-4(b)(2), 54.4974-2, A-4(b)(3).

The amount of the payments will be determined using the interest rate and mortality tables prescribed under IRC Section 7520, using the distribution commencement date determined under Treas. Reg. §1.401(a)(9)-3, A-3 and using the age of the beneficiary as of his birthday in the calendar year that contains that date. Treas. Reg. §54.4974-2, A-4(b)(2)(ii).

State Insurer Delinquency Proceedings

There is no violation of the minimum distribution requirements (and thus no excise tax) if a shortfall occurs because assets are invested in a contract issued by an insurance company that is in the midst of state insurer delinquency proceedings. The RMD rules are not violated merely because payments were reduced or suspended by reason of state insurer delinquency proceedings against the life insurance company issuing the annuity. This amount and any additional amount accrued during this period will be treated as though it is not vested during such proceedings. Any distributions with respect to such amounts must be made under the relevant rules for nonvested benefits described in Treas. Regs. §§1.401(a)(9)-5, A-8 or 1.401(a)(9)-6, A-6. See Q 341, Q 342. *ASRS, Sec. 59, ¶960.1.*

ALIENATION OF BENEFITS

348. What restrictions apply to the assignment or alienation of a participant's qualified plan benefit?

The plan must provide that benefits under the plan generally may not be assigned or alienated or subject to garnishment or execution. IRC Sec. 401(a)(13), ERISA Sec. 206(d). Limited exceptions are provided, including in the case of a qualified domestic relations order (QDRO–see Q 349), for collection of taxes or certain federal judgments, or when a participant has committed a breach of fiduciary duty to, or a criminal act against, the plan. IRC Sec. 401(a)(13)(C). The U.S. Supreme Court has held that for purposes of the anti-alienation provision, a working business owner and the owner's spouse are ERISA-protected participants, provided the plan covers one or more employees other than the owner and spouse. *Yates v. Hendon*, 124 S. Ct. 1330 (2004).

2006 Tax Facts on Insurance & Employee Benefits   389

Bankruptcy protection. Qualified plan interests generally are protected from the reach of plan participants' creditors in bankruptcy. *Patterson v. Shumate*, 112 S.Ct. 2242 (1992). Even where it was unclear whether a plan was tax qualified, the reach of *Patterson* extended to an "ERISA employee pension benefit plan" and trust that contained an ERISA-enforceable restriction on transfers. *Traina v. Sewell*, 180 F.3d 707 (5th Cir. 1999), citing *Baker v. LaSalle*, 114 F.3d 636 (7th Cir. 1997). The U.S. Supreme Court has also extended the protection offered to qualified plan assets under the federal Bankruptcy Code to an IRA containing a rolled over lump sum distribution from a qualified plan. See *Rousey v. Jacoway*, 125 S. Ct. 1561 (2005).

Payment of a participant's accrued benefit to a bankruptcy trustee pursuant to a bankruptcy court order, even with the participant's consent, is a prohibited alienation for qualification purposes. Let. Ruls. 9011037, 8910035, 8829009. A plan administrator may, however, plan permitting, draw a loan check or a hardship withdrawal check payable to the participant but, pursuant to an agreement between the participant and bankruptcy trustee, send such checks directly to the bankruptcy trustee, to be endorsed over to the trustee by the participant, without violating the anti-alienation prohibition. Let. Rul. 9109051.

A bankruptcy code requirement that debtors apply all "projected disposable income to be received ... to make payments under the [bankruptcy] plan" does not require a plan participant to take out a plan loan to pay toward his debt, because plan loans are not "income" for bankruptcy purposes. *In re Stones*, 157 Bankr. 669 (Bankr. S.D.Ca. 1993). However, once a participant has already taken a plan loan and subsequently files bankruptcy, amounts used to repay the loan do not receive preferential treatment merely because the loans are secured by plan assets. In at least two rulings, the payments were not deemed necessary for the participant's "maintenance and support." *In re Cohen*, 2000 Bankr. LEXIS 268; *In re Estes*, 2000 Bankr. LEXIS 1264.

QDRO exception. A plan may not distribute, segregate, or otherwise recognize the attachment of any portion of a participant's benefits in favor of the participant's spouse, former spouse or dependents unless such action is mandated by a QDRO. IRC Secs. 401(a)(13)(B), 414(p). The basic requirements for a QDRO are explained at Q 349. The voluntary partition of a participant's vested account balance between his spouse and himself in a community property state is an alienation of benefits. Let. Rul. 8735032. The Tax Court ruled that a participant's voluntary waiver of his benefits was a prohibited alienation, despite the PBGC's approval of the plan's termination; the waiver resulted in the plan being disqualified and the participant, who was the sole shareholder, being taxed on benefits he did not receive. *Gallade v. Comm.*, 106 TC 355 (1996).

Federal taxes and judgments. An anti-alienation provision will not prevent collection of federal taxes from the plan benefits. Treas. Reg. §1.401(a)-13(b)(1); *Iannone v. Comm.*, 122 TC 287 (2004). However, the IRS determined that a retirement plan was not obligated to honor an IRS levy on the benefits of a participant who was not yet entitled to receive a distribution; instead, the levy could be ignored until such time as the participant was eligible for a distribution. FSA 199930039. The Service's ability to attach pension benefits ended with the participant's death, since benefits payable to his son as beneficiary did not constitute "property" to which a tax lien could attach. *Asbestos Workers Local No. 23 Pension Fund v. U.S.*, 303 F.Supp. 551 (D.C. Pa. 2004).

In some cases, the IRS has permitted the collection of criminal fines and restitution against plan assets. See Let. Rul. 200342007. The Service has privately ruled that

PENSION AND PROFIT SHARING: QUALIFICATION   Q 348

for individuals already in "pay status," benefits may be subject to garnishment under the Federal Debt Collections Procedures Act (FDCPA), whether the defendant is the plan participant or a beneficiary. The IRS noted that such collections could be made whether the recipient was a government entity or a private party; the government, in effect, "steps into the shoes of the taxpayer," receiving funds the taxpayer would have received and applying them toward a valid debt of the taxpayer. However, such collections did not extend to individuals not yet in pay status, since they were not yet eligible for a distribution under the terms of the plan. Let. Rul. 200426027.

Crime or fiduciary violation. Generally, a plan may offset a participant's benefit under a qualified plan to recover certain amounts that the participant is ordered or required to pay. IRC Sec. 401(a)(13). For this exception to apply, the order or requirement to pay must arise under a judgment of conviction for a crime involving the plan, under a civil judgment entered by a court in an action brought in connection with a violation of the fiduciary responsibility provisions of ERISA, or pursuant to a settlement agreement between the Department of Labor (or the Pension Benefit Guaranty Corporation) and the participant in connection with a fiduciary violation. The judgment, order, decree or settlement must specifically provide for the offset of all or part of the amount required to be paid to the plan.

If the plan is subject to the survivor annuity rules (see Q 335), the offset will be permitted if (i) the spouse has consented to the offset or signed a waiver of the survivor annuity rules, (ii) the spouse is ordered or required to pay an amount to the plan in connection with a fiduciary violation (e.g., the spouse is held responsible for the fiduciary violation), or (iii) the judgment, order, decree, or settlement provides that the spouse retains the right to the minimum survivor annuity. IRC Sec. 401(a)(13)(C)(iii). Special rules are provided for determining the amount of the minimum survivor annuity. See IRC Sec. 401(a)(13)(D).

Other Exceptions

A plan may provide that after a benefit is in pay status, the participant or beneficiary receiving such benefit may make a voluntary and revocable assignment not to exceed 10% of any benefit payment, provided the assignment is not for the purpose of defraying plan administrative costs. IRC Sec. 401(a)(13)(A); Treas. Reg. §1.401(a)-13(d)(1).

Payment pursuant to a court order that is the result of a judicial determination that benefits cannot be paid to a beneficiary who murdered the plan participant is also permitted if the order conforms with the terms of the plan for directing payments when there is an ineligible beneficiary. Let. Rul. 8905058.

A disclaimer of qualified plan benefits that satisfies the requirements of state law and IRC Section 2518(b) (qualified disclaimers—see Q 908) is not a prohibited assignment or alienation. GCM 39858 (9-9-91).

An anti-alienation provision also will not prevent a plan from holding a rolled over distribution from another plan subject to an agreement to repay a part of the distribution in the event of early termination of the other plan. *Francis Jungers, Sole Proprietorship v. Comm.*, 78 TC 326 (1982), acq. 1983-1 CB 1.

A loan from the plan (but not from a third party) made to a participant or beneficiary and secured by the participant's accrued nonforfeitable benefit is not treated as an assignment or alienation if the loan is exempt from the excise tax on prohibited transactions or would be exempt if the participant or beneficiary were a disqualified person. Treas. Reg. §1.401(a)-13(d)(2); Rev. Rul. 89-14, 1989-1 CB 111.

A participant or beneficiary may direct payment of his plan benefit payment to a third party (including the employer) if the arrangement is revocable and the third party files with the plan administrator a written acknowledgement stating that he has no enforceable right to any plan benefit other than payments actually received. The written acknowledgement must be filed within 90 days after the arrangement is entered into. Treas. Regs. §§1.401(a)-13(d), 1.401(a)-13(e); TD 7534. After the death of a participant, an assignment made pursuant to a bona fide settlement between good faith adverse claimants to the participant's pension plan benefits was not invalidated by ERISA's anti-alienation provision. *Stobnicki v. Textron, Inc.*, 868 F.2d 1460 (5th Cir. 1989). *ASRS, Sec. 13, ¶110, Sec. 59, ¶490.3(a).*

349. What is a "qualified domestic relations order"?

A "qualified domestic relations order" (QDRO) is a judgment, decree, or order (including an approval of a property settlement agreement) that meets all the requirements under the Code for being "qualified." A plan may distribute, segregate, or otherwise recognize the attachment of any portion of a participant's benefits in favor of the participant's spouse, former spouse, or dependents without violating the restrictions on alienation of benefits (see Q 348) only if such action is mandated by a QDRO. IRC Secs. 401(a)(13)(B), 414(p). (Only a spouse, former spouse, child, or other dependent of a participant may be an "alternate payee" under a QDRO.)

The following requirements must be met for a domestic relations order (DRO) to be qualified: (1) it must relate to the provision of child support, alimony, or property rights to a spouse, former spouse, child, or other dependent; (2) it must be made under a state's community property or other domestic relations law; (3) it must create, recognize, or assign to the spouse, former spouse, child, or other dependent of the participant (i.e., to an alternate payee) the right to receive all or a portion of a participant's plan benefits; and (4) it must clearly specify (a) the names and, unless the plan administrator has reason to know them, the addresses of the participant and each alternate payee, (b) the amount or percentage of the participant's benefit to be paid to each alternate payee (or a method for determining such amount), (c) the number of payments or the period to which such order applies, and (d) each plan to which such order applies. IRC Sec. 414(p)(1).

A distribution from a governmental plan, a church plan or an eligible 457 governmental plan (see Q 124) will be treated as made pursuant to a QDRO as long as the domestic relations order meets requirements (1) through (3). IRC Sec. 414(p)(11). Model language for a QDRO is set forth in Notice 97-11, 1997-1 CB 379.

A marital settlement agreement that was incorporated into a divorcing couple's dissolution agreement constituted a QDRO, not merely a property settlement. *Hawkins v. Comm.* 86 F.3d 982 (10th Cir. 1996), rev'g 102 TC 61. However, a state court order modifying an earlier divorce order and requiring that an ex-wife receive payments from her ex-husband's pension was not a QDRO, because prior to the modification, the husband had retired and the surviving spouse benefit had "vested" in his second wife; thus, enforcement of the order would have required the plan to provide increased

PENSION AND PROFIT SHARING: QUALIFICATION Q 349

benefits. *Hopkins v. AT&T Global Information Solutions Co.*, 914 F. Supp. 1362 (E.D. W.Va. 1996).

An amendment to a divorce decree did not constitute a QDRO, and thus could not confer on the ex-wife a 50% interest in the participant's preretirement survivor annuity, because prior to the amendment the participant had died and the benefits had lapsed. As a result, the amendment impermissably provided for increased benefits. *Samaroo v. Samaroo*, 193 F.3d 185 (3rd Cir. 1999). Similarly, a divorce decree ordering a plan distribution as part of the marital settlement did not meet the qualifications for a QDRO where the payout predated the decree and was not made directly to the spouse. *Burton v. Comm.*, TC Memo 1997-20. A correction of a QDRO that at first did not meet the QDRO requirements related back to the original date of the order; thus, an intervening tax lien was insufficient to defeat the spouse's claim. See *U.S. v. Taylor*, 338 F.3d 947 (8th Cir. 2003).

In a private ruling, the IRS approved the use of a second QDRO to secure other marital obligations (in addition to a first QDRO ordering the segregation of a portion of the husband's retirement plan benefit for the wife's benefit). See Let. Rul. 200252097.

There is no clear consensus among the federal courts as to whether a QDRO is enforceable after a participant's death. In the Court of Appeals for the Eighth Circuit, a post-death QDRO was upheld where the employer was already on notice before participant's death as to the decree and the domestic relations order. The court noted that ERISA allows an 18-month period for issuance of a QDRO and held that the employer could not deny benefits during that period. *Hogan v. Raytheon*, 2002 U.S. App. Lexis 18724 (8th Cir. 2002); see also IRC Sec. 414(p)(7), ERISA Sec. 206(d)(3)(H). The Court of Appeals for the Ninth Circuit reached the same result, enforcing a child support order in a case where the plan benefit would have been payable to a different beneficiary in the absence of the QDRO. Neither the beneficiary designation, nor the participant's death before the QDRO was finalized, precluded an alternate payee from enforcing the child support order against the pension plan benefit. *Trustees of the Directors Guild of America-Producer Pension Benefits Plans v. Tise*, 2000 U.S. App. Lexis 31161 (9th Cir. 2000). Other courts have reached a similar result. See *IBM Savings Plan v. Price*, 349 F.Supp.2d 854 (D.Vt. 2004).

A different result was reached when an ex-spouse attempted to enforce a QDRO only when the employee died eight years after his divorce. In denying the spouse's claim, the district court ruled that the decedent's surviving spouse became "vested" in the plan's survivor annuity upon his death and, thus, a qualified domestic relations order (QDRO) could not be entered thereafter in favor of an earlier spouse. *Stahl v. Exxon Corp.*, 2000 U.S. Dist. LEXIS 13720 (S.D. Texas 2002).

The applicability of the QDRO provisions to benefits other than those provided by qualified plans is not fully clear. After having ruled in 1992 that they were inapplicable to nonqualified deferred compensation plans and welfare benefit plans (including life insurance), a Michigan district court reversed itself in 1996, holding that a QDRO provision should be followed with respect to the disposition of a welfare plan, such as life insurance. See *Metropolitan Life Ins. Co. v. Fowler*, 922 F. Supp. 8 (E.D. MI 1996), rev'g *Metropolitan Life Ins. Co. v. Person*, 805 F. Supp. 1411 (E.D. MI 1992). See also, Let. Rul. 9334032. The Court of Appeals for the Seventh Circuit has ruled that the QDRO provisions of ERISA were applicable to group term life insurance and other

Q 349   FEDERAL INCOME TAX

welfare plans. See *Metropolitan Life Ins. Co. v. Wheaton*, 42 F.3d 1080 (7th Cir. 1994). Final regulations governing 403(b) plans extend the application of the QDRO rules to tax-sheltered annuity contracts, at least with respect to taxable years beginning after 2005. See Treas. Regs. §§1.403(b)-10(c); 1.403(b)-11(a).

A QDRO generally may not require that the plan provide any form of benefit not otherwise provided under the plan and may not require that the plan provide increased benefits (as determined actuarially). However, within certain limits, it is permissible for a QDRO to require that payments to the alternate payee begin on or after the participant's earliest retirement age, even though the participant has not separated from service at that time. For these purposes, a participant's "earliest retirement age" is defined as the earlier of (1) the date that the participant is entitled to a distribution under the plan or (2) the later of (i) the date the participant attains age 50 or (ii) the earliest date on which the participant could begin receiving benefits under the plan if the participant separated from service. IRC Sec. 414(p)(4)(B).

A plan may provide for payment to an alternate payee prior to the earliest retirement age as defined in the Code. Treas. Reg. §1.401(a)-13(g)(3).

Planning Point: Employers should consider drafting their retirement plans to offer in-service distributions to alternate payees, so as not to be burdened with administering the benefits of employees' ex-spouses—a group that by its nature may be hostile to the employer. *Martin Silfen, J.D., Brown Brothers Harriman Trust Co., LLC.*

A domestic relations order requiring payment of benefits to an alternate payee is not qualified if such benefits are required to be paid to another alternate payee under a previous QDRO. The IRS has determined that the assignment of a participant's retirement account (or placement of a lien on it) to secure payment of obligations under the terms of a QDRO was not a prohibited alienation. Let. Ruls. 9234014, 200252093.

The Code provides that, to the extent specified in a QDRO, the former spouse of a participant (and not the current spouse) may be treated as a surviving spouse for purposes of the survivor benefit requirements and, for that purpose, a former spouse will be treated as married to the participant for the requisite 1-year period if such former spouse and the participant had been married for at least one year (see Q 336). IRC Sec. 414(p)(5); Treas. Reg. §1.401(a)-13(g)(4). In the absence of such a provision, a former spouse was not entitled to receive any benefits where the husband died before becoming entitled to receive retirement benefits and the preretirement survivor annuity was payable to the current spouse. *Dugan v. Clinton*, 1987 U.S. Dist. LEXIS 4276 (N.D. Ill. 1987).

The plan administrator is required to make the determination as to whether an order is a QDRO. All plans must establish reasonable procedures for making such determinations. IRC Secs. 414(p)(6), 414(p)(7). In addition, a plan administrator who has reason to believe an order is a sham or is questionable in nature must take reasonable steps to determine its credibility. DOL Adv. Op. 99-13A. However, the plan administrator is not required under the Code or ERISA to review the correctness of the determination that an individual is a surviving spouse under state domestic relations law. DOL Adv. Op. 92-17A. Moreover, a plan administrator is not required to, and should not, "look beneath the face" of a state court order to determine whether amounts to which it relates were properly awarded. *Blue v. UAL Corp.*, 160 F.3d 383 (7th Cir. 1998).

PENSION AND PROFIT SHARING: QUALIFICATION   Q 351

The DOL has stated that nothing in ERISA Section 206(d)(3) precludes a state court from altering or modifying an earlier QDRO of a couple petitioning the court for such a change, provided the new order satisfies the requirements of a QDRO. In such a case, the DOL noted that the new order would operate on a prospective basis only. DOL Adv. Op. 2004-02A.

A plan may provide for a "hold" to be placed on a participant's account while the determination is being made as to whether an order is a QDRO; however, where a plan with such a provision went beyond its written procedures to place a hold on an account before the order was received (but after the divorce was final), the hold violated ERISA. *Schoonmaker v. The Employee Sav. Plan of Amoco Corp.*, 987 F.2d 410 (7th Cir. 1993). The Department of Labor has also stated that plans are not permitted to impose separate fees for the costs of such procedures to individual participants or alternate payees. DOL Adv. Op. 94-32A.

For the taxation of payments made pursuant to a QDRO, see Q 426 and Q 428. For an explanation of the effect of a QDRO on the minimum distribution requirements, see Q 345. *ASRS, Sec. 59, ¶490.3(b).*

TOP-HEAVY PLAN REQUIREMENTS

350. What do the top-heavy rules require with respect to a qualified plan?

In any plan year in which the plan is a "top-heavy" plan (see Q 351), additional qualification requirements must be met. Plans established and maintained by the United States, by state governments and political subdivisions thereof, and by agencies and instrumentalities of any of these, are exempt from the top-heavy requirements. IRC Sec. 401(a)(10)(B). See Q 352 for details.

Moreover, except to the extent provided in the regulations, all non-exempt plans *(whether or not actually top-heavy)* must contain provisions that meet the additional top-heavy qualification requirements and that will become effective should the plan become top-heavy. For rules and exemptions, see Treas. Regs. §§1.416-1, T-35 to 1.416-1, T-38.

Plans established and maintained by the United States, by state governments and political subdivisions thereof, and by agencies and instrumentalities of any of these, are exempt from the top-heavy requirements. IRC Sec. 401(a)(10)(B). Also, the top-heavy rules are not applicable to SIMPLE IRA plans (see Q 242), SIMPLE 401(k) plans (see Q 400), or safe harbor 401(k) plans (see Q 399). IRC Secs. 416(g)(4)(G), 416(g)(4)(H), 401(k)(11)(D)(ii).

For the definition of a "top-heavy" plan, see Q 351. As to when a participant is a "key employee" for purposes of the top-heavy rules, see Q 357. For the additional qualification requirements applicable to top-heavy plans, see Q 352. *ASRS, Sec. 59, ¶440.*

351. When is a plan top-heavy?

Single Plans

In the simplest case, where an employer maintains only one qualified plan, that plan is a top-heavy plan with respect to a *plan* year if the present value of the cumulative accrued benefits under the plan (or the aggregate account balances if the plan is a defined contribution plan) for *key employees* (see Q 357) exceeds 60% of the present value of the cumulative accrued benefits under the plan (or the aggregate account balances) for *all* employees. IRC Sec. 416(g)(1)(A).

For purposes of determining the present values of accrued benefits (or the sums of account balances), benefits derived from both employer contributions and nondeductible employee contributions are taken into account; benefits derived from deductible employee contributions are disregarded. (*Deductible employee contributions* are certain contributions made before 1987; the term does not refer to salary reductions or employee deferrals.) Any *reasonable* interest rate assumption may be used to calculate these present values; however, the Service will automatically accept as reasonable a rate which is not less than 5%, nor greater than 6%. The interest rate used need not be the same as other assumptions used in the plan (e.g., the rate assumed for funding purposes). Where an aggregation group consists of two or more defined benefit plans, the interest rate assumptions used to calculate the present values must be the same in all plans. Treas. Regs. §§1.416-1, T-26, 1.416-1, T-28.

Present values and account balances are generally determined on the last day of the *prior* plan year; however, when testing for top-heaviness with respect to the first plan year (as well as the second) of a *new* plan, the determination date is the last day of the first plan year. IRC Sec. 416(g)(4)(C).

In the case of a defined contribution plan, the balance in each account on the determination date is calculated by adjusting the balance of each account as of the most recent valuation date occurring within 12 months prior to the determination date for contributions due as of the determination date. Treas. Reg. §1.416-1, T-24. For defined benefit plans, the present value of an accrued benefit as of the determination date is generally determined as of the most recent valuation date occurring in the previous 12 months. (Special rules apply in the case of a new defined benefit plan in its first and second plan years.) Treas. Reg. §1.416-1, T-25. The cumulative accrued benefit of non-key employees must be determined under the method used for accrual purposes for all plans of the employer or, if there is no such method, as if such benefit accrued not more rapidly than under the fractional method (see Q 373). IRC Sec. 416(g)(4)(F).

In determining these present values and account balances, any distribution (generally including death benefits) made from the plan with respect to any employee during the 1-year period ending on the determination date (and which is not already reflected in the present value or account balance) must be added back to the present value of that employee's accrued benefit or to his account balance, whichever is applicable. IRC Sec. 416(g)(3)(A); Reg. §1.416-1, T-30, T-31. In the case of a distribution made for a reason other than severance from employment, death, or disability, a 5-year lookback period applies for this purpose. IRC Sec. 416(g)(3)(B).

If an individual has not performed any services for the employer during the 1-year period ending on the determination date, his accrued benefit and his account are not to be taken into account for purposes of determining whether the plan is top-heavy. IRC Sec. 416(g)(4)(E). Also, if an individual was a key employee in a previous plan year but is currently a non-key employee for purposes of the top-heavy test, his cumulative accrued benefit (or account balance) is totally disregarded.

PENSION AND PROFIT SHARING: QUALIFICATION   Q 351

The terms "key employee" and "employee" should be read to include their "beneficiaries," so that the beneficiary of a key employee is treated as a key employee and the beneficiary of a former key employee is treated as a former key employee. IRC Sec. 416(i)(5); Treas. Reg. §1.416-1, T-12. (For the definition of *key employee*, see Q 357.) This apparently means that for purposes of testing top-heaviness, an individual's accrued benefit or account balance must be considered in its entirety and not allocated between the individual and his beneficiaries. For plan years beginning before January 1, 2002, it also meant that the accrued benefit or account balance of a deceased key employee, even though payable (or paid) to his beneficiary, continued to be treated as that of a key employee for four years. See IRC Sec. 416(i)(1)(A), prior to amendment by EGTRRA 2001.

A plan will not be treated as violating the top-heavy rules merely on account of the making of (or right to make) catch-up contributions by participants age 50 or over, under the provisions of IRC Section 414(v), so long as a universal availability requirement is met. IRC Sec. 414(v)(3)(B). See Q 397 for details on the requirements for catch-up contributions. For the effect of rollover contributions on the top-heavy calculation, see "Rollovers," below.

Multiple Plans

Generally, where an employer maintains more than one qualified plan, some or all of those plans will be aggregated and tested as a group for top-heaviness. Specifically, (1) all qualified plans (including collectively-bargained plans) of an employer which cover at least one key employee (i.e., key employee plans) and (2) any qualified plans which enable an otherwise discriminatory key employee plan to satisfy the nondiscrimination requirements of IRC Sections 401(a)(4) or 410 (see Q 324 to Q 330, Q 404 to Q 399) are *required* to be aggregated into a single group.

In addition, the employer may designate any other qualified plan or plans (including collectively-bargained plans) not required to be aggregated under (1) or (2) to be included in an existing aggregation group, provided that the resulting group, taken as a whole, would continue to satisfy IRC Sections 401(a)(4) and 410.

If an aggregation group is top-heavy, all plans required to be included in the group under (1) or (2) will be considered top-heavy plans; any plan included in the group solely because of the employer's designation will not be treated as top-heavy. (Even though a collectively-bargained plan covering a key employee might be part of a top-heavy aggregation group because it was required to be aggregated, that collectively-bargained plan will be excepted from the fast vesting, minimum benefits, and maximum compensation requirements discussed in Q 352.) See Treas. Reg. §1.416-1, T-3. If the aggregation group is *not* top-heavy, no plan in the group will be considered top-heavy, even though one or more plans composing the group would be top-heavy if tested alone. Treas. Reg. §1.416-1, T-9.

The procedure for testing top-heaviness of an aggregation group is the same as that discussed above for a single plan, except that the values tested are the sums of the respective present values and account balances determined for each plan (as of its determination date) composing the group. When plans composing the aggregation group have different plan years, the test is carried out using the determination dates which fall within the same calendar year. Treas. Reg. §1.416-1, T-23.

2006 Tax Facts on Insurance & Employee Benefits

If only one of the employer's plans is a key employee plan and that plan, by itself, satisfies the nondiscrimination requirements of IRC Sections 401(a)(4) and 410, that plan will be tested as a "single" plan unless the employer elects to designate another plan for aggregation with the key employee plan.

Simplified Employee Pension Plans

For purposes of testing for top-heaviness, a simplified employee pension plan, including a SAR-SEP (see Q 241), is treated as a defined contribution plan. An employer may elect to use aggregate employer contributions to the simplified employee pension plan, rather than aggregate account balances, for purposes of the top-heavy test. IRC Sec. 416(i)(6).

Rollovers

How amounts rolled over *(or otherwise transferred)* to or from a qualified plan are treated for purposes of determining whether the plan is top-heavy depends on the surrounding circumstances. If the rollover or transfer is initiated other than by the employee (as in the case of a merger or division of plans) or is made between plans of the same employer (or related employers required to be aggregated under IRC Section 414), the amount rolled over is counted as part of the employee's accrued benefits by the receiving plan, but disregarded by the distributing plan. If the rollover or transfer is initiated by the employee (regardless of who initiated the *distribution*) and is made between plans of unrelated employers, the rollover distribution generally must be added back to the distributing plan for a 1-year period and generally disregarded by the receiving plan. IRC Sec. 416(g)(4)(A); Treas. Reg. §1.416-1, T-32.

Simplified Calculation Methods

Precise top-heavy ratios need not be computed every year so long as the plan administrator knows whether or not the plan is top-heavy. For this purpose, and for the purpose of demonstrating to IRS that a plan is not top-heavy, an employer may use computations that are not precisely in accordance with the top-heavy rules but which mathematically prove that the plan is not top-heavy. (Several such methods are provided in the regulations.) Treas. Reg. §1.416-1, T-39. *ASRS, Sec. 59, ¶440.2.*

352. What are the special qualification requirements that apply to top-heavy plans?

In addition to the qualification requirements that apply to qualified plans generally (see Q 322), special requirements are imposed by the Code on top-heavy plans. Also, top-heavy simplified employee pension plans are required to meet certain minimum contribution requirements. In applying these requirements the *common control*, *controlled group*, and *affiliated service group* aggregation rules apply. See Q 359, Q 360. Also, under some circumstances, "leased" employees may be imputed to the employer (see Q 355). Guidelines for applying the top-heavy rules may be found in Treas. Reg. §1.416-1.

The following requirements must be met by top-heavy plans in general (top-heavy simplified employee pensions need meet only the minimum contribution requirements discussed in Q 352B, below):

PENSION AND PROFIT SHARING: QUALIFICATION   Q 352

Fast Vesting

A. A top-heavy plan must provide that an employee has a nonforfeitable right to his accrued benefit derived from employer contributions in accordance with *one* of the two following requirements:

1. *Three-year vesting.* An employee who has completed at least three years of service with the employer must have a nonforfeitable right to 100% of his accrued benefit. IRC Sec. 416(b)(1)(A).

2. *Six-year graded vesting.* An employee who has completed at least two years of service must have a nonforfeitable right to at least the following percentages of his accrued benefit: 20% after two years of service, 20% additional for each of the following years of service, reaching 100% after six years of service with the employer. IRC Sec. 416(b)(1)(B).

Except to the extent that they are inconsistent with these fast vesting schedules, the rules that pertain to vesting in qualified plans generally (including years of service and breaks in service, etc.) apply for purposes of the fast vesting requirements. IRC Sec. 416(b)(2); see Treas. Regs. §§1.416-1, V-1; 1.416-1, V-2. Thus, the fast vesting schedules are *not* safe harbors; even faster vesting may be required by IRC Section 411(d) where there is a pattern of abuse. See Q 333.

When a plan becomes top-heavy, fast vesting under one of the two schedules must generally be applied to all benefits accrued under the plan for the current plan year and *all* prior plan years (including benefits accrued in years before the plan became top-heavy and benefits accrued before the effective date of the top-heavy rules). However, the accrued benefit of any employee who does not have an hour of service after the plan became top-heavy, and any accrued benefits that were forfeited before the plan became top-heavy, need not be covered by the fast vesting schedule. Treas. Reg. §1.416-1, V-3.

Although the Code does not require that fast vesting be applied to benefits accrued in *future* plan years in which the plan is *not* top-heavy, a return to the plan's slower vesting when the plan ceases to be top-heavy may, in many cases, be impractical or impossible. For example, IRC Section 411(a)(10) requires that a change in vesting schedules not reduce a participant's nonforfeitable percentage in his accrued benefit and that certain participants be allowed to elect to be covered by the previous vesting schedule. See Q 333. See Treas. Reg. §1.416-1, V-7. For additional rules regarding vesting in a top-heavy plan, see Treas. Regs. §§1.416-1, V-5; 1.416-1, V-6.

Minimum Benefits and Contributions

B. For any top-heavy plan year, a plan generally must provide a minimum benefit or contribution for each *non-key* employee who is a participant. IRC Sec. 416(c); Treas. Reg. §1.416-1, M-1. Integration (i.e., permitted disparity) must be disregarded for purposes of determining a minimum benefit or contribution (see Q 352C, below).

Defined benefit plans. A top-heavy defined benefit plan generally must provide an accrued benefit (derived from employer contributions) for each non-key employee participant which when expressed as an annual retirement benefit is not less than the participant's *average compensation* multiplied by the lesser of 2% for each *year of service*

Q 352   FEDERAL INCOME TAX

with the employer or 20%. (For the non-key employees for which a minimum benefit is not required, see Treas. Reg. §1.416-1, M-4.)

Years of service are the same as the "years of service" taken into account for the ordinary vesting rules (see Q 333), but years of service in which non-top-heavy plan years end are not counted for this purpose, nor are years in which no key employee (or former key employee) benefits under the plan. IRC Sec. 416(c)(1)(C)(iii).

Average compensation is a participant's average annual compensation for the period of consecutive years (not exceeding five) during which the participant had the greatest aggregate compensation from the employer. IRC Sec. 416(c)(1)(D)(i). However, compensation for any year which is not a "year of service" is disregarded. IRC Sec. 416(c)(1)(D)(ii). Similarly, unless the plan provides otherwise, compensation for any year beginning after the plan has ceased forever to be top-heavy, is not counted. IRC Sec. 416(c)(1)(D)(iii). For the definition of *compensation*, see Q 331. *Annual retirement benefit* means a benefit payable annually in the form of a single life annuity (with no ancillary benefits) beginning at the normal retirement age under the plan. IRC Sec. 416(c)(1)(E); Treas. Regs. §§1.416-1, M-2, 1.416-1, M-3.

For the application of the minimum benefit requirement to a defined benefit plan funded exclusively by level premium insurance contracts, see Treas. Reg. §1.416-1, M-17.

Defined contribution plans. For each plan year in which a defined contribution plan or simplified employee pension plan is top-heavy, employer contributions and forfeitures allocated to the account of each non-key employee participant must not be less than the amount which is calculated by multiplying the participant's compensation by the lesser of (a) 3%, or (b) that percentage which is the highest contribution rate made for a key employee. IRC Sec. 416(c)(2); Treas. Reg. §1.416-1, M-7 to M-9.

For purposes of determining the highest contribution rate received by a key employee, employer contributions and forfeitures made on behalf of each key employee under the plan (or if the plan is part of a required aggregation group (see Q 351), all defined contribution plans included in the group) are divided by his total compensation for the year (but not more than $220,000, as indexed for 2006; see Appendix E for earlier years). IRC Sec. 401(a)(17); Treas. Reg. §1.416-1, M-7.

Although employer contributions attributable to salary reduction or similar arrangements may not be disregarded when calculating the minimum contribution requirement for a top-heavy defined contribution plan, such contributions may not be used to satisfy that top-heavy minimum contribution requirement. Treas. Reg. §1.416-1, M-20. Nonelective contributions and employer matching contributions may be used to satisfy the minimum contribution requirement, but such amounts generally cannot then be used in the ACP or ADP test (see Q 405, Q 404). Treas. Regs. §§1.416-1, M-18, 1.416-1, M-19. For application of the minimum contribution requirement in the case of a plan which has received a waiver of the *minimum funding requirements*, see Treas. Reg. §1.416-1, M-9.

If a top-heavy defined contribution plan required to be included in an aggregation group (see Q 351) with a discriminatory defined benefit plan enables that defined benefit plan to satisfy the nondiscrimination requirements of IRC Sections 401(a)(4) and 410, the minimum contribution is 3% of the participant's compensation (and the "highest contribution rate for key employees" is disregarded). IRC Sec. 416(c)(2)(B)(ii)(II).

Defined benefit and defined contribution plans. Although an employer who maintains both a top-heavy defined benefit plan and a top-heavy defined contribution plan is not required *by the top-heavy rules* to provide a non-key employee who participates in both plans with a minimum contribution *and* a minimum benefit, the non-key employee may not receive less under the combined plans than he would if he participated in only one of the plans. See TEFRA Conf. Rep., 1982-2 CB 677; see IRC Sec. 416(f). The regulations provide four safe harbor rules which a plan may use to determine which minimum an employee must receive. See Treas. Reg. §1.416-1, M-12.

Collective bargaining units. The minimum contribution and minimum benefit requirements do not apply in the case of any employee covered by a collective bargaining agreement if there is evidence that retirement benefits were the subject of good faith bargaining. IRC Sec. 416(i)(4).

Integration

C. Although the Code does not prohibit integration in a top-heavy plan, the fast vesting and minimum benefit (and contribution) requirements discussed in Q 352A and Q 352B, above, must be satisfied without taking into account employer payments of FICA taxes or contributions or benefits made or received under any other federal or state law. IRC Sec. 416(e). *ASRS, Sec. 59, ¶440.3.*

MISCELLANEOUS QUALIFICATION RULES

353. What other qualification requirements must be met in order for a plan to be qualified?

A. A qualified plan must be a permanent, as distinguished from a temporary, program. Thus, although an employer may reserve the right to amend or terminate the plan, the abandonment of the plan for any reason other than business necessity within a few years after its establishment will be evidence that the plan from its inception was not a bona fide program for the exclusive benefit of employees in general. This will especially be true if, for example, a pension plan is abandoned soon after pensions have been funded for the highly-paid or stockholder employees. Treas. Reg. §1.401-1(b)(2).

B. The plan must provide that in the case of any merger or consolidation with, or transfer of assets or liabilities to, any other plan, each participant in the plan would (if the plan then terminated) receive a benefit immediately after the merger, consolidation, or transfer which is equal to or greater than the benefit he would have been entitled to receive immediately before the merger, consolidation, or transfer (if the plan had then terminated). IRC Sec. 401(a)(12). (This requirement does not apply to certain multiemployer plans.) Shifting assets between funding media used for a single plan (e.g., between trusts and annuity contracts) is not a transfer of assets or liabilities. Treas. Reg. §1.414(l)-1.

C. *Early retirement benefit.* If a plan provides for payment of an early retirement benefit, a vested participant who terminates his employment after having satisfied the service requirements, but not the age requirement for the early benefit, must be entitled, upon satisfaction of the age requirement, to receive a benefit not less than the benefit to which he would be entitled at normal retirement age, actuarially reduced in accordance with reasonable actuarial assumptions. IRC Sec. 401(a)(14); Treas. Reg. §1.401(a)-14(c). In the case of a defined contribution plan, the employee, upon reaching early retirement age following termination after having satisfied service requirements, must be entitled to receive a benefit equal in value to the vested portion of his account balance at early retirement age. TIR 1334 (1/8/75), M-3.

D. *Social Security offset.* The plan must not permit benefits to be reduced by reason of any increase in Social Security benefit levels or wage base occurring (1) after separation from service, in the case of a participant who has separated from service with nonforfeitable rights to benefits, or (if earlier) (2) after first receipt of benefits, in the case of a participant or beneficiary who is receiving benefits under the plan. IRC Sec. 401(a)(15). This requirement also applies to plans that supplement benefits provided under state or federal laws other than the Social Security Act, such as the Railroad Retirement Act of 1937. Treas. Reg. §1.401(a)-15(d).

E. *Withdrawal of employee contributions.* The plan must preclude forfeitures of accrued benefits derived from employer contributions (whether forfeitable or nonforfeitable) solely because a benefit derived from the participant's contributions is voluntarily withdrawn by him after he has a nonforfeitable right to 50% of his accrued benefit derived from employer contributions. IRC Sec. 401(a)(19); Treas. Reg. §1.401(a)-19(b).

F. *Compensation.* Generally, a plan will not be qualified unless (for the purpose of any of the qualification rules) not more than $220,000 (as indexed for 2006) of annual compensation of any employee is taken into account under the plan for any plan year. IRC Sec. 401(a)(17)(A). (See Appendix E for the amounts for earlier plan years.) This amount is indexed for inflation in increments of $5,000. See IRC Sec. 401(a)(17)(B); Treas. Reg. §1.401(a)(17)-1(a). Special rules apply to governmental plans (see Q 467). *ASRS, Sec. 59.*

EMPLOYEES AND EMPLOYERS

354. What individuals are treated as "employees" of an employer for purposes of meeting the qualification requirements?

Generally, the term "employee" includes any individual who performs services for a person or entity that has the right to control and direct his work, not only as to the result to be accomplished but also as to the details and means by which the result is accomplished. Treas. Reg. §31.3121(d)-1(c)(2); *Packard v. Comm.*, 63 TC 621 (1975). These individuals are referred to as "common law employees." The Supreme Court has set forth a 20-factor test for determining whether an individual is a common law employee. See *Nationwide Mutual Ins. Co. v. Darden*, 503 U.S. 318 (1992). Self-employed individuals (including sole proprietors and partners operating trades, businesses, or professions), although clearly not "common law employees," are treated as employees for purposes of participating in qualified plans (see Q 358). IRC Sec. 401(c)(1).

To prevent abuses of the tax advantages of qualified retirement plans through the manipulation of separate employer entities, the Code provides several special rules that must generally be applied when testing plan qualification, as follows:

...All employees of all corporations that are members of a "controlled group" of corporations and all employees of trades or businesses under "common control" must

PENSION AND PROFIT SHARING: QUALIFICATION   Q 355

be treated as employed by a single employer. IRC Secs. 414(b), 414(c); Treas. Regs. §§1.414-1(b), 1.414(c)-1 to 1.414(c)-5. See Q 359.

...All employees of the members of an "affiliated service group" must be treated as employed by a single employer. IRC Sec. 414(m); Prop. Treas. Reg. §1.414(m)-1. See Q 360.

..."Leased employees" must be treated as employees. IRC Sec. 414(n). See Q 355 for an explanation of the special rules that apply to leased employees.

The aggregation rules for controlled groups and trades and businesses under common control also appear in ERISA; the aggregation rules for affiliated service groups do not. Except in the case of employees of an affiliated service group or certain leased employees, employees of a partnership need not be treated as employees of any partner who does not own more than a 50% interest in the capital or profits of the partnership. See *Garland v. Comm.*, 73 TC 5 (1979); *Thomas Kiddie, M.D., Inc. v. Comm.*, 69 TC 1055 (1978). *ASRS, Sec. 59, ¶490.4(d).*

355. What special rules apply to "leased employees" for purposes of the qualification requirements?

Generally, for purposes of most of the qualification requirements, an employer treats any individual who is a "leased employee" as though that individual were the employer's own employee; however, to the extent that contributions or benefits provided for the leased employee by the organization from which he is "leased" are attributable to services performed for the employer, such contributions or benefits are treated as if they were provided by the employer under a qualified plan. IRC Sec. 414(n)(1).

A *leased employee* is an individual who is not an "employee" of the recipient employer and who performs services for a recipient employer, if (1) his services are provided to the recipient under one or more agreements with a leasing organization, (2) he has performed his services for the recipient (or related employer) on a substantially full-time basis for a period of at least one year, and (3) the services are performed under primary direction or control by the recipient. IRC Sec. 414(n)(2). For purposes of this definition, the term "employee" means a "common law employee," as determined under the 20-factor test set forth in *Nationwide Mutual Ins. Co. v. Darden* (503 U.S. 318 (1992)), and that test must be applied before it can be determined whether an individual meets the definition of a "leased employee." *Burrey v. Pacific Gas and Elect. Co.*, 1998 U.S. App. Lexis 26594 (9th Cir. 1998); General Explanation of Tax Legislation Enacted in the 104th Congress (JCT-12-96), p. 173 (the 1996 Blue Book).

The fact that an individual is a leased employee, however, does not automatically mean he must be a participant in a plan maintained by the employer. At least two circuit courts have held that ERISA does not *per se* require the inclusion of leased employees in an employer's plan. See *Abraham v. Exxon Corp.*, 85 F.3d 1126 (5th Cir. 1996); *Bronk v. Mountain States Tel. & Tel., Inc.*, 21 EBC 2862 (10th Cir. 1998). In addition, guidance issued by the IRS has addressed this issue, stating that IRC Section 414(n)(1)(A) requires only that leased employees be treated as employees, not that they be participants in the plan. See Notice 84-11, 1984-2 CB 469, A-14. Despite its issuance prior to TRA '86, Notice 84-11 was cited favorably in *Bronk*, above, as controlling authority on this issue.

The determination of whether services are performed under the primary direction or control of the recipient is made on the basis of the facts and circumstances. Generally, such a finding will be made if the service recipient exercises the majority of direction and control over the individual; for example, if the individual is required to comply with the recipient's instructions as to (a) when, where and how the services are to be performed, (b) whether the services will be performed by a particular person, (c) whether the individual is subject to the recipient's supervision, and (d) whether the services must be performed in a particular order or sequence set by the recipient. For examples showing the application of the amended provision, see the 1996 Blue Book at pages 173-174.

The recipient may be a single employer or a group consisting of employers required to be aggregated under the controlled group, common control, or affiliated service group rules (see Q 359, Q 360). IRC Sec. 414(n)(6)(B). Employers are "related" if (1) a loss on a sale of property between them would be disallowed as a deduction under IRC Section 267 or 707(b), or (2) they are members of the same controlled group of corporations (using a 50% rather than 80% ownership test). IRC Secs. 414(n)(6)(A), 414(a)(3).

Even though an individual is a "leased employee" he may be disregarded by the employer for purposes of determining qualification *if* the individual is covered by a qualified money purchase pension plan maintained by the leasing organization and:

(1) the plan provides for employer contributions by the leasing organization at a nonintegrated rate which is not less than 10%,

(2) the plan provides for immediate participation on the first day an individual becomes an employee of the leasing organization (unless (i) the individual's compensation from the leasing organization in each plan year during the 4-year period ending with the plan year is less than $1,000, *or* (ii) the individual performs substantially all of his services for the leasing organization),

(3) the plan provides for full and immediate vesting of all contributions under the plan, *and*

(4) leased employees do not constitute more than 20% of the recipient's nonhighly compensated work force. IRC Sec. 414(n)(5).

(This "safe harbor" applies only for purposes of the leased employee provision; it does not permit an employer to disregard a common law employee who otherwise meets the definition of a leased employee. IRC Sec. 414(n)(2). See *Burnetta v. Comm.*, 68 TC 387 (1977).)

The recipient's *nonhighly compensated work force* is the aggregate number of individuals (who are not highly compensated—see Q 356) (1) who are common law employees of the recipient and have performed services for the recipient on a substantially full-time period of at least one year, or (2) who are leased employees with respect to the recipient. IRC Sec. 414(n)(5)(C)(ii).

A money purchase pension plan of a leasing organization is *not* qualified if it covers any individuals who are leased by the leasing organization to the recipient but who are not themselves employees (or, it would seem, leased employees) of the leasing

PENSION AND PROFIT SHARING: QUALIFICATION Q 356

organization; such a plan does not meet the "exclusive benefit" rule (see Q 323). See *Professional & Executive Leasing, Inc. v. Comm.*, 89 TC 225 (1987), *aff'd* Dkt. 87-7379 (9th Cir. 12-6-88). *ASRS, Sec. 59, ¶490.4(d)(2).*

356. Who are the "highly compensated" employees for purposes of the qualification requirements?

Generally, a *highly compensated employee* is any employee who is either a *highly compensated active employee* or a *highly compensated former employee.* Temp. Treas. Reg. §1.414(q)-1T, A-2. Under some circumstances, however, highly compensated active employees are considered separately from highly compensated former employees.

Status as a highly compensated active employee is determined by focusing on the determination year (i.e., the plan year for which the determination is being made) and the immediately preceding 12-month period (the "look-back" year).

An employee is a *highly compensated active employee* with respect to a plan year (i.e., the determination year) if he: (1) was a 5% owner (as defined for top-heavy purposes—see Q 357) at any time during either the determination year or look-back year, *or* (2) received compensation for the preceding year in excess of $100,000 (in 2006, as indexed) from the employer, *and* if the employer elects the application of this clause for the preceding year, was in the "top-paid group" (see below) for that year. IRC Sec. 414(q)(1). The income threshold ($80,000 as it appears in the Code) is indexed at the same time and in the same manner as the IRC Section 415 defined benefit dollar limitation; see Appendix E for the amounts for earlier years. IRC Sec. 414(q)(1). See Temp. Treas. Reg. §1.414(q)-1T, A-3(c)(1).

The applicable dollar amount for a particular determination or look-back year is the dollar amount for the calendar year in which the determination year or look-back year begins. Temp. Treas. Reg. §1.414(q)-1T, A-3(c)(2); Information Letter to Kyle N. Brown dated December 9, 1999.

Employers may identify which employees are highly compensated employees under IRC Section 414(q) using the same "snapshot" testing that is used for the non-discrimination requirements (i.e., use test results for a single day during the plan year, provided that day is representative of the employer's workforce and the plan's coverage throughout the plan year). Rev. Proc. 93-42, 1993-2 CB 540, as modified by Rev. Proc. 95-34, 1995-2 CB 385.

The IRS has stated that a fiscal year plan may make a calendar year data election. If the election is made, the calendar year beginning with or within the look-back year will be treated as the employer's look-back year for purposes of determining whether an individual is a highly compensated employee on account of his compensation (this election will not apply in determining whether a 5% owner is highly compensated). The effect of this election is that even though an employer maintains a plan on a fiscal year basis, it uses calendar year data. Once made, such an election applies for all subsequent years unless changed by the employer. Notice 97-45, 1997-2 CB 296.

The "top-paid group" of employees for a year is the group of employees in the top 20%, ranked on the basis of compensation paid for the year. IRC Sec. 414(q)(3). Once made, a top-paid group election remains in effect until it is changed by the employer.

2006 Tax Facts on Insurance & Employee Benefits

Notice 97-45, above. Former employees are not included in the top-paid group. Also, employees who are excluded in determining the number of the top-paid group by reason of the collective bargaining agreement exclusion (see below) are also excluded for purposes of identifying the members of the top-paid group. Temp. Treas. Reg. §1.414(q)-1T, A-9(c).

No special notification or filing of a top-paid group election or a calendar year data election is required; however, certain plan amendments may be necessary to incorporate a definition of highly compensated employees that reflects the election. Notice 97-45, above. Furthermore, a consistency requirement states generally that an election made by an employer operating more than one plan must apply consistently to all plans of the employer that begin with or within the same calendar year. Notice 97-45, above.

Nonresident aliens who receive no earned income from sources within the United States are disregarded for all purposes in determining the identity of the highly compensated employees. IRC Sec. 414(q)(8). An employer may adopt any rounding or tie-breaking methods which are reasonable, nondiscriminatory, and uniformly and consistently applied. Temp. Treas. Reg. §1.414(q)-1T, A-3(b). An employee who is highly compensated as a result of meeting two or more of the tests above is not disregarded for the purpose of applying any of those tests to other individuals. Temp. Treas. Reg. §1.414(q)-1T, A-3(d).

No employee of a church plan (as defined in IRC Section 414(e)) is considered an officer, a person whose principal duties consist of supervising the work of other employees, or a highly compensated employee for any year unless such an employee meets the definition of highly compensated employee. IRC Sec. 414(q)(9).

"Compensation" is the compensation received by the participant from the employer for the year, including elective or salary reduction contributions to a cafeteria plan, cash or deferred arrangement or a tax sheltered annuity. IRC Sec. 414(q)(4); Temp. Treas. Reg. §1.414(q)-1T, A-13.

In determining the *number* of employees in the top-paid group (but not for the purpose of identifying the particular employees in the group), the following employees may be excluded (IRC Sec. 414(q)(5); Temp. Treas. Reg. §1.414(q)-1T, A-9(b)): (1) employees with less than six months of service, including any service in the immediately preceding year; (2) generally, employees who normally work less than 17½ hours per week (if certain requirements are met; see Temp. Treas. Reg. §1.414(q)-1T, A-9(e)); (3) employees who normally work during not more than six months in any year, determined on the basis of the facts and circumstances as evidenced by the employer's customary experience in the years preceding the determination year; see Temp. Treas. Reg. §1.414(q)-1T, A-9(f); (4) employees under the age of 21; and (5) employees covered by a collective bargaining agreement if 90% or more of the employees of the employer are covered under the agreement and the plan being tested covers only employees who are not covered under the agreement. Temp. Treas. Reg. §1.414(q)-1T, A-9(b).

Except as provided by future IRS pronouncements, an employer may elect to use a shorter period of service, smaller number of hours or months, or lower age than those specified above (including a zero age or service requirement exclusion). IRC. Sec. 414(q)(5). See Temp. Treas. Reg. §1.414(q)-1T, A-9(b)(2)(i). Also, the employer may elect not to exclude members under the collective bargaining exclusion. Temp. Treas. Reg. §1.414(q)-1T, A-9(b)(2)(ii).

PENSION AND PROFIT SHARING: QUALIFICATION   Q 357

A *highly compensated former employee* for a determination year is any employee who had a separation year prior to the determination year and was a highly compensated active employee for either his separation year or any determination year ending on or after his 55th birthday. Temp. Treas. Reg. §1.414(q)-1T, A-4.

A separation year is any year during which the employee separates from service with the employer. For purposes of this rule, an employee who performs no services for the employer during a determination year is treated as having separated from service with the employer in the year that he last performed services for the employer. An employee will be deemed to have a separation year if, in a determination year prior to attainment of age 55, he receives compensation in an amount less than 50% of his average annual compensation for the three consecutive calendar years preceding the determination year in which he received the greatest amount of compensation from the employer (or the total period of his service with the employer, if less). Because an employee who is *deemed* to have a separation is still performing services for the employer during the determination year, he is treated as an active employee and the deemed separation year is relevant only for purposes of determining whether he will be a highly compensated former employee after he actually separates from service. However, an employee with a deemed separation year will not be treated as a highly compensated former employee (by reason of such deemed separation year) if he later has a significant increase in services and compensation and, thus, is deemed to have a resumption of employment. Temp. Treas. Reg. §1.414(q)-1T, A-5.

The controlled group, common control, and affiliated service group aggregation rules, as well as the employee leasing provisions, are applied before applying the highly compensated employee rules. IRC Sec. 414(q)(7). See Q 359, Q 360, and Q 355. However, the entity aggregation rules are not taken into account for purposes of determining who is a 5% owner. Also, the separate lines of business rules are not applicable in determining the highly compensated group. Temp. Treas. Reg. §1.414(q)-1T, A-6, A-8. *ASRS, Sec. 59, ¶490.4(d)(5).*

357. Who is a key employee for purposes of the top-heavy rules for qualified plans?

Generally, a key employee, for purposes of the top-heavy rules, is any employee (or, in some cases, a former or deceased employee) who *at any time during the plan year* containing the determination date for the plan year to be tested is:

(1) an officer (see below) of the employer whose annual compensation *from the employer* exceeds $140,000 (as indexed for 2006; this amount is indexed for inflation in increments of $5,000);

(2) a more-than-5% owner (see below) of the employer, or

(3) a more-than-1% owner of the employer having annual compensation from the employer for a plan year in excess of $150,000.

IRC Sec. 416(i); Treas. Reg. §1.416-1, T-12. (As to when the determination date occurs, see Q 351.)

The determination as to whether an individual is an *officer* is made on the basis of all facts and circumstances; job titles are disregarded. An officer is an administrative

2006 Tax Facts on Insurance & Employee Benefits   407

executive who is in regular and continuous service, not a nominal officer whose administrative duties are limited to special and single transactions. Treas. Reg. §1.416-1, T-13; Rev. Rul. 80-314, 1980-2 CB 152. Unincorporated associations (e.g., partnerships, sole proprietorships, etc.) may have officers. Treas. Reg. §1.416-1, T-15.

In any case, the number of individuals treated as key employees because of their "officer" status is limited to the greater of three (individuals) or 10% of all employees, but in any event, not more than 50. IRC Sec. 416(i), flush language.

Those employees who can be excluded when determining the number of employees in the "top-paid group" for purposes of identifying an employer's "highly compensated" employees (see Q 356) can also be disregarded in determining the number of officers to be taken into account in identifying "key employees." IRC Secs. 416(i)(1), 414(q)(5). It is unclear how ties in compensation should be resolved. Whether an individual is a key employee because of his "officer" status is determined without regard to whether he is a key employee for any other reason. Treas. Reg. §1.416-1, T-14.

An individual owns more than 5% of a corporate employer if he owns more than 5% of the outstanding stock of the corporation (by value) or stock possessing more than 5% of the total combined voting power of all stock of the corporation. In determining stock ownership, the attribution rules of IRC Section 318 apply (but stock is attributed *from* a corporation if a 5% rather than 50% ownership test is met). Only ownership in the particular employer is considered; the controlled group, common control, and affiliated service group aggregation rules of IRC Section 414 are disregarded. An individual owns more than 5% of a *noncorporate* employer if he owns more than 5% of the capital or profits interest in that employer. Rules similar to the attribution rules of IRC Section 318 apply for purposes of determining ownership in a noncorporate employer. The aggregation rules of IRC Section 414 are disregarded. IRC Sec. 416(i)(1)(B); Treas. Regs. §§1.416-1, T-17, 1.416-1, T-8.

The rules discussed in the previous paragraph also apply to determine whether an individual is a "more-than-1%" owner of the employer. Treas. Reg. §1.416-1, T-16. However, all employers who are under common control or who are members of a controlled or affiliated service group (see Q 359, Q 360) are treated as one employer for the purpose of determining whether a more-than-1% owner has annual compensation *from the employer* in excess of $150,000.

"Compensation," for purposes of identifying key employees generally, is the compensation taken into account for purposes of the IRC Section 415 limitations on contributions and benefits. Any elective or salary reductions contributions made on behalf of the employee to a 401(k) cash or deferred plan, simplified employee pension, 403(b) tax sheltered annuity, or cafeteria plan are included as compensation for IRC Section 415 purposes. IRC Secs. 416(i)(1)(D), 414(q)(4), 415(c)(3).

For purposes of determining an employee's ownership in the employer, the attribution rules of IRC Section 318 (presumably using a 5% rather than 50% test to determine whether there is attribution *from* a corporation) and the aggregation rules of IRC Section 414 apply. Treas. Reg. §1.416-1, T-19. If two employees have the same ownership interest in the employer, the employee who has the greater annual compensation from that employer will be treated as owning the larger interest. IRC Sec. 416(i)(1)(A).

Beneficiaries. The terms "employee" and "key employee" include their respective beneficiaries. IRC Sec. 416(i)(5). Treas. Reg. §1.416-1, T-12.

PENSION AND PROFIT SHARING: QUALIFICATION — Q 358

Governmental plans. The term "key employee" is applied under various provisions of the Internal Revenue Code (e.g., IRC Sections 401(h), 415(l), and 419A). For these purposes, the term does not include any officer or employee covered by a governmental plan. IRC Sec. 416(i). Thus, the separate accounting and nondiscrimination rules under those provisions do not apply to employees covered by governmental plans. *ASRS, Sec. 59, ¶440.1.*

358. Who is an owner-employee for purposes of the qualification requirements?

An *owner-employee* is an employee (as defined at Q 418) who (a) owns the entire interest in an unincorporated trade or business, or (b) in the case of a partnership, owns more than 10% of either the capital interest or the profits interest in the partnership. IRC Sec. 401(c)(3). Even if a partnership agreement does not specify a more than 10% interest in profits for any partner, if the formula for dividing profits (e.g., based on a partner's earnings productivity during the year) in operation actually produced at the end of the year a distribution of more than 10% of profits to a partner, the Tax Court has ruled he is an owner-employee for the year. *Hill, Farrer & Burrill v. Comm.*, 67 TC 411 (1976).

An individual who owns the entire interest in an unincorporated trade or business is treated as his own employer. IRC Sec. 401(c)(4). Thus, a proprietor or sole practitioner who has earned income (as defined in Q 418) can establish a qualified plan under which he is both employer and his own employee.

A partnership is treated as the employer of each partner who is an employee (as defined in Q 418). IRC Sec. 401(c)(4). Thus, partners individually cannot establish a qualified plan for the firm, but the partnership can establish a plan in which the partners can participate.

Persons who are shareholder-employees in professional corporations or associations or in business corporations (including S corporations) are not self-employed individuals. Such persons participate in a qualified plan of the corporation as regular employees of the corporation. Treas. Reg. §1.401-1(b)(3). This is true even of a shareholder-employee who is sole owner of the corporation. S corporation pass-through income may not be treated as self-employment earnings for purposes of a Keogh plan deduction, even where the shareholder performed services for the corporation. See *Durando v. U.S.*, 95-2 USTC ¶50,615 (9th Cir. 1995).

A "common law employee" (or "regular" employee) is one who is an employee under common law rules, as distinguished from a self-employed individual who is considered an employee only for qualified plan purposes. Generally speaking, an individual is considered an employee under the common law rules if the person or organization for whom he performs services has the right to control and direct his work not only as to the result to be accomplished, but also as to the details and means by which the result is accomplished. Treas. Reg. §31.3121(d)-1(c)(2).

The common law rules also apply generally in determining whether an individual is an "employee" for Social Security purposes. Ordinarily, therefore, an individual who is an "employee" under Social Security is a "common law employee" for self-employed plan purposes. However, a person's status for self-employed plan purposes is determined by the *definition* of "employee" under the Social Security law, irrespective of whether or how his *earnings* are covered under Social Security. Thus, if a person is an employee under the common law rules, it is immaterial that his earnings are treated as self-employment income under the Social Security law. For example, a minister or other clergy who is employed by a congregation on a salaried basis is a common law employee, and not a self-employed individual, even though for Social Security purposes his compensation is treated as net earnings from self-employment. But amounts received by him directly from members of the congregation, such as fees for performing marriages, baptisms, or other personal services, represent earnings from self-employment.

Furthermore, full-time life insurance salespersons are treated as common law employees for both Social Security and qualified retirement plan purposes even though, under the common law rules, they are self-employed. This is because of special statutory provisions in the Social Security Act and the Internal Revenue Code. Thus, a "full-time life insurance salesman" (as defined in the Social Security law) is prohibited from establishing a qualified plan for himself. Treas. Reg. §1.401-10(b)(3). See also IRC Sec. 7701(a)(20); IRS Pub. 560. However, it would appear that general agents and most general lines insurance agents and brokers are considered self-employed individuals and are eligible to establish qualified plans for themselves and their employees.

Attorneys with a law firm, depending on the circumstances, can either be self-employed or have the status of an "employee" of the firm. See Rev. Rul. 68-324, 1968-1 CB 433.

An individual may participate in a qualified plan as a self-employed person even though he performs work as a common law employee for another employer. For example, an attorney who is a common law employee of a corporation and who in the evenings maintains an office in which he practices law is eligible to establish a plan as a self-employed person with respect to his law practice. An individual may be self-employed with respect to some services he sells to a business even though he also provides other services to the same business as an employee. In either case, he may participate in a qualified plan as a self-employed person with respect to his self-employed earnings, even though his employer maintains a qualified plan under which he is covered as a common law employee. *Pulver v. Comm.*, TC Memo 1982-437; Treas. Reg. §1.401-10(b)(3)(ii). A tenured university professor who conducted seminars in a separate capacity at the university with which he was employed was determined by the Tax Court to be self-employed, despite objections by the IRS. As a result, he was permitted to establish a Keogh plan with amounts earned from his self-employment. *Reece v. Comm.*, TC Memo 1992-335.

Where a partnership's profit sharing plan which did not cover self-employeds permitted limited partners who were also employees of the partnership (and compensated as such in addition to their share of the partnership's profits) to participate, the IRS ruled that the plan failed to qualify. Rev. Rul. 70-411, 1970-2 CB 91. *ASRS, Sec. 60, ¶¶120, 130.*

359. What is a "controlled group" of corporations? When are trades or businesses under "common control"?

Generally, all employees of a group of employers that are members of a *controlled group* of corporations, or (in the case of partnerships and proprietorships) are under

PENSION AND PROFIT SHARING: QUALIFICATION   Q 359

common control will be treated as employed by a single employer, for purposes of the qualification, vesting and top-heavy rules, as well as the IRC Section 415 limits and the requirements for SEPs. IRC Secs. 414(b), 414(c).

Controlled Groups

A controlled group may be a *parent-subsidiary controlled group*, a *brother-sister controlled group*, or a *combined group*. Treas. Reg. §1.414(b)-1.

A *parent-subsidiary controlled group* is composed of one or more chains of subsidiary corporations connected through stock ownership with a common parent corporation. A parent-subsidiary group exists if at least 80% of the stock (by value or voting power) of each subsidiary corporation is owned by one or more of the other corporations in the group (either subsidiaries or parent) *and* the parent corporation owns at least 80% of the stock (by value or voting power) of at least one of the subsidiary corporations. When determining whether the parent owns 80% of the stock of a subsidiary corporation, all stock of that corporation owned directly by other subsidiaries is disregarded.

A *brother-sister controlled group* consists of two or more corporations in which five or fewer persons (individuals, estates, or trusts) own stock possessing (a) 80% or more (by value or voting power) of each corporation *and* (b) more than 50% (by value or voting power) of each corporation when taking into account each stockholder's interest only to the extent he has identical interests in each corporation. (For purposes of the 80% test, a stockholder's interest is considered only if he owns some interest in each corporation of the group. *U.S. v. Vogel Fertilizer Co.*, 49 AFTR 2d 82-491 (Sup. Ct. 1982); Treas. Reg. §1.1563-1(a)(3).)

A *combined group* consists of three or more corporations, each of which is a member of a parent-subsidiary group or a brother-sister group *and* one of which is both a parent of a parent-subsidiary group and a member of a brother-sister group. IRC Secs. 414(b), 1563; Treas. Reg. §1.414(b)-1.

Special rules for determining stock ownership, including special constructive ownership rules, apply when determining the existence of a controlled group. IRC Sec. 1563(d); Treas. Reg. §1.414(b)-1. Community property rules, where present, also apply. *Aero Indus. Co., Inc. v. Comm.*, TC Memo 1980-116. For purposes of qualification, the test for a controlled group is strictly mechanical; once the existence of the group is established, aggregation of employees is required and will not be negated by showing that the controlled group and plans were not created or manipulated for the purpose of avoiding the qualification requirements. *Fujinon Optical, Inc. v. Comm.*, 76 TC 499 (1981).

Trades or Businesses Under Common Control

Under the regulations, trades or businesses are under common control if they constitute a parent-subsidiary group of trades or businesses, a brother-sister group of trades or businesses, or a combined group of trades or businesses. The existence of these groups is determined under rules similar to those discussed above for controlled groups of corporations. "Trades or businesses" include sole proprietorships, partnerships, estates, trusts, *and* corporations. IRC Sec. 414(c); Treas. Regs. §§1.414(c)-1, 1.414(c)-2, 1.414(c)-3, 1.414(c)-4. *ASRS, Sec. 59, ¶490.4(c)(1)*.

360. What is an "affiliated service group"?

For purposes of certain qualification requirements, as well as the vesting requirements, top-heavy rules, IRC Section 415 limits and the requirements for SEPs, all employees of the members of an *affiliated service group* are generally treated as employed by a single employer. IRC Sec. 414(m)(1).

An "affiliated service group" is a group consisting of a service organization (referred to as "FSO" for "first service organization") and either or both of the following:

(1) an additional service organization (referred to as an "A" organization) that is a shareholder or partner in the FSO and regularly performs services for the FSO or is regularly associated with the FSO in the performance of services for third parties;

(2) an organization (referred to as a "B" organization) if a significant portion of the organization's business is the performance of services for the FSO or A organization (or both) and the services are of a type historically performed by employees in the service field of the FSO or A organization *and*

(3) 10% or more (in the aggregate) of the interests in the B organization is held by highly compensated employees of the FSO or A organization, or certain common owners. IRC Sec. 414(m); Prop. Treas. Reg. §1.414(m)-2(c)(1).

The term "affiliated service group" also includes a group consisting of (1) an organization the principal business of which is performing on a regular and continuing basis, management functions for another organization, and (2) the organization for which the functions are performed. IRC Sec. 414(m)(5).

An organization is a service organization if its principal business is the performance of services in one of the fields enumerated in the regulations (e.g., health, law, etc.) or if capital is not a material income-producing factor for the organization. IRC Sec. 414(m)(3); Prop. Treas. Reg. §1.414(m)-2(f). See Rev. Rul. 81-105, 1981-1 CB 256.

The performance of services for a first service organization or for an A organization (or both) will be assumed to constitute a significant portion of a B organization's business if 10% or more of its total gross receipts *from all sources* during the current year, or two preceding years, was derived from performing services for such organization(s). It will be assumed that the performance of services for such organization(s) is *not* a significant portion of a B organization's business if less than 5% of its gross receipts *derived from performing services* during the current year *and* two preceding years was derived from performing services for such organizations. Prop. Treas. Reg. §1.414(m)-2(c)(2). Services are of a type historically performed by employees in a particular field if it was not unusual for such services to be performed by employees of organizations in that service field in the United States on December 13, 1980. Prop. Treas. Reg. §1.414(m)-2(c)(3).

The principles of the constructive stock ownership rules of IRC Section 318(a) apply. Thus, ownership will generally be attributed to an individual from his spouse, children, grandchildren and parents, between a partner and his partnership, between a trust or estate and its beneficiaries, and between a corporation and a more-than-50% shareholder (including a corporate shareholder). IRC Sec. 414(m)(6)(B).

PENSION AND PROFIT SHARING: QUALIFICATION   Q 361

Two or more affiliated service groups will not be aggregated merely because an organization is an A organization or a B organization with respect to each affiliated service group. However, all organizations which are A organizations or B organizations with respect to a *single* FSO must, together with that FSO, be treated as a single affiliated service group. Prop. Treas. Reg. §1.414(m)-2(g).

Taxpayers may rely on the proposed regulations covering service-type affiliated groups until final rules are published. Examples explaining the tests for a "service-type" affiliated service group can be found in Rev. Rul. 81-105, 1981-1 CB 256. *ASRS, Sec. 59, ¶490.4(c)(2).*

RETROACTIVE DISQUALIFICATION

361. Can IRS apply retroactively its finding that a plan does not meet qualification requirements?

Yes. The IRS has broad discretion to determine the extent to which rulings and regulations will be given retroactive effect. *Automobile Club of Mich. v. Comm.*, 353 U.S. 180 (1957); IRC Sec. 7805(b). However, the wide array of correction procedures established by the IRS in the past decade offers a choice of less severe remedies and suggests that the Service is reluctant to disqualify plans, except under the most egregious circumstances.

The IRS may also retroactively correct its own mistaken application of law, even where a taxpayer may have relied to his detriment on the Service's mistake. *Dixon v. U.S.*, 381 U.S. 68 (1965). However, concerning determination letters, the IRS has voluntarily limited its authority by the issuance of revenue procedures stating the standards by which the continuing effect of a determination letter will be judged. The standards are in substance as follows:

1. If a published revenue ruling is issued which is applicable to a previously approved plan, the plan, in order to retain its qualified status, must be amended to conform with that ruling before the end (and effective at least as of the beginning) of the first plan year following the one in which the ruling was published. Rev. Proc. 80-30, 1980-1 CB 685, at Sec. 13.04. Thus, with respect to the approved plan, the revenue ruling is not given retroactive effect and becomes effective only at the beginning of the next plan year. (See also *Wisconsin Nipple and Fabricating Corp. v. Comm.*, 78-2 USTC 84,934 (7th Cir. 1978).)

2. If no applicable published ruling affecting the qualification of the plan has intervened between the approval and the revocation of the approval, the revocation will ordinarily not have retroactive effect with respect to the taxpayer to whom the ruling was originally issued or to a taxpayer whose tax liability was directly involved in such ruling if (a) there has been no misstatement or omission of material facts, (b) the facts subsequently developed are not materially different from the facts on which the ruling was based, (c) there has been no change in the applicable law, (d) the ruling was originally issued with respect to a prospective or proposed transaction, and (e) the taxpayer directly involved in the ruling acted in good faith in reliance upon the ruling and the retroactive revocation would be to his detriment. Rev. Proc. 83-36, 1983-1 CB 763, Sec. 13.05. See also *Lansons, Inc. v. Comm.*, 622 F.2d 774 (5th Cir. 1980); *Oakton Distributors, Inc. v. Comm.*, 73 TC 182 (1979); *Pittman Construction v. U.S.*, 437 F. Supp. 1215 (E.D. La. 1977). *ASRS, Sec. 59, ¶400.2.*

PENSION AND PROFIT SHARING: EMPLOYER DEDUCTION

OVERVIEW

362. How are the limits on the employer's deduction for qualified plan contributions applied?

The *amount* of an employer's deduction for contributions to a qualified plan depends on the type of plan being maintained. The maximum amounts an employer may deduct are explained at Q 383 for pension plans, Q 392 for profit sharing or stock bonus plans, and Q 415 for employee stock ownership plans (ESOPs). If an employer contributes to two or more plans covering any common participants, it will be subject to the limits explained in Q 366.

Rules that govern the *timing* of an employer's deduction are explained at Q 364. Other more specific requirements that may affect an employer's ability to deduct contributions or plan expenses are explained at Q 365.

Special rules governing contributions of property are explained at Q 363. The 10% penalty on nondeductible contributions is explained at Q 367. *ASRS, Sec. 59, ¶540.*

CONTRIBUTIONS OF PROPERTY

363. Can an employer contribute property other than money to a qualified plan trust?

The United States Supreme Court has held that an employer's transfer of unencumbered property to a defined benefit plan in satisfaction of a funding obligation is a prohibited transaction. *Keystone Consol. Indus., Inc. v. Comm.*, 113 S.Ct. 2006 (1993). The Court left open the question of whether a transfer of unencumbered property that is *not* in satisfaction of a funding obligation might be permissible without violating the prohibited transaction rules. The Department of Labor has also expressed the view that a contribution of property other than cash that reduces a sponsor's funding obligation would be a prohibited transaction (in the absence of a statutory or administrative exemption), whether it is made to a defined benefit or a defined contribution plan; however, such a contribution in excess of amounts needed to meet the plan's funding requirements may be permissible, provided that acceptance of the contribution is consistent with the general standards of fiduciary conduct under ERISA. DOL Interpretive Bulletin 94-3, 59 Fed. Reg. 66735 (December 28, 1994).

Certain contributions of employer stock are exempt from the prohibited transaction rules. See Q 443. Furthermore, there is an administrative exemption for the contribution of a life insurance policy to a plan if certain conditions are met (see Q 437 on the transfer for value aspect). This exemption also protects self-employed "owner-employees" and more-than-5% shareholder-employees of S corporations from the prohibited transaction rules of Title I of ERISA. PTE 92-5, 57 Fed. Reg. 5019, (formerly PTE 77-7, 1977-2 CB 423). See Q 443. If only a sole proprietor or partners (and their spouses) participate in the plan, Title I of ERISA does not apply. See Labor Reg. §2510.3-3.

A contribution of the employer's promissory note to the trust does not constitute payment, and no deduction is allowable until the note is paid. Rev. Rul. 55-608, 1955-2 CB 546; Rev. Rul. 80-140, 1980-1 CB 89; *Don E. Williams Co. v. U.S.*, 429 U.S. 569 (1977). The IRS has taken the position that the contribution of an employer's own term promissory note is a prohibited transaction. Rev. Rul. 80-140, above.

Planning Point: One way to deal with a plan's inability to distribute illiquid assets may be for the plan to contribute the illiquid assets to a separate trust and distribute certificates of interest in that trust to its participants as part of their lump sum distributions. *Martin Silfen, J.D., Brown Brothers Harriman Trust Co., LLC.*

A sale by plan fiduciaries of some of their customers' promissory notes to the plan was a prohibited transaction, notwithstanding the fact that the notes generated a competitive rate of return. See *Westoak Realty and Inv. Co., Inc. v. Comm.*, 93-2 USTC ¶50,395 (8th Cir. 1993). However, an earlier letter ruling indicated that a contribution of a third party promissory note was payment and its fair market value could be deducted. Let. Rul. 7852116. Contribution of a check is only conditional payment; if the check is not paid, the deduction will be disallowed. *Springfield Prod., Inc., v. Comm.*, TC Memo 1979-23.

The fair market value of contributed property is considered to be the amount contributed for purposes of calculating annual additions within the overall IRC Section 415 limits. Treas. Reg. §1.415-6(b)(4). See Q 332, Q 372 and Q 377. For special rules applying to the sale of employer securities to a defined contribution plan, see Q 400. The requirements for a 1042 election upon the sale of employer stock to an ESOP are explained at Q 401. *ASRS, Sec. 59, ¶¶540.6, 710.2.*

DEDUCTION OF EMPLOYER CONTRIBUTIONS

364. When does an employer take a deduction for its contributions to a pension, profit sharing, or stock bonus plan?

Generally, an employer's contribution is deductible only in the taxable year it is paid (except for certain carryforwards; see Q 383). IRC Sec. 404(a). However, both cash and accrual basis employers (including self-employed individuals) are deemed to have made a contribution in the *preceding tax year* if the payment is on account of that year and is made no later than the due date (including extensions) of the employer's tax return. IRC Sec. 404(a)(6). See, e.g., Let. Rul. 199935062. In contrast, the minimum funding rules may require that a contribution be made earlier than the time at which it is deductible. (See Q 385.) The payment will be considered made on account of the preceding tax year if the plan treats it as if received on the last day of that year and either the employer designates, in writing, that the payment is made on account of the previous year, or the employer claims it as a deduction on his tax return for the preceding tax year. Such a designation or deduction is irrevocable. Rev. Rul. 76-28, 1976-1 CB 106, as modified by Rev. Rul. 76-77, 1976-1 CB 107. (But see Q 375 for requirements of quarterly estimated contribution payments applicable to certain plans.)

Of course, the delayed payment is deductible for the prior year only if the payment would have been deductible had it actually made on the last day of the prior taxable year. Rev. Rul. 90-105, 1990-2 CB 69; *Lucky Stores, Inc. v. Comm.*, 28 AFTR 2d ¶98-5188 9th Cir. (1998), *cert. denied*, 119 S.Ct. 1755 (1999). Thus, where an employer's taxable year ended June 30 and the plan year ended December 31, the employer could not deduct elective deferrals and matching contributions attributable to compensation earned by plan participants after June 30, because such contributions were not compensation for services rendered in the prior taxable year of the employer (see Q 365). Rev. Rul. 90-105, above. See also *American Stores Co. v. Comm.* 108 TC 178 (1997), aff'd, 170 F.3d 1267 (10th Cir. 1999), *cert. denied* 120 S. Ct. 182 (1999). Where an employer's taxable year ended January 31, 1998 and the plan year was the calendar year, the employer could deduct elective deferrals and matching contributions attributable to compensation earned by plan participants during January 1998 on its return for its fiscal year ending January 31, 1998, even though that was the first month of the 1998 plan year. CCA 200038004, 2000 IRS CCA LEXIS 101.

Regulations under Section 401(k) provide that contributions made in anticipation of future performance of services generally will not be treated as elective contributions; thus, no deduction is available for such amounts. The regulations essentially make it clear that contributions made pursuant to a cash or deferred election must be made after the employee's performance of services with respect to which the compensation is payable. See Treas. Reg. §1.401(k)-1(a)(3)(iii)(B); see Q 395.

The liability to make the contribution need not have accrued in the preceding year, but the plan must have been in existence before the end of such preceding tax year. Rev. Rul. 76-28, above; *Engineered Timber Sales, Inc. v. Comm.*, 74 TC 808 (1980), appeal dismissed, (5th Cir. 1981). Likewise, the trust must be in existence within the taxable year for which deductions for contributions are claimed. *Catawba Indus. Rubber Co. v. Comm.*, 64 TC 1011 (1975); *Attardo v. Comm.*, TC Memo 1991-357. See Q 322. If a plan trust is complete in all respects on the last day of the taxable year except that it has no corpus, the trust is deemed to have been in existence in the taxable year if the initial contribution is made within the grace period. Rev. Rul. 81-114, 1981-1 CB 207.

In the case of a non-trusteed annuity plan evidenced only by the contract with the insurance company, the plan is not in effect until the contract is executed and issued. But where the plan is separate from the insurance contract, the plan will be considered in effect by the close of the taxable year if: (1) the contract has been applied for and the application accepted by the insurance company; (2) a contract or abstract has been prepared outlining the terms of the plan; (3) a part payment of premium has been made; and (4) the plan has been communicated to the employees. Rev. Rul. 59-402, 1959-2 CB 122; *Becker v. Comm.*, TC Memo 1966-55.

If the plan year of a defined benefit plan and the employer's tax year are not the same, the employer may claim a deduction for a contribution made for the plan year that either ends or begins in the tax year, or may use a weighted average, such as the number of months in each plan year falling in the tax year. However, the same method must be used consistently. Treas. Reg. §1.404(a)-14(c). Where a short taxable year with no plan year beginning or ending within it resulted when an employer changed its taxable year to a calendar year, the IRS approved a method giving the employer a prorated deduction for the length of the short year. See Let. Rul. 8806053. *ASRS, Sec. 59, ¶540.2.*

365. What other specific rules affect an employer's deduction for its contributions to a qualified plan?

Generally, if the plan is qualified, the employer may deduct its contributions currently, regardless of whether the rights of the individual participants are forfeitable or

PENSION AND PROFIT SHARING: EMPLOYER DEDUCTION Q 365

nonforfeitable. IRC Sec. 404. To be deductible, a contribution on behalf of a participant must qualify as reasonable compensation for services actually rendered to the contributing employer (not to a previous employer) by the participant as an employee. IRC Sec. 404(a); *Bianchi v. Comm.*, 66 TC 324 (1976), aff'd 77-1 USTC 86,545 (2d Cir. 1977); *La Mastro v. Comm.*, 72 TC 377 (1979); *Edwin's Inc. v. U.S.*, 501 F.2d 675 (7th Cir. 1974); *Chas. E. Smith & Sons Co. v. Comm.*, 184 F.2d 1011 (6th Cir. 1950); *Bardahl Mfg. Co. v. Comm.*, TC Memo 1960-223; *Acme Pie Co. v. Comm.*, TC Memo 1951. The IRS has discussed the limitations on deductions and carryovers for contributions to a qualified profit sharing plan when an employee's total compensation is unreasonable. Rev. Rul. 67-341, 1967-2 CB 156. It has been held that the part of a contribution attributable to unreasonable compensation may be reallocated (if the plan so permits) and deducted; if reallocation is not possible, deduction will be disallowed only as to that part of the contribution allocated on the basis of unreasonable compensation. *Quinn v. U.S.*, 1977-1 USTC 86,863 (D. Md. 1976).

Where reasonableness of compensation was not in question, the Tax Court ruled that a newly formed corporation could deduct its full contribution to a defined benefit plan for the plan year which began in the corporation's short first tax year; it rejected the IRS argument that only 4.5/12 of the contribution should be deductible because the short year was only 4.5 months long. *Plastic Eng'g & Mfg. Co. v. Comm.*, 78 TC 1187 (1982).

Deductions with respect to a *multiemployer* plan maintained pursuant to a collective bargaining agreement are determined as if all participants were employed by a single employer. IRC Sec. 413(b)(7); see Let. Rul. 8743077. In the case of a *multiple employer* plan, the deduction limit is generally applied as if each employer maintained a separate plan. IRC Sec. 413(c)(6). Different rules apply to a plan adopted by two or more corporations that are members of the same controlled group (see Q 359); in such case, the deduction limits are determined as if all such employers were a single employer. IRC Sec. 414(b).

Certain employer liability to the Pension Benefit Guaranty Corporation (PBGC) as a result of plan termination, or withdrawal from a multiemployer plan, will be treated as a contribution to be deducted when paid, without regard to the usual limits on the deduction of employer contributions to qualified plans. IRC Sec. 404(g).

Contributions to fund post-retirement medical benefits under IRC Section 401(h) for common law employees may be currently deducted by the employer if they are reasonable, ascertainable, and distinct from contributions to fund retirement benefits, provided such benefits are subordinate to the retirement benefits provided by the plan. IRC Sec. 404(a)(2); Treas. Reg. §1.404(a)-3(f); see Q 369. Contributions to fund post-retirement medical benefits are not taken into account in determining the amount deductible with respect to contributions for retirement benefits. The amount of any excess pension assets transferred in a "qualified transfer" (see Q 370) to an IRC Section 401(h) account is not deductible. IRC Sec. 420(d)(1)(A).

Any allocable portion of past service and current pension costs that must be included in the basis of property produced by the employer or held for resale by the employer under the uniform capitalization rules is not deductible by the employer. OBRA '87, Sec. 10204. See also, Notice 88-86, 1988-2 CB 401.

Plan Expenses

Brokers' fees paid by a qualified plan are not separately deductible by the employer and are subject to the deduction limits of IRC Section 404(a) (see Q 383, Q 392). Rev. Rul. 86-142, 1986-2 CB 60. Amounts that an employer reimburses a plan trustee for amounts paid to an investment manager to manage and invest plan assets also *are not* deductible under IRC Sections 162 or 212. However, amounts that an employer pays directly to the investment manager in connection with the management of the plan's assets apparently *are* deductible, and are not treated as plan contributions under IRC Section 404. See Let. Ruls. 9124036, 9124035, 8941009, 8940013. The distinction appears to be that brokers' fees are directly related to the purchase of an asset and are thus part of the cost of the securities, while investment managers' fees (as well as legal, accounting, and trustee fees) are recurring administrative expenses, which do not vary with the number or volume of investment transactions. Let. Rul. 9252029.

Some plans allocate plan expenses to the accounts of participants. The IRS has issued guidance permitting such plans to pay these expenses on behalf of active employees while charging the accounts of former employees their proportionate share of such expenses. See Rev. Rul. 2004-10, 2004-7 IRB 484. *ASRS, Sec. 59, ¶540.1.*

366. How much may an employer deduct if it contributes to more than one type of qualified plan?

An employer that sponsors two or more qualified retirement plans of different types (e.g., a profit sharing and a money purchase plan, or a defined benefit and a defined contribution plan) *covering any common participants* may deduct no more than 25% of participant payroll for the year or, if greater (i.e., in the case where one of the plans is a defined benefit plan) the contribution necessary to satisfy the minimum funding requirements for the plan year. IRC Sec. 404(a)(7)(A).

This combined limit does not apply if the only amounts contributed to the defined contribution plan are elective deferrals (see Q 394, Q 395, Q 396). IRC Sec. 404(a)(7)(C)(ii). Nonetheless, contributions or benefits may not be deducted in the year of contribution to the extent that they exceed the Section 415 limits (see Q 332, Q 372, Q 377), even if they are required by the minimum funding requirements. IRC Sec. 404(j); Notice 83-10, 1983-1 CB 536, F-3. However, the excess may be deducted in succeeding years as a contribution carry-over (but see Q 367 for an excise tax on nondeductible contributions). The deduction for current contributions and carry-overs in a tax year cannot exceed 25% of aggregate compensation. IRC Sec. 404(a)(7)(B); see Q 392.

For purposes of the deduction limitations, a Section 412(i) fully insured plan (see Q 407 to Q 408) is treated as a defined benefit plan. IRC Sec. 404(a)(7)(D); see Q 383.

If no employee (or former employee) benefits under both plans, then the limits that would apply to such plans separately (see Q 383, Q 392) are not reduced by this overall limit. IRC Sec. 404(a)(7)(C).

Generally, for purposes of the overall 25% limit, a simplified employee pension plan is treated as if it were a separate profit sharing or stock bonus plan. IRC Sec. 404(h)(3). If an employer maintains both a simplified employee pension plan and a profit shar-

PENSION AND PROFIT SHARING: EMPLOYER DEDUCTION   Q 367

ing or stock bonus plan, the 25% deductible limit applicable to qualified profit sharing and stock bonus plans must be reduced by the amount of any employer deduction for contributions to the simplified employee pension plan on behalf of a participant also covered under the profit sharing or stock bonus plan. IRC Sec. 404(h)(2). An employer sponsoring both a stock bonus and a profit sharing plan is considered to have a single plan. Let. Rul. 7916102. *ASRS, Sec. 59, ¶540.5.*

367. Is there a penalty if an employer contributes more to its qualified plan than it can deduct in a year?

Yes. The employer sponsoring the plan is generally subject to a tax equal to 10% of the nondeductible contributions (determined as of the close of the employer's tax year) under a qualified pension, profit sharing, or stock bonus plan, a simplified employee pension plan, or a SIMPLE IRA plan. IRC Sec. 4972(a).

Nondeductible contributions are the *sum of* (1) the amounts that the employer contributes to such plans in excess of the deduction limit for the taxable year (see Q 364 through Q 366, Q 383 and Q 392); plus (2) the total amount of employer contributions for each preceding year that were not allowable as a deduction, *reduced by* the sum of (a) the portion of such amounts that is returned to the employer during the taxable year; and (b) the portion of such amounts that became deductible for a preceding taxable year or for the current year. IRC Sec. 4972(c). The amount allowable as a deduction for any taxable year is treated as coming first from carry-forwards from preceding taxable years (in chronological order), and then from contributions made during the taxable year. IRC Sec. 4972(c)(2).

Certain defined benefit plan contributions (within the accrued liability full funding limit—see Q 386) may be disregarded in determining whether the employer has made nondeductible contributions. IRC Secs. 4972(c)(6), 4972(c)(7).

Contributions that are nondeductible solely because of the combined plan deduction limits are exempt from the excise tax to the extent of *the greater of*: (1) the amount of contributions not exceeding 6% of compensation; or (2) the sum of matching contributions (under IRC Section 401(m)(4)(A)) plus elective deferrals (under IRC Section 402(g)(3)(A); see Q 396). IRC Sec. 4972(c)(6)(A).

Where amounts contributed in one year to satisfy the preceding year's funding requirement under a conditional waiver would exceed the deductible limit for that prior year, the employer was permitted to report some of those contributions as contributions for the current year for deduction purposes and avoid the nondeductible contributions penalty. Let. Rul. 9107033.

Excess contributions can be eliminated by the withdrawal of the excess contribution (if the plan permits, see Q 323) or deduction of the excess contribution in a later year. Apparently, an excess contribution is also eliminated upon plan termination, because the plan no longer exists.

The excise tax does not apply in the case of (1) a governmental plan; or (2) an employer that has been exempt from income tax at all times. IRC Sec. 4972(d)(1)(B). However, to the extent that the employer has been subject to unrelated business income tax, this exception is inapplicable. See Let. Ruls. 9622037; 9304033. Contributions by

2006 Tax Facts on Insurance & Employee Benefits

a tax-exempt employer that was part of a controlled group including at least one nonexempt employer were subject to the excise tax. See Let. Rul. 9236026.

If a self-employed individual contributes more than he is permitted to deduct in a year, he is subject to a tax penalty, equal to 10% of nondeductible contributions under the plan (determined as of the close of his tax year). This tax is payable by the employer, which is the sole proprietor or the partnership, in the case of a plan that provides contributions or benefits for self-employed individuals. IRC Sec. 4972. Note that contributions required in order to meet the minimum funding standards are not subject to this tax, even if the self-employed individual cannot deduct them because they exceed his earned income. IRC Sec. 4972(c)(4). *ASRS, Sec. 59, ¶540.7.*

PENSION AND PROFIT SHARING: PLAN TYPES AND FEATURES

OVERVIEW

368. What requirements are specific to each type of plan?

While the requirements explained in Q 322 to Q 360, and the deduction limitations in Q 362 to Q 367 generally affect all qualified plans, there are additional qualification requirements and deduction limits that are specific to certain types of plans.

As a general rule, qualification requirements can be divided either of two ways: (a) between defined benefit (see Q 371 to Q 375) and defined contribution (see Q 376 to Q 380) plans, or (b) between pensions (see Q 381 to Q 390) and profit sharing plans (see Q 391 to Q 393). To some degree, these categories overlap; for example, all defined benefit plans are pensions, but not all pensions are defined benefit plans (see Q 381). Similarly, all profit sharing plans are defined contribution plans, but not all defined contribution plans are profit sharing plans; some are pensions.

Furthermore, special qualification, design and nondiscrimination requirements apply to 401(k) plans (see Q 394 to Q 406). Section 412(i) plans, while subject to the general requirements for defined benefit plans, must meet special requirements (see Q 407, Q 408) to be exempt from the minimum funding standard (Q 385 to Q 390). Stock bonus plans and ESOPs are subject to the special requirements explained at Q 409 to Q 416. Special rules for Keogh plans and S corporations are explained at Q 417 to Q 419.

Limitations on the employer's deduction for plan contributions are generally based on whether the plan is a pension (Q 383) or a profit sharing plan (Q 392).

Plans that offer insurance benefits are subject to the special rules explained in Q 369 (for plans that offer life or health insurance to participants) and Q 370 (for plans that transfer pension assets to Section 401(h) accounts). *ASRS, Sec. 59, ¶¶110, 200.*

INSURANCE BENEFITS

369. To what extent can a qualified plan provide life or health insurance benefits for its participants?

According to Treasury Regulations, such benefits must be merely "incidental" to the primary purpose of the plan. A pension plan exists primarily to provide retirement benefits but it "may also provide for the payment of incidental death benefits through insurance or otherwise ..." Treas. Reg. §1.401-1(b)(1)(i). A profit sharing plan is "primarily a plan of deferred compensation, but the amounts allocated to the account of a participant may be used to provide for him or his family incidental life or accident or health insurance." Treas. Reg. §1.401-1(b)(1)(ii).

The IRS has ruled that a profit sharing plan containing a medical reimbursement account does not satisfy the qualification requirements where distributions are available only for reimbursement of substantiated medical expenses of the participant

2006 Tax Facts on Insurance & Employee Benefits

and spouse or dependents. The Service noted that the plan would violate the nonforfeitability requirement of IRC Section 401(a)(7) and may violate other qualification requirements. The fact that only 25% of the plan contributions were used to fund the medical reimbursement account did not change this result. See Rev. Rul. 2005-55, 2005-33 IRB 284.

In 2004 guidance, the IRS specifically described as "excessive" life insurance coverage on a participant that provided for death benefits in excess of the death benefit provided to the participant under the plan (see Q 408 for details). See Rev. Rul. 2004-20, 2004-10 IRB 546. The IRS added that transactions substantially similar to the example are classified as "listed transactions," if the employer has deducted amounts used to pay premiums on a life insurance contract with a death benefit exceeding the participant's death benefit under the plan by more than $100,000. See Rev. Rul. 2004-20, above.

Applicability of Limitation

A profit sharing plan may provide for distribution of the funds accumulated under the plan after a fixed number of years (no fewer than two), the attainment of a stated age, or upon the prior occurrence of some event such as layoff, illness, disability, retirement, death, or severance of employment. Rev. Rul. 71-295, 1971-2 CB 184. The IRS has also ruled that a plan could permit participants with at least five years of participation to withdraw all employer contributions (including those made during the last two years). Rev. Rul. 68-24, 1968-1 CB 150.

If life or health insurance may be purchased only with funds that have been accumulated for the period required by the plan for the deferment of distributions, there is no limit on the amount of such funds that can be used to purchase life or health insurance; the "incidental" limitation applies, however, if the plan permits the use of funds that have not been so accumulated to purchase such insurance. Rev. Rul. 61-164, 1961-2 CB 99; Rev. Rul. 66-143, 1966-1 CB 79. The incidental limitation does not apply to life or health insurance bought with nondeductible *voluntary* employee contributions. Rev. Rul. 69-408, 1969-2 CB 58. Furthermore, the IRS determined that where the demutualization of a company that had been placed in rehabilitation resulted in traditional whole life contracts being restructured into flexible adjustable life contracts, the restructuring would not, of itself, result in a violation of the incidental death benefit requirements. See Let. Rul. 9339024.

Aside from the foregoing exceptions, the "incidental" limitation applies to insurance when it is purchased by a qualified plan on the life of a participant and benefits are payable to or for the participant, his estate, or his named beneficiary. The limitation also applies to contracts purchased under a qualified annuity plan. Treas. Reg. §1.403(a)-1(d). It would seem a necessary inference from this regulation that the incidental rule would not be applied to the purchase of insurance bought by a profit sharing plan on the life of a key individual responsible for employer profits to indemnify the plan for the premature loss by death of the insured.

The Basic 25% Rule

The basic approach taken by the IRS in determining whether life insurance benefits in a pension plan, or life or health insurance in a profit sharing plan, are "incidental" is by determining what proportion the cost of providing such benefits is of the cost of providing all benefits under the plan. In general, if the cost of providing current life and

PENSION AND PROFIT SHARING: PLAN TYPES AND FEATURES Q 369

health insurance benefits is less than 25% of the cost of providing all the benefits under the plan (both deferred and current) the incidental limitation is satisfied.

Despite the fact that an element of savings is involved in universal life coverage, the IRS has taken the position that universal life coverage must be treated under the rules applicable to term coverage, and thus, is subject to the 25% rule. FSA 1999-633. For purposes of the incidental rule, the IRS defines permanent insurance as insurance on which the premium does not increase and the death benefit does not decrease. Ira Cohen, Director, Employee Plans Technical and Actuarial Division, Internal Revenue Service, in response to a question asked at the 29th Annual Meeting of the AALU, 3-4-86. However, the IRS has informally ruled that a variable contract in which (1) the death benefit might decrease as a result of a decline in cash values and the operation of IRC Section 7702 (see Q 273), and (2) unscheduled extra premiums were permitted, would be treated as permanent insurance. See Let. Rul. 9014068. The IRS has also ruled for an insurer that where an adjustable life contract was to be used as a funding vehicle for a defined contribution plan, the Service would apply the incidental rule it applied in Rev. Rul. 61-164, below (see last paragraph under the following heading); in other words, one-half the premiums paid while the contract was providing lifetime protection plus the whole premium paid while the policy was providing term protection must total less than 25% of the total plan contributions to date. Let. Rul. 8725088.

In the case of a plan that provides life insurance benefits, the 25% rule is applied to the portion of the premium used to provide current life insurance protection (the cost of the "amount at risk"). In the case of a profit sharing plan that provides health insurance benefits, the 25% rule is applied to the entire cost of providing current health insurance protection for participants and their families. Rulings discussed and cited below illustrate the application of the 25% requirement in various circumstances.

Profit Sharing Plans–The 50% Test

A profit sharing plan which provides that less than one-half the amount allocated annually to each participant's account will be used to purchase ordinary life insurance on his life meets the 25% requirement (assuming the plan provides no other current benefits purchased with nondeferred funds). The reason is that by IRS reckoning, on the average, during an employee's working years, about one-half of each annual premium on ordinary life contracts bought by the plan on his life is required to pay the cost of current life insurance protection. In a profit sharing plan funded by a combination of ordinary life policies and a side fund, the aggregate premiums that have been paid (with nonaccumulated funds) for insurance on a participant's life must be at all times less than 50% of the aggregate employer contributions and forfeitures (without regard to trust earnings and capital gains and losses) that have been allocated to him. Also, the plan must require the trustee, at or before each employee's retirement, either (a) to convert the employee's policies into cash to provide income (without life insurance protection that continues past the employee's retirement), or (b) to distribute the policies to the employee. Rev. Rul. 60-84, 1960-1 CB 159; Rev. Rul. 57-213, 1957-1 CB 157; Rev. Rul. 54-51, 1954-1 CB 147; Letter Ruling, 3-14-66, signed by I. Goodman, Chief, Pension Trust Div. of IRS, Spencer's RPS 241-2.

If the 25% requirement is met with respect to insurance purchased by the plan, the plan may pay as a death benefit both the face amount of the insurance and the amount accumulated in the side fund allocated to the participant. Rev. Rul. 73-501, 1973-2

2006 Tax Facts on Insurance & Employee Benefits

CB 128. There appears no reason why a profit sharing plan could not provide for the purchase of term insurance (individual or group) rather than ordinary life, so long as aggregate premiums paid for insurance on each participant are less than 25% of aggregate employer contributions and forfeitures allocated to him. The IRS has applied the 25% limitation in the manner just described to an ordinary life contract to which was added a 10-year decreasing term rider in a ratio of one-to-one (i.e., $1,000 initial face amount of term for each $1,000 face amount of ordinary life). Rev. Rul. 76-353, 1976-2 CB 112. The Service has also applied the 25% limitation as described to a policy combining 70% participating whole life and 30% one year term insurance under which dividends are used to purchase paid-up additions; as the additions total increases, the amount of term insurance is reduced, so that a level death benefit is provided. Let. Rul. 8029100.

If a profit sharing plan provides for the purchase of both ordinary life and health insurance for participants from funds that have not been accumulated for the period required by the plan for deferment of distributions, the amount expended on health insurance premiums plus *one-half* the amount expended on ordinary life premiums must not exceed 25% of such accumulated funds. For example, assume the account of an employee has been allocated $1,000, no part of which has been accumulated for the requisite period. If $300 is expended for the purchase of ordinary life, not more than $100 may be expended on health insurance. Rev. Rul. 61-164, 1961-2 CB 99.

Employee Stock Ownership Plans

In general, the rules applicable to purchases of life insurance by qualified plans apply to employee stock ownership plans (see Q 410). TD 7506, 1977-2 CB 449. Thus, if assets are invested primarily in qualifying employer securities, life insurance may be purchased on the lives of participants for the benefit of their estates or named beneficiaries within the limits of the 25% "incidental" rule described above. However, proceeds of an exempt loan (see Q 410) may not be used by an employee stock ownership plan to purchase life insurance. TD 7506, 1977-2 CB 449 (Major Revision (9)); Treas. Reg. §54.4975-7(b)(4).

There appears no reason why, so long as assets are invested primarily in qualifying employer securities, an employee stock ownership plan may not purchase key person life insurance in the same way profit sharing plans do, and for essentially the same purpose. Also, should a key person insured be a shareholder, there appears no reason why the death proceeds could not be used to purchase employer stock from his estate. However, an employee stock ownership plan "must not ... obligate itself to acquire securities from a particular security holder at an indefinite time determined upon the happening of an event such as the death of the holder." Treas. Reg. §54.4975-11(a)(7)(i).

Money Purchase Pension Plans

Where life insurance is purchased on the lives of participants in a money purchase pension plan, the 25% rule is applied in basically the same way as if the plan were a profit sharing plan. However, since a money purchase pension plan is primarily a retirement plan, the "incidental" limitation applies regardless of whether the plan provides that funds used to purchase insurance must have been accumulated at least two years. Rev. Rul. 66-143, 1966-1 CB 79. In a plan funded by a combination of life insurance and a side fund, if the 25% requirement is met with respect to the premiums, the plan may provide for a death benefit consisting of both the face amount of the insurance and the amount credited to the participant's account at death. Rev. Rul. 74-307, 1974-2 CB 126.

PENSION AND PROFIT SHARING: PLAN TYPES AND FEATURES   Q 369

Defined Benefit Pension Plans

Death benefits under a pension plan *of any type* will be considered incidental if either (1) less than 50% of the employer contribution credited to each participant's account is used to purchase ordinary life insurance even if the total death benefit consists of both the face amount of the insurance and the amount credited to the participant's account at time of death, or (2) such death benefits would be incidental under the "100-to-1" test described below. Rev. Rul. 74-307, 1974-2 CB 126. It is clear, therefore, not only from the foregoing but also from dicta in prior rulings, that the 25% rule is intended to apply to life insurance benefits provided in defined benefit pension plans as well as in defined contribution plans. Since in a pension plan "death benefits" must be incidental, it would seem that the 25% rule would be applied to the cost of providing the entire death benefit the plan actually pays. However, at least where a plan purchases life insurance on participants' lives and participants have separate accounts, it appears that the 25% rule is applied only to the cost of providing current life insurance protection (i.e., the portion of premium paying for the "amount at risk"). See also Rev. Rul. 61-164, 1961-2 CB 99; Rev. Rul. 66-143, 1966-1 CB 79; Rev. Rul. 70-611, 1970-2 CB 89.

The "100-to-1" Test

In a pension plan of any type (and in a profit sharing plan, on the assumption that there is no other current benefit to be considered), the incidental limitation is automatically satisfied if a death benefit is provided which does not exceed the amount of death benefit that would be paid if all benefits under the plan were funded by retirement income endowment policies that have a death benefit of $1,000, or the reserve, if greater, for each $10 per month of life annuity the policy guarantees at retirement age. The reason is that the IRS has determined that the cost of providing such a death benefit will not in any case exceed 25% of the cost of providing all benefits under the plan. Rev. Rul. 60-83, 1960-1 CB 157 (profit sharing plan funded by single premium endowment policies maturing at retirement age); Rev. Rul. 61-121, 1961-2 CB 65 (pension plan death benefits based on employee's anticipated retirement income and the past service credits); Rev. Rul. 68-31, 1968-1 CB 151 (money purchase pension plan funded by retirement income policies); Rev. Rul. 68-453, 1968-2 CB 163 (pension plan funded by ordinary life contracts with face amount equaling 100 times anticipated monthly retirement benefit, plus side fund); Rev. Rul. 74-307, 1974-2 CB 126. This so-called 100-to-1 ratio test is therefore merely a "safe harbor" rule; it is not a limitation on the amount of death benefit that may be provided.

Miscellaneous Rulings

Postretirement death benefits in a pension plan are subject to the incidental limitation, presumably in the same way preretirement death benefits are. Rev. Rul. 60-59, 1960-1 CB 154. Such benefits are to be distinguished from postdeath payments derived from amounts accumulated under the plan for payment to a retired employee or his beneficiaries (e.g., the annuity paid to the survivor under a joint and survivor annuity). These latter type payments are subject to entirely different rules (see Q 346).

A plan providing only such benefits as are afforded through the purchase of ordinary life contracts which are converted to annuities at retirement is not a pension plan within the meaning of the regulations and will not qualify. Rev. Rul. 81-162, 1981-1 CB 169; Rev. Rul. 65-25, 1965-1 CB 173. A prototype pension plan providing for funding solely through ordinary life contracts will not qualify even if it requires the

2006 Tax Facts on Insurance & Employee Benefits

adopting employer to maintain a second plan containing provisions such that, when the two plans are considered as one, the death benefit does not exceed 100 times the monthly retirement annuity. Rev. Rul. 71-25, 1971-1 CB 115.

A pension plan that permits a participant to invest a portion of his account in life insurance on the life of anyone in whom he has an insurable interest will not qualify since it would provide a benefit that is not "definitely determinable" (see Q 384). Rev. Rul. 69-523, 1969-2 CB 90.

Health Insurance Benefits in Pension Plans

A pension plan may provide for the payment of a pension due to disability, but it may not provide benefits for sickness, accident, hospitalization, or medical expenses for active plan participants or their beneficiaries. Treas. Reg. §1.401-1(b)(1)(i). Such benefits may be provided for *retired* employees, their spouses, and their dependents, but only if (1) the benefits are subordinate to the retirement benefits provided by the plan, (2) a separate account is established and maintained for the benefits, (3) the employer's contributions to the separate account are reasonable and ascertainable, (4) no part of the account may be diverted to any other purpose, (5) the plan calls for return to the employer of any amounts remaining after satisfaction of all liabilities, and (6) in the case of an employee who is a key employee (see Q 357) at any time during the plan year (or any preceding plan year when contributions were made on behalf of such employee), a separate account is established and maintained for the benefits payable to the employee, his spouse, and dependents. IRC Sec. 401(h); (see Q 370 for details).

Generally, medical benefits are considered subordinate to retirement benefits as required under (1) above if, at all times, the aggregate of employer contributions (made after the date on which the plan first includes such medical benefits) to provide such medical benefits and any life insurance protection does not exceed 25% of the aggregate pension contributions made after such date (other than contributions to fund past service credits). IRC Sec. 401(h); Treas. Reg. §1.401-14(c)(1). Details as to the calculation of this limit, as well as the coordination of benefits between an IRC Section 401(h) account and a VEBA (see Q 504) have been explained by the IRS. See Let. Rul. 9834037.

See Q 423 and Q 436 for the tax aspects of IRC Section 401(h) contributions and benefits; and see Q 372 for the effect of IRC Section 401(h) contributions on behalf of key employees on the IRC Section 415 limitation on benefits in a defined benefit plan. *ASRS, Sec. 59, ¶475.*

370. May excess pension assets be transferred to Section 401(h) accounts?

Yes, under certain circumstances. A "qualified transfer" of "excess pension assets" (see below) from a defined benefit plan (other than a multiemployer plan) to an IRC Section 401(h) account of the same plan will not violate the qualification rules of IRC Section 401(a). Such a transfer will not be treated as an employer reversion (see Q 442) or as a prohibited transaction (see Q 443). IRC Sec. 420(a). A "qualified transfer" is one that does not contravene any other provision of law (e.g., a collective bargaining agreement under relevant law) and that meets the use, vesting and minimum cost requirements described below. See IRC Sec. 420(b)(1)(C). The rules permitting transfers to 401(h) accounts apply for taxable years beginning before January 1, 2014. IRC Sec. 420(b)(5).

PENSION AND PROFIT SHARING: PLAN TYPES AND FEATURES   Q 370

The amount transferred in a qualified transfer may not exceed an amount that is reasonably estimated to be the amount the employer maintaining the plan will pay (directly or through reimbursement) out of the 401(h) account during the taxable year for qualified current retiree health liabilities. IRC Sec. 420(b)(3). The amount of the qualified transfer may be based on amounts the employer paid during the taxable year before the date of the transfer and prior to the establishment of the 401(h) account as long as the account is established prior to the transfer and before the end of such taxable year. See IRS General Information Letter, 5 Pens. Pl. Guide (CCH) ¶17,381I (July 5, 1991). In addition, no more than one transfer per plan per taxable year may be treated as a qualified transfer. IRC Sec. 420(b)(2).

A qualified transfer must meet the following three requirements:

(1) *Use requirement*–Assets transferred to the 401(h) account may be used only to pay qualified current retiree health liabilities for the taxable year of the transfer. IRC Sec. 420(c)(1). (Qualified current retiree health liabilities do not include amounts provided for health benefits to retired key employees. IRC Sec. 420(e)(1)(D).) Amounts not used to pay for health benefits must be transferred back to the transferor plan. Such amounts are not includable in the gross income of the employer for such taxable year but are treated as an employer reversion and subject to the 20% penalty. IRC Sec. 420(c)(1)(B).

(2) *Vesting requirement*–The plan must generally provide that the accrued pension benefits of any participant or beneficiary under the plan become nonforfeitable as if the plan had terminated immediately before the qualified transfer (or in the case of a participant who separated during the 1-year period ending on the date of the transfer, immediately before such separation). IRC Sec. 420(c)(2).

(3) *Minimum cost requirement*–Each group health plan or arrangement under which applicable health benefits are provided must provide that the *applicable employer cost* (see below) for each taxable year during the "cost maintenance period" will not be less than the higher of the applicable employer cost for each of the two taxable years immediately preceding the taxable year of the qualified transfer. The "cost maintenance period" means the period of five taxable years beginning with the taxable year in which the qualified transfer occurs. (If a taxable year is in two or more overlapping cost maintenance periods, the highest applicable employer cost required during the taxable year will be taken into account for purposes of this rule.) IRC Sec. 420(c)(3).

Regulations state that an employer who significantly reduces retiree health coverage during the cost maintenance period will not satisfy the minimum cost requirement. Treas. Reg. §1.420-1(a). For this purpose, a retiree health coverage reduction is "significant" if for any taxable year during the cost maintenance period, either (i) the employer-initiated reduction percentage for the taxable year exceeds 10%, or (ii) the sum of such percentages for that taxable year and all prior taxable years during the cost maintenance period exceeds 20%. See Treas. Reg. §1.420-1(b).

"Excess pension assets" means the *excess of* the lesser of the fair market value of the plan's assets or the value of such assets determined under the minimum funding rules *over* (1) 125% of the current liability of the plan (as determined for purposes of the full funding limitation) if the accrued liability of the plan is less than 150% of the current liability or (2) 150% of the current liability if the accrued liability of the plan is greater than 150% of the current liability (see Q 386). IRC Sec. 420(e)(2).

"Applicable employer cost" means the amount determined by dividing (a) the qualified current retiree health liabilities of the employer for the taxable year *by* (b) the number of individuals to whom coverage for applicable health benefits was provided during the taxable year. For this purpose, the amount of qualified current retiree health liabilities is determined without regard to reductions for amounts previously set aside. If there was no qualified transfer during the taxable year, the qualified current retiree health liabilities amount is determined as though there had been such a transfer at the end of the taxable year. IRC Sec. 420(c)(3)(B).

An employer generally may not contribute to an IRC Section 401(h) account or a welfare benefit fund with respect to qualified current retiree health liabilities for which transferred assets are required to be used. IRC Sec. 420(d)(2). In addition, the amount that can be transferred in a qualified transfer is reduced if the employer has previously made a contribution to a 401(h) account or welfare benefit fund for the same liabilities. See IRC Sec. 420(e)(1)(B); see also, IRS General Information Letter, above.

In addition, ERISA requires that notice of any qualified transfer be given to plan participants, the DOL, and the IRS at least 60 days before the date of the qualified transfer (ERISA Sec. 101(e)); however, the Department of Labor and Treasury have agreed that one notice filed with the DOL within the requisite period will satisfy this requirement. Ann. 92-54, 1992-13 IRB 35. Penalties of up to $100 a day may be imposed on any plan administrator and/or employer for failure to provide the required notice. ERISA Sec. 502(c). *ASRS, Sec. 59, ¶475.3.*

Defined Benefit Plans

371. What is a defined benefit plan?

A defined benefit plan is a qualified retirement plan that expresses the participant's benefit as a certain amount (or formula for determining the amount) that will be paid at retirement. Defined benefit plans are a key type of pension (see Q 381), but a pension can also be a defined contribution plan (see Q 376). The Internal Revenue Code states that the term "defined benefit plan" means any plan that is not a defined contribution plan. IRC Sec. 414(j).

Variations on the traditional defined benefit plan include Section 412(i) (fully insured) plans (see Q 407) and cash balance plans (see Q 374). See Q 377 for the application of the Section 415 requirements to defined benefit plans, and Q 373 for special qualification requirements. *ASRS, Sec. 59, ¶¶200.4, 240.*

372. How are the Section 415 limits applied to defined benefit plans?

In a defined benefit plan, the highest *annual benefit* payable under the plan (or under all such plans aggregated, if the employer has more than one) must not exceed the lesser of: (a) 100% of the participant's average compensation in his *high three years of service*, or (b) $175,000 (in 2006, as indexed). IRC Sec. 415(b)(1). This limit is effective for limitation years ending in 2006; see Appendix E for the limits in prior years. IRC Sec. 415(d). Proposed regulations specify that this limit also applies to the annual benefit *payable* to a participant. See Prop. Treas. Reg. §1.415(b)-1(a)(1). The proposed regulations referenced throughout this question were issued in May, 2005 and are proposed to be effective for limitation years beginning on or after January 1, 2007. REG-130241-04,

PENSION AND PROFIT SHARING: PLAN TYPES AND FEATURES   Q 372

70 Fed. Reg. 31214 (May 31, 2005). For general rules affecting the application of the Section 415 limits, see Q 332; for the defined contribution plan limits, see Q 377.

High three years of service. A participant's high three years of service is the period of three consecutive calendar years during which the participant both was an active participant in the plan and had the greatest aggregate compensation from the employer. IRC Sec. 415(b)(3); Prop. Treas. Reg. §1.415(b)-1(a)(5). Under earlier regulations, a participant's highest 3-year average compensation could be determined by reference to years of service that occurred before the plan was effective (provided the definition was applied uniformly and consistently; see Treas. Reg. §1.415-3(a)(3)). Proposed regulations would state that a plan may not base accruals on compensation in excess of the 401(a)(17) limit ($220,000 in 2006, as indexed). See Prop. Treas. Reg. §1.415(b)-1(a)(5).

Annual benefit. For purposes of the defined benefit limits, "annual benefit" means a benefit that is payable annually in the form of a straight annuity. If the benefit is payable in a form other than a straight life annuity, the annual benefit is determined as the straight life annuity that is actuarially equivalent to the form in which the benefit is paid. See Prop. Treas. Reg. §1.415(b)-1(b)(1). The application of the 415(b) limit to a benefit that is not payable in the form of an annual straight life annuity is explained at Prop. Treas. Reg. §1.415(b)-1(c). Earlier guidance appeared at Rev. Rul. 2001-51, 2001-2 CB 427, A-3. The "annual benefit" does not include employee contributions and rollover contributions. See Prop. Treas. Reg. §1.415(b)-1(b)(1)(ii).

The annual benefit does not include employer contributions to an individual medical account (under IRC Section 401(h), see Q 370) of any individual under a defined benefit pension plan. Such amounts are treated as annual additions to a separate defined contribution plan. See IRC Sec. 415(l); Q 377.

Multiple annuity starting dates. Special rules have been proposed requiring an adjustment of the annual benefit where a participant has more than one annuity starting date (for example, where benefits under one plan are aggregated with benefits under another plan under which distributions have already commenced, *or* where benefits are increased under a cost of living adjustment). See Prop. Treas. Reg. §1.415(b)-2.

Adjustments to dollar limitation. The $175,000 limit (as indexed for 2006) is adjusted downward if the annuity starting date occurs before the participant reaches age 62. IRC Sec. 415(b)(2)(C). If the annuity starting date occurs after the participant reaches age 65, the limit is adjusted upward. IRC Sec. 415(b)(2)(D). The calculation of the adjustments is explained at IRC Sec. 415(b)(2)(E) and Prop. Treas. Reg. §1.415(b)-1(d) and (e). Earlier guidance on implementing these adjustments was provided at Rev. Rul. 2001-51, above, A-4.

An adjustment is also required for certain other forms of benefit, as well as for employee contributions and rollover contributions (see Q 444 to Q 456), so that such benefits are converted to the actuarial equivalent of a straight life annuity. IRC Sec. 415(b)(2)(B); see Prop. Treas. Reg. §1.415(b)-1(b)(2). Under earlier guidance this adjustment is more complex, generally following the manner in which Social Security benefits are reduced for Social Security purposes. The interest rate assumption used for making this adjustment must be no less than the greater of 5% or the rate specified in the plan; however, in the case of benefits subject to IRC Section 417(e)(3), the interest rate must be the rate set forth in IRC Section 417(e)(3). IRC Sec. 415(b)(2)(E)(i); IRC

Sec. 415(b)(2)(E)(ii). Guidance and detailed rules for making this calculation appear in Notice 2004-78, 2004-48 IRB 879 and at Prop. Treas. Reg. §1.415(b)-1(c)(3). Proposed simplification for amounts not subject to minimum present value rules of IRC Section 417(e)(3) is set forth at Prop. Treas. Reg. §1.415(b)-1(c)(2).

Adjustments to the ceiling do not need to be made for ancillary benefits not directly related to retirement benefits (such as preretirement death and disability benefits and postretirement medical benefits). Treas. Reg. §1.415-3(c)(2); Prop. Treas. Reg. §1.415(b)-1(c)(4). See also, IRS Information Letter, 18 Pens. Rep. (BNA) 1552 (1991); Let. Rul. 9636030. If the benefit is paid in the form of a joint and survivor annuity for the benefit of the participant and his spouse, the value of the feature will not be taken into consideration in reducing the ceiling unless the survivor benefit is greater than the joint benefit. IRC Sec. 415(b)(2)(B).

The 100% of compensation limit generally does not apply to governmental plans, multiemployer plans, or certain collectively bargained plans. Prop. Treas. Reg. §1.415(b)-1(a)(6).

10-year phase-in of limitation. The dollar limit and 100% compensation limit are subject to a 10-year phase-in rule. The $175,000 limit (as indexed for 2006) is reduced by multiplying it by a fraction: the numerator is the participant's years of participation in the defined benefit plan, and the denominator is 10. IRC Sec. 415(b)(5)(A). The 100% of compensation limit is reduced in the same manner, but based on years of service, rather than years of participation. IRC Sec. 415(b)(5)(B). "Years of service," for this purpose, includes employment with a predecessor employer, including affiliated employers. See Prop. Regs. §§1.415(b)-1(g)(2)(ii)(B), 1.415(f)-1(c), 1.415(a)-1(f); see also *Lear Eye Clinic, Ltd. v. Comm.*, 106 TC 418 (1996). Neither reduction will reduce the limitations to less than 10% of the otherwise applicable limitation amount. IRC Sec. 415(b)(5)(C).

Annual $10,000 benefit. A benefit of up to $10,000 in any limitation year may be provided to a participant without violating the IRC Section 415 limits, notwithstanding the 100% limit or required adjustments for ancillary benefits; however, this benefit is subject to the 10-year phase-in rule described above, based on years of service. The participant must not at any time have also participated in a defined contribution plan maintained by the employer. IRC Secs. 415(b)(4), 415(b)(5)(B).

Cost of living adjustments. A plan may incorporate by reference the automatic adjustments of plan benefits to the extent of the annual cost-of-living increases provided under the Internal Revenue Code; however, the scheduled benefit increases may not take effect earlier than the year in which the dollar limit adjustment becomes effective. Treas. Reg. §1.415-5(c); Prop. Treas. Regs. §§1.415(a)-1(d)(3)(v), 1.415(d)-1. Proposed rules state that the annual increase does not apply in limitation years beginning after the annuity starting date to a participant who has previously commenced receiving benefits *unless* the plan so specifies. See Prop. Treas. Reg. §1.415(a)-1(d)(3)(v)(C). Earlier regulations stated that a plan could provide for automatic freezing or reduction of the rate of benefit accrual to prevent the limitations from being exceeded. Treas. Reg. §1.415-1(d)(1).

A defined benefit plan may maintain a qualified cost-of-living arrangement under which employer and employee contributions may be applied to provide cost-of-living

PENSION AND PROFIT SHARING: PLAN TYPES AND FEATURES   Q 373

increases to the primary benefit under the plan. Such an arrangement is qualified if the adjustment is based on increases in the cost-of-living after the annuity starting date, determined by reference to one or more indexes prescribed by the Secretary (or a minimum of 3%). Among the requirements the arrangement must meet are that it must (1) be elective, (2) be available to all participants under the same terms, (3) provide for such election at least in the year the participant attains the earliest retirement age under the plan (determined without regard to any requirement of separation from service) or separates from service, and (4) not cover key employees. IRC Sec. 415(k)(2). *ASRS, Sec. 59, ¶470.*

373. What special qualification requirements apply to defined benefit pension plans?

A defined benefit pension plan may not exclude from participation in the plan employees who are beyond a specified age; however, the benefit of employees who are within five years of normal retirement age when they begin employment is computed using a retirement age which is the fifth anniversary of the time that plan participation begins for that employee. IRC Secs. 410(a)(2), 411(a)(8). In addition, a defined benefit plan must benefit a minimum number or percentage of employees (i.e., the 50/40 test) as explained below.

A defined benefit plan must contain a limit on the projected "annual benefit" under the plan (or under all such plans aggregated if the employer has more than one defined benefit plan). See Q 332, Q 372 for details.

Cash balance plans, where each employee has a hypothetical account or "cash balance" to which contributions and interest payments are credited, are treated as defined benefit plans. See Q 374.

A defined benefit plan (except certain insured plans) must satisfy one of the following three accrued benefit tests:

a. 3% test. The accrued benefit to which a participant is entitled upon his separation from service must be not less than (1) 3% of the normal retirement benefit to which he would be entitled if he commenced participation at the earliest entry age under the plan and served continuously until the earlier of age 65 or the normal retirement age specified under the plan, multiplied by (2) the number of years (not in excess of 33⅓) of his participation in the plan. IRC Sec. 411(b)(1)(A); Treas. Reg. §1.411(b)-(1)(b)(1).

b. 133⅓% test. In any particular plan year when qualification of the plan is tested, the plan must not allow for the annual rate of accrual of an individual's normal retirement benefit in any later plan year to exceed 133⅓% of the annual rate of accrual in the particular plan year or in any year between the particular plan year and such later plan year. IRC Sec. 411(b)(1)(B); Treas. Reg. §1.411(b)-1(b)(2).

c. Fractional (or pro rata) test. The accrued benefit to which a participant is entitled upon his separation from service must be not less than a fraction of his assumed retirement benefit. His assumed retirement benefit is computed as though the participant continued to earn the same rate of compensation annually that he had earned during the years which would have been taken into account under the plan (but not in excess of 10 years of service immediately preceding separation) had the employee reached normal retirement age at the date of his separation. The assumed retirement benefit is then multiplied by a fraction, the numerator of which is the total number of years of the employee's participation in the plan and the denominator of which is the total number of years he would have participated in the plan had he separated from service at normal retirement age. IRC Sec. 411(b)(1)(C); Treas. Reg. §1.411(b)-1(b)(3). For the calculation method (and examples) which will produce the lowest accrued benefit satisfying the fractional test where benefits are accrued following a break in service, see Rev. Rul. 81-11, 1981-1 CB 227.

A *412(i) fully insured plan* automatically satisfies any of the foregoing accrued benefit tests if (1) the plan is funded exclusively by insurance contracts calling for level annual premiums from the date the insured becomes a participant in the plan to not later than retirement age, (2) benefits provided by the plan are equal to the benefits provided under each contract at normal retirement age and are guaranteed by the insurer, and (3) an employee's accrued benefit at any time is not less than the cash surrender value his insurance contracts would have on the assumption that all premiums currently due are paid and there is no indebtedness against the contracts. IRC Sec. 411(b)(1)(F). See Q 407 and Q 408 for details on 412(i) plans.

A plan funded exclusively by a *group insurance or group annuity contracts* is considered a 412(i) fully insured plan if the contract has the requisite characteristics of individual contracts. IRC Sec. 412(i). Regulations take the position that, for example, amounts received by the insurer under a group contract must be allocated to purchase individual benefits for participants. "A plan which maintains unallocated funds in an auxiliary trust fund or which provides that an insurance company will maintain unallocated funds in a separate account, such as a group deposit administration contract, does not satisfy the requirements of ... [a fully insured plan]." Treas. Reg. §1.412(i)-1(c)(2)(v).

If at the time an employee separates from service the value of his employee contributions exceeds the cash surrender value of the insurance contract(s) funding his retirement benefit, the plan could supplement the cash surrender value(s) in order to satisfy the minimum vesting standard and the plan would not fail to be a fully insured plan. Treas. Reg. §1.412(i)-1(b).

A defined benefit plan that provides a stated benefit offset by the benefits of a profit sharing plan will satisfy the benefit accrual requirements if the benefit determined without the offset satisfies the requirements and if the offset is equal to the amount deemed provided by the vested portion of the account balance in the profit sharing plan on the date the amount of offset is determined. Rev. Rul. 76-259, 1976-2 CB 111.

A defined benefit plan must require separate accounting for the portion of each employee's accrued benefit derived from any voluntary employee contributions permitted under the plan. IRC Sec. 411(b)(2). See Rev. Rul. 78-202, 1978-1 CB 124 for rules relating to calculation of accrued benefits derived from mandatory employee contributions. See also Rev. Rul. 79-259, 1979-2 CB 197. Generally, a plan may not be amended to reduce a participant's accrued benefit. Treas. Reg. §1.411(d)-4, A-1. Procedures for obtaining approval of a retroactive plan amendment reducing a participant's accrued benefit are specified in Rev. Proc. 94-42, 1994-1 CB 353.

In addition, if a defined benefit plan subject to the minimum funding rules adopts an amendment that would increase current liability under the plan, and the funded

PENSION AND PROFIT SHARING: PLAN TYPES AND FEATURES   Q 373

current liability percentage under the plan (the ratio of the value of the plan's assets to its current liability) is less than 60%, the plan must require that the amendment will not become effective until the employer (or a member of the employer's controlled group) provides adequate security in favor of the plan. IRC Sec. 401(a)(29). See also Q 322 to Q 384 for other qualification requirements.

50/40 participation test. A defined benefit plan must also benefit the lesser of (a) 50 employees, or (b) the greater of 40% of all employees or two employees (or if there is only one employee, that employee). IRC Sec. 401(a)(26). However, state and local government plans are not subject to the 50/40 test, and plans maintained by the United States government are treated as satisfying it until the first plan year beginning on or after the date final regulations are issued. See IRC Sec. 401(a)(26)(H); Notice 2003-6, 2003-1 CB 298.

Defined benefit plans must meet the participation requirement on each day of the plan year; however, under a simplified testing method, a plan is treated as satisfying this test if it satisfies it on any single day during the plan year so long as that day is reasonably representative of the employer's workforce and the plan's coverage. A plan does not have to be tested on the same day each plan year. Treas. Reg. §1.401(a)(26)-7(b). Final regulations provide that a plan that does not satisfy the test for a plan year may be amended by the 15th day of the 10th month after the close of the plan year to satisfy the test retroactively. Treas. Reg. §1.401(a)(26)-7(c), Treas. Reg. §1.401(a)(4)-11(g). Comparable plans may not be aggregated for purposes of meeting this test. General Explanation–TRA '86, p. 683.

The 50/40 test may be applied separately with respect to each separate line of business if the employer makes such an election and the Secretary gives his consent. IRC Sec. 401(a)(26)(G). Furthermore, the requirement that a separate line of business have at least 50 employees generally does not apply in determining whether a plan satisfies the 50/40 test on a separate line of business basis. IRC Sec. 401(a)(26)(G).

A defined benefit plan's prior benefit structure must also satisfy the minimum participation rule. Treas. Reg. §1.401(a)(26)-1(a). The prior benefit structure under a defined benefit plan for a plan year includes all benefits accrued to date under the plan, and each defined benefit plan has only one prior benefit structure. A prior benefit structure satisfies the minimum participation rule if the plan provides meaningful benefits to a group of employees that includes the lesser of 50 employees or 40% of the employer's employees. Whether a plan is providing meaningful benefits, or whether the employees have meaningful accrued benefits under a plan, is determined on the basis of all the facts and circumstances. Treas. Regs. §§1.401(a)(26)-3(b), 1.401(a)(26)-3(c).

Generally, the same employees who are excludable under the coverage tests (see Q 325) may be excluded from consideration in meeting the 54/40 participation test. IRC Sec. 401(a)(26)(B)(i); Treas. Reg. §1.401(a)(26)-6. If employees who do not meet a plan's minimum age and service requirements are covered under a plan which meets the 50/40 test separately with regard to such employees, those employees may be excluded from consideration in determining whether other plans of the employer meet the 50/40 test, *but only if* (1) the benefits for the excluded employees are provided under the same plan as benefits for other employees, (2) the benefits provided to the excluded employees are not greater than comparable benefits provided to other employees under the plan, and (3) no highly compensated employee is included in the group of excluded employees for more than one year. IRC Sec. 401(a)(26)(B)(ii); Treas. Reg. §1.401(a)(26)-6(b)(1).

Generally, an employee is treated as benefiting under a plan for a plan year if the employee actually accrues a benefit for the plan year. An employee who fails to accrue a benefit merely because of the IRC Section 415 limits (see Q 332, Q 372) or a uniformly applicable benefit limit under the plan's structure is treated as benefiting under a plan for the plan year. Treas. Regs. §§1.401(a)(26)-5(a), 1.410(b)-3(a)(2)(iii).

As to which individuals must be treated as "employees" and which organizations make up an employer, see Q 354, Q 355, Q 359, and Q 360. *ASRS, Sec. 59, ¶¶410.4; 485.3.*

374. What is a cash balance plan?

A cash balance plan is a defined benefit plan that calculates benefits in a manner similar to defined contribution plans. It resembles a defined contribution plan in that each employee has a hypothetical account or "cash balance" to which contributions and interest payments are credited; however, since the actual funds are pooled, directed investing is not available. As with other defined benefit plans, the employer bears both the risk and the benefits of investment performance.

In a typical cash balance plan, the employee's benefit accrues evenly over his years of service, with annual service or pay credits to a hypothetical account (usually a fixed percentage of pay, such as 4% to 5%). The amount is determined actuarially to insure that the plan has sufficient funds to provide the promised benefits. In addition, interest is credited at a rate specified in the plan document, and compounded at least annually. The rate may be a standard interest rate or a variable interest rate (within specified limitations), but the interest rate must be the same for all employees in the plan for all plan years in order to meet certain nondiscrimination safe harbor requirements. Treas. Reg. §1.401(a)(4)-8(c)(3)(iv). (See Q 384 regarding what constitutes a definitely determinable benefit.) In contrast, since benefits under a traditional defined benefit plan are generally based on years of service and final pay, the accrual of benefits accelerates more in the later years as retirement approaches.

While the cash balance design itself may be an attractive feature to younger employees, the conversion of defined benefit plans to cash balance plans has been an issue of significant controversy in recent years. The IRS stopped issuing letter rulings on cash balance plan conversions in 1999, and in 2003 both houses of Congress passed amendments limiting appropriations to the Treasury Department with respect to any time it spends to develop cash balance plan regulations. In June, 2004, the Treasury and IRS announced the withdrawal of proposed regulations that had been issued in late 2002 (see http://www.ustreas.gov/press/releases/js1724.htm).

Most significantly, two federal courts issued judgments in 2003 against employers sponsoring cash balance plans. See *Berger v. Xerox Corp.* 338 F.3d 755 (7th Cir. 2003); *Cooper v. IBM Personal Pension Plan*, 274 F.Supp. 2d (S.D. Ill. 2003). An earlier attack on the conversion of a defined benefit plan to a cash balance plan was unsuccessful, focusing on the issue of age discrimination under the ADEA. See *Eaton v. Onan Corp.*, 117 F. Supp. 812 (S.D. Ind. 2000).

PENSION AND PROFIT SHARING: PLAN TYPES AND FEATURES Q 375

Earlier regulations include special safe harbors for cash balance plans to satisfy various nondiscrimination requirements. See Treas. Reg. §1.401(a)(4)-8(c)(3). *ASRS, Sec. 59, ¶265.*

375. How are the required annual and quarterly payments to defined benefit plans determined?

Contributions to certain defined benefit plans (other than multiemployer plans) subject to the minimum funding standard (see Q 385 to Q 390) must be made, on an estimated basis, at least quarterly. The quarterly contribution requirement is imposed on plans with a *funded current liability percentage* (see IRC Sec. 412(l)(8)(B)) of less than 100%. IRC Sec. 412(m); Rev. Rul. 95-31, 1995-1 CB 76.

The required amount for each quarterly installment is 25% of the required annual payment (RAP). IRC Sec. 412(m)(4)(C). The RAP is the lesser of:

(1) 90% of the amount the employer is required to contribute for the plan year under the minimum funding requirements (other than the unpredictable contingent event benefit liabilities); or

(2) 100% of the amount the employer was required to contribute for the preceding plan year (other than the unpredictable contingent event benefit liabilities), but only if the preceding plan year consisted of 12 months. IRC Sec. 412(m)(4)(B). A portion of the unpredictable contingent event benefit liabilities is required to be contributed in addition to each required installment. IRC Sec. 412(m)(4)(D).

Defined benefit plans subject to the quarterly contributions requirement must also meet a liquidity requirement. IRC Sec. 412(m)(5). Such plans generally must maintain liquid plan assets at an amount approximately equal to three times the total disbursements from the plan trust during the 12-month period ending on the last day of each quarter for which the plan must pay a required quarterly installment. See Rev. Rul. 95-31, 1995-1 CB 76.

The minimum funding requirement for a plan year is generally determined without regard to any credit balance as of the beginning of the plan year. However, an employer may treat all or a portion of the credit balance in the plan's funding standard account as a payment of a quarterly installment. Likewise, the overpayment of a quarterly installment may be used to reduce the payments necessary to satisfy a subsequent quarterly installment for the same plan year. Notice 89-52, 1989-1 CB 692, A-6, A-12, A-14.

If a required installment is not paid to the plan by its due date, the funding standard account is charged with interest on the amount by which the required installment exceeds the amount, if any, paid on or before such due date. Such interest is charged for the period from the due date until the date when such installment is actually paid. Due dates are April 15, July 15, October 15, and January 15 of the following year, or, if the plan year is not a calendar year, the 15th of each corresponding month in the plan year. The rate of interest charged is the *greater of* 175% of the federal mid-term rate (see Q 805) at the beginning of the plan year *or* the rate of interest used to determine current liability. IRC Secs. 412(m)(1), 412(b)(5).

A statutory lien may be imposed on an employer (determined on a controlled group basis–see Q 359) for failure to make a required installment or any other payment required by the minimum funding rules if the aggregate unpaid balance of such contributions or payments (including interest) exceeds $1,000,000 and the plan has an unfunded current liability for the plan year. See IRC Sec. 412(n). *ASRS, Sec. 59, ¶500.2.*

DEFINED CONTRIBUTION PLANS

376. What is a defined contribution plan?

A defined contribution plan is a qualified retirement plan that (1) provides an individual account for each participant, (2) provides benefits based solely on the amount contributed to the participant's account, plus any income, expenses, gains, losses and forfeitures allocated to the account. IRC Sec. 414(i). A defined contribution plan specifies the amount (or a formula for determining the amount) that the employer will contribute to the participant's account.

A defined contribution plan can be either a pension (see Q 381) or a profit sharing plan (see Q 391). Defined contribution plans include Section 401(k) plans (see Q 394), stock bonus plans (see Q 409) and employee stock ownership plans (see Q 410), as well as money purchase and target benefit plans (see Q 382).

See Q 377 for the application of the Section 415 limits to defined contribution plans, and Q 378 for special qualification requirements. *ASRS, Sec. 59, ¶200.5.*

377. How are the Section 415 limits applied to defined contribution plans?

The "annual additions" to a participant's account (or all such accounts aggregated, if the employer has more than one defined contribution plan) must not exceed the lesser of: (a) 100% of the participant's compensation, or (b) $44,000 (as indexed for 2006). IRC Sec. 415(c). (For the dollar limitations on annual additions in earlier limitation years, see Appendix E.) This limit is indexed for inflation in increments of $1,000. IRC Sec. 415(d)(4)(B).

Limitations applicable when an individual is a participant in one or more elective deferral plans (including 401(k) plans, SIMPLE IRAs, SAR-SEPs and tax sheltered annuities) are explained in Q 396. For general rules affecting the application of the Section 415 limits, see Q 332; for the defined benefit plan limits, see Q 372. The proposed regulations referenced throughout this question were issued in May, 2005 and are proposed to be effective for limitation years beginning on or after January 1, 2007. REG-130241-04, 70 Fed. Reg. 31214 (May 31, 2005).

The following amounts will not give rise to annual additions: (a) catch-up contributions (see Q 397); (b) payments made to restore losses resulting from a breach of fiduciary duty; (c) excess deferrals that are distributed as required in regulations (see Q 396), and (d) certain restorations of accrued benefits. Prop. Treas. Reg. §1.415(c)-1(b)(2)(ii); IRC Sec. 414(v)(3)(A); see also Rev. Rul. 2002-45, 2002-2 CB 116.

Earlier regulations provide for corrective measures when contributions in excess of the IRC Section 415 limits (i.e., excess annual additions) are made due to the allocation of forfeitures, due to reasonable error in estimating a participant's compensation, or under certain other limited circumstances. Treas. Reg. §1.415-6(b)(6). The preamble to the

PENSION AND PROFIT SHARING: PLAN TYPES AND FEATURES   Q 377

2005 proposed regulations states that future guidance on this subject will be included in the Employee Plans Compliance Resolution System (EPCRS).

Compensation to which the limit is applied is the compensation for the limitation year from the employer maintaining the plan. IRC Sec. 415(c)(3)(A). It includes wages, salaries, fees for professional services, and other amounts for services actually rendered (such as commissions, percentage of profits, tips, and bonuses). Prop. Treas. Reg. §1.415(c)-2(b)(1). Compensation also includes (i) elective deferrals to 401(k) plans, SAR-SEPs, SIMPLE IRAs and 457(b) plans to the extent not includable in the employee's income, and (ii) any amounts contributed or deferred by the election of the employee and excluded from gross income of the employee under IRC Sections 125 (cafeteria plans), 132(f) (qualified transportation fringe benefit plans) or 457 (deferred compensation plan of a government or tax-exempt organization). See IRC Secs. 415(c)(3), 402(g). The foregoing items may be used as a simplified safe harbor definition of compensation. Prop. Treas. Reg. §1.415(c)-2(d)(2).

The proposed regulations also permit the following to be included as compensation, to the extent they are includable in the gross income of the employee: certain payments received under an employer's accident and health plan, certain moving expense reimbursements, the value of nonqualified options in the year granted, and certain property transferred in connection with the performance of services. Prop. Treas. Reg. §1.415(c)-2(b)(3) to (6); see also Prop. Treas. Reg. §1.415(c)-2(d)(2).

In the case of a self-employed person, his earned income is compensation. IRC Sec. 415(c)(3)(B).

Except as noted above, compensation does not include nontaxable employer contributions toward deferred compensation plans, qualified or nonqualified, in the year in which they were contributed. Furthermore, deferred compensation distributions are not compensation when received whether or not excludable from gross income, except that distributions of unfunded nonqualified deferred compensation may be considered compensation in the year in which they are includable in gross income. Treas. Reg. §1.415-2(d)(3)(i); Prop. Treas. Reg. §1.415(c)-2(c)(1). Excludable premiums for group term life insurance are not compensation. Treas. Reg. §1.415-2(d)(3)(iv). Foreign source income generally will be treated as compensation even though excluded from gross income. Treas. Reg. §1.415-2(d)(2); Prop. Treas. Reg. §1.415(c)-2(c)(4).

The compensation must be *actually paid or made available* to be taken into account within the limitation year. Treas. Reg. §1.415-2(d)(4); Prop. Treas. Reg. §1.415(c)-2(e)(1)(i). Compensation includes compensation from all employers that are members of a controlled group of corporations or a group of trades or businesses under common control. Treas. Reg. §1.415-2(d)(6); Prop. Treas. Reg. §1.415(c)-2(g)(2). Regulations also provide for safe harbors based on wages for income tax withholding or wages as reported in Box 1 on Form W-2. See Treas. Reg. §1.415-2(d)(11); Prop. Treas. Reg. §1.415(c)-2(d)(2) and (3).

Post-severance compensation of the following amounts is included as compensation if it is paid within 2½ months following severance from employment: (1) payment for unused sick or vacation leave the employee would have been able to use, had employment continued, or (b) amounts that would have been paid had employment continued, such as compensation and overtime, commissions, bonuses or similar compensation. It

Q 377 FEDERAL INCOME TAX

should be noted that this treatment will not apply to other types of post-severance packages, such as parachute payments under IRC Section 280G and unfunded nonqualified deferred compensation. Prop. Treas. Reg. §1.415(c)-2(e)(3).

Any amount allocated to a separate account that is required to be established in a welfare benefit fund (see Q 499) to provide postretirement medical or life insurance benefits to a key employee (see Q 357) must be treated as an annual addition to a separate defined contribution plan for purposes of calculating the annual additions to defined contribution plans of an employer. IRC Sec. 419A(d)(2). Such amounts are not subject to the 100% of compensation limit under IRC Section 415(c)(1)(B) discussed above.

Annual additions means the sum credited to a participant's account for any limitation year, of (1) employer contributions, (2) employee contributions, and (3) forfeitures. "Employee contributions" do not include rollovers from another qualified plan or from an IRA (see Q 444), contributions under Section 457(e)(6), or employee contributions to a SAR-SEP (see Q 240) that are excludable from the employee's gross income. See IRC Sec. 415(c)(2). A direct transfer of funds or employee contributions from one defined contribution plan to another will not be considered an annual addition for the limitation year in which the transfer occurs. See Treas. Reg. §1.415-6(b)(2)(iv); Prop. Treas. Reg. §1.415(c)-1(b)(1); Let. Ruls. 9111046, 9052058.

A corrective allocation to a participant's account because of an erroneous forfeiture or a failure to make a required allocation in a prior limitation year will not be considered an annual addition for the limitation year in which the allocation is made, but will be considered an annual addition for the limitation year to which the corrective allocation relates. See Rev. Proc. 2001-17, above, 6.02(4)(b); Prop. Treas. Reg. §1.415(c)-1(b)(6)(ii)(A).

Restorative payments made to a defined contribution plan, to the extent they restore plan losses that result from a fiduciary breach (or a reasonable risk of liability for a fiduciary breach), are not contributions for purposes of Section 415(c). In contrast, payments made to a plan to make up for losses due to market fluctuations, but not due to a fiduciary breach, *will* be treated as contributions, not as restorative payments. Rev. Rul. 2002-45, 2002-2 CB 116; Prop. Treas. Reg. §1.415(c)-1(b)(2)(ii)(C); see also Let. Ruls. 9506048, 9628031.

Earlier regulations stated that if an allocation of forfeitures or a reasonable error in estimating a participant's annual compensation would cause additions to exceed the limit, they may, under certain circumstances, be held in suspense, be used to reduce employer contributions for that participant or be returned to the participant. Treas. Reg. §1.415-6(b)(6). (A return of mandatory contributions could result in discrimination.) Certain other transactions between a plan and an employer, or certain allocations to participants' accounts could be treated as giving rise to annual additions. Treas. Reg. §1.415-6(b)(2)(i).

Generally, an employer may elect to continue contributions under a profit sharing or stock bonus plan on behalf of permanently and totally disabled (see Q 833) participants. IRC Sec. 415(c)(3)(C). For the purpose of determining whether such contributions comply with the limitation on contributions, the disabled participant's compensation is deemed to be the amount of compensation he would have received for the year if paid at the rate of compensation he received immediately before becoming permanently and totally disabled. Contributions made under this provision *must* be nonforfeitable when made. IRC Sec. 415(c)(3)(C). The IRS has privately ruled that a 401(k) plan that purchased a group long term disability income policy to insure the continuation of benefit accumulation for disabled employees would not be required to include amounts paid under the policy as annual additions. Let. Ruls. 200031060, 200235043.

A defined contribution plan may provide for an automatic adjustment which reflects the cost-of-living increases in the limit on annual additions. Treas. Reg. §1.415-6(d). Like defined benefit plans, the plan may provide for automatic freezing or reduction in the rate of annual additions to prevent exceeding the limitation. Treas. Reg. §1.415-1(d)(1); see Prop. Treas. Reg. §1.415(d)-1(d).

In the case of an ESOP, if no more than one-third of the deductible employer contributions applied by the plan to the repayment of principal and interest on loans incurred to acquire qualifying employer securities are allocated to highly compensated employees (see Q 356), forfeitures of employer securities acquired with such loans and deductible employer contributions applied by the plan to the payment of interest on such loans may be excluded for purposes of the limitations on contributions. IRC Sec. 415(c)(6); see Prop. Treas. Reg. §1.415(c)-1(f). Where an employer reversion is transferred to an ESOP, amounts in excess of the Section 415 limit which are held in a reversion suspense account are not deemed to be annual additions until the limitation year in which they are allocated to the participants' accounts. IRC Sec. 4980(c)(3)(C); Let. Ruls. 8935056, 8925096. *ASRS, Sec. 59, ¶470.*

378. What special qualification requirements apply to defined contribution plans?

A defined contribution plan (money purchase pension plan, profit sharing plan or a stock bonus plan) may not exclude from participation in the plan employees who are beyond a specified age. IRC Sec. 410(a)(3).

A defined contribution plan must require separate accounting for each employee's accrued benefit. IRC Sec. 411(b)(2).

A defined contribution plan must contain the limitation on "annual additions" to a participant's account (or all such accounts aggregated, if the employer has more than one defined contribution plan). See Q 332, Q 377.

Target benefit plans (see Q 382), where the actual pension is based on the amount in the participant's account, are to be treated as defined contribution plans. Hybrid plans which are part target and part defined benefit will be treated as defined contribution to the extent that benefits are based on the individual account.

A defined contribution plan must provide for (1) allocation of contributions and trust earnings to participants in accordance with a definite formula; (2) distributions in accordance with an amount stated or ascertainable and credited to participants; and (3) a valuation of investments held by the trust, at least once a year, on a specified inventory date, in accordance with a method consistently followed and uniformly applied. Rev. Rul. 80-155, 1980-1 CB 84. Requirement (3) may, however, be satisfied in a plan where contributions are invested solely in insurance contracts or in mutual fund shares even if there is no provision in the plan for periodic valuation of assets. Rev. Rul. 73-435, 1973-2 CB 126; Rev. Rul. 73-554, 1973-2 CB 130.

A defined contribution plan will not fail to satisfy the participation, coverage and vesting requirements merely because it does not unconditionally provide for an allocation to a participant with respect to a computation period in which he completes 1,000 hours of service (see Q 324 and Q 333). (However, such a participant will not be treated as "benefiting" under the plan for purposes of the coverage requirement—see Q 325.) Thus, for example, a plan may require that a participant be employed as of the last day of a computation period in order to receive an allocation. See Treas. Regs. §§1.410(b)-3(a)(1), 1.410(b)-6, 1.401(a)(26)-5(a)(1); Rev. Rul. 76-250, 1976-2 CB 124 (to the extent not superseded by the regulations). Such a provision also will not violate the nondiscrimination requirements (see Q 326).

A money purchase pension plan or a profit sharing plan will not be qualified unless the plan designates which type of plan it is. IRC Sec. 401(a)(27)(B). The IRS has ruled that amounts transferred or directly rolled over from a money purchase pension plan to an otherwise qualified profit sharing plan must continue to be subject to the restrictions on money purchase pension plans. In the absence of such restrictions, the profit sharing plan would fail to qualify under IRC Section 401(a). Rev. Rul. 94-76, 1994-2 CB 46.

Plans That Provide for Acquisition of Employer Stock

A qualified defined contribution plan, other than a profit sharing plan, that is established by an employer whose stock is not readily tradable on an established market, and that holds more than 10% of its assets in employer securities must provide that the plan participants are entitled to exercise voting rights with respect to employer stock held by the plan with regard to approval of corporate mergers, consolidations, recapitalizations, reclassifications, liquidation, dissolution, sales of substantially all of the business's assets, and similar transactions as provided in future regulations. Each participant must be given *one* vote with respect to an issue, and the trustee must vote the shares held by the plan in a proportion which takes into account the one participant/one vote requirement. IRC Secs. 401(a)(22), 409(e). *ASRS, Sec. 59, ¶485.4.*

379. What are savings and thrift plans?

Savings and thrift plans are defined contribution plans in which employee contributions generally make up a relatively large part of total contributions. Employer contributions generally equal a percentage of at least some part of the employee contributions. The Code makes no specific provision for these plans, but they may be tax qualified if they meet the requirements for a pension, profit sharing, or stock bonus plan. A savings or thrift plan may qualify as a pension plan (e.g., a money purchase plan) unless there are preretirement privileges to withdraw benefits. Frequently they qualify as profit sharing plans by providing for employer contributions out of current or accumulated profits. *ASRS, Sec. 59, ¶270.3.*

380. What special rules apply to the sale of employer securities to a defined contribution plan?

The IRS will issue rulings as to whether a proposed sale of employer stock to a qualified defined contribution plan will be a sale of stock rather than a distribution of property taxable under IRC Section 301, if certain information and representations are provided. The representations must be stated in the precise language described by the IRS; however, they basically require that: (1) there is no intention that the employer will

PENSION AND PROFIT SHARING: PLAN TYPES AND FEATURES   Q 382

redeem any of the stock from the plan; (2) the selling shareholder and certain related persons may not have more than a 20% interest in the plan (this includes a 20% interest in (a) covered compensation, (b) total account balances, or (c) any separately managed fund in the plan, except a fund that at no time may be credited with employer stock); and (3) any restrictions on the sale of the stock held by the plan and by participants are no more onerous than restrictions on a majority of shares held by other shareholders (a right of first refusal will not be considered a restriction on disposition if it meets the conditions set forth in the revenue procedure). Rev. Proc. 87-22, 1987-1 CB 718. *ASRS Sec. 59, ¶485.7.*

PENSIONS

381. What is a pension plan?

A pension plan is a qualified plan established and maintained *by an employer* primarily to provide systematically for the payment of *definitely determinable benefits* (see Q 384) to its employees over a period of years, usually for life, after retirement. The requirement that the benefits be definitely determinable may be met by providing for either fixed benefits or fixed contributions; thus, a pension plan can be either a defined benefit plan or a defined contribution plan (see, e.g., Q 382).

Under a plan that provides fixed benefits (a "defined benefit" plan), the size of the pension, or a formula to determine size, is set in advance, and by actuarial methods the annual contributions are determined which will gradually accumulate a fund sufficient to provide each employee's pension when he retires. The size of an employee's pension is usually related to his compensation, years of service, or both. Under a plan that provides for fixed contributions (a "defined contribution" or "money purchase" plan), the annual *contribution* to an employee's account (rather than his future pension) is fixed or definitely determinable, and the employee receives whatever size retirement benefit can be purchased with the funds accumulated in his account. Usually the annual contribution is a fixed percentage of the employee's compensation; in any event, it must not be related to the employer's profits. IRC Sec. 401; Treas. Reg. §1.401-1. Contributions are not considered "fixed" where an employer intentionally overfunds a money purchase pension plan. *William Bryen Co., Inc. v. Comm.*, 89 TC 689 (1987).

A pension plan cannot provide regular temporary disability income or medical expense benefits (except medical expense benefits for retired employees). However, a pension plan may provide incidental death benefits, through life insurance or otherwise (see Q 369), and disability pensions. Treas. Regs. §§1.401-1(a)(2)(i), 1.401-1(b)(1)(i); IRC Sec. 401(h); Treas. Reg. §1.401-14.

The employer deduction limit for pension plans is explained at Q 404. For the minimum funding standard that applies to pension plans, see Q 385 to Q 390. *ASRS, Sec. 59, ¶200.3.*

382. What is a target benefit plan?

A target benefit plan is a money purchase pension plan under which contributions to an employee's account are determined by reference to the amounts necessary to fund the employee's stated benefit under the plan. Treas. Reg. §1.401(a)(4)-8(b)(3)(i). Consequently, allocations under a target plan are generally weighted for both age and compensation. Although a target benefit plan is a type of defined contribution plan, it is subject to the minimum funding requirements set forth in Q 385 to Q 388.

Safe harbor requirements for target plans are set forth in the cross testing regulations under Section 401(a)(4), under which a target plan will be deemed to be nondiscriminatory. See Treas. Reg. §1.401(a)(4)-8(b)(3).

Special rules apply to target plans for meeting the requirements of IRC Section 411(b)(2) (which states that a plan may not discontinue or reduce a participant's benefit accruals or allocations because of the participant reaching a particular age). See Prop. Treas. Reg. §1.411(b)-2(c)(3)(iii). *ASRS, Sec. 59, ¶200.3.*

383. What is the maximum amount that an employer may deduct annually for contributions on behalf of employees to a qualified pension trust or annuity plan?

The maximum annual limit on deductions by an employer, including a self-employed person, for contributions to a pension trust or annuity plan is determined under rules set forth below.

(1) The employer may deduct the amount needed to fund each employee's past and current service credits distributed as a level amount or level percentage of compensation over the remaining period of his anticipated future service. However, if more than one-half of the remaining unfunded cost is attributable to three or fewer participants, the deduction of such unfunded cost for them must be spread over at least five years. IRC Sec. 404(a)(1)(A)(ii).

(2) The employer may deduct the plan's normal cost for the year, plus an amount necessary to amortize the past service credits equally over 10 years. IRC Sec. 404(a)(1)(A)(iii); Treas. Reg. §1.412(c)(3)-1(e)(3). The "normal cost" is the level annual amount that would be required to fund the employee's pension from his date of employment to his retirement date. For an illustration, see Rev. Rul. 84-62, 1984-1 CB 121. The amortizable base is limited to the unfunded costs attributable to past service liability.

(3) The employer may deduct the amount necessary to satisfy the minimum funding requirements for the plan year, if that amount is greater than the deduction allowed under either (1) or (2) above. IRC Secs. 404(a)(1)(A)(i), 404(a)(1)(D). See Q 385. This limit includes any waived funding deficiencies outstanding as of the last day of the plan year. Rev. Rul. 78-223, 1978-1 CB 125; Let. Rul. 8919073.

(4) A defined contribution plan that is subject to the funding standards of Section 412 (e.g., a money purchase plan) is treated as a stock bonus or profit sharing plan for purposes of the deduction limits; thus, it is generally subject to a deduction limit of 25% of compensation. See IRC Sec. 404(a)(3)(A)(v).

Nonetheless, in computing the deduction for a contribution to a defined benefit plan, no benefit in excess of the IRC Section 415 limit may be taken into consideration. Similarly, in computing the deduction to a defined contribution plan, the contribution taken into account must be reduced by any annual additions in excess of the IRC Section 415 limit for the year. IRC Sec. 404(j)(1).

PENSION AND PROFIT SHARING: PLAN TYPES AND FEATURES   Q 383

No more than the full funding limit (see Q 386) may be deducted. Thus, no deduction is allowed for a contribution in excess of the amount needed to fully fund the plan. IRC Sec. 404(a)(1)(A). In determining the deductible amount, the same funding method and actuarial assumptions must be used as those used for the minimum funding standard. IRC Sec. 404(a)(1)(A); Treas. Reg. §1.404(a)-14(d). The IRS has denied the deduction where it believes contributions are based on unreasonable actuarial assumptions. See TAMs 9250002, 9249003, 9244006. The question of what constitutes reasonable actuarial assumptions was once the subject of extensive litigation; however, after a steady stream of losses in the Tax Court and federal courts, the IRS announced its concession on the issues that it lost in those cases. See IR-95-43, June 7, 1995; *Vinson & Elkins v. Comm.*, 93-2 USTC ¶50,632 (5th Cir. 1993); *Rhoades, McKee & Boer v. U.S.*, 93-2 USTC ¶50,425 (W.D.MI 1993); *Wachtell, Lipton, Rosen & Katz v. Comm.*, TC Memo 1992-392, aff'd 94-1 USTC ¶50,272 (2d Cir. 1994))

In guidance for Section 412(i) plans (see Q 407, Q 408), the IRS has also stated that the portion of contributions attributable to "excess life insurance coverage" does not constitute "normal cost" and, thus, is not deductible. Similarly, contributions to pay premiums for the disability waiver of premium feature with respect to such excess coverage are not deductible. Instead, such amounts are carried over to later years (but may be subject to a nondeductible contribution penalty; see Q 367). Generally "excess" coverage refers to contracts held on behalf of a participant whose benefit payable at normal retirement age is not equal to the amount provided at normal retirement age with respect to the contracts held on behalf of that participant, *or* contracts providing for a death benefit with respect to a participant in excess of the death benefit provided to that participant under that plan. See Rev. Rul. 2004-20, 2004-10 IRB 546.

In computing the deduction under (1), (2), or (3) above and the amount of the full funding limit, a plan may not take into consideration any adjustments to the IRC Section 415 limits before the year in which the adjustment takes effect. IRC Sec. 404(j)(2); Treas. Reg. §1.412(c)(3)-1(d)(i). However, the deductible limit for a defined benefit plan may reflect costs based on up to 100% of projected high three-year average compensation, even if it exceeds 100% of the employee's current high three-year average compensation (provided it does not exceed the current dollar limitation). Costs may also reflect a lower than current defined contribution fraction, provided that the projected fraction does not anticipate future increases in the defined contribution dollar limit. Notice 83-10, 1983-1 CB 536, F-1.

If the employer contributes more than the maximum deductible amount in any year, the excess amount may be carried over and deducted in succeeding years within the same limitations, even if the plan is no longer qualified in those succeeding years. IRC Secs. 404(a)(1)(E), 404(a)(2). (But see Q 367 for an excise tax on employer contributions that exceed the deduction limits.) However, a contribution to a defined contribution plan in excess of the IRC Section 415 limits (see Q 332, Q 377) may not be carried over and deducted in a subsequent year, even if the contribution is required under the minimum funding rules. Notice 83-10, above, F-1, F-3.

If, in the case of a defined benefit plan, more than one plan year is associated with the taxable year of the employer due to a change in plan years, then the deductible limit for the employer's taxable year must be adjusted as described in Rev. Proc. 87-27, 1987-1 CB 769. Certain collectively bargained plans may elect a special deduction rule. IRC Secs. 404(a)(1)(B), 404(a)(1)(C). See also, GCM 39677 (10-30-87). If an employer

2006 Tax Facts on Insurance & Employee Benefits

transfers funds from one pension plan to another, the employer realizes income if the previous deduction resulted in a tax benefit. Rev. Rul. 73-528, 1973-2 CB 13. *ASRS, Sec. 59, ¶540.3.*

384. What special qualification requirements apply to pension plans but not to profit sharing plans?

Definitely Determinable Benefits

A pension plan must provide for the payment of definitely determinable benefits to employees upon retirement or over a period of years after their retirement, or to their beneficiaries, benefits to be determined without regard to the employer's profits. Treas. Regs. §§1.401-1(a)(2)(i), 1.401-1(b)(1)(i). Benefits actually payable need not be definitely determinable, provided the contributions can be determined actuarially on the basis of definitely determinable benefits. This is the theoretical basis for defined benefit plans of the "assumed benefit" or "variable benefit" type (so-called "target" plans). Benefits are "definitely determinable" under a money purchase pension plan that calls for contributions of a fixed percentage of each employee's compensation. Treas. Reg. §1.401-1(b)(1)(i).

Benefits that vary with the increase or decrease in the market value of the assets from which such benefits are payable or that vary with the fluctuations of a specified and generally recognized cost-of-living index are consistent with a plan providing for definitely determinable benefits. Rev. Rul. 185, 1953-2 CB 202. Also, a plan provides a definitely determinable benefit if, in the case of an insured plan, the practice of the insurer is to provide a retirement annuity that is the higher of (1) an annuity bought at an annuity rate guaranteed in the contract surrendered in exchange therefor, or (2) the same type of annuity purchased at current annuity rates. Rev. Rul. 78-56, 1978-1 CB 116. The IRS determined that a governmental cash balance plan in which the interest rate credited on contributions was set by a board appointed under state law nonetheless provided a definitely determinable benefit. Let. Rul. 9645031.

A defined benefit plan will not be treated as providing definitely determinable benefits unless the actuarial assumptions used to determine the amount of any benefit (including any optional or early retirement benefit) are specified in the plan in a way that precludes employer discretion. IRC Sec. 401(a)(25); Rev. Rul. 79-90, 1979-1 CB 155.

Under certain plans a participant receives not only a defined benefit specified in the plan but amounts which have been credited to individual accounts each year based on excess earnings, in other words, actual trust earnings in excess of the investment yield assumption used in the valuation of the cost of providing the defined benefit (an excess earnings plan). Where contributions to such plans are discretionary, the amount of excess interest allocations to the defined contribution portion of the plan is not definitely determinable, and the plan will not qualify. Rev. Rul. 78-403, 1978-2 CB 153.

Retirement benefits would not be definitely determinable under a plan that permitted the withdrawal of employer contributions. Hence, a pension plan may not permit the withdrawal of employer contributions or earnings thereon, even in the case of financial need, before death, retirement, disability, severance of employment, or termination of the plan. See Rev. Rul. 69-277, 1969-1 CB 116; Rev. Rul. 74-417, 1974-2 CB 131. (Withdrawals may be made once the employee has reached normal retirement age even if the employee has not actually retired. See Rev. Rul. 71-24, 1971-1 CB 114; Rev.

PENSION AND PROFIT SHARING: PLAN TYPES AND FEATURES   Q 384

Rul. 73-448, 1973-2 CB 136.) For the same reason, a pension plan may not permit the withdrawal of mandatory employee contributions or, under a money purchase thrift plan, employee contributions to which employer contributions are geared before such stated events. Rev. Rul. 56-693, 1956-2 CB 282; Rev. Rul. 74-417, above. However, a pension plan may permit withdrawal of all or part of an employee's own contributions when he discontinues participation in the plan, even though he continues to work for the employer. Rev. Rul. 60-281, 1960-2 CB 146.

A pension plan may permit an employee to withdraw his nondeductible *voluntary* contributions without terminating his membership in the plan, provided the withdrawal will not affect the member's participation in the plan, the employer's past or future contributions on his behalf, or the basic benefits provided by both the participant's and the employer's compulsory contributions. Rev. Rul. 60-323, 1960-2 CB 148; Rev. Rul. 69-277, 1969-1 CB 116.

The IRS takes the position that all benefits payable under the plan, including early retirement, disability pension, and preretirement death benefits, must be definitely determinable. Thus, a pension plan funded by a combination of life insurance and an auxiliary fund, which provided a pension upon early retirement or disability, the amount of which was based in part on the participant's interest in the auxiliary fund, failed to qualify because the employer was not required to maintain the fund at a particular level or to make contributions at any particular time. Rev. Rul. 69-427, 1969-2 CB 87. Similarly, a defined benefit pension plan that provided a preretirement death benefit equal to the amount of the pension benefit funded for a participant as of the date of his death failed to qualify. Rev. Rul. 72-97, 1972-1 CB 106. Likewise, a change in actuarial factors that affects the calculation of a participant's optional or early retirement benefit would result in plan disqualification. Rev. Rul. 81-12, 1981-1 CB 228.

Benefits under a defined benefit plan will be considered definitely determinable even if they are offset by benefits provided by a profit sharing plan, if determination of the amount of offset is not subject to the employer's discretion. The actuarial basis and the time for determining the offset must be specified in the defined benefit plan in order to preclude employer discretion. Rev. Rul. 76-259, 1976-2 CB 111.

Pension benefits will not fail to be definitely determinable because a factor or condition, determinable only after retirement, is used to compute benefits in accordance with an express provision in the plan, if the factor or condition is not subject to the discretion of the employer. Rev. Rul. 80-122, 1980-1 CB 84.

Forfeitures

Related to the definitely determinable benefits rule is the requirement that a pension plan provide that forfeitures must not be applied to increase the benefits any employee would otherwise receive under the plan. IRC Sec. 401(a)(8).

Retirement Age

Pension and annuity plans are retirement plans; thus, they must be established primarily to provide definitely determinable benefits at normal retirement age.

The normal retirement age in a pension or annuity plan is the lowest age specified in the plan at which the employee has the right to retire without the consent of the employer and receive retirement benefits based on service to date of retirement at the full rate set forth in the plan (i.e., without actuarial or similar reduction because of retirement before some later specified age). Ordinarily, the normal retirement age under pension and annuity plans is 65, but a pension plan may provide for a normal retirement age of any age less than 65.

If normal retirement age is less than age 62, and benefits begin before that age, the defined benefit dollar limit must be actuarially reduced for purposes of the IRC Section 415 limits on benefits (see Q 332, Q 377). IRC Sec. 415(b)(2)(C). The Code also requires that the accrued benefit of an employee who retires after age 70½ be actuarially increased to take into account any period after age 70½ in which the employee was not receiving any benefits under the plan. See IRC Sec. 401(a)(9)(C)(ii). Guidance for implementing this requirement is set forth in regulations finalized in 2004 (Treas. Reg. §1.401(a)(9)-6, A-7). See Q 342.

An actuarial assumption that employees will retire at a normal retirement age specified in the plan that is a lower age than they normally retire, could result in computation of amounts that are not currently deductible if the assumption causes the actuarial assumptions in the aggregate not to be reasonable. Rev. Rul. 78-331, 1978-2 CB 158. The IRS has challenged the use of normal retirement ages under age 65 in small defined benefit plans (i.e., plans covering from one to five employees). See Q 383. However, a pension plan may permit early retirement, and any reasonable optional early retirement age will generally be acceptable.

While a pension plan must provide primarily retirement benefits, it has been determined that a plan could provide for a lump sum distribution to an employee who has reached both 59½ and normal retirement age, even if he continues to work for the employer. Special ruling, 10-29-76; Let. Rul. 7740031. Furthermore, a pension plan may provide for payment of the balance to the credit of an employee on plan termination. IRC Sec. 401(a)(20). A plan which permits an employee to elect death benefits to the exclusion of retirement benefits will not qualify. Rev. Rul. 56-656, 1956-2 CB 280. However, this rule does not prevent a plan from providing "incidental" death benefits. See Q 346, Q 369.

Phased retirement. Proposed regulations were issued in late 2004 that would allow pension plan participants (other than key employees—see Q 357) at least 59½ years of age to *voluntarily* reduce their hours (at least 20%) and receive a pro rata portion of their pension annuity. Under the proposal, all early retirement benefits, retirement type subsidies and optional forms of benefit available upon full retirement would have to be offered in the event of a phased retirement, except that payment could not be made in the form of a single-sum distribution or other eligible rollover distribution. An employee engaged in phased retirement essentially would have a "dual status"; he would remain an employee for purposes of plan participation, with full-time status imputed, except for the proportionate reduction in compensation for the lower number of hours worked, but he would receive a portion of his pension annuity corresponding to the reduction in his hours. The regulations do not take effect and may not be relied upon until they are finalized. See REG-114726-04, 69 Fed. Reg. 65108 (November 10, 2004); Prop. Treas. Regs. §§1.401(a)-3, 1.401(a)-1(b)(1)(i). *ASRS, Sec. 59, ¶485.1.*

Minimum Funding Standard

385. What is the minimum funding standard for pension plans?

In order to assure that pension plans are adequately funded, the Code provides for a *minimum funding standard;* that is, the employer must contribute at least a minimum

PENSION AND PROFIT SHARING: PLAN TYPES AND FEATURES   Q 385

amount to its qualified defined benefit, money purchase pension, or annuity plan. Profit sharing and stock bonus plans (see Q 391 to Q 409), certain government and church plans, certain employee-pay-all plans, and certain fully insured plans (i.e., Section 412(i) plans; see Q 408) are exempt from this minimum funding requirement. IRC Sec. 412(h). Relief from the minimum funding standard was provided for certain employers located in (or with record keepers in) the Hurricane Katrina disaster area. See Notice 2005-84, 2005-46 IRB 959; see also KETRA 2005, Sec. 403(b).

The minimum funding standard is *not* a qualification requirement. *Anthes v. Comm.*, 81 TC 1 (1983). See Q 322. Waiver of the minimum funding standard because of hardship may be available in some circumstances. See Q 389.

To determine its minimum contribution, an employer must establish a separate *funding standard account* for each separate plan. IRC Sec. 412(b); Rev. Rul. 81-137, 1981-1 CB 232. A plan that has a funding method requiring contributions at least equal to those required under the entry age normal cost method may also maintain an *alternative minimum funding standard account*. IRC Sec. 412(g).

Under the regular funding rules, the funding standard account (and alternative account, if one is maintained) is to be charged with certain liabilities and credited with certain amounts each plan year. If the charges to the funding standard account for all plan years beginning after the standard is first applicable to the plan, exceed the credits (or, if less, the excess of the charges to the alternative minimum funding standard account for the same years over the credits) the plan has an "accumulated funding deficiency" to the extent of the excess. The minimum funding standard is satisfied when there is no accumulated funding deficiency; that is, when the balance in the funding standard account (or the alternative minimum funding standard account) at the end of the year is zero. IRC Sec. 412(a).

Charges: The liabilities that must be currently funded and charged to the funding standard account under the regular funding rules are: (1) "normal cost" (the level annual amount that would be required to fund the employee's pension from his date of employment to his retirement); and (2) the amounts required to *amortize*, in equal installments, until fully amortized: (a) the unfunded past service liability that existed on the first day the section applied to the plan over a period of 30 years (40 years if the plan was in existence on January 1, 1974), (b) any net increase in unfunded past service liability because of plan amendments in the year over a period of 30 years, (c) any net experience loss over a period of five years (15 years if a multiemployer plan), (d) any net loss from changes in actuarial assumptions over a period of 10 years (30 years if a multiemployer plan), (e) each previously waived funding deficiency over a period of five years (15 years if a multiemployer plan), and (f) any amount previously credited to the account as a result of using the alternative minimum funding standard account as the funding standard over a period of five years. See IRC Sec. 412(b)(2). Employers must generally amortize the amount that they would have been required to contribute, but for the increase, over 20 years. IRC Sec. 412(b)(2)(E) (see Q 375). Special rules apply to funding methods that do not provide for amortization bases. Rev. Rul. 2000-20, 2000-1 CB 880.

Credits: Amounts that are credited to the funding standard account under the regular funding rules include: (1) employer contributions; (2) amounts necessary to *amortize*, in equal installments, (a) any net decrease in unfunded past service liability arising from amendments over a period of 30 years, (b) any net experience gain over a period of five years (15 years if a multiemployer plan), and (c) any gain from changes in actuarial assumptions over a period of 10 years (30 years if a multiemployer plan); (3) the amount of the funding standard that has been waived by the Secretary of Treasury because of substantial business hardship; and (4) an adjustment, if the alternative minimum funding standard was used in a previous year. IRC Sec. 412(b)(3). Amortization periods may be longer in certain circumstances. See IRC Secs. 412(e), 412(b)(6).

Guidelines for determining experience gains and losses are set forth in Rev. Rul. 81-213, 1981-2 CB 101. Dividends, rate credits, and forfeitures are treated as experience gains if the plan is funded solely through a group deferred annuity contract, the annual single premium is treated as the normal cost, *and* an amount necessary to pay, in equal annual installments over the amortization period, the single premium necessary to provide all past service benefits not initially funded, is treated as the annual amortization amount. Treas. Reg. §1.412(b)-2.

Alternative minimum funding standard account. The alternative minimum funding standard account is charged only with (1) the lesser of (a) normal cost under the plan's funding method, or (b) normal cost under the unit credit method; (2) any excess of the value of accrued benefits over the fair market value of plan assets; and (3) any excess of credits over charges to the account in all prior years. The alternative funding standard account is credited with the employer's contribution and is also charged or credited with interest. IRC Sec. 412(g)(2); Prop. Treas. Reg. §1.412(g)-1.

Interest. The funding standard account is also charged or credited with interest at a rate consistent with that used to determine plan costs. IRC Sec. 412(b)(5)(A). A funding method that does not properly charge or credit interest is not a reasonable method. Rev. Rul. 81-214, 1981-2 CB 105. The rate of interest used to determine current liability is a blended corporate rate based on investment grade long-term corporate bonds. See IRC Secs. 412(l)(7)(C)(i)(IV); 412(b)(5)(B)(i)(II); Notice 2004-34, 2004-18 IRB 848.

Deficit reduction contributions. An additional charge to the funding standard account (and, thus, increased contributions) are required for certain defined benefit plans (other than multiemployer plans) that have more than 100 participants; *and* (2) have a *funded current liability percentage* for any plan year below certain limits. See IRC Secs. 412(l)(1), 412(l)(6). However, relief from this requirement is available for certain airlines and steel manufacturers. See 412(i)(12).

Other provisions. Charges and credits in the case of a change in benefit structure are discussed in Rev. Rul. 77-2, 1977-1 CB 120. Guidelines for adjusting the funding standard requirements upon the spinoff of plan assets to a new plan are provided in Rev. Rul. 81-212, 1981-2 CB 99.

The minimum amount that an employer is required to contribute in order to fund a money purchase pension plan or target benefit plan is generally the contribution amount for each year as stated in the plan formula. *ASRS, Sec. 59, ¶¶500-530.*

386. What is the full funding limitation for pension plans?

In some instances, a plan might be overfunded if the employer contributed the full amount of the minimum funding standard. In this case, the employer is required

PENSION AND PROFIT SHARING: PLAN TYPES AND FEATURES   Q 388

to contribute only the excess, if any, of the accrued liability (including normal cost) under the plan, *over* the fair market value of the plan's assets. See IRC Secs. 412(c)(6), 412(c)(7). This limit on required contributions is called the *full funding limitation*. All amounts being amortized under the funding standard account will be considered fully amortized. IRC Secs. 412(c)(6), 412(c)(7). See Prop. Treas. Reg. §1.412(c)(6)-1.

"Accrued liability" is determined under the entry age normal funding method *if* it cannot be directly calculated under the funding method used for the plan by meeting conditions set forth in Rev. Rul. 81-13, 1981-1 CB 229. *ASRS, Sec. 59, ¶500.3*.

387. When are pension plan contributions credited for funding standard account purposes?

The funding standard account is credited with the contributions *for* the plan year. IRC Sec. 412(b)(3)(A). The employer has a grace period of 8½ months after the plan year ends to make contributions for that plan year. IRC Sec. 412(c)(10); Temp. Treas. Reg. §11.412(c)-12(b). This is true even with respect to the plan year in which the plan terminates. Rev. Rul. 79-237, 1979-2 CB 190, as modified by Rev. Rul. 89-87, 1989-2 CB 81. A contribution was not considered timely made where, prior to the expiration of the 8½ months, an employer merely segregated a sum sufficient to fund its plan contributions in an extra checking account in the name of the employer, not in the name of the plan. *D.J. Lee, M.D., Inc. v. Comm.*, 92 TC 291 (1989), *aff'd on other grounds*, 91-1 USTC 87,881 (6th Cir. 1991).

The rules governing the time when a contribution is deemed made for the purposes of crediting the funding standard account are generally independent of the rules governing the time when a contribution is deemed made for deduction purposes. Temp. Treas. Reg. §11.412(c)-12(b)(2); Prop. Treas. Reg. §1.412(c)(10)-1(c). Thus, contributions made for one plan year but carried over to a later tax year for deduction purposes may not be credited to the account as a contribution for the later year. Rev. Rul. 77-151, 1977-1 CB 121. However, a contribution made during the grace period on account of the preceding tax year may be made for and credited to the account for the current plan year. Rev. Rul. 77-82, 1977-1 CB 121. Likewise, a contribution made in and deducted for the current plan year may be credited for the previous year for purposes of the funding rules if made during the grace period. See Let. Rul. 9107033. *ASRS, Sec. 59, ¶530.3*.

388. What other special requirements apply when a qualified plan is subject to the minimum funding standard?

Funding for expected increases. Under the full funding limitation, a plan generally must fund for certain expected increases due to benefits accruing during the plan year. See IRC Sec. 412(c)(7)(E)(i)(I). Any resulting increase in unfunded liability must be amortized over 30 years. Although a change in benefit provisions of a plan may not be assumed under a reasonable funding method, future salary may be assumed to change without being considered a benefit change. Thus, funding must be based on projected benefits reflecting expected salary history, but only to the extent that the projected benefits do not exceed the maximum benefit permitted under the current plan provisions. For example, funding for a benefit of 90% of the participant's salary for his high three consecutive years may be based on 90% of projected salary, but not in excess of the maximum dollar benefit provided under the plan for the current year. Rev. Rul. 81-195, 1981-2 CB 104.

2006 Tax Facts on Insurance & Employee Benefits

Annual valuation. Experience gains and losses are to be determined and plan liability valued at least once a year. IRC Sec. 412(c)(9). Normal costs, accrued liabilities, and experience gains and losses are to be determined under the funding method used to determine costs under the plan. Plan assets are to be valued by any reasonable actuarial method that takes into account fair market value and is permitted under regulations (see Treas. Reg. §1.412(c)(2)-1(b)(6)). However, asset valuations may not be based on a range of 85% to 115% of average value. OBRA '87, Sec. 9303(c).

Ordinarily, the annual valuation must be made during the plan year or within one month prior to the beginning of the plan year. However, a valuation date from the immediately preceding plan year may be used, provided that, as of that date, the plan assets are not less than 100% of the plan's current liability. IRC Sec. 412(c)(9)(B). A change to a prior year valuation may not be made unless plan assets are not less than 125% of the plan's current liability. IRC Section 412(c)(9)(B)(iv).

Each actuarial assumption must be reasonable, or when aggregated, result in a total contribution equivalent to the amount that would be determined if each were reasonable. In the case of multiemployer plans, actuarial assumptions need only be reasonable in the aggregate. Of course, all actuarial assumptions must offer the actuary's best estimate of anticipated experience. IRC Sec. 412(c)(3).

Change in funding method. Automatic approval is available for certain changes in a plan's funding method. Examples of such changes would include approvals: (1) to remedy unreasonable allocation of costs; (2) for fully funded terminated plans; (3) for takeover plans; (4) for changes in valuation software; (5) for *de minimis* mergers; (6) for certain mergers with the same plan year and a merger date of first or last day of plan year; (7) for certain mergers involving a designated transition period. See Rev. Proc. 2000-40, 2000-2 CB 357.

The IRS will automatically approve a change in the plan's funding method made in order to take advantage of the plan valuation exception (discussed above) if it is made within the first three years during which the plan is eligible to make the change. EGTRRA 2001 Conf. Rep., *reprinted in* the General Explanation of EGTRRA 2001, p. 184.

For a funding method change that is not covered by the automatic approval procedures above, the plan sponsor (or its authorized representative) must request approval in writing directly from the IRS. The request must contain identifying information about the plan and the employer sponsoring it, as well as a description of the previous funding method, a brief statement of the reason for the change, an explanation of why the change does not qualify for automatic approval, certain actuarial information, a statement of the plan's unfunded liability, and the plan's basic funding formula. A request should be submitted no later than the close of the plan year for which the change in funding method is to be effective. Rev. Proc. 2000-41, 2000-2 CB 371.

Plan amendments. Defined benefit pension plans generally are not permitted to anticipate amendments (even if adopted within the remedial amendment period) in determining funding, except as specifically required by IRC Section 412(c)(12). Rev. Proc. 98-42, 1998-2 CB 55.

Multiemployer plan. For a multiemployer plan maintained pursuant to a collective bargaining agreement, the minimum funding standard is determined as if all participants

PENSION AND PROFIT SHARING: PLAN TYPES AND FEATURES   Q 389

in the plan were employed by a single employer. IRC Sec. 413(b)(5). Projected benefit increases scheduled to take effect during the term of the agreement must be taken into account. IRC Sec. 412(c)(12). In contrast, each employer in a *multiple employer plan* is generally treated as maintaining a separate plan for purposes of the minimum funding rules, unless the plan uses a method for determining required contributions under which each employer contributes at least the amount that would be required if each employer maintained a separate plan. IRC Sec. 413(c)(4).

Controlled groups. If the employer maintaining the plan is a member of a group treated as a single employer under the controlled group, common control, or affiliated service provisions (see Q 359, Q 360), then each member of the group is jointly and severally liable for the amount of any contributions required under the minimum funding standard or the amount of any required installments to the plan. IRC Sec. 412(c)(11).

Year of termination. The minimum funding standard continues to apply even if the plan later becomes nonqualified. However, it does not apply in years after the end of the plan year in which the plan terminates completely. For guidelines as to the application of the minimum funding standard to the plan year in which a plan terminates, see Rev. Rul. 79-237, 1979-2 CB 190, as modified by Rev. Rul. 89-87, 1989-2 CB 81. See also, Prop. Treas. Reg. §1.412(b)-4. The minimum funding standard must be re-established if the terminated plan is restored to the sponsoring employer by the PBGC. See Treas. Reg. §1.412(c)(1)-3, TD 8494, 1993-2 CB 203. *ASRS, Sec. 59, ¶¶500-530.*

389. What is the penalty for underfunding a qualified plan that is subject to the minimum funding standard?

If a plan subject to the "minimum funding standard" (see Q 385 to Q 388) fails to meet it, the employer sponsoring the plan is penalized by an excise tax, but the plan will not be disqualified. TIR 1334 (1/8/75), M-5. Imposition of the tax is automatic; there is no exception for unintentionally or inadvertently failing to meet the standard, nor for having intended to terminate the plan. See *D.J. Lee, M.D., Inc. v. Comm.*, 91-1 USTC ¶50,218 (6th Cir. 1991); *Lee Eng'g Supply Co., Inc. v. Comm.*, 101 TC 189 (1993).

An initial tax of 10% (5% in the case of multiemployer plans) of the amount of the accumulated funding deficiency (see Q 385 to Q 375), determined as of the end of the plan year, must be paid each tax year by the employer responsible for contributing to the plan. IRC Sec. 4971(a). An employer was liable for the 10% tax where a contribution was made timely according to the terms of the plan, but not within the period specified in IRC Section 412. *Wenger v. Comm.*, TC Memo 2000-156.

An additional tax of 100% is imposed on the employer to the extent that this accumulated funding deficiency is not corrected by the earlier of: (1) the date of mailing of a notice of deficiency with respect to the 10% tax; or (2) the date on which the 10% tax is assessed. IRC Sec. 4971(b). However, this tax will be abated if the deficiency is corrected within 90 days after the date when of the notice of deficiency with respect to the additional 100% tax is mailed. This period may be extended by the Secretary of the Treasury. IRC Secs. 4961, 4963(e).

An additional tax is applied to certain defined benefit plans with a funded current liability percentage of less than 100% that have a "liquidity shortfall" for any quarter during a plan year. IRC Secs. 4971(f), 412(m)(5). Such a plan may be subject to a tax of 10% of the excess of the amount of the liquidity shortfall for any quarter over the amount of such shortfall paid by the required installment for the quarter. IRC Sec. 4971(f). However, if the shortfall was due to reasonable cause and not willful neglect, and reasonable steps have been taken to remedy the liquidity shortfall, the Secretary of the Treasury has the discretion to waive part or all of the penalty. IRC Sec. 4971(f)(4).

An uncorrected deficiency will continue in later years and will be increased by interest charges until it is paid. IRC Sec. 412(b)(5). When an employer fails to contribute a plan's normal cost in any year, that amount will not, thereafter, become a past service cost to be amortized. The funding standard account will show the amount as a deficiency subject to tax each year until corrected.

If the employer is a member of a group that is treated as a single employer under the controlled group, common control, or affiliated services group provisions (see Q 359, Q 360), then each member of the group is jointly and severally liable for any tax payable under IRC Section 4971. IRC Sec. 4971(e). The tax is due for the tax year in which (or with which) the plan year ends. The IRS determined that general partners were jointly and severally liable for a partnership's excise tax obligation resulting from failure to satisfy the minimum funding standard. Let. Rul. 9414001.

Where a plan chooses to keep both a funding standard account and an alternative minimum funding standard account, the tax will be based on the lower minimum funding requirement. IRC Secs. 4971(c)(1), 412(a).

None of the excise taxes payable under IRC Section 4971 are deductible. IRC Sec. 275(a)(6).

If a plan is maintained: (1) pursuant to a collective bargaining agreement; or (2) by more than one employer, the liability of each employer will be based first on the employers' respective delinquencies in meeting their required contributions, and then on the basis of the employers' respective liabilities for contributions. IRC Secs. 413(b)(6), 413(c)(5).

The tax does not apply in years after the end of the plan year in which the plan terminates. However, if the accumulated funding deficiency has not been reduced to zero as of the end of that plan year, then the 100% tax is due for the plan year in which the plan terminates. Rev. Rul. 79-237, 1979-2 CB 190, as modified by Rev. Rul. 89-87, 1989-2 CB 81.

For further guidance on the tax penalty for underfunding, see Treas. Reg. §54.4971-1, and Prop. Treas. Regs. §§54.4971-2 to 54.4971-3. *ASRS, Sec. 59, ¶500.4.*

390. Can the minimum funding standard for qualified plans be waived?

Under limited circumstances, the IRS may grant a waiver of the minimum funding standard. In order to obtain such a waiver, the employer sponsoring the plan must demonstrate that imposition of the 100% tax would be (1) a substantial business hardship; and (2) adverse to the interest of plan participants in the aggregate. See IRC Sec. 412(d). Updated procedures for requesting a waiver of the 100% tax are set forth in Rev. Proc. 2004-15, 2004-7 IRB 490. See, e.g., Let. Ruls. 200349005, 9849024. The IRS may

PENSION AND PROFIT SHARING: PLAN TYPES AND FEATURES   Q 391

grant a waiver contingent upon certain conditions being met; if they are not met, the waiver is void retroactively. An employer sponsoring a plan may request a modification of a conditional waiver of the minimum funding requirements by private letter ruling request. See, e.g., Let. Ruls. 9852051, 9849031. The IRS has privately ruled that waiver is appropriate where the hardship is likely to be temporary (Let Rul. 9846047), but not where the hardship is of a permanent nature (Let. Rul. 9846049). Under certain circumstances, the IRS may approve a retroactive plan amendment reducing plan liabilities due to substantial business hardship. See Let. Rul. 9736044.

Employers sponsoring certain terminated single-employer defined benefit plans may obtain a waiver of the 100% tax imposed on an accumulated funding deficiency. In order to obtain the waiver, these conditions must be met: (1) the plan must be subject to Title IV of ERISA; (2) the plan must be terminated in a standard termination under ERISA section 4041; (3) plan participants must not be entitled to any portion of residual assets remaining after all liabilities of the plan to participants and their beneficiaries have been satisfied; (4) excise taxes that have been (or could be) imposed under IRC Section 4971(a) must have been paid for all taxable years (including the taxable year related to the year of plan termination); and (5) the plan must have filed all applicable forms in the 5500 series (including Schedule B) for all plan years (including the year of plan termination). See Rev. Proc. 2000-17, 2000-1 CB 766. *ASRS, Sec. 59, ¶530.4*

PROFIT SHARING PLANS

391. What is a profit sharing plan?

A profit sharing plan, as the name implies, is a plan for sharing employer profits with the employees. A profit sharing plan need not provide a definite, predetermined formula for determining the amount of profits to be shared. But in the absence of a definite formula, there must be recurring and substantial contributions, and contributions must not be made at such times and in such amounts that the plan *in operation* discriminates in favor of highly compensated employees. See Treas. Reg. §1.401-1(b)(1)(ii). A profit sharing plan may explicitly provide for investment primarily in qualifying employer securities. ERISA Secs. 407(b)(1), 407(d)(3). See Q 411.

For an explanation of specific qualification requirements applicable to profit sharing plans, see Q 393. The qualification requirements that apply to 401(k) plans are explained at Q 394 to Q 406. The employer deduction limit for profit sharing contributions is explained at Q 392.

A profit sharing plan *must* provide a definite, predetermined formula for allocating the contributions among the participants, and for distributing the accumulated funds to the employees after a fixed number of years (at least two), the attainment of a stated age, or upon prior occurrence of some event such as layoff, illness, disability, retirement, death, or severance of employment. The allocation formula is generally related to compensation, although age, service and other factors may be given consideration (see Q 329). A profit sharing plan cannot provide for allocations or distributions based on predetermined benefits, since such a plan would be a pension plan. Although a profit sharing plan is primarily a plan of deferred compensation, the plan may use funds in an employee's account to provide incidental life or health insurance for him or his family; see Q 358 to Q 359. Treas. Reg. §1.401-1(b)(1)(ii); Rev. Rul. 68-24, 1968-1 CB 150; Rev. Rul. 69-414, 1969-2 CB 59; Rev. Rul. 71-295, 1971-2 CB 184; *Bernard McMe-*

namy Contractors, Inc. v. Comm., 27 AFTR 2d 71-1307 (8th Cir. 1971); *Auner v. U.S.*, 27 AFTR 2d 71-796 (7th Cir. 1971).

A tax-exempt "non-profit" charitable organization may maintain a profit sharing plan, including a 401(k) plan. IRC Sec. 401(k)(4)(B); GCM 38283 (2-15-80). *ASRS, Sec. 59, ¶210.*

392. How much may an employer deduct for its contributions to a qualified profit sharing or stock bonus plan?

The employer's deduction for contributions to a profit sharing or stock bonus plan is the greater of (1) 25% of the compensation otherwise paid or accrued during the taxable year to the employees participating in the plan; or (2) the amount that the employer is required to contribute to the trust under the SIMPLE 401(k) requirements for the year (see Q 400). IRC Sec. 404(a)(3)(A); Treas. Reg. §1.404(a)-9.

The amount of annual compensation of each employee taken into account for purposes of this limitation may not exceed $220,000 (in 2006, as indexed). IRC Sec. 404(l). *Compensation* for this purpose is Section 415(c)(3) compensation, which includes elective deferrals under Section 401(k) and Section 457 plans, salary reduction contributions to Section 125 cafeteria plans, and qualified transportation fringe benefits under Section 132(f). IRC Section 404(a)(12). In the case of a self-employed person, "earned income" is used instead of "compensation." See Q 418.

"Contributions," for purposes of the deduction limit, do not include elective deferrals (see Q 396), and elective deferrals are not themselves subject to any limitation contained in Section 404. IRC Secs. 404(a)(3), 404(a)(7), 404(a)(9).

Contributions allocated to life and health insurance are included in the 25% limit. A terminating employee's compensation for the final year is included in the 25% only if he shares in profits for the final year. See Rev. Rul. 65-295, 1965-2 CB 148. Compensation paid to seasonal and part-time employees who are not eligible to participate in the plan may not be included in calculating the 25% limit; neither can compensation paid to employees who terminate before any allocation is ever made and whose allocations made after termination would be immediately forfeitable. See *Dallas Dental Labs v. Comm.*, 72 TC 117 (1979).

Where contributions are made to the trusts of two or more profit sharing or stock bonus plans, the trusts are considered a single trust for purposes of the 25% limit. IRC Sec. 404(a)(3)(A)(iv). The limit is applied by aggregating all contributions to such plans and limiting the total to 25% of the aggregate compensation of the employees covered by the plans. See Let. Rul. 9635045.

If more than the 25% limit is contributed in any year, the excess (called a *contribution carry-over*) may be deducted in succeeding years. However, nondeductible contributions are generally subject to a 10% excise tax. See Q 367. For any succeeding year, however, the deduction for current contributions and contribution carry-overs cannot exceed 25% of participating payroll for the taxable year. See Treas. Reg. §1.404(a)-9(e). Excess contributions made in a year when the trust is exempt may be carried over and deducted in a succeeding year even though the trust is no longer exempt in the succeeding year. Treas. Reg. §1.404(a)-9(a).

PENSION AND PROFIT SHARING: PLAN TYPES AND FEATURES   Q 393

The amount of contributions taken into account by profit sharing or stock bonus plans must be reduced by any annual additions in excess of the IRC Section 415 limits. IRC Sec. 404(j)(1). The excess amount may not be carried over and deducted in a later year. Notice 83-10, 1983-1 CB 536, F-1.

Contributions do not need to be made from current or accumulated profits to be deductible. See IRC Sec. 401(a)(27).

Restorative payments. Amounts paid to a defined contribution plan, to the extent they restore plan losses that result from a fiduciary breach (or a reasonable risk of liability for a fiduciary breach), are not contributions for purposes of the deduction limit. Rev. Rul. 2002-45, 2002-2 CB 116; see Let. Ruls. 9506048, 9628031. The same reasoning was applied in a 1998 private ruling where an employer made a restorative contribution to replace plan losses in derivatives, in order to avoid litigation with plan participants. See Let. Rul. 9807028. In contrast, payments that are made to a plan to make up for losses due to market fluctuations, but not due to a fiduciary breach, *will* be treated as contributions subject to the limit, not as restorative payments. Rev. Rul. 2002-45, above. Payments back to a plan to offset annuity surrender charges were treated as contributions in one ruling (Let. Rul. 200317048) but as restorative payments in another (Let. Rul. 200337017). *ASRS, Sec. 59, ¶540.4.*

393. What special qualification requirements apply to profit sharing plans but not to pension plans?

A profit sharing plan is a plan for sharing employer profits with employees or their beneficiaries. The plan must provide (1) a definite predetermined *formula* for allocating contributions and trust earnings among the participants, (2) for periodic valuation of trust assets, and (3) for distribution of the funds accumulated under the plan after a fixed number of years (meaning at least two years), the attainment of a stated age or upon the prior occurrence of some event such as layoff, illness, disability, retirement, death, or severance of employment. Treas. Reg. §1.401-1(b)(1)(ii); Rev. Rul. 71-295, 1971-2 CB 184; Rev. Rul. 80-155, 1980-1 CB 84. See also Q 391.

The IRS has also ruled that a plan could permit participants with at least five years of participation to withdraw all employer contributions (including those made during the last two years). Rev. Rul. 68-24, 1968-1 CB 150. With respect to amounts rolled over from another qualified plan, the receiving profit sharing plan must comply with the "fixed number of years" requirement without reference to the number of years such amounts were accumulated in the previous plan. Let. Rul. 8134110. However, where a participant's entire account balance is transferred to another qualified plan, the years of participation in both plans may be aggregated. Let. Rul. 8825130.

"...It is not necessary that the employer contribute every year or that he contribute the same amount or contribute in accordance with the same ratio every year. However, merely making a single or occasional contribution ... for employees does not establish a plan of profit-sharing. To be a profit-sharing plan, there must be recurring and substantial contributions ... for the employees." Treas. Reg. §1.401-1(b)(2). See Q 333.

A provision for offsetting contributions under a profit sharing plan by contributions made to a money purchase pension plan will not prevent either plan from qualifying. Rev. Rul. 81-201, 1981-2 CB 88.

In a profit sharing plan, any age lower than 65 may be specified as retirement age. Rev. Rul. 80-276, 1980-2 CB 131.

Withdrawal of Contributions

If a plan provides that employer contributions are allocated on the basis of employee contributions that may be withdrawn immediately after they are made, the plan will not qualify because such a withdrawal provision "could reasonably be expected to result in the manipulation of the allocation and contravention of the definite predetermined allocation formula requirement of Section 1.401-1(b)(1)(ii) of the regulations." Rev. Rul. 72-275, 1972-1 CB 109, as modified by Rev. Rul. 74-55, 1974-1 CB 89.

If, on the other hand, the withdrawal provision imposes a "substantial limitation" on the right of a participant to withdraw his own contributions, so that the provision "cannot reasonably be expected to result in the manipulation of the allocation" as described above, such provision will not cause a plan to fail to qualify. Rev. Rul. 74-56, 1974-1 CB 90. See also Let. Rul. 7816022.

Valuation of Assets

If the amounts to be allocated or distributed to a particular participant are to be ascertainable, the plan must provide for a valuation of investments held by the trust at least once a year, on a specified inventory date, in accordance with a method consistently followed and uniformly applied. The fair market value on the inventory date is to be used for this purpose. The respective accounts of the participants are to be adjusted in accordance with the valuation. Rev. Rul. 80-155, 1980-1 CB 84. However, if a fully insured profit sharing plan provides that all trust assets are to be invested immediately in individual annuity or retirement income contracts, the cash value of which at any particular time is contained in a schedule supplied by the insurance company, the plan need not provide for the periodic valuation of trust investments. Rev. Rul. 73-435, 1973-2 CB 126. *ASRS, Sec. 59, ¶485.2.*

401(K) PLANS

394. What is a 401(k) plan?

A 401(k) plan generally is a profit sharing plan or stock bonus plan that provides for contributions to be made pursuant to a "cash or deferred arrangement" (CODA) under which individual participants elect to take amounts in cash or to have the amounts deferred under the plan.

In addition to the general qualification requirements (Q 322 through Q 361), special qualification rules apply to 401(k) plans; see Q 395 to Q 406. The requirements for safe harbor plans are explained at Q 399, and the requirements for SIMPLE 401(k) plans are explained at Q 400. For an overview, see the 401(k) Navigator on p. xx.

The elective deferral limits apply to individuals participating in more than one salary reduction plan (e.g., a 401(k) plan and a 403(b) tax sheltered annuity or SIMPLE IRA); see Q 396. For the requirements that pertain to catch-up contributions by participants age 50 or over, see Q 397.

Amounts deferred under a 401(k) plan are referred to as elective deferrals (see Q 396). Generally, elective deferrals are excluded from a participant's gross income for

PENSION AND PROFIT SHARING: PLAN TYPES AND FEATURES   Q 395

the year of the deferral (in other words, the contributions are made with before-tax dollars) and treated as employer contributions to the plan. Treas. Regs. §1.401(k)-1(a). However, in the case of contributions to a qualified Roth contribution program (see Q 401), deferrals are made on an after-tax basis (i.e., they are treated as includable in income for withholding purposes). See IRC Sec. 402A.

A 401(k) plan may provide that all employer contributions are made pursuant to the election (a stand-alone plan) or may provide that the cash or deferred arrangement is in addition to ordinary employer contributions. Typically, the employer contributions are in the form of a percentage match for each dollar deferred by an employee. For the requirements that apply to matching contributions, see Q 405 and Q 406. *ASRS, Sec. 59, ¶260.*

395. What special qualification requirements apply to 401(k) plans?

In order to qualify, a 401(k) plan (or a plan that provides a 401(k) cash or deferred arrangement) generally must first be a qualified profit sharing or stock bonus plan. IRC Sec. 401(k); Treas. Reg. §1.401(k)-1(a)(1). Final regulations governing Sections 401(k) and 401(m) are effective for plan years beginning after December 31, 2005. Treas. Reg. § 1.401(k)-1(g)(1), (g)(2).

Contributions to the plan made under a cash or deferred arrangement (see below) that satisfies the nondiscrimination in amount requirement as explained in Q 404, that imposes the withdrawal restrictions explained in Q 402, and that meets the other requirements that follow will not be included in the employee's gross income, unless the employee elects to treat the contributions as designated Roth contributions (see Q 401).

Eligibility to offer 401(k) plan. Tax-exempt employers, such as 501(c)(3) organizations, are eligible to offer a 401(k) arrangement. IRC Sec. 401(k)(4)(B). State and local government employers (including political subdivisions and agencies thereof) are generally prohibited from offering 401(k) arrangements to their employees, however, certain rural cooperatives may do so. See IRC Secs. 401(k)(1), 401(k)(2).

Cash or deferred arrangement defined. A "cash or deferred arrangement" (CODA) is, by definition, an arrangement under which an eligible employee may make a cash or deferred election with respect to contributions, accruals or other benefits in a qualified plan. See Treas. Reg. §1.401(k)-1(a)(2). A cash or deferred *election* is any direct or indirect election (or modification of an earlier election) by an employee to have the employer either (a) provide an amount to the employee in the form of cash (or some other taxable benefit) that is not currently available; or (b) contribute an amount to a trust, or provide an accrual or other benefit under a plan deferring the receipt of compensation. Treas. Reg. §1.401(k)-1(a)(3).

With respect to timing, the final regulations provide that "a contribution is made pursuant to a cash or deferred election only if the contribution is made after the election is made." Treas. Regs. §§1.401(k)-1(a)(3)(iii)(B). See Q 364 with regard to deduction timing. Thus, under the final regulations amounts contributed in anticipation of future performance of services generally are not treated as elective contributions. However, a very limited exception is provided for administrative convenience (e.g., a company bookkeeper is absent the day the funds would normally be transmitted to the plan). See Treas. Regs. §§1.401(k)-1(a)(3)(iii)(C)(2). Special penalties and reporting requirements apply to listed transactions. See IRC Sec. 6707A; for details see Q 503.

Automatic enrollment. For purposes of determining whether an election is a cash or deferred election, it is irrelevant whether the default that applies in the absence of an affirmative is that the employee receives cash or that the employee contributes the specified amount to the trust. See Treas. Reg. §1.401(k)-1(a)(3)(ii).

A cash or deferred arrangement does not qualify as such if any *other benefit* provided by the employer, except for matching contributions, is conditioned on the employee's making an election under the plan. (What constitutes "other benefits" for this purpose is illustrated in the regulations.) IRC Sec. 401(k)(4)(A); Treas. Reg. §1.401(k)-1(e)(6); see Let. Rul. 9250013. The IRS has privately ruled that the purchase of a group long-term disability income policy that provided continuation of benefit accumulation for disabled employees did not violate this rule. Let. Ruls. 200235043, 200031060.

The IRS has repeatedly approved plans involving a "wraparound" arrangement, whereby contributions consisting of current year salary deferrals were held initially in a nonqualified deferred compensation plan; see Q 119 for details. The Service concluded that such deferrals were not impermissably conditioned on the deferral election. See e.g., Let. Ruls. 199924067, 9807010, 9752017, 9530038. Final regulations state that a plan will not fail to be qualified merely because it includes a nonqualified cash or deferred arrangement, but special requirements will apply to its nondiscrimination testing. See Treas. Reg. §1.401(k)-1(a)(5)(iv).

Elective deferral contributions to a 401(k) cash or deferred arrangement, including Roth contributions (see Q 401), are treated as employer contributions (except when they are recharacterized, see Q 406). Treas. Reg. §1.401(k)-1(a)(4)(ii). Contributions need not come from employer profits. IRC Sec. 401(a)(27).

Elective Deferral Limit. The plan must provide that the amount any employee can elect to defer for any calendar year under the cash or deferred arrangement of that plan (or any other plan or arrangement of that employer) is limited to $15,000 in 2006, and is subject to indexing for inflation thereafter. (For limitation amounts in earlier years, see Appendix E.) IRC Sec. 401(a)(30); IRC Sec. 402(g)(1); see Q 396. Plans may also allow additional elective deferrals, known as catch-up contributions, by participants age 50 or over. IRC Sec. 414(v). Such catch-up contributions, if made under the provisions of IRC Section 414(v), are not subject to the Section 401(a)(30) limit. IRC Sec. 414(v)(3)(A). See Q 397 for details.

Participation and coverage. A plan may not require, as a condition of participation in the cash or deferred arrangement, that an employee complete a period of service beyond the later of (1) age 21, or (2) the completion of one year of service. IRC Sec. 401(k)(2)(D).

A cash or deferred arrangement must satisfy one of the nondiscriminatory coverage tests explained in Q 325. IRC Sec. 401(k)(3)(A)(i). However, for purposes of applying those tests, all *eligible employees* are treated as benefiting under the arrangement, regardless of whether they actually make elective deferrals. Treas. Reg. §1.410(b)-3(a)(2)(i). An "eligible employee" is any employee who is directly or indirectly eligible to make a cash or deferred election under the plan for all or a portion of the plan year. An employee is not ineligible merely because he elects not to participate, is suspended from making an election under the hardship withdrawal rules, is unable to make an election because his compensation is less than a specified dollar amount, or because he may receive no

PENSION AND PROFIT SHARING: PLAN TYPES AND FEATURES   Q 395

additional annual additions under the IRC Section 415 limits (see Q 332, Q 377). Treas. Reg. §1.401(k)-6.

Employers may apply an early participation test for certain younger or newer employees permitted to participate in a plan. If a plan separately satisfies the minimum coverage rules of IRC Section 410(b), taking into account only those employees who have not completed one year of service or are under age 21, the employer may elect to exclude any eligible employees who have not satisfied the age and service requirements (assuming they are nonhighly compensated) for purposes of the ADP test (see Q 404). IRC Sec. 401(k)(3)(F); Treas. Reg. §1.401(k)-2(a)(1)(iii). This provision is designed to encourage employers to allow newer and younger employees to participate in the plan, without having the plan's ADP results "pulled down" by their often-lower rates of deferral. By making this election, the employer will be able to apply a single ADP test comparing the highly compensated employees who are eligible to participate in the plan to the nonhighly compensated who have completed one year of service and reached age 21.

If an employer includes a tax-exempt 501(c)(3) organization and sponsors both a 401(k) (or 401(m)) plan and a 403(b) plan, employees eligible to participate in the 403(b) plan can generally be treated as excludable employees for purposes of the 401(k) plan under proposed regulations, if: (1) no employee of the 501(c)(3) organization is eligible to participate in the 401(k) (or 401(m)) plan, and (2) at least 95% of the employees who are not 501(c)(3) employees are eligible to participate in the 401(k) or 401(m) plan. Prop. Treas. Reg. §1.410(b)-6(g).

Guidelines and transition rules for satisfying the coverage requirement during a merger or acquisition are set forth at Rev. Rul. 2004-11, 2004-7 IRB 480.

Nonforfeitability. An employee must be fully vested at all times in his elective contributions (even if he will make no additional elective contributions), and cannot be subject to the forfeitures and suspensions that are permitted by the Code for benefits derived from employer contributions (see Q 333). Furthermore, such amounts cannot be taken into consideration in applying the vesting rules to other contributions. IRC Sec. 401(k)(2)(C); Treas. Reg. §1.401(k)-1(c); see also Treas. Reg. §1.401(k)-1(c).

Employer matching contributions and nonelective employer contributions that are taken into account for purposes of satisfying the special nondiscrimination rules applicable to cash or deferred arrangements (see Q 404) must be immediately nonforfeitable and subject to the withdrawal restrictions explained in Q 402. See Treas. Regs. §1.401(k)-1(c), 1.401(k)-1(d). All other contributions to a plan that includes a cash or deferred arrangement are also subject to these restrictions unless a separate accounting is maintained. Treas. Reg. §1.401(k)-1(e)(3). Contributions made under a SIMPLE 401(k) plan are subject to special nonforfeitability requirements; see Q 400.

Aggregation of Plans and Deferral Percentages. Generally, all cash or deferred arrangements included in a plan are treated as a single cash or deferred arrangement for purposes of meeting the requirements discussed above, and for purposes of the coverage requirements of IRC Section 410(b). See Treas. Reg. §1.401(k)-1(b)(4)(ii). The deferral percentage taken into account under the ADP tests for any highly compensated employee who is a participant in two or more cash or deferred arrangements under plans of his employer which are required to be aggregated (as discussed above) is the average of the deferral percentages for the employee under each of the arrangements. IRC Sec. 401(k)(3)(B).

Restructuring may not be used to demonstrate compliance with the requirements of IRC Section 401(k). Treas. Reg. §1.401(k)-1(b)(4)(iv)(B). *ASRS, Sec. 59, ¶483.1(a)*.

396. What is the limit on elective deferrals to employer-sponsored plans?

The Code limits the total amount of "elective deferrals" any individual can exclude from income in a year. Elective deferrals, for this purpose, generally include all salary deferral contributions to: all 401(k) plans (see Q 394 through Q 401), tax sheltered annuities (see Q 473), SAR-SEPs (see Q 241), and SIMPLE IRAs (see Q 242). IRC Sec. 402(g)(3); Treas. Reg. §1.402(g)-1(b). Contributions under a Roth 401(k) feature (see Q 401) are subject to the same elective deferral limit as other 401(k) contributions. See IRC Sec. 402A(a)(1).

For tax years beginning in 2006, the elective deferral limit for traditional and safe harbor 401(k) plans and for 403(b) tax sheltered annuities is $15,000. IRC Sec. 402(g)(1). This limit will be indexed for inflation after 2006.

Elective deferral contributions to SIMPLE IRAs (see Q 242) and SIMPLE 401(k) plans (see Q 400) are subject to a limit of $10,000 in 2006, which will also be indexed for inflation after 2006. (See Appendix E for the amounts for earlier years). (The limit on elective deferrals to tax sheltered annuity plans may be further increased in the case of certain long-term employees of certain organizations. See Q 473.) Treas. Reg. §1.402(g)-1(c).

Year	SIMPLE IRAs and SIMPLE 401(k) Plans	Traditional and Safe Harbor 401(k) Plans, SAR-SEPs, 403(b) Plans
2005	$10,000	$14,000
2006	$10,000	$15,000

The Section 402(g) elective deferral limit is *not* required to be coordinated with the limit on Section 457 plans. As a result, an individual participating in both a 401(k) plan and a 457 plan in 2006 may defer as much as $30,000. See IRC Sec. 457(c); Q 124.

Generally, matching contributions made on behalf of self-employed individuals are not treated as elective deferrals for purposes of IRC Section 402(g); however this treatment does not apply to qualified matching contributions (QMACs) that are treated as elective contributions for purposes of the ADP test. See IRC Sec. 402(g)(9); Q 404.

Excess deferrals. Amounts deferred in excess of the ceiling (i.e., excess deferrals) are not excludable and, therefore, must be included in the individual's gross income for the taxable year. IRC Sec. 402(g)(1); Treas. Reg. §1.402(g)-1(a). However, in the case of participants age 50 or over, catch-up contributions permitted under Section 414(v) are not treated as excess elective deferrals under Section 402(g)(1). Treas. Reg. §1.414(v)-1(g); see Q 397.

If any amount is included in an individual's income under these rules and plan language permits distributions of excess deferrals, the individual may, prior to March

PENSION AND PROFIT SHARING: PLAN TYPES AND FEATURES Q 397

1 of the following year, allocate the excess deferrals among the plans under which the deferrals were made, and the plans may distribute such excess deferrals (including any income allocated thereto, provided the plan uses a reasonable method of allocating income) prior to April 15 of that year. Treas. Regs. §§1.402(g)-1(e)(2), 1.402(g)-1(e)(5). The amount of excess deferrals distributed under these rules is not included in income a second time as a distribution; however, any income on the excess deferral is treated as earned and received, and therefore includable in income, in the taxable year in which distributed. IRC Sec. 402(g)(2)(C); Treas. Reg. §1.402(g)-1(e)(8). Also, if the plan so provides, distributions of excess deferrals may be made during the taxable year of the deferral if the individual and the plan designate the distribution as an excess deferral and the correcting distribution is made after the date on which the plan received the excess deferral. Treas. Reg. §1.402(g)-1(e)(3).

Excess amounts that are not timely distributed are *not* included in the cost basis of plan distributions, even though they have previously been included in income. IRC Sec. 402(g)(2); Treas. Reg. §1.402(g)-1(e)(8). Thus, such amounts will be subjected to a second tax upon distribution in the future. Any corrective distribution of less than the entire amount of the excess deferral is treated as a pro rata distribution of excess deferrals and income. IRC Sec. 402(g)(2)(D); Treas. Reg. §1.402(g)-1(e)(10).

Planning Point: Due to this potential for double taxation, excess elective deferrals should be avoided, and, if they inadvertently occur, they should be corrected by the applicable deadline. One common trap for the unwary may occur where an individual participates in more than one plan that allows elective deferrals. Perhaps he participates in a 401(k) plan at his regular place of employment, and also participates in a SIMPLE IRA plan sponsored by his side business. The limits on elective deferrals are applied to the individual and not just to the plan, so he might easily stay within the terms of the two plans and still violate the elective deferral limits by contributing the maximum amount to both plans. *Martin Silfen, J.D., Brown Brothers Harriman Trust Co., LLC.*

For rules on coordinating distributions of excess contributions (see Q 406) and excess deferrals, see Treas. Reg. §1.401(k)-1(f)(5)(i). *ASRS, Sec. 59, ¶483.2.*

397. What are the rules for catch-up contributions to employer sponsored retirement plans?

Catch-up contributions are defined as *additional elective deferrals* by an eligible participant in an *applicable employer plan*, as those terms are defined in IRC Section 414(v) and regulations thereunder. "Elective deferral" for this purpose refers to the amounts described in IRC Section 402(g)(3) (see Q 396), but also includes amounts deferred to eligible IRC Section 457 governmental plans. IRC Secs. 414(v)(5)(B), 414(u)(2)(C); Treas. Reg. §1.414(v)-1(g)(2).

For purposes of Section 414(v), an "applicable employer plan" means: (1) employer plans qualified under Section 401(a) (see Q 322), (2) 403(b) tax sheltered annuities (see Q 473), (3) eligible Section 457 governmental plans, (4) salary reduction simplified employee pensions (i.e., SAR-SEPs, see Q 241), and (5) SIMPLE IRAs (see Q 242). IRC Sec. 414(v)(6). For this purpose, qualified plans, 403(b) plans, SAR-SEPs and SIMPLE IRAs that are maintained by a controlled group of corporations, a group of trades or businesses under common control, or members of an affiliated service group (see Q 360) are considered one plan. Also, if more than one eligible Section 457 governmental plan is maintained by the same employer, the plans will be treated as one plan. IRC Sec. 414(v)(2)(D).

Catch-up contributions permitted under Section 414(v) do not apply to a catch-up eligible participant for any taxable year in which a higher catch-up amount is permitted under Section 457(b)(3) during the last three years prior to the plan's normal retirement year–see Q 124. IRC Sec. 414(v)(6)(C); Treas. Reg. §1.414(v)-1(a)(3).

Dollar limit. A plan may not permit additional elective deferrals for any year in an amount greater than *the lesser of* (1) the amount in the appropriate table below, or (2) the excess (if any) of the participant's compensation (as defined in Section 415(c)(3)–see Q 332, Q 377) over any other elective deferrals for the year made without regard to the catch-up limits. IRC Sec. 414(v)(2)(A). An employer who sponsors more than one plan must aggregate the elective deferrals treated as catch-up contributions for purposes of the dollar limit. Treas. Reg. §1.414(v)-1(f)(1). An individual participating in more than one plan is subject to one annual dollar limit for all catch-up contributions during the taxable year. Treas. Regs. §§1.402(g)-2(b), 1.414(v)-1(f)(3).

The dollar limit on catch-up contributions to *SIMPLE IRAs and SIMPLE 401(k) plans* is:

For taxable years beginning in:	The applicable dollar amount is:
2005	$2,000
2006	$2,500

The dollar limit on catch-up contributions to *all other 401(k) plans, and to 403(b) plans, eligible Section 457 plans, and SAR-SEPs* is:

For taxable years beginning in:	The applicable dollar amount is:
2005	$4,000
2006	$5,000

Eligible participant. An "eligible participant," with respect to any plan year, is a plan participant who would attain age 50 before the end of the taxable year, and with respect to whom no other elective deferrals may be made to the plan for the plan (or other applicable) year as a result of any *limit or other restriction* (see below). IRC Sec. 414(v)(5). For this purpose, every participant who will reach age 50 during a plan year is treated as having reached age 50 on the first day of the plan year, regardless of the employer's choice of plan year, and regardless of whether the participant survives to age 50 or terminates employment prior to his or her birthday. See Treas. Reg. §1.414(v)-1(g)(3).

A "limit or other restriction" for purposes of the eligible participant definition may be a *statutory limit* (set forth in the Internal Revenue Code), an *employer-provided limit* (contained in the terms of the plan), or an *ADP limit* resulting from the application of the actual deferral percentage test under Section 404(k)(3) (see Q 404). Treas. Reg. §1.414(v)-1(b)(1). A participant need not have made elective deferrals above any other limit in order to be a catch-up eligible participant. See T.D. 9072, 2003-2 CB 527. Thus, for example, if a participant makes elective deferrals under two different employer plans during a year, amounts in excess of the $15,000 limit (in 2006) under

PENSION AND PROFIT SHARING: PLAN TYPES AND FEATURES   Q 397

IRC Section 402(g) may be excluded from gross income as catch-up contributions, even though they might not have exceeded a statutory or plan limit under either plan. See Treas. Reg. §1.414(v)-1(b).

Universal availability. A plan will not satisfy the nondiscrimination requirements of Section 401(a)(4) unless all catch-up eligible participants who participate in any applicable plan maintained by the employer are provided with the effective opportunity to make the same election with respect to the dollar limits described above. IRC Sec. 414(v)(4)(A); Treas. Reg. §1.414(v)-1(e). This is known as the universal availability requirement. However, a plan will not fail to satisfy this requirement merely because it allows participants to defer an amount equal to a specified percentage of compensation for each payroll period, and permits each catch-up eligible participant to defer a pro rata share of the dollar catch-up limit in addition to that amount. Treas. Reg. §1.414(v)-1(e).

For purposes of the universal availability requirement, all plans maintained by employers who are treated as a single employer under the controlled group, common control or affiliated service group rules (see Q 359, Q 360) generally must be aggregated. IRC Sec. 414(v)(4)(B). However, exceptions to the aggregation rule apply to 457 plans and certain newly acquired plans. See Treas. Reg. §1.414(v)-1(e)(2) and (3).

Calculation of catch-up contributions. Catch-up contributions are excluded from income in the same manner as elective deferrals. See IRC Sec. 402(g)(1)(C). The calculation of which elective deferrals will be considered catch-up contributions is generally made as of the end of the plan year, by comparing the total elective deferrals for the plan year with the applicable plan year limit. Treas. Reg. §1.414(v)-1(b)(2). Elective deferrals in excess of the plan, ADP or Code limits, but not in excess of the amount limitations described above will be treated as catch-up contributions as determined on the last day of the plan year. Treas. Reg. §1.414(v)-1(c).

Treatment of contributions. Catch-up contributions that meet the foregoing requirements are not subject to any of the otherwise-applicable limitations on (1) elective deferrals under Section 401(a)(30) (see Q 395); (2) distributions of and exclusion for SAR-SEP contributions under Section 402(h) (see Q 241); (3) deferrals for tax sheltered annuities under Section 403(b) (see Q 473); (4) SAR-SEP or SIMPLE IRA contributions under Section 408–see Q 241, Q 242; (5) contributions or benefits under Section 415(c) (see Q 332, Q 377); or (6) contributions under Section 457(b)(2) (determined without regard to Section 457(b)(3); see Q 124). Similarly, catch-up contributions are not counted in applying these limitations to other contributions or benefits provided under a plan. IRC Sec. 414(v)(3)(A).

Furthermore, so long as the plan meets the universal availability requirement described above, it will not be treated, merely on account of the catch-up contributions, as failing the requirements for: (1) nondiscrimination under Section 401(a)(4) (see Q 326 to Q 330, Q 404 to Q 399); (2) nondiscrimination and the ADP test under Section 401(k)(3) (see Q 404); (3) SIMPLE 401(k) plans under Section 401(k)(11); (4) nondiscrimination in tax sheltered annuity plans under Section 403(b)(12) (see Q 467); (5) SEPs under Section 408(k) (see Q 240, Q 241); (6) minimum coverage under Section 410(b) (see Q 325); or (7) top-heavy plans under Section 416 (see Q 351, Q 352). IRC Sec. 414(v)(3)(B).

An employer may, but is not required to, make matching contributions on catch-up contributions. However, if the employer does so, the contributions must satisfy the ACP test of IRC Section 402(m). See T.D. 9072 above; see Q 405. Reporting requirements for catch-up contributions are set forth in Announcement 2001-93, 2001-44 IRB 416. *ASRS: Sec. 59, ¶483.3.*

398. What is a solo 401(k) plan?

The term "solo 401(k) plan" refers to any 401(k) plan that covers only one participant. Solo 401(k) plans are a product of qualified plan reforms implemented by EGTRRA 2001, which substantially improved the tax favored treatment for employers sponsoring 401(k) plans. These changes were designed to encourage greater savings for retirement and to provide more incentive to businesses funding 401(k) plans.

First, EGTRRA 2001 increased the deduction limit for profit sharing and stock bonus plans (which includes 401(k) plans) to 25% of compensation. See IRC Section 404(a)(3)(A). In years beginning before 2002, profit sharing and stock bonus plans were subject to a deduction limit of 15% of compensation.

Second, the definition of compensation for purposes of the preceding paragraph includes elective deferrals to a qualified plan, 403(b) plan, 457 plan, SEP, SIMPLE, or Section 125 FSA plan. See IRC Section 404(A)(12). This means that the payroll upon which the 25% is based is higher than it was before 2002, resulting in a higher deduction limit for employer contributions to the plan.

Third, elective deferrals do not reduce the amount of employer contributions for purposes of calculating the 25% deduction limit. See IRC Section 404(n). This means that a higher amount can be attributable to matching contributions, nonelective contributions or other amounts paid by the employer. The elective deferral limits increased as well, with a maximum permitted deferral of $15,000 in 2006 (see IRC Sec. 402(g)(1); Q 396), and, for individuals age 50 or older, catch-up contributions ($5,000 in 2006; see IRC Sec. 414(v)(2)(B), Q 397).

These changes to the calculation of the employer deduction for all profit sharing plans, including 401(k) plans, led to a proliferation of solo 401(k) plans. While the advantages to a sole proprietor or one-person corporation can be significant, it is important to note that the plan is subject to the same minimum participation, coverage, nondiscrimination, and other requirements that apply to any other qualified defined contribution plan, in the event one or more employees are later added to the sponsoring employer. *ASRS, Sec. 60, ¶140.*

399. What are the requirements for a 401(k) safe harbor plan?

IRC Sections 401(k) and 401(m) provide for safe harbor designs for cash or deferred arrangements and matching contributions, respectively, which are deemed to satisfy the ADP and ACP tests. See IRC Secs. 401(k)(12), 401(m)(11); Treas. Reg. §1.401(k)-3(a). The final regulations cited throughout this question were published in December, 2004 and are effective for plan years beginning on or after January 1, 2006. See Treas. Reg. §1.401(k)-1(g).

The attraction of safe harbor plans is that in exchange for meeting notice and funding requirements, the employer is free of the requirement of annual testing of salary deferral and matching contributions (however, the safe harbor does not eliminate

PENSION AND PROFIT SHARING: PLAN TYPES AND FEATURES — Q 399

the requirement of ACP testing for employee after-tax contributions; see Q 405). Furthermore, safe harbor plans are generally exempt from the top-heavy requirements, except as explained below. IRC Sec. 416(g)(4)(H).

In addition, the contributions required under the safe harbor need not be made to the 401(k) plan; an employer meeting the contribution requirements with respect to *any* other defined contribution plan will be treated as having satisfied the safe harbor. IRC Sec. 401(k)(12)(F); see Treas. Reg. §1.401(k)-3(h)(4). Except for the provisions described below, a safe harbor plan is generally subject to the same requirements as a traditional 401(k) plan. Certain lower income taxpayers may be eligible to claim the saver's credit for elective deferrals to a safe harbor plan. See Q 213.

A safe harbor plan must meet a notice requirement and either a matching contribution or nonelective contribution requirement, as explained below. IRC Secs. 401(k)(12), 401(m)(11); Treas. Reg. §1.401(k)-3(a). The dollar limit on elective deferrals to a safe harbor plan is the same as for a traditional 401(k) plan; see Q 396.

A safe harbor plan generally may also permit *catch-up contributions* by participants who reach age 50 (or more) by the end of the plan year. See IRC Sec. 414(v). The limit on catch-up contributions to safe harbor plans is the lesser of (1) a specified dollar limit, or (2) the excess (if any) of the participant's compensation over any other elective deferrals for the year made without regard to the catch-up limits. IRC Sec. 414(v)(2)(A). The dollar limit for catch-up contributions is $5,000 in 2006. IRC Sec. 414(v)(2)(B)(i). See Q 397 for details on the requirements for catch-up contributions.

Notice requirement. Under the notice requirement, each employee eligible to participate must, before the plan year begins, be given written notice that describes: (a) the safe harbor matching contribution or safe harbor nonelective contribution formula used under the plan (including a description of the levels of safe harbor matching contributions, if any, available under the plan); (b) any other contributions under the plan or matching contributions to another plan on account of elective contributions or employee contributions under the plan (including the potential for discretionary matching contributions) and the conditions under which such contributions are made; (c) the plan to which safe harbor contributions will be made (if different than the plan containing the cash or deferred arrangement); (d) the type and amount of compensation that may be deferred under the plan; (e) how to make cash or deferred elections, including any administrative requirements that apply to such elections; (f) the periods available under the plan for making cash or deferred elections; (g) withdrawal and vesting provisions applicable to contributions under the plan; and (h) information that makes it easy to obtain additional information about the plan (including an additional copy of the summary plan description) such as telephone numbers, addresses and, if applicable, electronic addresses, of individuals or offices from whom employees can obtain such plan information. See Treas. Reg. §1.401(k)-3(d)(2)(ii).

The *timing requirement* for the notice is satisfied if the notice is provided within a reasonable period before the beginning of the plan year. This requirement is deemed to be met if the notice is provided to each eligible employee at least 30 days, and not more than 90 days, prior to the end of the plan year (i.e., by December 1 for a calendar year). See Treas. Reg. §1.401(k)-3(d)(3).

In the alternative, a *contingent* notice may be provided setting forth the same information as above, but stating that (a) the plan may be amended during the plan year to include the 3% safe harbor contribution, and (b) if the amendment is made, a follow-up notice will be provided. If the plan is amended, the follow-up notice must then be provided to each eligible employee at least 30 days prior to the end of the plan year (i.e., by December 1 for a calendar year). See Treas. Reg. §1.401(k)-3(f).

Much of the information in the summary plan description can be cross referenced rather than set forth again in the notice. Treas. Reg. §1.401(k)-3(d)(2)(iii). In either case, the notice must be (1) sufficiently accurate and comprehensive to inform the employee of his rights and obligations, *and* (2) written in a manner calculated to be understood by the average employee eligible to participate. IRC Secs. 401(k)(12)(D), 401(m)(11)(A)(ii); see Treas. Reg. §1.401(k)-3(d)(2)(i).

The *matching contribution* requirement is met if a matching contribution is made to each nonhighly compensated employee in an amount equal to: 100% of elective contributions to the extent they do not exceed 3% of compensation, *plus* an amount equal to 50% of the elective contributions that exceed 3% but do not exceed 5% of the compensation. IRC Secs. 401(k)(12)(B)(i), 401(m)(11)(A)(i). (Matching of catch-up contributions is not required. See REG-142499-01, 66 Fed. Reg. 53555 (10-23-01).) For administrative convenience, a plan may require elective contributions to be made in whole percentages of pay or whole dollar amounts. Treas. Reg. §1.401(k)-3(c)(6)(iii).

In no event may the rate of matching contributions for a highly compensated employee exceed that for a nonhighly compensated employee. IRC Secs. 401(k)(12)(B)(ii), 401(m)(11)(A)(i). The Code allows some variation on the basic formula described in the preceding paragraph, but it states that the end result must essentially be the same as under these percentages, and the rate of the match cannot go up with the rate of contributions. See IRC Secs. 401(k)(12)(B)(iii), 401(m)(11)(A)(i); see Treas. Reg. §1.401(k)-3(c)(3).

Matching contributions may be offered on both elective deferrals and employee after-tax contributions, provided that (a) the match on elective deferrals is not affected by the amount of employee contributions, *or* (b) matching contributions are made with respect to the sum of an employee's elective deferrals and employee contributions under the same terms as they are made with respect to elective deferrals. Treas. Reg. §1.401(k)-3(c)(5)(i).

The IRS has stated that matching contributions may be made on the basis of compensation for a payroll period, a month, or a quarter. Treas. Reg. §1.401(k)-3(c)(5)(ii). (Thus, if the employee stops making deferrals for any reason, the employer would not be obligated to continue making matching contributions after deferrals cease.) In addition, the IRS has clarified that if an employee takes an inservice (e.g., hardship) distribution, the plan may impose a 6-month suspension on his participation to the same extent as permitted by a traditional 401(k) plan. See Treas. Reg. §1.401(k)-3(c)(6)(v)(B); see Q 403.

A plan that satisfies the ADP test matching contribution safe harbor under Treas. Reg. §1.401(k)-3(c) will automatically satisfy the ACP test matching contribution safe harbor (see Q 405). Likewise, a plan that satisfies the ADP test nonelective contribution safe harbor under Treas. Reg. §1.401(k)-3(b) will automatically satisfy the corresponding ACP test safe harbor. Treas. Regs. §§1.401(m)-3(b), 1.401(m)-3(c). However, if the plan provides for additional matching contributions, special limitations apply, as described below. See IRC Sec. 401(m)(11)(B).

PENSION AND PROFIT SHARING: PLAN TYPES AND FEATURES   Q 399

The *nonelective contribution* requirement is met if a nonelective contribution is made (as an alternative to matching contributions) on behalf of all nonhighly compensated employees eligible to participate in the plan (not merely those making elective contributions) in an amount equal to at least 3% of the employee's compensation. IRC Secs. 401(k)(12)(C), 401(m)(11)(A)(i).

In either case, contributions must be fully vested and subject to the withdrawal restrictions on IRC Section 401(k) plans (see Q 402). IRC Sec. 401(k)(12)(E)(i). Generally, safe harbor nonelective contributions may be used to satisfy other nondiscrimination requirements; thus they are not subject to the limitations that apply to QNECs (see Q 404). However, contributions used to satisfy the nonelective contribution safe harbor may not be taken into account in determining whether a plan satisfies the permitted disparity rules (i.e., Social Security integration – see Q 330). IRC Sec. 401(k)(12)(E)(ii); Treas. Reg. §1.401(k)-3(h)(2).

Matching contribution limitation: The safe harbor requirement for matching contributions has a ceiling as well as the floor described above. It states that: (1) matching contributions on behalf of any employee may not be made with respect to an employee's contributions or elective deferrals in excess of 6% of the employee's compensation, (2) the rate of the employer's matching contribution does not increase with the rate of the employee's elective deferral or contribution, *and* (3) the matching contribution with respect to any highly compensated employee at any rate of employee contribution or rate of elective deferral is not greater than that made with respect to a nonhighly compensated employee. IRC Sec. 401(m)(11)(B).

If matching contributions are made in excess of this limitation, they will be subject to separate nondiscrimination testing as explained in Q 405. Furthermore, if employee after-tax contributions are permitted, they will be tested in the same manner. See 1996 Blue Book, p. 153.

Top heavy exemption: Safe harbor 401(k) and 401(m) plans are generally exempt from the top-heavy requirements; however, certain variations on the plan provisions set forth above (e.g., vesting requirements, additional discretionary contributions by the employer) may trigger the application of the top heavy rules. See IRC Sec. 416(g)(4)(H); Rev. Rul. 2004-13, 2004-7 IRB 485.

Comparison With SIMPLE 401(k) Plan

SIMPLE 401(k) plans (see Q 400) also provide a design-based alternative to the use of a safe harbor plan. Some of the differences between safe harbor plans and SIMPLE 401(k) plans are: (1) employees covered by a SIMPLE 401(k) plan may not be participants in any other plan offered by the employer, while employees participating in a safe harbor plan may be covered by more than one plan; (2) SIMPLE 401(k) plans are subject to lower dollar limits on elective deferrals and catch-up contributions than safe harbor plans; (3) employers offering a SIMPLE 401(k) plan may not offer any contributions other than those provided under the SIMPLE 401(k) requirements, while employers maintaining a safe harbor plan may do so within the limitations described above; (4) safe harbor plans may be offered by any employer, while SIMPLE 401(k) plans are available only to employers with 100 or fewer employees earning $5,000 or more in the preceding year, and (5) contributions required under a safe harbor design may be made to a separate plan of the employer, while contributions required under a SIMPLE 401(k) design must be made to the SIMPLE 401(k) plan. *ASRS, Sec. 59, ¶¶ 430.3, 483.5.*

400. What are the requirements for a SIMPLE 401(k) plan?

SIMPLE 401(k) plans allow an *eligible employer* to satisfy the actual deferral percentage test for 401(k) plans (see Q 404) by meeting the plan design requirements described below, instead of performing annual ADP testing. See IRC Sec. 401(k)(11); Treas. Reg. §1.401(k)-4(a). The final regulations cited throughout this question were published in December, 2004 and are effective for plan years beginning on or after January 1, 2006. See Treas. Reg. §1.401(k)-1(g). For a comparison of the features of a SIMPLE 401(k) plan to those of a safe harbor 401(k) plan, see Q 399.

An *eligible employer* is defined as one who had no more than 100 employees earning at least $5,000 of compensation from the employer for the preceding year. IRC Secs. 401(k)(11)(D)(i), 408(p)(2)(C)(i). Generally, an eligible employer who establishes a SIMPLE 401(k) plan for a plan year and later ceases to be eligible will be treated as eligible for the following two years. However, if the failure to remain eligible was due to an acquisition, disposition or similar transaction, special rules apply. See IRC Sec. 408(p)(10); IRC Secs. 401(k)(11)(D)(i), 408(p)(2)(C)(i)(II); Treas. Reg. §1.401(k)-4(b)(2).

A SIMPLE 401(k) plan must meet: (1) a contribution requirement, (2) an exclusive plan requirement, and (3) a vesting requirement; however, certain other requirements for SIMPLE IRAs (see IRC Sec. 408(p), explained at Q 242 to Q 243) are imposed on SIMPLE 401(k) plans by incorporating their definitions by reference. IRC Secs. 401(k)(11)(A), 401(k)(11)(D)(i).

Under the SIMPLE 401(k) contribution requirement: (i) employees must be able to elect to have the employer make elective contributions for the year on behalf of the employee to a trust under the plan; (ii) the amount to which the election applies must be expressed as a percentage of compensation and may not exceed $10,000 (in 2006), and (iii) the employer must make matching contributions or nonelective contributions under one of the formulas described below. IRC Sec. 401(k)(11)(B). Certain lower income taxpayers may be eligible to claim the saver's credit for elective deferrals to a SIMPLE 401(k) plan. See Q 213.

A SIMPLE 401(k) plan may also permit *catch-up contributions* by participants who reach age 50 (or more) by the end of the plan year. See IRC Sec. 414(v). The limit on catch-up contributions to SIMPLE 401(k) plans is the lesser of (1) a specified dollar limit, or (b) the excess (if any) of the participant's compensation over any other elective deferrals for the year made without regard to the catch-up limits. IRC Sec. 414(v)(2)(A). The dollar limit is $2,500 in 2006. IRC Sec. 414(v)(2)(B)(ii); Treas. Reg. §1.414(v)-1(c)(2)(ii).

A plan will not be treated as violating any of the applicable limitations of Section 401(k)(11) merely on account of the making of (or right to make) catch-up contributions, so long as a universal availability requirement is met. IRC Sec. 414(v)(3)(B); Treas. Reg. §1.414(v)-1(e). See Q 397 for details on the requirements for catch-up contributions.

Under the matching formula, the employer must match employee elective contributions dollar-for-dollar up to 3% of the employee's compensation. Treas. Reg. §1.401(k)-4(e)(3). (Earlier guidance stated that matching of catch-up contributions is not required. See REG-142499-01, 66 Fed. Reg. 53555 (10-23-01).) Under the nonelective contribution formula, instead of making matching contributions, an employer

PENSION AND PROFIT SHARING: PLAN TYPES AND FEATURES   Q 401

can elect to make a 2% of compensation nonelective contribution on behalf of each employee who is eligible to participate and who has at least $5,000 in compensation from the employer for the year, provided notice of the election is given prior to the 60-day election period. IRC Sec. 401(k)(11)(B)(ii); Treas. Reg. §1.401(k)-4(e)(4).

The plan must also provide that no other contributions may be made to the plan other than those described above. IRC Sec. 401(k)(11)(B)(i)(III); Treas. Reg. §1.401(k)-4(e)(1). All contributions to a SIMPLE 401(k) plan must be nonforfeitable. IRC Sec. 401(k)(11)(A)(iii).

The exclusive plan requirement for a SIMPLE 401(k) plan is met if no contributions were made, or benefits accrued, for services during the year under any qualified plan of the employer on behalf of any employee eligible to participate in the cash or deferred arrangement, other than the contributions made under the SIMPLE 401(k) requirements described above. IRC Sec. 401(k)(11)(C); Treas. Reg. §1.401(k)-4(c). However, the receipt of an allocation of forfeitures under another plan of the employer will not cause a SIMPLE 401(k) participant to violate this rule. Treas. Reg. §1.401(k)-4(c)(2).

Generally, employees must have the right to terminate participation at any time during the year; however, the plan may preclude the employee from resuming participation thereafter until the beginning of the next year. Treas. Reg. §1.401(k)-4(d)(2)(iii). Furthermore, each employee eligible to participate must have 60 days before the first day of any year (and 60 days before the first day the employee is eligible to participate) to elect whether to participate in the plan, or to modify his deferral amount. The foregoing requirements are met only if the employer notifies each eligible employee of such rights within a reasonable time before the 60-day election period. IRC Secs. 401(k)(11)(B)(iii), 408(p)(5)(B), 408(p)(5)(C); Treas. Reg. §1.401(k)-4(d)(3).

A SIMPLE 401(k) plan that meets the requirements set forth in IRC Section 401(k)(11) is not subject to the top-heavy rules (see Q 351), provided the plan allows only the contributions required under IRC Section 401(k)(11). IRC Sec. 401(k)(11)(D)(ii); Treas. Reg. §1.401(k)-4(h). However, SIMPLE 401(k) plans are subject to the other qualification requirements of a 401(k) plan, including the $220,000 compensation limit (as indexed for 2006), the 415 limits (see Q 332, Q 377), and the prohibition on state and local governments operating a 401(k) plan (see Q 395). Rev. Proc. 97-9, 1997-1 CB 624. The IRC Section 404(a) limit on the deductibility of contributions (25% of compensation; see Q 392) is increased in the case of SIMPLE 401(k) plans to *the greater of* (a) 25% of compensation, or (b) the amount of contributions required under IRC Section 401(k)(11)(B). IRC Sec. 404(a)(3)(A)(ii). *ASRS, Sec. 59, ¶483.4.*

401. What are the requirements for a Roth 401(k) feature?

Beginning in 2006, employers will be able to offer a Roth 401(k) feature, which combines certain advantages of the Roth IRA with the convenience of 401(k) plan elective deferral-style contributions. The Internal Revenue Code states that if a qualified plan trust or a 403(b) annuity includes a *qualified Roth contribution program*, contributions to it that are so designated by the employee, while not excluded from gross income, will otherwise be treated as an elective deferral (as defined in IRC Sec. 402(g)). A qualified plan or 403(b) plan will not be treated as failing to meet any qualification requirement merely on account of including a qualified Roth contribution program. IRC Secs. 402A(a), 402A(e)(1). Proposed regulations governing the operation of the

Roth 401(k) feature were issued in March 2005, and are proposed to take effect for plan years beginning on or after January 1, 2006. See REG-152354-04, 70 Fed. Reg. 10062 (March 2, 2005). Final regulations under Section 401(k) were published in December, 2004 and are also effective for plan years beginning on or after January 1, 2006. See Treas. Reg. §1.401(k)-1(g).

A *qualified Roth contribution program* means a program under which an employee may elect to make *designated Roth contributions* in lieu of all or a portion of elective deferrals that the employee is otherwise eligible to make. IRC Sec. 402A(b)(1). For this purpose, a "designated Roth contribution" is any elective deferral that would otherwise be excludable from the gross income of the employee, but that the employee designates as not being excludable. IRC Sec. 402A(c)(1). Proposed regulations set forth the following requirements for designated Roth contributions: (1) the contribution must be designated irrevocably by the employee at the time of the cash or deferred election as a designated Roth contribution, (2) the contribution must be treated by the employer as includable in the employee's income at the time the employee would have received the amount in cash, were it not for the election (i.e., it must be treated as subject to applicable withholding requirements), and (3) the contribution must be maintained by the plan in a separate account, as provided under additional requirements set forth below. Prop. Treas. Reg. §1.401(k)-1(f)(1).

The program must provide for separate accounts ("designated Roth accounts") for the designated Roth contributions of each employee and any earnings properly allocable thereto, and must maintain separate recordkeeping with respect to each account. IRC Sec. 402A(b)(2). Under proposed regulations, contributions and withdrawals must be credited and debited to a designated Roth contribution account, and the plan must maintain a record a record of the employee's investment in the contract (i.e., designated Roth contributions that have not yet been distributed. Furthermore, gains, losses and other credits and charges must be separately allocated on a reasonable and consistent basis to the designated Roth contribution account and other accounts under the plan. Forfeitures may not be allocated to the designated Roth contribution account. The separate accounting requirement applies from the time the designated Roth contribution is made until the designated Roth contribution account is completely distributed.

The maximum amount an employee may designate as a designated Roth contribution is limited to the maximum amount of elective deferrals permitted for the tax year, reduced by the aggregate amount of elective deferrals for the tax year for which no designation is made. IRC Sec. 402A(c)(2).

Proposed regulations also specify that designated Roth contributions must satisfy the rules applicable to elective deferral contributions. Thus, for example, the nonforfeitability requirements and distribution limitations of Treas. Reg. §1.401(k)-1(c) and (d) must be satisfied, and the contributions will be treated as an employer contribution for many purposes. Designated Roth contributions are treated as elective deferral contributions for purposes of the actual deferral percentage (ADP) test. See Prop. Treas. Reg. §1.401(k)-1(f)(3).

A designated Roth contribution account is subject to the minimum distribution requirements of IRC Section 401(a)(9) (see Q 338 to Q 346). Treas. Reg. §1.401(k)-1(f)(3). However, a payment or distribution otherwise allowable from a designated Roth account may be rolled over to (a) another designated Roth account of the individual

PENSION AND PROFIT SHARING: PLAN TYPES AND FEATURES   Q 402

from whose account the payment or distribution was made, or (b) a Roth IRA of the individual. IRC Sec. 402A(c)(3). Rollover contributions to a designated Roth account under this provision are not taken into account for purposes of the limit on designated Roth contributions. See IRC Sec. 402(A(c)(3)(B). Funds in a Roth IRA are not subject to the lifetime minimum distribution requirements; see Q 234.

The Code states that any *qualified distribution* from a designated Roth account is excluded from gross income. IRC Sec. 402A(d)(1). A qualified distribution, for this purpose is defined in the same manner as for Roth IRAs (except that the provision for "qualified special purpose distributions" at IRC Sec. 408A(d)(2)(A)(iv) is disregarded). IRC Sec. 402A(d)(2)(A). See Q 228. However, the term *qualified distribution* does not include distributions of excess deferrals (amounts in excess of the IRC Sec. 402(g) limit) or excess contributions (under IRC Sec. 401(k)(8)), nor any income on them. IRC Sec. 402A(d)(2)(C).

Nonexclusion period. A payment or distribution from a designated Roth account will not be treated as a qualified distribution if it is made within the 5-year nonexclusion period. This period begins with the earlier of (a) the first taxable year for which the individual made a designated Roth contribution to any designated Roth account established for that individual under the same retirement plan, or (b) if a rollover contribution was made to the designated Roth account from another designated Roth account previously established for the individual under another retirement plan, the first taxable year for which the individual made a designated Roth contribution to the previously established account. IRC Sec. 402A(d)(2)(B).

The Code states that notwithstanding Section 72, if any excess deferral attributable to a designated Roth contribution is not distributed on or before the first April 15 after the close of the taxable year in which the excess deferral was made, the excess deferral (a) will not be treated as investment in the contract, and (b) will be included in gross income for the taxable year in which such excess is distributed. IRC Sec. 402A(d)(3). Furthermore, it adds that "Section 72 shall be applied separately with respect to distributions and payments from a designated Roth account and other distributions and payments from the plan." IRC Secs. 402A(d)(3), 402A(d)(4).

Effective date. The requirements for Roth 401(k) plans were enacted by EGTRRA 2001, but take effect January 1, 2006. EGTRRA 2001, Sec. 617(a). Like all provisions of EGTRRA 2001, unless Congress takes action to make them permanent, the Roth 401(k) provisions are scheduled to sunset (expire) in 2010. *ASRS, Sec. 59, ¶483.8.*

402. What restrictions apply to distributions from 401(k) plans?

Amounts held by the trust that are attributable to employer contributions made pursuant to the election to defer may not be distributed to participants or beneficiaries prior to (1) the employee's death, disability or severance from employment, (2) certain plan terminations, without the establishment or maintenance of another defined contribution plan, or (3) in the case of a profit sharing or stock bonus plan, the employee's experiencing financial hardship (see Q 403) or attaining age 59½. Treas. Reg. §1.401(k)-1(d)(1). The final regulations cited in this question were published in December, 2004 and are effective for plan years beginning on or after January 1, 2006. See Treas. Reg. §1.401(k)-1(g).

2006 Tax Facts on Insurance & Employee Benefits   471

These occurrences are referred to as "distributable events." Such amounts may not be distributable merely by reason of completion of a stated period of participation or the lapse of a fixed number of years. IRC Sec. 401(k)(2)(B). A qualified Hurricane Katrina distribution (as defined in KETRA 2005; see Q 417) will be treated as satisfying the distribution requirements of IRC Sec. 401(k)(2)(B). KETRA 2005, Sec. 101(f)(2).

The cost of life insurance protection (Table 2001 or P.S. 58 costs, see Q 424) provided under the plan is not treated as a distribution for purposes of these rules. Neither is the making of a loan that is treated as a deemed distribution, even if the loan is secured by the employee's elective contributions or is includable in the employee's income under IRC Section 72(p). However, the reduction of an employee's accrued benefit derived from elective contributions (i.e., an offset distribution) by reason of a default on a loan is treated as a distribution; see Q 420. Treas. Reg. §1.401(k)-1(d)(5)(ii). The IRS has privately ruled that a transfer of 401(k) elective deferrals or rollovers to purchase service credits would not constitute an impermissible distribution from the plan, nor a violation of the separate accounting requirement. Let. Ruls. 200335035, 199914055.

These restrictions on distributions of elective contributions generally continue to apply even if such amounts are transferred to another qualified plan of any employer. Treas. Reg. §1.401(k)-1(d)(2). However, amounts transferred to a 401(k) plan by a direct rollover from another plan do not have to be subject to these restrictions. Treas. Reg. §1.401(k)-1(d)(5)(iv). Final regulations state that rollover amounts may be excepted from the timing restrictions on distribution applicable to a receiving plan, provided such amounts are separately accounted for. Treas. Reg. §1.401(k)-1(d)(5)(iv); see also Rev. Rul. 2004-12, 2004-7 IRB 478. *ASRS, Sec. 59, ¶483.7.*

403. What requirements apply to hardship withdrawals from a 401(k) plan?

Hardship withdrawals may be made from a 401(k) plan only if (1) the distribution is made on account of an immediate and heavy financial need, and (2) the distribution is necessary to satisfy the financial need. Treas. Reg. §1.401(k)-1(d)(3)(i). Furthermore, the distribution may not exceed the employee's *maximum distributable amount*. Hardship withdrawals generally may not be rolled over (see Q 445). IRC Sec. 402(c)(4); see also IRC Sec. 401(k)(2)(B). Final regulations that included changes to the hardship provisions (see below) were published in December, 2004 and are effective for plan years beginning on or after January 1, 2006. See Treas. Reg. §1.401(k)-1(g).

In relief for victims of Hurricane Katrina, the IRS announced that certain plans that would otherwise be permitted to make hardship distributions but do not contain the necessary enabling language could make such distributions to employees or former employees with a principal residence or place of employment (as of August 29, 2005) in one of the hurricane disaster areas. Such plans had to be amended by December 31, 2005 to add the appropriate language. See Ann. 2005-70, 2005-40 IRB 682. Certain participants who received a hardship distribution after February 28, 2005 and before August 29, 2005 for the purchase or construction of a principal residence in the disaster areas, but did not purchase or construct the residence because of Hurricane Katrina, may be permitted to recontribute the distribution to the plan on or before February 28, 2006. See KETRA 2005, Secs. 102, 101(d)(1); Notice 2005-92, 2005-51 IRB ___.

An employee's *maximum distributable amount* is generally equal to the employee's total elective contributions as of the date of distribution reduced by the amount of previous distributions on account of hardship. Treas. Reg. §1.401(k)-1(d)(3)(ii).

The determinations of whether the participant has "an immediate and heavy financial need" and whether other resources are "reasonably available" to meet the need are to be made on the basis of all relevant facts and circumstances. An example of "an immediate and heavy financial need" is the need to pay funeral expenses of a family member. A financial need will not fail to qualify as an immediate and heavy financial need merely because it was foreseeable or voluntarily incurred by the employee. Treas. Reg. §1.401(k)-1(d)(3)(iii)(A).

A distribution will be *deemed* to be made on account of "an immediate and heavy financial need" if it is made on account of any of the following: (1) "medical expenses" (see Q 826) incurred by the employee, his spouse or dependents; (2) the purchase (excluding mortgage payments) of the employee's principal residence; (3) payment of tuition, related educational fees, and room and board expenses for the next 12 months of post-secondary education for the employee, his spouse, children or dependents; (4) the need to prevent eviction of the employee from his principal residence or foreclosure on the mortgage on his principal residence; *and for plan years beginning after January 1, 2006*, (5) funeral or burial expenses for the employee's deceased parent, spouse, children or other dependents (as defined prior to 2005); and (6) expenses for the repair or damage to the employee's principal residence that would qualify for the casualty deduction under Section 165 (without regard to the 10% floor). Treas. Reg. §1.401(k)-1(d)(3)(iii)(B). This list may be expanded by the IRS but only by publication of documents of general applicability. Treas. Reg. §1.401(k)-1(d)(3)(v). Apparently, to be the taxpayer's "principal residence" for this purpose, the home must be the residence of the employee, not merely that of his family. See ABA Joint Committee on Employee Benefits, Meeting with IRS and Department of Treasury Officials, May 7, 2004 (Q&A-18).

A distribution is not necessary to satisfy such an immediate and heavy financial need (*and will not qualify as a hardship withdrawal*) to the extent the amount of the distribution exceeds the amount required to relieve the financial need. However, the amount of an immediate and heavy financial need may include any amounts necessary to pay any federal, state, or local income taxes or penalties reasonably anticipated to result from the distribution. Treas. Reg. §1.401(k)-1(d)(3)(iv).

The distribution also will not be treated as necessary to satisfy an immediate and heavy financial need to the extent the need can be satisfied from other resources that are reasonably available. Generally, a distribution may be treated as necessary if the employer reasonably relies upon the employee's written representation that the need cannot be relieved: (1) through reimbursement or compensation by insurance or otherwise, (2) by reasonable liquidation of the employee's assets, (3) by cessation of elective contributions or employee contributions, (4) by other distributions or nontaxable loans from any plans, or (5) by loans from commercial sources. Notwithstanding these provisions, an employee need not "take counterproductive actions" (such as a plan loan that might disqualify him from obtaining other financing) if the effect would be to increase the amount of the need. Treas. Reg. §1.401(k)-1(d)(3)(iv).

Regulations state that a distribution will be *deemed* to be "necessary" to meet a financial need (deemed or otherwise) if the employee has obtained all other distributions and nontaxable loans currently available under all of the employer's plans, and the employee is prohibited from making elective contributions and employee contributions to the plan and all other plans of the employer for a period of at least six months after receipt of the hardship distribution. See Treas. Reg. §1.401(k)-1(d)(3)(iv)(E). *ASRS, Sec. 59, ¶483.7(a).*

404. How does a 401(k) plan satisfy the nondiscrimination in amount requirement?

A cash or deferred arrangement will be treated as meeting the nondiscrimination requirement of IRC Section 401(a)(4) if it satisfies the actual deferral percentage (ADP) test. IRC Sec. 401(k)(3)(C). A plan can satisfy the ADP test in any of the following three ways: (1) by annually meeting the requirements of the ADP test itself, as explained below, (2) by satisfying the design-based requirements for a SIMPLE 401(k) plan (see Q 400), or (3) by satisfying the design-based requirements for a safe harbor plan (see Q 399). IRC Secs. 401(k)(3)(A)(ii), 401(k)(11)(A), 401(k)(12)(A); Treas. Reg. §1.401(k)-1(b)(1). The final regulations cited throughout this question were published in December, 2004 and are effective for plan years beginning on or after January 1, 2006. See Treas. Reg. §1.401(k)-1(g).

A plan will not be treated as violating the ADP test merely on account of the making of (or right to make) catch-up contributions by participants age 50 or over, under the provisions of IRC Section 414(v), so long as a universal availability requirement is met. IRC Sec. 414(v)(3)(B). See Q 397 for details.

Salary reductions that give rise to the saver's credit (see Q 213) may, nonetheless, be taken into account for purposes of satisfying the ADP test. Ann. 2001-106, 2001-44 IRB 416, A-10. If the plan provides for employee after-tax contributions or employer matching contributions, those contributions must meet the requirements of IRC Section 401(m) explained in Q 405. If the plan includes a profit sharing component (i.e., nonelective contributions that are not QNECs, other than as part of one of the designs explained in Q 400 and Q 399), that portion of the plan will be subject to nondiscrimination in amount testing; see Q 326.

A cash or deferred arrangement in which all of the eligible employees for a plan year are highly compensated employees (see Q 356) will be deemed to satisfy the ADP test for the plan year. Treas. Reg. §1.401(k)-2(a)(1)(ii). A 401(k) plan is also subject to the age and service, coverage, and other requirements explained in Q 395.

Final regulations treat all governmental plans (within the meaning of Section 414(d)) as meeting the coverage and nondiscrimination requirements. Treas. Reg. §1.401(k)-1(b)(2). The IRC states that state and local governmental plans (to the limited extent that they are eligible to offer a cash or deferred arrangement—see Q 395) meet the requirements of IRC Section 401(k)(3). IRC Sec. 401(k)(3)(G); see Notice 2001-46, 2001-2 CB 122, as modified by Notice 2003-6, 2003-3 IRB 298. Under earlier guidance, plans established and maintained for its employees by the government of the United States or by any agency or instrumentality of it are treated as meeting the requirements of IRC Section 401(k)(3) until the first day of the first plan year beginning on or after the date final regulations are issued. Notice 2003-6, above.

Actual Deferral Percentage Test

The actual deferral percentage test requires that the actual deferral percentage (ADP) of eligible highly compensated employees (HCEs—see Q 356) be compared to the ADP of all other eligible employees, and that it satisfy one of the following tests:

Test 1. The actual deferral percentage for eligible highly compensated employees (see Q 356) for the plan year does not exceed the actual defer-

PENSION AND PROFIT SHARING: PLAN TYPES AND FEATURES   Q 404

ral percentage of all other eligible employees for the preceding plan year, multiplied by 1.25; OR

Test 2. The actual deferral percentage for eligible highly compensated employees for the plan year does not exceed by more than 2% that of all other eligible employees for the preceding plan year and the actual deferral percentage for highly compensated employees for the plan year is not more than the actual deferral percentage of all other eligible employees for the preceding plan year multiplied by two.

The Code provides two methods of applying the ADP test: a *prior year testing method*, and a *current year testing method*. The foregoing method is the prior year testing method (as set forth in the Code), but the current year method is available by election. See IRC Sec. 401(k)(3)(A). Under the current year testing method, the ADP results of nonhighly compensated employees for the *current year* (instead of the preceding year) are used in each test.

Changes in testing method. Regulations limit the ability of plan sponsors to switch between the current and prior year testing methods. These limits are designed to curb abuses. Generally, the election to use the current year testing method is irrevocable except with the permission of the IRS; however, a plan is permitted to change from the current year testing method to the prior year testing method under certain limited circumstances. IRC Sec. 401(k)(3)(A); see Treas. Reg. §1.401(k)-2(c)(1)(ii). A plan that changes from the current year testing method to the prior year testing method is also subject to limitations designed to prevent double counting of certain contributions. Treas. Reg. §401(k)-2(a)(6)(vi).

Plans using the prior year testing method may change back to the current year method for any subsequent testing year. IRC Sec. 401(k)(3)(A); Treas. Reg. §1.401(k)-2(c)(1)(i). The plan document must reflect which testing method the plan is using for a testing year. Treas. Reg. §1.401(k)-1(e)(7).

Changes in nonhighly compensated employee population. As a general rule, the ADP for the nonhighly compensated employees in the prior year is determined without regard to minor changes in the group of nonhighly compensated employees who are eligible under the plan in the testing year. Thus, for example, the fact that some individuals who are eligible in the testing year were not eligible in the prior year, that some who were eligible in the prior year are no longer employed by the employer, or that some have become highly compensated employees will not preclude the use of the prior year's ADP results. Treas. Reg. §1.401(k)-2(c)(4)(i).

On the other hand, special rules apply where there is a plan coverage change that becomes effective during the testing year (generally, a change is considered minor if it affects 10% or fewer of the nonhighly compensated employees). See Treas. Reg. §1.401(k)-2(c)(4)(ii).

Use of QMACs and QNECs to Satisfy ADP Test

Qualified matching contributions (QMACs) and *qualified nonelective contributions* (QNECs) are employer matching contributions and nonelective contributions (respectively) that are subject to the same nonforfeitability (see Q 395) and withdrawal restrictions (see Q 402) as elective deferral contributions. Under certain circumstances, elective contributions used to pass the ADP test may include QMACs and QNECs that are made with respect to employees eligible under the cash or deferred arrangement. IRC Sec. 401(k)(3)(D)(ii). Specific requirements for such use are set forth in regulations. See Treas. Reg. §1.401(k)-2(a)(6).

QMACs and QNECs may be used only once. In other words, such contributions that are treated as elective contributions for purposes of the ADP test may not be taken into account for purposes of the ACP test under IRC Section 401(m) and are not otherwise taken into account in determining whether any other contributions or benefits are nondiscriminatory under IRC Section 401(a)(4). Similarly, QNECs that are treated as matching contributions for purposes of the ACP test may not be used to satisfy the ADP test. See Treas. Reg. §1.401(k)-2(a)(6)(vi).

Calculation of Actual Deferral Percentage

The actual deferral percentage for a group of eligible employees is the average of the *actual deferral ratios* of employees in the group for the plan year, as calculated separately for each employee and to the nearest 1/100 of 1%. Treas. Reg. §1.401(k)-2(a)(2)(i).

An employee's actual deferral ratio is determined by dividing the amount of elective contributions (including amounts treated as elective contributions) made to the trust on his behalf for the plan year by his compensation for the plan year. Treas. Reg. §1.401(k)-2(a)(3). Only contributions allocated to the employee's account for the plan year and related to compensation which would, but for the election to defer, have been received during the plan year (or, if attributable to services performed during the plan year, within 2½ months after the close of the plan year) are considered in applying the ADP test. Designated Roth contributions (see Q 401) are treated as elective deferral contributions for purposes of the ADP test. See Treas. Reg. §1.401(k)-1(f)(3).

Compensation, for purposes of calculating actual deferral percentages, generally means compensation for services performed for an employer which is includable in gross income (see Q 331). An employer may, however, limit the period taken into account to that portion of the plan year (or calendar year) in which the employee was an eligible employee, provided that this limit is applied uniformly to all eligible employees. See Treas. Reg. §1.401(k)-6.

Miscellaneous Provisions

Although a plan must, by its terms, provide that the ADP test will be met, it may incorporate by reference the 401(k) nondiscrimination provisions of the Code and regulations. Treas. Reg. §1.401(k)-1(e)(7). *ASRS, Sec. 59, ¶483.6.*

405. What special rules apply to employer matching contributions? What rules apply to employee contributions?

A defined contribution plan that provides for employee contributions or matching contributions (e.g., typically a 401(k) plan; see Q 395) must satisfy the actual contribution percentage (ACP) test (or one of the alternatives to it, as explained below) in order to meet the nondiscrimination in amount requirement of IRC Section 401(a)(4). IRC Sec. 401(m)(1). With respect to matching contributions *only*, two alternative plan designs are available that are deemed to satisfy the ACP test: (1) a SIMPLE 401(k) plan—see Q 400, or (2) the safe harbor design explained in Q 399. See IRC Secs. 401(m)(10),

PENSION AND PROFIT SHARING: PLAN TYPES AND FEATURES   Q 405

401(m)(11). Matching contributions are subject to special vesting requirements. IRC Sec. 411(a)(12); see Q 333. The final regulations cited throughout this question were published in December, 2004 and are effective for plan years beginning on or after January 1, 2006. See Treas. Reg. §1.401(m)-1(d).

A plan will not be treated as violating the ACP test merely on account of the making of (or right to make) catch-up contributions by participants age 50 or over, under the provisions of IRC Section 414(v), so long as a universal availability requirement is met. IRC Sec. 414(v)(3)(B). See Q 397 for details on the requirements for catch-up contributions.

All after-tax *employee contributions* are subject to ACP testing even if one of the design-based alternatives is used; however, "employee contributions" for this purpose, do not include designated Roth contributions (see Q 401). The term also does not include rollover amounts, repayment of loans, or any other amounts transferred from another plan. See Treas. Reg. §1.401(m)-1(a)(3)(ii).

The contributions that are required under a safe harbor plan (see Q 399) may not be used to satisfy the ACP test for after-tax employee contributions. However, any employer matching or nonelective contributions *in excess* of the amount required to satisfy the safe harbor rules for a qualified cash or deferred arrangement can be taken into account for purposes of satisfying the ACP test. See General Explanation of Tax Legislation Enacted in the 104th Congress (JCT-12-96), p. 153 (the 1996 Blue Book). Voluntary after-tax employee contributions that give rise to the saver's credit (see Q 213) may, nonetheless, be taken into account for purposes of satisfying the ACP test. Ann. 2001-106, 2001-44 IRB 416, A-10.

Of course, the plan must satisfy the general nondiscrimination requirements applicable to all qualified plans (see Q 326). In particular, the *availability* of matching and employee contributions, as well as any other benefits, rights and features under the plan, must be nondiscriminatory (see Q 327). Treas. Reg. §1.401(m)-1(a)(1)(ii).

Actual Contribution Percentage (ACP) Test

The Code provides two methods of applying the ACP test, a *prior year testing method* and a *current year testing method*. The prior year method is specified in the Code, but the current year method is available by election. See IRC Sec. 401(m)(2)(A); Treas. Reg. §1.401(m)-2(a)(2)(ii). Generally, a plan must specify which of these two methods it is using. Treas. Reg. §1.401(m)-1(c)(2).

Prior year testing method. Under the prior year testing method, a defined contribution plan that provides for employee or matching contributions meets the ACP test if the contribution percentage for eligible highly compensated employees for the plan year does not exceed the greater of (1) 125% of the contribution percentage for all other eligible employees *for the preceding plan year*, or (2) the lesser of (a) 200% of the contribution percentage for all other eligible employees *for the preceding plan year*, or (b) such contribution percentage for all other employees *for the preceding plan year* plus two percentage points. IRC Sec. 401(m)(2)(A); Treas. Reg. §1.401(m)-2(a)(2)(ii).

Current year testing method. Under the current year testing method, the ACP results of nonhighly compensated employees for the *current year* (also known as the "testing year") are compared with those of highly compensated employees for the current year.

The plan satisfies the ACP test if the contribution percentage for eligible highly compensated employees for the plan year does not exceed the greater of: (1) 125% of the contribution percentage for all other eligible employees for the plan year, or (2) the lesser of (a) 200% of the contribution percentage for all other eligible employees for the plan year, or (b) such contribution percentage for all other employees for the plan year plus two percentage points. See IRC Sec. 401(m)(2)(A); Treas. Regs. §§1.401(m)-2(a)(1), 401(m)-2(a)(2)(ii).

A plan is not required to use the same (current or prior year) method under the ACP test as it uses under the ADP test (see Q 404), but special rules must be followed if different methods are used. See Treas. Reg. §1.401(m)-2(c)(3).

Changes in Testing Method

Change from current year testing method to prior year testing method. A plan that elects to continue using the current year testing method may be subject to certain restrictions should the employer wish to change to the prior year testing method: one governs the revocability of the election, and a second limits the "double counting" of certain contributions.

The election to use the *current year* testing method ordinarily will not be revocable except with the permission of the IRS. IRC Sec. 401(m)(2)(A). However, regulations provide for limited circumstances under which a plan will be permitted to change from the current year testing method to the prior year testing method. See Treas. Reg. §1.401(m)-2(c)(1), 1.401(k)-2(c)(1)(ii). A plan that changes from the current year testing method to the prior year testing method is also subject to limitations designed to prevent double counting of certain contributions. See Treas. Reg. §1.401(m)-2(a)(6)(vi). Plans using the *prior year* testing method may change back to the current year method for any subsequent testing year. IRC Sec. 401(m)(2)(A); see Treas. Reg. §1.401(m)-2(c)(1).

Special rules apply in the first plan year; essentially a plan (other than a successor plan) may designate the ACP of nonhighly compensated employees at 3% in the first plan year that the plan uses the prior year testing method; however, the employer may elect to use the plan's first year ACP results instead. See Treas. Reg. §1.401(m)-2(c)(2)(i). The plan document must specify which of these methods will be used. Treas. Reg. §1.401(m)-1(c)(2).

Coverage changes in nonhighly compensated employee population. As a general rule, the ACP for the nonhighly compensated employees in the prior year is determined without regard to changes in the group of nonhighly compensated employees who are eligible under the plan in the testing year. Thus, for example, the fact that some individuals who are eligible in the testing year were not eligible in the prior year, that some who were eligible in the prior year are no longer employed by the employer, or that some have become highly compensated employees will not preclude the use of the prior year's ACP results. See Treas. Reg. §1.401(m)-2(a)(2)(ii). On the other hand, special rules apply where there is a plan coverage change that becomes effective during the testing year (unless the change is minor, generally affecting 10% or fewer of the nonhighly compensated employees). A plan coverage change is a change in the group or groups of eligible employees under a plan as a result of such events as the establishment or amendment of a plan, certain plan mergers, consolidations or spinoffs, or changes in the way plans are permissively aggregated. Special rules apply if such a plan uses the prior

PENSION AND PROFIT SHARING: PLAN TYPES AND FEATURES Q 405

year testing method. See Treas. Reg. §1.401(m)-2(c)(4). For the definition of "highly compensated employee" see Q 356.

Use of QNECs to Satisfy ACP Test

Elective and qualified nonelective contributions (QNECs) may be taken into account in determining whether a plan satisfies the ACP test, provided certain requirements are met. See Treas. Reg. §1.401(m)-2(a)(6). A "QNEC" is any employer contribution (other than elective contributions and matching contributions) (1) with respect to which the employee does not have an election to receive the amount in cash, and (2) that satisfies the nonforfeitability and withdrawal restrictions applicable to elective deferrals to qualified cash or deferred (401(k)) arrangements (see Q 395 and Q 402). IRC Sec. 401(m)(4); Treas. Regs. §§1.401(m)-5, 1.401(k)-1(c)-(d).

Employer matching contributions that are treated as elective contributions for purposes of the actual deferral percentage (ADP) test applicable to cash or deferred arrangements (see Q 404) are not subject to the ACP test above and may not be used to help employee contributions or other matching contributions to satisfy this test. Similarly, a QNEC that is treated as an elective contribution is subject to the ADP test and is not taken into account as a matching contribution for purposes of the ACP test. Treas. Reg. §1.401(m)-2(a)(6)(vi).

Under limited circumstances set forth in regulations, an employer may elect to include certain elective contributions and QNECs in computing the contribution percentage. IRC Sec. 401(m)(3); Treas. Reg. §1.401(m)-2(a)(6). In order to be taken into account in the calculation of the ACP for a year under the prior year testing method, a QNEC must be contributed no later than the end of the 12-month period following the applicable year, even though that year is different than the plan year being tested. Treas. Reg. §1.401(m)-2(a)(6)(i).

Calculation of Actual Contribution Percentage

The ACP for a group of eligible employees is the average of their *actual contribution ratios* (ACRs) for the year, computed separately for each employee and to the nearest one-hundredth of one percent. An employee's ACR is (a) the sum of matching contributions and employee contributions (including any QNECs taken into account), *divided by* (b) the employee's compensation (as defined in Q 339). Treas. Reg. §1.401(m)-2(a)(3)(i). Special rules apply for the first year a plan is in existence (other than a successor plan); see above. IRC Secs. 401(m)(3), 401(k)(3)(E). Compensation, for this purpose is generally the same as under IRC Sec. 414(s) (see Q 331), based on the plan year or the calendar year ending within the plan year (whichever period is selected must be applied uniformly for every eligible employee under the plan). Treas. Reg. §1.401(m)-5.

A *matching contribution* is (1) any employer contribution, including a discretionary contribution, to a defined contribution plan on account of an employee contribution to a plan maintained by the employer; (2) any employer contribution, including a discretionary contribution, to a defined contribution plan on account of an elective deferral (as defined in Treas. Reg. §1.402(g)-1(b), see Q 396); and (3) any forfeiture allocated on the basis of employee contributions, matching contributions, or elective contributions. IRC Sec. 401(m)(4)(A); Treas. Reg. §1.401(m)-1(a)(2).

For purposes of the ACP test, employee contributions are generally contributions that are designated or treated at the time of contribution as after-tax employee contributions, and are allocated to an individual account for each eligible employee. See Treas. Reg. §1.401(m)-1(a)(3) for details.

Matching contributions are taken into account for a plan year only if such contributions (a) are allocated to the employee's account under the terms of the plan as of a date within the plan year, (b) are made on behalf of an employee on account of the employee's contributions (elective or otherwise) for the plan year, and (c) are actually paid to the trust no later than the end of the 12-month period immediately following the close of the plan year. Treas. Reg. §1.401(m)-2(a)(4)(iii) Matching contributions that do not satisfy these requirements may not be considered in applying the ACP test for *any* plan year, but instead must meet the general test for the nondiscriminatory amount requirement (see Q 326) by treating them as if they were nonelective contributions and were the only nonelective employer contributions for the year. Treas. Reg. §1.401(m)-2(a)(5).

An *eligible employee* is generally any employee who is directly or indirectly eligible to make a contribution or to receive a matching contribution (including those derived from forfeitures) for all or a portion of the plan year. Employees who would be eligible to make contributions were it not for a suspension or an election not to participate are also considered eligible. See IRC Sec. 401(m)(5); Treas. Reg. §1.401(m)-5.

Under a special rule for early participation, a plan that separately satisfies the minimum coverage rules (see Q 325), taking into account only those employees who have not completed one year of service or are under age 21, may ignore, for purposes of the ACP test, eligible nonhighly compensated employees who have not met the age and service requirements in applying the ACP test. IRC Sec. 401(m)(5)(C); Treas. Reg. §1.401(m)-4(j)(3). (This provision is designed to encourage employers to include younger employees in the plan without the concern that they will "pull down" the ACP test results.)

Although a plan must, by its terms, provide that the ACP test will be met, it may incorporate by reference the IRC Section 401(m) nondiscrimination provisions of the Code and regulations. Treas. Reg. §1.401(m)-1(c)(2).

Miscellaneous Rules

Plans that accept rollover contributions generally assume the risk that the contributions qualify for rollover treatment; however, see Q 444. The IRS determined that where a plan accepted a rollover contribution that, in fact, did not qualify for rollover, the amount involved was received by the plan as a voluntary employee contribution, which had to be considered for purposes of the ACP test explained above. See Let. Rul. 8044030.

Generally, matching contributions (other than QMACs–see Q 404) on behalf of self-employed individuals are not be treated as an elective employer contribution for purposes of the limit on elective deferrals under IRC Section 402(g). IRC Sec. 402(g)(9). *ASRS, Sec. 59, ¶430.3.*

406. What happens if a 401(k) plan fails its nondiscrimination testing?

In the event that the ratio of salary deferrals or matching contributions of highly compensated employees to those of nonhighly compensated employees exceeds the

PENSION AND PROFIT SHARING: PLAN TYPES AND FEATURES   Q 406

limits set forth in the Code, the plan must make timely distributions of the excess contributions or excess aggregate contributions as described below. The complexity of the ADP and ACP tests, as well as that of the rules which follow, have led many employers to implement design-based plans that are deemed to satisfy these tests (see Q 400, Q 399). The final regulations cited throughout this question were published in December, 2004 and are effective for plan years beginning on or after January 1, 2006. See Treas. Regs. §§1.401(k)-1(g), 1.401(m)-1(d).

Corrective distributions may not be treated as qualified Hurricane Katrina distributions. Notice 2005-92, 2005-51 IRB ___; see KETRA 2005, Secs. 2, 101, 103.

Excess Contributions

An otherwise qualified cash or deferred arrangement will not be disqualified if, before the end of the following plan year, any excess contributions are (1) distributed along with any allocable income, or (2) recharacterized by treating them as if they had been distributed to the employee and then contributed by the employee to the plan (or other plan of the employer which has the same plan year) on an after-tax basis. Excess contributions may not remain unallocated or held in a suspense account for allocation in future years. IRC Sec. 401(k)(8); Treas. Reg. §1.401(k)-2(b)(1). Nevertheless, unless the excess is distributed or otherwise corrected *within 2½ months after the end of the plan year*, the employer will be subject to a 10% excise tax. IRC Sec. 4979; Treas. Regs. §§1.401(k)-2(b)(5), 54.4979-1.

Excess contributions, with respect to a plan year, are the aggregate amount of employer contributions (i.e., including elective contributions, QNECs and QMACs treated as elective contributions) made on behalf of highly compensated employees in excess of the maximum amount permitted under the ADP test (see Q 404). IRC Sec. 401(k)(8)(B); see Treas. Regs. §§1.401(k)-6, 1.401(k)-2(b)(2)(iii). Amounts contributed in excess of the $15,000 (in 2006) ceiling on elective deferrals are "excess deferrals" (see Q 396) and should not be confused with excess contributions. Special rules apply for coordinating distributions of excess contributions and excess deferrals. See Treas. Reg. §1.401(k)-2(b)(4)(i).

Excess contributions (and income thereon) actually distributed to the employee are generally treated as received in the taxable year for which the original contribution was made; however, if the total excess amount (including any excess aggregate contributions–see below) distributed to the recipient for the plan year is less than $100, such amounts are includable in the taxable year distributed. IRC Sec. 4979(f)(2).

Corrective distributions of excess contributions (and any "gap period" income allocable thereto) must be designated as such by the employer and must be distributed to the appropriate highly compensated employees within the 12-month period following the close of the plan year for which the excess contribution was made. Treas. Reg. §1.401(k)-2(b)(2)(v). If the corrective distribution is made within 2½ months after the end of the plan year, the distribution will be includable in the employee's income for the year the amounts would have been received had he elected to receive the distribution in cash. If the corrective distribution is *not* made within 2½ months after the end of the plan year, it will be includable as income in the taxable year in which it is distributed, and the employer may be subject to an excise tax under IRC Section 4979, as explained above. However, regardless of when the corrective distribution is made, the employee will not be subject to the premature distribution penalty on it under Section 72(t) (see Q 428). Treas. Reg. §1.401(k)-2(b)(2)(vi).

Distributions of excess contributions to highly compensated employees must be made on the basis of the dollar amount of contributions by, or on behalf of, each such employee. IRC Sec. 401(k)(8)(C). For examples of this allocation, see Treas. Reg. §1.401(k)-2(b)(2)(viii). Corrective distributions of excess contributions may be made without regard to the spousal consent rules discussed in Q 336. Treas. Reg. §1.401(k)-1(b)(2)(vii)(A). Corrective distributions may not be considered for purposes of satisfying the minimum distribution requirements (see Q 338 to Q 346). Treas. Reg. §1.401(k)-2(b)(2)(vii)(C).

Recharacterization. With respect to any highly compensated employee, excess contributions may be recharacterized as after-tax employee contributions only to the extent that the recharacterized amount, together with the amount of any actual after-tax contributions, does not exceed the amount of after-tax contributions otherwise permitted by the terms of the plan. Treas. Reg. §1.401(k)-2(b)(3)(iii)(B).

Recharacterized excess contributions must be included in the employee's gross income on the earliest date any elective contributions made on behalf of the employee during the plan year would have been received. The payor or plan administrator must report such amounts as employee contributions to the IRS and the employee. See Treas. Reg. §1.401(k)-2(b)(3)(ii). These recharacterized contributions continue to be treated as *employer* contributions that are elective contributions for all other purposes under the Code (for example, they remain subject to the nonforfeitability and withdrawal requirements applicable to elective contributions); however, for purposes of nondiscrimination testing and for purposes of determining the employee's cost basis in plan distributions recharacterized excess contributions are treated as *employee* contributions, and thus are subject to the ACP test, see Q 405. See Treas. Reg. §1.401(k)-2(b)(3)(ii).

Excess Aggregate Contributions

A plan will not be disqualified under the ACP test for any plan year if, within the 12-month period following the close of that plan year, any *excess aggregate contributions* (including any income thereon) are designated as such and distributed by the plan. IRC Sec. 401(m)(6); Treas. Reg. §1.401(m)-2(b)(1).

Excess aggregate contributions are the excess of the aggregate amount of employee contributions and employer matching contributions (including any QNECs or elective deferrals treated as matching contributions) made on behalf of highly compensated employees over the maximum amount permitted under the ACP test (see Q 405). IRC Sec. 401(m)(6)(B); see Treas. Reg. §1.401(m)-5. Distributions of excess aggregate contributions must be made to highly compensated employees on the basis of the amount of contributions on behalf of (or by) that employee. IRC Sec. 401(m)(6)(C). For an example of this allocation, see Treas. Reg. §1.401(m)-2(b)(5).

Any corrective distribution of less than the entire amount of the excess aggregate contributions is treated as a pro rata distribution of excess aggregate contributions and income. Treas. Reg. §1.401(m)-2(b)(3)(iv). No premature distribution penalty tax is imposed on the distribution. Treas. Reg. §1.401(m)-2(b)(2)(vi). Corrective distributions may be made without regard to the spousal consent rules discussed in Q 336. Furthermore,

PENSION AND PROFIT SHARING: PLAN TYPES AND FEATURES   Q 407

corrective distributions may not be considered for purposes of satisfying the required minimum distribution rules (see Q 338 to Q 346). Treas. Reg. §1.401(m)-2(b)(3).

If the total amount of excess aggregate contributions (and income) is not distributed within the 12-month period following the close of the plan year, the plan will be disqualified for the year for which the excess contributions were made and all subsequent plan years in which the excess remains undistributed. Treas. Reg. §1.401(m)-2(b)(4)(ii). Furthermore, unless the excess is distributed within 2½ months after the end of the plan year, the employer will be subject to a 10% excise tax. IRC Sec. 4979; Treas. Reg. §1.401(m)-2(b)(4)(i).

Distributions of excess aggregate contributions (and income) are treated as received by the recipient in the taxable year of the employee ending with or within the plan year for which the original contribution was made; however, if the total excess amount (including any excess contributions to a 401(k) plan—see above) distributed to the recipient under the plan for the plan year is less than $100, such amount is includable in the taxable year distributed. IRC Sec. 4979; see Treas. Reg. §1.401(m)-2(b)(2)(vi)(B). Amounts distributed more than 2½ months after the plan year are includable in gross income for the taxable year of the employee in which distributed. Treas. Reg. §1.401(m)-2(b)(2)(vi)(A).

Instead of distributing excess aggregate contributions, an employer may, to the extent permitted by the terms of the plan, correct the excess by making additional QNECs that when combined (as explained in Q 405) with employee contributions and matching contributions satisfy the ACP test. Excess aggregate contributions may *not* be corrected by forfeiting vested matching contributions, through recharacterization, by failing to make matching contributions required under the plan, by refusing to allocate the excess aggregate contributions, nor by holding contributions in a suspense account for allocation in future years. Treas. Reg. §1.401(m)-2(b)(1)(iii).

In the case of a plan that includes a cash or deferred arrangement, the determination of excess aggregate contributions is made after determining excess deferrals (see Q 396) and excess contributions to the cash or deferred arrangement (see Q 404). IRC Sec. 401(m)(6)(D). *ASRS, Sec. 59, ¶¶483.6(d), 490.4(e).*

412(i) PLANS

407. What is a 412(i) plan?

A 412(i) plan, or "fully insured plan" is a defined benefit plan that is entirely funded by life insurance and annuity contracts. For an overview, see the 412(i) Navigator on p. xxi. The Internal Revenue Code provides that if the plan and contracts meet certain requirements, the plan will be exempt from the minimum funding requirements that otherwise apply to defined benefit plans. See Q 408 for details as to the requirements the contracts must meet for this exemption to apply, and Q 373 as to how 412(i) plans may satisfy the defined benefit plan accrued benefit requirements. A 412(i) plan is also subject to all of the same qualification requirements as any other defined benefit plan (note that the funding arrangement is not a qualification requirement). The general qualification requirements are explained at Q 322 to Q 360 and the plan-specific qualification requirements are explained at Q 371 to Q 373, Q 381 and Q 384.

If properly structured, a 412(i) plan offers a useful retirement planning tool by providing for level funding of defined benefit plans, based on scheduled premium payments. Since larger contributions are necessary to fully fund a plan with life insurance and/or annuities, a larger amount is deductible (within limits), as compared with other defined benefit plans.

The IRS has issued extensive guidance designed to target certain abusive 412(i) arrangements on three issues: (1) the valuation of life contracts held by and distributed out of 412(i) plans, (2) the issue of discrimination in the types of contracts provided to highly compensated employees, versus the rank and file, and (3) the ability of employers to purchase and deduct premiums paid for amounts of life insurance the Service views as excessive. For details on the application of these standards in the 412(i) plan context, see Q 408. See TD 9223, 70 Fed. Reg. 50967 (August 29, 2005); Rev. Proc. 2005-25, 2005-17 IRB 962; Rev. Rul. 2004-20, 2004-10 IRB 546; Rev. Rul. 2004-21, 2004-10 IRB 544. *ASRS, Sec. 59, ¶240.6.*

408. What requirements must a Section 412(i) plan meet in order to be exempt from the minimum funding requirements?

A 412(i) plan (i.e., a fully insured plan) is a defined benefit plan that is funded entirely by a combination of life insurance and annuity contracts. The Internal Revenue Code provides that in order to be an exempt fully insured plan, the plan must satisfy the following requirements during the plan year:

(1) it must be funded exclusively with individual insurance or annuity contracts (or a combination of both);

(2) the contracts must provide for payment of level annual or more frequent premiums over a period ending no later than the normal retirement age of each participant, or the date when he ceases participation in the plan, if earlier, and beginning on the date (or the first payment date occurring thereafter) when the individual became a participant, or the time an increase in benefits became effective;

(3) the benefits provided each individual by the plan must equal the benefits provided under each contract at normal retirement age and must be guaranteed by an insurance carrier to the extent premiums have been paid;

(4) all premiums must have been paid before the lapse, or there must be reinstatement of the policy during the plan year of the lapse and before benefits commence to any participant whose benefits are reduced because of the lapse;

(5) no rights under the contract may have been subject to a security interest at any time during the plan year; and

(6) no policy loans (including loans to individual participants) may be outstanding at any time during the plan year (loans may be made after the policy is distributed). IRC Sec. 412(i).

Regulations add that a plan funded exclusively with *group contracts*, which has the same characteristics as described above, will also be exempt. IRC Sec. 412(i); Treas. Reg. §1.412(i)-1(c). A plan may be funded by a combination of individual contracts

PENSION AND PROFIT SHARING: PLAN TYPES AND FEATURES Q 408

and a group contract, if the combination, in the aggregate, satisfies the requirements. Treas. Reg. §1.412(i)-1(d).

Valuation. Regulations issued in 2004 and finalized in 2005 require that life insurance contracts distributed from any qualified plan be valued at their *fair market value.* For details, see Q 431.

Nondiscrimination. Like any other qualified plan, a 412(i) plan is subject to Code requirements prohibiting discrimination against nonhighly compensated employees. This requirement applies to contributions and benefits (see Q 326), as well as the availability of any other benefits, rights and features (see Q 327). Generally plans providing uniform benefits and meeting the safe harbor requirements will satisfy the "nondiscriminatory in amount" requirement of IRC Sec. 401(a)(4) (see Q 326). Treas. Reg. §1.401(a)(4)-3(b)(5). However, the IRS has stated that a plan that provides highly compensated employees the right to purchase life insurance contracts from the plan at cash surrender value, but does not provide that right (or rights of equal value) to nonhighly compensated employees violates the nondiscrimination requirement. See Rev. Rul. 2004-21, 2004-10 IRB 544.

The Service has also ruled that differences in cash value growth terms or different exchange features among life insurance contracts can create an optional form of benefit, or distinctly different rights and features (see Q 327), even if the terms under which the contracts can be purchased from the plan are the same. The IRS noted that one benefit right or feature is of inherently equal or greater value than another benefit, right or feature (i.e., it is nondiscriminatory) *only if,* at any time and under any conditions, it is impossible for any employee to receive a smaller amount or a less valuable right under the first benefit, right or feature than under the second benefit right, or feature. If this "inherently equal to or greater than" standard is not met, when comparing the benefits, rights and features available to nonhighly versus highly compensated employees, the plan is discriminatory. See Rev. Rul. 2004-21, above.

Excessive amount of life insurance. The IRS has provided guidance illustrating two circumstances under which 412(i) plans have purchased excessive amounts of life insurance. See Rev. Rul. 2004-20, 2004-10 IRB 546. In the first example, the participant's benefit payable at normal retirement age is not equal to the amount provided at normal retirement age with respect to the contracts held on behalf of that participant. The Service ruled that such a plan fails to satisfy the requirements of Section 412(i)(3) (see above). Accordingly, while the plan can still be a qualified defined benefit plan, it must satisfy the other requirements of IRC Section 412, including reasonableness of actuarial assumptions.

In the second example, the life insurance contracts on the life of a participant provide for death benefits in excess of the death benefit provided to that participant under the plan. In the example, upon the employee's death, proceeds in excess of the death benefit payable to his beneficiary were applied to the payment of premiums with respect to other participants.

The Service ruled that the portion of contributions attributable to such excess coverage does not constitute "normal cost" and thus, is not deductible. Similarly, contributions to pay premiums for the disability waiver of premium feature with respect to such excess coverage were not deductible. Instead, such amounts are carried over to later

2006 Tax Facts on Insurance & Employee Benefits

years. With respect to the excess coverage, the Service stated that such premiums could be carried over and treated as contributions in later years; they are deductible in years when excess death benefits are used to satisfy the employer's obligation to pay future premiums on other participants. It should be noted that nondeductible contributions are subject to a 10% excise tax under IRC Section 4972 (see Q 367).

Transactions that are substantially similar to the example in which excessive death benefit coverage is held are classified as "listed transactions," if the employer has deducted amounts used to pay premiums on a life insurance contract with a death benefit exceeding the participant's death benefit under the plan by more than $100,000. See Rev. Rul. 2004-20, above.

Miscellaneous Rules

Premium payments will be considered level even though experience gains and dividends are applied against premiums. Treas. Reg. §1.412(i)-1(b)(2)(ii). The requirement that a plan be funded exclusively by insurance contracts does not prevent an employer from making payments in order to satisfy minimum vesting requirements with respect to accrued benefits derived from employee contributions. For example, an employer may pay the "load factor" on insurance contracts in order to meet requirements that an employee be 100% vested in the accrued benefit derived from his own contributions. Treas. Regs. §§1.412(i)-1(b)(2)(i), 1.412(i)-1(c)(2)(i). Furthermore, if certain conditions are met, a side fund may be used to fund the additional benefits required when a plan is top-heavy. See Treas. Reg. §1.416-1, M-17. See Q 351, Q 352.

An existing defined benefit plan can be converted to a fully insured plan, and the requirement that payment of level annual premiums commence with the beginning of plan participation will be considered satisfied if:

(a) the plan otherwise satisfies the requirements under IRC Sections 412(i), 403(a), and 404(a)(2) for the plan year containing the conversion date;

(b) all benefits accruing for each participant on and after the conversion date are funded by level annual premium contracts under which payments begin at the time when the increased accrual becomes effective, and end not later than the individual's normal retirement age;

(c) all benefits accrued for each participant prior to the conversion date are guaranteed through insurance or annuity contracts, the purchase price of which equals the minimum amount required by the life insurance company for a contract that guarantees to provide the accrued benefits, including any optional forms of benefit;

(d) there are meaningful continuing benefit accruals under the plan after the conversion date (i.e., for at least three years); and

(e) the following are accomplished before the conversion date: (1) the contracts are purchased guaranteeing the benefits, (2) any remaining plan assets are applied to the payment or prepayment of premiums described in (b) above, and (3) any necessary plan amendments are adopted and made effective. Rev. Rul. 94-75, 1994-2 CB 59. The IRS determined that where a defined benefit plan was terminated and plan assets were used to purchase fully insured annuity contracts for participants, no "meaningful benefit accruals" would occur after the date of the conversion; thus, the plan could not meet the requirements for conversion. TAM 9234004.

PENSION AND PROFIT SHARING: PLAN TYPES AND FEATURES Q 410

Final nondiscrimination regulations under IRC Section 401(a)(4) include a safe harbor for insurance contract plans under IRC Section 412(i). For an overview of defined benefit and pension plans, see Q 407 and Q 381. For the general qualification requirements that apply to all qualified plans, see Q 322 to Q 360, and for specific qualification requirements applying to pensions and defined benefit plans, see Q 384, and Q 371 to Q 373. For the special requirements as to how 412(i) plans may satisfy the defined benefit plan accrued benefit requirements, see Q 373. *ASRS, Sec. 59, ¶450.2(c)*.

STOCK BONUS AND EMPLOYEE STOCK OWNERSHIP PLANS

409. What is a stock bonus plan?

A stock bonus plan provides benefits similar to those of a profit sharing plan but they are distributable in stock of the employer, and employer contributions are not necessarily dependent on profits. Traditionally, the IRS has taken the position that the distribution must be in the form of employer stock (except for the value of a fractional share). Rev. Rul. 71-256, 1971-1 CB 118. The Tax Court has upheld this requirement. *Miller v. Comm.*, 76 TC 433 (1981). However, a stock bonus plan may provide for payment of benefits in cash if certain conditions are met. See Q 412. For the purpose of allocating contributions and distributing benefits, the plan is subject to the same requirements as a profit sharing plan. For additional qualification requirements, see Q 412. *ASRS, Sec. 59, ¶220*.

410. What is an employee stock ownership plan?

An employee stock ownership plan (ESOP) is a defined contribution plan that must be a qualified stock bonus plan or a qualified stock bonus plan and a qualified money purchase pension plan. IRC Sec. 4975(e)(7); ERISA Sec. 407(c)(6). For additional rules that apply to ESOPs, see Q 412 to Q 416.

An ESOP must be designed to invest primarily in "qualifying employer securities." IRC Sec. 4975(e)(7). "Qualifying employer securities" are: shares of common stock issued by the employer (or a member of the same controlled group) (a) readily tradable on an established securities market, or, (b) in case there is no such readily tradable stock, having a combination of voting power and dividend rights at least equal to the class of common stock having the greatest voting power and the class of common stock having the greatest dividend rights. Noncallable preferred shares qualify also, if they are convertible into stock meeting the requirements of (a) or (b) (as appropriate) and if the conversion price is reasonable at the time the shares are acquired by the plan. IRC Secs. 4975(e)(8), 409(l). The IRS determined that the common stock of a corporation did not constitute employer securities with respect to employees of a partnership owned by the corporation's subsidiary, because a partnership is not a corporate entity. As a result, the employees of the partnership could not participate in the corporation's ESOP. GCM 39880 (10-8-92).

Certain tax-exempt entities (such as a qualified retirement plan trust) are eligible to be shareholders of S corporations; consequently, S corporations may adopt ESOPs. See IRC Sec. 1361(c)(6); Senate Committee Report for SBJPA '96. However, special limits apply to S corporation ESOPs. See Q 380, Q 415, Q 416.

An ESOP is an "eligible individual account plan" (see Q 411) that meets additional, stricter requirements. The significant tax advantages of meeting the stricter requirements for an ESOP are: (1) certain loan transactions, including a loan guarantee, between the plan and the employer are exempt from the prohibited transaction rules against loans between plans and parties-in-interest (IRC Sec. 4975(d)(3); ERISA Sec. 408(b)(3)); (2) certain forfeitures and contributions are excluded from the annual additions limit (see Q 332, Q 377); and (3) increased deductions by a C corporation employer are permitted on loan repayments (see Q 415).

For loans made prior to August 21, 1996, certain lenders were permitted to exclude from income 50% of the interest received on certain loans to an ESOP or sponsoring corporation used to purchase employer securities. IRC Sec. 133, prior to repeal by SBJPA '96. This exclusion was repealed; however, certain refinancings and loans pursuant to a written contract in effect on June 10, 1996 are treated as having been made prior to the effective date of the repeal. SBJPA '96, Sec. 1602(c). *ASRS, Sec. 59, ¶270.1.*

411. May plans other than employee stock ownership plans be invested primarily in employer securities?

Yes, under limited circumstances. If immediately after the acquisition the aggregate fair market value of the employer securities and of employer real property held by the plan exceeds 10% of the fair market value of the assets of the plan, then only an "eligible individual account plan" which explicitly provides for the acquisition and holding of "qualifying employer securities" may acquire the employer securities. ERISA Sec. 407.

An *eligible individual account plan* is an individual account plan which is (1) a profit sharing, stock bonus, thrift, or savings plan; (2) an employee stock ownership plan (see Q 410); or (3) a money purchase plan (defined contribution pension plan) which was in existence on September 2, 1974, and which on that date invested primarily in qualifying employer securities. *Qualifying employer securities* are employer's stock and certain marketable obligations. ERISA Secs. 407(a)(2), 407(b)(1), 407(d).

Generally, S corporation (see Q 839) stock may be held by an exempt plan or tax-exempt organization; thus, S corporations may establish a plan designed to invest primarily in employer securities, including an ESOP. IRC Sec. 1361(b)(1)(B), see Q 410, Q 412, Q 416. Such plans may also be installed by other small closely held corporations as well as corporations whose shares are publicly traded. The transfer of stock to such a plan by the employer is exempt from the prohibited transaction restrictions if the transfer is for an adequate value and no commission is charged. IRC Sec. 4975(d)(13).

However, the investment in employer securities must satisfy ERISA's fiduciary standards that an investment in employer stock be prudent. An individual account plan (whether profit sharing, stock bonus, thrift or savings, and whether qualified or not) designed to invest in more than 10% of qualifying employer securities is exempt from the requirement that a plan trustee diversify the trust's investments. ERISA Sec. 404(a)(2).

Furthermore, a plan (other than an ESOP) in which more than 1% of elective deferrals under a cash or deferred arrangement are *required* to be invested in qualifying employer securities, qualifying employer real property, or both will not be treated as an eligible individual account plan. ERISA Sec. 407(b). (However, this rule does not apply to elective deferrals that are used to acquire an interest in the income or gain from employer securities or employer real property acquired: (1) before January 1, 1999; or

PENSION AND PROFIT SHARING: PLAN TYPES AND FEATURES   Q 412

(2) after January 1, 1999, but pursuant to a written contract that was binding on January 1, 1999 and at all times thereafter. ERISA Sec. 407(b).)

Investments in employer securities by qualified plans must satisfy IRS requirements that the plan be for the exclusive benefit of employees or their beneficiaries. Rev. Rul. 69-494, 1969-2 CB 88. However, the Conference Committee Report on ERISA indicates that to the extent a fiduciary meets the prudent investment rules of ERISA, he will be deemed to meet the exclusive benefit requirements of Rev. Rul. 69-494.

To qualify, such a plan must meet the applicable requirements set forth in Q 322, Q 393, and Q 378. (Notice in Q 378 that profit sharing plans are not required to pass through voting rights.) If the plan is not qualified, it is subject to the rules in Q 110 to Q 113. *ASRS, Sec. 59, ¶¶485.2, 485.4, 485.6, 710.2(c), 730.*

412. What special qualification requirements apply to stock bonus plans and employee stock ownership plans?

Both stock bonus plans and employee stock ownership plans (ESOPs, see Q 413) must meet certain distribution, payout and pass-through voting requirements. IRC Secs. 401(a)(23), 4975(e)(7). Furthermore, an ESOP that holds stock in an S corporation must provide that no "prohibited allocation" will take place with respect to any portion of the assets of the plan attributable to such securities. IRC Secs. 409(p), 4975(e)(7). For additional requirements that apply only to ESOPs, see Q 413; for requirements applying to S corporation ESOPs, see Q 416.

A stock bonus plan or ESOP generally is required to give participants the right to demand benefits in the form of employer securities, and if employer securities are not readily tradable on an established market, the participant must have the right to require the *employer* (not the plan) to repurchase employer securities under a fair valuation formula (a put option). IRC Sec. 409(h).

The requirement that participants have the right to demand benefits in the form of employer securities does not apply to the portion of a participant's ESOP account that has been reinvested under the diversification rules discussed at Q 413. IRC Sec. 409(h)(7). The requirement also does not apply in the case of (i) an employer whose charter or bylaws restrict the ownership of substantially all outstanding employer securities to employees or to a qualified plan trust, or (ii) an S corporation. See Q 417. IRC Sec. 409(h)(2)(B). Anti-cutback relief is generally available for ESOPs that are amended to eliminate the right of participants to demand benefits in the form of employer securities. See Q 334; Treas. Reg. §1.411(d)-4, A-2(d)(2)(ii), A-11.

The put option must be available for at least 60 days following distribution of the stock and, if not exercised within that time, for another 60-day (minimum) period in the following year. IRC Sec. 409(h)(4).

Planning Point: Regulations have not yet been issued governing when the second option period should begin. One realistic approach is for the second 60-day period to begin after the next plan year's appraisal has been obtained by the plan trustee. *Martin Silfen, J.D., Brown Brothers Harriman Trust Co., LLC.*

The plan may repurchase the stock instead of the employer, but may not be required to do so. Banks prohibited by law from redeeming or purchasing their own shares are excused from the requirement that they give participants a put option. IRC Sec. 409(h)(3).

If an employer is required, pursuant to the put option, to repurchase securities distributed to an employee as part of a "total distribution," the amount paid for the securities must be paid in substantially equal periodic payments (at least annually), over a period beginning within 30 days after the exercise of the put option, and not exceeding five years. Also, adequate security must be provided, and a reasonable interest paid on unpaid amounts. A *total distribution* is a distribution to the recipient within one taxable year of the balance to the credit in his account. IRC Sec. 409(h)(5). If an employer is required to repurchase securities distributed to an employee as part of an "installment distribution," the amount paid for the securities must be paid within 30 days after the put option is exercised. IRC Sec. 409(h)(6). (These requirements generally apply only with respect to stock acquired after 1986; however, a plan may elect to have such rules apply to all distributions after October 22, 1986. TRA '86, Sec. 1174(c).)

Generally, distributions are subject to mandatory 20% withholding, unless the employee elects a direct rollover. IRC Sec. 3405(c). However, the mandatory withholding requirement does not apply to any distribution that consists only of securities of the employer corporation and cash of up to $200 in lieu of stock. The maximum amount to be withheld under the mandatory withholding rules may not exceed the sum of (i) the amount of money received and (ii) the fair market value of property other than securities of the employer corporation, received in the distribution. IRC Sec. 3405(e)(8).

The plan must provide that if a participant with the consent of his spouse so elects, the distribution of his account balance will commence *within one year* after the plan year (1) in which he separates from service by reason of attainment of the normal retirement age under the plan, disability, or death, or (2) which is the fifth plan year following the plan year in which the participant otherwise separated from service. (Distribution under (2) will not be required, if the participant is re-employed by the employer before distributions actually begin under (2).) IRC Sec. 409(o)(1)(A). Special rules, explained below, apply to leveraged ESOPs where the loan(s) used to acquire the employer securities remain outstanding. See IRC Sec. 409(o)(1)(B).

The plan must also provide that, unless the participant elects otherwise, distribution of his account balance will be in substantially equal periodic payments (at least annually) over a period not longer than the greater of (a) five years, or (b) in the case of a participant with an account balance in excess of $885,000 (in 2006, as indexed), five years plus one additional year (not to exceed five additional years) for each $175,000 (in 2006), or fraction thereof, by which the employee's account balance exceeds $885,000. IRC Sec. 409(o)(1)(C). (See Appendix E for the amounts for earlier years.) IRC Sec. 409(o)(2). However, if employer securities in an ESOP are acquired with the proceeds of a loan and repayments of principal are deductible under IRC Section 404(a)(9) (see Q 415), the securities are not considered to be part of a participant's account balance for purposes of these rules until the close of the plan year in which the loan is fully repaid. IRC Sec. 409(o)(1)(B).

Planning Point: An employer whose stock is not publicly traded, and is therefore subject to the employer's potential obligation to repurchase its stock from terminating plan participants, should be concerned about the impact that obligation could have on its cash flow. The employer should consider writing its plan to take the maximum time

PENSION AND PROFIT SHARING: PLAN TYPES AND FEATURES Q 413

allowed–generally five years–to begin the process of distributing stock from the plan and then repurchasing that stock from former employees. *Martin Silfen, J.D., Brown Brothers Harriman Trust Co., LLC.*

Notwithstanding these requirements, if the general rules for commencement of distributions from qualified plans (see Q 338) require distributions to begin at an earlier date, those general rules control. See General Explanation of TRA '86, p. 840.

A stock bonus plan or ESOP must pass through certain voting rights to participants or beneficiaries. Generally, if the employer's securities are "registration-type," each participant or beneficiary must be entitled to direct the plan as to how securities allocated to him are to be voted. IRC Secs. 401(a)(28), 4975(e)(7), 409(e)(2). ("Registration-type" securities are securities that must be registered under section 12 of the Securities and Exchange Act of 1934 or would be required to be registered except for an exemption in that Act, Sec. 12(g)(2)(H).)

If the securities are not "registration-type" *and* more than 10% of the plan's assets are invested in securities of the employer, each participant (or beneficiary) must be permitted to direct voting rights under securities allocated to his account with respect to approval of corporate mergers, consolidations, recapitalizations, reclassifications, liquidation, dissolution, sale of substantially all of the business's assets, and similar transactions as provided in future regulations.

A plan meets this requirement in the case of non-registration-type securities if each participant is given *one* vote with respect to an issue and the trustee votes the shares held by the plan in a proportion which takes this into account. IRC Secs. 401(a)(22), 409(e)(3), 409(e)(5). The IRS has ruled that an ESOP will not fail to comply in operation with these pass-through voting requirements merely because the trustee of the ESOP votes the shares of stock allocated to participants' accounts for which no voting directions are timely received (whether the securities are registration type or non-registration-type). Rev. Rul. 95-57, 1995-2 CB 62. *ASRS, Sec. 59, ¶485.6.*

413. What special qualification requirements apply to employee stock ownership plans (ESOPs)?

Both stock bonus plans and employee stock ownership plans (ESOPs) must meet the requirements set forth in Q 412; S corporation ESOPs must meet the special requirements described in Q 416. In addition, an ESOP must meet the following requirements:

Qualified sales. Provisions of the plan must insure that, in the case of certain "qualified sales" of employer securities by a participant or executor to the ESOP, no portion of the assets of the plan (or any other qualified plan of the employer) attributable to the securities purchased by the plan may accrue or be allocated for the benefit of any of the following persons–

  a. a taxpayer who has elected to have the gain on the sale and replacement of employer securities deferred under the qualified sales rules of IRC Section 1042 (see Q 380).

  b. any individual who is a member of the family (brothers, sisters, spouse, ancestors, lineal descendants) or is related under the other rules of IRC Section 267(b) to the taxpayer described in (a).

c. any person not described in (a) or (b) who owns, or is considered as owning under the attribution rules of IRC Section 318(a), more than 25% (by number or value) of any class of outstanding stock of the employer or of any corporation which is a member of the same controlled group of corporations as is the employer (see Q 359). For purposes of determining whether this limitation applies, an individual is treated as owning any securities he owned during the 1-year period ending on the date of the sale to the plan, or as of the date the securities are allocated to participants in the plan. IRC Secs. 409(n)(1)(B), 409(n)(3)(B).

No employer securities acquired by the plan in *any* transaction to which IRC Section 1042 applied can be allocated to such persons. Thus, an employee who sold his employer securities to an ESOP and elected nonrecognition under IRC Section 1042 could not receive allocations based on other employer securities acquired by the plan in a different IRC Section 1042 transaction. Let. Rul. 9041071.

Nonallocation period: After the later of (1) the date which is 10 years after the date of the sale of securities, or (2) the date of the plan allocation attributable to the final payment on indebtedness incurred in connection with the sale, a plan may permit accruals or allocations for individuals described in (a) or (b), above, but not individuals described in (c). This 10-year period is referred to as the "nonallocation period." IRC Secs. 409(n)(1)(A), 409(n)(3)(C). (This time period should not be confused with the "nonallocation year" explained in Q 416.)

A special rule provides that the prohibition does not have to be applied under (b) to a lineal descendant of the taxpayer if the aggregate amount allocated for the benefit of all lineal descendants of the taxpayer during the nonallocation period is not more than 5% of the employer securities (or amounts allocated in lieu thereof) held by the plan which are attributable to a qualified sale by a member of any of the descendants' families (brothers, sisters, spouse, ancestors, lineal descendants). IRC Sec. 409(n)(3)(A).

If a plan fails to meet these requirements, not only is the plan likely to be disqualified, but a penalty tax equal to 50% of the amount of any prohibited accrual or allocation will generally be levied against the plan. Also, the amount of any prohibited accrual or allocation will be treated as if distributed to the individual involved and taxed as such. IRC Secs. 409(n)(2), 4979A.

Diversification. Generally, an ESOP must provide for diversification of investments by permitting a plan participant (including one who has already separated from service with the employer) who has completed 10 years of participation in the plan and attained age 55 to elect to direct the investment (allowing at least three investment options) of a portion of his account balance. IRC Sec. 401(a)(28).

Planning Point: An employer sponsoring an ESOP that does not otherwise offer directed investments complying with these diversification requirements may wish to design the ESOP to offer a distribution election in lieu of a diversification election, rather than make the administration of the plan needlessly complex. *Martin Silfen, J.D., Brown Brothers Harriman Trust Co., LLC.*

In the case of an ESOP that had not existed for 10 years, the IRS permitted a plan participant to count years of participation in a terminated predecessor ESOP to meet the 10 years of participation requirement. Let. Rul. 9213006.

PENSION AND PROFIT SHARING: PLAN TYPES AND FEATURES Q 413

The election is made within 90 days after the close of each plan year in the 6-plan-year period which begins with the plan year in which the employee becomes eligible to make the election. Generally, *at least* 25% of the account balance attributable to employer securities acquired by or contributed to an ESOP must be subject to the election; however, in the last year of the 6-plan-year period the 25% is increased to 50%. IRC Sec. 401(a)(28)(B)(i).

The amount that must be subject to the election at the end of a given year is generally equal to: (1) 25% (or 50% in the last year) of the total number of shares of employer securities acquired by or contributed to the plan that have ever been allocated to the participant's account on or before the most recent plan allocation date, minus (2) the number of shares previously diversified. Notice 88-56, above, A-9. Employer securities may not be one of the three investment options. See General Explanation of TRA '86, p. 838.

A plan may meet this diversification requirement by distributing the portion of an account for which an election is made. IRC Sec. 401(a)(28)(B)(ii); Notice 88-56, above. The diversification requirement can also be satisfied by allowing a participant to transfer that portion of an account for which an election is made into a qualified defined contribution plan which provides for employee directed investment and in which the required diversification options are available. Notice 88-56, above, A-13.

Any form of diversification elected (i.e., the distribution, transfer, or implementation of an investment option) must be completed within 90 days after the close of the election period. IRC Sec. 401(a)(28)(B)(i); Notice 88-56, above, A-13. An election to diversify may be revoked or amended, or a new election made, at any time during the 90-day election period. See General Explanation of TRA '86, p. 835.

Independent appraiser. With respect to plan activities, all valuations of employer securities that are not readily tradable on an established securities market must be made by an independent appraiser whose name is reported to the IRS. IRC Sec. 401(a)(28)(C). See General Explanation of TRA '86, p. 840.

Planning Point: If the company hires an appraiser and decides the appraised value is too high, that information is discoverable in any subsequent legal dispute, such as with the IRS. However, if the company's attorney hires the appraiser, the appraisal remains in the files of the law firm and is subject to attorney-work product privilege. This allows the attorney to seek a lower appraisal, without fear that the appraisal for the higher amount will be discoverable and will create support for a finding of undervaluation. *Lawrence Brody, J.D., LL.M, Bryan Cave LLP.*

Regulations. An ESOP must meet requirements set forth in Treasury regulations. IRC Sec. 4975(e)(7); ERISA Sec. 407(c)(6). The regulations require that an exempt loan must be primarily for the benefit of participants and their beneficiaries. The proceeds of an exempt loan may not be used to buy life insurance (otherwise the general rules applicable to the purchase of life insurance by qualified plans apply–see Q 369). The plan or employer may have a right of first refusal if the stock is not publicly traded. Stock that is acquired after September 30, 1976 with the proceeds of an exempt loan, and that is not publicly traded or is subject to a trading restriction, must be subject to a put option exercisable only by a plan participant or by the participant's donees or successors. The option must permit a participant to "put" the security to the employer but must not bind the plan. Nonetheless, the plan may have the right to assume the employer's obligation when the put option is exercised. An ESOP may not otherwise obligate itself to a put option or to acquire securities from a particular security holder upon the happening of an event such as the death of the holder (e.g., a buy-sell agreement). The regulations provide rules for the current distribution of income. ESOPs generally may not be integrated with Social Security. Treas. Regs. §§54.4975-7, 54.4975-11. *ASRS*, Sec. 59, ¶485.7.

414. What is a Section 1042 election? What rules apply to qualified sales to an employee stock ownership plan?

A taxpayer or executor who sells *qualified securities* to an employee stock ownership plan (ESOP–see Q 410), and purchases *qualified replacement property* may be able to elect to defer recognition of long-term capital gain on the sale. See IRC Sec. 1042(a). This is referred to as a Section 1042 election. If the election is made, the taxpayer or estate recognizes gain on the sale only to the extent that the amount realized on the sale exceeds the cost of the securities purchased to replace the stock sold to the ESOP. IRC Secs. 1042(a), 1042(b)(3).

The election must be made in a written "statement of election" and filed with the taxpayer's return for the year of sale (including extensions). IRC Sec. 1042(c)(6); Temp. Treas. Reg. §1.1042-1T, A-3(a). The statement of election must contain specific information set forth in the regulations. See Temp. Treas. Reg. §1.1042-1T, A-3(b). The election cannot be made on an amended return, and once made, is irrevocable. Temp. Treas. Reg. §1.1042-1T, A-3(a). In the absence of such an election, the Tax Court denied the deferral of gain to a taxpayer whose estate argued unsuccessfully that he had "substantially complied" with the election requirements. *Estate of J.W. Clause*, 122 TC 115 (2004). Similarly, where a taxpayer failed, through his accountant's error, to make a timely election, the IRS strictly construed the statutory deadline. See Let. Rul. 9438016.

In addition, the taxpayer must file a statement from the employer whose employees are covered by the ESOP consenting to the application of (1) an excise tax (under IRC Sec. 4978, see below) if the transferred securities are disposed of prematurely; and (2) a tax (under IRC Sec. 4979A) on prohibited allocations of securities acquired in the sale. IRC Sec. 1042(b)(3). Failure to substantially comply with the statement of election and statement of consent requirements has resulted in denial of nonrecognition treatment. Let. Rul. 9733001.

The qualified replacement property must be purchased during the period that begins three months before the sale and ends 12 months after the sale. IRC Sec. 1042(c)(3). If the replacement property has not yet been purchased when the statement of election is required, the taxpayer must file a notarized *statement of purchase* with his income tax return for the tax year following the year for which the election was made. The statement of purchase must contain specific information and be notarized within 30 days of the purchase. See Temp. Treas. Reg. §1.1042-1T, A-3.

Qualified securities, for purposes of a Section 1042 exchange, means stock (1) in a domestic C corporation (i.e., not an S corporation) that has no stock outstanding that is readily tradable on an established securities market; and (2) that was *not* (a) acquired from a qualified pension, profit sharing, or stock bonus plan, (b) acquired under an

PENSION AND PROFIT SHARING: PLAN TYPES AND FEATURES   Q 414

employer stock option plan or an employee stock purchase plan, or (c) transferred to the individual in connection with his performance of services to the corporation. IRC Sec. 1042(c)(1). In addition, the taxpayer must have held the qualified securities for at least three years before the sale to the ESOP. IRC Sec. 1042(b)(4). Nonrecognition does not apply to any gain on the sale of any qualified securities that is includable in the gross income of any C corporation. IRC Sec. 1042(d)(7).

Qualified replacement property means securities issued by a domestic operating corporation that (1) did not have more than 25% of its gross receipts in certain passive investment income (including, generally, receipts from rents, royalties, dividends, interest, annuities, and sales and exchanges of stock or securities) for the taxable year preceding the tax year in which the security was purchased; and (2) is not the corporation (or a member of its controlled group–see Q 359) that issued the qualified securities being replaced. IRC Sec. 1042(c)(4)(A).

If a taxpayer does not intend to reinvest the total amount required, under IRC Section 1042, to completely defer the gain on the sale in replacement securities, the installment method may be available for the gain that does not qualify for nonrecognition, provided that the sale otherwise qualifies as an installment sale. The amount of gain is the same proportion of the installment payment actually received in such year that the total gain to be recognized under IRC Section 1042 bears to the total amount realized. Such gain is recognized in the taxable year in which the installment payment is made. Let. Ruls. 9102021, 9102017. See Q 806.

The taxpayer's basis in his replacement securities is reduced by the amount of gain not recognized. If more than one item is purchased, the unrecognized gain is apportioned among them. IRC Sec. 1042(d). However, if a taxpayer dies while still holding replacement securities, the basis provisions of IRC Section 1014 (see Q 816) would prevail, and the replacement securities would receive a stepped-up basis. Let. Rul. 9109024. The holding period of the replacement property will include the holding period of the securities sold. IRC Sec. 1223(13).

To qualify for nonrecognition, the sale must meet certain additional requirements. Generally, the ESOP must own, immediately after the sale, at least 30% of (1) each class of outstanding stock of the corporation that issued the qualified securities; or (2) the total value of outstanding employer securities. IRC Sec. 1042(b)(2).

The IRS has determined that where a note acquired by a company's owners from an ESOP in exchange for stock was a cash equivalent for tax purposes, the stock in a separate corporation acquired in exchange for the note constituted qualified replacement property. Let. Rul. 9321067.

If a taxpayer disposes of any qualified replacement property, he will generally recognize gain (if any) to the extent that it was not recognized when the replacement property was acquired. IRC Sec. 1042(e). If a taxpayer owns stock representing control of a corporation that issued the replacement property, he will be treated as having disposed of his qualified replacement property if that corporation disposes of a substantial portion of its assets (other than in the ordinary course of its trade or business).

The recapture rules do not apply if the transfer of the qualified replacement property is (1) in a reorganization (if certain requirements are met); (2) by reason of

2006 Tax Facts on Insurance & Employee Benefits

the death of the person making the original election; (3) by gift (even if a charitable deduction is obtained; see TAM 9515002); or (4) in a subsequent transfer that is eligible for an election not to recognize gain under the rules discussed above. IRC Sec. 1042(e)(3). A transfer to a revocable trust by the taxpayer will not trigger recapture where the grantor (i.e., the taxpayer) will continue to be treated as the owner of the property transferred to the grantor trust. Let. Ruls. 9141046, 9130027. The IRS has also determined that the distribution of qualified replacement property by a trust to its beneficiary was not a "disposition" for purposes of IRC Section 1042(e); thus, the recapture rules did not apply. Let. Rul. 9226027. Although the transfer of qualified replacement property to a charitable remainder unitrust was technically a "disposition," it did not result in recapture of the deferred gain, because the donors did not realize gain on the transaction. Let. Rul. 9234023. See also Let. Ruls. 9438012 and 9438021.

Subsequent Dispositions by the ESOP

If, within three years, the ESOP disposes of stock acquired in a sale in which the seller was permitted to defer the recognition of income (as discussed above) and, as a result, the number of the ESOP's shares falls below the number of employer securities held immediately after the sale, or the value is less than 30% of the total value of all employer securities, the disposition will be subject to a tax equal to 10% of the amount realized on the disposition, unless the disposition is a distribution made by reason of (1) the death or disability of an employee; (2) retirement of the employee after age 59½; or (3) separation of the employee from service for any period which results in a 1-year break in service. IRC Sec. 4978. *ASRS Sec. 59, ¶485*.7.

415. How much may an employer deduct for its contributions to an ESOP?

The deduction limits and related rules applicable to profit sharing and stock bonus plans (see Q 392) also generally apply to employee stock ownership plans (ESOPs—see Q 410). However, C corporation ESOPs are permitted to deduct additional amounts without regard to the deduction limits for profit sharing, stock bonus, and pension plans of the same employer, to the extent such additional amounts do not exceed the IRC Section 415 limits. (The rules that follow are not available to S corporation ESOPs. IRC Secs. 404(a)(9)(C), 404(k)(1).)

An employer's ESOP contributions that are used to repay the *principal* of a loan incurred in order to acquire employer securities are deductible up to 25% of the compensation paid to covered employees in the tax year for which the deduction is taken. To be deductible, the contribution must have been both paid to the trust and applied by the trust to the repayment of the principal by the due date (including extensions) of the tax return for that year. For contributions exceeding 25%, a contribution carryover is permitted to succeeding years in which the 25% limit is not fully used (but contributions to a defined contribution plan in excess of the IRC Section 415 limits may not be carried over—Notice 83-10, 1983-1 CB 536, F-1). See IRC Sec. 404(a)(9)(A).

Contributions applied by the plan to the repayment of *interest* on a loan used to acquire employer securities may be deducted without limit in the tax year for which it is contributed, if the contribution is paid by the due date (including extensions) for filing the tax return for that year. IRC Sec. 404(a)(9)(B).

PENSION AND PROFIT SHARING: PLAN TYPES AND FEATURES Q 416

An employer sponsoring an ESOP may also deduct the amount of any dividend paid on stock held by the ESOP on the record date if, in accordance with the plan provisions, the dividend is:

(1) paid in cash to the plan participants or their beneficiaries;

(2) paid to the plan and distributed in cash to the participants or their beneficiaries within 90 days after the close of the plan year;

(3) at the election of the participants or their beneficiaries (a) payable as provided in (1) or (2), or (b) paid to the plan and reinvested in qualifying employer securities (in which case the amounts must be fully vested–see IRC Sec. 404(k)(7)); *or*

(4) used to make payments on the loan used to acquire the employer securities with respect to which the dividend is paid.

IRC Sec. 404(k)(2)(A). See also Let. Ruls. 9840048, 9523034, 9439019. Dividend payments described in IRC Section 404(k)(2) are not treated as distributions subject to withholding. IRC Sec. 3405(e)(1)(B)(iv). Furthermore, it is important to note that dividends on Section 404(k) stock are not subject to the lower income tax rates enacted in 2003 for other types of dividend payments. See IRC Sec. 1(h)(11)(B)(ii)(III).

The IRS has issued guidance on numerous issues related to the election that employers can offer participants or their beneficiaries, as described in (3), above. See Notice 2002-2, 2002-1 CB 285.

The deduction for dividends that the participant elects to reinvest in qualifying employer securities (as described in (3) above) is allowable for the taxable year in which (a) the reinvestment occurs; or (b) the election is made, whichever is later. Section 404(k)(4)(B).

The IRS may disallow the deduction for a dividend under Section 404(k)(1) if the dividend constitutes, in substance, an avoidance or evasion of taxation. IRC Sec. 404(k)(5)(A); see also Let. Rul. 9304003.

The authority of the IRS to recharacterize excessive dividends paid on ESOP stock as employer contributions was upheld by the Court of Appeals for the Eighth Circuit, in a ruling that resulted in disqualification of the ESOP for its resulting failure to meet the IRC Section 415 limits. *Steel Balls, Inc. v. Comm.* 96-1 USTC ¶50,309 (8th Cir. 1996), aff'g TC Memo 1995-266. *ASRS, Sec. 59, ¶540.4.*

416. What requirements apply when an S corporation maintains an ESOP?

Certain tax-exempt entities (such as a qualified retirement plan trust) are eligible to be shareholders of S corporations; as a result, an S corporation can adopt an ESOP. See IRC Sec. 1361(c)(6); Senate Committee Report for SBJPA '96. However, special rules apply to the allocation of stock from an S corporation ESOP to certain individuals, and certain tax treatment otherwise available to ESOP sponsors, such as the deductions for employer contributions to the plan and for dividends paid on employer securities, or the rollover of gain on the sale of stock to an ESOP (see Q 415, Q 380) are not available to S corporations sponsoring an ESOP.

The IRS has stated that an ESOP may direct certain rollovers of distributions of S corporation stock to an IRA, in accordance with a distributee's election, without terminating the corporation's S election, provided certain requirements are met. See Rev. Proc. 2004-14, 2004-7 IRB 489.

S corporations that maintain an ESOP are subject to special rules with respect to the deduction of certain employer contributions and dividends paid on employer securities (see Q 415), the rollover of gain on the sale of stock to an ESOP (see Q 380), and the sale of employer securities by a shareholder-employee (as defined in IRC Sec. 4975(f)(6)) to an ESOP. See IRC Sec. 1361(c)(6); Senate Committee Report for SBJPA '96; Q 443. An S corporation that maintains an ESOP also is generally exempt from the requirement that employees be able to demand distribution of employer securities. See IRC Sec. 409(h)(2)(B); see also Q 412. Furthermore, an ESOP maintained by an S corporation will not be treated as receiving unrelated business income on items of income or loss of the S corporation in which it holds an interest. IRC Sec. 512(e)(3).

Prohibited Allocations of Stock

An ESOP that holds securities consisting of stock in an S corporation must also provide that no portion of the assets of the plan attributable to such securities will accrue or be allocated, directly or indirectly, to a "disqualified person" during a "nonallocation year." IRC Secs. 409(p), 4975(e)(7); Temp. Treas. Reg. §1.409(p)-1T(b)(1). Such an allocation is referred to as a prohibited allocation.

A *disqualified person* is any person for whom: (i) the number of the person's deemed-owned ESOP shares is at least 10% of the number of deemed-owned ESOP shares of the S corporation; (ii) the aggregate number of the person's deemed-owned ESOP shares and synthetic equity shares is at least 10% of the aggregate number of deemed-owned ESOP shares and synthetic equity shares of the S corporation; (iii) the aggregate number of deemed-owned ESOP shares of the person and his family is at least 20% of the number of deemed-owned ESOP shares of stock in the S corporation; *or* (iv) the aggregate number of deemed-owned ESOP shares and synthetic equity shares of the person and his family is at least 20% of the aggregate number of deemed-owned ESOP shares and synthetic equity shares of the S corporation. Temp. Reg. §1.409(p)-1T(d)(1); see IRC Secs. 409(p)(4)(A), 409(p)(4)(B).

"Family member" means the individual's spouse, an ancestor or lineal descendant of the individual or spouse, a sibling of the individual or spouse, and lineal descendants of any siblings, as well as spouses of the aforementioned individuals (except in the case of a legal separation or divorce). IRC Sec. 409(p)(4)(D); Temp. Reg. §1.409(p)-1T(d)(2). "Deemed-owned shares" with respect to any person are: (1) the stock in the S corporation constituting employer securities of an ESOP which is allocated to such person's account under the plan, and (2) such person's share (based on the same proportions as of the most recent allocation) of the stock in the corporation which is held by the ESOP but which is not allocated under the plan to participants. IRC Sec. 409(p)(4)(C), Temp. Reg. §1.409(p)-1T(e).

A *nonallocation year* means any plan year of the ESOP, if at any time during the year the ESOP holds any employer securities that are shares in an S corporation; and disqualified persons own at least 50% of (a) the number of outstanding shares in the

PENSION AND PROFIT SHARING: PLAN TYPES AND FEATURES — Q 416

S corporation (including deemed owned shares), *or* (b) the aggregate number of outstanding shares of stock (including deemed owned shares) and synthetic equity in the S corporation. IRC Sec. 409(p)(3)(A); Temp. Reg. §1.409(p)-1T(c)(1). For purposes of determining whether there is a nonallocation year, the attribution rules of Code section 318(a) apply in determining stock ownership, except that the broader "family member" rules above apply, the IRC Section 318(a) rules regarding options do not apply, and an individual is treated as owning "deemed-owned" shares. IRC Sec. 409(p)(3)(B); Temp. Reg. §1.409(p)-1T(c)(2).

In the event that a "prohibited allocation" is made in a "nonallocation year" to a "disqualified person," the plan will be treated as having distributed the amount of the allocation to the disqualified person on the date of the allocation. IRC Sec. 409(p)(2)(A). In other words, the allocation is a taxable distribution to the individual. For details on the application of this rule, see Temp. Reg. §1.409(p)-1T(b). Furthermore, an excise tax of 50% of the amount involved is imposed on the allocation, and a 50% excise tax is imposed on any "synthetic equity" owned by a disqualified person. IRC Sec. 4979A(a). The 50% excise taxes are imposed against the employer sponsoring the plan. IRC Sec. 4979A(c).

"Synthetic equity" includes any stock option, warrant, restricted stock, deferred issuance stock right, stock appreciation right payable in stock, or similar interest or right that gives the holder the right to acquire or receive stock of the S corporation in the future. Synthetic equity also includes a right to a future payment (payable in cash or any other form other than stock of the S corporation) that is based on the value of the stock of the S corporation or appreciation in such value, or a phantom stock unit. IRC Sec. 409(p)(6)(C); Temp. Reg. §1.409(p)-1T(f)(2).

Synthetic equity also includes any remuneration under certain nonqualified deferred compensation arrangements for services rendered to the S corporation, or a related entity. See Temp. Reg. §1.409(p)-1T(f)(2)(iv). The stock upon which "synthetic equity" is based will be treated as outstanding stock of the S corporation and deemed-owned shares of the person owning the synthetic equity, if such treatment results in (a) the treatment of any person as a disqualified person or (b) the treatment of any year as a nonallocation year. See IRC Sec. 409(p)(5).

Effective date. The Code provisions governing prohibited allocations generally apply to plan years beginning after 2004. A delayed effective date for application of the prohibited allocation rules may be permitted under the Code in the case of: (1) an ESOP established after March 14, 2001, or (2) an ESOP established on or before March 14, 2001 that was holding stock in a corporation for which an S election was not in effect on that date, the rules apply to plan years ending after March 14, 2001. EGTRRA 2001, Sec. 565(d)(2). However, the delayed effective date applies only to S corporations that provide broad-based employee coverage and that benefit rank-and-file employees as well as highly compensated employees and historical owners. See Rev. Rul. 2003-6, 2003-3 IRB 286.

Temporary regulations explaining the prohibited allocation rules of the Code were first issued in 2003 and restated in 2005. The temporary regulations are generally applicable for plan years beginning on or after January 1, 2005. For details and extensive transition rules, see Temp. Reg. §1.409(p)-1T(i). *ASRS, Sec. 59, ¶485.7(f)*.

2006 Tax Facts on Insurance & Employee Benefits

S Corporation Plans

417. What special requirements apply to plans covering shareholder-employees of S corporations?

With respect to qualification, plans of an S corporation (whether defined benefit or defined contribution) generally must meet the same requirements applicable to other corporate plans. See Q 322. For an explanation of the income tax treatment of S corporations see Q 839, and for the general requirements for an ESOP, see Q 410, Q 412 and Q 413.

The special rules that apply to S corporation ESOPs are explained at Q 416. Certain abusive S corporation ESOPs will not be treated as qualified plans, will be subject to prohibited transaction penalties (see Q 443) and are among the "listed transactions" treated as corporate tax shelters (subject to additional penalties). See Rev. Rul. 2003-6, 2003-3 IRB 286. *ASRS, Sec. 59, ¶490.4(b).*

Keogh Plans

418. What special qualification rules apply to Keogh plans?

A Keogh (or HR-10) plan is a qualified plan that covers self-employed individuals. As a general rule, a qualified trust must be established by an *employer* for the exclusive benefit of the employer's *employees* or their beneficiaries. IRC Sec. 401(a)(2). Obviously, self-employed individuals (proprietors or partners operating a trade, business, or profession) are not employees in the commonly accepted sense of the term (see Q 354). However, for the limited purpose of allowing such individuals to participate in qualified plans and to enjoy the principal tax advantages available to other participants in such plans, the law confers employee status on them. Thus, the Internal Revenue Code says that for purposes of section 401, the term "employee" includes for any taxable year an individual who has "earned income." IRC Sec. 401(c)(1).

The term "earned income" means, in general, net earnings from self-employment in a trade or business in which personal services of the individual are a material income-producing factor. IRC Sec. 401(c)(2). Thus, a partner who has contributed capital to the firm but renders no personal services for it has no "earned income" from the firm and cannot participate in a qualified plan of the partnership. Treas. Reg. §1.401-10(c)(3).

In arriving at net earnings, business expenses, including contributions to the plan on behalf of regular employees, must be deducted. In computing the earned income of a self-employed person, employer contributions to the plan on his own behalf must be deducted. IRC Secs. 401(c)(2)(A)(v), 404(a)(8)(C). In addition, the employer's share of the self-employment tax must be subtracted. A partner's earned income is his share of partnership net income, including any draw or "salary" he receives. IRC Secs. 401(c)(2), 1402(a).

Most of the rules for qualified retirement plans covering common law employees apply equally to plans that cover self-employed individuals. Certain limitations apply if a plan is top-heavy (see Q 351 to Q 352, Q 428), or if the individuals are "key employees" or are "5% owners," even if the plans are not top-heavy.

PENSION AND PROFIT SHARING: PLAN TYPES AND FEATURES   Q 419

The following special rules apply to plans covering self-employed individuals:

(1) Contributions on behalf of a self-employed individual may be made only with respect to his "earned income" (as defined above). In computing his earned income, a self-employed individual must deduct employer contributions made to the plan on his own behalf. Thus, for example, while a common law employee would need only $176,000 of compensation to support a deductible contribution of $44,000 to a defined contribution plan (see Q 392), a self-employed individual would need net earnings of $220,000 ($176,000 plus $44,000) or more in order to receive a contribution of the same amount. See IRC Sec. 401(d).

(2) Generally, matching contributions (other than QMACs, see Q 327) made on behalf of self-employed individuals are not treated as elective deferrals for purposes of the limit on such deferrals under IRC Section 402(g). See Q 396, Q 404. IRC Sec. 402(g)(9). *ASRS, Sec. 60.*

419. What are the rules governing the deduction for Keogh plan contributions?

For purposes of the deduction limit, "earned income" of a self-employed individual *does not* include the contribution on behalf of the self-employed person. IRC Sec. 404(a)(8)(D).

In determining his adjusted gross income, a self-employed person deducts his plan contributions directly from gross income–the deduction is allowable whether or not he itemizes deductions. A partner deducts the portion of the contribution made by the partnership on his behalf on his own individual return, and such contributions are not treated as expenses of the partnership. IRC Sec. 62(a)(6); Treas. Regs. §§1.62; 1.404(e)-1A(f).

Contributions on behalf of a self-employed individual may not be used to create or increase a net operating loss. IRC Sec. 172(d)(4)(D).

Employer contributions allocable to the purchase of life, accident, health, or other insurance on behalf of self-employed persons are not deductible. The cost of such coverage (see Q 424) is subtracted from the full contribution to determine the amount deductible. IRC Sec. 404(e); Treas. Reg. §1.404(e)-1A(g).

If life insurance protection is provided under the plan, the amount to be subtracted is the Table 2001 (or P.S. 58) cost, as explained in Q 424, plus the cost of any contract extras, such as a waiver of premium. If amounts attributable to deductible employee contributions are used to purchase life insurance, the amount to be subtracted is the amount so used. *ASRS, Sec. 60, ¶410.*

PENSION AND PROFIT SHARING: TAXATION OF DISTRIBUTIONS

PLAN LOANS

420. What are the tax and qualification consequences of a loan from a qualified plan?

A loan from a plan to a participant or beneficiary will be treated as a taxable distribution unless it meets certain requirements regarding (1) the enforceability of the agreement; (2) the term of the loan; (3) repayment; *and* (4) the dollar limitation, all of which are discussed in detail in Q 421. IRC Sec. 72(p)(2); Treas. Reg. §1.72(p)-1, A-3.

The repayment of a loan treated as a distribution will be considered a nondeductible employee contribution for tax purposes. Sen. Rept. 97-494, 97th Cong. 2nd Sess. When the recipient's benefit is later distributed to him, the amount already taxed will not be taxed again. Such repayments constitute investment in the contract (i.e., basis). Let. Rul. 9122059. They are not considered annual additions subject to the IRC Section 415 limits. Notice 82-22, 1982-2 CB 751.

A reduction or offset of a participant's account balance in order to repay a plan loan can be a "qualified Hurricane Katrina distribution," if the participant is a *qualified individual*. See Notice 2005-92, 2005-51 IRB ___. A qualified individual is an individual whose principal place of abode on August 28, 2005 was located in the Hurricane Katrina disaster area (i.e., Louisiana, Mississippi, Alabama or Florida, for purposes of KETRA 2005 relief), *and* who sustained an economic loss by reason of Hurricane Katrina. KETRA 2005, Sec. 103(c); Notice 2005-92, above. The definition and tax treatment of qualified Hurricane Katrina distributions is explained at Q 427 and Q 429.

Plan Qualification

The rules relating to the taxation of loans ordinarily do not affect the plan qualification rules, except as described below. Generally, a qualified plan can provide for loans to participants if they are adequately secured, bear a reasonable rate of interest, have a reasonable repayment schedule and are made available on a nondiscriminatory basis. IRC Sec. 4975(d)(1); Notice 82-22, 1982-2 CB 751; Rev. Rul. 71-437, 1971-2 CB 185; Rev. Rul. 67-288, 1967-2 CB 151. Plan loans are generally subject to the automatic survivor benefit requirements, and thus may require spousal consent. See Q 336.

Treatment of a loan as a distribution for tax purposes does not generally affect plan qualification. A *bona fide* loan that is not a prohibited transaction (see Q 443) will not cause a pension plan to fail to satisfy the requirement that a pension plan primarily provide benefits for employees or their beneficiaries over a period of years or for life after retirement. Notice 82-22, above. However, when a plan loaned out almost all of its assets to the company president, without seeking adequate security, a fair return, or prompt repayment, the plan was held not to have been operated for the exclusive benefit of the employees, and plan disqualification was justified. *Winger's Dept. Store, Inc. v. Comm.*, 82 TC 869 (1984).

A deemed distribution under IRC Section 72(p) will not be treated as an actual distribution for purposes of the qualification requirements of IRC Section 401; thus,

PENSION AND PROFIT SHARING: TAXATION OF DISTRIBUTIONS   Q 420

plan qualification will not be affected by reason of a deemed distribution. However, if a participant's accrued benefit is reduced (offset) in order to repay a plan loan, an actual distribution occurs for purposes of IRC Section 401. An *offset distribution* from a 401(k) plan at a time when the plan is not otherwise permitted to make a distribution would result in plan disqualification. See Treas. Reg. §1.72(p)-1, A-12, A-13.

A plan loan that is secured by the participant's (or beneficiary's) interest in the plan, but that is not a prohibited transaction, will not generally be an assignment or alienation of plan benefits that would disqualify a plan. Treas. Reg. §1.401(a)-13(d)(2). See Q 348. See also Notice 82-22, above. However, if there is a tacit understanding that collection of a loan is not intended, the loan may be treated as a disqualifying distribution if made at a time when the plan is not permitted to make distributions. See Rev. Rul. 71-437, 1971-2 CB 185.

If an actual distribution follows a deemed distribution, a plan must treat the "loan transition amount" (the amount by which the initial default amount, attributed as tax basis, exceeds the tax basis immediately preceding the transition date, plus any increase in tax basis thereafter) as an outstanding loan, taxable upon actual distribution. The plan may not attribute investment in the contract (tax basis–see Q 435) based upon the initial default amount, and, to the extent that a tax basis has been attributed, it must be reduced by the initial default amount.

Cash repayments made after a loan is deemed to have been distributed increase the participant's tax basis as if they were after-tax contributions (although they are not treated as after-tax contributions for other purposes). Treas. Reg. §1.72(p)-1, A-19 through A-21, see also Treas. Reg. §1.72(p)-1, A-1 through A-18.

Prohibited transactions. Plan loans that do not meet any of the requirements for a prohibited transaction exemption (see Q 443) could result in plan disqualification. The prohibited transaction rules apply to a loan that does not meet the exemption requirements, even if it is treated as (and taxed as) a distribution. *Medina v. U.S.*, 112 TC 51 (1999) (see Q 443).

Loans from a qualified plan to certain S corporation shareholders, partners, and sole proprietors are no longer, by definition, prohibited transactions (see Q 443). IRC Sec. 4975(f)(6)(B)(iii). Prior to 2002, a loan from a qualified plan made to an owner-employee (including his spouse, brothers, sisters, ancestors, and lineal descendants) was a prohibited transaction. IRC Sec. 4975(d), flush language, prior to amendment by EGTRRA 2001.

Investments in residential mortgages. Plan investments in residential mortgages (other than to officers, directors, or owners, or their beneficiaries) are permitted, but they are subject to the limitations of IRC Section 72(p) unless they are made in the ordinary course of a plan investment program (as defined in the regulations), which is not limited to participants and their beneficiaries. Treas. Reg. §1.72(p)-1, A-18. A longer term may be permitted. See Q 421.

Mandatory Withholding

Generally, distributions from a qualified plan are subject to mandatory income tax withholding at the rate of 20%, unless the participant elects a direct rollover. IRC Sec. 3405(c). The IRS has stated that since a deemed distribution attributable to a plan loan that does not meet the requirements of IRC Section 72(p), above, it will not be subject to the 20% mandatory withholding requirement, because such a distribution cannot be an "eligible rollover distribution." However, where a participant's accrued benefit is reduced (i.e., offset) in order to repay a plan loan, such as when employment is terminated, the offset amount may constitute an eligible rollover distribution. See Notice 93-3, 1993-1 CB 293. Mandatory withholding is required on a deemed distribution of a loan, or a loan repayment by benefit offset only to the extent that a transfer of cash or property (other than employer securities) is made to the participant or beneficiary from the plan at the same time. Treas. Reg. §1.72(p)-1, A-15. *ASRS, Sec. 59, ¶980.*

421. What requirements must a qualified plan loan meet in order to avoid taxation as a distribution?

In order to avoid being taxed as a distribution, a loan made from a plan to a participant (or beneficiary) must be made pursuant to an enforceable agreement, and the agreement must meet certain requirements with respect to the term of the loan, its repayment, and the dollar amount loaned. IRC Sec. 72(p)(2); Treas. Reg. §1.72(p)-1, A-3(a).

Loan Agreement

A plan loan must be evidenced by a legally enforceable agreement, which may be composed of more than one document. The agreement must specify the date, amount, and term of the loan, as well as the repayment schedule. The agreement need not be signed if it is enforceable without a signature under applicable law. Treas. Reg. §1.72(p)-1, A-3(b). Generally, the date of the loan is the date the loan is funded (i.e., the date of delivery of the check to the participant). ABA Joint Committee on Employee Benefits, Meeting with IRS and Department of Treasury Officials, May 7, 2004 (Q&A-4).

The agreement must be set forth in (1) a written paper document; (2) an electronic medium; or (3) such other form as approved by the IRS commissioner. Treas. Reg. §1.72(p)-1, A-3(b). If the loan agreement is in the form of an electronic medium, the medium must be reasonably accessible to the participant (or beneficiary), and be provided under a system that is reasonably designed to preclude any individual other than the participant (or beneficiary) from requesting a loan. Treas. Reg. §1.72(p)-1, A-3(b)(2).

The system must also provide the participant (or beneficiary) with a reasonable opportunity to review the terms of the loan, and to confirm, modify, or rescind the terms of the loan before it is made. Treas. Reg. §1.72(p)-1, A-3(b)(2)(ii). Finally, the system must provide a confirmation to the participant (or beneficiary) within a reasonable time after the loan is made. The confirmation may be made on a written paper document or through an electronic medium that meets the accessibility requirements above. The electronic confirmation must be no less understandable than a written paper document, and must inform the participant (or beneficiary) of his right to receive the confirmation via a written paper document at no charge. Treas. Reg. §1.72(p)-1, A-3(b)(2)(iii).

Term Requirement

Generally, the term of the loan must be no longer than five years. If the loan does not meet the term requirement, the entire loan is a distribution. IRC Sec. 72(p)(2)(b)(i). A distribution is deemed to occur the first time the term requirement is not met in form or operation; thus, it may occur at the time the loan is made, or at a later date. Treas. Reg. §1.72(p)-1, A-4.

PENSION AND PROFIT SHARING: TAXATION OF DISTRIBUTIONS Q 421

In the case of a plan loan to a "qualified individual" (see Q 420) affected by Hurricane Katrina, the period during which repayment is suspended (see below) may be disregarded for purposes of the 5-year term requirement. See Notice 2005-92, 2005-51 IRB ___.

If a loan initially satisfies the term requirement but payments are not made under the terms of the loan, a deemed distribution occurs as a result of the failure to make the payments. Treas. Reg. §1.72(p)-1, A-4. While such a failure will constitute an immediate violation of the loan provisions, the plan may allow for a "cure" period of up to three months beyond the calendar quarter in which the payment was due. A distribution in the amount of the entire outstanding balance of the loan will be deemed to have occurred on the last day of the cure period. Treas. Reg. §1.72(p)-1, A-10. Legislative history suggests that a loan treated as a distribution because its repayment period was not limited to five years cannot be corrected by renegotiation or repayment. Sen. Rept. 97-760, 97th Cong. 2nd Sess. If a loan is outstanding when a total distribution is made to a participant, the loan is treated as repaid (and the amount included in the distribution) on the date of distribution; thus, inclusion in income cannot be deferred until the end of the 5-year period. Let. Rul. 8433065.

An exception to the 5-year rule exists for residence loans, that is, those used to "acquire a dwelling unit which is to be, within a reasonable time, the principal residence of the participant." IRC Sec. 72(p)(2)(B)(ii); see Q 422 for details.

Repayment

The loan agreement must specify the amount and term of the loan and the repayment schedule. Treas. Reg. §1.72(p)-1, A-3(b). Failure to make a timely payment of a plan loan installment when due will generally result in a deemed distribution; however, the agreement may provide for a "cure" period, so long as such cure period does not extend beyond the end of the calendar quarter following the quarter in which the payment was due. Treas. Reg. §1.72(p)-1, A-10.

Special repayment terms may apply to individuals affected by Hurricane Katrina. If a "qualified individual" (see Q 420) has an outstanding plan loan after August 24, 2005, the due date for any repayment due after August 24, 2005 and before January 1, 2007 is delayed for one year. See KETRA 2005, Sec. 103(b); Notice 2005-92, 2005-51 IRB ___. Subsequent payments are also adjusted for the delay. The IRS has published safe harbor guidance for satisfying these provisions. See Notice 2005-92, above.

A loan that was not repayable in full within five years, and that had a balloon payment at the end was held to be a premature distribution subject to the 10% penalty (see Q 428) because it violated both the term requirement and the level amortization requirement. However, the participant was not subject to the substantial understatement or negligence components of the accuracy-related penalty, because he relied in good faith on the plan administrator's representations that the plan loan was in compliance. *Plotkin v. Comm.*, TC Memo 2001-71.

It should be noted that U.S. bankruptcy courts have held that a debtor's repayment of a participant loan from a 401(k) plan is not necessary for support, and thus is not exempt from the bankruptcy estate. *In re Darcy I. Estes*, 2000 Bankr. LEXIS 1264, *In re Cohen*, 2000 Bankr. LEXIS 268. See also Q 348.

Repayment during Military Service

A participant may suspend repayment of a loan during any period that he serves in the uniformed services. IRC Sec. 414(u)(4). This rule applies regardless of whether the service performed is "qualified military service" under the Uniformed Services Employment and Reemployment Rights Act of 1994 (USERRA '94). The suspension of repayment under these circumstances may extend beyond one year (unlike the suspension rules for other leaves of absence). Treas. Reg. §1.72(p)-1, A-9.

The participant must resume loan repayment once he completes his service with the uniformed services, at which time payments must be made as frequently and in an amount no less than was made before the suspension. The latest permissible term of the loan is five years from the date of the original loan, plus any period during which repayment was suspended due to military service. Treas. Reg. §1.72(p)-1, A-9.

Dollar Limit

Generally, the amount of the loan (when added to the outstanding balance of all other loans, whenever made, from all plans of the employer) may not exceed the lesser of (1) $50,000 (reduced by the *excess* of the highest outstanding balance of plan loans during the 1-year period ending on the day before the date when the loan is made *over* the outstanding balance of plan loans on the date when the loan is made); or (2) one-half of the present value of the employee's nonforfeitable accrued benefit under such plans (determined without regard to any accumulated deductible employee contributions). But a plan may provide that a minimum loan amount (up to $10,000) may be borrowed, even if it is more than one-half of the present value of the employee's nonforfeitable accrued benefit. IRC Sec. 72(p)(2)(A). For valuation purposes, a valuation within the past 12 months may be used, if it is the latest available. Notice 82-22, 1982-2 CB 751.

Increased limits apply to certain individuals affected by Hurricane Katrina. In the case of a loan to a qualified individual (see Q 420) occurring after September 23, 2005 and before January 1, 2007, the $50,000 limit, as described above, is increased to $100,000 and the 50% limit on the amount of the employee's vested accrued benefit is increased to 100%. See KETRA 2005, Sec. 103(a); Notice 2005-92, 2005-51 IRB ___.

If the loan does not meet the dollar limitation, a distribution of the amount in excess of the dollar limit is deemed to occur when the loan is made. Treas. Reg. §1.72(p)-1, A-4(a). If the outstanding loan balance meets the dollar limitation immediately after the date when the loan is made, the loan will not be treated as a distribution merely because the present value of the employee's nonforfeitable accrued benefit subsequently decreases. General Explanation–TEFRA, p. 296.

In determining the outstanding balance and the present value of the nonforfeitable accrued benefit under the plan, the employer's plans include plans of all members of a controlled group of employers, of trades and businesses under common control, and of members of an affiliated service group (see Q 359 and Q 360 for definitions). IRC Sec. 72(p)(2)(D)(i). The plans include all qualified pension, profit sharing, and stock bonus plans, all IRC Section 403(b) tax sheltered annuities, and all IRC Section 457 deferred compensation plans of aggregated employers. IRC Sec. 72(p)(2)(D)(ii). Outstanding loans made before August 14, 1982 are included in determining whether loans made thereafter exceed the limit. It is possible that the IRS may interpret "outstanding loans" to include any loans that have not been repaid and have been previously treated as distributions. *ASRS, Sec. 59, ¶980.*

PENSION AND PROFIT SHARING: TAXATION OF DISTRIBUTIONS   Q 422

422. What other rules apply to loans from a qualified plan?

Residence loans. Plan investments in residential mortgages (other than to officers, directors, or owners, or their beneficiaries) are permitted, but they are subject to the limitations of IRC Section 72(p) (see Q 421) unless they are made in the ordinary course of a plan investment program (as defined in the regulations), which is not limited to participants and their beneficiaries. Treas. Reg. §1.72(p)-1, A-18.

Provided the loan is to "acquire a dwelling unit which is to be, within a reasonable time, the principal residence of the participant," it will not be subject to the term requirement explained in Q 421. See IRC Sec. 72(p)(2)(B)(ii). The determination of whether the unit is to be used, within a reasonable time, as the participant's principal residence is made when the loan is made. Legislative history indicates that a dwelling unit includes a house, apartment, condominium, or mobile home not used on a transient basis. The determination of whether plan loan proceeds are used for the purchase or improvement of a principal residence is made using the tracing rules under IRC Section 163(h)(3)(B). Treas. Reg. §1.72(p)-1, A-7.

Planning Point: While a mortgage is not required for this purpose (see Treas. Reg. §1.72(p)-1, A-6), the participant may want to give the trustee a mortgage in order to qualify the interest as deductible interest. Treasury Department regulations require that in order for interest to be deductible as "qualified residence interest," (see Q 422, Q 823) the borrower must give the lender a mortgage, and the lender must actually take the step of recording the mortgage. *Martin Silfen, J.D., Brown Brothers Harriman Trust Co., LLC.*

No specific time limit is placed on residential loans; however, the loans must provide for substantially level amortization, with payments to be made at least quarterly. See IRC Sec. 72(p)(2)(C). This requirement does not preclude repayment or acceleration of the loan prior to the loan period, nor the use of a variable interest rate. General Explanation–TRA '86, p. 728. Of course, all loans (regardless of when made) must provide for a reasonable repayment schedule in order to qualify as a loan exempt from the prohibited transaction rules (see Q 443). A loan need not be secured by the residence in order to be considered a principal residence plan loan. Treas. Reg. §1.72(p)-1, A-6.

Assuming that the loan is otherwise a bona fide debt, a taxpayer may deduct interest paid on a mortgage loan from his qualified plan, even though the amount by which the loan exceeded the $50,000 limit of IRC Section 72(p) was deemed to be a taxable distribution. FSA 200047022.

Plan loan defined. Both direct and indirect loans are considered loans. A participant's (or beneficiary's) assignment, agreement to assign, pledge, or agreement to pledge any portion of his interest in the plan is considered to be a loan of that portion. However, if a participant's interest in a plan is pledged or assigned as security for a loan, only the amount of the loan, not the amount assigned or pledged, is treated as a loan. Treas. Reg. §1.72(p)-1, A-1.

Any amount received as a loan under a contract purchased under a plan (and any assignment or pledge with respect to such a contract) is treated as a loan under the plan. IRC Secs. 72(p)(1)(B), 72(p)(3). This would appear to treat a policy loan by a trustee as a loan to the participant. However, "if a premium which is otherwise in default is paid in the form of a loan against the contract, the loan is not considered made to the participant unless the contract has been distributed to the participant." General Explanation–TEFRA, p. 295.

The IRS has stated, in a general information letter, that where plan participants received mortgage loans from a bank, which were contingent upon the plan making deposits equal to the loan amounts, the loans were indirect plan loans for purposes of IRC Section 72(p). See IRS General Information Letter, 5 Pens. Pl. Guide (CCH) ¶17,383J (August 12, 1992).

A loan received by a beneficiary is treated as received by the participant if he is alive at the time the loan is treated as a distribution. General Explanation–TEFRA, p. 295.

Renegotiation, extension, renewal, or revision. Any loan balance outstanding on August 13, 1982 (September 3, 1982, in the case of certain government plans) that is renegotiated, extended, renewed, or revised is treated as a loan made on the date it is renegotiated, extended, renewed, or revised. TRA '86, Sec. 1134(e). See e.g., TAM 9344001. A consolidation of two qualified plans is not a renegotiation, extension, renewal, or revision that would subject a loan to the provisions of IRC Section 72(p). Let. Rul. 8542081. Similarly, the transfer of a participant's account balance, including an outstanding loan, in a trustee-to-trustee transfer is not treated as such a renegotiation, extension, renewal, or revision. Let. Rul. 8950008. A plan loan offset against the participant's account balance when the plan terminated was treated as a constructive distribution, subject to income tax and penalties. *Caton v. Comm.*, TC Memo 1995-80.

Interest deduction. An employee is not allowed an interest deduction with respect to a loan (otherwise meeting the requirements in Q 421) made after 1986 during the period (1) on or after the first day on which the borrower is a key employee (see Q 357); or (2) in which such loan is secured by elective contributions made to a 401(k) plan or tax sheltered annuity. IRC Sec. 72(p)(3). Loans from a qualified retirement plan do not qualify as a "qualified education loan" for which an interest deduction is available. Prop. Treas. Reg. §1.221-1(f)(3) (see Q 823). For rules affecting residence loans, see "Residence Loans" above.

Refinancing transactions. A refinancing transaction is any transaction in which one loan replaces another. For example, a refinancing may exist if the outstanding loan amount is increased, or if the interest rate or the repayment term of the loan is renegotiated. Treas. Reg. §1.72(p)-1, A-20(a).

If the term of the replacement loan ends later than the term of the loan it replaces, then both loans are treated as outstanding on the date of the refinancing transaction. This means generally that the loans must collectively satisfy the requirements of IRC Section 72(p). Treas. Reg. §1.72(p)-1, A-20(a)(2). There is an exception where the replacement loan would satisfy IRC Section 72(p)(2) if it were treated as two separate loans. Under this exception, the amount of the replaced loan, amortized over a period ending no later than the end of the original term of the replaced loan (or five years, if later), is treated as one loan. The other loan is for an amount equal to the difference between the amount of the replacement loan and the outstanding balance of the replaced loan. Treas. Reg. §1.72(p)-1, A-20(a)(2).

The IRS will not view the transaction as circumventing IRC Section 72(p) if the replacement loan effectively amortizes an amount equal to the replaced loan within

PENSION AND PROFIT SHARING: TAXATION OF DISTRIBUTIONS   Q 423

the original term of the replaced loan (or within five years, if later). For this reason, the outstanding balance of the replaced loan need not be taken into account in determining whether the limitations of IRC Section 72(p)(2) have been met—only the amount of the replacement loan (plus any existing loans that are not being replaced) is considered. Treas. Reg. §1.72(p)-1, A-20(a)(2). If the term of the replacement loan does not end later than the term of the replaced loan, then only the amount of the replacement loan (plus the outstanding balance of any existing loans that are not being replaced) must be taken into account in determining whether IRC Section 72(p) has been satisfied. Treas. Reg. §1.72(p)-1, A-20(a)(1).

Multiple loans. Where a participant receives multiple loans from a qualified retirement plan, each such loan must separately satisfy IRC Section 72(p), taking into account the outstanding balance of each existing loan. The refinancing rules do not apply, because the new loan is not used to replace any existing loan. Treas. Reg. §1.72(p)-1, A-20(a)(1). Earlier proposed regulations set a limit of two loans per participant within a single year; however, final regulations contain no such limit. Treas. Reg. §1.72(p)-1, A-20(a)(2).

Deemed distributions as outstanding loans. For purposes of the dollar limitation on loans under IRC Section 72(p) (see Q 421), a loan treated as a deemed distribution is considered an outstanding loan until it is repaid. Treas. Reg. §1.72(p)-1, A-19.

Regulations place two conditions on loans made while a deemed distribution loan remains unpaid: (1) the subsequent loan must be repayable under a payroll withholding arrangement enforceable under applicable law (the arrangement may be revocable, but should the participant revoke it, the outstanding loan balance is treated as a deemed distribution); and (2) the participant must provide the plan with adequate security (collateral for the loan in addition to the participant's accrued benefit). If, for any reason, the additional collateral ceases to be in force before the subsequent loan is repaid, the outstanding balance of the subsequent loan is treated as a deemed distribution. If these conditions are not satisfied, the entire subsequent loan is treated as a deemed distribution under IRC Section 72(p). Treas. Reg. §1.72(p)-1, A-19.

Generally, the final plan loan regulations took effect for loans made on or after January 1, 2004. Prior to that date, a reasonable, good faith compliance standard applied. Treas. Reg. §1.72(p)-1, A-22. *ASRS, Sec. 59, ¶980.*

INCOME TAXATION OF PARTICIPANTS AND BENEFICIARIES

Contributions to a Plan

423. Is an employee taxed currently on his employer's contributions to a qualified plan?

Unlike a nonqualified plan, a participant in a *qualified* retirement plan generally does not have to include contributions in gross income when his rights in the plan become fully vested, nor will he be taxed simply because amounts are made available to him (i.e., constructively received). Rather, he pays no tax until benefits are actually distributed to him. Delaying distribution will postpone taxation, unless it is delayed too long (see Q 338 to Q 346). IRC Secs. 402(a), 403(a); Treas. Regs. §§1.402(a)-1(a), 1.403(a)-1.

If life insurance protection is provided under the plan by deductible employer contributions or trust earnings, the employee must include the cost of the protection in income. For the method of determining the "cost" of such insurance protection taxable to the employee, see Q 424.

Premiums paid by a profit sharing trust on current accident or health insurance for an employee are currently taxable to the employee as distributions from the trust. Rev. Rul. 61-164, 1961-2 CB 99. Likewise, a direct distribution from profit sharing funds to reimburse an employee for medical expenses is a taxable distribution to the employee. Rev. Rul. 69-141, 1969-1 CB 48. The same principle was applied more recently to amounts distributed from a qualified retirement plan to reimburse participants' medical expenses or to pay health insurance premiums under a cafeteria plan; both were includable in the income of the distributee. Rev. Rul. 2003-62, 2003-1 CB 1034.

Employer contributions used to provide post-retirement medical benefits under a pension trust or annuity plan (see Q 370) are not taxable to the employees. Thus, if a trustee of a qualified trust uses employer contributions (or trust earnings) to purchase insurance to provide the post-retirement medical benefits, the amounts so applied are not taxable income to the employee for whom the insurance is purchased. Treas. Reg. §1.72-15(h).

Where a governmental employer "picks up" plan contributions otherwise designated as employee contributions, the contributions are treated as employer contributions. IRC Sec. 414(h)(2). Such contributions are excluded from the employee's income and are not subject to withholding. Rev. Rul. 77-462, 1977-2 CB 358; Let. Rul. 8845051. A state statute authorizing various retirement systems to "pick up" contributions is not sufficient to effectuate a "pick up" of employee contributions. *Howell v. U.S.*, 85-2 USTC 90,120 (7th Cir. 1985); *Foil v. Comm.*, 92 TC 376 (1989). The governmental employer must specify that contributions designated as employee contributions are being paid by the employer in lieu of employee contributions, and the employee must not have the option of choosing to receive the contribution directly. Rev. Rul. 81-35, 1981-1 CB 255; Rev. Rul. 81-36, 1981-1 CB 255; Let. Rul. 9441042. The required specification of payment of designated employee contributions by the employer must be completed before the period to which such contributions relate; retroactive "pick up" is not permitted. Rev. Rul. 87-10, 1987-1 CB 136; *Alderman v. Comm.*, TC Memo 1988-49. The employer may "pick up" either pre-tax or after-tax contributions used to repurchase service credit. Let. Rul. 200035033.

Contributions to a plan that has ceased to be qualified are taxed to an employee in the first year in which his right to such amounts is no longer subject to a substantial risk of forfeiture. IRC Secs. 402(b)(1), 83. Thus, the employee is taxed on such contributions to the extent that he is vested. However, if a plan fails to qualify solely because it does not satisfy either (1) the minimum participation rule (in the case of a defined benefit plan–see Q 373); or (2) the coverage requirements (see Q 325), then contributions on behalf of nonhighly compensated employees will not be includable in their income. Highly compensated employees, on the other hand, must include in income their vested accrued benefits (other than the investment in the contract). IRC Sec. 402(b)(4).

Social Security Taxes

Generally, payments to, from, or under a qualified retirement plan are specifically excluded from the definition of "wages" under the Social Security tax law. Consequently, neither employer contributions to, nor distributions from, a qualified retirement plan are subject to Social Security taxes. IRC Sec. 3121(a)(5). This exclusion does not extend to

PENSION AND PROFIT SHARING: TAXATION OF DISTRIBUTIONS   Q 424

amounts that a regular (i.e., common law) employee elects to contribute under a "cash or deferred" arrangement under IRC Section 401(k) (see Q 396), or to salary reduction contributions made to governmental plans and "picked up" by the employer. Thus, elective deferrals under a 401(k) plan and the amount of salary reductions "picked up" by a governmental employer are treated as "wages" subject to Social Security tax. IRC Sec. 3121(v)(1). *ASRS, Sec. 59, ¶900.1, ¶900.3.*

Cost of Life Insurance Protection Taxable to Employee

424. What method is used to determine the cost of current life insurance protection provided in a qualified plan and taxed to common law employee participants?

The cost of life insurance protection provided under a qualified pension, annuity, or profit sharing plan must be included in the employee's gross income for the year in which deductible employer contributions or trust income is applied to purchase life insurance protection. IRC Sec. 72(m)(3)(B); Treas. Reg. §1.72-16(b). This rule applies whether the insurance is provided under group permanent or individual cash value life insurance policies or term insurance, and whether it is provided under a trusteed or nontrusteed plan. Treas. Regs. §§1.402(a)-1(a)(3), 1.403(a)-1(d). According to letter rulings, the rule applies as well to the protection under a life insurance policy on a third party if the proceeds are allocable to the employee's account (for example, to fund a buy-sell arrangement). See Let. Ruls. 8426090, 8108110.

The employee is taxed currently on the cost of life insurance protection if the proceeds are either: (1) payable to the employee's estate or beneficiary; or (2) payable to the plan's trustee, if the plan requires the trustee to pay them to the employee's estate or beneficiary. Treas. Reg. §1.72-16(b)(1). On the other hand, the insured is not taxed on the insurance cost if the trustee has the right to retain any part of the death proceeds. Treas. Reg. §1.72-16(b)(6). Thus, the insured is not taxed on the cost of key person insurance purchased by the trustee as a trust investment. Likewise, participants are not taxed on the cost of a group indemnity policy purchased to indemnify the trust against excessive death benefit payments. Rev. Rul. 66-138, 1966-1 CB 25. But the insured does not avoid tax on the current cost of the insurance protection merely because, under the terms of the plan, his interest in the policy may be forfeited before his death, and the trust may receive the cash surrender value of the contract. *Funkhouser v. Comm.*, 58 TC 940 (1972).

The cost of life insurance protection may not be treated as a qualified Hurricane Katrina distribution. Notice 2005-92, 2005-51 IRB ___; see KETRA 2005, Secs. 2, 101, 103.

Cash Value Insurance

Only the cost of the "pure amount at risk" is treated as a currently taxable distribution. This cost (the amount of taxable income) is determined by applying the 1-year premium term rate at the insured's age to the difference between the face amount of insurance and the cash surrender value at the end of the year. Treas. Regs. §§ 1.72-16(b), 1.402(a)-1(a)(3); 1.403(a)-1(d). The applicable rate is that for the insured's age on his birthday nearest the beginning of the policy year (although his age on his last birthday would probably be acceptable to IRS, if used consistently).

2006 Tax Facts on Insurance & Employee Benefits   511

The manner in which the value of current life insurance provided under a qualified plan must be determined is not entirely clear. Guidance issued in 2001 and revised in 2002 provided "Table 2001," which sets forth premium rates that replaced the earlier P.S. 58 Table. See Notice 2002-8, 2002-1 CB 398. This table is reproduced in Appendix C. Table 2001 will be used until additional guidance, which was authorized by final regulations in 2003, is published in the Internal Revenue Bulletin. See Treas. Reg. §1.61-22(d)(3).

Until future guidance takes effect, taxpayers may be permitted to use the insurer's lower published premium rates that are available to all standard risks for initial issue 1-year term insurance. See Notice 2002-8, 2002-1 CB 398. The IRS does not consider an insurer's published premium rates to be available to all standard risks who apply for term insurance unless (i) the insurer generally makes the availability of such rates known to persons who apply for term insurance coverage from the insurer, and (ii) the insurer regularly sells term insurance at such rates to individuals who apply for term insurance coverage through the insurer's normal distribution channels. See Notice 2002-8, above.

Earlier guidance stated that if the insurer published rates for individual, initial issue, 1-year term policies (available to all standard risks), and these rates were lower than the then-applicable P.S. 58 (now Table 2001) rates, these insurer rates could be substituted to the extent provided by Rev. Rul. 66-110, 1966-1 CB 12, as amplified by Rev. Rul. 67-154, 1967-1 CB 11. However, this ability to use the insurer's lower published rates was limited to arrangements entered into before the effective date of the final regulations (i.e., generally, September 17, 2003). See Notice 2002-8, above.

For many years, "P.S. 58" rates were used to calculate the value of the protection. Rev. Rul. 55-747, 1955-2 CB 228. However, the IRS revoked Revenue Ruling 55-747 for most purposes. See Notice 2002-8, above.

If a profit sharing plan permits a participant to direct the trustee to purchase term insurance riders on either the participant's spouse or dependent children, the "cost" of such a rider must be measured using the P.S. 58 rates (currently Table 2001), not the actual cost of the rider. See Let. Rul. 9023044. The premium paid during the employee's taxable year may cover a period extending into the following year. However, the employee will not be permitted to apportion the cost between the two years; he must include the entire P.S. 58 (currently Table 2001) cost in his gross income for the taxable year during which the premium is paid. But if only a portion of the premium is paid during the taxable year, the cost may be apportioned for that year. See Special Ruling, 1946, Pension Plan Guide (CCH), Pre-1986 IRS Tax Releases, ¶17,303. An employee who leaves before the end of the year for which the premium has been paid must include in gross income the annual term cost reduced by the unearned premium credit reallocated to pay premiums for remaining employee-participants. Rev. Rul. 69-490, 1969-2 CB 11.

Term Insurance

Where individual or group term life insurance is provided under a qualified plan, the cost of the entire amount of protection is taxable to the employees. No part of the coverage of group term insurance is exempt under IRC Section 79 (see Q 142). IRC Sec. 79(b)(3). Moreover, the cost of the insurance protection cannot be determined by

PENSION AND PROFIT SHARING: TAXATION OF DISTRIBUTIONS Q 425

use of the special group term rates that are applicable to taxing excess group term life insurance purchased by the employer directly. Treas. Regs. §§1.79-1(a)(3), 1.79-3(d)(3). It is not settled whether the taxable amount is the actual premium, or the P.S. 58 (currently Table 2001) cost.

Contributory Plans

Life insurance protection purchased under a contributory plan is considered to have been paid first from employer contributions and trust earnings, unless the plan provides otherwise. Thus, the P.S. 58 (currently Table 2001) costs are taxed to the employee unless the plan provides that employee contributions are to be applied to the insurance cost. Rev. Rul. 68-390, 1968-2 CB 175.

If amounts *attributable to* deductible employee contributions, including net earnings allocable to them, are used to purchase life insurance, the amount used, not the P.S. 58 (currently Table 2001) cost, is included in the employee's gross income. IRC Sec. 72(o)(3). It is unclear whether such amounts are subject to a premature distribution penalty; the IRS has specifically exempted P.S. 58 (currently Table 2001) costs of life insurance protection included in income from such a penalty. See Q 428. While the deduction for any contribution so used is not disallowed, it is, in effect, offset. Loans under such a policy would be considered a distribution, including automatic premium loans on default of payment of a premium. *ASRS, Sec. 59, ¶900.2(a)*.

425. May the cost of life insurance protection be recovered tax free from qualified plan benefits?

If the life insurance protection under the plan is provided by a cash value policy, the aggregate costs that have been taxed to the employee (currently under Table 2001, formerly P.S. 58 rates, see Q 424) are a part of the employee's basis, which may be recovered tax free from the benefits received under the policy. Treas. Reg. §1.72-16(b). (It would seem that deductible employee contributions that have been applied to purchase life insurance and taxed to the employee would also be recovered tax free from benefits received under the policy. See IRC Sec. 72(o)(3)(B).) The amount recoverable is the total amount of income that has been reported, and not just the tax paid. However, the taxable cost can be recovered only from benefits under the contract. Treas. Reg. §1.72-16(b)(4). See Let. Rul. 8539066.

The regulations say that "each separate program of the employer consisting of interrelated contributions and benefits" is a single contract. Generally, where retirement benefits and life insurance are separately provided (e.g., through retirement income contracts and a side fund) they are separate programs. Thus, if the insurance is provided under a separate term policy, the taxable cost cannot be recovered from the retirement benefits. Treas. Reg. §1.72-2(a)(3), Ex. 6. But where a plan was amended to eliminate death benefits for employees dying prior to age 65 and its trustees redeemed the whole life insurance policies and invested the proceeds in various securities, the plan became a single program of interrelated contributions and benefits; the employees could recover their taxable insurance cost from distributions from the plan. Let. Rul. 8721083.

Where, under a combination plan, the trustee surrendered the life insurance policy and used both the policy's cash surrender value and the auxiliary fund to purchase an immediate annuity for a retiring employee, the employee could *not* recover the taxable insurance costs from the annuity payments (the result would have been different had the auxiliary fund been applied to a settlement under the life insurance policy). Rev. Rul. 67-336, 1967-2 CB 66. Similarly, where life insurance policies were surrendered and the value used to provide a cash lump sum distribution, the costs taxed to the employee (under Table 2001 or P.S. 58, see Q 424) were not part of his cost recoverable from the distribution. Thus, they could be included in the amount rolled over (see Q 446). Let. Ruls. 7902083, 7830082.

If insurance is purchased with employer contributions and trust earnings (other than those attributable to deductible employee contributions), both the employee's nondeductible contributions and insurance costs (under Table 2001 or P.S. 58, see Q 424) are recoverable from the plan distributions. Where nondeductible employee contributions have been earmarked, under plan provisions, for payment of the cost of life insurance protection, a letter ruling provided the following guidelines: (1) if the life insurance contracts are surrendered by the trustee and payment is made as a lump sum distribution or otherwise, the employee's basis is the amount of his nondeductible contributions to the plan that were not applied to the cost of life insurance protection; and (2) if the life insurance contract is distributed as part of the distribution, the employee's basis is (a) the amount of his nondeductible contributions to the plan, including those applied to the cost of life insurance protection, plus (b) any additional amounts taxed to him as the cost of life insurance protection (under Table 2001 or P.S. 58, see Q 424). Let. Rul. 7922109. For estate tax results, see Q 673.

Keogh Plans

A self-employed individual does not include any costs he paid for life insurance protection (under Table 2001 or P.S. 58, see Q 424) in his cost basis of benefits received under the contract. Treas. Reg. §1.72-16(b)(4).

A self-employed individual cannot deduct the part of the employer's contribution that is allocable to the cost of pure insurance protection for himself. In other words, the income tax deduction must be based on the balance of the premium after subtracting the 1-year term cost of the current life insurance protection. IRC Sec. 404(e); Treas. Reg. §1.404(e)-1(b)(1). The premium attributable to a waiver of premium provision may not be deducted. Treas. Reg. §1.404(e)-1(b)(1). But if any trust earnings are applied to purchase life insurance protection under a trusteed plan, the self-employed individual must include the cost (determined under Table 2001 or P.S. 58, see Q 424) in gross income. IRC Sec. 72(m)(3)(B); Treas. Reg. §1.72-16(b)(2). The life insurance cost is determined in the same manner as for regular employees (under Table 2001 or P.S. 58, see Q 424). The cost of life insurance protection included in income may not be included in an owner-employee's cost basis. Treas. Reg. §1.72-16(b)(4). *ASRS, Sec. 59, ¶900.2(b), Sec. 60, ¶410.2.*

Overview: Distributions

426. How are distributions from a qualified plan taxed?

The taxation of distributions from qualified plans generally depends on the timing and nature (e.g., "lump sum" or periodic) of the distribution.

...Amounts received preretirement are taxed as explained in Q 427.

...Certain premature distributions are subject to a 10% penalty (see Q 428).

PENSION AND PROFIT SHARING: TAXATION OF DISTRIBUTIONS   Q 427

...The treatment of amounts received postretirement is described in Q 429.

...The taxation of lump sum distributions is discussed in Q 430.

...Distribution of an annuity contract or life insurance policy is discussed in Q 431.

...Distribution of employer securities is discussed in Q 432.

...The taxation of periodic retirement payments is explained in Q 433 to Q 435.

...Disability payments are taxed as explained in Q 436.

...Payments to beneficiaries are taxed as explained in Q 437 to Q 439.

Loans to employees that do not meet the requirements explained at Q 420 to Q 422 are generally taxed as distributions. The treatment of corrective distributions of excess contributions and excess aggregate contributions is explained in Q 406; corrective distributions of excess deferrals are explained in Q 396.

Distribution to alternate payee. A spouse (or other) alternate payee under a qualified domestic relations order (see Q 349) is treated as a distributee for most purposes of the rules relating to the taxation of distributions from qualified plans, and, to the extent still available to participants, any special treatment of lump sum distributions (see Q 430, Q 432). IRC Secs. 402(e)(1); 402(d)(4)(J). See Let. Ruls. 8751040, 8744023.

Planning Point: A divorcing or separating spouse who is negotiating a qualified domestic relations order and who is not yet 59½ should weigh the relative advantages and disadvantages of (i) a lump sum distribution which can be rolled over to an IRA in his or her own name, and (ii) a series of distributions directly from his spouse's plan (if available). Distributions from the spouse's plan pursuant to the QDRO would be exempt from the 10% tax, whereas distributions from his or her own IRA made before age 59½ would not be exempt, unless another exception (such as the substantially equal periodic payment exception) applies. *Martin Silfen, J.D., Brown Brothers Harriman Trust Co., LLC.*

If any assets of an individually directed account under a qualified plan are used to purchase collectibles (works of art, gems, antiques, metals, certain coins, etc.), the amount so used will be treated as distributed from the account. IRC Sec. 408(m). *ASRS, Sec. 59, ¶¶900-990.*

Preretirement Distributions

427. How is an employee taxed on preretirement distributions from a qualified plan?

Preretirement distributions (i.e., those received before the "annuity starting date") made to an employee from a qualified plan are fully included in gross income *except* to the extent allocated to investment in the contract, as described below. IRC Secs. 72(e)(8), 72(e)(2)(B). Premature distributions are generally subject to an additional tax. See Q 428.

Special tax treatment applies to "qualified Hurricane Katrina distributions." A qualified Hurricane Katrina distribution is a distribution from a qualified plan, individual retirement plan, IRC Section 403(b) tax sheltered annuity or eligible governmental plan under IRC Section 457 that is made after August 24, 2005 and before January 1, 2007 to an individual whose principal place of abode on August 28, 2005 was located in the Hurricane Katrina disaster area (i.e., Louisiana, Mississippi, Alabama or Florida, for purposes of KETRA 2005), *and* who sustained an economic loss by reason of Hurricane Katrina. The aggregate amount that may be treated as qualified Hurricane Katrina distributions of an individual (from all eligible retirement plans) is $100,000. Notice 2005-92, 2005-51 IRB ___; KETRA 2005, Secs. 2, 101, 103.

Unless the taxpayer elects otherwise, qualified Hurricane Katrina distributions are included in gross income ratably over a 3-year period beginning with the first year of distribution (i.e., 2005 or 2006). KETRA 2005, Sec. 101(e); Notice 2005-92, above. Furthermore, if a qualified Hurricane Katrina distribution is an eligible rollover distribution (for example, it is not a periodic payment or a required minimum distribution, see Q 445), it may be recontributed to an eligible rollover plan (see Q 446) at any time in the 3-year period that begins the date after the distribution. KETRA 2005, Sec. 101(c); Notice 2005-92, above. Qualified Hurricane Katrina distributions are exempt from the 10% premature distribution penalty under IRC Sec. 72(t). See KETRA 2005, Sec. 101(a); Notice 2005-92, above.

A participant who has an investment in the contract (i.e., a cost basis, see Q 435) under a pension, profit sharing, or stock bonus plan, or under an annuity contract purchased by any such plan, is taxed under a rule that provides for pro rata recovery of cost. See IRC Sec. 72(e)(8). The employee excludes the portion of the distribution that bears the same ratio to the total distribution as his investment in the contract bears to the total value of the employee's accrued benefit on the date of the distribution. Generally, the total value of an employee's account balance is the fair market value of the total assets under the account, excluding any net unrealized appreciation attributable to employee contributions (whether or not all of such securities are distributed). Notice 87-13, 1987-1 CB 432, A-11, as modified by Notice 89-25, 1989-1 CB 662. The "annuity starting date" is the first day of the first period for which an amount is received as an annuity under the plan or contract. IRC Sec. 72(c)(4). See Q 10.

Employee contributions under a defined contribution plan may be treated as a separate contract for purposes of these rules. IRC Sec. 72(d)(2). And a defined benefit plan is treated as a defined contribution plan to the extent that employee contributions (and earnings thereon) are credited to a separate account, to which actual earnings and losses are allocated. IRC Sec. 414(k)(2); Notice 87-13, above, A-14. See also, Let. Ruls. 9618028, 8916081. Conversely, the IRS privately ruled that there was a single contract in the case of a defined benefit plan that did not credit earnings on employee after-tax contributions and allowed single sum withdrawal of such contributions at retirement (in exchange for actuarially reduced lifetime pension payments); the withdrawn amounts were taxed as preretirement distributions under IRC Section 72(e)(8)(B), and the investment in the contract with respect to the remaining benefit was reduced by the amount of such distribution. Let. Rul. 9847032. A lump sum distribution received under the alternative form of the Civil Service Retirement System annuity did not qualify as a defined contribution plan or a hybrid plan under these rules; thus it was not subject to separate contract treatment. *George v. U.S.*, 96-2 USTC ¶50,389 (Fed. Cir. 1996); *Logsdon v. Comm.*, TC Memo 1997-8.

PENSION AND PROFIT SHARING: TAXATION OF DISTRIBUTIONS Q 428

Grandfather Rule

If, on May 5, 1986, a plan permitted in-service withdrawal of employee contributions, the pro rata recovery rules do not apply to investment in the contract prior to 1987. Instead, investment in the contract prior to 1987 will be recovered first, and the pro rata recovery rules will apply only to the extent that amounts received before the annuity starting date (when added to all other amounts previously received under the contract after 1986) exceed the employee's investment in the contract as of December 31, 1986. IRC Sec. 72(e)(8)(D); see also Let. Ruls. 9652031, 8747061. If employee contributions are transferred after May 5, 1986 from a plan that permitted in-service withdrawals to another plan permitting such withdrawals, the pre-1987 investment in the contract under both plans continues to qualify for this grandfather treatment. If the transferor plan did not permit such in-service withdrawals, only the pre-1987 investment in the contract under the transferee plan qualifies. Notice 87-13, above, A-13. See also, Let. Ruls. 8829017, 8829006.

An employee who cashed out prior to 1986 and buys back after 1986 cannot use the grandfather rule, because there is no pre-1987 investment in the contract. However, even if the cash-out occurs after 1986 and there was investment in the contract as of December 31, 1986, the cash-out causes a permanent reduction in the grandfathered investment, which may not be restored by a later buy-back. Notice 89-25, above, A-5.

Where an employer amended its plan to provide that employees could receive distributions at their request "but not less than the minimum amounts that must be distributed by the applicable distribution date" under IRC Section 401(a)(9), distributions were not annuity payments, and there was no annuity starting date, so distributions were treated as amounts received before the annuity starting date and were subject to grandfather rule of IRC Section 72(e)(8)(D). Let. Ruls. 200117044, 20011045.

Where a state's defined benefit plan allowed eligible participants to elect optional retirement with partial lump sum distributions (PLSDs), and PLSDs were received within the window of eligibility specified in TAMRA '88, Sec. 1011A(b)(11), the PLSDs were taxable, on a pro-rata basis under IRC Section 72(e), only to the extent that they exceeded recipient's investment in the plan. Let. Rul. 200114040. *ASRS, Sec. 59, ¶940.*

428. What is a "premature distribution" from a qualified plan, and what penalties relate to it?

Except as noted below, amounts distributed from qualified retirement plans before the participant reaches age 59½ are premature distributions, subject to an additional tax equal to 10% of the amount of the distribution includable in gross income. IRC Sec. 72(t).

"Qualified Hurricane Katrina distributions" are exempt from the penalty. KETRA 2005, Sec. 101(a). A qualified Hurricane Katrina distribution is a distribution from a qualified plan, individual retirement plan, IRC Section 403(b) tax sheltered annuity or eligible governmental plan under IRC Section 457 that is made after August 24, 2005 and before January 1, 2007 to an individual whose principal place of abode on August 28, 2005 was located in the Hurricane Katrina disaster area (Louisiana, Mississippi, Alabama or Florida, for purposes of KETRA 2005), *and* who sustained an economic loss by reason of Hurricane Katrina. The aggregate amount that may be treated as qualified

Q 428 FEDERAL INCOME TAX

Hurricane Katrina distributions of an individual (from all eligible retirement plans) is $100,000. Notice 2005-92, 2005-51 IRB ___; KETRA 2005, Secs. 2, 101, 103.

To the extent that they are attributable to rollovers from a qualified retirement plan or IRC Section 403(b) plan, amounts distributed from IRC Section 457 plans (see Q 124) generally will be treated as distributed from a qualified plan, for purposes of the premature distribution penalty. IRC Sec. 72(t)(9).

The 10% penalty tax does *not* apply to distributions:

(1) made to a beneficiary, or the employee's estate, on or after the death of the employee;

(2) attributable to the employee's disability (as defined in IRC Section 72(m)(7));

(3) that are part of a series of substantially equal periodic payments made (at least annually) for the life or life expectancy of the employee or the joint lives or joint life expectancies of the employee and his designated beneficiary, and *beginning after* the employee separates from the service of the employer (see Q 232 for methods of calculation; see also further discussion below);

(4) made to an employee after separation from service during or after the year in which he attained age 55, or made to certain employees who had separated from service as of March 1, 1986 (TRA '86, Sec. 1123(e)(3));

(5) made to an alternate payee under a qualified domestic relations order (see Q 349);

(6) made to an employee for medical care, but not in excess of the amount allowable as a deduction to the employee under IRC Section 213 for amounts paid during the year for medical care (see Q 826) (determined without regard to whether the employee itemizes deductions for the year);

(7) made to reduce an excess contribution under a 401(k) plan (IRC Sec. 401(k)(8)(D); see Q 406);

(8) made to reduce an excess employee or matching employer contribution, (i.e., an excess aggregate contribution; see IRC Sec. 401(m)(7) and Q 406);

(9) made to reduce an excess elective deferral (IRC Sec. 402(g)(2)(C); see Q 396);

(10) which are dividends paid with respect to stock of a corporation described in IRC Section 404(k) (see "Employee Stock Ownership Plans," Q 415); or

(11) made on account of certain levies against a qualified plan (under IRC Sec. 6331).

The IRS has approved three methods for determining what constitutes a "series of substantially equal periodic payments" in the exception discussed in item (3), above. But if the series of payments is later "modified" (other than under 2002 guidance, or because of death or disability) before the employee reaches age 59½, or if after he reaches

PENSION AND PROFIT SHARING: TAXATION OF DISTRIBUTIONS Q 428

age 59½, within five years of the date of the first payment, the employee's tax for the year in which the modification occurs is increased by an amount equal to the tax that would have been imposed in the absence of the exception, plus interest for the deferral period. For an explanation of the calculation under each method, the 2002 guidance, the definition of "modified," and related rulings, see Q 232.

The exception for distributions pursuant to a QDRO (see item (5) above), was not applicable where a participant took a distribution from the plan following a "trade" of other marital property rights for his spouse's waiver of rights in his plan benefits. *O'Brien v. Comm.*, TC Summary Opinion 2001-148.

The Tax Court determined that the penalty tax was applicable to a distribution made to a teacher as a result of her participation in a state retirement system, even though the retirement plan was not necessarily the source of the entire distribution. See *O'Connor v. Comm.*, TC Memo 1994-169. Likewise, a distribution originating from an arbitration award was held to be subject to the 10% penalty, because the amounts attributable to the award were thoroughly integrated with benefits provided under the state retirement plan. *Kute v. U.S.*, 191 F.3d 371 (3rd Cir. 1999). Furthermore, the "involuntary" nature of a distribution does not preclude the application of the tax, provided that the participant had an opportunity (e.g., by a rollover) to avoid the tax. *Swihart v. Comm.*, TC Memo 1998-407.

The IRS has stated that the garnishment of an individual's plan interest under the Federal Debt Collections Procedures Act (FDCPA) to pay a judgment for restitution or fines (see item 11, above) will not trigger the application of the 10% penalty. See Let. Rul. 200426027.

Planning Point: An individual who is facing an IRS levy against his plan benefit and who is not yet age 59½ should allow the IRS to follow through on the levy rather than voluntarily taking a plan distribution and paying it over to the IRS in satisfaction of the unpaid taxes. Such a "voluntary" distribution would be subject to the 10% tax, whereas any amount distributed directly to the IRS pursuant to the levy would not. *Martin Silfen, J.D., Brown Brothers Harriman Trust Co., LLC.*

The cost of life insurance protection included in the employee's income (see Q 424) is not considered a distribution for purposes of applying the 10% penalty. Notice 89-25, 1989-1 CB 662, A-11. The Civil Service Retirement System is a qualified plan for purposes of the premature distribution penalty. *Roundy v. Comm.*, 97-2 USTC ¶50,625, aff'g TC Memo 1995-298; *Shimota v. U.S.*, 90-2 USTC ¶50,489 (Cl. Ct. 1990), aff'd 91-2 USTC ¶50,400 (Fed. Cir. 1992).

A plan is not required to withhold the amount of the additional income tax on an early withdrawal. General Explanation–TRA '86, p. 716. Distributions that are rolled over (see Q 444 to Q 456) generally are not includable in income, and, thus, the 10% penalty does not apply. However, in the case of a distribution subject to 20% mandatory withholding, the 20% withheld will be includable in income (to the extent required by IRC Section 402(a) or IRC Section 403(b)(1)), even if the participant rolls over the remaining 80% of the distribution within the 60-day period (see Q 454). Thus, an employee who rolls over only 80% of a distribution may be subject to the 10% penalty on the 20% withheld. See Treas. Regs. §§1.402(c)-2, A-11, 1.403(b)-2, A-1. *ASRS*, Sec. 59, ¶960.2.

2006 Tax Facts on Insurance & Employee Benefits

Postretirement Distributions

429. How is an employee taxed on postretirement distributions from a qualified plan?

The tax treatment of distributions received at or after retirement depends on the time and manner of distribution. If the distribution is rolled over to an IRA or other eligible retirement plan, the taxation of it is deferred until it is distributed in the future (see Q 444). If a lump sum distribution is made, it is subject to the treatment explained in Q 430 and, in the case of net unrealized appreciation on employer securities, as explained in Q 432. If the employee receives annuity payments, the benefits are taxed as explained in Q 433 and Q 434. The employee's cost basis, if any, is determined under the rules set forth in Q 435. If the distribution is received prior to age 59½, it may trigger the 10% penalty on premature distributions, unless one of the exceptions applies. See Q 428.

In the case of a "qualified Hurricane Katrina distribution," special rules apply. A qualified Hurricane Katrina distribution is a distribution from a qualified plan, individual retirement plan, IRC Section 403(b) tax sheltered annuity or eligible governmental plan under IRC Section 457 that is made after August 24, 2005 and before January 1, 2007 to an individual whose principal place of abode on August 28, 2005 was located in the Hurricane Katrina disaster area (i.e., Louisiana, Mississippi, Alabama or Florida, for purposes of KETRA 2005), *and* who sustained an economic loss by reason of Hurricane Katrina. The aggregate amount that may be treated as qualified Hurricane Katrina distributions of an individual (from all eligible retirement plans) is $100,000. Notice 2005-92, 2005-51 IRB ___; KETRA 2005, Secs. 2, 101, 103.

Unless the taxpayer elects otherwise, qualified Hurricane Katrina distributions are included in gross income ratably over a 3-year period beginning with the first year of distribution (i.e., 2005 or 2006). KETRA 2005; Sec. 101(e), Notice 2005-92, above. Furthermore, if a qualified Hurricane Katrina distribution is an eligible rollover distribution (for example, it is not a periodic payment or a required minimum distribution, see Q 445), it may be recontributed to an eligible rollover plan (see Q 446) at any time in the 3-year period that begins the date after the distribution. KETRA 2005, Sec. 101(c); Notice 2005-92, above. Qualified Hurricane Katrina distributions are exempt from the 10% premature distribution penalty under IRC Sec. 72(t). See KETRA 2005, Sec. 101(a); Notice 2005-92, above. *ASRS, Sec. 59, ¶¶910.1, 910.2, 910.3.*

Lump Sum Distributions

430. What is a lump sum distribution? What special tax treatment is available for a lump sum distribution from a qualified plan?

A distribution is a "lump sum distribution" if it is: (1) made in one taxable year; (2) of the *balance to the credit* of an employee; (3) payable (a) on account of the employee's death, (b) after the employee attained age 59½, or (c) on account of the employee's separation from service; and (4) made from a qualified pension, profit sharing, or stock bonus plan. IRC Sec. 402(e)(4)(D).

The same definition applies to distributions to self-employed individuals, except that distributions made after the a self-employed person has become disabled *are* considered lump sum distributions, and distributions made on account of separation from service *are not*. The balance to the credit includes all amounts in the participant's

PENSION AND PROFIT SHARING: TAXATION OF DISTRIBUTIONS   Q 430

account (including nondeductible employee contributions) as of the first distribution received after the triggering event. Let. Ruls. 9031028, 9013009.

Distributions meeting the requirements of a lump sum distribution are subject to special tax treatment only in limited circumstances (see Q 430); otherwise, they are generally taxed as ordinary income. However, special treatment applies for net unrealized appreciation in employer securities distributed in a lump sum distribution (see Q 432).

An "eligible employee" may elect 10-year averaging of lump sum distributions, and special treatment of certain capital gains. For this purpose, an eligible employee is an employee who attained age 50 before January 1, 1986 (i.e., who was born before 1936). Earlier Internal Revenue Code provisions that allowed for 5-year averaging of lump sum distributions were repealed, for tax years beginning after 1999.

10-Year Averaging. An eligible employee makes a special averaging election by filing Form 4972 with his tax return; the election may be revoked by filing an amended return. Temp. Treas. Reg. §11.402(e)(4)(B)-1. An eligible employee can make this election only once, and it must apply to all lump sum distributions he receives for that year.

Under 10-year averaging, the tax on the ordinary income portion of the distribution is 10 times the tax on 1/10 of the "total taxable amount," reduced by the "minimum distribution allowance." 1986 tax rates must be used, taking into account the prior law zero bracket amount. TRA '86, Sec. 1122(h)(5); TAMRA '88, Sec. 1011A(b)(15)(B). Generally, the larger the distribution, the less likely that 10-year averaging will be advantageous.

Planning Point: A distributee who is eligible for special tax treatment on a lump sum distribution should complete his entire income tax return more than once to determine the true tax costs and savings attributable to special tax treatment. In addition to the low nominal tax rate on lump sum distributions, the distributee may benefit from the fact that the distribution is deducted in determining adjusted gross income. This may have the effect of reducing or eliminating the phase-out of various tax benefits, which occurs at higher levels of adjusted gross income; for example, the reduction of itemized deductions and personal exemptions. *Martin Silfen, J.D., Brown Brothers Harriman Trust Co., LLC.*

Long-term Capital Gain Treatment. An eligible employee may also elect capital gain treatment for the portion of a lump sum distribution allocable to his pre-1974 plan participation. TRA '86, Sec. 1122(h)(3). This portion is determined by multiplying the "total taxable amount" by a fraction, the numerator of which is the number of pre-January 1, 1974 calendar years of active plan participation and the denominator of which is the total number of calendar years of active plan participation.

For these purposes, the *minimum distribution allowance* is the lesser of (1) $10,000; or (2) one-half of the total taxable amount. However, this must be reduced by 20% of the total taxable amount in excess of $20,000. Thus, if the total taxable amount is $70,000 or more, there is no minimum distribution allowance. The *total taxable amount* is the employee's cost basis (see Q 435), reduced by any previous distributions excludable from his gross income. *ASRS, Sec. 59, ¶910.1; Sec. 60, ¶430.*

2006 Tax Facts on Insurance & Employee Benefits

Distribution of Annuity or Life Insurance Contract

431. If a qualified plan trust distributes an annuity contract or life insurance policy to an employee, is the value of the contract taxable to the employee in the year of distribution?

Annuities

If the contract distributed is an *annuity* contract, the employee will not be taxed on its value (including cash surrender value that may be available to the employee upon surrender) unless and until he surrenders the contract. Treas. Reg. §1.402(a)-1(a)(2). He will be taxed on the annuity payments as he receives them (see Q 433, Q 434). A contract issued after 1962, however, must be nontransferable in order to qualify for this tax deferred treatment. IRC Sec. 401(g); Treas. Reg. §1.401-9(b)(1). The transfer of an annuity to a divorced spouse pursuant to a divorce decree will not violate the nontransferability requirement. Let. Rul. 8513065.

The IRS determined that the nontransferability requirement was not violated by a Section 1035 exchange of an annuity contract distributed from a qualified plan, where the taxpayer was simply uncomfortable with the amount of funds invested with a single insurer. Let. Rul. 9233054, GCM 39882 (10-30-92). Both the old and new contracts were materially similar, were nontransferable, and were subject to the spousal consent requirements, as well as meeting the other applicable IRC Section 401 requirements. See also Let. Rul. 9241007.

If the employee surrenders the annuity contract after the year of distribution, the gain realized on surrender is taxable as ordinary income and will not qualify for taxation as a lump sum distribution. Rev. Rul. 81-107, 1981-1 CB 201. However, the unsurrendered annuity contract will affect the taxation of any lump sum distribution of which it is a part, or that is made in the same year, as explained below. If the annuity is surrendered in the year of distribution, the proceeds will either be taxed as ordinary income, or, if the distribution of the annuity is all or part of a lump sum distribution, under the lump sum distribution rules (see Q 430). If the annuity is distributed in an eligible rollover distribution, tax may be deferred by rollover. See Q 446.

According to proposed regulations, the employee's cost basis is deducted first from the cash and property other than the annuity. Any excess is used to reduce the value of the annuity. Prop. Treas. Reg. §1.402(e)-2(c)(1)(ii)(C).

Amounts that become payable in cash under qualified plans are not includable in income simply because they are available. IRC Sec. 402(a). Thus, where a plan provides that an employee, upon termination of employment, may take either a single sum payment in cash or have the trustee purchase an annuity for him with cash, his election does not have to be made within any specific time after the cash became available. (However, plan distribution provisions must satisfy the distribution requirements discussed in Q 338 to Q 346.)

Life Insurance Contract

If the contract distributed is a life insurance, retirement income, endowment, or other contract providing life insurance protection, the *fair market value* of the contract at the time of distribution must be included in the distributee's income to the extent that it exceeds his basis (see Q 425, Q 435). Treas. Reg. §1.402(a)-1(a)(1)(iii). However,

PENSION AND PROFIT SHARING: TAXATION OF DISTRIBUTIONS — Q 432

inclusion of the contract's fair market value in the distributee's income is not required at the time of distribution to the extent that within 60 days after it is distributed: (1) all or any portion of the contract is irrevocably converted to an annuity (with no life insurance element); or (2) the contract is treated as a rollover contribution under IRC Section 402(c) (see Q 444). Treas. Reg. §1.402(a)-1(a)(2).

The fair market value standard also applies if the contract is sold by the plan to a participant or beneficiary. If the fair market value of the contract exceeds the value of the consideration, then such excess (i.e., the "bargain element") is treated as a distribution to the distributee under the plan for all purposes under the Internal Revenue Code. This treatment of the "bargain element" as a distribution applies for transfers occurring after August 28, 2005. For transfers occurring before August 29, 2005, the "bargain element" is includable in the distributee's gross income, but is not treated as a distribution for qualification purposes. See Treas. Reg. §1.402(a)-1(a)(1)(iii).

The fair market value standard is effective for distributions or sales occurring after February 12, 2004. See Rev. Proc. 2005-25, 2005-17 IRB 962. Fair market value includes the policy cash value and all other rights under the contract (including any supplemental agreements thereto, and whether or not guaranteed). Treas. Reg. §1.402(a)-1(a)(2)(iii). The IRS has issued safe harbor guidance for determining the fair market value of life insurance contracts. See Rev. Proc. 2005-25, above. Under the safe harbor, fair market value may be the greater of: (1) the interpolated terminal reserve and any unearned premiums, plus a pro rata portion of a reasonable estimate of dividends expected to be paid for that policy year, or (2) the product of the "PERC amount" (PERC stands for premiums, earnings, and reasonable charges) and the applicable "Average Surrender Factor." For details on these calculations, see Q 303.

Conversion to annuity contract. If the policy is converted, it will then be subject to the rules for annuity contracts (provided the annuity is nontransferable; see above). The IRS has taken the position that the mere elimination of the element of risk in a retirement income contract when the reserve exceeds the face amount does not convert the contract of insurance into an annuity contract. According to the IRS, the insured must act to convert the contract into an annuity contract that has at no time contained an element of life insurance protection. Rev. Rul. 66-322, 1966-2 CB 123. If the policy is distributed in a lump sum distribution, the taxable amount is eligible for favorable capital gains and special averaging treatment to the extent that such rules are still applicable; see Q 430.

Death benefit. When a life insurance contract matures by reason of the insured's death *after* the policy has been distributed from the plan, the proceeds are wholly tax-exempt to the beneficiary. Rev. Rul. 63-76, 1963-1 CB 23. See Q 273 with regard to the definition of a "life insurance contract." *ASRS, Sec. 59, ¶¶910.2, 910.3.*

Distribution of Employer Securities

432. How is net unrealized appreciation taxed when employer securities are distributed from a qualified plan?

"Net unrealized appreciation" (NUA) is the excess of the fair market value of employer securities at the time of a lump sum distribution over the cost (or other basis) of the securities to a qualified plan trust. See Treas. Reg. §1.402(a)-1(b)(2)(i). "Employer securities" for this purpose includes shares of a parent or subsidiary corporation. IRC Sec. 402(e)(4)(E).

If employer securities are distributed as part of a lump sum distribution (see Q 430) from a qualified plan, the net unrealized appreciation is excluded from the employee's income at the time of distribution, to the extent that the securities are attributable to employer and nondeductible employee contributions. Taxation of NUA following a lump sum distribution is deferred until the securities are sold or disposed of, unless the employee elects out of NUA treatment. See IRC Sec. 402(e)(4)(B). The election is made on the tax return for the year in which the distribution must be included in gross income, and does not preclude an election for special income averaging. IRC Sec. 402(e)(4).

Upon sale or other disposition of the employer securities, the NUA amount is treated as long-term capital gain, regardless of the distributee's actual holding period. The taxpayer's basis in the stock is the same as the basis in the hands of the qualified plan trust; that is, it does not include the NUA amount. Treas. Reg. §1.402(a)-1(b)(1)(i). Gain accruing after distribution of the securities and before the later disposition of them is treated as long-term or short-term capital gain (see Q 815), depending on the holding period after distribution. See Treas. Reg. §1.402(a)-1(b); Notice 98-24, 1998-1 CB 929; see also Rev. Rul. 81-122 1981-1 CB 202. The distributee's holding period begins the day after the day the plan trustee delivers the stock to the transfer agent with instructions to reissue the stock in the distributee's name. Rev. Rul. 82-75, 1982-1 CB 116.

Planning Point: The portion of the fair market value of the employer securities in excess of (i) their net unrealized appreciation and (ii) the amount of the participant's after-tax contributions to the plan, if any, is included in income and potentially subject to the 10% tax, so that tax should be taken into account in determining whether and how much of the distribution should be rolled over to an IRA if the participant has not yet attained age 59½, and has separated from service before age 55. *Martin Silfen, J.D., Brown Brothers Harriman Trust Co., LLC.*

An employer's shares, if acquired and credited to an employee's account, are still considered employer's stock, even if later transferred to the trust of an acquiring or subsidiary corporation. Rev. Rul. 73-29, 1973-1 CB 198. The basis does not change. Rev. Rul. 80-138, 1980-1 CB 87. The balance of the value of the stock is taxable to the recipient under the regular rules for taxing lump sum distributions (see Q 430). See Rev. Rul. 57-514, 1957-2 CB 261.

Unrealized appreciation that is excluded from income is not includable in the recipient's basis in the stock for the purpose of computing gain or loss upon a later sale or other taxable disposition. Prop. Treas. Reg. §1.402(a)-1(b). However, if part or all of the unrealized appreciation is excluded as something other than unrealized appreciation, only the part excluded as unrealized appreciation is not added to basis. Rev. Rul. 74-398, 1974-2 CB 136.

Excluded appreciation prior to distribution, which is realized on sale of the stock by the recipient of a distribution on account of the death of the employee or by a person inheriting the stock from the employee, is income in respect of a decedent. See Q 827. As such, it is taxed as long-term capital gain, and a deduction may be taken for the estate tax attributable to the inclusion of any part of the appreciation prior to distribution in the deceased employee's estate. Rev. Rul. 69-297, 1969-1 CB 131; Rev. Rul. 75-125, 1975-1 CB 254.

PENSION AND PROFIT SHARING: TAXATION OF DISTRIBUTIONS   Q 433

Net unrealized appreciation in employer securities distributed in other than a lump sum distribution is excludable only to the extent that the appreciation is attributable to nondeductible employee contributions. IRC Sec. 402(e)(4)(A). Thus, a rollover of employer securities to an IRA will preclude the taxpayer from receiving NUA treatment. However, a transfer to an IRA of less than all of a participant's account under an ESOP, with a distribution of the balance to the participant, does not bar treatment as a lump sum distribution. The IRS determined that a participant could exclude the net unrealized appreciation on the stock distributed until he disposes of it. Let. Ruls. 9721036, 200038057. Similarly, a participant who had received a series of substantially equal periodic payments (see Q 428, Q 232) from his plan account prior to retirement was not precluded thereafter from treating a distribution of the remaining amounts (including stock) in his plan account as a lump sum distribution (see Q 429), nor from excluding net unrealized appreciation on the stock. See Let. Rul. 200315041. *ASRS, Sec. 59, ¶910.4.*

Annuity Payments

433. How is an employee taxed on his periodic retirement benefits under a qualified pension, annuity, or profit sharing plan?

If the employee (whether a regular employee or a self-employed individual) has no cost basis for his interest in the plan, the full amount of each payment is taxable to him as ordinary income. Treas. Reg. §1.61-11(a); IRC Secs. 402(a), 403(a), 72; Treas. Reg. §1.72-4(d)(1). If the employee has a cost basis for his interest in the plan, the payments are taxed as discussed below, depending upon his annuity starting date. To determine the employee's cost basis, see Q 435.

The tax treatment is the same whether payment is made directly from the qualified trust or annuity plan, or the trust buys an annuity and distributes it to the employee. IRC Secs. 402(a), 403(a)(1). However, distribution of an annuity contract itself affects the tax on lump sum distributions (see Q 431). If the employee does have a cost basis for his interest, the payments are taxed as discussed below, depending on his annuity starting date.

Annuity payments may be "qualified Hurricane Katrina distributions" (see Q 429). Qualified Hurricane Katrina distributions are included in gross income ratably over a 3-year period beginning with the first year of distribution (i.e., 2005 or 2006). KETRA Sec. 101(e), Notice 2005-92, above.

Annuity Starting Date After December 31, 1997

For an employee who has a cost basis for his interest, and whose annuity starting date is after December 31, 1997, the investment in the contract is recovered according to one of two schedules set forth in the Code, instead of using the exclusion ratio. For purposes of this rule, the employee's investment in the contract does not include any adjustment for a refund feature under the contract. IRC Secs. 72(d)(1)(C), 72(c)(2); see Notice 98-2, 1998-1 CB 266.

These tables operate in the same manner as the simplified safe harbor announced in 1988. See IRC Sec. 72(d); Notice 98-2, 1998-1 CB 266. If the annuity is payable over one life, the payments will be taxed as described below for annuities with a starting date after November 18, 1996. If the annuity is payable over two or more lives, the excludable portion of each monthly payment is determined by dividing the employee's investment in the contract by the number of anticipated payments, as follows:

If the combined ages of the annuitants are:	Number of payments:
Not more than 110	410
More than 110 but not more than 120	360
More than 120 but not more than 130	310
More than 130 but not more than 140	260
More than 140	210

IRC Sec. 72(d)(1). According to the Conference Committee Report for TRA '97, this table applies to benefits based on the life of more than one annuitant, even if the amount of the annuity varies by annuitant. It does not apply to an annuity paid on a single life merely because it has additional features, such as a term certain. In the case of a term certain annuity without a life contingency, the expected number of payments is the number of monthly payments provided under the contract. Notice 98-2, 1998-1 CB 266. In the case of payments made other than monthly, an adjustment must be made to take into account the period on the basis of which payments are made. Two methods of making such an adjustment are set forth in Notice 98-2, above.

For purposes of this rule, if the annuity is payable to a primary annuitant and more than one survivor annuitant, the combined ages of the annuitants is the sum of the age of the primary annuitant and the youngest survivor annuitant. If the annuity is payable to more than one survivor annuitant but there is no primary annuitant, the combined ages of the annuitants is the sum of the age of the oldest survivor annuitant and the youngest survivor annuitant. Any survivor annuitant whose entitlement to payments is based on an event other than the death of the primary annuitant is disregarded. For an explanation of the basis recovery rules under IRC Section 72(d), see Let. Rul. 200009066.

Annuity Starting Date After November 18, 1996 and Before January 1, 1998

If the employee has a cost basis for his interest, and his annuity starting date is after November 18, 1996 and before January 1, 1998 (or if the annuity is payable over one life and has a starting date after December 31, 1997, as described above), the investment in the contract is recovered according to the schedule below. For purposes of this rule, the employee's investment in the contract does not include any adjustment for a refund feature under the contract. IRC Secs. 72(d)(1)(C), 72(c)(2); see Notice 98-2, 1998-1 CB 266.

The excludable portion of each monthly payment is determined by dividing the employee's investment in the contract by the number of anticipated payments contained in the following table:

Age	Number of payments:
Not more than 55	360
More than 55 but not more than 60	310
More than 60 but not more than 65	260
More than 65 but not more than 70	210
More than 70	160

PENSION AND PROFIT SHARING: TAXATION OF DISTRIBUTIONS Q 433

IRC Sec. 72(d)(1)(B). This table does not apply if the annuitant is age 75 or older unless there are fewer than five years of guaranteed payments under the annuity. IRC Sec. 72(d)(1)(E). It would appear that for an annuitant who is 75 or older and whose contract provides for five or more years of guaranteed payments, the rules for annuities with a starting date after July 1, 1986 and before November 19, 1996 would be applied.

If the contract provides for a fixed number of installment payments, the number of monthly annuity payments provided under the contract is used instead of the number listed on the table. See IRC Secs. 72(d)(1)(B)(i)(II), 72(c)(3)(B). If payments under the contract are not made on a monthly basis, appropriate adjustments must be made to the number of payments determined above to reflect the basis on which payments are made. IRC Sec. 72(d)(1)(F); see Notice 98-2, 1998-1 CB 266, for two such methods.

The excluded amount remains constant, even where the amount of the annuity payments changes. If the amount to be excluded from each payment is greater than the amount of the annuity payment (e.g., because of decreased survivor payments), then each annuity payment will be completely excluded from gross income until the entire investment is recovered. As noted below, under earlier law, for distributees with annuity starting dates after December 31, 1986, annuity payments received after the investment is recovered are fully includable in gross income. If two annuitants are receiving payments at the same time, each may exclude his pro rata portion of the amount provided under these rules. Notice 98-2, 1998-1 CB 266.

If a lump sum is paid to the taxpayer in connection with the commencement of the annuity payments, it will be taxable as an amount not received as an annuity under IRC Section 72(e), and treated as received before the annuity starting date. Such a taxpayer's investment in the contract will be determined as if the lump sum payment has been received. IRC Sec. 72(d)(1)(D). Where a defined benefit plan requiring after-tax contributions permitted participants to withdraw their aggregate after-tax contributions in a single sum at retirement in exchange for an actuarial reduction in their lifetime pension benefits, the IRS ruled that the single sum payment constituted a "lump sum payment" under IRC Sections 72(d)(1)(D) and 72(d)(1)(G). Let. Rul. 9847032.

The total amount that the employee can exclude may not exceed his investment in the contract, and if the employee dies prior to recovering his full investment in the contract, any unrecovered investment will be allowable as a deduction on his final return. IRC Secs. 72(d)(1)(B)(ii), 72(b)(2), 72(b)(3); see Notice 98-2, 1998-1 CB 266.

Special transition rules are provided for payors and distributees who continued using the simplified safe harbor contained in Notice 88-118 with respect to annuities with annuity starting dates after November 18, 1996. See Notice 98-2, 1998-1 CB 266.

Annuity Starting Date After July 1, 1986 and Before November 19, 1996

If the employee has a cost basis for his interest, and his annuity starting date is after July 1, 1986 and before November 19, 1996, the payments are taxed either under the regular annuity rules, or, if certain requirements are met, under the simplified safe harbor method described below. IRC Secs. 402(a), 72, 403(a). Under the regular annuity rules, an exclusion ratio is determined as of the annuity starting date. IRC Sec. 72(b); Treas. Reg. §1.72-4(a). Basically, the exclusion ratio is determined by dividing

Q 433　　　　　　　　　　　　　　　　　　　FEDERAL INCOME TAX

the *investment in the contract* by the *expected return* under the contract. The resulting quotient is the percentage of each payment that may be excluded from gross income. With respect to distributions from qualified plans, the employee's cost basis in the plan is his *investment in the contract*. (See Q 7, Q 435.) The total amount that it is estimated he will receive under the plan is his *expected return*. See Q 9. In the case of a straight life annuity, this expected return is determined by multiplying the total amount he will receive each year by the number of years in his life expectancy, according to Table I or Table V of the Annuity Tables, whichever is applicable (see Appendix A). For an explanation of the basic annuity rule and its application to various types of payments (e.g., straight life annuity, refund or period-certain life annuity, joint and survivor annuity, or payments for a fixed period), see Q 7 to Q 19. If the employee's annuity starting date is after December 31, 1986, the total amount that he can exclude during his lifetime is limited to his investment in the contract. With respect to earlier starting dates, the exclusion ratio continues to apply, even to amounts received in excess of the employee's investment in the contract.

> *Example.* Mr. Cochran retired on October 9, 1996, at the age of 65. He had the option under his employer's qualified contributory pension plan to elect an annuity for a period certain, but chose instead to receive a life annuity. On January 1, 1997, he started receiving payments under the plan. The pension arrangement will pay him $800 a month for life. Mr. Cochran's cost basis in the plan (including his own contributions and amounts that have been taxed to him) is $12,000. Mr. Cochran made contributions both before July 1, 1986 and after June 30, 1986, but because Mr. Cochran could have elected an annuity for a period certain, he may not elect to calculate his excludable amount separately with respect to the pre-July and post-June portions. (See Appendix A.) The life expectancy for age 65 is 20 years (Table V, Appendix A). So, the total expected return from the plan is $192,000 (20 × $9,600). Mr. Cochran's exclusion ratio is therefore $12,000/$192,000, or 6.3%. Each year he will exclude $604.80 (6.3% of $9,600) from gross income, until he has excluded the full $12,000, and each year he will include in gross income $8,995.20 ($9,600 - $604.80), until the full $12,000 has been recovered, after which he will include the full $9,600.

If an employee dies prior to recovering his full investment in the contract, the unrecovered investment will be allowed as a deduction on his final return. If payments are guaranteed and the refund beneficiary does not recover the amount unrecovered at decedent's death, the beneficiary may deduct the remaining unrecovered investment in the contract. IRC Sec. 72(b)(3).

Annuity Starting Date on or Before July 1, 1986

If the employee's annuity starting date was on or before July 1, 1986, payments were taxed according to the 3-year cost recovery rule or the regular annuity rules. IRC Sec. 72(d)(1), prior to repeal. The 3-year cost recovery rule was repealed for employees with an annuity starting date after July 1, 1986. TRA '86, Sec. 1122(c)(1). Certain premature distributions are subject to an additional tax (see Q 428). Excess retirement distributions were subject to an additional tax in years beginning before 1997.

Simplified "Safe Harbor" Method

In the case of an annuity starting date before November 19, 1996, a simplified safe harbor method can be used if the annuity payments depend upon the life of the employee or the joint lives of the employee and a beneficiary. If the employee was age 75 or older when the annuity payments commenced, this method could be used only if fewer than five years of payments were guaranteed. Notice 88-118, 1988-2 CB 450. Under this method, investment in the contract is the employee's cost basis in the plan. No refund feature adjustment has to be made. Investment in the contract is divided by the total number of monthly annuity payments expected. This number is taken from the following table and is based on the employee's age at the annuity starting date:

Age	Number of Payments
55 and under	300
56-60	260
61-65	240
66-70	170
71 and over	120

The same expected number of payments applies regardless of whether the employee is receiving a single life annuity or a joint and survivor annuity. The dollar amount excluded from each payment does not change, even if the amount of the payments increases or decreases. Notice 88-118, above. (Of course, if the annuity starting date is after December 31, 1986, annuity payments received after the investment in the contract is recovered are fully includable in income.)

An employee made the election to use the safe harbor method by reporting the taxable portion of the annuity payments received in the year (including the annuity starting date under that method) on the income tax return for that year and for succeeding years. An employee may change the method used to report the tax treatment of annuity payments (i.e., from the safe harbor method to the actual calculation of an exclusion ratio or vice versa) by filing an amended return for all open tax years, as long as the year containing the annuity starting date is an open year. Notice 88-118, above. *ASRS, Sec. 59, ¶910.5.*

434. How are variable annuity benefits, payable under a qualified pension or profit sharing plan, taxed to an employee?

If the employee has no cost basis for his interest in the plan, each payment, regardless of amount, is fully taxable as ordinary income. Generally, an employee's cost basis consists of any nondeductible contributions he has made to the plan and any employer contributions that have been taxed to him, other than excess deferrals (see Q 396) not timely distributed. See Q 435.

Annuity payments may be "qualified Hurricane Katrina distributions" (see Q 429). Qualified Hurricane Katrina distributions are included in gross income ratably over a 3-year period beginning with the first year of distribution (i.e., 2005 or 2006). KETRA Sec. 101(e), Notice 2005-92, above.

When the employee has a cost basis for his interest in the plan and the annuity starting date is after June 30, 1986, the payments are taxed under the annuity rules as expressly applied to variable payments. See Q 22 to Q 24. Thus, the amount excludable from the employee's gross income each year is determined by dividing his cost basis (adjusted for any refund or period-certain guarantee) by the number of years in the payment period. If the annuity is payable for a life or lives, the payment period is determined by use of the IRS annuity tables.

For annuities with a starting date after December 31, 1986, the present value of any refund feature is not to be taken into account in calculating the unrecovered investment in the contract; however, such amounts are still taken into account in calculating an

Q 434　　　　　　　　　　　　　　　FEDERAL INCOME TAX

individual's exclusion ratio. IRC Sec. 72(b)(2)(A). The unrecovered investment in the contract affects only those annuitants who die before the annuity payments end (i.e., the amount of their deduction on their final year return; see Q 27) and the annuitant's cost recovery date (i.e., the date upon which the annuity holder recovers his investment in the contract).

Example. Mr. Kinzie, age 65, retired on August 31, 2002. He is to receive monthly variable annuity payments for life under his employer's contributory pension plan. In the event of Mr. Kinzie's death before having received payments for at least five years, payments on the same variable basis will be continued to his beneficiary for the remainder of the 5-year period. Mr. Kinzie has contributed $6,000 to the plan ($5,000 representing investment in the contract before July 1, 1986; $1,000 representing investment in the contract after June 30, 1986). Payments for the first year begin in September, and during the last four months of the year, Mr. Kinzie receives a total of $640. Mr. Kinzie elects to determine his excludable amount by making separate calculations for his pre-July 1986 and post-June 1986 investment in the contract. (The value of the refund feature determined under Table VII is not more than 50%, and Mr. Kinzie had only life annuity options available.) On the basis of these facts, Mr. Kinzie's annual exclusion from gross income will be $343.60. The first step is to adjust the investment in the contract for the value of the refund feature, as follows:

Pre-July 1986 adjustment:
Unadjusted investment in the contract	$5,000
Allocable part of amount to be received annually (($5,000 ÷ $6,000) x $1,920)	$1,600
Duration of guaranteed amount (years)	5
Guaranteed amount (5 x $1,600)	$8,000
Percentage in Table III for age 65 and 5 years	7%
Present value of refund feature rounded to nearest dollar (7% of $8,000)	$ 560
Adjusted pre-July 1986 investment in the contract ($5,000 - $560)	$4,440

Post-June 1986 adjustment:
Unadjusted investment in the contract	$1,000
Allocable part of amount to be received annually (($1,000 ÷ $6,000) x $1,920)	$ 320
Duration of guaranteed amount (years)	5
Guaranteed amount (5 x $320)	$1,600
Percentage in Table VII for age 65 and 5 years	3%
Present value of refund feature rounded to nearest dollar (3% of $1,600)	$ 48
Adjusted post-June 1986 investment in the contract	$ 952

Once the investment in the contract has been adjusted by subtracting the value of the period-certain guarantee, an excludable amount is determined by dividing the adjusted investment in the contract by the life expectancy taken from Table I or V. Taking the example above, the excludable amount is determined as follows:

Pre-July 1986 investment in the contract (adjusted for period certain guarantee)	$ 4,440
Life expectancy from Table I (male age 65)	15 years
Excludable amount ($4,440 ÷ 15)	$ 296
Post-June 1986 investment in the contract (adjusted for period certain guarantee)	$ 952
Life expectancy from Table V (age 65)	20 years
Excludable amount ($952 ÷ 20)	$ 47.60
Amount excludable from gross income each year ($296 + $47.60)	$343.60

If the annuity starting date was before November 19, 1996, a simplified safe harbor method may be available. See Q 433.

With respect to annuities with starting dates prior to July 1, 1986, payments are taxed under the annuity rules or under the "3-year cost recovery" rule (see Q 433).

PENSION AND PROFIT SHARING: TAXATION OF DISTRIBUTIONS   Q 435

Certain premature distributions are subject to an additional tax (see Q 428). *ASRS, Sec. 59, ¶910.5(b)*.

435. How is an employee's cost basis for his interest in a qualified plan determined?

Normally, the employee will have no cost basis if the plan is noncontributory and no life insurance protection has been provided thereunder. However, if life insurance protection has been provided under a cash value policy, the employee usually will have some cost basis (the aggregate 1-year term costs that have been taxed to him), even though the plan is noncontributory. IRC Sec. 61(a)(1); Treas. Reg. §1.61-2(a)(1). But a self-employed person who is an owner-employee cannot include in his cost basis the annual 1-year costs of life insurance protection under Table 2001 (or previously under P.S. 58), see Q 424), even though these costs were not deductible. IRC Sec. 72(m)(2); Treas. Reg. §1.72-16(b)(4). And no self-employed person (whether or not an owner-employee) can include in his cost basis the cost of any health insurance features under the plan.

A common law employee's cost basis consists of: (1) total nondeductible contributions made by the employee (if the plan is contributory) and amounts contributed by an S corporation for years beginning before January 1, 1984 on behalf of a more-than-5% shareholder-employee in excess of the excludable amount; (2) the sum of the annual 1-year term costs of life insurance protection under Table 2001 (or previously P.S. 58, see Q 424) that have been includable as taxable income (if payment is being received under the contract that provided the life insurance protection–see Q 425); (3) any other employer contributions (other than excess deferrals–see Q 396) that have already been taxed to him, such as where a nonqualified plan was later qualified; (4) certain employer contributions attributable to foreign services performed before 1963; and (5) the amount of any loans included in income as taxable distributions (see Q 420). In addition, while amounts attributable to deductible employee contributions are not part of basis, to the extent that they have been taxable to the employee because they were used to purchase a life insurance contract, it would seem they should be included in basis (if benefits are received under the contract)–see Q 425. This cost basis must be reduced by any amounts previously distributed to the employee that were excludable from gross income as a return of all or part of his basis. IRC Sec. 72(f); Treas. Regs. §§1.72-8, 1.72-16(b)(4), 1.402(a)-1(a)(6), 1.403(a)-2. See also Rev. Rul. 72-149, 1972-1 CB 218.

A self-employed person's cost basis consists of: (1) the nondeductible 50% of contributions made before 1968, after subtracting the cost of incidental benefits, if any, such as waiver of premium and health insurance benefits, and, in the case of an owner-employee, the costs of life insurance protection under Table 2001 (or previously P.S. 58, see Q 424); (2) contributions on behalf of owner-employees under the 3-year average rule for determining contributions to level premium insurance and annuity contracts in excess of the deductible limit (in effect for years beginning before 1984); and (3) nondeductible voluntary contributions, if any, to a contributory plan. In addition, any amounts taxed to the individual because they were attributable to deductible voluntary employee contributions used to purchase life insurance (if benefits are received under the contract) should probably be included. *ASRS, Sec. 59, ¶910.5(b)*.

2006 Tax Facts on Insurance & Employee Benefits

Disability Benefits

436. How are disability pension payments from a qualified pension or profit sharing plan taxed?

Disability payments from a qualified plan receive different tax treatment, depending upon whether such payments are made to common law employees or self-employed individuals.

Payments to Common Law Employees

If the disability pension is derived from *employer* contributions and is made in lieu of wages to an employee who retired on account of permanent and total disability, the employee may be entitled to a tax credit. See Q 833. He is not entitled to exclude from income any part of such a disability benefit derived from employer contributions. Sec. 122(b), Social Security Amendments Act of 1993.

In a contributory plan, it will be presumed that the disability pension is derived from *employer* contributions unless the plan expressly provides otherwise. But if the plan does provide that *nondeductible employee* contributions are to be used for the disability pension, the disability payments will be excludable from gross income. However, any such employee contributions that were allocated to provide disability payments cannot be included in the employee's cost basis in figuring the tax on his retirement pension payments. Treas. Reg. §1.72-15(c); *Butler v. Comm.*, TC Memo 1987-463.

In the case of a plan that required employees to pay the premiums for the first six months of disability coverage, subject to a right of reimbursement from the employer, the Tax Court determined that the benefits were provided on a noncontributory basis. As a result, an employee who failed to take advantage of the reimbursement option could not exclude the disability benefits from income. *Andrews v. Comm.*, TC Memo 1992-668.

The payment of post-retirement medical expense benefits is tax-free to the employee. Treas. Reg. §1.72-15(h).

A few courts have held that a profit sharing plan can also be an "accident or health plan," so that payment of the full amount in the employee's account on termination of employment because of permanent disability for loss of a bodily function is entirely excludable under IRC Section 105(c). *Wood v. U.S.*, 590 F.2d 321 (9th Cir. 1979); *Masterson v. U.S.*, 79-2 USTC 88,469 (N.D. Ill. 1979); *Berner v. U.S.*, 81-2 USTC 88,468 (W.D. Pa. 1981). However, absent clear evidence to the contrary, other courts have been reluctant to find deferred compensation profit sharing plans to be dual purpose plans intended to provide both retirement and health or accident benefits. *Caplin v. U.S.*, 83-2 USTC 88,242 (2d Cir. 1983); *Berman v. Comm.*, 91-1 USTC 87,327 (6th Cir. 1991); *Gordon v. Comm.*, 88 TC 630 (1987); *Paul v. U.S.*, 88-1 USTC 83,110 (E.D. Mich. 1988). Distributions from such plans have been held to be taxable because they were not computed in reference to taxpayer's disability (as is the case in an accident or health plan), but to his length of service. *Est. of Hall v. Comm.*, 97-1 USTC 87,023 (3rd Cir. 1996), aff'g TC Memo 1996-93; *Dorroh v. Comm.*, 96-1 USTC 83,453 (11th Cir. 1996), aff'g TC Memo 1994-373; *Armstrong v. Comm.*, TC Memo 1993-579; *Maller v. Comm.*, TC Memo 1984-614. See also, Let. Rul. 8824013. An individual who terminated employment on account of disability after his normal retirement date, but prior to a deferred retirement date, could not claim the IRC Section 105(c) exclusion,

PENSION AND PROFIT SHARING: TAXATION OF DISTRIBUTIONS Q 437

because the plan provided that payments after normal retirement age would be paid on account of age and years of service, rather than on account of injury or sickness. Let. Rul. 9504041.

The IRS has taken the position that if a profit sharing plan makes medical expense reimbursement payments, the amounts are not excludable because they represent deferred compensation or retirement benefits. Rev. Rul. 69-141, 1969-1 CB 48.

Payments to Self-Employed Individuals

If a self-employed individual draws benefits from the plan because he has become permanently disabled, the disability payments will be taxed under the same rules that apply to retirement benefits (see Q 433). But if the self-employed individual receives the disability payments through *health insurance*, he may exclude from his gross income any amounts attributable to nondeductible contributions as a self-employed person. IRC Sec. 105(g); Treas. Reg. §1.105-1(a); Treas. Reg. §1.105-5(b); IRC Sec. 104(a)(3). Where contributions under a qualified plan are applied to provide incidental accident and health insurance for a self-employed individual, the insurance is treated as if he had purchased it directly from the insurance company. Treas. Reg. §1.72-15(g). *ASRS, Sec. 59, ¶930.1; Sec. 60, ¶430.5.*

Death Benefits

437. When an employee dies before retirement, how is his beneficiary taxed on a single sum cash payment of the death benefit payable under his qualified plan?

If the death benefit is payable *from the proceeds of a life insurance policy*, the difference between the cash surrender value and the face amount is treated as death proceeds of life insurance, and is excluded from income under IRC Section 101(a), but only if the insurance cost under Table 2001 (or previously under P.S. 58, see Q 424) has been paid with nondeductible employee contributions or has been taxable to the employee. Treas. Reg. §1.72-16(c)(4). The balance of the proceeds (representing the cash surrender value) is treated as a distribution from the plan. IRC Sec. 72(m)(3)(C); Treas. Reg. §1.72-16(c).

The following amounts may be subtracted from the cash surrender value and also excluded from gross income: (1) the sum of the annual term costs of life insurance protection previously taxed to the employee (see Q 425; however, if the deceased was a self-employed owner-employee, his beneficiary cannot subtract these costs, even though they were not deductible by the owner-employee); (2) if the plan is contributory, the employee's nondeductible contributions toward the cost of the insurance; (3) the amount of any loans included in the employee's income as taxable distributions (see Q 420); and (4) any employer contributions (other than excess deferrals—see Q 396) that have been taxed to the employee, including contributions in pre-1984 years on behalf of a more-than-5% shareholder-employee in an S corporation in excess of excludable amounts. The balance (if any) of the cash surrender value is taxable according to the rules applicable to lump sum distributions (see Q 430).

If the employer has purchased an existing policy from the employee for contribution to the trust, or if the employee has contributed it directly to the trust, the transfer for value rule (see Q 63) does not apply so long as neither the employer nor the trustee

2006 Tax Facts on Insurance & Employee Benefits

has the right to change the beneficiary. Rev. Rul. 73-338, 1973-2 CB 20; Rev. Rul. 74-76, 1974-1 CB 30. Similarly, if a trustee of one plan purchases a life insurance policy from the trustee of another plan, there is no transfer for value where the beneficiary is entitled to designate the beneficiary both before and after the transfer, since there has been no change in beneficial ownership. Let. Rul. 7844032.

If the contract is a retirement income contract, and the cash surrender value before death equals or exceeds the face amount, no portion of the proceeds is excludable as death proceeds of life insurance. *Jeffrey v. U.S.*, 11 AFTR 2d 1401 (D. N.J. 1963). However, the annual term costs of life insurance protection previously taxed to the employee would be excludable, except by the beneficiary of an owner-employee. If the contract has been distributed to the employee before his death, the IRS has previously considered the proceeds entirely tax-exempt as life insurance proceeds, while the Tax Court has considered them taxable as proceeds payable under an annuity contract, because death occurs after the element of risk has disappeared. See *Evans v. Comm.*, 56 TC 1142 (1971). However, if the contract distributed before death is subject to the definition of life insurance in IRC Section 7702 or IRC Section 101(f), the treatment of the death benefit would be as discussed in Q 273.

If the death benefit is *not from life insurance proceeds*, the beneficiary may subtract and receive tax free: (1) any nondeductible employee contributions; (2) the amount of any loans included in income; and (3) any employer contributions (other than excess deferrals–see Q 396) that have been taxed to the employee. The balance, if any, of the death benefit (other than amounts attributable to deductible employee contributions) is taxable according to the rules applicable to lump sum distributions (see Q 430).

A distribution to an employee's beneficiary on account of plan termination, rather than on account of death, may not be treated as a lump sum distribution nor as payment of an employee death benefit. *Est. of Stefanowski v. Comm.*, 63 TC 386 (1974).

The beneficiary may be entitled to an income tax deduction for any estate tax attributable to the distribution (see Q 673). IRC Sec. 691(c). See Q 827. *ASRS, Sec. 59, ¶930.3(a)*.

438. How is a beneficiary taxed on life income or installment payments of the death benefit under a qualified plan when an employee dies before retirement?

If the beneficiary *has no* cost basis for the payments, each payment will be fully taxable as ordinary income when received. In general, the beneficiary's cost basis is the same as the employee's cost basis (see Q 435). (In the case of decedents dying before August 21, 1996, the $5,000 death benefit exclusion was included in the beneficiary's cost basis. Rev. Rul. 58-153, 1958-1 CB 43. See Q 134.)

If the beneficiary *does* have a cost basis, the payments are subject to the rules that follow, depending on whether the death benefits come from life insurance proceeds:

If the death benefit payments *do not* come from life insurance proceeds, the beneficiary is taxed as the employee would have been taxed had he lived and received the periodic payments (see Q 433 to Q 434). However, the beneficiary's cost basis, rather than the employee's cost basis, is used. Depending on the annuity starting date, an

PENSION AND PROFIT SHARING: TAXATION OF DISTRIBUTIONS   Q 438

exclusion ratio may have to be determined; if so, the beneficiary's cost basis is used as the *investment in the contract* for an explanation of the basic annuity rule and its application to various types of payments (see Q 7 to Q 24). If the beneficiary elected the simplified safe harbor method for taxing annuity payments (see Q 433), and increased the investment in the contract by any employee death benefit exclusion allowable, the beneficiary had to attach a signed statement to his income tax return, stating that he was entitled to such exclusion in applying the safe harbor method. Notice 88-118, 1988-2 CB 450. When more than one beneficiary is to receive payments under the plan, the cost basis (including the $5,000 exclusion, if available) is apportioned among them, according to each one's share of the total death benefit payments.

If the death benefit payments *do* come from life insurance proceeds, the proceeds are divided into two parts: (1) the "amount at risk" (proceeds in excess of the cash surrender value immediately before death); and (2) the cash surrender value. Treas. Reg. §1.72-16(c).

The portion of the payments attributable to the "amount at risk" is taxable under IRC Section 101(d) as life insurance proceeds settled under a life income or installment option, as the case may be (see Q 276). Generally, the "amount at risk" is prorated over the payment period (whether for a fixed number of years or for life), and the prorated amounts are excludable from the beneficiary's gross income as a return of principal. Where payments are for life, the beneficiary's life expectancy is generally taken from IRS unisex annuity tables V and VI. See Appendix A; Treas. Reg. §1.101-7.

The portion of the payments attributable to the cash surrender value is taxed in the same manner as any other periodic payments from a qualified plan (see explanation above, and see Q 433 to Q 434).

Example. The widow of an employee who died on June 1, 2002 elects to receive $25,000 of life insurance proceeds in 10 annual installments of $3,000 each. The cash surrender value of the policy immediately before insured's death was $11,000. The employee made no contributions to the plan, and the aggregate 1-year term costs of life insurance protection that were taxed to the employee amounted to $940. The widow must include $1,506 of each $3,000 installment, computed in the following manner.

Face amount of insurance contract	$ 25,000
Cash value immediately before death	11,000
Excludable as life insurance proceeds	$ 14,000
Portion of each installment attributable to life insurance proceeds (14/25 of $3,000)	$ 1,680
Excludable as return of principal ($14,000 ÷ 10)	1,400
Includable in gross income	$ 280

(If beneficiary is surviving spouse of an employee who died before October 23, 1986, the $280 would be excludable under the $1,000 annual interest exclusion)

Portion of each installment attributable to cash surrender value of the contract (11/25 of $3,000)	$ 1,320
Beneficiary's cost basis ($940)	$ 940
Expected return (10 x $1,320)	$ 13,200
Exclusion ratio ($940/$13,200)	7.12%
Amount excludable each year (7.12% of $1,320)	$ 93.98
Includable in gross income ($1,320 - $93.98)	$ 1226.02

The beneficiary may be entitled to an income tax deduction for any estate tax attributable to the decedent's interest in the plan (see Q 673) IRC Sec. 691(c). See

2006 Tax Facts on Insurance & Employee Benefits

Q 827. It would seem that the deduction would be prorated over the beneficiary's life expectancy, in the case of life income payments, or over a fixed period, in the case of installment payments. See, for example, Q 17. *ASRS, Sec. 59, ¶930.3(a).*

439. How is the employee's beneficiary taxed on death benefit payments from a qualified plan when the employee dies after retirement?

If the employee had no cost basis for his interest, or has recovered his cost basis from benefits received during his life, all amounts received by the beneficiary will be fully taxable. The beneficiary may be entitled to an income tax deduction for any estate tax attributable to the employee's interest in the plan. IRC Sec. 691(c). See Q 827.

Joint and survivor annuity. The method of taxing the survivor annuity payments to the beneficiary will depend upon how the employee was taxed (see Q 433). If the employee was taxed on everything, the survivor annuitant will be. Treas. Reg. §1.72-4(d). If the employee was taxed under the 3-year cost recovery rule (in existence with respect to annuities with starting dates prior to July 1, 1986) and had not recovered his full cost basis, the survivor will receive the guaranteed payments tax free until the total of the employee's and survivor's tax free receipts equals the employee's cost basis; thereafter everything will be includable in gross income. Treas. Reg. §1.72-13. If the employee was taxed under the regular annuity rules, or under the safe harbor method, the survivor will continue with the same exclusion ratio (Treas. Regs. §§1.72-4, 1.72-5); however, if the employee's annuity starting date was after December 31, 1986, no amount is excludable by the employee or beneficiary after the investment in the contract has been recovered. IRC Sec. 72(b)(2).

Refund beneficiary under life annuity with refund or period-certain guarantee. If the employee had a cost basis for his interest, and had not recovered the full amount tax free, the beneficiary can exclude the balance of the cost basis from gross income (see Q 433). Otherwise, everything received by the beneficiary is taxable. Treas. Reg. §1.72-11; Treas. Reg. §1.72-13. If the beneficiary receives the refund in a lump sum distribution, the lump sum distribution rules apply (see Q 430). However, if the beneficiary surrenders an annuity contract that has been previously distributed to the employee, the payment does not qualify for lump sum treatment, because it is not viewed as a distribution from the trust, but a payment in settlement of the insurer's liability to make future payments. Rev. Rul. 68-287, 1968-1 CB 174. If the beneficiary receives the refund in installments, the taxable payments are ordinary income. If the refund beneficiary of a decedent whose annuity starting date was after July 1, 1986 does not fully recover the cost basis unrecovered at the decedent's death, he may take a deduction for the remaining unrecovered amount. IRC Sec. 72(b)(3).

Installment payments. Where payments for a fixed period or of a fixed amount (not involving life contingency) had commenced to the employee, tax consequences to the beneficiary can differ, depending upon whether the installments are continued, or are commuted and paid to the beneficiary in a lump sum. Also, the balance, if any, of the lump sum payment is taxable under the lump sum distribution rules. If the installments are continued, the method of taxing the payments will then depend upon how the employee was taxed (see Q 433). If the employee was taxed on everything, the beneficiary will be also. Treas. Reg. §1.72-4(d). If the employee was taxed under the 3-year cost recovery rule (in existence for annuities with starting dates prior to July 1, 1986), and had not recovered his full cost basis tax free, the beneficiary can exclude the

PENSION AND PROFIT SHARING: TAXATION OF DISTRIBUTIONS Q 441

balance from the first payments received. Thereafter, everything is taxable. Treas. Reg. §1.72-13. If the employee was taxed under the regular annuity rules or under the safe harbor method, the beneficiary will continue to exclude the same portion of each payment from gross income. Treas. Reg. §1.72-4(a). If the annuity starting date was after December 31, 1986, the beneficiary can exclude amounts only until the investment in the contract has been fully recovered; thereafter all amounts are included in income. IRC Sec. 72(b)(2). *ASRS, Sec. 59, ¶930.3(b)*.

WITHHOLDING ON BENEFITS

440. What general rules apply to withholding of income tax from qualified retirement plan benefits?

The withholding rules that apply to a distribution depend upon whether it constitutes an "eligible rollover distribution" (see Q 445). An "eligible rollover distribution" from a qualified retirement plan is subject to mandatory income tax withholding at the rate of 20%, unless the distribution is directly rolled over to an *eligible retirement plan* (see Q 446). An employee receiving an eligible rollover distribution may not otherwise elect out of this withholding requirement. IRC Sec. 3405(c).

On the other hand, a recipient may elect out of withholding with respect to distributions that do not qualify as eligible rollover distributions. IRC Secs. 3405(a)(2), 3405(b)(2). The amount to be withheld on periodic payments that are not eligible rollover distributions is determined at the rate applicable to wages. IRC Sec. 3405(a)(1). Nonperiodic payments that are not eligible rollover distributions are subject to income tax withholding at the rate of 10%. IRC Sec. 3405(b)(1).

Withholding applies to amounts paid to the beneficiary of a participant as well as to the participant. Withholding does not apply to amounts that it is reasonable to believe are not includable in income.

The maximum amount withheld cannot exceed the sum of the money plus the fair market value of property received other than employer securities. IRC Sec. 3405(e)(8). Thus, a payor will not need to dispose of employer securities to meet the withholding tax liability. Loans treated as distributions (i.e., "deemed distributions") continue to be subject to withholding as nonperiodic distributions at a rate of 10%. The IRS has stated that loans deemed to be distributions are not subject to the 20% mandatory withholding requirement, because such a deemed distribution cannot be an "eligible rollover distribution." However, where a participant's accrued benefit is reduced (i.e., offset) in order to repay a plan loan, such as when employment is terminated, the offset amount may constitute an eligible rollover distribution. See Notice 93-3, 1993-1 CB 293. Withholding is not required on the costs of current life insurance protection taxable to plan participants under Table 2001 (previously P.S. 58, see Q 424). *ASRS, Sec. 59, ¶990*.

TAXATION OF TRUST FUNDS

441. Are the earnings of a qualified pension or profit sharing trust taxable to the trust? Are they currently taxable to the plan participants?

Normally, the trustee pays no tax on earnings from the trust's investments; the trust is tax-exempt under IRC Section 501(a). Except in the case of government and

Q 441   FEDERAL INCOME TAX

non-electing church plans, the trust does not lose its tax-exempt status as a result of engaging in a prohibited transaction. IRC Sec. 503(a)(1)(B).

There is an exception to the tax exemption rule for unrelated business income, which is taxable to the trust. IRC Sec. 511.

Unrelated business income is taxable income from a trade or business regularly carried on by the trust. IRC Sec. 512. An exempt trust that is a limited partner may receive unrelated business income to the same extent as if it were a general partner. *Service Bolt & Nut Co. Profit Sharing Trust v. Comm.*, 84-1 USTC 83,078 (6th Cir. 1983). A specific deduction of up to $1,000 is allowed against unrelated business income. IRC Sec. 512(b)(12).

Income from any type of property will be taxable as unrelated business income if the property has been acquired with borrowed funds (i.e., is "debt-financed property"). Thus, income from property (such as employer securities or life insurance policies) purchased with the proceeds of a life insurance policy loan may be taxed as unrelated business taxable income. See *Siskin Memorial Found., Inc. v. U.S.*, 790 F.2d 480 (6th Cir. 1986), aff'g 603 F. Supp. 91 (E.D. Tenn. 1984). See also Let. Ruls. 7918095; 8028002.

Where a pension fund, in an attempt to increase the rate of return on three certificates of deposit, borrowed funds from a savings and loan with the three old certificates as collateral and was issued a new certificate in an amount equal to the borrowed amount, the net interest earned on the new certificate was income from debt-financed property and not exempt as additional interest on the old certificates. *Kern County Elec. Pension Fund v. Comm.*, 96 TC 845 (1991).

Generally, an exempt trust or 501(c)(3) organization may be a shareholder in an S corporation (see Q 411). Ordinarily, such an interest would be treated as an interest in an unrelated trade or business; thus, items of S corporation income could result in unrelated business income. However, an employee stock ownership plan (ESOP) (see Q 410, Q 416) maintained by an S corporation is not treated as receiving unrelated business income on items of income or loss of the S corporation in which it holds an interest. IRC Sec. 512(e)(3).

Bank trustees commonly invest the assets of separate qualified plans in a common trust fund maintained by the bank, in order to enhance diversification of investment. Income from a common trust is treated as unrelated business income of an otherwise tax-exempt trust, to the extent that the trust would have been taxed had the investment been made directly. Rev. Rul. 98-41, 1998-2 CB 256. This ruling resolved a conflict between Rev. Rul. 67-301, 1967-2 CB 146 (trust's income from a common trust was not unrelated business income), and Treas. Reg. §1.584-2(c)(3) (income from a common trust is unrelated business income to the extent it would have been had the investments been made directly).

Employer securities purchased by an ESOP with borrowed funds are also not within the rule taxing income from debt-financed property, because the indebtedness that an ESOP incurs to purchase employer securities is inherent in the purpose of the trust's tax exemption. Rev. Rul. 79-122, 1979-1 CB 204.

Income from certain debt-financed real estate will not be taxable. IRC Sec. 514(c)(9). Securities purchased on margin by a profit sharing trust and by a pension trust have

PENSION AND PROFIT SHARING: TAXATION OF DISTRIBUTIONS   Q 442

been held to be debt-financed property. *Elliot Knitwear Profit Sharing Plan v. Comm.*, 614 F.2d 347 (3rd Cir. 1980); *Ocean Cove Corp. Retirement Plan and Trust v. U.S.*, 87-1 USTC ¶9232 (S.D. Fla. 1987). The trust will be taxed on its unrelated business income at the tax rates applicable to trusts. IRC Sec. 511(b); *Marprowear Profit Sharing Trust v. Comm.*, 74 TC 1086 (1980), affirmed without opinion (3rd Cir. 1981).

Plan participants are not taxed on trust earnings derived from either employer or employee contributions until such earnings are distributed or made available to them (or their beneficiaries). IRC Secs. 402(a), 403(a).

The tax exemption applies to trusts including self-employed individuals, as well as to trusts including only common law employees. *ASRS, Sec. 59, ¶760.*

REVERSIONS

442. What is the penalty if money or property reverts to the employer from a qualified plan?

The amount of any cash and/or the fair market value of any property reverting to an employer (other than a tax-exempt employer or a governmental employer) from a qualified plan is includable in the employer's gross income, and is generally subject to a nondeductible excise tax. IRC Sec. 4980. The tax is 20% if the employer (1) establishes or maintains a "qualified replacement plan"; (2) provides for pro rata benefit increases for generally all participants and certain beneficiaries; or (3) is in Chapter 7 bankruptcy liquidation as of the termination date of the qualified plan. If none of the above apply, the tax is 50%.

A "qualified replacement plan," for this purpose, is any qualified plan established or maintained by the employer in connection with a qualified plan termination in which (1) at least 95% of the active participants in the terminated plan (who remain employed by the employer) are active participants; (2) a direct transfer of assets is made from the terminated plan to the replacement plan equal to 25% of the maximum reversion that could have been received under prior law (reduced, dollar-for-dollar, by the present value of certain increases in participants' accrued benefits, if any, made pursuant to a plan amendment adopted during the 60-day period ending on the date of termination and taking effect on such date) before any reversion occurs; *and* (3) the portion of the amount transferred to a defined contribution replacement plan is allocated to participants' plan accounts in the plan year in which the transfer occurs, or is credited to a suspense account and allocated to participants' accounts no less rapidly than ratably over the 7-year period beginning with the year of the transfer. If any amount credited to a suspense account cannot be allocated to a participant's account within the 7-year period, such amount must generally be allocated to the accounts of other participants. IRC Sec. 4980(d)(2).

The IRS has determined that where the above requirements were met, amounts transferred to a replacement plan could be used to make employer matching contributions. Let. Ruls. 200045031, 200031055, 9837036, 9834036, 9302027. If the entire surplus is transferred to a 401(k) plan that meets the requirements of a "qualified replacement plan," the employer's excise tax on the reversion will be eliminated. Let. Rul. 9837036. A profit sharing plan with a 401(k) feature has also been approved as a qualified replacement plan. Let. Ruls. 9834036, 9627030, 9252035.

Any amount transferred to a qualified replacement plan is not includable in the employer's gross income and is not treated as a reversion. No deduction is allowed with respect to the transferred amount. IRC Sec. 4980(d)(2)(B)(iii).

An employer is considered to provide for pro rata benefit increases for generally all plan participants and certain beneficiaries under the terminated plan if (1) a plan amendment is adopted in connection with the termination of the plan; (2) the pro rata benefit increases have an aggregate present value of not less than 20% of the maximum amount that the employer would otherwise have received as a reversion; and (3) the pro rata benefit increases take effect immediately on termination of the plan. IRC Sec. 4980(d)(3).

Benefits may not be increased, nor amounts allocated in contravention of the qualification requirements of IRC Section 401(a) or the IRC Section 415 limits (see Q 332, Q 372, Q 377). Any such increases or allocations must be treated as annual benefits or annual additions under IRC Section 415. IRC Sec. 4980(d)(4). The employer is determined on a controlled group basis and the Secretary of the Treasury may provide that two or more plans may be treated as one plan or that a plan of a successor may be taken into account. IRC Secs. 4980(d)(5)(D), 4980(d)(5)(E).

The tax applies to both direct and indirect reversions. An indirect reversion occurs where plan assets are used to satisfy an obligation of the employer. See, e.g., Let. Rul. 9136017.

The employer maintaining the plan must pay the tax, which is due on the last day of the month following the month in which the reversion occurs. IRC Sec. 4980(c)(4). Where money or property reverts to a sole proprietorship or partnership, the employer is the sole proprietor or the partners.

A distribution to any employer by reason of (1) a mistake of fact; (2) the failure of the plan to qualify initially; or (3) failure of employer contributions to be deductible is not a reversion subject to the tax. A reversion from a multiemployer plan will also not be subject to the tax if made because of (1) a mistake of law; or (2) the return of any withdrawal liability payment. IRC Sec. 4980(c)(2)(B).

A transfer of excess assets from a defined benefit plan to a defined contribution plan constitutes a reversion of assets to the employer followed by their contribution to the defined contribution plan. Thus, the excess assets are included in the employer's income and subject to the penalty tax. Notice 88-58, 1988-1 CB 546; GCM 39744 (7-14-88). While a qualified transfer of excess pension assets (see Q 370) from a defined benefit plan to an IRC Section 401(h) account of such a plan is not treated as a reversion to the employer, any amount transferred and not used to pay for qualified current retiree health benefits must be returned to the transferor plan and is treated as a reversion subject to the 20% excise tax. IRC Sec. 420(c)(1)(B). *ASRS, Sec. 59, ¶490.1(b)*.

PROHIBITED TRANSACTIONS

443. What are prohibited transactions? What is the tax penalty if a prohibited transaction takes place?

Generally, any of the following transactions, whether direct or indirect, between a plan and a "disqualified person" (see below) will constitute a *prohibited transaction* under the Internal Revenue Code: (1) a sale, exchange, or leasing of any property, including a transfer of property subject to a security interest assumed by the plan or placed on it within

PENSION AND PROFIT SHARING: TAXATION OF DISTRIBUTIONS   Q 443

10 years prior to the transfer (see IRC Sec. 4975(f)(3)); (2) lending of money or other extension of credit; (3) furnishing of goods, services, or facilities; and (4) the transfer of plan assets or income to, or use of them by or for the benefit of a disqualified person.

In addition, it is a prohibited transaction for a disqualified person who is a fiduciary to deal with income or assets of a plan in his own interest, or to receive consideration for his own personal account from a party dealing with the plan in connection with a transaction involving plan income or assets. IRC Sec. 4975(c)(1).

Title I of ERISA also prohibits a fiduciary from acting, in any transaction involving the plan, on behalf of anyone having interests adverse to those of the plan or plan participants or beneficiaries. ERISA Sec. 406(b)(2).

The definition of a "plan" for this purpose includes not only any qualified pension, profit sharing, stock bonus, or annuity plan, but also an individual retirement plan (see Q 210), Archer medical savings account (see Q 209), or education savings account (see Q 810). The term "plan" includes such plans even after they are no longer qualified. Government and church plans are excluded. IRC Sec. 4975(e)(1).

The Tax Court determined that a loan between a plan and a corporation partially owned by a disqualified person (see below) did not constitute a prohibited transaction where the loan was approved by and made at the sole discretion of the plan's independent bank trustee. *Greenlee v. Comm.* TC Memo 1996-378. However, a transfer of property to a plan in satisfaction of a participant loan was treated as a prohibited transaction where the borrower was a disqualified person. *Morrissey v. Comm.*, TC Memo 1998-443.

"Disqualified Person"

A "disqualified person" is: (1) a fiduciary (see below); (2) a person providing services to the plan; (3) an employer or employee organization, any of whose employees or members are covered by the plan; (4) a 50% owner (directly or indirectly) of an employer or employee organization described in (3); (5) a family member (see below) of any person described in (1) through (4); (6) a corporation, partnership, trust or estate that is 50% or more owned by any person described in (1), (2), (3), or (5); (7) an officer, director, 10% or more shareholder, or highly compensated employee (see below) of a person described in (3), (4), or (6); or (8) a 10% or more (in capital or profits) partner or joint venturer of a person described in (3), (4), or (6). IRC Sec. 4975(e)(2).

Fiduciary. A fiduciary is a person who has discretionary authority over plan management or administration or disposition of plan assets, or who renders investment advice for a fee or other compensation with respect to any money or other property of the plan. IRC Sec. 4975(e)(3).

A person renders investment advice if he advises as to the value of property or makes recommendations about the advisability of buying or selling property, *and*, directly or indirectly: (1) has discretionary authority with respect to buying or selling property; or (2) renders advice on a regular basis to the plan, pursuant to a mutual understanding that (a) the services will be the primary basis for investment decisions, and (b) he will render individualized advice regarding investment policies. Treas. Reg. §54.4975-9(c). Whether advice and recommendations regarding plan purchases of insurance contracts and annuities constitute investment advice depends upon the facts in each situation. Prohibited Transaction Exemption (PTE) 77-9 (Discussion of Major Comments). A "fee or other compensation" can include insurance sales commissions.

ERISA does not modify the definition of a fiduciary under IRC Section 4975; consequently, an individual who is not a fiduciary under ERISA can still be a fiduciary for purposes of IRC Section 4975. *Flahertys Arden Bowl, Inc. v. Comm.*, 115 TC 269 (2000), aff'd, 88 AFTR 2d 2001-5547 (8th Cir. 2001).

Family Member. A family member is defined, for this purpose, as a spouse, ancestor, lineal descendant, or any spouse of a lineal descendant. IRC Sec. 4975(e)(6).

Highly Compensated Employee. A highly compensated employee is defined, for this purpose, as any employee earning 10% or more of the yearly wages of an employer. IRC Sec. 4975(e)(2)(H).

Exemptions Provided by the Code

The Code lists specific exemptions from these broad prohibitions. These include: (1) the receipt of benefits under the terms of the plan; (2) the distribution of the assets of the plan meeting allocation requirements; (3) loans available to all plan participants or beneficiaries under certain circumstances (see below); (4) a loan to an employee stock ownership plan (see Q 410); (5) the acquisition or sale of qualifying employer securities by an individual account profit sharing, stock bonus, thrift, savings plan, or employee stock ownership plan for adequate consideration and without commission; and (6) the provision of office space or services necessary for the establishment or operation of the plan under a reasonable arrangement for no more than reasonable compensation.

This last exemption shields only the provision of services that would be prohibited transactions under (1), (3), and (4) in the first paragraph of this answer, not fiduciary self-dealing. IRC Sec. 4975(d). Thus, if an insurance agent is not a fiduciary, his sale of insurance to a plan and receipt of a commission is within this statutory exemption. But, if he is a fiduciary (for example, if the trustee relies on his investment advice), receipt of a commission for sale of insurance or annuities to a plan may be a prohibited transaction. PTE 77-9 (Discussion of Major Comments). See explanation below; also Treas. Reg. §54.4975-6(a)(5). However, certain administrative exemptions permit receipt of fees or commissions by fiduciaries in connection with the sale of insurance and annuity contracts to plans and the transfer of insurance contracts between plan and plan participants or employers. See "Administrative Exemptions," below.

Except for the first two exemptions listed above, these statutory exemptions do not apply where a plan: (1) lends assets or income; (2) pays any compensation for personal services rendered to the plan; or (3) except as described in the following paragraph, acquires property from or sells property to: (a) an owner-employee (as defined in Q 358) or an employee who owns more than 5% of the outstanding shares of an S corporation, an individual retirement plan participant, beneficiary, or sponsoring employer or association, as the case may be, (b) a family member of a person described in (a), or (c) a corporation controlled by a person described in (a), through ownership of 50% or more of total combined voting power of all classes of stock, or 50% or more of total shares of all classes of stock of the corporation. IRC Sec. 4975(f)(6)(A).

A transaction consisting of a sale of employer securities to an ESOP (see Q 412) by a *shareholder-employee* (as defined below), a member of his family, or a corporation in which he owns 50% or more of the stock will generally be exempt from the prohibited transaction rules. For this purpose, a shareholder-employee is an employee or officer of an S corporation who owns (or is deemed to own, under the constructive ownership

PENSION AND PROFIT SHARING: TAXATION OF DISTRIBUTIONS   Q 443

rules of IRC Section 318(a)(1)) more than 5% of the outstanding stock of the corporation on any day during the corporation's taxable year. IRC Secs. 4975(f)(6)(B)(ii), 4975(f)(6)(C). For special rules applying to S corporation ESOPs that the IRS views as abusive, see Q 416.

Plan Loans

Loans made to plan participants and beneficiaries are generally exempted from the prohibited transaction rules if the loans: (1) are made available to all participants and beneficiaries on a reasonably equivalent basis; (2) are not made available to highly compensated employees (as defined in Q 356) in an amount greater than the amount made available to other employees; (3) are made in accordance with specific provisions regarding such loans set forth in the plan; (4) bear reasonable rates of interest; and (5) are adequately secured. ERISA Sec. 408(b)(1); IRC Sec. 4975(d)(1); Labor Reg. §2550.408b-1.

A reasonable rate of interest is one that provides the plan with a return commensurate with the interest rates charged by persons in the business of lending money for loans made under similar circumstances. Labor Reg. §2550.408b-1(e).

Security for participant loans is considered adequate if it is such that it may reasonably be anticipated that loss of principal or interest will not result if default occurs. Labor Reg. §2550.408b-1(f)(1). The effect of this "no loss" requirement varies depending upon the type of plan; a plan in which the investment experience of the plan's assets is shared by all participants may require additional loan conditions, such as mandatory payroll deduction repayment upon stated events or additional collateral. Generally, no more than 50% of the present value of a participant's vested accrued benefit under a plan may be considered as security for the outstanding balance of all plan loans made to the participant. Labor Reg. §2550.408b-1(f)(2). Except in the case of directed investment loans, this loan exemption is not an exemption from the other fiduciary standards of ERISA. The prohibited transaction rules apply to a loan that does not meet the exemption requirements, even if it is treated (and taxed) as a distribution. *Medina v. U.S.*, 112 TC 51 (1999) (see Q 420).

Loans from a qualified plan to S corporation shareholders, partners, and sole proprietors are generally exempt from the prohibited transaction rules (see Q 420). IRC Sec. 4975(f)(6)(B)(iii). However, for rules applying to certain S corporation ESOPs the IRS views as abusive, see Q 416.

Administrative Exemptions

Prohibited Transaction Exemption 84-24, 1984-2 CB 231 (formerly PTE 77-9, 1977-2 CB 428, as amended by 1979-1 CB 371) provides administrative relief in addition to the statutory provisions. It permits a life insurance agent, broker, or pension consultant (and affiliates), including a fiduciary, who is a disqualified person (1) to receive sales commissions for insurance and annuity sales to a plan; or (2) to effect a transaction for the purchase of an insurance or annuity contract from an insurance company. The exemption also permits an investment company principal underwriter to effect a transaction for the purchase of an insurance or annuity contract. Furthermore, it allows the purchase of insurance or annuities from an insurance company that is a disqualified person. This class exemption is available only if certain conditions are met, as follows:

Q 443 FEDERAL INCOME TAX

First, the transaction must be effected in the ordinary course of business of the agent, broker, or consultant on terms at least as favorable to the plan as an arm's length transaction with an unrelated party would be. Also, the total fees and commissions must not be in excess of "reasonable compensation," determined on a facts and circumstances basis.

Second, the agent, broker, consultant, or insurance company (including its affiliates) may not act as a plan trustee (other than a nondiscretionary trustee who does not render investment advice with respect to any assets of the plan), plan administrator, or a fiduciary authorized to manage, acquire, or dispose of plan assets on a discretionary basis, or an employer, any of whose employees are covered by the plan (however see below for a proposed amendment that may change this requirement).

The term "affiliates" includes (1) any person controlled by or under common control with the agent, broker, consultant, or insurance company; (2) any officer, director, employee, or relative of or a partner in (but not of) the agent, broker, consultant, or insurance company; and (3) any corporation or partnership of which the agent, broker, consultant, or insurance company is an officer, director, or employee, or in which he is a partner.

The transaction must be approved, in writing, by an independent fiduciary, who may be the employer. Prior to the sale, the agent, broker, or consultant must disclose to the independent fiduciary: (a) the nature of the affiliation between the agent and the insurer whose contract is being recommended; (b) any limitations on the agent's ability to recommend insurance or annuity contracts; (c) the amount of sales commission, expressed as a percentage of gross annual premium payments for the first and renewal years; and (d) a description of any charges, fees, discounts, penalties, or adjustments that may be imposed in connection with the purchase, holding, exchange, termination, or sale of such contracts. Finally, the agent, broker, or consultant must retain records relating to the transaction for six years, but no filing with either the IRS or the Department of Labor is required. Such records must, however, be available for examination by those two federal agencies, plan participants, beneficiaries, and any employer or employee organization whose employees or members are covered by the plan.

An insurance company that is a service provider or fiduciary solely because it sponsors a master or prototype plan need satisfy only the first set of conditions. An agent, broker, or consultant who is a fiduciary and who sells insurance in connection with the master or prototype plan must meet both sets of conditions.

A proposed amendment to PTE 84-9 would extend the same relief to situations where an affiliate of the insurance agent or broker, pension consultant, or investment company principal underwriter is a trustee with investment discretion over plan assets that are not involved in the transaction. See Notice of Proposed Amendment to PTE 84-24, 69 Fed. Reg. 55463 (September 14, 2004).

Prohibited Transaction Exemption 79-60, 44 Fed. Reg. 59018, permits an insurance agent or broker who is the employer (or related, in certain ways listed below, to the employer) maintaining a plan to sell an insurance or annuity contract (including a contract providing only for the provision of administrative services) to the plan and receive a commission. A general agent who is the employer (or related to the employer in one of the listed ways) may receive override commissions on such sales by another agent.

PENSION AND PROFIT SHARING: TAXATION OF DISTRIBUTIONS   Q 443

The following three conditions must be met in order for a transaction to come within the exemption. First, the agent or broker must be (1) an employer with employees covered by the plan (including a sole proprietor who is the only plan participant); (2) a 10% or more partner of such an employer; (3) an employee, officer, or director (or an individual having powers or responsibilities similar to those of officers or directors), or a 10% or more stockholder of such an employer; (4) a 50% or more owner of the employer; *or* (5) a corporation or partnership that is 50% or more owned by (a) a plan fiduciary, (b) a person providing services to the plan, (c) the employer, (d) a 50% owner of the employer, or (e) an employee organization with members covered under the plan. Second, the plan may pay no more than adequate consideration for the policy or contract. Finally, the total commissions received in each taxable year of the agent or broker as a result of sales under this exemption must not exceed 5% of the total insurance commission income received by the agent or broker in that taxable year. There are no record keeping requirements.

Prohibited Transaction Exemption 80-26, 1980-2 CB 323, permits a disqualified person (other than another plan) to make unsecured interest-free loans to a plan in order to pay ordinary operating expenses (including the payment of benefits and periodic premiums under an insurance or annuity contract) or, for a period no longer than three days, for a purpose incidental to the ordinary operation of the plan. The Department of Labor proposed an extension of PTE 80-26 to include interest-free loans made to plans affected by the September 11th terrorist attacks. Proposed Amendment to PTE 80-26, 66 Fed. Reg. 49703 (September 28, 2001).

Prohibited Transaction Exemptions 92-5 and 92-6, 57 Fed. Reg. 5019, 5189 (formerly PTEs 77-7 and 77-8, 1977-2 CB 423, 425) establish conditions for the transfer of life insurance and annuity contracts to and from plans. PTEs 92-5 and 92-6 extended the relief granted under PTEs 77-7 and 77-8 to owner-employees and to shareholders owning more than 5% of the outstanding stock in an S corporation. PTE 92-5 permits individual contracts to be transferred to a plan by participants or employers, any of whose employees participate in the plan. Generally, the plan must pay no more than the lesser of the cash surrender value of the contract or the value of the participant's accrued benefit at the time of the transaction (or account balance, in the case of a defined contribution plan), and the contract must not be subject to any loan that the plan assumes. The DOL has stated that where participants transfer individual policies that have no cash surrender value, the transfer will not violate the prohibited transaction rules where the plan pays no consideration for the policies. DOL Adv. Op. 2002-12A.

PTE 92-6 enables a plan to sell insurance contracts and annuities to a plan participant insured under such policies, a relative of such participant who is a beneficiary under the contract, an employer whose employees are covered by the plan, or another employee benefit plan for the cash surrender value of the contracts, provided certain conditions are met. In the absence of these exemptions, such transfers would be prohibited transactions.

PTE 92-6 was first clarified in 1998 so that, if all of its other conditions are met, two or more relatives who are the sole beneficiaries under the contract may be considered a single "relative," and "individual life insurance contract" may be read to include a contract covering the life of the participant and his spouse (if permitted by applicable state insurance law, other applicable law, and "pertinent plan provisions"). In addition,

Q 443   FEDERAL INCOME TAX

a sale of a partial interest in a life insurance contract qualifies as a sale of an "individual life insurance contract" if certain requirements are met with both the portion sold and the portion retained. See DOL Adv. Op. 98-07A.

In 2002, PTE 92-6 was retroactively amended to permit transfers of life insurance contracts directly to life insurance trusts and certain other trusts. In addition, the DOL clarified that second to die policies covering spouses are included within the scope of PTE 92-6. See 67 Fed. Reg. 31835 (10-18-02).

Planning Point: This expansion and liberalization by the Department of Labor adds trusts to the list of those to whom life insurance owned by a qualified plan can safely be sold. But it is important to note that the exemption is conditioned on the fact that the plan, but for the sale, would have surrendered the life insurance contract. Furthermore, the plan must be paid what the policy is worth at the time it is sold. *Stephan R. Leimberg, Leimberg Information Services, Inc.*

The preamble to PTE 77-8 (citing Rev. Rul. 59-195; 1959-1 CB 18) noted that, for federal income tax purposes, the value of an insurance policy is not the same as, and may exceed, its cash surrender value, and that a purchase of an insurance policy at its cash surrender value may therefore be a purchase of property for less than its fair market value. In 2004 guidance, the Treasury Department clarified that under new proposed regulations, any such bargain element will be treated as a distribution under section 402(a), as well as for other purposes of the Code, including the limitations on in-service distributions from certain qualified plans and the limitations of section 415. See REG-126967-03, 69 Fed. Reg. 7384 (February 17, 2004).

Prohibited Transaction Exemption 93-33, 58 Fed. Reg. 31053 and *Prohibited Transaction Exemption 97-11,* 62 Fed. Reg. 5855 allow banks and brokerages, respectively, to offer no or low cost services based upon account balances in IRAs and Keogh plans, if certain requirements are met: (1) the services offered must be those that could be offered under applicable state and federal law, and that are available, in the ordinary course of business, to other customers who do not maintain an IRA or Keogh plan; (2) the eligibility requirements, based upon the account value or the amount of fees incurred, must be as favorable as any such requirements imposed upon any other account included in determining eligibility to receive such services; (3) the IRA or Keogh plan must be established for the exclusive benefit of the participant, his spouse, or their beneficiaries; (4) the investment performance of the IRA or Keogh plan must equal or exceed that of a like investment made at the same time by a customer ineligible to receive such low or no cost services. In addition, PTE 97-11 requires that the services offered by brokerages be the same as those offered to non-IRA or non-Keogh plan customers with like account values or like fees generated and that the combined total of all fees for the provision of services to the IRA or Keogh plan may not exceed "reasonable compensation," within the meaning of IRC Section 4975(d)(2).

The Department of Labor subsequently adopted amendments expanding these exemptions to Coverdell education savings accounts (see Q 810) and SIMPLE IRAs (see Q 242). See 64 Fed. Reg. 11044 and 64 Fed. Reg. 11042 (March 8, 1999). PTE 97-11 was similarly amended to extend its provisions to Roth IRAs (assuming they are not part of an employee benefit plan covered by Title I of ERISA, other than a SEP or a SIMPLE IRA). See 67 Fed. Reg. 76425 (December 12, 2002).

PENSION AND PROFIT SHARING: TAXATION OF DISTRIBUTIONS Q 443

Penalty Tax

Generally, a "first tier" tax equal to 15% of the amount involved is imposed on each prohibited transaction for each year (or part thereof) from the time the transaction occurs until the earliest to occur of the date when (1) it is corrected; (2) a deficiency notice is mailed; or (3) the tax is assessed. IRC Sec. 4975(a); IRC Sec. 4975(f)(2).

All disqualified persons who participate in the prohibited transaction (other than a fiduciary acting only as such) are jointly and severally liable for the full amount of the tax. A trustee was held liable for the tax even though he did not vote to approve the payment that was determined to be a prohibited transaction; the Seventh Circuit Court of Appeals determined that he had benefited from the payments and thus had "participated" in the transaction. *O'Malley v. Comm.*, 1992-2 USTC ¶50,411 (7th Cir. 1992).

An act of self-dealing involving the use of money or property (e.g., the leasing of property) may be treated as giving rise to multiple transactions—one on the day the transaction occurs and separate ones on the first day of *each* taxable year within the above period—and, thus, may result in multiple penalties. Temp. Treas. Reg. §141.4975-13; Treas. Reg. §53.4971(e)-1(e)(1)(i). See *Lambos v. Comm.*, 88 TC 1440 (1987).

If the transaction is not corrected within the above period, there is a "second tier" tax of 100% of the amount involved. However, this tax will be abated if the transaction is corrected within 90 days after the notice of deficiency with respect to the additional tax is mailed. This 90-day period may be extended in certain circumstances.

To "correct" a transaction, it must be undone to the extent possible, but, in any event, so as to place the plan in a financial position no worse than it would have been in had the disqualified person acted under the highest fiduciary standards. IRC Secs. 4975(b), 4961.

A prohibited transaction was held to be self-correcting, and thus not subject to the second tier tax (nor to the first tier tax in subsequent tax years) where the extraordinary success of the investment was such that to "undo" the transaction would have put the plan in a worse position than if the disqualified persons had acted under the highest fiduciary standards. Essentially, the transaction involved a sale of mineral rights that were producing over a million dollars a year in royalties to an ESOP by the employees of the employer in return for a private annuity. *Zabolotny v. Comm.*, 7 F.3d 774 (8th Cir. 1993), nonacq. 1994-1 CB 1. The Tax Court has indicated that it considers *Zabolotny* to be an anomaly, and that, in general, prohibited transactions cannot be self-correcting. See *Morrissey v. Comm.*, TC Memo 1998-443.

If the owner of an individual retirement account, or his beneficiary, engages in a prohibited transaction, and, as a result, the account ceases to be an individual retirement account, the tax does not apply (see Q 214). Similar rules apply to beneficiaries of health and Archer medical savings accounts (see Q 195 to Q 209) and to beneficiaries of and contributors to education savings accounts (see Q 810). IRC Sec. 4975(c)(3).

The IRS has the authority to impose tax penalties as a result of prohibited transactions, even when the Department of Labor has entered into a consent judgment concerning the plan. *Baizer v. Comm.*, 204 F.3d 1231 (9th Cir. 2000). *ASRS, Sec. 59,* ¶¶*710, 740.*

2006 Tax Facts on Insurance & Employee Benefits

ROLLOVER

444. What is a rollover, or rollover contribution? What are its tax effects?

A rollover or rollover contribution is the transfer of a distribution from a qualified plan, an IRC Section 403(b) tax sheltered annuity, an individual retirement plan or an eligible Section 457 governmental plan, *following the rules set out in the Code and Regulations*. Distributions that are rolled over according to these rules are not included in gross income until receipt at some time in the future. For the definition of "eligible rollover distribution," see Q 445; for the defintion of "eligible retirement plan," see Q 446.

Once funds or properties are rolled over to an "eligible retirement plan," they are generally subject to the tax treatment given that plan. See IRC Sec. 408(d). However, different rules apply to distributions made from a traditional IRA to an eligible retirement plan other than an IRA. Generally, the portion of the distribution that is rolled over to such an eligible retirement plan will be treated as coming first from non-after-tax contributions and earnings in all of the IRAs of the owner. IRC Sec. 408(d)(3). This rule effectively allows the owner to roll over the maximum amount permitted. See Q 227.

Generally, it is the responsibility of the plan administrator to determine whether a rollover it accepts is an eligible rollover distribution (see Q 445), and plans that accept invalid rollovers can face disqualification. However, regulations state that a receiving plan will not be disqualified for accepting a rollover that fails to meet the requirements for an eligible rollover distribution, if (a) the plan administrator reasonably concluded such requirements would be met, and (b) certain corrective measures are taken once the error is discovered. Treas. Reg. §1.401(a)(31)-1, A-14. It is not necessary that the distributing plan have a determination letter with respect to its status as a qualified plan for the administrator of the receiving plan to reasonably conclude that the contribution is a valid rollover contribution. Treas. Reg. §1.401(a)(31)-1, A-14(a).

Although the Service generally takes the position that the right to a rollover is personal to the employee and cannot be exercised by anyone else—except in the case of a spousal rollover (see Q 453)—at least one court has held that where an employee received a qualifying rollover distribution but died before making the rollover, his executor could complete the rollover (as long as the 60-day period had not expired). *Gunther v. U.S.*, 82-2 USTC ¶13,498 (W.D. Mich. 1982).

For an explanation of the requirement of a direct rollover option, see Q 447. For rules regarding the application of a mandatory income tax withholding rate of 20% on rollovers not made through a direct rollover, see Q 448. In some cases, a non-participant in a qualified plan may roll over amounts received from the plan by reason of a divorce or separation agreement. See Q 449. *ASRS, Sec. 62, ¶¶910, 920.*

445. What is required to roll over a distribution received from a qualified retirement plan or an eligible IRC Section 457 governmental plan?

Generally, if any portion of the balance to the credit of an employee in a qualified retirement plan is paid to the employee in an *eligible rollover distribution*, and the distributee transfers any portion of the property received to an *eligible retirement plan* (see Q 446), then the amount of the distribution so transferred will not be includable

ROLLOVER

Q 445

in income. IRC Sec. 402(c)(1). Unless otherwise indicated, the rules that apply to qualified plans are incorporated by reference into the requirements for eligible Section 457 governmental plans.

An *eligible rollover distribution* is defined as any distribution made to an employee of all or any portion of the balance to the credit of the employee in a qualified trust, except that the term does not include: (1) any distribution that is part of a series of substantially equal payments (at least annually) made over the life expectancy of the employee or the joint life expectancies of the employee and his designated beneficiary; (2) any distribution made for a specified period of 10 years or more; (3) any distribution that is a required minimum distribution under IRC Section 401(a)(9); and (4) any hardship distribution. IRC Secs. 402(c)(4), 457(e)(16).

Regulations specify other items that are not considered eligible rollover distributions, including any portion of a distribution excludable from gross income (other than net unrealized appreciation), the Table 2001 (or P.S. 58) cost of life insurance (see Q 424), corrective distributions of excess contributions and excess aggregate contributions (see Q 406), excess deferrals (see Q 396), and dividends paid on employer securities under IRC Section 404(k) (see Q 415). Treas. Regs. §§1.402(c)-2, A-3, 1.402(c)-2, A-4. (See Treas. Regs §§1.402(c)-2, A-9, 1.401(a)(31)-1 for guidance on the treatment of plan loans for purposes of the rollover and withholding rules.)

If a qualified retirement plan distributes an annuity contract to a participant, amounts paid under that contract are considered to be payments of the balance of the participant's credit and may be treated as eligible rollover distributions to the extent they would otherwise qualify. Therefore, the participant may surrender the annuity contract and treat the sum received as an eligible rollover distribution to the extent that it is includable in income and is not a required distribution under IRC Section 401(a)(9). Treas. Reg. §1.402(c)-2, A-10; Let. Rul. 9338041. The IRS determined that a separate lump-sum settlement payment to the widow of a plan participant who was already receiving monthly payments under the plan was eligible for rollover treatment under IRC Section 402(c)(4). Let. Rul. 9718037.

A distribution of property other than money is treated in the same manner. The amount transferred equals the property distributed. IRC Sec. 402(c)(1)(C). A taxpayer may not retain the property received in the distribution and simply roll over a cash amount representing the fair market value of the property. Rev. Rul. 87-77, 1987-2 CB 115. Conversely, the taxpayer may not take the cash received in a distribution, convert it into stock (or any other type of investment) and then contribute the converted cash investment into an IRA as a rollover. *Lemishow v. Comm.*, 110 TC 11 (1998). This rule applies to IRA and qualified retirement plan rollovers, including rollovers into Roth IRAs.

Where a distribution includes property and exceeds the rollover contribution, the participant, following a sale, may designate (irrevocably) which portion of the money received, and which portion of the proceeds of the sale, are to be treated as included in the rollover and which portions are to be deemed attributable to nondeductible employee contributions, if any. If he fails to make a designation, allocations will be made on a ratable basis. IRC Secs. 402(c)(6), 457(e)(16)(B). Under the basis recovery rules of IRC Section 72(e), the nondeductible employee contributions are recovered first from the amounts not rolled over. Notice 87-13, 1987-1 CB 432, A-18; Let. Rul. 9043056.

2006 Tax Facts on Insurance & Employee Benefits

The IRS determined that the mistaken transfer by a broker of an otherwise eligible rollover distribution from a qualified plan into a brokerage account and then into an IRA failed to qualify as an eligible rollover and was includable in the taxpayer's gross income. Let. Rul. 9847031. Taxpayers who were defrauded by their investment advisor of IRA distributions intended to be rollovers were not permitted to replace the stolen assets from other funds and treat the replacement assets as rollover contributions. FSA 199933038.

Generally, the maximum amount that may be rolled over is the amount that would be includable in income if not rolled over. IRC Secs. 402(c)(2), 457(e)(16)(B). However, *after-tax contributions* can be (1) rolled over from a qualified plan to a traditional IRA, or (2) transferred in a direct trustee-to-trustee transfer to a defined contribution plan, provided the plan separately accounts for after-tax contributions. After-tax contributions (including nondeductible contributions to a traditional IRA) may not be rolled over from a traditional IRA into a qualified plan, 403(b) tax sheltered annuity, or eligible Section 457 governmental plan. IRC Secs. 402(c)(2), 457(e)(16)(B). Rollover amounts will be treated as first consisting of taxable amounts. See IRC Sec. 402(c)(2).

A rollover must generally be completed within 60 days after receipt of the distribution. IRC Sec. 402(c)(3)(A), 457(e)(16)(B); see Q 454 regarding the application of the 60-day rule. However, the IRS has the authority to *waive* the 60-day requirement where failure to waive it would be against equity or good conscience, including casualty, disaster, or other events beyond the reasonable control of the individual subject to the requirement. IRC Sec. 402(c)(3)(B). Guidance on the requirements for a hardship waiver of the 60-day requirement was provided by the IRS in early 2003. See Rev. Proc. 2003-16, 2003-1 CB 359.

Unless a rollover is carried out by means of a "direct rollover," the distribution amount will be subject to a mandatory income tax withholding rate of 20%. IRC Sec. 3405(c)(1). See Q 447, Q 448.

Rollover contributions may be divided among several traditional IRAs. See Rev. Rul. 79-265, 1979-2 CB 186; Let. Rul. 9331055. These may be either existing plans or plans newly created to receive the rollover. See Q 452. However, a traditional IRA inherited from someone who died after 1983 (other than a deceased spouse) is ineligible to receive a rollover. If an individual retirement annuity is used, it may not be an endowment contract. Although property may normally be rolled over, a rollover to a traditional individual retirement account may not include a retirement income, endowment or other life insurance contract, because IRC Section 408(a)(3) prohibits investment of individual retirement account funds in life insurance contracts. Rev. Rul. 81-275, 1981-2 CB 92. A rollover may be made from a qualified plan even though the participant is an active participant in another plan. *ASRS, Sec. 62, ¶920.1(a).*

446. What is an eligible retirement plan?

The definition of "eligible retirement plan" depends on the plan from which the rollover is made. The availability of rollovers between various types of plans was considerably expanded by EGTRRA 2001.

Qualified plan. An eligible retirement plan with respect to a qualified plan means a traditional IRA, another qualified plan, an IRC Section 403(a) annuity, an IRC Section 403(b) tax sheltered annuity, and an eligible IRC Section 457 governmental plan (provided it agrees to separately account for funds received from any eligible retirement plan, except another eligible Section 457 governmental plan). IRC Secs. 402(c)(8), 402(c)(10). For taxpayers wishing to preserve any capital gains or special averaging treatment (see Q 430), a distribution must be made to a "conduit IRA" and rolled back over to another qualified plan. For this purpose, money from a qualified plan may not be commingled with other money. See Q 452.

Traditional IRAs. An eligible retirement plan with respect to a traditional IRA (individual retirement account or individual retirement annuity) means another traditional IRA, a qualified plan, a 403(a) annuity, an eligible IRC Section 457 governmental plan (provided it agrees to separately account for funds received from any eligible retirement plan, except another eligible Section 457 governmental plan), and a Section 403(b) tax sheltered annuity. IRC Secs. 408(d)(3)(A), 402(c)(10). See Q 452.

IRC Section 403(b) annuity. An eligible retirement plan with respect to an IRC Section 403(b) tax sheltered annuity includes a traditional IRA, a qualified plan, a 403(a) annuity, an eligible IRC Section 457 governmental plan (provided it agrees to separately account for funds received from any eligible retirement plan, except another eligible Section 457 governmental plan), and another 403(b) annuity. IRC Secs. 403(b)(8)(A)(ii), 402(c)(10).

SIMPLE IRA. Amounts paid or distributed out of a SIMPLE IRA during the first two years of participation may be rolled over only to another SIMPLE IRA. IRC Sec. 408(d)(3)(G). *ASRS, Sec. 62, ¶920.1.*

447. Must a participant receiving an eligible rollover distribution have the option of making the rollover by means of a "direct rollover"?

Yes. A qualified plan, an IRC Section 403(b) tax sheltered annuity, and an eligible IRC Section 457 governmental plan must provide a participant receiving an eligible rollover distribution the option to have the distribution transferred in the form of a direct rollover to another eligible retirement plan. IRC Secs. 401(a)(31), 403(b)(10), 457(d)(1)(C). Generally, this direct rollover option must be provided to any participant receiving a distribution. Treas. Reg. §1.402(c)-2, A-1.

A direct rollover is defined as an eligible rollover distribution (see Q 445) that is paid directly to an eligible retirement plan (see Q 446) for the benefit of the distributee. Such a rollover may be accomplished by any reasonable means of direct payment including the use of a wire transfer or a check that is negotiable only by the trustee of the eligible retirement plan. Treas. Reg. §1.401(a)(31)-1, A-3. Giving the check to the distributee for delivery to the eligible retirement plan is considered reasonable provided that the check is made payable to the trustee of the eligible retirement plan for the benefit of the distributee. Treas. Reg. §1.401(a)(31)-1, A-4. However, certain amounts may be rolled over only in the form of a trustee-to-trustee transfer. See IRC Sec. 402(c)(2). Qualified plans and tax sheltered annuities are not required to accept rollovers, direct or otherwise.

If a participant's total distribution is expected to be less than $200, the participant need not be offered the option of a direct rollover. Treas. Reg. §1.401(a)(31)-1, A-11. While a participant must be permitted to elect a direct rollover of only a portion of the distribution, the plan administrator may require that this direct rollover portion equal at least $500. (In the case of 403(b) tax sheltered annuities, the payor of the eligible rollover distribution is treated as the plan administrator. Treas. Reg. §1.403(b)-2, A-2.) Further, the plan administrator is not required to permit the participant to make a direct rollover of only a portion of the distribution at all if the full amount of the distribution totals less than $500. Treas. Reg. §1.401(a)(31)-1, A-9. A plan administrator may permit a participant to divide his distribution into separate distributions to be paid to two or more eligible retirement plans in direct rollovers but is not required to do so. Treas. Reg. §1.401(a)(31)-1, A-10.

If an eligible rollover distribution from a qualified retirement plan or a tax sheltered annuity is not handled by means of a direct rollover, the distribution will be subject to a mandatory income tax withholding rate of 20%. IRC Sec. 3405(c)(1). See Q 448.

Automatic Rollovers. Under new Department of Labor regulations effective March 28, 2005, plans subject to the direct rollover rules are required to provide that a cash-out distribution (see Q 333) in excess of $1,000, and less than $5,000, will automatically be transferred to an individual retirement plan unless the distributee affirmatively elects to have it transferred to another eligible retirement plan, or elects to receive it directly. The new regulations provide a safe harbor for plan fiduciaries who comply with the requirements. Labor Reg. §2550.404a-2; IRC Sec. 401(a)(31)(B); EGTRRA 2001, Sec. 657(a).

To qualify for the safe harbor, a plan fiduciary must generally meet six conditions:

1. The distribution must not exceed $5,000, not including balances rolled into the plan from another qualified plan or an IRA. The safe harbor applies to balances of $1,000 or less, even though those balances are not subject to the automatic rollover rules.

2. The distribution must be to an individual retirement account or annuity pursuant to a written agreement with the individual retirement plan provider that addresses the default investments and related fees and expenses.

3. The distribution must be invested in a manner designed "to preserve principal and provide a reasonable rate of return, whether or not such returned is guaranteed, consistent with liquidity." The investment must be offered by a state or federally regulated financial institution and must seek to maintain a stable dollar value (e.g., money market funds, interest-bearing savings accounts, certificates of deposit, and stable value products).

4. The fees and expenses charged to the IRA may not be higher than fees charged by the IRA custodian for other rollover IRAs.

5. The summary plan description provided to plan participants must provide an explanation of the plan's automatic rollover provisions, including an explanation of the expenses and default investments in the rollover IRA and a plan contact for further information.

6. The selection of the IRA custodian and investment options must not result in a prohibited transaction under ERISA Section 406. However, the DOL has finalized a class exemption that will allow financial institutions to establish IRAs for their own employees.

ROLLOVER   Q 448

Notice Requirements

A plan administrator, within a reasonable time before a distribution is made, must provide the recipient of the distribution with a written explanation of the options available for transferring the funds. The explanation must include the provisions under which the recipient may have the funds transferred by means of a direct rollover and under which circumstances the income tax withholding requirements will apply. Where applicable, the notice must explain that the automatic rollover rules apply to certain distributions. IRC Secs. 402(f), 457(e)(16)(B).

With respect to qualified plans and eligible IRC Section 457 governmental plans, the IRC Section 402(f) notice generally must be given no less than 30 days and no more than 90 days before the date of distribution. See Treas. Reg. §1.402(f)-1, A-2. However, if the recipient elects a distribution, the plan will not fail to comply with these notice requirements merely because the distribution is made less than 30 days after the notice is given if the plan administrator provides information to the recipient that clearly indicates that he has the opportunity to consider the direct rollover decision for at least 30 days after receiving notice. Treas. Reg. §1.402(f)-1, A-2. With respect to IRC Section 403(b) annuities, Treas. Reg. §1.402(f), A-2, is not applicable in determining what is considered to be a "reasonable time" for providing the IRC Section 402(f) notice. However, the payor of an IRC Section 403(b) annuity will be deemed to have provided the explanation within a reasonable time if he complies with the time period in this section of the regulations. Treas. Reg. §1.403(b)-2, A-3.

The IRS has issued a "safe harbor explanation" that plan administrators may use to satisfy the notice requirements of IRC Section 402(f), and that incorporates the amendments of EGTRRA 2001. Notice 2002-3, 2002-2 IRB 289.

The IRS has issued final regulations that permit the use of electronic media to satisfy the IRC Section 402(f) notice requirements. Under the regulations, the IRC Section 402(f) notice may be provided either in written form on paper or through an electronic medium. Any electronic notice issued must utilize a medium that is reasonably accessible to the participant such as e-mail or a plan website. The participant may request the notice on a written paper document that must be provided free of charge. Treas. Reg. §1.402(f)-1, A-5. *ASRS, Sec. 62, ¶910.3.*

448. If a rollover is not made through a direct rollover, must income tax be withheld from the distribution?

Distributions from qualified retirement plans, tax sheltered annuities, and eligible IRC Section 457 governmental plans are subject to a mandatory income tax withholding rate of 20% unless the transfer is handled by means of a direct rollover. IRC Secs. 3405(c)(1), 457(e)(16)(B). The employee receiving the distribution may not elect out of the withholding requirement. Distributions from traditional IRAs are not subject to mandatory 20% withholding. See Q 230.

Note that if a participant's total distribution is expected to be less than $200, the participant need not be offered the option of a direct rollover. Treas. Reg. §1.401(a)(31)-1, A-11.

If a participant receives an eligible rollover distribution that is subject to the 20% withholding rate, the 20% withheld will be includable in income—to the extent required by IRC Section 402(a), IRC Section 403(b)(1), or IRC Section 457(a)(1)(A)—even if the participant rolls over the remaining 80% of the distribution within the 60-day period (see Q 454). Treas. Regs. §§1.402(c)-2, A-11, 1.403(b)-2, A-1. Because the amount withheld is considered to be an amount distributed under such sections, the participant may add an amount equal to the 20% withheld to the 80% he has received, resulting in a rollover of the full distribution amount. The 10% premature distribution penalty (see Q 231, Q 485) may apply to the amount withheld where only the remaining 80% of the distribution is rolled over from a qualified plan or IRC Section 403(b) plan. Treas. Reg. §1.402(c)-2, A-11.

A distribution from an eligible IRC Section 457 governmental plan is treated as a premature distribution from a qualified plan to the extent that it represents funds rolled over from a qualified plan, IRC Section 403(b) plan, or traditional IRA. IRC Sec. 72(t)(9).

Where a distributee elects to transfer a portion of the distribution by a direct rollover and receive the remainder, the 20% withholding requirement applies only to the portion of the distribution that the distributee actually receives. It does not apply to the portion of the distribution that is transferred directly to another eligible retirement plan. Treas. Reg. §31.3405(c)-1, A-6. *ASRS, Sec. 62, ¶920.1(c).*

449. May an individual who is not a participant in a qualified plan roll over amounts received from the plan by reason of a divorce or separation agreement?

Yes, if the agreement is a "qualified domestic relations order," (QDRO), and certain requirements are met. Let. Ruls. 9109052, 8744023, 8712066, 8608055. A QDRO is, generally, a decree or judgment under state domestic relations law that recognizes or creates the right of another individual (spouse or child) to receive, or have set aside, a portion of a participant's interest in a qualified plan or an eligible IRC Section 457 governmental plan. IRC Secs. 414(p)(1)(A), 414(p)(12). See Q 349, Q 124.

If an alternate payee who is the spouse or former spouse of the participant receives a distribution by reason of a QDRO, the rollover rules apply to the alternate payee as if the alternate payee were the participant. IRC Sec. 402(e)(1). Thus, the alternate payee can avoid the requirement of including the distribution in income to the extent any portion of an eligible rollover distribution is rolled over to an eligible retirement plan within 60 days. IRC Sec. 402(c)(1).

It appears that a qualified retirement plan may be an eligible retirement plan for an alternate payee who is a spouse or former spouse of the participant and who receives the distribution by reason of a QDRO. See IRC Sec. 402(e)(1)(B). (For the rules applicable to surviving spouses, see Q 453.) Generally, such a rollover must be handled through a "direct rollover" to avoid a mandatory income tax withholding rate of 20%. IRC Sec. 3405(c)(1). See Q 447, Q 448. *ASRS, Sec. 62, ¶940.1.*

450. May a participant who receives a distribution of an annuity from a qualified pension or profit sharing plan surrender the annuity and roll over the proceeds?

Where a qualified pension or profit sharing plan distributes an ordinary annuity contract (deferred or otherwise) to a participant, the annuity contract or cash amount received on surrender of the contract may be rolled over if the distribution is an eligible rollover distribution, and meets the requirements necessary for rollover of such a distribution. IRC Sec. 402(c). See Q 445. For purposes of the 60-day rule, the distribution takes place upon distribution of the annuity contract from the plan, not on its surrender or transfer to the receiving plan. See Let. Ruls. 8014034, 8035054. See Q 454. *ASRS, Sec. 62, ¶920.*

451. Under what circumstances may a participant roll over permitted distributions from a Section 403(b) tax sheltered annuity?

For distributions received from tax sheltered annuities, any portion of the balance to the credit of an employee that is paid to the employee in the form of an eligible rollover distribution (see Q 445) and transferred to an eligible retirement plan (see Q 446) is not includable in income by the employee. IRC Secs. 402(c)(1), 403(b)(8). Rollover distributions from tax sheltered annuities may be made to another tax sheltered annuity, a traditional IRA, a qualified plan, an IRC Section 403(a) plan, or an eligible IRC Section 457 governmental plan (provided the IRC Section 457 plan agrees to separately account for such funds). IRC Sec. 403(b)(8)(A)(ii).

A trustee-to-trustee transfer from an IRC Section 403(b) plan to a defined benefit governmental plan that is used to purchase permissive service credits will be excluded from income. IRC Sec. 403(b)(13). Under a 1991 ruling, rollover treatment was disallowed for such a transfer. See *Tolliver v. Comm.*, TC Memo 1991-460. A proper rollover was not achieved where a taxpayer invested a tax sheltered annuity distribution in a certificate of deposit. *Adamcewicz v. Comm.*, TC Memo 1994-361.

Distributions excepted from the term "eligible rollover distribution" include (1) any distribution that is part of a series of substantially equal payments made over the life expectancy of the employee or the joint life expectancies of the employee and his designated beneficiary, (2) any distribution made for a specified period of 10 years or more, (3) any distribution that is a required minimum distribution under IRC Section 401(a)(9), and (4) any hardship distribution. IRC Secs. 402(c)(4), 408(b)(8)(B).

Regulations specify other items not considered to be eligible rollover distributions, including any portion of a distribution excludable from gross income, the Table 2001 or P.S. 58 cost of life insurance (see Q 481), and corrective distributions of excess deferrals (see Q 473) and excess employer matching contributions (see Q 467). Treas. Regs. §§1.402(c)-2, A-3, 1.402(c)-2, A-4, 1.403(b)-2, A-1. (See Treas. Regs. §§1.402(c)-2, A-9, 1.401(a)(31)-1 for guidance on the treatment of plan loans for purposes of the rollover and withholding rules.)

A distribution of property other than money is treated in the same manner. The amount transferred equals the property distributed. IRC Sec. 402(c)(1)(C).

Generally, the maximum amount that may be rolled over is the amount that would be includable in income if not rolled over. IRC Sec. 402(c)(2). However, *after-tax contributions* can be (1) rolled over to a traditional IRA, or (2) transferred in a direct trustee-to-trustee transfer to a defined contribution plan, provided the plan separately accounts for after-tax contributions. After-tax contributions (including nondeductible contributions to a traditional IRA) may not be rolled over from a traditional IRA into a qualified plan, 403(b) tax sheltered annuity, or eligible Section 457 governmental plan.

IRC Secs. 402(c)(2), 403(b)(8)(B). Rollover amounts will be treated as first consisting of taxable amounts. See IRC Sec. 402(c)(2).

The Service has indicated that a direct rollover may not be made of amounts that are not eligible for distribution from an IRC Section 403(b) annuity due to the distribution restrictions of IRC Section 403(b)(11). Such amounts may be transferred between tax sheltered annuities if the requirements of Revenue Ruling 90-24, 1990-1 CB 97, can be met. IRS Information Letter, May 19, 1995. Reaching a similar conclusion, a federal district court held that funds in a tax sheltered annuity attributable to a salary reduction agreement were not eligible for rollover treatment unless the requirements of IRC Section 403(b)(11) were satisfied. *Frank v. Aaronson*, 1996 U.S. Dist. LEXIS 15617. See Q 466. However, funds subject to such distribution requirements may be transferable to another tax sheltered annuity in a "direct transfer;" see Q 478. A deemed distribution under IRC Section 72(p) is not eligible to be rolled over to an eligible retirement plan. Prop. Treas. Reg. §1.72(p)-1, A-12.

A rollover generally must be completed within 60 days after the distribution is received. See Q 454. IRC Sec. 402(c)(3). However, the IRS has the authority to waive the 60-day requirement where failure to waive it would be against equity or good conscience, including casualty, disaster, or other events beyond the reasonable control of the individual subject to the requirement. IRC Sec. 402(c)(3)(B). Guidance on the requirements for this hardship waiver was issued in early 2003. See Rev. Proc. 2003-16, 2003-1 CB 359.

Unless a rollover is effected by means of a direct rollover, the distribution amount will be subject to a mandatory income tax withholding rate of 20%. IRC Secs. 403(b)(10), 3405(c)(1). See Q 447, Q 448. *ASRS, Sec. 62, ¶¶920.1(b), 920.2(b).*

452. Under what circumstances may rollover contributions be made from an individual retirement plan by the owner of the plan?

This is entirely dependent on the type of individual retirement plan owned and the source from which the funds in the plan originated.

No rollover from a traditional or Roth IRA is permitted if the individual for whose benefit the plan is maintained acquired such plan by reason of the death of another individual (i.e., in the case of an inherited plan) who died after 1983. This, however, does not apply where the plan is maintained for the benefit of the surviving spouse of the deceased individual. IRC Secs. 408(d)(3)(C), 408A(a).

A "qualified rollover contribution" may be made from a Roth IRA to another Roth IRA or from a traditional IRA to a Roth IRA. A "qualified rollover contribution" means a rollover contribution to a Roth IRA from another Roth IRA or from a traditional IRA but only if the rollover contribution meets the requirements discussed below under "Rollover to Another IRA." IRC Sec. 408A(e). For special rules applicable to rollovers of traditional IRAs to Roth IRAs, see Q 222.

No rollover contribution from a tax sheltered annuity or a qualified plan—other than a designated Roth account in a 401(k) plan (see Q 401)—may be made to a Roth IRA, and, thus, no rollover contribution may be made from a Roth IRA to a tax sheltered annuity or to a qualified plan—other than a designated Roth account. See IRC Sec.

408A(c)(6)(A). A distribution from a designated Roth account may be rolled over to (a) another designated Roth account of the individual from whose account the payment or distribution was made, or (b) a Roth IRA of the individual. IRC Sec. 402A(c)(3).

A rollover may be made from one SIMPLE IRA (see Q 242) to another SIMPLE IRA, but a rollover from a SIMPLE IRA to a traditional IRA or to a Roth IRA is permitted only in the case of distributions to which the 25% early distribution penalty does not apply (generally the penalty applies during the first two years of participation, but see Q 428). IRC Secs. 408(d)(3)(G), 408A(a); Temp. Treas. Reg. §1.408A-4, A-4. To the extent that an employee is no longer participating in a SIMPLE IRA plan and two years have expired since the employee first participated in the plan, the employee may treat the SIMPLE IRA account as a traditional IRA. General Explanation of Tax Legislation Enacted in the 104th Congress (JCT-12-96), p. 141 (the Blue Book).

A required minimum distribution from an IRA is not eligible for rollover. If a minimum distribution is required for a calendar year, any amounts distributed during a calendar year from an IRA are first treated as the required minimum distribution for the year. Treas. Reg. §1.408-8, A-4,

Rollover to a Qualified Retirement Plan

Generally, an individual may receive a distribution from his traditional IRA and, to the extent that the distribution would be includable in income if not rolled over, he may roll it over within 60 days into a qualified pension, profit sharing or stock bonus plan. IRC Sec. 408(d)(3)(A). After-tax contributions (including nondeductible contributions to a traditional IRA) may not be rolled over from a traditional IRA into a qualified plan. IRC Sec. 402(c)(2).

The Secretary of the Treasury may waive the 60-day rollover requirement if failure to waive it would be against equity or good conscience, including casualty, disaster, or other events beyond the reasonable control of the individual subject to the requirement (see Q 454). IRC Sec. 402(c)(3)(B); Rev. Proc. 2003-16, 2003-1 CB 359.

An IRA owner who mixes a rollover contribution from a qualified plan with funds from other sources will forfeit any capital gain or special averaging treatment that might otherwise have been available for the qualified plan money. See EGTRRA 2001, Secs. 641(f)(3), 642(c)(2); see Let. Rul. 8433078.

A terminated vested employee who rolled over her account balance to an IRA and began receiving substantially equal periodic payments from the IRA was permitted to roll over the remaining IRA account balance back into her employer's plan when she returned to her former job. Let. Rul. 9818055.

A surviving spouse who receives a distribution from a qualified plan and rolls it over into a traditional IRA is subject to the same treatment as would be applied to the employee. IRC Sec. 402(c)(9). See Q 453.

Rollover to a Tax Sheltered Annuity

An individual may receive a distribution from his traditional IRA and within 60 days roll it over into a tax sheltered annuity, to the extent that the distribution would be includable in income if not rolled over. IRC Secs. 408(d)(3)(A), 402(c)(8)(B)(vi).

After-tax contributions (including nondeductible contributions to a traditional IRA) may not be rolled over from a traditional IRA into an IRC Section 403(b) tax sheltered annuity. IRC Secs. 402(c)(2), 403(b)(8)(B).

The Secretary of the Treasury may waive the 60-day rollover requirement if failure to waive it would be against equity or good conscience, including casualty, disaster, or other events beyond the reasonable control of the individual subject to the requirement (see Q 454). IRC Sec. 402(c)(3); Rev. Proc. 2003-16, 2003-1 CB 359.

Rollover to IRC Section 457 Plan

An individual may receive a distribution from his traditional IRA and within 60 days roll it over into an eligible IRC Section 457 governmental plan, to the extent that the distribution would be includable in income if not rolled over. IRC Secs. 408(d)(3)(A), 402(c)(8)(B)(v). However, the IRC Section 457 plan must agree to separately account for the funds. IRC Sec. 402(c)(10). After-tax contributions (including nondeductible contributions to a traditional IRA) may not be rolled over from a traditional IRA into an eligible IRC Section 457 governmental plan. IRC Secs. 402(c)(2), 457(e)(16).

The IRS may waive the 60-day rollover requirement if failure to waive it would be against equity or good conscience, including casualty, disaster, or other events beyond the reasonable control of the individual subject to the requirement (see Q 454). IRC Sec. 402(c)(3); Rev. Proc. 2003-16, 2003-1 CB 359.

Rollover to Another IRA

An owner of a traditional IRA (other than a SIMPLE IRA during the first two years of participation–see Q 243) may receive a distribution of *any* amount from it and within 60 days roll that amount, or any part of that amount, over into any other traditional IRA (i.e., a receiving plan.) IRC Sec. 408(d)(3). Likewise, an owner of a Roth IRA may receive such a distribution from it and within 60 days roll that amount, or any part of that amount, over into any other Roth IRA. IRC Secs. 408(d)(3), 408A(a), 408A(e).

The IRS is authorized to waive the 60-day rollover requirement where failure to waive it would be against equity or good conscience, including casualty, disaster, or other events beyond the reasonable control of the individual subject to the requirement (see Q 454). IRC Sec. 402(c)(3)(B); Rev. Proc. 2003-16, 2003-1 CB 359.

The "owner," for purposes of these rules, includes a spouse who has made a rollover–see Q 453. The receiving plan may be an existing plan or one newly created (however, an endowment contract or an individual retirement plan inherited from a decedent who died after 1983, other than a deceased spouse, may not be used as a receiving individual retirement plan).

The distributing plan or any other eligible retirement plan (see Q 446) may receive any or all of the distribution as a rollover amount. See IRC Sec. 402(c)(8)(B). Mixing of funds from different sources in a single traditional IRA will not prevent further rollover to another eligible retirement plan; however, it will prevent the owner from preserving any capital gains or special averaging treatment (see Q 430) available on a plan distribution. See EGTRRA 2001, Secs. 641(f)(3), 642(c)(2).

Only one rollover *from* a particular traditional IRA to any other traditional IRA (or from a particular Roth IRA to any other Roth IRA) may be made in any 1-year period.

ROLLOVER

Q 453

See IRC Secs. 408(d)(3)(B), 408A(a). This limitation is applied separately to each IRA; thus, an individual who owns more than one IRA may roll over funds from IRA #1 to IRA #3 and from IRA #2 to any other IRA, including to IRA #3, within a single 12-month period. Prop. Treas. Reg. §1.408-4(b)(4)(ii); Let. Ruls. 9308050, 8731041. However, where a taxpayer made a rollover from one IRA (IRA #1) to another (IRA #2), then within the same year made a withdrawal from IRA #2 and replaced most of the funds within 60 days, the Tax Court ruled that rollover treatment was unavailable for the second transaction on the grounds that the second rollover violated the 1-year lookback limitation. *Martin v. Comm.*, TC Memo 1992-331. In other words, where amounts are rolled over from one IRA to a second IRA, a rollover may not be made within a 1-year period from the second IRA. See IRS Pub. 590. The 1-year lookback limitation of IRC Section 408(d)(3)(B) applies only to distributions from an individual retirement plan; a rollover from a qualified plan to an IRA is not counted. Let. Rul. 8745054. Also, a rollover from a traditional IRA to a Roth IRA does not count towards this limit. See IRC Sec. 408A(e).

Payment of an arbitration award, designed to replace wasted IRA assets, into a new individual retirement account was a valid rollover. Let. Rul. 8739034. Likewise, a court-ordered payment of the diminished value of an IRA resulting from the investment company's error was eligible for rollover treatment. Let. Rul. 8814063. *ASRS, Sec. 62, ¶930.*

453. May a surviving spouse make a rollover contribution?

Yes. Where any portion of an eligible distribution from a qualified plan is paid to the spouse of a participant after that participant's death, the spouse may make a rollover contribution of *all or any part* of that portion within 60 days of receipt. IRC Sec. 402(c)(9). (The Secretary of the Treasury is authorized to waive the 60-day rule under certain circumstances; see Q 454.)

A qualified plan, a traditional IRA, a tax sheltered annuity, or an eligible IRC Section 457 governmental plan (provided it agrees to separately account for funds received from any eligible retirement plan, except another eligible IRC Section 457 governmental plan) is treated as an eligible retirement plan with respect to a surviving spouse. IRC Secs. 402(c)(9), 402(c)(10). In other words, the surviving spouse may roll over an eligible distribution into his or her own plan account, provided the plan accepts rollover contributions. See Treas. Reg. §1.402(c)-2, A-11.

The other rules applicable to rollovers in general apply to rollovers by a deceased participant's spouse. See Q 446, Q 447, Q 448, Q 451, Q 454. IRC Secs. 402(c)(9), 403(a)(4), 403(b)(8). Thus, unless the spouse elects the direct rollover option, the distribution will be subject to mandatory withholding at 20%. See Q 448.

Planning Point: An IRA beneficiary who is a surviving spouse has the option of rolling over a distribution to his own IRA. If he exercises his rollover option and he is under age 59½, then future distributions from his IRA before he reaches age 59½ will be subject to the 10% tax, whereas distributions directly from the deceased spouse's IRA would not. The surviving spouse's need for distributions before age 59½ is one factor in his rollover decision. *Martin Silfen, J.D., Brown Brothers, Harriman Trust Co., LLC.*

Since the surviving spouse of an owner of a traditional IRA is not subject to the inherited account rules, the surviving spouse may make rollovers to and from the plan.

See IRC Sec. 408(d)(3)(C). Generally, this has held true whether the spouse was the beneficiary designated under the plan or inherited the account as sole beneficiary of the owner's estate. See e.g., Let. Ruls. 9820010, 9502042, 9402023, 8925048. Furthermore, a proper rollover was considered made by a surviving spouse who, as her deceased husband's executrix, transferred the right to receive the benefits due her husband from his profit sharing plan to herself under the residuary bequest in the husband's will and then transferred this amount into an IRA already established on her behalf. Let Rul. 9351041.

In a number of private rulings during the 1990s, the IRS stated that if a decedent's IRA or tax sheltered annuity passed through a third party, such as a trust, and then was distributed to the decedent's surviving spouse, the spouse was treated as acquiring the IRA or tax sheltered annuity from the trust rather than from the decedent; thus, no rollover was possible. See e.g., Let. Ruls. 9515041, 9427035, 9416045. However, the Service also determined on several occasions that if the trustee had no discretion as to the allocation of IRA proceeds to a trust or the payment of the proceeds directly to the surviving spouse, the surviving spouse would be treated as having acquired the IRA proceeds from the decedent rather from the trust. In other words, a rollover was possible. See e.g., Let. Ruls. 200324059, 9813018, 9649045, 9533042, 9445029. In numerous rulings, the Service has treated a surviving spouse as having acquired the IRA from the decedent and not the trust where the surviving spouse had the power to revoke the trust. Let. Ruls. 199910067, 9815050, 9721028, 9427035.

The Preamble to the 2002 final regulations under IRC Section 401(a)(9) (see Q 339) clarifies that if a surviving spouse receives a distribution from a deceased spouse's IRA, "the spouse is permitted to roll that distribution over within 60 days into an IRA in the spouse's own name to the extent that the distribution is not a required distribution, regardless of whether or not the spouse is the sole beneficiary of the IRA owner." See TD 8987, 67 Fed. Reg. 18988 (4-17-02). In other words, it appears that for rollover purposes, the final regulations were intended to put to rest the distinction between trusts that provide discretion to the surviving spouse and those that do not.

The surviving spouse does not receive a stepped up basis with respect to the decedent's plan interest or tax sheltered annuity. See Q 827. *ASRS, Sec. 62, ¶940.2.*

454. How is the 60-day time limitation on rollovers applied?

Once a distribution eligible for rollover treatment is received by a participant, he must make the rollover contribution within 60 days. IRC Sec. 402(c)(3). If more than one distribution is received by an employee from a qualified plan during a taxable year, the 60-day rule applies separately to each distribution. Treas. Reg. §1.402(c)-2, A-11.

The IRS has the authority to waive the 60-day requirement where failure to waive it would be against equity or good conscience, including casualty, disaster, or other events beyond the reasonable control of the individual subject to the requirement. IRC Sec. 402(c)(3)(B).

The IRS has issued guidelines for requesting a waiver of the 60-day requirement. See Rev. Proc. 2003-16, 2003-1 CB 359. Under the guidelines, a taxpayer may request a private letter ruling from the IRS waiving a failure to meet the 60-day requirement. The Service will consider "all relevant facts and circumstances," such as whether financial institutions committed any errors; whether an incomplete rollover was due to death, disability, hospitalization, incarceration, or postal error; how an amount distributed was used by the taxpayer, including whether a check was cashed; and how much time has elapsed since the distribution. The guidelines grant automatic waivers in cases where the failure to timely complete a rollover is "solely due to an error on the part of the financial institution." If the taxpayer followed the institution's required procedures within the 60-day rollover period, and the error is ultimately corrected within one year of the distribution, no waiver request is necessary.

The IRS has liberally applied the new guidelines, granting waivers for alcohol and drug treatment, blizzards, bank errors, dementia, health problems, hurricanes, mistakes of fact—confusing an IRA distribution for a life insurance or annuity payment—and mistakes of law—not understanding the tax consequences of the distribution. Let. Ruls. 200405014, 200406050, 200406052, 200406055, 200406056, 200543063, 200544025, 200544026. The IRS has denied waivers where a taxpayer used a distribution as a short-term loan and made no actual attempt to rollover the distribution within the 60-day limit. Let. Ruls. 200544027, 200544030.

The 60-day rollover time limit does not apply to qualified Hurricane Katrina distributions. Qualified Hurricane Katrina distributions are distributions not exceeding $100,000 in the aggregate from qualified retirement plans, individual retirement plans, tax sheltered annuities under IRC Section 403(b), or eligible governmental plans under IRC Section 457 made at any time on or after August 25, 2005 and before January 1, 2007 by an individual whose principal place of abode on August 28, 2005 was located in the Hurricane Katrina disaster area and who sustained an economic loss by reason of Hurricane Katrina. Taxpayers may complete a rollover of a qualified Hurricane Katrina distribution that was an eligible rollover distribution no later than 3 years from the day after such distribution was received. Section 101, KETRA 2005.

Prior to EGTRRA 2001, no waivers of the 60-day time limitation were permitted, even where the failure to meet it was the result of mistake, erroneous advice, the inaction of third parties, or reliance on prior rulings by the Service itself (see e.g., *Orgera v. Comm.*, TC Memo 1995-575; Let. Ruls. 9826036, 9211035, 9145036, 8608049, 8420083, 8207004, 8001067).

Where a stock certificate representing the participant's distribution was sent by registered mail but the participant was away from home, the 60-day period did not begin until the taxpayer signed the registered mail claim check at the post office and took physical receipt of the stock distribution. Let. Rul. 8804014. Likewise, the 60-day period began upon the taxpayer's receipt of a distribution check even though the check had been issued 10 months earlier but delivery was delayed because of an incorrect address. Let. Rul. 8833043.

The 60-day period does not include any period during which the amount transferred to the individual is a "frozen deposit" (i.e., cannot be withdrawn because of the bankruptcy or insolvency of the financial institution or any state-imposed requirement based on the bankruptcy or insolvency (or threat thereof) of institutions in the state). Also, the 60-day period will not be considered to expire any earlier than 10 days after the account ceases to be "frozen." IRC Secs. 402(c)(7)(A), 403(a)(4)(B), 403(b)(8)(B), 408(d)(3)(F), 457(e)(16)(B).

The inclusion of a distribution as income is not deferred into another calendar year merely because the 60-day rollover period extends into the succeeding year. *Robinson v. Comm.*, TC Memo 1996-517.

A timely rollover occurred where a corrective bookkeeping entry was made after the 60-day period but, based upon the facts of the case, the Tax Court concluded that the transfer itself had actually occurred within the required period. *Wood v. Comm.*, 93 TC 114 (1989). *ASRS, Sec. 62, ¶¶920, 920.5.*

455. May an individual who has attained age 70½ make a rollover?

Although there was considerable confusion on this issue at one time, it now seems clear that such rollovers may be made to traditional IRAs as long as the minimum distribution requirements are met. See Q 233 to Q 237. See Rev. Rul. 82-153, 1982-2 CB 86; Let. Rul. 9534027. But see Let. Rul. 8450068. (Rollovers, as well as contributions in general, may be made to Roth IRAs by individuals who have attained age 70½. See IRC Sec. 408A(c)(4).) It would appear that the same rationale would also permit rollovers to qualified plans and IRC Section 403(b) tax sheltered annuities after age 70½ if the minimum distribution requirements were met. See Q 339 to Q 345 and Q 486 to Q 489. *ASRS, Sec. 62, ¶930.3.*

456. May the recipient of a distribution roll the amount over into another person's individual retirement plan?

No. IR-1809, Q17, 5-9-77; IRC Sec. 408(d)(3)(A). Where a plan participant received a distribution from a qualified retirement plan and, within 60 days, the funds were placed in a traditional IRA held in his wife's name only—but not pursuant to a valid QDRO (see Q 449)—the Tax Court found that a valid rollover had not occurred. *Rodoni v. Comm.*, 105 TC 29 (1995). *ASRS Sec. 62, ¶910.1.*

SPLIT DOLLAR PLAN

457. What is a split dollar plan?

Split dollar insurance is an arrangement generally between an employer and an employee under which the policy benefits are split, and the costs (premiums) may be split. Split dollar plans can also be set up between corporations and shareholders ("shareholder split dollar") or between parents and their children ("private split dollar"). Under the traditional plan, the employer pays part of the annual premium equal to the current year's increase in the cash surrender value of the policy and the employee pays the balance, if any, of the premium. From this basic concept, hybrid plans have evolved; for example, "employer pay all" plans under which the employer pays the entire premium, and level contribution plans under which the employee pays a level amount each year. (See Q 461 for a discussion of reverse split dollar plans.) If the employee dies while the split dollar plan is in effect, the employer receives from the proceeds an amount equal to the cash value of the policy or at least its premium payments (under a basic plan), and the employee's beneficiary receives the balance of the proceeds.

After passage of the Sarbanes-Oxley Act of 2002 (P.L. 107-204), there is now a question of whether it is legal for a publicly traded company to set up a split dollar plan, or continue paying premiums on an already existing plan. Many publicly traded compa-

SPLIT DOLLAR PLAN
Q 457

nies have stopped paying premiums on split dollar plans. Some of these companies are instead paying bonuses to employees covered by split dollar plans so that the employees can pay the premiums. For more information on the Sarbanes-Oxley Act, see Q 805.

The split dollar arrangement may be in the form of an endorsement plan where the employer owns the policy and the benefit-split is provided by endorsement, or a collateral assignment plan under which the employee owns the policy and the employer's interest is secured by collateral assignment of the policy.

Plans Entered Into After September 17, 2003

Treasury regulations issued in 2003 define a split dollar life insurance arrangement as any arrangement between an owner and a non-owner of a life insurance contract satisfying the following criteria: (1) either party to the arrangement pays all or a portion of the premiums on the life insurance contract, including payment by means of a loan to the other party that is secured by the life insurance contract; (2) at least one of the parties to the arrangement that is paying premiums is entitled to recover all or a portion of the premiums and the recovery is to be made from or secured by the proceeds of the life insurance contract; and (3) the arrangement is not part of a group-term life insurance plan unless the plan provides permanent benefits. Treas. Reg. §1.61-22(b)(1).

Certain "compensatory arrangements" and "shareholder arrangements" are treated as split dollar arrangements even if they do not meet the general definition of a split dollar arrangement. A compensatory arrangement is one where: (1) the arrangement is entered into in connection with the performance of services and is not part of a group-term life insurance plan; (2) the employer pays all or a portion of the premiums; and (3) either (a) the beneficiary of any portion of the death benefit is designated by the employee or is a person the employee would reasonably be expected to designate as a beneficiary, or (b) the employee has any interest in the cash value of the policy. The definition of a shareholder agreement is similar, but with "corporation" substituted for "employer" and "shareholder" for "employee." Treas. Reg. §1.61-22(b)(2).

These definitions are effective for split dollar arrangements entered into after September 17, 2003, or split dollar arrangements entered into before September 18, 2003, that are materially modified after September 17, 2003. Treas. Reg. §1.61-22(j). For when a split dollar plan is considered entered into, see Q 458.

Plans Entered into Before September 18, 2003

The following discussion applies to split dollar plans that were entered into before September 18, 2003.

If a transaction is cast in a form that results in similar benefits to an employee as in a traditional split dollar plan, it will be treated as a split dollar plan. Rev. Rul. 64-328, 1964-2 CB 11. Thus, an arrangement dividing interests in the policy on an employee between the employer and the insured employee's wife was ruled a split dollar plan providing an taxable economic benefit to the employee (see Q 459; see Q 700 for gift tax consequences). Similarly, where the insured was the employee's father, the plan was held to provide a benefit to the employee taxable as a split dollar plan. Rev. Rul. 78-420, 1978-2 CB 67. A split dollar plan between a corporation and an insured non-employee shareholder was ruled to provide a taxable dividend to the shareholder. Rev. Rul. 79-50, 1979-1 CB 138.

2006 Tax Facts on Insurance & Employee Benefits

In a case before the Tax Court, a taxpayer claimed that life insurance policies insuring his life but owned by his wife should be treated as part of a split dollar arrangement. His solely-owned corporation was paying the premiums on the policies. Finding no documents or other evidence of either a split dollar arrangement, the court ruled against the taxpayer. *Goos v. Comm.*, TC Memo 1991-146. Whether or not an employer is entitled to recover a portion of its annual premium payments is one factor that the Tax Court has found significant in deciding whether an arrangement may be considered a split dollar plan. *Young v. Comm.*, TC Memo 1995-379.

A split dollar plan may exist between a limited partnership and its general partner. In this instance, the IRS determined that the general partner would derive no economic benefit from the agreement and would not receive a partnership distribution so long as the general partner contributed to the partnership an amount equal to the value of the insurance protection provided under the policy. Let. Rul. 9639053.

Other Considerations

A split dollar arrangement offered as a fringe benefit to employees of an S corporation in which the employer agreed to pay the total premium less the term insurance cost did not violate the one class of stock restriction applicable to S corporations under IRC Section 1361(b)(1)(D). Let. Rul. 9248019. Similarly, a split dollar arrangement for shareholders in which the employer agreed to pay the full premium and the shareholders agreed to reimburse the employer for the economic benefit amount did not violate the one class of stock restriction. Let. Rul. 9318007, Let. Rul. 9331009. See Q 839.

The cash values of policies in an endorsement-type split dollar plan that made use of an independent fiduciary to select the policies were not considered "plan assets" for purposes of ERISA. DOL Adv. Op. 92-22A.

For information on charitable split dollar, see Q 283. *ASRS, Sec. 65, ¶¶110-130.*

458. What are the income tax results of a split dollar plan entered into, or materially modified, after September 17, 2003?

The tax treatment of a split dollar arrangement depends on when the arrangement is first entered into. Generally, for split dollar arrangements entered into after September 17, 2003, the taxation of the arrangement is governed by regulations that were issued in 2003. Split dollar arrangements entered into before September 18, 2003, are generally governed by revenue rulings and other guidance issued by the IRS between 1964 and the issuance of the final regulations. For a discussion of the tax treatment of split dollar arrangements not subject to the split dollar regulations, see Q 459.

For split dollar arrangements entered into after September 17, 2003, the tax treatment will be under one of two mutually exclusive regimes; the arrangement will be treated either as the life insurance policy owner providing economic benefits to the non-owner, or as the non-owner making loans to the owner. Treas. Reg. §1.61-22(b)(3). The person named on the policy as the owner is generally considered the owner of the policy. A non-owner is any person (other than the owner) having an interest in the policy (except for a life insurance company acting only as the issuer of the policy). Treas. Reg. §1.61-22(c). A split dollar arrangement will be treated as a loan if: (1) payment is made by the non-owner to the owner; (2) the payment is a loan under general principles of federal tax law or a reasonable person would expect the payment to be repaid to the non-owner; and (3) the repayment is made from, or secured by, either the policy's death benefit, cash value, or both. Treas. Reg. §1.7872-15(a)(2). Loan treatment will generally occur in a collateral assignment arrangement.

Economic Benefit Treatment

If the split dollar arrangement is not treated as a loan, the contract's owner is treated as providing economic benefits to the non-owner. Economic benefit treatment will generally occur in an endorsement arrangement. The non-owner (and the owner for gift and employment tax purposes) must take into account the full value of the economic benefits provided to the non-owner by the owner, reduced by any consideration paid by the non-owner. Depending on the relationship between the owner and the non-owner, the economic benefits may consist of compensation income, a dividend, a gift, or some other transfer under the tax code. Treas. Reg. §1.61-22(d)(1). The value of the economic benefits is equal to: (1) the cost of life insurance protection provided to the non-owner; (2) the amount of cash value the non-owner has current access to (to the extent that amounts were not taken into account in previous years); and (3) the value of other benefits provided to the non-owner. The cost of life insurance protection will be determined by a life insurance premium factor put out by the IRS. Treas. Reg. §1.61-22(d)(2)-(3). Presumably, Table 2001 will be used until the IRS issues another table. See Notice 2002-8, 2002-1 CB 398.

Under the economic benefit regime, the non-owner will not receive any investment in the contract with respect to a life insurance policy subject to a split dollar arrangement. Premiums paid by the owner will be included in the owner's investment in the contract. Also, any amount the non-owner pays toward a policy will be included in the income of the *owner* and increase the *owner's* investment in the contract. Treas. Reg. §1.61-22(f).

Death benefits paid to a beneficiary (other than the owner of the policy) by reason of the death of an insured will be excluded from income to the extent that the amount of the death benefit is allocable to current life insurance protection provided to the non-owner, the cost of which was paid by the non-owner or the benefit of which the non-owner took into account for income tax purposes. Treas. Reg. §1.61-22(f)(3).

Upon the transfer of the policy to a non-owner, the non-owner is considered to receive generally the cash value of the policy and the value of all other rights in the policy, minus any amounts paid for the policy and any benefits that were previously included in the non-owner's income. However, amounts that were previously included in income due to the value of current life insurance protection that was provided to the non-owner may not be used to reduce the amount the non-owner is considered to receive upon roll-out. Thus, the taxation on the value of current life insurance protection will not provide the non-owner with any basis in the policy, while taxation for a previous increase in cash value will add basis for the non-owner. Treas. Reg. §1.61-22(g).

Loan Treatment

If the split dollar arrangement is treated as a loan, the owner is considered the borrower, and the non-owner is considered the lender. Treas. Reg. §1.7872-15(a)(2). If the split dollar loan is a below market loan, then interest will be imputed at the applicable federal rate (AFR), with the owner and the non-owner of the policy considered to transfer imputed amounts to each other. See IRC Sec. 7872. In a split dollar arrangement between an employer and employee, the lender would be employer and the borrower the employee. Each payment under the split dollar arrangement will be treated as a separate loan. The employer is considered to transfer the imputed interest to the employee. This amount is considered taxable compensation, and generally will be deductible to the employer (however, no deduction will be allowed in a corporation-shareholder arrangement). The employee is then treated as paying the imputed interest back to the employer, which will be taxable income to the employer. This imputed interest payment by the employee will generally be considered personal interest and therefore not deductible.

The calculation of the amount of imputed interest differs depending on the type of below market loan involved. A below market loan is either a "demand loan" or a "term loan." A demand loan is a loan that is payable in full upon the demand of the lender. IRC Sec. 7872(f)(5). All other below market loans are term loans. IRC Sec. 7872(f)(6). Generally, a split dollar term loan will cause more interest to be imputed in the early years of the arrangement, with the amount of imputed interest decreasing each year. In a split dollar demand loan, the imputed interest will be smaller in the early years of the arrangement, but will increase each year the arrangement is in place.

For more information on below market loans, see Q 805.

Effective Date of Regulations

These regulations apply to split dollar arrangements entered into after September 17, 2003, and arrangements entered into on or before September 17, 2003, that are materially modified after September 17, 2003. Treas. Regs. §§1.61-22(j), 1.7872-15(n). The final regulations provide a "non-exclusive list" of changes that will not be considered material modifications. This list includes: (1) a change solely in premium payment method (for example, from monthly to quarterly); (2) a change solely of beneficiary, unless the beneficiary is a party to the arrangement; (3) a change solely in the interest rate payable on a policy loan; (4) a change solely necessary to preserve the status of the life insurance contract under Code section 7702; (5) a change solely to the ministerial provisions of the life insurance contract (such as a change in the address to send premiums); and (6) a change made solely under the terms of the split dollar agreement (other than the life insurance contract) if the change is dictated by the arrangement, is non-discretionary to the parties, and was made under a binding commitment in effect on or before September 17, 2003. Treas. Reg. §1.61-22(j)(2). An exchange of policies under Code section 1035 is not on the list of non-material modifications. Note that the Service will not issue rulings or determination letters on whether a modification is material. Rev. Proc. 2005-3, Sec. 3.01(2), 2005-1 IRB 118.

The final regulations also contain rules on when a split dollar arrangement is considered to be entered into. A split dollar arrangement is entered into on the *latest* of the following dates: (1) the date the life insurance contract is issued; (2) the effective date of the life insurance contract under the arrangement; (3) the date the first premium on the life insurance contract is paid; (4) the date the parties to the arrangement enter into an agreement with regard to the policy; or (5) the date on which the arrangement satisfies the definition of a split-dollar life insurance arrangement. Treas. Reg. §1.61-22(j)(1)(ii). *ASRS, Sec. 65, ¶140.*

459. What are the income tax results of a split dollar plan entered into before September 18, 2003?

Split dollar arrangements that were entered into before September 18, 2003, are governed by various rulings and other guidance that have been issued by the IRS between 1964 and the issuance of final regulations on split dollar arrangements in 2003. This guidance includes Notice 2002-8, 2002-1 CB 398, which provides transition rules for arrangements not subject to the split dollar regulations. However, no inference is to be drawn from Notice 2002-8, or the proposed or final regulations regarding the appropriate tax treatment of split dollar arrangements entered into before September 18, 2003.

For the treatment of split dollar arrangements entered into after September 17, 2003, see Q 458.

Notice 2002-8

For split dollar arrangements entered into before September 18, 2003:

(1) The IRS will not treat an employer as having made a transfer of a portion of the cash value of a life policy to an employee for purposes of Section 83 solely because the interest or other earnings credited to the cash value of the policy cause the cash value to exceed the portion payable to the employer.

(2) Where the value of current life insurance protection is treated as an economic benefit provided by an employer to an employee, the IRS will not treat the arrangement as having been terminated (and thus will not assert that there has been a transfer of property to the employee by reason of termination of the arrangement) as long as the parties to the arrangement continue to treat and report the value of the life insurance protection as an economic benefit provided to the employee. This treatment will be accepted without regard to the level of the remaining economic interest that the employer has in the life insurance contract.

(3) The parties to the arrangement may treat premium or other payments by the employer as loans. The IRS will not challenge reasonable efforts to comply with the rules regarding original issue discount and below-market loans. (See Q 805 for more information on below market loans.) All payments by the employer from the beginning of the arrangement (reduced by any repayments to the employer) before the first taxable year in which payments are treated as loans for tax purposes must be treated as loans entered into at the beginning of the first year in which payments are treated as loans.

For split dollar arrangements entered into before January 28, 2002, under which an employer has made premium or other payments under the arrangement and has received or is entitled to receive full repayment, the IRS will not assert that there has been a taxable transfer of property to an employee upon termination of the arrangement if: (1) the arrangement is terminated before January 1, 2004; or (2) for all periods beginning on or after January 1, 2004, all payments by the employer from beginning of the arrangement (reduced by any repayments to the employer) are treated as loans for tax purposes, and the parties to the arrangement report the tax treatment in a manner consistent with this loan treatment, including the rules for original issue discount and below-market loans. Any payments by the employer before the first taxable year in which payments are treated as loans for tax purposes must be treated as loans entered into at the beginning of the first year in which payments are treated as loans.

Notice 2001-10

Notice 2001-10 was revoked by Notice 2002-8. However, for split dollar arrangements entered into before September 18, 2003, taxpayers may rely on the guidance contained in Notice 2001-10. Under Notice 2001-10, the IRS will generally accept the parties' characterization of the employer's payments under a split dollar plan, provided that: (1) the characterization is not clearly inconsistent with the substance of the arrangement; (2) the characterization has been consistently followed by the parties from the inception of the agreement; and (3) the parties fully account for all economic benefits conferred on the employee in a manner consistent with that characterization. Notice 2001-10, 2001-1 CB 459.

Under Notice 2001-10, there are three different ways that a split dollar plan may be characterized. First, the plan can be characterized as a loan, subject to the below market loan rules. Second, the plan could be characterized so as to be governed under the "traditional" split dollar rules of Revenue Ruling 64-328, 1964-2 CB 11. Finally, the plan could be characterized in such a way so that the employer's payments are treated as compensation.

Value of Economic Benefit

The employee is taxed on the value of the economic benefit he receives from his employer's participation in the split dollar arrangement. See Rev. Rul. 64-328, 1964-2 CB 11. One of the benefits the employee receives is current life insurance protection under the basic policy. The value of this benefit to the employee may be calculated by using government premium rates. For many years, "P.S. 58" rates were used to calculate the value of the protection. See Rev. Rul. 55-747, 1955-2 CB 228. However, the IRS revoked Rev. Rul. 55-747 and provided new "Table 2001" rates. P.S. 58 rates may generally be used prior to 2002; Table 2001 rates may generally be used starting in 2001. Notice 2002-8, 2002-1 CB 398. Notice 2002-8 does provide for some "grandfathering" of P.S. 58 rates. For split dollar arrangements entered into before January 28, 2002, in which a contractual agreement between an employer and employee provides that P.S. 58 rates will be used to determine the value of current life insurance protection provided to the employee (or the employee and one or more additional persons), the employer and employee may continue to use P.S. 58 rates. Notice 2002-8, 2002-1 CB 398.

If the insurer publishes rates for individual, initial issue, one-year term policies (available to all standard risks), and these rates are lower than the P.S. 58 or Table 2001 rates (as applicable), these insurer rates may be substituted. See Rev. Rul. 66-110, 1966-1 CB 12. Only standard rates may be substituted, not preferred rates (e.g., those offered to non-smoking individuals). Let. Rul. 8547006. The substituted rate must be a rate charged for initial issue insurance and must be available to all standard risks. Rev. Rul. 67-154, 1967-1 CB 11.

For arrangements entered into before September 18, 2003, taxpayers may use the insurer's lower published premium rates that are available to all standard risks for initial issue one-year term insurance. However, for arrangements entered into after January 28, 2002, and before September 18, 2003, for periods after December 31, 2003, an insurer's rates may not be used unless: (1) the insurer generally makes the availability of the rates known to those who apply for term insurance coverage from the insurer; and (2) the insurer regularly sells term insurance at those rates to individuals who apply for term insurance coverage through the insurer's normal distribution channels. Notice 2002-8, 2002-2 CB 398.

SPLIT DOLLAR PLAN   Q 459

The IRS concluded that five-year term insurance rates available only to non-smokers on policies of at least $1,000,000 did not meet the requirements of Revenue Ruling 66-110 and Revenue Ruling 67-154 for one-year, initial issue, individual term insurance. Additionally, rates issued by a parent insurance company could not be applied to a split dollar policy issued by a subsidiary insurance company since the rates were not issued by the same insurer. TAM 9452004. Whether the rates used were "published" and "available to all standard risks" was resolved in favor of the taxpayer through testimony from the insurance company that the rates were published and were available to anyone who applied and met the company's underwriting standards for a term insurance policy (which paid only a 2% first-year commission). *Healy v. U.S.*, 94-1 USTC ¶50,105 (D.S.D. 1994). The insurance company's dividend option rates may *not* be used to calculate the value of the insurance protection. Rev. Rul. 67-154, 1967-1 CB 11.

There are no rulings on the amount of economic benefit to be included when the employee has not had a full year's benefit under a policy (e.g., the policy was purchased on September 1 for a calendar year employee). It would seem that the IRS would accept any reasonable attempt at allocating the cost in such a year. Also, there has been no formal guidance from the IRS as to which rates should be used to measure the economic benefit resulting from a split dollar arrangement using a policy which insures more than one life. The IRS has said that taxpayers should make appropriate adjustments to premium rates if life insurance protection covers more than one life. Notice 2002-8, 2002-4 CB 398. Where the policy death benefit is payable at the second death, it is generally believed that following the first death, the Table 2001 or P.S. 58 rates for single lives should be used to measure the survivor's economic benefit. See Appendix C.

Where the employee's portion of the premium for a particular year exceeds the value of the benefits he receives for that year, no provision is made for carrying the excess over and applying it against taxable income in succeeding years.

The insured employee must pay income tax each year on the economic benefits where ownership of the portion in excess of cash value belongs to a trust for his family. *Johnson v. Comm.*, 74 TC 1316 (1980).

The rules on the nondeductibility of interest with respect to financed "whole dollar" life insurance explained at Q 245 apply as well to split dollar life insurance. Furthermore, there are other limits on the deduction of policy loan interest. See Q 260. See also Let. Rul. 9235020. See also Q 823.

Employer's Premiums Nondeductible

The employer cannot take a business expense deduction for its share of the annual premium because the employer is a beneficiary under the policy, within the meaning of IRC Section 264(a)(1). See Rev. Rul. 64-328 above. Moreover, it appears that the employer cannot deduct the value of the economic benefit (Table 2001 or P.S. 58 cost) that is taxable to the employee because the employer has not "paid or incurred" any expense other than nondeductible premium expense. See IRC Sec. 162.

Death Proceeds

Upon death of the employee, both the portion of the proceeds received by the employer and the portion of the proceeds received by the employee's beneficiary are exempt from federal income tax under IRC Section 101(a) as life insurance proceeds received by reason of the insured's death. Rev. Rul. 64-328, *supra*. However, death proceeds of split dollar life insurance payable to a corporation may affect the calculation of the alternative minimum tax (see Q 95).

Stockholder-Employees

Although the issue was not litigated, the IRS treated the (P.S. 58) benefit of a substantial stockholder-employee as a dividend in *Johnson v. Comm.*, 74 TC 1316 (1980). The IRS had already ruled that in the case of a split dollar arrangement between a nonemployee stockholder and the corporation, the economic benefit flowing from the corporation to the insured stockholder is taxed as a corporate distribution (dividend). Rev. Rul. 79-50, 1979-1 CB 138. *ASRS, Sec. 65, ¶140*.

460. What are the income tax consequences of the transfer or "rollout" of a policy subject to a split dollar arrangement?

Under the split dollar regulations, upon the transfer of the policy to a non-owner, the non-owner is considered to receive generally the cash value of the policy and the value of all other rights in the policy, minus any amounts paid for the policy and any benefits that were previously included in the non-owner's income. However, amounts that were previously included in income due to the value of current life insurance protection that was provided to the non-owner may not be used to reduce the amount the non-owner is considered to receive upon roll-out. Thus, the taxation on the value of current life insurance protection will not provide the non-owner with any basis in the policy, while taxation for a previous increase in cash value will add basis for the non-owner. Treas. Reg. §1.61-22(g).

No inference is to be drawn regarding the tax treatment of split dollar arrangements entered into before September 18, 2003 (see Q 459). See Notice 2002-8, 2002-1 CB 398.

Arrangements Entered before September 18, 2003

The following discusses rollout from a split dollar arrangement entered into before September 18, 2003.

The IRS considered this issue in two private letter rulings. In the first, the split dollar plan provided that the insured employee would be entitled to a portion of the life insurance policy's cash surrender value annual increase equal to his share of the annual premium. His portion of the annual premium was determined by a payment schedule which entitled him to a portion of the cash surrender value of the policy. The plan's rollout provision stated that if the employee remained employed for a specified time, the policy would then be transferred to him without cost. The net cash value of the policy transferred to him at that time would equal the employee's cumulative premium, or, if greater, the cash surrender value less the employer's cumulative premiums.

The IRS concluded that when the policy is transferred to the employee, he would have taxable income to the extent the cash value in the policy exceeded the amounts he contributed. The IRS reasoned that the cash surrender value would be property transferred in connection with the performance of services and therefore the amount exceeding the employee's basis (his contributions) would be immediately taxable under IRC Section 83. Under IRC Section 83(h), the employer would be entitled to a deduction equal to the amount included in the employee's income. However, this deduction would be offset by the employer's recognition of a gain equivalent to the amount received in

SPLIT DOLLAR PLAN   Q 461

excess of its basis. Further, the insured employee must include in his income each year the annual P.S. 58 cost of life insurance protection he received, to the extent paid for by the employer. Let. Rul. 7916029.

The employee was not entitled to use his contributions to offset the employer-provided insurance protection. The ruling does not indicate how the amount of protection provided by the employer is calculated, but it has been suggested that the calculation should be made in a manner consistent with Revenue Ruling 64-328, 1964-2 CB 11.

The second private letter ruling involved an "endorsement" arrangement, in which the employer owned all the cash values, but was to receive death benefits limited to its premium contributions. At the eighth policy year, the employer borrowed an amount equal to its premium contribution from the policy, leaving some amount of cash value in the policy, which was then rolled out to the employee. The IRS, once again, applied IRC Section 83, and found that in the year of the rollout the employer recognized gain in the policy to the extent the cash value exceeded its cumulative premium basis. Treas. Reg. §1.83-6(b). The employer was entitled to an IRC Section 162 business deduction equal to the total cash value less the employee's premium contributions. The employee must likewise include under IRC Section 83 the full amount of the policy cash value less the premiums he paid over the first seven years. Let. Rul. 8310027.

The IRS has not ruled on the more customary split dollar plan in which the employer's interest is limited to its aggregate premium outlay both during lifetime and at death. Under these circumstances the employer's contractual rights to cash values are limited to the premiums it has paid, which is exactly the amount borrowed from or withdrawn out of the policy in the year of rollout. Typically, the employee pays premiums to offset the economic benefit, and contractually owns cash values in excess of the employer's aggregate premium outlay. The 1979 ruling suggested the employee's premium outlay could not be used to offset both the economic benefits and serve as his basis in mitigating the tax on the cash values. The 1983 ruling does not clearly respond to this issue. Neither ruling considered the policy loan in measuring the value transferred to the employee.

Although there are no IRS rulings on point, whether the policy has failed the seven pay test of IRC Section 7702A(b) and is therefore classified as a modified endowment contract should be considered in determining the income tax consequences of a split dollar rollout. Generally, any policy distributions, including policy loans, may be taxed less favorably if the policy is a modified endowment contract than if it is not. See Q 250 for a more detailed discussion.

Where a split dollar arrangement provides a "permanent benefit" (discussed in Q 148) to a member of a group covered by group term life insurance issued by the same insurer (or an affiliate), the arrangement may be considered part of "a policy" providing group term life insurance and its taxation subject to rules discussed in Q 147. *ASRS, Sec. 65, ¶140.1.*

461. What is reverse split dollar and how is it taxed?

Reverse split dollar is a variation on the traditional split dollar arrangement discussed in Q 457 in which the ownership of the policy cash value and death proceeds is split between the corporation and the insured employee, but the traditional roles of the two parties to the arrangement are reversed. In the typical reverse split dollar plan, the employer pays a portion of the policy premium equal to the annual P.S. 58 cost (or Table 2001 cost) each year while the difference between this cost and the full premium is contributed by the employee. Notice 2002-59, 2002-2 CB 481, is believed to have ended the viability of reverse split dollar.

In Notice 2002-59, the IRS stated that a party to a split dollar arrangement may use Table 2001 or the insurer's rates only for the purpose of valuing current life insurance protection when the protection is conferred as an economic benefit by one party on another party, determined without regard to consideration or premiums paid by the other party. Thus, if one party has the right to current life insurance protection, neither Table 2001 not the insurer's rates can be used to value that party's insurance protection for purposes of establishing the value of policy benefits to which another party may be entitled.

Notice 2002-59 provides one example where the premium rates are properly used and one where they are not properly used. In the first example, a donor is assumed to pay the premiums on a life insurance policy that is part of a split dollar arrangement between the donor and a trust, with the trust having the right to the current life insurance protection. The current life insurance protection has been conferred as an economic benefit by the donor on the trust and the donor is permitted to value the life insurance protection using either Table 2001 or the insurer's lower term rates.

However in the second example, if the donor or the donor's estate has the right to the current life insurance protection, neither Table 2001 nor the insurer's lower term rates may be used to value the donor's current life insurance protection to establish the value of economic benefits conferred upon the trust. Results will be similar if the trust pays for all or a portion of its share of benefits provided under the life insurance arrangement.

Notice 2002-59 does not contain an effective date, which indicates that the IRS does not consider it "new" guidance, but a restatement by the IRS of current law. If that is the case, it will affect reverse split dollar arrangements that were in place before the notice was issued.

462. What is private split dollar and how is it taxed?

"Private" split dollar is yet another variation on the traditional split dollar arrangement (see Q 457). The label of "private" comes from the fact that this type of split dollar arrangement does not include the participation of an employer. Rather, a private split dollar arrangement is typically between two family members or one family member and a trust. When two family members are involved the label "family" split dollar is often used. A common example of family split dollar involves a father assisting his son in setting up a policy insuring the son's life.

The IRS has said that the same principles that govern the tax treatment of employer-employee split dollar plans (see Q 458 and Q 459) should also govern arrangements that provide benefits in gift contexts, which presumably would include private split dollar plans. See Notice 2002-8, 2002-1 CB 398.

The regulations regarding split dollar also apply to private split dollar arrangements (see Q 458). For the estate tax consequences of private split dollar, see Q 615 (under "Non-Employer-Employee Relationship"). For gift tax implications, see Q 700. *ASRS, Sec. 65, ¶140.*

TAX SHELTERED ANNUITIES FOR EMPLOYEES OF SECTION 501(C)(3) ORGANIZATIONS AND PUBLIC SCHOOLS

463. What are the tax benefits of a tax sheltered annuity?

The tax sheltered annuity is a deferred tax arrangement expressly granted by Congress in IRC Section 403(b). Under the provisions of IRC Section 403(b), an employee can exclude from his gross income, within limits, the premiums paid on a contract that will provide him with an annuity for his retirement or amounts paid to a custodian for purchase of stock in regulated investment companies (see Q 465). The plan may be used by only certain employers (see Q 464). The employee must generally report the payments received under the contract or custodial account as taxable income (see Q 490).

The plan must meet specific requirements (see Q 466, Q 467); however, certain failures to meet such requirements may be subject to correction under the Employee Plans Compliance Resolution System (EPCRS). See Rev. Proc. 2003-44, 2003-25 IRB 1051. *ASRS, Sec. 61, ¶430.*

464. What types of organizations can make tax sheltered annuities available to their employees?

The organization must be either: (1) a tax-exempt organization of one of the types described in IRC Section 501(c)(3), or (2) a public school system. IRC Sec. 403(b)(1)(A)(i), 403(b)(1)(A)(ii). An organization in either of these two categories may make the tax sheltered annuity benefits available to one or more of its full-time or part-time employees.

Note, however, the annuitant must be an *employee* (see below); persons working for the organization in a self-employed capacity are generally not eligible. IRC Sec. 403(b)(1).

A tax sheltered annuity may also be purchased for a duly ordained, commissioned, or licensed minister of a church by (1) the minister himself if he is self-employed, or (2) an organization other than one described in IRC Section 501(c)(3) that employs the minister and with respect to which the minister shares common religious bonds. IRC Secs. 403(b)(1)(A)(iii), 414(e)(5). This definition includes chaplains. See Q 474.

IRC Section 501(c)(3) organizations are nonprofit organizations that are organized and operated exclusively for religious, charitable, scientific, literary, educational or safety testing purposes, or for the prevention of cruelty to children or animals. Generally, organizations (other than public schools) that are wholly owned by a state or other local government are not eligible employers. However, some such organizations will qualify as 501(c)(3) organizations if they are separately organized, are not an integral part of the government, and meet the description of a 501(c)(3) organization (e.g., some state or city hospitals). Rev. Rul. 55-319, 1955-1 CB 119, as modified by Rev. Rul. 60-384, 1960-2 CB 172; Rev. Rul. 67-290, 1967-2 CB 183.

A school or college that is operated exclusively for educational purposes by a separate educational instrumentality may qualify doubly, both as a public school and as an

IRC Section 501(c)(3) organization. See *Est. of Johnson v. Comm.*, 56 TC 944 (1971), *acq.*, 1973-2 CB 2; Let. Rul. 7817098. A state department of education may qualify as a part of a public school system if its services involve the operation or direction of the state's public school program. Rev. Rul. 73-607, 1973-2 CB 145. Likewise, a state agency that administers a guaranteed student loan program and is part of a state department of insurance may qualify. See Let. Rul. 9438031. Thus, annuities may be purchased for employees such as public school teachers, teachers in private and parochial schools, school superintendents, college professors, clergymen and social workers.

A doctor who works as an employee for a hospital is eligible, provided the hospital is a qualified employer. Generally, the doctor is not eligible, however, unless he is an employee of the hospital for all purposes, such as Social Security and withholding tax purposes. If his relationship to the hospital is that of an independent contractor, he is not eligible, and any premiums paid on his behalf for an annuity will be currently taxable. Rev. Rul. 66-274, 1966-2 CB 446; Rev. Rul. 70-136, 1970-1 CB 12; *Azad v. U.S.*, 388 F.2d 74 (8th Cir. 1968); see also Rev. Rul. 73-417, 1973-2 CB 332; *Ravel v. Comm.*, TC Memo 1967-182; *Haugen v. Comm.*, TC Memo 1971-294. Although teachers who are under a state teachers retirement system may also participate in a tax sheltered annuity plan, the employees of the retirement system itself are not eligible. Rev. Rul. 80-139, 1980-1 CB 88. The Uniformed Services University of the Health Sciences will be treated as a 501(c)(3) employer for purposes of providing tax sheltered annuities for employee members of the civilian faculty or staff with respect to service after December 31, 1979. P.L. 96-613.

Proposed Regulations

Editor's Note: The effective date for the 403(b) regulations was originally set for "taxable years beginning after December 31, 2005" (i.e., January 1, 2006). However, the Service has announced that the final regulations, when released (presumably in 2006), will delay the effective date one year (i.e., until January 1, 2007). See *Employee Plans News*, p. 4 (Fall 2005), at: http://www.irs.gov/pub/irs-tege/fall05.pdf.

The proposed regulations provide rules for the federal income tax treatment of an annuity purchased for an employee by an employer that is either: (1) a tax-exempt entity under IRC Section 501(c)(3) (relating to certain religious, charitable, scientific, or other types of organizations); (2) a public school; or (3) a minister described in IRC Section 414(e)(5)(A). Prop. Treas. Reg. §1.403(b)-1.

"Eligible employer" means: (1) a state, but only with respect to an employee of the state performing services for a public school; (2) a Section 501(c)(3) organization with respect to any employee of the 501(c)(3) organization; (3) any employer of a minister described in IRC Section 414(e)(5)(A), but only with respect to the minister; and (4) a minister described in IRC Section 414(e)(5), but only with respect to a retirement income account established for the minister. Prop. Treas. Reg. §1.403(b)-2(a)(8).

"Employee" means a common law employee performing services for the employer, and does not include a former employee, or an independent contractor. The term "employee" also includes a minister described in IRC Section 414(e)(5) when performing services in the exercise of his or her ministry. Prop. Treas. Reg. §1.403(b)-2(a)(9).

"Employee performing services for a public school" means an employee performing services as an employee of a public school of a state. This definition does not

TAX SHELTERED ANNUITIES   Q 465

apply unless the employee's compensation for performing services for a public school is paid by the state. Furthermore, a person occupying an elective or appointive office is not an employee performing services for a public school unless such office is one to which an individual is elected or appointed only if the individual has received training, or is experienced, in the field of education. Prop. Treas. Reg. §1.403(b)-2(a)(10). "Public office" includes any elective or appointive office of a state. Prop. Treas. Reg. §1.403(b)-2(a)(10).

"Public school" means a state-sponsored educational organization as described in IRC Sec. 170(b)(1)(A)(ii) (relating to educational organizations that normally maintain a regular faculty and curriculum and normally have a regularly enrolled body of pupils or students in attendance at the place where educational activities are regularly carried on). Prop. Treas. Reg. §1.403(b)-2(a)(14).

"Church" means a church as defined in IRC Section 3121(w)(3)(A) and a qualified church-controlled organization as defined in IRC Section 3121(w)(3)(B). *ASRS, Sec. 61, ¶¶120, 130.1(b).*

465. What are the various methods of funding a tax sheltered annuity plan?

Editor's Note: The effective date for the 403(b) regulations was originally set for "taxable years beginning after December 31, 2005" (i.e., January 1, 2006). However, the Service has announced that the final regulations, when released (presumably in 2006), will delay the effective date one year (i.e., until January 1, 2007). See *Employee Plans News*, p. 4 (Fall 2005), at: http://www.irs.gov/pub/irs-tege/fall05.pdf.

Annuity Contracts

IRC Section 403(b) provides that the tax sheltered annuity rules apply if "an annuity contract" is purchased for the employee. The proposed regulations provide that "annuity contract" means a contract that is issued by an insurance company qualified to issue annuities in a state and that includes payment in the form of an annuity. Prop. Treas. Reg. §1.403(b)-2(a)(2). A "custodial account" (see below) is also treated as an annuity contract. Prop. Treas. Reg. §1.403(b)-8(d)(1). "Retirement income accounts" (see below) are also treated as annuity contracts. Prop. Treas. Reg. §1.403(b)-9(a).

An insurance company annuity contract (individual or group) that provides fixed retirement benefits may be used. A single group annuity contract that pools the assets of an employer's tax sheltered annuity plan and defined contribution plan may also be used where the assets of each plan are separately accounted for at the plan level and at the participant level through the use of sub-accounts. Let. Rul. 9422053.

The IRS has ruled that a variable annuity contract will qualify. Rev. Rul. 68-116, 1968-1 CB 177. A variable annuity contract in which the contract holder directs the investments in *publicly available securities* (i.e., mutual funds) will be treated as an "annuity contract," and the contract holder will *not* be treated as owning the underlying assets, if certain conditions are met. For contracts intended to qualify as annuity contracts under IRC Section 403(b), such status will be granted *if* no additional federal tax liability would have been incurred if the employer of the contract holder had instead paid an amount into a custodial account in an arrangement under IRC Section 403(b)(7)(A). In other words, the contract holder will receive the same favorable tax treatment whether the

2006 Tax Facts on Insurance & Employee Benefits   575

investment in publicly available mutual fund shares is made through a mutual fund custodial account or variable annuity contract. The diversification rules under IRC Section 817(h) for variable annuity contracts are not applicable to IRC Section 403(b) contracts. The revenue procedure, which was effective on November 16, 1999 with respect to all taxable years, will not be applied adversely to an issuer or holder of a contract issued before November 16, 1999. Rev. Proc. 99-44, 1999-48 IRB 598, *modifying* Rev. Rul. 81-225, 1981-2 CB 12.

Face Amount Certificates

The Code expressly provides that so-called face amount certificates are to be treated as annuity contracts. IRC Sec. 401(g). See also Treas. Reg. §1.401-9(a).

Regulated Investment Company Stock

According to proposed regulations (effective after 2006 – see *Editor's Note*, above), the term "custodial account" means a plan (or a separate account under a plan) in which an amount attributable to 403(b) contributions (or amounts rolled over to 403(b) contracts) is held by a bank (or certain other entities – see below) *if*: (1) all of the amounts held in the account are invested in stock of a regulated investment company; (2) the distribution restrictions that apply to custodial accounts are satisfied with respect to the amounts held in the account; (3) the assets held in the account cannot be used for, or diverted to, purposes other than for the exclusive benefit of plan participants or their beneficiaries; *and* (4) the account is not part of a retirement income account. The custodial account rule is not satisfied if the account includes any assets other than regulated investment company stock. Prop. Treas. Reg. §1.403(b)-8(d). The custodian must be a bank, insured federal credit union, building and loan association or other person satisfactory to the Secretary of the Treasury. IRC Sec. 403(b)(7).

State Teachers' Retirement System

According to proposed regulations (effective after 2006—see *Editor's Note*, above), the requirement that a contract be issued by an insurance company qualified to issue annuities in a state does *not* apply if one of the following two conditions is, and has continuously been, satisfied since May 17, 1982: (1) benefits are provided from a separately funded retirement reserve that is subject to supervision of the state insurance department; *or* (2) benefits are provided from a fund that is separate from the fund used to provide statutory benefits payable under a state teachers' retirement system to purchase benefits that are unrelated to the basic benefits provided under the retirement system, and the death benefit under the contract does not at any time exceed the larger of the reserve or the contribution made for the employee. Prop. Treas. Reg. §1.403(b)-8(c)(3).

Contributions of additional amounts to a state teachers' retirement system or to a separately funded employee retirement reserve subject to the supervision of the state insurance department will not be considered contributions to "annuity contracts." Rev. Rul. 82-102, 1982-1 CB 62, *revoking*, Rev. Rul. 67-361, 1967-2 CB 153 and Rev. Rul. 67-387, 1967-2 CB 153. However, such arrangements properly established in reliance on these two revoked rulings on or before May 17, 1982 may continue to cover employees covered on May 17, 1982 and may cover employees entering the plan after that date if the IRS had not previously advised the employer (or financial institution) that the arrangement did not meet the requirements of IRC Section 403(b). See Prop. Treas. Reg. §1.403(b)-8(c)(3); Let. Rul. 9511040.

TAX SHELTERED ANNUITIES   Q 465

Credit Union Share Accounts

The IRS takes the position that separate nonforfeitable share accounts in a credit union may not be considered annuity contracts for purposes of IRC Section 403(b). Rev. Rul. 82-102, 1982-1 CB 62. See *Corbin v. U.S.*, 760 F.2d 234 (8th Cir. 1985).

Retirement Income Accounts of Churches

Churches are permitted to maintain an account that will be treated as a tax sheltered annuity (see Q 474).

Treatment of Insurance under Proposed Regulations

According to the proposed regulations (issued 11-15-2004), life insurance contracts, endowment contracts, health or accident contracts, and property, casualty, or liability insurance contracts do *not* meet the definition of "annuity contract" (see above). Prop. Treas. Reg. §1.403(b)-8(c)(2). Consequently, unless such insurance is grandfathered by February 15, 2005 (according to unofficial IRS comments), incidental insurance may *not* be part of a 403(b) plan. (*Editor's Note:* The conclusion stated in the proposed regulations appears to run contrary to an earlier ruling from the Service. See Revenue Ruling 74-115, below.) This rule does not apply to a contract issued before February 14, 2005. Prop. Treas. Reg. §1.403(b)-11(d). These plans may terminate and distribute assets with full rollover ability, as well as recognize the occurrence of an employment severance where an employee no longer works for an employer eligible to maintain a 403(b). See *Employee Plans News Extra Special Edition*, p. 2 (11-17-2004) at: www.irs.gov.

Guidance issued prior to proposed regulations. Multiple contracts are considered a single contract for purposes of applying the 403(b) rules; consequently, separate insurance contracts may be purchased as part of a 403(b) annuity contract. However, such insurance contracts must meet the form requirements and all the limitations of an IRC Section 403(b) annuity contract. It does not appear to matter whether the form requirements and limitations are imposed by means of an endorsement to the insurance policy (see Let. Ruls. 9713022 (variable universal life policy), 9626042, 9336054, 9336053, 9327025, 9324042, 9303024), an addendum to the salary reduction agreement (see Let. Rul. 9324044), or a trust agreement (see Let. Ruls. 9324043, 9106022). (It should be noted, however, that most of the rulings do not address whether such an insurance investment would be permissible if the amounts were invested in a custodial account.) Where an insurance policy endorsement failed to adequately restrict the premiums to meet the incidental benefit limit and the elective deferral limit and also contained conflicting provisions that rendered the agreement revocable, the Service ruled that the life policy as endorsed did not constitute a 403(b) annuity contract. Let. Rul. 9242022.

In Letter Ruling 9215055, the Service concluded that it is irrelevant whether the premiums under the insurance contract are paid by contributions made by the employer on behalf of the participant under a salary reduction agreement or by dividends (and interest thereon) accumulated under the contract so long as the incidental benefit limit is not exceeded. A series of transfers of funds from the accumulation value of a pre-existing annuity contract held by one insurance company may be used to purchase incidental life insurance from another insurance company so long as the transfers are made in accordance with the procedures described in Revenue Ruling 90-24 for direct transfers (see Q 478). Let. Rul. 9327025.

The life insurance protection contained in a retirement income or pension plan endowment type of policy comes within the incidental limitation. An endowment policy with an annuity rider which, combined, provided in later policy years a death benefit greater than under a typical retirement income policy qualified as an annuity contract when actuarial comparison of only the endowment contract with the retirement income contract indicated the cost of the death benefit under the endowment contract was less than that of the retirement income contract. Rev. Rul. 74-115, 1974-1 CB 100.

However, a contract of the "family plan" type—that is, one that includes term insurance on the lives of members of the employee's family—will not be treated as an annuity contract. Rev. Rul. 69-146, 1969-1 CB 132. A pre-existing contract, whether originally purchased by the employee or by a former eligible employer, may be used. Rev. Rul. 66-254, 1966-2 CB 125. If other insurance protection is provided (e.g., waiver of premium or disability income), either with or without life insurance protection, the total insurance protection is deemed to be "incidental" if the level premium for the entire contract is no more than one-third larger than the level premium for a retirement annuity contract issued by the same company at the same age and in the same year. Letter Ruling, 3-15-66, signed I. Goodman, Chief, Pension Trust Branch, 1968 MDRT Proceedings, p. 221. *ASRS, Sec. 61, ¶140.*

Plan Requirements

466. What requirements must a tax sheltered annuity meet?

Editor's Note: Under the proposed regulations, amounts contributed by an eligible employer for the purchase of an annuity contract for an employee are excluded from the gross income of the employee under IRC Section 403(b) only if each of the requirements in the nine paragraphs, below, are satisfied. Prop. Treas. Reg. §1.403(b)-3(a). (If a proposed regulation provision indicates a new position by the IRS that will be indicated by showing the effective date for the proposed regulations. Alternatively, if the proposed regulation merely reiterates a current position of the Service, then the effective date will not be shown.) *Effective date postponed:* The effective date for the 403(b) regulations was originally set for "taxable years beginning after December 31, 2005" (i.e., January 1, 2006). However, the Service has announced that the final regulations, when released (presumably in 2006), will delay the effective date one year (i.e., until January 1, 2007). See *Employee Plans News,* p. 4 (Fall 2005), at: http://www.irs.gov/pub/irs-tege/fall05.pdf.

Purchase by Employer

1. A tax sheltered annuity contract must be purchased by an eligible employer (see Q 464). IRC Sec. 403(b)(1). Proposed regulations provide that the contract cannot be purchased under a qualified plan (under IRC Section 401(a) – see Q 322; or IRC Section 404(a)(2) – see Q 365), *or* an eligible governmental plan under IRC Section 457(b) (see Q 126). Prop. Treas. Reg. §1.403(b)-3(a)(1).

Thus, the employer must agree to pay the premiums. Rev. Rul. 66-254, 1966-2 CB 125. Although the employer must pay the premiums, the premiums may be derived either directly from the employer as additional compensation to the employee, or indirectly from the employee through a reduction in his salary. If the premiums are to come from a reduction in the employee's salary, the reduction must be made under a

TAX SHELTERED ANNUITIES Q 466

legally binding agreement between the employer and the employee, and the agreement must be irrevocable as to salary earned while the agreement is in effect.

An employee is permitted to enter into multiple salary reduction agreements with the same employer during any one taxable year of the employer. In general, for purposes of IRC Section 403(b), the frequency that an employee is permitted to enter into a salary reduction agreement, the salary to which such an agreement may apply, and the ability to revoke such an agreement is determined under the rules of IRC Section 401(k). SBJPA '96, Sec. 1450(a).

All annuity contracts (including custodial accounts and retirement income accounts) purchased by an employer on behalf of an employee are treated as a single annuity contract for purposes of applying the requirements of IRC Section 403(b). See IRC Sec. 403(b)(5); see also Prop. Treas. Reg. §1.403(b)-3(b)(1).

Tax deferment will be achieved only for premium payments attributable to amounts earned by the employee after the agreement becomes effective; premium payments attributable to salary earned prior to the effective date, or after termination of the agreement, are includable in the employee's gross income. For this purpose, salary is considered earned when the services for which it is compensation are performed, even though payment is deferred and subject to a risk of forfeiture. GCM 39659 (9-8-87). Contributions made by payroll deduction instead of salary reduction are not excludable. *Bollotin v. U.S.*, 76-2 USTC ¶9604 (S.D. N.Y. 1976), aff'd, 77-1 USTC ¶9,450 (2d Cir. 1977).

Premiums may be paid on a single premium, annual premium or monthly premium basis. Some companies provide a flexible premium arrangement under which the amount of premium need not be uniform. According to the IRS, the premium may be paid on an annual basis even though, under the salary reduction agreement, amounts are withheld monthly from the employee's salary. Rev. Rul. 67-69, 1967-1 CB 93.

However, the Department of Labor argues that amounts withheld under a salary reduction agreement must be promptly transmitted to the annuity contract; unreasonable delay in transmitting such amounts could inadvertently cause the plan to be subject to ERISA. Ironically, if a tax sheltered annuity plan is subject to Title I of ERISA, the Department of Labor requires that amounts an employee pays to the employer or has withheld from his salary by the employer for contribution to a plan become plan assets as soon as such amounts can reasonably be segregated from the employer's general assets. In order to meet that requirement, amounts contributed by an employee or withheld from an employee's wages must be transmitted to the plan no later than the 15th business day of the month following the month in which the contributions are received or withheld by the employer. Labor Reg. §2510.3-102. See also Prop. Treas. Reg. §1.403(b)-8(b).

Nonforfeitable Rights

2. In order to take advantage of the applicable limit under IRC Section 415 (see Q 469, Q 471), the employee's rights under the contract must be nonforfeitable (except for failure to pay future premiums). See IRC Sec. 403(b)(1)(C). According to proposed regulations (effective after 2006; see *Editor's Note*, above), an employee's rights under a contract are not nonforfeitable unless the participant for whom the contract is purchased has at all times a fully vested and nonforfeitable right to *all* benefits provided under the contract. Prop. Treas. Reg. §1.403(b)-3(a)(2).

The effect of this requirement is that salary reduction contributions to a tax sheltered annuity must be immediately vested. However, actual employer contributions can be subjected to delayed vesting. For the vesting rules applicable to employer contributions in plan years beginning after December 31, 2001, see Q 333. With exceptions for governmental and certain church plans, tax sheltered annuity plans with actual employer contributions are generally subject to ERISA and must comply with ERISA's minimum vesting schedules if they delay vesting.

Participation and Coverage

3. Except for contracts purchased by a church or certain governmental plans, tax sheltered annuity contracts generally must be provided under a plan that meets minimum participation, coverage and nondiscrimination requirements. IRC Sec. 403(b)(1)(D); Prop. Treas. Reg. §1.403(b)-3(a)(3). These requirements are explained in Q 467.

Limits on Elective Deferrals

4. Under proposed regulations (effective after 2006; see *Editor's Note*, above), the contract must satisfy IRC Section 401(a)(30), relating to limits on elective deferrals. A contract does not satisfy such limit *unless* the contract requires all elective deferrals for an employee not to exceed the limits of IRC Section 402(g)(1), including (1) elective deferrals for the employee under the contract, (2) any other elective deferrals under the plan under which the contract is purchased *and* under all other plans, contracts, or arrangements of the employer. Prop. Treas. Reg. §1.403(b)-3(a)(4).

There are essentially two limits restricting the amount of elective deferrals that may be made on behalf of a participant: (1) a *participant limit* under IRC Section 402(g); and (2) a *contract limit* under IRC Section 403(b)(1)(E). The participant limit applies to all the elective deferrals made on behalf of a participant. See Q 473. The contract requirement applies to limit elective deferrals made on behalf of employees by a single employer. A failure to satisfy the contract requirement results in the loss of 403(b) status of the annuity contract. See Sec. V(A.1)(1)(e)-(g), and Sec. V(A.1)(4) of the final tax sheltered annuity audit guidelines, *reprinted in* ASRS, Sec. 61, ¶440.2.

The contract limit has two components, a form and an operational requirement. Sec. V(A.1)(1)(e) of the final tax sheltered annuity audit guidelines, *reprinted in* ASRS, Sec. 61, ¶440.2. With respect to *form*, see the explanation above. The exclusion of elective deferrals from an employee's gross income will not be affected to the extent other employees exceed the annual limit. IRC Sec. 403(b)(1)(E). The participant limit and contract *operational* requirements are explained in Q 473.

Nontransferable

5. A contract must be expressly nontransferable. Prop. Treas. Reg. §1.403(b)-3(a)(5). An agreement between employer and employee that the employee will not transfer the contract is not sufficient. Rev. Rul. 74-458, 1974-2 CB 138. (For this purpose, an employer is considered to have purchased a new contract when it pays the first premium on a previously issued contract. Rev. Rul. 68-33, 1968-1 CB 175.) Although the contract must be nonassignable, the employee can surrender the contract to the insurer, borrow against the loan value, and exercise all other ownership rights. Cash value is not constructively received by the employee merely because he could receive it by surrendering the contract. Rev. Rul. 68-482, 1968-2 CB 186. But for the tax results of a policy loan, see Q 483, Q 484.

Minimum Required Distributions

6. Effective with regard to benefits accruing after December 31, 1986, tax sheltered annuity contracts and custodial accounts must provide that distributions of at least a minimum amount must be made. IRC Sec. 403(b)(10); Prop. Treas. Reg. §1.403(b)-3(a)(6). These requirements may be incorporated in a plan by reference. TAMRA '88, Sec. 1101A(a)(3). See Q 486.

Direct Rollover Option

7. Generally, a plan must provide that if a distributee of any eligible rollover distribution (see Q 451) elects to have the distribution paid directly to a traditional IRA, another tax sheltered annuity (if applicable), or an eligible retirement plan (see Q 446) and specifies the plan to which the distribution is to be paid, then the distribution will be paid to that plan in a direct rollover (see Q 447). IRC Secs. 403(b)(10), 401(a)(31); Prop. Treas. Reg. §1.403(b)(a)(7). Amounts held in an annuity contract or account described in IRC Section 403(b) cannot be converted directly to a Roth IRA. Treas. Reg. §1.408A-4, A-5. The payor of a 403(b) annuity contract or custodial account must withhold 20% from any eligible rollover distribution that the distributee does not elect to have paid in a direct rollover (see Q 448). IRC Sec. 3405(c). A safe harbor explanation that a payor may give to recipients of "eligible rollover distributions" from tax sheltered annuities is provided in Notice 2002-3, 2002-2 IRB 289.

Limitation on Incidental Benefits

8. Under the proposed regulations (effective after 2006; see *Editor's Note*, above), the contract must satisfy the incidental benefit requirements of IRC Section 401(a). Prop. Treas. Reg. §1.403(b)-3(a)(8). See Q 369, Q 481, and Q 488.

Maximum Annual Additions

9. According to the proposed regulations (effective after 2006; see *Editor's Note*, above), the annual additions to the contract must not exceed the applicable limitations of IRC Section 415(c) (treating contributions and other additions as annual additions). Prop. Treas. Reg. §1.403(b)-3(a)(9). See Q 471 and Q 472.

Plan in Form and Operation

According to the proposed regulations (effective after 2006; see *Editor's Note*, above), a 403(b) contract must be maintained pursuant to a "plan." For this purpose, a "plan" is a written document that satisfies certain requirements (set forth in Prop. Treas. Regs. §§1.403(b)(4) - 1.403(b)-10)). Thus, the plan must contain all of the material terms and conditions for eligibility, benefits, applicable limitations, the contracts available under the plan, and the time and form under which benefit distributions would be made. A plan may contain options and features not required under IRC Section 403(b), such as hardship withdrawal distributions, loans, plan-to-plan or annuity contract-to-annuity contract transfers, and acceptance of rollovers to the plan. But if a plan contains any optional provisions, the optional provision must meet, in both form and operation, the relevant requirements. Prop. Treas. Reg. §1.403(b)-3(b)(3). However, this rule does not require that there be a single plan document. For example, this requirement would be satisfied by complying with the plan document rules applicable to qualified plans (see Q 322). Preamble, REG-155608-02, 69 Fed. Reg. 67075, 67077 (11-16-2004).

The Department of Labor has advised the IRS and the Treasury Department that, although it does not appear that the proposed regulations would mandate the "establishment or maintenance" of an employee pension benefit plan in order to satisfy the above requirements, it leaves open the possibility that an employee may undertake responsibilities that would constitute "establishing or maintaining" an ERISA-covered plan. Whether the manner in which any particular employer decides to satisfy particular responsibilities under the proposed regulations will cause the employer to be considered to have "established or maintained" an ERISA-covered plan must be analyzed on a case-by-case basis applying the criteria set forth in Labor Reg. §2510.3-2(f), including the employer's involvement as contemplated by the plan documents and operation. To the extent that the proposed regulations may raise questions for employers concerning the scope and application of the labor regulation, the Treasury Department is requesting comments. Preamble, REG-155608-02, 69 Fed. Reg. 67075, 67077 (11-16-2004).

Prohibited Distributions

A *custodial account* invested in mutual funds must provide that amounts will not be made available before the employee dies, attains age 59½, has a severance from employment, becomes disabled (within the meaning of IRC Section 72(m)(7)) or encounters financial hardship. IRC Sec. 403(b)(7)(A)(ii). According to final regulations (effective for plan years beginning on or after January 1, 2006), hardship withdrawals may be made only on account of "an immediate and heavy" financial need." See Q 403. In years beginning after December 31, 1988, financial hardship distributions may be made only from assets held as of the close of the last year beginning before 1989 and from amounts contributed thereafter under a salary reduction agreement (not including earnings on such amounts).

An *annuity contract* must provide that distributions *attributable to salary reduction* contributions (including the earnings on them) may be made only after the employee attains age 59½, has severance from employment, dies, becomes disabled, or in the case of hardship (but the earnings on salary reduction contributions may not be distributed for financial hardship). IRC Sec. 403(b)(11). These restrictions apply for years beginning after 1988, but only with respect to distributions attributable to assets other than assets held as of the close of the last year beginning before 1989. TAMRA '88, Sec. 1011A(c)(11). See Let. Rul. 9442030; see also Prop. Treas. Reg. §1.403(b)-6(d)(1)(ii).

Timely distributions of excess elective deferrals (see Q 473) and excess aggregate contributions (see Q 467) may be made without regard to the above restrictions. IRC Secs. 402(g)(2), 401(m)(6). For the restrictions affecting retirement income accounts, see Q 474.

Loans. Amounts borrowed from a tax sheltered annuity and treated as a deemed distribution under IRC Section 72(p) (see Q 483) are not treated as actual distributions for purposes of these distribution restrictions and will not violate these restrictions. Treas. Reg. §1.72(p)-1, A-12. However, if a participant's accrued benefit is reduced (offset) to repay a loan, an actual distribution occurs for purposes of these distribution restrictions. Prop. Treas. Reg. §1.403(b)-6(g). (See also Sec. VIII(A)(2)(b) of the final tax sheltered annuity audit guidelines, reprinted in ASRS, Sec. 61, ¶440.2.) Accordingly, a plan may be prohibited from making such an offset to enforce its security interest in a participant's account balance attributable to salary reduction contributions until a date on which a distribution is permitted under IRC Section 403(b)(11). Treas. Reg. §1.72(p)-1, A-13(b);

TAX SHELTERED ANNUITIES   Q 466

see also Sec. X(A)(3)(f) of the final tax sheltered annuity audit guidelines (executing on a security interest in the event of default is a distribution for purposes of IRC Section 403(b)(11)), reprinted in ASRS, Sec. 61, ¶440.2; IRS General Information Letter to J. McKeever III and B. Mattox dated 1/26/94 (non-binding) (foreclosure, upon default on participant loan, on cash value of tax sheltered annuity contract used as security for loan would constitute distribution for purposes of IRC Section 403(b)(11)).

Similarly, it would seem that servicing a plan loan with tax sheltered annuity funds before a distribution is permitted would constitute a prohibited distribution. Even though a distribution may be permitted under these rules (e.g., for hardship or after severance from employment), it may nonetheless be subject to a 10% tax (in addition to income tax) as a premature distribution (see Q 485). These rules would also apply in the case of custodial accounts. See Sec. X(A)(4)(c) of the final tax sheltered annuity audit guidelines, reprinted in ASRS, Sec. 61, ¶440.2 (stating that if the participant's account balance is reduced to satisfy the loan balance, there is an actual distribution that could violate IRC Section 403(b)(7)). See also, Sec. X(A)(3)(f) of the final tax sheltered annuity audit guidelines (the executing on a security in the event of default on a loan is an impermissible distribution under IRC Section 403(b)(7)).

QDROs. A distribution to a former spouse pursuant to a qualified domestic relations order (QDRO) will be permitted under certain circumstances (see Q 349) even though the distribution might otherwise be prohibited under the prohibited distribution rules. IRC Sec. 414(p)(10); Prop. Treas. Reg. §1.403(b)-10(c).

Plan terminations. According to the proposed regulations (effective after 2006; see *Editor's Note*, above), an employer *may* amend its 403(b) plan to eliminate future contributions for existing participants. Alternatively, an employer may amend its 403(b) plan to limit participation to existing participants and employees. A 403(b) plan may contain provisions that permit plan termination and permit accumulated benefits to be distributed on termination. However, in the case of a 403(b) contract that is subject to certain distribution restrictions (i.e., those applicable to custodial accounts or elective deferrals) termination of the plan and the distribution of accumulated benefits is permitted only if the employer does not make contributions to an alternate section 403(b) contract that is not part of the plan. A distribution includes delivery of a fully paid individual insurance annuity contract. Prop. Treas. Reg. §1.403(b)-10(a)(1).

Protection of retirement savings in bankruptcy. To the extent that retirement funds are in a fund or account that is exempt from tax under IRC Section 403, such funds are generally *exempt* from the bankruptcy estate (effective 10-17-2005). Sec. 224(a), BAPCPA 2005. (See also Sec. 323, BAPCPA 2005.) If the subject funds are in a retirement fund that has received a favorable determination regarding qualification of the fund for purposes of tax-exempt status, those funds will be *presumed* to be exempt from the bankruptcy estate. However, if the subject funds are in a retirement fund that has *not* received a favorable determination regarding qualification, those funds will be exempt from the bankruptcy estate only if the debtor demonstrates both of the following: (1) no prior determination to the contrary [concerning qualification] has been made by a court or the Service; *and* (2) the retirement fund is in substantial compliance with the applicable requirements of the Code (or the retirement fund is not in compliance with the applicable requirements, but the debtor is not materially responsible for that failure). Sec. 224(a), BAPCPA 2005. Under BAPCPA, loans are *not* excepted from discharge (i.e., such loans remain in effect). See Sec. 224(c), BAPCPA 2005. However,

2006 Tax Facts on Insurance & Employee Benefits

loan repayments, through payroll deduction, can continue under the new law. *ASRS, Sec. 61, ¶¶135, 440.2.*

467. What nondiscrimination requirements must a tax sheltered annuity meet?

Editor's Note: According to the proposed regulations, under IRC Section 403(b)(12)(A)(i), employer contributions and employee after-tax contributions must satisfy all of the nondiscrimination requirements in the same manner as a qualified plan under IRC Section 401(a) (i.e., IRC Secs. 401(a)(4), 401(a)(5), 401(a)(17), 401(m), and 410(b)). Prop. Treas. Reg. §1.403(b)-5(a). The proposed regulations do *not* adopt the good faith reasonableness standard of Notice 89-23, 1989-1 CB 654 for purposes of satisfying the nondiscrimination requirements of IRC Section 403(b)(12)(A)(i). Preamble, REG-155608-02, 69 Fed. Reg. 67075, 67080 (11-16-2004). The proposed regulations further provide that an annuity contract does *not* satisfy the requirements unless the contributions are made pursuant to a plan (see Q 466), and the terms of the plan satisfy the nondiscrimination rules. *Effective date postponed*: The proposed regulations will be effective for taxable years beginning after December 31, 2006, and cannot be relied upon until adopted in final form. Prop. Treas. Reg. §1.403(b)-11(a). The effective date for the 403(b) regulations was originally set for "taxable years beginning after December 31, 2005" (i.e., January 1, 2006). However, the Service has announced that the final regulations, when released (presumably in 2006), will delay the effective date one year (i.e., until January 1, 2007). See *Employee Plans News*, p. 4 (Fall 2005), at: http://www.irs.gov/pub/irs-tege/fall05.pdf.

Prior to 1989, there was no requirement that all employees, or that all of any class of employees, be made eligible for participation in an employer's tax sheltered annuity plan. In years beginning after 1988, (except for contracts purchased by certain churches or church-controlled organizations) tax sheltered annuities must be provided under a plan that meets certain nondiscrimination requirements. IRC Secs. 403(b)(1)(D), 403(b)(12). Various employees, including students employed by a school in which they are enrolled and regularly attending classes and employees who normally work less than 20 hours in a week, may be excluded. See IRC Sec. 403(b)(12)(A). But if any such students or part-time employees are excluded, all must be. IRC Sec. 403(b)(12)(A).

Notice 89-23 provides that, until further guidance is issued, a tax sheltered annuity plan will be deemed to be in compliance with these requirements if the employer operates the plan in accordance with a reasonable, good faith interpretation of such requirements (but see *Editor's Note*, above). Notice 89-23, 1989-1 CB 654, as modified by Notice 90-73, 1990-2 CB 353, Notice 92-36, 1992-2 CB 364 and Notice 96-64, 1996-2 CB 229; see also Announcement 95-48, 1995-23 IRB 13. Pending the issuance of regulations or other guidance, Notice 89-23 (extended by Notice 96-64) provides guidance for complying with the nondiscrimination rules. Sec. VI(A)(1)(d) of the final tax sheltered annuity audit guidelines, *reprinted in* ASRS, Sec. 61, ¶440.2.

Also, until further guidance is issued under IRC Section 403(b)(12) by the IRS, transitional safe harbors (see below) are generally available for tax sheltered annuities to meet most of these requirements. In applying the safe harbors, an employer must take into account all of its nonexcludable employees; it may not use a statistically valid random sample of employees. Notice 89-23, 1989-1 CB 654, as extended by

TAX SHELTERED ANNUITIES   Q 467

Notice 90-73, 1990-2 CB 353, Notice 92-36, 1992-2 CB 364, and by Notice 96-64, 1996-2 CB 229.

There is no requirement that employees who have completed a certain number of years of service or who have reached a certain age must be allowed to participate. In the case of plans subject to the Employee Retirement Income Security Act (ERISA), if the employer does require a minimum age or a minimum number of years of service, the employer may not require that the employee complete a period of service extending beyond the date the employee becomes 21 years old or, if later, completes one year of service. However, if the employee is given a nonforfeitable right to 100% of his accrued benefits (as would normally be the case with a tax sheltered annuity), the "waiting period" may be as much as two years instead of one. In the case of employees of an educational institution, the age may be 26 instead of 21 if after one year of service the employee is 100% vested and his rights are nonforfeitable. ERISA Sec. 202.

Title I of ERISA (reporting and disclosure, participation and vesting, etc.) does not apply to governmental and certain church plans. ERISA Sec. 4(b). Also, ERISA generally does not apply to tax sheltered annuities of other employers unless the plan is "established or maintained" by the employer. See ERISA Sec. 3(2). A salary reduction plan will generally not be considered "established or maintained" by an employer if, among other things, employee participation is voluntary, employer involvement is limited to such things as requesting and providing information and collecting and remitting premiums, and the employer permits employees at least a reasonable choice among products and annuity contractors (he need not seek out products and contractors). Labor Reg. §2510.3-2(f). (*Editor's Note*: But see Q 466 explaining the new written plan requirement under the proposed regulations.) An employer was found to exceed the limited involvement permitted under the regulation where the employer evaluated circumstances and exercised its judgment in determining eligibility for in-service withdrawals on account of disability or financial hardship. DOL Adv. Op. 94-30A.

Salary Reduction Plans

Tax sheltered annuity plans offering salary reduction contributions are generally subject to a single nondiscrimination rule with respect to salary reduction contributions (the requirement does not apply to contracts purchased by certain churches or church-controlled organizations). In general, if any employee may elect to have the employer make contributions to a TSA under a salary reduction agreement, then all employees of the organization (other than certain excludable employees) must be allowed to elect to have the employer make contributions of more than $200 annually pursuant to a salary reduction agreement. IRC Secs. 403(b)(1)(D), 403(b)(12)(A)(ii), 403(b)(12)(B). See also Prop. Treas. Reg. §1.403(b)-5(b)(1).

While the general thrust of this rule is to require that all employees be eligible to make salary reduction contributions if the opportunity to make salary reduction contributions is offered to any employee, the rule is most likely intended to allow employers to impose a minimum, or threshold, annual salary reduction contribution for participation in a salary reduction agreement; the employer may require a minimum annual salary reduction contribution of $200.01, and may exclude from participation in a salary reduction agreement any employee who is not willing to reduce his salary by more than $200 per year. See, e.g., H.R. Rep. No. 99-426 (Tax Reform Act of 1986), at 715, *reprinted in* 1986-3 CB (vol. 2), at 715; H.R. Conf. Rep. No. 99-841 (TRA '86), at II-420, *reprinted in* 1986-3 CB (vol.4), at 420; Sec. VI(A)(2)(b)(5) of the final audit guidelines for tax sheltered annuities, *reprinted in* ASRS, Sec. 61, ¶440.2. The rule probably also prohibits employer efforts to cap an employee's annual salary reduction contributions at $200 or less.

In addition, the nondiscrimination rule applicable to salary reduction contributions allows an employer to exclude certain other employees, including those who are participants in an IRC Section 457 deferred compensation plan of the employer, a qualified cash or deferred IRC Section 401(k) arrangement of the employer, or another tax sheltered annuity; certain ministers (described in IRC Section 414(e)(5)(C)) may be excluded as well. IRC Sec. 403(b)(12)(A); Sec. VI(A)(2)(b)(7) of the final tax sheltered annuity audit guidelines, *reprinted in* ASRS, Sec. 61, ¶440.2. See also Prop. Treas. Reg. §1.403(b)-5(b)(4). If, in addition to elective deferrals, the employer also provides nonelective contributions, the nondiscrimination rules discussed below, apply to those contributions. General Explanation of TRA '86, p. 680; Notice 89-23, 1989-1 CB 654. See also Q 480.

A contribution is considered not made pursuant to a salary reduction agreement if under the agreement it is made pursuant to a one-time irrevocable election by the employee at the time of initial eligibility to participate. IRC Sec. 403(b)(12)(A); Notice 89-23, 1989-1 CB 654. See Section VI(A)(2)(d) of the final tax sheltered annuity audit guidelines, *reprinted in* ASRS, Sec. 61, ¶440.2. The legislative history provides that if an employee has a one-time election to participate in a program that requires an employee contribution, such contribution will not be considered an elective deferral to the extent that the employee is not permitted subsequently to modify the election in any manner. H.R. Conf. Rep. No. 99-841 (TRA '86), at II-420, *reprinted in* 1986-3 CB (vol. 4), at 420; General Explanation of TRA '86, p. 680.

Under Notice 89-23, "employer" means the common law employer (and not the controlled group) for purposes of testing salary reduction contributions for nondiscrimination. A good faith, reasonable interpretation as to the identity of the employer is sufficient for this purpose. Section VI(A)(2)(d) of the final tax sheltered annuity audit guidelines, *reprinted in* ASRS, Sec. 61, ¶440.2.

Safe Harbor

Until further specific guidance is issued by the IRS, a 403(b) annuity plan that provides for salary reduction contributions is deemed to satisfy the nondiscrimination requirements with respect to such contributions only if each employee of the employer sponsoring or maintaining the plan is eligible to defer annually more than $200 pursuant to a salary reduction agreement *and* the opportunity to make such contribution is available to all employees on the same basis (but see the *Editor's Note* at the beginning of this question). See Prop. Treas. Reg. §1.403(b)-5(b)(1). According to the final audit guidelines, until further guidance is issued, both public education institutions and 501(c)(3) organizations *must* currently operate their 403(b) plans in accordance with a good faith/reasonable interpretation of the nondiscrimination requirement for salary reduction contributions. Sec. VI(A)(2)(a) of the final tax sheltered annuity audit guidelines, *reprinted in* ASRS, Sec. 61, ¶440.2.

If a common law employer historically has treated its various geographically distinct units as separate organizations for employee benefit purposes, then each unit may be considered a separate organization for purposes of this safe harbor so long as the units are operated independently on a day-to-day basis. Units located within the same Standard

TAX SHELTERED ANNUITIES   Q 467

Metropolitan Statistical Area are generally not "geographically distinct." Notice 89-23, above, as extended by Notice 90-73, 1990-2 CB 353, Notice 92-36, 1992-2 CB 364, and by Notice 96-64, 1996-2 CB 229. See also Prop. Treas. Reg. §1.403(b)-5(b)(3)(ii).

For purposes of this safe harbor, certain employees can be excluded when testing to see whether the opportunity to make salary reduction contributions is available to all employees on the same basis. Notice 89-23, Sec. V(B)(3), 1989-1 CB 654, at 659-660; and Sec. VI(A)(2)(b) of the final tax sheltered annuity audit guidelines, *reprinted in* ASRS, Sec. 61, ¶440.2. See also Prop. Treas. Reg. §1.403(b)-5(b)(4). See Notice 89-23 for definitions of employer and other terms used in applying the safe harbors.

Contributions Other Than by Salary Reduction

With respect to contributions other than by salary reduction, plans (other than those of certain churches or church controlled organizations) must meet many of the same minimum participation and coverage and nondiscrimination rules that apply to qualified plans – specifically, they must meet the requirements of IRC Sections 401(a)(4), 401(a)(5), 401(a)(17), 401(m), and 410(b) (see Q 325 through Q 331 for details of these requirements). IRC Secs. 403(b)(1)(D), 403(b)(12)(A)(i), 403(b)(12)(B). (IRC Section 401(a)(26), although listed in IRC Section 403(b)(12)(A)(i), no longer applies to defined contribution plans.) A plan will not be treated as violating the requirements under IRC Section 403(b)(12) merely on account of the making of (or right to make) catch-up contributions by participants age 50 or over, under the provisions of IRC Section 414(v), so long as a universal availability requirement is met. IRC Sec. 414(v)(3)(B). See Q 397 for details on the requirements for catch-up contributions.

A *governmental plan* is one established by the United States government, the government of any state or political subdivision or any agency or instrumentality of any of them. IRC Sec. 414(d). The minimum participation and coverage and nondiscrimination requirements described in IRC Section 403(b)(12)(A)(i) (other than IRC Section 401(a)(17)) do not apply to state and local governmental plans – specifically, the requirements of IRC Sections 401(a)(4), 401(a)(5), 401(m), and 410(b) do not apply to such plans. IRC Sec. 403(b)(12)(C).

Sponsors of governmental 403(b) plans may not continue to rely on a reasonable, good faith interpretation of IRC Section 401(a)(17) as permitted under Notice 89-23, but rather must comply with the regulations under IRC Section 401(a)(17). Announcement 95-48, 1995-23 IRB 13; Treas. Reg. §1.401(a)(17)-1(d)(4)(i).

Regulations under IRC Sections 401(a)(4), 401(a)(5), and 410(b) are generally effective for plans maintained by tax-exempt organizations (as defined in Notice 92-36, 1992-2 CB 364, as modified by Rev. Proc. 94-13, 1994-1 CB 566) (delayed effective dates for the regulations under IRC Sections 401(a)(4) and 401(a)(5) apply to certain church plans). Announcement 95-48, 1995-23 IRB 13; Notice 96-64, 2 CB 229, as modified by Notice 98-39, 1998-2 CB 205, Notice 2001-9, 2001-1 CB 375, and Notice 2001-46, 2001-42 IRB 122. However, since there has been no further guidance with respect to the application of these IRC Sections to tax sheltered annuity plans, 403(b) plans maintained by 501(c)(3) tax-exempt organizations remain able to satisfy these IRC Sections by operating in accordance with a reasonable, good faith interpretation of these IRC Sections under Notice 89-23, as modified (but see the *Editor's Note* at the beginning of this question). Sec. VI(A)(3)(c) of the final tax sheltered annuity audit guidelines, *reprinted in* ASRS, Sec. 61, ¶440.2.

Q 467   FEDERAL INCOME TAX

Plans maintained by tax-exempt organizations may apparently continue to rely on a reasonable, good faith interpretation of IRC Section 401(m) (but see the *Editor's Note* at the beginning of this question). See Sec. VI(A)(3)(c) of the final tax sheltered annuity audit guidelines, *reprinted in* ASRS, Sec. 61, ¶440.2. Tax-exempt sponsors of 403(b) plans may not continue to rely on a reasonable, good faith interpretation of IRC Section 401(a)(17) as permitted under Notice 89-23, but rather must comply with the regulations under IRC Section 401(a)(17). Announcement 95-48, 1995-23 IRB 13. But see Sec. VI(A)(3)(c) of the final tax sheltered annuity guidelines, *reprinted in* ASRS, Sec. 61, ¶440.2.

For plans maintained by 501(c)(3) tax-exempt organizations, Notice 89-23, as modified, provides certain safe harbors under which the IRS will consider an employer to be operating a tax sheltered annuity plan in accordance with a reasonable, good faith interpretation of the coverage, participation, and nondiscrimination requirements (but see the *Editor's Note*, at the beginning of this question). See Sec. VI(A)(3)(c) of the final tax sheltered annuity audit guidelines, *reprinted in* ASRS, Sec. 61, ¶440.2. See "Safe Harbors," below.

Generally, all employees of a group of employers that are members of a *controlled group* of corporations or all employees of trades or businesses that are under *common control* will be treated as employed by a single employer for purposes of the minimum participation, coverage and nondiscrimination rules (see Q 359). IRC Secs. 403(b)(12)(A)(i), 414(b), 414(c). Until further guidance is issued, a good faith, reasonable interpretation applies in defining the employer for this purpose (but see the *Editor's Note* at the beginning of this question). Sec. VI(A)(3)(e) of the final tax sheltered annuity audit guidelines, *reprinted in* ASRS, Sec. 61, ¶440.2. In the case of nonstock nonprofit corporations, an entity has a controlling interest in such an organization if at least 80% of the directors or trustees of such organization are either representatives of such entity (i.e., a trustee, director, agent or employee of such entity) or directly or indirectly controlled by such entity. See Prop. Treas. Reg. §1.414(c)-5(b). A trustee or director is controlled by the controlling entity if such entity has the power to remove such trustee or director and designate a new trustee or director. See Let. Rul. 9442031. Because of the difficult issues that arise for tax-exempt employers in determining which entities must be aggregated under IRC Sections 414(b) and 414(c), tax-exempt employers may – until further guidance is issued – apply a reasonable, good faith interpretation of IRC Sections 414(b) and 414(c) in determining which entities must be aggregated (but see the *Editor's Note* at the beginning of this question). Notice 96-64, 1996-2 CB 229. Any future guidance will be prospective and not effective before plan years beginning in 2001. See, e.g., Prop. Treas. Reg. §1.414(c)-5(c). See Q 325 through Q 331 for the actual requirements of IRC Section 401(a)(4), IRC Section 401(a)(5), IRC Section 401(a)(17), IRC Section 401(m), and IRC Section 410(b).

Safe Harbors

Until further guidance is issued under IRC Section 403(b)(12) by the IRS, a 403(b) annuity plan that provides for non-salary reduction contributions other than employer matching contributions or after-tax employee contributions is deemed to satisfy the minimum participation, coverage and nondiscrimination requirements applicable to such contributions if the aggregated 403(b) annuity program satisfies one of three safe harbors with respect to such contributions (but see the *Editor's Note* at the beginning of this question). Notice 89-23, 1989-1 CB 654, as extended by Notice 90-73, 1990-2 CB 353, Notice 92-36, 1992-2 CB 364, and by Notice 96-64, 1996-2 CB 229. An aggregated 403(b) program generally means all tax sheltered annuity contracts, all custodial accounts, and all retirement income contracts under IRC Section 403(b)

TAX SHELTERED ANNUITIES   Q 467

to which an employer makes contributions. The employer may also aggregate other plans (e.g., a qualified plan or a governmental or church plan) covering the employer's employees, so long as each plan satisfies the general qualified plan nondiscrimination requirements (see Q 326). If a plan or plans included in the aggregated program provides for matching contributions or employee contributions, the plan or plans must meet the nondiscrimination requirements of IRC Section 401(m) and the regulations thereunder (see above). Notice 89-23, 1989-1 CB 654, 655-656.

While it is not clear, use of the safe harbors presumably will not satisfy the requirements of IRC Section 401(a)(17). See Announcement 95-48, 1995-23 IRB 13. Furthermore, tax sheltered annuity plans maintained by 501(c)(3) organizations must comply with the regulations under IRC Section 401(a)(4), IRC Section 401(a)(5), and IRC Section 410(b). Notice 96-64, 1996-2 CB 229. However, such plans may continue to rely on the safe harbor rules with respect to IRC Sections 401(a)(4), 401(a)(5), 410(a)(26), 401(m), 410(b)(but see the *Editor's Note* at the beginning of this question). See Sec. VI(A)(3)(c) of the final tax sheltered annuity guidelines, *reprinted in* ASRS, Sec. 61, ¶440.2.

The first safe harbor is met if (1) the highest percentage of compensation for a year contributed on behalf of any highly compensated employee currently accruing benefits under the program is not more than 180% of the lowest percentage of compensation for a year contributed on behalf of any nonhighly compensated employee currently accruing benefits; (2) at least 50% of the nonhighly compensated employees are currently accruing benefits under the program; and (3) the percentage of employees who are currently accruing benefits under the program and who are nonhighly compensated employees is at least 70%. The second safe harbor is similar to the first except that the percentages in (1) through (3) are changed—the percentages are 140%, 30% and 50% respectively.

The last safe harbor is met if there is no disparity between the percentage of compensation contributed for a year on behalf of any highly compensated and nonhighly compensated employee *and* if either (1) at least 20% of the nonhighly compensated employees are currently accruing benefits under the program and the percentage of participants in the program who are nonhighly compensated employees is at least 70%, *or* (2) at least 80% of the nonhighly compensated employees are currently accruing benefits under the program and the percentage of participants in the program who are nonhighly compensated employees is at least 30%.

For purposes of the safe harbors, Notice 89-23 allows an employer to include in its class of highly compensated employees only those employees who, during the plan year, are more-than-5% owners (but see below) of any entity within the same controlled group as the employer, or receive compensation in excess of $50,000 (as indexed for inflation – for 1996, $66,000, Notice 95-55, 1995-2 CB 336.) For tax years beginning after December 31, 1996, the above amount was adjusted to $80,000 and will be indexed annually for inflation. IRC Sec. 414(q)(1); see Appendix E. The applicable dollar amount for a particular determination or look-back year is the dollar amount for the calendar year in which such determination or look-back year begins. Temp. Treas. Reg. §1.414(q)-1T, A-3(c)(2). Thus for example, to determine HCE status for a plan year beginning in 2006, based on a look-back year beginning in 2005, the applicable income threshold would be $95,000, the amount in effect for 2005. See Information Letter to Kyle N. Brown dated December 9, 1999. See also Q 356.

The safe harbors are to be applied as of the last day of the plan year, taking into account employees who are employed by the employer on such day. However, highly compensated employees who terminate employment with the employer during the last quarter of such year must generally be included for purposes of determining the highly compensated employee with the highest percentage of compensation. If the employer chooses to include other types of plans in the aggregate 403(b) program, adjustments will be required for any difference between the various vesting schedules. See Notice 89-23 for definitions of plan year, employer, excludable employees and other terms used in applying the safe harbors. *ASRS, Sec. 61, ¶135.1.*

468. What are the requirements for an automatic enrollment provision in a 403(b) plan?

In an effort to encourage employee participation in retirement plans, the Service has approved automatic enrollment provisions for 403(b) plans. Rev. Rul. 2000-35, 2000-31 IRB 138. These arrangements, which are also referred to as "negative elections," are available to 501(c)(3) organizations and state and local school systems. Under an automatic salary reduction election provision in a 403(b) plan, each employee's compensation is automatically reduced by a fixed percentage and this amount is contributed towards the purchase of an annuity contract *unless* the employee affirmatively elects to (1) receive cash or (2) have a different percentage contributed.

Automatic salary reduction contributions must satisfy certain requirements to be treated as contributions made under a salary reduction agreement and, thus, excludable from gross income. An employee must receive notice explaining the right to receive cash in lieu of having it contributed towards the purchase of an annuity contract, mutual fund custodial account, or retirement income account. In addition, an employee must have a reasonable period before the cash is currently available to make the election. Finally, the employee must not be able to receive amounts contributed towards the purchase of an annuity contract before the occurrence of certain events (see Q 466).

Automatic salary reduction features are available to current and newly hired employees. According to the revenue ruling, an election to "opt out" of the automatic salary reduction (i.e., to take the cash instead of making the contribution) or to contribute a different percentage can be made at any time. Salary reduction contributions made in this manner are not contributions made under a one-time irrevocable election because the employee can change the election in the future.

The IRS has stated in a general information letter that there is no special maximum limit on the automatic compensation reduction percentage, and no safe harbor automatic compensation reduction percentage. The compensation reduction percentage under an automatic compensation reduction election for a 403(b) annuity or custodial account is permitted to be *any* percentage of compensation that would be permitted in the case of an elective contribution or elective deferral made pursuant to an affirmative, explicit election (i.e., in which the default is no elective contribution or elective deferral). General Information Letter to J. Mark Iwry, 1775 Massachusetts Ave., N.W., Washington, D.C., 20036-2188, dated March 17, 2004.

CONTRIBUTIONS

Limits

469. What limits are there on excludable contributions to a tax sheltered annuity?

Generally speaking, an employee can exclude from his gross income the contributions paid by his IRC Section 501(c)(3) or public school employer on a retirement

TAX SHELTERED ANNUITIES   Q 471

annuity for his benefit. IRC Sec. 403(b)(1). However, the amount that he may exclude in his tax year is limited.

For taxable years beginning after 2001, there are two limits to be considered: (1) the overall limit (see Q 471), and (2) the limit on the amount that may be excluded under a salary reduction agreement (see Q 473). IRC Sec. 403(b)(1). (For taxable years beginning after 2001, the exclusion allowance is *repealed*. IRC Sec. 403(b)(2), repealed by EGTRRA 2001.) If the entire contribution in the year is by salary reduction, only the lowest of the two limits may be excluded. If the contribution is partly salary reduction and partly additional contribution, the salary reduction portion is limited to the salary reduction limit, and the excludable contribution may not exceed the IRC Section 415 limit. See Treas. Reg. §1.415-6(e)(1). The effect of contributions that exceed these limits are explained in Q 472, Q 473, and Q 475.

The IRC Section 415 overall limit applies to contributions (and other additions) regardless of whether they are vested or not. See IRC Sec. 403(b)(1). *ASRS, Sec. 61, ¶¶135.2, 170.1.*

470. What was the exclusion allowance for a tax sheltered annuity? How was it calculated?

For taxable years beginning after 2001, the exclusion allowance is *repealed*. IRC Sec. 403(b)(2), as repealed by EGTRRA 2001. For details, see *ASRS Sec, 61, ¶170.3.*

471. How does the Section 415 overall limit affect the excludable amount for a tax sheltered annuity?

The limit on contributions and benefits applicable to qualified pension plans applies to tax sheltered annuities. IRC Sec. 415(a)(2) (see Q 469). For the purpose of this limit, tax sheltered annuities will generally be treated as defined contribution plans. Treas. Reg. §1.415-6(e)(1)(i). Thus, they are subject to a limit of the lesser of (a) 100% of the "participant's compensation" (defined below) or (b) the applicable dollar limit, $44,000 in 2006 ($42,000 in 2005). IRC Sec. 415(c); IRS News Releases IR-2005-120, IR-2004-127. (For the dollar limitations on annual additions in earlier limitation years, see Appendix E.) This limit is indexed for inflation in increments of $1,000. IRC Sec. 415(d)(4)(B). See Q 332.

The limit is on the amount of "annual additions" that may be made in any "limitation year" to a participant's account. *Annual additions* are employer contributions (including salary reduction amounts) and employee after-tax contributions. Excess elective deferrals (see Q 473) that are correctly distributed under the regulations are not included as annual additions. Treas. Regs. §§1.402(g)-1(e)(1)(ii); 1.415-6(b)(1)(i). However, excess matching employer contributions (see Q 467) are included, even if the excess is corrected by distribution from the plan. Treas. Regs. §§1.401(m)-1(e)(3)(iv); 1.415-6(b)(1)(i). Earnings attributable to distributed elective deferrals that are not themselves distributed will be considered as an employer contribution for the limitation year in which the distributed elective deferral was made. Treas. Reg. §1.415-6(b)(6)(iv). A contribution made during a tax year is treated as if made on the last day of the limitation year that ends in or with the tax year. Treas. Reg. §1.415-6(e)(1)(iii). A *limitation year* is the calendar year or any other 12-month period that may be elected by the individual by attaching a statement to his income tax return. If the employee controls an employer, his limitation year must

2006 Tax Facts on Insurance & Employee Benefits   591

be the same as that of the controlled employer. Treas. Reg. §1.415-2(b). Contributions in excess of the overall limit are discussed in Q 472.

Includable Compensation

In the context of a 403(b) annuity contract, *participant's compensation* means the participant's "includable compensation" determined under IRC Section 403(b)(3). IRC Sec. 415(c)(3)(E). *Includable compensation* is based on compensation earned by the employee for the most recent period (ending not later than the close of the taxable year for which the limitation is being determined) that constitutes a full year of service *and* that precedes the taxable year by no more than five years. IRC Sec. 403(b)(3). Thus, for a full-time employee, includable compensation is generally his salary for the current taxable year. But for a part-time employee, fractional years' earnings are required to be aggregated. IRC Sec. 403(b)(4)(B). To illustrate, assume that as of the end of 2006, an employee had worked 3 years half-time and had the following earnings: $11,500 in 2004, $12,000 in 2005, and $12,500 in 2006. In computing his exclusion allowance for 2005, his includable compensation would be $24,500 (12,000 + $12,500).

The definition of *includable compensation* includes: (1) any elective deferrals (see Q 473) made to the plan and (2) any amount that has been contributed or deferred by the employer at the election of the employee and that is not includable in gross income by reason of IRC Sections 125, 132(f)(4), or IRC Section 457 (see Q 99 concerning cafeteria plans and Q 123 concerning IRC Section 457 deferred compensation plans). IRC Sec. 403(b)(3). Only compensation from the employer who paid the premiums can be included; compensation from any other employer or any other source cannot be included. The "employer" is generally the common law employer.

For purposes of determining the limits on contributions under IRC Section 415(c), amounts paid to a minister as a tax-free housing allowance may not be treated as compensation under the general or alternative definitions of compensation under the regulations. Let. Rul. 200135045; Treas. Reg. §1.415-2(d).

Post-severance compensation. Under proposed regulations, the exclusion from gross income under IRC Section 403(b) applies to contributions made for former employees with respect to certain compensation paid within 2½ months following severance from employment. Prop. Treas. Regs. §§1.403(b)-3(b)(4)(ii), 1.415(c)-2(e)(3)(ii). Certain payments made within 2½ months after an employee's severance from employment will not fail to be "compensation" within the meaning of IRS Section 415(c) simply because of timing *if* those payments are paid within 2½ months following severance from employment and are: (1) payments that – absent a severance from employment – would have been paid to the employee while the employee continued in employment and are regular compensation; or (2) payments for accrued bona fide sick, vacation, or other leave, but only if the employee would have been able to use the leave if employment had continued. Prop. Treas. Reg. §1.415(c)-2(e)(3)(ii). An IRS official has stated that the post-severance compensation provision in the proposed regulations – when finalized – will be effective for limitation years beginning on or after January 1, 2005, but, taxpayers can rely on this portion of the proposed regulations until the final regulations are issued. See IRS Employee Plans News Special Edition (June 2, 2005), at: www.irs.gov.

Multiple Plans

A tax sheltered annuity is generally considered to be the plan of any employer controlled by the individual for whom the annuity is bought. As such, it must be

TAX SHELTERED ANNUITIES   Q 473

aggregated with other plans (i.e., defined contribution plans, simplified employee pensions) of employers under his control, such as sole proprietorships or more than 50%-owned corporations or partnerships. IRC Sec. 415(k)(4). Thus, a 403(b) participant is *not* required to aggregate contributions to his tax sheltered annuity with other defined contribution plans of the employer who provides the annuity when he does *not* control that employer. IRC Sec. 415(k)(4).

In applying the IRC Section 415 limit to a combination of a 403(b) annuity and a defined contribution plan of an employer controlled by the individual, each plan must separately meet the limitation applicable to it taking into consideration only the compensation from the employer providing the plan. In determining the combined limit, compensation from the controlled employer may be aggregated with that from the employer providing the annuity. Treas. Reg. §1.415-2(d)(7). *ASRS, Sec. 61, ¶170.2.*

472. What is the effect of making contributions to a tax sheltered annuity in excess of the "overall limit"?

To the extent a contribution in a limitation year exceeds the overall (IRC Section 415) limit, it must be included in gross income for the tax year with which (or in which) the limitation year ends. Treas. Regs. §§1.415-6(e)(1)(ii), 1.403(b)-1(d)(3)(v); Prop. Treas. Reg. §1.403(b)-4(f). See also GCM 39071 (12-1-83); Sec. V(B)(6) of the final tax sheltered annuity audit guidelines, *reprinted in* ASRS, Sec. 61, ¶440.2.

As a result of excess IRC Section 415 amounts, the annuity contract or custodial account is bifurcated into a non-qualified annuity (comprised of the excess and earnings thereon) and a qualifying 403(b) annuity. See Sec. X(A)(4)(b) of the final tax sheltered annuity audit guidelines, *reprinted in* ASRS, Sec. 61, ¶440.2. See also Prop. Treas. Reg. §1.403(b)-3(b)(2)(referring to See IRC Sec. 415(a)(2) (flush language). The entire contract fails to be a 403(b) contract if an excess annual addition is made and a separate account is not maintained with respect to the excess.

An excess contribution made to a custodial account may also be subject to an excise tax (see Q 475). *ASRS, Sec. 61, ¶170.2.*

473. What is the limit on excludable amounts that may be contributed to tax sheltered annuity plans under salary reduction agreements? What are the consequences of exceeding the limit?

The amount of "elective deferrals" that an individual can exclude from income for his tax year is limited. Elective deferrals are: (1) amounts contributed to tax sheltered annuity plans under salary reduction agreements; (2) amounts contributed under cash or deferred arrangements to 401(k) plans (see Q 393), and salary reduction SEPs (SAR-SEPs) (see Q 241); and (3) amounts contributed under salary reductions to SIMPLE IRAs (see Q 242). IRC Sec. 402(g). Elective deferrals do not include elective contributions made pursuant to a one-time irrevocable election that is made at initial eligibility to participate in the salary reduction agreement (or pursuant to certain other one-time irrevocable elections to be specified in regulations, or pre-tax contributions made as a condition of employment). IRC Sec. 402(g)(3).

For 2006, the aggregate limit on elective deferrals is $15,000 ($14,000 in 2005). IRC Sec. 402(g)(1); IRS News Releases IR-2005-120, IR-2004-127. For tax years

2006 Tax Facts on Insurance & Employee Benefits

Q 473   FEDERAL INCOME TAX

beginning after 2006, the elective deferral limit will again be indexed for inflation, in increments of $500. IRC Sec. 402(g)(4).

A *special increased limit* is provided for amounts contributed to 403(b) plans under a salary reduction agreement in the case of an employee who has completed 15 years of service with an educational institution, hospital, home health service agency, church (or a convention or association of churches), or a health and welfare service agency. The limit for any one year is increased by the lesser of (1) $3,000, (2) $15,000, reduced by amounts already excluded for prior taxable years by reason of this special exception, or (3) the *excess* of $5,000 multiplied by the number of years of service the employee has with the organization *over* all elective deferrals (to 403(b) plans, 401(k) plans, SEPs, and SIMPLE IRAs). IRC Sec. 402(g)(7). It is the current limit (i.e., $15,000 in 2006) that is increased by the above amount.

The "15 years of service" requirement takes into account *only* employment with the qualified organization. Prop. Treas. Reg. §1.403(b)-4(c)(3)(iii). (For the rule coordinating the 15-years of service catch-up with the age 50 catch-up, see below.) The final audit guidelines state that in theory, an employee who has 15 years of service with *another* qualified organization could use the full amount of the "catch-up" election with respect to the *new* organization. Section V(A.1.)(3) of the final tax sheltered annuity audit guidelines, *reprinted in* ASRS, Sec. 61, ¶440.2. According to comments by an IRS official, this does not mean that the years worked at a prior organization may be added to the years with a new organization; instead, the employee starts over again in amassing the years required to qualify for the second election.

Any elective deferral in excess of the applicable limit is included in the individual's gross income for the year of deferral. If any such amount is included, the individual may, no later than April 15 of the following year, allocate the excess deferrals among the plans under which the deferrals were made, and, if plan language permits it, the plans may distribute to the individual the amounts so allocated (together with income allocable to the amounts) no later than April 15 of that year. IRC Sec. 402(g)(2); Treas. Reg. §1.402(g)-1(e)(2); Prop. Treas. Reg. §1.403(b)-4(f)(2). Such a timely distribution may be made regardless of prohibitions on distributions otherwise applicable (see Q 466). IRC Sec. 402(g)(2).

Because an excess deferral is not excluded from gross income, the excess amount distributed under these rules by April 15 is not included in income as a distribution. Any income on the excess deferral is included in income in the taxable year in which distributed. Treas. Reg. §1.402(g)-1(e)(8). A distribution of less than the entire amount of excess (and income) is treated as a pro rata distribution of deferral amount and income. Treas. Reg. §1.402(g)-1(e)(10). A timely (by April 15) distribution of excess deferrals and income is not subject to tax as a premature distribution under IRC Section 72(t). Treas. Reg. §1.402(g)-1(e)(8). A distribution of an excess deferral is not a distribution for purposes of meeting the minimum distribution requirements. IRC Sec. 402(g)(2)(C); Treas. Reg. §1.402(g)-1(e)(9).

If the excess deferral is not distributed by April 15, it is subject to the regular prohibitions on withdrawals and is *not* included in the "investment in the contract" (basis) even though it has been included in income. Thus, excess deferrals are includable in gross income when later distributed. IRC Sec. 402(g)(6). A withdrawal that occurs before the excess deferral was made does not count as a distribution of an excess deferral. Treas. Reg. §1.402(g)-1(e)(3).

TAX SHELTERED ANNUITIES   Q 474

The amount of salary reduction excludable in a year may actually be less than the amount permitted under the limit if the overall limit is less (see Q 469). Contributions by salary reduction are not deductible employee contributions; they are *employer* contributions that are *excludable* within limits (see Q 466, Q 469).

Age 50 catch-up. The otherwise applicable dollar limit on elective deferrals under a Section 403(b) annuity can be increased for individuals who would attain age 50 by the end of the taxable year. IRC Secs. 414(v)(1), 414(v)(5). The applicable dollar limit is $5,000 in 2006 ($4,000 in 2005) and thereafter. IRC Sec. 414(v)(2)(B)(i); IRS News Releases IR-2005-120, IR-2004-127. After 2006, these limits will be indexed for inflation in $500 increments.

Catch-up contributions by participants age 50 or over made under the provisions of IRS Section 414(v) are *not* subject to the elective deferral limit. See IRC Section 414(v)(3)(A); Treas. Reg. §1.414(v)-1(d). The elective deferral limit of $15,000 in 2006 ($14,000 in 2005) is increased by (1) the special catch-up limit (under IRC Section 402(g)(7)), and is further increased by the catch-up limit under Treas. Reg. §1.414(v)-1(c)(2). Treas. Reg. §1.402(g)-2(a). According to proposed regulations (effective after 2006), any catch-up amount contributed by an employee who is eligible for both an age 50 catch-up and the special 403(b) catch-up for certain organizations (see above) is treated *first* as an amount contributed as a special 403(b) catch-up to the extent that type of catch-up is permitted, and *second* as an amount contributed as an age 50 catch-up (to the extent the catch-up amount exceeds the maximum special 403(b) catch-up after taking into account IRC Sections 402(g) and 415(c), the special 403(b) catch-up, and any limits on the special 403(b) catch-up that are imposed by the terms of the plan). Prop. Treas. Reg. §1.403(b)-4(c)(3)(iv). For details on the requirements for catch-up contributions, see Q 397.

Coordination with IRC Section 457 deferral limit. For taxable years beginning *after 2001*, the rules requiring that the contribution limits under IRC Section 457 be coordinated with elective deferral limits are *repealed*. IRC Sec. 457(c). Consequently, an individual who participates in a 403(b) and 457 plan could conceivably defer a total of $30,000 in 2006 (i.e., $15,000 in each plan). See Q 124. *ASRS, Sec. 61, ¶¶165, 170.5, 170.6.*

474. What special rules apply to tax sheltered annuities for church employees?

A duly ordained, commissioned or licensed minister of a church, or a lay person, who is an employee of a church, or a convention or association of churches, including a tax-exempt organization controlled by or associated with a convention or association of churches, may be able to increase his excludable tax sheltered annuity contributions under the special rules explained below. For these purposes, a duly ordained, commissioned or licensed minister who is self-employed or who is employed by an organization other than one described in IRC Section 501(c)(3) but with respect to which the minister shares common religious bonds is considered a church employee. See IRC Sec. 414(e)(5). This definition includes chaplains.

A church employee may make an election that may provide a higher IRC Section 415 annual additions limit than discussed in Q 471. He may elect an annual addition limit of as much as $10,000 in any one year. Employer contributions under this election (i.e., payments in excess of the otherwise applicable annual addition limit) may not aggregate more than $40,000 over the employee's lifetime. IRC Sec. 415(c)(7).

A church employee with 15 years of service is eligible for the higher elective deferral limit explained in Q 473.

Contributions to a defined contribution program ("retirement income account") established or maintained by a church are considered contributions for a tax sheltered annuity contract. (However, a program in existence on August 13, 1982 will not fail to be a tax sheltered annuity merely because it is a defined benefit plan, even if it is later amended or extended to other employees.) IRC Sec. 403(b)(9); TEFRA, Sec. 251(e)(5); Let. Rul. 8837061. See Prop. Treas. Reg. §1.403(b)-9(a). Retirement income accounts can be established for self-employed ministers and chaplains and ministers who are employed by an organization other than one described in IRC Section 501(c)(3), but with respect to which the ministers share common religious bonds.

The proposed regulations clarify that retirement income accounts will be expected to be maintained pursuant to a plan that affirmatively states the intent to be a retirement income account. See Prop. Treas. Regs. §§1.403(b)-3(b)(3), 1.403(b)-9(a)(2)(ii). *Effective date postponed*: The effective date for the 403(b) regulations was originally set for "taxable years beginning after December 31, 2005" (i.e., January 1, 2006). However, the Service has announced that the final regulations, when released (presumably in 2006), will delay the effective date one year (i.e., until January 1, 2007). See *Employee Plans News*, p. 4 (Fall 2005), at: http://www.irs.gov/pub/irs-tege/fall05.pdf.

Contributions made by a minister to a retirement income account *after 2001* will be allowed to the extent they do not exceed the limit on elective deferrals or the limit on annual additions. IRC Secs. 404(a)(10)(B), 414(e)(5).

A church plan does not have to meet the participation and nondiscrimination requirements applicable to other employer tax sheltered annuity plans (see Q 467). IRC Sec. 403(b)(1)(D); see also IRC Sec. 403(b)(12)(B).

In figuring his Section 415 annual additions limit, a church employee must count all years of service with organizations that are part of a particular church as years of service with one employer. Similarly, he must treat contributions by such churches as made by one employer. IRC Sec. 415(c)(7)(B). In the case of a foreign missionary, contributions (and other additions) for an annuity contract or retirement income contract, when expressed as an annual addition to the employee's account, are not treated as exceeding the IRC Section 415 annual additions limit *if* the annual addition is not in excess of the greater of (i) $3,000 or (ii) the employee's includable compensation under IRC Section 403(b)(3). IRC Sec. 415(c)(7)(C). *ASRS, Sec. 61, ¶¶170.3(a), 170.3(c), 170.4.*

Excess Contributions

475. What is an excess contribution to a tax sheltered annuity? What is an excess aggregate contribution? What excise taxes apply to them?

There are several different limitations applicable to amounts contributed to 403(b) annuities. Contributions that exceed any of these particular limits may be thought of as "excess" contributions, but they are treated differently depending on the limit that is exceeded and, sometimes, depending on whether the excess amount is contributed to a custodial account or toward the purchase of an annuity contract.

TAX SHELTERED ANNUITIES   Q 476

Contributions that exceed the lesser of the excludable amount or the overall limit. When such contributions are made to a *custodial account* for the purchase of regulated investment company stock (or a retirement income account to the extent funded through custodial accounts), they are properly called "excess contributions" and are subject to an excise tax. IRC Sec. 4973(c). See Sec. V(E)(1) of the final tax sheltered annuity audit guidelines, *reprinted in* ASRS, Sec. 61, ¶440.2. The tax is 6% (not to exceed 6% of the value of the account) of (1) the amount by which the contributions (other than a permissible rollover contribution–see Q 451) exceed the lesser of the amount excludable from gross income under IRC Section 403(b) or the overall limitation under IRC Section 415 (or, whichever is applicable if only one is applicable), *plus* (2) any such excess carried over from the preceding tax year. An excess carried over from a previous year may be reduced by contributing in a year less than the excludable amount or the contribution limit, whichever is lower. An excess may also be reduced by income taxable distributions. IRC Sec. 4973(c). The tax is on the employee.

If such contributions are made toward the purchase of an *annuity contract*, the excess is not subject to an excess contributions tax (because annuity earnings are tax free whether or not bought under IRC Section 403(b)).

Contributions in excess of the overall limit of IRC Section 415 (see Q 472).

Salary reduction contributions in excess of the limit on elective deferrals. These are not subject to a tax, but the amount above the limit is not excludable from income and, if not timely distributed, does not increase basis and is included in gross income when later distributed (even though it was originally included, as well) (see Q 473). See also Q 469.

Matching employer contributions in excess of a nondiscriminatory amount. If an employer makes certain discriminatory matching contributions toward an annuity contract or to a custodial account, amounts in excess of nondiscriminatory amounts are called "excess aggregate contributions" and are subject to a 10% excise tax if not timely distributed. IRC Sec. 4979. These requirements and the tax are explained in Q 406. *ASRS, Sec. 61, ¶¶190.1, 190.6.*

Post-Retirement Employer Contributions

476. Can an employer make post-retirement contributions to a tax sheltered annuity on behalf of a retired employee?

Yes, but time limits apply. Under the Code, the term *includable compensation* (defined in Q 471) means compensation earned by the employee for the most recent period (ending not later than the close of the taxable year for which the limitation is being determined) that constitutes a full year of service *and that precedes the taxable year by no more than five years.* IRC Sec. 403(b)(3).

Under proposed regulations (effective after 2006—see *Editor's Note*, below), the exclusion from gross income provided by IRC Section 403(b) does not apply to contributions made for former employees. A contribution is not made for a former employee if the contribution is with respect to compensation that would otherwise be paid for a payroll period that begins before severance from employment. Prop. Treas. Reg. §1.403(b)-3(b)(4). A former employee is deemed to have monthly includible compensation (see Q 471) for the period through the end of the taxable year in which

2006 Tax Facts on Insurance & Employee Benefits   597

he ceases to be an employee and through the end of each of the next five taxable years. The amount of the monthly includable compensation is equal to one-twelfth of the former employee's includable compensation during the former employee's most recent year of service. Accordingly, nonelective employer contributions for a former employee must not exceed the IRC Section 415(c) limit up to the lesser of the dollar amount in IRC Section 415(c), *or* the former employee's annual includable compensation based on the former employee's average monthly compensation during his most recent year of service. Prop. Treas. Reg. §1.403(b)-4(d)(1). *Editor's Note*: The effective date for the 403(b) regulations was originally set for "taxable years beginning after December 31, 2005" (i.e., January 1, 2006). However, the Service has announced that the final regulations, when released (presumably in 2006), will delay the effective date one year (i.e., until January 1, 2007). See *Employee Plans News*, p. 4 (Fall 2005), at: http://www.irs.gov/pub/irs-tege/fall05.pdf.

Roth 403(b)

477. What is a Roth 403(b) Contribution Program?

Effective in 2006, 403(b) plans will be allowed to offer a *qualified Roth contribution program*, which is basically a Roth account for elective deferrals. IRC Secs. 402A(b), 402A(e). Essentially, participants of 403(b) plans establishing such a program will be able to designate all, or a portion, of their elective deferrals as Roth contributions. The Roth contributions will be included in the participant's gross income in the year the contribution is made, and then be held in a separate account with separate recordkeeping. IRC Sec. 402A(b).

For years beginning after December 31, 2002, a 403(b) tax sheltered annuity plan may allow employees to make voluntary employee contributions to a separate account or annuity established under the plan (i.e., deemed IRA). For more details, see Q 213. *ASRS, Sec. 61, ¶170.7*

CHANGING ISSUERS

478. May an employee transfer his tax sheltered annuity to another carrier or to a custodial account?

A *direct transfer* between issuers of an amount representing *all or part* of an individual's interest in an IRC Section 403(b) annuity or custodial account is not a distribution subject to tax or to the premature distribution penalty, provided the funds transferred continue after the transfer to be subject to distribution requirements at least as strict as those applicable to them before the transfer. Rev. Rul. 90-24, 1990-1 CB 97. See also, Sec. IX(A)(2) of the final tax sheltered annuity audit guidelines, *reprinted in* ASRS, Sec. 61, ¶440.2; Let. Rul. 9043042. The proposed regulations (effective after 2006—see below) clarify that Revenue Ruling 90-24 is intended to be limited to situations where the employee is a participant of the receiving plan. See Prop. Treas. Regs. §§1.403(b)-10(b)(1), 1.403(b)-10(b)(2). A direct transfer is not considered a distribution or a rollover and, thus, is not subject to the direct rollover option requirement (see Q 466) or 20% mandatory withholding (see Q 448). See Prop. Treas. Reg. §1.403(b)-10(b)(1). See Q 466 for the distribution restrictions applicable to 403(b) annuity contracts, custodial accounts, and retirement income accounts. *Effective date postponed*: The effective date for the 403(b) regulations was originally set for "taxable years beginning after December

TAX SHELTERED ANNUITIES   Q 478

31, 2005" (i.e., January 1, 2006). However, the Service has announced that the final regulations, when released (presumably in 2006), will delay the effective date one year (i.e., until January 1, 2007). See *Employee Plans News*, p. 4 (Fall 2005), at: http://www.irs.gov/pub/irs-tege/fall05.pdf.

The IRS ruled that Revenue Ruling 90-24 would not apply to an employer's transfer of funds from a 403(b) plan to a profit-sharing plan. The employer wanted to consolidate the assets of its retirement plan participants into one unified investment and reporting system in order to simply plan administration. According to the IRS, nontaxability of transfers under Revenue Ruling 90-24 does not encompass transfers from 403(b) arrangements to arrangements not described in IRC Section 403(b), such as IRC Section 401(a). Consequently, the proposed transfer or rollover of plan assets from the 403(b) plan to the profit-sharing plan would cause the participants' assets to be includable in income as a taxable distribution. Let. Rul. 200317022; see also Prop. Treas. Reg. §1.403(b)-10(b)(1).

Revenue Ruling 90-24 permits amounts subject to distribution restrictions to be accounted for separately for purposes of retaining the distribution restrictions applicable to them. Thus, transfers to and from 403(b)(1) contracts and 403(b)(7) accounts are permitted so long as the distribution limits are retained. Furthermore, the transferring individual may be a current employee, a former employee or a beneficiary of a former employee. See also Let. Rul. 9104021. Where only a part of an individual's interest in the annuity is transferred and the individual has a cost basis in the annuity, a pro rata portion of the basis is considered transferred to the second annuity.

With respect to a "two-tier" annuity that credits a lower rate of interest on funds withdrawn in a lump sum and a higher rate on those that are annuitized, the IRS has privately ruled that transfers of interest-only over three years, followed in the third year by a transfer of the principal remaining in the annuity, will be direct transfers so long as the funds continue to be subject to the same distribution requirements. Let. Rul. 9224042.

Amounts transferred from one annuity contract to another will retain any grandfathered status as long as such amounts are accounted for separately and continue to be clearly identified under the new contract. Let. Rul. 9045052. Thus, pre-1989 amounts will continue to *not* be subject to IRC Section 403(b)(11) distribution restrictions (see Q 466), and pre-1987 amounts will continue to *not* be subject to the regular minimum distribution rules (see Q 486).

Revenue Ruling 90-24 can be used to facilitate transfers of funds and interests from insolvent insurers. See Let. Ruls. 9442030, 9348051, 9339024. Also, an individual who receives cash from the surrender of a tax sheltered annuity contract issued by a troubled insurance company (i.e., one that is subject to a rehabilitation, conservatorship, insolvency or similar state proceeding at the time of the distribution) and who reinvests the cash in another annuity or custodial account may receive nonrecognition treatment under Revenue Ruling 90-24 if certain conditions are met. Rev. Proc. 92-44, 1992-1 CB 875, as modified by Rev. Proc. 92-44A, 1992-1 CB 876. See Q 30 for more details.

Employers and issuers of 403(b) annuity contracts and custodial accounts are not required to allow direct transfers. See Prop. Treas. Reg. §1.403(b)-10(b)(1). *ASRS, Sec. 61, ¶220.*

2006 Tax Facts on Insurance & Employee Benefits

AMOUNTS RECEIVED UNDER THE PLAN

479. May an employee or his surviving spouse roll over a distribution from a tax sheltered annuity?

Yes, but under the rules set forth in "Rollovers" (see Q 451, Q 453) only certain distributions may be rolled over.

480. May an employee transfer funds from a 403(b) account to purchase past service credits?

Yes. Effective for transfers made after December 31, 2001, plan participants may exclude from income amounts directly transferred (i.e., from trustee to trustee) from an IRC Section 403(b) tax sheltered annuity or IRC Section 457 plan to a governmental defined benefit plan that are used to purchase "permissive service credits." Likewise, a participant may use such directly transferred amounts to repay contributions or earnings that were previously refunded because of a forfeiture of service credit, under either the transferee plan or another IRC Section 457 plan or an IRC Section 403(b) tax sheltered annuity maintained by a governmental employer in the same state. IRC Secs. 403(b)(13), 457(e)(17). See also Prop. Treas. Reg. §1.403(b)-10(b)(4).

For this purpose, *permissive service credit* means credit for a period of service recognized by the plan only if the employee contributes an amount, determined by the plan, that does not exceed the amount necessary to fund the benefit attributable to such period of service. Such contributions must be voluntary and in addition to regular employee contributions; they are subject to the limits of IRC Section 415. *ASRS, Sec. 61, ¶170.10; Sec 64, ¶420.2(b).*

Incidental Life Insurance Protection

481. Is the employee taxed on incidental life insurance protection and waiver of premium benefits under a tax sheltered annuity contract?

Editor's Note: The proposed regulations provide that unless grandfathered, incidental insurance may *not* be part of a 403(b) plan. For details on this change from current law, see Q 465.

The 1-year term cost of the pure life insurance protection provided by the employer must be included each year in the employee's gross income. This cost is computed in the same manner, and with use of the same rates, as under a qualified plan (see Q 424). Treas. Reg. §1.72-16(b). Thus, the applicable rate is applied to the amount at risk each year to determine the amount includable in gross income.

Where the insurance is provided through a group contract, the insurance company issuing the group contract is responsible for reporting the 1-year term costs on Form 1099-R in accordance with IRC Section 6047(d). See Let. Rul. 9007001. The sum of these annual 1-year term costs that have been taxed to the employee will constitute all or part of his cost basis in computing the tax on the payments he receives under the contract (see Q 490). Treas. Reg. §1.72-16(b)(4). In other words, the aggregate cost of insurance protection (the amount reported by the employee as taxable income) can be recovered tax free from the annuity payments. Rev. Rul. 68-304, 1968-1 CB 179.

TAX SHELTERED ANNUITIES   Q 483

Since a waiver of premium provision and a disability income provision are not pure annuity features, their cost is not within the overall limit provided by the Code. The extra premiums for such provisions must be included in the employee's gross income. Let. Rul., 3-15-66, signed I. Goodman, Chief Pension Trust Branch, 1968 MDRT Proceedings, p. 221. See Q 491 for the taxation of the death benefit. *ASRS, Sec. 61, ¶180.2.*

Dividends

482. How are dividends under a tax sheltered annuity treated for income tax purposes?

The regulations do not cover this point. Under the general rule, dividends received under a contract described in IRC Section 403(b) are taxed under a rule that provides for a pro rata recovery of cost. IRC Sec. 72(e)(5); Treas. Reg. §1.72-11(b). In the case of a tax sheltered annuity, the premiums are considered paid by the employer even when they are derived from a reduction in the employee's salary. Consequently, if the premiums have all been excludable from the employee's gross income, he will have no cost basis, and any dividends received by him will constitute taxable income. In that case, dividends that are paid to the employee in cash are taxable.

If dividends are used to reduce current premiums, apparently they are not taxable to the employee, and the overall limit should be applied to the net premium. Even though accumulated dividends are subject to withdrawal, constructive receipt by the employee is not a problem in tax years beginning after December 31, 1986. IRC Sec. 403(b)(1). The IRS is treating interest on accumulated dividends as part of the retirement fund and not taxed until the participant begins to receive distributions from the fund. General Information Letter, January 20, 1978. *ASRS, Sec. 61, ¶180.4.*

Loans

483. Are amounts borrowed under a tax sheltered annuity taxable income?

Loans made after August 13, 1982, under IRC Section 403(b) tax sheltered annuity plans (including IRC Section 403(b)(7) custodial accounts) are subject to the same rules that apply to loans under qualified plans (see Q 420, including the effective date of the final regulations). IRC Sec. 72(p)(4)(A). Therefore, unless certain requirements are met, amounts borrowed from a tax sheltered annuity will be taxed as a deemed distribution under the plan. Specifically, a loan will be treated as a deemed distribution under the plan unless it satisfies (1) the repayment term requirement, (2) the substantially level amortization requirement, (3) certain dollar limitations, and, according to final loan regulations, (4) the enforceable agreement requirement. IRC Secs. 72(p)(1), 72(p)(2); Treas. Reg. §1.72(p)-1, A-3.

According to proposed regulations (effective after 2006—see below), a facts and circumstances inquiry must be made when determining whether (1) the availability of a loan, (2) the making of a loan, or (3) failure to repay a loan is treated as a distribution, directly or indirectly. Among the facts and circumstances to be considered are whether the loan has a fixed repayment schedule, bears a reasonable rate of interest, and whether there are repayment safeguards to which a prudent lender would adhere. Thus, for example, a loan must bear a reasonable interest rate to *not* be treated as a distribution. Prop. Treas. Reg. §1.403(b)-6(f). *Effective date for proposed regulations postponed*: The effective date for the proposed 403(b) regulations was originally set for January 1, 2006. However, the Service has announced that the final regulations will delay the effective date until January 1, 2007. See *Employee Plans News*, p. 4 (Fall 2005), at: http://www.irs.gov/pub/irs-tege/fall05.pdf.

If there is an express or tacit understanding that the loan will not be repaid or, for any reason, the transaction does not create a debtor-creditor relationship, then the amount transferred is treated as an actual distribution from the plan rather than as a loan or a deemed distribution. Treas. Reg. §1.72(p)-1, A-17. If a participant pledges or assigns any portion of his interest in a plan as security for a loan, the amount pledged or assigned is subject to the deemed distribution rule. Treas. Reg. §1.72(p)-1, A-1(b).

Repayment Term Requirement

Generally, to avoid treatment as a deemed distribution, a loan must, by its terms, be required to be repaid within five years. However, a loan used to acquire a dwelling that within a reasonable time is to be used as the participant's "principal residence" (as defined in IRC Section 121) is not subject to the 5-year repayment term requirement. IRC Sec. 72(p)(2)(B); Treas. Reg. §1.72(p)-1, A-5. While the Code puts no specific limit on the term of such principal residence loans, it is likely that the Service will impose at least a reasonable term on the theory that the "loan" is not in fact a loan if there is no obligation to repay. Compare Treas. Reg. §1.72(p)-1, A-17, above. But see *Dean v. Comm.*, TC Memo 1993-226 (suggesting that the term of principal residence loans extends to maturity of the tax sheltered annuity contract; deciding treatment of principal residence loans taken out before effective date of level amortization requirement). See also the example under Treas. Reg. §1.72(p)-1, A-8 (involving the application of the tracing requirement to a 15-year loan used to repay a bank loan for the purchase of a principal residence). A loan need not be secured by the dwelling that is to be the participant's principal residence to qualify as a principal residence loan exempt from the 5-year term requirement. Treas. Reg. §1.72(p)-1, A-6. (But see Q 484 if there is a desire to render the interest on such a loan deductible as "qualified residence interest.") Also, the tracing rules under IRC Section 163(h)(3)(B) apply in determining whether a loan is treated as for the acquisition of a principal residence and, therefore, exempt from the 5-year term requirement. Treas. Reg. §1.72(p)-1, A-7. Finally, a refinancing generally cannot qualify as a principal residence loan exempt from the 5-year term requirement. However, a loan used to repay a loan from a third party will qualify as a principal residence loan if it qualifies as such a loan without regard to the loan from the third party. Treas. Reg. §1.72(p)-1, A-8. *Editor's Note.* Under KETRA 2005, special rules apply with respect to repayments. See Q 420, Q 421.

Substantially Level Amortization Requirement

Generally, to avoid treatment as a deemed distribution, a loan must provide for substantially level amortization over the term of the loan, with loan repayments to be made at least quarterly. IRC Sec. 72(p)(2)(C); see *Est. of Gray v. Comm.*, TC Memo 1995-421. However, the level amortization requirement does not apply – and payments may be suspended – for a period up to one year while a participant is on a leave of absence and his pay from the employer is insufficient to service the debt; a participant taking advantage of such a suspension must still repay the loan by the "latest permissible term of the loan" (see below) and the installments due after payments resume must be at least as great as those required under the terms of the original loan. The *latest permissible term of the loan* is the latest date permitted under IRC Section 72(p)(2)(B) (i.e., five years from

TAX SHELTERED ANNUITIES Q 483

the date of the loan, subject to the exception for principal residence loans – see above), *plus* any additional period of suspension permitted under a military service leave (see below). Treas. Regs. §§1.72(p)-1, A-9(a), 1.72(p)-1, A-9(c), 1.72(p)-1, A-19(c).

Military service. With respect to a leave of absence due to military service, IRC Section 414(u)(4) allows a participant to suspend repayment of a loan during any period that he serves in the uniformed services. The suspension of repayment under these circumstances may extend beyond one year (unlike the suspension rules for other leaves of absence). The participant must resume loan repayment once he completes his military service, at which time payments must be made as frequently and in an amount no less than was made before the suspension. The full amount of the loan, including interest accrued during the suspension, must be repaid by the end of the "latest permissible loan term." The *latest permissible loan term* under these circumstances is the latest permissible date under IRC Section 72(p)(2)(B) (i.e., five years from the date of the loan, subject to the exception for principal residence loans, see above), *plus* any additional period of suspension permitted for military service. For example, if a military reservist obtained a 3-year loan, and then served two years on active duty, the officer would have up to seven years to repay the loan (i.e., the 5-year maximum permissible loan term *plus* the 2-year suspension period). An example in the regulations illustrates the application of a 6% interest rate cap (under the Soldier's and Sailor's Civil Relief Act Amendments of 1942) on a reservist's monthly installments and payment period. Treas. Reg. §1.72(p)-1, A-9.

Failure to make any installment payment when due generally results in a deemed distribution of the entire outstanding balance of the loan at the time of such failure. However, a plan may provide a "cure period" for payments, so long as the cure period does not extend beyond the last day of the calendar quarter following the calendar quarter in which the required payment was due (the cure period was referred to as a grace period under the proposed regulations). Treas. Reg. §1.72(p)-1, A-10.

Enforceable Agreement Requirement

To avoid treatment as a deemed distribution, a loan must be evidenced by a legally enforceable agreement (which may include more than one document) set forth either in writing *or* in an electronic medium specifying the amount of the loan, the term of the loan, and the repayment schedule. The agreement does not have to be signed if it is enforceable under applicable law without being signed. Treas. Reg. §1.72(p)-1, A-3(b). If the agreement is set forth in an electronic medium, it must be one that is reasonably accessible to the participant *and* provided under a system that: (1) is reasonably designed to preclude anyone other than the participant from requesting a loan; (2) provides the participant with a reasonable opportunity to review, confirm, modify, or rescind the terms of the loan before it is made; and (3) provides the participant with confirmation of the loan terms within a reasonable time after it is made. The confirmation may be provided in an electronic format *or* in a written paper document. If it is provided electronically, it must be done in a manner that is no less understandable to the participant than a written document and at the time the confirmation is provided, the participant must be advised that he may request and receive a written paper document at no charge. Treas. Reg. §1.72(p)-1, A-3(b).

Dollar Limit

Loans made after 1986 are taxable as distributions from the plan to the extent the amount of the loan, when added to the outstanding balance of all other loans, whenever made, from all tax sheltered annuities, IRC Section 457 deferred compensation plans, and qualified pension, profit sharing, stock bonus and bond purchase plans of the employer, exceeds the lesser of (1) $50,000 (but see "Hurricane Katrina tax relief below"), reduced by the excess of the highest outstanding balance of loans from the plans during the 1-year period ending on the day before the date the loan is made over the outstanding balance of loans from the plans on the date the loan is made, or (2) one-half of the present value of the employee's nonforfeitable accrued benefit under the plans (nonetheless, at least $10,000). IRC Sec. 72(p)(2)(A); see also Let. Rul. 8742008. *Hurricane Katrina tax relief.* For "qualified individuals" (see above), the maximum loan amount is increased to $100,000. See Sec. 103(a), KETRA 2005. See also Q 414 and Q 415.

Loans subject to the above dollar limitations are those that by their terms require repayment within five years (or if they are "principal residence" loans, within a reasonable time), and satisfy the substantially level amortization requirement and the enforceable agreement requirement. All plans of all other members of a controlled group of employers, of an affiliated service group, or businesses under common control are counted as plans of the employer. IRC Sec. 72(p)(2)(D).

Deemed Distributions

The entire amount of a loan will be treated as a distribution from the outset if the terms of the loan do not satisfy the repayment term requirement or the level amortization requirement, or if the loan is not evidenced by an appropriate enforceable agreement. Treas. Reg. §1.72(p)-1, A-4(a); see IRC Secs. 72(p)(1), 72(p)(2); *Est. of Gray v. Comm.*, above.

If the loan satisfies the other requirements but the amount loaned exceeds the applicable dollar limitation, the amount of the loan in excess of the limit is a deemed distribution at the time the loan is made. Treas. Reg. §1.72(p)-1, A-4(a); see IRC Secs. 72(p)(1), 72(p)(2). If the loan initially satisfies all of the requirements to avoid treatment as a deemed distribution, but payments are not made in accordance with the terms of the loan, a deemed distribution of the entire outstanding balance (including accrued interest) generally results at the time of such failure. Treas. Regs. §§1.72(p)-1, A-4(a), 1.72(p)-1, A-10(b). However, a plan may provide a "cure period" for payments, so long as the cure period does not extend beyond the last day of the calendar quarter following the calendar quarter in which the required payment was due (the cure period was referred to as a grace period under the proposed regulations). In such a case, a failure to make a payment will not trigger a deemed distribution of the outstanding balance until the end of the cure period. Treas. Regs. §§1.72(p)-1, A-4(a), 1.72(p)-1, A-10(a).

Once a loan is deemed distributed under IRC Section 72(p), the interest that accrues thereafter on that loan is not included in income (i.e., for purposes of determining the amount that is taxable under IRC Section 72). In addition, neither the income that results from the deemed distribution nor the interest that accrues thereafter increases the participant's investment in the contract (i.e., his tax basis) under IRC Section 72. However, to the extent the deemed distribution is repaid, his investment in the contract will be increased. See Treas. Regs. §§1.72(p)-1, A-19(a), 1.72(p)-1, A-21(a).

A loan that is deemed distributed under IRC Section 72(p) (including interest accruing thereafter) and that has not been repaid (such as by a plan loan offset) is still considered outstanding for purposes of determining the maximum amount of any sub-

TAX SHELTERED ANNUITIES   Q 483

sequent loans to the participant or the beneficiary. Treas. Reg. §1.72(p)-1, A-19(b)(1). Thus, for example, the *amount* limitation would be reduced by an outstanding loan even after a deemed distribution has occurred. To the extent that a participant repays by cash any portion of a loan that has been deemed distributed, he does acquire a tax basis in the contract in the same manner as if the repayments were after-tax contributions; however, loan repayments are not treated as after-tax contributions for other purposes, including the nondiscrimination requirements and IRC Section 415 limits). See Treas. Reg. §1.72(p)-1, A-21(a).

The final regulations place two conditions on loans made while the loan treated as a distribution remains unpaid. First, the subsequent loan must be repayable under a payroll withholding arrangement enforceable under applicable law. This arrangement may be revocable, but should the participant revoke it, then the outstanding balance of the loan is treated as a deemed distribution. Second, the participant must provide the plan with adequate security (in the form of collateral for the loan) in addition to the participant's accrued benefit. If, for any reason, the additional collateral is no longer in force before the subsequent loan is repaid, the outstanding balance of the subsequent loan is treated as a deemed distribution. If these conditions are not satisfied, the entire subsequent loan is treated as a distribution under IRC Section 72(p). Treas. Reg. §1.72(p)-1, A-19(b).

Where a loan fee is withheld from net loan proceeds actually received by a participant but is included in the participant's outstanding loan balance, the deemed distribution upon a default may include the withheld loan fee. See *Earnshaw v. Comm.*, TC Memo 1995-156.

Multiple Loans

Where a participant receives multiple loans, each such loan must separately satisfy IRC Section 72(p), taking into account the outstanding balance of each existing loan. Under the final regulations, there is no limit on the number of loans a participant is permitted to take out. Treas. Reg. §1.72(p)-1, A-20(a)(3).

Refinancing Transactions

A refinancing transaction is any transaction in which one loan replaces another. For example, a refinancing may exist if the outstanding loan amount is increased, or if the interest rate or the repayment term of the loan is renegotiated. Treas. Reg. §1.72(p)-1, A-20(a).

If the term of the replacement loan ends after the "latest permissible term" (see above) of the loan it replaces, then both loans are treated as outstanding on the date of the refinancing transaction. This means generally that the loans must collectively satisfy the requirements of IRC Section 72(p). Treas. Reg. §1.72(p)-1, A-20(a)(2). There is an exception where the replacement loan would satisfy IRC Section 72(p)(2) if it were treated as two separate loans. Under this exception, the amount of the replaced loan, amortized in substantially level payments over a period ending not later than the last day of the "latest permissible term" of the replaced loan, is treated as one loan. The other loan is for an amount equal to the difference between the amount of the replacement loan and the outstanding balance of the replaced loan. Treas. Reg. §1.72(p)-1, A-20(a)(2).

The IRS will not view the transaction as circumventing IRC Section 72(p) provided that the replacement loan effectively amortizes an amount equal to the replaced loan

2006 Tax Facts on Insurance & Employee Benefits

over a period ending not later than the last day of the "latest permissible term" of the replaced loan. For this reason, the outstanding balance of the replaced loan need not be taken into account in determining whether the limitations of IRC Section 72(p)(2) have been met—only the amount of the replacement loan (plus any existing loans that are not being replaced) is considered. Treas. Reg. §1.72(p)-1, A-20(a)(2).

If the term of the replacement loan does not end later than the "latest permissible term" of the replaced loan, then only the amount of the replacement loan (plus the outstanding balance of any existing loans that are not being replaced) must be taken into account in determining whether IRC Section 72(p) has been satisfied. Treas. Reg. §1.72(p)-1, A-20(a)(1).

Actual Distributions

Loans to participants can give rise to two kinds of taxable distributions: (1) deemed distributions under IRC Section 72(p), discussed above, and (2) actual distributions. As noted above, sham loans are treated as actual distributions. But even bona fide loans can result in actual distributions through distributions of plan loan offset amounts. A distribution of a plan loan offset amount occurs when the accrued benefit of the participant is reduced (offset) in order to repay the loan. The amount of the account balance that is offset against the loan is an actual distribution of plan benefits. Treas. Reg. §1.72(p)-1, A-13. See also Prop. Treas. Reg. §1.403(b)-6(f), stating that a plan loan offset is a distribution. Compare *Caton v. Comm.*, TC Memo 1995-80. Accordingly, a plan may be prohibited from making such an offset under the distribution restrictions of IRC Sections 403(b)(7) and 403(b)(11) (see Q 466). Treas. Reg. §1.72(p)-1, A-13(b). The final audit guidelines state that if the participant's account balance is reduced to satisfy the loan balance, there is an actual distribution which could violate IRC Section 403(b)(11) and IRC Section 403(b)(7). Sec. (X)(A)(4)(c) of the final tax sheltered annuity audit guidelines, *reprinted in* ASRS, Sec. 61, ¶440.2.

Taxation

If a loan is treated as a deemed distribution it is includable in gross income under the rules discussed in Q 490 as if it were an actual distribution. See Treas. Reg. §1.72(p)-1, A-11(a). A loan treated as a deemed distribution may be subject to the 10% tax on early distributions imposed by IRC Section 72(t) (see Q 485) as if it were an actual distribution. Treas. Reg. §1.72(p)-1, A-11(b); see also *Dean v. Comm.*, above.

It would seem that the outstanding balance of a "tax-free" loan (that is, one not treated as a distribution under IRC Section 72(p)) will be includable in income upon maturity or termination of the tax sheltered annuity contract before the end of the loan's term. See *Dean v. Comm.*, above.

To the extent a loan, when made, is a deemed distribution or an account balance is reduced to repay a loan (apparently at the time a loan is made), the amount includable in income is subject to withholding. If a deemed distribution or a loan repayment by benefit offset results in income after the date the loan is made, withholding is required only if a transfer of cash or property (excluding employer securities) is made from the plan at the same time. Treas. Reg. §1.72(p)-1, A-15. For further guidance on withholding rules, see Temp. Treas. Reg. §35.3405-1T, Q&A F-4 and Treas. Regs. §§31.3405(c)-1, A-9, and 31.3405(c)-1, A-11. Deemed distributions under IRC Section 72(p) are not "eligible rollover distributions" and are not subject to the mandatory 20% withholding applicable to certain eligible rollover distributions. Treas. Regs. §§1.402(c)-2, A-4,

TAX SHELTERED ANNUITIES   Q 485

31.3405(c)-1, A-1(a); Treas. Reg. §1.72(p)-1, A-12. Plan loan offset amounts can be eligible rollover distributions. Treas. Reg. §1.402(c)-2, A-9. For withholding rules relevant to plan loan offset amounts that are eligible rollover distributions, see Treas. Reg. §31.3405(c)-1, especially A-11.

Other considerations. Tax sheltered annuity plans that are subject to ERISA are subject to the prohibited transaction requirements applicable to loans: they must be adequately secured, bear a reasonable rate of interest, be available to all participants or beneficiaries on a reasonably equivalent basis, be made in accordance with specific provisions regarding such loans set forth in the plan, and not discriminate in favor of a prohibited group (see Q 443). ERISA Sec. 408(b); Labor Reg. §2550.408b-1. In addition, to the extent a tax sheltered annuity is not funded by salary reduction, the plan must meet nondiscrimination rules which would generally require that loans be available on a nondiscriminatory basis (see Q 467).

See Q 484 for deduction of interest on a loan. See Q 466 for a discussion of deemed distributions, plan loan offsets, and the distribution restrictions of IRC Sections 403(b)(7) and 403(b)(11). *ASRS, Sec. 61, ¶180.5.*

484. Is interest on a loan under a tax sheltered annuity deductible?

Interest on a loan not treated as a distribution (see Q 483) made, renewed, renegotiated, modified or extended after December 31, 1986 is not deductible during the period the loan is secured by amounts attributable to salary reduction contributions, or the period on or after the individual to whom the loan is made becomes a key employee as defined in Q 357. IRC Sec. 72(p)(3). (Certain salary reduction contributions made under a one-time election at the time of initial eligibility are not considered salary reduction contributions. IRC Sec. 402(g)(3); Sec. VI(A)(2)(d) of the final tax sheltered annuity audit guidelines, *reprinted in* ASRS, Sec. 61., ¶440.2.) No basis is created in a participant's account with respect to such nondeductible interest paid to the plan. General Explanation of TRA '86, p. 729. Where the loan is not secured by salary reduction amounts, see also Q 260, Q 823.

Interest paid on amounts borrowed under a tax sheltered annuity for the purchase or improvement of a principal residence is deductible as "qualified residence interest" (see Q 823) where the loan is secured by a recorded deed of trust and not the participant's account balance. See Let. Ruls. 8935051, 8742025; see also Earnshaw v. Comm., TC Memo 1995-156. Assuming that the loan is otherwise a bona fide debt, a taxpayer may deduct interest paid on a mortgage loan from his qualified plan, even though the amount by which the loan exceeded the $50,000 limit of IRC Section 72(p) was deemed to be a taxable distribution. FSA 200047022. *ASRS, Sec. 61, ¶180.5.*

DISTRIBUTIONS

Premature Distributions

485. What distributions from a tax sheltered annuity are subject to a penalty for early, or premature, distributions?

If a taxpayer receives an amount from a tax sheltered annuity (including any amount attributable to accumulated deductible contributions and including plan loan amounts treated as deemed distributions—see Q 483), his regular income tax will be increased by 10% of the portion of the distribution includable in income *unless* the distribution is:

2006 Tax Facts on Insurance & Employee Benefits

(1) made on or after the date on which the employee attains age 59½ (IRC Sec. 72(t)(2)(i));

(2) made to a beneficiary, or the employee's estate, on or after the death of the employee (IRC Sec. 72(t)(2)(ii));

(3) attributable to the employee's disability (IRC Sec. 72(t)(2)(iii));

(4) part of a series of substantially equal periodic payments made (not less frequently than annually) for the life or life expectancy of the employee or the joint lives or joint life expectancies of the employee and his beneficiary and beginning after the employee separates from the service of the employer. IRC Secs. 72(t)(2)(A)(iv), 72(t)(3). (See Q 232 for acceptable methods for meeting this exception.) But if the series of payments is later modified (other than because of death or disability) before the employee reaches age 59½ or, if after he reaches age 59½, within five years of the date of the first payment, the employee's tax for the year the modification occurs is increased by an amount equal to the tax which, but for the exception, would have been imposed plus interest for the deferral period (IRC Sec. 72(t)(4));

(5) made to an employee on account of separation from service after attaining age 55 (IRC Sec. 72(t)(2)(A)(v)). A distribution will be treated as falling within this exception if the distribution is made *after* the employee has separated from service and the separation occurs during *or* after the calendar year in which the employee attains age 55. Notice 87-13, 1987-1 CB 432, A-20;

(6) properly made to an alternate payee under a "qualified domestic relations order" (IRC Sec. 72(t)(2)(C); see Q 466);

(7) made to an employee for medical care, but not in excess of the amount allowable as a medical expense deduction to the employee for amounts paid during the taxable year for medical care (determined without regard to whether the employee itemizes deductions for the year). Apparently, this exempts from the penalty only amounts in excess of the 7.5% floor on deductible medical expenses (IRC Sec. 72(t)(2)(B); see Ann. 87-2, 1987-2 IRB 38);

(8) timely made to correct an excess aggregate contribution (IRC Sec. 401(m)(7); see Q 467); *or*

(9) timely made to reduce an excess elective deferral (see Q 473). IRC Sec. 402(g)(2)(C).

The costs of life insurance protection that are included in the employee's income are not considered as distributions for purposes of applying the premature distribution penalty. Notice 89-25, 1989-1 CB 662, A-11. See Q 424 regarding the proper measure of the value of current life insurance protection.

Hurricane Katrina tax relief. Under KETRA 2005, special rules apply with respect to the following: (1) non-application of the 10% early withdrawal tax to premature distributions (see Q 427, Q 428, Q 429); (2) permissible re-contributions of distributions (see Q 427, Q 429); and (3) ratable taxation of distributions over a 3-year period (see Q 427, Q 429). *ASRS, Sec. 61, ¶190.3.*

TAX SHELTERED ANNUITIES   Q 486

Required Distributions

486. When must distributions from a tax sheltered annuity begin? What is the effect of failure to meet the requirements?

Tax sheltered annuities (including custodial accounts and church retirement income contracts) are subject to the minimum distribution rules set forth in IRC Section 401(a)(9), both in form and operation. IRC Sec. 403(b)(10); Prop. Treas. Reg. §1.403(b)-6(e)(1). Generally, except as described below and at Q 487 to Q 489, Section 403(b) contracts are treated as IRAs for purposes of applying the minimum distribution requirements. Prop. Treas. Reg. §1.403(b)-6(e)(2); see Treas. Reg. §1.408-8. Proposed regulations issued in November, 2004 would codify a number of issues concerning the application of these rules to tax sheltered annuities; however, the proposed rules are not effective until finalized, and taxpayers are technically not permitted to rely on the proposed regulations. See REG-155608-02, 69 Fed. Reg. 67075 (November 16, 2004).

If the custodian has adequate records to distinguish between amounts accruing before January 1, 1987 (the pre-1987 account balance) and amounts accruing after December 31, 1986 (i.e., the post-1986 account balance, which includes earnings on the pre-1987 account balance), the minimum distribution requirements are imposed only on the post-1986 account balance. Prop. Treas. Reg. §1.403(b)-6(e)(6)(i); Treas. Reg. §1.403(b)-3, A-2(a). The issuer or custodian of the contract must be able to identify the pre-1987 balance, maintain accurate records of changes in it, and provide such information upon request to the participant or beneficiaries with respect to the contract. If the issuer or custodian does not keep such records, the entire balance will be treated as subject to IRC Section 401(a)(9). Treas. Reg. §1.403(b)-3, A-2(b); Prop. Treas. Reg. §1.403(b)-6(e)(ii).

The characterization of distributions as coming from pre-1987 or post-1986 balances has no relevance for purposes of determining the portion of a distribution that is includable in income under Section 72. Prop. Treas. Reg. §1.403(b)-6(e)(6)(v).

The application of the IRC Section 401(a)(9) rules to tax sheltered annuities is explained in Q 487 for lifetime distributions, and Q 489 for after-death distributions. The application of the minimum distribution incidental benefit rule is explained in Q 488.

Guidance on the application of the minimum distribution requirements under IRC Section 401(a)(9) is found in regulations finalized in April 2002 and June 2004, as well as proposed regulations under Section 403(b) issued in November 2004. See TD 8987, 67 Fed. Reg. 18988 (4-17-02); REG-155608-02, above; TD 9130, 2004-26 IRB 1082; REG-155608-02, 69 Fed. Reg. 67075. The proposed 2004 regulations made minimal changes to the preexisting requirements, but would clarify the treatment of pre-1987 balances. See Prop. Treas. Reg. §1.403(b)-6(e)(6).

Distributions that are required under IRC Section 401(a)(9) reduce the post-1986 balance to the extent they are necessary to meet the requirements; to the extent they exceed the minimum, they permanently reduce the pre-1987 balance. Treas. Reg. §1.403(b)-3, A-2(b); Prop. Treas. Reg. §1.403(b)-6(e)(3).

Under earlier rules that are still in effect, distributions, *regardless of when the amounts accrued*, must also satisfy the "incidental benefit" or "minimum distribution incidental benefit" (MDIB) rule. IRC Sec. 403(b)(10); Treas. Regs. §§1.401-1(b)(1)(i); 1.403(b)-3, A-3. The application of the MDIB rule is explained in Q 488.

2006 Tax Facts on Insurance & Employee Benefits

The distribution requirements under the two sets of rules are different. First, the MDIB requirement affects only distributions required to be made to the participant during his lifetime (although distributions to be made after death are considered in determining the minimum required to be distributed to him during his lifetime). Second, the amounts required under the two rules may be different. If the two requirements call for different minimums, the larger is the amount that must be distributed.

According to both the final 2002 regulations and the proposed 2004 regulations, distributions attributable to the pre-1987 account balance are treated as satisfying the MDIB requirement if all distributions from the Section 403(b) contract (including distributions attributable to the post-1986 account balance) satisfy the requirements of Treasury Regulation §1.401-1(b)(1)(i) (which the regulations cite as authority for the "old" MDIB rule) without regard to distributions under the 2002 regulations, *and* distributions from the post-1986 account satisfy the requirements of IRC Section 401(a)(9). Treas. Reg. §1.403(b)-3, A-3; Prop. Treas. Reg. §1.403(b)-6(e)(6)(vi).

In the alternative, distributions attributable to the pre-1987 account will be treated as satisfying the MDIB requirement if all distributions from the contract (whether pre-1987 or post-1986 amounts) satisfy the regulations under IRC Section 401(a)(9). Treas. Reg. §1.403(b)-3, A-3; Prop. Treas. Reg. §1.403(b)-6(e)(6)(vi).

The IRS has previously ruled privately that for purposes of determining the minimum distribution where amounts are transferred, in installments, from an insolvent insurer to another insurer pursuant to an exchange agreement between the two insurers and a court-appointed receiver, all amounts (subject to any grandfathering of unrecovered pre-1987 account balances) under all annuity contracts of the individual must be taken into account including any amounts not yet transferred under the agreement. Let. Rul. 9442030.

Rollovers and transfers. If a distribution is made from a participant's pre-1987 balance and rolled over to another tax sheltered annuity, it will be treated as part of the post-1986 balance in the second contract. However, if a direct transfer of pre-1987 funds is made from one contract to another, the amount transferred retains its character as part of the pre-1987 balance, provided the issuer of the second contract meets the recordkeeping requirements described above. Prop. Treas. Reg. §1.403(b)-6(e)(6)(iv).

Multiple tax sheltered annuities. If an individual has more than one tax sheltered annuity, each must meet the requirements separately; however, after determining the required minimum for each 403(b) annuity separately, the amounts may be totalled and the total taken from any one or more of the annuities. Only amounts that an individual holds as a participant may be aggregated under this rule. If an individual account holder is also the beneficiary of the tax sheltered annuity of a decedent, the required distribution from that account may not be aggregated with amounts required under contracts held by the individual, for purposes of meeting the distribution requirements. Treas. Reg. §1.403(b)-3, A-4; Prop. Treas. Reg. §1.403(b)-6(e)(7).

Failure to Make Minimum Distributions

Technically, a tax sheltered annuity that fails in its operation to meet the minimum distribution requirements with respect to all required distributions is subject to loss of its tax-exempt status. The preamble to the 2001 proposed regulations noted that such failures may be corrected through the Employee Plans Compliance Resolution System

TAX SHELTERED ANNUITIES   Q 487

(EPCRS); however neither the final 2002 regulations nor the proposed 2004 regulations mention this alternative. See REG-130477-00, REG-130481-00, 66 Fed. Reg. 3928 (January 17, 2001).

If an amount distributed from a tax sheltered annuity is less than the required minimum distribution, an excise tax equal to 50% of the shortfall is generally levied against the individual (not the plan). IRC Sec. 4974; see Q 347. However, the tax may be waived if the payee establishes to the satisfaction of the IRS that the shortfall was due to reasonable error, and that reasonable steps are being taken to remedy the shortfall. Treas. Reg. §54.4974-2, A-7(a). Generally, the excise tax will be waived automatically in the case of a beneficiary who receives the entire benefit to which he is entitled under the 5-year rule. Treas. Reg. §54.4974-2, A-7(b).

The minimum distribution requirements will not be treated as violated and, thus, the 50% excise tax will not apply where a shortfall occurs because assets are invested in a contract issued by an insurance company in state insurer delinquency proceedings. To the extent that a distribution otherwise required under IRC Section 401(a)(9) is not made during the state insurer delinquency proceedings, this amount and any additional amount accrued during this period will be treated as though it is not vested. Treas. Reg. §1.401(a)(9)-8, A-8. *ASRS, Sec. 61, ¶135.3(b)*.

487. What minimum distributions must be made from a tax sheltered annuity during the life of the participant under Section 401(a)(9)?

If the post-1986 account balance is not totally distributed to the participant by his *required beginning date* (see below), distributions of the balance must begin by that date and must, at a minimum, be distributed over one of the following periods: the life of the participant, the lives of the participant and his beneficiary, or a period not extending beyond the life expectancy of the participant or the life expectancy of the participant and a designated beneficiary. IRC Secs. 403(b)(10), 401(a)(9). If the issuer or custodian of the account does not keep adequate records to distinguish between pre-1987 and post-1986 balances, the entire account will be treated as subject to IRC Section 401(a)(9). Treas. Reg. §1.403(b)-3, A-2(b); Prop. Treas. Reg. §1.403(b)-6(e)(6)(ii).

The minimum distribution requirements include the rules prescribed by the IRS and Treasury for meeting the Code's requirements in final regulations issued in 2002. See TD 8987, 67 Fed. Reg. 18988 (4-17-02). Additional regulations finalized in June, 2004, govern annuity distributions under Section 403(b) plans. See TD 9130, 2004-26 IRB 1082. Proposed regulations issued in November, 2004 would, if adopted as final, take effect for distributions after 2005. See REG-155608-02, 69 Fed. Reg. 67075 (November 16, 2004).

The IRS has stated that future regulations will provide a special effective date for the application of these requirements to governmental plans. Until that date, such plans are subject to a "reasonable, good faith interpretation" standard, and compliance with the 2002 regulations, the 2001 regulations or the 1987 regulations will be considered to meet that standard. See Rev. Proc. 2003-10, 2003-1 CB 259; Notice 2003-2, 2003-1 CB 257.

Generally, a participant's *required beginning date* is April 1 of the calendar year following the later of (a) the calendar year in which the participant attains age 70½ or (b) the calendar year in which the participant retires. IRC Sec. 401(a)(9)(C); Prop.

2006 Tax Facts on Insurance & Employee Benefits

Treas. Reg. §1.403(b)-6(e)(3). For any part of a Section 403(b) contract that is not part of a government plan or church plan, the proposed regulations state that the required beginning date for a 5% owner is April 1 of the calendar year following *the earlier of* the calendar year in which the employee reaches age 70½ or retires from employment with the employer maintaining the plan. Prop. Treas. Reg. §1.403(b)-6(e)(3).

Under the 2002 regulations (as under earlier guidance), a plan is permitted to provide that the required beginning date for *all participants* is April 1 of the calendar year following the calendar year in which the participant attains age 70½. See Treas. Reg. §1.401(a)(9)-2, A-2(e). (Governmental or church plan participants are permitted under the Code to delay distributions until April 1 of the calendar year following the later of the year in which the participant retires or turns 70½; consequently, this provision is not applicable to them. IRC Sec. 401(a)(9)(C).)

The distribution for the calendar year the participant becomes age 70½ (or retires, if applicable) must be made by April 1 of the following calendar year. The distribution for each calendar year after the year the participant becomes 70½ (or retires, as applicable) must be made by December 31 of that year. Thus, it is possible that the distributions for the calendar year in which the participant becomes 70½, or retires, and the following calendar year will be made in the same calendar year.

Nonannuity payments. Under the 2002 regulations, if the distributions are not made as annuity payments under an annuity contract, the account balance is distributed according to a *uniform lifetime table*, set forth below. Treas. Reg. §1.401(a)(9)-9, A-2. The minimum required to be distributed each year is determined by dividing the post-1986 account balance as of the end of the preceding year by the applicable distribution period of the participant as follows:

Uniform Lifetime Table

Age of Employee	Distribution Period	Age of Employee	Distribution Period	Age of Employee	Distribution Period
70	27.4	86	14.1	101	5.9
71	26.5	87	13.4	102	5.5
72	25.6	88	12.7	103	5.2
73	24.7	89	12.0	104	4.9
74	23.8	90	11.4	105	4.5
75	22.9	91	10.8	106	4.2
76	22.0	92	10.2	107	3.9
77	21.2	93	9.6	108	3.7
78	20.3	94	9.1	109	3.4
79	19.5	95	8.6	110	3.1
80	18.7	96	8.1	111	2.9
81	17.9	97	7.6	112	2.6
82	17.1	98	7.1	113	2.4
83	16.3	99	6.7	114	2.1
84	15.5	100	6.3	115	1.9
85	14.8				

For an example of a calculation under this method, see Q 234. The amount of an individual's lifetime required distribution is calculated without regard to the beneficiary's age, except in the case of a spouse beneficiary who is more than 10 years younger than the participant. Treas. Reg. §1.401(a)(9)-5, A-4.

TAX SHELTERED ANNUITIES   Q 487

If the sole designated beneficiary is the participant's spouse, the distribution period during the participant's lifetime is the longer of (a) the uniform lifetime table, above, or (b) the joint and survivor life expectancy of the participant and spouse using their attained ages in the distribution calendar year. Treas. Reg. §1.401(a)(9)-5, A-4(b). See Appendix F for the joint and survivor life expectancy table set forth in the 2002 final regulations (Treas Reg. §1.401(a)(9)-9, A-3). As a practical matter, the joint and survivor life expectancy table will produce a longer (and thus, lower) payout only if the spouse beneficiary is more than 10 years younger than the participant.

Account balance. For purposes of calculating minimum distributions, the account balance is determined as of the last valuation date in the immediately preceding calendar year (i.e., the valuation calendar year). Treas. Reg. §1.401(a)(9)-5, A-3(a). Distributions in excess of the amount required in one year may not be used to reduce the amount required in subsequent years. Treas. Reg. §1.401(a)(9)-5, A-2.

Payments under annuity contract. Regulations finalized under Section 401(a)(9) in June, 2004, govern annuity distributions under Section 403(b) plans. See TD 9130, 2004-26 IRB 1082. Under those regulations, annuity distributions must be periodic payments made at least annually, for a life (or lives), or over a period certain not longer than a life expectancy (or joint and survivor life expectancy) of the participant (or the participant and a beneficiary), as set forth in the Code's provisions for lifetime and after death distributions. Treas. Regs. §§1.401(a)(9)-6, A-1(a); 1.401(a)(9)-6, A-3; IRC Sec. 401(a)(9)(A); see Q 342 for details. The annuity may also be a life annuity with a period certain, so long as the life (or lives) and period certain each meet the foregoing requirements. Treas. Reg. §1.401(a)(9)-6, A-1(b). The distribution of an annuity contract is not a distribution for purposes of meeting the required minimum distribution requirements of IRC Section 401(a)(9). Treas. Reg. §1.401(a)(9)-8, A-10.

Commencement of distributions. Distributions from an annuity contract must begin on or before the participant's required beginning date. The first payment must be the payment that is required for one payment interval. The regulations state that the second payment need not be made until the end of the next payment interval, even if the interval ends in the next calendar year. (Examples of payment intervals include monthly, bimonthly, semi-annually and annually.) Treas. Reg. §1.401(a)(9)-6, A-1(c). All benefit accruals as of the last day of the first distribution calendar year must be included in the calculation of the amount of the life annuity payments for payment intervals ending on or after the participant's required beginning date. Treas. Reg. §1.401(a)(9)-6, A-1(c)(1).

Exceptions to nonincreasing annuity requirement. Except as otherwise provided (see below) annuity payments must be nonincreasing, or increase only in accordance with: (1) an annual percentage not exceeding that of an eligible cost-of-living index (e.g., one issued by the Bureau of Labor Statistics, or certain others defined in the regulations) (2) a percentage increase that occurs at specified times (e.g., at specified ages) and does not exceed the cumulative total of annual percentage increases in an eligible cost of living index (see (1)) since the annuity starting date; (3) increases to the extent of the reduction in the amount of the employee's payments to provide for a survivor benefit upon death (if the beneficiary dies or is no longer subject to a QDRO—see Q 349), (4) increases that result from a plan amendment; or (5) increases to allow a beneficiary to convert the survivor portion of a joint and survivor annuity into a single sum distribution upon the employee's death. See Treas. Reg. §1.401(a)(9)-6, A-14(a).

2006 Tax Facts on Insurance & Employee Benefits

Additional permitted increases for annuity contracts purchased from insurance companies. If the total future expected payments from an annuity purchased from an insurance company exceed the total value being annuitized, payments under the annuity will not fail to satisfy the nonincreasing payment requirement merely because the payments are increased in accordance with one or more of the following: (1) by a constant percentage, applied not less frequently than annually; (2) to provide a final payment upon the employee's death that does not exceed the excess of the total value being annuitized over the total of payments before the death of the employee; (3) as a result of dividend payments or other payments resulting from certain actuarial gains; and (4) an acceleration of payments under the annuity (as defined in the regulations). See Treas. Regs. §§1.401(a)(9)-6, A-14(c), 1.401(a)(9)-6, A-14(e).

Period certain limitations. Generally, the period certain for annuity distributions commencing during the life of a participant, with an annuity starting date on or after the required beginning date, may not exceed the "Uniform Lifetime Table" explained above. However, if a participant's spouse is the sole beneficiary as of the annuity starting date, and the annuity provides only a period certain and no life annuity the period certain may be as long as the joint and survivor life expectancy of the participant and spouse, based on their ages as of their birthdays in the calendar year that contains the annuity starting date. Treas. Reg. §1.401(a)(9)-6, A-3(a).

The IRS privately ruled under the 1987 regulations that an IRC Section 403(b) annuity contract that offered a settlement option under which the retirement benefit payment was determined in accordance with the individual account rules (i.e., the nonannuity payments rule, above) and provided for nonlevel retirement income benefits satisfied the minimum distribution rules. Let. Rul. 9128035.

Designated beneficiary. A "designated beneficiary" means any individual designated as a beneficiary by the participant. IRC Sec. 401(a)(9)(E). However, under the 2002 final regulations, a participant's designated beneficiary is determined based on the beneficiaries designated as of *September 30* of the calendar year following the year of the participant's death. Treas. Reg. §1.401(a)(9)-4, A-4(a). Thus, for example, a beneficiary who disclaims his interest after the death of the participant but before the September 30 deadline would not be a considered a beneficiary for this purpose. Exceptions apply if the account is payable as an annuity, or if a surviving spouse beneficiary dies after the participant but before distributions have begun. See Q 344 for details.

Under the 2002 final regulations, a beneficiary designated as such under the plan is an *individual* (or certain trusts, see Q 344) who is entitled to a portion of a participant's benefit, contingent on the participant's death or another specified event. A designated beneficiary need not be specified by name in the plan or by the participant to the plan in order to be a designated beneficiary so long as the individual who is to be the beneficiary is identifiable under the plan as of the date the beneficiary is determined.

The 2002 final regulations state that an individual may be designated as a beneficiary under the plan either by the terms of the plan or, if the plan so provides, by an affirmative election by the participant (or the participant's surviving spouse) specifying the beneficiary. Treas. Reg. §1.401(a)(9)-4, A-1. The fact that a participant's interest under the plan passes to a certain individual under applicable state law, however, does not make that individual a designated beneficiary unless the individual is designated as a beneficiary under the plan. Treas. Reg. §1.401(a)(9)-4, A-1. *ASRS, Sec. 61, ¶135.3(b)(1).*

488. What are the requirements of the minimum distribution incidental benefit rule with respect to tax sheltered annuities?

The minimum distribution incidental benefit (or MDIB) requirement constitutes a second set of minimum distribution rules that must be considered in determining the minimum amount required to be distributed during the participant's lifetime. See IRC Sec. 403(b)(10); Treas. Reg. §1.401-1(b)(1)(i). The MDIB rules apply to the pre-1987 account balance as well as the post-1986 balance. The reason they apply to the pre-1987 account balance, while the minimum distribution rules under IRC Section 401(a)(9) do not, is that unlike those requirements, the incidental benefit rule existed in regulations for many years before it was enacted into the Code in 1986, and amounts accumulated before 1987 were subject to its requirements. Regulations under IRC Section 403(b) required that the death benefit under a tax sheltered annuity be merely incidental to its primary purpose of providing retirement benefits.

In November, 2004, regulations under Section 403(b) were proposed which briefly addressed the application of the older MDIB rule. These regulations do not take effect until after 2005, if finalized, and may not be relied upon until they become final. See REG-155608-02, 69 Fed. Reg. 67075 (November 16, 2004). However, they generally restated rules contained in early regulations, to the effect that the post-1986 balance is subject to the IRC Section 401(a)(9) regulations and that both the pre-1987 balance and the post-1986 balance are subject to the MDIB rule. Treas. Reg. §1.403(b)-3, A-2, A-3; Prop. Treas. Reg. §1.403(b)-6(e)(6). See Q 486 for details.

The proposed (2004) regulations do not interpret the old MDIB rule, but describe two ways it can be satisfied. First, distributions attributable to the pre-1987 account balance are treated as satisfying the MDIB requirement if all distributions from the Section 403(b) contract (including distributions attributable to the post-1986 account balance) satisfy the requirements of Treasury Regulation §1.401-1(b)(1)(i) (which the regulations cite as authority for the "old" MDIB rule) without regard to distributions under the 2002 regulations, *and* distributions from the post-1986 account satisfy the requirements of IRC Section 401(a)(9). Treas. Reg. §1.403(b)-3, A-3; Prop. Treas. Reg. §1.403(b)-6(e)(6)(vi).

Second, and in the alternative, distributions attributable to the pre-1987 account will be treated as satisfying the MDIB requirement if all distributions from the contract (whether pre-1987 or post-1986 amounts) satisfy the regulations under IRC Section 401(a)(9). Treas. Reg. §1.403(b)-3, A-3; Prop. Treas. Reg. §1.403(b)-6(e)(6)(vi).

Under much earlier rulings, the old rule was generally interpreted as requiring a distribution arrangement under which the present value of the aggregate payments to be made to the participant must be more than 50% of the present value of the total payments to be made to the participant and his beneficiaries. Rev. Rul. 72-241, 1972-1 CB 108; Rev. Rul. 73-239, 1973-1 CB 201; see also Let. Ruls. 8642072, 7843043, 7825010. Generally, the old rules required that distributions commence by age 75. See Let. Ruls. 9345044, 7825010. It would appear that the old rules may continue to apply in determining distributions required from the pre-1987 balance. See Let. Rul. 9345044. (Of course, nothing would prevent a participant from choosing to apply the Section 401(a)(9) rules. See Treas. Reg. §1.403(b)-3, A-3; Prop. Treas. Reg. §1.403(b)-6(e)(6)(vi).

Nonannuity distributions. The final 2002 regulations state that if distributions are made in accordance with the individual account rules set forth therein (see Q 488), the MDIB requirement will be satisfied. Treas. Reg. §1.401(a)(9)-5, A-1(d).

Annuity Distributions

If the participant's benefit is payable in the form of a life annuity for the life of the participant that satisfies the requirements of IRC Section 401(a)(9), the MDIB requirement will be satisfied. Treas. Reg. §1.401(a)(9)-6, A-2(a). If the participant's sole beneficiary as of the annuity starting date is the participant's spouse, and the distributions satisfy IRC Section 401(a)(9), the MDIB requirement will be satisfied. Treas. Reg. §1.401(a)(9)-6, A-2(b). But payments under the annuity must be nonincreasing, except as explained at Q 487. See Rev. Proc. 2003-10, 2003-1 CB 259; Notice 2003-2, 2003-1 CB 257.

If distributions begin under a particular distribution option that is in the form of a joint and survivor annuity for the joint lives of the participant and a nonspouse beneficiary, the MDIB requirement will *not* be satisfied as of the date distributions begin unless the distribution option provides that annuity payments to be made to the participant on and after his required beginning date will satisfy the conditions set forth in Treas. Reg. §1.401(a)(9)-6, A-2(c). Under those provisions, the periodic annuity payment payable to the survivor must not at any time on and after the participant's required beginning date exceed the applicable percentage of the annuity payment payable to the participant using the following table:

Excess of Participant's Age over Beneficiary's Age	Applicable Percentage	Excess of Participant's Age over Beneficiary's Age	Applicable Percentage	Excess of Participant's Age over Beneficiary's Age	Applicable Percentage
10 or less	100	22	70	34	57
11	96	23	68	35	56
12	93	24	67	36	56
13	90	25	66	37	55
14	87	26	64	38	55
15	84	27	63	39	54
16	82	28	62	40	54
17	79	29	61	41	53
18	77	30	60	42	53
19	75	31	59	43	53
20	73	32	59	44 and greater	52
21	72	33	58		

Treas. Reg. §1.401(a)(9)-6, A-2(c)(2). The applicable percentage is based on how much older the participant is than the beneficiary as of their attained ages on their birthdays in the first calendar year for which distributions to the participant are required. For example, if the beneficiary is 10 or fewer years younger, the survivor annuity may be 100%. If the age difference is greater than 10 years, the maximum survivor annuity permitted is less than 100%. If there is more than one beneficiary, the age of the youngest beneficiary is used. Treas. Reg. §1.401(a)(9)-6, A-2(c)(1).

If a distribution form includes a life annuity and a period certain, the amount of the annuity payments payable to the beneficiary need not be reduced during the period certain, but in the case of a joint and survivor annuity with a period certain, the amount of the annuity payments payable to the beneficiary must satisfy the foregoing requirements *after* the expiration of the period certain. Treas. Reg. §1.401(a)(9)-6, A-2(d).

Period certain limitations. The period certain for annuity distributions commencing during the life of the participant with an annuity starting date on or after his required

TAX SHELTERED ANNUITIES   Q 489

beginning date generally may not exceed the applicable distribution period for the participant (see Q 487) for the calendar year that contains the annuity starting date. However, if the participant's spouse is his sole beneficiary, and the annuity provides only a period certain and no life annuity, the period certain may last as long as the joint and survivor life expectancy of the participant and spouse, if that period is longer than the applicable distribution period for the participant. Treas. Reg. §1.401(a)(9)-6, A-3(a). If distributions commence after the death of the participant under the life expectancy rule explained in Q 343, the period certain for any distributions commencing after death cannot exceed the distribution period determined under the life expectancy provisions of Treas. Reg. §1.401(a)(9)-5, A-5(b).

Application of penalty. If the amount required to be distributed under the MDIB requirements exceeds the amount required under the regular minimum distribution rules (see Q 339 to Q 345), the shortfall is subject to a 50% excise tax (levied on the individual, not the plan). See IRC Sec. 4974. For details, see Q 347. *ASRS, Sec. 61, ¶135.3(b)(2)*

489. How are the minimum distribution requirements met after the death of a tax sheltered annuity participant?

A tax sheltered annuity must satisfy the requirements set forth in IRC Section 401(a)(9) for qualified plans, with respect to minimum distributions. IRC Sec. 403(b)(10). Most of the requirements were explained in final regulations published in April 2002. See TD 8987, 67 Fed. Reg. 18988 (4-17-02). However, regulations governing annuity payouts from defined benefit plans were finalized in June, 2004 (see Q 487 and Q 342), and proposed regulations addressing additional matters were issued under Section 403(b) in November, 2004. See REG-155608-02, 69 Fed. Reg. 67075 (November 16, 2004).

The final 2002 regulations simplified the calculation process and included longer life expectancy tables (see Appendix F). The Preamble to the regulations stated that the final regulations apply for determining required minimum distributions for calendar years beginning on or after January 1, 2003; however, governmental plans may be subject to a later effective date. See Rev. Proc. 2003-10, 2003-1 CB 259; Notice 2003-2, 2003-1 CB 257; see Q 342, Q 487.

After the death of a tax sheltered annuity participant, the application of the minimum distribution requirements depends on whether he died before or after his required beginning date. Generally, for this purpose, distributions are treated as having begun in accordance with the minimum distribution requirements under IRC Section 401(a)(9)(A)(ii), without regard to whether payments have been made before that date. Treas. Reg. §1.401(a)(9)-2, A-6(a). However, if distributions *irrevocably* (except for acceleration) began prior to the required beginning date in the form of an annuity that meets the minimum distribution rules, the annuity starting date will be treated as the required beginning date for purposes of calculating lifetime and after death minimum distribution requirements. Treas. Reg. §1.401(a)(9)-6, A-10, A-11.

Death Before Required Beginning Date

If a participant dies *before* his required beginning date, distributions must be made under one of two methods:

(1) *Five year rule*: the entire interest must be distributed within five years after the death of the participant (regardless of who or what entity receives the distribution). IRC

Sec. 401(a)(9)(B)(ii), Treas. Reg. §1.401(a)(9)-3, A-1(a). In order to satisfy this rule, the entire interest must be distributed by the end of the calendar year that contains the fifth anniversary of the date of the participant's death. Treas. Reg. §1.401(a)(9)-3, A-2.

(2) *Life expectancy rule:* if any portion of the interest is payable to, or for the benefit of, a designated beneficiary, that portion must be distributed over the life (or life expectancy) of the beneficiary, beginning within one year of the participant's death. IRC Sec. 401(a)(9)(B)(iii); Treas. Reg. §1.401(a)(9)-3, A-1(a).

To the extent that the interest is payable to a *nonspouse beneficiary*, distributions must begin by the end of the calendar year immediately following the calendar year in which the participant died. Treas. Reg. §1.401(a)(9)-3, A-3(a). The nonspouse beneficiary's life expectancy for this purpose is measured as of his birthday in the year following the year of the participant's death. In subsequent years, this amount is reduced by one for each calendar year that has elapsed since the year immediately following the year of the participant's death. See Treas. Reg. §1.401(a)(9)-5, A-5(c)(1).

If the sole designated beneficiary is the participant's *surviving spouse*, distributions must begin by the later of (i) the end of the calendar year immediately following the calendar year in which the participant died, or (ii) the end of the calendar year in which the participant would have reached age 70½. See IRC Sec. 401(a)(9)(B)(iv); Treas. Reg. §1.401(a)(9)-3, A-3(b). The payout period during the surviving spouse's life is measured by the surviving spouse's life expectancy as of his or her birthday in each distribution calendar year for which a minimum distribution is required after the year of the participant's death. Treas. Reg. §1.401(a)(9)-5, A-5(c)(2). After the surviving spouse's death, the distribution period is based on his or her remaining life expectancy. This is determined using the age of the surviving spouse in the calendar year of his or her death, reduced by one for each calendar year that has elapsed after the calendar year of the surviving spouse's death. See Treas. Reg. §1.401(a)(9)-5, A-5(c)(2).

The 2002 final regulations set forth tables containing single and joint and survivor life expectancies for calculating required minimum distributions, as well as a "Uniform Lifetime Table" for determining the appropriate distribution periods. See Q 487; Treas. Reg. §1.401(a)(9)-9; Appendix F.

Unless a plan adopts a provision specifying otherwise, if distributions to a participant have not begun prior to his death, they must be made automatically either under the life expectancy rule described above, or, if there is no designated beneficiary, under the 5-year rule. Treas. Regs. §§1.401(a)(9)-1, A-3(c), 1.401(a)(9)-3, A-4(a). A plan may adopt a provision specifying that the 5-year rule will apply after the death of a participant, or a provision allowing participants (or beneficiaries) to elect whether the 5-year rule or the life expectancy rule will be applied. Treas. Regs. §§1.401(a)(9)-3, A-4(b), 1.401(a)(9)-3, A-4(c).

Death on or After Required Beginning Date

If the participant dies *on or after* the date distributions have begun (i.e., generally on or after his required beginning date), but before his entire interest in the plan has been distributed, the Code states that the entire remaining balance must generally be distributed at least as rapidly as under the method of distribution in effect as of the participant's date of death. See IRC Sec. 401(a)(9)(B)(i). Generally, this method of distribution will depend on whether the distribution was in the form of distributions from an individual account or annuity payments. See Treas. Reg. §1.401(a)(9)-2, A-5.

TAX SHELTERED ANNUITIES   Q 489

Under the 2002 regulations, a beneficiary determination is made as of *September 30* of the year after the year of the participant's death. Treas. Reg. §1.401(a)(9)-4, A-4(a). If the participant does not have a "designated beneficiary" (see below) as of that date, his interest is distributed over his remaining life expectancy, using the age of the participant in the calendar year of his death, reduced by one for each calendar year that elapses thereafter. See Treas. Reg. §1.401(a)(9)-5, A-5(c)(3). If the participant *does* have a designated beneficiary as of the determination date, the beneficiary's interest is distributed over the longer of (i) the beneficiary's life expectancy, calculated as described above at "Life Expectancy Rule" (i.e., under Treas. Reg. §1.401(a)(9)-5, A-5(c)(1) or (2)) *or* (ii) the remaining life expectancy of the participant, determined using the age of the participant in the calendar year of his death, reduced by one for each calendar year that elapses thereafter (i.e., under Treas. Reg. §1.401(a)(9)-5, A-5(c)(3)). Treas. Reg. §1.401(a)(9)-5, A-5(a)(1).

Designated Beneficiary

In order to be a designated beneficiary, an individual must be a beneficiary on the date of the participant's death. However, the determination of the existence and identity of a designated beneficiary for purposes of minimum distributions is made on September 30 of the calendar year following the year of the participant's death. Treas. Reg. §1.401(a)(9)-4, A-4(a). (Exceptions may apply if the account is payable as an annuity, or if a surviving spouse beneficiary dies after the participant but before distributions have begun.) This is in order that a distribution may be calculated and made by the deadline of December 31 following the year of the participant's death. Consequently, an individual who was a beneficiary as of the date of the participant's death, but is not a beneficiary as of September 30 of the following year (e.g., because he disclaims entitlement to the benefit or because he receives the entire benefit to which he is entitled before that date) is not taken into account for purposes of determining the distribution period for required minimum distributions after the participant's death. Treas. Reg. §1.401(a)(9)-4, A-4(a).

Under the 2002 final regulations, special rules apply if more than one beneficiary is designated as of the date on which the determination is made. Generally, the beneficiary with the shortest life expectancy will be the designated beneficiary for purposes of determining the distribution period. Treas. Reg. §1.401(a)(9)-5, A-7(a).

If a surviving spouse beneficiary dies after the participant, but before distributions to the spouse have begun, the 5-year rule and the life expectancy rule described above for surviving spouses will be applied as though the surviving spouse were the participant. See IRC Sec. 401(a)(9)(B)(iv)(II); Treas. Reg. §1.401(a)(9)-3, A-5. However, this provision will not allow a new spouse of the deceased participant's surviving spouse to delay distributions under the surviving spouse rules of IRC Section 401(a)(9)(B)(iv). Treas. Reg. §1.401(a)(9)-3, A-5.

Proposed regulations issued in November, 2004 would provide that the special rule allowing surviving spouse to treat an IRA interest as the spouse's own (see Treas. Reg. §1.408-8, A-5) does not apply to a Section 403(b) contract, even if the spouse is the sole beneficiary. See Prop. Treas. Reg. §1.403(b)-6(e)(4).

If the beneficiary is not an individual or a permitted trust (see Q 344), the participant will be treated as having no beneficiary. A participant's estate may not be a designated beneficiary. Treas. Reg. §1.401(a)(9)-4, A-3. *ASRS, Sec. 61, ¶135.3(b)(1).*

2006 Tax Facts on Insurance & Employee Benefits

Taxation of Benefits

490. Are the payments received under a tax sheltered annuity taxable income to the employee?

Yes, except to the extent the amounts are a recovery of the employee's investment in the contract or to the extent he rolls over an eligible distribution to another tax sheltered annuity, a qualified retirement plan, an eligible governmental 457 plan, or a traditional individual retirement plan (see Q 451).

Where an annuity contract (without life insurance protection) is used for funding, all payments received are normally taxable in full as ordinary income to the employee. This is the result regardless of whether premiums were paid by the employer as additional compensation to the employee, were derived from a reduction in the employee's salary, or were paid in part by deductible voluntary employee contributions. Since premiums derived from salary reduction have not been previously taxed to the employee (where they have come within the overall limit), they cannot be treated as a cost basis for the contract. IRC Sec. 403(b)(1).

In some instances, however, the employee will have a cost basis for the contract. An employee's cost basis consists of any nondeductible premiums he has paid and any portion of the premiums paid by his employer on which he has paid tax, except that excess salary reduction amounts not distributed from the plan by April 15 of the year following the contribution are not included in basis even though they were included in income (see Q 473). Where a life insurance policy is used (see Q 465 for the new restrictions under the proposed regulations), the sum of the annual 1-year term costs that have been taxed to the employee are included in his cost basis. Rev. Rul. 68-304, 1968-1 CB 179. (See Q 481 regarding the proper measure of the value of current life insurance protection.) Likewise, any portion of the employer's premiums that have been included in the employee's gross income because they exceeded his overall limit are included in his cost basis (see Q 469). The amount of any policy loans included in income as a taxable distribution (see Q 483) would also constitute part of the employee's cost basis. His basis should also include amounts attributable to deductible employee contributions that were included in his income as constructive distributions, such as life insurance premiums or amounts pledged (see Q 425 and Q 420).

Once a loan is deemed distributed under IRC Section 72(p), the interest that accrues thereafter on that loan is not included in income (i.e., for purposes of determining the amount that is taxable under IRC Section 72). In addition, neither the income that results from the deemed distribution nor the interest that accrues thereafter increases the participant's investment in the contract (i.e., his tax basis) under IRC Section 72. To the extent that a participant repays by cash any portion of a loan that has been deemed distributed, he does acquire a tax basis in the contract in the same manner as if the repayments were after-tax contributions. See Treas. Regs. §§1.72(p)-1, A-19(a), 1.72(p)-1, A-21(a).

If the employee takes the maturity values in a one lump sum cash payment, the full amount received will be ordinary income to him in the year of receipt unless he has a cost basis (except as provided in Q 478, Q 479). If he has a cost basis, the amount in excess of the cost basis will be ordinary income. IRC Sec. 72(e)(5). Likewise, if the employee surrenders his contract before it matures, all amounts received in excess of his cost basis (if any) will be taxable as ordinary income.

TAX SHELTERED ANNUITIES   Q 490

Amounts received before the annuity starting date (i.e., an in-service distribution) by an employee who has a cost basis are taxed under a rule that provides for pro rata recovery of cost. IRC Sec. 72(e)(8). The employee excludes that portion of the distribution that bears the same ratio to the total distribution as his investment in the contract bears to the total value of the employee's accrued benefit as of the date of the distribution. (Amounts received prior to July 2, 1986 were taxed under a "cost recovery" rule permitting recovery of basis before taxing any of the distribution as interest. IRC Sec. 72(e)(5)(D).) The "annuity starting date" is the first day of the first period for which an amount is received as an annuity under the contract (see Q 10). IRC Sec. 72(c)(4). If a plan on May 5, 1986 permitted in-service withdrawal of employee contributions, the pro rata recovery rules do not apply to investment in the contract prior to 1987. Instead, investment in the contract prior to 1987 will be recovered first, and the pro rata recovery rules will apply only to the extent that amounts received before the annuity starting date (when added to all other amounts previously received under the contract after 1986) exceed the employee's investment in the contract as of December 31, 1986. IRC Sec. 72(e)(8)(D).

If an employee who has a cost basis for his contract receives life annuity or installment payments, the payments are taxed as discussed in Q 433, depending on his annuity starting date.

An employee who terminates his employment may wish to continue to pay the premiums rather than surrender the contract or take a paid-up annuity. The premiums he pays thereafter will be nondeductible, included in his cost basis and can be recovered tax free from the annuity payments. If the employee goes to work for another eligible employer, he can continue to use his existing contract. Rev. Rul. 66-254, 1966-2 CB 125. However, his annual maximum contribution thereafter will be based entirely upon his service with the new employer. If he elects an extended term option, he will be taxed on the policy reserve in the taxable year the option is elected. Rev. Rul. 68-648, 1968-2 CB 49.

Where the 403(b) annuity contract or custodial account is solely liable for the payment of investment expenses, the direct payment of investment advisor fees from a participant's annuity or account is not treated as a distribution. Let. Ruls. 9332040, 9316042, 9047073. Likewise, where an annuity contract consists of different subaccounts for which a financial advisor provides asset allocation advice, if the annuity contract expenses are assessed directly against the contract value itself, those payments are then expenses of the contract itself and are, therefore, not distributions from the contract includable in the annuity contract owner's gross income. Furthermore, assessing expenses against a contract in this manner does not cause the contract to lose its qualified status under IRC Section 403(b). Let. Rul. 9845003.

Withholding

With respect to distributions other than eligible rollover distributions (see Q 451), amounts will be withheld from annuity (periodic) payments at the rates applicable to wage payments and from other distributions at a 10% rate. The employee may elect not to have income tax withheld from these payments. Tax will not be withheld on amounts distributed that it is reasonable to believe will not be includable in income. IRC Sec. 3405; Temp. Treas. Reg. §35.3405-1, A-20.

Generally, any eligible rollover distribution made after December 31, 1992 is subject to mandatory income tax withholding at the rate of 20% unless the distributee elects to have the distribution paid by means of a direct rollover. IRC Sec. 3405(c); Treas. Reg. §31.3405(c)-1, A-1(a). This mandatory withholding applies even if the employee's employment terminated prior to January 1, 1993 and even if the eligible rollover distribution is part of a series of payments that began before January 1, 1993. Treas. Reg. §31.3405(c)-1, A-1(c)(1)(i). For distributions after 1992 but before October 19, 1995, slightly different rules may be applicable under temporary regulations (see Q 446). *ASRS, Sec. 61, ¶200.*

491. How is a death benefit under a tax sheltered annuity taxed to the employee's beneficiary?

In general, a death benefit under a tax sheltered annuity is taxed in the same manner as a death benefit under a qualified pension or profit sharing plan, except that there is no special treatment for a lump sum payment (see Q 437 to Q 439). In the case of a *single sum payment where no life insurance is involved,* all amounts received by the beneficiary are taxable as ordinary income except that the beneficiary may exclude from gross income the employee's unrecovered cost basis, if any. *If the death benefit consists of life insurance proceeds,* the amount of the proceeds in excess of the cash surrender value of the policy immediately before the insured's death is excludable from gross income under IRC Section 101(a)(1). (*Editor's Note*: For the rule under the proposed regulations restricting the availability of life insurance in 403(b) arrangements, see Q 465.) The cash surrender value is taxable as ordinary income to the extent that it exceeds the portion of the premiums taxed to the employee as being the cost of life insurance protection (see Q 481 regarding the proper measure of the value of current life insurance protection), and any other unrecovered cost basis of the employee. IRC Secs. 403(c), 72(m)(3)(C); Treas. Reg. §1.72-16(c).

Withholding

With respect to distributions other than eligible rollover distributions (see Q 451), payments to a surviving spouse or beneficiary are subject to income tax withholding unless the spouse or beneficiary elects not to have withholding apply. Amounts need not be withheld on any part of the distribution that it is reasonable to believe is not includable in gross income. Annuity payments are subject to withholding at the rate applicable to wages; other payments are subject to withholding at a 10% rate. IRC Sec. 3405; Temp. Treas. Regs. §§35.3405-1, A-17; 35.3405-1, A-28. In the case of an eligible rollover distribution, a surviving spouse or other beneficiary is subject to the same mandatory withholding rules as the employee (see Q 490). *ASRS, Sec. 61, ¶230.*

SOCIAL SECURITY AND WITHHOLDING TAXES

492. How is a reduction in salary for a tax sheltered annuity treated for Social Security tax and income tax withholding purposes?

Excludable amounts paid into a tax sheltered annuity are not "wages" subject to *income tax* withholding, even if the amounts are derived from a salary reduction agreement. Rev. Rul. 65-208, 1965-2 CB 414.

The amount of salary reduction used for premium payments is subject to *Social Security taxes* even though it is excludable from the employee's gross income; but if the employer uses non-salary reduction funds for the premium payments, such payments are not includable in "wages" for Social Security purposes. IRC Sec. 3121(a)(5); Rev.

TAX SHELTERED ANNUITIES Q 493

Rul. 65-208, 1965-2 CB 383; Rev. Rul. 181, 1953-2 CB 111. See also CCA 200333003; TAM 200305006; Let. Ruls. 200318074, 200234009, 200210014.

"Salary reduction agreement" means a plan or arrangement under which payment will be made by an employer on behalf of an employee under or to an annuity contract: (1) if the employee elects to reduce his compensation under a cash or deferred election; (2) if the employee elects to reduce his or her compensation pursuant to a one-time irrevocable election made at or before the time of initial eligibility to participate in such plan or arrangement; *or* (3) if the employee agrees as a condition of employment to make a contribution that reduces his compensation. Temp. Treas. Reg. §31.3121(a)(5)-2T.

Apparently, amounts contributed by salary reduction by a minister (or by church employees whose organizations have chosen to be exempt from FICA) are not treated as wages subject to Social Security taxes to the extent the contributions are not more than the employer contribution limit. See IRS Pub. No.517.

Amounts of salary reduction treated as "wages" for Social Security tax are creditable to the individual's Social Security account for benefit purposes. SSR 64-59. *ASRS, Sec. 61, ¶¶400, 410.*

EXCISE TAXES

493. What excise taxes and additional taxes apply to tax sheltered annuity contributions and distributions?

Excess contributions to custodial accounts. Contributions to a custodial account for the purchase of regulated investment company stock (and to a retirement income account to the extent funded through custodial accounts) are subject to a tax of 6% (not to exceed 6% of the value of the account) on (1) the amount by which the contributions (other than a permissible rollover contribution—see Q 451) exceed the lesser of the amount excludable from gross income under IRC Section 403(b) or the overall limitation under IRC Section 415 (or, whichever is applicable if only one is applicable), *plus* (2) any such excess carried over from the preceding tax year (see Q 475). IRC Sec. 4973; Sec. V(E)(1) of the final tax sheltered annuity audit guidelines, *reprinted in* ASRS, Sec. 61, ¶440.2.

Early (premature) distributions. If a taxpayer receives a premature distribution from a tax sheltered annuity, his tax will be increased by 10% of the portion of the distribution includable in income. IRC Sec. 72(t). Distributions subject to this penalty are described in Q 485.

Excess accumulations. If the amount distributed during a tax year is less than the minimum required distribution for the year, there is generally a tax equal to 50% of the amount that the distribution made in the year falls short of the required amount. The tax is on the payee (see Q 486). IRC Sec. 4974.

Excess aggregate contributions (excess matching employer contributions). If an employee makes after-tax contributions or the employer makes contributions that match contributions under an employee's salary reduction agreement or match employee after-tax contributions and the aggregate amount of such contributions exceeds the nondiscriminatory amount explained in Q 405, a tax of 10% of the amount in excess of the permitted (nondiscriminatory) maximum is imposed on the employer to the extent the excess amount (and income attributable to it) is not distributed within 2½ months after the end of the plan year. IRC Sec. 4979; see Q 406. *ASRS, Sec. 61, ¶190.*

2006 Tax Facts on Insurance & Employee Benefits 623

WELFARE BENEFIT FUNDS

General

494. May an employer make deductible contributions to a welfare benefit fund to provide medical, disability and life insurance benefits (including postretirement medical and death benefits) for employees and independent contractors?

The deduction of contributions paid by an employer to a fund under a plan to provide such benefits to employees and their beneficiaries is generally limited. These limitations also apply to contributions to provide benefits for independent contractors and their beneficiaries. See IRC Secs. 419(a), 419(b), 419(g).

As a general rule, the limits apply to contributions to any fund that is part of a plan (or method or arrangement having the effect of a plan) of an employer and through which the employer provides welfare benefits to employees or their beneficiaries. A "welfare benefit" is rather cryptically defined as any benefit other than one subject to the deduction rules applicable to (1) property transferred in connection with performance of services (IRC Section 83 property) and (2) qualified and nonqualified deferred compensation. Any such fund is called, for tax purposes, a "welfare benefit fund." IRC Secs. 419(e)(1), 419(e)(2).

A welfare benefit fund can be (1) any tax-exempt organization that is a voluntary employees' beneficiary association (VEBA), a trust providing for payment of supplemental unemployment compensation benefits (SUB), a qualified group legal services organization (GLSO) (the tax exemption for GLSOs is not available in taxable years beginning after June 30, 1992), or a social club, or (2) any taxable organization that is a corporation, a trust, or other organization. IRC Secs. 419(e)(3), 120(e).

Certain accounts held by an insurance company for an employer will also be considered funds. See IRC Sec. 419(e)(3)(C); TRA '86, Sec. 1851(a)(8)(B); Temp. Treas. Reg. §1.419-1T, A-3(c); Ann. 86-45, 1986-15 IRB 52.

However, amounts held by an insurance company are not considered a fund subject to the limitation if they are held pursuant to a contract that is (1) a life insurance contract covering the life of an officer, employee or any person financially interested in any trade or business carried on by the policyholder if the policyholder is directly or indirectly a beneficiary, or (2) not guaranteed renewable and the only payments (other than insurance protection) to which the employer or employees are entitled are experience-rated refunds or policy dividends that are not guaranteed and are determined by factors other than the amount of welfare benefits paid to or on behalf of employees or their beneficiaries. The experience refund or policy dividend in (2) must furthermore be treated by the employer as paid or accrued in the taxable year in which the policy year ends. IRC Sec. 419(e)(4).

An employer's ability to contribute to a welfare benefit fund with respect to certain retiree health liabilities may be limited if the employer has made a qualified transfer of excess pension assets to a 401(h) retiree health account. IRC Sec. 420(d)(2). In addition, setting assets aside in a welfare benefit fund to pay for retiree health liabilities may limit an employer's ability to make a qualified transfer of excess pension assets to a

WELFARE BENEFIT FUNDS   Q 496

401(h) retiree health account (see Q 370). IRC Sec. 420(e)(1)(B). The rules permitting transfers to 401(h) accounts apply for taxable years beginning before January 1, 2014. IRC Sec. 420(b)(5), as amended by PFEA 2004. Details of the coordination of benefits between an IRC Section 401(h) account and a VEBA have been explained by the IRS. See Let. Rul. 9834037. *ASRS, Sec. 66, ¶¶610, 620; Sec. 59, ¶475.3(b)*.

495. When is a deduction allowed for contributions to a welfare benefit fund?

Contributions paid or accrued by an employer to a welfare benefit fund will generally be deductible when paid to the fund (if they are otherwise deductible), but subject to the limitation discussed in Q 496. IRC Sec. 419(a). If the contributions paid by an employer during a taxable year exceed the deduction limitation, the excess is treated as paid to the fund in the next taxable year. IRC Sec. 419(d). *ASRS, Sec. 66, ¶620.2*.

496. What is the limit on the amount an employer may deduct for contributions to a welfare benefit fund to provide disability, medical, death and other benefits to employees and independent contractors?

Qualified Cost

An amount, otherwise deductible, contributed by an employer to a welfare benefit fund may be deducted up to the fund's "qualified cost" for the taxable year of the fund that ends with or within the employer's taxable year. IRC Secs. 419(a), 419(b); Temp. Treas. Regs. §§1.419-1T, A-1, 1.419-1T, A-4. A fund's qualified cost for any taxable year generally is its (1) "qualified direct cost" for that taxable year, *plus* (2) any additions to a "qualified asset account" for that taxable year to the extent such additions do not cause the account to exceed its "account limit" for the taxable year, *minus* (3) the fund's after-tax income for the taxable year. IRC Secs. 419(c)(1), 419(c)(2), 419A(b); Temp. Treas. Reg. §1.419-1T, A-5(a). However, the deductible amount may be further reduced by additional rules. See Temp. Treas. Reg. §1.419-1T, A-5(b).

In determining whether a company's contributions to a proposed trust to fund postretirement medical benefits for union retirees under a plan would be treated as not exceeding the trust's "qualified cost" under IRC Section 419(b) and IRC Section 419(c), and would be deductible without regard to the limits of IRC Section 419A(b) and IRC Section 419A(c), the Service determined that if the amount of the contribution satisfies the requirements of IRC Section 419, the deduction of such amount is generally not limited by IRC Section 162. However, if the contribution is such that the assets exceed the amount needed to provide postretirement benefits to all current and future retirees (from current active employees)(i.e., the present value of future benefits), then the contribution would fail to satisfy the requirements of IRC Section 162. Let. Rul. 199945066.

When the taxable year of a fund is different from the taxable year of the employer, special rules determine the deduction limit for the taxable year of the employer in which the fund is established and for the employer's next taxable year. See Temp. Treas. Reg. §1.419-1T, A-7. Special rules also require contributions made after the close of a fund's taxable year but during the employer's taxable year to be treated as an amount in the fund as of the last taxable year of the fund that relates to the taxable year of the employer. See Temp Treas. Reg. §1.419-1T, A-5(b). Accordingly, an employer with a differing tax year than its welfare benefit trust cannot accelerate its deduction for its contribution to the trust to an earlier tax year by making its contribution after the end of the trust's tax year but before the end of the employer's tax year and, therefore, prefunding the trust for benefits to be provided in the following tax year. *Square D Co. v. Comm.*, 109 TC 200 (1997).

A fund's "qualified direct cost" for a taxable year is generally the amount (including administrative expenses) a cash basis employer with the same taxable year as the fund could deduct had it provided the benefits directly instead of through an intermediary fund. Any rules limiting the deduction for benefits provided directly by the employer apply even though the benefits are provided through a fund. The benefit is considered provided in the year the benefit is includable in income by the employee (or would be includable except for Code provisions excluding the benefit from income). IRC Sec. 419(c)(3); Temp. Treas. Regs. §§1.419-1T, A-6(a), 1.419-1T, A-6(c).

A "qualified asset account" is an account consisting of assets *set aside* to provide for the payment of disability benefits, medical benefits, supplemental unemployment benefits (SUB), severance pay benefits, or life insurance benefits (including any other death benefits). IRC Sec. 419A(a). The "account limit" on a qualified asset account for a taxable year is generally the amount reasonably and actuarially necessary to fund *claims incurred but unpaid* (as of the close of the fund's taxable year) for such benefits, as well as the administrative costs with respect to those claims. IRC Sec. 419A(c)(1).

In one case, the Tax Court concluded that assets must actually be set aside for the payment of future long-term disability benefits that were incurred but unpaid; thus, an employer could not deduct contributions for such benefits where the employer had failed to accumulate the necessary assets in the VEBA trust. However, the Sixth Circuit Court of Appeals determined that the Tax Court had erroneously "interpreted the term 'set aside' in IRC Section 419A(a) as having the same meaning as the term 'reserve' in IRC Section 419A(c)(2)." The Sixth Circuit held that an employer has "set aside" assets for purposes of IRC Section 419A(a) when it has made an irrevocable contribution to a welfare benefit fund providing those benefits specified in IRC Section 419A(a). *Parker-Hannifin Corp. v. Comm.*, TC Memo 1996-337, *aff'd in part, rev'd in part*, 139 F.3d 1090 (6th Cir. 1998). In other words, "set aside" with respect to an account for disability, medical, supplemental unemployment, severance, or life insurance benefits under IRC Section 419A(a) has a different, less restrictive meaning than "reserve" as it applies to an account for postretirement medical or life insurance benefits. *Internal Revenue Service Exempt Organizations Continuing Professional Education Text for Fiscal Year 1999*, Chapter F, Voluntary Employees' Beneficiary Associations. (Apparently, the amount reasonably and actuarially necessary to fund incurred but unpaid claims in a fully insured plan is zero. See Let. Rul. 9325050.)

Under certain circumstances, the account limit may also include an amount to fund (over their working lives) postretirement medical or life insurance benefits (including any other death benefit) to be provided to covered employees. See IRC Secs. 419A(c)(2), 419A(e)(1). Such a reserve may not be included in the account limit, though, unless such a reserve is actually established and funded – that is, unless assets are actually accumulated in the fund to cover postretirement obligations. *General Signal Corp. v. Comm.*, 103 TC 216 (1994), *aff'd*, 142 F.3d 546 (2nd Cir. 1998); *Parker-Hannifin Corp. v. Comm.*, TC Memo 1996-337, *aff'd in part, rev'd in part*, 139 F.3d 1090 (6th Cir. 1998). See also *Square D Co. v. Comm.*, 109 TC 200 (1997). The present value of projected

WELFARE BENEFIT FUNDS   Q 496

postretirement medical benefits for employees who are retired at the time the reserve is created may be deducted in the year the reserve is created (approving the use of the individual level premium cost method to compute the reserve and rejecting the use of the aggregate cost method). *Wells Fargo v. Comm.*, 120 TC 69 (2003). The IRS privately ruled that where a company's VEBA intended to purchase a retiree health insurance policy to fund retiree benefits under the VEBA: (1) the VEBA would not be taxed on any income from the policy; (2) the company would not be required to recognize any income on the amount of the policy; and (3) the benefit payments under the policy to the VEBA would be excluded from the VEBA's gross income. Let. Rul. 200404055.

Whether deductions may be claimed under IRC Section 419A(c)(2) turns on the intent of the employer at the time that the reserve is established. *General Signal Corp. v. Comm.*, 142 F.3d 546 (2nd Cir. 1998). A reserve for postretirement benefits is not required to be segregated from the general assets of the fund into a separate account. See *General Signal Corp. v. Comm.*, 103 TC 216 (1994) (agreeing in dicta with Service attorneys' argument that a postretirement reserve need not be maintained in a separate account), *aff'd*, 142 F.3d 546 (2nd Cir. 1998); *Parker-Hannifin Corp. v. Comm.*, 139 F.3d 1090 (6th. Cir. 1998).

One special rule provides that certain employee pay-all VEBAs have no account limits. IRC Sec. 419A(f)(5)(B). Another special rule provides that welfare benefit funds under collective bargaining agreements have no account limits. IRC Sec. 419A(f)(5)(A); see Temp. Treas. Reg. §1.419A-2T, A-2. (Certain arrangements purportedly qualifying as collectively-bargained welfare benefit funds excepted from the account limits of IRC Sections 419 and 419A have been identified as "listed transactions." Notice 2003-24, 2003-18 IRB 853. See Q 503 for the rules applicable to listed transactions.) The Department of Labor has released criteria for determining when a plan is established and maintained under a collective bargaining agreement for purposes of the exception from the multiple employer welfare arrangement (MEWA) rules under ERISA. See Labor Reg. §2510.3-40; 68 Fed. Reg. 17471 (4-9-2003).

Maintenance of a separate welfare benefit fund for union employees is required. A fund for union employees must not only be separate from the employer and its creditors, but it must also be "distinct and apart from any funds provided for non-collectively bargained employees." *Parker-Hannifin Corp. v. Comm.*, 139 F.3d 1090 (6th Cir. 1998). But see Let. Ruls. 200137066, 199945066.

A fund's after-tax income is generally the fund's gross income, including employee contributions, but excluding employer contributions, reduced by allowable deductions directly connected with production of gross income and by the tax on the income. IRC Sec. 419(c)(4).

Employer contributions that are not deductible in one year because they exceed the limit on allowable deductions are carried over and treated as contributed in the next year. IRC Sec. 419(d).

If a welfare benefit fund is part of a 10 or more employer plan, see Q 503.

Account Limit

Claims incurred but unpaid. "Claims are incurred only when an event entitling the employee to benefits, such as a medical expense, a separation, a disability, or a death actually occurs. The allowable reserve includes amounts for claims estimated to have been incurred but which have not yet been reported, as well as those claims [that] have been reported but have not yet been paid." H.R. Conf. Rep. 861 (TRA '84), 98th Cong., 2d Sess. 1156, *reprinted in* 1984-3 CB (vol. 2) 410. Incurred but unpaid claims would include the present value of a future stream of payments under a long-term disability or death claim, using reasonable actuarial assumptions, according to that conference report. See *id.* The report of the Senate committee (TRA '86) notes that no more than 12 months of disability benefits may be deemed incurred with respect to a short-term disability expected to last more than five months. S. Rep. No. 313, 99th Cong., 2d Sess. 1006, *reprinted in* 1986-3 CB (vol. 3) 1006.

The account limit to fund for disability claims incurred but unpaid may not take into account disability benefits to the extent they are payable at an annual rate in excess of the lower of 75% of the individual's average high 3-years' compensation or the dollar limit on an annual benefit of a defined benefit plan ($175,000 in 2006; $170,000 in 2005). IRC Sec. 419A(c)(4)(A); Rev. Proc. 2005-70, 2005-47 IRB 979; IRS News Release IR-2005-127 (10-20-2004). In applying this limit, all welfare benefit funds of the employer are treated as one fund. IRC Sec. 419A(h)(1)(A).

The account limit with respect to reserves set aside to provide postretirement medical or life insurance benefits may not take into account life insurance benefits in excess of $50,000, except to the extent a higher amount may be provided tax free under grandfathering provisions of Section 79 for certain individuals. IRC Sec. 419A(e)(2); TRA '86, Sec. 1851(a)(3)(B), as amended by TAMRA '88, Sec. 1018(t)(2)(D). For this purpose, all welfare benefit funds of the employer are treated as one. IRC Sec. 419A(h). In funding for postretirement medical benefits, current cost assumptions must be used; future inflation may not be assumed. IRC Sec. 419A(c)(2).

Furthermore, the account limit generally may not include a reserve to provide postretirement medical or death benefits under a plan that fails to meet the nondiscriminatory benefit requirements discussed in Q 500. See IRC Sec. 419A(e)(1); TRA '86, Sec. 1851(a)(3)(B), as amended by TAMRA '88, Sec. 1018(t)(2)(D). If postretirement benefits are provided for key employees, see Q 499.

Unless there is an actuarial certification of the account limit by a qualified actuary, the account limit for a taxable year may not exceed certain "safe harbor limits." See IRC Sec. 419A(c)(5)(A); H.R. Conf. Rep. 861 (TRA '84), above, *reprinted in* 1984-3 CB (vol. 2) 412. The Code's reference to safe harbor limits here is potentially confusing because these limits are not true safe harbors. See *General Signal Corp. v. Comm.*, 103 TC 216 (1994), *aff'd*, 142 F.3d 546 (2nd Cir. 1998); *Square D Co. v. Comm.*, 109 TC 200 (1997); TAMs 9818001, 9446002, 9334002. That is, the safe harbor limits do not establish a minimal reserve level (or, account limit) that an employer can automatically fund on a currently deductible basis. An employer claiming an account limit equal to or less than the applicable safe harbor limit(s) must still show that its claimed reserve satisfies the generally applicable restrictions of IRC Section 419A. That is, the claimed reserve must still be reasonably and actuarially necessary to pay incurred but unpaid claims (plus administrative costs). See, e.g., Let. Rul. 9818001. Any reserve for postretirement medical or life insurance benefits must be actuarially determined on a level basis to fund the postretirement benefits over the working lives of the covered employees. Claiming an account limit at or below the applicable safe harbor limit(s) simply relieves the employer of the obligation to obtain an actuarial certification justifying its reserve

WELFARE BENEFIT FUNDS   Q 496

computations. See *General Signal*, above; *Square D Co.*, above; H.R. Conf. Rep. No. 861, above, *reprinted in* 1984-3 CB (vol. 2) 412. Actuarial valuation *reports* do not constitute an actuarial *certification* for purposes of IRC Section 419A. Let. Rul. 9818001.

The *"safe harbor limit"* for any taxable year for short-term disability claims is 17.5% of the "qualified direct costs" (other than insurance premiums) for short-term disability benefits for the immediately preceding taxable year. IRC Sec. 419A(c)(5)(B)(i).

The *"safe harbor limit"* for any taxable year for long-term disability or life insurance benefits is to be prescribed by regulations. IRC Sec. 419A(c)(5)(B)(iv).

The *"safe harbor limit"* for any taxable year for medical claims is 35% of the "qualified direct costs" (other than insurance premiums) for medical benefits for the immediately preceding taxable year. IRC Sec. 419A(c)(5)(B)(ii). The TRA '84 conference report explains that insurance premiums may not be taken into account because the conferees did not intend that a fund be used as a vehicle for prepayment of insurance premiums for current benefits. H.R. Conf. Rep. 861, above, *reprinted in* 1984-3 CB (vol. 2) 412.

In determining the employer's deduction, no item may be taken into account more than once. IRC Sec. 419(c)(5).

Supplemental Unemployment Compensation (SUB) and Severance Pay Benefits

Where contributions are made to the fund to provide supplemental unemployment compensation (SUB) or severance pay benefits, the account limit for SUB or severance pay benefits is 75% of the average "qualified direct costs" for any two of the immediately preceding seven taxable years (as selected by the fund). IRC Sec. 419A(c)(3)(A). If the benefit to any individual is payable at an annual rate in excess of 150% of the IRC Section 415 dollar limit on contributions to defined contribution plans, the excess cannot be taken into account in determining the account limit. IRC Sec. 419A(c)(4)(B). In applying this latter limit, all welfare benefit funds of the employer are treated as one fund. IRC Sec. 419A(h)(1)(A). Treasury regulations are to provide an interim limit for new SUB or severance pay plans that do not cover key employees. IRC Sec. 419A(c)(3)(B).

The "safe harbor limit" for SUB or severance pay benefits is the amount as determined above. IRC Sec. 419A(c)(5)(B)(iii).

For the explanation of how certain severance benefits are treated in light of the deferred compensation rules set forth in IRC Section 409(A), see Q 505.

Aggregation Rules

An employer must treat all of its welfare benefit funds as one fund for certain purposes. IRC Sec. 419A(h)(1)(A). For other purposes, an employer may elect to treat two or more of its funds as one. IRC Sec. 419A(h)(1)(B). An election to aggregate must be consistent for deduction and nondiscrimination purposes (see Q 500, Q 504 for a discussion of nondiscrimination rules applicable to certain welfare benefit funds), the conference report to TRA '84 notes. H.R. Conf. Rep. 861, above, *reprinted in* 1984-3 CB (vol. 2) 413. Aggregation rules similar to those of IRC Section 414 (controlled groups of corporations, employers under common control, affiliated service groups) and rules similar to the employee leasing rules apply. IRC Sec. 419A(h)(2). *ASRS, Sec. 66, ¶¶620, 680.*

497. What are the tax consequences to the employer and to the welfare benefit fund if the employer contributes excess amounts to the fund?

First, the deduction for the excess contribution is disallowed currently, although the excess contribution may be carried over and may be deductible in a later year. This carryover appears to be unlimited in time. See IRC Sec. 419(d).

Second, the fund's income-based tax liability may be increased. If the contributions are made to a tax-exempt fund, the fund's liability for unrelated business income tax may increase: (1) to the extent that the excess contributions reduce any difference between the qualified asset account and the qualified asset account limit (calculated with some modification), the excess contributions will limit the fund's ability to protect some of its income from treatment as UBTI; (2) excessive contributions to the fund may ultimately increase the fund's earnings, which may cause an increased exposure to unrelated business income tax (see Q 498).

Third, any increase in the fund's after-tax income (including employee contributions but not employer contributions) reduces the amount the employer can deduct (see Q 496). Thus, the Code forces the fund's earnings to be used to provide benefits. The amount of tax imposed on the employer attributable to income of the fund is treated as a contribution to the fund as of the last day of the employer's taxable year. The amount of the tax is treated as a tax on the fund for purposes of determining the fund's after-tax income.

Finally, efforts to retrieve excessive contributions may be costly: the Code imposes an excise tax of 100% on any portion of the fund that reverts to the benefit of the employer to the extent it is attributable to deductible contributions (see Q 501). IRC Sec. 4976. It is not clear whether efforts to retrieve excessive contributions to a voluntary employees' beneficiary association (VEBA) would violate the prohibition against private inurement (see Q 504). *ASRS, Sec. 66, ¶¶620.2(a), 620.2(f), 630, 640, 690.5.*

498. What income of a tax-exempt welfare benefit fund is taxable as unrelated business taxable income?

A tax-exempt welfare benefit fund is subject to a tax on its "unrelated business taxable income" (UBTI); a corporate fund is taxed at corporate rates and a trust at rates applicable to trusts. IRC Sec. 511. See, e.g., *Sherwin-Williams Co. Employee Health Plan Trust v. U.S.*, 2005-1 USTC ¶50,286 (6th Cir. 2005), *aff'g*, 2002-2 USTC ¶50,271 (ND Ohio 2002). Income (less certain deductions) from an unrelated trade or business regularly carried on by the organization is taxable. Other income of a tax-exempt organization (excluding member contributions, and less certain deductions) is taxable *except* to the extent it is set aside for certain purposes and, at least in some cases, within certain limits. IRC Sec. 512(a)(3).

A VEBA or SUB may protect income from treatment as UBTI by setting it aside for the payment of life, sick, accident, or other benefits (and reasonable, directly connected administrative costs). IRC Sec. 512(a)(3)(B)(ii). But the amount that may be so protected is expressly limited to the amount that may be set aside without causing the total assets set aside for such purposes to exceed the fund's "account limit" (see Q 496) for the taxable year. IRC Sec. 512(a)(3)(E)(i). (This limitation *does* apply to a fund that is part of a 10 or more employer plan.) In determining the account limit for

WELFARE BENEFIT FUNDS — Q 498

this purpose, a reserve for postretirement medical benefits generally may not be taken into consideration. IRC Sec. 512(a)(3)(E)(ii). Income in excess of the amount properly set aside is taxable as unrelated business income. Obviously, to the extent the account limit is already satisfied, the fund's income cannot be set aside tax free.

If any amount attributable to income set aside tax free is used for any purpose other than one entitling the set-aside to tax-free treatment, the amount will generally be treated as UBTI. IRC Sec. 512(a)(3)(B). But see Let. Ruls. 200126035, 200126034, 200023052, 9401033, 9147059.

Where there are existing reserves as of the close of the last plan year ending before July 18, 1984, or, if greater, on July 18, 1984, set aside to provide postretirement medical or life insurance benefits, special rules apply. See IRC Sec. 512(a)(3)(E)(ii); Temp. Treas. Reg. §1.512(a)-5T, A-4.

In *Sherwin-Williams Co. Employee Health Plan Trust v. Comm.*, the Sixth Circuit Court of Appeals reversed the Tax Court and held that the IRC Section 512(a)(3)(E)(i) limit on accumulating set-aside income does *not* apply to income that was set aside *and spent* on the reasonable costs of administering health care benefits under IRC Section 512(a)(3)(B) over the course of the year. Instead, the limit is on the amount of income that is still set aside at the end of the year. The appeals court reasoned that the limit does not apply to such spent income because that income is exempt function income, which is not subject to tax under IRC Section 512(a)(3)(A). *Sherwin-Williams Co. Employee Health Plan Trust v. Comm.*, 330 F.3d 449 (6th Cir. 2003), *rev'g*, 115 TC 440 (2000). The Service did *not* acquiesce in the above decision, but did recognize the decision's precedential effect on other cases appealed to the Sixth Circuit. Therefore, with respect to cases within the Sixth Circuit, the Service announced that it will follow the *Sherwin-Williams* decision if the opinion cannot be meaningfully distinguished. See Action on Decision 2005-2 (released 9-12-2005) at: http://www.irs.gov/pub/irs-aod/aod200502.pdf.

In technical advice, the Service stated that all income of a VEBA, other than income from an existing reserve, is included in computing the UBTI of a VEBA even though the VEBA consists of four separate claims reserves that are accounted for separately. Also, in computing UBTI, income from tax-exempt bonds is not treated as exempt function income of the VEBA. However, such income affects the amount of assets available to pay benefits and, thus, may indirectly affect the computation of UBTI. Finally, amounts set aside in existing reserves and additional reserves for postretirement medical or life insurance benefits are taken into account in accordance with Treasury Regulation Sections 1.512(a)-5T, Q&A-4(a) and 1.512(a)-5T, Q&A-4(d) when computing the UBTI of the VEBA. TAM 199932050. In other technical advice, the IRS determined that an employer could aggregate two welfare benefit funds (a VEBA and a non-tax exempt welfare benefit fund) for the purpose of computing UBTI. TAM 200317036.

The set aside limitation does not apply to any funds to which substantially all contributions are made by employers who were tax-exempt throughout the five-taxable year period ending with the taxable year in which the contributions are made. IRC Sec. 512(a)(3)(E)(iii). And because they have no account limits, welfare benefit funds under collective bargaining agreements and certain employee pay-all VEBAs (those with at least 50 employees and in which no employee is entitled to a refund other than one based on the experience of the entire fund) are not subject to the Code's express set-aside limitation. *ASRS, Sec. 66, ¶640.1.*

Postretirement Medical and Life Insurance Benefits

499. If postretirement medical or life insurance benefits are provided to a key employee through a welfare benefit fund, what special rules apply?

1. In the first year a reserve for postretirement medical or life insurance benefits (including any other death benefits) is taken into account in determining the applicable account limit (see Q 496), a separate account must be established for any medical or life insurance benefits provided with respect to a key employee after retirement. The separate account must be maintained for all subsequent taxable years. Medical or life insurance benefits provided with respect to such employee after retirement must be paid from that separate account only. IRC Sec. 419A(d)(1).

A "key employee" is one who at any time during the plan year or any preceding plan year is or was a key employee as defined for "top-heavy" qualified retirement plans (see Q 357 for the definition of "key employee" under IRC Sec. 416(i)). IRC Sec. 419A(d)(3). The separate account is to include amounts contributed to the plan with respect to service after the employee becomes a key employee as well as a reasonable allocation (under regulations) of amounts contributed on his behalf before he became a key employee. H.R. Conf. Rep. 861 (TRA '84), 98th Cong., 2d Sess. 1157, *reprinted in* 1984-3 CB (vol.2) 411.

2. Any amount allocated to an account of a key employee for postretirement medical benefits must be counted as an "annual addition" for purposes of the IRC Section 415 dollar (but not percentage of compensation) limit as if it were a contribution to a qualified defined contribution plan; all welfare benefit funds of the employer are treated as one fund for this purpose. IRC Secs. 419A(d)(2), 419A(h)(1)(A). Therefore, any such amount allocated to a key employee's account can have a significant effect on the qualification of any pension, profit sharing or stock bonus plan in which he is a participant. Presumably, amounts allocated for periods before he became a key employee can be disregarded. *ASRS, Sec.66, ¶620.2(c)*.

500. Must a welfare benefit fund providing postretirement life insurance or medical benefits meet nondiscrimination requirements?

A reserve for such postretirement benefits generally may not be included in determining a fund's qualified asset account limit if the plan of which the fund is a part is discriminatory with respect to those benefits; thus, in effect, a deduction is not available for contributions to prefund such discriminatory benefits. IRC Sec. 419A(e)(1).

A plan is discriminatory with respect to postretirement medical or life insurance benefits (including any other death benefits) unless it meets the nondiscrimination requirements, if any, specifically applicable to the benefit it provides or, if none, satisfies the following requirements: (1) each class of such benefits must be provided under a classification of employees that is set forth in the plan and that is found by the IRS not to be discriminatory in favor of "highly compensated individuals"; and (2) the benefits provided under each class of benefits must not discriminate in favor of "highly compensated individuals." IRC Secs. 419A(e)(1), 505(b). These nondiscrimination requirements also apply to VEBAs and are explained in Q 504. *ASRS, Sec. 66, ¶¶620.2(c), 630, 660.*

Excise Tax on "Disqualified Benefits"

501. What is the penalty for providing certain "disqualified benefits" through a welfare benefit fund?

Generally, an employer will be subject to a tax equal to 100% of: (1) any postretirement medical or life insurance benefit (including any other death benefit) provided to a key employee other than from a separate account (if a separate account was required) (see Q 499); (2) any postretirement medical or life insurance benefit (including any other death benefit) provided with respect to an individual in whose favor discrimination is prohibited unless the plan is nondiscriminatory with respect to such benefit (for the applicable nondiscrimination requirements, see Q 500 and Q 504); or (3) any portion of the fund reverting to the benefit of the employer that is attributable to contributions that were deductible in the current or any prior year. IRC Sec. 4976.

One exception provides that postretirement medical or life insurance benefits charged against amounts in a reserve up to the greater of the amount in the reserve as of the close of the last plan year ending before July 18, 1984, or on July 18, 1984, or charged against the income on such amounts, are not subject to the tax referred to in (1) and (2) above. IRC Sec. 4976(b)(4). Another exception provides that certain welfare benefit funds maintained pursuant to collective bargaining agreements are not subject to the tax described in (2) above. IRC Sec. 4976(b)(2).

With respect to item (3) above, the Service has concluded that a transfer of assets from an employer's VEBA to a 401(h) arrangement under a qualified pension plan of the same employer created income to the extent the employer derived a tax benefit from contributions in prior years, and the receipt of that income constituted a taxable reversion. See GCM 39785 (3-24-89). However, the transfer of assets from one welfare benefit fund to another for the purpose of providing welfare benefits to the employees of the employer generally should not be a reversion. See the General Explanation of TRA '84, p.794; see also GCM 39774 (8-1-88).

The transfer of assets from a retired lives reserve (or similar retirement funding account) to a VEBA (or to another retiree life insurance funding account) should not cause a taxable reversion where (1) the policy (or other controlling document(s)) prohibits any portion of the reserve (or similar account) from reverting to the employer while any covered employee remains alive and (2) the integrity of the reserve (or similar account) is preserved after the transfer. See, e.g., Let. Ruls. 200113009, 200037052, 199932032; compare Rev. Rul. 73-599, 1973-2 CB 40; Rev. Rul. 77-92, 1977-1 CB 41. One way to preserve the integrity of the reserve (or similar account) is for the VEBA and the plan under which it is administered to require that the amounts transferred to the VEBA be credited to a separate account for postretirement life insurance benefits and be used exclusively for such benefits. See, e.g., Let. Ruls. 200113009, 200037052.

A loan by a VEBA to its members' employer is not necessarily a prohibited reversion, but any such transaction will apparently be carefully reviewed to determine whether it is a genuine, commercially viable loan. See GCM 39884 (10-29-92). *ASRS, Sec. 66, ¶630.*

502. Must a tax-exempt welfare benefit fund apply for recognition of its tax-exempt status?

A VEBA or SUB must give notice to the IRS, in the manner required in the regulations, that it is applying for recognition of its tax-exempt status. IRC Sec. 505(c). An organization not giving required notice will not be tax-exempt, at least until it does give notice. Requirements for giving notice are set forth in Temp. Treas. Reg. §1.505(c)-1T. *ASRS, Sec. 66, ¶670.*

503. What is the exception for a welfare benefit fund that is part of a 10 or more employer plan?

IRC Sections 419 and 419A do not apply to a welfare benefit fund that is part of a 10 or more employer plan that does not maintain experience rating arrangements with respect to individual employers. A 10 or more employer plan is one to which more than one employer contributes, and to which no employer normally contributes more than 10% of the total contributions made under the plan by all employers. IRC Sec. 419A(f)(6).

A variety of multi-employer plans have been marketed to take advantage of the 10 or more employer plan exception; some of these plans were very aggressive and did not qualify for the exception. In 1995, the IRS claimed to have uncovered significant tax problems in multi-employer arrangements, and warned taxpayers that arrangements claiming to qualify for the multi-employer plan exception may suffer from various defects, including the following ones: (1) The arrangements may actually be providing deferred compensation rather than welfare benefits. This issue seems to arise most often in connection with plans purporting to provide severance benefits. See, e.g., *Wellons v. Comm.*, 31 F.3d 569, 94-2 USTC ¶50,402 (7th Cir. 1994) (severance pay arrangement is more akin to deferred compensation plan than welfare benefit plan where five years of service must be given before benefits accrue, benefit amount is linked to level of compensation and length of service, and benefits can be paid at virtually any termination of employment), *aff'g*, TC Memo 1992-704. (2) The arrangements may be, in fact, separate plans maintained for each employer although nominally linked together as part of multi-employer arrangements. (3) The arrangements may be experience-rated with respect to individual employers in form or operation because, among other things, the trusts may maintain, formally or informally, separate accounting for each employer and the employers may have reason to expect that their contributions will benefit only their employees. See Notice 95-34, 1995-1 CB 309.

The IRS successfully argued before the Tax Court points (2) and (3) with respect to the multi-employer plan in question in *Booth v. Comm.*, 108 TC 524 (1997). The court held that the multi-employer plan did not fall within the scope of IRC Section 419A(f)(6)(A) because the plan was an aggregation of separate welfare benefit plans each having an experience-rating arrangement with the related employer. The court stated, "We interpret the word 'plan' to mean that there must be a single pool of funds for use by the group as a whole (i.e., to pay the claims of all participants), and we interpret the phrase '10 or more employer plan' to mean that 10 or more employers must contribute to this single pool. We do not interpret the statutory language to include a program like the instant one where multiple employers have contributed funds to an independent party to hold in separate accounts until disbursed primarily for the benefit of the contributing employer's employees in accordance with unique terms established by that employer." *Id.*, at 571. As a result, the deductions of the employers participating in the plan were subject to the deduction limitations of IRC Sections 419 and 419A.

In *Neonatology Assoc., P.A., et al. v. Comm.*, 115 TC 43 (2000) (19 consolidated cases), *aff'd*, 299 F.3d 221 (3rd Cir. 2002), the Tax Court denied deductions for the portion of VEBA contributions in excess of the cost of current-year (term) life insurance under IRC Section 162. (Contributions to a welfare benefit fund can be deducted only in the amount (see Q 496) and at the time permitted by IRC Section 419 (see Q 495), but they must also satisfy the requirements of IRC Section 162 or IRC Section 212. See IRC Sec. 419(a), Temp. Treas. Reg. §1.419-1T, A-10.) In this case, the two VEBAs were structured so that each employer established and contributed to its own plan. The premiums on the underlying insurance policies were substantially greater than the cost of conventional term life insurance because they funded both the costs of term life insurance *and* credits that would be applied to conversion universal life policies of the individual insureds. Policyholders generally could withdraw any earned amount or borrow against their policies without any out-of-pocket costs.

The Tax Court in *Neonatology* determined that the VEBAs were not designed, marketed, purchased or sold as a means for an employer to provide welfare benefits to its employees. The court held that the VEBAs were primarily vehicles that were designed and served in operation to distribute surplus cash surreptitiously in the form of excess contributions from the medical corporations for the employee/owners' ultimate use and benefit. Although the plans provided term life insurance to the employee/owners, the excess contributions were not attributable to that current-year protection. The court further held that the excess contributions were constructive distributions of cash to the employee/owners that did not constitute deductible ordinary and necessary business expenses under IRC Section 162(a).

10 or More Employer Plan Regulations

Requirements

A valid 10 or more employer plan is a single plan (1) to which more than one "employer" (see below) contributes, (2) to which no employer normally contributes more than 10% of the total contributions of all employers under the plan, and (3) that does not maintain an "experience-rating arrangement" (see below) with respect to any individual employer. Treas. Reg. §1.419A(f)(6)-1(a)(1).

To qualify as a valid 10 or more employer plan, the purported plan must also satisfy certain compliance requirements. A plan satisfies the requirements if it is maintained pursuant to a written document that: (1) requires the "plan administrator" (see below) to maintain records sufficient for the IRS or any participating employer to readily verify the plan's compliance with the requirements of IRC Section 419A(f)(6) and Treasury Regulation §1.419A(f)(6)-1(a)(2)); and (2) provides the IRS and each participating employer with the right (upon written request to the plan administrator) to inspect and copy all such records. Treas. Reg. §1.419A(f)(6)-1(a)(2).

In order to qualify as a valid 10 or more employer plan, a plan must satisfy the requirements of the regulations in both form and operation. Treas. Reg. §1.419A(f)(6)-1(a)(3)(i). The term "plan" includes the totality of the arrangement and all related facts and circumstances, including any related insurance contracts. Thus, all agreements and understandings (including promotional materials and policy illustrations) and the terms of any insurance contracts will be taken into account in determining whether the requirements are satisfied in form and in operation. Treas. Reg. §1.419A(f)(6)-1(a)(3)(ii).

Experience-Rating Arrangements

A plan maintains an "experience-rating arrangement" with respect to an individual employer if, for any period, the relationship of contributions under the plan to the benefits or other amounts payable under the plan (i.e., the "cost of coverage") is or can be expected to be based, in whole or in part, on the "benefits experience" (see below) or the "overall experience" (see below) of that employer or one or more employees of that employer. Treas. Reg. §1.419A(f)(6)-1(b)(1). In the Preamble, the Service states that this determination is not intended to be purely a computational one (although actual numbers often can be used to demonstrate the existence of an experience-rating arrangement). Preamble, TD 9079, 68 Fed. Reg. 42254, 42256 (7-17-2003).

For these purposes, an employer's contributions include all contributions made by or on behalf of the employer or the employer's employees. The prohibition against experience-rating applies under all circumstances, including employer withdrawals and plan terminations. Treas. Reg. §1.419A(f)(6)-1(b)(1).

An example of a plan that maintains an experience-rating arrangement with respect to an individual employer is a plan that entitles the employer to (or for which the employer can expect) a reduction in future *contributions* if that employer's overall experience is positive, or an increase in future contributions if that employer's overall benefits experience is negative. Treas. Reg. §1.419A(f)(6)-1(b)(2). Another example of a plan that maintains an experience-rating arrangement with respect to an individual employer is a plan under which *benefits* for an employer's employees are (or can be expected to be) increased if that employer's overall experience is positive, or decreased if that employer's overall experience is negative. Treas. Reg. §1.419A(f)(6)-1(b)(3).

Use of insurance contracts. In the Preamble, the Service recognizes that if whole life insurance contracts (or other insurance contracts that provide for level premiums or otherwise generate a savings element) are purchased under an arrangement, the economic values reflected under those contracts (e.g., cash values, reserves, conversion credits, high dividend rates, or the right to continue coverage at a premium that is lower than the premium that would apply in the absence of that savings element) reflect the overall experience of the employers and employees who participate under the plan. Preamble, TD 9079, 68 Fed. Reg. 42254, 42256 (7-17-2003).

The Service also states in the Preamble that neither IRC Section 419A(f)(6) nor the regulations regulate the investments of a welfare benefit fund, including investments by a trust in cash value policies. Instead, the Service is concerned with the economic relationship between a fund and participating employers, and whether the pass-through of premiums based on the insurance contracts associated with an employer's employees has the effect of creating experience-rating arrangements with respect to individual employers. Furthermore, the Service believes that the exception is still viable for many life and health benefit arrangements that are self-insured in accordance with the Employee Retirement Income Security Act of 1974 (ERISA) or state law. Preamble, TD 9079, 68 Fed. Reg. 42254, 42257 (7-17-2003).

Special Rules

Treatment of insurance contracts. In general, insurance contracts will be treated as assets of the fund. Thus, the value of the insurance contracts (including non-guaranteed elements) is included in the value of the fund, and amounts paid between the fund and the insurance company are disregarded (except to the extent they generate gains or losses, as explained below). Treas. Reg. §1.419A(f)(6)-1(b)(4)(i)(A).

WELFARE BENEFIT FUNDS   Q 503

Payments to and from an insurance company. Payments from a participating employer or its employees to an insurance company with respect to insurance contracts will be treated as contributions made to the fund. Amounts paid under the arrangement from an insurance company will be treated as payments from the fund. Treas. Reg. §1.419A(f)(6)-1(b)(4)(i)(B).

Gains and losses from insurance contracts. As of any date, if the sum of the benefits paid by the insurer and the value of the insurance contract (including non-guaranteed elements) is greater than the cumulative premiums paid to the insurer, the excess is treated as a gain to the fund. As of any date, if the cumulative premiums paid to the insurer are greater than the sum of the benefits paid by the insurer and the value of the insurance contract (including non-guaranteed elements), the excess is treated as a loss to the fund. Treas. Reg. §1.419A(f)(6)-1(b)(4)(i)(C).

Treatment of flexible contribution arrangements. Solely for purposes of determining the "cost of coverage" under a plan, if contributions for any period can vary with respect to a benefit package, the Service may treat the employer as contributing the minimum amount that would maintain the coverage for that period. Treas. Reg. §1.419A(f)(6)-1(b)(4)(ii).

Experience-rating by group of employers (or employees). A plan will not be treated as maintaining an experience-rating arrangement with respect to an individual employer merely because the cost of coverage under the plan is based, in whole or in part, on the benefits experience or the overall experience of a "rating group" (see below) provided that no employer normally contributes more than 10% of all contributions with respect to that rating group. Treas. Reg. §1.419A(f)(6)-1(b)(4)(iii).

Characteristics Indicating a Plan is *Not* a 10 or More Employer Plan

The presence of any of the characteristics listed below generally indicates that the plan is *not* a 10 or more employer plan under IRC Section 419A(f)(6). It is important to note that a plan's lack of all of the following characteristics does not create any inference that it is a 10 or more employer plan described in IRC Section 419A(f)(6). Treas. Reg. §1.419A(f)(6)-1(c)(1). The characteristics are as follows:

(1) *Allocation of plan assets.* Assets of the plan or fund are allocated to a specific employer or employers through separate accounting of contributions and expenditures for individual employers, or otherwise. §1.419A(f)(6)-1(c)(2).

(2) *Differential pricing.* The amount charged under the plan is not the same for all the participating employers, and those differences are not merely reflective of differences in current risk or rating factors that are commonly taken into account in manual rates used by insurers (such as current age, gender, geographic locale, number of covered dependents, and benefit terms) for the particular benefit or benefits being provided. Treas. Reg. §1.419A(f)(6)-1(c)(3).

(3) *No fixed welfare benefit package.* The plan does not provide for fixed welfare benefits for a fixed coverage period for a fixed cost. Treas. Reg. §1.419A(f)(6)-1(c)(4).

(4) *Unreasonably high cost.* The plan provides for fixed welfare benefits for a fixed coverage period for a fixed cost, but that cost is unreasonably high for the covered risk for the plan as a whole. Treas. Reg. §1.419A(f)(6)-1(c)(5).

(5) *Nonstandard benefit triggers.* The plan provides for benefits (or other amounts payable) that can be paid, distributed, transferred or otherwise provided from a fund that is part of a plan by reason of any event other than the illness, personal injury, or death of an employee or family member, or the employee's involuntary separation from employment. For example, a plan exhibits this characteristic if the plan provides for the payment of benefits to an employer's employees on the occasion of the employer's withdrawal from the plan. A plan will not be treated as having this characteristic merely because upon cessation of participation in the plan, an employee is provided with the right to convert coverage under a group life insurance contract to coverage under an individual life insurance contract without demonstrating evidence of insurability, but only if there is an additional economic value association with the conversion right. Treas. Reg. §1.419A(f)(6)-1(c)(6).

For examples of arrangements classified as experience-rating arrangements, see Treas. Reg. §1.419A(f)(6)-1(f).

Definitions

The term *benefits or other amounts payable* includes all amounts payable or distributable (or that will be otherwise provided) directly or indirectly to employers, to employees or their beneficiaries, or to another fund as a result of a spin-off or transfer, regardless of the form of the payment or distribution (i.e., whether provided as welfare benefits, cash, dividends, credits, rebates of contributions, property, promises to pay, or otherwise). Treas. Reg. §1.419A(f)(6)-1(d)(1). *Benefits experience* of an employer (or of an employee, or a group of employers or employees) means the benefits and other amounts incurred, paid, or distributed (or otherwise provided), directly or indirectly, including to another fund as a result of a spin-off or transfer, with respect to the employer regardless of the form of payment or distribution. Treas. Reg. §1.419A(f)(6)-1(d)(2).

The *overall experience* of an employer (or group of employers) is the balance that would have accumulated in a welfare benefit fund if that employer were the only employer providing benefits under the plan. The *overall experience* of an employee (or group of employees, whether or not employed by the same employer) is the balance that would have accumulated in a welfare benefit fund if that employee were the only employee being provided benefits under the plan. Overall experience as of any date may be either a positive or a negative number. Treas. Reg. §1.419A(f)(6)-1(d)(3).

The term *employer* means the employer whose employees are participating in the plan and those employers required to be aggregated under IRC Sections 414(b), 414(c), or 414(m). Treas. Reg. §1.419A(f)(6)-1(d)(4). *Rating group* means a group of participating employers that includes the employer or a group of employees covered under the plan that includes one or more employees or that employer. Treas. Reg. §1.419A(f)(6)-1(b)(4)(iii).

A plan provides a *fixed welfare benefit package* (i.e., fixed welfare benefits for a fixed coverage period for a fixed cost) if it: (1) defines one or more welfare benefits, each of which has a fixed amount that does not depend on the amount or type of assets held by the fund; (2) specifies fixed contributions to provide for those welfare benefits; and (3) specifies a coverage period during which the plan agrees to provide specified welfare benefits, subject to the payment of the specified contributions by the employer. Treas. Reg. §1.419A(f)(6)-1(d)(5)(i). For the treatment of actuarial gains or losses, see Treas. Reg. §1.419A(f)(6)-1(d)(5)(ii).

WELFARE BENEFIT FUNDS   Q 504

Plan administrator is defined the same as in Treasury Regulation §1.414(g)-1. Treas. Reg. §1.419A(f)(6)-1(a)(2). The "plan administrator" of a plan that is intended to be a 10 or more employer plan described in IRC Section 419A(f)(6) is required to maintain permanent records and other documentary evidence sufficient to substantiate that the plan satisfies the requirements of IRC Section 419A(f)(6) and the regulations. Treas. Reg. §1.419A(f)(6)-1(e).

Multi-Employer Plans and Tax Shelters

Certain trust arrangements under Notice 95-34, 1995-1 CB 309, which are purported to qualify as multiple employer plans exempt from the IRC Section 419 and IRC Section 419A limits, have been classified by the IRS as listed transactions. See Notice 2004-67, 2004-41 IRB 600, *supplementing and superseding*, Notice 2003-76, 2003-49 IRB 1181.

"Reportable transaction" means any transaction with respect to which information is required to be included with a return or statement because (as determined under regulations prescribed under IRC Section 6011) the transaction is of a type that the Secretary determines as having a potential for tax avoidance or evasion. IRC Section 6707A(c)(1). One category of reportable transactions is a "listed transaction" – that is, a transaction that is the same as, or substantially similar to, one of the types of transactions that the Service has determined to be a tax avoidance transaction and has identified by notice, regulation, or other form of published guidance. See Treas. Reg. §1.6011-4(b)(2); see also IRC Sec. 6707A(c)(2).

Under AJCA 2004, the penalty for failing to disclose a listed transaction is $100,000 in the case of a natural person ($200,000 in any other case). IRC Sec. 6707A. A 20% penalty applies when a taxpayer has a reportable transaction understatement attributable to a listed transaction. IRC Secs. 6662A(a), 6662A(b). A 30% penalty applies to undisclosed listed transactions. IRC Sec. 6662A(c). For guidance on the penalty assessed under IRC Section 6707A, see Notice 2005-11, 2005-7 IRB 493. Guidance on the penalty assessed under IRC Section 6662A is provided in Notice 2005-12, 2005-7 IRB 494. See also IRS News Release IR-2005-10 (1-19-2005).

For other tax shelter provisions, see IRC Sec. 6111, (disclosure of reportable transactions by material advisors); IRC Sec. 6112 (list maintenance requirements for material advisors); and IRC Sec. 6502(c) (statute of limitations). For guidance on material advisor reporting (and exceptions to tax shelter reportable transactions), see Notice 2004-80, 2004-50 IRB 963, *clarified and modified by*, Notice 2005-17, 2005-8 IRB 606, *and* Notice 2005-22, 2005-12 IRB 756.

For the final regulations outlining the requirements applicable to tax shelters, see TD 9046, 68 Fed. Reg. 10161 (3-4-2003). For the final requirements for tax shelter opinion letters, see TD 9165, 69 Fed. Reg. 75839 (12-20-2004). *ASRS, Sec. 66,* ¶¶*620.2(g), 680.*

VOLUNTARY EMPLOYEES' BENEFICIARY ASSOCIATIONS (501(C)(9) TRUSTS)

504. What is a "501(c)(9) trust" (VEBA)?

A Voluntary Employees' Beneficiary Association (VEBA) is a tax-exempt entity created to fund life, sick, accident, or certain other benefits (see Q 505) for members, their dependents, or their designated beneficiaries. A VEBA may be established by an employer or through collective bargaining. A trust created to provide benefits to one employee does not qualify as an employees' association for purposes of exemption from federal income tax under IRC Section 501(c)(9). Rev. Rul. 85-199, 1985-2 CB 163. Some of the requirements for tax-exempt VEBA status are discussed below.

Membership Eligibility

Generally, membership must be limited to employees (including certain former employees). See Treas. Regs. §§1.501(c)(9)-2(a)(1), 1.501(c)(9)-2(b)(2), 1.501(c)(9)-2(b)(3). Membership may include some non-employees, as long as such people share an employment-related bond with the employee-members and as long as at least 90% of the members are employees. Treas. Reg. §1.501(c)(9)-2(a)(1); GCM 39834 (12-26-90). See, e.g., Let. Rul. 200137066.

Eligibility for membership must be defined by reference to objective standards that constitute an employment-related common bond. Such a common bond could be, for example, a common employer or common coverage under a collective bargaining agreement. Treas. Reg. §1.501(c)(9)-2(a)(1). The Service believes that employees whose only connection is that their employers are engaged in the same line of business will have the requisite common bond only if their employers are in the "same geographic locale." See, e.g., GCM 39817 (5-9-90). The Service sticks to this position in spite of *Water Quality Assoc'n Employees' Benefit Corp. v. U.S.*, 795 F.2d 1303 (7th Cir. 1986), which held that such a geographic locale restriction is invalid. See, e.g., the preamble to Prop. Treas. Reg. §1.501(c)(9)-2(d), 57 Fed. Reg. 34886 (8-7-92).

Currently, the Service believes that an area is a single "geographic locale" if it does not exceed the boundaries of three contiguous states. The Service also believes that larger areas can be considered a single "geographic locale" under the appropriate facts and circumstances. See Prop. Treas. Reg. §1.501(c)(9)-2(d).

Membership may be limited by objective criteria reasonably related to employment, such as a limitation based on a reasonable minimum period of service or a requirement that members be full-time employees. But any criteria used to restrict membership may not be used to limit membership to officers, shareholders, or highly compensated employees. Treas. Reg. §1.501(c)(9)-2(a)(2).

Nondiscrimination Requirements

While eligibility for membership and benefits may generally be restricted by objective conditions, any objective criteria used to restrict eligibility for membership or for benefits may not limit membership or benefits to officers, shareholders, or highly compensated employees of a contributing employer, and they may not entitle any of that prohibited group to "disproportionate" benefits. Treas. Reg. §1.501(c)(9)-2(a)(2)(i). Generally, a plan will not run afoul of the prohibition against disproportionate benefits by basing life or disability income benefits on a uniform percentage of compensation. Treas. Regs. §§1.501(c)(9)-2(a)(2)(ii)(F), 1.501(c)(9)-2(a)(2)(ii)(G). In the context of associations with a small number of members receiving disparate levels of compensation, General Counsel Memoranda have concluded that severance benefits may be based on a uniform percentage of compensation; these memoranda have also concluded that severance benefits may be based on length of service requirements as long as those

WELFARE BENEFIT FUNDS   Q 504

requirements do not limit benefits to members of the prohibited group. GCMs 39818 (5-10-90), 39300 (10-30-84).

However, if by virtue of basing death and disability benefits on uniform percentages of compensation, or by basing severance benefits on a percentage of compensation and determining that percentage by reference to length of service, an association provides a dominant share of benefits to a member of the prohibited group, and if the association provides that upon termination of the association the members will be entitled to their allocable share of the association's assets, and if the member of the prohibited group effectively controls the association, the association may violate the prohibition against inurement. See *id.* See also GCM 39801 (10-26-89). For further important information, see the inurement discussion below, especially the references to the *Lima Surgical* litigation. Also note that courts have pointed to the basing of severance benefits on both level of compensation and length of service in ruling that the benefits were really impermissible retirement benefits. See *Lima Surgical Assoc., Inc. v. U.S.*, 90-1 USTC ¶50,329 (U.S. Claims Court 1990), *aff'd*, 944 F.2d 885, 91-2 USTC ¶50,473 (Fed. Cir. 1991). See Q 505.

Generally, a VEBA will not be tax-exempt unless the plan meets the nondiscrimination rules applicable to the particular benefits provided or, if none, the following nondiscrimination requirements: (1) each class of benefits under the plan must be provided under a classification of employees that is set forth in the plan and that is found by the IRS not to be discriminatory in favor of employees who are "highly compensated individuals," and (2) the benefits provided under each class of benefits must not discriminate in favor of employees who are "highly compensated individuals." See IRC Secs. 505(a)(1), 505(b)(1). See also IRC Sec. 505(a)(2) (providing an exception for certain collectively bargained VEBAs); and Let. Ruls. 200119064, 199920044 (a VEBA maintained pursuant to a collective bargaining agreement, which was the subject of good faith bargaining between the company and the union, was not subject to the nondiscrimination requirements). (A "highly compensated individual" is similar to a "highly compensated employee" for qualified plan purposes (see Q 356).)

For purposes of applying the nondiscrimination standards, certain employees may be excluded from consideration. See IRC Sec. 505(b)(2); H.R. Conf. Rep. 861 (TRA '84), 98th Cong., 2d Sess. 1164, *reprinted in* 1984-3 CB (vol. 2) 418; the General Explanation of TRA '84, p. 800. For purposes of testing for discrimination, an employer may elect to treat two or more plans as one plan. IRC Sec. 505(b)(4). An election to aggregate must be consistent for deduction and discrimination purposes (see Q 496). H.R. Conf. Rep. 861 (TRA '84), above, *reprinted in* 1984-3 CB (vol. 2) 413. Also, employers related under the common control, controlled group, and affiliated service group aggregation rules (see Q 359, Q 360) must be treated as a single employer, *and* the employee leasing provision (other than the safe harbor rule) must be applied (see Q 355). IRC Secs. 414(n)(3)(C), 414(t).

A life insurance, disability, severance, or supplemental unemployment compensation benefit is not considered discriminatory merely because the benefits bear a uniform relationship to total (or basic, or regular rate of) compensation of employees covered by the plan. IRC Sec. 505(b)(1).

A plan generally will not satisfy the nondiscrimination requirements of IRC Section 505(b) unless the annual compensation of each employee taken into consideration for any year does not exceed $220,000 in 2006 ($210,000 in 2005) IRC Sec. 401(a)(17)); Rev. Proc. 2005-70, 2005-47 IRB 979; IRS News Release IR-2004-127. This limitation does not apply in determining whether the nondiscrimination rules of IRC Section 79 are met. IRC Sec. 505(b)(7).

If the VEBA plan provides postretirement medical or group term life insurance benefits, see Q 499 and Q 500.

Control Requirements

The association must be controlled by its membership (that is, by its participants), or by independent trustees, or by trustees some of whom are designated by or on behalf of the members. Treas. Reg. §1.501(c)(9)-2(c)(3). Requisite control was held lacking where the trustees were appointed by a self-perpetuating board of directors, new members of which were appointed by current members from among a group only indirectly selected by employees. *American Assn. of Christian Schools v. U.S.*, 87-1 USTC ¶9328 (M.D. Ala. 1987), *aff'd*, 850 F.2d 1510, 88-2 USTC ¶9452 (11th Cir. Ala. 1988). A bank may not necessarily be considered an independent trustee. See *Lima Surgical Assoc., Inc. v. U.S.*, 90-1 USTC ¶50,329 (U.S. Claims Court 1990), *aff'd on other grounds*, 944 F.2d 885, 91-2 USTC ¶50,473 (Fed. Cir. 1991).

Inurement of Earnings Prohibited

Except in payment of permissible benefits, no part of the earnings of a VEBA may inure to the benefit of any private shareholder or individual. Treas. Regs. §§1.501(c)(9)-1(d), 1.501(c)(9)-4(a). A return of excess insurance premiums to their payor, based on mortality or morbidity experience, is not prohibited. Treas. Reg. §1.501(c)(9)-4(c); Let. Rul. 9006051. See also Let. Rul. 9214030 (the rebate of excess insurance premiums to professional associations whose members contributed premiums to the VEBA for disability protection and agreed that any excess funds in the VEBA could go to the professional associations was not prohibited inurement as long as the professional associations could use the money to provide VEBA benefits to their members). In addition, the refund of contributions to an employer, which had been paid after the collective bargaining agreement had ended but during the pendency of a labor dispute with the union, did not constitute inurement. Let. Rul. 199930040.

On termination of a plan, there is no prohibited inurement if, after satisfaction of all liabilities to existing beneficiaries, remaining assets are applied to provide permitted benefits pursuant to criteria that do not provide for disproportionate benefits to officers, shareholders, or highly compensated employees. A distribution to members on dissolution of the VEBA made on an objective and reasonable basis not resulting in unequal payments to similarly situated employees or disproportionate distributions to officers, shareholders, or highly compensated employees will not be prohibited inurement. Assets of a VEBA may not be distributable to contributing employers on dissolution, either under the trust document or by operation of law, unless the distribution is applied to provide permissible benefits in a manner that does not result in disproportionate benefits for officers, shareholders, or highly compensated employees of the employers. Treas. Reg. §1.501(c)(9)-4(d).

A transfer of assets from a VEBA to a separate nonexempt trust resulting from the termination of the sick leave/severance plan component of the VEBA and then to a bank account to be distributed to employees who participated in the terminated trust was not considered prohibited inurement as funds were apparently used to pay qualifying 501(c)(9) benefits. TAM 9647001. In terminating a VEBA, use of the assets in a postretirement medical reserve to pay health care claims of employees who had retired prior to the effective date of the VEBA did not constitute prohibited inurement or a reversion of plan assets to the employer because the use of the reserves for an additional class of retirees was consistent with the purpose of the reserve. Let. Rul. 9720034. The termination of the life insurance portion (the Retiree Life Plan) of a welfare benefit plan (a non-exempt trust) and subsequent transfer to a VEBA of the assets remaining after the purchase of individual paid-up policies to satisfy the obligation of the Retiree Life Plan and the subsequent use of those remaining assets to provide payment of permitted benefits other than life insurance did not result in prohibited inurement to the employer. Let. Rul. 9740024. Where an employer intended to reactivate a previously inactive VEBA by using the remaining assets to purchase one or more insurance policies that would provide accidental death, disability, and long-term care benefits to the current employees and then terminate the VEBA upon exhaustion of such assets, the proposed use of the net assets would not affect the tax-exempt status (i.e., no prohibited inurement) since the assets would be used to provide benefits contemplated by IRC Section 501(c)(9). See Let. Rul. 9446036, Treas. Reg. §1.501(c)(9)-4(d).

A General Counsel Memorandum concluded that a transfer of assets from an employer's VEBA to a 401(h) arrangement under a qualified pension plan of the same employer (providing retiree health benefits) would result in inurement of earnings from the VEBA to the employer, inasmuch as a 401(h) arrangement is required to provide for return to the employer of assets remaining in the account after satisfaction of all liabilities under the plan (see Q 369). GCM 39785 (3-24-89). However, the transfer of excess assets from a terminating VEBA to a successor VEBA to fund permissible VEBA benefits for the employer's employees generally should not result in prohibited inurement. See, e.g., Let. Ruls. 200122051, 200122047 (assets transferred from a terminated VEBA to another VEBA would be used to provide permissible welfare benefits in a nondiscriminatory manner, a common employment-related bond was present, and the transfer was not being used to avoid any of the statutory VEBA requirements). See also Let. Ruls. 200024054, 200009051, 9812035, 9551007, 9505019, 9438017, 9414011, 9322041, 9115035, and 9014065; in each situation, the Service ruled that the transfer did not result in inurement or trigger excise tax).

The transfer of a terminated VEBA's remaining assets to an exempt educational trust fund did not result in prohibited inurement. Let. Rul. 200136028. No inurement resulted from the termination of a VEBA and transfer of assets back to its original tax-exempt sponsor (formerly operating as a charity hospital and currently operating as a charity only) since the assets were to be distributed by the charity for charitable purposes, with the remaining assets to be distributed to the charity's former employees who were currently working for the new hospital. Let. Rul. 200003054. The termination of a VEBA and distribution of the remaining assets to a 501(c)(3) private foundation did not result in a reversion since the foundation was not an employer with respect to the trust, nor was it an organization that otherwise was merely an alter ego of the employer; instead, the foundation was a charitable organization whose assets were dedicated to charitable purposes and that could not be used for the private benefit of the employer. Let. Rul. 199908054.

The substitution of a successor company for the original company in a VEBA trust document did not constitute prohibited inurement. Let. Rul. 200041035.

The Service has indicated tax-exempt status may be denied where the principal shareholders receive a dominant share of aggregate benefits and effectively control the organization. See, e.g., GCMs 39818 (5-10-90), 39801 (10-26-89), 39300 (10-30-84).

In the *Lima Surgical* case, above, where highly compensated owner-employees stood to receive a dominant share of severance benefits, the Claims Court found a violation of the prohibition against private inurement because the dominant benefits were based on both level of compensation *and* length of service, but did not explicitly analyze whether owner-employees also effectively controlled the plan trust. 90-1 USTC ¶50,329, at pp. 84,145-84,146. (In administrative proceedings prior to litigation, the Service found a violation of the inurement proscription because the owner-employees were entitled to a dominant share of benefits *and* controlled the corporation. 90-1 USTC ¶50,329, at p. 84,145, n.6.) On appeal, the Federal Circuit did not address the Claims Court's inurement ruling, but the Service conceded that the arrangement did *not* violate the prohibition against inurement. 91-2 USTC ¶50,473, at p. 89,800. It is not clear why the Service concluded there was not prohibited inurement.

A loan from a VEBA to its members' employer might violate the prohibition against private inurement. See GCM 39884 (10-29-92) (whether the loan violated the prohibition was not an issue in the memorandum, but the Service noted nonetheless that the loan at issue might have been a sham transaction for the employer's benefit and was "tainted by the type of economic domination by a controlling person...that (has been) found to constitute private inurement"). *ASRS, Sec. 66, ¶¶690.1 - 690.7.*

505. What benefits can a 501(c)(9) trust (VEBA) provide?

The trust may provide "for the payment of life, sick, accident, or other benefits" to its members, their dependents or their designated beneficiaries. (A dependent can be, among others, a spouse, a child of the member or the member's spouse who is a minor or a student (for income tax dependent exemption purposes), or any other minor child residing with the member. Treas. Reg. §1.501(c)(9)-3(a).) Provision of an insubstantial or "de minimis" amount of impermissible benefits will not disqualify an arrangement from tax-exempt VEBA status. See, e.g., GCM 39817 (5-9-90); TAM 9139003.

A "life benefit" is one payable by reason of death of a member or dependent; it may be provided directly or through insurance. It generally must consist of current protection, but it may include "a permanent benefit as defined in, and subject to the conditions in, the regulations under section 79" (see Q 147, Q 148). Treas. Reg. §1.501(c)(9)-3(b). In addition, the IRS has indicated that life benefits may be provided through employer-funded whole-life policies that are not group-permanent policies under IRC Section 79 if (1) the policies are owned by the VEBA, (2) the policies are purchased through level premiums over the expected lives or working lives of the individual members, and (3) the accumulated cash reserves accrue to the VEBA. GCM 39440 (11-7-85). (However, the purchase of individual whole life insurance by VEBAs funding ERISA plans may violate ERISA. Compare *Reich v. Lancaster*, 55 F.3d 1034 (5th Cir. 1995), *aff'g* 843 F. Supp. 194 (N.D. Tex. 1993) (purchases of individual whole life insurance by self-funded welfare benefit plan violated various provisions of ERISA); *Reich v. McDonough*, Civ. Action No. 91-12025 H (D. Mass. Dec. 10, 1993) (consent judgment and order settling the case of *Martin v. Feingold*, Civ. Action No. 91-12025 H (D. Mass. filed July 31, 1991), and in part recognizing that individual whole life insurance can be an appropriate investment for ERISA plans.) A reserve for future retirees' life insurance held by a

WELFARE BENEFIT FUNDS	Q 505

postretirement trust was found to provide an impermissible benefit similar to deferred compensation, and the trust was not tax-exempt under 501(c)(9). Let. Rul. dated May 25, 1982. (Also consider the conference report to TRA '84, which admonishes that a plan providing medical or life insurance benefits exclusively for retirees would be considered a deferred compensation plan rather than a welfare benefit plan. H.R. Conf. Rep. 861, 98th Cong., 2d Sess. 1157, *reprinted in* 1984-3 CB (vol. 2) 411. But consider Let. Rul. 9151027 (see Q 494).)

The payment of self-funded, paid-up life insurance constituted a qualifying benefit for purposes of IRC Section 501(c)(9) regardless of how self-funded, paid-up life insurance was characterized under state law where: (1) payment of the benefit only came due upon the occurrence of an unanticipated event (i.e., the death of the insured), and protected a member and his family or beneficiary against a contingency that interrupted or impaired the member's earning power; and (2) it was clear that unlike an annuity or retirement benefit, the self-funded, paid-up life insurance benefit was not payable merely by reason of passage of time. Let. Rul. 199930040.

"Sick and accident benefits" may be reimbursement for medical expenses. They may be amounts paid in lieu of income during a period a member is unable to work because of sickness or injury. Sick benefits include benefits designed to safeguard or improve the health of members and their dependents. They may be provided directly, or through payment of premiums to an insurance company, or to another program providing medical services. Treas. Reg. §1.501(c)(9)-3(c). Home health care benefits provided under a VEBA qualified as medical care benefits and, thus, were excludable from gross income. Let. Rul. 200028007. Supplemental medical benefits qualified as "sick and accident benefits." Let. Rul. 200003053. Reimbursement of union members' health insurance premiums constituted a permitted benefit where benefits would be paid only as reimbursement for health premiums, and under no circumstances could employees take the contributions as unrestricted cash. Let. Rul. 199902016. Paid sick days and short-term disability wage replacement benefits have been considered "sick and accident benefits." See TAM 9126004. Health benefits provided by a VEBA to nondependent, nonspousal domestic partners of participants did not adversely affect the VEBA's tax-exempt status because such coverage/benefits would constitute no more than a "de minimis" amount of the VEBA's total benefits under Treas. Reg. §1.501(c)(9)-3(a). Let. Rul. 200108010.

"Other benefits" are limited to those similar to life, sick or accident benefits. A benefit is "similar" if it is "intended to safeguard or improve the health of a member or a member's dependents or it protects against a contingency that interrupts or impairs a member's earning power." Treas. Reg. §1.501(c)(9)-3(d). The Service understands a "contingency" to be an unanticipated event beyond the control of the beneficiary. See GCM 39879 (9-15-92). Other benefits may include vacation benefits, child care facilities, supplemental unemployment compensation benefits, severance benefits (*but see below*), and education benefits. Treas. Reg. §1.501(c)(9)-3(e). Holiday pay and paid personal days have been considered "other benefits." See TAM 9126004. Social, recreational, and cultural benefits provided to retirees, designed to promote their physical, mental and/or emotional well-being, or to provide them with information relating to retirement and asset management, constituted permissible benefits. Let. Rul. 9802038.

Other benefits do not include, among other things, any benefit that is similar to a pension or annuity payable at the time of mandatory or voluntary retirement, or a benefit that is similar to the benefit provided under a stock bonus or profit-sharing plan. In other words, other benefits do not include deferred compensation payable by reason of the passage of time rather than because of an unanticipated event. Treas. Reg. §1.501(c)(9)-3(f). See also *Lima Surgical Assoc., Inc. v. U.S.*, 90-1 USTC ¶50,329 (U.S. Claims Court 1990) (severance benefits based on length of service and level of compensation and payable upon retirement were impermissible deferred compensation), *aff'd*, 944 F.2d 885, 91-2 USTC ¶50,473 (Fed. Cir. 1991); Let. Rul. 9249027 (severance benefits payable upon any voluntary or involuntary termination, including retirement, are deferred compensation or retirement benefits and are not qualifying other benefits). Compare *Wellons v. Comm.*, 31 F.3d 569, 94-2 USTC ¶50,402 (7th Cir. 1994) (severance pay arrangement is more akin to deferred compensation plan than welfare benefit plan where five years of service must be given before benefits accrue, benefit amount is linked to level of compensation and length of service, and benefits can be paid at virtually any termination of employment), *aff'g*, TC Memo 1992-704. (For a discussion of the manner in which plans that provide medical and death benefits, but require participants to contribute a portion of the cost, may violate Treas. Reg. §1.501(c)(9)-3(f), see *Internal Revenue Service Exempt Organizations Continuing Professional Education Text for Fiscal Year 1999*, Chapter F, Voluntary Employees' Beneficiary Associations.) A benefit payable by reason of death may be settled in the form of an annuity to the beneficiary. Treas. Reg. §1.501(c)(9)-3(b).

Severance Pay Arrangements and Deferred Compensation under AJCA 2004

IRC Section 409A creates requirements governing whether and when employees are to be taxed on deferred compensation. Under the general rule, if a nonqualified deferred compensation plan (1) fails to meet certain requirements (regarding distributions, acceleration of benefits, and interest on tax liability payments; see Q 115) or (2) is not operated in accordance with such requirements, all compensation deferred under the plan for the taxable year and all preceding taxable years is includible in gross income for the taxable year to the extent not subject to a substantial risk of forfeiture and not previously included in gross income. IRC Sec. 409A(a)(1).

Unlike certain welfare benefits (bona fide vacation leave, sick leave, compensatory time, disability pay, or death benefits), severance pay plans are *not* excluded from the definition of "nonqualified deferred compensation plan." See IRC Sec. 409A(d); Prop. Treas. Reg. §1.409A-1(a)(5).

According to the proposed regulations, a separation pay arrangement does not provide for a deferral of compensation if the arrangement is a collectively bargained separation pay arrangement that provides for separation pay upon an actual involuntary separation from service or pursuant to a "window program" (see below). Prop. Treas. Reg. §1.409A-1(b)(9)(ii). The term "window program" refers to a program established by the service recipient to provide for separation pay in connection with a separation from service, for a limited period of time (no greater than one year), to service providers who separate from service during that period or to service providers who separate from service during that period under specified circumstances. Prop. Treas. Reg. §1.409A-1(b)(9)(v).

The Treasury Department and the Service recognize that separation pay arrangements providing for short-term payments upon an involuntary separation from service are common arrangements, and that compliance with the provisions of IRC Section

409A may be burdensome. In addition, the Treasury Department and the Service recognize that where both the amount of the payments and the time over which such payments may be made are limited, these arrangements create fewer concerns with respect to manipulation of the timing of compensation income. Accordingly, the proposed regulations generally exempt such arrangements where the entire amount of separation payments does not exceed two times the service provider's annual compensation *or*, if less, two times the limit on annual compensation that may be taken into account for qualified plan purposes under IRC Section 401(a)(17) ($220,000 for 2006; $210,000 for 2005), each for the calendar year preceding the year in which the service provider separates from service. The separation pay must be paid no later than December 31 of the second calendar year following the calendar year in which the service provider teriminates service. See Preamble, REG-158080-04, 70 Fed. Reg. 57930, 57940 (10-4-2005); see also Prop. Treas. Reg. §1.409A-1(b)(9)(iii).

According to IRS interim guidance (released in January 2005), provided that plans were otherwise amended in compliance with IRC Section 409A(a), plans that provide severance pay benefits, and that are collectively bargained plans or do not cover any service providers who are key employees, such plans were not required to meet the requirements of IRC Section 409A during the calendar year 2005 with respect to such severance pay benefits. See Notice 2005-1, 2005-2 IRB 274, Q&A 19. The good faith compliance period originally provided under Q&A 19 has been extended through December 31, 2006. See REG-158080-04, 70 Fed. Reg. 57930, 57954 (10-4-2005).

The proposed regulations are generally applicable January 1, 2007. For further explanation of IRC Section 409A, see Q 115. *ASRS, Sec. 66, ¶690.4.*

506. Are an employer's contributions to a 501(c)(9) trust (VEBA) deductible?

As a general rule, contributions to an employer-funded VEBA are deductible to the extent contributions to an employee welfare benefit fund are deductible (see Q 494 through Q 497). See, e.g, *National Presto Indus., Inc. v. Comm.*, 104 TC 559 (1995); Let. Ruls. 9401033, 9351042, 9322041. *ASRS, Sec. 66, ¶¶620, 690.8(a).*

507. How are contributions to and benefits payable under 501(c)(9) trusts (VEBAs) taxed to participants?

Contributions

Whether an employer's contributions to a VEBA to provide particular benefits are taxable to participants would seem to be determined under generally applicable tax rules. The presence of the VEBA would not seem to require special treatment. For example, employer contributions to trusts providing accident and health benefits have been privately ruled to be excludable from participants' gross income as provided in IRC Section 106. See, e.g., Let. Ruls. 9513007, 9340054, 9151017, 9046023, 8534048, 8507024, 8445019.

Similarly, whether contributions to a VEBA are wages for FICA, FUTA, and federal income tax withholding purposes is generally determined under the FICA, FUTA, and withholding rules applicable to the kind(s) of benefit(s) at issue. See, e.g., Let. Ruls. 9340054, 8824030, 8534048.

Benefits

Both cash and noncash benefits provided through the association are included in (or excluded from) income under general tax rules. They are not given special tax treatment simply because they are provided by a 501(c)(9) association. Treas. Reg. §1.501(c)(9)-6.

Medical expense benefits and dismemberment and disability benefits appear to be tax-free or taxable to the participant under the rules applicable to employer-provided health insurance (see Q 159, Q 160) to the extent such benefits are attributable to *employer* contributions. Such benefits appear to be excludable from gross income to the extent allowed under the rules applicable to personal health insurance (see Q 155) to the extent such benefits are attributable to *participant* contributions. See, e.g., Let. Ruls. 9340054, 9151017, 9046023, 8534048, 8507024, 8445019, 8352022, 8344069. See also Let. Rul. 199930015 (long-term disability coverage purchased under either of two options would be attributable to employee contributions for purposes of IRC Section 104(a)(3); accordingly, if the union employees could be treated as a separate class of employees, the long-term disability benefits received by participants in new plans created under two different options would be excludable from the participants' gross income under IRC Section 104(a)(3)).

Fully insured group term life insurance coverage provided by an employer through a VEBA has been privately ruled to be excludable from the employee's gross income to the extent permitted by IRC Section 79. See Let. Ruls. 8302034, 8248108, 8226062, 8225147. (The exclusion rules of IRC Section 79 are discussed in Q 142.)

Fully insured group term life insurance coverage provided by employees to themselves through a VEBA has been considered not to be subject to the inclusion rules of IRC Section 79 where the insurance is not carried directly or indirectly by the employer. See Let. Ruls. 9549029, 8906023. Employees who purchased fully insured group term life insurance for their dependents through a VEBA were not required to include the cost of that coverage in their income as a fringe benefit where the employer's involvement with the arrangement was limited to providing reimbursed administrative services and the insurance was arranged and financed on an after-tax basis entirely by the employees. See Let. Ruls. 9549029, 9151033.

Fully insured group term life insurance death benefits payable by reason of the employee's death are excludable under IRC Section 101(a), at least where the benefits are paid directly from the insurance company to the beneficiary. See Let. Ruls. 8507024, 8352022, 8248108, 8226062, 8225147. After "extensive study," the IRS announced it would issue rulings on whether the death benefit under self-insured life insurance provided through a 501(c)(9) trust will be tax-exempt under IRC Section 101(a). Rev. Proc. 89-36, 1989-1 CB 919. See e.g., Let. Rul. 199921036 (general and accidental death benefits paid by a self-insured VEBA constituted amounts received under a life insurance contract and, therefore, were excludable from gross income under IRC Section 101(a); the arrangement was found to possess the requisite risk-shifting and risk-distributing elements necessary to establish the existence of a life insurance arrangement under *Helvering v. LeGierse*, 312 U.S. 531 (1941).) See also Let. Rul. 200002030. Uninsured death benefits payable under a private plan created under federal law constituted amounts received under a life insurance contract and were excludable from gross income under IRC Section 101(a). Let. Rul. 9840040 (as corrected by Let. Rul. 199903026).

WELFARE BENEFIT FUNDS
Q 507

Reimbursement of health insurance premiums under a collectively bargained "Retiree Premium Reimbursement Plan" would be excludable from the gross income of members under IRC Section 106. Let. Rul. 199902016.

Whether benefits provided through a VEBA are wages for FICA, FUTA, and federal income tax withholding purposes is generally determined under the FICA, FUTA, and withholding rules applicable to the kind(s) of benefit(s) at issue. See, e.g., Let. Ruls. 200043007, 9340054, 8824030, 8534048.

Rebates and Termination Distributions

Payments made by a company to its employees from its general assets to reimburse the employees for excess pre-tax and after-tax contributions to a VEBA were wages for FICA, FUTA, and income tax withholding purposes, the Service has ruled in a private letter ruling. If the employer had made the payments on behalf of the VEBA and then received reimbursement from the VEBA, the portion of the rebate attributable to employee after-tax contributions would have escaped such treatment. Let. Rul. 9203033.

Participants in an employee pay-all VEBA who were receiving disability benefits were not required to recognize income when, upon termination of the VEBA, they received disability insurance policies (purchased with VEBA assets) providing precisely the same benefits. Further, disability benefits under the policies were ruled excludable from income under IRC Section 104(a)(3) to the extent that disability benefits from the VEBA were excludable under that section. E.g., Let. Ruls. 9244035, 9219016, 9219014, 9219013.

Upon the termination of employee pay-all VEBAs and the distribution of their assets in cash, all participants were considered to have received income to the extent the distributions exceeded their contributions; those who had taken deductions for their contributions were considered to have received additional income in the amount of any contributions for which they had taken a deduction that reduced their tax liability in earlier years. Let. Ruls. 9147059, 9039009. See also 200023052. Where the distributions did not exceed the employees' contributions, the distributions were not wages for FICA or FUTA purposes. Let. Rul. 9039009.

Compare *Sheet Metal Workers Local 141 Supplemental Unemployment Benefit Trust Fund v. U.S.*, 64 F.3d 245 (6th Cir. 1995) (distributions at termination of supplemental unemployment benefit fund of amounts representing earnings on contributions to the fund were wages for FICA and FUTA purposes where the distributions derived solely from employer contributions and where eligibility for distribution payments was based on satisfaction of work requirements or their equivalents), *cert. denied*, 116 S. Ct. 713 (1996). *ASRS, Sec. 66, ¶690.8.*

PART II

FEDERAL ESTATE TAX

on

INSURANCE AND EMPLOYEE BENEFITS

ANNUITIES AND LIVING PROCEEDS

600. What, in general, are the estate tax results when decedent has been receiving payments under an annuity contract, or under an optional settlement of endowment maturity proceeds or life insurance cash surrender values?

If the decedent was receiving a straight life annuity, there is no property interest remaining at his death to be included in his gross estate. But if the contract provides a survivor benefit (as under a refund life annuity, joint and survivor annuity, or installment option), tax results depend upon whether the survivor benefit is payable to decedent's estate or to a named beneficiary and, if payable to a named beneficiary, upon who paid for the contract. If payable to decedent's estate, the value of the post-death payment or payments is includable in his gross estate under IRC Section 2033, as a property interest owned by him at the time of his death. If payable to a named beneficiary, generally the provisions of IRC Section 2039(a) and IRC Section 2039(b) apply, and inclusion in the gross estate is determined by a "premium payment" test. Thus, if the decedent purchased the contract (after March 3, 1931), the value of the refund or survivor benefit is includable in his gross estate. But in the event the decedent furnished only part of the purchase price, his gross estate includes only a proportional share of this value. (See Q 601 to Q 605.) The foregoing rules do not apply to death proceeds of life insurance on the life of the decedent (see Q 626). And special statutory provisions apply to employee annuities under qualified pension and profit-sharing plans (see Q 673, Q 674), to certain other employee annuities (see Q 672, Q 686), and to individual retirement plans (see Q 648).

Life insurance or annuity proceeds payable to a surviving spouse qualify for the marital deduction if certain conditions are met (see Q 663). If the proceeds used the marital deduction in the first spouse's estate and the contract provides a survivor benefit to the surviving spouse's estate or to a person surviving the surviving spouse, then the proceeds are usually includable in the surviving spouse's estate. However, if the surviving spouse receives a straight life annuity, there is no property interest remaining at his death to be included in his gross estate. *ASRS, Sec. 54, ¶24.1.*

601. If an individual purchases a deferred or retirement annuity and dies before the contract matures, is the death value of the contract includable in his estate?

Generally, yes; the amount payable upon death before maturity is not life insurance; the estate tax rules for annuities apply. The same rules apply to the proceeds of a retirement income endowment if the insured dies after the terminal reserve value equals or exceeds the face value. Treas. Reg. §20.2039-1(d). If the death benefit is payable to annuitant's estate, its value is includable in his gross estate, under IRC Section 2033, as a property interest owned by him at the time of his death. If the death benefit is payable to a named beneficiary and annuitant purchased the contract (after March 3, 1931), the value of the death benefit is generally includable in his gross estate under IRC Section 2039–whether or not the right was reserved to change the beneficiary. However, if the individual purchased the annuity as a gift for another person, and retained no interest in the annuity payments, incidents of ownership, or refunds, the value of the annuity will ordinarily not be includable in the individual's gross estate (see Q 606). *ASRS, Sec. 54, ¶24.7.*

602. In the case of a joint and survivor annuity, what value is includable in the gross estate of the annuitant who dies first?

The value of the survivor's annuity is includable in the deceased annuitant's gross estate in proportion to his contribution toward the purchase price of the contract. IRC Sec. 2039(a) and (b). (But this rule applies only to contracts purchased after March 3, 1931.) Thus, if the deceased annuitant purchased the contract, the full value of the survivor's annuity is includable in his gross estate. But if the *survivor* purchased the contract, no part of the value is includable in the deceased annuitant's estate. If both contributed to the purchase price, only a proportionate part of the value is includable in deceased's estate. For example, suppose that decedent and his wife each contributed $15,000 to the purchase price of a joint and survivor annuity payable for their joint lives and the life of the survivor. If the value of the survivor's annuity is $20,000 at decedent's death, the amount to be included in his gross estate is one-half of $20,000 ($10,000) since he contributed one-half of the cost of the contract. Treas. Reg. §20.2039-1(c)(Ex. 1). In accord with this rule, if a joint and survivor annuity is purchased with community funds, only one-half of the value of the survivor's annuity is includable in the gross estate of the spouse who dies first. *Est. of Mearkle v. Comm.*, 129 F.2d 386 (3rd Cir. 1942); *Comm. v. Est. of Wilder*, 118 F.2d 281 (5th Cir. 1941). (For estate tax value of survivor's annuity, see Q 603.) Where a joint and survivor annuity between spouses is treated as qualifying terminable interest property for gift tax purposes (see Q 731) and the donee spouse dies before the donor spouse, nothing is included in the donee spouse's estate by reason of the qualifying interest. IRC Sec. 2523(f)(6). Where decedent has paid a gift tax in connection with the irrevocable designation of a survivor annuitant, see Q 870. Where the survivor is the deceased annuitant's spouse, the value of the survivor's annuity will qualify for the marital deduction if the contract satisfies the conditions discussed at Q 663.

Planning Point: A joint and survivor annuity between spouses will usually escape estate tax in both spouse's estates because of the marital deduction and because the annuity ends at the survivor's death.

ASRS, Sec. 54, ¶24.5.

603. What is the estate tax value of a survivor's annuity under a joint and survivor annuity contract?

The amount the same insurance company would charge the survivor for a single life annuity as of the date of the first annuitant's death. Treas. Reg. §20.2031-8; *Est. of Mearkle v. Comm.*, 129 F.2d 386 (3rd Cir. 1942); *Christiernin v. Manning*, 138 F. Supp.

ANNUITIES AND LIVING PROCEEDS

Q 605

923 (D.N.J. 1956); *Est. of Pruyn v. Comm.*, 12 TC 754 (1949); *Est. of Welliver v. Comm.*, 8 TC 165 (1947). However, where it can be proved that the survivor's life expectancy is below average, it may be possible to obtain a valuation based upon the survivor's actual life expectancy at date of decedent's death. *Est. of Jennings v. Comm.*, 10 TC 323 (1948); *Est. of Dalton v. Comm.*, 52 AFTR 1919 (S.D. Ind. 1956). For example, lower valuation has been obtained upon proof that the surviving annuitant's life expectancy was short because of an incurable disease. *Est. of Denbigh v. Comm.*, 7 TC 387 (1946), acq., 1953-1 CB 4; *Est. of Hoelzel v. Comm.*, 28 TC 384 (1957), acq., 1957-2 CB 5.

Even if the executor elects to value estate assets as of six months after death (alternate valuation), the survivor's annuity is valued at date of death. (Date of death value is used, despite election of alternate valuation, where any change in value after death is due only to lapse of time.) But if the surviving annuitant dies during the six months following the first annuitant's death, a lower valuation may be obtained by electing alternate valuation. Thus, in one case, where the survivor died before the optional valuation date, the value at optional valuation date was determined by subtracting the cost of an annuity as of the survivor's date of death from the cost of an annuity as of the first annuitant's date of death. *Est. of Hance v. Comm.*, 18 TC 499 (1952). *ASRS, Sec. 54, ¶24.5.*

604. In the case of a refund or period certain annuity, is the balance of the guaranteed amount, payable after annuitant's death, includable in the annuitant's gross estate?

If payable to the annuitant's estate, it is includable in his gross estate under IRC Section 2033, as a property interest owned by him at death. If payable to a named beneficiary, and *annuitant* purchased the contract (after March 3, 1931), it is includable in his gross estate under IRC Section 2039(a); it is immaterial whether the beneficiary designation was revocable or irrevocable. If the refund beneficiary is a charitable organization, the estate is entitled to a deduction for the value of the transfer to a charitable organization. IRC Sec. 2055. But where a decedent has directed his executor to purchase a refund annuity for a personal beneficiary and to name a charitable organization as refund beneficiary, decedent's estate is not entitled to a charitable deduction for the value of the refund. Treas. Reg. §20.2055-2(b); *Choffin's Est. v. U.S.*, 222 F. Supp. 34 (S.D. Fla. 1963). *ASRS, Sec. 54, ¶24.3.*

605. Are the death proceeds payable under a single premium annuity and life insurance combination includable in the annuitant's gross estate?

It has been held that even though the insured-annuitant holds no incidents of ownership in the life insurance policy at death, the proceeds of the policy are nevertheless includable in his gross estate, under IRC Section 2039, as a payment under an annuity contract purchased by him. *Est. of Montgomery v. Comm.*, 56 TC 489 (1971), aff'd 458 F.2d 616 (5th Cir. 1972), cert. den., 409 U.S. 849 (1972); *Sussman v. U.S.*, 76-1 USTC ¶13,126 (E.D. N.Y. 1975). In a case decided before IRC Section 2039 was enacted, the U.S. Supreme Court held that the proceeds were not includable in the insured-annuitant's gross estate, under IRC Section 2036, as property transferred by him in which he retained a right to income for life. *Fidelity-Philadelphia Trust Co. v. Smith*, 356 U.S. 274 (1958). If the insured-annuitant transfers the life insurance policy within three years before his death, the proceeds may be includable in his gross estate, under IRC Section 2035 (see Q 642). *U.S. v. Tonkin*, 150 F.2d 531 (3rd Cir. 1945). If the insured-annuitant owns the life insurance policy at death, the proceeds are includable in his gross estate either as property owned by him at time of death (IRC Sec. 2033), or as a payment under an annuity contract purchased by him (IRC Sec. 2039). *ASRS, Sec. 54, ¶40.*

606. If the decedent purchased an annuity on the life of another person, will the value of the contract be includable in his gross estate?

If the decedent purchased the annuity as a gift for the other person, and retained no interest in the annuity payments, incidents of ownership, or refunds, the value of the annuity will ordinarily not be includable in his gross estate. See *Wishard v. U.S.*, 143 F.2d 704 (7th Cir. 1944). See Q 860 for the rules pertaining to gifts of property (including annuities) made within 3 years of death. But if the decedent has named himself as refund beneficiary, the value of the refund may be taxable in his estate as a transfer intended to take effect at death. IRC Sec. 2037(a). This rule is not applicable, however, unless the value of the refund exceeds 5% of the value of the annuity immediately before the donor's death. Moreover, if the donee-annuitant has the power to surrender the contract or to change the refund beneficiary, it would appear that such a power would preclude taxation in the donor's estate as a transfer to take effect at death (see Q 853(5)). IRC Sec. 2037(b); see *Est. of Hofford v. Comm.*, 4 TC 542 (1945). Where the decedent retains ownership of the contract until his death, the value in the gross estate would apparently be the cost of a comparable contract at the time of his death. In one case, however, where decedent and his wife paid one-half the cost of an annuity for their son, reserving to themselves the right to surrender the contract, only one-half the surrender value was included in the decedent's gross estate. *Wishard v. U.S.*, supra. *ASRS, Sec. 54, ¶24.9.*

607. If a person makes a gift of an annuity, will the value of any refund be includable in the donee-annuitant's estate?

If the donor irrevocably names one person to receive the income for life, and irrevocably names another to receive the refund, the value of the refund at the donee-annuitant's death should not be includable in the donee-annuitant's gross estate. IRC Section 2039 is not applicable because the donee-annuitant is not the purchaser of the contract (see Q 600). *ASRS, Sec. 54, ¶24.9.*

608. If decedent has been receiving payments under a private annuity, what is includable in his estate?

In the usual private annuity transaction (see Q 41), where the decedent is the sole annuitant, the annuity ceases at the decedent's death and there is nothing to be taxed in his estate. If, however, under the terms of the private annuity agreement, benefits are payable to a survivor, the value of such benefits is includable in decedent's estate. (See Q 910, for valuation of private annuities.) Survivor benefits paid to a surviving spouse under a joint and survivor annuity should qualify for the marital deduction.

If the transaction resulted in a gift from the annuitant to the obligor (see Q 705), annuitant's death within three years of the transaction may result in the value of the gift (plus gift tax paid) being included in the deceased annuitant's gross estate (see Q 860). If annuitant's death does not occur within three years, but the gift was a *taxable* gift, the gift will be an *adjusted taxable* gift for purposes of the estate tax computation in the annuitant's estate (see Q 852).

In the usual private annuity transaction, the annuitant's transfer of the property given in exchange for the annuity is complete and absolute. Under such circumstances, no part of the transferred property is includable in the annuitant's estate. If, however, the annuitant retains at his death an interest in the property transferred, the value of the property could be includable in his gross estate under such of IRC Sections 2033, 2036, 2037 or 2038 as may be appropriate under the circumstances (see Q 853(1), (4), (5), (6)). *ASRS, Sec. 54, ¶24.10.*

LIFE INSURANCE IN BUSINESS

INSURANCE ON KEY PERSONS, PARTNERS, STOCKHOLDERS

609. If a partnership purchases and owns life insurance on the life of a partner, are the proceeds includable in the insured partner's estate?

If the partnership is both policyowner and beneficiary, the insurance proceeds, as such, are not includable in the insured's gross estate under the incidents of ownership test (Q 630). *Est. of Knipp v. Comm.*, 25 TC 153 (1955), acq. in result, 1959-1 CB 4; *Est. of Atkins v. Comm.*, 2 TC 332 (1943); Rev. Rul. 83-147, 1983-2 CB 158. Proceeds received by the partnership will be included with other partnership assets in determining the value of decedent's partnership interest for estate tax purposes; consequently, his gross estate will reflect a share of the proceeds proportionate to his partnership interest. IRC Sec. 2033. If the insured has personal incidents of ownership in the policy, such as the right to change the beneficiary, the entire value of the proceeds will be includable in his gross estate. See IRC Sec. 2042(2); *Hall v. Wheeler*, 174 F. Supp. 418 (D. Me. 1959); *Est. of Piggott v. Comm.*, TC Memo 1963-61, aff'd 340 F.2d 829 (6th Cir. 1965). Where the death proceeds are payable to the partner's personal beneficiary, the insured is deemed to own an incident of ownership in the insurance in his capacity as a partner for purposes of IRC Sec. 2042(2), regardless of the percentage of his partnership interest; consequently, if the partnership owns the insurance at his death, the entire proceeds will be includable in his estate. Rev. Rul. 83-147, 1983-2 CB 158; GCM 39034 (9-21-83). (But see Q 645 for estate tax treatment of group term life insurance covering the life of a partner.) *ASRS, Sec. 54, ¶¶41.4, 43.*

610. If a corporation purchases life insurance on the life of a key person to indemnify the business against loss on account of his death, are the proceeds includable in the insured's estate?

If, at insured's death, the policy was owned by and payable to the corporation and insured possessed no "incidents of ownership" in the policy (see Q 630 to Q 631), the proceeds are not includable in insured's gross estate. But if insured possessed at his death any incidents of ownership in the policy, the proceeds are includable in his gross estate even though the corporation has been named owner and beneficiary. IRC Sec. 2042(2); *Est. of Piggott v. Comm.*, 340 F.2d 829 (6th Cir. 1965), aff'g TC Memo 1963-61; *Hall v. Wheeler*, 174 F. Supp. 418 (D. Me. 1959); *Kearns v. U.S.*, 399 F.2d 226 (Ct. Cl. 1968); *Est. of Cockrill v. O'Hara*, 302 F. Supp. 1365 (M.D. Tenn. 1969).

Death proceeds of life insurance owned by and payable to a corporation are considered, along with the other nonoperating assets, as a relevant factor in valuing the corporation's stock for estate tax purposes (but see Q 612). Treas. Reg. §20.2031-2(f).

Consequently, where the insured is a stockholder, the value of such proceeds will be reflected in valuing the stock includable in his gross estate. *Est. of Blair v. Comm.*, 4 BTA 959 (1926); *Est. of Doerken v. Comm.*, 46 BTA 809 (1926); *In re Patton's Will*, 278 N.W. 866 (Wisc. 1938); *In re Reed's Est.*, 153 N.E. 47 (N.Y. 1926); *Kennedy v. Comm.*, 4 BTA 330 (1926); *Est. of Carew v. Comm.*, 311 A2d 185 (N.J. 1973). It is not correct to value the stock first, without considering the insurance proceeds, and then simply add the amount of proceeds to such value. *Est. of Huntsman v. Comm.*, 66 TC 861 (1976), acq. 1977-1 CB 1. Factoring life insurance proceeds into the valuation of the stock may or may not, depending on the appropriate valuation method, result in an increase in value equal to the full value of the insurance proceeds. *Est. of Blount v. Comm.*, TC Memo 2004-116.

It may be possible to obtain some reduction in the value of the stock to reflect the loss to the business of the key person's services. Rev. Rul. 59-60, Sec. 4.02(b), 1959-1 CB 237; *Newell v. Comm.*, 66 F.2d 102 (7th Cir. 1933); *Est. of Huntsman*, supra. However, the executor must offer proof to establish that the insured's death did actually cause a loss; a loss does not result *per se* from the death of the owner and manager of a corporation. *Est. of Scherer v. Comm.*, 1940 P-H BTA Memorandum Decisions ¶40,530. Also, it has been held that no decrease in value for loss of insured's services will be allowed if the stock is stock of a personal holding company whose assets consist almost entirely of stocks and bonds; the corporation must be an operating business requiring management, with going value and good will. *In re Patton's Will*, above.

If the insured is a *controlling* stockholder (i.e., one who owns stock possessing more than 50% of the total combined voting power of the corporation), then to the extent proceeds are payable *other* than to or for the benefit of the corporation, any incidents of ownership in the insurance held by the corporation as to such proceeds will be attributed to the insured and thereby cause such proceeds to be includable in insured's gross estate. Treas. Reg. §20.2042-1(c)(6). In Rev. Rul. 82-141, 1982-2 CB 209, X corporation owned insurance on the life of its controlling stockholder, D. The corporation assigned all its incidents of ownership in the policy to A. D died in 1981 within three years of the assignment, and the proceeds of the policy were paid to A. The Service held that the proceeds were includable in D's estate under IRC Section 2035 (see Q 642) by reason of attribution to D of the incidents of ownership held by the corporation. The ruling failed to state who was beneficiary under the policy before the assignment. The Service also held that proceeds were includable in the insured's estate under IRC Section 2035 where a corporation transferred a policy insuring the controlling shareholder to a third person within three years of the insured's death even though the insured disposed of his stock after the transfer of the policy and prior to his death. Rev. Rul. 90-21, 1990-1 CB 172, Situation 1. Proceeds were also includable in an insured's estate where the corporation retained ownership of the policy and the insured transferred enough stock so as to cease being a controlling shareholder within three years of death. Rev. Rul. 90-21, 1990-1 CB 172, Situation 2. (See also Q 615.) *ASRS, Sec. 54, ¶41.*

611. If partners or stockholders enter into a buy-and-sell agreement, and each purchases life insurance on the lives of the others to fund the agreement, are the proceeds includable in an insured's gross estate?

If, under this cross-purchase arrangement, proceeds are not payable to insured's estate, and the insured has no incidents of ownership in the policies on his life, the

LIFE INSURANCE IN BUSINESS

Q 612

proceeds are not includable in his gross estate. IRC Sec. 2042; Rev. Rul. 56-397, 1956-2 CB 599. In one case the Tax Court held that a provision in the agreement that prohibited the policy owner from surrendering the policy, borrowing against the policy, or changing the beneficiary of the policy without the insured's consent did not give the insured incidents of ownership in the policy. *Est. of Infante v. Comm.*, TC Memo 1970-206 (appeal dismissed). (But see Q 631.) The value of his partnership interest or corporate stock is includable. *Est. of Riecker v. Comm.*, TC Memo 1944. The value of any unmatured policies he owns on the life of his associates will also be includable.

If the proceeds are payable to insured's estate, or if the insured has incidents of ownership in a policy on his life, the proceeds are includable in his gross estate. However, where the proceeds are includable in the gross estate but the estate is obligated to apply them to the purchase price of the insured's business interest, the value of the business interest will be includable in the gross estate only to the extent that it exceeds the value of the proceeds. In other words, there will be no double taxation. *Est. of Mitchell v. Comm.*, 37 BTA 1 (1938), acq.; *Est. of Tompkins v. Comm.*, 13 TC 1054 (1949), acq.; *Est. of Ealy v. Comm.*, TC Memo 1951; *Dobrzensky v. Comm.*, 34 BTA 305 (1936); *Boston Safe Deposit & Trust Co. v. Comm.*, 30 BTA 679 (1934). However, there is some legal authority to the effect that the terms of the policy can be modified by the terms of the business agreement. Thus, where the agreement gave all beneficial ownership in the proceeds to insured's co-partners and obligated the parties to apply them to the purchase of insured's business interest, the proceeds were not included in insured's gross estate despite a policy provision giving insured the right to change the beneficiary. *Est. of Fuchs v. Comm.*, 47 TC 199 (1966), acq. 1967-2 CB 2; *First Nat'l Bank of Birmingham v. U.S.*, 358 F.2d 625 (5th Cir. 1966). *ASRS, Sec. 54, ¶¶42.1, 42.3.*

612. If life insurance is owned by and payable to a partnership or corporation to fund the purchase of an owner's business interest, are the proceeds includable in the insured owner's estate?

Since the proceeds are not payable to insured's estate and the insured has no incidents of ownership in the policy (at least in his capacity as an individual), the proceeds are not includable in his gross estate. IRC Sec. 2042; *Est. of Knipp v. Comm.*, 25 TC 153 (1955), acq. in result, 1959-1 CB 4; Rev. Rul. 83-147, 1983-2 CB 158. The same result should obtain where the business owns the insurance but the proceeds are payable to a trustee who must use them to purchase insured's business interest for the partnership or corporation.

The value of the business interest is, of course, includable in insured's gross estate. *Wilson v. Crooks*, 52 F.2d 692 (W.D. Mo. 1931); *Est. of Ealy v. Comm.*, TC Memo 5-9-51; *Est. of Riecker v. Comm.*, TC Memo 12-11-44; *Est. of Atkins v. Comm.*, 2 TC 332 (1943); *Est. of Knipp*, supra.

In valuing the insured's business interest, a part of the proceeds, proportionate to the insured's interest in the business, will be included unless: (1) the proceeds are excluded from the purchase price under the terms of the agreement, and (2) the agreement is effective in fixing the value of the business interest for estate tax purposes (see Q 613). *Newell v. Comm.*, 66 F.2d 102 (7th Cir. 1933); *Kennedy v. Comm.*, 4 BTA 330 (1926); see also *Est. of Salt v. Comm.*, 17 TC 92 (1952); *Est. of Littick v. Comm.*, 31 TC 181 (1958), acq. in result 1984-2 CB 1; *Rubel v. Rubel*, 75 So. 2d 59 (Miss. 1954).

2006 Tax Facts on Insurance & Employee Benefits

Where the insured is a controlling stockholder, incidents of ownership in the insurance owned by the corporation are not attributable to the insured so as to cause the death proceeds to be includable in the decedent's gross estate under IRC Section 2042 (see Q 610). Treas. Reg. §20.2042-1(c)(6); Rev. Rul. 82-85, 1982-1 CB 137. See also *Est. of Huntsman v. Comm.*, 66 TC 861 (1976), acq. 1977-1 CB 1. *ASRS, Sec. 54,* ¶42.2.

613. How is a closely held business interest valued for federal estate tax purposes?

Fixing Value by Purchase Agreement

For purchase agreements entered into after October 8, 1990, or substantially modified after such date, the value of a closely held business interest is to be determined without regard to any purchase agreement exercisable at less than fair market value (determined without regard to such purchase agreement) unless the purchase agreement (1) is a bona fide business arrangement, (2) is not a device to transfer the property to members of the decedent's family for less than full or adequate consideration in money or money's worth, and (3) has terms comparable to those entered into by persons in an arm's length transaction. IRC Sec. 2703. See Q 915.

Whether or not the agreement is subject to IRC Section 2703, case law has established the additional following rules: (1) the estate must be obligated to sell at death (under either a mandatory purchase agreement or an option held by the business or survivors); (2) the price must be fixed by the terms of the agreement or the agreement must contain a formula or method for determining the price; (3) the agreement must prohibit the owner from disposing of his interest during life without first offering it to the other party or parties at no more than the contract price; (4) the price must be fair and adequate when the agreement is made. *May v. McGowan*, 194 F.2d 396 (2nd Cir. 1952); *Comm. v. Child's Est.*, 147 F.2d 368 (3rd Cir. 1945); *Comm. v. Bensel*, 100 F.2d 639 (3rd Cir. 1938); *Lomb v. Sugden*, 82 F.2d 166 (2nd Cir. 1936); *Wilson v. Bowers*, 57 F.2d 682 (2nd Cir. 1932); *Third Nat'l Bank v. U.S.*, 64 F. Supp. 198 (M.D. Tenn. 1946); *Est. of Mitchell v. Comm.*, 37 BTA 1 (1938); *Est. of Newman v. Comm.*, 31 BTA 772 (1934); *Est. of Riecker v. Comm.*, TC Memo 12-11-44; *Est. of Strange v. Comm.*, BTA Memo 4-29-42; *Citizens Fidelity & Trust Co. v. Comm.*, 209 F. Supp. 254 (W.D. Ky. 1962); *Est. of Littick v. Comm.*, 31 TC 181 (1958), acq. in result 1984-2 CB 1; *Est. of Salt v. Comm.*, 17 TC 92 (1951), acq.; *Brodrick v. Gore*, 224 F.2d 892 (10th Cir. 1955); *Davis v. U.S.*, 5 AFTR 2d 1902 (D. Utah 1960); *Mandel v. Sturr*, 52 AFTR 1585; *Fiorito v. Comm.*, 33 TC 440 (1959), acq.; *Est. of Weil v. Comm.*, 22 TC 1267 (1954), acq.; *Mathews v. U.S.*, 226 F. Supp. 1003 (E.D.N.Y. 1964); *Est. of Caplan v. Comm.*, TC Memo 1974-39; *Est. of Bischoff v. Comm.*, 69 TC 32 (1977); *Est. of Davis v. Comm.*, TC Memo 1978-69; *Est. of Seltzer v. Comm.*, TC Memo 1985-519; see also Treas. Reg. §20.2031-2(h); Treas. Reg. §20.2031-3; TAMs 8541005, 8710004. If a business purchase agreement calls for shares to be purchased from the estate with installment purchase notes bearing a rate of interest lower than the market rate at date of death, the executor may be allowed to discount the value of the shares by the difference between the interest rate called for in the buy-sell agreement and the rate prevailing at date of death. Let. Rul. 8245007.

A "first-offer" agreement, under which the survivors have no enforceable right to purchase the business interest, and can buy only if the executor wishes to sell, does not fix the value of the interest for estate tax purposes. *Worcester County Trust Co. v. Comm.*,

LIFE INSURANCE IN BUSINESS

Q 613

134 F.2d 578 (1st Cir. 1943); *City Bank Farmers Trust Co. v. Comm.*, 23 BTA 663 (1931); *Michigan Trust Co. v. Comm.*, 27 BTA 556 (1933). Or, if the agreement is between closely related persons and is merely a scheme for avoiding estate taxes, the price set in the agreement will not control. *Slocum v. U.S.*, 256 F. Supp. 753 (S.D.N.Y. 1966). A buy-sell agreement is not binding unless it represents a bona fide business agreement and is not testamentary in nature. *Est. of True v. Comm.*, 2004-2 USTC ¶60,495 (10th Cir. 2004). An agreement may be found to be a scheme for avoiding estate taxes even where it serves a bona-fide business purpose. *St. Louis County Bank v. U.S.*, 49 AFTR 2d ¶148,515 (8th Cir. 1982).

No effect will be given to an option or contract under which the decedent is free to dispose of the interest or shares at any price he chooses during life. *Est. of Caplan v. Comm.*, TC Memo 1974-39; *Est. of Gannon v. Comm.*, 21 TC 1073 (1954); *Est. of Trammell v. Comm.*, 18 TC 662 (1952); *Est. of Mathews v. Comm.*, 3 TC 525 (1944); *Hoffman v. Comm.*, 2 TC 1160 (1943); *Est. of Tompkins v. Comm.*, 13 TC 1054 (1949); Rev. Rul. 59-60, 1959-1 CB 237; Rev. Rul. 157, 1953-2 CB 255. On the other hand, an agreement that restricts sale during life, but not at death, will also fail to fix estate tax value. *Land v. U.S.*, 303 F.2d 170 (5th Cir. 1962). *ASRS, Sec. 54, ¶42.4.*

Value Where Not Covered by Purchase Agreement

Valuation of closely held corporation stock requires a determination of fair market value. The estate tax regulations define this as "the price at which the property would change hands between a willing buyer and a willing seller, neither being under compulsion to buy or sell and both having reasonable knowledge of the relevant facts." Treas. Reg. §20.2031-1(b).

Factors that should be considered when determining fair market value include: the company's net worth, prospective earning and dividend paying capacity, goodwill, the economic outlook in the particular industry and its management, the degree of control of the business represented by the block of stock to be valued, and the value of securities of corporations engaged in the same or similar lines of business which are listed on the stock exchange. Treas. Reg. §20.2031-2. See also Rev. Rul. 59-60, 1959-1 CB 237.

If a block of stock represents a controlling interest in a corporation, a "control premium" generally adds to the value of the stock. If, however, the shares constitute a minority ownership interest, a "minority discount" is often used. A premium may also attach for swing vote attributes where one block of stock may exercise control by joining with another block of stock. TAM 9436005. One memorandum valued stock included in the gross estate at a premium as a controlling interest, while applying a minority discount to the marital deduction portion which passed to the surviving spouse. TAM 9403005. Just because an interest being valued is a minority interest does not mean that a minority discount is available. *Godley v. Comm.*, 2002-1 USTC ¶60,436 (4th Cir. 2002) (partnerships held housing projects subject to long-term government contracts). However, one case valued stock with voting rights at no more than stock without voting rights. *Est. of Simplot v. Comm.*, 2001-1 USTC ¶60,405 (9th Cir. 2001).

The Tax Court has held that if real estate is specially valued for estate tax purposes under IRC Section 2032A (see Q 862), an estate may not take a minority discount with respect to stock in a corporation which held such real estate. *Est. of Maddox v. Comm.*, 93 TC 228 (1989). However, in a split decision, the Tenth Circuit has ruled

2006 Tax Facts on Insurance & Employee Benefits

659

that minority discounts and special use valuation under IRC Section 2032A are not mutually exclusive; it would apply the minority discount to the fair market value of the real estate (as owned through a partnership) and then apply the $750,000 cap on special use valuation to the difference between the fair market value as discounted and the special use value of the real estate. *Est. of Hoover v. Comm.*, 95-2 USTC ¶60,217 (10th Cir. 1995) (acq. 1998-2 CB xix), rev'g 102 TC 777 (1994).

The Fifth Circuit Court of Appeals has ruled that shares of stock in a decedent's estate were to be valued as a minority interest when the decedent himself owned less than 50%, despite the fact that control of the corporation was within the decedent's family, even when, immediately before death, the decedent and his spouse owned more than 50% of the stock as community property. The court also ruled that family attribution (see Q 82) would not apply to lump a decedent's stock with that of related parties for estate tax valuation purposes, both because of prior case law and because, to apply attribution would be inconsistent with the "willing buyer-willing seller" rule. *Est. of Bright v. Comm.*, 658 F.2d 999 (5th Cir. 1981). A minority discount will not be disallowed solely because a transferred interest would be part of a controlling interest if such interest were aggregated with interests held by family members. Rev. Rul. 93-12, 1993-1 CB 202. A minority discount was allowed even when the person to whom the interest was transferred was already a controlling shareholder. TAM 9432001. However, a couple of deathbed transactions were aggregated into a single integrated transfer to which a control premium attached rather than minority discounts where a parent (a 60% shareholder) sold a 30% interest in the corporation to a child (a 20% shareholder) and the parent had the corporation redeem the remaining 30% interest in the corporation held by the parent. TAM 9504004.

The Tax Court has determined that an estate would not be allowed a minority discount where the decedent transferred a small amount of stock immediately prior to death for the sole purpose of reducing her interest from a controlling interest to a minority interest for valuation purposes. *Est. of Murphy v. Comm.*, TC Memo 1990-472. Similarly, the Service has disallowed minority discounts while disregarding partnerships or LLCs created on the decedent's deathbed presumably to obtain minority discounts. TAMs 9719006, 9723009, 9725002, 9730004, 9735003, 9736004, 9842003. A couple of courts have rejected the idea that the partnership can be ignored for purposes of IRC Section 2703 (see Q 915).

However, a partnership or LLC entity may be included in the gross estate under IRC Section 2036 without benefit of discounts under a number of circumstances: e.g., if a decedent puts everything he owns in the entity, retains complete control over the income of the entity, uses the entity as a personal pocket book, or fails to follow entity formalities. *Est. of Strangi v. Comm.*, 2005-2 USTC ¶60,506 (5th Cir. 2005), aff'g TC Memo 2003-145; *Est. of Bongard v. Comm.*, 124 TC No. 8 (2005); *Est. of Bigelow v. Comm.*, TC Memo 2005-65; *Kimbell v. U.S.*, 2003-1 USTC ¶60,455 (N.D. Tex. 2003), rev'd 2004-1 USTC ¶60,486 (5th Cir. 2004); *Est. of Abraham v. Comm.*, TC Memo 2004-39; *Est. of Hilgren v. Comm.*, TC Memo 2004-46 (discount for business loan agreement was allowed); *Est. of Thompson v. Comm.*, 2004-2 USTC ¶60,489 (3rd Cir. 2004), aff'g TC Memo 2002-246. One case has held that IRC Section 2036 did not apply because the court concluded that the transfer to the partnership was a bona fide sale for an adequate consideration. *Kimbell v. U.S.*, 2004-1 USTC ¶60,486 (5th Cir. 2004), rev'g 2003-1 USTC ¶60,455 (N.D. Tex. 2003).

LIFE INSURANCE IN BUSINESS   Q 615

For more information on valuing property for estate tax purposes, see Q 862.

For additional special valuation rules contained in Chapter 14 of the IRC, see Q 912 to Q 916.

PARTNERSHIP INCOME CONTINUATION

614. Will the value of payments to a deceased partner's spouse, under a partnership income continuation agreement, be includable in the partner's estate?

Yes, whether the payments are of a guaranteed amount or a share of partnership profits for a certain number of years. Rev. Rul. 66-20, 1966-1 CB 214; Rev. Rul. 71-507, 1971-2 CB 331; *Est. of Riegelman v. Comm.*, 253 F.2d 315 (2nd Cir. 1958); *McClennen v. Comm.*, 131 F.2d 165 (1st Cir. 1942); *Est. of Beal v. Comm.*, 47 TC 269 (1966); *Winkle v. U.S.*, 160 F. Supp. 348 (W.D. Pa. 1958); *Est. of Degener v. Comm.*, 26 BTA 185 (1932); *Est. of Wood v. Comm.*, 26 BTA 533 (1932); *Est. of England v. Comm.*, BTA Memo 1941-181; *Est. of Lincoln v. Comm.*, BTA Memo 1942-685. The value of guaranteed payments is their present value at date of death. The value of a share in future partnership profits is based on past profits known as of the valuation date. *Est. of Hull v. Comm.*, 38 TC 512 (1962). Such payments are "income in respect of a decedent." IRC Secs. 753, 736(a). Consequently, the beneficiary will be entitled to an income tax deduction for any estate tax attributable to including the value of the payments in decedent's gross estate (see Q 827).

SPLIT DOLLAR INSURANCE PLAN

615. Are the proceeds of life insurance under a split dollar plan (or reverse split dollar plan) includable in the insured's gross estate?

A close reading of IRC Section 2042(2) (see Q 626) seems to call for the conclusion that if the insured in a split dollar plan (see Q 457), including a reverse split dollar plan (see Q 461), has any incident of ownership in the policy at his death (e.g., the right to name the beneficiary of proceeds in excess of the cash value, or the right to name the beneficiary of the cash value in the case of a reverse split dollar plan) the *entire* proceeds would be includable in his gross estate. IRC Section 2042(2) says, in pertinent part, "The value of the gross estate shall include the value of all property …. To the extent of the amount receivable by all other beneficiaries as insurance under policies on the life of the decedent with respect to which the decedent possessed at his death any of the incidents of ownership, exercisable either alone or in conjunction with any other person." Notice in particular the phrases "*all* other beneficiaries" (i.e., beneficiaries other than the insured's estate) and "*any* of the incidents of ownership" (emphasis added). The language certainly seems inclusive enough to call for the conclusion suggested. (See Rev. Ruls. 79-129, 82-145, discussed below.) Moreover, this seems to be the position of the Tax Court on the proper application of IRC Section 2042(2) to split dollar life insurance. (See the discussion of *Est. of Levy*, below.)

Estate tax results depend upon the substance of the arrangement (who has what incidents of ownership), not on whether the endorsement form or the collateral assignment form is used (see Q 457). Neither are estate tax results altered depending upon the source or purpose of premium payments. Rev. Rul. 76-274, 1976-2 CB 278.

2006 Tax Facts on Insurance & Employee Benefits

Non-Employer-Employee Relationship

In a 1979 ruling on a split dollar arrangement not in the employer-employee context, the trustee of a funded irrevocable insurance trust created by the insured, D, for the benefit of his spouse and children was designated policyowner and beneficiary of proceeds (of an ordinary life policy) in excess of the cash surrender value at death. The trust provided that D would pay the portion of the annual premium equal to the annual increase in cash value. The policy gave the insured the right to borrow against the cash surrender value up to the total of premiums paid by him (the trustee owned all other policy rights), and designated D's estate as beneficiary of the portion of proceeds equal to the cash value at death less outstanding indebtedness. The IRS ruled that the entire proceeds, both the portion payable to D's estate and the portion payable to the trustee, were includable in D's estate under IRC Section 2042. Rev. Rul. 79-129, 1979-1 CB 306. (See Q 655 for information on the estate taxation of funds remaining from a premium payment fund upon the death of the grantor insured of an irrevocable funded life insurance trust.)

However, proceeds would not be includable in an insured's estate under IRC Section 2042(2) where the insured's spouse and an irrevocable trust created by the insured but over which the insured retained no powers entered into a split dollar arrangement and the insured held no incidents of ownership in the policy. Let. Rul. 9636033. Nor would a husband and wife be treated as holding incidents of ownership under IRC Section 2042(2) where the husband and wife transferred cash to an irrevocable trust, the trust purchased a second to die policy on the life of the husband and wife, and the husband and wife entered into a collateral assignment split dollar arrangement with the trust whereby the trust would pay a portion of the premium equal to term rates, the husband and wife would pay the balance of the premium, and the only right held by the husband and wife was to be reimbursed for their premium payments through receipt of cash surrender values in excess of cash surrender values at the end of the initial policy year. Let. Rul. 9745019.

Employer-Employee Relationship

In *Schwager v. Comm.*, 64 TC 781 (1975), a sole proprietor applied for and owned a policy on the split dollar (endorsement) plan on the life of an employee. The beneficiary of proceeds equal to the cash value at death was designated in the policy as the "part A" beneficiary, and in this case was the employer. The beneficiary of proceeds in excess of the cash value, the "part B" beneficiary, was the employee's wife. By policy amendment, the "part B" beneficiary could not be changed without the insured's consent. The Tax Court decided that the insured's right to consent to a change of beneficiary was an incident of ownership, and held that the portion of proceeds paid to his widow was includable in his estate. (The opinion does not make it clear that only the portion of proceeds payable to the insured's widow was includable in the estate, but counsel for the taxpayer confirmed the fact for us. Apparently, the Commissioner did not try for the includability of more.)

In *Est. of Tomerlin v. Comm.*, TC Memo 1986-147, a corporation owned insurance on the life of the decedent, a 50% shareholder of the corporation. The policy provided that the corporation was the sole owner of the policy and that the death proceeds were to be divided between the corporation and the decedent's children. The corporation was to receive the proceeds equal to the premiums it had paid, and the decedent's children were to receive the balance. However, the decedent had been given incidents of ownership in the policy by agreement with the corporation, including the right to designate the beneficiaries of the policy. The Commissioner sought includability in the decedent's estate under IRC Section 2042(2) of the portion of the proceeds payable to the decedent's children, and the court found for the Commissioner.

Letter Ruling 9026041 held that the full value of the proceeds of a life insurance policy to be held subject to an endorsement reverse split dollar agreement would be included in the estate of the insured key person. The insured key person would hold incidents of ownership in the policy. However, the estate would be allowed to deduct the portion of the proceeds which would be payable to the corporate participant in the reverse split dollar arrangement.

Split Dollar Insurance on Controlling Stockholders

In the case of split dollar insurance owned by a corporation on the life of a controlling stockholder, special rules apply. Estate tax regulations provide that "if any part of the proceeds of the policy are not payable to or for the benefit of the corporation, ... any incidents of ownership held by the corporation as to that part of the proceeds will be attributed to the decedent through his stock ownership when the decedent is the sole or controlling stockholder. Thus, for example, if the decedent is the controlling stockholder in a corporation, and the corporation owns a life insurance policy on his life, the proceeds of which are payable to the decedent's spouse, the incidents of ownership held by the corporation will be attributed to the decedent through his stock ownership and the proceeds will be included in his gross estate under section 2042. If in this example the policy proceeds had been payable 40% to the decedent's spouse and 60% to the corporation, only 40% of the proceeds would be included in decedent's gross estate under section 2042." Treas. Reg. §20.2042-1(c)(6), as amended April 29, 1974.

Note that the above-quoted regulation attributes to the stockholder incidents of ownership held by the corporation "as to that part of the proceeds" not payable to or for the corporation. Apparently, the quoted phrase led IRS originally to take a position as to which it later reversed itself. In a 1976 ruling, the Service held that if under a split dollar agreement the corporation's incidents of ownership were limited to those appropriate to protecting its (IRS characterized) position as a lender of premium dollars (an incident such as the right to borrow against the policy but only to the extent of the portion of premiums it has advanced), so that the corporation's exercise of those rights could not impair the interests of the insured or his personal beneficiary, the corporation's incidents of ownership would not be attributed to the insured. Rev. Rul. 76-274 (Situation 3), 1976-2 CB 278.

In 1982, the Service ruled that its conclusion in Situation 3 of Rev. Rul. 76-274 was incorrect and indeed was inconsistent with Rev. Rul. 79-129 (discussed under "Non-Employer-Employee Relationship," above). IRS concluded that the incident of ownership described in Situation 3 of the 1976 ruling was attributable to the insured and that this attribution warrants inclusion of the entire amount of policy proceeds under IRC Section 2042(2). *However*, the Service added, "pursuant to the rule in section 20.2042-1(c)(6) adopted to prevent double taxation, to the extent that the proceeds are payable to the corporation, they are considered in valuing the decedent's stock under section 2031, rather than included under section 2042(2)." A grandfathering provision in the ruling reads as follows: "the conclusion in this revenue ruling reversing the holding in *Situation 3* of Rev. Rul. 76-274 will not be applied with respect to insurance policies obtained before [4 August 1982], except to the extent, if any, that there has been an increase, after [4 August 1982], in the amount of the insurance proceeds payable other than to or for the benefit of the corporation." Rev. Rul. 82-145, 1982-2 CB 213. (See Q 610.)

Est. of Thompson v. Comm., TC Memo 1981-200, a 1981 Tax Court case that supports the Service's position announced in Rev. Rul. 82-145, concerned an employer-pay-all split dollar whole life policy owned by a corporation on the life of its president and sole owner, the decedent. Under the plan, the death proceeds were divided between the corporation (the cash value portion) and the beneficiaries designated by decedent (the balance). The court found that the decedent owned incidents of ownership in the policy and concluded that an amount equal to the insurance proceeds payable to the beneficiary designated by decedent was includable in decedent's estate under IRC Section 2042(2). The portion of the proceeds payable to the corporation would of course be reflected in the value of the corporation's stock all of which was owned by decedent and therefore includable in his estate under IRC Section 2031.

The Tax Court agrees that in the split dollar context, *any* incident of ownership (see Q 631) owned by the corporation is attributable to the sole or controlling stockholder under Treas. Reg. §20.2042-1(c)(6). *Est. of Dimen v. Comm.*, 72 TC 198 (1979), aff'd without published opinion (3rd Cir. 1980). See also *Est. of Carlstrom v. Comm.*, 76 TC 142 (1981), acq. 1981-2 CB 1.

Letter Ruling 9348009 appears to conclude that an S corporation does not have incidents of ownership in insurance on the life of its owners held in a split dollar arrangement if the only interest the corporation has in the policy is to be reimbursed for its outlay for premiums made. This conclusion appears to be inconsistent with the official position of the IRS and of courts which have addressed this issue. It may be, although the ruling does not say so, that the ruling concluded that since the owners were not controlling shareholders, incidents of ownership held by the corporation would not be attributed to the owners. However, the issues of whether a corporation holds incidents of ownership and whether an owner is treated as holding incidents of ownership held by the corporation are ordinarily treated as separate issues. A later letter ruling involving a collateral assignment split dollar life insurance arrangement determined that a corporation would not be treated as holding incidents of ownership in the policy where the only right the corporation would hold would be, in essence, the right to be reimbursed for premiums paid by the corporation. As a result, the life insurance proceeds would not be includable in a controlling shareholder's estate. The importance of the ruling may have been undercut by its reliance on Rev. Rul. 76-274, see above, which was later reversed by Rev. Rul. 82-145, see above. Let. Rul. 9511046. Nevertheless, several rulings have since stated that a corporation or S corporation which has no interest in a collateral assignment split dollar arrangement other than to be reimbursed for its outlay for premiums made does not hold incidents of ownership (an issue which need not be reached where there is no controlling shareholder). Let. Rul. 9651030, 9709027, 9746006, 9808024.

Any transfer by the corporate employer of incidents of ownership in a split dollar policy on the life of the controlling stockholder to the insured's transferee within three years of the insured's death is considered a transfer by the insured for purposes of the bringback rule of IRC Section 2035 (see Q 642). Let. Rul. 8252016.

CHARITABLE GIFTS Q 616

In another Tax Court decision dealing with estate taxation of split dollar life insurance, a corporation owned two split dollar policies on the life of a stockholder who owned 80.4% of the voting stock. The corporation owned all incidents of ownership except that it could not change the beneficiary (for any amount in excess of the cash value, at least) without the approval of the insured's wife. The corporation was beneficiary of proceeds equal to the net cash value at death; the insured's widow was beneficiary of the excess proceeds. The executors of the insured's estate did not include any of the insurance proceeds in the estate since the insured at his death did not own directly any incidents of ownership in the policies. The Commissioner, in his deficiency notice, determined that the portion of policy proceeds payable to the insured's widow was includable in the estate. The court strongly supported the position of the government, that the incidents of ownership owned by the corporation were properly attributable to the insured. Moreover, the court indicated that had the Commissioner's deficiency notice called for inclusion in the estate of the entire proceeds (rather than just the portion payable to the insured's widow), the court would have supported the Commissioner. As it was, only the proceeds payable to the insured's widow were held includable in the insured's estate. *Est. of Levy v. Comm.*, 70 TC 873 (1978).

Does Plan Create True Indebtedness?

In the usual split dollar plan, the portion of the premium paid by the employer (or one who occupies his position in the arrangement) is not a true loan. Although the employer or his successor expects ultimately to recover such amount from death proceeds, the usual agreement does not obligate the insured to "repay" from any source other than the policy or otherwise to treat such amount as a debt.

For estate tax purposes, it may make a real difference whether or not a split dollar plan creates a true indebtedness. If there is an indebtedness, and if the entire proceeds are brought into the insured's gross estate under the incidents of ownership rule, the estate will be allowed a deduction under IRC Section 2053 (see Q 863) for the amount of the debt repaid from the insurance proceeds. In such case, the net result will be the same as if only the portion of proceeds payable to the insured's beneficiary were included in the insured's gross estate in the first place. But if there is no true indebtedness, and if the entire proceeds are brought into the insured's gross estate under the incidents of ownership rule, the portion of the proceeds going to the employer (or to whoever occupies his place in the arrangement) cannot be taken as an IRC Section 2053 deduction by the estate.

For estate taxation on the death of a third party owner of a policy on the split dollar plan, see Q 676. *ASRS, Sec. 65, ¶140.3.*

CHARITABLE GIFTS

616. If life insurance proceeds are payable to a religious, charitable or educational organization, is their value taxable in insured's gross estate?

Generally, no. If the insured has any incident of ownership in the policy at the time of his death, the proceeds are includable in his gross estate, but a charitable deduction is allowable for their full value. IRC Secs. 2042(2), 2055; *McKelvy v. Comm.*, 82 F.2d 395 (3rd Cir. 1936); *Comm. v. Pupin*, 107 F.2d 745 (2nd Cir. 1939).

However, if the law in the state of the donor's domicile does not recognize that a charity has an insurable interest (see ASRS, section 12, ¶20.24) in the life of the donor, complications may arise. In some states, a charity may not have an insurable interest with respect to a newly issued insurance policy given to charity or for a policy applied for and issued to the charity as owner and beneficiary. If the charity does not have an insurable interest and the insurer or the insured's estate raise the question of lack of an insurable interest, the insured's estate may be able to recover the proceeds (or the premiums paid). The proceeds are includable in the insured's estate to the extent that the proceeds could be received by the insured's estate. However, no charitable deduction may be allowed if the executor recovers the proceeds for the estate or if the executor were to fail to recover the proceeds and the proceeds passed to charity. See Let. Rul. 9110016 (revoked by Let. Rul. 9147040 when state law was amended to permit an insured to immediately transfer a newly purchased life insurance policy to charity). *ASRS, Sec. 54, ¶31.*

COLLECTION OF ESTATE TAXES FROM BENEFICIARY

617. To what extent can a beneficiary of life insurance proceeds be held liable for payment of federal estate tax falling on the insured's estate?

The executor has primary liability for paying the federal estate tax and he is expected to pay it from the probate estate before distribution. IRC Secs. 2002, 2205. However, under IRC Section 2206, unless the decedent has directed otherwise, the executor may ordinarily recover from a named beneficiary such portion of the total tax paid as the proceeds included in the gross estate and received by the beneficiary bear to the taxable estate (see Q 852). However, in the case of insurance proceeds receivable by the surviving spouse and qualifying for the marital deduction, IRC Section 2206 applies, if at all, only to proceeds in excess of the aggregate amount of marital deduction allowed the estate (see Q 864). Most states also have apportionment laws under which life insurance beneficiaries share the estate tax burden with estate beneficiaries. It is not entirely clear whether IRC Section 2206 imposes a duty on the executor to seek apportionment, or only gives him the power to do so. But, where the executor is unable to recover a pro-rata share of the estate tax from the beneficiary of the life insurance proceeds, the estate cannot claim a deduction under IRC Section 2054. It is a bad debt and as such is not deductible under IRC Section 2054. However, a legatee whose share of the estate bears the burden of tax attributable to the proceeds does get a bad debt deduction. Rev. Rul. 69-411, 1969-2 CB 177.

If the government is unable to collect the estate tax from the insured's estate, the tax can be collected from the beneficiary of the life insurance proceeds up to the full amount of the proceeds if the value of the proceeds was includable in the gross estate. Any person who receives property includable in a decedent's gross estate under IRC Sections 2034 to 2042 (see Q 853) is liable for the tax. IRC Secs. 6324(a), 6901; Treas. Reg. §20.2205-1; *U.S. v. Melman*, 398 F. Supp. 87 (E.D. Mo. 1975), aff'd 530 F.2d 790 (8th Cir. 1976). It is immaterial that insured's will directed payment from his general estate. *Lansburgh v. Comm.*, 35 BTA 928 (1937); *Matthews v. Comm.*, TC Memo 1950. However, an insurance company holding the proceeds under a settlement option is not liable for the tax. *John Hancock Mut. Life Ins. Co. v. Comm.*, 128 F.2d 745 (D.C. Cir. 1942). There is a split of authority as to whether transferee liability for interest on any unpaid tax is limited to the amount of proceeds received from the decedent's estate. *Baptiste v. Comm.*, 94-2 USTC ¶60,178 (11th Cir. 1994), aff'g in part 100 TC 252

(1993); *Baptiste v. Comm.*, 94-2 USTC ¶60,173 (8th Cir. 1994), cert. den., rev'g in part 100 TC 252 (1993). *ASRS, Sec. 54, ¶39.*

COMMUNITY (MARITAL) PROPERTY

618. How are proceeds of community property life insurance treated in the insured's estate?

Generally speaking, community property is recognized for federal tax purposes as belonging one-half to the husband and one-half to the wife. Consequently, if life insurance proceeds are community property, when the insured spouse dies first, only one-half of the proceeds are includable in his gross estate regardless of whether they are payable to his estate, his surviving spouse, or some other beneficiary. Treas. Reg. §20.2042-1(b)(2); *DeLappe v. Comm.* (La.) 113 F.2d 48 (5th Cir. 1940); *Howard v. U.S.* (La.) 125 F.2d 986 (5th Cir. 1942); *Est. of Moody v. Comm.* (Tex.) 42 BTA 987 (1940); *Lang v. Comm.* (Wash.) 304 U.S. 264 (1938); *Est. of Levy v. Comm.* (Cal.) 42 BTA 991 (1940); *McCoy v. Comm.* (Cal.) 29 BTA 822 (1934); *Nance v. U.S.* (Ariz.) 430 F.2d 662 (9th Cir. 1970). Where community proceeds are payable to insured's estate only one-half is considered receivable by or for the benefit of decedent's estate, the other half is received on behalf of his spouse. Where community proceeds are payable to a beneficiary other than insured's estate, the fact that under local community property law the insured had management powers over the insurance is not construed to mean that he possessed incidents of ownership (see Q 631) in his spouse's community half. Treas. Reg. §20.2042-1(c)(5). Local community property law determines the nature and extent of ownership of policy proceeds and policy rights. (With respect to life insurance issued under U.S. Government programs, see Q 644. See Q 621 for estate tax results where deaths of insured and spouse occur simultaneously.)

By way of contrast with the law in other community property states, it has been held under Louisiana law that the presumption of community *generally applicable to property acquired with community funds during marriage* does not apply to life insurance acquired by a spouse (a) on his own life payable to his spouse irrevocably, or (b) on his spouse's life where he has named himself policy owner and revocable beneficiary. In these cases, the policies were held to be the separate property of the noninsured spouse. *Catalano v. U.S.*, 429 F.2d 1058 (5th Cir. 1969); *Est. of Saia v. Comm.*, 61 TC 515 (1974), nonacq. 1978-2 CB 4; *Bergman v. Comm.*, 66 TC 887 (1976), acq. in result, 1976-2 CB 1. Under Louisiana law, life insurance proceeds were excluded entirely from an insured decedent's estate where the policy was treated as the separate property of the decedent's spouse and the proceeds were not payable to decedent's estate. Rev. Rul. 94-69, 1994-2 CB 241. According to the Supreme Court of Louisiana, "It is well settled in Louisiana that the proceeds of life insurance, if payable to a named beneficiary other than the estate of the insured, are not considered to be a part of the estate of the insured ... nor are they subject to community claims." *T.L. James & Co., Inc. v. Montgomery*, 332 So. 2d 834 (1976). However, in Louisiana, the presumption of community where the policy is purchased with community property does apply if one spouse is both the insured and named owner. *Est. of Burris v. Comm.*, TC Memo 2001-210. Therefore, if a Louisiana decedent purchased a life insurance policy during marriage, named the decedent as owner, and does not transfer ownership of the policy, the proceeds are presumed to be community property and one-half the proceeds are includable in decedent's estate. Rev. Rul. 2003-40, 2003-17 IRB 813. *ASRS, Sec. 54, ¶32.1.*

619. Where life insurance on the life of a spouse is bought with community funds and one of the spouses is designated policy owner, is the policy community property, or the separate property of the spouse designated as owner?

Generally, life insurance acquired after marriage, with community funds, is presumed to be community property, notwithstanding that only one of the spouses is designated policy owner. The mere act of designating the noninsured spouse as policy owner, say for the purpose of achieving certain tax results, will not of itself rebut the presumption; there must in addition be clear and convincing evidence that the policy was intended by the spouses to be the separate property of the spouse designated as owner and under his or her sole control. In the following cases, and a revenue ruling, the presumption was *not* rebutted: *Comm. v. Fleming*, 155 F.2d 204 (5th Cir. 1946); *Freedman v. U.S.*, 382 F.2d 742 (5th Cir. 1967); *First Nat'l Bank of Midland, Texas (Mathers) v. U.S.*, 291 F. Supp. 348 (1968), rev'd on other grounds 423 F.2d 1286 (5th Cir. 1970); *Lutich v. U.S.*, 29 AFTR2d 72-1583 (N.D. Cal. 1972); *Est. of Meyer v. Comm.*, 66 TC 41 (1976); *Est. of Madsen v. Comm.*, TC Memo 1979-289, 659 F.2d 897 (9th Cir. 1981); 82-2 USTC ¶13,495 (S.C. Wash. 1982); 82-2 USTC ¶13,500 (9th Cir. 1982), aff'g TC Memo 1979-289; *Daubert v. U.S.*, 533 F. Supp. 66 (W.D. Tex. 1981); Rev. Rul. 67-228, 1967-2 CB 331. In the following cases, the presumption *was* rebutted: *Parson v. U.S.*, 460 F.2d 228 (5th Cir. 1972); *Waite v. U.S.*, 32 AFTR2d 73-6238 (N.D. Tex. 1973); *Est. of McKee v. Comm.*, TC Memo 1978-108, appeals dismissed; *Kern v. U.S.*, 491 F.2d 436 (9th Cir. 1974); *Est. of Wilmot v. Comm.*, TC Memo 1970-240; *Kroloff v. U.S.*, 487 F.2d (9th Cir. 1973); *Est. of Crane v. Comm.*, TC Memo 1982-174; *Miner v. U.S.*, 50 AFTR2d ¶148,529 (S.D. Tex. 1982), gov't will not appeal; *Est. of Hutnik v. U.S.*, 83-2 USTC ¶13,539 (S.D. Tex. 1983). In Louisiana, the general presumption that property acquired with community funds during marriage is community property does not apply to life insurance acquired by one spouse under some circumstances (see Q 618).

In a 1986 case involving Nevada residents, the Tax Court came to the conclusion that although the decedent/husband/insured and his wife had succeeded in making the insurance policy the separate property of the wife, one-half the death proceeds payable to the wife as beneficiary was nonetheless included in the decedent's estate. Two circumstances accounted for this unusual result: First, the premiums were paid entirely with community property, and second, the insured died in 1978 and within three years of the date the policy was purchased. Following the reasoning in the line of cases represented by *Bel, Detroit Bank & Trust Co.*, and *First Nat'l Bank of Oregon* (see Q 642), the court held that the payment of the premium with community funds amounted to a transfer by the decedent to his wife of his community half of the funds so used, and therefore also amounted to a transfer of the policy itself for purposes of IRC Section 2035. *Est. of Hass v. Comm.*, TC Memo 1986-63.

620. What are the estate tax results in insured's estate where life insurance premiums have been paid with both community and separate funds?

Where premiums have been paid partly with the insured's separate funds and partly with community funds, one of two basic approaches is taken, depending on local law. Under California and Washington law, a "premium tracing rule" is applied, which says that the proceeds are part separate and part community in proportion that the premiums were paid with separate and community funds. Accordingly, in estate tax cases involving

COMMUNITY (MARITAL) PROPERTY   Q 621

California and Washington residents where this issue is presented, includable in the insured's estate is the proportion of proceeds considered paid for with the insured's separate property and one half the proportion of proceeds considered paid for with community property. *Lang v. Comm.*, 304 U.S. 264 (1938). Louisiana, Texas and probably New Mexico (possibly also Arizona) apply the "inception of title" doctrine in determining whether such proceeds are separate or community: Proceeds of life insurance bought initially as separate property remain separate property, although the community is entitled to be reimbursed for premiums paid from community funds; conversely, proceeds of insurance bought initially as community property remain community property, although the separate estate is entitled to be reimbursed for premiums paid from separate funds. In the case of a Texas decedent who purchases life insurance as his separate property, the amount includable in the gross estate as life insurance proceeds under IRC Section 2042 (see Q 625) is the face amount of policy proceeds less the amount of premiums paid with community funds. In addition, one-half the premiums paid with community funds is separately includable in the gross estate under IRC Section 2033 (see Q 853(1), (2)) as the decedent's interest in community property. Rev. Rul. 80-242, 1980-2 CB 276, modifying Rev. Rul. 54-272, 1954-2 CB 298; *Est. of Wildenthal v. Comm.*, TC Memo 1970-119. Apparently, in the case of Louisiana decedents, if the proceeds are community property and payable to the insured's estate or to a named beneficiary other than the surviving spouse, the entire proceeds are includable in the gross estate, but a deduction under IRC Section 2053 (see Q 863) for a claim by the marital community for reimbursement will be allowed if such claim is presented and actually paid by the insured's estate representatives. Rev. Rul. 232, paragraph (E), 1953-2 CB 268, revoked by Rev. Rul. 94-69, 1994-2 CB 241. But where the beneficiary is the surviving spouse, the treatment will be the same as in the case of a Texas decedent. Rev. Rul. 80-242, above. Nothing is included in the insured's estate if the policy is treated as the separate property of the noninsured spouse and the proceeds are not payable to the insured's estate. Rev. Rul. 94-69, 1994-2 CB 241 (and see Q 618). There are no rulings or cases on this issue concerning New Mexico or Arizona decedents.

If the resident of a community property state whose law provides that the income from a spouse's separate property is community property makes a gift of property (e.g., life insurance or premium dollars) to his spouse, the donor spouse does not, by operation of that law, retain an interest that will cause any portion of the transferred property to be included in the donor's gross estate under IRC Section 2036 (see Q 853(4)). *Est. of Wyly v. Comm.*, 610 F.2d 1282 (5th Cir. 1980). *ASRS, Sec. 54, ¶¶32, 44.3(k).*

621. Under what circumstances can death proceeds of community property life insurance payable to someone other than the surviving spouse be includable in the surviving spouse's gross estate?

If the insured elects to have death proceeds held under an interest or installment option for his surviving spouse with proceeds remaining at her death payable to another, a portion of such remaining proceeds may be includable in the surviving spouse's gross estate under IRC Section 2036 as a transfer by her of her community property interest with life income retained (see Q 853(4)). Such a transfer will be imputed to her if under state law the insured's death makes the transfer absolute (see Q 710). The amount includable is the value of the surviving spouse's community half of the remaining proceeds going to the beneficiary of the remainder interest, less the value (at the insured's death) of the surviving spouse's income interest in the *insured's* community half of the proceeds. *U.S. v. Gordon*, 406 F.2d 332 (5th Cir. 1969). In states where the noninsured spouse has a vested interest in the proceeds of community property life insurance (e.g., California and Washington), a gift of her community property interest should not be imputed to the surviving spouse unless she has consented to or acquiesced in the insured's disposition of the proceeds. See *Whiteley v. U.S.*, 214 F. Supp. 489 (W.D. Wash. 1963). But see, also, *Est. of Bothun v. Comm.*, TC Memo 1976-230, decided under California law, where an IRC Section 2036 transfer was imputed to the surviving spouse-primary beneficiary when, because she failed to survive a 15-day delayed payment clause, proceeds were paid to the contingent beneficiary. The opinion contained no suggestion of any evidence that the noninsured spouse had consented to the delayed payment clause.

IRS has ruled that where community property life insurance is payable to a named beneficiary other than the noninsured spouse, if deaths of the insured and spouse occur simultaneously when both possess the power to change beneficiary in conjunction with the other, one-half the proceeds is includable in each spouse's estate without regard to whether local law provides a presumption as to survivorship. Rev. Rul. 79-303, 1979-2 CB 332. *ASRS, Sec. 54, ¶¶32.1, 32.3.*

622. How is community property life insurance taxed where the spouse who is not the insured dies first?

One-half the value of the unmatured policy is includable in the non-insured spouse's gross estate. *U.S. v. Stewart* (Cal.) 270 F.2d 894 (9th Cir. 1959); *California Trust Co. v. Riddell* 136 F. Supp. 7 (S.D. Cal. 1955); Rev. Rul. 74-284, 1974-1 CB 276 (N.M.). The value of the policy is determined under Treasury Regulation Section 20.2031-8 (see Q 676). Rev. Rul. 75-100, 75-1 CB 303. The amount includable in the estate of the surviving insured spouse upon his or her subsequent death is determined by applying state law to the facts presented to ascertain the extent to which the proceeds are treated as community property or as separate property of the insured. See *Scott v. Comm.* (Cal.) 374 F.2d 154 (9th Cir. 1967); *Est. of Cavenaugh v. Comm.* (Tex.) 95-1 USTC ¶60,195 (5th Cir. 1995), rev'g in part 100 TC 407 (1993); *Est. of Cervin v. Comm.*, 97-1 USTC ¶60,274 (5th Cir. 1997), rev'g TC Memo 1994-550; Rev. Rul. 75-100, above (Tex.). *ASRS, Sec. 54, ¶32.2.*

CREDITOR INSURANCE

623. If a policy has been assigned as collateral security for insured's loan, are the life insurance proceeds includable in insured's gross estate?

Yes, regardless of policy ownership or beneficiary designation. To the extent that the creditor has a right to collect the debt from the proceeds, the proceeds are considered to be receivable for the benefit of the estate (see Q 626). IRC Sec. 2042(1); Treas. Reg. §20.2042-1(b); *Fidelity Trust Co. (Matthews) v. Comm.*, 3 TC 525 (1944); *Est. of Hofferbert v. Comm.*, 46 BTA 1101 (1942); *Morton v. Comm.*, 23 BTA 236 (1931); cf. *Prichard v. U.S.*, 397 F.2d 60 (5th Cir. 1968) and *Bintliff v. U.S.*, 462 F.2d 403 (5th Cir. 1972). It is immaterial whether the debt is actually paid from estate assets or that the beneficiary has a right to recover from the estate the amount of proceeds paid to the creditor. *Est. of Gwinn v. Comm.*, 25 TC 31 (1955); *Hornstein (Reinhold) v. Comm.*, TC Memo 1944. However, the amount of the debt outstanding at date of insured's death, with interest accrued to that date, is deductible in determining the taxable estate even

DEATH PROCEEDS OF LIFE INSURANCE   Q 626

though the debt is paid from the proceeds. Treas. Regs. §§20.2042-1(b)(1), 20.2053-4. (For policy loan, see Q 659). *ASRS, Sec. 54, ¶29.2.*

624. If a policy under which insured's spouse is the named beneficiary has been assigned as collateral security, will the full amount of the life insurance proceeds qualify for the marital deduction?

As a general rule, if a property interest passing to a surviving spouse is subject to an encumbrance, only the value of the property interest in excess of the amount of the encumbrance will qualify for the marital deduction. IRC Sec. 2056(b)(4)(B). But if the debt which is secured by the policy is actually paid from estate assets, or if the spouse-beneficiary has a right of subrogation against the estate and the estate is solvent, the full amount of the proceeds will qualify for the marital deduction despite the collateral assignment. *Est. of Gwinn v. Comm.*, 25 TC 31 (1955), acq. 1956-1 CB 4; *Wachovia Bank & Trust Co. v. U.S.*, 163 F. Supp. 832 (Ct. Cl. 1958); Treas. Reg. §20.2056(b)-4(b). (But for policy loans, see Q 659.)

DEATH PROCEEDS OF LIFE INSURANCE

625. What benefits payable at death are included in the term "life insurance" for estate tax purposes?

IRC Section 2042 deals specifically with the estate taxation of proceeds from insurance on the life of the decedent. According to regulations, the term "insurance," as used in IRC Section 2042, means life insurance of every description, including death benefits paid by fraternal societies operating under the lodge system. Treas. Reg. §20.2042-1(a). In the case of a retirement income endowment, the death proceeds are treated as insurance proceeds under IRC Section 2042 if the insured dies before the terminal reserve value equals or exceeds the face value; if the insured dies after that time, the proceeds are treated as death proceeds of an annuity contract (see Q 600, Q 601). Treas. Reg. §20.2039-1(d).

With respect to the proceeds of "no-fault" automobile liability insurance, the IRS has ruled on three categories of benefits: (1) *Survivors' loss benefits.* These are benefits payable only to certain named dependent survivors of the insured; if the insured dies leaving no such eligible dependents, no benefits are paid. The value of any such benefit is not includable in the insured's gross estate under IRC Section 2033 (see Q 853), nor under IRC Section 2042(2) because if the proceeds are life insurance (an issue the ruling did not decide) the insured would not have owned any incidents of ownership (Q 631) at his death. Rev. Rul. 82-5, 1982-1 CB 131. (2) *Basic economic loss benefit.* This benefit covers the insured's medical expenses and loss of income arising from his injury while operating an automobile. The value of this benefit is includable in the insured's gross estate under IRC Section 2033, but not under IRC Section 2042(1) (life insurance proceeds payable to or for insured's estate). Rev. Rul. 83-44, 1983-1 CB 228. (3) *Death benefit.* This is a benefit payable unconditionally to the estate of the insured and to the estate of any passenger in the insured's car killed in a covered accident. The value of this benefit is includable under IRC Section 2042(1) in the estate of each insured receiving the benefit. Rev. Rul. 83-44, above. *ASRS, Sec. 54, ¶¶24.8, 25.2, 44.3(a).*

626. Under what circumstances are death proceeds of life insurance includable in the insured's gross estate?

1. When the proceeds are payable to insured's estate, or are receivable for the benefit of his estate. IRC Sec. 2042(1). (See Q 627 to Q 629.)

2. When the proceeds are payable to a beneficiary other than insured's estate but the insured possessed one or more incidents of ownership in the policy at the time of his death (whether exercisable by insured alone or only in conjunction with another person). IRC Sec. 2042(2). (See Q 630 to Q 634.)

3. When the insured has made a gift of the policy on his life within 3 years before his death. IRC Sec. 2035. (See Q 642.)

4. When the insured has transferred the policy for less than an adequate consideration (i.e., the transaction was not a bona fide sale) and the transfer falls within one of the rules for includability contained in IRC Sections 2035, 2036, 2037, 2038, and 2041 (see Q 853). Under these circumstances, the value of the proceeds in excess of the value of the consideration received is includable in insured's estate. IRC Sec. 2043. *ASRS, Sec. 54, ¶25.*

PROCEEDS RECEIVABLE BY OR FOR THE BENEFIT OF INSURED'S ESTATE

627. If life insurance proceeds are payable to the insured's estate, is their value includable in his estate?

Yes, the entire value of the proceeds must be included in insured's gross estate even if insured possessed no incident of ownership in the policy, and paid none of the premiums. IRC Sec. 2042(1); *Est. of Bromley v. Comm.*, 16 BTA 1322 (1929). But see Q 619 to Q 620 for the rule in community property states. Proceeds payable to an executor in her individual capacity rather than as executor for the insured's estate were not treated as payable to the insured's estate. *Est. of Friedberg v. Comm.*, TC Memo 1992-310. *ASRS, Sec. 54, ¶25.3.*

628. Under what circumstances are life insurance proceeds includable in insured's gross estate even though the insured has no incident of ownership in the policy, and the proceeds are not payable to his estate?

Proceeds are includable in an insured's gross estate if they are receivable by or *for the benefit of* his estate. Thus, if the beneficiary is under a legally binding obligation to pay debts or taxes of insured's estate, the amount of proceeds required to discharge these debts and taxes (to the extent of the beneficiary's obligation) is includable in insured's gross estate. This is so, even though insured possessed no incidents of ownership in the policy at his death. Treas. Reg. §20.2042-1(b)(1); *Hooper v. Comm.*, 41 BTA 114 (1940); *Est. of Rohnert v. Comm.*, 40 BTA 1319 (1939); *Pacific Nat'l Bank of Seattle (Morgan) v. Comm.*, 40 BTA 128 (1939); *Davidson's Est. (Fourth Nat'l Bank in Wichita) v. Comm.*, 158 F.2d 239 (10th Cir. 1946). State law generally requires a life insurance beneficiary to forfeit the proceeds if he is convicted of feloniously killing the insured. Where state law further provides that in such case proceeds will be distributed to beneficiaries of the insured's estate (other than the felon), it has been held that the proceeds are treated for federal estate tax purposes as payable to the insured's estate. *Est. of Draper v. Comm.*, 536 F.2d 944 (1st Cir. 1976); *First Kentucky Trust Co. v. U.S.*, 84-2 USTC ¶13,581 (6th Cir. 1984); Let. Rul. 7909056. See also Q 623, with respect to insurance assigned as collateral. (For discretionary powers that may be granted to trustee, see Q 654.) (See also Q 642.) *ASRS, Sec. 54, ¶¶25.3, 36.*

DEATH PROCEEDS OF LIFE INSURANCE   Q 631

629. Is life insurance that is taken out to pay insured's death taxes includable in his estate?

The proceeds are includable in insured's gross estate if the beneficiary has a legally binding obligation to use them to pay insured's death taxes. Treas. Reg. §20.2042-1(b)(1). But the proceeds should not be includable in the gross estate merely because the beneficiary lends the proceeds to the estate, or uses the proceeds to buy assets from the estate. For powers that may be given to a trustee, see Q 654. *ASRS, Sec. 54, ¶25.3.*

PROCEEDS RECEIVABLE BY BENEFICIARIES
OTHER THAN INSURED'S ESTATE

630. Under what circumstances are life insurance proceeds that are payable to a beneficiary other than insured's estate includable in insured's estate?

The proceeds are includable in insured's gross estate if the insured *legally possessed* and could *legally exercise* any incidents of ownership at the time of his death. It does not matter that decedent did not have possession of the policy and therefore was unable to exercise his ownership rights at the time of his death (*Comm. v. Est. of Noel*, 380 U.S. 678 (1965)), or that decedent was unable as a practical matter to effect any change in the policy because the policy was collaterally assigned (*Est. of Goodwyn v. Comm.*, TC Memo 1973-153). The proceeds are includable even if the insured cannot exercise his ownership rights alone, but only in conjunction with another person. IRC Sec. 2042(2); *Goldstein's Est. v. U.S.*, 122 F. Supp. 677 (Ct. Cl. 1954). It has been held, however, that an insured who succeeded to ownership of insurance on his life as residuary legatee under the policyowner's will but died an hour after the policyowner died did not possess incidents of ownership in the policies; inasmuch as legal title and possession of personal property passed to the personal representative, insured did not have legal power to exercise the incidents of ownership. *Est. of Dawson v. Comm.*, 57 TC 837 (1972), aff'd by 3rd Cir. in unpublished decision. It has also been held that an insured did not possess incidents of ownership where he had paid no premiums, did not regard the policy as his own and had made an irrevocable designation of beneficiary and mode of payment of proceeds. *Morton v. U.S.*, 29 AFTR 2d 72-1531 (4th Cir. 1972). (For what constitutes an incident of ownership, see Q 631.) But even if the proceeds are payable to a beneficiary other than the insured's estate, and the insured possesses no incidents of ownership in the policy, the proceeds are nevertheless includable in his gross estate if they are receivable for the benefit of his estate (see Q 628). And even though insured retains no incidents of ownership in the policy, the proceeds may be includable in his estate if he has transferred the policy within 3 years before his death (see Q 642). See also Q 651. *ASRS, Sec. 54, ¶25.4.*

631. What are the incidents of ownership which, if held by the insured, will cause life insurance proceeds to be includable in his estate?

The proceeds will be includable in insured's gross estate if he possesses any of the following incidents of ownership at his death: the right to change the beneficiary; the right to surrender or cancel the policy; the right to assign the policy; the right to revoke an assignment; the right to pledge the policy for a loan; the right to obtain a policy loan. Treas. Reg. §20.2042-1(c)(2); *Chase Nat'l Bank v. U.S.*, 278 U.S. 327 (1929);

2006 Tax Facts on Insurance & Employee Benefits   673

Est. of DeVos v. Comm., TC Memo 1975-216; *Est. of Riefberg v. Comm.*, TC Memo 1982-70; *Liebmann v. Hassett*, 148 F.2d 247 (1st Cir. 1945); *Allentown Nat'l Bank v. Comm.*, 37 BTA 750 (1938). The reservation of a right to make premium loans has been held to be an incident of ownership. *Est. of McCoy v. Comm.*, TC Memo 1961-40. A right to change contingent beneficiaries who are to receive benefits after the primary beneficiary's death, is an incident of ownership. *Broderick v. Keefe*, 112 F.2d 293 (1st Cir. 1940); *Est. of Newbold v. Comm.*, TC Memo 6-4-45. The mere right to change the time or manner of payment of proceeds to the beneficiary, as by electing, changing or revoking settlement options, has been held an incident of ownership. *Est. of Lumpkin v. Comm.*, 474 F.2d 1092 (5th Cir. 1973). The Tax Court and the Third Circuit have held to the contrary: *Lumpkin v. Comm.*, 56 TC 815 (1971), rev'd by 5th Cir. (above); *Billings v. Comm.*, 35 BTA 1147 (1937), acq. withdrawn 1972-1 CB 3; *Est. of Connelly v. U.S.*, 551 F.2d 545 (3rd Cir. 1977). (In 1981, the IRS reiterated its opposition to the Third Circuit's holding in *Connelly*, and indicated its intent to continue to oppose that result in all circuits except the Third (Pa., Del., N.J., Virgin Islands). Rev. Rul. 81-128, 1981-1 CB 469.)

Trust provisions which changed beneficial interest from a decedent's spouse to the decedent's children if the decedent and his spouse became divorced was not the equivalent to a retained incident of ownership that would bring the life insurance proceeds into the decedent's estate. TAM 8819001. The memorandum implies that the result would have been different if the trust had provided that the beneficial interest would revert to the decedent upon divorce.

The right to receive disability income is an incident of ownership if payment of disability benefits would reduce the face amount payable at death. *Old Point Nat'l Bank v. Comm.*, 39 BTA 343 (1939). But where an employer corporation owned the policy and the insured employee was entitled to benefits under a disability income rider, the Commissioner did not claim that the right to the disability income was an incident of ownership which would cause the proceeds to be includable in insured's gross estate. *Est. of Morrow v. Comm.*, 19 TC 1068 (1953), acq. 1954-1 CB 5, nonacq. 1979-2 CB 2; *Est. of Dorson v. Comm.*, 4 TC 463 (1944).

An employee insured's right to designate the beneficiary of an employer-paid death benefit is not treated as an incident of ownership in the insurance funding the benefit if the employer is sole owner of the policy and sole beneficiary for its exclusive use. *Est. of Morrow*, above. IRS has taken the position that if the insured under a corporation-owned policy has an agreement with the corporation giving him first right to purchase the policy for its cash surrender value if the corporation decides to discontinue the coverage, the purchase option is an incident of ownership. Rev. Rul. 79-46, 1979-1 CB 303. However, the Tax Court has held that the insured's contingent purchase option as described in Rev. Rul. 79-46 is not an incident of ownership within the meaning of IRC Section 2042(2). *Est. of Smith v. Comm.*, 73 TC 307 (1979), acq. in result, 1981-1 CB 2. Also, the IRS has ruled that where, under an insured stock redemption agreement, a stockholder had the right to purchase the policies the corporation owned on his life if he ceased being a stockholder, such contingent purchase option was not an incident of ownership in the insurance. Let. Rul. 8049002. An insured who held the right to purchase a policy upon termination of a buy-sell agreement did not possess incidents of ownership so long as the contingency had not occurred, but would possess incidents once the agreement was terminated. TAM 9127007. Also, a shareholder was not treated as holding incidents of ownership in a life insurance policy where

DEATH PROCEEDS OF LIFE INSURANCE   Q 631

the shareholder could purchase a corporate-owned policy upon disability, or upon a cross-purchase of his stock if he dissented to sale of the corporation to a third party or a public offering. Let. Rul. 9233006. However, an insured was treated as holding incidents of ownership in a policy held in a trusteed buy-sell arrangement where the insured was considered to have transferred the policy to the trust and retained the right to purchase the policy for its cash surrender value. TAM 9349002. The right to receive dividends has been held *not* to be an incident of ownership in the policy. *Est. of Bowers v. Comm.*, 23 TC 911 (1955), acq.; *Old Point Nat'l Bank*, supra. It has been held that if the insured has the power to terminate the interest of the primary beneficiary with only the consent of the secondary beneficiary, the insured has an incident of ownership. *Est. of Goodwyn v. Comm.*, TC Memo 1973-153. However, a sole shareholder would not be treated as holding incidents of ownership in a life insurance policy on his own life where a collateral consequence of a termination of an employee's employment would be a termination of the employee's option agreement to purchase the shareholder's stock with a corresponding change in beneficiary of the insurance proceeds held in an irrevocable life insurance trust created by the employee. TAM 9421037. The assignment of a life insurance policy by a third party owner as an accommodation to the insured to cover his debts does not in itself create in the insured an incident of ownership. *Est. of Goodwyn*, supra. But if a policyowner collaterally assigns a policy as security for a loan and then makes a gift of the policy subject to the assignment, the donor will be deemed to have retained an incident of ownership. *Est. of Krischer v. Comm.*, TC Memo 1973-172.

Where an insurance funded buy-sell agreement prohibited each partner from borrowing against, surrendering or changing the beneficiary on the policy he owned on the life of his partner, without the insured's consent, it was held that the decedent-insured did not possess an incident of ownership in the policy insuring his life. *Est. of Infante v. Comm.*, TC Memo 1970-206 (appeal dismissed). However, it has been reported that IRS, citing an internal ruling from the Commissioner, dated January 7, 1971, has declined to follow the *Infante* decision. 55 *Taxes* (CCH) 146 (Feb. 1977). An insured was treated as holding incidents of ownership in a policy held in a trusteed buy-sell arrangement where the trust could only act as directed by the shareholders through the buy-sell agreement and the insured could thus withhold her consent to the exercise of policy rights. TAM 9349002 (cf. Let. Ruls. 9511009 and 9622036, in which no estate inclusion was required for life insurance held in a trust to fund a corporate buy-sell agreement).

Where insured absolutely assigned a policy which required his consent before the policy could be assigned to or the beneficiary changed to someone who had no insurable interest in his life, it was ruled that he had retained an incident of ownership. Rev. Rul. 75-70, 1975-1 CB 301. Similarly, the Tax Court has held that an employee's right to consent to a change of beneficiary on a split dollar policy owned by his employer on the employee's life is an incident of ownership. *Schwager v. Comm.*, 64 TC 781 (1975). The Tax Court has also held that where the insured assigned policies, retaining the right to consent to the assignee's designating as beneficiary, or assigning the policies to, anyone who did not have an insurable interest in the insured's life, the assignee's act of designating an irrevocable beneficiary did not eliminate the insured's retained incidents of ownership. However, the Third Circuit reversed the Tax Court in this case, taking the position that since under the facts presented the insured could not have enjoyed any economic benefit from exercising his veto power over the designation of beneficiaries or assignees, his retained power did not amount to an incident of ownership. *Est. of Rockwell v. Comm.*, 86-1 USTC ¶13,651 (3rd Cir. 1985), rev'g TC Memo 1984-654.

2006 Tax Facts on Insurance & Employee Benefits

The insured's right to purchase the policy from an assignee was treated as equivalent to the right to revoke an assignment which is an incident of ownership. TAM 9128008.

A more than 5% reversionary interest in the proceeds is an incident of ownership. IRC Sec. 2042(2). (See Q 634). Where a wife who owned insurance on her husband's life and who was the primary beneficiary changed the contingent beneficiary from her estate to whomever the insured named in his will, it was held that the insured did not possess at his death an incident of ownership. Rev. Rul. 79-117, 1979-1 CB 305. Cf. *Est. of Margrave v. Comm.*, Q 633. *ASRS, Sec. 54, ¶25.4.*

632. If the insured holds incidents of ownership at his death, but only as a fiduciary or by reason of a retained right to remove a trustee and appoint another, will the life insurance proceeds be includable in his estate?

The position of the IRS is that incidents of ownership held by the insured in a fiduciary capacity will cause includability of the proceeds in his estate only if (1) the incidents are exercisable for the insured's personal benefit, *or* (2) the insured transferred the policy or at least some of the consideration for purchasing or maintaining the policy to the trust from personal assets *and* the incidents of ownership devolved upon the insured as part of a prearranged plan involving the participation of the insured. The IRS states that this position is consistent with *Skifter, Fruehauf,* and *Hunter*, courts of appeals decisions discussed below. Rev. Rul. 84-179, 1984-2 CB 195, revoking Rev. Rul. 76-261, 1976-2 CB 276.

The regulations say that "A decedent is considered to have an 'incident of ownership' in an insurance policy on his life held in trust if, under the terms of the policy, the decedent (either alone or in conjunction with another person or persons) has the power (as trustee or otherwise) to change the beneficial ownership in the policy or its proceeds, or the time or manner of enjoyment thereof, even though the decedent has no beneficial interest in the trust." Treas. Reg. §20.2042-1(c)(4). The IRS says it will read this regulation in accordance with its position adopted in Rev. Rul. 84-179, above. The courts have taken three different views of the foregoing regulation:

(1) The U.S. Court of Appeals for the Sixth Circuit has held that the possession by the insured of incidents of ownership in a fiduciary capacity is not enough to bring the proceeds into his estate under IRC Section 2042(2) unless the insured had the power at his death to benefit himself or his estate by exercising any of the incidents. *Est. of Fruehauf v. Comm.*, 427 F.2d 80 (6th Cir. 1970). This also appears to be the view of the Tax Court. *Est. of Skifter v. Comm.*, 56 TC 1190 (1971), rev'd 468 F.2d 699, nonacq. 1978-1 CB 3 (see below). See, also, *Est. of Jordahl v. Comm.*, 65 TC 92 (1975), acq. 1977-1 CB 1, where the Tax Court held that the decedent's right, as trustee of a funded life insurance trust of which he was grantor and in which he had an income interest, to borrow against the policies to keep them in effect if trust income was insufficient, was not an incident of ownership because in fact the income never was insufficient. The court, in *Jordahl*, also ruled that decedent's reservation of the right, as grantor, to substitute "other policies of equal value" for those held in trust at any time was not an incident of ownership.

(2) The Second Circuit has limited the application of the foregoing regulation as follows: If an insured at his death possesses incidents of ownership in the insurance only as a consequence of having received them by transfer from a third party policyowner

DEATH PROCEEDS OF LIFE INSURANCE   Q 632

long after the insured had divested himself of all interest in the insurance (if he ever had any interest), then the proceeds are not includable in the insured's estate under 2042(2) unless the insured possessed the power to benefit himself or his estate by exercising any of the incidents he possessed; but if an insured is also policyowner and is the transferor of the insurance to a trust, then any incidents of ownership he possesses at his death, as trustee or otherwise, will cause includability of the proceeds in his estate, even if he cannot benefit himself economically by exercising those incidents. *Est. of Skifter v. Comm.*, 468 F.2d 699 (2nd Cir. 1972).

(3) The Fifth Circuit takes the view that the insured's mere possession at death of an incident of ownership (even the limited right, as trustee, to alter the time or manner of payment of death proceeds to the beneficiary), regardless of whether the insured could have benefited himself or his estate by exercising the incident, and regardless of how he came into possession of such incident, is sufficient to cause the proceeds to be included in his estate under IRC Section 2042(2). *Rose v. U.S.*, 511 F.2d 259 (5th Cir. 1975); *Terriberry v. U.S.*, 517 F.2d 286 (5th Cir. 1975), cert. denied 424 U.S. 977. In Rev. Rul. 84-179, above, IRS revoked Rev. Rul. 76-261, which supported the Fifth Circuit's position.

The Fifth Circuit seems to stand alone in its broad scope view of IRC Section 2042(2). Courts outside the Fifth Circuit (in addition to the Tax Court and Second and Sixth Circuits) have generally taken the view that an insured who receives fiduciary powers over policies of insurance on his life from a third party policyowner does not (merely by reason of possessing those powers) possess incidents of ownership in such policies within the meaning of the statute unless it is possible for the insured to benefit himself or his estate economically by exercising any of those powers. *Gesner v. U.S.*, 79-2 USTC ¶13,305 (Ct. Cl. 1979); *Hunter v. U.S.*, 46 AFTR 2nd ¶148,409 (8th Cir. 1980). See also *Est. of Connelly v. U.S.*, 551 F.2d 545 (3rd Cir. 1977). Where the decedent insured as executor was given the power to surrender policies for cash to pay death taxes and settlement costs, because such costs were paid with nonprobate assets it was held that the decedent did not possess incidents of ownership but only a power over a contingency which never arose. *Hunter*, above. It has been held, however, that if the insured has the power to benefit himself by exercising his fiduciary power, it does not matter that he can exercise the power only with the consent of co-trustees whose interests in the trust are adverse to his own. *Gesner*, above. If an insurance trust gives the trustee-insured the power to deal with the insurance policies held by the trust as if he were the absolute owner and without the necessity to account to anyone for his dealings, he still has only fiduciary powers which must be exercised only for the exclusive benefit of the trust beneficiaries. If he violates his fiduciary duty by, say, pledging the policies to secure a personal loan, his wrongful act does not convert his powers into incidents of ownership for purposes of IRC Section 2042. *Est. of Bloch v. Comm.*, 78 TC 850 (1982).

A technical advice memorandum advised that if a trustee possessed incidents of ownership in a life insurance policy held for the trust and the insured/grantor retained the right to remove trustees and appoint anyone other than himself as trustee, the insured/grantor retained incidents of ownership in the policy which would cause the insurance proceeds to be included in his estate under IRC Section 2042(2). TAM 8922003. However, for purposes of IRC Sections 2036 or 2038, the Service will no longer include trust property in a decedent grantor's estate where the grantor retains the right to replace the trustee but can replace the trustee with only an independent corporate trustee. Rev. Rul. 95-58, 1995-2 CB 191; *Est. of Wall v. Comm.*, 101 TC 300 (1993).

2006 Tax Facts on Insurance & Employee Benefits

Hopefully, the Service will extend its new policy with regard to trustee removal under IRC Sections 2036 and 2038 to IRC Section 2042. A later letter ruling determined that the right to replace a trustee *for cause* with someone other than the insured/grantor was not an incident of ownership. Let. Rul. 9832039.

The issue of incidents of ownership in a trust can generally be avoided by providing that an insured cannot exercise any incident of ownership in a policy on his life (even as a trustee). See Let. Rul. 9348028. Letter ruling 9748020 concluded that where a spouse resigned as trustee of a credit shelter bypass trust (in which the decedent had given spouse an income interest) prior to purchase of life insurance by the trust on the spouse's life, proceeds of the life insurance would not be includable in spouse's estate provided that (1) spouse has not transferred any assets to the trust, (2) the premiums for the policy are paid from trust corpus, (3) spouse does not maintain the policy with personal assets, and (4) the spouse is not reinstated as trustee. *ASRS, Sec. 54, ¶35.6.*

633. Are life insurance proceeds includable in the insured's estate if someone other than the insured took out the policy and owns it at insured's death?

Ordinarily the proceeds are not includable in the insured's gross estate if the insured has never owned the policy and the proceeds are not payable to or for the benefit of his estate. IRC Sec. 2042. (But see Q 628.) However, if the terms of the policy give the insured any legal incidents of ownership, the proceeds may be included in his gross estate even though a third party purchased the policy and has always retained physical possession of it. *U.S. v. Rhode Island Hosp. Trust Co.*, 335 F.2d 7 (1st Cir. 1966). Even though the policy says clearly that incidents of ownership belong to the insured, if it is also clear from facts outside the policy that it was the intention and belief of the parties involved in purchasing the insurance that these ownership rights were to be, and were, placed in another, courts may allow the "intent facts" to override the "policy facts"; i.e., they may find that the insured did not actually possess the incidents of ownership the policy said were exercisable by him. *National Metropolitan Bank v. U.S.*, 87 F. Supp. 773 (Ct. Cl. 1950); *Schongalla v. Hickey*, 149 F.2d 687 (2d Cir. 1945), cert. denied 326 U.S. 736; *Watson v. Comm.*, TC Memo 1977-268; *First Nat'l Bank of Birmingham v. U.S.*, 358 F.2d 625 (5th Cir. 1966); Let. Rul. 8610068. On the other hand, even though the policy does not give the insured any incidents of ownership, an incident of ownership may be given to the insured by an outside document, such as a corporate resolution, or a trust indenture, or other agreement between the insured and the third party. *Est. of Thompson v. Comm.*, TC Memo 1981-200; *St. Louis Union Trust Co. (Orthwein) v. U.S.*, 262 F. Supp. 27 (E.D. Mo. 1966); *Est. of Tomerlin v. Comm.*, TC Memo 1986-147. The fact that the insured has had no opportunity to exercise his legal incidents of ownership is immaterial. *Comm. v. Est. of Noel*, 380 U.S. 678 (1965). Also, if the insured causes insurance to be bought on his life by another with funds supplied by insured and then dies within 3 years of the purchase, the proceeds may be includable in insured's estate (see Q 642). The Eighth Circuit has affirmed a 9-7 decision of the Tax Court holding that the proceeds of a wife-owned policy, payable revocably to the trustee of a revocable trust created by the insured husband, were not includable in the insured's estate under either IRC Section 2042 (incidents of ownership test—see Q 631) or IRC Section 2041 (general power of appointment—see Q 853(9)). *Est. of Margrave v. Comm.*, 71 TC 13 (1978), aff'd 45 AFTR 2d ¶148,393 (8th Cir. 1980). IRS has agreed to follow the holding in *Margrave*. Rev. Rul. 81-166, 1981-1 CB 477. *ASRS, Sec. 54, ¶¶25.4, 25.6, 35.1 and 36.*

634. Can an insured remove existing life insurance from his gross estate by an absolute assignment of the policy?

Yes (assuming the insured lives for at least 3 years after the assignment—see Q 642), provided the insured assigns *all* incidents of ownership and the assignee is not legally obligated to use the proceeds for the benefit of insured's estate. Treas. Regs. §§20.2042-1(b)(1), 20.2042-1(c)(1); *Lamade v. Brownell*, 245 F. Supp. 691 (M.D. Pa. 1965). If the form of the assignment reserves any incidents of ownership to the insured, the proceeds may be included in his gross estate despite his clear intention to transfer all ownership rights. *Est. of Piggott v. Comm.*, 340 F.2d 829 (6th Cir. 1965). It has been held that where the insured had paid no premiums and had never treated the policy as his own that his irrevocable designation of beneficiaries and mode of payment of proceeds was an effective assignment of all his incidents of ownership in the policy. *Morton v. U.S.*, 29 AFTR 2d 72-1531 (4th Cir. 1972). The amount of any *premiums* paid on the assigned policy by insured may be included to the extent they are paid within 3 years of death (see Q 642). (But for indirect possession of incidents of ownership, see Q 610, Q 631 and Q 651. See Q 645 for information on the assignment of group term insurance coverage.)

A reversionary interest in a policy is an incident of ownership if, immediately before insured's death, the value of the reversionary interest is worth more than 5% of the value of the policy. IRC Sec. 2042(2). However, the insured will have no such reversionary interest if the policy is purchased and owned by another person, or if the policy is absolutely assigned to another person by the insured. The regulations state that the term "reversionary interest" does not include the possibility that a person might receive a policy or its proceeds by inheritance from another person's estate, or by exercising a surviving spouse's statutory right of election, or under some similar right. They state also that, in valuing a reversionary interest, there must be taken into consideration interests held by others which would affect the value. For example, a decedent would not have a reversionary interest in a policy worth more than 5% of the policy's value, if, immediately before his death, some other person had the unrestricted power to obtain the cash surrender value of the policy; the value of the reversionary interest would be zero. Treas. Reg. §20.2042-1(c)(3).

An insured was treated as holding a reversionary interest in a policy held in a trusteed buy-sell arrangement where the insured was considered to have transferred the policy to the trust and retained the right to purchase the policy for its cash surrender value upon termination of the buy-sell agreement. TAM 9349002. However, a policy held in a trusteed buy-sell arrangement would not be includable in an insured's estate under IRC Section 2042 where (1) proceeds would be received by a partner's estate only in exchange for purchase of the partner's stock, and (2) all incidents of ownership would be held by the trustee of the irrevocable life insurance trust. Let. Rul. 9511009. *ASRS*, Sec. 54, ¶25.5.

635. Are the general rules for including life insurance proceeds in the insured's gross estate applicable to proceeds payable under a qualified pension or profit-sharing plan?

Yes, generally, for estates of decedents dying after 1984; but see Q 673 for details.

636. May a life insurance beneficiary be required to pay estate tax attributable to the death proceeds?

Yes, under either of two circumstances: (1) Where the decedent/insured has directed in his will that the life insurance beneficiary pay the share of death taxes attributable to the proceeds; and (2) where the state of the decedent's domicile has a statute that apportions the burden of death taxes among probate and nonprobate beneficiaries in absence of any direction from the decedent regarding where the burden of death taxes should fall.

Most states have statutes that apportion death taxes (federal, state, or both) among the beneficiaries of an estate, probate and nonprobate, under circumstances where the decedent has not directed otherwise. (See ASRS, section 49, for a current listing). At this writing, the states which place the death tax burden on the probate estate (technically, the residuary estate) are Alabama, Arizona, Georgia, Iowa, Michigan, Mississippi, and Wisconsin.

A federal apportionment statute provides in pertinent part as follows: "Unless the decedent directs otherwise in his will, if any part of the gross estate on which tax has been paid consists of proceeds of policies of insurance on the life of the decedent receivable by a beneficiary other than the executor, the executor shall be entitled to recover from such beneficiary such portion of the total tax paid as the proceeds of such policies bear to the taxable estate." IRC Sec. 2206.

In *McAleer v. Jernigan*, 86-2 USTC ¶13,705 (11th Cir. 1986), rev'g and remanding 86-2 USTC ¶13,704 (S.D. Ala. 1986), the decedent's former wife was the beneficiary of insurance on the decedent's life. The decedent, who died domiciled in Alabama, did not direct in his will where the burden of death taxes should fall. The Alabama statute said that unless the decedent directed otherwise, the executor was to pay death taxes out of estate property (i.e., from the residuary estate). The statute also said that the executor was under no duty to recover any pro rata portion of such taxes from the beneficiary of any nonprobate property. In a suit by the executor to recover from the life insurance beneficiary a pro rata share of the estate tax due (the insurance proceeds having been found includable in the gross estate for federal estate tax purposes), the Eleventh Circuit held that the federal statute (IRC Section 2206) prevailed over the state statute and allowed the executor to recover. *ASRS, Sec. 49, ¶400.8(h).*

637. May a life insurance beneficiary make a qualified disclaimer of an amount equal to his proportionate share of death taxes when the decedent directed that death taxes be paid entirely out of the probate estate?

Yes, it has been so held. In *Est. of Boyd v. Comm.*, 87-1 USTC ¶13,720 (7th Cir. 1987), rev'g 85 TC 1056 (1985), in an unusual fact situation, the decedent's son was left the entire probate estate, $153,000, plus $389,000 of life insurance proceeds (as named beneficiary). The decedent's second wife (the son's step mother) received nothing. The decedent's will directed his executor to pay out of the probate estate the tax (an estimated $78,000) allocable to the life insurance proceeds. The son disclaimed the entire probate estate *and* any right to have the probate estate pay any death tax attributable to the life insurance proceeds. The IRS refused to give effect to the second disclaimer, which had the effect of reducing the amount of marital deduction the estate claimed. The disclaimer statute (see Q 908) says that a qualified disclaimer means an irrevocable and unqualified refusal to accept an *interest in property*. The court recognized the subject of the second disclaimer as an interest in property for purposes of the statute and allowed the claimed marital deduction. *ASRS: Sec. 49; Sec. 55, ¶57.5(f).*

DIVIDENDS

638. How are life insurance paid-up additions purchased with dividends treated for estate tax purposes?

In the same manner as other insurance. Proceeds are includable in insured's estate if they are payable to or for the benefit of his estate, or if insured has any incidents of ownership in the policy at the time of his death (see Q 626). IRC Sec. 2042.

639. What rules are applicable to including life insurance accumulated and post-mortem dividends in insured's estate?

Accumulated dividends (including interest thereon) and post-mortem dividends are reported together with the face amount of the policy on Schedule D of the insured's estate tax return.

DIVORCE

640. If life insurance proceeds are required under terms of a property settlement agreement or a divorce decree to be paid to certain beneficiaries, are the proceeds includable in insured's estate? Is an offsetting deduction allowable?

Includability of Proceeds or Premiums

The Internal Revenue Service has ruled that where a divorced wife had an absolute right, under terms of a property settlement agreement incorporated by reference in a divorce decree, to annuity payments after the death of her former husband, such payments to be provided by insurance on his life maintained by him for that purpose, the former husband possessed no incidents of ownership in the insurance at his death; no part of the insurance proceeds was includable in his estate. Rev. Rul. 54-29, 1954-1 CB 186. (See Q 626 for the general rules of includability.) Also the Tax Court has held that where a divorced husband was required under a property settlement agreement to maintain insurance on his life payable to his former wife, if living, otherwise to their surviving descendants, otherwise to his former wife's estate—the insurance, in other words, was not merely security for other obligations—the insured possessed no incidents of ownership in the insurance. *Est. of Bowers v. Comm.*, 23 TC 911 (1955), acq. 1955-2 CB 4. The Tax Court has also held that where an insured was subject to a court order requiring him to maintain insurance on his life payable to his minor children, such court order, operating in conjunction with other applicable state law, effectively nullified incidents of ownership the insured would otherwise possess by policy terms. *Est. of Beauregard v. Comm.*, 74 TC 603 (1980), acq. 1981-1 CB 1.

Where, on the other hand, the divorced husband was merely required to maintain a stated sum of insurance on his life payable to his former wife so long as she lived and remained unmarried, the insured was held to have retained a reversionary interest sufficient in value to make the proceeds includable in his estate (see Q 631). Rev. Rul. 76-113, 1976-1 CB 276. It has also been held that where, pursuant to a divorce decree, the proceeds of insurance maintained by a divorced husband on his own life to secure alimony payments, are paid following the insured's death directly to the former wife, the proceeds are includable in the insured's estate. It was reasoned that since the proceeds satisfy a debt of the decedent or his estate, the result is the same as if the proceeds are received by the decedent's executor (see Q 626). *Est. of Mason v. Comm.*, 43 BTA 813 (1941).

Availability of Estate Tax Deduction

Where insurance proceeds payable to a divorced spouse are required to be included in the insured's estate, it is sometimes possible to secure an offsetting deduction either (1) on the basis that the beneficiary's right to the proceeds amounts to a claim against the estate representing a personal obligation of the decedent existing at the time of his death (IRC Sec. 2053(a)(3)), or (2) on the basis that the beneficiary's interest in the proceeds amounts to an indebtedness against the proceeds included in the estate (IRC Sec. 2053(a)(4)). However, a deduction is not allowed on either basis if the claim or indebtedness is founded on an agreement between the spouses in the nature of a property settlement agreement not supported by "adequate and full consideration in money or money's worth." IRC Sec. 2053(c)(1)(A). But where property is transferred from a decedent or from a decedent's estate to a former spouse of the decedent pursuant to a property settlement agreement, and divorce occurred within a three-year period measured from the date one year before the agreement was entered into, and where the property is includable in the decedent's gross estate, the transfer is considered to be made for an adequate and full consideration in money or money's worth. IRC Sec. 2043(b)(2). A relinquishment or promised relinquishment of marital rights in property is not consideration in money or money's worth. IRC Secs. 2053(e), 2043(b). Although it has been held that a wife's right to support is a "marital right in property" within the meaning of the statute (*Meyer's Est. v. Helvering*, 110 F.2d 367 (2nd Cir. 1940), cert. den. 310 U.S. 651), IRS has declined to follow the decision (Rev. Rul. 68-379, 1968-2 CB 414) and declares instead that a release of support rights by a wife constitutes a consideration in money or money's worth. Rev. Rul. 71-67, 1971-1 CB 271; Rev. Rul. 75-395, 1975-2 CB 370. The Tax Court has consistently agreed that a wife's relinquishment or promised relinquishment in a separation agreement of her support rights is a consideration in money or money's worth. *McKeon v. Comm.*, 25 TC 697 (1956); *Est. of Glen v. Comm.*, 45 TC 323 (1966); *Est. of Iverson v. Comm.*, 65 TC 391 (1975), rev'd and remanded on another issue, 552 F.2d 977 (3rd Cir. 1977); *Est. of Satz v. Comm.*, 78 TC 1172 (1982). See also *Bowes v. U.S.*, 77-2 USTC ¶13,212 (N.D. Ill. 1977).

But even though it is found that the relinquishment or promised relinquishment of support rights is consideration in money or money's worth, it must also be found that the claim or indebtedness against property was "contracted bona fide and for an adequate and full consideration in money or money's worth." IRC Sec. 2053(c)(1)(A). It must be found, in other words, that that which is sought to be deducted from the estate was bargained for in exchange for support rights. Thus, the executor of the estate must be prepared to show, according to applicable local law, just what was the value of the wife's support rights at the time the separation agreement was entered into. If he is unable to establish a dollar value by any reasonable approach, such as taking into account the value of the marital assets and the former spouses' incomes and their expenses, the deduction sought will be denied. *Est. of Iverson*, *Est. of Satz*, both cited above. If a dollar value of the support rights is established, the deduction allowed cannot exceed that amount or, if less, the amount of the claim.

If, then, insurance proceeds are payable to a former spouse pursuant to the terms of a property settlement agreement (but not pursuant to a court decree), the insured's

DIVORCE

Q 640

estate may be permitted an offsetting deduction to the extent of the value of any support rights relinquished by the wife under the agreement. *Gray v. U.S.*, 78-1 USTC ¶13,244 (C.D. Cal. 1978), on remand; *Est. of Fenton v. Comm.*, 70 TC 263 (1978). But to the extent the proceeds exceed the value of such support rights, no deduction is allowable if the only other consideration given by the wife was relinquishment or promised relinquishment of inheritance rights in the decedent's property. For information on how to value support rights, see Rev. Rul. 71-67, 1971-1 CB 271, and *Est. of Fenton v. Comm.*, 70 TC 263 (1978).

Where a property settlement agreement is incorporated in a divorce decree, and where the divorce court is free to ignore the allowances made in the agreement and to set different allowances in its own discretion instead, the obligations of the parties are not "founded upon a promise or agreement" but upon the divorce decree. In this case, a deduction of a proper claim or indebtedness under IRC Section 2053 is allowable without regard to the nature of the consideration given by the wife. *Comm. v. Maresi*, 156 F.2d 929 (2nd Cir. 1946); *Comm. v. Est. of Watson*, 216 F.2d 941 (2nd Cir. 1954), acq. 1958-1 CB 6; *Young v. Comm.* 39 BTA 230 (1939); *Est. of Mason v. Comm.*, 43 BTA 813 (1941). Even if both the agreement and the court decree provide that the covenants in the agreement shall survive any decree of divorce that may be entered, the obligations of the parties are still founded on the court decree, not on a promise or agreement. *Harris v. Comm.*, 340 U.S. 106 (1950); *Est. of Robinson v. Comm.*, 63 TC 717 (1975).

On the other hand, where a property settlement agreement is incorporated in a divorce decree, but under applicable state law the divorce court is not free to disregard the provisions of a valid property settlement agreement, the obligations of the parties are held to be founded upon a promise or agreement and not upon the divorce decree. In such case, the availability of the offsetting estate tax deduction is limited as previously explained. *Est. of Bowers v. Comm.*, 23 TC 911 (1955), acq. 1955-2 CB 4; *Est. of Barrett v. Comm.*, 56 TC 1312 (1971); *Gray v. U.S.*, 541 F.2d 228 (9th Cir. 1976), reversing and remanding 391 F. Supp. 693; *Est. of Satz v. Comm.*, 78 TC 1172 (1982); Rev. Rul. 60-160, 1960-1 CB 374; Rev. Rul. 75-395, 1975-2 CB 370. Also, IRS has ruled that where life insurance proceeds were payable to insured's minor children pursuant to a divorce decree, the deduction was not allowable because (1) the decree exceeded the support obligation imposed by state law in requiring the spouse to maintain insurance on his life payable to his children, and (2) the maintenance of the insurance was not contracted for a full and adequate consideration. Rev. Rul. 78-379, 1978-2 CB 238.

Deduction as Claim Against the Estate

IRS has held that availability of the deduction under IRC Section 2053(a)(3) depends upon the nature of the insured's legal obligation under the divorce decree. If the insured's obligation was simply to keep the policy in full force and effect with all premiums paid as long as the former spouse lived and remained unmarried, and he did that, then no obligation survived his death and his estate would not be entitled to a deduction. If, on the other hand, the divorce decree provided for the payment, upon the decedent's death, to his former spouse of a specific sum of money and he provided funds therefor by the purchase of life insurance, then the payment of the required amount would be a personal obligation of the decedent, and should the insurer be unable to meet its obligation, would be payable from his estate; under these circumstances, any proceeds payable to the former spouse to discharge the decedent's obligation would be deductible under IRC Section 2053(a)(3). Rev. Rul. 76-113, 1976-1 CB 276.

Deduction as Indebtedness Against Proceeds

The Tax Court has allowed an offsetting deduction under IRC Section 2053(a)(4) where a divorced husband was required under the terms of a property settlement agreement incorporated in a divorce decree to maintain a certain amount of insurance on his life payable to his former wife, and where the proceeds were paid upon his death directly from the insurer to the former wife as beneficiary. The court held that the proceeds were property included in the estate and subject to an indebtedness even though, because the proceeds were paid directly to the former wife, it was not necessary for her to file a claim against the estate. *Est. of Robinson v. Comm.*, 63 TC 717 (1975), acq. 1976-2 CB 2. The Tax Court has also allowed a deduction under IRC Section 2053(a)(4) where the decedent had been ordered through a divorce decree to assign two policies to his former wife. *Est. of DeVos v. Comm.*, TC Memo 1975-216.

The position of the Internal Revenue Service now is that where a divorced spouse is required by the terms of a divorce decree to maintain insurance on his life payable to his former spouse, until the beneficiary spouse dies or remarries, an offsetting deduction *is* allowed the estate under IRC Section 2053(a)(4). Rev. Rul. 76-113, 1976-1 CB 276. (On these facts, the deduction would not be allowed under IRC Section 2053(a)(3)—see above.) The IRS has ruled similarly where in a paternity action adjudicating custody and support rights the insured was required by court decree to maintain insurance on his life for the benefit of his child. Let. Rul. 8128005. *ASRS, Sec. 54, ¶30.*

DOUBLE INDEMNITY

641. Are life insurance proceeds paid under a double indemnity clause includable in insured's gross estate?

They are subject to the same rules as other life insurance proceeds (see Q 626, Q 645). *Est. of Ackerman v. Comm.*, 15 BTA 635 (1929); *Est. of Wright v. Comm.*, 8 TC 531 (1947); see *Comm. v. Est. of Noel*, 380 U.S. 678 (1965).

GIFTS WITHIN THREE YEARS OF DEATH

642. Under what circumstances are the death proceeds of life insurance given away by the insured within three years of his death includable in his gross estate?

The proceeds are automatically includable in the insured's gross estate without regard to the insured's motives in making the gift. Also includable is the amount of any gift tax paid by the decedent or his estate on the transfer. The provision which excepts from includability gifts as to which the decedent was not required to file a gift tax return does not apply to a "transfer with respect to a life insurance policy." IRC Sec. 2035. The quoted language, part of the amendment of IRC Sec. 2035 made by the Revenue Act of 1978, seems broad enough to include gifts of both policies and premium payments. (However, committee reports explaining the provision indicate that it was not the intention to treat as a "transfer with respect to a life insurance policy" any gifts of premium payments made more than three years after the donor has made a gift of the policy. See Congressional committee explanation of section 702(f) of the Revenue Act of 1978.) See Q 645 for special rules applicable to group insurance.

GIFTS WITHIN THREE YEARS OF DEATH

Q 642

Where the insured makes a gift of the policy within three years of his death, the value of any premiums he pays gratuitously after making the gift is not added to the proceeds includable in his estate. *Peters v. U.S.*, 78-1 USTC ¶13,239 (Ct. Cl. 1978). It had been held under earlier versions of IRC Section 2035 that if any premiums paid after the transfer are paid by the donee rather than by the insured, only proceeds in the ratio of premiums paid by donor to total premiums paid are includable in donor's estate. *Liebmann v. Hassett*, 148 F.2d 247 (1st Cir. 1945); *Est. of Silverman v. Comm.*, 61 TC 338 (1973), aff'd 521 F.2d 574 (2nd Cir. 1975); Treas. Reg. §20.2035-1(e). The proportional proceeds rule where the donee pays premiums after the transfer has also been applied to deaths occurring after 1981 even though payment of premiums no longer determines includability of proceeds under the transfers within three years of death rule. *Est. of Friedberg v. Comm.*, TC Memo 1992-310; TAM 9128008. If premiums are paid from property owned jointly by decedent and donee, the burden is on the donee to prove the extent to which the premiums were paid out of property originally owned by the donee. *Peters v. U.S.*, above.

What estate tax result should we expect, when a policy is purchased on the initiative of the insured with funds provided by the insured, a third party is designated owner of the policy, and the insured dies within three years of the purchase? In order for the bringback rule of Section 2035 to apply, there would have to be found a transfer for the purposes of one of the following IRC Sections: 2036, 2037, 2038, or 2042.

The courts have determined that insurance proceeds are not included in an insured's estate, even though death occurred within three years of purchase of the policy, if the policy is owned by a third party, the policy is not made payable to the insured's estate, and the insured held no incidents of ownership in the policy under IRC Section 2042. *Est. of Leder v. Comm.*, 90-1 USTC ¶60,001 (10th Cir. 1989); *Est. of Headrick v. Comm.*, 90-2 USTC ¶60,049 (6th Cir. 1990); *Est. of Perry v. Comm.*, 91-1 USTC ¶60,064 (5th Cir. 1991); *Est. of Richins v. Comm.*, TC Memo 1991-23; *Est. of Ard v. Comm.*, TC Memo 1990-294; *Est. of Chapman v. Comm.*, TC Memo 1989-105; *Est. of Litman v. U.S.*, 90-1 USTC ¶60,023 (W.D. Pa. 1990). Indeed, attorney fees were awarded to the taxpayers in the *Perry* case because the position of the United States was not substantially justified. *Est. of Perry v. Comm.*, 91-1 USTC ¶60,073 (5th Cir. 1991). Due to the adverse court decisions, the IRS has announced that it will no longer litigate its position (although it still believes that substance should prevail over form and that the "beamed transfer" theory should be applied to such "indirect transfers" of life insurance within three years of death). AOD 1991-012.

In TAM 9323002, life insurance proceeds were not included in an insured's estate where (1) the insured applied for the policy, (2) the insured then had the policy split into two policies and named her two sons as owners and beneficiaries prior to paying any premiums, (3) the insured's sons paid all premiums, and (4) the insured died within three years of purchase of the policy. The memorandum determined that under the terms of the contract and state law no contract existed prior to the time that the first premium was paid and the life insurance contract was issued and delivered. The memorandum also concluded that although it appeared that the decedent passed something of value to her two sons (i.e., although the insurance company's premium rates had increased between steps 1 and 2, the earlier lower premium rates were obtained by the sons), it was unlikely that such transfer constituted a transfer of incidents of ownership.

An exchange of policies by an irrevocable trust was not treated as a transfer within three years of death where the original transfer of the policy had occurred more than three years before death, the decedent possessed no interest in the policy at the time of the exchange, and the decedent's signature was not essential to the exchange. TAM 8819001. Decedent insured did not transfer a policy within three years of death, even though a policy was amended within three years of death to provide that a trust, rather than the decedent, was the owner, where the intent of the parties clearly indicated through extrinsic evidence that the decedent had ceased being the owner of the policy more than three years before death. Let. Rul. 9651004.

Life insurance owned by a corporation on its majority shareholder was not included in such shareholder's estate where the shareholder sold her interest in the corporation within three years of death. The corporation had always owned the policy, paid the premiums, and been beneficiary of the proceeds. Let. Rul. 8906002. However, where a majority shareholder reduced his interest in a corporation to 40% within three years of death and proceeds of life insurance owned by the corporation on such shareholder were payable to the shareholder's daughter, proceeds were included in the shareholder's estate. Rev. Rul. 90-21, 1990-1 CB 172, situation 2. Also, where a corporation transferred a life insurance policy to the beneficiary within three years of the controlling shareholder's death, proceeds were included in the controlling shareholder's estate even though the shareholder transferred his interest in the corporation to his son after the corporation's transfer of the life insurance policy and prior to his death. Rev. Rul. 90-21, 1990-1 CB 172, situation 1. (See also Q 610.) Where a non-majority shareholder held the right to purchase a policy on his life from a corporation upon termination of a buy-sell agreement and the shareholder caused the corporation to transfer the policy to an irrevocable trust within three years of the shareholder's death, the proceeds were included in the shareholder's estate. TAM 9127007.

An exception is provided to the transfers within three years of death rules for any bona fide sale for adequate and full consideration. IRC Sec. 2035(d). It is unclear whether consideration equal to the interpolated terminal reserve of a policy plus any unexpired premiums is adequate to avoid the transfers within three years of death rule. TAM 8806004 interpreted full consideration as requiring that the consideration must be adequate relative to what would be included in the estate (i.e., the proceeds), not relative to what is transferred (i.e., the policy). See *Est. of Pritchard v. Comm.*, 4 TC 204 (1944) (consideration equal to cash surrender value was inadequate). However, TAM 9413045 accepted the interpolated terminal reserve plus any unexpired premiums as adequate consideration. *ASRS, Sec. 54, ¶25.8.*

643. If a donor dies within three years of making a gift of a life insurance policy he owned on the life of another, is the value of the policy includable in the donor's gross estate?

IRC Section 2035 is the section which brings back into a decedent's estate certain gifts made within three years of death. The bringback rule of Section 2035 (see Q 860) applies to a transfer of an interest in property which is included in the value of the gross estate under IRC Sections 2036, 2037, 2038, or 2042, or would have been included under any of such sections if such interest had been retained by the decedent. IRC Section 2042 has to do with proceeds of insurance *on the life of the decedent*. The IRC section under which the value of a policy owned by the decedent on the life of *another* is includable in the decedent's estate is IRC Section 2033. A transfer of an interest in property included in the value of the gross estate under IRC Section 2033, or which would have been included under such section if the interest had been retained by the decedent, is not among the enumerated sections under the bringback rule of IRC Section 2035. Thus, the value of a policy owned by a decedent on the life of another and transferred by the decedent within three years of his death (death occurring after 1981) will not be brought back into the decedent's estate under IRC Section 2035, except for the limited purposes described at Q 860. *ASRS, Sec. 54, ¶25.8.*

GOVERNMENT LIFE INSURANCE

644. Are proceeds of life insurance issued under U.S. Government programs includable in insured's estate?

Yes, despite a federal law which provides that no tax can be levied on government life insurance. The estate tax is not a tax *on* property, but a tax on the right to transfer property at death. Hence, the exemption from taxes does not apply to the estate tax. Proceeds of a policy owned by the insured at the time of his death are includable in his estate (government life insurance is nonassignable). IRC Sec. 2042; *U.S. Trust Co. of N.Y. v. Helvering*, 307 U.S. 57 (1939); Rev. Rul. 55-622, 1955-2 CB 385.

The U.S. Supreme Court has held that community property laws cannot interfere with the right of an insured to name his own beneficiary of his National Service Life Insurance. *Wissner v. Wissner*, 338 U.S. 655 (1949). Consequently, it has been held that even though an insured and his spouse are residents of a community property state and all premiums have been paid with community funds, the entire proceeds of government life insurance issued to servicemen and veterans are includable in insured's gross estate for federal estate tax purposes as if they were his separate property. *Est. of Hutson v. Comm.*, 49 TC 495 (1968) (NSLI); *Hunt's Estate v. U.S.*, 4 AFTR 2d 6051 (E.D. Tex. 1959) (USGLI); Rev. Rul. 56-603, 1956-2 CB 601 (USGLI, NSLI, and policies issued under the Servicemen's Indemnity Act of 1951). The Supreme Court of California has held that the *Wissner* decision is not authority with respect to Federal Employees Group Life Insurance, that community property rights can be asserted in the proceeds of such insurance notwithstanding the insured's beneficiary designation. *Carlson v. Carlson*, 11 Cal. 3d 474, 521 P.2d 1114 (1974). If the *Carlson* decision is followed in the federal courts, then the proceeds of FEGLI (and probably Servicemen's Group Life Insurance as well) are includable in the insured's estate on the same basis as the proceeds of regular group life insurance. (See Q 619 to Q 620.) In the case of FEGLI, the master policy used to specifically prohibit assignment, but assignment is now permissible (generally, effective October 3, 1994).

Life insurance proceeds were includable in a federal judge's estate where the judge attempted to assign a FEGLI policy which was not assignable at the time of the attempted assignment. The judge also attempted to assign the policy after a limited 1984 change in the FEGLI law permitted some assignments. However, such attempts were made within three years of the judge's death and were caught by the gifts within three years of death rule (see Q 642). The assignments made after the 1984 change in FEGLI law were not permitted to relate back to the pre-1984 attempted assignment because assignments were not permissible before 1984. *Hays v. U.S.*, 95-2 USTC ¶60,203 (S.D. Ill. 1995).

The IRS has held that in community property states which determine whether life insurance is separate or community property according to the "inception of title" doctrine (see Q 620), the proceeds of NSLI purchased initially as the insured's separate property are separate property even though later premiums were paid with community funds. Rev. Rul. 74-312, 1974-2 CB 320. *ASRS, Sec. 54, ¶33.*

GROUP LIFE INSURANCE

645. Are the proceeds of group term life insurance includable in insured's estate?

The general rules for including life insurance proceeds in the gross estate apply (see Q 626). Accordingly, the proceeds are includable if they are payable to or for the benefit of insured's estate, or if the insured possesses any incident of ownership in the policy at the time of his death. There is no question, for example, that if at the employee's death he possessed the right to designate or change the beneficiary of his group life insurance, he possessed an incident of ownership within the intendment of IRC Section 2042(2). *Chase Nat'l Bank v. U.S.*, 278 U.S. 327 (1929); *Est. of Henry v. Comm.*, TC Memo 1987-119. In addition to the general rules concerning incidents of ownership, in group life insurance, the insured's right to convert to an individual policy on termination of employment is *not* an incident of ownership. *Est. of Smead v. Comm.*, 78 TC 43 (1982), acq. in result, 1984-2 CB 2; Rev. Rul. 84-130, 1984-2 CB 194, modifying Rev. Rul. 69-54, Situation 2, 1969-1 CB 221; GCM 39272 (8-16-84); AOD 056. Moreover, the power of an employee to effect cancellation of his coverage by terminating his employment is *not* an incident of ownership. Rev. Rul. 72-307, 1972-1 CB 221; *Landorf v. U.S.*, 408 F.2d 461 (Ct. Cl. 1969); *Est. of Lumpkin v. Comm.*, 56 TC 815 (1971), rev'd on other grounds, 474 F.2d 1092 (5th Cir. 1973). Also, estate tax regulations which attribute to an insured who is a stockholder-employee, under certain circumstances, corporate held incidents of ownership (see Q 610), provide (as amended in 1979): "In the case of group-term life insurance, as defined in the regulations under section 79, the power to surrender or cancel a policy held by a corporation shall not be attributed to any decedent through his stock ownership." Treas. Reg. §20.2042-1(c)(6). (See Q 139 for the definition of group-term life insurance.) Drawing somewhat of a parallel to the controlling stockholder regulations, the IRS has held that a partnership's power to surrender or cancel its group term life insurance policy is not attributable to any of the partners. It does not matter, says the Service, that partners, in that they are not employees, do not qualify for the income exclusion provided in IRC Section 79 (Q 142). Under the facts of the ruling, the insured partner was one of 35 partners. Rev. Rul. 83-148, 1983-2 CB 157. GCM 39034 (9-21-83). IRS has ruled on an optional contributory plan of group life insurance which provided that if an employee opted not to participate on his own, any one of certain specified relatives of the employee could, with the employee's consent, apply and pay for the insurance on the employee's life and own all incidents of ownership. The plan also provided that should the third party applicant-owner cease to qualify as such, the insurance would terminate, in which event the employee would be eligible again to apply for coverage on his own. The Service held that the employee did not possess an incident of ownership within the meaning of IRC Section 2042. Rev. Rul. 76-421, 1976-2 CB 280. The Tax Court has held that the death proceeds of a combination group term life and disability income policy are taxable for estate tax purposes under IRC Section 2042 as proceeds of life insurance. *Est. of Perl v. Comm.*, 76 TC 861 (1981).

Assignment of Group Term Life

It is possible for an employee to assign all his incidents of ownership in group term life insurance so long as both the policy and state law permit an absolute assignment of all the insured's interest in the insurance including the conversion privilege, if any. If he completes such an assignment during his lifetime, he will be deemed not to have retained an incident of ownership in the insurance under IRC Section 2042(2). Rev. Rul. 69-54, 1969-1 CB 221, as modified by Rev. Rul. 72-307, 1972-1 CB 307, and Rev. Rul. 84-130, 1984-2 CB 194. In a contributory plan, there is apparently the additional requirement that the assignment must give the assignee the right to continue to pay the insured's share of the premiums. Almost all states have enacted laws which specifically permit the assignment of a group policy, including assignment of the conversion privilege. An assignment (including the conversion privilege) of a group policy was held to be effective even though state law neither expressly permitted nor prohibited the assignment. *Landorf v. U.S.*, 408 F.2d 461 (1969). In another case, an assignment was upheld where the master contract permitted the assignment but the individual certificates contained provisions against assignment. *Est. of Gorby v. Comm.*, 53 TC 80 (1969), acq. 1970-1 CB xvi. But, an attempted assignment will fail where the terms of the master contract specifically prohibit assignment. *Est. of Bartlett v. Comm.*, 54 TC 1590 (1970). In the absence of express statutory permission, establishment of the law may require case-by-case litigation.

Assignment Within Three Years of Death

An assignment of group term life insurance made within three years before the death of the insured will cause the proceeds to be included in the insured's gross estate under IRC Section 2035 (see Q 642). Let. Rul. 8022025. It has been held that where a prospective insured, when he applied for group coverage, had ownership of the certificate placed in another, he made a transfer of his insurance within the meaning of IRC Section 2035. *Kahn v. U.S.*, 449 F. Supp. 806 (N.D. Ga. 1972). Similarly, in *Levine v. U.S.*, 86-1 USTC ¶13,667 (Cl. Ct. 1986), where the decedent/insured's controlled corporation procured the insurance and where the insured had his wife sign as applicant and beneficiary (insured died in 1978 within three years of the insurance purchase). IRS has ruled that annual renewal of group term insurance by mere payment of the renewal premium does not create a new agreement but merely continues the old agreement, and that therefore, as to an employee who has assigned his coverage, renewal is not a new transfer of insurance coverage for purposes of IRC Section 2035; therefore, if the insured has transferred his coverage under such a plan more than three years before his death, the death proceeds will not be brought back into his estate under IRC Section 2035. Rev. Rul. 82-13, 1982-1 CB 132. IRS has also ruled that while (1) an employee cannot, by agreement with an assignee of his life coverage, effectively assign also life coverage he may receive in the future furnished by a new insurance carrier, (2) if a change of insurance carriers necessitates a new assignment of an employee's coverage to the same assignee "and the new arrangement is identical in all relevant aspects to the previous arrangement" with the old carrier, the new assignment will not cause the proceeds to be includable in the employee's estate under IRC Section 2035 if he dies within three years after the new assignment but more than three years after the first assignment. Rev. Rul. 80-289, 1980-2 CB 270, revoking Rev. Rul. 79-231.

A later private ruling dealt with the assignment of the insured's rights in a group life policy which was later replaced by a policy virtually identical in all material respects with the prior policy but issued by a different carrier. The new policy provided that an employee's irrevocable assignment of his rights in the old policy would be effective to vest in the assignee the insured's rights under the new policy. No new assignment was made after issuance of the new policy. The Service stated that if applicable local law would not recognize the provision in the new policy as constituting a valid assignment of rights in the new policy, the insured would be treated as the owner of the policy at his death. Let. Rul. 8230038. The Seventh Circuit Court of Appeals held that the proceeds of a group life policy were includable in the decedent's gross estate where the insured died within three years of the issuance of a policy offered by the employer in exchange for an earlier group life insurance policy. In this case, the insured was required to execute a new assignment when the second policy was issued. *American Nat'l. Bank v. U.S.*, 87-2 USTC ¶13,738 (7th Cir. 1987).

Where the issuance of a life insurance policy to a trust created by the insured's children was treated as an exercise of the conversion rights under a group policy in which the insured had held incidents of ownership that he had not previously assigned and the insured died within three years of the conversion, the insured was considered to have transferred incidents of ownership in the policy within three years of death, and the proceeds were included in the insured's estate. TAM 9141007. *ASRS, Sec. 66, ¶360.*

HEALTH INSURANCE

646. Is an accidental death benefit payable under a health insurance policy includable in the insured's gross estate?

Such benefits are "life insurance" proceeds, and are subject to the same rules as proceeds under regular life insurance policies (see Q 626). *Comm. v. Est. of Noel*, 380 U.S. 678 (1965); *Est. of Ackerman v. Comm.*, 15 BTA 635 (1929); see Rev. Rul. 66-262, 1966-2 CB 105. When insured purchased a one year accidental death policy and arranged for the policy to be owned by his children from the beginning, the proceeds were includable in his estate as a transfer in contemplation of death when he died within the policy term. Rev. Rul. 71-497, 1971-2 CB 329; *Bel v. U.S.*, 452 F.2d 683 (5th Cir. 1971), cert. den. 406 U.S. 919. *ASRS, Sec. 54, ¶37.*

647. Are medical expense reimbursement insurance proceeds received by the insured decedent's estate includable in the gross estate?

IRS has ruled that such payments are includable under IRC Section 2033 (see Q 853(1)) if the insured had an enforceable right to the proceeds at his death. Rev. Rul. 78-292, 1978-2 CB 233. *ASRS, Sec. 54, ¶37.*

INDIVIDUAL RETIREMENT PLANS

648. Is the value of a survivor benefit payable under an individual retirement plan (IRA) includable in the decedent's gross estate?

Yes, generally, in the case of decedents dying after 1984. For details, see below. Benefits payable to a surviving spouse will generally qualify for the marital deduction, see Q 649.

The value of an IRA account is not discounted for income tax payable by beneficiaries or for lack of marketability. However, an income tax deduction may be available for estate tax attributable to the IRA (see Q 827). *Est. of Smith v. U.S.*, 2004-2 USTC ¶60,493 (5th Cir. 2004), aff'g 2004-1 USTC ¶60,476 (S.D. Tex. 2004), TAM 200247001.

Estates of Decedents Dying After 1984

The value of an annuity or other payment receivable under an individual retirement plan or arrangement (IRA) by the beneficiary of a deceased individual is

INDIVIDUAL RETIREMENT PLANS   Q 648

includable in the decedent's gross estate under the rules discussed in Q 600 to Q 607. In reading those rules, be aware that any contribution to the purchase of an annuity made by the decedent's employer or former employer (as under a SEP–see Q 240) is considered to be contributed by the decedent if made by reason of his employment. IRC Sec. 2039(b).

The Tax Reform Act of 1984 repealed the estate tax exclusion discussed below generally for estates of decedents dying after 1984. However, the repeal does not apply to the estate of any decedent who (a) was a plan participant in pay status on December 31, 1984, and (b) irrevocably elected the form of benefit before July 18, 1984. For the meaning of "in pay status" and the requirements for an irrevocable election of the form of benefit, see Temp. Treas. Reg. §20.2039-IT. Qualified plan benefits rolled over to an IRA are treated as subject to the transitional rules for IRAs rather than those for qualified plans (see Q 673). Rev. Rul. 92-22, 1992-1 CB 313.

Estates of Decedents Dying After 1976 and Before 1985

With respect to the estate of a decedent dying after 1982 and before 1985, the aggregate estate tax exclusion applicable to survivor benefits payable under a qualified plan (see Q 321 to Q 418), a tax sheltered annuity (see Q 463 to Q 493), an individual retirement plan, a Retired Serviceman's Family Protection Plan, or a Survivor Benefit Plan (see ASRS section 18) *cannot exceed $100,000.* IRC Sec. 2039(c), (e), (g), as amended and added by the Tax Equity and Fiscal Responsibility Act of 1982 (TEFRA) and before repeal by the Tax Reform Act of 1984. The Tax Reform Act of 1984 also amended TEFRA to provide that the $100,000 limit shall not apply to the estate of any decedent who was a plan participant on pay status on December 31, 1982, and irrevocably elected, before January 1, 1983, the form of benefit. For estates of decedents dying after 1976 and before 1983, the exclusion (as described below) is unlimited.

Subject to the limitation just described and to the following three conditions, the value of a survivor benefit payable under an individual retirement plan is excludable from the individual's gross estate.

First, the benefit must be payable other than to or for the benefit of the estate (see Q 627 to Q 629). Treas. Reg. §20.2039-5(a)(2)(ii). Second, the exclusion applies only to amounts attributable to (1) payments that were allowable as a deduction under IRC Section 219 (see Q 220), and (2), subject to the following exceptions and qualifications, rollover contributions (see Q 446). Amounts attributable to rollover contributions from a tax sheltered annuity are not excludable unless the employer is a so-called REC organization, as described in Q 686. Amounts attributable to a rollover contribution from a surviving spouse are not excludable from the surviving spouse's estate (though the rollover secures the exclusion in the first spouse's estate (see Q 673). Amounts attributable to rollover contributions from another individual retirement plan are not excludable to the extent those contributions are in turn attributable to rollover contributions described in the preceding two sentences which the decedent made to the transferor plan. Treas. Reg. §20.2039-5(c). An individual has 60 days from his receipt of a qualifying distribution to make his rollover contribution (see Q 450). It has been held that where an employee receives a qualifying rollover distribution but then dies before the end of the 60-day period without having made a rollover into an IRA, his estate may make the rollover for him. *Gunther v. U.S.*, 82-2 USTC ¶13,498 (W.D. Mich. 1982). See also Let. Rul. 8351119.

2006 Tax Facts on Insurance & Employee Benefits   691

Third, the benefit must be in the form of a "qualifying annuity." The term "qualifying annuity" means an annuity contract or other arrangement providing for a series of substantially equal periodic payments to be made to a beneficiary for the beneficiary's life or over a period ending at least 36 months after the decedent's death. The term "annuity contract" includes an annuity purchased for a beneficiary and distributed to the beneficiary, if the contract is not included in the gross income of the beneficiary upon distribution (see Q 214). The term "other arrangement" includes any arrangement arising by reason of the decedent's participation in the program providing the individual retirement plan. Payments are considered "periodic" if under the arrangement or contract (including a distributed contract) payments are to be made to the beneficiary at regular intervals. If the contract or arrangement provides optional payment provisions, not all of which provide for periodic payments, payments are considered periodic only if an option providing periodic payments is elected not later than the date the estate tax return is filed. For this purpose, the right to surrender a contract (including a distributed contract) for a cash surrender value will not be considered an optional payment provision. Payments are considered "substantially equal" even though the amounts receivable by the beneficiary may vary. Payments are not considered substantially equal, however, if more than 40% of the total amount payable to the beneficiary under the individual retirement plan, determined as of the date of the decedent's death and excluding any postmortem increase, is payable to the beneficiary in any 12-month period. Treas. Reg. §20.2039-5(b). See also Let. Rul. 8318015.

The exclusion applies only with respect to the gross estate of a decedent on whose behalf the plan was established; it does not apply to the estate of a decedent who was only a beneficiary under the plan. Treas. Reg. §20.2039-5(a)(2)(i); Let. Rul. 8141082 (same as Let. Rul. 8410182). Under circumstances described in Q 233, a beneficiary who is receiving benefits under an IRA following the death of the one on whose behalf the plan was established (or death of his surviving spouse) may, however, elect to have the plan treated as his own plan. He can do this in one of two ways: (1) by failing to meet the distribution requirements applicable to a beneficiary under the plan and by meeting instead the distribution requirements applicable to the one on whose behalf the plan was established (see Q 233), or (2) by contributing an amount (or amounts) which is subject to the distribution requirements applicable to the one on whose behalf the plan was established. If the election is made, the estate tax exclusion will not apply in the estate of the electing beneficiary to the amounts as to which the election was made. Treas. Reg. §20.2039-5(c). *ASRS, Sec. 62, ¶510.2.*

649. Is a marital deduction available for the value of a survivor benefit payable under an individual retirement plan (IRA) that is includable in the decedent's gross estate?

Yes, if benefits pass to the surviving spouse in a form that qualifies for the marital deduction (see Q 864). IRC Sec. 2056. Thus, an outright transfer of the IRA account balance to the surviving spouse should qualify for the marital deduction. Also, a marital deduction should be available if any income or principal distributed while the surviving spouse is alive is distributed to such spouse and principal and income, if any, is distributed to such spouse's estate at death. A marital deduction should also be available if all income from the IRA is distributed at least annually to the surviving spouse and such spouse is given a general power to appoint the IRA to himself or his estate. IRC Sec. 2056(b)(5). Additionally, a marital deduction should be available if all income from the IRA is distributed at least annually to the surviving spouse, no one has the power to distribute any part of the IRA to anyone other than the surviving spouse, and the executor makes a qualified terminable interest property (QTIP) election. IRC Sec. 2056(b)(7). If the surviving spouse is given a survivor annuity where only the spouse has the right to receive payment's during such spouse's lifetime, such interest would qualify for the QTIP marital deduction. IRC Sec. 2056(b)(7)(C). In the case of a surviving spouse who is not a U.S. citizen, a qualified domestic trust would generally be required to obtain the marital deduction. IRC Secs. 2056(d), 2056A; Let. Ruls. 9544038, 9322005.

An executor can elect to treat an IRA and a trust as QTIP if (1) the trustee of the trust is the beneficiary of the IRA, (2) the surviving spouse can compel the trustee to withdraw all income earned by the IRA at least annually and distribute that amount to the spouse, and (3) no person has the power to appoint any part of the trust to any person other than the spouse. Rev. Rul. 2000-2, 2000-1 CB 305. Prior to Revenue Ruling 2000-2, where IRA proceeds were to be distributed to a trust benefiting the survivor spouse, marital deduction requirements had to be generally met at both the IRA and the trust level. Thus, in Revenue Ruling 89-89, 1989-2 CB 231, obsoleted by Revenue Ruling 2000-2, a decedent's executor was permitted to elect to treat a decedent's IRA as eligible for the QTIP marital deduction where (1) the distribution option elected by the decedent for the IRA required the principal balance of the IRA be distributed in annual installments to a testamentary QTIP trust and the income earned on the undistributed balance of the IRA be distributed annually to the trust, and (2) all trust income was payable annually to decedent's spouse. However, a QTIP marital deduction was not available for an IRA with distributions payable to a marital trust where none of the IRA options provided that all income would be distributed at least annually to the marital trust. TAM 9220007.

A marital deduction may also be available if IRA proceeds are paid to a charitable remainder annuity trust or unitrust (see Q 825) and the surviving spouse is the only noncharitable beneficiary (other than certain ESOP remainder beneficiaries). IRC Sec. 2056(b)(8). Presumably, the IRA would have to incorporate all the charitable deduction requirements for such a trust.

For the income tax implications of distributions from a traditional IRA, see Q 227, from a Roth IRA, see Q 228.

LIFE INSURANCE TRUSTS

650. If a grantor creates a revocable life insurance trust with a policy on his life, will the proceeds be includable in his estate?

Yes, the entire value of the proceeds is includable in his gross estate. If he has funded the trust, the funding property is also includable. IRC Sec. 2038(a); Treas. Reg. §20.2042-1(c)(4). *ASRS, Sec. 54, ¶35.1.*

651. If policies on insured's life are placed in an irrevocable life insurance trust, are the proceeds includable in his estate?

Ordinarily, no. *Est. of Crosley v. Comm.*, 47 TC 310 (1966), acq. 1967-2 CB 2. However, the proceeds will be included in the insured's gross estate if he retains any incident of ownership in the policy at the time of his death, whether the ownership right is exercisable by him alone or only in conjunction with another person (see Q 626). Treas.

Reg. §20.2042-1(c)(4); *Farwell v. U.S.*, 243 F.2d 373 (7th Cir. 1957); *In re Rhodes' Est.*, 174 F.2d 584 (3rd Cir. 1949); *Est. of Seward v. Comm.*, 164 F.2d 434 (4th Cir. 1947). Even though the insured has assigned the policy to the trustee, the proceeds will be included in his gross estate if, under the terms of the trust instrument, he has a right to the cash surrender values. *St. Louis Union Trust Co. (Orthwein) v. U.S.*, 262 F. Supp. 27 (E.D. Mo. 1966). The mere right to give investment advice, in the case of a funded trust, is not considered an incident of ownership in the policy. *Est. of Mudge v. Comm.*, 27 TC 188 (1956). However, see Q 642 for tax results where the trust was established within three years of death, or insured paid premiums within three years of death. On whether the right to control payment of the proceeds when such right is held by the insured as trustee is an incident of ownership, see Q 632. *ASRS, Sec. 54, ¶35.2.*

652. Under what circumstances might the death proceeds be includable in the estate of the life income beneficiary of a life insurance trust?

If upon the insured's death the life income beneficiary was owner of the policies of insurance payable to the trust, and if at the life income beneficiary's subsequent death she is still life income beneficiary of the trust, an amount equal to the death proceeds will be includable in her estate under IRC Section 2036(a)(1) as a transfer of the proceeds with a life income interest retained (see Q 853(4)). Rev. Rul. 81-166, 1981-1 CB 477. Where, on the other hand, a husband insured created a nonfunded, revocable life insurance trust under which his wife was life income beneficiary, and where the wife paid premiums out of her own funds, it was held that upon the wife's death following her husband's death, the wife's payment of premiums was not a transfer making the proceeds includable in her estate under IRC Section 2036(a)(1). *Goodnow v. U.S.*, 302 F.2d 516 (Ct. Cl. 1962). However, where the trust is irrevocable, there is a possibility that payment of premiums by the income-beneficiary may cause her to be considered a co-grantor of the trust. Thus, she may be considered to have made a transfer with a retained income interest. This would cause the portion of the proceeds attributable to such premiums to be includable in her estate on her subsequent death. IRC Sec. 2036(a)(1). Trust beneficiaries would not hold incidents of ownership in life insurance under IRC Section 2042 where (1) a beneficiary could not make contributions to a trust which might hold life insurance on the beneficiary's life and (2) a beneficiary's limited power of appointment could not be exercised if the trust held life insurance on the beneficiary's life. Let. Rul. 9602010. *ASRS, Sec. 54, ¶¶35.1, 35.5.*

653. If the income beneficiary is given a power to invade the corpus of the trust, will the value of the trust assets over which she has the power be includable in her gross estate when she dies?

If the income beneficiary, as the insured's surviving spouse, is given a "qualifying income interest for life" in the trust, the trust corpus (or the specific portion thereof in which she has her income interest) will be includable in her estate if the marital deduction election is made, whether or not she is given a power to invade the corpus of the trust (see Q 864). IRC Sec. 2044. But if the income beneficiary's interest is not a "qualifying income interest for life" in the trust, and if the power is deemed a general power of appointment within the meaning of IRC Section 2041, *and* if she either (1) possessed the power at her death (but see next sentence) or (2) exercised or released the power during life by a disposition of such nature that if it were a transfer of property she owned, the property would be includable in her estate under one of IRC Sections 2035-2038 (see Q 853(3)-(6)), the value of the trust assets will be includable in her

LIFE INSURANCE TRUSTS   Q 653

gross estate. In the case of a power created on or before October 21, 1942, property subject to the power would be includable in her estate under IRC Section 2041 only if she exercised the power by will or as in (2) above. IRC Sec. 2041(a). The lapse of a power during the power holder's lifetime is considered a release of such power (as in (2) above), but only to the extent that property that could have been appointed by exercise of the powers which lapsed in any calendar year exceeded in value at the time of the lapse the greater of (a) $5,000, or (b) 5% of the value of the assets over which the lapsed powers existed (see Q 681). IRC Sec. 2041(b)(2).

Subject to the exceptions noted below, the income beneficiary would be deemed to hold a general power of appointment if she had the power to invade the trust corpus for the benefit of herself, her estate, her creditors, or the creditors of her estate (any one of the foregoing is sufficient). The following powers if possessed by the income beneficiary would *not* be deemed general powers of appointment for purposes of IRC Section 2041:

   1. A power to invade the corpus for her benefit if the power is limited by an "ascertainable standard" relating to her "health, education, support, or maintenance."

   2. A power of appointment created on or before October 21, 1942, which is exercisable by her only in conjunction with another person.

   3. A power of appointment created after October 21, 1942, which is exercisable by her only in conjunction with the creator of the power or with a person having a substantial interest in the property subject to the power adverse to exercise of the power in favor of the income beneficiary. IRC Sec. 2041(b)(1).

Five percent of a family trust (as well as 100% of a marital trust) was includable in the surviving spouse's estate where the surviving spouse held a power of withdrawal over all of the marital trust and a contingent power to withdraw 5% annually from the family trust if the marital trust was exhausted. *Est. of Kurz v. Comm.*, 95-2 USTC ¶60,215 (7th Cir. 1995).

In the past, a number of letter rulings have determined that a beneficiary who has the power to remove a trustee will be treated as holding any powers held by the trustee for purpose of determining whether the beneficiary holds a general power of appointment. Let. Ruls. 8916032, 9113026 (does not apply to transfers in trust before October 29, 1979, if trust was irrevocable on October 28, 1979). However, for purposes of IRC Sections 2036 or 2038, the Service will no longer include trust property in a decedent grantor's estate where the grantor retains the right to replace the trustee but can replace the trustee with only an independent corporate trustee. Rev. Rul. 95-58, 1995-2 CB 191; *Est. of Wall v. Comm.*, 101 TC 300 (1993). More recently, the power to remove a trustee and replace the trustee with an independent corporate trustee was not treated as the retention of powers held by the trustee for purposes of IRC Section 2041. Let. Rul. 9607008. Hopefully, this represents an extension by the Service of its new policy with regard to trustee removal under IRC Sections 2036 and 2038 to IRC Section 2041. Similarly, a beneficiary's right to veto a replacement trustee and to petition a court for appointment of an independent replacement trustee was not treated as a general power of appointment. Let. Rul. 9741009.

See Q 658 regarding the reciprocal trust doctrine. *ASRS, Sec. 54, ¶44.3(i).*

654. Are life insurance proceeds includable in insured's estate if they are payable to an irrevocable trust, and the trustee has power to use them for payment of insured's estate debts and death taxes?

Yes, if the trustee is *required* to use the proceeds to discharge estate obligations. The amount of proceeds required for payment of such debts and taxes is includable in insured's gross estate, whether or not the proceeds are actually used for such purposes. Treas. Reg. §20.2042-1(b)(1); *Hooper v. Comm.*, 41 BTA 114 (1940); *Pacific Nat'l Bank of Seattle (Morgan Will) v. Comm.*, 40 BTA 128 (1939); *Est. of Rohnert v. Comm.*, 40 BTA 1319 (1939); *Est. of Logan v. Comm.*, 23 BTA 236 (1931). But if the trustee's power is merely discretionary, and the trust is for the benefit of named individuals, the proceeds are includable in insured's estate only to the extent they are actually used for such purposes. *Est. of Wade v. Comm.*, 47 BTA 21 (1942); *Old Colony Trust Co. (Flye's Est.) v. Comm.*, 39 BTA 871 (1939), acq. 1939-2 CB 27. (See also Q 628.)

Planning Point: Liquidity for insured's estate can be aided by authorizing the trustee to lend proceeds to insured's estate, or to use them to buy assets from insured's estate; such powers, if only discretionary, should not subject the proceeds to inclusion in insured's estate.

ASRS, Sec. 54, ¶35.3.

655. If a grantor funds his life insurance trust by transferring income-producing property to the trustee, is the value of the funding property includable in his gross estate?

It should not be includable in grantor's estate if, generally, (1) the trust is irrevocable and grantor has retained no power to alter or amend, (2) the grantor has retained no interest or control over enjoyment of the property or income, and (3) the grantor does not have a reversionary interest in excess of 5%. IRC Secs. 2036, 2037, 2038; *First Nat'l Bank of Birmingham (Est. of Sanson) v. Comm.*, 36 BTA 651 (1937), acq. 1937-2 CB 24; *Est. of Carlton v. Comm.*, 34 TC 988 (1960), nonacq. 1964-1 CB 9; Rev. Rul. 81-164, 1981-1 CB 458. If the grantor retains power to withdraw and surrender policies placed in the trust, the funding property may be includable in his gross estate. Treas. Reg. §20.2042-1(c)(4); *Est. of Resch v. Comm.*, 20 TC 171 (1953), acq. 1953-2 CB 6. *ASRS, Sec. 54, ¶35.2.*

656. If a grandfather creates a funded irrevocable life insurance trust with policies on the life of his son for the benefit of his grandchildren, is anything includable in the grantor's gross estate?

Perhaps. If the grandfather retains any interest in or control over the insurance or the funding property, the value of the trust assets at the grantor's death (or alternate valuation date), including the insurance policies or proceeds held in trust, could be includable in the gross estate under one or more of the following IRC Sections: 2036, 2037, 2038 or 2041 (see Q 853). *Comm. v. Est. of Arents*, 297 F.2d 894 (2nd Cir. 1962), cert. denied 369 U.S. 848. The incidents of ownership test of IRC Section 2042 (see Q 631) is inapplicable because the grantor is not the insured. *ASRS, Sec. 54, ¶35.6.*

657. How is a "reversionary interest trust" taxed under the estate tax law?

If the trust instrument provides that the trust will end upon grantor's death, the entire value of the property is includable in his gross estate. Otherwise, the grantor's reversionary interest is includable in his estate. The longer the trust has to go, the less will be the value of the reversion in grantor's estate. This value is determined by use of the Estate and Gift Tax Valuation Tables (see Q 910). If the gift of the income interest was a taxable gift, the amount of the gift, if not included in the gross estate, will be added to the taxable estate for purposes of computing the tentative estate tax (see Q 852). Nothing will be includable in the *beneficiary's* estate if the trust instrument provides for termination upon beneficiary's death. Otherwise, the value of the right to income will be includable. This value decreases as the trust term draws to a close. Treas. Reg. §20.2031-7(d)(2). (See Q 844 for description of a reversionary interest trust.) *ASRS, Sec. 54,* ¶35.

658. What is the reciprocal trust doctrine, and how does it affect life insurance trusts?

Assume there are two insureds, A and B, each of whom wishes to create funded life insurance trusts for the same beneficiaries, each retaining certain life interests in the property he transfers. Each realizes that the retention of such interests will cause the value of the property each transfers to be included in his gross estate (see Q 654, Q 655). They reason that if instead of each retaining interests in his own transferred property, each gives to the *other* these interests, there should be no basis for includability of the trust assets in their estates, assuming the trusts are irrevocable.

The reciprocal trust doctrine, developed by the courts, prevents the estate tax result the parties hoped for. If the parties were to go ahead with their plan, the doctrine would be applied so as to "uncross" the trusts: for estate tax purposes, A would be treated as grantor of the trusts in form created by B, and vice-versa. The doctrine is applied where trusts are interrelated and the arrangement, to the extent of mutual value, leaves the grantors in approximately the same economic position in which they would have been had each retained life interests in the trusts he in form created. There is no need to find that the trusts were exchanged in "payment" for each other, nor that there was a specific "tax avoidance" motive involved in their creation. *U.S. v. Grace,* 395 U.S. 316 (1969). See also *Est. of Moreno v. Comm.,* 260 F.2d 389 (8th Cir. 1958). The Sixth Circuit and the Tax Court, in split decisions, have held that application of the reciprocal trust doctrine does not require that the grantors have crossed *economic* interests in the trusts they have created. *Est. of Green v. U.S.,* 95-2 USTC ¶60,216 (6th Cir. 1995); *Est. of Bischoff v. Comm.,* 69 TC 32 (1977). The Federal Circuit appears to concur with the Tax Court in this view (see case cited below). The reciprocal trust doctrine has also been applied to uncross transfers of assets in custodianship under the Uniform Gifts to Minors Act (see Q 856). *Exchange Bank & Trust Co. of Fla. v. U.S.,* 82-2 USTC ¶13,505 (Fed. Cir. 1982).

A letter ruling uncrossed reciprocal discretionary distribution rights given to trustees where each trustee was given a discretionary power to make distributions to the other trustee. Consequently, the decedent was treated as holding a general power to appoint trust corpus to himself and the corpus was included in his estate. Let. Rul. 9235025. *ASRS, Sec. 54,* ¶35.

LOANS ON LIFE INSURANCE

659. Is a life insurance policy loan deductible as a claim against the estate?

No, a policy loan is considered as an advancement of part of the policy proceeds, and not an enforceable claim against the estate. Treas. Regs. §§20.2042-1(a)(3), 20.2053-4; *Est. of Waterman v. Comm.*, 45 BTA 1160 (1941); *Kennedy v. Comm.*, 4 BTA 330 (1926). Only the excess of the proceeds over the amount of the policy loan is includable in the gross estate. *ASRS, Sec. 54, ¶29.1.*

MARITAL DEDUCTION

660. May a trust intended to qualify for the marital deduction as a "power of appointment trust" authorize the trustee to retain or acquire life insurance policies?

Under a "power of appointment trust," the surviving spouse must be entitled for life to all the income (see Q 864). This condition contemplates a trust holding income-producing property. Thus, if the trustee is empowered to retain or acquire non-income-producing property (such as life insurance), the condition will probably not be satisfied unless the trustee is required to make payments to the surviving spouse out of other trust assets to replace the lost income, or unless the trust gives the surviving spouse the power to compel the trustee to convert the non-income-producing property to income-producing property. Treas. Regs. §§20.2056(b)-5(f)(4), 20.2056(b)-5(f)(5); Rev. Rul. 75-440, 1975-2 CB 372; *Est. of Robinson v. U.S.*, 46 AFTR 2d ¶148,414 (E.D. Tenn. 1980). *ASRS, Sec. 51, ¶280.*

661. May a trust intended to qualify for the marital deduction as "qualified terminable interest property" (QTIP) authorize the trustee to retain or acquire life insurance policies?

Under a "qualified terminable interest property (QTIP) trust," the surviving spouse must be entitled for life to all the income (see Q 864). This condition contemplates a trust holding income-producing property. Thus, if the trustee is empowered to retain or acquire non-income-producing property (such as life insurance), the condition will probably not be satisfied unless the trust gives the surviving spouse the power to compel the trustee to convert the non-income-producing property to income-producing property, or unless the trustee is restrained under a state law "prudent man rule" to treat the surviving spouse fairly by protecting the spouse's income interest. TAM 8745003. *ASRS, Sec. 51, ¶280.*

662. If a decedent directs his executor or a trustee to buy a nonrefund life annuity for his surviving spouse, will the annuity qualify for the marital deduction?

No. The surviving spouse's interest in the annuity is considered a non-deductible terminable interest even though no interest in the annuity has passed from the decedent to any other person (see Q 864). Treas. Reg. §20.2056(b)-1(c)(2)(i). However, such an annuity will not fail to qualify if it is bought under a general investment power authorizing

MARITAL DEDUCTION   Q 664

investments in both terminable interests and other property. IRC Sec. 2056(b)(1)(C); Treas. Reg. §20.2056(b)-1(f). *ASRS, Sec. 51, ¶280.*

663. Under what conditions will life insurance or annuity proceeds payable to the surviving spouse qualify for the marital deduction?

There are five basic arrangements for the payment of proceeds that will qualify: (1) proceeds payable in a lump sum to surviving spouse (regardless of whether contingent beneficiaries are named or whether the surviving spouse actually elects to receive the proceeds under a settlement option) (Treas. Reg. §20.2056(c)-2(b)(3)(ii)); (2) proceeds payable solely to surviving spouse or to her estate (see Q 664); (3) proceeds payable to surviving spouse under a settlement option with contingent beneficiaries named, provided surviving spouse is given a general power of appointment over the proceeds (see Q 665, Q 666); (4) (unless otherwise elected by the decedent spouse's executor) proceeds of a survivor annuity where only the surviving spouse has the right to receive payments during such spouse's lifetime (IRC Section 2056(b)(7)(C)); (5) (if executor elects to have proceeds qualify) proceeds held under the interest option for the surviving spouse for her lifetime, interest payable to her at least annually, no power in any person to appoint any of the proceeds to anyone other than the spouse during her lifetime. Arrangements (4) and (5) make the proceeds qualified terminable interest property (see Q 864); however, to the extent provided in the regulations, an *annuity* interest is to be treated in a manner similar to an income interest in property (regardless of whether the property from which the annuity is payable can be separately identified). IRC Sec. 2056(b)(7)(B)(ii). A specific portion must be determined on a fractional or percentage basis. IRC Sec. 2056(b)(10). The proceeds will likewise qualify for the marital deduction if they are payable outright to the surviving spouse under insured's or annuitant's will or intestate laws, or to a trust that qualifies for the marital deduction (see Q 864). The marital deduction is not available unless the insured or annuitant is actually survived by his spouse, or is legally presumed to have been survived by his spouse (see Q 669, Q 864). Thus, a provision in the disposing instrument that the proceeds are payable to the spouse on the sole condition that she survive the insured or annuitant will not disqualify the proceeds (Q 667, Q 668).

A marital deduction is generally not allowable where the surviving spouse is not a United States citizen unless the transfer is to a qualified domestic trust (see Q 864). *ASRS, Sec. 51, ¶280.*

664. Will the life insurance or annuity proceeds qualify for the marital deduction if they are payable to the surviving spouse under a settlement option with her estate designated as contingent beneficiary? If they are payable to her as a straight life annuity?

If the proceeds are payable only to the surviving spouse or her estate, they will qualify. IRC Sec. 2056(a); Treas. Reg. §20.2056(c)-2(b)(3). For example, the following settlement would qualify: life income to widow with 20-year certain period, and should she die within the 20-year period, the balance of the guaranteed payments to be commuted and paid to her estate. Or, interest to widow for life, and principal to her estate. Likewise, the proceeds will qualify if they are payable to the surviving spouse under a straight life annuity settlement with no refund or period-certain guarantee (no portion of the proceeds would be payable to any other person after her death). Treas.

2006 Tax Facts on Insurance & Employee Benefits

Reg. §20.2056(b)-1(g), Example (3). If proceeds are payable under a no-refund life annuity to surviving spouse, qualification is not affected by the fact that an annuity is also payable to another, so long as their respective rights to their annuities are not tied together in any way. Rev. Rul. 77-130, 1977-1 CB 289. Where only the surviving spouse has the right to receive payments from a survivor annuity during such spouse's lifetime, such proceeds are treated as qualified terminable interest property (see Q 864) unless otherwise elected by the decedent spouse's executor. IRC Sec. 2056(b)(7)(C). *ASRS, Sec. 51, ¶280.*

665. Can life insurance settlements naming the spouse as primary beneficiary and other persons as contingent beneficiaries be so arranged that the proceeds will qualify for the marital deduction?

Yes. Where there is a possibility that one or more persons may receive some unpaid proceeds after the spouse's death, the spouse receives only a *terminable interest* in the proceeds. And, as a rule, terminable interests do not qualify for the marital deduction (see Q 864). As an exception to the general rule, however, a settlement naming contingent beneficiaries will qualify if the spouse is given a general power of appointment over the proceeds and certain other requirements are met.

Specifically, an insured may elect an interest-only, life income, or installment option for his spouse, naming contingent beneficiaries to take after her death, and the proceeds will qualify, provided the settlement meets the following conditions: (1) the interest or installments must be payable annually or more frequently, the first payment must be payable no later than 13 months after the insured's death; (2) all amounts payable during the spouse's life must be payable only to her; (3) the spouse must have a *general power of appointment* over the proceeds (a power to appoint the proceeds to herself or to her estate—see Q 666); (4) the spouse's power to appoint must be exercisable by her alone and in all events, whether exercisable by will or during life; (5) the proceeds must not be subject to a power in any other person to appoint against the spouse. IRC Sec. 2056(b)(6); Treas. Reg. §20.2056(b)-6; *Est. of White v. Comm.*, 22 TC 641 (1954); *Est. of Zeman v. Comm.*, TC Memo 1958-68; *Est. of Fiedler v. Comm.*, 67 TC 239 (1976), acq. 1977-1 CB 1; Rev. Rul. 76-404, 1976-2 CB 294.

An alternative settlement naming contingent beneficiaries does not require that the spouse be given any power over the proceeds so long as she has a "qualifying income interest for life" in the proceeds, and so long as the executor elects to have such proceeds qualify for the marital deduction. The surviving spouse has a "qualifying income interest for life" if she is entitled to all the income from the proceeds, payable annually or more frequently, and no person has a power to appoint any part of the proceeds to any person other than the surviving spouse. The insured or anyone else, including the surviving spouse, can designate beneficiaries to receive proceeds remaining at the spouse's death, and the spouse may be (but need not be) given the right to withdraw proceeds during her lifetime. See Q 663.

It is not necessary that the entire proceeds qualify. If a specific portion of the proceeds meets the conditions outlined above, that specific portion will qualify for the deduction. IRC Secs. 2056(b)(6), 2056(b)(7); Treas. Reg. §20.2056(b)-6(b). However, a specific portion must be determined on a fractional or percentage basis. IRC Sec. 2056(b)(10). *ASRS, Sec. 51, ¶280.*

MARITAL DEDUCTION   Q 668

666. For purposes of the marital deduction, what constitutes a general power to appoint the proceeds of a life insurance policy?

For purposes of the marital deduction, the donee of a general power of appointment must have the power to appoint the property to himself or to his estate. IRC Sec. 2056(b)(6). Thus, if the widow-beneficiary has the power to revoke contingent beneficiaries and name her estate instead, she is deemed to have a general power to appoint to her estate. Or, if she can withdraw the principal sum for her own use, she is deemed to have a general power to appoint to herself. Treas. Reg. §20.2056(b)-6(e)(4); Rev. Rul. 55-277, 1955-1 CB 456. She need not possess both powers; either will suffice. And the term "power to appoint" need not be used in the insurance policy. Thus, even where the widow is not given the power to revoke contingent beneficiaries, the proceeds will qualify if she is given the power to withdraw the proceeds during her life and the power is exercisable *in all events*. Insurance companies normally impose some administrative restrictions on the exercise of withdrawal rights. However, the regulations state that limitations of a formal nature—such as requirements that reasonable intervals must elapse between partial exercise—will not cause disqualification. Treas. Reg. §20.2056(b)-5(g)(4). See also *Est. of Cornwell v. Comm.*, 37 TC 688 (1962), acq., *Est. of Jennings v. Comm.*, 39 TC 417 (1962), acq. *ASRS, Sec. 51, ¶280.*

667. Does the use of a "delay clause" disqualify life insurance proceeds for the marital deduction?

The "delay clause" will not disqualify the proceeds unless the delay period specified is for more than six months. For example, the beneficiary arrangement may provide that payment will be made to insured's wife if she is living at the end of 60 days after insured's death, otherwise to contingent beneficiaries.

Under the general rules, a delay clause would create a terminable interest and, accordingly, disqualify the proceeds. The reason for this is that such a clause creates a possibility that the surviving spouse's interest will end (if she dies within the delay period) and the contingent beneficiaries will receive the proceeds (see Q 864). Under a specific exception, however, such a clause will not disqualify the proceeds if: (1) the delay period does not exceed six months, and (2) the surviving spouse actually survives the delay period. However, any clause that creates the possibility that the surviving spouse may have to survive longer than six months to receive the proceeds will ordinarily disqualify them for the marital deduction—even though the spouse survives the period and actually receives the proceeds. IRC Sec. 2056(b)(3); Treas. Reg. §20.2056(b)-3(b); Rev. Rul. 54-121, 1954-1 CB 196; TAM 8747003; but see *Eggleston v. Dudley*, 257 F.2d 398 (3rd Cir.). See also Rev. Rul. 70-400, 1970-2 CB 196.

Planning Point: Although—because of the special exception—a delay clause does not always result in loss of the marital deduction, the clause should not be used when it is important to secure the marital deduction with respect to the proceeds for insured's estate. If the spouse does survive the delay period, the clause will have served no purpose. If she survives the insured, but does not survive the full delay period, the clause will cause loss of the marital deduction.

ASRS, Sec. 51, ¶280.

668. Does a common disaster clause disqualify life insurance proceeds for the marital deduction?

2006 Tax Facts on Insurance & Employee Benefits

Where a true common disaster clause is used, the beneficiary-spouse will not receive the proceeds if she dies of injuries sustained in the same accident (or other disaster) that causes the death of the insured—regardless of how long she actually survives the insured. A common disaster clause creates a terminable interest (see Q 864). But as a special exception to the terminable interest rule, a clause will not disqualify the proceeds unless the death of the insured and that of his spouse are actually caused by the same disaster. IRC Sec. 2056(b)(3). A true common disaster clause is seldom used in an insurance policy. *ASRS, Sec. 51, ¶280.*

669. Can operation of the Uniform Simultaneous Death Act result in loss of the marital deduction?

Yes. If the insured and spouse-beneficiary die under circumstances that make it impossible to determine the order of death (usually when both are killed in the same accident), the Uniform Simultaneous Death Act creates a presumption that the *beneficiary* died first. Since it is presumed that the spouse-beneficiary did *not* survive, the Act would result in loss of the marital deduction. However, it is possible to reverse the statutory presumption by inserting in the policy a so-called "reverse simultaneous death clause." This clause would provide that, if the order of death cannot be determined, it will be presumed that the insured died first. This would save the marital deduction. Treas. Reg. §20.2056(c)-2(e). However, it cannot save the marital deduction if there is evidence that the beneficiary actually died first. *ASRS, Sec. 51, ¶280.*

670. Can proceeds of community property life insurance passing to the surviving spouse qualify for the marital deduction?

Yes, and without limit as to amount (see Q 864). IRC Sec. 2056. *ASRS, Sec. 51, ¶280.*

MULTIPLE-LIFE LIFE INSURANCE

671. Does the estate taxation of a life insurance policy that insures more than one life differ from the taxation of a policy that insures a single life?

Basically, no. However, application of the rules generally depends on when proceeds are payable. With a "first-to-die" or "joint life" policy, proceeds are payable at the death of the first insured to die. With a "second-to-die," "survivorship," or "joint and survivor" policy, proceeds are payable at the death of the last survivor.

In general, proceeds of a first-to-die policy will be included in the insured's estate if (1) the proceeds are payable to or for the benefit of the insured's estate, or (2) the insured held incidents of ownership in the policy at death (or within three years of death). See Q 626. Also, the value of a first-to-die policy will be included in the estate of a policyowner who is not the insured. See Q 676.

The value of a second-to-die policy will be included in the estate of a policyowner who is not the insured. See Q 676. For the same reasons, at the first death, the value of a second-to-die policy will be included in the estate of the decedent/insured if he is a policyowner. At the second death, proceeds of a second-to-die policy will be included in the insured's estate if (1) the proceeds are payable to or for the benefit of the insured's

PENSION AND PROFIT SHARING PLANS (QUALIFIED)　　　　　Q 673

estate, or (2) the insured held incidents of ownership in the policy at death (or within three years of death). See Q 626.

Planning Point: Second-to-die policies are frequently used to provide for estate taxes deferred through use of the marital deduction until the surviving spouse's death. First-to-die policies are frequently used to provide funds for a buy-sell agreement or to provide some funds at the death of the first spouse to die.

For income taxation of multiple-life life insurance, see Q 302. For gift taxation of multiple-life life insurance, see Q 732.

NONQUALIFIED EMPLOYEE ANNUITY

672. Is the value of a death benefit payable under a nonqualified employee annuity includable in the employee's gross estate?

Yes; if the employee was receiving payments under the contract when he died, or if he would have had the right to receive payments had he lived, the value of the death benefit is includable in his gross estate. IRC Sec. 2039(a). It is immaterial whether employee's rights were forfeitable or nonforfeitable before death. Treas. Reg. §20.2039-1. Premiums paid by the employer are considered as having been paid by the employee himself. IRC Sec. 2039(b). *All v. McCobb*, 321 F.2d 633 (2nd Cir. 1963); *Est. of Bahen v. Comm.*, 305 F.2d 827 (Ct. Cl. 1962); *Est. of Wadewitz v. Comm.*, 39 TC 925 (1962), aff'd 339 F.2d 980 (7th Cir. 1964). (But for tax sheltered annuities purchased for employees of tax-exempt organizations and public schools, see Q 686.) *ASRS, Sec. 64, ¶540.2.*

PENSION AND PROFIT SHARING PLANS (QUALIFIED)

673. Is the value of a death benefit payable from a qualified plan includable in the employee's gross estate?

In general, yes, if the employee dies after 1984. For details, see below.

Estates of Decedents Dying After 1984

The present value (at date of decedent's death or alternate valuation date—see Q 862) of an annuity or any other benefit payable to any surviving beneficiary under a qualified plan upon the death of a participant (other than death proceeds of insurance on the life of the participant) is includable in the decedent's estate. IRC Secs. 2039(a), 2039(b).

The Tax Reform Act of 1984 repealed the estate tax exclusion discussed below generally for estates of decedents dying after 1984. However, the repeal does not apply to the estate of any decedent who (a) was a plan participant in pay status on December 31, 1984, and (b) irrevocably elected the form of the benefit before July 18, 1984. TRA '84, Sec. 525. The Tax Reform Act of 1986 provided that (a) and (b) are considered met if the decedent separated from service before January 1, 1985 and does not change the form of benefit before death. TRA '86, Sec. 1852(e)(3). Qualified plan benefits rolled over to an IRA are treated as IRA benefits (see Q 648) which are not eligible for the TRA '86 separation from service rule. Rev. Rul. 92-22, 1992-1 CB 313. For the meaning of the term "in pay status" and the requirements of an irrevocable election of the form of benefit, see Temp. Treas. Reg. §20.2039-1T.

Life insurance proceeds are includable under IRC Section 2042, assuming the participant held an incident of ownership in the insurance at his death or the proceeds are payable to or for the participant's estate. The right to name the beneficiary of the death proceeds is an incident of ownership–see Q 631.

Estates of Decedents Dying After 1982 and Before 1985

Up to $100,000 in value of an annuity or other benefit payable to any surviving beneficiary under a qualified plan upon the death of a participant, to the extent such value is attributable to employer contributions and to deductible employee contributions, is excludable from the gross estate (but special rules apply to a lump sum distribution). IRC Sec. 2039(c), (g), as amended and added by the Tax Equity and Fiscal Responsibility Act of 1982 (TEFRA), and before repeal by the Tax Reform Act of 1984. The $100,000 limitation is an *aggregate* limitation applicable to survivor benefits payable under a qualified plan, a tax sheltered annuity (see Q 686), an individual retirement plan (see Q 648), a Retired Serviceman's Family Protection Plan, or a Survivor Benefit Plan (see ASRS, section 18). The Tax Reform Act of 1984 also amended TEFRA to provide that the $100,000 limit shall not apply to the estate of any decedent who (a) was a plan participant on pay status on December 31, 1982, and (b) irrevocably elected before January 1, 1983, the form of benefit. TRA '84, Sec. 525. The Tax Reform Act of 1986 provided that (a) and (b) are considered met if the decedent separated from service before January 1, 1983 and does not change the form of benefit before death. TRA '86, Sec. 1852(e)(3).

Estates of Decedents Dying After 1953 and Before 1983

The value of an annuity or other benefit payable to any surviving beneficiary under a qualified plan upon the death of a participant, to the extent such value is attributable to employer contributions and to deductible employee contributions, is excludable from the gross estate (but special rules apply to a lump sum distribution). IRC Sec. 2039(c), before amendment by TEFRA. *ASRS, Sec. 59, ¶970.1.*

674. Is a death benefit payable under a Keogh plan includable in a self-employed individual's gross estate?

Yes, generally, as to decedents dying after 1984.

Estates of Decedents Dying After 1984

The federal estate taxation of survivor benefits payable under a Keogh plan (see Q 418) is the same in the estate of a self-employed individual/participant as in the estate of a participant covered under a "corporate" plan (see Q 673).

Estates of Decedents Dying After 1953 and Before 1985

The federal estate tax exclusion, as described at Q 673, is available as well to the estates of self-employed individuals covered under qualified plans. For purposes of the exclusion, contributions or payments on behalf of the decedent participant while he was covered as a self-employed individual (see Q 358) are treated as employer contributions to the extent they were deductible as contributions to a qualified plan (see Q 365); to the extent they were not so deductible, such contributions or payments are treated as employee contributions. IRC Sec. 2039(c); Treas. Reg. §20.2039-2(c)(iii). (The exclusion applies only to amounts that are attributable to employer contributions (Let. Rul. 8122024), and to "deductible employee contributions".) In an insured plan, for example, the cost of current life insurance protection for self-employed participants is not deductible (see Q 425H); therefore, the "amount at risk" portion of the death proceeds of life insurance payable under the plan is not eligible for the estate tax exclusion. As to common law employees, on the other hand, the entire proceeds are eligible for the exclusion where the cost is paid by the employer. *ASRS, Sec. 60, ¶450.*

675. How does community property law affect the estate taxation of qualified plan benefits?

If an employee's interest in his employer's qualified plan is community property, then such interest is considered to be owned one-half by the employee and one-half by his spouse. Accordingly, if the employee were to predecease his spouse, only his community interest in any death benefit would be includable in his estate (see Q 673). Likewise, if the employee's spouse were to die first, only her community interest in the plan would be includable in her gross estate. IRC Sec. 2033.

The extent to which employee interests in qualified plans are community property is a matter of local law. There appears to be little doubt that an employee's vested interest in a qualified plan, to the extent it is attributable to contributions made while the employee was married and living in a community property state, is community property. *Herring v. Blakeley*, 385 S.W. 2d 843 (Tex. 1965); *Lynch v. Lawrence*, 293 So. 2d 598 (La. App. 1974, writs ref'd.); *T.L. James & Co., Inc. v. Montgomery*, 332 So. 2d 834 (La. 1976); *Everson v. Everson*, 537 P. 2d 624 (Ariz. App. 1975); *Marriage of Ward*, 50 Cal. App.3d 150 (1975); *Fox v. Smith*, 531 S.W. 2d 654 (Tex. Civ. App. 1975); 50 *Texas L. Rev.* 334 (1972); 17 *Loyola L. Rev.* 162 (1970-71); 24 *So. Calif. Tax Inst.* 469 (1972); 94 ALR3d 176. Moreover, there appears to be increasing support for the view that *nonvested* benefits in a retirement plan are not mere expectancies but are property, and thus can be community property. *Johnson v. Johnson*, 638 P.2d 705 (Ariz. 1981); *Re Marriage of Brown*, 544 P.2d 561 (Cal. 1976); *Cearley v. Cearley*, 544 S.W. 2d 661 (Tex. 1976); *Wilder v. Wilder*, 534 P.2d 1353 (Wash. 1975); 94 ALR3d 176, §9(a).

POLICYHOLDER OTHER THAN INSURED

676. If a policyowner who is not the insured dies before the insured, is the value of the unmatured life insurance policy included in the policyowner's gross estate?

Yes. IRC Sec. 2033. The value of the policy is determined in the same manner as for gift tax purposes, substituting date of death for date of gift (see Q 744). Treas. Reg. §20.2031-8; *DuPont Est. v. Comm.*, 233 F.2d 210 (3rd Cir. 1956); *Est. of Donaldson v. Comm.*, 31 TC 729 (1959).

A revenue ruling involved the estate tax valuation of a third party owned policy on the split dollar plan (see Q 457). The policy had been in force for some time and premiums remained to be paid after the decedent policyowner's death. Premiums and proceeds were split between the decedent and the insured's employer, to whom the policy had been collaterally assigned. It was ruled that the amount includable in decedent's estate was the interpolated terminal reserve plus the proportionate part of the gross premium paid before the date of decedent's death that covered the period extending beyond that date, less the amount of the employer's interest in the policy. Rev. Rul. 79-429, 1979-2 CB 321.

Where the executor elects to value assets six months after death (alternate valuation), any increase in policy value due to payment of premiums or accrual of interest during the six months following death, is excluded in determining the estate tax value of the policy. Rev. Rul. 55-379, 1955-1 CB 449. But if the executor elects to value the estate by the alternative valuation method, and the insured dies before the optional valuation date (six months after the policyowner's death–see Q 862), the entire value of the proceeds is includable in the policyowner's gross estate. Rev. Rul. 63-52, 1963-1 CB 173. (See Q 862.)

Where the owner-beneficiary of a life insurance policy and the insured die simultaneously (to all appearances), and where policy proceeds are distributed as if the owner-beneficiary predeceased the insured (as provided in the Uniform Simultaneous Death Act, except where the policy or other controlling instrument provides otherwise), the value of the policy (valued as described above) is likewise included in the owner-beneficiary's estate under IRC Section 2033. *Chown v. Comm.*, 428 F.2d 1395 (9th Cir. 1970); *Old Kent Bank & Trust Co. v. U.S.*, 430 F.2d 392 (6th Cir. 1970); *Meltzer v. Comm.*, 439 F.2d 798 (4th Cir. 1971); *Wien v. Comm.*, 441 F.2d 32 (5th Cir. 1971); Rev. Rul. 77-181, 1977-1 CB 272; *Est. of Goldstone v. Comm.*, 78 TC 1143 (1982). In Rev. Rul. 77-181, A and B each owned policies on the other's life with proceeds payable to the owner or the owner's estate. A and B died under circumstances where the Uniform Act provisions applied, so that the proceeds of the policies on A's life were paid to B's estate and the proceeds of policies on B's life were paid to A's estate. The Service ruled that the amount to be included in the gross estate of each was the sum of the date-of-death interpolated terminal reserve value of the policies decedent owned at death and the proportionate part of the gross premium last paid covering the post-death period. Where, in the instrument controlling disposition of policy proceeds, the presumed order of the deaths is reversed (from that provided for in the Uniform Act), simultaneous deaths of the policyowner-beneficiary and the insured will cause the death proceeds to be includable in the policyowner's estate. Rev. Rul. 77-48, 1977-1 CB 292. (See also Q 735.) *ASRS, Sec. 54, ¶36.*

SETTLEMENT OPTIONS–BENEFICIARY'S ESTATE

677. If the insured elects a settlement option for his primary beneficiary, and names contingent beneficiaries, will the value of any unpaid life insurance proceeds be includable in the primary beneficiary's estate?

As a general rule, the proceeds are not includable in the primary beneficiary's estate unless she has a general power of appointment over the proceeds (see Q 666, Q 678) or unless she was the insured's surviving spouse and has a "qualifying income interest for life" in proceeds as to which the marital deduction was allowed (see Q 665). IRC Secs. 2041, 2044. The transfer to contingent beneficiaries is from the insured, not from the

SETTLEMENT OPTIONS–BENEFICIARY'S ESTATE   Q 680

primary beneficiary. (But for a limited, noncumulative power to withdraw, see Q 681.) With respect to community property insurance, however, one-half of the proceeds belongs to the noninsured spouse. Consequently, where she is primary beneficiary, one-half of the proceeds will be includable in the insured spouse's estate, and one-half of the value of the proceeds remaining at her death will be includable in her estate. IRC Sec. 2036. *Whiteley v. U.S.*, 214 F. Supp. 489 (W.D. Wash. 1963). See *Tyre v. Aetna Life Ins. Co.*, 353 P. 2d 725 (Cal. 1960). *ASRS, Sec. 54, ¶¶28.1, 32.*

678. If the surviving income beneficiary dies possessing the power during her lifetime to appoint the life insurance proceeds only to her children, are the proceeds includable in her estate?

If the surviving spouse has a "qualifying income interest for life" in the proceeds, the proceeds will be includable in her estate if the marital deduction election was made whether or not she has any power to appoint the proceeds. (See Q 665.) IRC Sec. 2044. If she does not have a "qualifying income interest for life" in the proceeds, according to a 1979 revenue ruling, the answer depends on whether the income beneficiary at her death could have discharged her legal duty to support her children, in whole or in part, by exercising her power to appoint the proceeds. To the extent she could have, her power would be treated as a general power of appointment and the proceeds would be includable. Under the facts of the ruling, it was held that no part of the proceeds was includable because all of the income beneficiary's children were adults at the time of her death and she was not obligated under local law to provide for their support. Rev. Rul. 79-154, 1979-1 CB 301. See Q 658 regarding the reciprocal trust doctrine. *ASRS, Sec. 54, ¶28.5.*

679. If life insurance proceeds remaining unpaid at the primary beneficiary's death are payable to her estate, are they includable in her gross estate?

Yes. Since the beneficiary can dispose of the remaining proceeds as she wishes through her will, she is deemed to have a general power of appointment over the proceeds (see Q 666). IRC Sec. 2041(a); Rev. Rul. 55-277, 1955-1 CB 456; *Keeter v. U.S.*, 29 AFTR 2d 72-1540 (5th Cir. 1972). Contra, *Second Nat'l Bank of Danville, Ill. v. Dallman*, 209 F.2d 321 (7th Cir. 1954). *ASRS, Sec. 54, ¶28.3.*

680. If the insured elects a settlement option, naming contingent beneficiaries, but giving the primary beneficiary power to withdraw the proceeds, are life insurance proceeds remaining unpaid at the primary beneficiary's death includable in her estate?

If the primary beneficiary has a "qualifying income interest for life" in the proceeds, the proceeds will be includable in her estate if the marital deduction election was made whether or not she has a power to withdraw any of the proceeds (see Q 665). IRC Sec. 2044. Otherwise, a full power of withdrawal constitutes a *general power of appointment* (see Q 666). Treas. Reg. §20.2056(b)-6(e)(4). Whether the possession of such a power by the primary beneficiary will cause the remaining proceeds to be taxable in her estate depends upon when the power was created. If the primary beneficiary has an unrestricted power to withdraw the proceeds, and the power was created after October 21, 1942, the value of any proceeds remaining unpaid at her death will be included in her gross estate. IRC Sec. 2041(a)(2). (But for a limited, noncumulative withdrawal right, see Q 681.)

2006 Tax Facts on Insurance & Employee Benefits

If the primary beneficiary's power of withdrawal was created before October 22, 1942, the value of the unpaid proceeds is not includable in her gross estate merely because she possessed the power. IRC Sec. 2041(a)(1). A power of appointment is created when the insured executes the supplementary contract electing the settlement option. This is the date the power is created even though insured retains the right to surrender the policy and to change the beneficiary. Treas. Reg. §20.2041-1; Rev. Rul. 61-129, 1961-2 CB 150. *ASRS, Sec. 54, ¶28.5.*

681. Can an insured give his primary beneficiary limited, noncumulative withdrawal rights without causing remaining unpaid life insurance proceeds to be includable in her estate?

If the insured gives his primary beneficiary (spouse) a "qualifying income interest for life" in the proceeds, the proceeds will be includable in her estate if the marital deduction election was made whether or not she has a power to withdraw any of the proceeds (see Q 665). IRC Sec. 2044. If she does not have such an interest in the proceeds, the insured can give his beneficiary a noncumulative right to withdraw each year up to $5,000 or 5% of the balance of the proceeds, whichever is greater. If the beneficiary's annual withdrawal right does not exceed these limits, the amounts she could have withdrawn but did not withdraw are not includable in her gross estate (except the unwithdrawn amount which she could have withdrawn in the year of her death). IRC Sec. 2041(b)(2).

> *Example.* The proceeds of a $100,000 life insurance policy are left with the insurer under the interest only option for insured's daughter. The daughter is given a noncumulative right to withdraw $5,000 a year. She does not have a power to appoint the proceeds to her estate. The daughter dies seven years later, having withdrawn none of the proceeds. Only $5,000, the amount she could have withdrawn in the year of death, is includable in her gross estate. Rev. Rul. 79-373, 1979-2 CB 331.

If the beneficiary's noncumulative withdrawal right exceeds the $5,000/5% limits, the aggregate withdrawable amounts in excess of these limits which she did not withdraw will be includable in her gross estate (but not in excess of the full proceeds). Thus, if the daughter in the example above had been given a power to withdraw $6,000 annually, the amount includable in her gross estate would be $12,000 [6 × $1,000 (amount in excess of $5,000) + $6,000 (year of death)]. *ASRS, Sec. 54, ¶28.6.*

682. If, under a settlement option, the primary beneficiary is given the power to revoke contingent beneficiaries and appoint to her estate, are life insurance proceeds remaining unpaid at her death includable in her estate?

A beneficiary who has power to appoint to her estate has a general power of appointment over the proceeds. Treas. Reg. §20.2056(b)-6(e)(4). Generally, such a power, given to a wife-beneficiary, will qualify the proceeds for the marital deduction in insured's estate (see Q 665), but will cause remaining unpaid proceeds to be includable in the beneficiary's estate. However, includability in the beneficiary's estate will depend upon when the power was created. If the power was created *after* October 21, 1942, the proceeds remaining unpaid at the primary beneficiary's death are includable in her estate. IRC Sec. 2041(a)(2). If the power was created *before* October 22, 1942, the proceeds remaining unpaid at beneficiary's death are includable in her estate only if she exercised the power. (See Q 680 with respect to when a power is created.) *ASRS, Sec. 54, ¶28.5.*

683. If the beneficiary elects the settlement option, are life insurance proceeds remaining unpaid at her death includable in her estate?

Yes. Thus, if the proceeds are payable to her in a lump sum and, after insured's death, she elects a settlement option for herself as primary beneficiary, the proceeds are includable in her estate. IRC Sec. 2036; *Est. of Tuohy v. Comm.*, 14 TC 245 (1950); *Est. of Morton v. Comm.*, 12 TC 380 (1949); *Rundle v. Welch*, 184 F. Supp. 777 (S.D. Ohio 1960); Let. Rul. 8051019. Likewise, if the beneficiary as *policyowner* elects a settlement for herself and contingent beneficiaries, the remaining proceeds are includable in her gross estate. *Est. of Pyle v. Comm.*, 313 F.2d 328 (3rd Cir. 1963). *ASRS*, Sec. 54, ¶28.4.

SURVIVOR INCOME BENEFIT

684. If an employer provides, under a nonqualified agreement or plan, an income benefit only for certain survivors designated by family or marital relationship to the employee, how is the benefit treated for estate tax purposes in the employee's estate?

The threshold issue in answering this question is whether the survivor income benefit plan is treated as insurance or as an annuity (see Q 153 for background).

If it is treated as life insurance, includability of the value of the survivor benefit in the employee's estate is determined under the rules applicable to death proceeds of insurance. The controlling statute in this case is usually IRC Section 2042 although IRC Section 2035 comes into play if the decedent insured has assigned any of his rights in the benefit within three years of death (see Q 626, Q 644). If the plan is treated as an annuity, includability is usually determined under IRC Section 2039(a), but not under IRC Section 2042 (see Q 685, particularly the discussion of death-benefit-only plans).

Case law and IRS rulings dealing with the estate taxation of survivor income benefits tend to support the view of the Second Circuit. In *All v. McCobb*, 321 F.2d 633 (2nd Cir. 1963), the Second Circuit held that a survivor income benefit plan that was uninsured and unfunded lacked the necessary insurance elements of risk-shifting and risk-distribution to be treated as insurance. (See also the cases cited at Q 153.) *Est. of Lumpkin v. Comm.*, 474 F.2d 1092 (5th Cir. 1973), *Est. of Connelly v. U.S.*, 551 F.2d 545 (3rd Cir. 1977), and *Est. of Smead v. Comm.*, 78 TC 43 (1982), acq. in result, 1984-2 CB 2, concern an insured plan and treat the plan as group insurance. In Let. Rul. 8046110, a plan funded by group life insurance was treated as insurance; following Rev. Rul. 69-54 (see Q 645), the Service ruled that because the decedent insured died possessing the right to convert his group life insurance into individual insurance, an incident of ownership according to IRS, the sum used by the insurance company in determining the amount of the survivor annuity payable was includable in the decedent's estate (see Treas. Reg. §20.2042-1(a)(3)). Rev. Rul. 77-183, 1977-1 CB 274; *Est. of Schelberg v. Comm.*, 70 TC 690 (1978), rev'd on other grounds, 79-2 USTC ¶13,321 (2nd Cir. 1979); *Est. of Van Wye v. U.S.*, 82-2 USTC ¶13,485 (6th Cir. 1982), all deal with an uninsured and unfunded plan and treat the plan as an annuity. No estate tax cases or rulings have been found which deal with *uninsured funded* plans (but see Q 153). *ASRS*, Sec. 66, ¶540.5.

685. Is the value of a survivor benefit payable by an employer under a nonqualified salary continuation or deferred compensation agreement includable in the employee's gross estate?

It is includable under IRC Section 2039(a) if, (1) it is provided for "under any form of contract or agreement," and (2) the decedent had a right to receive the payments himself "for his life or for any period not ascertainable without reference to his death or for any period which does not in fact end before his death."

Clearly the statute applies where the decedent was receiving payments and had a nonforfeitable right to future payments at the time of his death. However, regulations make it equally clear that IRS will consider the statute applicable whether the decedent had a right to present or future payments at the time of his death and whether the rights were forfeitable or nonforfeitable.

The regulations provide: "The term 'contract or agreement' includes any arrangement, understanding or plan, or any combination of arrangements, understandings or plans arising by reason of the decedent's employment."Treas. Reg. §20.2039-1(b). While the Tax Court has stated that an enforceable contract is a prerequisite to the application of IRC Section 2039 (*Est. of Barr v. Comm.*, 40 TC 227 (1963), acq. in result only, 1978-1 CB 1), later case law has led to a less rigid rule. Where there is lacking a legally enforceable contract, other circumstances may exist which would cause an annuity to be considered as having been paid under a contract or agreement for purposes of the statute. Thus, if the survivor annuitant has a controlling interest in the company, or if consideration for the annuity is found, or if the company has in the past consistently paid annuities pursuant to an unenforceable plan, the annuity may be considered as having been paid under a contract or agreement; but if no such circumstances are found, a legally enforceable contract must exist. *Neely v. U.S.*, 613 F.2d 802 (Ct. Cl. 1980); *Courtney v. U.S.*, 84-2 USTC ¶13,580 (N.D. Ohio, 1984). See also Let. Rul. 8005011.

It has been argued that payments under a deferred compensation contract have no estate tax value if they were forfeitable to the executive during his lifetime. This argument is based on the theory that the estate tax value is to be determined as of the moment prior to death. However, it is now pretty firmly established that the value is to be determined as of the moment after death when the contingencies have ceased to have an operative effect. *Goodman v. Granger*, 243 F.2d 264 (3rd Cir. 1957). In *Silberman v. U.S.*, 28 AFTR 2d 71-6282 (W.D. Pa. 1971), the commuted value of the widow's benefit was includable in the employee's estate even though the employee had to render consulting services in order to get retirement benefits.

The estate tax cannot be avoided by providing for the retirement pay and death benefit under separate contracts; the regulations interpret the statutory term "contract or agreement" to include "any combination of arrangements, understandings or plans arising by reason of the decedent's employment."Treas. Reg. §20.2039-1(b). However, under certain circumstances an unfunded deferred compensation agreement which provides death benefits only may escape inclusion in the employee's gross income. For a discussion of these plans, see below.

The death benefit is includable in the gross estate whether it is payable in a lump sum or in periodic payments, and whether it is forfeitable or nonforfeitable to the

SURVIVOR INCOME BENEFIT   Q 685

survivor. However, forfeitability will be taken into account in connection with the valuation of the benefit in the employee's estate. Treas. Reg. §20.2039-1(b)(2)(Ex. 2). For example, where the employer has a right to recover remaining unpaid benefits upon the death or remarriage of the employee's widow, the value of the death benefit in employee's estate will not include the value of this refund feature. *Allen v. Comm.*, 39 TC 817 (1963), acq. 1964-1 CB 4. (Such a forfeiture provision would, however, make the benefit ineligible for the marital deduction—see Q 864.) Where the death benefit is payable as an annuity, the commuted value of the payments is the proper estate tax value. *Est. of Beal v. Comm.*, 47 TC 269 (1966), acq. 1967-2 CB 1. The commuted value of annuity payments is determined by use of the Estate and Gift Tax Valuation Tables (see Q 910).

Thus, a widow's benefit under a typical deferred compensation agreement is includable in the gross estate by reason of IRC Section 2039(a). Even if it were not includable under IRC Section 2039(a), however, it would probably be includable under one of the other estate tax sections. See *Goodman v. Granger*, 243 F.2d 264; *Est. of Leoni v. Comm.*, TC Memo 1948; *Est. of Davis v. Comm.*, TC Memo 1952; Rev. Rul. 260, 1953-2 CB 262. *ASRS, Sec. 64, ¶420.6(b)*.

Death-Benefit-Only Plans

If the employee has no right to any post-employment retirement or disability benefits, other than benefits under a qualified pension or profit sharing plan (that is, only a pure survivor benefit is provided), the benefit is not subject to estate tax under IRC Section 2039(a). *Est. of Fusz v. Comm.*, 46 TC 214 (1966), acq. 1967-2 CB 2; Rev. Rul. 76-380, 1976-2 CB 270. In determining whether the deceased employee had any post employment benefits, all rights and benefits accruing to the employee and others by reason of his employment (except those under a qualified pension or profit-sharing plan) will be treated as one contract or plan under IRC Section 2039(a). Treas. Reg. §20.2039-1(b). The section cannot be avoided, for instance, by providing life-time benefits under one agreement, and the death benefit under another. Treas. Reg. §20.2039-1(b)(2)(Ex. 6); *Est. of Beal v. Comm.*, supra; *Gray v. U.S.*, 410 F.2d 1094 (3rd Cir. 1969). However, it has been held that the mere fact that at his death the employee was covered under a plan which, had he lived and been found totally and permanently disabled sometime in the future, would have paid him benefits, was not sufficient to bring the value of the survivor benefit under a death-benefit-only plan into the employee's estate under IRC Section 2039(a). *Est. of Schelberg v. Comm.*, 79-2 USTC ¶13,321 (2nd Cir. 1979), rev'g 70 TC 690 (1978); *Est. of Van Wye v. U.S.*, 82-2 USTC ¶13,485 (6th Cir. 1982). The IRS has announced that it will follow the *Schelberg* decision in all circuits. *Looney v. U.S.*, Docket No. 83-8709 (11th Cir., motion filed 1-26-84). If the agreement provides for payments to the employee after he becomes too incapacitated to perform services, or requires only nominal services after a certain age, payments will be treated as postretirement benefits of the employee. *Silberman v. U.S.*, 333 F. Supp. 1120 (W.D. Pa. 1971); *Gaffney v. U.S.*, 75-2 USTC 88,872 (Ct. Cl. 1972); *Hetson v. U.S.*, 75-2 USTC 88,873 (Ct. Cl. 1975). On the other hand, if substantial services are necessary to receive the payments, the payments have been held salary rather than retirement or disability benefits. *Kramer v. U.S.*, 406 F.2d 1363 (Ct. Cl. 1969). Similarly, a plan paying a wage-related benefit and designed to provide for disability resulting in only a temporary absence from work is considered to pay benefits in the nature of salary, not a post-employment benefit. Rev. Rul. 77-183, 1977-1 CB 274; *Est. of Siegel v. Comm.*, 74 TC 613 (1980); see also *Est. of Schelberg* and *Est. of Van Wye*, above.

A pure survivor benefit is not includable in decedent's gross estate under IRC Section 2033, because no interest is held by decedent at death. *Kramer v. U.S.*, 406 F.2d 1363 (Ct. Cl. 1969); *Est. of Porter v. Comm.*, 442 F.2d 915 (1st Cir. 1971); *Hinze v. U.S.*, 29 AFTR 2d 72-1553 (C.D. Cal. 1972); *Harris v. U.S.*, 29 AFTR 2d 72-1558 (C.D. Cal. 1972); see also *Worthen v. U.S.*, 192 F. Supp. 727 (D. Mass. 1961). Nonetheless, under certain circumstances the value of the pure survivor benefit may be included in the decedent's gross estate under other estate tax provisions. Courts have ruled that by giving consideration (e.g., agreeing to continue in employ) for the survivorship benefit, decedent makes a transfer of the benefit to the survivor. *Est. of Fried v. Comm.*, 445 F.2d 979 (2nd Cir. 1971); *Est. of Porter v. Comm.*, supra; *Est. of Bogley v. U.S.*, 75-1 USTC 87,454 (Ct. Cl. 1975); see also *Worthen v. U.S.*, supra and *Molter v. U.S.*, 146 F. Supp. 497 (E.D. N.Y. 1956); however, for a contrary view, see *Hinze v. U.S.*, supra, and *Harris v. U.S.*, supra. If the decedent holds a reversionary interest of more than 5% of the value of the benefit, its value is includable under IRC Section 2037. *Est. of Fried v. Comm.*, supra; *Est. of Bogley v. U.S.*, supra; Rev. Rul. 78-15, 1978-1 CB 289; Let. Rul. 7802002. If the decedent retains the power to alter, amend, revoke, or terminate the agreement or to change the beneficiary, either alone or with the consent of the employer or someone else, the value could be included under IRC Sections 2036 and 2038. Rev. Rul. 76-304, 1976-2 CB 269; *Est. of Siegel v. Comm.*, 74 TC 613 (1980); Let. Rul. 8943082. Generally, the mere possibility that an employee could negotiate a new agreement with his employer, or exert his influence as an officer, shareholder or director to secure desired changes, or terminate the plan by terminating employment, has not been held a retention of such powers. *Kramer v. U.S.*, supra; *Est. of Whitworth v. Comm.*, TC Memo 1963-41; *Hinze v. U.S.*, supra; *Harris v. U.S.*, supra; Let. Rul. 7827010. In TAM 8701003, which concerned a DBO plan between a corporation and its controlling stockholder, the Service agreed with the reasoning in the *Kramer*, *Hinze*, and *Harris* cases cited above, and concluded that the stockholder-employee's voting power did not give him rights that would make the value of the death benefit includable in his estate under IRC Sections 2036 or 2038. However, in *Est. of Levin v. Comm.*, 90 TC 723 (1988), an annuity payable under a DBO plan was included in the estate of the deceased controlling shareholder and Chairman of the Board under IRC Section 2038 because the decedent was considered to have held until his death the right to amend or revoke an annuity payable by the corporation to his wife if he should die while still in the employ of the controlled corporation and if certain eligibility requirements (tailor made for the decedent) were met. *ASRS, Sec. 64, ¶540.2.*

For the gift tax implications of DBO plans, see Q 711.

Voluntary Payments

If the payment is not made under a contract or plan, but is purely voluntary on the part of the employer, it is not subject to tax in the employee's estate. *Est. of Barr v. Comm.*, 40 TC 227 (1963), acq. in result only, 1978-1 CB 1; *Est. of Albright v. Comm.*, 42 TC 643 (1964); *Est. of Morrow v. Comm.*, 19 TC 1068 (1953), acq. 1954-1 CB 5, nonacq. 1979-2 CB 2; *Garber v. Comm.*, TC Memo 1958; *Worthen v. U.S.*, supra; *Est. of Bogley v. U.S.*, supra. *ASRS, Sec. 64, ¶540.2.*

TAX SHELTERED ANNUITIES

686. Is a death or survivor benefit under a tax sheltered annuity includable in the employee's gross estate?

TAX SHELTERED ANNUITIES   Q 686

Estates of Decedents Dying After 1984

The value of an annuity or other payment receivable under a TSA by the beneficiary of a deceased TSA annuitant is includable in the annuitant's estate under the rules discussed in Q 600 to Q 607. In reading those rules, remember that any contribution to the purchase of the annuity made by the decedent's employer or former employer is considered to be contributed by the decedent if made by reason of his employment. IRC Sec. 2039(b). Note that in the case of payments received *as insurance* on the life of the decedent (see Q 465), estate taxation is determined under the rules of IRC Section 2042 (see Q 625 to Q 635), not under IRC Section 2039.

The Tax Reform Act of 1984 repealed the estate tax exclusion discussed below generally for estates of decedents dying after 1984. However, the repeal does not apply to the estate of any decedent who (a) was a plan participant in pay status on December 31, 1984, and (b) irrevocably elected the form of the benefit before July 18, 1984. TRA '84, Sec. 525. The Tax Reform Act of 1986 provided that (a) and (b) are considered met if the decedent separated from service before January 1, 1985 and does not change the form of benefit before death. TRA '86, Sec. 1852(e)(3).

Estates of Decedents Dying After 1953 and Before 1985

Unless the employer is an organization described in IRC Section 170(b)(1)(A)(ii) or (vi) or a religious organization (other than a trust) and is exempt under IRC Section 501(a), there is no estate tax exclusion for the death or survivor benefit. IRC Sec. 2039(c)(3). Generally, these organizations (frequently referred to as REC organizations—religious, educational, charitable) include educational institutions (other than public schools), churches, and charities that receive substantial support from a government or the general public. IRS has taken the position that the exclusion does not apply to a contract purchased by an employer that is an integral part of a state or local government, such as a public school, college, university, or hospital. Rev. Rul. 60-384, 1960-2 CB 172; Rev. Rul. 68-294, 1968-1 CB 46 (obsoleted by Rev. Rul. 95-71, 1995-2 CB 323). The Tax Court, however, has held that the exclusion applied to contracts bought by a state university and a city board of education. *Est. of Johnson v. Comm.*, 56 TC 944 (1971), acq. 1973-2 CB 2 (followed in Let. Rul. 7817098); *Est. of Green v. Comm.*, 82 TC 843 (1984).

If the employer is one of the eligible types, an estate tax exclusion is available provided the benefit is payable to some beneficiary other than the employee's estate. However, the exclusion applies only to amounts attributable to *employer* contributions (that is, to premiums that were excludable from the employee's gross income under the exclusion allowance rule—see Q 469) and to "deductible employee contributions." Any portion of the premiums that were not excludable from the employee's gross income or were not "deductible employee contributions" are treated as *employee* contributions, and a corresponding portion of the value of the death or survivor benefit is includable in his gross estate. IRC Sec. 2039(c)(3). For this purpose, any one-year term costs of pure life protection that were includable in the employee's gross income are treated as *employee* contributions. Memorandum, 1967, Pension Plan Guide (CCH), Pre-1986 IRS Tax Releases, ¶17,337. The estate tax exclusion appears applicable whether payments are made in a single sum or in several payments. But if the benefit is payable to the employee's estate, the entire value is includable in his gross estate even though all premiums have come within the exclusion allowance. IRC Sec. 2039(c)(3).

2006 Tax Facts on Insurance & Employee Benefits   713

With respect to the estate of a decedent dying after 1982 and before 1985, the aggregate estate tax exclusion applicable to survivor benefits payable under a qualified plan (see Q 381 to Q 411), a tax sheltered annuity, or an individual retirement plan (see Q 210) *cannot exceed $100,000.* IRC Sec. 2039(c), (g), as amended and added by TEFRA, and before repeal by TRA '84. TRA '84 also amended TEFRA to provide that the $100,000 limit shall not apply to the estate of any decedent who (a) was a plan participant on pay status on December 31, 1982, and (b) irrevocably elected before January 1, 1983, the form of benefit. TRA '84, Sec. 525. The Tax Reform Act of 1986 provided that (a) and (b) are considered met if the decedent separated from service before January 1, 1983 and does not change the form of benefit before death. TRA '86, Sec. 1852(e)(3). For estates of decedents dying before 1983, the exclusion (as described) is unlimited.

The estate tax exclusion applies to the value of the death benefit receivable under a "retirement annuity contract." Payments to a retirement fund by an REC organization will be regarded as the purchase of a "retirement annuity contract" for the organization's employee if the payments are made pursuant to a contractual arrangement between the organization and the custodian of the fund whereby the custodian of the fund is obligated to provide an annuity to the employee. Thus, if a state university makes payments under such an arrangement to a state retirement system on behalf of a professor employed by the university, the value of survivor benefits payable from the system following the professor's death is eligible for the estate tax exclusion in the professor's estate. Rev. Rul. 79-301, 1979-2 CB 327.

Although it is clear that a tax sheltered annuity may provide incidental life insurance protection (see Q 465), it is not entirely clear what the estate tax results will be where the death benefit consists of life insurance proceeds payable by reason of insured's death prior to maturity of the contract. However, a technical advice memorandum indicates that the term costs of life insurance protection (unlike the results under a qualified pension plan) will be treated as (nondeductible) *employee* contributions for estate tax purposes. Memorandum, 1967, Pension Plan Guide (CCH), Pre-1986 IRS Tax Releases, ¶17,337.

The estate tax exclusion under IRC Section 2039(c) is applicable only to the estate of a decedent who was the employee and not to the estate of a non-employee beneficiary. *Est. of Kleemeier v. Comm.*, 58 TC 241 (1972). (See Q 648 for the estate tax exclusion applicable to amounts rolled over from a tax sheltered annuity to an IRA.) *ASRS, Sec. 61, ¶300.1.*

VALUATION

687. How are life insurance proceeds valued for insured's estate tax return?

The full face amount plus paid-up additions, accumulated dividends (with interest thereon), and post-mortem dividends, less policy loans, should be included in Schedule D of the estate tax return. See Estate Tax Form 706, Schedule D, and Form 712. Treas. Reg. §20.2042-1(a)(3). The date of death value is used, regardless of whether the executor elects the optional valuation date. Rev. Rul. 58-576, 1958-2 CB 625.

688. If the amount of life insurance proceeds collectible from the insurer is not determinable when the estate tax return is filed, what amount is reportable on the return?

The unsatisfactory answer appears to be that from the facts and circumstances of the particular case, a determination of the fair market value of the insurance claim or claims at date of death or alternate valuation date must be made, and that is the amount to be reported. *American Nat'l Bank & Trust Co. v. U.S.*, 594 F.2d 1141 (7th Cir. 1979); Let. Rul. 8308001. This problem is most likely to be encountered when an insured's death occurs during the policy's contestable period and there is a question whether either the insured made material misrepresentations in applying for the insurance or the insured's death resulted from suicide.

PART III

FEDERAL GIFT TAX

on

INSURANCE AND EMPLOYEE BENEFITS

700. What constitutes a gift of a life insurance policy or annuity contract? What constitutes a gift of a premium?

If a person purchases a life insurance policy or annuity contract the proceeds of which are payable to a beneficiary other than himself or his estate, and he retains no reversionary interest in himself or his estate, and no power to revest the economic benefits in himself or his estate, or to change the beneficiary, he has made a gift of the contract. Likewise, if he absolutely assigns a contract, or relinquishes by assignment every power he retained in a previously issued contract, he has made a gift. If he pays a premium on a contract in which he has no ownership rights, he has made a gift of the premium. Of course, if he receives an adequate consideration for the transfer, it is not a gift. Treas. Reg. §25.2511-1(h)(8); *Fletcher Trust Co. v. Comm.*, 1 TC 798 (1943), aff'd 141 F.2d 36 (7th Cir. 1944).

A divorced wife owned policies of insurance on the life of her former husband. Pursuant to the terms of a property settlement agreement calling for the insured to pay future premiums and any gift tax, the former wife assigned the policies to their children. It was held that the assignment constituted an indirect gift of the policies from the insured to his children. *du Pont v. Comm.*, TC Memo 1978-16.

See Q 741 regarding gifts with respect to split dollar arrangements.

The IRS has ruled that where an employee has irrevocably assigned his rights under a group term life policy, and the policy is later replaced by a policy identical in all material respects to the prior policy, and where the new policy provides that an employee's irrevocable assignment of his rights under the old policy is effective to vest in the assignee the insured's rights under the new policy, the replacement of the old policy with the new does not constitute a new gift of policy rights for federal gift tax purposes. Let. Rul. 8230038. *ASRS, Sec. 55, ¶45.*

ANNUITIES

701. Does the purchase of a joint and survivor annuity result in a taxable gift?

Yes, if the purchaser of the contract does not reserve the right to change the beneficiary of the survivor payments. Rev. Rul. 55-388, 1955-1 CB 233; Treas. Reg. §25.2511-1. On how to value the gift, see Q 704. *ASRS, Sec. 55, ¶56.2.*

702. Is the naming of an irrevocable beneficiary under a refund annuity a gift?

Yes, even though the refund beneficiary will get nothing unless the annuitant dies before receiving payments equal to his premium cost. Since the gift is contingent upon the annuitant's death within a specified period, it is the gift of a "future interest" and hence, does not qualify for the annual exclusion (see Q 712). *Morrow v. Comm.*, 2 TC 210 (1943). (Where gift is from one spouse to another, see Q 731.) The value of the gift is the present value of the contingent right to receive any remaining refund payments upon the death of the annuitant. *ASRS, Sec. 55, ¶56.*

703. Under what circumstances does the gift of an annuity between spouses qualify for the gift tax marital deduction?

A direct gift to the spouse of an annuity contract in which no one else has an interest would, like a similar gift of any other kind of property, qualify for the gift tax marital deduction (see Q 920). The interest of a donee spouse in a joint and survivor annuity in which only the donor and donee spouses have a right to receive payments during such spouses' joint lifetimes is treated as a "qualifying income interest for life" (see Q 920) for which the marital deduction is available unless the donor spouse irrevocably elects otherwise within the time allowed for filing a gift tax return. IRC Sec. 2523(f)(6). To the extent provided in the regulations, an annuity interest is to be treated in a manner similar to an income interest in property (regardless of whether the property from which the annuity is payable can be separately identified). IRC Sec. 2523(f)(3). If, however, an election is made to not have the donee spouse's interest treated as a "qualifying income interest for life," the marital deduction is not allowed if (1) the donor gives an interest in the contract to a third party, or keeps an interest for himself, and (2) there is a possibility that the donor or the third party could receive some benefits from this interest after the donee's interest ends. Thus, if the donee spouse's interest is not treated as a "qualifying income interest for life," the gift of a refund annuity will not qualify if the refund is payable to the donor or a third party in event of donee's death during the refund period. Treas. Reg. §25.2523(b)-1(b)(6)(iii); §25.2523(b)-1(c)(2). An annual exclusion (see Q 917) may be allowed instead of the marital deduction if the donee spouse is not a United States citizen (see Q 920). *ASRS, Sec. 51, ¶280.*

704. What is the gift tax value of an annuity contract or of a donee's interest in a joint and survivor annuity?

Where an annuity is purchased by a donor on his own life and immediately given to another, or is purchased by one person for another on the latter's life, the value of the gift is the premium paid for the contract. But if a person purchases an annuity, and at a later date gives this contract to another person, the gift tax value is the single premium the company would charge for an annuity providing payments of the same amount on the life of a person who is annuitant's age at the time of the gift. Treas. Reg. §25.2512-6. The value of a deferred premium-paying annuity is the terminal reserve, adjusted to date of gift, plus the unearned portion of the last premium payment (see Q 744). *Comm. v. Edwards*, 135 F.2d 574 (5th Cir. 1942).

Joint and Survivor Annuity

Where a donor purchases a joint and survivor annuity for the benefit of himself and another, the gift tax value is the cost of the annuity less the cost of a single life annuity for the donor. Treas. Reg. §25.2512-6.

Example. A donor purchases from a life insurance company for $15,198 a joint and survivor annuity contract which provides for the payment of $60 a month to the donor during his lifetime, and then to his sister for such time as she may survive him. The premium which would have been charged by the company for an annuity of $60 monthly payable during the life of the donor alone is $10,690. The value of the gift is $4,508 ($15,198 less $10,690). Treas. Reg. §25.2512-6(Ex. 5).

ASRS, Sec. 55, ¶56.

705. Can the purchase of a private annuity result in a taxable gift?

There is no gift if the purchase of the annuity is a bona fide ordinary business transaction. Rev. Rul. 69-74, 1969-1 CB 43, Treas. Regs. §§25.2511-1(g)(1), 25.2512-8. However, where closely related parties are involved, a gift is made to the promisor of the amount by which the fair market value of the property exchanged for the annuity exceeds the *present value of the annuity*. Rev. Rul. 69-74, above; *Est. of Bell v. Comm.*, 60 TC 469 (1973); *Fehrs v. U.S.*, 79-2 USTC ¶13,324 (Ct. Cl. 1979); *La Fargue v. Comm.*, 800 F.2d 936 (9th Cir. 1986). Likewise, a gift is made to the purchaser of the amount by which the present value of the annuity exceeds the fair market value of the property transferred. But even in an intra-family transaction, if substantially equal values are exchanged and there is no donative intent found, there will be no gift. *Ellis Sarasota Bank & Trust Co. v. U.S.*, 77-2 USTC ¶13,204 (M.D. Fla. 1977). See also Rev. Rul. 76-491, 1976-2 CB 301. Present value of the annuity is generally determined by use of the current estate and gift tax valuation tables (see Q 910). Notice 89-60, 1989-1 CB 700; Treas. Regs. §§20.2031, 25.2512; *Est. of Cullison v. Comm.*, 2000-1 USTC ¶60,376 (9th Cir. 2000). See Q 41. After November 23, 1984, those same tables are used in valuing an annuity issued by an organization, other than an insurance company, such as a corporation, trust, fund, or foundation, which from time to time issues annuities in exchange for money or other property. Rev. Rul. 84-162, 1984-2 CB 200. However, the estate and gift tax valuation tables are not used where the decedent is terminally ill. *ASRS, Sec. 55, ¶56.3.*

BUSINESS LIFE INSURANCE

706. Does a life insurance funded buy-and-sell agreement fix the value of a business interest for gift tax purposes?

No. However, an agreement restricting lifetime sale may be considered with all other pertinent factors, and may tend to lower the value of the close corporation or other business interest (but see Q 915). *Est. of James v. Comm.*, 148 F.2d 236 (2nd Cir. 1945); *Kline v. Comm.*, 130 F.2d 742 (3rd Cir. 1942); *Krauss v. U.S.*, 140 F.2d 510 (5th Cir. 1944); *Comm. v. McCann*, 146 F.2d 385 (2nd Cir. 1944); *Spitzer v. Comm.*, 153 F.2d 967 (8th Cir. 1946); Rev. Rul. 189, 1953-2 CB 294.

On the other hand, failure to exercise rights under a buy-and-sell agreement could result in a taxable gift. See Q 903.

CHARITABLE GIFTS

707. Are gifts of life insurance to charitable organizations subject to gift tax?

Generally, no. An individual may take a gift tax deduction for the full value of gifts to qualified charities of life insurance and annuity contracts, and of premiums or consideration paid for such contracts owned by qualified charities. IRC Sec. 2522. (See Q 921.) However, such a deduction is not allowed where an insured assigns (even irrevocably) to a charity the cash surrender value of a life insurance policy (either paid-up or premium paying), including a right to death proceeds equal to the cash surrender value immediately before death, if the donor retains the right to name or change the beneficiary of proceeds in excess of the cash surrender value and to assign the balance of the policy subject to the charity's right to the cash surrender value. According to the Internal Revenue Service, such a gift is neither one of the donor's entire interest in the property nor one of an undivided portion of the donor's entire interest in the property, and so the deduction is disallowed under IRC Section 2522(c). Rev. Rul. 76-200, 76-1 CB 308. (See Q 283.)

If the law in the state of the donor's domicile does not recognize that a charity has an insurable interest (see ASRS, section 12, ¶20.24) in the life of the donor, a charitable deduction may not be allowed for a gift of a newly issued insurance policy (or premiums paid thereon) or for gifts of premium payments on a policy applied for and issued to the charity as owner and beneficiary. See Let. Rul. 9110016 (revoked by Let. Rul. 9147040 when state law was amended to permit an insured to immediately transfer a newly purchased life insurance policy to charity). *ASRS, Sec. 55, ¶46.*

COLLECTION OF GIFT TAX

708. Can the gift tax be collected from the donee of a life insurance policy or proceeds?

Yes. If the gift tax is not collected from the donor, the donee is liable for the tax. The government can collect the gift tax from the donee-beneficiary, and the latter's liability is not limited to the policy's cash value. IRC Secs. 6324(b), 6901; *Comm. v. Chase Manhattan Bank*, 259 F.2d 231 (5th Cir. 1958). *ASRS, Sec. 55, ¶57.4.*

COMMUNITY PROPERTY

709. Does a taxable gift occur when a donor spouse assigns community property life insurance to a donee spouse?

Generally, no. The assignment generally qualifies for the unlimited gift tax marital deduction applicable to interspousal gifts, even though the policy is community property. IRC Sec. 2523. (The assignment is actually of the donor spouse's one-half community property interest, since the donee spouse already owns the other one-half.) An annual exclusion (see Q 917) may be allowed instead of the marital deduction if the donee spouse is not a United States citizen (see Q 920). *ASRS, Sec. 55, ¶54.*

710. If one spouse uses community property to purchase life insurance on either spouse's life, and names a child as beneficiary, does the death of the insured spouse give rise to a taxable gift from the noninsured spouse?

Perhaps. If under state law the insured spouse's death makes the transfer of the noninsured spouse's community interest absolute, a gift will be imputed to the noninsured spouse, equal in value to one-half the proceeds payable to the child. Treas. Reg. §25.2511-

GIFT TAX ANNUAL EXCLUSION   Q 712

1(h)(9). This result has been held to follow under Texas and Louisiana law. Rev. Rul. 48, 1953-1 CB 392 (La.); Rev. Rul. 232, 1953-2 CB 268 (Texas); *Comm. v. Chase Manhattan Bank*, 259 F.2d 231 (5th Cir. 1958). In Louisiana, life insurance owned by one spouse may be either separate or community property even if community property is used to purchase the policy. As a result, a noninsured spouse could be treated as making a gift of all or one-half of the proceeds when the insured spouse dies and proceeds are paid to the child. See Rev. Rul. 94-69, 1994-2 CB 241, revoking Rev. Rul. 48, above; Rev. Rul. 232, above; Rev. Rul. 2003-40, 2003-17 IRB 813. However, where the noninsured spouse receives as beneficiary her community share or more, no gift is imputed to her of amounts also payable to a third party beneficiary unless there is evidence of donative intent. *Kaufman v. U.S.*, 462 F.2d 439 (5th Cir. 1972). *ASRS, Sec. 55, ¶54*.

DEATH-BENEFIT-ONLY PLANS

711. Are death-benefit-only (DBO) plans subject to gift tax?

No, at least not at the time of death. Rev. Rul. 92-68, 1992-2 CB 257, revoking Revenue Ruling 81-31, 1981-1 CB 475 (in which the Service treated an employee as making a gift of the benefit from a DBO plan in the year of the employee's death); *Est. of DiMarco v. Comm.*, 87 TC 653 (1986), acq. in result, 1990-2 CB 1. Note that neither Revenue Ruling 81-31 nor *Est. of DiMarco v. Comm.* addressed whether an employee should be treated each year as (1) receiving compensation equal to the value of providing a death benefit or survivor income benefit to an eligible survivor if the employee died during the year, and (2) transferring such value to the eligible survivor. Of course, the use of the annual exclusion (Q 917) and the marital deduction (Q 920) might protect such a gift from any gift tax. (See Q 685 for estate tax aspects.) *ASRS, Sec. 64, ¶540.3*.

GIFT TAX ANNUAL EXCLUSION

712. May the annual exclusion of $10,000 as indexed for gifts to each donee be applied against gifts of life insurance policies and premiums?

Yes, if the gifts are made in such manner that they are gifts of present interests. The annual exclusion of $12,000 (in 2006, see Appendix B) is not available for gifts of future interests (see Q 713). If the gift of the policy is a gift of present interest, premiums subsequently paid by the donor will also qualify for the exclusion (see Q 717). The annual exclusion is effectively $24,000 in 2006 (2 × $12,000, see Appendix B) if the donor makes a gift to a third party with the consent of his spouse—see Q 742. For gifts from one spouse to another, see Q 730. IRC Sec. 2503(b), Treas. Regs. §§25.2503-3(a), 25.2503-3(c)(Ex. 6).

> *Example.* Donor, a widower, assigns a policy on his life to his son in 2006. The policy's value is $10,000. The gift tax annual exclusion of $12,000 (in 2006, see Appendix B) can be applied against the gift of the policy. The donor may continue to pay the annual premium of $1,500 in subsequent years and need not report the premium payments for gift tax purposes so long as they fall within the gift tax annual exclusion for such subsequent year (unless he gives his son other gifts in any one year which together with the premium payments exceed the annual exclusion for such year).

Where the value of a policy exceeds the annual exclusion, the insurance company may consent to split it into two or more smaller policies; by giving the donee one policy in each of several succeeding years, the entire value can fall within the annual

2006 Tax Facts on Insurance & Employee Benefits   721

exclusions. In some instances, however, such a split would result in a higher premium. *ASRS, Sec. 55, ¶48.*

713. When is the gift of a life insurance policy considered the gift of a future interest, so as to deprive the donor of the gift tax annual exclusion?

A future interest is created when restrictions are placed upon the donee's right to receive benefits or to exercise ownership rights under the policy. The gift of a policy is not considered a gift of a future interest merely because the obligations under the contract are payable at some time in the future. However, a future interest in such contractual obligations can be created by limitations contained in a trust or other instrument of transfer used in effecting a gift (see Q 724). Treas. Reg. §25.2503-3. (But see Q 725 for gifts in trust to minors.) A gift of a policy to a corporation is a gift of a future interest to its shareholders. Rev. Rul. 71-443, 1971-2 CB 337. Gifts made to individual partnership capital accounts were treated as gifts of a present interest which qualified for the gift tax annual exclusion where the partners were free to make immediate withdrawals of the gifts from their capital accounts. *Wooley v. U.S.*, 90-1 USTC ¶60,013 (S.D. Ind. 1990). *ASRS, Sec. 55, ¶48.1.*

714. Is the annual exclusion available where an insured transfers ownership of a life insurance policy to two or more donees jointly?

No; if joint action is required to exercise ownership rights in the policy, it is a gift of a future interest. *Skouras v. Comm.*, 188 F.2d 831 (2nd Cir. 1951). *ASRS, Sec. 55, ¶48.3.*

715. Will the gift of a life insurance policy fail to qualify for the annual exclusion merely because the policy has no cash value?

No. Rev. Rul. 55-408, 1955-1 CB 113. *ASRS, Sec. 55, ¶48.2.*

716. Does the outright gift of a life insurance policy qualify for the gift tax annual exclusion even if the gift is to a minor?

Yes. The exclusion can be applied against the value of the policy at the time of gift and to subsequent premium payments. IRC Sec. 2503(b); Treas. Regs. §§25.2503-3(c)(Ex. 6), 25.2511-1(a), 25.2511-1(g). An outright gift of a policy to a minor qualifies for the exclusion even though a guardian is not appointed. *Baer v. Comm.*, ¶43,294 P-H TC Memo (1943), aff'd 149 F.2d 637 (8th Cir. 1945); Rev. Rul. 54-400, 1954-2 CB 319; see *Daniels v. Comm.*, ¶51,044 P-H TC Memo (1951). A gift of life insurance under a Uniform Gifts to Minors Act or a Uniform Transfers to Minors Act generally qualifies for the gift tax annual exclusion (but see Q 919). All but a few states have modified the Uniform Act to include gifts of life insurance. Any transfer of property to a minor under statutes patterned after either the Model Act or the Uniform Act constitutes a complete gift for federal gift tax purposes to the extent of the full fair market value of the property transferred. Such a gift generally qualifies for the gift tax annual exclusion authorized by IRC Section 2503(b) (but see Q 919). Rev. Rul. 56-86, 1956-1 CB 449; Rev. Rul. 59-357, 1959-2 CB 212; Rev. Rul. 73-287, 1973-2 CB 321. If the subject of the gift is life insurance, its "full fair market value" would presumably be established by the same rules applicable to gifts of life insurance generally (see Q 744). *ASRS, Sec. 55, ¶48.5.*

717. Where a life insurance policy has been given away, are premiums subsequently paid by the donor gifts of present interest qualifying for the annual exclusion or future interest?

The payment of premiums will be gifts of present interest if the gift of the policy was a present interest gift. Likewise, the premiums will be future interest gifts if the gift of the policy was a future interest gift. *Baer v. Comm.*, ¶43,294 P-H TC Memo (1943), aff'd 149 F.2d 637 (8th Cir. 1945); *Roberts v. Comm.*, 2 TC 679 (1943); *Comm. v. Boeing*, 123 F.2d 86 (9th Cir. 1941); *Bolton v. Comm.*, 1 TC 717 (1943). (See Q 733.) *ASRS, Sec. 55, ¶48.4.*

GIFTS WITHIN THREE YEARS OF DEATH

718. If an insured, within three years of his death, makes a gift of life insurance on which he pays a gift tax, is the gift also subject to estate tax?

Both the insurance proceeds and the gift tax paid will be included in the gross estate (see Q 860). IRC Sec. 2035. *ASRS, Sec. 54, ¶44.2.*

LIFE INSURANCE TRUSTS

719. Is there a gift for gift tax purposes when a grantor transfers a life insurance policy to an irrevocable trust in which he has no interest?

Yes. Treas. Reg. §25.2511-1(h)(8). The value of the gift will be the fair market value of the policy as of the date of the transfer (see Q 744). There is no gift if the trust is revocable. Treas. Reg. §25.2511-2(c). An employee's assignment of a group life policy to an irrevocable trust was held to be not a taxable gift because the policy had no ascertainable value (see Q 733, Q 724, Q 744). Rev. Rul. 76-490, 1976-2 CB 300. *ASRS, Sec. 55, ¶55.2.*

720. If income-producing property is transferred to an irrevocable life insurance trust to fund premium payments, does the value of the property constitute a gift?

Generally, the full value of the property, in addition to the value of the policy, constitutes a gift. (But see Q 721, relating to reversionary interest trusts.) However, subsequent premium payments by the trustee from trust income will not constitute additional gifts from the grantor. This is true, even though the insurance is on the life of the grantor, and the grantor therefore remains personally liable for the income tax on the trust income which may be used to pay premiums. *Comm. v. Est. of Beck*, 129 F.2d 243 (2d Cir. 1942); *Lockard v. Comm.*, 166 F.2d 409 (1st Cir. 1948). *ASRS, Sec. 55, ¶55.2.*

721. How is the gift tax value of a "reversionary interest trust" measured?

In a reversionary interest trust (see Q 844), the gift is the right to receive *trust income* during the trust term. The value of this right is determined and taxed in the year the trust is established. Generally, the value of the gift is the value of the property transferred less the value of the grantor's retained interest. Treas. Reg. §25.2512-9(a)(1)(i). The value of these income and reversionary (or remainder) interests is determined using the estate and gift tax valuation tables (see Q 910). For example, assuming a valuation table interest rate of 10% and a trust term of 32 years, the value of the gift of income is .952638 times the value of the property (1 - .047362) (see Appendix D). However, if the reversionary interest is not a qualified interest, the value of the gift is generally the full value of the property transferred to trust (see Q 914). To avoid this result, an annuity or unitrust interest should generally be given rather than an income interest. *ASRS, Sec. 55, ¶57.3(a).*

722. Does the transfer of a life insurance policy to an irrevocable trust for the benefit of the grantor's spouse qualify for the gift tax marital deduction?

Generally, the gift tax marital deduction is not available for a gift in trust unless the donee spouse has at least the right to all the income from the property and a general power of appointment over the principal, or unless her income interest is a "qualifying income interest for life" in the property transferred, in which case she does not usually have to have a general power of appointment over the principal (see Q 920). Since a life insurance policy ordinarily does not produce income before maturity, the requirement that the donee spouse receive all the income for life will not be met unless the donee spouse has the power to compel the trustee to convert the policy to income-producing property, or the power to terminate the trust and demand the policy. Treas. Regs. §§25.2523(e)-1(f)(4), 25.2523(e)-1(f)(6). An annual exclusion (see Q 917) may be allowed instead of the marital deduction if the donee spouse is not a United States citizen (see Q 920). *ASRS, Sec. 51, ¶282.4(1).*

723. If a grantor creates a revocable trust with a life insurance policy on the life of another person, and names third parties as trust beneficiaries, does a gift take place when insured dies and the trust becomes irrevocable?

Yes. In one case, a wife placed a policy on her husband's life in a revocable trust for their children. It was held that a gift from the wife to the children took place when insured died and the trust became irrevocable. The value of the gift was the full amount of the death proceeds. *Goodman v. Comm.*, 156 F.2d 218 (2d Cir. 1946). If the trust had been irrevocable, the annual premiums paid by the wife, instead of the proceeds, would have constituted gifts. *Watkins v. Comm.*, ¶43,282 P-H TC Memo (1943).

724. Does the gift of a life insurance policy in trust (and/or a gift of subsequent premiums) qualify for the gift tax annual exclusion?

In the usual case, no annual exclusions are allowable either upon the creation of the trust or upon the payment of premiums (Q 713, Q 717). Treas. Reg. §25.2503-2; *Comm. v. Boeing*, 123 F.2d 86 (9th Cir. 1941).

> *Example.* C transfers certain insurance policies on his own life to a trust created for the benefit of D. Upon C's death the proceeds of the policies are to be invested, and the net income therefrom paid to D during his lifetime. Since the income payments to D will not begin until after C's death, the transfer in trust represents a gift of a future interest in property against which no exclusion is available. Treas. Reg. §25.2503-3(c)(Ex. 2).

LIFE INSURANCE TRUSTS

Q 726

If the beneficiary were given the power to demand trust principal, apparently the annual exclusion would be available. *Halsted v. Comm.*, 28 TC 1069 (1957), acq. 1958-2 CB 5. However, such a power would cause the trust principal to be includable in the beneficiary's gross estate.

Where an employee assigned his group life insurance policy to an irrevocable trust, IRS ruled that subsequent premiums paid by the employer qualified for the annual exclusion as gifts of a present interest by the *employee*. Under the terms of the trust, the beneficiary or the beneficiary's estate was to receive the full proceeds of the policy immediately on the insured's death. Rev. Rul. 76-490, 1976-2 CB 300. In a later ruling, the facts were essentially the same as in Rev. Rul. 76-490, except that the trust terms directed the trustee to retain the insurance proceeds, paying income to the insured's children for life, remainder to grandchildren; the employer's premium payments following the assignment were held gifts of a future interest in property, not therefore qualifying for the annual exclusion. Rev. Rul. 79-47, 1979-1 CB 312. (See also Q 620, Q 625.)

IRS has also allowed the gift tax annual exclusion where a grantor created a trust with an initial contribution of a $50,000 group term policy on his life and $1,000 in cash. The trust gave the grantor's wife a $3,000 annual noncumulative withdrawal right and provided that any asset in the trust, including the insurance policy, could be used to satisfy the demand. The ruling held that the grantor's initial contribution, as well as his employer's subsequent premium payments on the group term insurance would qualify for the exclusion. Let. Rul. 8006109.

But for special provision with respect to gifts in trust to minors, see Q 725. *ASRS*, Sec. 55, ¶55.2.

725. Is the annual exclusion available when a life insurance policy is placed in an irrevocable trust for a minor beneficiary?

IRC Section 2503(c) provides that there is a gift of a present interest if the property which constitutes the gift and all income from the property (1) *may* be expended for the benefit of the minor, and (2) will, to the extent not so expended pass to the minor when he is 21, or, if he dies before reaching 21, be payable to his estate or as he may appoint under a general power of appointment. IRC Sec. 2503(c). The fact that under local law a minor is legally unable to exercise a power or to execute a will does not cause the transfer to fail to satisfy the conditions. Treas. Reg. §25.2503-4. Thus, the gift of a policy in trust for a minor should qualify as one of present interest if policy values may be used for his benefit, and the policy will be given to him when he is 21, or, if he dies before that age, the policy or proceeds will go to his estate or to any beneficiary he may appoint during life or by will. Any premiums paid on the policy by the grantor should also qualify as gifts of present interest (see Q 717). (See also Q 918.) *ASRS*, Sec. 55, ¶55.3.

726. Can transfers, to the trustee of an irrevocable life insurance trust, of amounts to be used by the trustee to pay premiums, qualify for the gift tax annual exclusion?

Although such transfers would ordinarily be future interest gifts (see Q 918), it has been held that they will be present interest gifts, qualifying for the exclusion, to the extent the trust beneficiaries are given immediate withdrawal rights with respect

2006 Tax Facts on Insurance & Employee Benefits

to the amounts transferred. *Crummey v. Comm.*, 397 F.2d 82 (9th Cir. 1968); Rev. Rul. 73-405, 1973-2 CB 321; Let. Ruls. 7826050, 7902007, 7909031, 7947066, 8007080, 8118051, 8445004, 8712014, 9625031.

> *Example.* G creates an irrevocable insurance trust for each of his four children, transferring to the trusts amounts (additions) from year to year to fund the trusts. Two of the children are minors when the trusts are created and for several years thereafter but neither has a court appointed guardian during his minority. The trusts provide that with respect to the additions, each child may demand in writing at any time (up to the end of the calendar year in which an addition is made) the sum of $5,000 or the amount of the addition, whichever is less, payable immediately in cash. If a child is a minor when an addition is made, his guardian may make such demand on his behalf and hold the amount received for the benefit and use of the child. To the extent demands for payment are not made by the beneficiaries, the trustee is directed to use the additions to pay insurance premiums as needed and to purchase additional insurance and investments for the trust. G transfers to each trust $5,000 each year the trusts are in existence. Each trust provides that it is irrevocable for the lifetime of the beneficiary and that the trust assets will revert to the grantor only if the beneficiary dies before age 21. All children survive past age 21. By the rule of the Crummey case, G is entitled under present law to $20,000 in gift tax annual exclusions each year ($5,000 for each child). It does not matter that the minor children never had guardians appointed. Had the trusts given the beneficiaries immediate payment rights of no more than $2,000 each with respect to the additions, G's exclusions would be limited to $8,000 per year (assuming he made no other present interest gifts to his children during the year).

The IRS has ruled that where the beneficiary of a discretionary trust was a competent adult, contributions to the trust did not qualify for the annual exclusion because the beneficiary did not receive timely notice or have actual knowledge of his right to demand immediate distribution of contributions. Rev. Rul. 81-7, 1981-1 CB 474; Let. Rul. 7946007. Another ruling allowed the annual exclusion where the trust provided for timely written notice to the beneficiaries of their withdrawal rights, and where the beneficiaries were given a 30-day period within which to exercise their withdrawal rights. Let. Rul. 8003033. See also Let. Ruls. 8517052, 8813019. Yet another ruling allowed the exclusion where the trust required the trustee to notify the beneficiaries within seven days of receipt of additional contributions and further required that the beneficiaries be given 30 days after receipt of notice within which to exercise their withdrawal rights. Let. Rul. 8004172. If the beneficiary is given reasonable notice of his withdrawal right and a reasonable time within which to exercise the right, the fact that a calendar year ends between the date of the transfer and the date the beneficiary received notice does not transform a present interest gift into a future interest gift. Rev. Rul. 83-108, 1983-2 CB 167.

However, the annual exclusion was not allowed where the beneficiaries waived their right to receive notice of contributions to trust with respect to which their withdrawal rights could be exercised. Furthermore, the annual exclusion was not allowed because the grantor set up a trust which provided that notice was to be given to the trustee as to whether a beneficiary could exercise a withdrawal power with respect to a transfer to trust and the grantor never notified the trustee that the withdrawal powers could be exercised with respect to any of the transfers to trust. TAM 9532001.

The value of a withdrawal right may be reduced or nil if the trustee has discretion to invade the trust corpus for the benefit of non-Crummey beneficiaries. TAM 8107009, Let. Rul. 8213074. The exclusion is allowed only to the extent there is cash, or assets reducible to cash, in the trust to satisfy any beneficiary demand rights, or to the extent the trustee is required to maintain sufficient liquidity to meet immediate withdrawal demands. Let. Ruls. 8126047, 8134135. But see also Let. Ruls. 7909031,

8007080, 8006109, 8021058, which allowed the exclusion where liquidity requirements were not clearly stated.

Where appointment of a legal guardian would be necessary to enable a beneficiary to exercise his withdrawal right, sufficient time, at least 30 days, should be allowed to make the appointment before the right to withdraw terminates. Let. Ruls. 8022048, 8134135, 8326074, 8517052, 8610028, 8616027. If "there is no impediment under the trust or local law to the appointment of a guardian and the minor donee has a right to demand distribution, the transfer is a gift of a present interest that qualifies for the annual exclusion allowable under" IRC Section 2503(b). Rev. Rul. 73-405, 1973-2 CB 321. See also Let. Ruls. 8326074, 8335050, 8517052, 8610028, 8616027, 8701007. But see also *Naumoff v. Comm.*, TC Memo 1983-435, and Let. Rul. 8229097.

Reciprocal Crummey trusts have been unsuccessfully tried in an attempt to increase each donor's annual exclusion. In Rev. Rul. 85-24, 1985-1 CB 329, A, B, and C, partners in the X partnership, each created a Crummey trust for his child, each contributing $20,000 to the trust initially. A's trust gave his child, F, a power to withdraw $10,000 of the contribution within 60 days, and gave B and C each the power to withdraw $5,000 on the same terms. B's trust gave his child, G, the power to withdraw $10,000, and gave A and C each the power to withdraw $5,000. C's trust gave his child, H, the power to withdraw $10,000, and gave A and B each the power to withdraw $5,000. A, B, and C each claimed a $20,000 gift tax exclusion for the year in which the trusts were created. The Service ruled that each of A, B, and C was entitled to only a $10,000 exclusion for the gift to his child. No gift tax exclusions were allowable with respect to the Crummey powers the partners gave one another; these transfers were not gifts because they were based on adequate consideration. The consideration for the reciprocal transfers among the partners was each partner's foregoing of the exercise of the right of withdrawal in consideration of the other partner's similar forbearance. The Service said further that upon the lapse of a partner's withdrawal power the child's gift (from his parent) was increased by $5,000, but the failure of the partner to exercise the power was not considered a lapse of a general power of appointment (i.e., not a gift) because the transfer to the partner was not a gift.

Since August 24, 1981, the IRS has had under extensive study the following type of Crummey insurance trust and has stated that it will not issue rulings or determination letters on the allowability of the gift tax annual exclusion for transfers of property to such trusts until the Service resolves the issues through publication of a revenue ruling, revenue procedure, regulation, or otherwise: Where (1) the trust corpus consists or will consist substantially of insurance policies on the life of the grantor or the grantor's spouse, (2) the trustee or any other person has a power to apply the trust's income or corpus to the payment of premiums on policies of insurance on the life of the grantor or the grantor's spouse, (3) the trustee or any other person has a power to use the trust's assets to make loans to the grantor's estate or to purchase assets from the grantor's estate, (4) the trust beneficiaries have the power to withdraw, on demand, any additional transfers made to the trust, and (5) there is a right or power in any person that would cause the grantor to be treated as the owner of all or a portion of the trust under IRC Sections 673 to 677. Rev. Proc. 2005-3, Sec. 4.45, 2005-1 IRB 118.

The IRS has ruled with respect to Crummey trusts that the annual exclusion could not be applied to trust contributions on behalf of trust beneficiaries who had withdrawal rights as to the contributions (except to the extent they exercised their withdrawal rights) but who had either no other interest in the trust (a naked power) or only remote contingent interests in the remainder. TAMs 9141008, 9045002, 8727003. However, the Tax Court has rejected the IRS's argument that a power holder must hold rights other than the withdrawal right to obtain the annual exclusion. The withdrawal right (assuming there is no agreement to not exercise the right) is sufficient to obtain the annual exclusion. *Est. of Cristofani v. Comm.*, 97 TC 74 (1991), acq. in result, 1996-2 CB 1. (Language in *Cristofani* appears to support use of naked powers although case did not involve naked powers). In an Action On Decision, the Service stated that, applying the substance over form doctrine, the annual exclusions should not be allowed where the withdrawal rights are not in substance what they purport to be in form. If the facts and circumstances show an understanding that the power is not meant to be exercised or that exercise would result in undesirable consequences, then creation of the withdrawal right is not a bona fide gift of a present interest and an annual exclusion should not be allowed. AOD 1996-010. In TAM 9628004, annual exclusions were not allowed where transfers to trust were made so late in the first year that *Crummey* withdrawal powerholders had no opportunity to exercise their rights, most powerholders had either no other interest in the trust or discretionary income or remote contingent remainder interests, and withdrawal powers were never exercised in any year. However, annual exclusions were allowed where the IRS was unable to prove that there was an understanding between the donor and the beneficiaries that the withdrawal rights should not be exercised. *Est. of Kohlsaat*, TC Memo 1997-212; *Est. of Holland v. Comm.*, TC Memo 1997-302. In TAM 97310004, annual exclusions were denied where eight trusts were created for eight primary beneficiaries, but *Crummey* withdrawal powers were given to 16 or 17 persons who never exercised their powers and most powerholders held either a remote contingent interest or no interest other than the withdrawal power in the trusts in which the powerholder was not the primary beneficiary.

Substance over form analysis may be applied to deny annual exclusions where indirect transfers are used in an attempt to obtain inappropriate annual exclusions for gifts to intermediate recipients. *Heyen v. U.S.*, 91-2 USTC ¶60,085 (10th Cir. 1991). For example, suppose A transfers $12,000 to each of B, C, and D in 2006. By arrangement, B, C, and D each immediately transfer $12,000 to E. The annual exclusion for A's indirect transfers to E is limited to $12,000 and A has made taxable gifts of $24,000 to E. Under the appropriate circumstances, the substance over form analysis might even be used to deny annual exclusions for Crummey powers. *ASRS, Sec. 51, ¶230.2(b)*.

727. If the beneficiary of a Crummey trust allows his right to withdraw a contribution to the trust to go unexercised, under what circumstances will he be deemed to have made a transfer subject to gift or estate tax?

The withdrawal power held by a Crummey trust beneficiary is a general power of appointment. If a Crummey trust provides for a contingent beneficiary to succeed to the interest of the primary beneficiary in the event of the primary beneficiary's death before the trust terminates, the primary beneficiary's failure to exercise his withdrawal right acts as a transfer to the contingent beneficiary, either at the time of the lapse of the withdrawal right or at the time of the primary beneficiary's death. The amount thus transferred is subject to federal gift or estate tax to the extent it exceeds the greater of $5,000 or 5% of the aggregate value of the assets out of which, or the proceeds of which, the exercise of the withdrawal right could be satisfied. IRC Sec. 2514(e).

A spouse who was given a withdrawal power would be treated as making gifts to remainder persons each time the spouse allows a withdrawal power to lapse to the

LIFE INSURANCE TRUSTS   Q 727

extent that the lapsed power exceeds the greater of $5,000 or 5% of the trust principal. Furthermore, the value of the gift would not be reduced by the spouse's retained income interest or the spouse's interest in principal subject to an ascertainable standard because such interests are not qualified retained interests under IRC Section 2702 (see Q 914). Let. Rul. 9804047.

In those cases, then, where (1) the primary beneficiary's gift or estate tax liability is to be avoided, and (2) the trust value is under $240,000, in the case of a $12,000 withdrawal right, or under $480,000, in the case of a $24,000 withdrawal right (husband and wife grantors splitting the gift), the "5 or 5" limitation must be dealt with.

A hanging power is one method that has been used in an attempt to manage the "5 or 5" limitation. A hanging power is designed to lapse in any year only to the extent that the power does not exceed the "5 or 5" limitation. Any excess is carried over to succeeding years and lapses only to the extent that the power does not exceed the "5 or 5" limitation in such years.

> *Example.* Beginning in 1997, parents transfer an amount equal to eight (2 donors × 4 donees) times the annual exclusion to a trust each year. Four children are each given a right to withdraw an amount equal to two (2 donors) times the annual exclusion annually. [The annual exclusion was $10,000 from 1997 to 2001 and $11,000 from 2002 to 2005, and is $12,000 in 2006, see Appendix B.] Upon nonexercise of the power to withdraw, the power lapses in any year to the extent of the greater of $5,000 or 5% of corpus. To the extent that a power does not lapse in a year, it is carried over and added to any power arising in the succeeding year. The hanging power is eliminated in the tenth year (i.e., when carryover equals zero).

YEAR	CORPUS	POWER	LAPSE	CARRYOVER
1997	$ 80,000	$20,000	$ 5,000	$15,000
1998	160,000	35,000	8,000	27,000
1999	240,000	47,000	12,000	35,000
2000	320,000	55,000	16,000	39,000
2001	400,000	59,000	20,000	39,000
2002	488,000	61,000	24,400	36,600
2003	576,000	58,600	28,800	29,800
2004	664,000	51,800	33,200	18,600
2005	752,000	40,600	37,600	3,000
2006	848,000	27,000	27,000	0

In Letter Ruling 8901004, a hanging *Crummey* withdrawal power written in the form of a tax savings clause was ruled invalid. Many commentators believe that a hanging power which lapses only to the extent that the power does not exceed the "5 or 5" limitation (rather than by reference to whether there would be a taxable gift) would be valid.

A powerholder is not treated as making a gift upon the lapse of a general power if the powerholder is, in effect, still the owner of the property after the lapse. Consequently, other methods used in an attempt to manage the "5 or 5" limitation include (1) giving the powerholder a testamentary limited power to appoint the property to other than the powerholder or the powerholder's estate, and (2) vesting the property in the powerholder.

Under each of these methods for managing the "5 or 5" limitation for gift tax purposes, estate tax inclusion could result. See Q 681, Q 653, Q 853(1).

2006 Tax Facts on Insurance & Employee Benefits

Since August 24, 1981, the IRS has had under extensive study the following type of Crummey insurance trust and has stated that it will not issue rulings or determination letters on the applicability of IRC Section 2514(e) to a beneficiary's lapse of a withdrawal power when (1) the trust corpus consists or will consist substantially of insurance policies on the life of the grantor or the grantor's spouse, (2) the trustee or any other person has a power to apply the trust's income or corpus to the payment of premiums on policies of insurance on the life of the grantor or the grantor's spouse, (3) the trustee or any other person has a power to use the trust's assets to make loans to the grantor's estate or to purchase assets from the grantor's estate, (4) the trust beneficiaries have the power to withdraw, on demand, any additional transfers made to the trust, and (5) there is a right or power in any person that would cause the grantor to be treated as the owner of all or a portion of the trust under IRC Sections 673 to 677. Rev. Proc. 2005-3, Sec. 4.46, 2005-1 IRB 118. *ASRS, Sec. 51, ¶230.2(b).*

728. May dividends paid on a life insurance policy in trust be gifts of present interest even though the policy itself was a gift of future interest?

Yes. If the trustee is directed to pay the dividends to the trust beneficiary, the value of probable dividends will be considered a gift of a present interest. *Tidemann v. Comm.*, 1 TC 968 (1943). *ASRS, Sec. 55, ¶55.2.*

LOANS

729. If the beneficiary of life insurance pays the interest on a policy loan, is this a gift to the insured?

Not unless the insured owns the policy. *Seligmann v. Comm.*, 9 TC 191 (1947).

MARITAL DEDUCTION

730. If a person gives his spouse a life insurance policy, is he entitled to a gift tax marital deduction?

An outright gift of a life insurance policy to the donor's spouse qualifies for the gift tax marital deduction on the same basis as the gift of a bond or any other similar property. *Kidd v. Patterson*, 230 F. Supp. 769 (N.D. Ala. 1964). The same should hold for subsequent premiums paid on the policy by the donor. See Q 920. An annual exclusion (see Q 917) may be allowed instead of the marital deduction if the donee spouse is not a United States citizen (see Q 920). See Q 722 for gift of policy in trust. *ASRS, Sec. 51, ¶282.4(1).*

731. Does the interest of a donee spouse in a joint and survivor annuity qualify for the marital deduction?

The interest of a donee spouse in a joint and survivor annuity in which only the donor and donee spouses have a right to receive payments during such spouses' joint lifetimes is treated as qualifying terminable interest property (QTIP) for which the marital deduction is available unless the donor spouse irrevocably elects otherwise within the time allowed for filing a gift tax return. IRC Sec. 2523(f)(6).

MULTIPLE-LIFE LIFE INSURANCE

732. Does the gift taxation of a life insurance policy which insures more than one life differ from the taxation of a policy which insures a single life?

Basically, no. However, application of the rules may depend on when proceeds are payable. With a "first-to-die" or "joint life" policy, proceeds are payable at the death of the first insured to die. With a "second-to-die," "survivorship," or "joint and survivor" policy, proceeds are payable at the death of the last survivor.

Thus, with a "first-to-die" policy, a policyowner who is not the insured may be treated as making a gift to beneficiaries when an insured dies. Also, with a "second-to-die" policy, at the second death, a policyowner who is not the insured may be treated as making a gift to beneficiaries. See Q 735.

Planning Point: Second-to-die policies are generally viewed as providing low-cost premiums for gift tax purposes; conversely, first-to-die premiums should generally appear high compared to premiums to insure one life.

For income taxation of multiple-life life insurance, see Q 302. For estate taxation of multiple-life life insurance, see Q 671.

PREMIUMS

733. Do premiums gratuitously paid on life insurance owned by and payable to another constitute gifts?

Generally, yes; if an individual pays a premium on a life insurance policy in which he has no ownership rights, he has made a gift of the premium. *Comm. v. Boeing*, 123 F.2d 86 (9th Cir. 1941). Where, for example, a wife paid premiums on a policy owned by her husband and payable to his estate, she was held to have made a gift to her husband even though she had a contingent interest in the policy as a beneficiary of his estate. (Under present law, however, such a gift would qualify for the unlimited marital deduction (see Q 920).) *Harris v. Comm.*, 10 TC 741 (1948) (see also Q 730). A gift of premiums may also qualify for the gift tax annual exclusion (see Q 712).

Ordinarily the premium payer will be considered the donor. However, where an employee assigned his group life insurance policy to an irrevocable trust he had created for his beneficiary, IRS ruled that premiums subsequently paid by the employer were gifts from the *employee* to the trust. Rev. Rul. 76-490, 1976-2 CB 300; Rev. Rul. 79-47, 1979-1 CB 312. (See also Q 719, Q 724.) *ASRS, Sec. 55, ¶45; Sec. 66, ¶370.*

734. Do premiums paid by one of several beneficiaries of an irrevocable life insurance trust constitute gifts to the other beneficiaries?

Yes; premiums paid in excess of the amount necessary to protect one beneficiary's actuarially determined interest constitute gifts to the other beneficiaries. *Comm. v. Berger*, 201 F.2d 171 (2nd Cir. 1953). *ASRS, Sec. 55, ¶45.*

PROCEEDS

735. If a life insurance policy is owned by someone other than the insured, is there a gift when the insured dies and the proceeds are paid to the owner's designated beneficiary?

Yes. For example, if a wife owns a policy on the life of her husband, and their children are named beneficiaries, subject to wife's right to change the beneficiaries, there is a gift from the wife to the children when insured dies. The value of the gift would be the value of the entire proceeds. See *Goodman v. Comm.*, 156 F.2d 218 (2d Cir. 1946). Under such circumstances the gift of the proceeds will *not* be considered a split-gift between the wife and her late husband-insured under IRC Section 2513 (see Q 742), even if the executor signs a "consent of spouse" and files a gift tax return on behalf of the deceased spouse. Rev. Rul. 73-207, 1973-1 CB 409.

Another example: A bought insurance on the life of B, revocably designating as beneficiary Y, trustee of a trust established by A. The trust provided (1) that trust income was payable to B for life, then to A for life, then trust corpus to children of A and B; and (2) that for purposes of the trust agreement, if A and B died simultaneously, A would be presumed to have survived B. A and B died simultaneously. It was held that there was a taxable gift of the proceeds from A to the children of A and B. Rev. Rul. 77-48, 1977-1 CB 292; *Est. of Goldstone v. Comm.*, 78 TC 1143 (1982). (See also Q 676).

Another example: D created an unfunded revocable insurance trust under which the life income was payable to B for life and the remainder to E and F. B purchased a life insurance policy on D's life designating the trust as beneficiary and paying all the premiums. While B was alive, D died and the insurance proceeds were paid to the trust. B, until the death of D, possessed all the incidents of ownership in the policy, including the right to change the beneficiary. It was held that B made a completed gift for gift tax purposes to E and F on D's death; the value of the gift was the amount of the policy proceeds less the present value of B's life estate (determined by use of the Estate and Gift Tax Valuation Tables, see Q 910). Rev. Rul. 81-166, 1981-1 CB 477. *ASRS, Sec. 55, ¶52.*

QUALIFIED PLANS, TAX SHELTERED ANNUITIES AND INDIVIDUAL RETIREMENT PLANS

736. Is there a taxable gift when an individual covered under a qualified plan, a tax sheltered annuity, or an individual retirement plan (IRA) irrevocably designates a beneficiary to receive a survivor benefit payable under the plan?

Such a designation would appear to be a gift falling under the broad sweep of IRC Section 2511, applying the gift tax "whether the transfer is in trust or otherwise, whether the gift is direct or indirect, and whether the property is real or personal, tangible or intangible–." IRC Sec. 2511(a); Treas. Reg. §25.2511-1(a). The IRS has ruled, for example, that a retiring federal employee who receives a reduced annuity in order to provide a survivor annuity for his beneficiary makes a gift subject to gift tax of the value of the survivor annuity by the mere act of his retiring. Let. Ruls. 8715010,

SETTLEMENT OPTIONS—PRIMARY BENEFICIARY   Q 740

8715035, 8811017. The gift is clearly one of a future interest, so it does not qualify for the gift tax annual exclusion (Q 918). Treas. Reg. §25.2503-3(c)(Ex. 2). However, if the beneficiary of the survivor annuity is the employee's spouse, the gift will generally qualify for the marital deduction (see Q 731).

737. Is there a taxable gift when a nonparticipant spouse waives the right to receive a qualified joint and survivor annuity or a qualified preretirement survivor annuity?

Waiver of the right to receive a qualified joint and survivor annuity or a qualified preretirement survivor annuity (see Q 336) by a nonparticipant spouse is not treated as a taxable transfer by such spouse if the waiver is made before the death of the participant spouse. IRC Sec. 2503(f).

738. Can community property law create a taxable gift by the spouse of an individual who designates a third party beneficiary to receive a survivor benefit payable under a qualified plan, a tax sheltered annuity, or an individual retirement plan (IRA)?

If an employee's interest in a qualified plan is community property (Q 675) and he gratuitously and effectively designates someone other than his spouse to receive a survivor benefit, the value of the benefit conveyed comes equally from the employee's community half and his spouse's community half. (Community property law varies from state to state with respect to the power of a spouse to make a gift of community property without the express consent of the other spouse.) The effect of the transaction is to create a gift from the employee's spouse of one-half the value of the benefit conveyed when the conveyance is complete. Such gift is considered by IRS to be subject to gift tax. See Rev. Rul. 75-240, 1975-1 CB 315 (obsoleted by Rev. Rul. 95-71, 1995-2 CB 323, due to repeal of IRC Section 2517 which contained an exemption from gift tax for this kind of gift).

739. If one who is covered under an individual retirement plan (IRA) contributes to a similar plan covering his nonemployed spouse, are such contributions considered gifts?

Yes. However, such contributions generally qualify for the marital deduction and do not require filing of a gift tax return (see Q 920). There should be no question that an individual's contributions to a spousal IRA would qualify for the marital deduction, so long as the donee spouse is the one who names a beneficiary to receive account proceeds remaining at her death. However, if the donor spouse (i.e., the contributing individual) designates a beneficiary, the donee spouse's interest in the IRA would be a nondeductible terminable interest and the marital deduction would not be allowed, except in the case of certain joint and survivor annuities (see Q 731). *ASRS, Sec. 62, ¶510.2.*

SETTLEMENT OPTIONS–PRIMARY BENEFICIARY

740. If a primary beneficiary of life insurance proceeds payable under a settlement option has a power to withdraw part of the proceeds, does the beneficiary's failure to exercise the power constitute a taxable gift to contingent beneficiaries?

Where the primary beneficiary has an annual, limited, noncumulative right of withdrawal, the beneficiary has made a gift to contingent beneficiaries when the beneficiary fails to exercise the right. However, a lapse of the right is subject to gift tax only to the extent that the right to withdraw exceeded the greater of $5,000 or 5% of the value of the proceeds at the time of lapse. IRC Sec. 2514(e). (See Q 681.) *ASRS, Sec. 55, ¶53.*

SPLIT DOLLAR

741. How are split dollar life insurance arrangements treated for gift tax purposes?

Gifts may arise in a split dollar arrangement where a donor provides a benefit to a donee. For example, an employee or shareholder who irrevocably assigns his interest in a compensatory or shareholder split dollar arrangement (see Q 457) to a third party (such as a family member) may make gifts to such third party (including annual gifts of the amount the employee or shareholder is required to include in income). Also, a donor may make gifts to an irrevocable life insurance trust under a private split dollar arrangement.

The treatment of split dollar arrangements may differ depending on whether the split dollar arrangement was entered into or modified after September 17, 2003.

Post-September 17, 2003 Arrangements

Regulations provide generally that treatment of a split dollar arrangement depends on whether the donor is the owner of the life insurance contract. TD 9092, 2003-46 IRB 1055; Treas. Regs. §§1.61-22, 1.7872-15. Even if the donee is named as the policy owner, the donor may be treated as the owner if the only economic benefit provided to the donee is the value of current life insurance protection.

If a life insurance trust is the owner of the policy, the donor makes premium payments, and the donor is entitled to recover an amount equal to the premiums, the donor is treated as making a loan to the trust in the amount of the premium payment. If the loan is repayable on the death of the donor, the term of the loan is equal to the donor's life expectancy on the date of the payment [under Treasury Regulation Section 1.72-9 (see Table V in Appendix B)]. The value of the gift equals the premium payment less the present value (determined under IRC Section 7282, see Q 904) of the donor's right to receive repayment. If there is no right to repayment, the value of the gift would equal the premium payment.

If the donor is treated as the owner of the policy, the donor is treated as making a gift to the trust. The value of the gift equals the economic benefits provided to the trust, less the amount of premium paid by the trustee. If the donor's estate is entitled to receive the greater of aggregate premiums paid by the donor or cash surrender value, the gift is equal to the cost of life insurance protection less premiums paid by the trustee. If the donor's estate is entitled to receive the lesser of aggregate premiums paid by the donor or cash surrender value, the gift is equal to the cost of life insurance protection, plus the amount of cash surrender value to which the trust has current access (except to the extent taken into account in an earlier year), plus any other economic benefit provided to the trust (except to the extent taken into account in an earlier year), less premiums paid by the trustee. If the donor is treated as the owner of the policy, amounts received by the life insurance trust under the contract (e.g., dividends or policy loan) are treated as gifts from the donor to the trust.

No matter who is treated as owner of the life insurance policy, there may be a gift upon transfer of an interest in a policy to a third party. See Rev. Rul. 81-198, below.

Pre-September 18, 2003 Arrangements

In a 1978 ruling, a wife owned a policy on the split dollar plan on the life of her husband. The husband's employer paid the portion of the premiums equal to annual cash value increases and was entitled to reimbursement from death proceeds. IRS ruled that the value of the life insurance protection provided by the employer, which the Service also ruled was included in the husband's income (see Q 457), was deemed to be a gift from the husband to his wife, subject to the gift tax. Rev. Rul. 78-420, 1978-2 CB 67, revoked by Rev. Rul. 2003-105, 2003-40 IRB 696, for split dollar arrangements entered into or modified after September 17, 2003.

Where an employee makes a gift of his rights under a basic plan of split dollar insurance (as described in Q 457) in which the insurance is premium paying and has been in force some time, the IRS has ruled that three elements are valued. First, the value of the insured's rights in the policy at the date of gift is the interpolated terminal reserve plus the proportionate part of the last premium paid before the date of gift covering the period beyond that date, reduced by the total of premiums paid by the employer. Second, the premiums paid by the insured following the date of gift are gifts on the date paid. Third, the value of the life insurance protection provided by the employer, included in the employee's gross income, is deemed to be a gift by the employee. Rev. Rul. 81-198, 1981-2 CB 188.

One letter ruling provided that a gift of the amount at risk under a split dollar plan is valued as the greater of: (1) the value of the insurance protection as computed for income tax purposes (see Q 458); or (2) the difference between the premium payment and the increase in the cash surrender value of the policy. Letter Ruling dated December 4, 1972, reproduced in ASRS, section 65. A later technical advice memorandum stated that, with respect to a split dollar plan, a gift may be made of (1) the value of the insurance protection and (2) increases in cash surrender values in excess of premiums paid by and returnable to the corporation. TAM 9604001.

SPLIT-GIFT

742. What is the advantage of the "split-gift" law where either husband or wife gives a life insurance, endowment or annuity contract to a third person?

See generally Q 907. If the gift qualifies as a present interest gift (Q 712), each spouse's annual exclusion ($12,000 in 2006, see Appendix B) can be applied to reduce or eliminate the gift tax. Thus, $24,000 (in 2006, 2 × $12,000) can be subtracted from the value of the contract given and from premiums paid by the donor as gifts in subsequent years (so long as the spouse consents each year) in computing taxable gifts for years in which the gifts are made. The consenting spouse's unified credit (Q 922) can also be availed of to apply against any gift tax imposed on the spouse's gift where the gift is in excess of the allowable exclusion or is a future interest gift. (See also Q 735.) *ASRS, Sec. 55, ¶50.*

SURVIVOR INCOME BENEFIT PLANS

743. Does an employee covered under a survivor income benefit plan make a gift of the survivor benefit for federal gift tax purposes?

Under a survivor income benefit plan, an employer provides an income benefit only for certain survivors designated by family or marital relationship to the employee.

An employee does not make a gift of the survivor benefit at the time of death. Rev. Rul. 92-68, 1992-2 CB 257, revoking Rev. Rul. 81-31, 1981-1 CB 475 (in which the Service treated an employee as making a gift of the benefit from a DBO plan in the year of the employee's death); *Est. of DiMarco v. Comm.*, 87 TC 653 (1986), acq. in result, 1990-2 CB 1. Note that neither Revenue Ruling 81-31 nor *Est. of DiMarco v. Comm.* addressed whether an employee should be treated each year as (1) receiving compensation equal to the value of providing a death benefit or survivor income benefit to an eligible survivor if the employee died during the year, and (2) transferring such value to the eligible survivor. Of course, the use of the annual exclusion (Q 917) and the marital deduction (Q 920) might protect such a gift from any gift tax. (See Q 684 for estate tax aspects and Q 153 for income tax aspects.) *ASRS, Sec. 66, ¶540.6.*

VALUATION

744. How are life insurance policies and endowment contracts valued for gift tax purposes?

Generally, the value of a gift of life insurance is established through the sale by the company of comparable contracts. Treas. Reg. §25.2512-6.

(1) If a new policy is purchased for another, or is transferred as a gift immediately after purchase, its gift value is the gross premium paid by the donor to the insurance company. Treas. Reg. §25.2512-6(a), Example 1.

(2) If a person makes a gift of a previously purchased policy, and the policy is single-premium or paid-up, its gift value is the single premium which the company would charge currently for a comparable contract of equal face value on the life of a person who is insured's age at the time of the gift. Treas. Reg. §25.2512-6(a), Example 3. A 1978 ruling concerned a single premium life policy in force for 20 years, where the replacement cost of a single premium life policy of the same face value on the same insured was substantially less than the cash surrender value of the existing policy. The Service ruled that the replacement contract would not be "comparable" and that in the absence of information pertaining to a "comparable contract" the value of the policy would be determined by reference to the interpolated terminal reserve value (see (3) below). Rev. Rul. 78-137, 1978-1 CB 280.

(3) If the gift is of a policy on which further premiums are payable, the value is established by adding the "interpolated terminal reserve" (the reserve adjusted to the date of the gift) and the value of the unearned portion of the last premium. Treas. Reg. §25.2512-6(a), Example 4.

VALUATION Q 744

Example. A gift is made four months after the last premium due date of an ordinary life insurance policy issued nine years and four months prior to the gift thereof by the insured, who was 35 years of age at date of issue. The gross annual premium is $2,811. The computation is as follows:

Terminal reserve at end of tenth year	$14,601.00
Terminal reserve at end of ninth year	12,965.00
Increase	$ 1,636.00
One-third of such increase (the gift having been made four months following the last preceding premium due date) is	$ 545.33
Terminal reserve at end of ninth year	12,965.00
Interpolated terminal reserve at date of gift	$13,510.33
Two-thirds of gross premium ($2,811)	1,874.00
Value of gift	$15,384.33

The amount of a policy loan outstanding at time of gift would be subtracted. IRS Form 712, Part II.

The effect of the circumstance that the insured is uninsurable at time of gift is uncertain; there is no case directly in point. See *U.S. v. Ryerson*, 312 U.S. 260 (1941); 54 Harvard L. Rev. 895 (1941); *Est. of Pritchard v. Comm.*, 4 TC 204 (1944); Treas. Reg. §25.2512-1.

See Q 741 regarding gifts with respect to split dollar arrangements.

If gift of the policy or contract is conditioned upon payment of the gift tax by the donee, the value of the gift is reduced by the amount of the gift tax paid by the donee. Rev. Rul. 75-72, 1975-1 CB 310. See Q 911. See also Rev. Rul. 76-104, 76-1 CB 301; Rev. Rul. 76-105, 76-1 CB 304.

A group term life policy assigned by an employee to an irrevocable trust on the day before a monthly premium was due was held to have no ascertainable value for gift tax purposes, but it was also held that after the assignment the employee would be deemed to have made a gift to the assignee whenever the employer paid a premium. Rev. Rul. 76-490, 1976-2 CB 300. A 1984 ruling valued the gift as follows: If the plan of group term insurance is nondiscriminatory or the employee is not a key employee, the Table I rates may be used. If the employee chooses not to use Table I, or if the plan is discriminatory and the employee is a key employee, the employee should use the actual cost allocable to the employee's insurance by obtaining the necessary information from the employer. The rates apply to the full face amount of the insurance. Rev. Rul. 84-147, 1984-2 CB 201. Projecting the holding of the 1984 ruling to the nondiscrimination rules applicable to taxable years ending after October 22, 1986 (see Q 143) it would seem that if the plan of group term insurance is discriminatory with respect to the employee, the employee must use the higher of Table I rates or actual cost. *ASRS Sec. 55, ¶47; Sec. 66, ¶370.*

PART IV

GENERATION-SKIPPING TRANSFER TAX

on

INSURANCE AND EMPLOYEE BENEFITS

750. Can arrangements for payment of the proceeds of life insurance and annuity contracts attract the generation-skipping transfer tax?

Yes. Regardless of what form an arrangement may take (whether, for example, a life insurance trust or an agreement with the insurer for payment of proceeds under settlement options, or an outright payment to a beneficiary), if an insured (or annuitant) transfers benefits to a "skip person," (see Q 950), generally, he has made a generation-skipping transfer. (See Q 950 to Q 955 for details.)

For purposes of the generation-skipping transfer tax, the following definitions (taken verbatim from the IRC) apply:

"(1) **Trust.** The term 'trust' includes any arrangement (other than an estate) which, although not a trust, has substantially the same effect as a trust.

"(2) **Trustee.** In the case of an arrangement that is not a trust but which is treated as a trust under this subsection, the term 'trustee' shall mean the person in actual or constructive possession of the property subject to such arrangement.

"(3) **Examples.** Arrangements to which this subsection applies include arrangements involving life estates, estates for years, and insurance and annuity contracts." IRC Sec. 2652(b).

The IRS has been given authority to issue regulations which may modify the generation-skipping rules when applied to trust equivalents, such as life estates and remainders, estates for years, and insurance and annuity contracts. IRC Sec. 2663(3). The Committee Report states that such authority might, for example, be used to provide that the beneficiary of an annuity or insurance contract be required to pay any generation-skipping tax.

Regulations provide that the executor is responsible for filing and paying the GST tax if (1) a direct skip (see Q 950) occurs at death, (2) the property is held in a trust arrangement (includes arrangements having the same effect as an explicit trust), and (3) the total value of property subject to the direct skip is less than $250,000. The executor is entitled to recover the GST tax attributable to the transfer from the trustee (if the property continues to be held in trust) or from the recipient of the trust property (if transferred from the trust arrangement). The regulations provide a number of examples which treat insurance proceeds as a trust arrangement. Where insurance proceeds held by an insurance company are to be paid to skip persons in a direct skip at death (a direct skip can occur whether proceeds are paid in a lump sum or over a period of time) and the aggregate value of such proceeds held by the company is less than $250,000, the executor is responsible for filing and paying the GST tax; consequently, the insurance company can pay out the proceeds without regard to the GST tax (apparently, the insurance company could not do so if the executor attempts to recover the GST tax while the company still holds proceeds). However, where the value of the proceeds in the aggregate equals or exceeds $250,000, the insurance company is responsible for filing and paying the GST tax. Treas. Reg. §26.2662-1(c)(2).

For general rules relating to filing and payment of GST tax, see Q 956 and Q 955. *ASRS, Sec. 56.*

751. Can the transfer to an irrevocable life insurance trust of an amount used to make premium payments qualify for the generation-skipping transfer tax annual exclusion?

Yes, if certain requirements are met, a transfer to an irrevocable life insurance trust can qualify for the annual exclusion (and thus avoid generation-skipping transfer tax). A nontaxable gift which is a direct skip (see Q 950) has an inclusion ratio of zero (i.e., it is not subject to GST tax). Nontaxable gifts means gifts eligible for the annual exclusion (see Appendix B for amounts) [doubled if gifts are split between spouses–see Q 907], as well as certain transfers for educational or medical expenses (see Q 917). However, with respect to transfers after March 31, 1988, the nontaxable gift which is a direct skip to a trust for the benefit of an individual has an inclusion ratio of zero only if (1) during the life of such individual no portion of the trust corpus or income may be distributed to or for the benefit of any other person, and (2) the trust would be included in such individual's estate if the trust did not terminate before such individual died. IRC Sec. 2642(c). Thus, separate shares or separate trusts, as described in the preceding sentence, must be created for each such individual if premium payments are to be covered by the annual exclusion for generation-skipping transfer tax purposes. *ASRS, Sec. 56.*

Planning Point: Because of the separate share requirement, the annual exclusion is generally not used for generation-skipping life insurance trusts. Instead, the trust is usually protected by allocating GST exemption to all transfers to the trust.

752. How can the generation-skipping transfer (GST) tax exemption be leveraged using an irrevocable life insurance trust?

Leveraging of the $2,000,000 (in 2006, see Appendix B) GST tax exemption (see Q 951) can be accomplished by allocating the exemption against the discounted dollars which the premiums represent when compared with the ultimate value of the insurance proceeds. However, in the case of inter vivos transfers in trust, allocation of the GST exemption is postponed until the end of an estate tax inclusion period (ETIP) (see Q 951). In general, an ETIP would not end until the termination of the last interest held by either the transferor or the spouse of the transferor during the period in which the property being transferred would have been included in either spouse's estate if that spouse died. Of course, the transferor should be given no interest which would cause the trust property to be included in the transferor's estate. Furthermore, the transferor's spouse should be given no interest which would cause the trust property to be included in the transferor spouse's estate if the transferor spouse were to die. The property is not considered as includable in the estate of the spouse of the transferor by reason of

INSURANCE AND EMPLOYEE BENEFITS — Q 752

a withdrawal power limited to the greater of $5,000 or 5% of the trust corpus if the withdrawal power terminates no later than 60 days after the transfer to trust. Also, the property is not considered as includable in the estate of the transferor or the spouse of the transferor if the possibility of inclusion is so remote as to be negligible (i.e., less than a 5% actuarial probability). Furthermore, the ETIP rules do not apply if a reverse QTIP election (see Q 951) is made. Otherwise, if proceeds are received during the ETIP, the allocation of the GST exemption must be made against proceeds rather than premiums and the advantage of leveraging is lost. *ASRS, Sec. 56.*

Example 1. G creates a trust for the benefit of his children and grandchildren. Each year he transfers to the trust $50,000 (to be used to make premium payments on a $2 million insurance policy on his life) and allocates $50,000 of his GST exemption to each transfer. Assuming G makes no other allocations of his GST exemption, the trust will have a zero inclusion ratio (i.e., it is not subject to GST tax) during its first 20 years. At the end of 20 years, G will have used up his GST exemption and the trust's inclusion ratio (see Q 951) will increase slowly with each additional transfer of $50,000 to the trust. If G died during the 20 year period, the insurance proceeds of $2 million would not be subject to GST tax. Part of the $2 million proceeds may be subject to GST tax if G died in a later year. In order to insure that the trust has a zero inclusion ratio, use of a policy which becomes paid-up before the transfers to trust exceed the GST exemption may be indicated. Twenty years in the example is based upon the $1 million GST exemption prior to any inflation or other adjustment after 1998 (see Q 951).

Example 2. Same facts as in Example 1, except that the trust is created for G's spouse, S, during her lifetime, and then, to benefit children and grandchildren. If the trust is intended to qualify for the marital deduction (apparently, other than if a reverse QTIP election, see Q 951, is used), the valuation of property for purpose of the ETIP rule (see Q 951) is generally delayed until G or S dies because the property would have been included in S's estate if she died during the ETIP. Consequently, if the $2 million insurance proceeds are received during the wife's lifetime, the GST exemption is allocated against the $2 million proceeds, and a substantial amount of GST tax may be due upon subsequent taxable distributions and taxable terminations from the trust. Because allocation of the exemption must be made against the proceeds if they are received during the ETIP, the advantage of leveraging enjoyed in Example 1 is lost.

PART V

FEDERAL INCOME TAX

GENERAL

INDIVIDUALS

FILING REQUIREMENTS

800. Who must file an income tax return?

A return must be filed for taxable year 2006 by every individual whose gross income equals or exceeds the following limits:

(1) Married persons filing jointly–$16,900 (if one spouse is blind *or* elderly–$17,900; if both spouses are blind *or* elderly–$18,900; if both spouses are blind *and* elderly–$20,900). IRC Sec. 63(c). (See "Marriage penalty relief," Q 817.) A married taxpayer with gross income of $3,300 or more (in 2006) must file a return if he and his spouse are living in different households at the end of the taxable year.

(2) Surviving spouse (see Q 830)–$13,600 (if elderly *or* blind–$14,600; if elderly *and* blind–$15,600). IRC Sec. 63(c). (See "Marriage penalty relief," Q 817.)

(3) Head-of-household (see Q 831)–$10,850 (if blind *or* elderly–$12,100; if elderly *and* blind–$13,350).

(4) Single persons–$8,450 (if blind *or* elderly–$9,700; if blind *and* elderly–$10,950).

(5) Married filing separately–if neither spouse itemizes, a return must be filed if gross income equals or exceeds $8,450 in 2006 (if blind *or* elderly–$9,450; if blind *and* elderly–$10,450). IRC Sec. 63(c). (See "Marriage penalty relief," Q 817.) If either spouse itemizes–$3,300.

(6) Dependents–every individual who may be claimed as a dependent of another must file a return for 2006 if he has unearned income in excess of $850 (plus any additional standard deduction if the individual is blind or elderly) or total gross income that exceeds the sum of any additional standard deduction if the individual is blind or elderly plus the greater of (a) $850 or (b) the lesser of (i) $300 plus earned income, or (ii) $5,150.

(7) Taxpayers who are non-resident aliens or who are filing a short year return because of a change in their annual accounting period–$3,300. IRC Secs. 6012(a), 63(c), 151; Rev. Proc. 2005-70, 2005-47 IRB 979.

Certain parents whose children are required to file a return may be permitted to include the child's income over $1,700 on their own return, thus avoiding the necessity of the child filing a return. See Q 818.

A taxpayer with self-employment income must file a return if *net* self-employment income is $400 or more. See Q 837. *ASRS, Sec. 53, ¶20.14(a).*

801. Who must pay the estimated tax and what penalties are imposed for underpayment of the tax?

Taxpayers are generally required to pay estimated tax if failure to pay would result in an underpayment (see below) of federal income tax. IRC Sec. 6654. Taxpayers must include the alternative minimum tax and estimated self-employment tax in their calculation of estimated tax (see Q 829 and Q 837, respectively). IRC Sec. 6654(d)(2)(B)(i). An underpayment is the amount by which a required installment exceeds the amount, if any, paid on or before the due date of that installment (due dates are April 15, June 15, September 15 and January 15 of the following year). IRC Secs. 6654(b), 6654(c). The required amount for each installment is 25% of the *required annual payment.* IRC Sec. 6654(d)(1)(A).

Generally, the "required annual payment" is the lower of (a) 90% of the tax shown on the return for the taxable year (or, if no return is filed, 90% of the tax for the year), or (b) 100% of the tax shown on the return for the preceding year (but only if the preceding taxable year consisted of 12 months and a return was filed for that year). IRC Sec. 6654(d)(1)(B). However, for an individual whose adjusted gross income for the previous tax year exceeded $150,000 ($75,000 in the case of married individuals filing separately), the required annual payment is the lesser of (a) 90% of the current year's tax, as described above, or (b) the *applicable percentage* of the tax shown on the return for the preceding year. The applicable percentage for tax years beginning in 2003 or later is 110%. (Different rules applied for installments due in tax years prior to 2000.) IRC Sec. 6654(d)(1)(C).

As an alternative to the required annual payment methods in the preceding paragraph, taxpayers can pay estimated tax by paying a specified percentage of the current year's tax, computed by annualizing the taxable income for the months in the taxable year ending before the month in which the installment falls due. The percentages that apply under the annualization method are: 22.5% (1st quarter), 45% (2nd quarter), 67.5% (3rd quarter), and 90% (4th quarter). IRC Sec. 6654(d)(2).

However, regardless of the method used to calculate estimated taxes, there is no interest penalty imposed if (1) the tax shown on the return for the taxable year (or, if no return is filed, the tax) after reduction for withholdings, is less than $1,000; or (2) the taxpayer owed no tax for the preceding year (a taxable year consisting of 12 months) and the taxpayer was a U.S. citizen or resident for the entire taxable year. IRC Sec. 6654(e). Otherwise, underpayment results in imposition of an interest penalty, compounded daily, at an annual rate that is adjusted quarterly so as to be three percentage points over the short-term applicable federal rate. IRC Sec. 6621(a)(2). (See Q 805).

If the taxpayer elects to apply an overpayment to the succeeding year's estimated taxes, the overpayment is applied to unpaid installments of estimated tax due on or after the date(s) the overpayment arose in the order in which they are required to be paid to avoid an interest penalty for failure to pay estimated income tax with respect to such tax year. Rev. Rul. 99-40, 1999-40 IRB 441. For application of the estimated tax to trusts and estates, see Q 843.

INDIVIDUALS   Q 802

Hurricane tax relief. For detailed information on the extended estimated tax payment deadline (February 28, 2006) and other tax relief available to taxpayers affected by hurricanes in 2005, see: (1) *Hurricane Katrina* – Notice 2005-81, 2005-47 IRB 977, Notice 2005-73, 2005-42 IRB 723, and IR-2005-112; *Hurricane Rita* — Notice 2005-82, 2005-47 IRB 978, and IR-2005, IR-2005-110; and *Hurricane Wilma* – IR-2005-128. *ASRS, Sec. 53, 20.13(b).*

GROSS INCOME

802. What items are included in gross income? What items are excluded from gross income?

Gross income includes all income (whether derived from labor or capital) *less* those items that are excludable by law. Thus, gross income includes salary, fees, commissions, business profits, interest and dividends, rents, alimony received, and gains from sale of property–but not mere return of capital. IRC Sec. 61(a).

Some of the items that can be *excluded* from gross income and received tax free by an individual taxpayer include: gifts and inheritances (IRC Sec. 102); damages received by suit or settlement for personal injury, other than punitive damages (see Q 157); death proceeds of life insurance (see Q 271) and up to $1,000 annually of interest on death proceeds received under a life income or installment option by a surviving spouse of an insured who died before October 23, 1986 (see Q 276); certain amounts paid or expenses incurred by an employer for qualified adoption expenses in connection with the adoption of a child by an employee if the amounts are furnished pursuant to an adoption assistance program (IRC Sec. 137); certain qualifying expenses paid under an employer-provided educational assistance plan (IRC Sec. 127); dividends on unmatured life insurance policies (see Q 252); gain (within limits) from the sale of a personal residence (IRC Sec. 121); 50% of gain (within limits) from the sale of certain qualified small business stock (IRC Sec. 1202); group term life insurance premiums paid by an employer on coverage up to $50,000 (see Q 142); health insurance proceeds (see Q 155); interest on many bonds of a state, city or other political subdivision (IRC Sec. 103); premiums paid by an employer on health insurance for employees (see Q 159); most benefits under employers' accident and health plans (see Q 197); Social Security benefits (within limits–see Q 807); railroad retirement benefits (within limits–see Q 807); veterans' benefits (but retirement pay is taxable) (IRC Sec. 104(a)(4)); certain contributions to a "Medicare Advantage MSA" by the Secretary of Health and Human Services (IRC Sec. 138); interest on certain U.S. savings bonds used to pay higher education expenses (within limits – see IRC Sec. 135); contributions (within limits) paid by an employer to Health Savings Accounts (IRC Sec. 106(d)); distributions from Health Savings Accounts used to pay qualified medical expenses (IRC Sec. 223(f)(1)); and federal subsidies for prescription drug plans (IRC Sec. 139A).

Military. The tax-free treatment of the death gratuity paid to survivors of U.S. military members for deaths occurring after October 7, 2001 is $100,000. Sec. 1013, Emergency Supplemental Appropriations Act for Defense, the Global War on Terror, and Tsunami Relief, 2005 (P.L. 109-13). In addition, military personnel on qualified official extended duty can suspend the 5-year qualifying period for the home sale gain exclusion for up to 10 years. See IRC Secs. 121(d)(9), 134(b)(3)(C).

Victims of terrorist attacks. Employee death benefits that are payable by reason of the death of certain terrorist attack victims are excludable from gross income. IRC. Sec.

101(i). Lump-sum *and* periodic payments from the September 11th Victim Compensation Fund are excludable from income; similarly, any payments to an estate or secondary beneficiary are also excludable from the gross income of the successor beneficiary. Rev. Rul. 2003-115, 2003-46 IRB 1052. Certain cancellations of debt of certain taxpayers, which occurred as a result of the death of an individual because of terrorist attacks, are also excludable from gross income. See Sec. 105, VTTRA 2001. See also Pub. 3920, *Tax Relief for Victims of Terrorist Attacks* at: http://www.irs.gov. For guidance on how to have tax forgiven, how to claim tax refunds, or the procedures by which the IRS will determine whether a terrorist or military act has occurred, see Rev. Proc. 2004-26, 2004-19 IRB 890.

Disaster relief payments. Gross income generally does not include "qualified disaster relief payments" received by an individual. IRC Sec. 139(a). "Qualified disaster relief payments" are amounts paid to or for the benefit of an individual: (1) to reimburse or pay reasonable and necessary personal, family, living, or funeral expenses incurred as a result of a "qualified disaster"(see below); (2) to reimburse or pay reasonable and necessary expenses incurred for the repair or rehabilitation of a personal residence, or repair or replacement of its contents, to the extent that the need for such repair, rehabilitation, or replacement is attributable to a qualified disaster; (3) by a person engaged in the furnishing or sale of transportation as a common carrier by reason of the death or personal physical injuries incurred as a result of a qualified disaster; or (4) if such amount is paid by a federal, state, or local government (or agency or instrumentality) in connection with a qualified disaster in order to promote the general welfare. However, payments are excludible *only* to the extent any expense compensated by such payment is not otherwise compensated for by insurance (or otherwise). IRC Sec. 139(b). "Qualified disaster" means: (1) a disaster that results from a terroristic or military action (as defined in IRC Section 692(c)(2)); (2) a Presidentially declared disaster (as defined in IRC Section 1033(h)(3)); (3) a disaster that results from an accident involving a common carrier, or from any other event that is determined by the Secretary to be of a catastrophic nature; or (4) with respect to amounts described in item (4), above, a disaster that is determined by an applicable federal, state, or local authority to warrant assistance from the federal, state, or local government (or agency or instrumentality). IRC Sec. 139(c).

The Service has ruled that grants individuals receive under a state program, or under a program sponsored by their employer, to pay (or reimburse) unreimbursed reasonable and necessary medical, temporary housing, or transportation expenses they incur as a result of a flood are excludible from gross income. Payments that individuals receive under a charitable organization's program to pay (or reimburse) unreimbursed medical, temporary housing, or transportation expenses they incur as a result of a flood are also excludible from gross income. Rev. Rul. 2003-12, 2003-3 IRB 283.

Hurricane Katrina Tax Relief

Cancellations of debt. Under KETRA 2005, gross income does not include any amount that, without this exclusion, would otherwise be includible in gross income because of the discharge of indebtedness of a "natural person" (see below). A "natural person" is one whose principal place of abode on August 25, 2005, was located: (1) inside the "core disaster area" (see below); *or* (2) outside the core disaster area, but in the "Hurricane Katrina disaster area" (see below), *and* the individual suffered economic loss as a result of Hurricane Katrina. Secs. 401(a), 401(b), KETRA 2005. "Hurricane Katrina disaster area" means an area with respect to which a major disaster has been declared by the President before September 14, 2005, under the Robert T. Stafford

INDIVIDUALS   Q 803

Disaster Relief and Emergency Assistance Act by reason of Hurricane Katrina. "Core disaster area" means that portion of the Hurricane Katrina disaster area determined by the President to warrant individual or individual and public assistance from the federal government. Sec 2, KETRA 2005. The debt discharge exclusion does *not* apply to debt incurred in connection with a trade or business, or to any discharge of debt to the extent that real property constituting security for the debt is located outside of the Hurricane Katrina disaster area. Sec. 401(c), KETRA 2005. The exclusion applies to discharges made on or after August 25, 2005, and before January 1, 2007. Sec. 401(e), KETRA 2005.

Mileage reimbursements to charitable volunteers. KETRA 2005 provides that for tax years ending on or after August 25, 2005, gross income of an individual generally does not include amounts received from a qualified charity as reimbursement of operating expenses with respect to use of a passenger vehicle for the benefit of a charity providing relief relating to Hurricane Katrina during the period beginning on August 25, 2005, and ending on December 31, 2006. This exclusion applies *only* to the extent the reimbursed expenses would be deductible if IRC Section 274(d) (i.e., the rule for substantiating certain business expenses) were applied (1) by using the standard business mileage rate in effect at the time of such use, and (2) as if the individual were an employee of an organization *not* described in IRC Section 170(c) (i.e., *not* a qualified charity). Sec 304(a), KETRA 2005.

Leave donation programs. The Service has announced that it will not assert that cash payments an employer makes to charitable organizations in exchange for vacation, sick, or personal leave that its employees elect to forgo constitute gross income or wages of the employees *if* the payments are: (1) made to the charitable organizations for the relief of victims of Hurricane Katrina; *and* (2) paid to the charitable organizations before January 1, 2007. Similarly, the Service will not assert that the opportunity to make such an election results in constructive receipt of gross income or wages for employees. Electing employees may not claim a charitable contribution deduction with respect to the value of foregone leave excluded from compensation and wages. Notice 2005-68, 2005-40 IRB 622. See also IRS News Release IR-2005-97. *ASRS, Sec. 53, ¶¶20.3-20.4.*

803. How are the commissions of a sales representative taxed?

Commissions are generally taxable as ordinary income in the year received, regardless of whether the taxpayer is on a cash or accrual method of accounting, and regardless of whether the taxpayer has a contingent obligation to repay them. Commissions on insurance premiums, however, are a special situation. (See Q 108 regarding the $1 million limitation on the employer's deduction.)

General rule for insurance commissions. First year and renewal commissions are taxable to the agent as ordinary income in the year received. If the agent works on commission with a drawing account, the amount he reports depends upon his contract with the company. If the drawing account is a loan that must be repaid (or upon which he remains personally liable) if he leaves, he reports only commissions actually received. If the drawing account is guaranteed compensation, he reports this compensation and any commissions received in excess of the amount that offsets his draw. This rule applies even if the agent uses the accrual method of accounting. See Rev. Rul. 75-541, 1975-2 CB 195; *Security Assoc. Agency Ins. Corp. v. Comm.*, TC Memo 1987-317; *Dennis v. Comm.*, TC Memo 1997-275. The procedure by which an insurance company may obtain au-

2006 Tax Facts on Insurance & Employee Benefits

tomatic consent to change its method of accounting for cash advances on commissions paid to its agents is set forth in Revenue Procedure 2001-24, 2001-10 IRB 788.

The Tax Court held that an agent's advance commissions were not compensation where they were repayable on demand, bore interest, and were secured by earned commissions as well as by the personal liability of the agent. Thus, even though the amounts were reported to the taxpayer as income on Form 1099-MISC, they were not income. *Gales v. Comm.*, TC Memo 1999-27; acq. in result, 1999-2 CB 3. The IRS determined that cash advances made to an agent by an insurance company *were* income in the year of receipt where the agent was not unconditionally obligated to repay the advances, and any excess in advances over commissions earned would be recovered by the insurance company only by crediting earned commissions and renewals against such advances. TAM 9519002. These positions are consistent with other IRS rulings and prior case law. See Rev. Rul. 83-12, 1983-1 CB 99 (also released as IR 82-150); *Geo. Blood Enter., Inc. v. Comm.*, TC Memo 1976-102. (See Rev. Proc. 83-4, 1983-1 CB 577 for guidance in complying with these rules.) A salesman who was discharged from the obligation to repay advance commissions received in previous years was required to recognize income in the year of discharge. *McIsaac v. Comm.*, TC Memo 1989-307. See also *Cox v. Comm.*, TC Memo 1996-241; *Diers v. Comm.*, TC Memo 2003-229.

The Tax Court has held that amounts received by a district manager upon the termination of his agency contract are treated as ordinary income, and not capital gain resulting from the sale of a capital asset, if the money received was compensation for the termination of the right to receive future income in the form of commissions. *Clark v. Comm.*, TC Memo 1994-278. See also *Farnsworth v. Comm.*, TC Memo 2002-29, *Parker v. Comm.*, TC Memo 2002-305.

The Tax Court also held that where a retired insurance agent did not actually own any company assets he returned to the insurance company upon his retirement, termination payments received by the agent were not proceeds from a sale of capital assets subject to capital gain treatment, but instead were ordinary income. *Baker v. Comm.*, 118 TC 452 (2002), *aff'd*, 2003 U.S. App. LEXIS 15509 (7th Cir. 2003). See also *Trantina. v. United States*, 95 AFTR 2d ¶2005-2830 (D. Ariz. 2005).

Commissions on agent's own policies. Commissions on policies purchased by the agent for himself, on his own life or on the life of another, are taxable to him as ordinary income. Such commissions are considered compensation, not a reduction in the cost of the policies. *Ostheimer v. U.S.*, 264 F.2d 789 (3rd Cir. 1959); Rev. Rul. 55-273, 1955-1 CB 221. This rule applies to brokers as well as to other life insurance salesmen. *Comm. v. Minzer*, 279 F.2d 338 (5th Cir. 1960); *Bailey v. Comm.*, 41 TC 663 (1964); *Mensik v. Comm.*, 37 TC 703 (1962), *aff'd*, 328 F.2d 147 (7th Cir. 1964).

Deferred income plan. If, before he retires, an insurance agent enters into an irrevocable agreement with the insurance company to receive his renewal commissions in level installments over a period of years, only the amount of the annual installment will be taxable to him each year—instead of the full amount of commissions as they accrue. *Comm. v. Oates*, 207 F.2d 711 (7th Cir. 1953); Rev. Rul. 60-31, 1960-1 CB 174; Let. Ruls. 9540033, 9245015. Although the *Oates* case and Rev. Rul. 60-31 concern deferred compensation arrangements during retirement years, the same principle should apply if the agent during his lifetime elects a level commission arrangement for payments after his death. The IRS determined that an insurance agent's contributions of commissions

INDIVIDUALS   Q 803

to his company's nonqualified deferred compensation plan will not be includable in the agent's gross income or subject to self-employment tax until actually distributed. Let. Rul. 9609011. In another case, the insurance company, by agreement with the agent, substituted an annuity contract for its obligation to pay future renewal commissions. The Tax Court and the U.S. Court of Appeals for the Eighth Circuit held that the agreement was effective to defer tax until payments were received under the annuity. *Comm. v. Olmsted Inc. Life Agency*, 35 TC 429 (1960), *aff'd*, 304 F.2d 16 (8th Cir. 1962). However, the IRS did not acquiesce to the *Olmsted* decision (Non-acq., 1961-2 CB 6).

Assignment of renewal commissions. If the agent assigns his right to renewal commissions as a gift, he still must pay income tax on them as they are received by the donee. *Helvering v. Eubank*, 311 U.S. 122 (1940); *Hall v. U.S.*, 242 F.2d 412 (7th Cir. 1957). The Tax Court determined that an insurance agent had to pay income tax on his commission income despite the assignment of that income to his S corporation. The court noted that the agent was the true earner of the income and that he made no valid assignment of his employment agreement with the insurance company. *Isom v. Comm.*, TC Memo 1995-383. In a 1998 memorandum decision, the Tax Court held that an agent's transfer to a corporation of his right to receive renewal commissions was ineffective for tax purposes, since it constituted an anticipatory assignment of income rather than a sale of property. Citing *Helvering v. Eubank*, above, the court held that the commission income continued to be taxable to the agent, not to the corporation to which he transferred the rights. *Zaal v. Comm.*, TC Memo 1998-222.

Sale of renewal commissions. It appears likely that a bona fide, arm's length *sale* of a right to receive renewal commissions can successfully transfer the federal income taxation of renewal commissions to the purchaser. The Court of Appeals for the Second Circuit has held that in the event of a sale of the right to receive renewal commissions, the sale price would constitute ordinary income to the agent in the year received. *Cotlow v. Comm.*, 228 F.2d 186 (2nd Cir. 1955); see also, *Turner v. Comm.*, 38 TC 304 (1962). The court in *Cotlow* added that the purchaser receives the renewals tax free until he recovers his cost; then the excess is taxable to him as ordinary income as it is received. Other cases have held that the purchaser must amortize his cost. In other words, he can exclude from gross income each year only that portion of the purchase price that the renewals received in that year bear to the total anticipated renewals. *Latendresse v. Comm.*, 243 F.2d 577 (7th Cir. 1957); *Hill v. Comm.*, 3 BTA 761 (1926).

Commissions received after agent's death. Commissions owed to an agent before he died, but paid after his death, are includable in his gross income on his final return. Renewal commissions payable after his death are "income in respect of a decedent" (see Q 827); consequently, the value of the right to the commissions is includable in the agent's gross estate. The renewal commissions are taxable income to whomever receives them (e.g., his estate, beneficiaries, or a trust). *Latendresse v. Comm.*, above; *Est. of Goldstein v. Comm.*, 33 TC 1032 (1960), *aff'd*, 340 F.2d 24 (2nd Cir. 1965); *Est. of Remington v. Comm.*, 9 TC 99 (1947). However, the person who receives the commissions is entitled to take an income tax deduction against them for any portion of federal estate taxes and generation-skipping transfer taxes attributable to their value (see Q 827). If the decedent has purchased renewal commissions from another agent, the recipient will be allowed to amortize any portion of the decedent's cost unrecovered at his death. *Latendresse v. Comm.*, above. If the recipient of the right to commissions sells or otherwise disposes of his right to receive them, he is taxed on the fair market value of the right in the year of sale or other disposition (e.g., gift). But if the recipient dies, the fair market value of the right to commissions will not be included in his final return; the person who receives the income right from the second decedent by will or inheritance pays tax on the commissions as they are received by him. IRC Sec. 691(a); Treas. Reg. §1.691(a)-1.

Self-employment tax. Termination payments received by former insurance salesmen are not included in self-employment income if: (1) the amount is received after the termination of the agent's agreement to perform for the company; (2) the agent does not perform services for the company after the date of the termination of the service agreement and before the end of the taxable year; (3) the agent enters into a covenant not to compete with the company for at least a 1-year period beginning on the date of the termination; and (4) the amount of the payment (a) depends primarily on policies sold by or credited to the agent's account during the last year of the service agreement or to the extent such policies remain in effect for some period after termination of service, or both, and (b) does not depend to any extent on the length of service or overall earnings from services performed for such company (without regard to whether eligibility for payment depends on length of service). IRC Sec. 1402(k). For termination payments that do not fall within the above description, earlier case law and rulings may apply.

The Eleventh Circuit Court of Appeals held that the FICA statute does not impliedly provide a private cause of action to purported "employees" – in this case, insurance agents claiming they had been improperly classified as independent contractors – to sue their purported "employer" for nonpayment of the employer's portion of FICA taxes. See *McDonald v. Southern Farm Bureau Life Ins. Co.*, 2002 U.S. App. LEXIS 9110 (11th Cir. 2002). *ASRS, Sec. 53, ¶20.16(b-h).*

804. What is an insurance premium rebate? What are the income tax consequences of rebating premiums?

Generally

Insurance premium rebates are unlawful in most states. A premium rebate is a transaction in which a life insurance agent returns all or a portion of his commission to the purchaser of a life insurance policy, or simply pays the policy's first-year premium without contribution from the purchaser. The amount of the commission, allowance and/or bonus paid by the insurance company to the agent for the sale of the policy often exceeds the policy premium. The purchaser of the policy receives free or less expensive life insurance coverage.

Income Tax to the Agent

As mentioned above, almost all states have anti-rebating statutes that prohibit the sharing of insurance commissions with unlicensed persons. The tax consequences to the agent may vary, depending on the laws of the state in which the agent resides, as well as the position of the respective circuit court. In one state where such an anti-rebating statute was in force, the Ninth Circuit Court of Appeals found that an agent who rebated a premium was considered to have received taxable income in the amount of the total commission earned on the sale of the policy, including any portion used by the agent to rebate the premium to the insured. *Alex v. Comm.*, 628 F.2d 1222 (9th Cir. 1980), *aff'g* 70 TC 322 (1978). The agent in that case argued that the portion of the premium rebated should be excluded from income since the rebate was in the nature of a price adjustment. The court did not agree with this characterization. See also *Custis v. Comm.*, TC Memo 1982-296; *Kreisberg v. Comm.*, TC Memo 1979-420.

Furthermore, the agent in the *Alex* case was not permitted to offset commission income earned on the sale of the policy with a business expense deduction for the payment of premiums because the Code disallows deductions for any payment that is illegal under a generally enforced state law that subjects the payor to a criminal penalty or to the loss of a license or privilege to engage in a trade or business. IRC Sec. 162(c)(2). See *Kreisberg*, above. However, in the *Custis* case, above, an agent who rebated premiums was allowed to deduct the amount of the rebates under IRC Section 162 as business expenses since he was able to show that the state anti-rebating statute was not generally enforced.

The Court of Appeals for the Tenth Circuit decided that an insurance agent who expressly agreed with his clients to waive his right to collect basic commissions on policies sold by him was not in receipt of taxable income. The agent was required to collect and remit only the net premiums due on the policies he sold, which he did. The court found that since he was never in receipt of the basic commissions, taxable income could not be imputed to him. The court did not address the issue of whether the transactions violated state anti-rebating laws. *Worden v. Comm.*, 2 F.3d 359 (10th Cir. 1993).

Income Tax to the Purchaser

A federal district court and the Tax Court have determined that the purchasers of universal and whole life policies are subject to tax on the full amount of any premiums illegally rebated to them by the agents who sold the policies. *Woodbury v. U.S.*, 93-2 USTC ¶50,528 (D. N.D. 1993), *aff'd per curium*, 27 F.3d 572 (8th Cir. 1994); *Wentz v. Comm.*, 105 TC 1 (1995); *Haderlie v. Comm.*, TC Memo 1997-525. The courts rejected the purchasers' argument that the agents' reimbursements were really price adjustments. The court in *Woodbury* stated that the reimbursements were analogous to kickbacks and, as such, were includable in the purchasers' gross income. The court also rejected the purchasers' argument that their tax liability should be limited to the term element of the universal life policies. The fact that the purchasers did not intend to renew the policies did not convert the universal policies into term life insurance for tax purposes. The Tax Court has expressed its agreement with the district court's conclusions set forth in the *Woodbury* decision. In *Wentz*, it noted that the insurance agent was, in effect, a purchaser of the policies, and that he realized income in the amount of the kickbacks. Both the Tax Court and the *Woodbury* district court stated that the taxation of both the seller and the purchaser engaged in such an illegal scheme was permissible.

The Service has concluded that the purchaser of a life insurance policy is subject to income tax on the value of the free insurance coverage obtained as a result of receiving a premium rebate. TAMs 9214008, 9214007, 9214006. However, the Service stated that the valuation process itself was outside the scope of the memoranda; thus, it is unclear how the Service will calculate the actual value of the free coverage. (See Q 458 and Q 424 for an explanation of how employer-provided life insurance coverage is valued under split dollar arrangements and qualified retirement plans, respectively.) *ASRS, Sec. 53, ¶¶20.5(a), 20.16(a), 20.16(b).*

805. What are the income tax consequences of below market loans?

Editor's Note: The Sarbanes-Oxley Act of 2002 (P.L. 107-204) adopts new securities law provisions intended to deter and punish corporate and accounting fraud and corruption, ensure justice for wrongdoers, and protect the interests of workers and shareholders of publicly-traded corporations. However, it would appear that one provision of the Act indirectly impacts below market loans made to executives of publicly-traded corporations. See "Securities law restrictions on personal loans," below.

A below market loan is generally a demand loan with an interest rate that is below the *applicable federal rate* or a term loan in which the amount received by the borrower exceeds the present value of all payments due under the loan (in other words, a below market loan is a loan in which some amount of interest is deemed to have been forgone by the lender). A demand loan is a loan that is payable in full at any time on the demand of the lender, or that has an indefinite maturity; generally, all other loans are term loans. IRC Secs. 7872(e), 7872(f). The Code essentially recharacterizes a below market loan as two transactions: (1) an arm's-length loan requiring payment of interest at the applicable federal rate, and (2) a transfer of funds by the lender to the borrower ("imputed transfer"). Prop. Treas. Reg. §1.7872-1(a).

If the forgoing of interest on a below market demand or term loan is in the nature of a gift, the lender is deemed to have transferred to the borrower and the borrower is deemed to have transferred to the lender an amount equal to the forgone interest. IRC Sec. 7872(a)(1). As a result, the amount of forgone interest must be included in the gross income of the lender. On the other hand, deductibility by the borrower depends on how the interest is classified for tax purposes (i.e., personal, passive, etc.–see Q 823). For the gift tax consequences of below market gift loans, see Q 904.

For the treatment of below market split dollar loans, see Treas. Reg. §1.7872-15 and Notice 2002-8, 2002-1 CB 398. For the treatment of split dollar loans, generally, see Q 458.

If a *demand* loan is compensation-related (e.g., employer to employee) or a corporation-shareholder loan, a transfer and retransfer of forgone interest is also deemed to have occurred. Prop. Treas. Regs. §§1.7872-4(c), 1.7872-4(d). The lender has interest income to the extent of the forgone interest and generally a corresponding deduction for compensation paid (but there is no deduction in the case of a corporation-shareholder loan). The borrower has includable compensation (or dividend) income, but a deduction for the forgone interest is subject to the limitations on interest deductions (see Q 823). If a *term* loan is compensation-related or a corporation-shareholder loan, the lender is deemed to have transferred to the borrower and the borrower is deemed to have received a cash payment equal to the *excess of* the amount loaned *over* the present value (determined as of the date of the loan, discounted at the applicable federal rate) of all payments required to be made under the terms of the loan. This excess is treated as original issue discount transferred on the day the loan was made. IRC Sec. 7872(b). The lender deducts the amount treated as original issue discount as compensation (but no deduction is available in the case of a corporation-shareholder loan) and includes the amount as interest income as it accrues over the term of the loan. The borrower has includable compensation (or dividend) income on the day the loan is made, but deductions (if allowed–see Q 823) for the "imputed" interest can be taken only as such interest accrues over the loan period.

In a case of first impression involving below market loans made to noncontrolling shareholders, the Tax Court held that the below market loan rules may apply to a loan to a majority *or* a minority shareholder. The court also held that direct *and* indirect loans are subject to these rules. *Rountree Cotton, Inc. v. Comm.*, 113 TC 422 (1999), *aff'd per curiam*, 87 AFTR2d ¶2001-718 (10th Cir. 2001).

INDIVIDUALS Q 805

Below market loans (other than those discussed above) in which one of the principal purposes is tax avoidance or, to the extent provided for in regulations, in which the interest arrangements have a significant effect on the federal tax liability of either party, are also subject to these rules. IRC Secs. 7872(c)(1)(D), 7872(c)(1)(E). (The Service has determined that certain loans, including life insurance policy loans, do not have such an effect, and, unless one of the principal purposes is tax avoidance, such transactions are not subject to the below market loan rules. Temp. Treas. Reg. §1.7872-5T.)

Certain de minimis rules limit the application of the below market loan rules. With respect to gift loans, the below market loan rules apply only to individuals between whom the aggregate total of all loans exceeds $10,000 (however, special rules govern gift loans that are directly attributable to the purchase or carrying of income-producing assets). IRC Sec. 7872(c)(2). Compensation-related loans and corporation-shareholder loans, whether demand or term, are not subject to either of the above rules if the aggregate outstanding amount does not exceed $10,000 (see IRC Sec. 7872(c)(3)); however, with respect to term loans that are not gift loans, once the aggregate outstanding amount exceeds $10,000, this de minimis exception no longer applies, even if the outstanding balance is later reduced below $10,000. IRC Sec. 7872(f)(10).

Applicable federal rates are determined and published by the Secretary on a monthly basis. IRC Sec. 1274(d). A blended annual rate is published annually in July. The blended annual rate for calendar year 2005 is 3.11%. Rev. Rul. 2005-38, 2005-27 IRB 6. The Secretary may by regulation permit a rate that is lower than the applicable federal rate to be used under certain circumstances. See IRC Sec. 1274(d)(1)(D).

For additional IRS guidance on arm's length issues, the timing of interest recognition and the allocation of interest and principal, see Market Specialization Program (MSSP) Audit Technique Guide on Shareholder Loans. This IRS guide can be viewed or downloaded at the following address: www.irs.gov/pub/irs-mssp/a8shloan.pdf.

Securities law restrictions on personal loans. Section 402 of the Sarbanes-Oxley Act of 2002 (P.L. 107-204) amends Section 13 of the Securities and Exchange Act of 1934 (15 USC 78m) to prohibit "issuers" (i.e., publicly-traded companies) from directly or indirectly (1) extending or maintaining credit, or (2) arranging for the extension of credit, or renewing an extension of credit, in the form of a personal loan to or for any director or executive officer (or equivalent) of that issuer. The narrow exceptions to this rule are loans made for the following purposes: home improvement; consumer credit; any extension of credit under an open-end credit plan; a charge card; or any extension of credit by a broker or dealer to buy, trade, or carry securities. To fall within the exception, the loan must also be (1) made or provided in the ordinary course of business of the company, (2) of a type that is generally made available by the company to the public, and (3) made on market terms, or terms that are no more favorable than those offered by the issuer to the general public for such extensions of credit.

Thus, it would appear that a below market loan made by a publicly-traded company to a director or executive officer for a purpose other than those outlined in the exceptions would be prohibited under the new securities law. Extensions of credit maintained by a company on July 30, 2002 are not subject to the prohibition so long as no material modification is made to any term of the loan and the loan is not renewed on or after that date. *ASRS, Sec. 53, ¶20.3(a); Sec. 63, ¶150.*

2006 Tax Facts on Insurance & Employee Benefits

806. What is an installment sale? How is it taxed?

An installment sale is a disposition of property (other than marketable securities, certain real property, and "inventory") where at least one payment is to be received by the seller after the close of the taxable year in which the disposition occurs. IRC Sec. 453(b). It is not necessary that there be more than one payment. Loss cannot be reported on the installment method. See IRC Sec. 453.

Unless the taxpayer *elects out* on or before the due date, including extensions, for filing his federal income tax return for the taxable year in which the disposition occurred, any gain must be reported under this method. IRC Secs. 453(a), 453(d); *Bolton v. Comm.*, 92 TC 303 (1989). An election out is made by reporting all of the gain on the transaction in the year of the sale. A decision by the taxpayer not to elect out is generally irrevocable unless the IRS finds that the taxpayer had good cause for failure to make a timely election. Temp. Treas. Reg. §15A.453-1(d); Rev. Rul. 90-46, 1990-1 CB 107. Good cause will not be found if the purpose of a late election out is tax avoidance. Let. Rul. 9230003. However, where a taxpayer intended to use the installment method but failed to do so through his accountant's error, the IRS permitted the taxpayer to revoke his election out of the installment method. Let. Rul. 9218012. See also Let. Rul. 200226039. Similarly, the IRS has granted permission to revoke an election out where the election was not the result of a conscious choice by the taxpayer. Let. Ruls. 9419012, 9345027. But see *Krause v. Comm.*, TC Memo 2000-343 (holding that an election out will not be revoked when one of the purposes for the revocation is the avoidance of federal income taxes).

Under the installment method, the total payment is divided into (a) return of the seller's investment, (b) profit, and (c) interest income. Generally, where the sale price is over $3,000 and any payment is deferred more than one year, interest must be charged on payments due more than six months after the sale at least at 100% of the "applicable federal rate," compounded semiannually, or it will be imputed at that rate. IRC Sec. 483.

The applicable federal rate (see Q 805) will be the lowest of the AFRs in effect for any month in the 3-month period ending with the first calendar month in which there is a binding contract in writing. IRC Sec. 1274(d)(2)(B).

All interest received by the taxpayer is ordinary income. Treas. Reg. §1.483-1. In some cases, depending on the property and amount involved, the interest (or imputed interest) to be paid over the period of the loan must be reported as "original issue discount" that accrues in daily portions; in other cases the interest is allocated among the payments and that much of each payment is treated as interest includable and deductible according to the accounting method of the buyer and seller.

Interest surcharge. In the case of installment sales obligations arising from the dispositions of any property with a sales price exceeding $150,000 (with three exceptions) there is generally an interest surcharge to the extent that deferred payments for sales during the taxable year exceed $5,000,000. The exceptions to this rule are: (1) property used or produced in the trade or business of farming, (2) timeshares and residential lots, and (3) personal use property. IRC Sec. 453A(b).

INDIVIDUALS

Q 807

Planning Point: This interest surcharge on installment sales with deferred payments can be minimized in some cases by splitting the sale between a husband and wife, and in two taxable years. For example, a $20 million business owned by a couple could be split into two $10 million sales, and the transaction could be completed in two stages: $5 million per spouse in December, followed by $5 million per spouse in January. Structured this way, the sale would not trigger the interest surcharge. – *Robert S. Keebler, CPA, MST, Virchow, Krause & Company, LLP, Green Bay, Wisconsin.*

Depreciation recapture. Once interest is segregated, recapture of depreciation is recognized as ordinary income in the year of sale to the extent of gain on the sale. IRC Sec. 453(i). Any gain in excess of recaptured depreciation is allocated to each payment by determining a profit percentage (ratio of total profit to be realized to total selling price, exclusive of interest) that is applied to the noninterest portion of each installment. See IRC Sec. 453(c). Thus, if the selling price (the principal amount or imputed principal amount) is $10,000 and the total profit to be realized after depreciation recapture is $2,000, 20% ($2,000/$10,000) of each dollar collected (after segregating interest) is gain that must be reported as income for that taxable year. Whether the gain is capital gain or ordinary income is determined by the type of asset sold.

Sales between related parties. There are strict rules governing installment reporting of sales between "related" parties. If a related purchaser disposes of the property before the related seller has received the entire selling price, a special "second disposition" rule applies. This rule provides that the amount realized on the second disposition (to the extent it exceeds payments already received by the related seller) will be treated as though it had been received by the related seller *on the date of the second disposition*. In other words, his gain is accelerated. However, this rule generally does not apply if: the second disposition occurs more than two years after the first disposition; the second disposition is an involuntary conversion, the threat of which did not exist at the time of the first disposition; the second disposition occurs after the death of either of the related parties; or neither disposition had as one of its principal purposes the avoidance of income tax. IRC Sec. 453(e). If an installment sale between related parties is canceled or payment is forgiven, the *seller* must recognize gain in an amount equal to the difference between the fair market value of the obligation on the date of cancellation (but in no event less than the face amount of the obligation) and the seller's basis in the obligation. IRC Sec. 453B(f).

A sale of depreciable property between related parties may not be reported on the installment method, unless it is shown that avoidance of income tax was not a principal purpose. For purposes of this rule only, "related persons" refers generally to controlled business entities, not natural persons related by family. IRC Sec. 453(g).

JGTRRA 2003 reduced capital gain rates for sales or exchanges occurring on or after May 6, 2003 and before January 1, 2009. IRC Sec. 1(h). For the tax treatment of installment payments, see Q 815. *ASRS, Sec. 53, ¶20.9.*

807. Are Social Security and railroad retirement benefits taxable?

If a taxpayer's modified adjusted gross income plus one-half of the Social Security benefits (including tier I railroad retirement benefits) received during the taxable year *exceeds* certain base amounts, then a portion of the benefits received must be included in gross income and taxed as ordinary income. "Modified adjusted gross income" is a taxpayer's adjusted gross income (disregarding the foreign income, savings bond and adoption assistance program exclusions, the deduction for education loan interest, and the deduction for qualified tuition and related expenses) plus any tax-exempt interest income received or accrued during the taxable year. IRC Sec. 86(b)(2).

A taxpayer whose modified adjusted gross income plus one-half of his Social Security benefits exceed a base amount is required to include in gross income the *lesser* of (a) 50% of the excess of such combined income over the base amount, *or* (b) 50% of the Social Security benefits received during the taxable year. IRC Sec. 86(a)(1). The "base amount" is $32,000 for married taxpayers filing jointly, $25,000 for unmarried taxpayers, and zero ($0) for married taxpayers filing separately who have not lived apart for the entire taxable year. IRC Sec. 86(c)(1).

In a case of first impression, the Tax Court held that for purposes of IRC Section 86(c)(1)(C)(ii), the term "live apart" means living in separate residences. Thus, where the taxpayer lived in the same residence as his spouse for at least 30 days during the tax year in question (even though maintaining separate bedrooms), the Tax Court ruled that he did not "live apart" from his spouse at all times during the year; therefore, the taxpayer's base amount was zero. *McAdams v. Comm.*, 118 TC 373 (2002).

In addition to the initial tier of taxation as discussed above, a percentage of Social Security benefits that exceed an adjusted base amount will be includable in a taxpayer's gross income. The "adjusted base amount" is $44,000 for married taxpayers filing jointly, $34,000 for unmarried taxpayers, and zero ($0) for married individuals filing separately who did not live apart for the entire taxable year. IRC Sec. 86(c)(2). If a taxpayer's modified adjusted gross income plus one-half of his Social Security benefits exceed the adjusted base amount, his gross income will include the *lesser* of (a) 85% of the Social Security benefits received during the year, *or* (b) the sum of – (i) 85% of the excess over the adjusted base amount, plus (ii) the smaller of – (A) the amount that is includable under the initial tier of taxation (see above), or (B) $4,500 (single taxpayers) or $6,000 (married taxpayers filing jointly). IRC Sec. 86(a)(2).

Example 1. Mr. and Mrs. Franklin are a married couple who file a joint return. During the taxable year, the Franklins received $12,000 in Social Security benefits and had a modified adjusted gross income of $35,000 ($28,000 plus $7,000 of tax-exempt interest income). Their modified adjusted gross income plus one-half of their Social Security benefits [$35,000 + (1/2 of $12,000) = $41,000] is greater than the applicable *base amount* of $32,000 but less than the applicable *adjusted base amount* of $44,000; therefore, $4,500 [the lesser of one-half of their benefits ($6,000) or one-half of the excess of $41,000 over the base amount (1/2 × ($41,000 - $32,000), or $4,500)] is included in gross income.

Example 2. During the taxable year, Mr. Murray, a single individual, had a modified adjusted gross income of $33,000 and received $8,000 in Social Security benefits. Mr. Murray's modified adjusted gross income plus one-half of his Social Security benefits [$33,000 + (1/2 of $8,000) = $37,000] is greater than the applicable *adjusted base amount* of $34,000. Thus, $6,550 [the lesser of 85% of his benefits ($6,800), or 85% of the excess of $37,000 over the adjusted base amount (85% × ($37,000 - $34,000), or $2,550) plus the lesser of $4,000 (the amount includable under the initial tier of taxation) or $4,500] is included in gross income.

An election is available that permits a taxpayer to treat a lump sum payment of benefits as received in the year to which the benefits are attributable. IRC Sec. 86(e).

Any workers' compensation pay that reduced the amount of Social Security received and any amounts withheld to pay Medicare insurance premiums are included in the figure for Social Security benefits. Rev. Rul. 84-173, 1984-2 CB 16.

Tax-exempt interest is included in the calculation made to determine whether Social Security payments are includable in gross income. IRC Sec. 86(b)(2)(B). It has been determined that although this provision may result in indirect taxation of tax-exempt interest, it is not unconstitutional. *Goldin v. Baker*, 809 F.2d 187 (2nd Cir. 1987), *cert. denied*, 484 U.S. 816 (1988).

Railroad retirement benefits (other than tier I benefits) are taxed like benefits received under a qualified pension or profit sharing plan. For this purpose, the tier II portion of the taxes imposed on employees and employee representatives is treated as an employee contribution, while the tier II portion of the taxes imposed on employers is treated as an employer contribution. See Q 430, Q 433. Legislation enacted in 2001 provides increased benefits for surviving spouses and adjustments to the tier II tax rates. See Secs. 101 and 204, The Railroad Retirement and Survivors' Improvement Act of 2001. *ASRS, Sec. 15, ¶50.1; Sec. 16, ¶50.4.*

808. Are alimony payments included in the gross income of the recipient? May the payor spouse take a deduction for these payments?

Alimony and separate maintenance payments generally are taxable to the recipient and deductible from gross income by the payor (even if he does not itemize). IRC Secs. 71(a), 215(a). Payments of arrearages from prior years are taxed to a cash basis taxpayer in the year of receipt. *Coleman v. Comm.*, TC Memo 1988-442. Arrearages paid to the estate of a former spouse are taxed as income in respect of a decedent (see Q 827). *Kitch v. Comm.*, 97-1 USTC ¶50,124 (10th Cir. 1996).

A payment received by (or on behalf of) a recipient spouse pursuant to a divorce or separation instrument executed after 1984 is an alimony or separate maintenance payment if: (1) the payment is made in cash; (2) the divorce or separation instrument does not designate the payment as *not* includable or deductible as alimony (see *Richardson v. Comm.* 125 F.3d 551 (7th Cir. 1997), *aff'g* T.C. Memo 1995-554; see also Let. Rul. 200141036); (3) there is no liability to make the payments after the death of the recipient (see, e.g., *Okerson v. Comm.*, 123 TC No. 14 (2004)); and (4) if the individuals are legally separated under a decree of divorce or separate maintenance, the spouses are not members of the same household at the time the payment is made. IRC Sec. 71(b). Lump sum payments made by a husband to his former wife under a consent judgment were not deductible under IRC Section 215(a) except to the extent the lump sum constituted past due alimony. *Barrett v. U.S.*, (unpublished opinion) No. 95-60114 (5th Cir. Feb. 9, 1996).

The failure of the divorce or separation instrument to provide for termination of payments at the death of the recipient will *not* disqualify payments from alimony treatment. See IRC Sec. 71(b)(1)(D); TRA '86 Conf. Rept. at page 849. However, if both the divorce instrument and state law fail to provide for termination of payments at death, such payments may be disqualified from receiving alimony treatment. *Hoover v. Comm.*, 97-1 USTC ¶50,111 (6th Cir. 1996); *Ribera v. Comm.*, TC Memo 1997-38. See also *Thomas D. Berry v. Comm.*, 2002 U.S. App. LEXIS 10785 (10th Cir. 2002), *aff'g*, TC Memo 2000-373; *Lovejoy v. Comm.*, 293 F.3d 1208 (10th Cir. 2002), *aff'g*, *Miller v. Comm.*, TC Memo 1999-273. But see *Kean v. Comm.*, 2005-1 USTC ¶50,397 (3rd Cir. 2005), *aff'g*, TC Memo 2003-163; *Michael K. Berry v. Comm.*, TC Memo 2005-91.

The deduction for alimony paid is limited to the amount required under the divorce or separation instrument. *Ritchie v. Comm.*, TC Memo 1989-426. A divorce or separation instrument includes any decree of divorce or separate maintenance or a written instrument incident to such, a written separation agreement, or other decree requiring spousal support or maintenance payments. IRC Sec. 71(b). An attorney's letter detailing a settlement agreement was held to constitute a separation instrument for purposes of determining whether payments made thereunder were alimony. *Azenaro v. Comm.*, TC Memo 1989-224. However, a list of expenses by the former wife, negotiation letters between attorneys, notations on the husband's check to his former wife indicating support, and the fact that the husband actually provided support did not constitute a written separation agreement for purposes of IRC Sections 71(b)(2) and 215. *Ewell v. Comm.*, TC Memo 1996-253.

Payments made voluntarily by a husband to his spouse, which were not mandated by a qualifying divorce decree or separation instrument, were not deductible to the husband. *Meyer v. Comm.* TC Memo 2003-12. The Tax Court held that a contract for deed is a third-party debt instrument; consequently, the taxpayer could not deduct the value of the contract for deed transferred to his former spouse as alimony because it did not constitute a cash payment. *Lofstron v. Comm.*, 125 TC No. 13 (2005). In deciding whether the transfer of ownership of an annuity contract itself constituted alimony, the Service determined that because IRC Section 71 and the Treasury regulations make it clear that in order to constitute alimony a payment must be in cash, the transfer of ownership of the annuity contract to the taxpayer in this instance did not constitute alimony includible in the taxpayer's gross income. Let. Rul. 200536014

Where a beneficial interest in a trust is transferred or created incident to a divorce or separation, the payments by the trust to the beneficiary spouse will be treated the same as payments to a trust beneficiary under IRC Section 682, disregarding that the payments may qualify as alimony. Thus, instead of including payments entirely as ordinary income, the beneficiary spouse may be entitled to the flow-through of tax-exempt income. In any event, no deduction will be allowed to the grantor for payments by the trust that are not includable as income to the beneficiary spouse. IRC Sec. 215(d).

When a payor spouse claims alimony payments as a deduction, he is required to furnish the recipient spouse's Social Security number on his tax return for each taxable year the payments are made. Temp. Treas. Reg. §1.215-1T(A-1). Alimony paid by a U.S. citizen spouse to a foreign spouse is deductible by the payor spouse even though the recipient is not taxable on the income under a treaty; however, the penalty for failing to include the recipient's Taxpayer Identification Number (TIN) on the payor's tax return may still apply. Legal Memo. 200251004.

Alimony recapture rules generally require recapture in the third post-separation year of "excess" payments (i.e., disproportionately large payments made in either the first or second years—or both—that are deemed to represent nondeductible property settlements previously deducted as alimony). The first post-separation year is the first calendar year in which payments are made; the second and third years are the second and third calendar years thereafter. The amount recaptured is included in the income of the payor spouse and deducted from the gross income of the recipient. The amount recaptured is determined by first comparing the alimony payments made for the second and third post-separation years. If payments during the second year exceed the payments during the third year by more than $15,000, the excess is "recaptured." Next, the payments during the first year are compared with the average of the payments made during the second year (as reduced by any recaptured excess) and the payments made during the third year. If the payments made during the first year exceed the average of the amounts paid during the second (as reduced) and third years by more than $15,000, the excess is also recaptured. IRC Sec. 71(f).

There are limited exceptions to the recapture rules; if payments cease because of the marriage of the recipient or the death of either spouse before the close of the third separation year, or to the extent payments required over at least a 3-year period are tied to a fixed portion of income from a business or property or compensation, the rule will not apply. Furthermore, payments under temporary support orders do not come within the recapture rules. IRC Sec. 71(f); Temp. Treas. Reg. §1.71-1T(d)(A-25).

Child support. Any portion of a payment specified in the divorce or separation instrument as payable for child support is not treated as alimony. IRC Sec. 71(c). In *Freyre v. U.S.*, No. 04-5580 (6th Cir. 2005.), the appeals court held that because the divorce court order did not specifically designate or fix the disputed monthly payments as child support, as required in the statute (IRC Sec. 71(c)(1)) and the treasury regulations (Treas. Reg. §1.71-1(e)), the payments had to be considered as alimony and, thus, were deductible by the taxpayer. See also *Preston v. Comm.*, 209 F.3d 1281 (11th Cir. 2000). Premiums paid by a husband on his former wife's whole life insurance policy (with their handicapped minor child named as beneficiary) were treated as alimony where the support decree had not specifically designated the premium payments as child support. *Marten v. Comm.*, TC Memo 1999-340, *on motion for reconsideration, holding reaffirmed in* TC Memo 2000-185; *aff'd per curiam, Comm. v. Lane*, 2002 U.S. App. LEXIS 8367 (9th Cir. 2002). Child support payments are considered a legal obligation of the payor and thus are taxable to the payor, not to the payee. A parent was required to include in his gross income the portion of a distribution from his pension plan that was used to satisfy a back child support obligation. *Stahl v. Comm.*, TC Memo 2001-22. Any payment that is less than the amount specified in the divorce or separation instrument is applied first as child support and treated as alimony only after the specified child support payment has been met. IRC Sec. 71(c)(3); *Blair v. Comm.*, TC Memo 1988-581. *ASRS, Sec. 53, ¶20.5(k).*

809. Who is taxed on the income from property that is transferred to a minor under a uniform "Gifts to Minors" act?

As a general rule, the income is taxable to the minor. However, in the case of *unearned* income of most children under age 14, the unearned income taxable to the child generally will be taxed at his parents' marginal rate (see Q 818). To the extent that income from the transferred property is used for the minor's support, it may be taxed to the person who is legally obligated to support the minor. Rev. Rul. 56-484, 1956-2 CB 23; Rev. Rul. 59-357, 1959-2 CB 212. State laws differ as to a parent's obligation to support. The income will be taxable to the parent only to the extent that it is actually used to discharge or satisfy the parent's obligation under state law. IRC Sec. 677(b). *ASRS, Sec. 48, ¶510.1; Sec. 53, ¶20.7.*

810. What is an Education Savings Account?

Education IRAs were renamed Coverdell Education Savings Accounts (ESAs) in 2001. P.L. 107-22 (7-26-2001). An ESA means a trust or custodial account created exclusively for the purpose of paying the "qualified education expenses" of the designated beneficiary of the trust, and that is designated as an ESA at the time it is created. IRC

Secs. 530(b), 530(g). The designated beneficiary of an ESA must be a life-in-being as of the time the account is established. IRC Sec. 530(b)(1). ESAs are exempt from taxation (except for unrelated business income tax, if applicable). IRC Sec. 530(a). Distributions from ESAs for "qualified education expenses" are not includable in income and contributions to ESAs are not deductible. IRC Sec. 530(d).

Annual contributions may be made up until the due date (excluding extensions) for filing the tax return for the calendar year for which such contributions were intended. IRC Sec. 530(b)(5).

Contributions must be made in cash and must be made on or before the date on which the beneficiary attains age 18 unless the beneficiary is a special needs beneficiary. A special needs beneficiary is to be defined in Treasury regulations; however, according to the Conference Report, a special needs beneficiary will include an individual who because of a physical, mental, or emotional condition (including learning disabilities) requires additional time to complete his or her education. IRC Sec. 530(b)(1).

In general, aggregate contributions to an ESA on behalf of a beneficiary (except in the case of rollover contributions) cannot exceed $2,000. IRC Sec. 530(b)(1)(A)(iii). The maximum contribution amount is phased-out for certain high-income contributors. The maximum contribution for single filers is reduced by the amount that bears the same ratio to such maximum amount as the contributor's *modified adjusted gross income* (MAGI) in excess of $95,000 bears to $15,000. IRC Sec. 530(c)(1). For joint filers, the maximum contribution is reduced by the amount that bears the same ratio to such maximum amount as the contributor's MAGI in excess of $190,000 bears to $30,000. IRC Sec. 530(c)(1). For this purpose, MAGI is adjusted gross income without regard to the exclusions for income derived from certain foreign sources or sources within United States possessions. IRC Sec. 530(c)(2). For taxable years beginning after 2001, contributions to an ESA are not limited due to contributions made to a qualified state tuition program in the same year.

Contributions in excess of the maximum annual contribution (as reduced for high-income contributors) that are not returned before the first day of the sixth month of the taxable year following the taxable year in which the contribution was made are subject to the 6% excess contribution excise tax under Code section 4973(a). IRC Sec. 4973(e)(2). Note that any excess contributions from previous taxable years, to the extent not corrected, will continue to be taxed as excess contributions in subsequent taxable years. IRC Sec. 4973(e).

A distribution from an ESA is subject to income tax using the IRC Section 72(b) exclusion ratio for investment in the contract. IRC Sec. 530(d)(1). However, distributions from an ESA are excludable from income tax if the distributions received during the year are used solely for the "qualified education expenses" (see below) of the designated beneficiary. IRC Sec. 530(d)(2)(A).

"Qualified education expenses" include both "qualified *higher* education expenses" and "qualified *elementary* and *secondary* education expenses." IRC Sec. 530(b)(2). "Qualified higher education expenses" include tuition, fees, costs for books, supplies, and equipment required for the enrollment or attendance of the student at any "eligible educational institution," and amounts contributed to a qualified tuition program. IRC Secs. 529(e)(3), 530(b)(2). Room and board (up to a certain amount) is also included if the student is enrolled at least half-time. IRC Sec. 530(b)(2). An "eligible educational institution" is any college, university, vocational school, or other postsecondary educational institution described in section 481 of the Higher Education Act of 1965. See IRC Sec. 529(e)(5). Thus, virtually all accredited public, nonprofit, and proprietary postsecondary institutions are considered eligible educational institutions. Notice 97-60, 1997-2 CB 310, at 16 (Sec. 3, A16).

Qualified education expenses must be reduced by any scholarships received by the individual, any educational assistance provided to the individual, or any payment for such expenses (other than a gift, devise, bequest, or inheritance) that is excludable from gross income. These expenses must also be reduced by the amount of any such expenses that were taken into account in determining the Hope Scholarship Credit or the Lifetime Learning Credit. IRC Sec. 530(d)(2)(C). (Note that for taxable years beginning before 2002 these education credits could not be claimed in a taxable year in which distributions from an ESA were excluded from income. IRC Sec. 25A(e)(2), prior to amendment by EGTRRA 2001.)

"Qualified elementary and secondary education expenses" include tuition, fees, and costs for academic tutoring, special needs services, books, supplies, and other equipment that are incurred in connection with the enrollment or attendance of the designated beneficiary at any public, private, or religious school that provides elementary or secondary education (K through 12) as determined under state law. Also included are expenses for room and board, uniforms, transportation, supplementary items and services (including extended day programs) that are required or provided by such schools, and any computer technology or certain related equipment used by the beneficiary and the beneficiary's family during any of the years the beneficiary is in school. IRC Sec. 530(b)(4).

If a designated beneficiary receives distributions from both an ESA and a qualified tuition program and the aggregate distributions exceed the qualified education expenses of the designated beneficiary, then the expenses must be allocated among such distributions for purposes of determining the amount excludable under each. IRC Sec. 530(d)(2)(C)(ii). Any qualified education expenses taken into account for purposes of this exclusion may not be taken into account for purposes of any other deductions, credits, or exclusions. IRC Sec. 530(d)(2)(D).

Where distributions from the ESA exceed the qualified education expenses of the designated beneficiary for the year, the amount includable is determined by: (1) calculating the amount subject to tax under IRC Section 72(b) (without regard to the following proration); (2) multiplying the amount in (1) by the ratio of qualified education expenses to total distributions; and (3) subtracting the amount in (2) from the amount in (1). IRC Sec. 530(d)(2)(B).

If a distribution from an ESA is includable in the income of the recipient, the amount includable in income will be subject to an additional 10% penalty tax unless the distribution is (1) made after the death of the beneficiary of the ESA, (2) attributable to the disability of such beneficiary (within the meaning of IRC Section 72(m)(7)), (3) made in an amount equal to a scholarship, allowance, or other payment under IRC Section 25A(g)(2), or (4) includable in income because expenses were reduced by the amount claimed as a Hope Scholarship Credit or a Lifetime Learning Credit. IRC Sec. 530(d)(4). The penalty tax also does not apply to any distribution of an excess contribution and the earnings thereon if such contribution and earnings are distributed before the first day of the sixth month of the taxable year following the taxable year in which the contribution was made. IRC Sec. 530(d)(4)(C). However, the earnings are includable in the contributor's income for the taxable year in which such excess contribution was made.

No part of the assets of the ESA can be used to purchase life insurance. IRC Sec. 530(b)(1)(C). Nor can the assets of the ESA be commingled with other property except in a common trust fund or common investment fund. IRC Sec. 530(b)(1)(D). If the beneficiary engages in a prohibited transaction, the account loses its status as an ESA and will be treated as distributing all of its assets. If the beneficiary pledges the account as security for a loan, the amount so pledged will be treated as a distribution from the account. IRC Sec. 530(e).

An amount may be rolled over from one ESA to another ESA, without being treated as a distribution (and without being subject to taxation) *only* if the beneficiary of the recipient ESA is the same as the beneficiary of the original ESA, or a member of such beneficiary's family. The new beneficiary must be under age 30 as of the date of such distribution or change, except in the case of a special needs beneficiary. IRC Sec. 530(b)(1). The rollover contribution must be made no later than 60 days after the date of the distribution from the original ESA. However, no more than one rollover may be made from an ESA during any 12-month period. IRC Sec. 530(d)(5). Similarly, the beneficiary of an ESA may be changed without taxation or penalty if the new beneficiary is a member of the family of the previous ESA beneficiary and has not attained age 30 or is a special needs beneficiary. IRC Secs. 530(b)(1), 530(d)(6). Transfer of an individual's interest in an ESA can be made from one spouse to another pursuant to a divorce (or upon the death of a spouse) without changing the character of the ESA. IRC Sec. 530(d)(7). Likewise, non-spouse survivors who acquire an original beneficiary's interest in an ESA upon the death of the beneficiary will be treated as the original beneficiary of the ESA as long as the new beneficiary is a family member of the original beneficiary. IRC Sec. 530(d)(7).

Upon the death of the beneficiary of the ESA, any balance to the credit of the beneficiary must be distributed to his estate within 30 days. The balance remaining in an ESA must also be distributed within 30 days after a beneficiary, other than a special needs beneficiary, reaches age 30. IRC Sec. 530(b)(1)(E). Any balance remaining in the ESA is deemed distributed within 30 days after such events. IRC Sec. 530(d)(8). The earnings on any distribution under this provision are includable in the beneficiary's gross income. IRC Sec. 530(d)(1).

Under Section 225 of BAPCPA 2005, funds placed in an "education individual retirement account" (as defined in IRC Section 530(b)(1)) no later than 365 days before the date of the filing of the bankruptcy petition may be excluded from the bankruptcy estate if certain conditions are met. 11 USC 541(b), as amended by BAPCPA 2005.

For guidance regarding certain reporting requirements and transition rules applicable to Coverdell ESAs, see Notice 2003-53, 2003-33 IRB 362. See Q 858 for the estate tax treatment and Q 905 for the gift tax treatment of ESAs. *ASRS, Sec. 62, ¶450.*

811. What is a qualified tuition program and how are contributions taxed?

A qualified tuition program (QTP) is a program established and maintained by a state (or agency or instrumentality thereof) *or* by one or more "eligible educational

INDIVIDUALS   Q 811

institutions" (see below) that meet certain requirements (see below) *and* under which a person may buy tuition credits or certificates on behalf of a "designated beneficiary" (see below) that entitle the beneficiary to a waiver or payment of "qualified higher education expenses" (see below) of the beneficiary. These plans are often collectively referred to as "529 plans." In the case of a state-sponsored qualified tuition program, a person may make contributions to an account established to fund the qualified higher education expenses of a designated beneficiary. IRC Sec. 529(b)(1); Prop. Treas. Reg. §1.529-2(b). Qualified tuition programs sponsored by "eligible educational institutions" (i.e., private colleges and universities) are *not* permitted to offer savings plans; these institutions may sponsor only pre-paid tuition programs. IRC Sec. 529(b)(1)(A).

To be treated as a qualified tuition program, a state program or privately sponsored program must: (1) mandate that contributions and purchases be made in cash only; (2) maintain a separate accounting for each designated beneficiary; (3) provide that no designated beneficiary or contributor may directly or indirectly direct the investment of contributions or earnings (but see below); (4) not allow any interest in the program or portion thereof to be used as security for a loan; *and* (5) provide *adequate safeguards* (see below) to prevent contributions on behalf of a designated beneficiary in excess of those necessary to provide for the beneficiary's "qualified higher education expenses." IRC Sec. 529(b). (The former requirement that a qualified state tuition program impose a "more than de minimis penalty" on any refund of earnings not used for certain purposes has been repealed. IRC Sec. 529(b)(3). See "Penalties," in Q 812.)

With respect to item (3), above, the IRS announced a special rule stating that state-sponsored qualified tuition savings plans may permit parents to change the investment strategy (1) once each calendar year and (2) whenever the beneficiary designation is changed. According to the IRS, final regulations are expected to provide that in order to qualify under this special rule, the state-sponsored qualified tuition program savings plan must: (1) allow participants to select among only broad-based investment strategies designed exclusively by the program; and (2) establish procedures and maintain appropriate records to prevent a change in investment options from occurring more frequently than once per calendar year, or upon a change in the designated beneficiary of the account. According to the IRS, qualified tuition programs and their participants may rely on the 2001 guidance pending the issuance of final regulations under IRC Section 529. Notice 2001-55, 2001-39 IRB 299.

A program established and maintained by one or more "eligible educational institutions" must satisfy two requirements to be treated as a qualified tuition program: (1) the program must have received a ruling or determination that it meets the applicable requirements for a qualified tuition program; *and* (2) the program must provide that assets are held in a "qualified trust." IRC Secs. 529(b)(1), 529(e)(5). "Eligible educational institution" means an accredited *post-secondary* college or university that offers credit towards a bachelor's degree, associate's degree, graduate-level degree, professional degree, or other recognized post-secondary credential and that is eligible to participate in federal student financial aid programs. See Prop. Treas. Reg. §1.529-1(c). For these purposes, "qualified trust" is defined as a domestic trust for the exclusive benefit of designated beneficiaries that meets the requirements set forth in the IRA rules, (i.e., a trust maintained by a bank, or other person who demonstrates that it will administer the trust in accordance with the requirements, and where the trust assets will not be commingled with other property, except in a common trust fund or common investment fund). IRC Sec. 529(b)(1).

2006 Tax Facts on Insurance & Employee Benefits   763

The term "qualified higher education expenses" means: (1) tuition, fees, books, supplies, and equipment required for a designated beneficiary's enrollment or attendance at an eligible educational institution (including certain vocational schools); and (2) expenses for special needs services incurred in connection with enrollment or attendance of a special needs beneficiary. IRC Sec. 529(e)(3)(A). Qualified higher education expenses also include reasonable costs for room and board, within limits. Generally, they may not exceed: (1) the allowance for room and board that was included in the cost of attendance in effect on the date that EGTRRA 2001 was enacted as determined by the school for a particular academic period, or *if greater* (2) the actual invoice amount the student residing in housing owned and operated by the private college or university is charged by such institution for room and board costs for a particular academic period. IRC Sec. 529(e)(3)(B).

A safe harbor provides the definition of what constitutes *adequate safeguards* to prevent contributions in excess of those necessary to meet the beneficiary's qualified higher education expenses. The safe harbor is satisfied if all contributions to the account are prohibited once the account balance reaches a specified limit that is applicable to all accounts of beneficiaries with the same expected year of enrollment. Prop. Treas. Reg. §1.529-2(i)(2). The total of all contributions may not exceed the amount established by actuarial estimates as necessary to pay tuition, required fees, and room and board expenses of the beneficiary for five years of undergraduate enrollment at the highest cost institution allowed by the program. Prop. Treas. Reg. §1.529-2(h)(2).

Coordination rules. A taxpayer may claim a Hope Scholarship or Lifetime Learning Credit and exclude distributions from a qualified tuition program on behalf of the same student in the same taxable year if the distribution is not used to pay the same educational expenses for which the credit was claimed. See IRC Sec. 529(c)(3)(B)(v). See Q 835. An individual is required to reduce his total qualified higher education expenses by certain scholarships and by the amount of expenses taken into account in determining the Hope or Lifetime Learning credit allowable to the taxpayer (or any other person). IRC Sec. 529(c)(3)(B)(v).

A contribution to a qualified tuition program can be made in the same taxable year as a contribution to a Coverdell Education Savings Account for the benefit of the same designated beneficiary without incurring an excise tax. (See Q 810.) IRC Sec. 4973(e). If the aggregate distributions from a qualified tuition program exceed the total amount of qualified higher education expenses taken into account after reduction for the Hope and Lifetime Learning credits, then the expenses must be allocated between the Coverdell Education Savings Account distributions and the qualified tuition program distributions for purposes of determining the amount of the exclusion. IRC Sec. 529(c)(3)(B)(vi).

Reporting. Each officer or employee having control over a qualified tuition program must report to the IRS and to designated beneficiaries with respect to contributions, distributions, and other matters that the IRS may require. The reports must be filed and furnished to the above individuals in the time and manner determined by the IRS. IRC Sec. 529(d); Prop. Treas. Reg. §1.529-4. In 2001, the IRS released guidance regarding certain recordkeeping, reporting, and other requirements applicable to qualified tuition programs in light of the amendments to IRC Section 529 under EGTRRA 2001. See Notice 2001-81, 2001-52 IRB 617. Qualified tuition programs and their participants may rely on Notice 2001-81 pending the issuance of final regulations under IRC Sec-

INDIVIDUALS   Q 812

tion 529. (Note that reporting was not required for calendar years before 1999. Notice 97-52, 1997-38 IRB 306.)

As a general rule, a qualified tuition program is exempt from federal income tax, except the tax on unrelated business income of charitable organizations imposed by IRC Section 511. IRC Sec. 529(a).

Under Section 225 of BAPCPA 2005, funds used to purchase a tuition credit or certificate or contributed to an account under a QTP no later than 365 days before the date of the filing of the bankruptcy petition may be excluded from the bankruptcy estate if certain conditions are met. 11 USC 541(b), as amended by BAPCPA 2005.

IRC Section 529 generally took effect for taxable years ending after August 20, 1996; special transitional rules applied for earlier programs. See Q 812 for the tax treatment of distributions from qualified tuition programs. See Q 859 for the estate tax treatment and Q 906 for the gift tax treatment of qualified tuition programs. *ASRS, Sec. 53, ¶20.3(b)*.

812. How are distributions from a qualified tuition program taxed?

Distributions from *state* qualified tuition programs are fully excludable from gross income if the distributions are used to pay "qualified higher education expenses" (see Q 811) of the designated beneficiary. IRC Sec. 529(c)(3)(B). (For the general rule governing nonqualified distributions, see below.) Beginning in 2004, distributions from pre-paid tuition programs sponsored by private colleges and universities are also fully excludable from gross income to the extent that those distributions are used to pay qualified higher education expenses of the designated beneficiary. IRC Sec. 529(c)(3)(B).

In the case of excess cash distributions, the amount otherwise includable in gross income must be reduced by a proportion that is equal to the ratio of expenses to distributions. IRC Sec. 529(c)(3)(B). In-kind distributions are not includable in gross income so long as they provide a benefit to the distributee which, if paid for by the distributee himself, would constitute payment of a qualified higher education expense. IRC Sec. 529(c)(3)(B).

Nonqualified distributions (i.e., distributions that are not used to pay "qualified higher education expenses") are includable in the gross income of the distributee under the rules of IRC Section 72 to the extent they are not excludable under some other Code provision. IRC Sec. 529(c)(3)(A). Distributions are treated as representing a pro rata share of the principal (i.e., contributions) and accumulated earnings in the account. IRC Sec. 72(e)(9). For purposes of applying IRC Section 72, the Code provides that: (1) all qualified tuition programs of which an individual is a designated beneficiary must generally be treated as one program; (2) all distributions during a taxable year must be treated as one distribution; and (3) the value of the contract, income on the contract, and investment in the contract must be computed as of the close of the calendar year in which the taxable year begins. IRC Sec. 529(c)(3)(D).

The IRS announced in 2001 that the final regulations are expected to provide that only those accounts maintained by a qualified tuition program and having the same account owner and the same designated beneficiary must be aggregated for purposes of computing the earnings portion of any distribution. The IRS also stated that the final regulations are expected to revise the time for determining the earnings portion of any distribution from a qualified tuition account. Specifically, for distributions made after 2002 such programs will be required to determine the earnings portion of each distribution as of the date of the distribution. A different effective date applies to direct transfers between qualified tuition programs. See Notice 2001-81, 2001-52 IRB 617.

Penalties on nonqualified distributions. For taxable years beginning before 2002, a qualified *state* tuition program was required to impose a "more than de minimis penalty" on any refund of earnings not used for qualified higher education expenses of the beneficiary. IRC Sec. 529(b)(3), prior to amendment by EGTRRA 2001. See Prop. Treas. Reg. §1.529-2 for the safe harbor definition of "more than de minimis." However, for taxable years beginning after 2001, the state-imposed penalty is repealed. IRC Sec. 529(b)(3). In place of that penalty, a 10% additional tax will be imposed on nonqualified distributions in the same manner as the 10% additional tax is imposed on certain distributions from Coverdell Education Savings Accounts; see Q 810. IRC Secs. 529(c)(6), 530(d)(4). The 10% additional tax will not apply to any payment or distribution in any taxable year before 2004 that is includable in gross income but used for qualified higher education expenses of the designated beneficiary. IRC Sec. 529(c)(6). According to the Conference Committee Report, this means that the earnings portion of a distribution from a qualified tuition program of a private institution that is made in 2003, and that is used for qualified higher education expenses, is not subject to the additional tax even though the earnings portion is includable in gross income. H.R. Conf. Rep. No. 107-84. The 10% additional tax also does not apply if the payment or distribution is (1) made to a beneficiary on or after the death of the designated beneficiary, or (2) attributable to the disability of the designated beneficiary. IRC Sec. 530(d)(4)(B).

With respect to any distributions made after 2001, a qualified tuition program is no longer required to verify how distributions are used or to collect any penalty, but the program must continue to verify whether the distribution is used for qualified higher education expenses of the beneficiary and to collect a "more than de minimis penalty" on nonqualified distributions made *before* 2002. Notice 2001-81, above.

Rollovers. Any portion of a distribution that is transferred within 60 days to the credit of a new "designated beneficiary" (see below) who is a "member of the family" (see below) of the designated beneficiary, is not includable in the gross income of the distributee. (In other words, a distribution generally can be "rolled over" within 60 days from one family member to another.) See Prop. Treas. Regs. §§1.529-3(a) and (b); Prop. Treas. Reg. §1.529-1(c). A change in designated beneficiaries with respect to an interest in the same qualified tuition program will not be treated as a distribution provided that the new beneficiary is a member of the family of the old beneficiary. IRC Sec. 529(c)(3)(C). A transfer of credits (or other amounts) for the benefit of the *same* designated beneficiary from one qualified tuition program to another is not considered a distribution; however, only one transfer within a 12-month period can receive such rollover treatment. IRC Sec. 529(c)(3)(C)(iii). According to the Conference Committee Report, a program-to-program transfer on behalf of the same beneficiary is intended to allow a transfer between a prepaid tuition program and a savings program maintained by the same state, or a transfer between a state-sponsored plan and a prepaid private tuition program. H.R. Conf. Rep. No. 107-84 (EGTRRA 2001).

Generally, "member of the family" means an individual's: (1) spouse; (2) child or his descendant; (3) stepchild; (4) sibling or step sibling; (5) parents and their ances-

INDIVIDUALS   Q 814

tors; (6) stepparents; (7) nieces or nephews; (8) aunts and uncles; or (9) in-laws; (10) the spouse of any of the individuals in (2) through (9); and (11) any first cousin of the designated beneficiary. IRC Sec. 529(e)(2); IRC Sec. 152(d). (However, for any contracts issued before August 20, 1996, IRC Section 529(c)(3)(C) will not require that a distribution be transferred to a member of the family or that a change in beneficiaries may be made only to a member of the family. TRA '97, Sec. 211(f)(6).) A "designated beneficiary" is: (1) the individual designated at the beginning of participation in the qualified tuition program as the beneficiary of amounts paid (or to be paid) to the program; (2) in the case of a rollover of a distribution or change in beneficiaries within a family (as described above), the new beneficiary; and (3) in the case of an interest in a qualified tuition program that is purchased by a state or local government (or its agency or instrumentality) or certain tax-exempt 501(c)(3) organizations as part of a scholarship program, the individual receiving the interest as a scholarship. IRC Sec. 529(e)(1). *ASRS, Sec. 53, ¶20.3(b)*.

ADJUSTED GROSS INCOME

813. How is adjusted gross income determined?

Adjusted gross income is determined by subtracting the following deductions from gross income: (a) expenses directly incurred in carrying on a trade, business or profession (not as an employee) (see Q 814); (b) the deduction for contributions made by a self-employed individual to a qualified pension, annuity, or profit sharing plan, SIMPLE IRA plan, or simplified employee pension plan; (c) certain reimbursed expenses of an employee in connection with his employment, provided the reimbursement is included in gross income (if the employee accounts to his employer and reimbursement does not exceed expenses, reporting is not required); (d) deductions related to property held for the production of rents and royalties (within limits); (e) deductions for depreciation and depletion by a life tenant, an income beneficiary of property held in trust, or an heir, legatee or devisee of an estate; (f) deductions for losses from the sale or exchange of property; (g) the deduction allowed for amounts paid in cash by an eligible individual to a traditional individual retirement account, or individual retirement annuity (see Q 220); (h) the deduction allowed for amounts forfeited as penalties because of premature withdrawal of funds from time savings accounts; (i) alimony payments made to the taxpayer's spouse (see Q 808); (j) certain reforestation expenses; (k) certain jury duty pay remitted to the taxpayer's employer; (l) moving expenses; (m) the deduction for Archer medical savings accounts under IRC Section 220(i) (*Editor's Note*: the deduction expires December 31, 2005); (n) the deduction for interest on education loans; (o) the deduction for qualified tuition and related expenses (*Editor's Note*: the deduction expires December 31, 2005); (p) the deduction for contributions (within limits) to Health Savings Accounts; (q) the deduction for attorneys' fees involving discrimination suits; and (r) the deduction for certain expenses of elementary and secondary school teachers up to $250 (*Editor's Note*: the deduction expires December 31, 2005). *ASRS, Sec. 53, 20.5*.

814. How are business expenses reported for income tax purposes?

A deduction is permitted for all ordinary and necessary expenses paid or incurred during the taxable year in carrying on a trade or business. Examples of deductible business expenses include: (1) expenditures for reasonable salaries, (2) traveling expenses (within limits), and (3) certain rental expenses incurred for purposes of a trade or business. IRC

Sec. 162(a). Illegal payments made in the course of business, such as bribes to government officials or illegal rebates (see Q 804), are not deductible. IRC Sec. 162(c).

The amount of the deduction for expenses incurred in carrying on a trade or business depends upon whether the individual is an independent contractor or an employee. Typically, whether an insurance agent is considered an independent contractor or employee is determined on the basis of all the facts and circumstances involved; however, where an employer has the right to control the manner and the means by which services are performed, an employer-employee relationship will generally be found to exist. See *Butts v. Comm.*, TC Memo 1993-478, *aff'd*, 49 F.3d 713 (11th Cir. 1995); Let. Rul. 9306029. The IRS has ruled that a full-time life insurance salesperson is not an "employee" for purposes of IRC Sections 62 and 67, even though he is treated as a "statutory employee" for Social Security tax purposes. Rev. Rul. 90-93, 1990-2 CB 33. See Q 358. Furthermore, according to decisions from the Sixth and Eleventh Circuit Courts of Appeals, the fact that an insurance agent received certain employee benefits did not preclude his being considered an independent contractor, based on all the other facts and circumstances of the case. See *Ware v. U.S.*, 67 F.3d 574 (6th Cir. 1995); *Butts v. Comm.*, above. The IRS has determined, however, that a district manager of an insurance company was an employee of the company, and not an independent contractor. TAM 9342001. On the other hand, the IRS has determined that individuals who were regional and senior sales vice presidents of an insurance company (but who were not officers of the company) were independent contractors and not employees of the insurance company. TAM 9736002.

Independent contractors may deduct all allowable business expenses from gross income (i.e., "above-the-line") to arrive at adjusted gross income. IRC Sec. 62(a)(1). The business expenses of an employee are deductible from adjusted gross income (i.e., "below-the-line) if he itemizes instead of taking the standard deduction (see Q 817), but only to the extent that they exceed 2% of adjusted gross income when aggregated with other "miscellaneous itemized deductions" (described in Q 822).

Industrial agents (or "debit agents") are treated as employees for tax purposes. Rev. Rul. 58-175, 1958-1 CB 28. Thus, as in the case of any employee, a debit agent can deduct transportation and away-from-home traveling expenses *from* adjusted gross income if he itemizes, only to the extent that the aggregate of these and other miscellaneous itemized deductions exceeds 2% of adjusted gross income. IRC Sec. 67.

Self-employed taxpayers are permitted a deduction equal to one-half of their self-employment (i.e., Social Security) taxes for the taxable year. This deduction is treated as attributable to a trade or business that does not consist of the performance of services by the taxpayer as an employee; thus it is taken "above-the line." IRC Sec. 164(f).

In a legal memorandum concerning the deductibility of medical insurance costs, the Service ruled as follows: (1) A sole proprietor who purchases health insurance in his individual name has established a plan providing medical care coverage with respect to his trade or business, and therefore may deduct the medical care insurance costs for himself, his spouse, and dependents under IRC Section 162(l), but only to the extent the cost of the insurance does not exceed the earned income derived by the sole proprietor from the specific trade or business with respect to which the insurance was purchased. (2) A self-employed individual may deduct the medical care insurance costs for himself and his spouse and dependents under a health insurance plan established for his trade

INDIVIDUALS   Q 815

or business up to the net earnings of the specific trade or business with respect to which the plan is established, but a self-employed individual may not add the net profits from all his trades and businesses for purposes of determining the deduction limit under IRC Section 162(l)(2)(A). However, if a self-employed individual has more than one trade or business, he may deduct the medical care insurance costs of the self-employed individual and his spouse and dependents under each specific health insurance plan established under each specific business up to the net earnings of that specific trade or business. CCA 200524001.

In *Allemeier v. Commissioner*, TC Memo 2005-207, the Tax Court held that the taxpayer could deduct his expenses ($15,745) incurred in earning a master's degree in business administration to the extent those expenses were substantiated and education-related. The court based its decision on the fact that the taxpayer's MBA did not satisfy a minimum education requirement of his employer, nor did the MBA qualify the taxpayer to perform a new trade or business.

Expenses for business meals and entertainment must meet one of two tests, as defined in regulations, in order to be deductible. The meal must be: (1) "directly related to" the active conduct of the trade or business, or (2) "associated with" the trade or business. Generally, the deduction for business meal and entertainment expenses is limited to 50% of allowable expenses. IRC Sec. 274(n)(1). The 50% otherwise allowed as a deduction is *then* subject to the 2% floor that applies to miscellaneous itemized deductions. Temp. Treas. Reg. §1.67-1T(a)(2). The taxpayer or his employee generally must be present for meal expenses to be deductible, and expenses that are lavish or extravagant may be disallowed. Substantiation is required for lodging expenses and, in the case of expenditures incurred on or after October 1, 1995, for most items of $75.00 or more. Treas. Reg. §1.274-5(c)(2)(iii). An employee must generally provide an "adequate accounting" of reimbursed expenses to his employer. Treas. Reg. §1.274-5(f)(4). *ASRS, Sec. 53, ¶20.5(a)*.

815. How is an individual taxed on capital gains and losses?

Adjusted net capital gain is generally subject to a maximum rate of 15%. (See "Reduction in Capital Gains Rates," below.) However, detailed rules as to the exact calculation of the capital gains tax result in some exceptions. IRC Sec. 1(h).

"Adjusted net capital gain" is *net capital gain* reduced (but not below zero) by the sum of: (1) *unrecaptured IRC Section 1250 gain*; and (2) *28% rate gain* (both defined below); *plus* (3) "qualified dividend income" (as defined in IRC Section 1(h)(11)(B); see "New Lower Rates for Qualified Dividend Income," below). IRC Sec. 1(h)(3).

Gain is determined by subtracting the adjusted basis of the asset sold or exchanged from the amount realized. Loss is determined by subtracting the amount realized from the adjusted basis of the asset sold or exchanged. See Q 816. The amount realized includes both money and the fair market value of any property received. IRC Sec. 1001. Gains and losses from the sale or exchange of capital assets are either short-term or long-term. Generally, in order for gain or loss to be long-term, the asset must have been held for more than one year.

Net capital gain is the excess of net long term capital gain for the taxable year over net short term capital loss for such year. IRC Sec. 1222(11). However, net capital gain for any taxable year is reduced (but not below zero) by any amount the taxpayer takes into account under the investment income exception to the investment interest deduction. IRC Secs. 1(h)(2), 163(d)(4)(B)(iii). See Q 823.

The Code provides that for a taxpayer with a net capital gain for any taxable year, the tax will not exceed the *sum* of the following five items:

(A) the tax computed at regular rates (without regard to the rules for capital gain) on the *greater* of (i) taxable income reduced by the net capital gain, or (ii) the *lesser* of (I) the amount of taxable income taxed at a rate below 25% (See Appendix B), *or* (II) taxable income reduced by the adjusted net capital gain;

(B) 5% (0% in the case of taxable years beginning after 2007) of so much of the taxpayer's adjusted net capital gain (or, if less, taxable income) as does not exceed the *excess* (if any) of (i) the amount of taxable income that would (without regard to this paragraph) be taxed at a rate below 25% (see Appendix B) *over* (ii) the taxable income reduced by the adjusted net capital gain;

(C) 15% of the taxpayer's adjusted net capital gain (or, if less, taxable income) in *excess* of the amount on which a tax is determined under (B) above;

(D) 25% of the *excess* (if any) of (i) the unrecaptured IRC Section 1250 gain (or, if less, the net capital gain (determined without regard to qualified dividend income)), *over* (ii) the *excess* (if any) of (I) the sum of the amount on which tax is determined under (A) above, *plus* the net capital gain, *over* (II) taxable income; *and*

(E) 28% of the amount of taxable income in *excess* of the sum of the amounts on which tax is determined under (A) through (D) above. IRC Secs. 1(h)(1)(D); IRC Secs. 1(h)(1)(A), 1(h)(1)(B), 1(h)(1)(C), 1(h)(1)(E).

It is important to note that as a result of this complex formula, generally, the maximum capital gains rate on *adjusted net capital gain* will be 15% to the extent an individual is taxed at the 25% or higher marginal rates (see Q 828), and 5% (0% in the case of taxable years beginning after 2007) to the extent the individual is taxed at the 15% or 10% rates. IRC Sec. 1(h).

"Unrecaptured IRC Section 1250 gain" means the *excess*, if any, of: (i) that amount of long-term capital gain (not otherwise treated as ordinary income) that would be treated as ordinary income if IRC Section 1250(b)(1) included all depreciation and the applicable percentage under IRC Section 1250(a) were 100%; *over* (ii) the excess, if any of (a) the sum of collectibles loss, net short-term capital loss and long-term capital loss carryovers, *over* (b) the sum of collectibles gain and IRC Section 1202 gain. However, at no time may the amount of unrecaptured IRC Section 1250 gain that is attributable to sales, exchanges, and conversions described in IRC Section 1231(a)(3)(A) for any taxable year exceed the net IRC Section 1231 gain, as defined in IRC Section 1231(c)(3) for such year. IRC Sec. 1(h)(6).

"28% rate gain" means the *excess*, if any, of (A) the *sum* of collectibles gain and IRC Section 1202 gain (i.e., gain on certain small businesses), *over* (B) the *sum* of (i) collectibles loss, (ii) net short-term capital loss, and (iii) long-term capital loss carried over under IRC Section 1212(b)(1)(B) (i.e., the excess of net long-term capital loss

INDIVIDUALS   Q 815

over net short-term capital gain, carried over to the succeeding taxable year). IRC Sec. 1(h)(4).

"Collectibles gain or loss" is gain or loss on the sale or exchange of a collectible that is a capital asset held for more than one year, but only to the extent such gain is taken into account in computing gross income and such loss is taken into account in computing taxable income. IRC Sec. 1(h)(5). Examples of collectibles include artwork, gems and coins. See IRC Sec. 408(m)(2).

"IRC Section 1202 gain" means the *excess* of (A) the gain that would be excluded from gross income under IRC Section 1202 but for the percentage limitation in IRC Section 1202(a) *over* (B) the gain excluded from gross income under IRC Section 1202 (i.e., 50% exclusion for certain qualified small business stock). IRC Sec. 1(h)(7). (For alternative minimum tax purposes, an amount equal to 7% of the amount excluded from gross income for the taxable year under IRC Section 1202 will be treated as a preference item. IRC Sec. 57(a)(7).)

The foregoing rules essentially establish four groups of capital assets (based upon pre-existing tax rates): (1) short-term capital assets, with no special tax rate; (2) 28% capital assets, generally consisting of collectibles gain or loss, and IRC Section 1202 gain; (3) 25% capital assets, consisting of assets that generate unrecaptured IRC Section 1250 gain; and (4) 15%/5% (0% in the case of taxable years beginning after 2007 for taxpayers in the 15%/10% ordinary income tax brackets) capital assets, consisting of all other long-term capital assets. Within each group, gains and losses are netted. The effect of this process is generally that if there is a net loss from (1), it is applied to reduce any net gain from (2), (3), or (4), in that order. If there is a net loss from (2) it is applied to reduce any net gain from (3) or (4), in that order. If there is a net loss from (4), it is applied to reduce any net gain from (2) or (3), in that order. IRC Sec. 1(h)(1); Notice 97-59, 1997-45 IRB 7.

After all of the netting above, if there are net losses, up to $3,000 ($1,500 in the case of married individuals filing separately) of losses can be deducted against ordinary income. IRC Sec. 1211(b). Apparently, any deducted loss would be treated as reducing net loss from (1), (2), or (4), in that order. Any remaining net losses could be carried over to other taxable years, retaining its group classifications. If there are net gains, such gains would generally be taxed as described above.

Reduction in Capital Gain Rates for Individuals

Long-term capital gains incurred on or after May 6, 2003 are subject to lower tax rates. For taxpayers in the 25% tax bracket and higher (28%, 33% and 35% in 2006 – see Q 828), the rate on long-term capital gains is reduced from 20% to 15% in 2003 through 2008. For taxpayers in the 15% and 10% brackets, the rate on long-term capital gains is reduced from 10% to 5% in 2003 through 2007, and all the way down to 0% in 2008. IRC Sec. 1(h)(1).

The lower capital gain rates are effective for taxable years ending on or after May 6, 2003 and beginning before January 1, 2009. (For the treatment of long-term capital gains incurred prior to May 6, 2003, see "Transitional rules," below.) After December 31, 2008, the lower rates on long-term capital gains will "sunset" (expire), at which time the prior capital gain rates (20%, 10%) will, once again, be effective. IRC Sec. 1(h); Act. Secs. 301(d), 303, JGTRRA 2003.

Q 815   FEDERAL INCOME TAX

Collectibles gain, IRC Section 1202 gain (i.e., qualified small business stock), and unrecaptured IRC Section 1250 gain continue to be taxed at their current tax rates (i.e., 28% for collectibles gain and IRC Section 1202 gain, and 25% for unrecaptured IRC Section 1250 gain). IRC Sec. 1(h).

Repeal of qualified 5-year gain. For tax years beginning after December 31, 2000, if certain requirements were met, the maximum rates on "qualified 5-year gain" could be reduced to 8% and 18% (in place of 10% and 20% respectively). Furthermore, a noncorporate taxpayer in the 25% bracket (or higher) who held a capital asset on January 1, 2001 could elect to treat the asset as if it had been sold and repurchased for its fair market value on January 1, 2001 (or on January 2, 2001 in the case of publicly traded stock). If a noncorporate taxpayer made this election, the holding period for the elected assets began after December 31, 2000, thereby making the asset eligible for the 18% rate if it was later sold after having been held by the taxpayer for more than five years from the date of the deemed sale and deemed reacquisition. IRC Secs. 1(h)(2), 1(h)(9), prior to amendment by JGTRRA 2003; Sec. 414(a) of JCWAA 2002, and Sec. 314(c) of the Community Renewal Tax Relief Act of 2000, amending Sec. 311(e) of TRA '97. Under JGTRRA 2003, the 5-year holding period requirement, and the 18% and 8% tax rates for qualified 5-year gain are repealed. When the 15%/5% rates for capital gains "sunset" (expire), the 5-year holding period requirement and 18% and 8% rates will, once again, be effective. IRC Secs. 1(h)(2), 1(h)(9), as repealed by JGTRRA 2003; Act Sec. 107, JGTRRA 2003.

Transitional rules. In the case of a taxable year that *includes* May 6, 2003, the amount of tax determined under (B) above, will generally be equal to the *sum* of:

(A)   5% of the *lesser* of: (i) the net capital gain determined by taking into account only gain or loss taken into account for the portion of the taxable year on or after May 6, 2003 (determined without regard to collectibles gain or loss and IRC Section 1202 gain); *or* (ii) the amount on which a tax is determined under (B), above (without regard to this subsection);

(B)   8% of the *lesser* of: (i) the qualified 5-year gain (as that term was defined on May 27, 2003 under IRC Section 1(h)(9)) taken into account for the portion of the taxable year before May 6, 2003; *or* (ii) the *excess* (if any) of (I) the amount on which a tax is determined under (B), above (without regard to this subsection), *over* (II) the amount on which a tax is determined under (A), above; *plus*

(C)   10% of the *excess* (if any) of: (i) the amount on which a tax is determined under (B), above (without regard to this subsection), *over* (ii) the sum of the amounts on which a tax is determined under (A) and (B), above. Act. Sec. 301(c)(1), JGTRRA 2003.

In the case of a taxable year that *includes* May 6, 2003, the amount of tax determined under (C), above, will generally be equal to the *sum* of:

(A)   15% of the *lesser* of: (i) the *excess* (if any) of the amount of net capital gain determined under subparagraph (A)(i) of paragraph (1) of this subsection, *over* the amount on which a tax is determined under subparagraph (A) of paragraph (1) of this subsection; *or* (ii) the amount on which a tax is determined under (C), above (without regard to this subsection); *plus*

INDIVIDUALS   Q 815

    (B)   20% of the *excess* (if any) of: (i) the amount on which a tax is determined under (C), above (without regard to this subsection); *over* (ii) the amount on which a tax is determined under (A), of this paragraph. Act Sec. 301(c)(2), JGTRRA 2003.

With respect to any pass-through entity (e.g., a mutual fund), the determination of when gains and losses are properly taken into account will be made at the entity level. Act Sec. 301(c)(4), JGTRRA 2003.

Dividends that are "qualified dividend income" (see below) will be treated as gain properly taken into account for the portion of the taxable year on or after May 6, 2003. Act Sec. 301(c)(5), JGTRRA 2003.

Lower Rates for Qualified Dividend Income

Under prior law, dividends were treated as ordinary income and, thus, were subject to ordinary income tax rates. Under JGTRRA 2003, "qualified dividend income" (see below) is treated as "net capital gain" (see below) and is, therefore, subject to new lower tax rates. For taxpayers in the 25% income tax bracket and higher (see Q 828), the maximum rate on qualified dividends paid by corporations to individuals is 15% in 2003 through 2008. For taxpayers in the 15% and 10% income tax brackets, the tax rate on qualified dividend income is reduced to 5% in 2003 through 2007, and all the way down to 0% in 2008. IRC Sec. 1(h)(1). The preferential treatment of qualified dividends as net capital gains will "sunset" (expire) after December 31, 2008, at which time the prior treatment of dividends will, once again, be effective. In other words, dividends will once again be taxed at ordinary income tax rates. Act. Sec. 303, JGTRRA 2003.

Qualified dividend income. Certain dividends are taxed as "net capital gain" for purposes of the reduction in the tax rates on dividends. "Net capital gain" for this purpose means net capital gain *increased* by "qualified dividend income" (without regard to this paragraph). IRC Sec. 1(h)(11)(A). "Qualified dividend income" means dividends received during the taxable year from domestic corporations and "qualified foreign corporations" (defined below). IRC Secs. 1(h)(11)(B).

The term qualified dividend income does *not* include the following:

    (1)   dividends paid by tax-exempt corporations;

    (2)   any amount allowed as a deduction under IRC Section 591 (relating to the deduction for dividends paid by mutual savings banks, etc.);

    (3)   dividends paid on certain employer securities as described in IRC Section 404(k);

    (4)   a share (or shares) of stock that the shareholder has not held for more than 60 days during the *121-day* period beginning 60 days before the ex-dividend date (as measured under section 246(c)). For preferred stock, the holding period is more than 90 days during the *181-day* period beginning 90 days before the ex-dividend date *if* the dividends are attributable to a period exceeding 366 days (note, however, that if the preferred dividends are attributable to a period totalling less than 367 days, the holding period stated in the preceding sentence applies). IRC Sec. 1(h)(11)(B)

Special rules. Qualified dividend income does not include any amount that the taxpayer takes into account as investment income under IRC Section 163(d)(4)(B). See also Temp. Treas. Reg. 1.163(d)-1T. If an individual, trust, or estate receives qualified dividend income from one or more dividends that are "extraordinary dividends" (within the meaning of IRC Section 1059(c)), any loss on the sale or exchange of such share(s) of stock will, to the extent of such dividends, be treated as long-term capital loss. IRC Sec. 1(h)(11)(D).

Mutual fund dividends. In general, ordinary income dividends paid by mutual funds are eligible for the 15%/5% tax rates *if* the income being passed from the fund to investors is "qualified dividend income" in the hands of the fund, and not short-term capital gain or interest from bonds (which continues to be taxed at ordinary income tax rates). See IRC Secs. 854(b)(1), 854(b)(2), 854(b)(5). Mutual funds report (on Form 1099-DIV) the nature of the dividend being distributed to shareholders (i.e., whether the dividend is "qualified dividend income" subject to the 15%/5% rates, or a nonqualifying dividend subject to ordinary income tax rates). Ordinary income dividends paid by REITS are generally *not* eligible for the 15%/5% rates. See IRC Sec. 857(c)(2).

The Service has clarified that mutual funds and REITs that pass through dividend income to their shareholders must meet the holding period test for the dividend paying stocks that they hold in order for corresponding amounts they pay out to be reported as qualified dividends on Form 1099-DIV. Investors must *also* meet the test relative to the share they hold directly, from which they received the qualified dividends that were reported to them. IRS News Release IR-2004-22; see also Pub. 564 (2004).

Pass through entities. In the case of partnerships, S corporations, common trust funds, trusts, and estates, the amendments made by JGTRRA 2003 apply to taxable years ending after December 31, 2002, except that dividends received by the entity prior to January 1, 2003 are *not* treated as qualified dividend income. Act Sec. 402(a)(6) of WFTRA 2004, amending, Act Sec. 302(f) of JGTRRA 2003.

Qualified foreign corporations. The term "qualified foreign corporation" means a foreign corporation incorporated in a possession of the United States, or a corporation that is eligible for benefits of a comprehensive income tax treaty with the United States. If a foreign corporation does not satisfy either of these requirements, it will nevertheless be treated as such with respect to any dividends paid by that corporation *if* its stock (or ADRs with respect to such stock) is readily tradable on an established securities market in the United States. IRC Sec. 1(h)(11)(C).

A distribution with respect to a security issued by a qualified foreign corporation also is subject to the other limitations in IRC Section 1(h)(11). In particular, the recipient must satisfy the holding period requirements of IRC Section 1(h)(11)(B)(iii). In addition, the distribution must constitute a dividend for U.S. federal income tax purposes. Accordingly, the security with respect to which the distribution is made must be equity rather than debt for U.S. federal income tax purposes (the "equity test"), and the distribution must be out of the corporation's earnings and profits rather than a return of capital (the "E&P test"). Notice 2003-79, 2003-50 IRB 1206.

The term "qualified foreign corporation" does not include any foreign corporation if, for the taxable year of the corporation in which the dividend was paid (or the preceding taxable year), the corporation is a passive foreign investment company (as defined in IRC Section 1297). IRC Sec. 1(h)(11)(C)(iii).

INDIVIDUALS   Q 816

Special rules apply in determining a taxpayer's foreign tax credit limitation under IRC Section 904 in the case of qualified dividend income. For these purposes, rules similar to the rules of IRC Section 904(b)(2)(B) (concerning adjustments to the foreign tax credit limitation to reflect any capital gain rate differential) will apply to any qualified dividend income. See IRC Sec. 1(h)(11)(C)(iv).

For other guidance on foreign stock dividends, see Notice 2004-71, 2004-45 IRB 793 (reporting guidance); Notice 2003-69, 2003-42 IRB 851 (current list of U.S. tax treaties that meet the "treaty test"), and Notice 2003-71, 2003-43 IRB 922 (when ordinary or common stock is considered "readily tradable on an established securities market in the United States"). *ASRS, Sec. 53, ¶¶20.8(b), 20.10.*

816. What basis is used to determine the amount of gain or loss upon the sale or exchange of a capital asset?

"Basis" is the starting point for determining gain or loss. The basis to be used depends upon the manner in which the taxpayer acquired the property. The basis of the property may be: (1) its cost, (2) its fair market value at a specified date, or (3) a substituted basis. In addition, this basis must be "adjusted" for certain things, such as depreciation and cost of improvements.

Property Acquired by Purchase or Exchange

With respect to property purchased or acquired in a taxable exchange on or after March 1, 1913, a taxpayer's basis is cost (the cash he paid for the property or the fair market value of the property he gave for it). IRC Sec. 1012. If the property was acquired by purchase before March 1, 1913, basis for determining gain is cost, or fair market value as of March 1, 1913, whichever is greater; for determining loss, the basis is cost.

For an explanation of how the holding period is determined for stock received by a policyholder or annuity holder in a demutualization transaction, see SCA 200131028.

Property Acquired From a Decedent

Decedent Dying in Year Other Than 2010

Stepped up basis. As a general rule, the basis of property that has been acquired from a decedent (other than a decedent dying in 2010, see below) is the fair market value of the property at the date of the decedent's death (i.e., the basis is "stepped up" or "stepped down," as the case may be, to the fair market value). This rule applies generally to all property includable in the decedent's gross estate for federal estate tax purposes (whether or not an estate tax return is required to be filed). It applies also to the survivor's one-half of community property where at least one-half of the value of the property was included in the decedent's gross estate. As an exception, however, the rule does not apply to "income in respect of a decedent" (see Q 827); normally the basis of such income is zero. IRC Sec. 1014(c). As another exception, the rule does not apply to appreciated property acquired by the decedent by gift within one year of his death where the one receiving the property from the decedent is the donor or the donor's spouse; in such case the basis of the property in the hands of the donor (or spouse) is the adjusted basis of the property in the hands of the decedent immediately before his death. IRC Sec. 1014(e). If an estate tax return is filed and the executor elects the alternative valuation, the basis is the fair market value on the alternative valuation date instead of its value on the date of death. IRC Sec. 1014(a).

Jointly held property. Note that the "stepped up" basis rule applies only to property includable in the decedent's gross estate for federal estate tax purposes. IRC Sec. 1014(b)(9). Thus, one acquiring property from a decedent who held the property jointly with another (or others) under the general rule of estate tax includability (i.e., the entire value of the property is includable in the estate of the first joint owner to die except to the extent the surviving joint owner(s) can prove contribution to the cost–see Q 853(8)) receives a stepped up basis in the property in accordance with that rule. By contrast, one who acquires property from a decedent spouse who with the surviving spouse had a *qualified joint interest* in the property (see Q 854) receives a stepped up basis equal to one-half the value of that interest.

Community property. The stepped up basis rule applies in the case of community property both to the decedent's one-half interest and to the surviving spouse's one-half interest. IRC Sec. 1014(b)(6).

Qualified terminable interest property. Upon the death of the donee spouse or surviving spouse, qualified terminable interest property (see Q 864) is considered as "acquired from or to have passed from the decedent" for purposes of receiving a new basis at death. IRC Sec. 1014(b)(10).

Decedent Dying in 2010

Modified carryover basis. In 2010, along with repeal of the estate tax for one year, a modified carryover basis regime (with limited step-up in basis) replaces the step-up in basis for property acquired from a decedent. That is, the basis of the person acquiring property from a decedent dying in 2010 will generally be equal to the lesser of (1) the adjusted basis of the decedent (i.e., carried over to recipient from decedent), or (2) the fair market value of the property at the date of the decedent's death. However, step-up in basis is retained for up to $1,300,000 of property acquired from a decedent. In the case of certain transfers to a spouse, step-up in basis will be available for an additional $3,000,000 of property acquired from a decedent. In the case of a decedent nonresident who is not a United States citizen, step-up in basis will be available for only $60,000 of property acquired from the decedent. IRC Secs. 1014(f), 1022, as added by EGTRRA 2001.

Property Acquired by Gift

If the property was acquired by gift after 1920 and before 1977, the basis for determining gain is the same as in the hands of the donor. This basis may be increased by the amount of any gift tax paid but total basis may not exceed the fair market value of the property at the time of the gift. In the case of property received by gift after 1976, the donee takes the donor's basis plus a *part* of the gift tax paid. The added fraction is the amount of the gift tax paid that is attributable to appreciation in the value of the gifted property over the donor's basis. IRC Sec. 1015. The amount of attributable gift tax bears the same ratio to the amount of gift tax paid as net appreciation bears to the value of the gift.

For the purpose of determining loss, the basis of property acquired by gift after 1920 is the foregoing substituted basis, or the fair market value of the property at the time of gift, whichever is lower. As to property acquired by gift before 1921, basis is the fair market value of the property at the time of acquisition. IRC Sec. 1015.

Property Acquired in a Generation-Skipping Transfer

Generally, in the case of property received in a generation-skipping transfer (see Q 950), the transferee takes the adjusted basis of the property immediately before the transfer plus a *part* of the generation-skipping transfer (GST) tax paid. The added fraction is the amount of the GST tax paid that is attributable to appreciation in the value of the transferred property over its previous adjusted basis. The amount of attributable GST tax bears the same ratio to the amount of GST tax paid as net appreciation bears to the value of the property transferred. Nevertheless, basis is not to be increased above fair market value. When property is acquired by gift in a generation-skipping transfer, the basis of the property is increased by the gift tax basis adjustment (see above) before the generation-skipping transfer tax basis adjustment is made. IRC Sec. 2654(a)(1).

However, where property is transferred in a taxable termination (see Q 950) that occurs at the same time and as a result of the death of an individual, the basis of such property is increased (or decreased) to fair market value, except that any increase (or decrease) in basis is limited by multiplying such increase (or decrease) by the inclusion ratio used in allocating the generation-skipping tax exemption (see Q 951). IRC Sec. 2654(a)(2).

Property Acquired From a Spouse or Incident to Divorce

If property is transferred between spouses, or former spouses incident to a divorce, after July 18, 1984 pursuant to an instrument in effect after that date, the transferee's basis in the property is the adjusted basis of the property in the hands of the transferor immediately before the transfer and no gain or loss is recognized at the time of transfer (unless, under certain circumstances, the property is transferred in trust). IRC Secs. 453B(g), 1041; Temp. Treas. Reg. §1.1041-1T, A-1.

In the case of a transfer to a third party incident to a divorce, no gain or loss will apply if (1) the transfer is required by the divorce or separation agreement (and not merely required by the circumstances of the divorce), (2) the transfer is at the request of the other or former spouse, and (3) the transferor receives the written consent or ratification of the transfer by the other or former spouse. Temp. Treas. Reg. §1.1041-1T, A-9. These rules may apply to transfers made after 1983 if both parties elect. Temp. Treas. Reg. §1.1041-1T, A-16. See Q 281.

Final regulations provide the tax treatment of certain stock redemptions, during marriage or incident to divorce, of stock owned by a spouse or former spouse ("transferor spouse"). Treas. Reg. §1.1041-2; TD 9035, 67 Fed. Reg. 1534 (1-13-2003). *ASRS, Sec. 53, ¶20.8(a).*

TAXABLE INCOME--CALCULATION OF TAX

817. How is taxable income calculated? What is the standard deduction?

In most cases, taxable income is calculated by one of two methods. Taxpayers may subtract from adjusted gross income (see Q 813) an amount for each personal exemption allowable to the taxpayer and the standard deduction (explained below). Alternatively, taxpayers can deduct from adjusted gross income their allowable personal exemptions (see Q 819, Q 820) and the total of their itemized deductions. IRC Sec. 63.

In the case of individuals, the standard deduction for taxable years beginning in 2006 is $10,300 for married individuals filing jointly and surviving spouses; $7,550 for heads of households, $5,150 for single individuals and married individuals filing separately. IRC Sec. 63(c); Rev. Proc. 2005-70, 2005-47 IRB 979. The standard deduction is adjusted annually for inflation. IRC Sec. 63(c)(4).

Individuals who do not itemize and who are elderly (age 65 or older) or blind are entitled to increase their standard deduction. For taxable years beginning in 2006, individuals who are married or are surviving spouses are each entitled to an additional deduction of $1,000 if they are elderly and an additional $1,000 deduction if they are blind. The extra standard deduction is $1,250 for unmarried elderly taxpayers and $1,250 for unmarried blind taxpayers. IRC Sec. 63(f); Rev. Proc. 2005-70, above. The additional amounts for elderly and blind individuals are indexed for inflation. IRC Sec. 63(c)(4).

The following taxpayers are ineligible for the standard deduction and thus must itemize their deductions or take a standard deduction of zero dollars: (1) married taxpayers filing separately, if either spouse itemizes (see e.g., Legal Memorandum 200030023), (2) non-resident aliens, (3) taxpayers filing a short year return because of a change in their annual accounting period, and (4) estates or trusts, common trust funds, or partnerships. IRC Sec. 63(c)(6).

For taxable years beginning in 2006, the standard deduction for an individual who *may* be claimed as a dependent by another taxpayer is the greater of $850 or the sum of $300 and the dependent's earned income (but the standard deduction so calculated cannot exceed the regular standard deduction amount above). IRC Sec. 63(c)(5); Rev. Proc. 2005-70, above. These dollar amounts are adjusted for inflation. IRC Sec. 63(c)(4).

"Marriage penalty" relief. EGTRRA 2001 increased the basic standard deduction for a married couple filing a joint return, providing for a phase-in of the increase until the standard deduction for a married couple filing jointly equaled twice the standard deduction for an unmarried individual filing a single return by 2009. JGTRRA 2003 accelerated the phase-in, providing that the basic standard deduction for a married couple filing a joint return equaled twice the standard deduction for an unmarried individual filing a single return for 2003 and 2004, then reverting to the lower, gradually increasing standard deduction amounts provided for under EGTRRA for 2005 through 2009 until the married filing jointly standard deduction was, once again, twice the size of the single standard deduction. However, under WFTRA 2004, the standard deduction for married individuals filing jointly is twice the amount of the standard deduction for unmarried individuals filing single returns for tax years beginning *after December 31, 2003 and continuing through 2010*. IRC Sec. 63(c). The larger standard deduction for married individuals filing jointly will "sunset" (expire) for taxable years beginning after December 31, 2010, at which time the standard deduction in effect prior to the enactment of EGTRRA 2001 will become effective (i.e., the standard deduction for married individuals filing jointly will, once again, be 167% of the standard deduction for single individuals). Act Sec. 107, JGTRRA 2003. *ASRS, Sec. 53, ¶20.6.*

818. How is the unearned income of children under age 14 taxed?

Children under the age of 14 must pay tax on their unearned income above a certain amount at their parents' marginal rate. IRC Sec. 1(g). (See Q 828 for the tax rates in 2006.) The tax applies to all unearned income, regardless of when the assets producing the income were transferred to the child.

The so-called "kiddie tax" applies to children who have not attained the age of 14 before the close of the taxable year, who have at least one parent alive at the close

INDIVIDUALS   Q 818

of the taxable year, and who have over $1,700 (in 2006) of unearned income. The tax is the greater of (A) the tax the child would pay at his own tax rate (i.e., in the absence of IRC Sec. 1(g)), or (B) the sum of (1) the tax he would pay on net unearned income at the parent's top rate, plus (2) the tax he would pay on all other income (other than "net unearned income") at his own rate. IRC Sec. 1(g)(1).

The tax applies only to "net unearned income." "Net unearned income" is defined as adjusted gross income that is not attributable to earned income, and that exceeds (1) the $850 standard deduction for a dependent child, *plus* (2) the greater of $850 or (if the child itemizes) the amount of allowable itemized deductions that are directly connected with the production of his unearned income. IRC Sec. 1(g)(4); Rev. Proc. 2005-70, 2005-47 IRB 979.

"Earned income," essentially, means all compensation for personal services actually rendered. IRC Secs. 911(d)(2), 1(g)(4)(A)(i). A child is therefore taxed at his own rate on reasonable compensation for services.

Regulations specify that "unearned income" includes any Social Security or pension payments received by the child, income resulting from a gift under the Uniform Gift to Minors Act, and interest on both earned and unearned income. Temp. Treas. Reg. §1.1(i)-1T, A-8, A-9, A-15. In the case of a trust, distributable net income that is includable in the child's net income can trigger the tax; however, most accumulation distributions received by a child from a trust will not be included in the child's gross income because of the minority exception under IRC Section 665(b). Temp. Treas. Reg. §1.1(i)-1T, A-16. Generally, the tax on accumulation distributions does not apply to domestic trusts (see Q 843). The source of the assets that produce unearned income need not be the child's parents. Temp. Treas. Reg. §1.1(i)-1T, A-8. The application of the "kiddie tax" to funds provided to a child by sources other than the child's parents was held constitutional. See *Butler v. U.S.*, 798 F. Supp. 574 (E.D. Mo. 1992).

> *Example:* Karl is a child who is under 14 years of age at the end of the taxable year beginning on January 1, 2006. Both of Karl's parents are alive at the end of the taxable year. During 2006, Karl receives $2,400 in interest from his bank account and $1,700 from a paper route. Some of the interest earned by Karl from the bank account is attributable to Karl's paper route earnings that were deposited in the account. The balance of the account is attributable to cash gifts from Karl's parents and grandparents and interest earned prior to 2006. Some cash gifts were received by Karl prior to 2006. Karl has no itemized deductions and is eligible to be claimed as a dependent on his parent's return. Therefore, for the taxable year 2006, Karl's standard deduction is $2,000, the amount of Karl's earned income, plus $300. Of this standard deduction amount, $850 is allocated against unearned income, and $1,150 is allocated against earned income. Karl's taxable unearned income is $1,550, of which $850 is taxed without regard to section 1(g). The remaining taxable unearned income of $700 is net unearned income and is taxed under section 1(g). The fact that some of Karl's unearned income is attributable to interest on principal created by earned income and gifts from persons other than Karl's parents or that some of the unearned income is attributable to property transferred to Karl prior to 2006, will not affect the tax treatment of this income under section 1(g).

The parent whose taxable income is taken into account is (a) in the case of parents who are not married, the custodial parent of the child (determined by using the support test for the dependency exemption) and (b) in the case of married individuals filing separately, the individual with the greater taxable income. Temp. Treas. Reg. §1.1(i)-1T, A-11, A-12. If the custodial parent files a joint return with a spouse who is not a parent of the child, the total joint income is applicable in determining the child's rate. "Child," for purposes of the kiddie tax, includes children who are adopted,

2006 Tax Facts on Insurance & Employee Benefits

related by the half-blood, or from a prior marriage of either spouse. Temp. Treas. Reg. §1.1(i)-1T, A-13, A-14.

If there is an adjustment to the parent's tax, the child's resulting liability must also be recomputed. In the event of an underpayment, interest, but not penalties, will be assessed against the child. Temp. Treas. Reg. §1.1(i)-1T, A-17, A-19. Any child subject to the tax imposed under IRC Section 1(g) is generally subject, to the same extent as his parents, to the alternative minimum tax provisions. IRC Sec. 59(j).

In the event that a child does not have access to needed information contained in the tax return of a parent, he (or his legal representative) may, by written request to the IRS, obtain such information from the parent's tax return as is needed to file an accurate return. Temp. Treas. Reg. §1.1(i)-1T, A-22. The IRS has stated that where the necessary parental information cannot be obtained before the due date of the child's return, no penalties will be assessed with respect to any reasonable estimate of the parent's taxable income or filing status, or of the net investment income of the siblings. Ann. 88-70, 1988-16 IRB 37.

Certain parents may elect to include their child's unearned income over $1,700 on their own return, thus avoiding the necessity of the child filing a return. The election is available to parents whose child has gross income of more than $850 and less than $8,500, all of which is from interest and dividends. IRC Sec. 1(g)(7); Rev. Prov. 2005-70, above.

The election will not be available if there has been backup withholding under the child's Social Security number or if estimated tax payments have been made in the name and Social Security number of the child. If the election is made, any gross income of the child in excess of $1,700 is included in the parent's gross income for the taxable year. (However, the inclusion of the child's income will increase the parent's adjusted gross income for purposes of certain other calculations, such as the 2% floor on miscellaneous itemized deductions and the limitation on medical expenses.) Any interest that is an item of tax preference of the child (e.g., private activity bonds) will be treated as a tax preference of the parent. For each child to whom the election applies, there is also a tax of 10% of the lesser of $850 or the excess of the gross income of such child over $850. If the election is made, the child will be treated as having no gross income for the year. IRC Sec. 1(g)(7)(B). The threshold and ceiling amounts for the availability of this election, the amount used in computing the child's alternative minimum tax, and a threshold amount used in computing the amount of tax are indexed for inflation. *ASRS Sec. 53, ¶20.2(c).*

EXEMPTIONS

819. What personal exemptions is an individual entitled to deduct in calculating his taxable income?

Taxpayers generally are permitted to deduct the following personal exemption amounts: (1) For taxable years beginning in 2006, $3,300 for husband and wife each on a joint return ($6,600 for both); (2) $3,300 for a taxpayer filing a single or separate return; (3) $3,300 for the spouse of a taxpayer filing a separate return, provided the spouse has *no gross* income and is not claimed as the dependent of another taxpayer. Rev. Proc. 2005-70, 2005-46 IRB 979. The personal exemption amount is adjusted annually for

INDIVIDUALS   Q 819

inflation. IRC Sec. 151. Generally, the exemption will not be allowed unless the Social Security number of the individual for whom the personal exemption is being claimed is provided. IRC Sec. 151(e).

The personal exemptions of certain upper income taxpayers are phased out over defined income levels. The dollar amount of personal and dependency exemptions of taxpayers with adjusted gross income above certain levels is reduced by an "applicable percentage" in the amount of two percentage points for every $2,500 (or fraction thereof; $1,250 in the case of a married individual filing separately) by which the taxpayer's adjusted gross income exceeds the following threshold amounts in 2006: Married filing jointly (and surviving spouses): $225,750; Head of household: $188,150; Single: $150,500; Married filing separately: $112,875. The phaseout is completed at the following income levels: Married filing jointly (and surviving spouses): $348,250; Head of household: $310,650; Single: $273,000; Married filing separately: $174,125. These amounts are adjusted annually for inflation. IRC Secs. 151(d)(3), 151(d)(4); Rev. Proc. 2005-70, above.

Editor's Note Beginning in 2006, the phaseout is gradually reduced each year until it is completely repealed in 2010. The amended phaseout amount is calculated by multiplying the otherwise applicable phaseout amount by the "applicable fraction." The applicable fraction for each year is as follows: 66.6% (2/3) in 2006 and 2007; 33.3% (1/3) in 2008 and 2009; and 0% in 2010. IRC Secs. 151(d)(3)(E), 151(d)(3)(F).

A child or other dependent (i.e., an individual who may be claimed as a dependent by another taxpayer) who files his own return cannot claim a personal exemption for himself. IRC Sec. 151(d)(2).

Hurricane Katrina tax relief. For tax years beginning in 2005 and 2006, individuals may reduce their taxable income by $500 for each "Hurricane Katrina displaced individual" (see below) of the taxpayer for the taxable year. Sec. 302(a), KETRA 2005. The reduction cannot exceed $2,000, reduced by the amount of the reduction for all prior taxable years. An individual cannot be taken into account if he was taken into account by the taxpayer for any prior taxable year. The taxpayer identification number of the displaced individual must be included on the taxpayer's return for the taxable year. Sec. 302(b), KETRA 2005.

A "Hurricane Katrina displaced individual" means (with respect to any taxpayer for any taxable year) any natural person *if:*

(1)   the individual's principal place of abode on August 28, 2005, was in the "Hurricane Katrina disaster area" (see below);

(2)   *either* (a) the individual is displaced from an abode located inside the "core disaster area" (see below); *or* (b) the individual is displaced from an abode located outside the core disaster area and (i) the abode was damaged by Hurricane Katrina, or (ii) or the individual was evacuated from his abode because of Hurricane Katrina; *and*

(3)   the individual is being provided free housing by the taxpayer in the taxpayer's principal residence for a period of 60 consecutive days ending in the taxable year. Sec. 302(c), KETRA 2005.

2006 Tax Facts on Insurance & Employee Benefits

The term "Hurricane Katrina displaced individual" does not apply to the taxpayer's spouse or any dependent of the taxpayer. Sec. 302(c), KETRA 2005. No deduction is allowed if the taxpayer receives any rent or other amount (from any source) in connection with the provision of such housing. Sec. 302(d), KETRA 2005. "Hurricane Katrina disaster area" means an area with respect to which a major disaster has been declared by the President before September 14, 2005, under the Robert T. Stafford Disaster Relief and Emergency Assistance Act. "Core disaster area" means that portion of the Hurricane Katrina disaster area determined by the President to warrant individual or individual and public assistance from the federal government. Sec 2, KETRA 2005. *ASRS, Sec. 53, ¶20.7.*

820. What conditions must be met to entitle the taxpayer to a dependency exemption?

A taxpayer may claim the dependency exemption for each dependent with respect to whom the following tests are met. IRC Secs. 151, 152. The term "dependent" means a "qualifying child" (see below) or a "qualifying relative" (see below). IRC Sec. 152(a).

Dependents may not claim a personal exemption for themselves in addition to the exemption claimed by the taxpayer who supports them. IRC Sec. 152(b)(1). The dependent, if married, must not file a joint return with his or her spouse. IRC Sec. 152(b)(2). In addition, the term "dependent" does not include an individual who is not a citizen or resident of the United States (or a resident of Canada or Mexico). However, a legally adopted child who does not satisfy the residency or citizenship requirements may, nevertheless, qualify as a dependent if certain requirements are met. IRC Sec. 152(b)(3).

The taxpayer may claim the exemption even though the dependent files a return. The taxpayer must include the Social Security number of any dependent claimed on his return. See, e.g., *Miller v. Comm.*, 114 TC 184 (2000).

Qualifying child. The term "qualifying child" means an individual who:

(1) is the taxpayer's "child" (see below) or a descendant of such child, *or* the taxpayer's brother, sister, stepbrother, stepsister or a descendant of any such relative;

(2) has the same principal place of abode as the taxpayer for more than one-half of the taxable year;

(3) has not attained the age of 19 as of the close of the calendar year in which the taxable year begins, *or* is a student who has not attained the age of 24 as of the close of the calendar year; *and*

(4) has *not* provided over one-half of the individual's own support for the calendar year in which the taxpayer's taxable year begins. IRC Sec. 152(c).

The term "child" means an individual who is: (1) a son, daughter, stepson, or stepdaughter of the taxpayer; or (2) an "eligible foster child" of the taxpayer. IRC Sec. 152(f)(1). An "eligible foster child" means an individual who is placed with the taxpayer by an authorized placement agency or by judgment decree, or other order of any court of

INDIVIDUALS   Q 820

competent jurisdiction. IRC Sec. 152(f)(1)(C). Any adopted children of the taxpayer are treated the same as natural born children. IRC Sec. 152(f)(1)(B).

Qualifying relative. The term "qualifying relative" means an individual who meets the following tests:

(1) who is the taxpayer's:

    (i) child or a descendant of a child,

    (ii) brother, sister, stepbrother, or stepsister,

    (iii) father or mother or an ancestor of either, or stepfather or stepmother,

    (iv) son or daughter of a brother or sister of the taxpayer,

    (v) brother or sister of the father or mother of the taxpayer,

    (vi) son-in-law, daughter-in-law, father-in-law, mother-in-law, brother-in-law, or sister-in-law, or

    (vii) an individual (other than a spouse) who, for the taxable year of the taxpayer, has the same principal place of abode as the taxpayer and is a member of the taxpayer's household;

(2) whose gross income for the calendar year in which the taxable year begins is less than the exemption amount (see below);

(3) for whom the taxpayer provides over one-half of the individual's support for the calendar year in which the taxable year begins; *and*

(4) who is *not* a qualifying child of the taxpayer (or of any other taxpayer) for any taxable year beginning in the calendar year in which the taxable year begins.

The amount of the personal exemption ($3,300 in 2006) is adjusted annually for inflation. The exemption is subject to phaseout for certain upper income taxpayers. For details, see Q 819.

Special rule for divorced parents. In the case of divorced parents who between them provide more than one-half of a child's support for the calendar year, and have custody of the child for more than one-half of the calendar year, the custodial parent (i.e., the one having custody for the greater portion of the year) is generally allowed the dependency exemption. However, the noncustodial parent can claim the exemption if the custodial parent signs a written declaration (i.e., Form 8332, or a statement conforming to the substance of Form 8332) agreeing not to claim the child as a dependent, *and* the noncustodial parent attaches the declaration to his tax return for the calendar year. (The noncustodial parent can also claim the exemption if a divorce decree or separation agreement executed before 1985 expressly provides such and he provides at least $600 for the support of the child during the calendar year. IRC Secs. 152(e)(1), 152(e)(2).) The Tax Court held that the special support rule under IRC Section 152(e) applies to parents who have never been married as well as divorced parents. *King v. Comm.*, 121 TC 245 (2003). The Service has clarified that a custodial parent may *revoke* the release of the dependency exemption and therefore, claim the dependency exemption himself, but only if the noncustodial parent agrees and does not claim the child. Legal Memorandum 200007031.

In *Miller v. Comm.*, 114 TC 184 (2000), the Tax Court denied the dependency exemption to the noncustodial parent where the custodial parent had not signed a release of the claim to the exemption; the court order, giving the noncustodial parent the right to claim the exemption was held not to be a valid substitute. In *Boltinghouse v. Comm.*, TC Memo 2003-134, the Tax Court held that there is no requirement in IRC Section 152(e) or the regulations that a spouse's waiver of his claim to a dependency exemption deduction be incorporated into a divorce decree to be effective; according to the court, a copy of the signed separation agreement attached to the income tax return satisfied the statutory requirements. In *Omans v. Comm.*, TC Summary Opinion 2005-110, the Tax Court determined that the custodial parent's certified signature on the settlement agreement signified her sworn agreement to the settlement agreement's contents, including her former spouse's entitlement to the dependency exemption.

Life insurance premiums on a child's life are not included in determining the cost of his support. *Kittle v. Comm.*, TC Memo 1975-150; *Vance v. Comm.*, 36 TC 547 (1961). A state appeals court held that federal law does not preempt a state family law court in its discretion from alternating the dependency exemption between the parents, even though one parent may have custody during the calendar year for less than half the year. *Rios v. Pulido*, 2002 Cal. App. LEXIS 4412 (2nd App. Dist. 2002). *ASRS, Sec. 53, ¶20.7.*

DEDUCTIONS

821. What itemized deductions may be taken by an individual taxpayer?

Itemized deductions are subtracted *from* adjusted gross income in arriving at taxable income; they may be claimed in addition to deductions *for* adjusted gross income (see Q 813). Itemized deductions are also referred to as "below-the-line" deductions.

In 2006, the aggregate of most itemized deductions is reduced dollar-for-dollar by the lesser of (1) 3% of the amount of the individual's adjusted gross income that exceeds $150,500 ($75,250 in the case of a married taxpayer filing separately) or (2) 80% of the amount of such itemized deductions otherwise allowable for the taxable year. IRC Sec. 68(a). The threshold income amounts at which the limit is imposed are adjusted annually for inflation. IRC Sec. 68(b); Rev. Proc. 2005-70, 2005-47 IRB 979. The Katrina Emergency Tax Relief Act of 2005 (KETRA 2005) provides an exception to the overall limitation on itemized deductions. The amount of any charitable contribution deduction allowed (under IRC Section 170) that does not exceed the "qualified contributions" (see Q 824) paid during 2005 will *not* be treated as an itemized deduction for purposes of IRC Section 68. Sec. 301(c), KETRA 2005.

For taxable years beginning after 2005 and before 2010, the limitation on itemized deductions is gradually reduced until it is completely repealed in 2010. The amended limitation amount is calculated by multiplying the otherwise applicable limitation amount by the "applicable fraction." The "application fraction" for each year is as follows: 66.6% (2/3) in 2006 and 2007; 33.3% (1/3) in 2008 and 2009; and 0% in 2010. IRC Sec. 68(f).

The limitation on itemized deductions is not applicable to medical expenses deductible under IRC Section 213, investment interest deductible under IRC Section 163(d), or certain casualty loss deductions. IRC Sec. 68(c). The limitation also is not applicable to estates and trusts. IRC Sec. 68(e). For purposes of certain other calculations, such as the limits on deduction of charitable contributions or the 2% floor on miscellaneous itemized deductions, the limitations on each separate category of deductions are applied *before* the overall ceiling on itemized deductions is applied. IRC Sec. 68(d). The deduction limitation is not taken into account in the calculation of the alternative minimum tax. IRC Sec. 56(b)(1)(F).

Among the itemized deductions taxpayers may be able to claim are the following:

...Interest, within limits (see Q 823).

...Personal taxes of the following types: state, local and foreign real property taxes; state and local personal property taxes; state, local and foreign income, war profits, and excess profits taxes; and the generation-skipping tax imposed on income distributions (see also "Sales tax deduction," below). If taxes other than these are incurred in connection with the acquisition or disposition of property, they must be treated as part of the cost of such property or as a reduction in the amount realized on the disposition. IRC Sec. 164(a).

...Uncompensated personal casualty and theft losses. But these are deductible only to the extent that the aggregate amount of uncompensated losses in excess of $100 (for each casualty or theft) exceeds 10% of adjusted gross income. IRC Sec. 165(h). The taxpayer must file a timely insurance claim for damage to property that is not business or investment property or else the deduction is disallowed to the extent that insurance would have provided compensation. IRC Sec. 165(h)(4)(E). Uncompensated casualty and theft losses in connection with a taxpayer's business or in connection with the production of income are deductible in full (see Q 813). *Hurricane Katrina tax relief – suspension of certain limitations on personal casualty losses.* Under KETRA 2005, the $100 limitation (see above) and the 10% limitation (see above) generally do not apply to the casualty or theft losses of individuals that arise in the "Hurricane Katrina disaster area" (see Q 802) on or after August 25, 2005, and that are attributable to Hurricane Katrina. In the case of any other losses, the rule set forth in IRC Section 165(h)(2)(A) – that net casualty losses are allowed only to the extent they exceed 10% of adjusted gross income – will be applied without regard to the losses referred to in the prior sentence. See Section 402, KETRA 2005. Casualty and theft losses are generally deductible only in the year the casualty occurred or the theft was discovered. See IRC Secs. 165(a), 165(e). However, because a Katrina loss qualifies as a "disaster loss" (under IRC Section 165(i)(1)), a taxpayer may *elect* to deduct his Katrina loss on his return for the preceding year, 2004. If a taxpayer has already filed his 2004 return, he may claim the loss by filing an amended return (Form 1040X) for 2004. If a taxpayer wishes to claim a loss for 2004, he generally has until the due date for filing his 2005 return to do so. Casualty losses should be reported on Form 4684 and Schedule A (Form 1040). The Service has noted that claiming a loss on an amended (or original) return for 2004 will provide an earlier refund, but waiting to claim a loss on a taxpayer's 2005 return could result in a greater tax savings, depending on the taxpayer's situation for 2005. See IRS News Release IR-2005-119.

...Contributions to charitable organizations, within certain limitations (see Q 824, Q 825).

...Unreimbursed medical and dental expenses and expenses for the purchase of prescribed drugs or insulin incurred by the taxpayer for himself and his spouse and dependents, to the extent that such expenses exceed 7.5% of his adjusted gross income (see Q 826).

...Expenses of an employee connected with his employment. Generally, such expenses are "miscellaneous itemized deductions" (see Q 822).

...Federal estate taxes and generation-skipping transfer taxes paid on "income in respect of a decedent" (see Q 827).

Generally, certain moving expenses permitted under IRC Section 217 are deductible directly from gross income (see Q 813).

Sales tax deduction. Individuals may (for a limited period of time) deduct state and local sales taxes instead of state and local income taxes. The deduction, which expires on December 31, 2005, may be based on actual sales taxes or on tables published by the Service. IRC Sec. 164(b)(5). See also Notice 2005-31, 2005-14 IRB 830, IRS Fact Sheet FS-2005-6, and Pub. 600, Optional State Sales Tax Tables, (2004). *ASRS, Sec. 53, ¶20.5.*

822. What are miscellaneous itemized deductions? What limits apply?

"Miscellaneous itemized deductions" are deductions *from* adjusted gross income ("itemized deductions") *other than* the deductions for: (1) interest; (2) taxes; (3) non-business casualty losses and gambling losses; (4) charitable contributions; (5) medical and dental expenses; (6) impairment-related work expenses for handicapped employees; (7) estate taxes on income in respect of a decedent; (8) certain short sale expenses; (9) certain adjustments under the Code's claim of right provisions; (10) unrecovered investment in an annuity contract (see Q 7); (11) amortizable bond premium; and (12) certain expenses of cooperative housing corporations. IRC Sec. 67(b).

"Miscellaneous itemized deductions" are allowed only to the extent that the aggregate of all such deductions for the taxable year exceeds 2% of adjusted gross income. IRC Sec. 67(a). For tax years beginning before 2010, miscellaneous itemized deductions are also subject to the reduction for certain upper income taxpayers (see Q 821).

Miscellaneous itemized deductions generally include unreimbursed employee business expenses, such as professional society dues or job hunting expenses, and expenses for the production of income, such as investment advisory fees or the cost for storage of taxable securities in a safe deposit box. Temp. Treas. Reg. §1.67-1T(a)(1). Expenses that relate to both a trade or business activity and a production of income or tax preparation activity (see Q 814) must be allocated between the activities on a reasonable basis. Temp. Treas. Reg. §1.67-1T(c).

INDIVIDUALS   Q 823

The Code prohibits the indirect deduction, through pass-through entities, of amounts (i.e., miscellaneous itemized deductions) that would not be directly deductible by individuals. IRC Sec. 67(c)(1); Temp. Treas. Reg. §1.67-2T. However, publicly offered mutual funds are not subject to this rule, and "pass-through entity," for this purpose, does not include estates, trusts (except for certain common trust funds established by banks) cooperatives or real estate investment trusts. IRC Sec. 67(c); Temp. Treas. Reg. §1.67-2T(g)(2). Affected pass-through entities (including partnerships, S corporations, nonpublicly offered mutual funds and REMICs) must generally allocate to each investor his respective share of such expenses; the investor must then take the items into account for purposes of determining his taxable income and deductible expenses, if any. Temp. Treas. Reg. §1.67-2T(a). *ASRS, Sec. 53, ¶¶20.2, 20.5.*

823. Is interest deductible?

The deductibility of interest depends on its classification, as described below. Furthermore, interest expense that is deductible under the rules below may be subject to the additional limitation on itemized deductions described in Q 821 (unless it is investment interest, which is not subject to that provision). Interest must be classified and is deductible within the following limitations:

(1) *Investment interest.* This includes any interest expense on indebtedness properly allocable to property held for investment. IRC Sec. 163(d)(3). Generally, investment interest is deductible only to the extent of investment income; however, investment interest in excess of investment income may be carried over to succeeding tax years. Under JGTRRA 2003, certain dividends are taxable at 15% rather than at higher ordinary income tax rates. See Q 815, Q 828. A dividend will be treated as investment income for purposes of determining the amount of deductible investment interest income only if the taxpayer elects to treat the dividend as *not* being eligible for the reduced rates. IRC Secs. 1(h)(11)(D)(i), 163(d)(4)(B). For the temporary regulations relating to an election that may be made by noncorporate taxpayers to treat qualified dividend income as investment income for purposes of calculating the deduction for investment interest, see Temp. Treas. Reg. §1.163(d)-1T; TD 9147, 69 Feg. Reg. 47364 (8-5-2004). See also REG-171386-03, 69 Fed. Reg. 47395 (8-5-2004).

(2) *Trade or business interest.* This includes any interest incurred in the conduct of a trade or business. Generally, such interest is deductible as a business expense. IRC Sec. 162.

(3) *Qualified residence interest.* Qualified residence interest is interest paid or accrued during the taxable year on debt that is secured by the taxpayer's qualified residence and that is either (a) "acquisition indebtedness" (that is, debt incurred to acquire, construct or substantially improve the qualified residence, or any refinancing of such debt), or (b) "home equity indebtedness" (any other indebtedness secured by the qualified residence). There is a limitation of $1,000,000 on the aggregate amount of debt that may be treated as acquisition indebtedness, *but* the amount of refinanced debt that may be treated as acquisition indebtedness is limited to the amount of debt being refinanced. The aggregate amount that may be treated as "home equity indebtedness" (that is, borrowing against the fair market value of the home less the acquisition indebtedness, or refinancing to borrow against the "equity" in the home) is $100,000. IRC Sec. 163(h)(3). Indebtedness incurred on or before October 13, 1987 (and limited refinancing of it) that is secured by a qualified residence is considered acquisition indebtedness. This pre-October 14,

2006 Tax Facts on Insurance & Employee Benefits

Q 823   FEDERAL INCOME TAX

1987 indebtedness is not subject to the $1,000,000 aggregate limit, but is included in the aggregate limit as it applies to indebtedness incurred after October 13, 1987. IRC Sec. 163(h)(3)(D).

A "qualified residence" is the taxpayer's principal residence and one other residence that the taxpayer (a) used during the year for personal purposes more than 14 days or, if greater, more than 10% of the number of days it was rented at a fair rental value, or (b) used as a residence but did not rent during the year. IRC Sec. 163(h)(4)(A). See, e.g., FSA 200137033.

Subject to the above limitations, qualified residence interest is deductible. If indebtedness used to purchase a residence is secured by property other than the residence, the interest incurred on it is not residential interest but is personal interest. Let. Ruls. 8743063 and 8742025. The Tax Court denied a deduction for mortgage interest to individuals renting a home under a lease with an option to purchase the property; although the house was their principal residence, they did not have legal or equitable title to the home and the earnest money did not provide ownership status. *Blanche v. Comm.*, TC Memo 2001-63, *aff'd without opinion*, 2002 U.S. App. LEXIS 6379 (5th Cir. 2002). An individual member of a homeowner's association was denied a deduction for interest paid by the association on a common building because the member was not the party primarily responsible for repaying the loan and the member's principal residence was not the specific security for the loan. Let. Rul 200029018. Assuming that the loan was otherwise a bona fide debt, a taxpayer could deduct interest paid on a mortgage loan from his qualified plan, even though the amount by which the loan exceeded the $50,000 limit of IRC Section 72(p) was deemed to be a taxable distribution. FSA 200047022.

(4) *Interest taken into account in computing income or loss from a passive activity.* A passive activity is generally an activity that involves the conduct of a trade or business but in which the taxpayer does not materially participate, or any rental activity. IRC Secs. 163(d), 469(c).

(5) *Interest on extended payments of estate tax.* Generally, this interest is deductible. See Q 851.

(6) *Interest on education loans.* An above-the-line deduction is available to certain taxpayers for interest paid on a "qualified education loan." IRC Secs. 163(h)(2)(F), 221. The deduction is subject to a limitation of $2,500 in 2006. The deduction is phased out over an income range of $30,000 for taxpayers with modified adjusted gross income (MAGI–see below) above $105,000 (married filing jointly) and over an income range of $15,000 for taxpayers with MAGI above $50,000 (single). The deduction is fully phased out at $135,000 for married taxpayers filing jointly and at $65,000 for other taxpayers. IRC Sec. 221(b); Rev. Proc. 2005-70, 2005-47 IRB 979. Certain other requirements must be met for the deduction to be available. See IRC Sec. 221; Treas. Reg. §1.221-1; 68 Fed. Reg. 25489 (5-7-2004).

(7) *Personal interest.* This is any interest expense not described in (1) through (6) above and is often referred to as "consumer" interest. IRC Sec. 163(h)(2). Personal interest includes interest on indebtedness properly allocable to the purchase of consumer items, and interest on tax deficiencies. Personal interest is not deductible. IRC Sec. 163(h)(1).

INDIVIDUALS   Q 824

The proper allocation of interest generally depends on the use to which the loan proceeds are put, except in the case of qualified residence interest. Detailed rules for classifying interest by tracing the use of loan proceeds are contained in temporary regulations. See Temp. Treas. Reg. §1.163-8T. The interest allocation rules apply to interest expense that would otherwise be deductible. Temp. Treas. Reg. §1.163-8T(m)(2).

Various provisions in the Code may prohibit or delay the deduction of certain types of interest expense. For example, no deduction is allowed for interest paid on a loan used to buy or carry tax-exempt securities or, under certain conditions, for interest on a loan used to purchase or carry a life insurance or annuity contract (see Q 245). *ASRS, Sec. 53, ¶20.5(c)*.

824. What is the maximum annual limit on the income tax deduction allowable for charitable contributions?

An individual who itemizes may take a deduction for certain contributions "to" or "for the use of" charitable organizations. The amount that may be deducted by an individual in any one year is subject to the income percentage limitations as explained below. The value that may be taken into account for various gifts of property depends on the type of property and the type of charity to which it is contributed; these rules are explained under separate headings below.

For an explanation of the phaseout of the deduction for certain upper income taxpayers, see Q 821. For an explanation of the deduction for charitable gifts of life insurance, see Q 282. For an explanation of the deduction for a contribution of a remainder interest or income interest in trust, see Q 825.

Income Percentage Limits

Fifty percent limit. An individual is allowed a charitable deduction of up to 50% of his adjusted gross income for a charitable contribution *to*: churches; schools; hospitals or medical research organizations; organizations that normally receive a substantial part of their support from federal, state, or local governments or from the general public and that aid any of the above organizations; federal, state, and local governments. Also included in this list is a limited category of private foundations (i.e., private operating foundations and conduit foundations–see IRC Sec. 170(b)(1)(E)) that generally direct their support to public charities. IRC Sec. 170(b)(1)(A). The above organizations are often referred to as "50%-type charitable organizations."

Hurricane Katrina relief – temporary suspension of 50% limit. KETRA 2005 provides that the percentage limitation set forth above does *not* apply to "qualified contributions" (see below). Sec. 301(a), KETRA 2005. However, qualified contributions are allowed only to the extent that the aggregate of those contributions does not exceed the excess of (1) the taxpayer's adjusted gross income over (2) the amount of all other charitable contributions allowed under IRC Section 170(b)(1). Sec. 301(b)(1), KETRA 2005. "Qualified contribution" means any charitable contribution: (1) paid during the period beginning on August 28, 2005, and ending on December 31, 2005, in *cash* to an organization described in IRC Section 170(b)(1)(A) (i.e., a "50%-type organization" – see above); and (2) with respect to which the individual taxpayer has *elected* to apply this treatment. Sec. 301(d)(1), KETRA 2005. The term "qualified contribution" does not include a contribution if it is for establishment of a new (or maintenance in an existing) segregated fund or account with respect to which the donor (or any person appointed

2006 Tax Facts on Insurance & Employee Benefits   789

or designated by the donor) has, or reasonably expects to have, advisory privileges with respect to distributions or investments by reason of the donor's status as a donor (i.e., donor advised funds, private non-operating foundations, and supporting organizations). Sec. 301(d)2), KETRA 2005. In addition, KETRA 2005 also provides an exception to the overall limitation on itemized deductions; see Q 821. Sec. 301(c), KETRA 2005.

Thirty percent limit. The deduction for contributions of most long-term capital gain property to the above organizations, contributions *for the use of* any of the above organizations, as well as contributions (other than long-term capital gain property) *to* or *for the use of* any other types of charitable organizations (i.e., most private foundations) is limited to the lesser of (a) 30% of the taxpayer's adjusted gross income, or (b) 50% of adjusted gross income minus the amount of charitable contributions allowed for contributions to the 50%-type charities. IRC Secs. 170(b)(1)(B), 170(b)(1)(C).

Twenty percent limit. The deduction for contributions of long-term capital gain property to most private foundations (see below) is limited to the lesser of (a) 20% of the taxpayer's adjusted gross income, or (b) 30% of adjusted gross income minus the amount of charitable contributions allowed for contributions to the 30%-type charities. IRC Sec. 170(b)(1)(D).

Deductions denied because of the 50%, 30% or 20% limits may be carried over and deducted over the next five years, retaining their character as 50%, 30% or 20% type deductions. IRC Secs. 170(d)(1), 170(b)(1)(D)(ii).

Gifts are "to" a charitable organization if made directly to the organization. "For the use of" applies to indirect contributions to a charitable organization (e.g., an income interest in property, but not the property itself; see Q 825). See Treas. Reg. §1.170A-8(a)(2). The term "for the use of" does not refer to a gift of the right to use property. Such a gift would generally be a nondeductible gift of less than the donor's entire interest.

Gifts of Long-term Capital Gain Property

If an individual makes a charitable contribution to a 50%-type charity of property the sale of which would have resulted in long-term capital gain (other than certain tangible personal property, see below), he is generally entitled to deduct the full fair market value of the property, but the deduction will be limited to 30% of adjusted gross income. IRC Sec. 170(b)(1)(C).

Long-term capital gain property. "Long-term capital gain" means "gain from the sale or exchange of a capital asset held for more than 1 year, if and to the extent such gain is taken into account in computing gross income." IRC Sec. 1222(3).

Any portion of a gift of long-term capital gain property to a 50%-type organization that is disallowed as a result of the adjusted gross income limitation may be carried over for five years, retaining its character as a 30% type deduction. IRC Sec. 170(b)(1)(C)(ii).

A taxpayer may elect in any year to have gifts of long-term capital gain property be subject to a 50% of adjusted gross income limit; if he does so, the gift is valued at the donor's adjusted basis. Once made, such an election applies to all contributions of capital gain property during the taxable year (except unrelated use gifts of appreciated tangible personal property, as explained below) and is generally irrevocable for that

INDIVIDUALS   Q 824

year. IRC Sec. 170(b)(1)(C)(iii); *Woodbury v. Comm.*, TC Memo 1988-272, *aff'd*, 90-1 USTC ¶50,199 (10th Cir. 1990).

Gifts of Tangible Personal Property

The treatment of a contribution of appreciated tangible personal property (i.e., property which, if sold, would generate long-term capital gain) depends on whether the use of the property is related or unrelated to the purpose or function of the (public or governmental) organization. If the property is related use property (e.g., a contribution of a painting to a museum), generally the full fair market value is deductible, up to 30% of the individual's adjusted gross income; however, if the property is unrelated use property, the deduction is generally limited to the donor's adjusted basis. IRC Secs. 170(e)(1)(B), 170(b)(1)(C); Treas. Reg. §1.170A-4(b).

Gifts to Private Foundations

Most private foundations are family foundations subject to restricted contribution limits. Certain other private foundations (i.e, conduit foundations and private *operating* foundations), which operate much like public charities, are treated as 50%-type organizations. See IRC Secs. 170(b)(1)(E), 170(b)(1)(A)(vii). The term "private foundations" as used under this heading refers to standard private (e.g., family) foundations.

The amount of the deduction for a contribution of appreciated property (tangible or intangible) contributed *to* or *for the use of* private foundations generally is limited to the donor's adjusted basis; however, certain gifts of *qualified appreciated stock* made to a private foundation are deductible at their full fair market value. IRC Sec. 170(e)(5).

Qualified appreciated stock is generally publicly traded stock which, if sold on the date of contribution at its fair market value, would result in a long-term capital gain. See IRC Sec. 170(e)(5). Such a contribution will not constitute qualified appreciated stock to the extent that it exceeds 10% of the value of all outstanding stock of the corporation; family attribution rules apply in reaching the 10% level. IRC Sec. 170(e)(5)(C). The Service has determined that shares in a mutual fund can constitute qualified appreciated stock. Let. Rul. 199925029. See also Let. Rul. 200322005 (ADRs are qualified appreciated stock).

Other Gifts of Property

The deduction for any charitable contribution of property is reduced by the amount of gain that would *not* be long-term capital gain if the property were sold at its fair market value at the time of the contribution. IRC Sec. 170(e)(1)(A).

In the case of a gift of S corporation stock, special rules (similar to those relating to the treatment of unrealized receivables and inventory items under IRC Section 751) apply in determining whether gain on such stock is long-term capital gain for purposes of determining the amount of a charitable contribution. IRC Sec. 170(e)(1).

A contribution of a partial interest in property is deductible only if the donee receives an undivided portion of the donor's entire interest in the property. Such a contribution was upheld even where the donee did not take possession of the property during the tax year. *Winokur v. Comm.*, 90 TC 733 (1988), acq. 1989-1 CB 1. Generally, a deduction is denied for the mere use of property or for any interest which is less than the donor's entire interest in the property, unless the deduction would have been allowable if the transfer had been in trust.

Substantiation

Charitable contributions of $250 or more (whether in cash or property) must be substantiated by a contemporaneous written acknowledgment of the contribution supplied by the charitable organization. Substantiation is not required if certain information is reported on a return filed by the charitable organization. IRC Sec. 170(f)(8). (Publication 1771 states that an organization can provide the acknowledgement electronically, such as via an e-mail addressed to the donor. Pub. 1771 (March 2002), p. 1.) Special rules apply to the substantiation and disclosure of quid pro quo contributions and contributions made by payroll deduction. See Treas. Regs. §§1.170A-13(f), 1.6115-1.

AJCA 2004 provides strict rules for charitable donations of patents and intellectual property, and tightens rules for donations of used motor vehicles, boats, and airplanes. See IRC Sec. 170(e)(1)(B); IRC Secs. 170(f)(11), 170(f)(12), 170(m), as added by AJCA 2004. See also IRS News Release IR-2004-142 (11-30-2004). For interim guidance on such contributions, see Notice 2005-25 IRB 1287. *ASRS, Sec. 53, ¶20.5(h)*.

825. Can a charitable deduction be taken for a contribution in trust of a remainder interest or a lead interest in property?

Yes, if certain requirements are met. An individual may make an immediately deductible gift in trust to a charity, but keep (or give to another person or persons) the right to receive regular payments from the trust, for life or a period of years, before the charity receives any amount. To receive this special treatment, the gift must be made to a *charitable remainder trust*, defined below, or to a pooled income fund. IRC Sec. 170(f)(2)(A). Any individual beneficiaries must be alive when the trust is created. To be immediately deductible, the gift must be of real property or intangibles; a gift of a remainder interest in tangible personal property is deductible only when all intervening interests have expired or are held by parties unrelated to the donor. IRC Sec. 170(a)(3); Treas. Reg. §1.170A-5(a)(1). The IRC also permits a deduction for a gift of an annuity or unitrust interest, generally referred to as a *charitable lead trust* (see below). IRC Sec. 170(f)(2)(B).

The Code narrowly defines these trusts in order to assure that an accurate determination can be made of the value of the contribution.

A *charitable remainder unitrust* provides to a noncharitable beneficiary a variable payout based on the annual valuation of the trust assets. The payout is paid at least annually to a noncharitable beneficiary or beneficiaries, and must generally be a fixed percentage of not less than 5% and not more than 50% of the net fair market value of the trust assets. IRC Sec. 664(d)(2)(A). Furthermore, the value of the remainder interest in property contributed to a unitrust must be at least 10% of the net fair market value of each contribution as of the date the property is contributed to the unitrust. (Different rules applied to transfers in trust and wills executed before July 29, 1997.) IRC Sec. 664(d)(2)(D).

The trust instrument may limit the payout to the net income of the trust, with any deficiency to be made up in later years; this is commonly referred to as a *net income unitrust*. Since the trust is valued annually, the donor may make additional contributions

INDIVIDUALS Q 825

to the trust. The payout may extend for a term of up to 20 years, or if the beneficiary is an individual, for life (or the lives of more than one beneficiary). Generally, no payments other than those described above may be made to anyone other than a qualified charity. IRC Sec. 664(d)(2)(B). Following the termination of all payments, the remainder interest generally is transferred to the charity or retained by the trust for the benefit of the charity. IRC Sec. 664(d)(1)(C).

A *charitable remainder annuity trust* provides to a noncharitable beneficiary a fixed payout at least annually of not less than 5% and not more than 50% of the initial net fair market value of all property placed in the trust. IRC Sec. 664(d)(1)(A). The value of a remainder interest in property contributed to an annuity trust generally must be at least 10% of the initial fair market value of all property placed in the trust. (Different rules applied to transfers in trust and wills executed before July 29, 1997.) IRC Sec. 664(d)(1)(D).

Because the payout amount is fixed at the inception of the trust, valuation occurs only once, and the payout cannot be limited to the net income of the trust. Furthermore, the donor cannot make additional payments to the trust. The payments may extend for a term of up to 20 years or, if the beneficiary is an individual, for life (or the lives of more than one beneficiary). No payments other than those described may be made to anyone other than a qualified charity. IRC Sec. 664(d)(1)(B). Following the termination of all payments, the remainder interest is generally transferred to the charity or retained by the trust for the benefit of the charity. IRC Sec. 664(d)(1)(C).

Spousal Election Rights and Charitable Remainder Trusts. The IRS and Treasury Department have issued guidance providing a safe harbor procedure to avoid the disqualification of a charitable remainder trust (CRAT or CRUT) if, under applicable state law, the grantor's surviving spouse has a right of election exercisable upon the grantor's death to receive an elective, statutory share of the grantor's estate, and that share could be satisfied in whole or part from assets of the CRAT or CRUT (in violation of IRC Section 664(d)). See Rev. Proc. 2005-24, 2005-16 IRB 909.

A *pooled income fund* is a trust maintained by the charity into which each donor transfers property and from which each named beneficiary receives an income interest. The remainder interest ultimately passes to the charity that maintains the fund. All contributions to a pooled income fund are commingled, and all transfers to it must meet the requirements for an irrevocable remainder interest. The pooled income fund cannot accept or invest in tax-exempt securities, and no donor or beneficiary of an income interest can be a trustee of the fund. The income to the beneficiaries is determined by the rate of return earned by the trust each year. IRC Sec. 642(c)(5); Treas. Reg. §1.642(c)-5.

A *charitable lead trust* is essentially the reverse of a charitable remainder trust; the donor gives an annuity or unitrust interest to the charity, with the remainder reverting to the donor (or his named beneficiaries). Such trusts are commonly called charitable "lead" trusts because the first or leading interest is in the charitable donee. Even though a gift of such an interest in property is less than the entire interest of the donor, its value will be deductible if the interest is in the form of a "guaranteed annuity interest" or a "unitrust interest." IRC Sec. 170(f)(2)(B).

A *guaranteed annuity interest* is an irrevocable right to receive at least annually payment of a determinable amount. A *unitrust interest* is an irrevocable right to receive payment at least annually of a fixed percentage of the fair market value of the trust assets, determined annually. In either case, payments may be made to the charity for a term of years or over the life or lives of an individual (who is living at the date of the transfer to the trust). Treas. Reg. §1.170A-6(c)(2). One or more of only the following individuals may be used as measuring lives: (1) the donor; (2) the donor's spouse; (3) a lineal ancestor of all the remainder beneficiaries; or (4) the spouse of a lineal ancestor of all the remainder beneficiaries. A trust will satisfy the requirement that all remainder beneficiaries are lineal descendants of the individual who is the measuring life (or that individual's spouse) if there is less than a 15% probability that individuals who are not lineal descendants will receive any trust corpus. Treas. Reg. §1.170A-6(c)(2).

A guaranteed annuity may be made to continue for the shorter of a term of years or lives in being plus a term of years. Rev. Rul. 85-49, 1985-1 CB 330. After termination of the income interest, the remainder interest in the property is returned to the donor or his designated beneficiaries. *ASRS, Sec. 53, ¶20.5(h)*.

826. What are the limits on the medical expense deduction?

A taxpayer who itemizes deductions can deduct unreimbursed expenses for "medical care" (the term "medical care" includes dental care) and expenses for *prescribed* drugs or insulin for himself, his spouse and his dependents, to the extent that such expenses exceed 7.5% of his adjusted gross income. (On a joint return, the 7.5% floor is based on the combined adjusted gross income of husband and wife.) The taxpayer first determines his net unreimbursed expenses by subtracting all reimbursements received during the year from total expenses for medical care paid during the year. He must then subtract 7.5% of his adjusted gross income from net unreimbursed medical expenses; only the balance, if any, is deductible. IRC Sec. 213. The deduction for medical expenses is not subject to the reduction in itemized deductions for certain upper income taxpayers. (See Q 821.) For more details on the deduction of health insurance premiums, see Q 154.

"Medical care" is defined as amounts paid: (a) for the diagnosis, cure, mitigation, treatment, or prevention of disease, or for the purpose of affecting any structure or function of the body; (b) for transportation primarily for and essential to such medical care; (c) for qualified long-term services; or (d) for insurance covering such care or for any qualified long-term care insurance contract. IRC Sec. 213(d)(1).

The term "medical care" does not include cosmetic surgery or other similar procedures unless necessary to correct a deformity resulting from a congenital abnormality, a personal injury resulting from accident or trauma, or a disfiguring disease. IRC Sec. 213(d)(9); see, e.g., Let. Rul. 200344010. But see *Al-Murshidi v. Comm.*, TC Summary Opinion 2001-185 (the surgical removal of excess skin from a formerly obese individual was not "cosmetic surgery" for purposes of IRC Section 213(d)(9)(A) because the procedures meaningfully promoted the proper function of the individual's body and treated her disease; thus, the costs of the surgical procedures were deductible despite the "cosmetic surgery" classification given to the procedures by the surgeon).

A taxpayer can deduct the medical expenses he pays for a dependent (within the specified limits) even though he is not entitled to a dependency exemption. The fact that the dependent's income exceeds $3,300 (in 2006) for the year is immaterial so long as the taxpayer has furnished over one-half of his support. A child of parents who are divorced (or in some situations, separated) *and* who between them provide more than

INDIVIDUALS   Q 826

one-half of the child's support for the calendar year and have custody of the child for more than one-half of the calendar year will be treated as a dependent of both parents for purposes of this deduction. IRC Sec. 213(d)(5). But in the case of a multiple support agreement, only the person designated to take the dependency exemption may deduct the dependent's medical expenses, and then only to the extent that he actually paid the expenses. Treas. Reg. §1.213-1(a)(3)(i). See Q 820.

Deductible medical expenses include amounts paid for lodging, up to $50 per individual per night, while away from home *primarily for and essential to* medical care if such care is provided by a physician in a licensed hospital (or similar medical care facility) and there is no element of personal pleasure, recreation or vacation in the travel away from home. No deduction is allowed if the lodgings are "lavish or extravagant." IRC Sec. 213(d)(2). A mother was permitted to deduct lodging expenses incurred when her child was receiving medical care away from home and her presence was essential to such care. Let. Rul. 8516025. A parent's costs of attending a medical conference (i.e., registration fee, transportation costs) to obtain information about a chronic disease affecting the parent's child were deductible so long as the costs were primarily for and essential to the medical care of the dependent. However, the costs of meals and lodging incurred by the parent while attending the conference were not deductible. Rev. Rul. 2000-24, 2000-19 IRB 963. The Service privately ruled that taxpayers could deduct special education tuition for their children as a medical care expense where the children attended a school primarily to receive medical care in the form of special education and in those years each child had been diagnosed as having a medical condition that handicapped the child's ability to learn. See Let. Rul. 200521003.

Generally, medical expenses are deductible only in the year they are paid, regardless of when the expenses were incurred. (But see *Zipkin v. U.S.*, 2000-2 USTC ¶50,863 (D. Minn. 2000), holding that expenses incurred by a taxpayer to build a home to meet his wife's special health needs were properly deducted in the year the home became habitable, even though the costs had been paid in earlier years.) Costs paid by parents to modify a van used to transport their handicapped child were deductible in the year those costs were paid; however, the court held that depreciation was not a deductible medical expense. *Henderson v. Comm.*, TC Memo 2000-321. However, medical expenses of a decedent paid out of his estate within one year from date of death are considered paid by the decedent at the time the expenses were incurred. IRC Sec. 213(c). A decedent's medical expenses cannot be taken as an income tax deduction unless a statement is filed waiving the right to deduct them for estate tax purposes. Amounts not deductible under IRC Section 213 may not be treated as deductible medical expenses for estate tax purposes. Thus, expenses that do not exceed the 7.5% floor are not deductible. Rev. Rul. 77-357, 1977-2 CB 328.

The Social Security hospital tax that an individual pays as an employee or self-employed person cannot be deducted as a medical expense. See IRC Sec. 213(d). But a 65-year-old who has signed up for the supplementary medical plan under Medicare can treat his monthly premiums as amounts paid for insurance covering medical care. See Q 154. Rev. Rul. 66-216, 1966-2 CB 100. Also, the unreimbursed portion of an entrance fee for life care in a residential retirement facility that is allocable to future medical care is deductible as a medical expense in the year paid (but, if the resident leaves the facility and receives a refund, the refund is includable in gross income to the extent it is attributable to the deduction previously allowed). Rev. Rul. 76-481, 1976-2 CB 82, *as clarified by* Rev. Rul. 93-72, 1993-2 CB 77; Let. Rul. 8641037. Either the percentage method or the actuarial method may be used to calculate the portions of monthly service fees (paid for lifetime residence in a continuing care retirement community) allocable to medical care. *Baker v. Comm.*, 122 TC 143 (2004).

Amounts paid by an individual for medicines and drugs, which can be purchased without a doctor's prescription, are not deductible. Rev. Rul. 2003-58, 2003-22 IRB 959. However, amounts paid by an individual for equipment (e.g., crutches), supplies (e.g., bandages), or diagnostic devices (e.g., blood sugar test kits) may qualify as amounts paid for medical care and may be deductible under IRC Section 213. (In this ruling, the IRS determined that the crutches were used to mitigate the effect of the taxpayer's injured leg and the blood sugar test kits were used to monitor and assist in treating the taxpayer's diabetes; accordingly, the costs were amounts paid for medical care and were deductible.) Rev. Rul. 2003-58, above; see also IRS Information Letter INFO-2003-169 (6-13-2003).

The costs of nutritional supplements, vitamins, herbal supplements, and "natural medicines" cannot be included in medical expenses unless they are recommended by a doctor as treatment for a specific medical condition diagnosed by a doctor. Pub. 502, Medical and Dental Expenses (2004). Certain expenses for smoking cessation programs and products are deductible as a medical expense. See Rev. Rul. 99-28, 1999-25 IRB 6.

Amounts paid by individuals for breast reconstruction surgery following a mastectomy for cancer, and for vision correction surgery are medical care expenses and are deductible. But amounts paid by individuals to whiten teeth discolored as a result of age are not medical care expenses and are not deductible. Rev. Rul. 2003-57, 2003-22 IRB 959.

Costs paid by individuals for participation in a weight-loss program as treatment for a specific disease or diseases (e.g., obesity, hypertension, or heart disease) diagnosed by a physician are deductible as medical expenses; however, costs of diet food are not deductible. Rev. Rul. 2002-19, 2002-16 IRB 778. According to Publication 502 (2004), this includes fees paid by a taxpayer for membership in a weight reduction group and attendance at periodic meetings. Membership dues for a gym, health club, or spa cannot be included in medical expenses, but separate fees charged for weight loss activities can be included as medical expenses. In informational guidance, the IRS has also stated that taxpayers may deduct exercise expenses, including the cost of equipment to use in the home, if required to treat an illness (including obesity) diagnosed by a physician. For an exercise expense to be deductible, the taxpayer must establish the purpose of the expense is to treat a disease rather than to promote general health, and that the taxpayer would not have paid the expense but for this purpose. Information Letter INFO 2003-0202.

Expenses for childbirth classes were deductible as a medical expense to the extent that the class prepared the taxpayer for an active role in the process of childbirth. Let. Rul. 8919009. Egg donor fees and expenses relating to obtaining a willing egg donor count as medical care expenses that are deductible. Let. Rul. 200318017; see also Information Letter INFO 2005-0102 (3-29-2005).

The Service has clarified that no deduction is allowed for the cost of drugs imported from Canada. See Information Letter INFO 2005-0011 (3-14-2005); see also Pub. 502 (2004). *ASRS, Sec. 53, ¶20.5(i).*

INDIVIDUALS   Q 827

827. What is income in respect of a decedent and how is it taxed? Is the recipient entitled to an income tax deduction for estate and generation-skipping transfer taxes paid on this income?

"Income in respect of a decedent" (IRD) refers to those amounts to which a decedent was entitled as gross income, but which were not includable in his taxable income for the year of his death. IRC Sec. 691(a). It can include, for example: renewal commissions of a sales representative (see Q 803); payment for services rendered before death or under a deferred compensation agreement (see Q 135); and, proceeds from sales on the installment method (see Q 806). Effective for decedents dying after August 20, 1996, if stock is acquired in an S corporation from a decedent, the pro rata share of any income of the corporation that would have been IRD if that item had been acquired directly from the decedent is IRD. IRC Sec. 1367(b).

The IRS has determined that a distribution from a qualified plan of the balance as of the employee's death is IRD. Rev. Rul. 69-297, 1969-1 CB 131; Rev. Rul. 75-125, 1975-1 CB 254. The Service has also privately ruled that a distribution from a 403(b) tax sheltered annuity is IRD. Let. Rul. 9031046. It also concluded that a death benefit paid to beneficiaries from a deferred variable annuity would be IRD to the extent that the death benefit exceeded the owner's investment in the contract. Let. Rul. 200041018. In addition, the Service has determined that distributions from a decedent's individual retirement account were IRD, including the portion of each distribution used to satisfy the decedent's estate tax obligation, since the individual retirement account was found to have automatically vested in the beneficiaries at the time of the decedent's death. Let. Rul. 9132021. See also Let. Rul. 200336020. However, a rollover of funds from a decedent's IRA to a marital trust and then to the surviving spouse's IRA was not IRD where the surviving spouse was the sole trustee and sole beneficiary of the trust.

The proceeds from the sale of real property where the decedent had failed to perform all of the substantial preconditions to the sale prior to death were not IRD. *Est. of Napolitano v. Comm.*, TC Memo 1992-316. Gain realized up on the cancellation at death of a note payable to a decedent has been held to be IRD to the decedent's estate. *Est. of Frane v. Comm.*, 998 F.2d 567 (8th Cir. 1993). Payment of an alimony arrearage to the estate of a former spouse was also IRD. *Kitch v. Comm.*, 97-1 USTC ¶50,124 (10th Cir. 1996).

Generally IRD must be included in the gross income of the recipient; however, a deduction is normally permitted for estate and generation-skipping transfer taxes paid on the income. The amount of the total deduction is determined by computing the federal estate tax (or generation-skipping transfer tax) with the net IRD included and then recomputing the tax with the net IRD excluded. The difference in the two results is the amount of the income tax deduction. However, if two or more persons receive IRD of the same decedent, each recipient is entitled to only a proportional share of the income tax deduction. Similarly, if the IRD is received over more than one taxable year, only a proportional part of the deduction is allowable each year. A beneficiary was allowed to claim a deduction for IRD attributable to annuity payments that had been received even though the estate tax had not yet been paid. FSA 200011023. Where the income would have been ordinary income in the hands of the decedent, the deduction is an itemized deduction. IRC Sec. 691(c); Rev. Rul. 78-203, 1978-1 CB 199. The recipient does not receive a stepped up basis. IRC Sec. 1014(c). See Q 816.

2006 Tax Facts on Insurance & Employee Benefits

Q 828   FEDERAL INCOME TAX

The Service has ruled that if the owner-annuitant of a deferred annuity contract dies *before* the annuity starting date, and the beneficiary receives a death benefit under the annuity contract, the amount received by the beneficiary in a lump sum in excess of the owner-annuitant's investment in the contract is includible in the beneficiary's gross income as IRD. If the death benefit is instead received in the form of a series of periodic payments, the amounts received are likewise includible in the beneficiary's gross income in an amount determined under IRC Section 72 as IRD. Rev. Rul. 2005-30, 2005-20 IRB 1015. See, e.g., Let. Rul. 200537019 (where the Service ruled that the amount equal to the excess of the contract's value over the decedent's basis, which would be received by the estate as the named beneficiary of the contract upon surrender of the contract, would constitute IRD includible by the estate in its gross income; however, the estate would be entitled to a deduction for the amounts of IRD paid to charities in the taxable year, or for the remaining amounts of IRD that would be set aside for charitable purposes).

In *Estate of Kahn*, 125 TC No. 11 (2005), the Tax Court held that in computing the gross estate value, the value of the assets held in the IRAs is not reduced by the anticipated income tax liability following the distribution of IRAs, in part because IRC Section 691(c) addresses the potential double tax issue. The Tax Court further held that a discount for lack of marketability is not warranted because the assets in the IRAs are publicly traded securities. Payment of the tax upon distribution is not a prerequisite to making the assets in the IRA marketable; consequently there is no basis for the discount. In technical advice the Service has also determined that a discount for lack of marketability is not available to an estate where the deduction for IRD is available to mitigate the potential income tax liability triggered by the IRD assets. TAM 200247001; see also TAM 200303010. *ASRS, Sec. 53, ¶20.15.*

RATES

828. What are the federal income tax rates for individuals?

EGTRRA 2001 reduced income tax rates above 15% for individuals, trusts and estates. EGTRRA 2001 also provided for subsequent rate reductions to occur in 2004 and 2006. IRC Secs. 1(i)(1), 1(i)(2), prior to amendment by JGTRRA 2003. JGTRRA 2003 accelerated the reductions that were scheduled to occur in 2004 and 2006. Thus, for 2003 and thereafter, the income tax rates above 15% are lowered to 25%, 28%, 33% and 35% (down from 27%, 30%, 35%, and 38.6%). IRC Sec. 1(i)(2), as amended by JGTRRA 2003. This provision is effective for taxable years beginning after December 31, 2002.

The income brackets to which each rate applies depend upon whether a separate return, joint return, head-of-household return, or single return is filed. (For an explanation of which taxpayers may file jointly or as a head-of-household, see Q 830 and Q 831.) Children under the age of 14 are generally taxed on unearned income at their parent's marginal rate (see Q 818). IRC Sec. 1(g). The income brackets are indexed annually for inflation. IRC Sec. 1(f). Separate tax rates may apply to capital gains (see Q 815).

Larger 10% tax bracket effective through 2010. EGTRRA created a new 10% bracket that applied to the first $12,000 of taxable income for married individuals filing jointly, $6,000 for single individuals, and $10,000 for heads of households. EGTRRA 2001 also provided a scheduled increase, beginning in 2008, under which the $6,000 level would have increased to $7,000, and the $12,000 level would have increased to $14,000

INDIVIDUALS   Q 829

(with those levels to be adjusted annually for inflation for taxable year beginning after December 31, 2008). JGTRRA 2003 accelerated the scheduled increases to 2003 and 2004. Consequently, in 2004 the taxable income levels (as indexed) were: $14,300 for married individuals filing jointly; $7,150 for single individuals and married individuals filing separately; and $10,200 for heads of households. Rev. Proc. 2003-85, 2003-2 CB 1184. (See Income Tax Tables, Appendix B.) For 2005 through 2010, the 10% brackets were scheduled to revert to the levels provided under EGTRRA 2001. Thus, in 2005 through 2007 the income levels would have dropped to $12,000 for married individuals filing jointly, $6,000 for single individuals, and $10,000 for heads of households. Not until 2008 would the income levels for the 10% brackets have once again increased to $14,000 for married individuals filing jointly and $7,000 for single individuals (with annual adjustments for inflation beginning after December 31, 2008).

WFTRA 2004 extends the expanded 10% brackets through 2010 at the 2003 levels (i.e., $14,000 for married individuals filing jointly, $7,000 for single individuals) with annual indexing from 2003. IRC Sec. 1(i)(1)(B). In 2006, the indexed 10% brackets are $15,100 (married filing jointly), $7,550 (single and married filing separately), and $10,750 (head of household). Rev. Proc. 2005-70, 2005-47 IRB 979. The 10% tax bracket will "sunset" (expire) for tax years beginning after December 31, 2010, at which time the 10% tax bracket will be eliminated and the portion of the income that was taxed in the 10% bracket will once again be subject to taxation in the 15% bracket. IRC Sec. 1(i)(1), as amended by JGTRRA 2003; Act Sec. 105, WFTRA 2004; Act Sec. 107, JGTRRA 2003.

"Marriage penalty" relief. EGTRRA 2001 increased the size of the 15% bracket for married couples filing joint returns to twice the size of the corresponding bracket for unmarried individuals filing single returns, phasing in the increase over four years, beginning in 2005. JGTRRA 2003 accelerated those increases, making the size of the 15% bracket for married individuals filing jointly equal to twice the size of the corresponding bracket for unmarried individuals filing single returns for taxable years beginning in 2003 and 2004. For taxable years beginning after 2004, the applicable percentages were scheduled to revert to those provided under EGTRRA 2001. Under WFTRA 2004, the 15% bracket for married individuals filing jointly is twice the size (200%) of the corresponding bracket for unmarried individuals filing single returns for tax years beginning *after December 31, 2003*. IRC Sec. 1(f)(8). The larger 15% bracket for married individuals filing jointly will "sunset" (expire) for taxable years beginning after December 31, 2010, at which time the tax bracket that was in effect prior to the enactment of EGTRRA 2001 will become effective (i.e., the 15% bracket for single individuals will, once again, be 160% of the 15% bracket for married individuals filing jointly). Act Sec. 105, WFTRA 2004; Act Sec. 107, JGTRRA 2003. *ASRS, Sec. 53, ¶20.10.*

829. What is the alternative minimum tax?

Generally

In addition to the tax calculated under the normal rates, it is sometimes necessary for a taxpayer to pay the *alternative minimum tax (AMT)*. The AMT is calculated by first determining the alternative minimum taxable income (AMTI), reducing this amount by the allowable exemption to determine taxable excess, and then applying a two-tier tax rate schedule to the amount of the taxable excess. The two-tier rate schedule applies a 26% rate to taxable excess that does not exceed $175,000 ($87,500 for married taxpayers filing separately), and a 28% rate to taxable excess over that amount. The resulting amount is the taxpayer's tentative minimum tax. The preferential tax rates on certain capital gains held for more than twelve months are also used when determining the taxpayer's tentative minimum tax (see Q 815). IRC Secs. 55(a), 55(b).

If the tentative minimum tax reduced by the AMT foreign tax credit exceeds the regularly calculated tax (with adjustments) for the tax year, the excess is the AMT. Regularly calculated tax for AMT purposes excludes certain taxes including: (1) the alternative minimum tax; (2) the tax on benefits paid from a qualified retirement plan in excess of the plan formula to a 5% owner; (3) the 10% penalty tax for certain premature distributions from annuity contracts; (4) the 10% additional tax on certain early distributions from qualified retirement plans; (5) the 10% additional tax for certain taxable distributions from modified endowment contracts; (6) taxes relating to the recapture of the federal subsidy from use of qualified mortgage bonds and mortgage credit certificates; (7) the additional tax on certain distributions from Coverdell education savings accounts; (8) the 15% additional tax on medical savings account distributions not used for qualified medical expenses; and (9) the 10% additional tax on health savings account distributions not used for qualified medical expenses. Regularly calculated tax is reduced by the foreign tax credit, the Puerto Rico and possession tax credit, and the Puerto Rico economic activity credit. IRC Secs. 55(c)(1), 26(b).

The American Jobs Creation Act of 2004 repealed the 90-percent limit on the AMT foreign tax credit for tax years beginning after 2004. AJCA 2004, Sec. 421. For tax years beginning before 2005, the AMT foreign tax credit is limited to the excess of the tentative minimum tax (determined without regard to such credit) over 10% of the tentative minimum tax (determined without regard to the AMT foreign tax credit, the AMT net operating loss deduction, and the tax preference exception for certain intangible drilling costs of independent producers). IRC Sec. 59(a)(2), prior to repeal by AJCA 2004.

For tax years from 2000 through 2005, certain nonrefundable personal credits (see Q 832) may be used to reduce the sum of a taxpayer's regular tax liability and AMT liability. IRC Sec. 26(a).

For tax years beginning after 2005, certain nonrefundable personal credits (except for the adoption expenses credit, the child tax credit, and the credit for elective deferrals and IRA contributions) may not reduce a taxpayer's regular tax liability to less than the taxpayer's tentative minimum tax. IRC Sec. 26(a).

Alternative Minimum Taxable Income

Alternative minimum taxable income is taxable income, with adjustments made in the way certain items are treated for AMT purposes, and increased by any items of tax preference. IRC Sec. 55(b)(2). In 2003 through 2005, a married individual filing a separate return must increase AMTI by the lesser of (a) 25% of the excess of the AMTI over $191,000, or (b) $29,000. After 2005, a married individual filing a separate return must increase AMTI by the lesser of (a) 25% of the excess of the AMTI over $165,000, or (b) $22,500. See IRC Sec. 55(d).

Generally, the provisions that apply in determining the regular taxable income of a taxpayer also generally apply in determining the AMTI of the taxpayer. Treas. Reg. §1.55-1(a). In addition, references to a noncorporate taxpayer's adjusted gross income

(AGI) or modified AGI in determining the amount of items of income, exclusion, or deduction must be treated as references to the taxpayer's AGI or modified AGI as determined for regular tax purposes. Treas. Reg. §1.55-1(b).

Exemption

Exemption amounts of $58,000 ($45,000 after 2005) on a joint return (or for a surviving spouse), $40,250 ($33,750 after 2005) on a single return, $29,000 ($22,500 after 2005) on a married filing separate return, and $22,500 on an estate or trust return, are available in calculating the taxable excess. These exemption amounts are reduced by 25% of the amount by which the AMTI exceeds $150,000 on a joint return, $112,500 on a single return and $75,000 on a separate return or in the case of an estate or trust. IRC Sec. 55(d). For children subject to the "kiddie tax" (Q 818) the exemption is the lesser of the above amounts or the child's earned income plus $6,050 (as indexed for 2006). IRC Sec. 59(j); Rev. Proc. 2005-70, 2005-47 IRB 979.

Adjustments

In general, the following adjustments are made to taxable income in computing alternative minimum taxable income: (1) generally, property must be depreciated using a less accelerated method or the straight line method over a period that is longer than that used for regular tax purposes, except that a longer period is not required for property placed in service after 1998; (2) the AMT net operating loss is deductible only up to 90% of AMTI determined without regard to such net operating loss (some relief was available for 2001 and 2002); (3) no deduction is allowed for miscellaneous itemized deductions; (4) generally, no deduction is allowed for state and local taxes unless attributable to a trade or business, or property held for the production of income (recovery of state tax disallowed for AMT purposes in a previous year is not added to AMTI in the year recovered); (5) medical expenses are allowed as a deduction only to the extent such expenses exceed 10% of adjusted gross income; (6) interest on indebtedness secured by a primary or second residence is generally deductible (within dollar limitations) if incurred in acquiring, constructing, or substantially improving the residence; however, the amount of refinanced indebtedness with regard to which interest is deductible is limited to the amount of indebtedness immediately prior to refinancing; (7) no standard deduction is allowed; (8) no deduction for personal exemptions is allowed; (9) the limitation on itemized deductions for upper-income taxpayers does not apply; (10) the taxpayer will include any amount realized due to a transfer of stock pursuant to the exercise of an incentive stock option; (11) AMTI is determined using losses from any tax shelter farm activity (determined by taking into account the AMTI adjustments and tax preferences) only to the extent that the taxpayer is insolvent or when the tax shelter farm activity is disposed of; and (12) passive activity losses (determined by taking into account the adjustments to AMTI and tax preferences) are not allowed in determining AMTI except to the extent that the taxpayer is insolvent. IRC Secs. 56, 58.

Preference Items

Items of tax preference that must be added to AMTI include: (1) the excess of depletion over the adjusted basis of property (except in the case of certain independent producers and royalty owners); (2) the excess of intangible drilling costs expensed (other than drilling costs of a nonproductive well) over the amount allowable for the year if the intangible drilling costs had been amortized over a 10 year period to the extent the excess is greater than 65% of the net income from oil, gas, and geothermal properties (with an exception for certain independent producers); (3) tax-exempt interest on specified private activity bonds (but reduced by any deduction not allowed in computing the regular tax if the deduction would have been allowable if the tax-exempt interest were includable in gross income); (4) accelerated depreciation or amortization on certain property placed in service before 1987; and (5) for dispositions after May 5, 2003, seven percent of the amount excluded under IRC Section 1202 (gain on sales of certain small business stock). IRC Sec. 57(a). For dispositions before May 6, 2003, the preference is 42% (28% for stock with a holding period beginning after 2000) of the amount excluded under IRC Section 1202.

Credit for Prior Year Minimum Tax Liability

A taxpayer subject to the AMT in one year may be allowed a minimum tax credit against regular tax liability in subsequent years. The credit is equal to the total of the *adjusted minimum taxes* imposed in prior years reduced by the amount of minimum tax credits allowable in prior years. However, the amount of the credit cannot be greater than the excess of the taxpayer's regular tax liability (reduced by certain credits such as certain business related credits and certain investment credits) over the tentative minimum tax. The adjusted net minimum tax for any year is the AMT for that year reduced by the amount that would be the AMT if: (1) the only adjustments were those concerning the limitations on certain deductions (such as state taxes, certain itemized deductions, the standard deduction and personal exemptions); and (2) the only preferences were those dealing with depletion, tax-exempt interest, and small business stock. The adjusted net minimum tax is increased by the amount of any nonconventional fuel source credit and qualified electric vehicles credit that was not allowed for that year due to the AMT (For tax years ending after 2005, only the qualified electric vehicles credit that was not allowed is added to the adjusted net minimum tax). IRC Sec. 53, as amended by ETIA 2005. *ASRS, Sec. 53, ¶20.10(b).*

830. Who may file a joint return?

(1) A husband and wife. Gross income and deductions of both spouses are included; however, a joint return may be filed even though one spouse has no income. (2) A widow or widower *with a dependent child* for two years after the taxable year in which the spouse died. Thus, the surviving spouse with a child continues to get the benefit of joint rates for these two years. But no personal exemption is allowed for the deceased spouse except in the year of death. IRC Secs. 2(a), 6013(a). *ASRS, Sec. 53, ¶¶20.14(c), (d).*

831. Who may use head-of-household rates?

An individual who meets the four requirements below.

1. He must be (a) unmarried, or legally separated from his spouse under a decree of divorce or of separate maintenance, or (c) married, living apart from his spouse during the last six months of the taxable year, and maintain as his home a household that constitutes the principal place of abode for a "qualifying child" (as defined in IRC Sec. 152(c); see Q 820) with respect to whom the individual is entitled to claim a deduction, and with respect to whom the taxpayer furnishes over one-half the cost of maintaining such household during the taxable year. IRC Sec. 2(b)(1); IRC Secs. 2(c), 7703(b).

2. He must maintain as his home a household in which one or more of the following persons lives: (a) a qualifying child (if that individual is unmarried, it is not necessary that he have less than $3,300 (in 2006) of income or that the head-of-household furnish

INDIVIDUALS

more than one-half his support; if the qualifying child is married, he must qualify as a dependent of the taxpayer claiming head-of-household status or would qualify except for the waiver of the exemption by the custodial parent (see Q 435)), *or* (b) any other person for whom the taxpayer can claim a dependency exemption except a cousin or unrelated person living in the household. IRC Sec. 2(b)(1); Treas. Reg. §1.2-2(b). An exception to this rule is made with respect to a taxpayer's dependent mother or father: so long as he maintains the household in which the dependent parent lives, it need not be his home. IRC Sec. 2(b)(1).

3. He must contribute over one-half the cost of maintaining the home. IRC Sec. 2(b)(1).

4. He must not be a nonresident alien. IRC Sec. 2(b); IRC Sec. 2(d). *ASRS, Sec. 53, ¶20.14(e).*

CREDITS

832. What credits may be taken against the tax?

After rates have been applied to compute the tax, certain payments and credits may be subtracted from the tax to arrive at the amount of tax payable. The refundable credits include taxes withheld from salaries and wages, payments of estimated tax, excess Social Security withheld (two or more employers), the earned income credit, and the 65% health care tax credit for uninsured workers displaced by trade competition. *Refundable* credits are recoverable regardless of the amount of the taxpayer's tax liability for the taxable year.

The *nonrefundable* credits are as follows: (1) the personal credits – such as the child and dependent care credit (IRC Sec. 21); the credit for the elderly and the permanently and totally disabled (IRC Sec. 22 – see Q 833), the qualified adoption credit (IRC Sec. 23), the Hope Scholarship and Lifetime Learning Credits (IRC Sec. 25A – see Q 835); the credit for elective deferrals and IRA contributions (the "saver's credit" – IRC Sec. 25B); the credit for certain non-business energy property (i.e., energy efficient improvements to existing homes; IRC Sec. 25C, as added ETIA 2005); the credit for residential energy efficient property (IRC Sec. 25D, as added by ETIA 2005); (2) other non-business credits; and (3) the general business credit (IRC Sec. 38, as amended by ETIA 2005). A portion of the child tax credit may be refundable for certain taxpayers (see Q 834). IRC Sec. 24.

ETIA 2005 provides a new alternative motor vehicle credit for qualified fuel cell vehicles, advanced lean-burn technology vehicles, qualified hybrid vehicles; and qualified alternative fuel vehicles. IRC Sec. 30B, as added by ETIA 2005. (This new credit replaces the prior deduction for qualified clean-fuel vehicle property, which sunsets on December 31, 2005. See Sec. 1348, ETIA 2005; IRC Sec. 179A, as amended by ETIA 2005.) The portion of the credit attributable to vehicles of a character subject to an allowance for depreciation is treated as a portion of the general business credit (IRC Sec. 38, as amended by ETIA 2005); the remainder of the credit is a personal credit allowable to the extent of the excess of the regular tax (reduced by certain other credits) over the alternative minimum tax for the taxable year. See IRC Sec. 30B(g), as added by ETIA 2005.

For tax years beginning in 2006 and thereafter, the only nonrefundable personal credits available for offset against the regular income tax and the alternative minimum tax are the (1) nonrefundable adoption credit, (2) nonrefundable child tax credit (see Q 834); and (3) nonrefundable saver's credit (which expires on December 31, 2006). For tax years beginning in 2004 and 2005, all of the nonrefundable personal credits were available for offset against the regular income tax and the alternative minimum tax. IRC Sec. 26(a). A credit may also be allowed for prior years' alternative minimum tax liability (see Q 829). *ASRS, Sec. 53, ¶20.12.*

833. Who qualifies for the tax credit for the elderly and the permanently and totally disabled and how is the credit computed?

The credit is available to taxpayers age 65 or older, *or* who are under age 65, retired on disability and were considered permanently and totally disabled when they retired. IRC Sec. 22(b).

> "An individual is permanently and totally disabled if he is unable to engage in any substantial gainful activity by reason of any medically determinable physical or mental impairment which can be expected to result in death or which has lasted or can be expected to last for a continuous period of not less than 12 months. An individual shall not be considered to be permanently and totally disabled unless he furnishes proof of the existence thereof in such form and manner, and at such times, as the Secretary may require." IRC Sec. 22(e)(3).

The credit equals 15% of an individual's IRC Section 22 amount for the taxable year, but may not exceed the amount of tax. This IRC Section 22 base amount is $5,000 for a single taxpayer or married taxpayers filing jointly if only one spouse qualifies for the credit; $7,500 for married taxpayers filing jointly if both qualify; and $3,750 for a married taxpayer filing separately. IRC Sec. 22(c). Married taxpayers must file a joint return to claim the credit, unless they lived apart for the entire taxable year. IRC Sec. 22(e)(1).

This base figure is limited for individuals under age 65 to the amount of the disability income (taxable amount an individual receives under an employer plan as wages or payments in lieu of wages for the period he is absent from work on account of permanent and total disability) received during the taxable year. IRC Sec. 22(c)(2)(B)(i). (Proof of continuing permanent and total disability may be required. GCM 39269 (8-2-84).) For married taxpayers who are both qualified and who file jointly, the base figure cannot exceed the total of both spouses' disability income if both are under age 65 or if only one is under age 65, the sum of $5,000 plus the disability income of the spouse who is under 65. IRC Sec. 22(c)(2)(B)(ii).

The base figure (or the amount of disability income in the case of individuals under age 65, if lower) is reduced dollar-for-dollar by one-half of adjusted gross income in excess of $7,500 (single taxpayers), $10,000 (joint return), or $5,000 (married filing separately). IRC Sec. 22(d). A reduction is also made for Social Security and railroad retirement benefits that are excluded from gross income, and certain other tax-exempt income. IRC Sec. 22(c)(3). *ASRS, Sec. 53, ¶20.12(a).*

834. What is the child tax credit?

A child tax credit is available for each "qualifying child" (defined below) of eligible taxpayers who meet certain income requirements. The child tax credit is $1,000 from 2006 through 2010. IRC Sec. 24(a). However, the increased child tax credit will "sunset"

INDIVIDUALS   Q 834

(expire) for tax years beginning after December 31, 2010, at which time the child tax credit will return to its pre-EGTRRA level (i.e., $500). Sec. 105, WFTRA 2004; Sec. 107, JGTRRA 2003; IRC Sec. 6429.

The term *qualifying child* means a "qualifying child" of the taxpayer (as defined under IRC Section 152(c) – see below) who has not attained the age of 17. IRC Sec. 24(c)(1).

"Qualifying child" means, with respect to any taxpayer for any taxable year, an individual:

(1) who is the taxpayer's "child" (see below), or a descendant of such a child, *or* the taxpayer's brother, sister, stepbrother, or stepsister or a descendant of any such relative;

(2) who has the same principal place of abode as the taxpayer for more than one-half of the taxable year; *and*

(3) who has *not* provided over one-half of such individual's own support for the calendar year in which the taxpayer's taxable year begins. IRC Sec. 152(c).

Additionally, a qualifying child must be either a citizen or a resident of the United States. IRC Sec. 24(c)(2).

The term "child" means an individual who is: (1) a son, daughter, stepson, or stepdaughter of the taxpayer; or (2) an "eligible foster child" of the taxpayer. IRC Sec. 152(f)(1). An "eligible foster child" means an individual who is placed with the taxpayer by an authorized placement agency or by judgment decree, or other order of any court of competent jurisdiction. IRC Sec. 152(f)(1)(C). Any adopted children of the taxpayer are treated the same as natural born children. IRC Sec. 152(f)(1)(B).

The amount of the credit is reduced for taxpayers whose modified adjusted gross income (MAGI) exceeds certain levels. A taxpayer's MAGI is his adjusted gross income without regard to the exclusions for income derived from certain foreign sources or sources within United States possessions. The credit amount is reduced by $50 for every $1000 or fraction thereof, by which the taxpayer's MAGI exceeds the following threshold amounts: $110,000 for married taxpayers filing jointly, $75,000 for unmarried individuals, and $55,000 for married taxpayers filing separately. IRC Sec. 24(b)(2).

The child tax credit is refundable to the extent of 15% of the taxpayer's earned income in excess of $10,000 (as indexed–see below). IRC Sec. 24(d)(1)(B)(i). For families with three or more qualifying children, the credit is refundable to the extent that the taxpayer's Social Security taxes exceed the taxpayer's earned income credit *if* that amount is greater than the refundable credit based on the taxpayer's earned income in excess of $10,000 (as indexed–see below). IRC Sec. 24(d)(1). The $10,000 amount is indexed for inflation ($11,300 in 2006). IRC Sec. 24(d)(3); Rev. Proc. 2005-70, 2005-47 IRB 979. (Prior to 2001, the child tax credit was refundable only for individuals with three or more qualifying children. IRC Sec. 24(d), prior to amendment by EGTRRA 2001.)

Hurricane Katrina tax relief – special "look-back" rule for determining refundable child tax credit. KETRA 2005 permits "qualified individuals" (see below) to elect to

Q 835　　　　　　　　　　　　　　　　　　FEDERAL INCOME TAX

calculate their refundable child tax credit for the taxable year that includes August 25, 2005, using their earned income from the *prior* taxable year. Qualified individuals are permitted to make the election only if their earned income for the taxable year that includes August 25, 2005, is less than their earned income for the preceding taxable year. A "qualified individual" is one whose principal place of abode August 25, 2005 was located in (1) the "core disaster area" (see Q 802) or (2) outside the core disaster area, but in the "Hurricane Katrina disaster area" (see Q 802), *and* the individual was displaced from his principal place of abode because of Hurricane Katrina. See Sec. 406, KETRA 2005; Joint Committee on Taxation, *Technical Explanation of H.R. 3768, the "Katrina Emergency Tax Relief Act of 2005," as Passed by the House and the Senate on September 21, 2005*, (JCX-69-05), September 22, 2005.

The nonrefundable child tax credit can be claimed against the individual's regular income tax *and* alternative minimum tax (see Q 832). The nonrefundable child tax credit cannot exceed the excess of (i) the sum of the taxpayer's regular tax plus the alternative minimum tax over (ii) the sum of the taxpayer's nonrefundable personal credits (other than the child tax credit, the adoption credit, and the saver's credit) and the foreign tax credit for the taxable year. IRC Sec. 24(b)(3). For tax years beginning after 2001, the refundable child tax credit is *not* required to be *reduced* by the amount of the taxpayer's alternative minimum tax. IRC Sec. 24(d). The nonrefundable credit must be reduced by the amount of the refundable credit. IRC Sec. 24(d)(1).

Some additional restrictions applying to the child tax credit include: (1) an individual's tax return must identify the name and taxpayer identification number (Social Security number) of the child for whom the credit is claimed; and (2) the credit may be claimed only for a full taxable year, unless the taxable year is cut short by the death of the taxpayer. IRC Secs. 24(e), 24(f).

For purposes of applying a uniform method of determining when a child attains a specific age, the Service has ruled that a child attains a given age on the anniversary of the date that the child was born (e.g., a child born on January 1, 1987, attains the age of 17 on January 1, 2004). Rev. Rul. 2003-72, 2003-33 IRB 346. The IRS has stated that it would apply Revenue Ruling 2003-72 retroactively and would notify those taxpayers entitled to a refund for 2002 as a result of Revenue Ruling 2003-72. Information Letter INFO-2003-0215 (8-29-2003).

The supplemental child tax credit, which was available before 2002 to certain lower income taxpayers, has been repealed. IRC Sec. 32(n), repealed by EGTRRA 2001. *ASRS Sec. 53 ¶20.12(f)*.

835. What are the Hope Scholarship and Lifetime Learning Credits?

The Hope Scholarship Credit and the Lifetime Learning Credit are education incentives available to certain eligible taxpayers who pay qualified tuition and related expenses. IRC Sec. 25A. The Hope Scholarship Credit applies to expenses paid after December 31, 1997 for education furnished in academic periods beginning after December 31, 1997. The Lifetime Learning Credit applies to expenses paid after June 30, 1998 for education furnished in academic periods beginning after June 30, 1998.

Hope Scholarship Credit

The Hope Scholarship Credit provides a credit for each *eligible student* equal to the sum of: (1) 100% of qualified tuition and related expenses up to $1,100; plus (2) 50%

INDIVIDUALS   Q 835

of qualified tuition and related expenses in excess of $1,100, up to the applicable limit. The applicable limit is two times the $1,100 amount. IRC Secs. 25A(b)(1), 25A(b)(4); Treas. Reg. §1.25A-3(a). The amounts used to calculate the credit are adjusted for inflation and rounded to the next lowest multiple of $100. IRC Sec. 25A(h)(1). The maximum credit for 2006 is $1,650 ($1,100 + (50% × $1,100)).

The Hope Scholarship Credit is available only for the first two years of postsecondary education, and can be used in only two taxable years. Treas. Reg. §1.25A-3(c). To qualify for the credit, the student must carry at least half of a full-time academic workload for an academic period during the taxable year. IRC Sec. 25A(b)(2); Treas. Reg. §1.25A-3(d)(ii).

An *eligible student* generally means a student who: (1) for at least one academic period beginning in the calendar year, is enrolled at least half-time in a program leading to a degree, certificate, or other recognized educational credential and is enrolled in one of the first two years of postsecondary education, and (2) is free of any conviction for federal or state felony offenses consisting of the possession of a controlled substance. IRC Sec. 25A(b)(3); Notice 97-60, 1997-46 IRB 310 (Sec. 1, A3); Treas. Reg. §1.25A-3(d)(1).

Qualified tuition and related expenses are tuition and fees required for the enrollment or attendance of the taxpayer, the taxpayer's spouse, or any dependent of the taxpayer (for whom he is allowed a dependency exemption) at an "eligible education institution."Treas. Reg. §1.25A-2(d)(1). Qualified tuition and related expenses do not include nonacademic fees such as room and board, medical expenses (including required student health fees), transportation, student activity fees, athletic fees, insurance expenses, and similar personal, living or family expenses unrelated to a student's academic course of instruction. Treas. Reg. §1.25A-2(d)(3). Additionally, qualified tuition and related expenses do not include expenses for a course involving sports, games or hobbies, unless it is part of the student's degree program. IRC Sec. 25A(f)(1); Treas. Reg. §1.25A-2(d)(5).

An *eligible educational institution* generally means a postsecondary educational institution that: (a) provides an educational program for which it awards a bachelor's degree, or a 2-year program that would be accepted for credit towards a bachelor's degree; (b) has at least a one year program that trains students for gainful employment in a recognized profession; (c) participates in a federal financial aid program under Title IV of the Higher Education Act of 1965 or is certified by the Department of Education as eligible to participate in such a program; or (d) meets requirements for certain postsecondary vocational, proprietary institutions of higher learning and certain institutions outside the United States. In any event, the institution must also be accredited or have been granted pre-accreditation status. See IRC Sec. 25A(f)(2); Section 481, Higher Education Act of 1965; Treas. Reg. §1.25A-2(b).

An *academic period* means a quarter, semester, trimester or other period of study (such as summer school session) as reasonably determined by an eligible educational institution. Treas. Reg. §1.25A-2(c).

Lifetime Learning Credit

The Lifetime Learning Credit is available in an amount equal to 20% of "qualified tuition and related expenses" (defined above) paid by the taxpayer during the taxable year for any course of instruction at an "eligible educational institution" (defined above)

2006 Tax Facts on Insurance & Employee Benefits

taken to acquire or improve the job skills of the taxpayer, his spouse or dependents. The Lifetime Learning Credit is a per-taxpayer credit and the maximum credit available does not vary with the number of students in the family. The maximum amount of the credit in 2006 is $2,000 (20% of up to $10,000 of qualified tuition and related expenses). IRC Sec. 25A(c); Treas. Reg. §1.25A-4(a).

Qualified tuition and related expenses, for the purposes of the Lifetime Learning Credit, include expenses for graduate as well as undergraduate courses. The Lifetime Learning Credit applies regardless of whether the individual is enrolled on a full-time, half-time, or less than half-time basis. Additionally, the Lifetime Learning Credit is available for an unlimited number of taxable years. Treas. Regs. §§1.25A-4(b), 1.25A-4(c).

Limitations and Phaseouts

The Code sets forth special rules coordinating the interaction of these credits. The Lifetime Learning Credit is not available with respect to a student for whom an election is made to take the Hope Scholarship Credit during the same taxable year. IRC Sec. 25A(c)(2)(A); Treas. Reg. §1.25A-1(b). However, the taxpayer may use the Hope Scholarship Credit for one student and the Lifetime Learning Credit for other students in the same taxable year.

Both credits are subject to the same phaseout rules based on the taxpayer's modified adjusted gross income (MAGI). MAGI is the taxpayer's adjusted gross income without regard to the exclusions for income derived from certain foreign sources or sources within United States possessions. The maximum credit in each case is reduced by the credit multiplied by a ratio. For single taxpayers, the ratio equals the excess of (i) the taxpayers MAGI over $40,000 to (ii) $10,000. For married taxpayers filing jointly, the ratio equals (a) the excess of the taxpayer's MAGI over $80,000 to (b) $20,000. IRC Sec. 25A(d); Treas. Reg. §1.25A-1(c). The $40,000 and $80,000 amounts are adjusted for inflation and rounded to the next lowest multiple of $1,000. IRC Sec. 25A(h)(2); Treas. Reg. §1.25A-1(c)(3). For 2006, the threshold amounts are $45,000 for single taxpayers and $90,000 for married taxpayers filing jointly. Rev. Proc. 2005-70, 2005-47 IRB 929.

The amount of qualified tuition and related expenses for both credits is limited by the sum of the amounts paid for the benefit of the student, such as scholarships, education assistance advances, and payments (other than a gift, bequest, devise, or inheritance) received by an individual for educational expenses attributable to enrollment. IRC Sec. 25A(g)(2); Treas. Reg. §1.25A-5(c). The IRS has determined that qualified tuition and related expenses paid with distributions of educational benefits from a trust could be used to compute Hope Scholarship and Lifetime Learning Credits if the distributions were included in the taxable income of the beneficiaries. Let. Rul. 9839037.

Neither credit is allowed unless a taxpayer elects to claim it on a timely filed (including extensions) federal income tax return for the taxable year in which the credit is claimed. The election is made by completing and attaching Form 8863, Education Credits (Hope and Lifetime Learning Credits), to the return. Treas. Reg. §1.25A-1(d). Neither credit is allowed unless the taxpayer provides the name and the taxpayer identification (i.e., Social Security) number of the student for whom the credit is claimed. Treas. Reg. §1.25A-1(e).

If the student is claimed as a dependent on another individual's tax return (e.g., parents) he cannot claim either credit for himself, even if he paid the expenses himself.

IRC Sec. 25A(g)(3); Treas. Reg. §1.25A-1(f)(1). (The Service has privately ruled that a student was entitled to claim a Hope Scholarship Credit on his own return even though his parents were eligible to claim him as a dependent, but chose not to do so. Let. Rul. 200236001.) However, if another individual is eligible to claim the student as a dependent, but does not do so, only the student may claim the Hope or Lifetime Learning Credit for his own qualified tuition and related expenses. Treas. Reg. §1.25A-1(f)(1). Both credits are unavailable to married taxpayers filing separately. IRC Sec. 25A(g)(6); Treas. Reg. §1.25A-1(g). Neither of these credits is allowed for any expenses for which there is a deduction available. IRC Sec. 25A(g)(5); Treas. Reg. §1.25A-5(d). Taxpayers are not eligible to claim a Hope or Lifetime Learning Credit and the deduction for qualified higher education expenses in the same year with respect to the same student. IRC Sec. 222(c)(2)(A).

A taxpayer may claim a Hope Scholarship or Lifetime Learning Credit *and* exclude distributions from a qualified tuition program on behalf of the same student in the same taxable year *if* the distribution is not used to pay the same educational expenses for which the credit was claimed. See IRC Sec. 529(c)(3)(B)(v). See Q 811.

A taxpayer can claim a Hope Scholarship or Lifetime Learning Credit *and* exclude distributions from a Coverdell Education Savings Account (ESA; see Q 810) on behalf of the same student in the same taxable year *if* the distribution is *not* used to pay the same educational expenses for which the credit was claimed. See IRC Sec. 530(d)(2)(C). A taxpayer may elect *not* to have the Hope Scholarship or Lifetime Learning Credit apply with respect to the qualified higher education expenses of an individual for any taxable year. IRC Sec. 25A(e).

Reporting. For the reporting requirements for higher education tuition and related expenses, see IRC Sec. 6050S, as amended by P.L. 107-131 (1-16-2002). For the reporting requirements for qualified tuition and related expenses, see Prop. Treas. Reg. §1.6050S-1, 67 Fed. Reg. 20923 (4-29-02). *ASRS Sec. 53 ¶20.12(g).*

SOCIAL SECURITY TAXES

836. What are the Social Security tax rates for 2006?

The rates for 2006, as adjusted by an automatic cost-of-living increase in the earnings base, are:

Self-employment tax: 15.30% (12.40% OASDI and 2.90% hospital insurance). In 2006, the OASDI tax is imposed on up to $94,200 of self-employment income for a maximum tax of $11,680.80. (In 2005, the tax is imposed on up to $90,000 of self-employment income for a maximum tax of $11,160.) The hospital insurance tax is imposed on all of a taxpayer's self-employment income. However, an above-the-line deduction is permitted for one-half of self-employment taxes paid by an individual and attributable to a trade or business carried on by the individual (not as an employee). IRC Sec. 164(f).

FICA tax (on employer and employee, each): 7.65% (6.20% OASDI and 1.45% hospital insurance). In 2006, the OASDI tax is imposed on up to $94,200 of wages for a maximum tax of $5,840.40 for the employer and $5,840.40 for the employee, or $11,680.80 for employer and employee together. (In 2005, the tax is imposed on up to $90,000 of wages for a maximum tax of $5,580 for the employer and $5,580 for the employee, or $11,160 for the employer and the employee together.) The hospital insurance tax is imposed on all of a taxpayer's wages. IRC Secs. 3101(b), 3121(u).

Back wages paid as the result of a settlement agreement are subject to FICA and FUTA taxes in the year the wages are actually paid, not in the year the wages were earned or should have been paid. *U.S. v. Cleveland Indians Baseball Co.*, 87 AFTR2d ¶2001-798 (U.S. 2001). See also *The Phillies v. U.S.* 87 AFTR2d 2001-983 (E.D. PA. 2001). *ASRS, Sec. 15.*

837. Who must pay the self-employment tax?

An individual whose net earnings from self-employment are $400 or more for the taxable year must pay the self-employment tax. IRC Sec. 6017. In 2006, such an individual must file a Schedule SE and pay Social Security taxes on up to $94,200 ($90,000 in 2005) of self-employment income. (The hospital insurance tax is imposed on all of a taxpayer's self-employment income.) However, an above-the-line deduction is permitted for one-half of the self-employment tax paid by an individual and attributable to a trade or business carried on by the individual (not as an employee). IRC Sec. 164(f). If the individual also works in covered employment as an *employee*, his self-employment income (subject to the self-employment tax) is only the difference, if any, between his "wages" as an employee and the maximum Social Security earnings base. *ASRS, Sec. 15.*

CORPORATIONS

838. How is a corporation taxed?

Any corporation, including a professional corporation or association, is considered a C corporation, taxable under the following rules, unless an election is made to be treated as an S corporation (see Q 839).

Graduated Tax Rates

A corporation pays tax according to a graduated rate schedule. The rates range from 15% to 35%, with higher effective rates of 38% and 39% applicable to income at certain levels. IRC Sec. 11(b). See Appendix B for the rates. A "personal service corporation" is subject to a different income tax rate. See Q 840.

Taxable income is computed for a corporation in much the same way as for an individual. Generally, a corporation may take the same deductions as an individual, except those of a personal nature (e.g., deductions for medical expenses and the personal exemptions). A corporation also does not receive a standard deduction. There are a few special deductions for corporations, however, including a deduction equal to 70% of dividends received from other domestic corporations, 80% of dividends received from a 20% owned company, and 100% for dividends received from affiliated corporations. IRC Sec. 243. A corporation may deduct contributions to charitable organizations to the extent of 10% of taxable income (with certain adjustments). IRC Sec. 170(b)(2). Generally, charitable contributions in excess of the 10% limit may be carried over for five years. IRC Sec. 170(d)(2).

A corporation is also allowed a deduction for production activities. When this deduction is fully phased in (in 2010) it will be equal to nine percent of a taxpayer's qualified production activities income (or, if less, the taxpayer's taxable income). The deduction is limited to 50 percent of the W-2 wages paid by the taxpayer for the year. The definition of "production activities" is broad and includes construction activities, energy production, and the creation of computer software. IRC Sec. 199.

Capital Gains

Capital gains and losses are netted in the same manner as for an individual and net short-term capital gain, to the extent it exceeds net long-term capital loss, if any, is taxed at the corporation's regular tax rates (see Q 815). A corporation reporting a "net capital gain" (i.e., where net long-term capital gain exceeds net short-term capital loss; see Q 815) is taxed under one of two methods, depending upon which produces the lower tax:

1. *Regular method.* Net capital gain is included in gross income and taxed at the corporation's regular tax rates.

2. *Alternative method.* First, a tax on the corporation's taxable income, exclusive of "net capital gain," is calculated at the corporation's regular tax rates. Then a second tax on the "net capital gain" (or, if less, taxable income) for the year is calculated at the rate of 35%. The tax on income exclusive of net capital gain and the tax on net capital gain are added to arrive at the corporation's total tax. IRC Secs. 1201, 1222.

Alternative Minimum Tax

A corporate taxpayer must calculate its liability under the regular tax and a tentative minimum tax, then add to its regular tax so much of the tentative minimum tax as exceeds its regular tax. The amount added is the alternative minimum tax. IRC Secs. 55-59. See Q 829.

To calculate its alternative minimum tax (AMT), a corporation first calculates its "alternative minimum taxable income" (AMTI). IRC Sec. 55(b)(2). Also, the corporation calculates its "adjusted current earnings" (ACE), increasing its AMTI by 75% of the amount by which ACE exceeds AMTI (or possibly reducing its AMTI by 75% of the amount by which AMTI exceeds ACE). IRC Sec. 56(g). The tax itself is a flat 20% of AMTI. IRC Sec. 55(b)(1)(B). Each corporation receives a $40,000 exemption; however, the exemption amount is reduced by 25% of the amount by which AMTI exceeds $150,000 (thus phasing out completely at $310,000). IRC Secs. 55(d)(2), 55(d)(3).

AMTI is regular taxable income determined with certain adjustments and increased by tax preferences. IRC Sec. 55(b)(2). *Tax preferences* for corporate taxpayers are the same as for other taxpayers (see Q 829). *Adjustments* to income include the following: (1) property is generally depreciated under a less accelerated or a straight line method over a longer period, except that a longer period is not required for property placed in service after 1998; (2) mining exploration and development costs are amortized over 10 years; (3) a percentage of completion method is required for long-term contracts; (4) net operating loss deductions are generally limited to 90% of AMTI (although some relief was available in 2001 and 2002); (5) certified pollution control facilities are depreciated under the alternative depreciation system except those that are placed in service after 1998, which will use the straight line method; and (6) the adjustment based on the corporation's adjusted current earnings (ACE). IRC Secs. 56(a), 56(c), 56(d).

To calculate ACE, a corporation begins with AMTI (determined without regard to ACE or the AMT net operating loss) and makes additional adjustments. These adjustments include adding certain amounts of income that are includable in earnings and profits but not in AMTI (including income on life insurance policies and receipt of key person insurance death proceeds). The amount of any such income added to AMTI is reduced by any deductions that would have been allowed in calculating AMTI had the item been included in gross income. The corporation is generally not allowed a deduction for ACE purposes which is not allowed for earnings and profits purposes. However, certain dividends received by a corporation are allowed to be deducted. Generally, for property placed into service after 1989 but before 1994, the corporation must recalculate depreciation according to specified methods for ACE purposes. For ACE purposes, earnings and profits are adjusted further for certain purposes such as the treatment of intangible drilling costs, amortization of certain expenses, installment sales, and depletion. IRC. Sec. 56(g).

Application of the adjustments for adjusted current earnings with respect to life insurance is explained in Q 95.

A corporation subject to the AMT in one year may be allowed a minimum tax credit against regular tax liability in subsequent years. The credit is equal to the excess of the adjusted net minimum taxes imposed in prior years over the amount of minimum tax credits allowable in prior years. IRC Sec. 53(b). However, the amount of the credit cannot be greater than the excess of the corporation's regular tax liability (reduced by certain credits such as certain business related credits and certain investment credits) over its tentative minimum tax. IRC Sec. 53(c).

Certain small corporations are deemed to have a tentative minimum tax of zero and thus are exempt from the AMT. To qualify for the exemption, the corporation must meet a gross receipts test for the three previous taxable years. To meet the test, a corporation's average annual gross receipts for the three years must not exceed $7.5 million. For purposes of the gross receipts test, only tax years beginning after 1993 are taken into account. For a corporation not in existence for three full years, those years the corporation was in existence are substituted for the three years (with annualization of any short taxable year). To initially qualify for the exemption, the corporation must meet the three-year gross receipts test but with $5 million substituted for $7.5 million. Generally, a corporation will be exempt from the AMT in its first year of existence. IRC Secs. 55(e), 448(c)(3).

If a corporation fails to maintain its small corporation status, it loses the exemption from the AMT. If that happens, certain adjustments used to determine the corporation's AMTI will be applied for only those transactions entered into or property placed in service in tax years beginning with the tax year in which the corporation ceases to be a small corporation and tax years thereafter. IRC Sec. 55(e)(2). A corporation exempt from the AMT because of the small corporation exemption may be limited in the amount of credit it may take for AMT paid in previous years. In computing the AMT credit, the corporation's regular tax liability (reduced by applicable credits) used to calculate the credit is reduced by 25% of the amount that such liability exceeds $25,000. IRC Sec. 55(e)(5).

Accumulated Earnings Tax

A corporation is subject to a penalty tax, in addition to the graduated tax, if, for the purpose of preventing the imposition of income tax upon its shareholders, it accumulates earnings instead of distributing them. IRC Secs. 531-537; *GPD, Inc. v. Comm.*, 75-1 USTC ¶9142 (6th Cir. 1974), rev'g 60 TC 480 (1973). The tax is 15% of the corporation's *accumulated taxable income*. IRC Sec. 531. Accumulated taxable income is taxable income for the year (after certain adjustments) less the federal income tax, dividends paid to stockholders (during the taxable year or within 2½ months after the close of the taxable year), and the "accumulated earnings credit." IRC Sec. 535.

The tax can be imposed only upon amounts accumulated beyond those required to meet the reasonable needs of the business since an accumulated earnings credit, generally equal to this amount, is allowed. A corporation must demonstrate a specific, definite and feasible plan for the use of the accumulated funds in order to avoid the tax. *Eyefull Inc. v. Comm.*, TC Memo 1996-238. The use of accumulated funds for the personal use of a shareholder and his family is evidence that the accumulation was to prevent the imposition of income tax upon its shareholders. *Northwestern Ind. Tel. Co. v. Comm.*, 97-2 USTC ¶50,859 (7th Cir. 1997). In deciding whether a family owned bank was subject to the accumulated earnings tax, the IRS took into account the regulatory scheme the bank was operating under to determine its reasonable needs. TAM 9822009. Most corporations are allowed a minimum accumulated earnings credit equal to the amount by which $250,000 ($150,000 in the case of service corporations in health, law, engineering, architecture, accounting, actuarial science, performing arts or consulting) exceeds the accumulated earnings and profits of the corporation at the close of the preceding taxable year. IRC Sec. 535(c)(2). Consequently, an aggregate of $250,000 ($150,000 in the case of the above listed service corporations) may be accumulated for any purpose without danger of incurring the penalty tax.

Tax-exempt income is not included in the accumulated taxable income of the corporation but will be included in earnings and profits in determining whether there has been an accumulation beyond the reasonable needs of the business. Rev. Rul. 70-497, 1970-2 CB 128. But, a distribution in redemption of stock to pay death taxes which is treated as a dividend does not qualify for the "dividends paid" deduction in computing accumulated taxable income (see Q 82, Q 85). Rev. Rul. 70-642, 1970-2 CB 131.

The accumulated earnings tax applies to all C corporations, without regard to the number of shareholders in taxable years beginning after July 18, 1984. IRC Sec. 532(c).

Personal Holding Company Tax

The personal holding company (PHC) tax is a second penalty tax designed to keep shareholders from avoiding personal income taxes on securities and other income-producing property placed in a corporation to avoid higher personal income tax rates. The PHC tax is 15% of the corporation's undistributed PHC income (taxable income adjusted to reflect its net economic income for the year, minus dividends distributed to shareholders), if it meets both the "stock ownership" and "PHC income" tests. IRC Secs. 541, 542, 545.

A corporation meets the "stock ownership" test if more than 50% of the value of its stock is owned, directly or indirectly, by or for not more than 5 shareholders. IRC Sec. 542(a)(2). Certain stock owned by families, trusts, estates, partners, partnerships, and corporations may be attributed to individuals for purposes of this rule. IRC Sec. 544.

A corporation meets the "PHC income" requirement if 60% or more of its adjusted ordinary gross income is PHC income, generally defined to include the following: (1)

dividends, interest, royalties, and annuities; (2) rents; (3) mineral, oil, and gas royalties; (4) copyright royalties; (5) produced film rents (amounts derived from film properties acquired before substantial completion of the production); (6) compensation from use of corporate property by shareholders ; (7) personal service contracts; and (8) income from estates and trusts. IRC Secs. 542(a)(1), 543(a).

Professional Corporations and Associations

Organizations of physicians, lawyers, and other professional people organized under state professional corporation or association acts are generally treated as corporations for tax purposes. Rev. Rul. 77-31, 1977-1 CB 409. However, to be treated as a corporation, a professional service organization must be both organized and *operated* as a corporation. *Roubik v. Comm.*, 53 TC 365 (1969). Although professional corporations are generally treated as corporations for tax purposes, they are not generally taxed the same as regular C corporations. See Q 840. Note that if a professional corporation has elected S corporation status, the shareholders will be treated as S corporation shareholders. See Q 839.

Although a professional corporation is recognized as a taxable entity separate and apart from the professional individual or individuals who form it, the IRS may under some circumstances reallocate income, deductions, credits, exclusions, or other allowances between the corporation and its owners in order to prevent evasion or avoidance of tax or to properly reflect the income of the parties. Under IRC Section 482, such reallocation may be made only where the individual owner operates a second business distinct from the business of the professional corporation; reallocation may not be made where the individual works exclusively for the professional corporation. *Foglesong v. Comm.*, 82-2 USTC ¶9650 (7th Cir. 1982), rev'g 77 TC 1102 (1981). However, note that the IRS has stated that it will not follow the *Foglesong* decision to the extent that it held that the two business requirement of IRC Section 482 is not satisfied where a controlling shareholder works exclusively for the controlled corporation. Rev. Rul. 88-38, 1988-1 CB 246. A professional corporation may also be subject to the special rules applicable to "personal service corporations," see Q 840. *ASRS, Sec. 43, ¶20.*

839. How is an S corporation taxed?

An S corporation is one that elects to be treated, in general, as a passthrough entity, thus avoiding most tax at the corporate level. See IRC Secs. 1361, 1362, 1363. To be eligible to make the election, a corporation must meet certain requirements as to the kind and number of shareholders, classes of stock, and sources of income. An S corporation must be a domestic corporation with only a single class of stock and may have up to 100 shareholders (none of whom are nonresident aliens) who are individuals, estates and certain trusts. An S corporation may not be an ineligible corporation. An ineligible corporation is one of the following: (1) a financial institution that uses the reserve method of accounting for bad debts; (2) an insurance company; (3) a corporation electing (under IRC Section 936) credits for certain tax attributable to income from Puerto Rico and other U.S. possessions; and (4) a current or former domestic international sales corporation (DISC). Qualified plans (see Q 417) and certain charitable organizations may be S corporation shareholders. IRC Sec. 1361.

Members of a family may elect to be treated as one shareholder. "Members of the family" are defined as "the common ancestor, lineal descendants of the common ancestor, and the spouses (or former spouses) of such lineal descendants or common ancestor."

Generally, the common ancestor may not be more than six generations removed from the youngest generation of shareholders who would be considered members of the family. IRC Sec. 1361(c)(1). A member of the family who is a shareholder in the S corporation may make this election. The election is made by notifying the S corporation. The notice must identify the family member making the election, the common ancestor of the family to which it applies, and the first taxable year to which the election applies. Notice 2005-91, 2005-51 IRB ____.

Trusts which may be S corporation shareholders include: (1) a trust all of which is treated as owned by an individual who is a citizen or resident of the United States under the grantor trust rules (see Q 844); (2) a trust which was described in (1) above immediately prior to the deemed owner's death and continues in existence after such death may continue to be an S corporation shareholder for up to two years after the owner's death; (3) a trust to which stock is transferred pursuant to a will may be an S corporation shareholder for up to two years after the date of the stock transfer; (4) a trust created primarily to exercise the voting power of stock transferred to it; (5) a qualified subchapter S trust (QSST); (6) an electing small business trust (ESBT); and (7) in the case of an S corporation that is a bank, an IRA or Roth IRA. IRC Secs. 1361(c)(2), 1361(d).

A QSST is a trust that has only one current income beneficiary (who must be a citizen or resident of the U.S.), requires that all income be distributed currently, and requires that corpus not be distributed to anyone else during the life of such beneficiary. The income interest must terminate upon the earlier of the beneficiary's death or termination of the trust, and if the trust terminates during the lifetime of the income beneficiary, all trust assets must be distributed to that beneficiary. IRC Sec. 1361(d)(3). The beneficiary must make an election for the trust to be treated as a QSST. IRC Sec. 1361(d)(2).

An ESBT is a trust in which all of the beneficiaries are individuals, estates, or certain charitable organizations. IRC Sec. 1361(e). Each potential current beneficiary of an ESBT is treated as a shareholder for purposes of the shareholder limitation. IRC Sec. 1361(c)(2)(B)(v). A potential current beneficiary is generally someone who is entitled to, or in the discretion of any person may receive a distribution of principal or interest of the trust. Treas. Reg. §1.1361-1(m)(4). Trusts exempt from income tax, QSSTs, charitable remainder annuity trusts, and charitable remainder unitrusts may not be ESBTs. An interest in an ESBT may not be obtained by purchase. IRC Sec. 1361(e). If any portion of a beneficiary's basis in the beneficiary's interest is determined under the cost basis rules, the interest was acquired by purchase. Treas. Reg. §1.1361-1(m)(1)(iii). An ESBT is taxed at the highest income tax rate under IRC Section 1(e). IRC Sec. 641(c).

An S corporation may own a qualified subchapter S subsidiary (QSSS). A QSSS is a domestic corporation that is not an ineligible corporation, if 100% of its stock is owned by the parent S corporation and the parent S corporation elects to treat the subsidiary as a QSSS. Except as may be provided in regulations, a QSSS is not treated as a separate corporation and its assets, liabilities and items of income, deduction and credit are treated as those of the parent S corporation. IRC Sec. 1361(b)(3). A QSSS may be required to file a separate information return. IRC Sec. 1361(b)(3)(A). Regulations provide special rules regarding the recognition of a QSSS as a separate entity for tax purposes in certain circumstances. Treas. Reg. §1.1361-4(a).

If a QSSS ceases to meet the above requirements, it will be treated as a new corporation acquiring all its assets and liabilities from the parent S corporation in exchange for its stock. If the corporation's status as a QSSS terminates, the corporation is generally prohibited from being a QSSS or an S corporation for five years. IRC Sec. 1361(b)(3). Regulations provide that in certain cases following a termination of a corporation's QSSS election, the corporation may be allowed to elect QSSS or S corporation status without waiting five years if, immediately following the disposition, the corporation is otherwise eligible to make an S corporation election or QSSS election, and the election is effective immediately following the termination of the QSSS election. Examples where this rule would apply include an S corporation selling all of its QSSS stock to another S corporation, or an S corporation distributing all of its QSSS stock to its shareholders. Treas. Reg. §1.1361-5(c).

A corporation will be treated as having one class of stock if all of its outstanding shares confer identical rights to distribution and liquidation proceeds. Treas. Reg. §1.1361-1(l)(1). However, a bona fide buy-sell agreement will be disregarded for purposes of the one-class rule unless a principal purpose of the arrangement is to circumvent the one-class rule and it establishes a purchase price that is not substantially above or below the fair market value of the stock. Agreements that provide for a purchase price or redemption of stock at book value or a price between book value and fair market value will not be considered to establish a price that is substantially above or below fair market value. Treas. Reg. §1.1361-1(l)(2)(iii). See IRC Secs. 1361, 1362. Agreements triggered by divorce and forfeiture provisions that cause a share of stock to be substantially nonvested will be disregarded in determining whether a corporation's shares confer identical rights to distribution and liquidation proceeds. Treas. Reg. §1.1361-1(l)(2)(iii)(B). Also, the typical unfunded deferred compensation plan should not be considered to create a second class of stock. See Treas. Reg. §1.1361-1(b)(4). See also Let. Rul. 9421011 (plan providing for payment at termination of employment of a fraction of corporation's book value and providing for payment of dividend equivalents taxed currently does not create second class of stock); Let. Rul. 9317021 (stock equivalency plan does not create a second class of stock); Let. Ruls. 9501032 and 9233005 (phantom stock plans do not create a second class of stock); Let. Rul. 9626033 (bonus deferral plan does not create a second class of stock). The Service has ruled privately that a split dollar arrangement offered as a fringe benefit to employees of an S corporation does not violate the one class of stock restriction. Let. Rul. 9248019. Likewise, a split dollar arrangement entered into between an S corporation and a trust holding a second-to-die policy on the life of the majority shareholder/employee does not alter rights to distribution and liquidation proceeds and does not create a second class of stock. Let. Rul. 9651017. See Q 457, Q 458. An employment agreement between an S corporation and its sole shareholder does not violate the provision. Let. Rul. 9442007. The fact that an S corporation continues to be registered as a corporation in a foreign country does not violate the one class of stock rule. Let. Rul. 9512001. Further, where distributions to shareholders were based on cumulative earnings instead of percentage of ownership, the S corporation avoided a violation of the one class of stock rule by correcting the distributions the following year. Let. Rul. 9519048.

An S corporation is generally not subject to tax at the corporate level. However, a tax is imposed at the corporate level on certain gains. For S elections made after 1986 where the corporation had previously been a C corporation, when an S corporation disposes of property within 10 years after an election has been made, gain attributable to pre-election appreciation of the property (built in gain) is taxed at the corporate level to the extent such gain does not exceed the amount of taxable income imposed on the

CORPORATIONS   Q 839

corporation if it were not an S corporation. IRC Sec. 1374. This includes the fair market value of work-in-process inventory of the corporation. *Reliable Steel Fabricators, Inc. v. Comm.*, TC Memo 1995-293. For S elections made before 1987, unless the corporation was an electing corporation for the three immediately preceding tax years (or had been in existence less than four taxable years and had been an electing corporation each of its taxable years), a tax is imposed at the corporate level on its net capital gain which exceeds $25,000 if the net capital gain exceeds 50% of the corporation's taxable income for the year and the taxable income is more than $25,000. IRC Sec. 1374, prior to amendment by TRA '86.

A corporation switching from a C corporation to an S corporation may be required to recapture certain amounts in connection with goods previously inventoried under a LIFO method. IRC Sec. 1363(d). In addition, a tax is imposed at the corporate level on *excess* "net passive income" of an S corporation but only if the corporation, at the end of the tax year, has accumulated earnings and profits and if passive investment income exceeds 25% of gross receipts. The rate is the highest corporate rate. IRC Sec. 1375(a). Passive investment income for this purpose is rents, royalties, dividends, interest, annuities, and proceeds from sales or exchanges of stock or securities. IRC Secs. 1362(d)(3), 1375(b)(3). However, passive investment income does not include rents for the use of corporate property if the corporation also provides substantial services in connection with the property (such as maid service in a hotel); interest derived in the ordinary course of any trade or business; or interest on obligations acquired in the ordinary course of business, such as interest earned on accounts receivable. Treas. Reg. §1.1362-2(c)(5)(ii)(B), (D). Passive investment income specifically does not include gross receipts derived in the ordinary course of a trade or business of lending or financing; dealing in property; purchasing or discounting accounts receivable, notes, or installment obligations; or servicing mortgages. Treas. Reg. §1.1362-2(c)(5)(iii)(B). Passive investment income does not include certain dividends from C corporations where the S corporation owns 80% or more of the C corporation. Treas. Reg. §1.1362-8. If amounts are subject to tax both as built in gain and as excess net passive income, an adjustment will be made in the amount taxed as passive income. IRC Sec. 1375(b)(4). Tax is also imposed at the corporate level on the recapture of investment credit which was allowed prior to the effective date of the S election. IRC Sec. 1371(d).

Like a partnership, an S corporation computes its taxable income in generally the same way as an individual, except that certain personal deductions are not allowed and the corporation may elect to amortize organizational expenses. The deduction for production activities is also allowed (see Q 838). Each shareholder then reports on his individual return his proportionate share of the corporation's items of income, loss, deductions and credits; these items retain their character on passthrough. Certain items of income, loss, deduction or credit must be passed through as separate items because they may have an individual effect on each shareholder's tax liability. For example, net capital gains and losses pass through as such to be included with the shareholder's own net capital gain or loss. Any gains and losses on certain property used in a trade or business are passed through separately to be aggregated with the shareholder's other section 1231 gains and losses. IRC Secs. 1366(a), 1366(b). If any tax is imposed on built in gains (described above), the amount of the tax imposed will be treated as a loss by the corporation. IRC Sec. 1366(f)(2). Charitable contributions pass through to shareholders separately subject to the individual shareholder's percentage limitations on deductibility. tax-exempt income passes through as such. Items involving determination of credits pass through separately. Items that do not need to be passed through separately are aggregated on the corporation's tax return and each shareholder reports his share of such nonseparately computed net income or loss on his individual return. IRC Sec. 1366(a)(1). Before passthrough, each item of passive investment income is reduced by its proportionate share of the tax at the corporate level on excess net passive investment income. IRC Sec. 1366(f)(3).

Thus, whether amounts are distributed to them or not, shareholders are taxed on the corporation's taxable income. Shareholders take into account their shares of income, loss, deduction and credit on a per-share, per-day basis. IRC Sec. 1377. Treasury Regulation Section 1.1377-1(a)(2) contains provisions for determining a shareholder's pro rata share. The S corporation income must also be included on a current basis by shareholders for purposes of the estimated tax provisions (see Q 801). Let. Rul. 8542034.

The Tax Court determined that when an S corporation shareholder files for bankruptcy, all the gains and losses for that year flowed through to the bankruptcy estate. The gains and losses should not be divided based on the time before the bankruptcy was filed. *Williams v. Comm.*, 123 TC No. 8 (2004).

The basis of each shareholder's stock is *increased* by his share of items of separately stated income (including tax-exempt income) and by his share of any nonseparately computed income, and by any excess of deductions for depletion over the basis of the property subject to depletion. IRC Sec. 1367(a)(1). An S corporation shareholder may *not* increase his basis due to excluded discharge of indebtedness income. IRC Sec. 108(d)(7)(A). The basis of each shareholder's stock is *decreased* (not below zero) by items of separately stated loss and deductions and nonseparately computed loss, any expense of the corporation not deductible in computing taxable income and not properly chargeable to capital account and any depletion deduction with respect to oil and gas property to the extent that the deduction does not exceed the shareholder's proportionate share of the property's adjusted basis. IRC Sec. 1367(a)(2). If the aggregate of these amounts exceeds his basis in his stock, the excess reduces the shareholder's basis in any indebtedness of the corporation to him. IRC Sec. 1367(b)(2).

A shareholder may not take deductions and losses of the S corporation which, aggregated, exceed his basis in his S corporation stock plus his basis in any indebtedness of the corporation to him. IRC Sec. 1366(d)(1). Such disallowed deductions and losses may be carried over indefinitely, but these losses may not be carried over by transferees of stock unless the transferees are certain divorced spouses. IRC Sec. 1366(d)(2). In other words, he may not deduct in any tax year more than he has "at risk" in the corporation. Basis is also reduced by distributions from the corporation which are not includable in income. IRC Sec. 1367(a)(2)(A).

Post-1982 earnings of an S corporation are not treated as earnings and profits. An S corporation may have accumulated earnings and profits for any year in which a valid election was not in effect or as the result of a corporate acquisition in which there is a carryover of earnings and profits under IRC Section 381. IRC Sec. 1371(c).

A distribution from an S corporation which does not have accumulated earnings and profits lowers the shareholder's basis in the corporation's stock. IRC Sec. 1367(a)(2)(A). Any excess is generally treated as gain. IRC Sec. 1368(b)(2).

If the S corporation does have earnings and profits, distributions are treated as distributions by a corporation without earnings and profits, to the extent of the shareholder's share of an accumulated adjustment account (generally, post-1982 gross receipts less deductible expenses, which have not been distributed). Any excess distribution is treated under the usual corporate rules. That is, it is a dividend up to the amount of the accumulated earnings and profits. Any excess is applied to reduce the shareholder's basis. Finally, any remainder is treated as a gain. IRC Sec. 1368(c). However, in any tax year, shareholders receiving the distribution may, if all agree, elect to have all distributions in the year treated first as dividends to the extent of earnings and profits and then as return of investment to the extent of adjusted basis and any excess as capital gain. IRC Sec. 1368(e)(3). If the IRC Section 1368(e)(3) election is made, it will apply to all distributions made in the tax year. Let. Rul. 8935013. A stock redemption may be treated as a distribution that reduces the S corporation's accumulated adjustments account. Rev. Rul. 95-14, 1995-1 CB 169.

If the S corporation distributes appreciated property to a shareholder, gain will be recognized to the corporation as if the property were sold at fair market value; the gain will pass through to shareholders like any other gain. IRC Sec. 311(b), 1366(a)(1).

The rules discussed above generally apply in tax years beginning after December 31, 1982. Nonetheless, certain casualty insurance companies and certain corporations with oil and gas production will continue to be taxed under the rules applicable to Subchapter S corporations prior to these rules. Subchapter S Revision Act of 1982, Sec. 6. *ASRS, Sec. 43, ¶¶ 20.10; 40.8(h).*

840. How is a "personal service corporation" taxed?

Certain personal service corporations are taxed at a flat rate of 35%. IRC Sec. 11(b)(2). In effect, this means that the benefit of the graduated corporate income tax rates is not available. (See Appendix B). A personal service corporation for this purpose is a corporation substantially all of the activities of which involve the performance of services in the fields of health, law, engineering, architecture, accounting, actuarial science, performing arts, or consulting. In addition, substantially all of the stock must be owned directly by employees, retired employees, or their estates or indirectly through partnerships, S corporations, or qualified personal service corporations. IRC Sec. 448(d)(2).

IRC Section 269A permits the IRS to reallocate income, deductions, credits, exclusions, and other allowances (to the extent necessary to prevent avoidance or evasion of federal income tax) between a personal service corporation (PSC) and its employee-owners if the corporation is formed for the principal purpose of securing tax benefits for its employee-owners (i.e., more than 10% shareholder-employees after application of attribution rules) and substantially all of its services are performed for a single other entity. For purposes of IRC Section 269A, a personal service corporation is a corporation the principal activity of which is the performance of personal services and such services are substantially performed by the employee-owners. IRC Sec. 269A(b)(1). A professional basketball player was considered to be an employee of an NBA team, not his personal service corporation, and all compensation therefrom was taxable to him individually, even though his PSC had entered into a contract with the team for his personal services. *Leavell v. Comm.*, 104 TC 140 (1995).

In addition, special rules apply to the tax year that may be used by a personal service corporation (as defined for purposes of IRC Section 269A, except that all owner-employees are included and broader attribution rules apply). IRC Secs. 441(i), 444. *ASRS, Sec. 43, ¶20.12(a)*.

LIMITED LIABILITY COMPANIES

841. What is a limited liability company and how is it taxed?

A limited liability company (LLC) is a statutory business entity that may be formed by at least two members (although one-member LLCs are permitted in some states) by drafting articles of organization and filing them with the appropriate state agency. There are no provisions for LLCs in the Code, but regulations provide rules to determine how a *business entity* is classified for tax purposes. A business entity is any entity recognized for federal tax purposes that is not a trust. Unlike an S corporation (see Q 839) an LLC has no restrictions on the number or types of owners and multiple classes of ownership are generally permitted. If the LLC is treated as a partnership, it combines the liability shield of a corporation with the tax advantages of a partnership.

An LLC may be treated as either a corporation (see Q 838), partnership (see Q 842), or sole proprietorship for federal income tax purposes. A sole proprietor and his business are one and the same for tax purposes. An *eligible entity* (a business entity not subject to automatic classification as a corporation) may elect corporate taxation by filing an entity classification form; otherwise it will be taxed as either a partnership or sole proprietorship depending upon how many owners are involved.

A separate entity must exist for tax purposes, in that its participants must engage in a business for profit. Trusts are not considered business entities. Treas. Reg. §301.7701-1. Certain entities, such as corporations organized under a federal or state statute, insurance companies, joint stock companies, and organizations engaged in banking activities, are automatically classified as corporations for federal tax purposes. A business entity with only one owner will be considered a corporation or a sole proprietorship. In order to be classified as a partnership, the entity must have at least two owners. Treas. Reg. §301.7701-2. If a newly-formed domestic eligible entity with more than one owner does not elect to be taxed as a corporation, it will be classified as a partnership. Likewise, if a newly-formed single-member eligible entity does not elect to be taxed as a corporation, it will be taxed as a sole proprietorship. Under most circumstances, a corporation in existence on January 1, 1997 does not need to file an election in order to retain its corporate status. Treas. Reg. §301.7701-3.

If a business entity elects to change its classification, rules are provided for how the change is treated for tax purposes. Treas. Reg. §301.7701-3(g).

Revenue Ruling 95-37, 1995-1 CB 130, provides that a partnership converting to a domestic LLC will be treated as a partnership-to-partnership conversion (and therefore be "tax free") provided that the LLC is classified as a partnership for federal tax purposes. The partnership will not be considered terminated under IRC Section 708(b) upon its conversion to an LLC so long as the business of the partnership is continued after the conversion. See also Let. Ruls. 9623016, 9538022, 9525058, 9443024, 9412030. Further, there will be no gain or loss recognized on the transfer of assets and liabilities so long as each partner's percentage of profits, losses and capital remains the same after the conversion. See also Let. Ruls. 9501033, 9443024, 9443018, 9434027, 9422034, 9412030. The same is true for a limited partnership converting to an LLC. Let. Rul. 9607006.

An LLC formed by two S corporations was classified as a partnership for federal tax purposes. Let. Rul. 9529015. An S corporation may merge into an LLC without adverse tax consequences provided the LLC would not be treated as an investment company under IRC Section 351 and the S corporation would not realize a net decrease in liabilities exceeding its basis in the transferred assets pursuant to Treasury Regulation Section 1.752-1(f). Neither the S corporation nor the LLC would incur gain or loss upon the contribution of assets by the S corporation to the LLC in exchange for interests therein pursuant to IRC Section 721. Let. Rul. 9543017. A corporation will retain its S election when it transfers all assets to an LLC, which is classified as a corporation for federal tax purposes due to a preponderance of corporate characteristics (see below), provided the transfer qualifies as a reorganization under IRC Section 368(a)(1)(F) and the LLC meets the requirements of an S corporation under IRC Section 1361. Let. Rul. 9636007.

An LLC that was in existence prior to January 1, 1997, may continue under its previous claimed classification if (1) it had a reasonable basis for the classification; (2) the entity and its members recognized the consequences of any change in classification within the sixty months prior to January 1, 1997; and (3) neither the entity nor its members had been notified that the classification was under examination by the IRS. Treas. Reg. §301.7701-3(h)(2).

Prior to January 1, 1997, whether an LLC was treated as a corporation or partnership for federal income tax purposes depended on the existence or nonexistence of a preponderance of six corporate characteristics: (1) associates; (2) an objective to carry on a business and divide the gains therefrom; (3) limited liability; (4) free transferability of interests; (5) continuity of life; and, (6) centralized management. Treas. Reg. §301.7701-2(a)(1), as in effect prior to January 1, 1997. Characteristics (1) and (2) above are common to both corporations and partnerships and were generally discounted when determining whether an organization was treated as a corporation or partnership. Treas. Reg. §301.7701-2(a)(2), as in effect prior to January 1, 1997. These former regulations provided an example of a business entity that possessed the characteristics of numbers (1), (2), (4) and (6) above, noting that since numbers (1) and (2) were common to both corporations and partnerships, these did not receive any significant consideration. The business entity did not possess characteristics (3) and (5) above and, accordingly, was labeled a partnership. Treas. Reg. §301.7701-2(a)(3), as in effect prior to January 1, 1997. *ASRS, Sec. 45.*

PARTNERSHIPS

842. How is the income from a partnership taxed?

With the exception of certain publicly traded partnerships, a partnership, as such, is not taxed. IRC Sec. 701. However, the partnership must file an information return on Form 1065, showing taxable ordinary income or loss and capital gain or loss. The partnership is regarded as an entity for the purpose of computing taxable income, and business expenses of the partnership may be deducted. In general, taxable income is computed in the same manner as for individuals; but the standard deduction, personal exemptions, and expenses of a purely personal nature are not allowed. IRC Secs. 703(a), 63(c)(6)(D). The deduction for production activities may also be allowed (see Q 838). Each partner must report his share of partnership profits, whether distributed or not, on his individual return. A partner's distributive share is determined either on the basis of the partner's interest or by allocation under the partnership agreement. Allocation by agreement must have a "substantial economic effect." Special allocation rules apply where the partner's interest changes during the year. IRC Secs. 706(d), 704(b).

A person is a partner if he owns a capital interest in a partnership in which capital is a material income-producing factor, whether he acquired his interest by purchase or gift. Generally, such a person will be taxable on his share of partnership profits. If capital is not an income-producing factor, the transfer of a partnership interest to a family member may be disregarded as an ineffective assignment of income, rather than an assignment of property from which income is derived. Where an interest is acquired by gift (an interest purchased by one family member from another is considered to have been acquired by gift), allocation of income among the partners according to the partnership agreement will not control to the extent that: (1) it does not allow a reasonable salary for the donor of the interest; or (2) the income attributable to the capital share of the donee is proportionately greater than the income attributable to the donor's capital share. IRC Sec. 704(e). The transfer must be complete and the family member donee must have control over the partnership interest consistent with the status of partner. If he is not old enough to serve in the capacity of partner, his interest must be controlled by a fiduciary for his benefit.

A partnership which is traded on an established securities market, known as a publicly traded partnership, is taxed differently than a partnership in some instances. IRC Sec. 7704. *ASRS, Sec. 42, ¶20.2*.

TRUSTS AND ESTATES

843. How is the federal income tax computed for trusts and estates?

Taxable income is computed by subtracting the following from gross income: allowable deductions; amounts distributable to beneficiaries; and the exemption. Estates are allowed a $600 exemption. For trusts that are required to distribute all their income currently, the exemption is $300; for all other trusts, $100. Certain trusts that benefit disabled persons may use the personal exemptions available to individuals. IRC Sec. 642(b). A standard deduction is not available. IRC Sec. 63(c)(6). Rates are determined from a table for estates and trusts (see Appendix B).

For estates of decedents dying after August 5, 1997, an election may be made to treat a *qualified revocable trust* as part of the decedent's estate for income tax purposes. The election must be made by both the executor of the estate and the trustee of the qualified revocable trust. A qualified revocable trust is a trust that was treated as a grantor trust during the life of the decedent due to his power to revoke the trust (see Q 844). If such an election is made, the trust will be treated as part of the decedent's estate for tax years ending after the date of the decedent's death and before the date that is two years after his death (if no estate tax return is required) or the date that is six months after the final determination of estate tax liability (if an estate tax return is required). IRC Sec. 645.

TRUSTS AND ESTATES

Q 843

Generally, income that is accumulated by a trust is taxable to the trust and income that is distributable to beneficiaries is taxable to the beneficiaries. IRC Secs. 641(a), 652(a). A beneficiary who may be claimed as a dependent by another taxpayer may not use a personal exemption, and his standard deduction may not exceed the greater of (1) $500 ($850 as indexed for 2006); or (2) $250 ($300 as indexed for 2006) plus earned income. IRC Secs. 151(d)(2), 63(c)(5); Rev. Proc. 2005-70, 2005-47 IRB 979. The amount of trust income that can be offset by the basic standard deduction will be reduced if the beneficiary has other income. See Q 819, Q 817. Also, trust income taxable to a beneficiary under 14 years of age may be taxed at his parents' marginal tax rate. See Q 818. (See Q 304 regarding life insurance trusts, Q 844 as to grantor trusts, and Q 307 as to when trust income is taxable to someone other than the grantor, the trust or the beneficiary.) IRC Secs. 651-652, 661-663.

Deductions available to an estate or trust are generally subject to the 2% floor on miscellaneous itemized deductions. IRC Sec. 67(a). However, deductions for costs incurred in connection with the administration of an estate or trust that would not have been incurred if the property were not held by the estate or trust are fully deductible from gross income. IRC Sec. 67(e).

It has been held that trust advisory fees incurred by a trust, due to the co-trustees' inexperience with large sums of money and their need to fulfill fiduciary duties imposed by state law, were fees incurred as a result of property being held in trust and, thus, were not subject to the 2% floor for miscellaneous itemized deductions. *O'Neill Irrev. Trust v. Comm.*, 93-1 USTC ¶50,332 (6th Cir. 1993), *nonacq.*, 1994-2 CB 1, *rev'g* 98 TC 227 (1992). However, other courts have held that payments for private investment advice *are* subject to the 2% floor for miscellaneous itemized deductions. *Scott v. U.S.*, 2003-1 USTC ¶50,428 (4th Cir. 2003); *Mellon Bank v. U.S.*, 2001-2 USTC ¶50,621 (Fed. Cir. 2001); *Rudkin Testamentary Trust v. Comm.*, 124 TC No. 19 (2005).

For distributions in taxable years beginning after August 5, 1997, the throwback rule for accumulation distributions from trusts in IRC Sections 665-667 has been eliminated for domestic trusts, except for certain domestic trusts that were once foreign trusts, and except in the case of trusts created before March 1, 1984 that would be aggregated with other trusts under the multiple trusts rules. IRC Sec. 665(c). Generally, for those trusts subject to the throwback rule, if a trust distributes income which it has accumulated after 1968, all of the income is taxed to the beneficiary upon distribution. The amounts distributed are treated as if they had been distributed in the preceding years in which the income was accumulated, but are includable in the income of the beneficiary for the current year. The "throwback" method of computing the tax in effect averages the tax attributable to the distribution over three of the five preceding taxable years of the beneficiary, excluding the year with the highest and the year with the lowest taxable income. IRC Secs. 666-667.

Excess taxes paid by the trust may not be refunded, but the beneficiary may take a credit to offset any taxes (other than the alternative minimum tax) paid by the trust. However, a beneficiary who receives accumulation distributions from more than two trusts may not take such an offset for taxes paid by the third and any additional trusts. But if distributions to a beneficiary from a trust total less than $1,000 for the year, this penalty will not apply to distributions from that trust. IRC Secs. 666-667.

2006 Tax Facts on Insurance & Employee Benefits

Distributions of income accumulated by a trust before the beneficiary is born or before he attains age 21 are not considered accumulation distributions and thus are not generally subject to the throwback rules. IRC Sec. 665(b).

Estates are required to file estimated tax for taxable years ending 2 years or more after the date of the decedent's death. IRC Sec. 6654(l). Trusts generally are required to pay estimated tax (see Q 801). However, there are two exceptions to this rule: (1) with respect to any taxable year ending before the date that is 2 years after the decedent's death, trusts owned by the decedent (under the grantor trust rules) and to which the residue of the decedent's estate will pass under his will need not file estimated tax (if no will is admitted to probate, this rule will apply to a trust which is primarily responsible for paying taxes, debts and administration expenses); and (2) charitable trusts (as defined in IRC Section 511) and private foundations are not required to file estimated tax. IRC Sec. 6654(l). A trustee may elect to treat any portion of a payment of estimated tax made by the trust for any taxable year as a payment made by a beneficiary of the trust. Any amount so treated is treated as paid or credited to the beneficiary on the last day of the taxable year. IRC Sec. 643(g). *ASRS, Sec. 53, ¶21.1.*

844. What is a grantor trust? How is a grantor trust taxed?

A grantor who retains certain interests in a trust he creates may be treated as the "owner" of all or part of the trust and thus taxed on the income of the trust in proportion to his ownership. There are five categories of interests for which the Code gives detailed limits as to the amount of control the grantor may have without being taxed on the trust income. These categories are: reversionary interests, power to control beneficial enjoyment, administrative powers, power to revoke, and income for benefit of grantor. IRC Secs. 673-677. With respect to any taxable year ending within two years after a grantor/decedent's death, any trust, all of which was treated under these grantor trust rules as owned by the decedent, is not required to file an estimated tax return (see Q 843). IRC Sec. 6654(l)(2)(B).

Reversionary Interests

Generally, a grantor will be treated as the owner of any portion of a trust in which he has a reversionary interest in either the corpus or the income, if, as of the date of inception of that portion of the trust, the value of such interest exceeds 5% of the value of the trust. IRC Sec. 673(a). There is an exception to this rule where the reversionary interest will take effect at the death before age 21 of a beneficiary who is a lineal descendant of the grantor. IRC Sec. 673(b). For transfers in trust made prior to March 2, 1986, the reversionary interest was not limited to a certain percentage, and so long as it took effect *after* 10 years it did not result in taxation of the grantor. IRC Sec. 673(a), prior to amendment by TRA '86. Using the 10% estate and gift tax valuation tables, the value of the reversionary interest of a term trust falls below 5% if the trust runs more than about 31 years. The value of a reversion will depend on the interest rate and the valuation tables required to be used (see Q 910).

Power to Control Beneficial Enjoyment

If the grantor has any power of disposition over the beneficial enjoyment of any portion of the trust, and such power is exercisable without the approval of an adverse party, he will be treated (i.e., taxed) as the owner of that portion. IRC Sec. 674(a). A grantor may do any of the following without such action resulting in his being treated

TRUSTS AND ESTATES   Q 844

as the owner of that portion of the trust: (1) reserve the power to dispose of the trust corpus by will, (2) allocate corpus or income among charitable beneficiaries (so long as it is irrevocably payable to the charities), (3) withhold income temporarily (provided the accumulated income must ultimately be paid to or for the benefit of the beneficiary), (4) allocate receipts and disbursements between corpus and income, and (5) distribute corpus by a "reasonably definite standard." IRC Sec. 674(b). An example of a "reasonably definite standard" is found in Treasury Regulation §1.674(b)-1(b)(5): "for the education, support, maintenance and health of the beneficiary; for his reasonable support and comfort; or to enable him to maintain his accustomed standard of living; or to meet an emergency." A grantor also may retain the power to withhold income during the disability or minority of a beneficiary. IRC Sec. 674(b)(7). However, if *any person* has the power to add or change beneficiaries, other than providing for the addition of after-born or after-adopted children, the grantor will be treated as the owner. IRC Sec. 674(c).

IRC Section 674(c) allows powers, solely exercisable by a trustee or trustees (none of whom is the grantor, and no more than half of whom are related or subordinate parties who are subservient to the wishes of the grantor), to distribute, apportion, or accumulate income to or for beneficiaries or pay out trust corpus to or for a beneficiary without the grantor being considered the owner of the trust. A related or subordinate party is a person who is not an adverse party and who is the grantor's spouse if living with the grantor; the grantor's father, mother, issue, brother or sister; an employee of the grantor; or a corporation or employee of a corporation if the grantor and the trust have significant voting control of the corporation. IRC Sec. 672(c). An adverse party is any person having a substantial beneficial interest in a trust which would be adversely affected by the exercise or nonexercise of the power the person possesses respecting the trust. IRC Sec. 672(a).

The grantor will also not be considered the owner of the trust due to a power solely exercisable by a trustee or trustees, none of whom are the grantor or the grantor's spouse living with the grantor, to distribute, apportion, or accumulate income to or for a beneficiary as long as the power is limited to a reasonably definite external standard set forth in the trust instrument. IRC Sec. 674(d). Regulations treat a reasonably definite external standard as synonymous with a reasonably definite standard, described above. Treas. Reg. §1.674(d)-1.

Income for Benefit of Grantor

If the trust income is (or, in the discretion of the grantor or a nonadverse party, or both, may be) distributed or held for the benefit of the grantor or his spouse, he will be treated as the owner of it. IRC Sec. 677(a). This provision applies to the use of trust income for the payment of premiums for insurance on the life of the grantor or his spouse, although taxation does not result from the mere power of the trustee to purchase life insurance. See Q 305. This provision is also invoked any time trust income is used *for the benefit of the grantor*, to discharge a legal obligation. Thus, when trust income is used to discharge the grantor's legal support obligations, it is taxable income to the grantor. IRC Sec. 677(b). State laws vary as to what constitutes a parent's obligation to support; however, such a determination may be based in part on the background, values and goals of the parents, as well as the children. *Stone v. Comm.*, TC Memo 1987-454; *Braun v. Comm.*, TC Memo 1984-285.

The mere power of the trustee to use trust income to discharge a legal obligation of the grantor will not result in taxable income to the grantor. Under IRC Section 677(b), there must be an actual distribution of trust income for the grantor's benefit in order for the grantor to be taxable on the amounts expended.

Other Grantor Powers

A grantor's power to revoke the trust will result in his being treated as owner of it. This may happen by operation of law in states requiring that the trust instrument explicitly state that the trust is irrevocable. Such a power will also be inferred where the grantor's powers are so extensive as to be substantially equivalent to a power of revocation, such as a power to invade the corpus. IRC Sec. 676.

Certain administrative powers retained by the grantor will result in his being treated as owner of the trust; these include the power to deal with trust funds for less than full and adequate consideration, the power to borrow without adequate interest or security, or borrowing from the trust without completely repaying principal and interest before the beginning of the taxable year. IRC Sec. 675. *ASRS, Sec. 53, ¶21.2.*

FEDERAL ESTATE TAX

GENERAL

850. What is the federal estate tax?

It is a tax on the right to transfer property at death, and is imposed on a decedent's "taxable estate" (see Q 852). EGTRRA 2001 repeals the estate tax for one year in 2010. Technically, EGTRRA 2001 repeals the estate tax for decedents dying after 2009. However, EGTRRA 2001 sunsets (or expires) after 2010. IRC Sec. 2210; EGTRRA 2001 Sec. 901. *ASRS, Sec. 54, ¶44.1.*

FILING AND PAYMENT

851. Who needs to file a return and pay the estate tax, and when are they due?

A federal estate tax return (Form 706), if required, must be filed, and the tax paid, by the executor within nine months after the decedent's death. IRC Secs. 6018(a), 6075(a), 6151(a). Whether or not a return is required depends on the size of the gross estate (see Q 853), and possibly also on what kinds of gifts were made by the decedent during life. Generally, a return must be filed if the gross estate of a decedent who is a U.S. citizen or resident exceeds the unified credit equivalent ($2,000,000 in 2006, see Appendix B). However, the $2,000,000 (in 2006) amount is reduced by the amount of *taxable* gifts (see Q 902) made by the decedent after December 31, 1976, except those includable in the decedent's gross estate. Also, the amount is further reduced by the amount allowed as a specific exemption (the old $30,000 lifetime gift tax exemption) on gifts made by the decedent after September 8, 1976. IRC Sec. 6018(a). An automatic six month extension is available for the Form 706 to anyone who applies for the extension. Treas. Reg. §20.6081-1.

The IRS may, for "reasonable cause," extend the time for payment of any part of the estate tax for a reasonable period not in excess of 10 years from the date the tax is due under the general rule (nine months after decedent's death). The "reasonable cause" extension also applies to any part of any installment payment of tax under the IRC Section 6166 election (see below), but the extension in this case may extend up to 12 months past the due date of the last installment. IRC Sec. 6161(a)(2). If the gross estate includes a reversionary or remainder interest, the executor may elect to postpone payment of the portion of the tax attributable to that interest until six months after termination of the precedent interest in the property; the Service may also grant a "reasonable cause" extension of up to three years beyond the expiration of the postponement period for payment of that portion of the tax. IRC Sec. 6163. In addition, the Service has been given authority to enter into written agreements to pay taxes in installments when the Service determines that such an agreement will facilitate the payment of taxes. IRC Sec. 6159. Interest on all the foregoing extensions and postponements is compounded daily and charged at an annual rate adjusted quarterly so as to be three percentage points over the short-term federal rate. IRC Secs. 6601(a), 6621(a)(2). The underpayment rate for the last quarter of 2005 is 7%. Rev. Rul. 2005-62, 2005-38 IRB 557.

Q 851 FEDERAL ESTATE TAX

The IRC Section 6166 Election

If the decedent's "interest in a closely held business," as defined below, exceeds 35% of the adjusted gross estate (the gross estate less deductions for estate expenses, indebtedness and taxes (IRC Sec. 2053) and for unreimbursed casualty and theft losses (IRC Sec. 2054)), the portion of the federal estate tax (including the generation-skipping tax if it is imposed on a direct skip transfer occurring as a result of decedent's death) attributable to that interest may be paid in annual installments (maximum of 10), and the executor may elect to delay the beginning of the installment payments up to five years, i.e., four annual installments of interest only, followed by ten annual installments of both interest and principal. IRC Sec. 6166. Where the decedent gratuitously transferred property within three years of death, the 35% requirement is met by the estate only if the estate meets the requirement both with and without the application of the bringback rule of IRC Section 2035 (see Q 860). IRC Sec. 2035(c)(2).

For decedents dying prior to 1998, a special 4% interest rate applies to the portion of tax on which payment is deferred under IRC Section 6166. However, if such portion exceeds $345,800, reduced by the amount of unified credit allowable against the tax, the excess amount will bear interest at the regular underpayment rate (see above). IRC Sec. 6601(j), prior to amendment by TRA '97. In 1997, the maximum amount of deferred tax eligible for the 4% interest rate was $153,000.

For decedents dying after 1997, a special 2% interest rate applies to the portion of tax on which payment is deferred under IRC Section 6166. However, if such portion exceeds the amount of tax which would be calculated on the sum of $1,000,000 ($1,200,000 as indexed for 2006) plus the unified credit equivalent, reduced by the amount of the unified credit (see Q 868) allowable against the tax, the excess amount will bear interest at 45% of the regular underpayment rate (see above). The $1,000,000 amount is adjusted for inflation, rounded down to the next lowest multiple of $10,000, after 1998. IRC Sec. 6601(j). No deduction is permitted for estate or income tax purposes for the interest payable on such deferred tax. IRC Secs. 163(k), 2053(c)(1)(D). In 2006, the maximum amount of deferred tax eligible for the 2% interest rate is $552,000. See Appendix B for amounts in other years.

If an election to defer taxes was made for a decedent dying before 1998, an irrevocable election could be made before 1999 to apply the lower interest rates (and the corresponding interest deduction disallowance) to payments due after the election was made (however, the 2% portion is equal to the amount which would be the 4% portion were it not for this election). TRA '97, Sec. 503(d)(2).

For purposes of determining whether an estate qualifies for an IRC Section 6166 extension, the term "interest in a closely held business" means–

(A) an interest as a proprietor in a trade or business carried on as proprietorship;

(B) an interest as a partner in a partnership carrying on a trade or business, if–

(i) 20% or more of the total capital interest in such partnership is included in determining the gross estate of the decedent, or

GENERAL   Q 851

(ii) such partnership had 45 (15 for decedents dying before 2002 and after 2010) or fewer partners; or

(C) stock in a corporation carrying on a trade or business if—

(i) 20% or more in value of the voting stock of such corporation is included in determining the gross estate of the decedent, or

(ii) such corporation had 45 (15 for decedents dying before 2002 and after 2010) or fewer shareholders. IRC Sec. 6166(b)(1).

For purposes of applying the foregoing rules, community property or property the income from which is community property and property held by a husband and wife as joint tenants, tenants by the entirety, or tenants in common is treated as though the property were owned by one shareholder or one partner, as the case may be. Also, property owned, directly or indirectly, by or for a corporation, partnership, estate, or trust is considered as being owned proportionately by or for its shareholders, partners, or beneficiaries. For purposes of the preceding sentence, a person is treated as a beneficiary of any trust only if he has a present interest in the trust. All stock and partnership interests owned by the decedent and his family are treated as owned by the decedent. The decedent's family for this purpose includes only his spouse, his ancestors, his lineal descendants, and his brothers and sisters. IRC Sec. 6166(b)(2). As to any capital interest in a partnership or any nonreadily-tradeable stock (i.e., stock for which at the time of decedent's death there was no market on a stock exchange or in an over-the-counter market) attributable to the decedent under the rules described in this paragraph, the value of such interest does not qualify for the five-year deferral or the special 2% or 4% interest rates. IRC Sec. 6166(b)(7).

The term "interest in a closely held business" means (with regard to a stockholder interest) "stock in a corporation carrying on a trade or business." "Business," for purposes of IRC Section 6166, according to the IRS, refers to a business such as manufacturing, mercantile or service enterprise, as distinguished from management of investment assets. Let. Ruls. 8352086, 8451014, 8524037, 8529026, 8942018.

For purposes of IRC Section 6166, at the executor's election, the portion of the stock of any holding company which represents direct ownership (or indirect ownership through one or more other holding companies) by such company in a "business company" (i.e., a corporation carrying on a trade or business) is deemed to be stock in such business company. However, as to such holding company stock, the five-year delay and the 2% or 4% interest provisions (see above) will not apply. IRC Sec. 6166(b)(8).

The value included in the computations necessary to determine if the estate qualifies for an IRC Section 6166 extension is the value determined for purposes of the estate tax. IRC Sec. 6166(b)(4). Thus, in the case of a farm or other business as to which the executor elected special use valuation (see Q 862), the special use valuation is treated as the value of the property as to which it applies, for purposes of IRC Section 6166. House Report No. 94-1380, pages 32-33.

Also, for purposes of such valuation, the value of passive assets held by the business is not includable. IRC Sec. 6166(b)(9). A technical advice memorandum states that using a life insurance policy as collateral to secure loans to purchase properties

2006 Tax Facts on Insurance & Employee Benefits

used in a business does not convert the policy to an asset actively used in a trade or business. TAM 8848002.

In general, the term "passive asset" includes any stock held in another corporation. However, holding company stock included in the executor's election, explained just above, is not considered a passive asset. Also, if a corporation owns 20% or more in value of the voting stock of another corporation, or such other corporation has 45 (15 for decedents dying before 2002 and after 2010) or fewer stockholders, and 80% or more of the value of the assets of each such corporation is attributable to active assets, then such corporations are treated as one corporation. In other words, if the foregoing conditions are met, then for purposes of the passive asset rule, the corporation is not considered to hold stock in another corporation. IRC Sec. 6166(b)(9).

Special rule: At the election of the executor, if (1) a corporation has 15 or fewer shareholders on June 22, 1984, and at all times thereafter before the date of decedent's death, and (2) stock of such corporation is included in the decedent's gross estate, then all other corporations, all of the stock of which is owned directly or indirectly by the corporation described above, are treated as one corporation for purposes of IRC Section 6166. P.L. 98-361, Sec. 1021(d).

For purposes of IRC Section 6166, interests in two or more closely held businesses, with respect to each of which there is included in determining the value of the decedent's gross estate 20% or more of the total value of each such business, are treated as an interest in a single closely held business. For purposes of this 20% requirement, an interest in a closely held business that represents the surviving spouse's interest in property held by the decedent and the surviving spouse as community property, joint tenants, tenants by the entirety, or tenants in common is treated as having been included in determining the value of the decedent's gross estate. IRC Sec. 6166(c). However, an interest so attributed will not qualify for the 5-year deferral or the special 2% or 4% interest rates. IRC Sec. 6166(b)(7).

In general, if any payment of principal or interest is not paid when due, the whole of the unpaid portion of the tax payable in installments must be paid upon notice and demand from the district director. However, if the full amount of the delinquent payment (principal and all accrued interest) is paid within six months of the original due date, the remaining tax balance is not accelerated. Rather, the payment loses eligibility for the special 2% or 4% interest rates and a penalty is imposed, equal to 5% per month based on the amount of the payment. IRC Sec. 6166(g)(3).

The IRC Section 6166 election terminates and the whole of the unpaid portion of the tax payable in installments becomes due and is payable upon notice and demand from the district director if (1) any portion of the business interest is distributed, sold, exchanged, or otherwise disposed of, or money and other property attributable to such an interest is withdrawn from the business, and (2) the aggregate of such distributions, sales, exchanges, or other dispositions and withdrawals equals or exceeds 50% of the value of such interest. IRC Sec. 6166(g)(1)(A). Transfer of the business interest by the executor or administrator to one entitled to receive it under the decedent's will or under the intestate succession laws is not counted as a distribution for this purpose. However, a subsequent transfer of the interest by the distributee does constitute a distribution, sale, exchange, or other disposition for such purpose. Treas. Reg. §20.6166A-3(e)(1). A sale of business assets by the estate to satisfy unpaid mortgages encumbering the business

GENERAL   Q 852

property is not considered a disposition for purposes of the IRC Section 6166 election; however, to the extent proceeds from such a sale exceed the amount used to satisfy the mortgages, the transaction is considered a disposition. Let. Rul. 8441029. A mere change in the operation of a business from a corporate form to an unincorporated form is not a disposition of the business interest. Rev. Rul. 66-62, 1966-1 CB 272. A sale of business property by the unincorporated business is not considered a disposition *if* sales proceeds are used solely to discharge debts of the unincorporated business attributable to the corporation. Let. Rul. 8452043. Distributions in redemption of stock under IRC Section 303 (see Q 85), are not counted as withdrawals or as disposals of decedent's interest in the business if an amount equal to any such distribution is paid in estate tax on or before the due date of the first installment of tax due after the distribution, or, if earlier, within one year after the distribution. (The position of the IRS is that payment of state death tax in an amount covered by the credit for state death taxes (see Q 869) is not considered payment of the federal estate tax for this purpose. Rev. Rul. 85-43, 1985-1 CB 356. See also GCM 39229.) However, an IRC Section 303 redemption does reduce the value of the business (as of the applicable valuation date) by the proportionate part which the redemption represents, for purposes of determining whether other withdrawals, distributions, sales, exchanges, or disposals meet the applicable 50% test. IRC Sec. 6166(g)(1)(B). *ASRS, Sec. 54, ¶44.7*.

CALCULATION OF TAX

852. How is the federal estate tax computed?

The tax is imposed on the transfer of the taxable estate. The taxable estate is the gross estate (Q 853) less allowable deductions (Q 863). The estate tax rates (see IRC Sec. 2001(c), Appendix B) are applied to the sum of (1) the amount of the taxable estate, and (2) the amount of adjusted taxable gifts (see below). For decedents dying before 2002 and after 2010, the unified tax rates are increased by a 5% additional tax in the case of certain large estates, see below. This produces a "tentative tax" from which is deducted the aggregate amount of gift tax which would have been payable by the decedent or his estate with respect to gifts made by the decedent after 1976 if the tax rate schedule as in effect at the decedent's death had been applicable at the time of such gifts. Included in the aggregate amount of gift tax for purposes of the preceding sentence are gift taxes paid by the decedent's spouse on gifts made by the decedent which are includable in the decedent's gross estate and were consented to by decedent's spouse; *not* included, however (i.e., not deducted from the tentative tax), are gift taxes paid on gifts made by the decedent's spouse which are includable in such spouse's gross estate as gifts made within three years of death and which were consented to by the decedent. IRC Sec. 2001; Rev. Rul. 82-198, 1982-2 CB 206. The result of the foregoing computation is the estate tax, against which allowable credits (Q 867) are applied to determine the final tax payable.

Adjusted taxable gifts are taxable gifts (the balance after subtracting allowable exclusions and deductions) made by the decedent after 1976 other than gifts includable in the decedent's gross estate. The term includes one-half the amount of any gift the decedent or his spouse made to a third party that was consented to by the donor's spouse (i.e., a split gift—see Q 907). IRC Sec. 2513(a)(1); Let. Rul. 8515005. The term does not include split gifts made by decedent's spouse and consented to by decedent which gifts were brought back into the donor spouse's estate as gifts made within three years of death (see Q 860). See Rev. Rul. 82-198, 1982-2 CB 206.

FEDERAL ESTATE TAX

A couple of federal district courts have ruled that in calculating adjusted taxable gifts for estate tax purposes, the Service may not revalue gifts made during life if the statute of limitations against revaluing gifts in IRC Section 2504(c) would apply for gift tax purposes. *Boatmen's First Nat'l Bank of Kansas City (Est. of Douthat) v. U.S.*, 89-1 USTC ¶13,795 (W.D. Mo. 1988); and see *Evanson* below. For contrary opinions, see *Levin v. Comm.*, 93-1 USTC ¶60,128 (4th Cir. 1993), cert. denied; *Evanson v. U.S.*, 94-2 USTC ¶60,174 (8th Cir. 1994), rev'g an unpublished opinion (D.N.D.); *Est. of Smith v. Comm.*, 94 TC 872 (1990), acq. 1990-2 CB 1 (taxpayer permitted to offset the tax on the revalued adjusted taxable gifts with the amount of tax which would be payable on such gifts); *Est. of Robinson v. Comm.*, 101 TC 499 (1993) (gifts for which annual exclusions were improperly taken were added to adjusted taxable gifts); *Stalcup v. U.S.*, 91-2 USTC ¶60,086 (W.D. Okla. 1991). A gift made after August 5, 1997, cannot be revalued, if the gift was adequately disclosed on a gift tax return and the gift tax statute of limitations (generally, three years) has passed. IRC Sec. 2001(f).

For decedents dying before 2002 and after 2010, the benefit of the graduated tax rates is phased out for cumulative taxable transfers in excess of $10 million through imposition of a 5% additional tax. IRC Sec. 2001(c). (See Appendix B.) *ASRS, Sec. 54, ¶44.2.*

GROSS ESTATE

853. What items are includable in a decedent's gross estate?

The gross estate consists of the value of:

1. *Property owned by decedent at death.* Generally, all property passing under the decedent's will or under the intestacy laws of the state if he died without a will. This category includes all types of property owned by the decedent: tangible and intangible personal property, and real estate, whether located in the U.S. or in a foreign country. IRC Sec. 2033.

2. *Dower and curtesy interests.* Property passing to surviving wife or husband as dower or curtesy, or under state statutes taking the place of dower or curtesy. IRC Sec. 2034.

3. *Gifts within three years of death.* Certain kinds of transfers and transfers for certain purposes made within three years of the donor's death. IRC Sec. 2035. See Q 860.

4. *Gifts with life interest retained.* Property given away by decedent (in trust or otherwise) but with respect to which he retained for life: the income from the property; the right to use or enjoy the property; the right to designate who should ultimately receive the property or the income from the property. The retention of the right to vote shares of stock of a controlled corporation (as defined in IRC Sec. 2036(b)(2)) is considered a retention of the enjoyment of the stock; also, for purposes of applying IRC Section 2035 (see Q 860), the relinquishment or cessation of voting rights is treated as a transfer of property made by the decedent.

Interspousal gifts in a state whose laws provide that the income from a spouse's separate property is community property have been held *not* to be gifts of property with a life interest retained within the meaning of IRC Section 2036. *Est. of Castleberry v. Comm.*, 45 AFTR 2d ¶148,381 (5th Cir. 1980), rev'g 68 TC 682 (1977), nonacq. 1978-2

GENERAL

Q 853

CB 3; *Est. of Wyly v. Comm.*, 45 AFTR 2d ¶148,381 (5th Cir. 1980), rev'g 69 TC 227 (1977); *Est. of McKee v. Comm.*, TC Memo 1978-108 (appeals dismissed); Rev. Rul. 81-221, 1981-2 CB 178, revoking Rev. Rul. 75-504, 1975-2 CB 363; *Est. of Deobald v. U.S.*, 444 F. Supp. 374 (E.D. La. 1977).

A trust is includable in a grantor's estate if the trustee is required, by the trust document or under state law, to reimburse the grantor for income tax payable by the grantor on trust income. A trust is not includable merely because the trustee has a discretionary reimbursement power. Rev. Rul. 2004-64, 2004-27 IRB 7.

5. *Gifts taking effect at death.* Property given away by the decedent (in trust or otherwise) if: (a) the person to whom the gift was made could obtain possession or enjoyment of the property only by surviving the decedent, and (b) the decedent had a reversionary interest in the property worth more than 5% of the value of the property at death. But a gift will not be taxable as a transfer taking effect at death if any beneficiary could have obtained possession of the property through the exercise of a power of appointment, and the power was exercisable immediately before decedent's death. IRC Sec. 2037.

6. *Revocable gifts.* Property given away by the decedent (in trust or otherwise) where he reserved the power to alter, amend, revoke, or terminate the gift. IRC Sec. 2038.

7. *Annuities* (see Q 600 to Q 608).

8. *Joint interests.* Property owned jointly by the decedent and another. Under the general rule, the entire value of the jointly owned property will be included in the decedent's gross estate except the part, if any, attributable to the portion of the purchase price furnished by the survivor. (The decedent's estate has the burden of proving the extent of consideration that was furnished by the surviving joint owner. For application of the general rule as to mortgaged property includable in a decedent joint owner's estate, see Rev. Rul. 79-302, 1979-2 CB 328.) However, if the property was acquired by the joint owners by gift or inheritance, only the decedent's fractional share of the property is includable in his gross estate. IRC Sec. 2040(a). See Q 854 for a special rule applicable to certain joint interests of husbands and wives.

9. *Power of appointment.* Property over which decedent possessed at his death a general power of appointment that was created on or after October 22, 1942. Property over which decedent possessed at his death a general power of appointment that was created before October 22, 1942–but only if decedent exercised the power by will or by a transfer during life that would come within any of the provisions of IRC Sections 2035-2038 (see 3-6 above). IRC Sec. 2041.

10. *Proceeds of life insurance.* (See Q 626.) IRC Sec. 2042.

11. *Transfers for insufficient consideration.* If any one of the transfers described in 3, 4, 5, 6, and 9 is made for consideration in money or money's worth, but the consideration is not adequate and full, the excess of the fair market value of the property transferred over the consideration received is the amount includable in the gross estate. IRC Sec. 2043(a). There is a split of authority over whether adequate and full consideration is measured by reference to what would otherwise be included in the estate or using time

value of money discounts. *Gradow v. U.S.*, 90-1 USTC ¶60,010 (Fed. Cir. 1990); *Pittman v. U.S.*, 95-1 USTC ¶60,186 (E.D.N.C. 1994); *Parker v. U.S.*, 95-1 USTC ¶60,199 (N.D. Ga. 1995); *Est. of D'Ambrosio v. Comm.*, 96-2 USTC ¶60,252 (3rd Cir. 1996), rev'g 105 TC 252 (1995); *Wheeler v. Comm.*, 97-2 USTC ¶60,278 (5th Cir. 1997), rev'g 96-1 USTC ¶60,226 (W.D. Tex. 1996); *Est. of Magnin v. Comm.*, 99-2 USTC ¶60,347 (9th Cir. 1999), rev'g TC Memo 1996-25. With regard to consideration and life insurance, see Q 642.

12. *Certain marital deduction property.* Property for which the marital deduction was previously allowed and in which the decedent had a qualifying income interest for life (see Q 864). IRC Sec. 2044. Such property is *not* included in the gross estate of the *donor* spouse. IRC Sec. 2523(f)(5)(A)(i). In the case of a joint and survivor annuity treated as a qualifying income interest for life (see Q 731), nothing is included in the donee spouse's estate if such spouse dies before the donor spouse. IRC Sec. 2523(f)(6).

13. *Community property.* Decedent's one-half interest in community property. IRC Sec. 2033.

14. *Recapture of qualified payments.* Additional estate tax due with respect to certain transfers of interests in corporations or partnerships to reflect cumulative but unpaid distributions on retained interests (see Q 913). IRC Sec. 2701.

15. *Certain lapsing rights.* Deemed transfers at death upon the lapse of certain voting or liquidation rights in a corporation or partnership (see Q 916). IRC Sec. 2704. *ASRS, Sec. 54, ¶44.3.*

854. What special estate tax includability rule applies to property interests held jointly by spouses?

In the case of joint interests created after 1976, notwithstanding the provisions of IRC Section 2040 explained above (Q 853(8)), only one-half the value of a *qualified joint interest* is included in a decedent's gross estate under IRC Section 2040. [The rule for inclusion in a decedent's estate for spousal jointly owned property is still based upon consideration furnished if the joint interest was created prior to 1977. *Gallenstein v. U.S.*, 92-2 USTC ¶60,114 (6th Cir. 1992); *Patten v. U.S.*, 97-2 USTC ¶60,279 (4th Cir. 1997); *Anderson v. U.S.*, 96-2 USTC ¶60,235 (D.C. Md. 1996); *Hahn v. Comm.*, 110 TC 140 (1998), acq. 2001-42 IRB iii.] A *qualified joint interest* means any interest in property held by the decedent and the decedent's spouse as (a) tenants by the entirety; or (b) joint tenants with right of survivorship, but only if the decedent and the spouse of the decedent are the only joint tenants. IRC Sec. 2040(b). However, if the decedent's spouse is not a United States citizen, interests in property held by the decedent and the decedent's spouse are not treated as a *qualified joint interest* (apparently unless the transfer to the surviving spouse is in a qualified domestic trust, see Q 864). IRC Sec. 2056(d). For purposes of applying the consideration furnished test (see Q 853(8)) where the *qualified joint interest* rule does not apply because the decedent's spouse is not a United States citizen, consideration furnished by the decedent to the decedent's spouse before July 14, 1988 is generally treated as consideration furnished by the decedent's spouse. OBRA '89, Sec. 7815(d)(16).

855. Are social security benefits includable in a decedent's gross estate?

GENERAL   Q 858

No. Neither the lump sum death benefit nor the value of monthly survivor benefits need be included in the gross estate. Rev. Rul. 81-182, 1981-2 CB 179; Rev. Rul. 67-277, 1967-2 CB 322; Rev. Rul. 55-87, 1955-1 CB 112. *ASRS, Sec. 54, ¶¶44.3(a), (g).*

856. Is the value of property transferred under a Uniform Gifts (or Transfers) to Minors Act includable in the donor's gross estate?

The value of property transferred to a minor donee under a Uniform Gifts to Minors Act or a Uniform Transfers to Minors Act is includable in the gross estate of the donor if the donor appoints himself custodian and dies while serving in that capacity and before the custodianship ends. Rev. Rul. 57-366, 1957-2 CB 618; Rev. Rul. 59-357, 1959-2 CB 212. *Est. of Prudowsky v. Comm.*, 55 TC 90 (1971), aff'd per curiam 465 F.2d 62 (7th Cir. 1972); *Stuit v. Comm.*, 452 F.2d 190 (7th Cir. 1971); *Eichstedt v. U.S.*, 30 AFTR 2d 72-5912 (N.D. Cal. 1972); *Est. of Jacoby v. Comm.*, TC Memo 1970-165. The results will be the same where the donor dies while serving as successor custodian (as, for example, where the husband donor is appointed successor custodian upon the death of his wife). Rev. Rul. 70-348, 1970-2 CB 193. However, if the wife of the donor dies while serving as custodian, the custodial property will not be included in her estate merely because she had consented to having the gift treated as if made one-half by her and one-half by her husband (see Q 907). Rev. Rul. 74-556, 1974-2 CB 300. See Q 658 for application of the reciprocal trust doctrine to crossed transfers of assets in custodianship. *ASRS, Sec. 48.*

857. Is the value of a life insurance agent's renewal commissions includable in his gross estate?

Yes, assuming that he owns the right to the renewal commissions at the time of his death. The value includable will be the fair market value of the renewals at the time of death. Following the agent's death, the actuaries of the company will value the renewal account using some appropriate persistency table and an assumed rate of interest. If desired, the renewal commissions can be made to qualify for the marital deduction. For example, the value of the commissions will qualify for the marital deduction if all commissions are payable to the surviving spouse during her lifetime, and to her estate at her death. They should also qualify if she has the right to all renewals payable during her lifetime and a power to appoint who shall receive the commissions payable after her death. But if the surviving spouse is given only a right to those commissions which are payable during her lifetime, and someone else will receive the remaining payments in event of her death during the renewal period, she will have only a "terminable interest" in the commissions, and they will not qualify unless a QTIP election is made. *Est. of Selling v. Comm.*, 24 TC 191 (1955); *Est. of Baker v. Comm.*, TC Memo 1988-483; Let. Rul. 9016084. (See Q 864.) The recipient must pay income tax on the renewals as received but is entitled to an income tax deduction for the estate tax attributable to including the value of the renewals in the agent's gross estate (see Q 827).

858. Is an education savings account includable in an individual's gross estate?

Upon the distribution of an education savings account (previously called an Education IRA) on account of the death of the beneficiary, the amount of the education savings account is includable in the estate of the beneficiary, not the contributor. However, where a donor elects to have contributions prorated over a five year period for gift tax purposes

2006 Tax Facts on Insurance & Employee Benefits   835

and dies during such period, the gross estate of the donor includes prorated contributions allocated to periods after the donor's death. IRC Secs. 530(d)(3), 529(c)(4).

See Q 905 for the gift tax treatment and Q 810 for the income tax treatment of education savings accounts.

859. Is a qualified tuition program includable in an individual's gross estate?

No interest in a qualified tuition program will be includable in the estate of any individual for purposes of the estate tax, with two exceptions: (1) a distribution to the estate of the beneficiary upon the beneficiary's death; and (2) if such a donor dies before the end of a 5-year gift tax proration period (see Q 906), the gross estate of the donor will include the portion of contributions allocable to periods after the death of the donor. IRC Sec. 529(c)(4).

See Q 906 for the gift tax treatment and Q 812 for the income tax treatment of qualified tuition programs.

860. Under what circumstances is the value of property transferred by gift within three years of the donor's death includable in the donor's gross estate?

Subject to two kinds of exceptions, gifts made within three years of death by donors who die after 1981 are not brought back into the donor's gross estate under the bringback rule of IRC Section 2035 (see below). *However*, gift tax paid on any post-1976 gifts made by a decedent within three years of his death is includable in the gross estate in any case, regardless of whether the value of the gift itself is includable under IRC Section 2035 or any other IRC section. IRC Sec. 2035(b); Rev. Rul. 81-229, 1981-2 CB 176. Gift tax paid by decedent's spouse on a split-gift within three years of decedent's death was included in decedent's estate where the decedent had funneled money to his spouse who then transferred the money to a life insurance trust (and to the IRS to pay gift tax); the transfers were treated as collapsed into one transaction under the step-transaction doctrine. *Brown v. U.S.*, 2003-1 USTC ¶60,462 (9th Cir. 2003).

The first kind of exception applies (1) where a donor gratuitously transfers property within three years of death but retains an interest in that property described in IRC Section 2036 (transfer with a retained life estate), IRC Section 2037 (transfer taking effect at death with reversionary interest retained), IRC Section 2038 (transfer with power retained to revoke or amend), or IRC Section 2042 (incidents of ownership in insurance on life of donor), or (2) where a donor transfers property subject to such a retained interest more than three years before death, but relinquishes that interest within three years of death (see Q 853(4), (5), (6), (10)). The bringback rule applies to these transfers whether or not a gift tax return was required to be filed. IRC Sec. 2035(a). The entire value of the property transferred under this exception is includable in the decedent's gross estate, including the value of the property, if any, transferred by the decedent's consenting spouse (i.e., a split gift—see Q 907). If the consenting spouse dies within three years of the gift and the entire value of the gift was includable in the donor spouse's estate under IRC Section 2035, the consenting spouse's portion of the gift is not an adjusted taxable gift and is not includable in the consenting spouse's gross estate. IRC Sec. 2001(e); Rev. Rul. 82-198, 1982-2 CB 206. The gift tax paid by

GENERAL   Q 861

the donor spouse or his estate is includable in the donor spouse's estate, and the gift tax paid by the consenting spouse or her estate is includable in the consenting spouse's estate. IRC Sec. 2035(b); Rev. Rul. 82-198, above. For the effect of this exception on transfers of life insurance, see Q 642, Q 643. However, gift tax paid by decedent's spouse on a gift split between the spouses within three years of decedent's death was included in decedent's estate where the spouse did not have sufficient assets to pay the spouse's share of the gift tax and the decedent transferred assets to the spouse to pay the taxes. TAM 9729005.

A transfer from a revocable trust is treated as made directly by the grantor. IRC Sec. 2035(e). Such a transfer will generally be subject to the three-year bringback rule only with respect to gift tax paid within three years of death and for the limited purpose of the second exception below.

The second kind of exception retains the three-year bringback rule of IRC Section 2035 for the purposes of (a) determining the estate's qualification for (1) IRC Section 303 stock redemptions (see Q 85), current use valuation for qualified real property (see Q 862), and (b) determining property subject to estate tax liens. IRC Sec. 2035(c)(1). With respect to the IRC Section 6166 extension of time to pay estate tax (see Q 851), the requirement that the decedent's interest in a closely held business must exceed 35% of the adjusted gross estate is met by an estate only if the estate meets the requirement both with and without the application of the bringback rule. IRC Sec. 2035(c)(2). An exception to this second exception is that any gifts (other than a transfer with respect to a life insurance policy, see Q 642, Q 643) not required to be reported on a gift tax return filed by the decedent for the year the gift was made are not includable in the gross estate. Gifts up to the limit of the gift tax annual exclusion and qualified transfers (see Q 917), but not split gifts, described at Q 907, do not require the filing of a return. Another exception to the second exception is a gift which qualifies for the gift tax marital deduction (see Q 920). IRC Sec. 2035(c)(3).

The bringback rule of IRC Section 2035, referred to in the opening sentence of this answer, operates as follows: In general, gifts made by the decedent (in trust or otherwise) after December 31, 1976, which are caught by the three-year rule are includable in the decedent's estate. Also includable is the amount of any gift tax paid by the decedent or his estate on any gifts made by the decedent or his spouse after December 31, 1976, and within three years prior to decedent's death; the gift tax is includable regardless of whether the value of the gift itself is includable under IRC Section 2035 or any other IRC section. IRC Sec. 2035(b); Rev. Rul. 81-229, 1981-2 CB 176; Rev. Rul. 82-198, 1982-2 CB 206. Where the decedent made a "net gift" (i.e., a gift made on the condition that the donee pay the gift tax—see Q 911), the amount includable in the gross estate is the total value of the property transferred. Let. Rul. 8317010. *ASRS, Sec. 54, ¶44.3(c).*

EXCLUSION

861. What estate tax exclusion is available for a qualified conservation easement?

An estate tax exclusion is provided for qualified conservation easements. IRC Sec. 2031(c). An irrevocable election must be made by the executor if the exclusion is to apply. The exclusion is available for the lesser of (1) the applicable percentage of the

2006 Tax Facts on Insurance & Employee Benefits   837

value of land subject to the qualified conservation easement, reduced by the amount of any charitable deduction for the easement under IRC Section 2055(f), or (2) the exclusion limitation. IRC Secs. 2031(c)(1), 2031(c)(6). The applicable percentage is equal to 40% reduced (but not below zero) by two percentage points for every percentage point (or fraction thereof) by which the value of the conservation easement is less than 30% of the value of the land (determined without regard to the easement and reduced by any development right). IRC Sec. 2031(c)(2). After 2001, the exclusion limitation is $500,000. See Appendix B for limitations in other years. IRC Sec. 2031(c)(3).

The land subject to the conservation easement must be located in the United States or its possessions (for decedents dying in 2001 to 2009). IRC Sec. 2031(c)(8)(A)(i), as amended by EGTRRA 2001. For decedents dying before 2000 and after 2010, the land subject to the conservation easement must generally on the date of the decedent's death be located (1) within 25 miles of a metropolitan area, (2) within 25 miles of part of the National Wilderness Preservation System, or (3) within 10 miles of an Urban National Forest.

The land subject to the conservation easement must be owned by decedent or members of decedent's family at all times during the three year period ending at decedent's death. IRC Sec. 2031(c)(8)(A)(ii).

The exclusion is not available to the extent that the land is subject to acquisition indebtedness or retained development rights (excludes certain farming uses). IRC Secs. 2031(c)(4), 2031(c)(5). Nor is the exclusion available if the easement is granted after the death of the decedent and anyone receives an income tax deduction with regard to granting of the easement. IRC Sec. 2031(c)(9). *ASRS: Sec. 54, ¶44.2A(b).*

VALUATION

862. How is property valued for estate tax purposes?

Once the property that makes up the gross estate is determined, the next step is the valuation of such property. As a general rule, the estate tax value is the fair market value of the property on the date of the decedent's death. Fair market value is defined as "the price at which the property would change hands between a willing seller and a willing buyer, neither being under any compulsion to buy or to sell and both having reasonable knowledge of relevant facts." IRC Sec. 2031; Treas. Reg. §20.2031-(1)(b). However, the law permits the executor or administrator to elect an "alternate valuation" method if the election will decrease the value of the gross estate and the amount of the federal estate tax and generation-skipping tax imposed; generally, this means that the property will be included in the gross estate at its fair market value as of *six months* after the decedent's death. IRC Sec. 2032.

Specifically, if the alternate valuation method is elected, the property will be valued under the following rules: (1) Any property distributed, sold, exchanged or otherwise disposed of within six months after decedent's death is valued as of the date of such distribution, sale, exchange or other disposition. (2) Any property not distributed, sold, exchanged or otherwise disposed of within six months after decedent's death is valued as of the date six months after death. (3) Any property interest whose value is affected by mere lapse of time is valued as of the date of decedent's death. But an adjustment is made for any change in value during the six-month period (or during the period

GENERAL
Q 862

between death and distribution, sale or exchange) which is not due to mere lapse of time. (4) Interest and dividends (other than extraordinary dividends) received during the six months are excluded. (5) The alternate valuation method must be applied to all the property included in the gross estate, and cannot be applied to only a portion of the property. Treas. Reg. §20.2032-1(b)(2). (6) The election to value property using the alternate valuation method must be made no later than one year after the due date (including extensions) for filing the estate tax return. The election is irrevocable, unless it is revoked no later than the due date (including extensions) for filing the estate tax return. If use of the alternate valuation method would not result in a decrease in both the value of the gross estate and the amount of estate tax and generation-skipping transfer tax on a filed return, a protective election can be made to use the alternate valuation method if it is later determined that such a decrease would occur. Prop. Treas. Reg. §20.2032-1(b).

The fair market value of mutual fund shares is considered to be their redemption value. Treas. Reg. §20.2031-8(b). Community property may be valued at less than one-half the fair market value of the whole if the executor can show by qualified appraisement or other evidence that the value of the decedent's interest should be discounted. *Propstra v. Comm.*, 50 AFTR 2d ¶148,534 (9th Cir. 1982).

Property includable in a surviving spouse's estate as qualified terminable interest property (see Q 864) under IRC Section 2044 (see Q 853) is not aggregated with other property includable in the estate for estate tax valuation purposes. *Est. of Bonner v. U.S.*, 96-2 USTC ¶60,237 (5th Cir. 1996), rev'g an unpublished decision (S.D. Tex.); *Est. of Mellinger v. Comm.*, 112 TC 26 (1999), acq. AOD 1999-006. However, property included in the gross estate because of a general power of appointment should be aggregated with property owned outright by the powerholder for estate tax valuation purposes. FSA 200119013; *Est. of Fontana v. Comm.*, 118 TC 318 (2002).

Life estates, reversions, remainders, and annuities (other than commercial contracts—see Q 603) are valued according to estate and gift tax valuation tables (see Q 910). Various courts have held, however, that in exceptional cases where there is strong evidence at the date of valuation that the life by which an interest is measured has an expectation of life longer or shorter than the tables indicate such interest may be valued according to the facts at hand rather than according to the tables. (See cases cited in ASRS, section 54, ¶¶44.3(e) and 44.4, and also cases cited in Q 910.) The government's position is that the tables must be applied in *every* case where a decedent's reversionary interest must be valued under IRC Sections 2042(2) (see Q 634) or 2037 (see Q 853(5)). In all other cases involving the valuation of an interest dependent on the life of one or more individuals, the standard valuation tables must generally be applied unless an individual who is a measuring life has an incurable illness or other deteriorating physical condition and at least a 50% probability of dying within one year (see Q 910). In valuing a decedent's life estate in property for purposes of the credit for estate taxes paid on prior transfers (see Q 871), if the executor of the transferor estate elects alternate valuation, the decedent's life estate is valued by applying the appropriate factor from the actuarial tables for the decedent's age at the date of the transferor's death to the value of the property (in which decedent had a life estate) at the valuation date. Rev. Rul. 81-118, 1981-1 CB 453.

Where life estates, reversions, remainders, and annuities are valued according to estate and gift tax valuation tables and an election is made to value property at the alternate valuation date (see above), the IRC Section 7520 interest rate to be used is the rate for the alternate valuation date (generally six months after death). TAM 9637006.

If the IRS makes a determination of the value of any item of property for purposes of the estate or gift tax laws or the generation-skipping tax, the executor or donor may request that the IRS furnish a written statement explaining the basis on which the valuation was determined. IRC Sec. 7517; Treas. Reg. §301.7517-1.

With respect to estate tax returns, 20% of an underpayment attributable to a substantial estate tax valuation understatement is added to tax. There is a substantial estate tax valuation understatement if (1) the value claimed was 50% or less of the correct amount, and (2) the underpayment exceeds $5,000. If the value claimed was 25% or less of the correct amount (and the underpayment exceeds $5,000), 40% of an underpayment attributable to such a gross estate tax valuation understatement is added to tax. IRC Sec. 6662. The 20% or 40% penalty is not imposed with respect to any portion of the underpayment for which it is shown that there was reasonable cause and the taxpayer acted in good faith. IRC Sec. 6664(c)(1).

Special Valuation for Qualified Real Property

Under certain conditions spelled out in IRC Section 2032A, an executor may elect to value, for federal estate tax purposes, real property (called "qualified real property") devoted to farming or other trade or business (called "qualified use") by the decedent or a member of the decedent's family on the date of decedent's death, on the basis of its actual use rather than by taking into account the "highest and best" use to which the property could be put. However, this special valuation cannot reduce the gross estate by more than $750,000 ($900,000 as indexed for 2006, see Appendix B for amounts in other years). The $750,000 amount is adjusted for inflation, rounded down to the next lowest multiple of $10,000, after 1998. IRC Sec. 2032A(a)(3). A decedent's estate may elect both alternate valuation and special use valuation. Rev. Rul. 83-31, 1983-1 CB 225. If both elections are made, the special use valuation is made as of the alternate valuation date. Also, in such case, the $750,000 as indexed limitation is applicable to the difference between fair market value and special use valuation on such date. Rev. Rul. 88-89, 1988-2 CB 333.

To qualify for this special valuation: (1) the "adjusted value" of the real and personal property used in the farming operation or other business as to which special valuation is sought must amount to at least 50% of the "adjusted value" of the property included in the gross estate ("adjusted value" means the value of the property concerned reduced by the amount of unpaid mortgages or other indebtedness against such property); (2) at least 25% of the adjusted value of the gross estate must be qualified real property; (3) this property must have been acquired from or passed from the decedent to a "qualified heir" (described below); (4) the real property must have been owned by the decedent or a member of his family and used for a qualified use by the decedent or a member of the decedent's family for five of the last eight years prior to decedent's death; and (5) there must have been material participation in the operation of the farm or other business by the decedent or a member of his family for five of the last eight years immediately preceding the earlier of the decedent's death or the date the decedent became disabled or started to receive social security retirement benefits, but only if on the date of decedent's death the material participation requirements were not met and the retirement benefits or disability had been continuous up to the date of death. IRC Secs.

GENERAL   Q 863

2032A(b)(1), 2032A(b)(4). Although at least 25% of the adjusted value of the gross estate must be qualified real property, the property for which the election is actually made may consist of less than 25% of the adjusted value of the gross estate. *Miller v. U.S.*, 88-1 USTC ¶13,757 (C.D. Ill. 1988). The term "qualified heir" means a member of the decedent's family, defined as: his spouse; his ancestors; lineal descendants of the decedent, of the decedent's spouse, or of a parent of the decedent; or the spouses of any of the foregoing lineal descendants; the term also includes the widow or widower of a lineal descendant of the decedent. IRC Secs. 2032A(e)(1), 2032A(e)(2); Rev. Rul. 81-236, 1981-2 CB 172.

In general, the tax benefits derived from the special valuation are recaptured if, within 10 years after the decedent's death, the qualified heir disposes of any interest in qualified real property to anyone other than a member of his family, or if the heir ceases to use the qualified real property for a qualified use. Also, certain "involuntary conversions" (IRC Sec. 2032A(h)) of qualified real property are excused from the recapture tax. The recapture takes the form of an additional estate tax for which the qualified heir is personally liable and as to which a tax lien attaches to the property interest. IRC Sec. 6324B.

The methods of valuing qualified real property are set forth in IRC Section 2032A(e)(7) and IRC Section 2032A(e)(8). (See also Treas. Reg. §20.2032A-4.) *ASRS, Sec. 54, ¶44.4.*

DEDUCTIONS

863. What deductions are allowed in computing the taxable estate of a decedent?

(1) To the extent allowable by the law (governing the administration of decedents' estates) under which the estate is being administered, (a) funeral expenses, (b) administration expenses, (c) claims against the estate, and (d) unpaid mortgages on or other indebtedness against property included at its full value in the gross estate; (2) casualty and theft losses incurred during settlement of the estate and not compensated for by insurance or otherwise; (3) bequests to charitable organizations (and state taxes paid on charitable bequests) (Q 865); (4) the marital deduction (Q 864); (5) the qualified family-owned business interest deduction (Q 866); and (6) state death taxes. IRC Secs. 2053-2058, as amended by EGTRRA 2001. (Deductions are not limited to the value of the *probate* estate. IRC Sec. 2053.)

Funeral and Administration Expenses, Claims, Indebtedness

Administration expenses include chiefly fees or commissions of executors and attorneys, and miscellaneous costs incurred in connection with the preservation and settlement of the estate, including determination and contest of death taxes. Interest paid on a loan from a private lender which enables the executor to pay the estate tax on its due date is deductible. *Est. of Todd v. Comm.*, 57 TC 288 (1971), acq. 1973-2 CB 4; *Hipp v. U.S.*, 72-1 USTC 84,678 (D.S.C. 1971). Interest payable with respect to an extension of time to pay estate taxes on closely held businesses under IRC Section 6166 (see Q 851) is not deductible for decedents dying after 1997 (or for decedents dying before 1998 if an election is made before 1999 to apply the lower TRA '97 interest rates). IRC Sec. 2053(c)(1)(D), TRA '97 Sec. 503(d)(2). Otherwise, authority is split as to whether statutory interest paid in connection with extensions of time to pay the tax granted under provisions of the Internal Revenue Code (see Q 851) is deductible. In the area covered by the U.S. Court of Appeals for the Seventh Circuit (Illinois, Indiana, Wisconsin), such interest is not deductible. *Ballance v. U.S.*, 347 F.2d 419 (7th Cir. 1965). On the other hand, a federal district court, the Tax Court and IRS have declined to follow *Ballance*, holding that such interest is deductible, so long as it is allowable as an administrative expense under local law. *Snyder v. U.S.*, 84-1 USTC ¶13,564 (D. Md. 1984); *Est. of Bahr v. Comm.*, 68 TC 74 (1977), acq. 1978-1 CB 1; Rev. Rul. 78-125, 1978-1 CB 292, revoking Rev. Rul. 75-239. Generally, such interest is deductible only when it accrues, although there is some authority for the proposition that it can be deductible when it is incurred. See, e.g., *Est. of Bahr v. Comm.*, above; *Snyder v. U.S.*, 84-1 USTC ¶13,564 (D. Md. 1984). The regulations say: "An item may be entered on the return for deduction though its exact amount is not then known, provided it is ascertainable with reasonable certainty, and will be paid. No deduction may be taken upon the basis of a vague or uncertain estimate." Treas. Reg. §20.2053-1(b)(3). If, under the terms of the loan, repayment could be accelerated at the option of the borrower or under certain conditions at the option of the lender, or, if the interest rates were subject to unpredictable fluctuation during the term of the loan, it has been held that such factors make the estimate of interest to be paid vague and uncertain and thus not deductible when the interest liability is incurred but not accrued. *Est. of Hoover v. Comm.*, TC Memo 1985-183; *Est. of Spillar v. Comm.*, TC Memo 1985-529; *Est. of Bailly v. Comm.*, 81 TC 246 (1983); Rev. Rul. 80-250, 1980-2 CB 278; Rev. Rul. 84-75, 1984-1 CB 193. Although interest accrues daily, for administrative convenience, the Service instructs taxpayers to claim the deduction only annually when the estate tax installments are due; each claim for deduction requires recomputation of the tax, the interest, and the installment payments. Rev. Rul. 80-250, 1980-2 CB 278. The recomputation is shown on a supplemental Form 706 filed by the executor with or after an annual installment payment. Rev. Proc. 81-27, 1981-2 CB 548. The IRS has also ruled that interest incurred on a federal estate tax deficiency is, to the extent allowable under local law, deductible. Rev. Rul. 79-252, 1979-2 CB 333. The penalty imposed on the failure to pay the estate tax or file the return is not deductible as a necessary administration expense even if the expense is allowable under local law; however, the interest incurred because of a late payment of tax is deductible to the extent it is allowable under local law. Rev. Rul. 81-154, 1981-1 CB 470. Likewise, interest incurred on the late payment of state death taxes is deductible as an administration expense, regardless of the reason for the interest charge. Rev. Rul. 81-256, 1981-2 CB 183.

As a rule, claims against the estate which are founded on a promise or agreement are not deductible unless they were contracted for an adequate consideration in money or money's worth. An exception is made for enforceable pledges to qualified charitable organizations. Such pledges are deductible even though not contracted for an adequate consideration in money or money's worth. A release of dower or other marital rights generally is not deemed an adequate consideration; but a claim for alimony is fully deductible if founded on a divorce decree. Also, where property is transferred from a decedent or from a decedent's estate to a former spouse of the decedent pursuant to a property settlement agreement, and divorce occurred within a three-year period measured from the date one year before the agreement was entered into, and where the property is includable in the decedent's gross estate, the estate is allowed a deduction for such value. IRC Sec. 2043(b)(2). See also Q 640. Life insurance proceeds, if payable to a beneficiary pursuant to an agreement supported by adequate consideration, can be deductible under IRC Section 2053. *Carlson v. U.S.*, 84-1 USTC ¶13,570 (D. Minn. 1984).

GENERAL   Q 864

A payment in settlement of a will contest is not deductible from the gross estate. A claim to share in the estate is to be distinguished from a claim against the estate. *Est. of Moore v. Comm.*, TC Memo 1987-587.

Unpaid mortgages are deductible provided the property subject to the mortgage is included at its full value in the gross estate.

Property taxes accrued prior to decedent's death, and taxes on income received during the decedent's life are deductible. The property taxes, however, must be enforceable obligations (a lien upon the property) at the time of death. Ordinarily, state death taxes are not deductible, but may be taken as a credit against the federal tax (see Q 869). As an exception, however, the executor may elect to deduct any state taxes paid on bequests which qualify as charitable deductions under the federal estate tax law. If deducted, they cannot, of course, be taken as a credit against the tax. An estate tax deduction is not allowed for death taxes paid to a city even though a credit is not allowed for such taxes (see Q 869). TAM 9422002.

In community property states, the extent to which administration expenses and claims are deductible depends upon their treatment under state law. If they are expenses or debts of the entire community, only one-half of them is deductible.

A deduction is allowed for expenses and debts attributable to non-probate property includable in the gross estate. They are deductible even though they exceed the property in the gross estate which under local law is subject to the claims against the estate. However, to the extent that they exceed such property they are not deductible unless actually paid before the due date for filing the estate tax return.

State Death Tax Deduction

A deduction is available for federal estate tax purposes for estate, inheritance, legacy, or succession taxes (i.e., death taxes) paid to any state or the District of Columbia with respect to the estate of the decedent. IRC Sec. 2058, as added by EGTRRA 2001. The deduction is available from 2005 to 2009, and the estate tax is repealed for one year in 2010. A credit for state death taxes (see Q 869) is available before 2005 and after 2010.

The deduction is available only for state death taxes actually paid and claimed as a deduction before the later of (1) 4 years after the filing of the federal estate tax return; (2) 60 days after a decision of the Tax Court with respect to a timely filed petition for redetermination of a deficiency; or (3) with respect to a timely filed claim for refund or credit of the federal estate tax, the later of (a) 60 days of the mailing of a notice of disallowance by the IRS, (b) 60 days after the decision of any court of competent jurisdiction on such claim, or (c) 2 years after the taxpayer files a notice of waiver of disallowance. *ASRS, Sec. 54, ¶44.5.*

864. What is the estate tax marital deduction and what is the limitation on the deductible amount?

The marital deduction is a deduction allowed from the gross estate for interests in property which pass from the decedent to his (or her) surviving spouse and which are included in determining the value of the gross estate, and limited only by the value of such interests. IRC Sec. 2056(a). If an estate values land under the special use valuation

2006 Tax Facts on Insurance & Employee Benefits

Q 864 FEDERAL ESTATE TAX

provisions of IRC Section 2032A (see Q 862) and distributes such land to decedent's spouse, the value to be used in determining the estate tax marital deduction is the special use value of such land and not its fair market value. *Est. of Evers v. Comm.*, TC Memo 1989-292. In general, a marital deduction is not available if the surviving spouse is not a United States citizen unless property passes to the surviving spouse in a qualified domestic trust (QDOT) (see below).

Property will be considered as passing from the decedent to the surviving spouse if the spouse receives it: (1) by bequest or devise; (2) by inheritance; (3) as dower or curtesy (or statutory substitute therefor); (4) by transfer during life in a manner which caused it to be included in deceased's gross estate; (5) by joint ownership with survivorship rights; (6) by exercise or nonexercise of a general power of appointment; or (7) as proceeds of life insurance. IRC Sec. 2056(c). In the case of a transfer within three years of death brought back into the decedent's estate under IRC Section 2035 (see Q 860), the transferee must have been married to the donor at the time of the donor's death (and must have survived the donor), whether or not she was married to the donor at the time of the transfer, in order for the property interest transferred to qualify for the marital deduction. Rev. Rul. 79-354, 1979-2 CB 334.

The marital deduction is reduced when death taxes are paid from the marital share or when the interest passing to the surviving spouse is encumbered in any manner. IRC Sec. 2056(b)(4). Prior to the issuance of regulations discussed below, the marital deduction was reduced where administration expenses were paid from the marital share principal, but not where administration expenses were paid from income from the marital share. *Comm. v. Est. of Hubert*, 97-1 USTC ¶60,261 (U.S. 1997).

Regulations, effective for estates of decedents dying after December 3, 1999, provide rules for reducing the marital share by administration expenses depending on the type of expense: transmission expenses or management expenses. Treas. Reg. §20-2056(b)-4.

Transmission expenses are defined as expenses that would not have been incurred but for the decedent's death. Transmission expenses are also defined as any administration expense that is not a management expense. Transmission expenses paid from the marital share reduce the marital share.

Management expenses are defined as expenses related to investment, preservation, and maintenance of the assets during a reasonable period of estate administration. Management expenses attributable to the marital share do not reduce the marital share except to the extent that the expense is deducted under IRC Section 2053 as an administration expense. Management expenses which are paid by the marital share but which are not attributable to the marital share reduce the marital share.

Generally speaking, a property interest will not qualify for the marital deduction unless it will be includable in the surviving spouse's gross estate if she still owns it at her death. (A duty of consistency may require that property be includable in the surviving spouse's estate where a marital deduction was claimed in the first spouse's estate even if the marital deduction was improperly claimed in the first spouse's estate. *Est. of Letts v. Comm.*, 2000-1 USTC ¶60,374 (11th Cir. 2000); TAM 200407018.) Thus, certain "terminable interests" passing to the surviving spouse do not qualify for the marital deduction.

The terminable interest rule provides that a property interest passing to the surviving spouse will not qualify for the marital deduction if it is only a life estate or other terminable interest *and* (1) an interest in the property passes or has passed to someone other than the spouse, or the spouse's estate, and (2) such other person may possess or enjoy the property after the spouse's interest ends. IRC Sec. 2056(b)(1). The Internal Revenue Code provides these exceptions to the terminable interest rule:

Common disaster or delay clause. The terminable interest rule does not cause disqualification of the property interest if: (1) the only condition that will terminate the surviving spouse's interest is (a) her death within six months after decedent's death, or (b) the surviving spouse's death as a result of a disaster that also caused decedent's death; and (2) the condition did not occur. IRC Sec. 2056(b)(3). (See Rev. Rul. 70-400, 1970-2 CB 196.)

Qualified terminable interest property. "Qualified terminable interest property (QTIP)" means property (1) which passes from the decedent, (2) in which the surviving spouse has a "qualifying income interest for life," and (3) as to which the executor makes an irrevocable election on the federal estate tax return to have the marital deduction apply. The surviving spouse has a "qualifying income interest for life" if (a) the surviving spouse is entitled to all the income from the property, payable annually or at more frequent intervals, or has a usufruct interest for life in the property, and (b) no person has a power to appoint any part of the property to any person other than the surviving spouse unless the power is exercisable only at or after the death of the surviving spouse. IRC Sec. 2056(b)(7)(B). Apparently, the last requirement is violated even if it is the surviving spouse who is given the lifetime power to appoint to someone other than the surviving spouse. TAM 200234017.

An income interest does not fail to qualify as a qualifying income interest for life merely because the income accumulated by the trust between the last date of distribution and the surviving spouse's death is not required to be either distributed to such spouse's estate or subject to a general power of appointment exercisable by such spouse. Treas. Reg. §20.2056(b)-7(d)(4). However, any income from the property from the date the QTIP interest is created to the death of the spouse with the QTIP interest that has not been distributed before such spouse's death is included in such spouse's estate under IRC Section 2044 to the extent it is not included in the estate under any other IRC provision. Treas. Reg. §20.2044-1(d)(2).

In Technical Advice Memorandum 9139001, the marital deduction was denied because (1) a son's right to purchase stock in a QTIP trust at book value was treated as the power to withdraw property from the trust (i.e., as a power to appoint property to someone other than the spouse), and (2) the spouse and the trustee lacked the right to make the closely held stock, in which the son held all voting rights, income productive. Similarly, a marital deduction was denied where the trustee could sell stock in a QTIP trust to a son at book value. *Est. of Rinaldi v. U.S.*, 97-2 USTC ¶60,281 (Ct. Cl. 1997). While Technical Advice Memorandum 9113009 had provided that a QTIP marital deduction would be denied if the non-QTIP portion of the estate were not funded with an amount equal to the face value of loans guaranteed by the decedent, it was withdrawn by Technical Advice Memorandum 9409018 which provided instead that the marital deduction would not be reduced by the entire unpaid balance of the guaranteed loans unless at the time of death it would appear that a default after the marital deduction were funded would be likely, that marital deduction property would be used to pay the entire unpaid balance of such loans, and that subrogation rights held by the marital portion would appear to be worthless. According to Technical Advice Memorandum

9206001, a QTIP marital deduction was not available where the spouse was given an income interest in only certain types of property held in a trust and the trustee could change the mix of assets in the trust.

The IRS has conceded the validity of the contingent QTIP marital deduction (i.e., where the surviving spouse's qualifying income interest is contingent upon the QTIP election being made), if the QTIP election is made. Treas. Regs. §§20-2056(b)-7(d)(3), 20-2056(b)-7(h)(Ex. 6).

The term "property" includes an interest in property, and a specific portion of property is treated as separate property. IRC Sec. 2056(b)(7). However, a specific portion must be determined on a fractional or percentage basis. IRC Sec. 2056(b)(10). The term "property" also contemplates income-producing property; the deduction will thus be disallowed as to nonincome-producing property (a life insurance policy, for example, is nonincome-producing property) if under local law the spouse has no power to convert the property to income-producing property or to compel such conversion. Let. Ruls. 8304040, 8339018, 8638004, 8745003. The value of the entire property subject to the surviving spouse's qualifying income interest qualifies for the marital deduction if the decedent's executor makes the election as described above. If the surviving spouse's income interest is limited to a term of years or is subject to termination upon the occurrence of some event such as remarriage, the deduction is not allowable. The surviving spouse may be given withdrawal rights with respect to the property supporting her income interest, or, if the property is in trust, the trustee may be given the power to invade the principal for the benefit of the surviving spouse (but not for the benefit of any other person during the spouse's lifetime). Qualified terminable interest property elected to qualify for the marital deduction is includable in the surviving spouse's gross estate to the extent she has not consumed it during her lifetime. IRC Sec. 2044. Also, one who receives such property upon the surviving spouse's death takes a new basis in the property (see Q 816). If the surviving spouse makes a gift of her qualifying income interest, for gift tax purposes the gift is considered a gift of the property supporting the income interest. IRC Sec. 2519. The executor's election may be made for all or any part of property which passes from the decedent and in which the surviving spouse has a qualifying income interest for life; however, any partial election must relate to a fractional or percentile share of the property so that the elective part will reflect its proportionate share of the increment or decline in the whole of the property for purposes of applying IRC Section 2044 or IRC Section 2519 (above). Treas. Reg. §20.2056(b)-7(b)(2).

A survivor annuity in which only the surviving spouse has a right to receive payments during such spouse's life is treated as a qualifying income interest for life unless otherwise elected on the decedent spouse's estate tax return. IRC Sec. 2056(b)(7)(C).

An estate tax QTIP election is ordinarily made by the executor. However, in the absence of a qualified executor, a QTIP election can be made by a person in actual or constructive possession of property. Treas. Reg. §20.2056(b)-7(b)(3). A protective QTIP election can be made with respect to property as to which there is a bona fide issue regarding whether the property is includable in the estate or regarding the amount or nature of the property the spouse is to receive. The election is irrevocable. Thus, if a protective election is made with respect to property as to which there is a bona fide issue regarding whether the property is includable in the estate and it is later determined that the property is includable in the estate, the election cannot be revoked. Treas. Reg. §20.2056(b)-7(c).

GENERAL   Q 864

Trusts. There are five kinds of trusts that will qualify for the marital deduction: (1) the "qualified terminable interest property trust," (2) the "power of appointment trust," (3) the "estate trust," (4) the "special rule charitable remainder trust," and (5) the "qualified domestic trust." The first two and the fourth are specific exceptions to the nondeductible terminable interest rule; the third does not come under the rule; the fifth is the only form permitted if the surviving spouse is not a United States citizen.

(1) *Qualified terminable interest property trust.* If qualified terminable interest property, as defined above, passes to the surviving spouse in trust, the trust is called a qualified terminable interest property trust (QTIP trust). The surviving spouse must have a qualifying interest for life in the trust property; neither the trustee nor anyone else must have the power to appoint any part of the trust property to anyone other than the surviving spouse during her lifetime; and the decedent's executor must make the election to have the trust qualify for the marital deduction.

(2) *Power of appointment trust.* It is specifically provided that property passing to the surviving spouse under a trust which meets the following requirements will qualify for the marital deduction: (a) the surviving spouse must be entitled for life to all the income; (b) such income must be payable at least annually; (c) the surviving spouse must have power to appoint the trust property to herself or to her estate; (d) the power (whether exercisable during life or by will) must be exercisable by the spouse alone, and in all events; (e) no other person must have a power to appoint to someone other than the surviving spouse. A specific portion of the trust can qualify if all requirements are met with respect to that specific portion. However, a specific portion must be determined on a fractional or percentage basis. IRC Secs. 2056(b)(5), 2056(b)(10). The marital deduction is equal to the lesser of the life estate (income) specific portion or the power of appointment specific portion. Treas. Reg. §20.2056(b)-5(c). The life estate with power of appointment marital deduction is not available if the power of appointment is contingent on the qualifying terminable interest property (QTIP) marital deduction not being elected. TAM 8924003. Nor is the life estate with power of appointment marital deduction available if the power of appointment or the income interest would terminate in favor of other beneficiaries if the surviving spouse became incompetent. *Est. of Walsh v. Comm.*, 110 TC 393 (1998).

(3) *Estate trust.* Under an estate trust (a) the income is either distributed to the surviving spouse or accumulated during her lifetime, and (b) the principal and accumulated income, if any, is payable to her estate.

(4) It is possible that a trust which combines the features of an estate trust with a power of appointment trust will qualify for the marital deduction. Rev. Rul. 72-333, 1972-2 CB 530.

(5) *Special rule charitable remainder trust.* If the surviving spouse is the only noncharitable beneficiary (other than certain ESOP remainder beneficiaries) of a "qualified charitable remainder trust" created by the decedent, the spouse's interest is not considered a nondeductible terminable interest and the value of such interest will qualify for the marital deduction. A "qualified charitable remainder trust" means a charitable remainder annuity trust or a charitable remainder unitrust (see Q 825 for definitions). IRC Sec. 2056(b)(8). Concerning the charitable contributions deduction, see Q 865, Q 921.

(6) *Qualified domestic trust.* In general, a marital deduction is not available for a transfer to a surviving spouse who is not a United States citizen unless the transfer is

to a qualified domestic trust (QDOT) for which the executor has made an election. IRC Sec. 2056(d). A QDOT must qualify for the marital deduction under (1), (2), (3), or (5), as well as meet the following requirements. At least one trustee of the QDOT must be a United States citizen or a domestic corporation and no distribution (other than a distribution of income) may be made from the trust unless that trustee has the right to withhold any additional gift or estate tax imposed on the trust. Additional gift tax is due on any distribution while the surviving spouse is still alive (other than a distribution to the surviving spouse of income or on account of hardship). Additional estate tax is due on any property remaining in the QDOT at the death of the surviving spouse (or at the time the trust ceases to qualify as a QDOT, if earlier). The additional gift or estate tax is calculated as if any property subject to the tax had been included in the taxable estate of the first spouse to die. IRC Sec. 2056A.

Regulations add additional requirements in order to ensure the collection of the deferred estate tax. If the fair market value (as finally determined for estate tax purposes, see Q 862, but determined without regard to any indebtedness with respect to the assets) of the assets passing to the QDOT exceeds $2,000,000, then the QDOT must provide that either (1) at least one U.S. trustee is a bank (as defined in IRC Section 581), (2) at least one trustee is a U.S. branch of a foreign bank and another trustee is a U.S. trustee, or (3) the U.S. trustee furnish a bond or security or a line of credit equal to 65% of the fair market value of the QDOT corpus. The line of credit must be issued by (1) a U.S. bank, (2) a U.S. branch of a foreign bank, or (3) a foreign bank and confirmed by a U.S. bank. Treas. Reg. §20.2056A-2(d)(1)(i).

A QDOT with assets of less than $2,000,000 must either (a) meet one of the requirements for a trust exceeding $2,000,000, or (b) provide that (1) no more than 35% of the fair market value (determined annually on last day of trust's taxable year) of assets consists of real property located outside the U.S., and (2) all other QDOT assets be physically located within the U.S. at all times during the trust term. All QDOTs for the benefit of a surviving spouse are aggregated for purposes of the $2,000,000 threshold. A QDOT owning more than 20% of the voting stock or value in a corporation with 15 or fewer shareholders (or 20% of the capital interest in a partnership with 15 or fewer partners) is deemed to own a pro rata share of the assets of the corporation (or the pro rata share of the greater of the QDOT's interest in the capital or profits of the partnership) for purposes of the 35% foreign real property limitation. All interests in the corporation (or partnership) held by or for the benefit of the surviving spouse or the surviving spouse's family (includes brothers, sisters, ancestors, and lineal descendants) are treated as one person for purpose of determining the number of shareholders (or partners) and whether a 20% or more interest exists. However, the attribution rules do not apply in determining the QDOT's pro rata share of the corporation's (or partnership's) assets. Interests in other entities (such as another trust) are treated similarly to corporations (and partnerships). Treas. Reg. §20.2056A-2(d)(1)(ii).

For purposes of the $2,000,000 QDOT threshold and the amount of a bond or letter of credit required, up to $600,000 in value attributable to the surviving spouse's personal residence and related furnishings held by the QDOT may be excluded. However, the personal residence exclusion does not apply for purposes of determining whether 35% of the fair market value of assets consists of real property located outside the U.S.. A personal residence is either the principal residence of the surviving spouse or one other residence of the surviving spouse. A personal residence must be available for use by the surviving spouse at all times and may not be rented to another party. Related

GENERAL   Q 865

furnishings include furniture and commonly used items within the value associated with normal household use; rare artwork, valuable antiques, and automobiles are not included. If a residence ceases to be used as the surviving spouse's personal residence or a residence is sold, the personal residence exclusion ceases to apply with regard to that residence. However, if part or all of the amount of the adjusted sales price of the residence is reinvested in a new personal residence within 12 months of the date of sale, the exclusion continues to the extent the adjusted sales price is reinvested in the new residence. Also, if a residence ceases to be used as the surviving spouse's personal residence or a residence is sold, the exclusion can be allocated to another personal residence of the surviving spouse that is held by a QDOT of the surviving spouse. In this instance, the exclusion can be up to $600,000 (less the amount previously allocated to a personal residence that continues to qualify for the exclusion). Treas. Reg. §20.2056A-2(d)(1)(iv).

A plan, annuity, or other arrangement which would qualify for the marital deduction except for the fact that the surviving spouse is not a U.S. citizen, and whose payments cannot be assigned to a QDOT because of federal, state, or foreign law, or because of the terms of the plan, annuity, or other arrangement (a "nonassignable annuity or other arrangement"—see, for example, Q 348) will be treated as meeting the QDOT requirements if the executor of the decedent spouse's estate submits an agreement by the noncitizen surviving spouse to either (1) remit deferred estate tax on the corpus portion of each annuity payment, or (2) roll over the corpus portion of each annuity payment to a QDOT. Treas. Regs. §§20.2056A-4(c), 20.2056A-4(d)(Ex. 4).

Legal life estate. An interest consisting of a legal life estate plus a general power of appointment over the remainder will qualify if it meets the requirements (a) to (e) for a "power of appointment trust" above. A life estate which is a "qualifying income interest for life" in "qualified terminable interest property," as described above, will also qualify the value of the whole property for the marital deduction.

Life insurance proceeds. Certain rules, similar to those for trusts, provide for settlement options that may qualify for the marital deduction (see Q 663 to Q 670). *ASRS, Sec. 51, ¶280.*

865. What is the estate tax charitable deduction and what is the limitation on the deductible amount?

An estate tax deduction is allowed for the full amount of bequests to charity (but not in excess of the value of the transferred property required to be included in the gross estate). The deduction is not subject to percentage limitations such as are applicable to the charitable deduction under the income tax.

Specifically, IRC Section 2055 provides a deduction for bequests:

(1) to or for the use of the United States, any state, territory, any political subdivision thereof, or the District of Columbia, for exclusively public purposes;

(2) to or for the use of corporations organized and operated exclusively for religious, charitable, scientific, literary, or educational purposes, or to foster amateur sports competition, and the prevention of cruelty to children or animals (and which meet certain other conditions);

2006 Tax Facts on Insurance & Employee Benefits

(3) to trustees, or fraternal societies, orders or associations operating under the lodge system, but only if the bequests are to be used exclusively for religious, charitable, scientific, literary, or educational purposes, or for the prevention of cruelty to children or animals (and if certain other conditions are met); and

(4) to or for the use of any veterans' organization incorporated by Act of Congress or to any of its components, so long as no part of the net earnings inures to the benefit of any private shareholder or individual. IRC Sec. 2055(a).

If any death taxes are, either by the terms of the will, by the law of the jurisdiction under which the estate is administered, or by the law of the jurisdiction imposing the particular tax, payable in whole or in part out of the bequests otherwise deductible as charitable contributions, then the amount deductible is the amount of such bequests reduced by the amount of such taxes. IRC Sec. 2055(c). Prior to the issuance of regulations discussed below, in a similar situation, it was held that the marital deduction (see Q 864) was reduced where administration expenses were paid from the marital share principal, but not where administration expenses were paid from income from the marital share. *Comm. v. Est. of Hubert*, 97-1 USTC ¶60,261 (U.S. 1997).

Regulations, effective for estates of decedents dying after December 3, 1999, provide rules for reducing the charitable share by administration expenses depending on the type of expense: transmission expenses or management expenses. Treas. Reg. §20.2055-3.

Transmission expenses are defined as expenses that would not have been incurred but for the decedent's death. Transmission expenses are also defined as any administration expense that is not a management expense. Transmission expenses paid from the charitable share reduce the charitable share.

Management expenses are defined as expenses related to investment, preservation, and maintenance of the assets during a reasonable period of estate administration. Management expenses attributable to the charitable share do not reduce the charitable share except to the extent that the expense is deducted under IRC Section 2053 as an administration expense. Management expenses which are paid by the charitable share but which are not attributable to the charitable share reduce the charitable share.

In *U.S. Trust Co. (Chisholm Est.) v. U.S.*, 86-2 USTC ¶13,698 (5th Cir. 1986), rev'g and remanding 85-2 USTC ¶9741 (S.D. Miss. 1985), the executors satisfied a charitable bequest by making the distribution out of estate income. The estate claimed and was allowed an estate tax deduction under IRC Section 2055 for the bequest. The estate could not claim an income tax charitable contributions deduction because the will did not specify that the bequest be paid out of estate income. IRC Sec. 642(c). The estate claimed but was not allowed an income tax distribution deduction under IRC Section 661(a)(2) for the same distribution.

Property that is transferred to the charity by the exercise or nonexercise of a general power of appointment is considered transferred by the donee of the power rather than by the donor of the power. Or, to paraphrase, property includable in the decedent's gross estate under IRC Section 2041 (see Q 853(9)) received by a charity is considered a bequest of such decedent. IRC Sec. 2055(b).

An estate tax charitable deduction was denied for the transfer of a residuary interest in the estate to charity where the amount of the charitable deduction was not ascertainable at the time of death because of discretionary powers given to personal representatives to distribute the estate to other potential beneficiaries. *Est. of Marine v. Comm.*, 93-1 USTC ¶60,131 (4th Cir. 1993). Also, in TAM 9327006, an estate tax charitable deduction was denied where a trustee was given discretion to select donees from among various charities, and not all of the charities were on the IRS list of charities for which a charitable deduction is permitted.

Where an interest in property (other than a remainder interest in a personal residence or farm or an undivided portion of the decedent's entire interest in property) passes from the decedent to a charity and an interest in the same property passes (for less than adequate and full consideration in money or money's worth) from the decedent to a non-charity, no estate tax charitable contributions deduction is allowed for the interest going to the charity unless—

(a) in the case of a remainder interest, such interest is in a trust which is a *charitable remainder annuity trust*, a *charitable remainder unitrust*, or a *pooled income fund* (these three trusts are described in Q 825), or

(b) in the case of any other interest, such interest is in the form of a guaranteed annuity or is a fixed percentage distributed yearly of the fair market value of the property (to be determined yearly). IRC Sec. 2055(e)(2).

If the decedent has created a qualified charitable remainder trust in which his surviving spouse is the only noncharitable beneficiary (see Q 864), the estate will receive a charitable contributions deduction for the value of the remainder interest. However, if the property in the trust is "qualified terminable interest property" and the surviving spouse's interest is a "qualifying income interest for life" (see Q 864), the charitable contributions deduction may be taken by the surviving spouse's estate upon her death, the decedent's estate having taken a marital deduction (assuming the executor's election) for the entire value of the property. Treas. Reg. §20.2044-1(b).

In certain kinds of cases it is necessary to look closely to see whether what might at first seem to be a gift to charity of a split interest in property is what it appears. In Let. Rul. 8506089, a decedent left the residue of his estate to a charity on the condition that the charity take on the obligation to pay an annuity equal to 7% of the value of the estate assets going to the charity to his brother for his lifetime. The Service ruled that because the annuity was payable out of the general assets of the charity rather than out of the assets in the decedent's estates going to the charity, the bequest was not a split interest gift in the same property; accordingly, a charitable contribution deduction was allowed equal to the amount by which the value of the property transferred by the decedent to the charity exceeded the present value of the annuity payable to the decedent's brother.

In *Oetting v. U.S.*, 83-2 USTC ¶13,533 (8th Cir. 1983), a trust receiving assets from the residue of an estate provided that the assets would be used first to provide life incomes of $100 per month for the lifetimes of three elderly ladies and the remainder paid to four qualified charities. Since the total assets received by the trust greatly exceeded expectations, the trustees petitioned the probate court for permission to buy annuities for the income beneficiaries with a fraction of the trust assets and to pay the balance immediately to the charities. The court so decreed, the trustees bought the annuities for $23,000 and paid the balance, $558,000, to the charities. The court allowed the estate a charitable contributions deduction for the amount paid to the charities, reasoning that since the amount going to the charities was certain, it was not a split interest in the same property for purposes of IRC Section 2055.

In general, a trust can be reformed to qualify for the estate tax charitable deduction if:

(1) the difference in actuarial value of the qualified trust at time of death and its value at time of reformation is no greater than 5% of its value at time of reformation;

(2) the term of the trust is the same before and after reformation (however, if the term of years for a trust exceeds 20 years, the term can be shortened to 20 years);

(3) any changes are effective as of date of death;

(4) the charitable deduction would have been allowable at death if not for the split-interest rules (which generally require use of annuity, unitrust, and pooled income interests); and

(5) any payment to a noncharitable beneficiary before the remainder vests in possession must have been an annuity or unitrust interest (the lower of income or the unitrust amount, with make-up provisions, is permitted). This fifth provision does not apply if judicial proceedings are started to qualify the interests for the estate tax charitable deduction no later than 90 days after (a) the due date (including extensions) for filing the estate tax return, or (b) if no estate tax return is required, the due date (including extensions) for filing the income tax return for the first taxable year of the trust for which such a return must be filed. IRC Sec. 2055(e)(3).

A reformation done solely to obtain a charitable deduction (in contrast to a reformation done pursuant to a will contest) must meet the requirements of IRC Section 2055(e)(3). *Est. of Burdick v. Comm.*, 92-2 USTC ¶60,122 (9th Cir. 1992). The amount of a charitable deduction taken with respect to property transferred to charity pursuant to a will contest cannot exceed the actuarial value of what the charity could have received under a will or through intestate succession. *Terre Haute First Nat'l Bank v. U.S.*, 91-1 USTC ¶60,070 (S.D. Ind. 1991). *ASRS, Sec. 54, ¶44.5(d)*.

866. What estate tax deduction is available for a qualified family-owned business interest?

For decedents dying before 2004 or after 2010, an estate tax deduction is available for up to $675,000 of qualified family-owned business interests. IRC Sec. 2057. If the deduction is taken, the unified credit equivalent (see Q 868) is changed to equal the lesser of (1) the regular unified credit equivalent, or (2) $1,300,000 minus the amount of the qualified family-owned business deduction. The deduction is not available for decedents dying in 2004 to 2010. IRC Secs. 2057(j), 2210, as added by EGTRRA 2001. However, the unified credit is increased substantially for 2004 to 2009 (see Appendix B) and the estate tax is repealed in 2010 (see Q 850).

In order to qualify for the family-owned business deduction, at least 50% of the value of the adjusted gross estate must consist of the sum of (1) family-owned business interests included in the estate and (2) certain gifts of family-owned business interests. IRC Sec. 2057(b)(1)(C). Gifts of family-owned business interests include family-owned

GENERAL   Q 866

business interests that decedent gave to members of decedent's family if the members of decedent's family retained such interests until decedent's death. IRC Sec. 2057(b)(3). The family-owned business interest is not reduced by an IRC Section 303 redemption for purposes of making the initial determination of qualifying for the family-owned business deduction. Rev. Rul. 2003-61, 2003-24 IRB 1015.

For this purpose, the adjusted gross estate means the gross estate reduced by the estate tax deductions for claims against the estate and debts under IRC Section 2053(a)(3) and IRC Section 2053(a)(4), and increased by certain gifts. These gifts include (to the extent not otherwise includable in the estate): (1) family-owned business interests that decedent gave to members of decedent's family if the members of decedent's family retained such interests until decedent's death; (2) gifts to spouse within 10 years of decedent's death (excluding those under (1)); and (3) gifts within three years of death (excluding annual exclusion gifts to family members and those under (1) or (2)). IRC Sec. 2057(c).

Family-owned means that either (1) 50% of the business must be owned by decedent and members of decedent's family, or (2) 30% of the business must be owned by decedent and members of decedent's family and (a) 70% of the business is owned by two families, or (b) 90% of the business is owned by three families. IRC Sec. 2057(e)(1).

However, family-owned business interests do not include (1) a business whose principal place of business is not in the United States; (2) any entity whose stock or debt is readily traded on an established securities or secondary market; (3) an entity, other than a bank or building and loan association, if more than 35% of the adjusted gross income of the entity for the year which includes the date of decedent's death is personal holding company income; and (4) the portion of the business which consists of (a) cash or marketable securities in excess of reasonably expected day-to-day working capital needs, and (b) assets held for the production of personal holding company income or foreign personal holding company income. IRC Sec. 2057(e)(2).

Personal holding company income generally includes dividends, interest, royalties, annuities, rents, personal property use by a shareholder, and personal service contracts. IRC Sec. 543(a). However, personal holding company income does not include income from a net cash lease of property to another family member who uses the property in a way which would not cause income from the property to be treated as personal holding company income if the lessor had engaged directly in the activity of the lessee. IRC Sec. 2057(e)(2).

Similar to the requirements for special use valuation, (1) for at least five of the eight years ending on decedent's death, the business interests must have been owned by decedent or members of decedent's family, and decedent or members of decedent's family must have materially participated in the business (IRC Sec. 2057(b)(1)(D)), and (2) for 10 years after decedent's death (or until the earlier death of the qualified heir), such business interests must be owned by qualified heirs, and qualified heirs must materially participate in the business (IRC Sec. 2057(f)(1)). Qualified heirs include members of decedent's family, as well as any employee who has been an active employee of the business for at least 10 years before the decedent's death. IRC Sec. 2057(j)(1).

Additional tax, plus interest thereon, is due if the ownership or material participation requirements are not met after decedent's death. IRC Sec. 2057(f). The additional tax is equal to the following percentage of the tax savings attributable to use of the family-owned business deduction, depending on when the failure to meet the requirements occurs.

Year	Recapture Percentage
1-6	100
7	80
8	60
9	40
10	20

For this purpose, an IRC Section 303 redemption is not treated as a disposition of the family-owned business interest. Rev. Rul. 2003-61, 2003-24 IRB 1015. ASRS: Sec. 54, ¶44.5(e).

CREDITS

867. What credits may be taken against the estate tax?

After the estate tax is computed (Q 852), the following credits may be taken against the tax: (1) unified credit (Q 868); (2) credit for state death taxes (Q 869) (replaced by a deduction from 2005 to 2009 – see Q 863); (3) gift tax credit (Q 870); (4) credit for estate tax on prior transfers (Q 871); (5) credit for foreign death taxes (IRC Sec. 2014). *ASRS, Sec. 54, ¶44.6.*

868. What is the unified credit, and how is it applied against the estate tax?

The unified credit is a dollar amount allocated to each taxpayer which can be applied against the gift tax (but see Q 922) and the estate tax. The estate tax unified credit is equal to $780,800 in 2006 which translates into a tentative tax base (or unified credit exemption equivalent or applicable exclusion amount) of $2,000,000 in 2006. See Appendix B for amounts in other years (and gift tax amounts). The credit is reduced directly by 20% of the amount of lifetime gift tax exemption the decedent elected to use on any gifts made after September 8, 1976 (see Q 922). The 20% reduction is made even though the value of the property to which the exemption applied is brought back into the estate for estate tax purposes; neither is the reduction a deprivation of property under the due process clause of the U.S. Constitution. *U.S. v. Hemme*, 86-1 USTC ¶13,671 (U.S. 1986); *Est. of Allgood v. Comm.*, TC Memo 1986-455. The credit is also reduced (but indirectly) by the amount of unified credit applied against any gift tax imposed on the decedent's post-1976 gifts. The indirect reduction is accomplished by adding to the taxable estate the amount of all taxable gifts made by the decedent after 1976, other than gifts includable in the estate, and then applying the unified tax rates to the sum (see Q 852). IRC Sec. 2010, as amended by EGTRRA 2001. *ASRS, Sec. 54, ¶44.6(a).*

869. What estate tax credit is allowed for state death taxes?

For decedents dying before 2005 and after 2010, the amount of all estate, inheritance, legacy or succession taxes actually paid to a state may be subtracted from the federal estate tax, but the credit cannot exceed the amounts set forth in IRC Section 2011(b) (see Appendix B). The maximum amount for which a credit can be taken was

GENERAL   Q 871

reduced by 25% in 2002, 50% in 2003, and 75% in 2004. IRC Sec. 2011(b)(2), as added by EGTRRA 2001. The credit is replaced by a deduction (see Q 863) for state death taxes in 2005 to 2009. IRC Sec. 2011(g), as added by EGTRRA 2001. The federal estate tax credit for state death taxes paid was not available where the property subject to state death taxes was not includable in the federal gross estate. *Est. of Owen v. Comm.*, 104 TC 498 (1995). *ASRS, Sec. 54, ¶44.6(b)*.

870. Is an estate tax credit allowed for gift taxes paid by the decedent on property which he transferred during life, but which is includable in his gross estate?

Not as to gifts made after December 31, 1976. IRC Sec. 2012(e). (But see Q 852.) As to gifts made on or before that date, such a credit may be taken, but the credit cannot exceed an amount which bears the same ratio to the estate tax actually paid as the value of the gift (at time of gift or at time of death, whichever is lower) bears to the value of the gross estate minus charitable and marital deductions allowed. IRC Sec. 2012(a). *ASRS, Sec. 54, ¶44.6(c)*.

871. Is an estate tax credit allowed for estate taxes previously paid on property included in the gross estate?

Yes; a credit is allowed against the decedent's estate tax for all or part of the estate tax paid with respect to the transfer of property from another decedent (the transferor) who dies within 10 years before or two years after the present decedent's death. If the transferor died within two years before or after the decedent, the credit will be equal to the full amount of estate tax paid by the transferor's estate with respect to the property transferred to the decedent. If the transferor died more than two years before the decedent, the credit will be the following percentages of such amount:

80% if within the 3rd or 4th years before death
60% if within the 5th or 6th years before death
40% if within the 7th or 8th years before death
20% if within the 9th or 10th years before death

No credit is allowable if the transferee predeceased the transferor by more than two years. IRC Sec. 2013(a).

The credit (before percentage reductions, if applicable) is the portion of the *transferor's* federal estate tax attributable to the value of the property transferred, *but limited to* the portion of the *transferee's* federal estate tax attributable to the value of the property transferred. IRC Secs. 2013(b), 2013(c)(1).

The credit is allowed with respect to property received from a spouse; however, the net value of the property transferred, for purposes of determining the estate tax liability of the transferor's estate, is reduced by the amount of marital deduction allowed. IRC Sec. 2013(d)(3). For valuation of property for purposes of the credit, see Q 862. The credit does not apply in the estate of a transferee insured if the insured had no direct beneficial interest in the transferred policy. Rev. Rul. 77-156, 1977-1 CB 269. *ASRS, Sec. 54, ¶44.6(d)*.

FEDERAL GIFT TAX

GENERAL

900. What is the federal gift tax?

The gift tax is an excise tax on an individual's right during life to transfer money or property by gift (see Q 902). IRC Sec. 2501(a)(1). *ASRS, Sec. 55, ¶¶57.1, 57.5.*

FILING AND PAYMENT

901. Who files the return and pays the gift tax, and when?

Filing the Return

The donor is responsible for filing the gift tax return (Form 709). A return needs to be filed for any calendar year in which the donor makes any gifts other than (a) those which come within the annual exclusion (Q 917), (b) qualified transfers (Q 917), (c) those which qualify for the marital deduction (Q 920), or (d) gifts to charity of the donor's entire interest in the property transferred where the donor does not (and has not) transferred any interest in the property to a noncharitable beneficiary. IRC Sec. 6019. The return is due on or before April 15 following the close of the calendar year, except that an extension of time granted for filing the income tax return serves also as an extension of time for filing the gift tax return. Where the donor's death occurs before the end of the calendar year in which a gift is made, the gift tax return is due at the time (including extensions) the estate tax return is due. IRC Sec. 6075(b)(3). However, should the time for filing the estate tax return fall later than the 15th day of April following the close of the calendar year, the time for filing the gift tax return is on or before the 15th day of April following the close of the calendar year, unless an extension (not extending beyond the time for filing the estate tax return) was granted for filing the gift tax return. If no estate tax return is required to be filed, the time for filing the gift tax return is on or before the 15th day of April following the close of the calendar year, unless an extension was given for filing the gift tax return. IRC Sec. 6075; Treas. Reg. §25.6075-1(b)(2). The IRS is authorized to grant a reasonable extension of time for filing the return. Except in the case of taxpayers who are abroad, no such extension may exceed six months. IRC Sec. 6081(a).

Paying the Tax

The tax is due and payable by the donor at the time fixed for filing the return (without regard to any extension of time for filing the return). IRC Secs. 2502(c), 6151(a). If the tax is not paid when due, the donee is personally liable for the tax to the extent of the value of the gift. IRC Sec. 6324(b); *Comm. v. Chase Manhattan Bank*, 259 F.2d 231 (5th Cir. 1958).

At the request of the donor, an extension of time for payment of the tax may be granted by the district director. The period of extension may not exceed six months, unless the donor is abroad. The time for payment of a gift tax deficiency may be extended up to 18 months if the donor shows that payment on the date fixed would result in undue hardship; in exceptional cases, an additional extension of up to 12 months may be granted. IRC Sec. 6161. In addition, the Service has been given authority to enter into written agreements to pay taxes in installments when the Service determines that such an agreement will facilitate the payment of taxes. IRC Sec. 6159. Interest compounded daily is charged on all extensions at an annual rate adjusted quarterly so as to be three percentage points over the short term federal rate. IRC Secs. 6601(a), 6621(a)(2). The underpayment rate for the last quarter of 2005 is 7%. Rev. Rul. 2005-62, 2005-38 IRB 557. *ASRS, Sec. 55, ¶57.4.*

CALCULATION OF TAX

902. How is the gift tax computed?

The tax is imposed on the value of gifts made in the calendar year after subtracting allowable exclusions and deductions. An *annual* exclusion of $12,000 (in 2006, see Appendix B for amounts in other years) is allowed against gifts to *each donee*, provided they are outright gifts or gifts of a "present interest" (see Q 917, Q 918). An exclusion is also available for "qualified transfers" for educational and medical purposes (see Q 917). A gift tax *marital deduction* may be available for a gift by a husband to his wife, or by a wife to her husband (see Q 920). A married couple may treat a gift made by one of them to a third person as having been made one-half by each (see Q 907). A deduction may be taken for the full value of gifts made to charitable organizations (see Q 921).

The tax is cumulative in effect: gifts in previous years (since June 6, 1932) must be taken into account in figuring the tax on gifts in the current calendar year. Consequently, taxable gifts in past years boost later gifts into higher tax brackets.

The tax is based on *taxable gifts* (the balance after subtracting allowable exclusions and deductions); in general the steps are as follows: (1) compute the tax on total gifts for the current calendar year and all preceding calendar periods (use appropriate rate schedule in Appendix B); (2) compute the tax on gifts made in previous calendar periods, leaving out gifts in the current calendar year (use same rate schedule); (3) the difference between (1) and (2) is the gift tax for the current calendar year. (But see Q 922 for the unified credit against the tax.) IRC Sec. 2502(a).

Example. Taxable amount of gifts in current calendar year, $20,000. Taxable amount of gifts in all calendar periods, including those in current calendar year, $50,000.

Tax on $50,000 (taxable amount of gifts in all periods) $10,600
Tax on $30,000 (taxable amount of gifts in earlier periods) 6,000

Tax on gifts for current calendar year (before applying unified credit) .... $ 4,600

ASRS, Sec. 55, ¶57.2.

GIFTS

903. What kinds of gifts are subject to gift tax?

The tax applies to transfers by way of gift whether in trust or otherwise, whether direct or indirect, and whether the property is real or personal, tangible or intangible. Treas. Reg. §25.2511-1(a). Where property is transferred, the tax is based on the fair market value of the property at the time of the gift. Treas. Reg. §25.2512-1. The tax attaches when the transfer occurs, even if the identity of the donee is not then known or ascertainable. Treas. Reg. §25.2511-2(a). Donative intent is not an essential element; for example, a gift made pursuant to state law by a guardian on behalf of an incompetent donor is subject to the gift tax; but the tax is applicable only to a transfer of a beneficial interest in property, not to a transfer of bare legal title to a trustee. Treas. Reg. §25.2511-1(g)(1); Let. Rul. 7838112; *Millard v. U.S.*, 84-2 USTC ¶13,597 (S.D. Ill. 1984); Let. Rul. 7921017.

An individual's waiver of a survivor benefit (as described at Q 336) made before the participant's death is not treated as a transfer of property for gift tax purposes. IRC Sec. 2503(f).

Where property is transferred for less than full consideration in money or money's worth, the amount by which the value of the property exceeds the value of the consideration is deemed a gift. IRC Sec. 2512(b). However, a sale or exchange made in the ordinary course of business (an arm's length transaction) is considered to have been made for full consideration in money or money's worth. Treas. Reg. §25.2512-8. On the other hand, an intra-family exchange is not considered an ordinary business transaction. (See Q 705.)

The gift tax is imposed only on completed gifts. A gift occurs when the donor parts with dominion and control over the property given. Treas. Reg. §25.2511-2. Where two stockholders in a buy-sell agreement set a price for their shares that was $100 a share less than the fair market value of the shares and agreed that a withdrawing shareholder would not sell his shares to a third party without first offering them to the other shareholder at the agreement price, it was ruled that the agreement did not create completed gifts for purposes of the federal gift tax. Let. Rul. 8140016. The gratuitous transfer by the maker of a legally binding promissory note is a completed gift (the transfer of a legally unenforceable promissory note is an incomplete gift); if the note is unpaid at the donor's death, the gift is not treated as an adjusted taxable gift in computing the tentative estate tax (see Q 852), and no deduction is allowable from the gross estate for the promisee's claim with respect to the note (see Q 863). Rev. Rul. 84-25, 1984-1 CB 191.

A transfer of a nonstatutory stock option which was not traded on an established market would be treated as a gift to a family member on the later of (1) the transfer or (2) the time when the donee's right to exercise the option is no longer conditioned on the performance of services by the transferor. Rev. Rul. 98-21, 1998-1 CB 975.

In the case of a gift by check, when is the gift complete, when the check is delivered, or when the check is cashed? In the litigation to date, the courts initially appeared to make a distinction between gifts to charitable donees and gifts to noncharitable donees. In the former case it has been held that at least where there is timely presentment and payment, payment of the check by the bank relates back to the date of delivery for purposes of determining completeness of the gift. *Est. of Spiegel v. Comm.*, 12 TC 524 (1942). In the latter case, the courts have shown less of a willingness to apply the "relation back" doctrine. In *Est. of Dillingham v. Comm.*, 90-1 USTC ¶60,021 (10th Cir. 1990), the noncharitable donees did not cash the checks until 35 days after their delivery, the donor's death having intervened. The court said that this delay cast doubt as to whether the checks were unconditionally delivered. Since the estate failed to prove unconditional delivery, the court declined to extend the relation back doctrine to the case before it. It then turned to local law to determine whether the decedent had parted with dominion and control upon delivery of the checks. It determined that under applicable local law (Oklahoma), the donor did not part with dominion and control until the checks were cashed. However, in *Est. of Gagliardi v. Comm.*, 89 TC 1207 (1987), checks written by a brokerage firm and charged against the decedent's account prior to decedent's death were treated as completed gifts to the noncharitable donees even though some checks were cashed after decedent's death. Also, in *Est. of Metzger v. Comm.*, 94-2 USTC ¶60,179 (4th Cir. 1994), aff'g 100 TC 204 (1993), the relation-back doctrine was applied to gifts made by check to noncharitable beneficiaries where the taxpayer was able to establish: (1) the donor's intent to make gifts, (2) unconditional delivery of the checks, (3) presentment of the check during the year for which a gift tax annual exclusion was sought and within a reasonable time after issuance, and (4) that there were sufficient funds to pay the checks at all relevant times. In *W. H. Braum Family Partnership v. Comm.*, TC Memo 1993-434, the relation-back doctrine was not applied where the taxpayer could not establish either (2) or (4). In response to *Metzger*, the Service has issued a revenue ruling providing that a gift by check to a noncharitable beneficiary will be considered complete on the earlier of (1) when the donor has so parted with dominion and control under state law such that the donor can no longer change its disposition, or (2) when the donee deposits the check, cashes the check against available funds, or presents the check for payment if the following conditions are met: (a) the check must be paid by the drawee bank when first presented for payment to the drawee bank; (b) the donor must be alive when the check is paid by the drawee bank; (c) the donor must have intended a gift; (d) delivery of the check by the donor must have been unconditional; (e) the check must be deposited, cashed or presented in the calendar year for which the completed gift tax treatment is sought; and (f) the check must be deposited, cashed or presented within a reasonable time of issuance. Rev. Rul. 96-56, 1996-2 CB 161.

The placing of title to property in joint names (but generally not between spouses—see Q 920) can create a taxable gift, either immediately or (as in the case of joint bank accounts and United States savings bonds) when the donee reduces some amount to his exclusive possession. Treas. Reg. §25.2511-1(h).

The exercise or lapse of a power of appointment, which results in another's receiving a beneficial interest in the appointive property, may be a gift subject to tax. IRC Sec. 2514. Similarly, a refusal to accept the transfer of property, which results in another's receiving a beneficial interest in the disclaimed property, may be a taxable gift. IRC Sec. 2518. (See Q 908.)

Where spouses enter into joint and mutual wills, the surviving spouse may be treated as making a gift of a remainder interest at the other spouse's death. *Grimes v. Comm.*, 88-2 USTC ¶13,774 (7th Cir. 1988).

The transfer of a qualifying income interest for life in qualified terminable interest property (QTIP) for which a marital deduction was allowed (see Q 864, Q 920) will be treated as a transfer of such property for gift tax purposes. IRC Sec. 2519. If a QTIP trust is severed into Trust A and Trust B and the spouse renounces her interest in Trust A, such renunciation will not cause the spouse to be treated as transferring Trust B under IRC Section 2519. Let. Ruls. 200116006, 200122036.

The spouse is entitled to collect from the donee the gift tax on the transfer of a QTIP interest. The amount treated as a transfer for gift tax purposes is reduced by the amount of the gift tax the spouse is entitled to recover from the donee. Thus, the transfer is treated as a net gift (see Q 911). The failure of a spouse to exercise the right to recover gift tax from the donee is treated as a transfer of the unrecovered amount to the donee when the right to recover is no longer enforceable. If a written waiver of the right of recovery is executed before the right becomes unenforceable, the transfer of the unrecovered gift tax is treated as made on the later of (1) the date of the waiver, or (2) the date the tax is paid by the transferor. Any delay in exercise of the right of recovery is treated as an interest-free loan (see Q 904) for gift tax purposes. Treas. Regs. §§25.2207A-1(b), 25.2519-1(c)(4).

Where a surviving spouse acquires a remainder interest in QTIP marital deduction property in connection with a transfer of property or cash to the holder of the remainder interest, the surviving spouse makes a gift to the remainder person under both IRC Section 2519 (disposition of QTIP interest) and IRC Sections 2511 and 2512 (transfers and valuation of gifts). The amount of the gift is equal to the greater of (1) the value of the remainder interest, or (2) the value of the property or cash transferred to the holder of the remainder interest. Rev. Rul. 98-8, 1998-1 CB 541. On the other hand, children would be treated as making a gift if the children transfer their remainder interest in a QTIP marital deduction trust to the surviving spouse. Let. Rul. 199908033.

Any subsequent transfer by the donor spouse of an interest in property for which a QTIP marital deduction was taken is not treated as a transfer for gift tax purposes, unless the transfer occurs after the donee spouse is treated as having transferred such property under IRC Section 2519 or after such property is includable in the donee spouse's estate under IRC Section 2044 (see Q 853(12)). IRC Sec. 2523(f)(5). Also, if property for which a QTIP marital deduction was taken is includable in the estate of the spouse who was given the QTIP interest and the estate of such spouse fails to recover from the person receiving the property any estate tax attributable to the QTIP interest being included in such spouse's estate, such failure is treated as a transfer for gift tax purposes unless (1) such spouse's will waives the right to recovery, or (2) the beneficiaries cannot compel recovery of the taxes (e.g., where the executor is given discretion to waive the right of recovery in such spouse's will). Treas. Reg. §20.2207A-1(a).

Transfers of property from a corporation to an individual, or from an individual to a corporation, may be taxable gifts from or to the individual stockholders. Treas. Reg. §25.2511-1(h)(1); Let. Rul. 8351137. (See Q 918.)

Shareholders of nonparticipating preferred stock in profitable family held corporations have been held to have made gifts to the common stockholders (typically descendants of the preferred shareholder) by waiving payment of dividends or simply by failing to exercise conversion rights or other options available to a preferred stockholder to preserve his position. TAMs 8723007, 8726005. The Tax Court has held that the failure to convert noncumulative preferred stock to cumulative preferred stock did not give rise to a gift, but that thereafter a gift was made each time a dividend would have accumulated. However, the failure to exercise a put option at par plus accumulated dividends plus interest was not treated as a gift of foregone interest. *Snyder v. Comm.*, 93 TC 529 (1989).

A transaction involving the nonexercise by a son of an option under a cross-purchase buy-sell agreement followed by the sale of the same stock by the father to a third party when the fair market value of the stock was substantially higher than the option price was treated as a gift from the son to the father. Let. Rul. 9117035. Also, a father indirectly made a gift to his son to the extent that the fair market value of stock exceeded its redemption price when the father failed to exercise his right under a buy-sell agreement to have a corporation redeem all of the available shares held by his brother-in-law's estate and the stock passed to the son. TAM 9315005.

With respect to a trust, the grantor/income beneficiary may be treated as making additional gifts of remainder interests in each year that the grantor fails to exercise his right to make nonproductive or underproductive property normally productive. Let. Rul. 8945006. A mother made gifts to her children to the extent that the children were paid excessive trustee fees from the marital deduction trust of which the mother was a beneficiary. TAM 200014004. However, a grantor of a trust does not make a gift to trust beneficiaries by paying the income tax on trust income taxable to the grantor under the grantor trust rules (see Q 844). Rev. Rul. 2004-64, 2004-27 IRB 7.

Letter Ruling 9113009 (withdrawn without comment by TAM 9409018) had ruled that a parent who guaranteed loans to his children made a gift to his children because, without the guarantees, the children could not have obtained the loans or, at the very least, would have paid a higher interest rate.

For recapture rules applicable where distributions are not timely made in connection with the transfer of an interest in a corporation or partnership which is subject to the Chapter 14 valuation rules, see Q 913. For deemed transfers upon the lapse of certain voting or liquidation rights in a corporation or partnership, see Q 916.

A gift may be made of foregone interest with respect to interest-free and bargain rate loans (see Q 904). *ASRS, Sec. 55, ¶57.5.*

904. Are gifts made of foregone interest with respect to interest-free and bargain rate loans?

An interest-free or low-interest loan within a family or in any other circumstances where the foregone interest is in the nature of a gift results in a gift subject to the federal gift tax. IRC Section 7872 applies in the case of term loans made after June 6, 1984 and demand loans outstanding after that date.

In general, IRC Section 7872 recharacterizes a below-market loan (an interest-free or low-interest loan) as an arm's length transaction in which the lender (1) made a loan to the borrower in exchange for a note requiring the payment of interest at a statutory rate, and (2) made a gift, distributed a dividend, made a contribution to capital, paid compensation, or made another payment to the borrower which, in turn, is used by the borrower to pay the interest. The difference between the statutory rate of interest and the rate (if any) actually charged by the lender, the "foregone interest," is thus either a gift to the borrower or income to him, depending on the circumstances. The income tax aspects of below-market loans are discussed in Q 805. The gift tax aspects of such loans are discussed here.

First, some definitions: The term "gift loan" means any below-market loan where the foregoing of interest is in the nature of a gift. The term "demand loan" means any loan which is payable in full at any time on the demand of the lender. The term "term loan" means any loan which is not a demand loan. The term "applicable federal rate"

GENERAL   Q 905

means: in the case of a demand loan or a term loan of up to three years, the federal short-term rate; in the case of a term loan over three years but not over nine years, the federal mid-term rate; in the case of a term loan over nine years, the federal long-term rate. In the case of a term loan the applicable rate is compounded semiannually. These rates are reset monthly. IRC Sec. 1274(d). The "present value" of any payment is determined (a) as of the date of the loan, and (b) by using a discount rate equal to the applicable federal rate. See Prop. Treas. Reg. §1.7872-14. The term "below-market loan" means any loan if (a) in the case of a demand loan, interest is payable on the loan at a rate less than the applicable federal rate, or (b) in the case of a term loan, the amount loaned exceeds the present value of all payments due under the loan. The term "foregone interest" means, with respect to any period during which the loan is outstanding, the excess of (a) the amount of interest that would have been payable on the loan for the period if the interest accrued on the loan at the applicable federal rate and were payable annually on the last day of the appropriate calendar year, over (b) any interest payable on the loan properly allocable to the period.

In the case of a demand gift loan, the foregone interest is treated as transferred from the lender to the borrower and retransferred by the borrower to the lender as interest on the last day of each calendar year the loan is outstanding. In the case of a term gift loan, the lender is treated as having transferred on the date the loan was made, and the borrower is treated as having received on such date, cash in an amount equal to the excess of (a) the amount loaned over (b) the present value of all payments which are required to be made under the terms of the loan. The provisions of the new law do not apply in the case of a gift loan between individuals (a husband and wife are treated as one person) that at no time exceeds $10,000 in the aggregate amount outstanding on *all* loans, whether below-market or not. The $10,000 de minimus exception does not apply, however, to loans attributable to acquisition of income-producing assets.

IRC Section 7872 does not apply to life insurance policy loans. Prop. Treas. Reg. §1.7872-5(b)(4). Neither does IRC Section 7872 apply to loans to a charitable organization if at no time during the taxable year the aggregate outstanding amount of loans by the lender to that organization does not exceed $250,000. Temp. Treas. Reg. §1.7872-5T(b)(9).

The Tax Court has held that IRC Section 483 and safe harbor interest rates contained therein do not apply for gift tax purposes. Consequently, the value of a promissory note given in exchange for real property was discounted to reflect time value of money concepts under IRC Section 7872 (without benefit of IRC Section 483). *Frazee v. Comm.*, 98 TC 554 (1992).

Prior to enactment of IRC Section 7872, the Supreme Court held that, in the case of an interest-free demand loan made within a family, a gift subject to federal gift tax is made of the value of the use of the money lent. *Dickman v. Comm.*, 104 S. Ct. 1086 (1984). The court did not decide how to value such a gift, but implicit in the decision was the assumption that low-interest or interest-free loans within a family context have, since the first federal gift tax statute was enacted in 1924, resulted in gifts. Rev. Proc. 85-46, 1985-2 CB 507, provided guidance in valuing and reporting gift demand loans not covered by IRC Section 7872. *ASRS, Sec. 55, ¶57.5(b)*.

905. When is a gift made with respect to an education savings account?

Contributions to an education savings account are treated as completed transfers to the beneficiary of a present interest in property which can qualify for the gift tax and generation-skipping transfer (GST) tax annual exclusions. If contributions for a year exceed the annual exclusion, the donor can elect to prorate the gifts over a five year period beginning with such year. A contribution to an education savings account does not qualify for the gift tax or GST tax exclusion for qualified transfers for educational purposes. IRC Secs. 530(d)(3), 529(c)(2). Distributions from an education savings account are not treated as taxable gifts. Also, if the designated beneficiary of an education savings account is changed, or if funds in a education savings account are rolled over to the account of a new beneficiary, such a transfer is subject to the gift tax or GST tax only if the new beneficiary is a generation below the old beneficiary. IRC Secs. 530(d)(3), 529(c)(5).

See Q 858 for the estate tax treatment and Q 810 for the income tax treatment of education savings accounts.

906. When is a gift made with respect to a qualified tuition program?

For gift tax and generation-skipping transfer (GST) tax purposes, a contribution to a qualified tuition program on behalf of a designated beneficiary is not treated as a qualified transfer for purposes of the gift tax and GST tax exclusion for educational expenses, but is treated as a completed gift of a present interest to the beneficiary which qualifies for the annual exclusion (see Q 917). If a donor makes contributions to a qualified tuition program in excess of the annual exclusion, the donor may elect to take the donation into account ratably over a 5-year period. IRC Sec. 529(c)(2). Distributions from a qualified tuition program are not treated as taxable gifts. Also, if the designated beneficiary of a qualified tuition program is changed, or if funds in a qualified tuition program are rolled over to the account of a new beneficiary, such a transfer is subject to the gift tax or GST tax only if the new beneficiary is a generation below the old beneficiary. IRC Sec. 529(d)(5)(B).

See Q 859 for the estate tax treatment and Q 811 for the income tax treatment of qualified tuition programs.

Split-gifts
907. When is the "split-gift" provision available?

When a husband or wife makes a gift to a *third* person, it may be treated as having been made one-half by each if the other spouse consents to the gift. IRC Sec. 2513; Treas. Reg. §25.2513-1.

Planning Point: The split-gift provision enables a spouse who owns most of the property to take advantage of the other spouse's annual exclusions (see Q 917) and unified credit (see Q 922). Thus, a spouse, with the other spouse's consent, can give up to $24,000 (2 × $12,000 annual exclusion in 2006, see Appendix B) a year to each donee free of gift tax, and, in addition, will have both their unified credits to apply against gift tax imposed on gifts in excess of the annual exclusion. Moreover, by splitting the gifts between husband and wife, they will fall in lower gift tax brackets.

GENERAL   Q 908

Where spouses elect to use the "split-gift" provision, the consent applies to all gifts made by either spouse to third persons during the calendar year. IRC Sec. 2513(a)(2). A technical advice memorandum permitted a taxpayer to elect after his spouse's death to split gifts with his spouse where the gifts were made by the taxpayer shortly before the spouse's death. TAM 9404023. *ASRS, Sec. 55,* ¶*57.8.*

Disclaimers

908. If a person refuses to accept a transfer of an interest in property, as a result of which the interest passes to another, is the one who disclaims considered to have made a gift?

Not if he makes a *qualified disclaimer*. A "qualified disclaimer" means an irrevocable and unqualified refusal to accept an interest in property created in the person disclaiming by a taxable transfer made after 1976. With respect to inter vivos transfers, for the purpose of determining when a timely disclaimer is made (see condition (3) below), a taxable transfer occurs when there is a completed gift for federal gift tax purposes regardless of whether a gift tax is imposed on the completed gift. Thus, gifts qualifying for the gift tax annual exclusion are regarded as taxable transfers for this purpose. Treas. Reg. §25.2518-2(c)(3). Furthermore, a disclaimer of a remainder interest in a trust created prior to the enactment of the federal gift tax was subject to the gift tax where the disclaimer was not timely and the disclaimer occurred after enactment of the gift tax. *U.S. v. Irvine*, 94-1 USTC ¶60,163 (U.S. 1994). In order to effectively disclaim property for transfer tax purposes, a disclaimer of property received from a decedent at death should generally be made within nine months of death rather than within nine months of the probate of the decedent's will. *Est. of Fleming v. Comm.*, 92-2 USTC ¶60,113 (7th Cir. 1992).

In general, the disclaimer must satisfy these conditions: (1) the disclaimer must be irrevocable and unqualified; (2) the disclaimer must be in writing; (3) the writing must be delivered to the transferor of the interest, his legal representative, the holder of the legal title to the property, or the person in possession of the property, not later than nine months after the later of (a) the day on which the transfer creating the interest is made, or (b) the day on which the disclaimant reaches age 21; (4) the disclaimant must not have accepted the interest disclaimed or any of its benefits; and (5) the interest disclaimed must pass either to the spouse of the decedent or to a person other than the disclaimant without any direction on the part of the person making the disclaimer. IRC Sec. 2518(b); Treas. Reg. §25.2518-2(a). With respect to condition (4), it has been held that a group life insurance beneficiary accepted the benefits of the proceeds by merely filing a completed claim form and death certificate with the employer, as a result of which the insurer established an account in the beneficiary's name and provided her with checks with which she could draw upon the account. Let. Rul. 8702024. Also, a person cannot disclaim a remainder interest in property while retaining a life estate or income interest in the same property. *Walshire v. Comm.*, 2002-1 USTC ¶60,439 (8th Cir. 2002).

If a person makes a qualified disclaimer, for purposes of the federal estate, gift, and generation-skipping transfer tax provisions, the disclaimed interest in property is treated as if it had never been transferred to the person making the qualified disclaimer. Instead it is considered as passing directly from the transferor of the property to the person entitled to receive the property as a result of the disclaimer. Accordingly, a person making a qualified disclaimer is not treated as making a gift. Similarly, the value of a decedent's gross estate for purposes of the federal estate tax does not include the value of property with respect to which the decedent or his executor has made a qualified disclaimer. Treas. Reg. §25.2518-1(b).

In the case of a joint tenancy with rights of survivorship or a tenancy by the entirety, the interest which the donee receives upon creation of the joint interest can generally be disclaimed within nine months of the creation of the interest and the survivorship interest received upon the death of the first joint tenant to die (deemed to be a one-half interest in the property) can be disclaimed within nine months of the death of the first joint tenant to die, *without regard to* (1) whether either joint tenant can sever unilaterally under local law, (2) the portion of the property attributable to consideration furnished by the disclaimant, or (3) the portion of the property includable in the decedent's gross estate under IRC Section 2040. However, in the case of a creation of a joint tenancy between spouses or tenancy by the entirety created after July 13, 1988 where the *donee spouse is not a U.S. citizen*, a surviving spouse can make a disclaimer within nine months of the death of the first spouse to die of any portion of the joint interest that is includable in the decedent's estate under IRC Section 2040. Also, in the case of a transfer to a *joint bank, brokerage, or other investment account* (e.g., mutual fund account) where the transferor can unilaterally withdraw amounts contributed by the transferor, the surviving joint tenant may disclaim amounts contributed by the first joint tenant to die within nine months of the death of the first joint tenant to die. Treas. Reg. §25.2518-2(c)(4).

For purposes of a qualified disclaimer, the mere act of making a surviving spouse's statutory election is not to be treated as an acceptance of an interest in the disclaimed property or any of its benefits. However, the disclaimer of a portion of the property subject to the statutory election must be made within nine months of the decedent spouse's death, rather than within nine months of the surviving spouse's statutory election. Rev. Rul. 90-45, 1990-1 CB 176.

A power with respect to property is treated as an interest in such property. IRC Sec. 2518(c)(2). The exercise of a power of appointment to any extent by the donee of the power is an acceptance of its benefits. Treas. Reg. §25.2518-2(d)(1); Let. Rul. 8142008.

A beneficiary who is under 21 years of age has until nine months after his 21st birthday in which to make a qualified disclaimer of his interest in property. Any actions taken with regard to an interest in property by a beneficiary or a custodian prior to the beneficiary's 21st birthday will not be an acceptance by the beneficiary of the interest. Treas. Reg. §25.2518-2(d)(3). This rule holds true even as to custodianship gifts in states which provide that custodianship ends when the donee reaches an age below 21. Treas. Reg. §25.2518-2(d)(4), Example 11.

If the person disclaiming is given by the instrument of transfer a power to appoint any disclaimed interest to others, his exercise of the power is considered a gift of the interest to the appointee(s) of the power. Rev. Rul. 76-156, 1976-1 CB 292; IRC Sec. 2518(c)(2).

A qualified disclaimer of an IRA can be made by the beneficiary even though the beneficiary receives a required minimum distribution for the year of the IRA owner's death. If the beneficiary accepts the required minimum distribution, the beneficiary cannot disclaim the income attributable to the required minimum distribution. The disclaimer can be with respect to all or a portion of the balance of the IRA, other than the income with respect to the required minimum distribution received by the beneficiary, provided that the disclaimed amount and the income attributable to the disclaimed amount is paid to the beneficiary entitled to the disclaimed amount, or segregated in a separate account for such beneficiary. Rev. Rul. 2005-36, 2005-26 IRB 1368.

A written transfer of the transferor's (disclaimant's) entire interest in property to the person or persons who would otherwise have received the property if an effective disclaimer had been made will be treated as a valid disclaimer for federal estate and gift tax purposes provided the transfer is timely made and the transferor has not accepted any of the interest or any of its benefits. IRC Sec. 2518(c)(3). *ASRS, Sec. 55, ¶57.5(f)*.

VALUATION

909. How is property valued generally for gift tax purposes?

The valuation of gifts of property is based on the same principles that apply to valuation of property for estate tax purposes (see Q 862). However, there is no alternate valuation date for the gift tax. The valuation is determined at the date of the gift. The value used is fair market value–the price at which the property would change hands between a willing buyer and a willing seller, neither being under any compulsion to buy or sell. IRC Sec. 2512(a); Treas. Reg. §25.2512-1. Gifts are valued without the benefit of hindsight; later events are generally ignored. *Okerlund v. U.S.*, 2004-1 USTC ¶60,481 (Fed. Cir. 2004).

In the case of any taxable gift which is a direct skip within the meaning of the generation-skipping transfer tax (GST tax) (see Q 950 et seq.), the amount of such gift is increased by the amount of the GST tax imposed on the transfer. IRC Sec. 2515.

If the IRS makes a determination of the value of any item of property for gift tax purposes, the donor may request that the Service furnish a written statement explaining the basis upon which the valuation was determined. IRC Sec. 7517.

With respect to gift tax returns, 20% of an underpayment attributable to a substantial gift tax valuation understatement is added to tax. There is a substantial gift tax valuation understatement if (1) the value claimed was 50% or less of the correct amount, and (2) the underpayment exceeds $5,000. If the value claimed was 25% or less of the correct amount (and the underpayment exceeds $5,000), 40% of an underpayment attributable to such a gross gift tax valuation understatement is added to tax. IRC Sec. 6662. The 20% or 40% penalty is not imposed with respect to any portion of the underpayment for which it is shown that there was reasonable cause and the taxpayer acted in good faith. IRC Sec. 6664(c)(1).

A gift which is disclosed on a gift tax return in a manner adequate to apprise the Service of the nature of the item may not be revalued after the statute of limitations (generally, three years after the return is filed) has expired. IRC Sec. 6501(c)(9). *ASRS, Sec. 55, ¶57.3*.

910. How are life estates, remainders, and private annuities valued?

Life estates, estates for a term of years, remainder interests, and private annuities are generally valued by use of the government's valuation tables (see below). *Fehrs v.*

U.S., 79-2 USTC ¶13,324 (Ct. Cl. 1979). However, it has been held that the tables are only *presumptively* correct, that in exceptional cases where there is strong evidence at the date of valuation that the life by which an interest is measured has an expectation of life longer or shorter than the tables indicate, that interest may be valued according to the facts at hand rather than according to the tables. *Est. of Carter v. U.S.*, 91-1 USTC ¶60,054 (5th Cir. 1991); *Dunigan v. U.S.*, 434 F.2d 892 (5th Cir. 1970); *Est. of Hoelzel v. Comm.*, 28 TC 384 (1957), acq. 1957-2 CB 5; *Est. of Jennings v. Comm.*, 10 TC 323 (1948), acq. 1953-1 CB 5; *Ellis Sarasota Bank & Trust Co. v. U.S.*, 77-2 USTC ¶13,204 (M.D. Fla. 1977); Rev. Rul. 66-307, 1966-2 CB 429; TAM 9133001. On the other hand, the government tables must be used even though the life tenant or life annuitant is in poor health at the date of valuation if the tenant's or annuitant's time of death is neither predictable nor imminent. *Miami Beach First Nat'l Bank v. U.S.*, 443 F.2d 116 (5th Cir. 1971); *Est. of Bell v. U.S.*, 46 AFTR 2d ¶148,406 (E.D. Wash. 1980); *Bank of Cal. (Est. of Manning) v. U.S.*, 82-1 USTC ¶13,461 (C.D. Cal. 1980); *Est. of Fabric v. Comm.*, 83 TC 932 (1984); *Est. of McDowell v. Comm.*, TC Memo 1986-27. Account may not be taken of facts later coming to light but not available at the date of valuation; i.e., the interest may not be valued through the aid of hindsight. *U.S. v. Provident Trust Co.*, 291 U.S. 272 (1934); *Est. of Van Horne v. Comm.*, 83-2 USTC ¶13,548 (9th Cir. 1983), aff'g 78 TC 728 (1982), *cert. den*. Regulations provide that the standard valuation tables are not to be used where the individual who is a measuring life is terminably ill (defined as a person with an incurable illness or other deteriorating physical condition and at least a 50% probability of dying within one year). However, if an individual survives for 18 months after the transaction, the individual is presumed to have not been terminally ill at the time of the transaction unless the contrary is established by clear and convincing evidence. Treas. Regs. §§1.7520-3(b)(3), 20.7520-3(b)(3), 25.7520-3(b)(3).

The estate and gift tax valuation tables are based on an assumed interest rate. Departure from strict application of the tables is permissible in exceptional cases where use of the tables would violate reason and fact: for example, where transferred property may yield no income at all or the income is definitely determinable by other means. *Morgan v. Comm.*, 42 TC 1080 (1964), aff'd 353 F.2d 209 (4th Cir. 1965); *Hanley v. U.S.*, 63 F. Supp. 73 (Ct. Cl. 1945). However, IRS will not allow such departure on a mere showing that past income yield from trust assets has been substantially lower than the rate assumed in the tables. Rev. Rul. 77-195, 1977-1 CB 295. Nor will departure be allowed simply because the property transferred as a gift in trust is nonincome producing if the trustee has power to convert it to income producing property. Rev. Rul. 79-280, 1979-2 CB 340.

Regulations provide that the standard valuation tables are not to be used to value an annuity, if considering the assumed interest rate the trust is expected to exhaust the fund before the last possible annuity payment is made in full (measuring life survival to age 110 is assumed for this purpose). For a fixed annuity (i.e., annuity amount is payable for a term certain, or for one or two lives) payable annually at the end of the year, the corpus is assumed to be sufficient to make all payments if the assumed interest rate is greater than or equal to the annuity payment percentage (i.e., the amount of the annual annuity payment divided by the initial value of the corpus). If the annuity payment percentage exceeds the assumed interest rate and the annuity is for a term certain, multiple the annual annuity payment by the term certain annuity factor (derived from the Term Certain Remainder Factors Table in Appendix D). If the annuity payment percentage exceeds the assumed interest rate and the annuity is for one or two lives, multiple the annual annuity payment by the term certain annuity factor (derived from

GENERAL   Q 910

the Term Certain Remainder Factors Table in Appendix D) for a term equal to 110 minus the age of the youngest measuring life. If the present value for a term certain annuity derived in either of the two preceding sentences exceeds the fund from which the annuity is to be paid, a special IRC Section 7520 valuation factor may be required to take into account the exhaustion of the fund. Adjustments in the computations described above would be required if payment terms differ from those described. Treas. Regs. §§1.7520-3(b)(2)(i), 20.7520-3(b)(2)(i), 25.7520-3(b)(2)(i).

> *Example.* Donor, age 60, transfers $1,000,000 to a trust. The trust will pay $100,000 a year to charity for the life of donor, with remainder to the donor's child. The IRC Section 7520 interest rate for the transfer is 6.8%. Since the annuity payment percentage of 10% ($100,000 annual payment divided by $1,000,000 initial value of trust fund) exceeds the 6.8% assumed interest rate, it can not be assumed the annuity payments will not exhaust the trust. Therefore, subtract donor's age 60 from 110, resulting in a term of 50 years. The remainder factor for a term of 50 years at 6.8% interest is .037277 (Term Certain Remainder Factors Table in Appendix D). The life income factor equals one minus the remainder factor of .037277, or .962723. The annuity factor equals the life income factor of .962723 divided by the assumed interest rate of 6.8%, or 14.1577. The present value of a term certain annuity equals $1,415,770 ($100,000 annual payment multiplied by 14.1577 annuity factor). Since this exceeds the value of the trust fund of $1,000,000, special IRC Section 7520 valuation factors will be required to take into account the exhaustion of the fund. See Treas. Reg. §25.7520-3(b)(2)(v)(Ex. 5).

Regulations provide that the standard valuation tables are not to be used to value an income interest, unless the income beneficiary is given an income interest which in light of the trust, will, or other instrument, or state law, is in accord with an income interest which the principles of the laws of trust would provide consistent with the value of the trust corpus and its preservation. Also, the standard valuation tables are not to be used to value a use interest, unless the beneficiary is given a use interest which in light of the trust, will, or other instrument, or state law, is in accord with an interest given to a life tenant or term holder. Standard valuation tables are not to be used for an income interest if (1) income or other enjoyment can be withheld, diverted, or accumulated for another's use without the consent of the income beneficiary, or (2) corpus can be withdrawn for another's use without the consent of the income beneficiary or accountability to such beneficiary. Thus, special factors may be required in conjunction with unproductive property, if the beneficiary has no right to require that the trustee make the trust income producing, and with Crummey withdrawal powers, if the power permits a diversion of income or principal to a person other than the income beneficiary during the income term. Treas. Regs. §§1.7520-3(b)(2)(ii), 20.7520-3(b)(2)(ii), 25.7520-3(b)(2)(ii).

A remainder or reversionary interest is to be valued using the standard valuation factors only if the preceding interest (e.g., an income or annuity interest) adequately preserves and protects the remainder or reversionary interest (e.g., from erosion, invasion, depletion, or damage) until the interest takes effect. Treas. Regs. §§1.7520-3(b)(2)(iii), 20.7520-3(b)(2)(iii), 25.7520-3(b)(2)(iii).

There is a split in the courts regarding lottery winnings includable in the gross estate as to whether they should be valued as an annuity under the standard valuation tables or whether a discount is available where state law prohibited the assignment of state lottery winnings. *Est. of Shackelford v. U.S.*, 2001-2 USTC ¶60,417 (9th Cir. 2001), aff'g 99-2 USTC ¶60,356 (E.D. Calif. 1999); *Est. of Cook v. Comm.*, 2003-2 USTC ¶60,471 (5th Cir. 2003), aff'g TC Memo 2001-170; *Est. of Gribauskas v. Comm.*, 2003-2 USTC ¶60,466 (2nd Cir. 2003), rev'g 116 TC 142 (2001); *Est. of Donovan v. Comm.*, 2005-1 USTC ¶60,500 (DC Mass. 2005). One court has ruled that structured settlement payments should be valued as an annuity under the standard valuation tables without discount for lack of marketability. *Est. of Anthony v. U.S.*, 2005-1 USTC ¶60,504 (M.D. La. 2005).

Valuation Tables

Valuation tables using up-to-date interest and mortality factors must be used where the valuation date occurs on or after May 1, 1989. The value of an annuity, an interest for life or term of years, or a reversionary or remainder interest, is determined using tables and an interest rate (rounded to the nearest 2/10ths of 1%) equal to 120% of the federal midterm rate in effect for the month in which the valuation date occurs. IRC Sec. 7520(a). An interest rate falling midway between any 2/10ths of a percent is rounded up. Treas. Reg. §20.7520-1(b)(1). However, the valuation tables are not to be used with respect to any of the income tax provisions relating to qualified pension plans (including tax sheltered annuities and IRAs) contained in IRC Sections 401 to 419A. IRC Sec. 7520(b). The Section 7520 interest rate for each month is published in *Tax Facts News*, a National Underwriter publication, as the rate becomes available. It can also be found at www.TaxFactsOnline.com.

See Appendix D for valuation tables (other than two-life factors or unitrust factors) and an explanation of their use. (See *Tax Facts 2* for selected unitrust tables.) IRS Publications 1457 and 1458 contain extensive valuation tables. Where the standard valuation table is to be used but the interest rate or payout rate to be used is between rates in the table, interpolation (an algebraic calculation of a number falling between table factors) is required. Treas. Regs. §§1.642(c)-6(e)(4), 1.664-4(e).

If an income, estate, or gift tax charitable deduction is allowable with respect to the property transferred, the taxpayer can elect to use the interest rate for either of the two months preceding the month in which the valuation date occurs. However, if a transfer of more than one interest in the same property is made with respect to which the taxpayer could use the same interest rate, such interest rate is to be used with respect to each such interest. IRC Sec. 7520(a).

911. What effect does it have on gift tax valuation if the donee agrees to pay the gift tax?

If a gift is made subject to the express or implied condition that the gift tax be paid by the donee (or by the trustee if the gift is in trust) the value of the gift is reduced by the amount of tax. Rev. Rul. 75-72, 1975-1 CB 310; *Lingo v. Comm.*, 13 TCM 436 (1959); *Harrison v. Comm.*, 17 TC 1350 (1952), acq. 1952-2 CB 2. The computation of the tax requires the use of an algebraic formula, since the amount of the tax is dependent on the value of the gift which in turn is dependent on the amount of the tax.

The formula is

$$\frac{\text{Tentative Tax}}{1 \text{ plus Rate of Tax}} = \text{True Tax.}$$

Examples illustrating the use of this formula, with the algebraic method, to determine the tax in a net gift situation are contained in IRS Publication 904 (rev. May 1985). Three of the examples show the effect of a state gift tax upon the computation. (See also Q 922.) *ASRS, Sec. 55, ¶57.3(c)*.

GENERAL   Q 913

Chapter 14 Special Valuation Rules

912. What are the Chapter 14 special valuation rules?

Special valuation rules are contained in Chapter 14 of the Internal Revenue Code. Chapter 14 generally focuses on establishing the value of various interests transferred to family members at the time of the transfer when the transferor retains certain interests in the property being transferred. Special rules apply to certain transfers of interests in corporations and partnerships (see Q 913); to certain transfers of interests in trusts and even remainder and joint purchase transactions (see Q 914); to certain agreements, options, rights or restrictions exercisable at less than fair market value (see Q 915); and to various lapsing rights and restrictions (see Q 916).

913. What special valuation rules apply to the transfer of an interest in a corporation or partnership under Chapter 14?

As a general rule, the value of a transferred residual interest is equal to the value of the transferor's entire interest prior to the transfer reduced by the value of the interest retained by the transferor. For the purpose of determining whether a transfer of an interest in a corporation or partnership to (or for the benefit of) a "member of the transferor's family" is a gift (and the value of the transfer), the value of any "applicable retained interest" that is held by the transferor or an "applicable family member" immediately after the transfer is treated as being zero unless the applicable retained interest is a "distribution right" which consists of the right to receive a "qualified payment." IRC Secs. 2701(a)(1), 2701(a)(3)(A). Where an applicable retained interest consists of a distribution right which consists of the right to receive a qualified payment and there are one or more liquidation, put, call, or conversion rights with respect to such interest, the value of all such rights is to be determined by assuming that each such liquidation, put, call, or conversion right is exercised in a manner which results in the lowest value. IRC Sec. 2701(a)(3)(B). IRC Section 2701 does not apply to distribution rights with respect to qualified payments where there is no liquidation, put, call, or conversion right with respect to the distribution right. IRC Sec. 2701(a)(3)(C). If the transfer subject to these rules is of a junior equity interest in a corporation or partnership, the transfer must be assigned a minimum value under the "junior equity rule." IRC Sec. 2701(a)(4).

These rules do not apply if for either the transferred interest or the applicable retained interest market quotations are readily available (as of the date of transfer) on an established securities market. Also, the rules do not apply if the applicable retained interest is of the same class as the transferred interest, or if the applicable retained interest is proportionally the same as the transferred interest (disregarding nonlapsing differences with respect to voting in the case of a corporation, or with respect to management and limitations on liability in the case of a partnership). IRC Sec. 2701(a)(2). An exception from the rules is also provided for a transfer of a vertical slice of interests in an entity (defined as a proportionate reduction of each class of equity interest held by the transferor and applicable family members in the aggregate). Treas. Reg. §25.2701-1(c)(4).

Definitions and Rules

Transfers

The rules apply to transfers with respect to new, as well as existing, entities. Treas. Reg. §25.2701-1(b)(2)(i). Transfers may be either direct or indirect. Furthermore, except as provided in regulations, a contribution to capital, a redemption, a recapitalization, or

2006 Tax Facts on Insurance & Employee Benefits

other change in capital structure of a corporation or partnership is treated as a transfer if the taxpayer or an applicable family member receives an applicable retained interest in the transaction, or as provided under regulations, holds such an interest immediately after the transfer. IRC Sec. 2701(e)(5). Any termination of an interest is also treated as a transfer. IRC Sec. 2701(d)(5).

Applicable Retained Interests

An "applicable retained interest" is any interest in an entity with respect to which there is (1) a distribution right and the transferor and applicable family members control the entity immediately before the transfer, or (2) a liquidation, put, call, or conversion right. IRC Sec. 2701(b). (Regulations or rulings may provide that any applicable retained interest be treated as two or more interests. IRC Sec. 2701(e)(7); Treas. Reg. §25.2701-7.) A "distribution right" is any right to a distribution from a corporation with respect to its stock, or from a partnership with respect to a partner's interest in the partnership, other than (1) a distribution with respect to any interest if such right is junior to the rights of the transferred interest, (2) any right to receive a guaranteed payment of a fixed amount from a partnership under IRC Section 707(c), or (3) a liquidation, put, call, or conversion right. IRC Sec. 2701(c)(1).

For these purposes, a liquidation, put, call, or conversion right is treated as a distribution right rather than as a liquidation, put, call, or conversion right if (1) it must be exercised at a specific time and at a specific amount, or (2) the liquidation, put, call, or conversion right: (a) can be converted into a fixed amount or fixed percentage of the same class of shares of stock as the transferred shares; (b) is nonlapsing; (c) is subject to proportionate adjustments for splits, combinations, reclassifications, and similar changes in the capital stock; and (d) is subject to adjustments for accumulated but unpaid distributions. (Similar rules are to apply to liquidation, put, call, or conversion rights in a partnership.) Where a liquidation, put, call, or conversion right is treated as exercised in a manner which produces the lowest value in the general rule above, such a right is treated as a distribution right which must be exercised at a specific time and at a specific amount. IRC Sec. 2701(c)(2).

Regulations provide that applicable retained interests consist of (1) extraordinary payment rights, and (2) distribution rights held in a controlled entity. Treas. Reg. §25.2701-2(b)(1). The term "extraordinary payment rights" is used to refer to liquidation, put, call, or conversion rights, the exercise or nonexercise of which affects the value of the transferred interests. Treas. Reg. §25.2701-2(b)(2). The following are treated as neither extraordinary payment rights nor distribution rights: (1) mandatory fixed payment rights; (2) liquidation participation rights (other than ones in which the transferor, members of the transferor's family, and applicable family members have the ability to compel liquidation); and (3) non-lapsing conversion rights subject to proportionate adjustments for changes in equity and to adjustments to take account of accumulated but unpaid qualified payments. Treas. Reg. §25.2701-2(b)(4).

Qualified Payments

A "qualified payment" means any dividend payable on a periodic basis at a fixed rate (including rates tied to specific market rates) on any cumulative preferred stock (or comparable payment with respect to a partnership). With respect to the transferor, an otherwise qualified payment is to be treated as such unless the transferor elects otherwise. With respect to applicable family members, an otherwise qualified payment is not to be treated as such unless the applicable family member so elects. A transferor or an applicable family member can make an irrevocable election to treat any distribution right (which is otherwise not a qualified payment) as a qualified payment, payable at such times and in such amounts as provided in the election (such times and amounts not to be inconsistent with any underlying legal instruments creating such rights). IRC Sec. 2701(c)(3). The value assigned a right for which an election is made cannot exceed fair market (determined without regard to IRC Section 2701). Treas. Reg. §25.2701-2(c)(2).

Attribution

A "member of the transferor's family" includes the transferor's spouse, lineal descendants of the transferor or transferor's spouse, and the spouse of any such descendant. IRC Sec. 2701(e)(1). An "applicable family member" with respect to a transferor includes the transferor's spouse, an ancestor of the transferor or transferor's spouse, and the spouse of any such ancestor. IRC Sec. 2701(e)(2). An individual is treated as holding interests held indirectly through a corporation, partnership, trust, or other entity. IRC Sec. 2701(e)(3). In the case of a corporation, "control" means 50% ownership (by vote or value) of the stock. In the case of a partnership, "control" means 50% ownership of the capital or profits interests, or in the case of a limited partnership, the ownership of any interest as a general partner. IRC Sec. 2701(b)(2). When determining control, an individual is treated as holding any interest held by an applicable family member (see above), including (for this purpose) any lineal descendant of any parent of the transferor or the transferor's spouse. IRC Sec. 2701(b)(2)(C). The application of IRC Section 2701 to transfers involving an ESOP will be determined by looking at the eligible beneficiaries of the ESOP. Let. Rul. 9253018.

Minimum Value/Junior Equity Rule

If the transfer subject to these rules is of a junior equity interest in a corporation or partnership, the value of the transferred interest cannot be less than the amount which would be determined if the total value of all junior equity interests in the entity were equal to 10% of the sum of (1) the total value of the equity interests in the entity, and (2) the total amount of debt owed the transferor or an applicable family member by the entity. IRC Sec. 2701(a)(4). For this purpose, indebtedness does not include (1) short term indebtedness incurred for the current conduct of trade or business, (2) indebtedness owed to a third party solely because it is guaranteed by the transferor or an applicable family member, and (3) amounts set aside for qualified deferred compensation to the extent such amounts are not available to the entity. While a properly structured lease is not treated as indebtedness, arrearages with respect to a lease are indebtedness. Treas. Reg. §25.2701-3.

Valuation Method

For purposes of IRC Section 2701, the amount of a gift is determined as follows: (1) determine the fair market value of all family-held equity interests in the entity (treat as if held by one individual); (2) subtract out the sum of (a) the fair market value of all family-held senior equity interests in the entity other than applicable retained interests (treat as if held by one individual) and (b) the value of applicable retained interests as valued under IRC Section 2701; (3) allocate the remaining value among the transferred interests and other family-held subordinate interests; (4) reduce the value allocated to the transferred interests to adjust for a minority or similar discount or for consideration received for the transferred interest. Treas. Reg. §25.2701-3(b).

Recapture

If "qualified payments" are valued under these rules, additional estate or gift tax may be due at the time of a later taxable event to reflect cumulative but unpaid distributions. The amount of an increase in estate or gift tax is equal to the excess (if any) of (1) the value of the qualified payments as if each payment had been timely made during the period beginning with the transfer subject to these rules and ending with the taxable event and each payment were reinvested at the (capitalization or discount) interest rate used to value the applicable retained transfer at the time of the transfer, over (2) the value of the qualified payments actually made adjusted to reflect reinvestment as in (1). For this purpose, any payment made within four years of its due date is treated as made on its due date. IRC Sec. 2701(d). The due date is the date specified in the governing instrument as the date on which the payment is to be made (or if no date is specified, the last day of each calendar year). Treas. Reg. §25.2701-4(c)(2). A transfer of a debt obligation bearing compound interest at a rate not less than the appropriate IRC Section 7520 discount rate from the due date of the payment and with a term of no more than four years is treated as payment. Treas. Reg. §25.2701-4(c)(5).

Regulations limit the amount of the increase in gift or estate tax attributable to recapture in order to prevent double inclusion of the same transfer in the transfer tax system. The mitigation provisions include reduction of the amount recaptured by the sum of (1) the portion of the fair market value of the qualified payment interest which is attributable to cumulative but unpaid distributions; (2) to the extent held by the individual at the time of a taxable event, the fair market value of any equity interest received by the individual in lieu of qualified payments; and (3) the amount by which the individual's aggregate taxable gifts were increased to reflect failure of the individual to enforce his rights to qualified payments. Treas. Reg. §25.2701-4(c)(1).

As an overall limitation, the amount of any increase in tax due to cumulative but unpaid distributions will not exceed the applicable percentage of the excess (if any) of (1) the value (determined as of the date of the taxable event) of all equity interests in the entity which are junior to the applicable retained interest, over (2) the value of such interests (determined as of the date of the earlier transfer subject to these rules). The numerator of the applicable percentage is equal to the number of shares in the corporation held (as of the date of the taxable event) by the transferor which are applicable retained interests of the same class. The denominator of the applicable percentage is equal to the total number of shares in the corporation (as of the date of the taxable event) which are of the same class as the shares used in the numerator. (A similar rule applies to partnerships.) IRC Sec. 2701(d)(2)(B). The applicable percentage equals the largest ownership percentage interest in any preferred interest held by the interest holder. Treas. Reg. §25.2701-4(c)(6)(iii). The appreciation limitation does not apply if the interest holder elects to treat the late payment of a qualified payment as a taxable event (see below). Treas. Reg. §25.2701-4(d)(2).

For purposes of an increase in tax due to cumulative but unpaid distributions, a "taxable event" includes (1) the death of the transferor if the applicable retained interest is included in the transferor's estate, (2) the transfer of an applicable retained interest, and (3) at the election of the taxpayer, the payment of a qualified payment which is made after its four-year grace period. IRC Sec. 2701(d)(3)(A). Also, a termination of a qualified payment interest is treated as a taxable event. Thus, a taxable event occurs with respect to an individual indirectly holding a qualified payment interest held by a trust on the earlier of (1) the termination of the individual's interest in the trust, or (2)

GENERAL   Q 913

the termination of the trust's interest in the qualified payment interest. However, if the value of the qualified payment interest would be included in the individual's federal gross estate if the individual were to die immediately after the termination, the taxable transfer does not occur until the earlier of (1) the time the interest would no longer be includable in the individual's estate (other than by reason of the gifts within three years of death rule of IRC Section 2035), or (2) such individual's death. Treas. Regs. §§25.2701-4(b)(1); 25.2701-4(b)(2).

A "taxable event" does not include an applicable retained interest includable in the transferor's estate and passing under the marital deduction. Nor does a "taxable event" include a lifetime gift to a spouse which does not result in a taxable gift because the marital deduction is taken, or the spouse pays consideration for the transfer. However, such a spouse is thereafter treated in the same manner as the transferor. IRC Sec. 2701(d)(3)(B).

An applicable family member is treated the same as the transferor with respect to any applicable retained interest retained by such family member. Also, if the transferor transfers an applicable retained interest to an applicable family member (other than the transferor's spouse), the applicable family member is treated the same as the transferor with respect to distributions accumulating after the time of the taxable event. In the case of a transfer of an applicable retained interest from an applicable family member to the transferor, IRC Section 2701 continues to apply as long as the transferor holds the interest. IRC Sec. 2701(d)(4).

Adjustment to Mitigate Double Taxation

As provided in regulations, if there is a later transfer or inclusion in the gross estate of property which was subject to IRC Section 2701, adjustments are to be made for gift, estate, and generation-skipping transfer tax purposes to reflect any increase in valuation of a prior taxable gift or any recapture under IRC Section 2701. IRC Sec. 2701(e)(6).

IRC Section 2701 interests transferred after May 4, 1994. An individual (the initial transferor) who has previously made a transfer subject to IRC Section 2701 (the initial transfer) may be permitted a reduction in his taxable gifts for gift tax purposes or adjusted taxable gifts for estate tax purposes. If the holder of the IRC Section 2701 interest (i.e., the applicable retained interest, see above) transfers the interest to an individual other than the initial transferor or an applicable family member of the initial transferor in a transfer subject to estate or gift tax during the lifetime of the initial transferor, then the initial transferor can reduce the amount upon which his tentative tax is calculated for gift tax purposes in the year of the transfer. The amount of the reduction is generally equal to the lesser of (1) the amount by which the initial transferor's taxable gifts were increased by reason of IRC Section 2701, or (2) the amount by which the value of the IRC Section 2701 interest at the time of the subsequent transfer exceeds its value at the time of the initial transfer (the duplicated amount). Any unused reduction can be carried over and applied in succeeding years; any reduction remaining at death can be applied in the initial transferor's estate. The amount upon which the initial transferor's tentative tax is calculated for estate tax purposes may also be reduced (generally occurs if the IRC Section 2701 interest is retained until the initial transferor's death or if there is a carryover of any unused reduction). If the holder of the IRC Section 2701 interest transfers the interest to an individual other than the initial transferor or an applicable family member of the initial transferor in an exchange for consideration during the lifetime of the initial transferor, then the reduction is taken by the initial transferor's

2006 Tax Facts on Insurance & Employee Benefits   875

estate and calculated as if the value of the consideration were included in the estate at its value at the time of the exchange. Property received in a nonrecognition exchange for an IRC Section 2701 interest is thereafter treated as the IRC Section 2701 interest for adjustment purposes. Reductions are calculated separately for each class of IRC Section 2701 interests. If spouses elected to treat the initial transfer as a split gift (see Q 907), then (1) each spouse may be entitled to reductions if there is a transfer of the IRC Section 2701 interest during their joint lives; and (2) if there is a transfer of the IRC Section 2701 interest at or after the death of either spouse, then (a) the donor spouse's estate may be entitled to reductions; and (b) the consenting spouse's aggregate sum of taxable gifts and gift tax payable on prior gifts are reduced to eliminate any remaining effect of IRC Section 2701 if the consenting spouse survives the donor spouse. In any event, no reduction is available to the extent that double taxation has otherwise been avoided. Treas. Reg. §25.2701-5.

IRC Section 2701 interests transferred before May 5, 1994. The initial transferor can use the final regulations (see above), the proposed regulations (see below), or any other reasonable interpretation of the statute. Treas. Reg. §25.2701-5(h).

A person who has previously made a transfer subject to IRC Section 2701 is permitted a reduction in his adjusted taxable gifts for estate tax purposes. Whether a person is a transferor is determined without regard to the split-gift provisions for spouses (see Q 907). If any portion of the transferor's IRC Section 2701 interest is transferred to the transferor's spouse in a nontaxable event (e.g., the marital deduction), any reduction in adjusted taxable gifts is taken by such spouse rather than the transferor. Prop. Treas. Reg. §25.2701-5(a).

The amount of the reduction is equal to the lesser of (1) the amount by which the transferor's taxable gifts were increased by reason of IRC Section 2701, or (2) the amount of the excess estate tax value of such interest multiplied by a fraction. The excess estate tax value equals the estate value of the IRC Section 2701 interest reduced by the value of such interest under IRC Section 2701 at the time of the transfer. In the case of an IRC Section 2701 interest transferred during life, the estate tax value equals the sum of (1) the increase in taxable gifts resulting from the transfer of the IRC Section 2701 interest, and (2) consideration received in exchange for the transfer. The numerator of the fraction above equals the value allocated under step 3 of the "Valuation Method" (see heading above); the numerator of the fraction equals the value allocated under step 2 of the "Valuation Method." Prop. Treas. Reg. §25.2701-5(b). However, no reduction is available to the extent that double taxation has otherwise been avoided. Prop. Treas. Reg. §25.2701-5(c).

Miscellaneous

These provisions apply to transfers after October 8, 1990. However, with respect to property transferred before October 9, 1990, any failure to exercise a right of conversion, to pay dividends, or to exercise other rights to be specified in regulations, is not to be treated as a subsequent transfer. OBRA '90, Sec. 11602(e)(1).

With respect to gifts made after October 8, 1990, the gift tax statute of limitations on a transfer subject to these provisions does not run unless the transaction is disclosed on a gift tax return in a manner adequate to apprise the IRS of the nature of the retained and transferred interests. IRC Sec. 6501(c)(9); OBRA '90, Sec. 11602(e)(2).

Effect on Corporate and Partnership Transactions

Recapitalizations and Transfers of Stock

If a parent recapitalizes a corporation into common and preferred stock and gives the common stock to his children, the value of the common stock is determined by subtracting from the value of the entire corporation the value of the preferred stock as determined under IRC Section 2701. If the parent treats the preferred stock's right to dividends as qualified payments, the right to such payments is assigned a present value. However, the value assigned to the common stock must be at least equal to the value determined under the junior equity rule above. If the parent does not receive the preferred dividends within four years of their due dates, the parent may be treated as making additional transfers of the accumulated, but undistributed dividends, at the time of a subsequent transfer of the preferred stock. On the other hand, if the parent does not treat the right to dividends as qualified payments, such a right is assigned a value of zero.

Similarly, if a parent owns 80% of a corporation and a child owns 20% of the same corporation and the parent's common stock is exchanged for preferred stock, the value of what the parent has transferred and what the parent has retained are determined under IRC Section 2701.

Even if the child pays consideration for the common stock, whether the parent has made a transfer (and the value of such transfer) is determined under IRC Section 2701.

If a parent and a child each contributes to the start up of a new business and the parent receives preferred stock while the child receives common stock, the parent is treated as if he received common stock and preferred stock and then exchanged the common stock for the balance of the preferred stock. The value of what the parent has transferred and what the parent has retained are determined under IRC Section 2701.

However, a gift or a sale of stock to a child is not subject to IRC Section 2701 if the stock is of the same class as that retained by the parent. Also, a gift or a sale of stock to a child is not subject to IRC Section 2701 if the stock is proportionately the same as that retained by the parent (e.g., retained stock is entitled to $2 of dividends for every $1 of dividends paid to transferred stock), without regard to nonlapsing voting rights (i.e., parent can retain control with nonlapsing voting right).

If applicable family members receive or retain applicable retained interests at the time of a gift or a sale of stock to a child, the transaction may be subject to IRC Section 2701 even though the parent is willing to terminate his equity relationship with the corporation.

IRC Section 2701 could be avoided by selling the common stock to a nonfamily member, such as a valuable employee. Proceeds of the sale could then be distributed to the children.

Of course, IRC Section 2701 does not apply if either the transferred interest (common stock) or retained interest (preferred stock) is publicly traded. Also, with regard to retained distribution rights, IRC Section 2701 does not apply if the transferor and applicable family members do not control the corporation immediately before the transfer. However, with regard to liquidation, put, call, or conversion rights (other than those treated as distribution rights, see above), IRC Section 2701 can apply even if the transferor and applicable family members do not control the corporation.

If the typical recapitalization is reversed (i.e., the parent retains the common stock and transfers the preferred stock), IRC Section 2701 should not apply (assuming no retention of applicable retained interests by parent or applicable family members).

Partnership Freezes

The traditional partnership freeze worked similarly to the traditional estate freeze recapitalization. It too is caught by the IRC Section 2701 special valuation rules. Most of the techniques employed to reduce the effect of, or to avoid, the valuation rules with respect to a recapitalization will also work with a partnership. Examination of the partnership agreement will be required to determine which partners hold which rights. Note that in the case of a limited partnership, "control" includes the holding of any interest as a general partner. Also, any right to receive a guaranteed payment of a fixed amount from a partnership under IRC Section 707(c) is not treated as a distribution right.

Other Changes in Capital Structure

Other changes in capital structure may also be caught by the IRC Section 2701 special valuation rules. Except as provided in regulations, a contribution to capital, a redemption, a recapitalization, or other change in capital structure of a corporation or partnership is treated as a transfer if the taxpayer or an applicable family member receives an applicable retained interest in the transaction, or as provided under regulations, holds such an interest immediately after the transfer.

Nonequity Interests

The IRC Section 2701 special valuation rules apply only to equity interests. Thus, for purposes of IRC Section 2701, none of the following should be treated as a retained interest: an installment sale of an interest in a corporation or partnership, an exchange of an interest in a corporation or partnership for a private annuity, an employment contract or deferred compensation, or debt owed by a corporation or partnership to a transferor or applicable family member. See TAM 9436006. However, the total amount of debt owed the transferor or an applicable family member by the entity is a factor in the junior equity rule above.

914. What special valuation rules apply to the transfer of an interest in trust, or to certain remainder or joint purchase transactions, under Chapter 14?

As a general rule, the value of a transferred remainder interest is equal to the value of the transferor's entire interest prior to the transfer reduced by the value of the interest retained by the transferor. For the purpose of determining whether a transfer of an interest in a trust to (or for the benefit of) a member of the transferor's family is a gift (and the value of the transfer), the value of any interest retained by the transferor or an applicable family member is treated as being zero unless the retained interest is a qualified interest. This rule does not apply to an incomplete gift (a transfer that would not be treated as a gift whether or not consideration was received), to a transfer to a trust if the only property to be held by the trust is a residence to be used as a personal residence by persons holding term interests in the trust (see below), or to the extent that regulations provide that a transfer is not inconsistent with IRC Section 2702. IRC Sec. 2702(a). Also, IRC Section 2702 does not apply to (1) certain charitable remainder trusts, (2) a pooled income fund, (3) a charitable lead trust in which the only interest in the trust other than the remainder interest or a qualified annuity or unitrust interest is the charitable lead interest, (4) the assignment of a remainder interest if the only interest retained by the transferor or an applicable family member is as a permissible recipient of income in the sole discretion of an independent trustee, and (5) a transfer in trust to a spouse for full and adequate consideration in connection with a divorce if any remaining interests in the trust are retained by the other spouse. Treas. Reg. §25.2702-1(c). For transfers to a trust made after May 18, 1997, regulations exempt charitable remainder unitrusts (CRUTs) from IRC Section 2702 only if the trust provides for simple unitrust payments, or in the case of a CRUT with a lesser of trust income or the unitrust amount provision, the grantor and/or the grantor's spouse (who is a citizen of the U.S.) are the only noncharitable beneficiaries. Treas. Reg. §25.2702-1(c)(3). Modified rules apply to certain qualified tangible property, see below.

For these purposes, a transfer in trust does not include (1) the exercise, release, or lapse of a power of appointment over trust property that would not be a transfer for gift tax purposes, or (2) the exercise of a qualified disclaimer. An interest in trust includes a power with respect to a trust which would cause any portion of the transfer to be incomplete for gift tax purposes. Treas. Reg. §25.2702-2(a).

Retained Interests

Retained is defined as the same person holds an interest both before and after the transfer in trust. Thus, a transfer of an income interest for life in trust to an applicable family member in conjunction with the transfer of a remainder interest in trust to a member of the transferor's family is not subject to IRC Section 2702. However, with respect to the creation of a term interest (e.g., a joint purchase creating a term and remainder interest), any interest held by the transferor immediately after the transfer is treated as held both before and after the transfer. Treas. Reg. §25.2702-2(a)(3). A negotiable note received in exchange for publicly traded stock sold to a trust was not treated as a retained interest in a trust. TAM 9436006.

Qualified Interests

A "qualified interest" is an annuity or unitrust interest, or, if all other interests in the trust are annuity or unitrust interests, a noncontingent remainder interest. A *qualified annuity interest* means a right to receive fixed amounts (or a fixed fraction or percentage of the property transferred to the trust) not less frequently than annually. A *qualified unitrust interest* means a right to receive amounts which are payable not less frequently than annually and are a fixed percentage of the fair market value of the property in the trust (determined annually). IRC Sec. 2702(b). A qualified annuity interest can provide for an annuity amount (or fixed fraction or percentage) which increases by not more than 120% of the stated dollar amount (or fixed fraction or percentage) payable in the preceding year. Treas. Reg. §25.2702-3(b)(1)(ii). A qualified unitrust interest can provide for a unitrust percentage which increases by not more than 120% of the fixed percentage payable in the preceding year. Treas. Reg. §25.2702-3(c)(1)(ii).

The retention of a power to revoke a qualified annuity or unitrust interest of the transferor's spouse is treated as retention of the qualified annuity or unitrust interest. Treas. Reg. §25.2702-2(a)(5). Contingent annuity interests retained by the grantor or given to the grantor's spouse were not qualified interests. TAMs 9707001, 9717008, 9741001; *Cook v. Comm.*, 2001-2 USTC ¶60,422 (7th Cir. 2001), aff'g 115 TC 15

(2000). Regulations treat an interest with the following characteristics as a qualified interest retained by the grantor: an annuity or unitrust interest that is (1) given to the spouse of the grantor; and (2) contingent only on (a) the spouse surviving, or (b) that the grantor does not revoke the spouse's interest. Treas. Reg. §25.2702-3(d)(2). The grantor makes an additional gift to the remainder person when the spouse's interest is revoked or the grantor survives the trust term without having revoked the interest.

A right to receive each year the *lesser of* an annuity interest or a unitrust interest is not treated as a qualified interest. The right to receive each year the *greater of* an annuity interest or a unitrust interest is treated as a qualified interest. However, the qualified interest is valued at the greater of the two interests. Treas. Reg. §25.2702-3(d)(1). A right of withdrawal, whether or not cumulative, is not a qualified annuity or unitrust interest. Treas. Regs. §§25.2702-3(b)(1)(i); 25.2702-3(c)(1)(i).

A qualified annuity or unitrust interest may permit the payment of income in excess of the annuity or unitrust amount to the transferor or applicable family member with the retained annuity or unitrust interest. However, the annuity or unitrust interest is valued without regard to the right to excess income (which is not a qualified annuity or unitrust interest). Treas. Regs. §§25.2702-3(b)(1)(iii); 25.2702-3(c)(1)(iii). Also, a qualified annuity interest may permit the payment of an amount sufficient to reimburse the grantor for any income tax due on income in excess of the annuity amount; the annuity interest is valued without regard to such reimbursement right. Let. Ruls. 9441031, 9345035. Distributions from the trust cannot be made to anyone other than the transferor or applicable family member who holds the qualified annuity or unitrust interest. Treas. Reg. §25.2702-3(d)(2).

The term of the annuity or unitrust interest must be for the life of the transferor or applicable family member, for a specified term of years, or for the shorter of the two periods. Treas. Reg. §25.2702-3(d)(3). There is a split of authority as to whether valuation may be based on two lives, or just one life. *Schott v. Comm.*, 2003-1 USTC ¶60,457 (9th Cir. 2003), rev'g TC Memo 2001-110; *Cook v. Comm.*, 2001-2 USTC ¶60,422 (7th Cir. 2001), aff'g 115 TC 15 (2000). Regulations permit certain revocable spousal interests (see above), but value the retained grantor and spouse's interests separately as for a single life. Treas. Reg. §25.2702-3(e)(Ex. 8).

An example in the regulations had provided that where a grantor retained the right to annuity payments for 10 years and the payments continued to his estate if he died during the 10-year term, the annuity was valued as for 10 years or until the grantor's prior death (i.e., as a temporary annuity). Former Treas. Reg. §25.2702-3(e)(Ex. 5). The Tax Court ruled that the example was invalid, that the annuity should be valued as for 10 years (i.e., as a term annuity). *Walton v. Comm.*, 115 TC 589 (2000). The IRS has changed the regulations so as to follow *Walton*. Treas. Reg. §25.2702-3(e)(Ex. 5). Note that if the trust property reverted to grantor's estate if the grantor died during the 10-year term, the annuity is valued as for 10 years or until the grantor's prior death. Treas. Reg. §25.2702-3(e)(Ex. 1). Similar results should apply likewise to unitrust payments.

Planning Point: A grantor retained annuity trust (GRAT) can be zeroed out (i.e., the value of the gift of the remainder reduced to zero) using an annuity payable to the grantor for a term of years with payments continuing to the grantor's estate for the balance of the term of years if the grantor dies during the term. In general, the GRAT is zeroed out if the annuity payment is made to equal the value of the property transferred to the trust divided by the appropriate annuity factor (including adjustments for frequency of payment).

The IRS will not issue rulings or determination letters on whether annuity interests are qualified interests under IRC Section 2702 where (1) the amount of the annuity payable annually is more than 50% of the initial fair market value of the property transferred to trust, or (2) the value of the remainder interest is less than 10% of the initial fair market value of the property transferred to trust. For purposes of the 10% test, the value of the remainder interest is determined under IRC Section 7520 without regard to the possibility that the grantor might die during the trust term, or that the trust property might revert to the grantor or the grantor's estate. Rev. Proc. 2005-3, Sec. 4.50, 2005-1 IRB 118.

Commutation (generally, an actuarially based acceleration or substitution of benefits) of a qualified annuity or unitrust interest is not permitted. Treas. Reg. §25.2702-3(d)(4). Additional contributions are not permitted with qualified annuity interests. Treas. Reg. §25.2702-3(b)(4).

The use of notes, other debt instruments, options or similar financial arrangements in satisfaction of the annuity or unitrust requirements under IRC Section 2702 is prohibited. Treas. Reg. §25.2702-3.

A remainder (or reversion) interest is treated as a *qualified remainder interest* if: (1) all interests in the trust (other than non-contingent remainder interests) are either qualified annuity interests or qualified unitrust interests (thus, an excess income provision is not permitted for this purpose); (2) each remainder interest is entitled to all or a fractional share of the trust property when all or a fractional share of the trust terminates (a transferor's right to receive the original value of the trust property, or a fractional share, would not qualify); and (3) the remainder is payable to the beneficiary or the beneficiary's estate in all events (i.e., it is non-contingent). Treas. Reg. §25.2702-3(f).

A qualified interest is to be valued using the valuation tables prescribed by IRC Section 7520. IRC Sec. 2702(a)(2)(B). For valuation rules for certain qualified tangible property, see below.

Qualified Tangible Property

If the nonexercise of rights under a term interest in tangible property would not have a substantial effect on the valuation of the remainder interest, the interest is valued at the amount for which it could be sold to an unrelated third person (i.e., market value is used instead of the valuation tables or zero valuation). IRC Sec. 2702(c)(4). *Qualified tangible property* is tangible property (1) for which a depreciation or depletion allowance would not be allowable if the property were used in a trade or business or held for the production of income, and (2) as to which the nonexercise of any rights under the term interest would not affect the value of the property passing to the remainderperson. A de minimis exception is provided at the time of the transfer to trust for improvements to the property which would be depreciable provided such improvements do not exceed 5% of the fair market value of the entire property. Treas. Reg. §25.2702-2(c)(2).

Term interests in qualified tangible property are valued using actual sales or rentals that are comparable both as to the nature and character of the property and the duration of the term interest. Little weight is given appraisals in the absence of comparables. Tables used in valuing annuity, unitrust, estate, and remainder interests under IRC Section 7520 are not evidence of what a willing buyer would pay a willing seller for an interest in qualified tangible property. Treas. Reg. §25.2702-2(c)(3). If the taxpayer cannot establish the value of the term interest, the interest is valued at zero. Treas. Reg. §25.2702-2(c)(1).

If, during the term, the term interest is converted into property other than qualified tangible property, the conversion is treated as a transfer of the unexpired portion of the term interest (valued as of the time of the original transfer) unless the trust is converted to a qualified annuity interest (see above). Treas. Reg. §25.2702-2(c)(4). If an addition or improvement is made to qualified tangible property such that the property would no longer be treated as qualified tangible property, the property is subject to the conversion rule above. If the addition or improvement would not change the nature of the qualified tangible property, the addition or improvement is treated as an additional transfer subject to IRC Section 2702. Treas. Reg. §25.2702-2(c)(5).

Personal Residences

IRC Section 2702 does not apply to the transfer of an interest in a personal residence trust or a qualified personal residence trust. IRC Sec. 2702(a)(3)(A)(ii); Treas. Reg. §25.2702-5(a). However, a person is limited to holding a term interest in only two such trusts. Treas. Reg. §25.2702-5(a). A personal residence trust or a qualified personal residence trust which does not meet the requirements in the regulations may be modified (by judicial modification or otherwise, so long as the modification is effective under state law), if the reformation commences within 90 days of the due date (including extensions) for filing the gift tax return and is completed within a reasonable time after commencement. Treas. Reg. §25.2702-5(a)(2).

A *personal residence* is defined as either (1) the principal residence of the term holder, (2) a residence of the term holder which the term holder uses for personal use during the year for a number of days which exceeds the greater of 14 days or 10% of the days during the year that the residence is rented at fair market value, or (3) an undivided fractional interest in either (1) or (2). A personal residence includes appurtenant residential structures and a reasonable amount of land (taking into account the residence's size and location). Personal property, such as household furnishings, are not included in a personal residence. A personal residence is treated as such as long as it is not occupied by any other person (other than the spouse or a dependent) and is available at all times for use by the term holder as a personal residence. A personal residence can be rented out if the rental use is secondary to the primary use as a personal residence (but see above). Use of the residence as transient lodging is not permitted if substantial services are provided (e.g., a hotel or a bed and breakfast). Spouses may hold interests in the same personal residence or qualified personal residence trust. Treas. Regs. §§25.2702-5(b); 25.2702-5(c)(2).

A *personal residence trust* is a trust that is prohibited for the entire term of the trust from holding any property other than one residence to be used as the personal residence of the term holder(s). A personal residence trust cannot permit the personal residence to be sold, transferred, or put to any other use. Expenses of the trust can be paid by the term holder. A personal residence trust can hold proceeds payable as a result of damage to, or destruction or involuntary conversion of, the personal residence for reinvestment in a personal residence within two years of receipt of such proceeds. Treas. Reg. §25.2702-5(b).

A personal residence trust created after May 16, 1996 must be prohibited from selling or transferring, directly or indirectly, the residence to the grantor, the grantor's spouse, or an entity controlled by the grantor or the grantor's spouse, at any time after the original term interest during which the trust is a grantor trust. A distribution upon or after the expiration of the original duration of the trust term to another grantor trust of the grantor or the grantor's spouse pursuant to the trust terms will not be treated as a sale or transfer to the grantor or grantor's spouse if the second trust prohibits sale or transfer of the property to the grantor, the grantor's spouse, or an entity controlled by the grantor or the grantor's spouse. This prohibition against a transfer to the grantor or the grantor's spouse does not apply to a transfer pursuant to the trust document or a power retained by the grantor in the event the grantor dies prior to the expiration of the original duration of the trust term. Nor does this prohibition apply to a distribution (for no consideration) of the residence to the grantor's spouse pursuant to the trust document at the expiration of the original duration of the trust term. Treas. Regs. §§25.2702-5(b)(1), 25.2702-7.

A *qualified personal residence trust* (QPRT) is generally prohibited for the entire term of the trust from holding any property other than one residence to be used as the personal residence of the term holder(s), but certain exceptions are available. Thus, a qualified personal residence trust is permitted to hold cash in a separate account, but not in excess of the amount needed (1) for payment of trust expenses (including mortgage payments) currently due or expected within the next six months, (2) for improvements to the residence to be paid within the next six months, and (3) for purchase of a personal residence either (a) within three months of the creation of the trust, or (b) within the next three months pursuant to a previously entered into contract to purchase. Improvements to the personal residence that meet the personal residence requirements are permitted. Treas. Reg. §25.2702-5(c)(5).

Generally, sales proceeds (including income thereon) may be held in a qualified personal residence trust in a separate account until the earlier of (1) two years from the date of sale, (2) termination of the term holder's interest, or (3) purchase of a new residence. Insurance proceeds (including, for this purpose, certain amounts received upon an involuntary conversion) paid to a qualified personal residence trust for damage or destruction to the personal residence may also be held in the trust in a separate account for a similar period of time. Treas. Regs. §§25.2702-5(c)(5)(ii); 25.2702-5(c)(7).

A qualified personal residence trust created after May 16, 1996 must be prohibited from selling or transferring, directly or indirectly, the residence to the grantor, the grantor's spouse, or an entity controlled by the grantor or the grantor's spouse, during the original trust term and at any time after the original term interest during which the trust is a grantor trust. A distribution upon or after the expiration of the original duration of the trust term to another grantor trust of the grantor or the grantor's spouse pursuant to the trust terms will not be treated as a sale or transfer to the grantor or grantor's spouse if the second trust prohibits sale or transfer of the property to the grantor, the grantor's spouse, or an entity controlled by the grantor or the grantor's spouse. This prohibition against a transfer to the grantor or the grantor's spouse does not apply to a transfer pursuant to the trust document or a power retained by the grantor in the event the grantor dies prior to the expiration of the original duration of the trust term. Nor does this prohibition apply to a distribution (for no consideration) of the residence to the grantor's spouse pursuant to the trust document at the expiration of the original duration of the trust term. Treas. Regs. §§25.2702-5(c)(9), 25.2702-7.

Cash held by a qualified personal residence trust in excess of the amounts permitted above must be distributed to the term holder at least quarterly. Furthermore, upon termination of the term holder's interest, any cash held by a qualified personal residence trust for payment of trust expenses must be distributed to the term holder within 30 days. Treas. Reg. §25.2702-5(c)(5)(ii)(A)(2).

The qualified personal residence trust must provide that any trust income be distributed at least annually to the term holder. Treas. Reg. §25.2702-5(c)(3). Distributions from a qualified personal residence trust cannot be made to anyone other than the term holder during any term interest. Treas. Reg. §25.2702-5(c)(4). Commutation (generally, an actuarially based acceleration or substitution of benefits) of a qualified personal residence trust is not permitted. Treas. Reg. §25.2702-5(c)(6).

A qualified personal residence trust ceases to be a qualified personal residence trust if the residence ceases to be used or held for use as the personal residence of the term holder. A residence is held by the trust for use as the personal residence of the term holder so long as the residence is not occupied by any other person (other than the spouse or a dependent of the term holder) and is available at all times for use by the term holder. A sale of a personal residence is not treated as a cessation of use as a personal residence if the personal residence is replaced by another within two years of the sale. The trust must provide that if damage to or destruction of the residence renders it unusable as a residence, the trust ceases to be a qualified personal residence trust unless the residence is repaired or replaced within two years. Treas. Reg. §25.2702-5(c)(7).

A qualified personal residence trust must provide that within 30 days of ceasing to be a qualified personal residence trust with respect to any assets, either (1) the assets must be distributed to the term holder; (2) the assets must be put into a separate share of the trust for the balance of the term holder's interest as a qualified annuity interest; or (3) the trustee may elect either (1) or (2). The amount of such an annuity must be no less than the amount determined by dividing the lesser of the original value of all interests retained by the term holder or the value of all the trust assets by an annuity valuation factor reflecting the valuation table rate on the date of the original transfer and the original term of the term holder's interest. If only a portion of the trust continues as a qualified personal residence trust, then the annuity determined in the preceding sentence is reduced in proportion to the ratio that assets which still qualify as a personal residence trust bear to total trust assets. Treas. Reg. §25.2702-5(c)(8).

Remainder Interest Transactions and Joint Purchases

The transfer of an interest in property with respect to which there are one or more term interests (e.g., transfer of a remainder interest) is to be treated as a transfer of an interest in trust. IRC Sec. 2702(c)(1). A leasehold interest in property is not treated as a term interest provided a good faith effort is made to set the lease at a fair rental value. Treas. Reg. §25.2702-4(b). If a person acquires a term interest in property in a joint purchase (or series of related transactions) with members of his family, then such person is treated as though he acquired the entire property and then transferred the interests acquired by the other persons in the transaction to such persons in return for consideration furnished by such persons. IRC Sec. 2702(c)(2). For this purpose, the amount considered transferred by such individual is not to exceed the amount which such individual furnished for such property. Treas. Reg. §25.2702-4(c). Special rules apply to "qualified tangible property" (see above).

GENERAL   Q 914

Attribution

A "member of the family" with respect to an individual includes such individual's spouse, any ancestor or lineal descendant of such individual or such individual's spouse, any brother or sister of the individual, and any spouse of the above. IRC Sec. 2702(e). An "applicable family member" with respect to a transferor includes the transferor's spouse, an ancestor of the transferor or transferor's spouse, and the spouse of any such ancestor. IRC Secs. 2702(a)(1), 2701(e)(2).

Adjustment to Mitigate Double Taxation

A gift tax and estate tax adjustment is provided to mitigate the double taxation of retained interests previously valued under IRC Section 2702. In the case of a transfer by gift of a retained interest previously valued under IRC Section 2702 using the zero valuation rule or the qualified tangible property rule, a reduction in aggregate taxable gifts is available in calculating gift tax. If a retained interest previously valued under IRC Section 2702 using the zero valuation rule or using the qualified tangible property rule is later included in the gross estate, a reduction in adjusted taxable gifts is available in calculating estate tax. The amount of the reduction in aggregate taxable gifts or adjusted taxable gifts is equal to the lesser of (1) the increase in the taxable gifts resulting from the retained interest being initially valued under the zero valuation rule or the qualified tangible property rule, or (2) the increase in taxable gifts or gross estate resulting from the subsequent transfer of the interest. For purposes of (2), the annual exclusion is applied first to transfers other than the transfer valued under the zero valuation rule or the qualified tangible property rule. One-half of the amount of reduction may be assigned to a consenting spouse if gifts are split under IRC Section 2513. Treas. Reg. §25.2702-6.

Miscellaneous

These provisions apply to transfers after October 8, 1990. However, with respect to property transferred before October 9, 1990, any failure to exercise a right of conversion, to pay dividends, or to exercise other rights to be specified in regulations, is not to be treated as a subsequent transfer. OBRA '90, Sec. 11602(e)(1).

With respect to gifts made after October 8, 1990, the gift tax statute of limitations on a transfer subject to these provisions does not run unless the transaction is disclosed on a gift tax return in a manner adequate to apprise the IRS of the nature of the retained and transferred interests. IRC Sec. 6501(c)(9); OBRA '90, Sec. 11602(e)(2).

Effect on Trust, Remainder Interest, and Joint Purchase Transactions

GRITs, GRATs, and GRUTs

Generally, a grantor retained income trust (GRIT) should no longer be used unless the only property to be held by the trust is a residence to be used as a personal residence by persons holding term interests in the trust. Under IRC Section 2702, the grantor is treated as though he transferred the entire property to the remainderman at the time of the creation of the GRIT since his retained income interest is valued at zero (except with respect to the personal residence exception or unless the remainderman is not a member of the transferor's family). See Let. Rul. 9109033.

Instead, grantor retained annuity trusts (GRATs) and grantor retained unitrusts (GRUTs) can be used to leverage gifts. The retained annuity or unitrust interest is valued using the government valuation tables provided under IRC Section 7520 (see Q 910). Notes, other debt instruments, options or similar financial arrangements cannot be used in satisfaction of the annuity or unitrust requirements. The value of the transferred remainder interest is equal to the value of the entire property reduced by the value of the retained interest. A reversion or general power of appointment retained by the grantor which is contingent upon the grantor dying during the trust term will no longer reduce the value of the transferred property. However, the value of the retained interest is reduced by such a contingency.

Charitable Trusts

Transfers to charitable remainder annuity trusts (CRATs), certain charitable remainder unitrusts (CRUTs), and pooled income funds are not subject to IRC Section 2702. Also, IRC Section 2702 does not apply to a charitable lead trust in which the only interest in the trust other than the remainder interest or a qualified annuity or unitrust interest is the charitable lead interest. For transfers to a trust made after May 18, 1997, regulations exempt CRUTs from IRC Section 2702 only if the trust provides for simple unitrust payments, or in the case of a CRUT with a lesser of trust income or the unitrust amount provision, the grantor and/or the grantor's spouse (who is a citizen of the U.S.) are the only noncharitable beneficiaries. Treas. Reg. §25.2702-1(c)(3).

Irrevocable Life Insurance Trusts

Irrevocable life insurance trusts should not be affected by IRC Section 2702. Generally, the full value of transfers to an irrevocable life insurance trust are already treated as gifts (except to the extent that annual exclusions are available).

Other Trusts

If a term interest (whether for life or term of years) is given to the transferor's spouse, an ancestor of the transferor or transferor's spouse, or the spouse of any such ancestor, and a remainder interest is given to any member of the transferor's family, IRC Section 2702 should not apply because the grantor has not retained a term interest.

Remainder Interest Transaction (RIT)

In general, if a person retains a term interest (whether for life or term of years) in property and sells or gives a remainder interest in the property to another family member, the value of the transferred property will be equal to the full value of the property unless the transferor retained an annuity or unitrust interest in the property (i.e., the value of a retained income interest is valued at zero).

However, if the nonexercise of rights under a term interest in tangible property would not have a substantial effect on the valuation of the remainder interest, the interest is valued at the amount for which it could be sold to an unrelated third person (i.e., market value is used instead of the valuation tables or zero valuation). The Senate Committee Report to OBRA '90 gives a painting, or undeveloped real estate, as examples of such tangible property. Depletable property is given as an example of property which would not qualify for this special rule. See "Qualified Tangible Property," above.

Split Purchases (Splits)

If a person acquires a term interest in property in a joint purchase (or series of related transactions) with members of his family, then such person is treated as though he acquired the entire property and then transferred the interests acquired by the other persons in the transaction to such persons in return for consideration furnished by such

GENERAL   Q 915

persons. Thus, if a father and son purchase rental property and the father receives an interest for life and the son receives a remainder interest, the father is treated as though he sold the remainder interest to his son for the consideration furnished by the son. The transaction is then essentially treated as a sale of a remainder interest (see above).

915. What special valuation rules apply to certain agreements, options, rights or restrictions exercisable at less than fair market value under Chapter 14?

For estate, gift, and generation-skipping transfer tax purposes, the value of any property is to be determined without regard to any restriction on the right to sell or use such property, or any option, agreement or other right to acquire or use the property at less than fair market value (determined without regard to such an option, agreement, or right). However, the previous sentence is not to apply if the option, agreement, right, or restriction (1) is a bona fide business arrangement, (2) is not a device to transfer the property to members of the decedent's family for less than full and adequate consideration in money or money's worth, and (3) has terms comparable to those entered into by persons in an arm's length transaction. IRC Sec. 2703. The three prongs of the test must be independently satisfied. Treas. Reg. §25.2703-1(b)(2). All three prongs of the test are considered met if more than 50% of the value of the property subject to the right or restriction is owned by persons who are not members of the transferor's family or natural objects of the transferor's bounty. The property owned by such other persons must be subject to the right or restriction to the same extent as the property owned by the transferor. Treas. Reg. §25.2703-1(b)(3).

To determine whether a buy-sell agreement or other restrictive agreement has terms comparable to those entered into by persons in an arm's length transaction, the following factors are to be considered: "the expected term of the agreement, the current fair market value of the property, anticipated changes in value during the term of the agreement, and the adequacy of any consideration given in exchange for the rights granted." Treas. Reg. §25.2703-1(b)(4)(i). The terms of a buy-sell agreement or other restrictive agreement must be comparable to those used as a general practice by unrelated persons under negotiated agreements in the same business. Isolated comparables do not meet this requirement. More than one recognized method may be acceptable. Where comparables are difficult to find because the business is unique, comparables from similar businesses may be used. Treas. Reg. §25.2703-1(b)(4)(ii).

In the case of a partnership (or LLC) created on a decedent's deathbed, the IRS has stated that the partnership was the agreement for purposes of IRC Section 2703, and the partnership should be ignored because the partnership was not a valid business arrangement and the partnership was a device to transfer the underlying property to the family members for less than adequate consideration. Even if the partnership was not ignored, the Service stated that it would ignore the restrictions on use of the property contained in the partnership's agreement; such restrictions also would fail IRC Section 2703. TAMs 9723009, 9725002, 9730004, 9735003, 9736004, 9842003. A few courts have rejected the idea that the partnership can be ignored for purposes of IRC Section 2703. *Est. of Strangi v. Comm.*, 2002 USTC ¶60,441 (5th Cir. 2002), aff'g 115 TC 478 (2000); *Church v. U.S.*, 2000-1 USTC ¶60,369 (W.D. Tex. 2000).

For more information on valuing a closely held business interest, see Q 613, Q 706.

2006 Tax Facts on Insurance & Employee Benefits

Effective Date and Transition Rules

This provision applies to agreements, options, rights or restrictions entered into or granted after October 8, 1990, and agreements, options, rights or restrictions substantially modified after October 8, 1990. OBRA '90, Sec. 11602(e)(1)((A)(ii). Any discretionary modification of an agreement that results in other than a de minimis change in the quality, value, or timing of the agreement is a substantial modification. Generally, a modification required by the agreement is not considered a substantial modification. However, if the agreement requires periodic modification, the failure to update the agreement is treated as a substantial modification unless the updating would not have resulted in a substantial modification. The addition of a family member as a party to a right or restriction is treated as a substantial modification unless (1) the addition is mandatory under the terms of the right or restriction or (2) the added family member is in a generation (using the generation-skipping transfer tax definitions of generations) no lower than the lowest generation of any individuals already party to the right or restriction. The modification of a capitalization rate in a manner that bears a fixed relationship to a specified market rate is not treated as a substantial modification. Furthermore, a modification that results in an option price that more closely approximates fair market value is not treated as a substantial modification. Treas. Reg. §25.2703-1(c).

Effect on Options and Buy-sell Agreements

In order to help fix values for estate, gift and generation-skipping transfer tax purposes, newly executed or substantially modified options and buy-sell agreements exercisable at less than fair market value between persons who are the natural objects of each others' bounty will generally have to meet all three requirements of IRC Section 2703. Otherwise, such agreement will be disregarded in valuing the property. Old options and buy-sell agreements which are not substantially modified after October 8, 1990 are not affected by IRC Section 2703. IRC Section 2703 applies to agreements involving either business or nonbusiness property.

916. What special valuation rules apply to certain lapsing rights and restrictions under Chapter 14?

In general, IRC Section 2704(a) provides that the lapse of certain voting or liquidation rights in a family owned business results in a taxable transfer by the holder of the lapsing right. IRC Section 2704(b) provides generally that certain restrictions on liquidating a family owned business are ignored in valuing a transferred interest. These provisions apply to restrictions or rights (or limitations on rights) created after October 8, 1990. OBRA '90, Sec. 11602(e)(1)(A)(iii).

For more information on valuing a closely held business interest, see Q 613.

Lapse of Certain Rights

For estate, gift, and generation-skipping transfer tax purposes, if there is a lapse of a voting or liquidation right in a corporation or partnership and the individual holding such right (the "holder") immediately before the lapse and members of the holder's family control the entity (both before and after the lapse), then the holder is treated as making a transfer. The value of the transfer is equal to the amount (if any) by which the value of all interests in the entity held by the holder immediately prior to the lapse (determined as if all voting and liquidation rights were nonlapsing) exceeds the sum of

GENERAL   Q 916

(1) the value of such interests immediately after the lapse (determined as if held by one individual), and (2) in the case of a lapse during the holder's life, any consideration in money or money's worth received by the holder with respect to such lapse. IRC Sec. 2704(a); Treas. Regs. §§25.2704-1(a), 25.2704-1(d).

A *voting right* is defined as a right to vote with respect to *any* matter of the entity. Also, with respect to a partnership, the right of a general partner to participate in partnership management is treated as a voting right. A *liquidation right* is the right to compel (including by aggregate voting power) the entity to acquire *all or a portion* of the holder's equity interest in the entity. Treas. Reg. §25.2704-1(a)(2). A lapse of a voting or liquidation right occurs when a presently exercisable right is restricted or eliminated. Treas. Regs. §§25.2704-1(b), 25.2704-1(c)(1).

The transfer of an interest which results in the lapse of a liquidation right is not subject to IRC Section 2704(a) if the rights with respect to the transferred interest are not restricted or eliminated. However, a transfer that results in the elimination of the transferor's right to compel the entity to acquire an interest of the transferor which is subordinate to the transferred interest is treated as a lapse of a liquidation right with respect to the subordinate interest. The lapse rule does not apply to the lapse of a liquidation right with respect to (1) a transfer that was previously valued in the hands of the holder as a transfer of an interest in a corporation or partnership under IRC Section 2701 (see Q 913), or (2) the lapse of a liquidation right to the extent that immediately after the lapse the holder (or the holder's estate) and members of the holder's family cannot liquidate an interest that the holder could have liquidated prior to the lapse. Whether an interest can be liquidated immediately after the lapse is determined under state law or, if the governing instruments are less restrictive than the state law which would apply in the absence of such instruments, the governing instruments. For this purpose, any applicable restriction under IRC Section 2704(b) (see below) is disregarded. Treas. Reg. §25.2704-1(c).

If a lapsed right may be restored only upon the occurrence of a future event not within the control of the holder or the holder's family, the lapse is deemed to occur at the time the lapse becomes permanent with respect to the holder (e.g., upon the transfer of the interest). Treas. Reg. §25.2704-1(a)(3).

For attribution rules, see below.

Transfers Subject to Applicable Restrictions

If there is a transfer of an interest in a corporation or partnership to (or for the benefit of) a member of the transferor's family and the transferor and members of transferor's family control the entity (immediately before the transfer), any applicable restriction is to be disregarded in valuing the transferred interest for estate, gift, or generation-skipping transfer tax purposes. IRC Sec. 2704(b)(1). If an applicable restriction is disregarded under this rule, the rights of the transferor are valued under the state law that would apply but for the limitation (which is treated as if it did not exist). Treas. Reg. §25.2704-2(c).

"Applicable restriction" means any restriction which effectively limits the ability of the corporation or partnership to liquidate if either (1) the restriction lapses (in whole or in part) after the transfer, or (2) the transferor or any member of the transferor's family, acting alone or collectively, can remove the restriction (in whole or in part) after the

2006 Tax Facts on Insurance & Employee Benefits   889

transfer. IRC Sec. 2704(b)(2). Applicable restriction treatment was avoided where the consent of all parties was required and a charity (a nonfamily member) had become a partner. *Kerr v. Comm.*, 2002-1 USTC ¶60,440 (5th Cir. 2002).

However, any restriction imposed or required by any federal or state law is not treated as an applicable restriction. IRC Sec. 2704(b)(3)(B). Thus, the definition of an applicable restriction has been limited to a restriction which is more restrictive than the limitations which would apply under state law if there were no restriction. Also, whether there is the ability to remove a restriction is determined under the state law which would apply in the absence of the restrictive provision in the governing instruments. Treas. Reg. §25.2704-2(b).

An applicable restriction does not include any commercially reasonable restriction which arises as part of any financing by the corporation or partnership with a person who is not related to the transferor or transferee, or a member of the family of either. IRC Sec. 2704(b)(3)(A). Regulations provide that an applicable restriction does not include any commercially reasonable restriction which arises as a result of any unrelated person providing capital in the form of debt or equity to the corporation or partnership for the entity's trade or business operations. For this purpose, the regulations apply the relationship rules of IRC Section 267(b), except that the term "fiduciary of a trust" under the relationship rules is modified to generally exclude banks, trust companies, and building and loan associations. Treas. Reg. §25.2704-2(b).

Furthermore, an applicable restriction does not include an option, right to use property, or other agreement subject to IRC Section 2703 (see Q 915). Treas. Reg. §25.2704-2(b).

With respect to a partnership (or LLC) created on a decedent's deathbed, the IRS has disregarded restrictions where the partnership provided that a partner could not liquidate his interest, while state law provided a less restrictive provision. TAMs 9723009, 9725002, 9730004, 9735003, 9736004, 9842003. For a few cases that have held that partnership liquidation provisions were no more restrictive than state law and should not be ignored under IRC Section 2704(b), see *Kerr v. Comm.*, 113 TC 449 (1999); *Knight v. Comm.*, 115 TC 506 (2000).

Attribution

The following attribution rules or definitions generally apply for purposes of the rules which apply to certain lapsing rights and applicable restrictions under IRC Section 2704.

In the case of a corporation, "control" means 50% ownership (by vote or value) of the stock. In the case of a partnership, "control" means 50% ownership of the capital or profits interests, or in the case of a limited partnership, the ownership of any interest as a general partner. IRC Secs. 2704(c)(1), 2701(b)(2).

A "member of the family" with respect to an individual includes such individual's spouse, any ancestor or lineal descendant of such individual or such individual's spouse, any brother or sister of the individual, and any spouse of the above. IRC Sec. 2704(c)(2).

An individual is treated as holding interests held indirectly through a corporation, partnership, trust, or other entity. IRC Secs. 2704(c)(3), 2701(e)(3). Thus, transfers may be either direct or indirect.

GENERAL   Q 917

EXCLUSIONS

917. What gift tax exclusions are available to a donor?

The Annual Exclusion

A donor can give up to $10,000 as indexed ($12,000 in 2006, see Appendix B for amounts in other years) in money or property to *each* donee in *each* calendar year free of gift tax using the gift tax annual exclusion. The $10,000 amount is adjusted for inflation, rounded down to the next lowest multiple of $1,000, after 1998. IRC Sec. 2503(b). However, the gifts must be outright gifts or gifts of "present interest" to qualify for these annual exclusions (see Q 918). The annual exclusions are available for gifts to *any number of donees* and *for an unlimited number of years*. For example, based upon the annual exclusion as indexed for 2006, a parent can give each of his four children $12,000 a year for 10 years (a total of $480,000), and none of the gifts would be subject to tax. The exclusions are not cumulative, however; exclusions unused in one year cannot be carried over and used in a succeeding year. A donor is not required to file a return for (or include in a filed return) outright gifts totaling no more than the annual exclusion ($12,000 in 2006, see Appendix B) to any one person in a calendar year; total gifts in excess of the annual exclusion to one person in one year must be reported, and the donor takes the annual exclusion against the total on his return.

If a donor transfers a specified portion of real property subject to an "adjustment clause" (i.e., under terms that provide that if the IRS subsequently determines that the value of the specified portion exceeds the amount of the annual exclusion, the portion of property given will be reduced accordingly, or the donee will compensate the donor for the excess), the adjustment clause will be disregarded for federal tax purposes. Rev. Rul. 86-41, 1986-1 CB 300.

A married donor can exclude gifts of up to $24,000 a year (2 × $12,000 annual exclusion in 2006) to each donee if his spouse consents to the gifts (see Q 907). Thus, the tax-free gifts to the four children in the example above could be doubled with consent of donor's spouse. However, if, say, the donor has a married brother with children, and the donor and his wife make gifts to his brother's children in exchange for similar gifts from the brother and his wife to the donor's children, the scheme will not effectively again double the exclusion. TAM 8717003; *Sather v. Comm.*, 2001-1 USTC ¶60,409 (8th Cir. 2001); *Schuler v. Comm.*, 2002-1 USTC ¶60,432 (8th Cir. 2002).

In the case of a present interest gift between spouses, the annual exclusion is applied before the gift tax marital deduction is taken, when computing taxable gifts for the calendar year (see Q 902, Q 920). IRC Sec. 2503(b).

If the spouse of the donor is not a United States citizen, the annual exclusion for a transfer from the donor spouse to the non-citizen spouse is increased from $10,000 to $100,000 ($120,000 as indexed in 2006, see Appendix B for amounts in other years) (provided the transfer would otherwise qualify for the marital deduction if the donee spouse were a United States citizen). The $100,000 amount is adjusted for inflation, as is the $10,000 amount (see above). IRC Sec. 2523(i). However, the marital deduction is not available for a transfer to a spouse who is not a United States citizen (see Q 920).

Exclusion for "Qualified Transfers"

A "qualified transfer" is not considered a gift for gift tax purposes. A "qualified transfer" means any amount paid on behalf of an individual—

(A) as tuition to an educational organization (described in IRC Section 170(b)(1)(A)(ii)) for the education or training of such individual, or

(B) to any person who provides medical care (as defined in IRC Section 213(e)) with respect to such individual as payment for such medical care. IRC Sec. 2503(e); Rev. Rul. 82-98, 1982-1 CB 141. A technical advice memorandum treated tuition payments for future years as qualified transfers where the payments were nonrefundable. TAM 199941013. *ASRS, Sec. 55, ¶57.6*.

918. What is a gift of a "future interest" that will not qualify for the gift tax annual exclusion?

An outright gift, or gift of a "present interest," will qualify for the gift tax annual exclusion (see Q 917), but the gift of a "future interest" will not. IRC Sec. 2503(b). Generally speaking, a "future interest" is a right to use property only in the future. But the mere fact that a bond, note, or insurance policy is *payable* in the future does not make ownership of it a "future interest." Treas. Reg. §25.2503-3(a). Ordinarily, the future interest question arises in connection with gifts in trust. The income beneficiary usually has a present interest, and the remainder beneficiary a future interest. But if the income is to be accumulated, everyone has a future interest (except in certain circumstances as, for example, where a beneficiary can demand the trust principal (see Q 726), or where a trust for a minor meets the requirements of IRC Section 2503(c) below). If the trust is revocable, the gift is not complete until an actual distribution is made to a beneficiary, at which time the gift is a present interest gift. If the grantor of a revocable trust dies before distribution is made, the value of the trust corpus and accumulated income is included in his gross estate for estate tax purposes and is not subject to the gift tax.

There is a special provision with respect to gifts to minors—IRC Section 2503(c). If a gift to a minor meets the conditions set forth in IRC Section 2503(c), the gift can qualify for the exclusion even though the income is to be accumulated during the beneficiary's minority. Under IRC Section 2503(c), a gift to a minor will qualify for the exclusion if, under the terms of the trust or other instrument of gift, the property given (1) may be expended by, or for the benefit of, the donee before his attaining age 21, and (2) will to the extent not so expended (a) pass to the donee on his attaining age 21, or (b) if he dies before age 21, be payable to his estate or as he may appoint under a general power of appointment. A gift in trust to a minor is separable for tax purposes. If trust provisions regarding income earned before the donee is age 21 meet the requirements of IRC Section 2503(c), the annual exclusion is available for the value of such income interest even though provisions for interest earned after the donee is 21 (if any) or provisions for disposition of the principal do not allow the interests in post-21 income or principal to qualify for the exclusion. *Herr v. Comm.*, 35 TC 732 (1961), aff'd 303 F.2d 780 (3rd Cir. 1962), acq. 1968-2 CB 2; *Konner v. Comm.*, 35 TC 727 (1961), acq. 1968-2 CB 2; *Weller v. Comm.*, 38 TC 790 (1962), acq. 1968-2 CB 3; *Rollman v. U.S.*, 342 F.2d 62 (Ct. Cl. 1965); *Thebaut v. Comm.*, TC Memo 1964-102, aff'd in part, rev'd in part 361 F.2d 428 (5th Cir. 1966); *Pettus v. Comm.*, 54 TC 10 (1970); *Est. of Levine v. Comm.*, 526 F.2d 717 (2nd Cir. 1976), rev'g 63 TC 136, nonacq. 1978-2 CB 3; Rev. Rul. 68-670, 1968-2 CB 413.

A gift of an income interest will not qualify for the annual exclusion if the donor is unable to prove that the income interest has any real value. Thus, the exclusion has been denied for gifts of an income interest in close corporation stock which had no dividend paying history and no likelihood of paying dividends in the foreseeable future. *Stark v. U.S.*, 477 F.2d 131 (8th Cir. 1973), aff'g 345 F. Supp. 1263 (W.D. Mo. 1972), cert. den. 94 S. Ct. 290; *Berzon v. Comm.*, 534 F.2d 528 (2nd Cir. 1976), aff'g 63 TC 601. Also, a gift of an income interest must be distinguished from a gift of periodic dollar amounts. Thus, for example, a gift of $100,000 to an irrevocable trust which directs the trustee to pay the income annually to B is a present interest gift. But the same gift to a trust which directs the trustee to pay $10,000 annually to B is a gift of a future interest that does not qualify for the exclusion. *Est. of Kolker v. Comm.*, 80 TC 1082 (1983). Annual exclusions were denied for gifts of limited partnership interests where (1) the general partner could retain income for any reason whatsoever, (2) limited partnership interests could not be transferred or assigned without the permission of a supermajority of other partners, and (3) limited partnership interests generally could not withdraw from the partnership or receive a return of capital contributions for many years into the future. TAM 9751003. Similarly, annual exclusions were denied for gifts of business interests where the beneficiaries were not free to withdraw from the business entity, could not sell their interests, and could not control whether any income would be distributed (and no immediate income was expected). *Hackl v. Comm.*, 2003-2 ¶USTC 60,465 (7th Cir. 2003), aff'g 118 TC 279 (2002).

A gift of property to a corporation is a gift of a future interest in the property to its shareholders and does not qualify for the annual exclusion. Rev. Rul. 71-443, 1971-2 CB 337; Treas. Reg. §25.2511-1(h)(1); *Stinson v. U.S.*, 2000-1 USTC ¶60,377 (7th Cir. 2000); *Hollingsworth v. Comm.*, 86 TC 91 (1986). Also a gift for the benefit of a corporation (transfer of stock to certain key employees) is a gift of a future interest in the property to its shareholders and does not qualify for the annual exclusion. Let. Rul. 9114023. However, gifts made to individual partnership capital accounts have been treated as gifts of a present interest which qualify for the annual exclusion where the partners were free to make immediate withdrawals of the gifts from their capital accounts. *Wooley v. U.S.*, 90-1 USTC ¶60,013 (S.D. Ind. 1990). Also, a donor's gratuitous payment of the monthly amount due on the mortgage on a house owned in joint tenancy by others has been held a present interest gift to the joint tenants in proportion to their ownership interests. Rev. Rul. 82-98, 1982-1 CB 141. *ASRS, Sec. 51, ¶230.*

919. Does a gift to a minor under a state's Uniform Gifts to Minors Act or Uniform Transfers to Minors Act qualify for the gift tax annual exclusion?

Generally, yes. Rev. Rul. 56-86, 1956-1 CB 449; Rev. Rul. 59-357, 1959-2 CB 212; Let. Rul. 8327060. The allowance of the exclusion is not affected by the amendment of a state's Uniform Act lowering the age of majority and thus requiring that property be distributed to the donee at age 18. Rev. Rul. 73-287, 1973-2 CB 321. These rulings base the allowance of the exclusion on the assumption that gifts under the Uniform Act come within the purview of IRC Section 2503(c). Gifts to minors under IRC Section 2503(c) must pass to the donee on his attaining age 21 (see Q 918). If a state statute varies from the Uniform Act by providing that under certain conditions custodianship may be extended past the donee's age 21, gifts made under those conditions would not qualify for the exclusion. *ASRS, Sec. 51, ¶230.2(d).*

DEDUCTIONS

920. What is the gift tax marital deduction?

It is a deduction allowed for gifts of interests in property (including cash) between spouses in an amount equal to the value of such gifts made after 1981. IRC Sec. 2523(a).

Outright gifts to the spouse qualify for the deduction. However, the marital deduction cannot be taken if the gift is of a life estate or other terminable interest unless it meets certain statutory requirements for qualification. In general, these are the same requirements necessary to qualify a terminable interest for the estate tax marital deduction; that is, the donee spouse must have (1) a right to the income from the property for life and a general power of appointment over the principal; or, (2) a "qualifying income interest for life" in "qualified terminable interest property," as to which the donor must make an election (on or before the date, including extensions, for filing a gift tax return with respect to the year in which the transfer was made – see Q 901) to have the marital deduction apply (see Q 864). As to qualifying a joint and survivor annuity for the marital deduction, see Q 731. The marital deduction will also apply to the value of a donee spouse's income interest in a "qualified charitable remainder trust" created by the donor spouse if the donee spouse is the only noncharitable beneficiary of the trust other than certain ESOP remainder beneficiaries (see Q 864). IRC Sec. 2523(e)-(g). A marital deduction has been disallowed for a transfer to an irrevocable trust where state law provided that the interest given the spouse would be revoked upon divorce and the grantor had not provided in the trust instrument that the trust would not be revoked upon divorce. TAM 9127005.

If the spouse of the donor is not a United States citizen, the marital deduction is not available for a transfer to such a spouse. However, in such a case, the annual exclusion (see Q 917) for the transfer from the donor spouse to the non-citizen spouse is increased from $10,000 to $100,000 as indexed ($120,000 in 2006, see Appendix B) (provided the transfer would otherwise qualify for the marital deduction if the donee spouse were a United States citizen). The $100,000 amount is adjusted for inflation, as is the $10,000 amount (see Q 917). IRC Sec. 2523(i). *ASRS, Sec. 51, ¶280.*

921. Is the federal gift tax imposed on gifts to charitable organizations?

No. A deduction is allowed for the value of the gift. However, no deduction is allowed for a lead interest in a trust unless the payments to the charity are in the form of a guaranteed annuity, or a fixed percentage distributed yearly of the fair market value of the property (to be determined yearly). No deduction is allowed for a remainder interest in a trust unless the interest is in the form of a charitable remainder annuity trust, a charitable remainder unitrust, or a pooled income fund (see Q 825). IRC Sec. 2522. A deduction is allowable for a gift to charity of a legal remainder interest in the donor's personal residence even though the interest conveyed to charity is in the form of a tenancy in common with an individual. Rev. Rul. 87-37, 1987-1 CB 295, revoking Rev. Rul. 76-544, 1976-2 CB 288. If an individual creates a qualified charitable remainder trust in which his spouse is the only noncharitable beneficiary other than certain ESOP remainder beneficiaries (see Q 864), the grantor will receive a charitable contributions deduction for the value of the remainder interest. IRC

GENERAL   Q 922

Sec. 2522(c)(2). However, if the property in the trust is "qualified terminable interest property" and the donee spouse's interest is a "qualifying income interest for life," (see Q 864), it would appear that the charitable contributions deduction could be taken by the donee spouse if and when she disposes of her income interest during life, assuming the donor spouse elected to take the marital deduction for the entire value of the property. H. Rep. 97-201, p. 162, n. 4. A gift tax charitable deduction is allowed for a gift to a qualified charity which is made in exchange for an annuity issued by the charity if (1) the value of the gift exceeds the value of the annuity, and (2) the annuity is payable out of the general funds of the charity. The annuity is valued by applying the estate and gift tax valuation tables (see Q 910). Rev. Rul. 84-162, 1984-2 CB 200. *ASRS, Sec. 55, ¶57.10.*

UNIFIED CREDIT

922. What is the unified credit, and how is it applied against the gift tax?

The unified credit is a dollar amount allotted to each taxpayer which can be applied against the gift tax and the estate tax (but see Q 868). The gift tax unified credit is equal to $345,800 in 2006 which translates into a tentative tax base (or unified credit exemption equivalent or applicable exclusion amount) of $1,000,000 in 2006. See Appendix B for amounts in other years (and estate tax amounts). Application of the credit against the gift tax reduces (by the amount used) the credit that would otherwise be available against future gifts and against any estate tax later imposed on transfers from the donor's estate (see IRC Sections 2505(a), 2001(b)). With respect to gifts made after September 8, 1976 and before January 1, 1977, if the donor elected to apply any of his $30,000 lifetime exemption to such gifts, the donor's unified credit is reduced by 20% of the amount of the exemption allowed against those gifts (see IRC Section 2505(b), and also Q 868). IRC Sec. 2505.

The following examples illustrate the application of the unified credit against the gift tax:

Example 1. D made a gift in October 1976. He elected to use $10,000 of his lifetime exemption to reduce the amount of the taxable gift. It was the only gift D made between September 8, 1976 and January 1, 1977, against which he elected to apply any of his lifetime exemption. In April 1977, D made his next taxable gift (the only gift he made in that quarter), on which the gift tax imposed was $5,000. The amount of unified credit allowable was $4,000 ($6,000 reduced by 20% of $10,000, or $2,000).

Example 2. In September 1977, D (same donor) made his next taxable gift (the only taxable gift he made in that quarter), on which the gift tax imposed was $50,000. The amount of unified credit allowable was $24,000 ($30,000 reduced by the sum of $4,000 and $2,000).

Example 3. In June 1980, D (same donor) made his next taxable gift (the only taxable gift he made in that quarter), on which the tax imposed was $10,000. The amount of unified credit allowable is $10,000. ($42,500 reduced by the sum of $24,000, $4,000 and $2,000 is $12,500; but the credit allowable cannot exceed the amount of the tax.)

Example 4. In January 2006, D (same donor) makes his next taxable gift (the only taxable gift he makes in the calendar year), on which the tax imposed is $100,000. The amount of unified credit allowable is $100,000. ($345,800 reduced by the sum of $10,000, $24,000, $4,000 and $2,000 is $305,800; but the credit allowable cannot exceed the amount of the tax.)

Where the donor makes a gift conditioned on the donee's paying the gift tax (see Q 911), it is the *donor's* unified credit that is applied against the tax, not the donee's. Let. Rul. 7842068. Moreover, use of the unified credit is not optional. That is, in the foregoing situation the donor may not require the donee to forego taking the credit, pay the tax, and thus save the unified credit undiminished for use against the tax on a subsequent gift or against the donor's estate tax; the unified credit must be applied when it is available. Rev. Rul. 79-398, 1979-2 CB 338; Let. Rul. 8132011. *ASRS, Sec. 55, ¶57.7.*

TAX ON GENERATION-SKIPPING TRANSFERS

GENERAL

950. What is a generation-skipping transfer (GST) on which a generation-skipping transfer tax (GST tax) is imposed?

In general, it is a transfer to a person two or more generations younger than the transferor (called a "skip person"; see Q 952 regarding generation assignments), and can take any one of three forms: (1) a taxable distribution, (2) a taxable termination, and (3) a direct skip. A trust is also a skip person if the trust can benefit only persons two or more generations younger than the transferor. IRC Secs. 2611(a), 2613. The GST tax is repealed for one year in 2010. Technically, EGTRRA 2001 repeals the GST tax for transfers after 2009. However, EGTRRA 2001 sunsets (or expires) after 2010. IRC Sec. 2664; EGTRRA 2001 Sec. 901.

Transferor

A "transferor," in the case of any property subject to the federal estate tax, is the decedent. In the case of any property subject to the federal gift tax, the transferor is the donor. IRC Sec. 2652(a)(1). Thus, to the extent that a lapse of a general power of appointment (including a right of withdrawal) is subject to gift or estate tax (see Q 727), the powerholder becomes the transferor with respect to such lapsed amount. Treas. Reg. §26.2652-1(a). Thus, a *Crummey* powerholder should not be treated as a transferor with respect to the lapse of a withdrawal power if the amount lapsing in any year is no greater than (1) $5,000, or (2) 5% of the assets out of which exercise of the power could be satisfied (see Q 727). Let. Rul. 9541029.

If there is a generation-skipping transfer of any property and immediately after such transfer such property is held in trust, a different rule (the "multiple skip" rule) applies to subsequent transfers from such trust. In such case, the trust is treated as if the transferor (for purposes of subsequent transfers) were assigned to the first generation above the highest generation of any person having an "interest" (see below) in such trust immediately after such transfer. IRC Sec. 2653(a). If no person holds an interest immediately after the GST, then the transferor is assigned to the first generation above the highest generation of any person in existence at the time of the GST who may subsequently hold an interest in the trust. Treas. Reg. §26.2653-1.

For the effect of making a "reverse QTIP election," see Q 951.

Direct Skip

A direct skip is a transfer subject to federal gift or estate tax to a skip person. IRC Sec. 2612(c). However, with respect to transfers before 1998, such a transfer was not a direct skip if the transfer was to a grandchild of the transferor or of the transferor's spouse or former spouse, and the grandchild's parent who was the lineal descendant of the transferor or his spouse or former spouse was dead at the time of the transfer. In other words, a person could be stepped-up in generations because a parent who had been in the line of descent predeceased such person. This rule could be reapplied to lineal descendants below that of a grandchild. Persons assigned to a generation under this rule were also assigned to such generation when such persons received transfers from the portion of a trust attributable to property to which the step-up in generation rule applied. IRC Sec. 2612(c)(2), prior to amendment by TRA '97. For purposes of this predeceased child rule, a living descendant who died no later than 90 days after a transferor was treated as predeceasing the transferor if treated as predeceased under the governing instrument or state law. Treas. Reg. §26.2612-1(a)(2)(i). For a more expansive predeceased parent rule after 1997, see Q 952.

In some circumstances, whether a step-up in generation was available could depend on whether a QTIP or a reverse QTIP marital election was made for GST tax purposes (see Q 951). If the parent of a grandchild-distributee died after the transfer by a grandparent to a generation-skipping trust but before the distribution from the trust to the grandchild and a reverse QTIP election had been made, the distribution was a taxable termination and the "step-up in generation" rule was not available. However, if the reverse QTIP election had not been made, the distribution was eligible for the "step-up in generation" exception from treatment as a direct skip and was not subject to GST tax. Rev. Rul. 92-26, 1992-1 CB 314.

Also, for purposes of the GST tax, the term "direct skip" did not include any transfer before January 1, 1990, from a transferor to a grandchild of the transferor to the extent that the aggregate transfers from such transferor to such grandchild did not exceed $2 million. This $2 million exemption was available with respect to a transfer in trust only if (1) during the life of such individual no portion of the trust corpus or income could be distributed to or for the benefit of any other person, (2) the trust would be included in such individual's estate if such individual were to die before the trust terminated, and (3) all of the income of the trust had to be distributed at least annually to the grandchild once he reached 21. Requirement (3) applied only to transfers after June 10, 1987. However, the Committee Report indicated that this requirement was not satisfied by a *Crummey* demand power. TRA '86, Sec. 1433(b)(3), as amended by TAMRA '88, Sec. 1014(h)(3).

The $2 million per grandchild exemption applied to transfers to grandchildren only; the step-up in generation rule for a predeceased parent did not apply. A transfer which would have been a direct skip were it not for the $2 million exemption was likewise exempted from being treated as a taxable termination or taxable distribution. However, the rules which apply to the taxation of multiple skips will apply to subsequent transfers from such trust.

Taxable Termination

A taxable termination occurs when an "interest in property" (see below) held in trust (or some arrangement having substantially the same effect as a trust) for a skip person is terminated by an individual's death, lapse of time, release of a power, or otherwise, unless either (1) a non-skip person has an interest in the trust immediately after such termination, or (2) at no time after the termination may a distribution be made from the trust to a skip person, other than a distribution the probability of which occurring is so remote as to be negligible (i.e., less than a 5% actuarial probability). If upon the termination of an interest in a trust by reason of the death of a lineal descendant of the transferor, a portion of the trust is distributed to skip persons (or to trusts for such persons), such partial termination is treated as taxable. If a transfer subject to estate or gift tax occurs at the time of the termination, the transfer is not a taxable termination (but it may be a direct skip). IRC Sec. 2612(a); Treas. Reg. §26.2612-1(b).

Taxable Distribution

A taxable distribution is any distribution from a trust to a skip person (other than a taxable termination or a direct skip). IRC Sec. 2612(b).

Generation-Skipping Transfer Exceptions

However, the following are not considered generation-skipping transfers:

(1) Any transfer which, if made during life by an individual, would be a "qualified transfer" (see Q 917); and

(2) Any transfer to the extent (a) the property transferred was subject to a prior GST tax, (b) the transferee in the prior transfer was in the same generation as the current transferee or a younger generation, and (c) the transfers do not have the effect of avoiding the GST tax. IRC Sec. 2611(b).

Interest in Property

A person has an "interest in property" held in trust if (at the time the determination is made) such person–

(1) has a present right to receive income or corpus from the trust (e.g., a life income interest);

(2) is a permissible current recipient of income or corpus from the trust (Ex: a beneficiary entitled to distribution of income or corpus, but only in the discretion of the trustee) and is not a charitable organization (specifically, one described in IRC Section 2055(a); or

(3) is such a charitable organization and the trust is a charitable remainder annuity trust, a charitable remainder unitrust, or a pooled income fund (see Q 825).

In determining whether a person has an interest in a trust, the fact that income or corpus may be used to satisfy a support obligation is disregarded if such use is discretionary or made pursuant to the Uniform Gifts to Minors Act (or similar state statute). In other words, a parent is not treated as having an interest in a trust merely because the parent acts as guardian for a child. However, a parent would be treated as having an interest in the trust if support obligations are mandatory. IRC Sec. 2652(c)(3).

An interest may be disregarded if it is used *primarily* to postpone or avoid the generation-skipping tax. IRC Sec. 2652(c)(2). The regulations provide that an interest is disregarded if *a significant purpose* for the creation of the interest is the postponement or avoidance of the generation-skipping tax. Treas. Reg. §26.2612-1(e)(2)(ii).

Effective Date and Transitional Rules

The rules explained here and in the succeeding questions apply generally to any generation-skipping transfer made after October 22, 1986. Also, any lifetime transfer after September 25, 1985, and on or before October 22, 1986, is treated as if made on October 23, 1986. These rules will not, however, apply to the following:

(1) Any GST under a trust that was irrevocable on September 25, 1985, but only to the extent that such transfer is not made out of corpus (or income attributable to such corpus) added to the trust after September 25, 1985;

(2) Any GST under a will or revocable trust executed before October 22, 1986, if the decedent died before January 1, 1987; and

(3) Any GST–

(a) under a trust to the extent such trust consists of property included in the gross estate of a decedent (other than property transferred by the decedent during his life after October 22, 1986), or reinvestments thereof, or

(b) which is a direct skip that occurs by reason of the death of any decedent;

but only if such decedent was, on October 22, 1986, under a mental disability to change the disposition of his property and did not regain his competence to dispose of such property before the date of his death. TRA '86, Sec. 1433(a), (b), as amended by TAMRA '88, Sec. 1014(h)(2). It appears that Congress does not intend for the third grandfathering rule to apply with respect to property transferred after August 3, 1990 to an incompetent person, or to a trust of such a person. OBRA '90, Sec. 11703(c)(3).

951. How is the amount of tax on a GST determined? What is the GST exemption and how is it applied in determining the GST tax?

The amount of tax is the "taxable amount" (based on the kind of GST involved–see Q 950) multiplied by the "applicable rate." IRC Sec. 2602. The applicable rate of tax applied to the taxable amount is itself a product. It is a product of the maximum federal estate tax rate in effect at the time of the GST (46% in 2006, see Appendix B) and the "inclusion ratio" with respect to the transfer. IRC Sec. 2641. The inclusion ratio, in turn, depends on allocations of the "GST exemption." IRC Sec. 2642. The GST tax is repealed for one year in 2010. IRC Sec. 2664; EGTRRA 2001 Sec. 901.

Taxable Amount

In the case of a taxable distribution, the taxable amount is the value of the property received by the transferee reduced by any expense incurred by the transferee with respect to the GST tax imposed on the distribution. If any portion of the GST tax with respect to a taxable distribution is paid out of the trust, the taxable distribution is increased by such an amount. IRC Sec. 2621.

In the case of a taxable termination, the taxable amount is the value of all property with respect to which the taxable termination has occurred, reduced by the expenses, similar to those allowed as a deduction under IRC Section 2053 in determining the taxable estate for estate tax purposes (see Q 863, the first heading), with respect to which the taxable termination has occurred. IRC Sec. 2622.

In the case of a direct skip, the taxable amount is the value of the property received by the transferee. IRC Sec. 2623. Where a life estate was given to a skip person and a

GENERAL   Q 951

remainder interest was given to a non-skip person, the value of the entire property (and not just the actuarial value of the life estate) was subject to GST tax. TAM 9105006.

GST Exemption

For purposes of determining the inclusion ratio, every individual is allowed a GST exemption of $2,000,000 (in 2006, see Appendix B) which may be allocated irrevocably by him (or his executor) to any property with respect to which he is the transferor. In 2004 to 2009, the GST exemption is equal to the estate tax unified credit equivalent (applicable exclusion amount) rather than to $1 million as indexed (see Appendix B). [The $1,000,000 amount is adjusted for inflation, rounded down to the next lowest multiple of $10,000, after 1998 and before 2004 (and after 2010). Any indexing increase in the GST exemption is available for all generation-skipping transfers occurring in the year of the increase and subsequent years in which the GST exemption is equal to $1 million as indexed up to the year of the decedent's death.] IRC. Sec. 2631, as amended by EGTRRA 2001. The GST tax is repealed for one year in 2010. In general, an individual or the individual's executor may allocate the GST exemption at any time from the date of the transfer until the time for filing the individual's federal estate tax return (including extensions actually granted), regardless of whether a return is required (see Q 851). IRC Sec. 2632.

The GST exemption is automatically allocated to lifetime direct skips unless otherwise elected on a timely filed federal gift tax return (see Q 901). IRC Sec. 2632(b).

In addition, any unused GST exemption is automatically allocated to indirect skips to a GST trust, effective 2001 to 2009. IRC Sec. 2632(c), as added by EGTRRA 2001. An indirect skip is a transfer (other than a direct skip) subject to gift tax to a GST trust. A transferor can elect to have the automatic allocation not apply to (1) an indirect skip, or (2) to any or all transfers made by the individual to a particular trust. The transferor can also elect to treat a trust as a GST trust with respect to any or all transfers made by the individual to the trust. Nevertheless, an allocation still cannot be made until the end of any estate tax inclusion period (see below).

A GST trust is a trust that could have a generation-skipping transfer with respect to the transferor unless:

1. The trust provides that more than 25% of the trust corpus must be distributed to, or may be withdrawn by, one or more individuals who are non-skip persons, either (a) before the individual's 46th birthday, (b) on or before a date prior to such birthday, or (c) an event that may reasonably be expected to occur before such birthday.

2. The trust provides that more than 25% of the trust corpus must be distributed to, or may be withdrawn by, one or more individuals who are non-skip persons and who are living on the date of death of an individual identified in the trust (by name or class) who is more than 10 years older than such individuals.

3. The trust provides that, if one or more individuals who are non-skip persons die before a date or event described in (1) or (2), more than 25% of the trust corpus must either (a) be distributed to the estate(s) of one

or more of such individuals, or (b) be subject to a general power of appointment exercisable by one or more of such individuals.

4. Any portion of the trust would be included in the gross estate of a non-skip person (other than the transferor) if such person died immediately after the transfer.

5. The trust is a charitable lead annuity trust (CLAT), charitable remainder annuity trust (CRAT), charitable remainder unitrust (CRUT), or a charitable lead unitrust (CLUT) with a non-skip remainder person.

For purposes of these GST trust rules, the value of transferred property is not treated as includable in the gross estate of a non-skip person nor subject to a power of withdrawal if the withdrawal right does not exceed the amount of the gift tax annual exclusion with respect to the transfer. It is also assumed that a power of appointment held by a non-skip person will not be exercised.

Regulations generally permit elections to allocate or not allocate GST exemption to individual transfers or to all current or future transfers to a trust or trusts, or any combination of these. An election with regard to all transfers to a trust can later be revoked with respect to future transfers to the trust. The regulations also permit elections with regard to individual transfers to a trust even where an election is in place with regard to all transfers to a trust. Treas. Reg. §26.2632-1.

Planning Point: It probably makes sense for grantors to make elections to allocate or not allocate GST exemption with respect to all transfers to a particular trust. GST exemption can be allocated to trusts benefiting skip persons; while allocations are not made to trusts benefiting non-skip persons. If need be, the election could be changed later, for future transfers.

A retroactive allocation of the GST exemption can be made when certain non-skip beneficiaries of a trust predecease the transferor, effective 2001 to 2009. The non-skip beneficiary must (1) have an interest or a future interest (for this purpose, a future interest means the trust may permit income or corpus to be paid to such person on a date or dates in the future) in the trust to which any transfer has been made, (2) be a lineal descendant of a grandparent of the transferor or of a grandparent of the transferor's spouse or former spouse, (3) be assigned to a generation lower than that of the transferor, and (4) predecease the transferor. In such a case, an allocation of the transferor's unused GST exemption (determined immediately before the non-skip person's death) can be made to any previous transfer or transfers to the trust (value of transfer is its gift tax value at the time of the transfer) on a chronological order. The allocation is made by the transferor on the gift tax return for the year of the non-skip person's death. The allocation is treated as effective immediately before the non-skip person's death. IRC Sec. 2632(d), as added by EGTRRA 2001.

Example. Grandparent creates a trust for the primary benefit of Child, with Grandchild as contingent remainder beneficiary. Grandparent doesn't expect Grandchild will receive anything, or that the trust will be generation-skipping; so he doesn't allocate GST exemption to the trust. (Or, perhaps, allocation of the GST exemption was simply overlooked.) Child dies unexpectedly before Grandparent. There is a GST taxable termination at Child's death. Grandparent can make a retroactive allocation of GST exemption to the trust to reduce or eliminate the GST tax on the taxable termination.

GENERAL   Q 951

With regard to lifetime transfers other than a direct skip, an allocation is made on the federal gift tax return. An allocation can use a formula (e.g., the amount necessary to produce an inclusion ratio of zero). An allocation on a timely filed gift tax return is generally effective as of the date of the transfer. An allocation on an untimely filed gift tax return is generally effective as of the date the return is filed and is deemed to precede any taxable event occurring on such date. (For certain retroactive allocations, see above.) An allocation of the GST exemption is irrevocable after the due date. However, an allocation of GST exemption to a trust (other than a charitable lead annuity trust, see below) is void to the extent the amount allocated exceeds the amount needed to produce an inclusion ratio of zero (see below). Treas. Reg. §26.2632-1(b).

An executor can make an allocation of the transferor's unused GST exemption on the transferor's federal estate tax return. An allocation with respect to property included in the transferor's estate is effective as of the date of death. A late allocation of the GST with respect to a lifetime transfer can be made by the executor on the estate tax return and is effective as of the date the allocation is filed. A decedent's unused GST exemption is automatically and irrevocably allocated on the due date for the federal estate tax return to the extent not otherwise allocated by the executor. The automatic allocation is made to nonexempt property: first to direct skips occurring at death, and then to trusts with potential taxable distributions or taxable terminations. IRC Sec. 2632(e), as redesignated by EGTRRA 2001, Treas. Reg. §26.2632-1(d).

Inclusion Ratio

In general, the inclusion ratio with respect to any property transferred in a GST is the excess of one minus (a) the "applicable fraction" for the trust from which the transfer is made, or (b) in the case of a direct skip, the applicable fraction determined for the skip. IRC Sec. 2642(a)(1).

The "applicable fraction" is a fraction (a) the numerator of which is the amount of the GST exemption allocated to the trust (or to the property transferred, if a direct skip), and (b) the denominator of which is the value of the property transferred reduced by (i) the sum of any federal estate or state death tax actually recovered from the trust attributable to such property, (ii) any federal gift tax or estate tax charitable deduction allowed with respect to such property, and (iii) with respect to a direct skip, the portion that is a nontaxable gift (see below). The fraction should be rounded to the nearest one-thousandth, with five rounded up (i.e., .2345 is rounded to .235). If the denominator of the applicable fraction is zero, the inclusion ratio is zero. IRC Sec. 2642(a)(2), Treas. Reg. §26.2642-1.

Example. In the year 2006, G transfers irrevocably in trust for his grandchildren $6 million and allocates all his $2,000,000 GST exemption to the transfer. The applicable fraction is 2,000,000/6,000,000, or .333. The inclusion ratio is 1 minus .333, or .667. The maximum estate tax rate, 46%, is applied against the inclusion ratio, .667. The resulting percentage, 30.7%, is applied against the value of the property transferred, $6,000,000, to produce a GST tax of $1,842,000. The tax is paid by G, the transferor, because this is a direct skip (other than a direct skip from a trust) (see Q 956).

Example. Same facts as in preceding example, except that for federal gift tax purposes G's wife consented to a split gift of the $6 million (see Q 953). Thus, for GST tax purposes as well, the gift is considered split between the spouses. If they both elect to have their respective GST exemptions allocated to the transfer, the applicable fraction for each is 2,000,000/3,000,000, or .667. The inclusion ratio is 1 minus .667, or .333. The maximum estate tax rate, 46%, is applied against the inclusion

2006 Tax Facts on Insurance & Employee Benefits   903

ratio, .333. The resulting percentage, 15.3%, is applied against the value of the property transferred, $3,000,000, to produce a GST tax of $459,000 for each, or a total GST tax of $918,000 on the $6 million transfer. The tax is paid ½ each by G and G's wife, the transferors, because each gift is a direct skip (other than a direct skip from a trust) (see Q 956).

Example. In 2006, G transfers $100,000 to a trust and allocates $100,000 GST exemption to the trust. The trust has an inclusion ratio of zero, and taxable distributions and taxable terminations can be made free of GST tax.

Example. In 2006, G transfers $100,000 to a trust and allocates no GST exemption to the trust. If all the trust beneficiaries are grandchildren of G, G has made a direct skip fully subject to GST tax. The GST tax is $46,000 ($100,000 transfer × 46% GST tax rate in 2006) and is payable by G. If the trust beneficiaries are children and grandchildren of G, the trust has an inclusion ratio of one, and GST transfers are fully subject to tax at the GST tax rate at the time of any later transfer.

If there is more than one transfer in trust the applicable fraction must be recomputed at the time of each transfer. Thus, if property is transferred to a preexisting trust, the "recomputed applicable fraction" is determined as follows: The numerator of such fraction is the sum of (1) the amount of the GST exemption allocated to the property involved in such transfer and (2) the nontax portion of the trust immediately before the transfer. (The nontax portion of the trust is the value of the trust immediately before the transfer multiplied by the applicable fraction in effect before such transfer.) The denominator of such fraction is the value of the trust immediately after the transfer reduced by (i) the sum of any federal estate or state death tax actually recovered from the trust attributable to such property, (ii) any federal gift tax or estate tax charitable deduction allowed with respect to such property, and (iii) with respect to a direct skip, the portion that is a nontaxable gift (see below). IRC Sec. 2642(d)(2), Treas. Reg. §26.2642-4.

Example. In the year 1995, G transfers irrevocably in trust for his children and grandchildren $4 million and allocates all his $1 million GST exemption to the transfer. The applicable fraction is 1,000,000/4,000,000, or .250. The inclusion ratio is 1 minus .250, or .750.

In 2001, the trust makes a taxable distribution to the grandchildren of $100,000. The maximum estate tax rate, 55% in 2001, is applied against the inclusion ratio, .750. The resulting percentage, 41.3%, is multiplied by the $100,000 transfer, resulting in a GST tax of $41,300. GST taxes in this example are paid by the grandchildren, the transferees, because the transfers are taxable distributions (see Q 956).

In 2006, the trust makes a taxable distribution to the grandchildren of $100,000. The maximum estate tax rate, 46% in 2006, is applied against the inclusion ratio, .750. The resulting percentage, 34.5%, is multiplied by the $100,000 transfer, resulting in a GST tax of $34,500.

Later in 2006, when the trust property has grown to $6 million, G transfers an additional $3 million to the trust. An additional $1,000,000 of GST exemption is available to G in 2006 ($2,000,000 GST exemption in 2006 minus $1,000,000 exemption already used). The numerator of the recomputed fraction is the value of the nontax portion of the trust immediately before the transfer, or $1.5 million (value of the trust, $6 million, multiplied by the applicable fraction of .250), plus $1,000,000 additional exemption, or $2,500,000. The denominator of the recomputed fraction is $9 million (the sum of the transferred property, $3 million, and the value of all the property in the trust immediately before the transfer, $6 million). The applicable fraction is 2,500,000/9,000,000, or .278. The inclusion ratio is 1 minus .278, or .722.

Later in 2006, the trust makes a taxable distribution to the grandchildren of $100,000. The maximum estate tax rate, 46% in 2006, is applied against the inclusion ratio, .722. The resulting percentage, 33.2%, is multiplied by the $100,000 transfer, resulting in a GST tax of $33,200.

GENERAL

Q 951

Planning Point: Trusts are usually created with an inclusion ratio of either one (GST transfers, if any, with respect to trust are fully taxable) or zero (fully exempt from GST tax). A trust has an inclusion ratio of zero if GST exemption is allocated to any transfer to the trust that is not a nontaxable gift [an allocation of GST exemption is not needed for a direct skip nontaxable gift (see below); it has an inclusion ratio of zero]. For information on severing a trust to create separate trusts with inclusion ratios of zero and one, see "Separate Trusts," below.

Valuation

"Value" of the property is its value at the time of the transfer. In the case of a direct skip of property that is included in the transferor's gross estate, the value of the property is its estate tax value. In the case of a taxable termination with respect to a trust occurring at the same time as and as a result of the death of an individual, an election may be made to value at the alternate valuation date (see Q 862). In any case, the value of the property may be reduced by any consideration given by the transferee. IRC Sec. 2624.

For purposes of determining the GST inclusion ratio, certain other valuation rules may apply in some instances. For purposes of determining the denominator of the applicable fraction (see above), the value of property transferred during life is its fair market value as of the effective date of the GST exemption allocation (see above). However, with respect to late allocations of the GST exemption to a trust, the transferor may elect (solely for purpose of determining the fair market value of trust assets) to treat the allocation as made on the first day of the month in which the allocation is made. This election is not effective with respect to a life insurance policy, or a trust holding a life insurance policy, if the insured individual has died. For purposes of determining the denominator of the applicable fraction, the value of property included in the decedent's gross estate is its value for estate tax purposes. However, special use valuation (see Q 862) is not available unless the recapture agreement under IRC Section 2032A specifically refers to the GST tax. There are special rules in the regulations concerning the allocation of post-death appreciation or depreciation with respect to pecuniary payments and residuary payments made after a pecuniary payment. IRC Sec. 2642(b)(2)(A), Treas. Reg. §26.2642-2.

Charitable Lead Annuity Trusts

With respect to property transferred after October 13, 1987, the GST tax exemption inclusion ratio for any charitable lead annuity trust is to be determined by dividing the amount of exemption allocated to the trust by the value of the property in the trust following the charitable term. For this purpose, the exemption allocated to the trust is increased by interest determined at the interest rate used in determining the amount of the estate or gift tax charitable deduction with respect to such a trust over the charitable term. With respect to a late allocation of the GST exemption (see above), interest accrues only from the date of the late allocation. The amount of GST exemption allocated to the trust is not reduced even though it is determined at a later time that a lesser amount of GST exemption would have produced a zero inclusion ratio. IRC Sec. 2642(e), Treas. Reg. §26.2642-3.

Estate Tax Inclusion Period (ETIP)

With respect to inter vivos transfers subject at some point in time to the GST tax, the allocation of any portion of the GST exemption to such a transfer is postponed until

2006 Tax Facts on Insurance & Employee Benefits

the earlier of (a) the expiration of the period (not to extend beyond the transferor's death) during which the property being transferred would be included in the transferor's estate (other than by reason of the gifts within three years of death rule of IRC Section 2035) if he died, or (b) the GST. For purposes of determining the inclusion ratio with respect to such exemption, the value of such property is: (a) its estate tax value if it is included in the transfer's estate (other than by reason of the three year rule of IRC Section 2035), or (b) its value determined at the end of the ETIP. However, if the allocation of the exemption under the second valuation method is not made on a timely filed gift tax return for the year in which the ETIP ends, determination of value is postponed until such allocation is filed. IRC Sec. 2642(f).

Example. Grantor sets up an irrevocable trust: income retained for 10 years, then life estate for children, followed by remainder to grandchildren. The valuation of property for purpose of the inclusion rule is delayed until the earlier of the expiration of the 10-year period or the transferor's death. If the grantor were to die during such time the property would be included in the grantor's estate under IRC Section 2036(a) (see Q 853(4)). However, if the grantor survived the 10-year period and failed to make an allocation of the exemption on a timely filed gift tax return, the determination of value is postponed until the earlier of the time an allocation is filed or death.

Except as provided in regulations, for purpose of the GST exemption allocation rules, any reference to an individual or a transferor is generally treated as including the spouse of such individual or transferor. IRC Sec. 2642(f)(4). Thus, an ETIP includes the period during which, if death occurred, the property being transferred would be included in the estate (other than by reason of the gifts within three years of death rule of IRC Section 2035) of the transferor or the spouse of the transferor. The property is not considered as includable in the estate of the transferor or the spouse of the transferor if the possibility of inclusion is so remote as to be negligible (i.e., less than a 5% actuarial probability). The property is not considered as includable in the estate of the spouse of the transferor by reason of a withdrawal power limited to the greater of $5,000 or 5% of the trust corpus if the withdrawal power terminates no later than 60 days after the transfer to trust. Apparently, the ETIP rules do not apply if a reverse QTIP election (see below) is made. The ETIP terminates on the earlier of (1) the death of the transferor; (2) the time at which no portion would be includable in the transferor's estate (other than by reason of IRC Section 2035) or, in the case of the spouse who consents to a split-gift, the time at which no portion would be includable in the other spouse's estate; (3) the time of the GST (but only with respect to property involved in the GST); or (4) in the case of an ETIP arising because of an interest or power held by the transferor's spouse, at the earlier of (a) the death of the spouse, or (b) the time at which no portion would be includable in the spouse's estate (other than by reason of IRC Section 2035). Treas. Reg. §26.2632-1(c).

Example. Grantor sets up an irrevocable trust: income retained for the shorter of nine years or life, remainder to grandchild. Grantor and spouse elect to split the gift. If spouse dies during trust term, spouse's executor can allocate GST exemption to spouse's deemed one-half of the trust. However, the allocation is not effective until the earlier of the expiration of grantor's income interest or grantor's death.

The election out of automatic allocation of GST exemption for either a direct skip or an indirect skip can be made at any time up until the due date for filing the gift tax return for the year the ETIP ends. If the transfer subject to an ETIP occurred in an earlier year, the election must specify the particular transfer. An affirmative allocation of GST exemption cannot be revoked after the due date for filing the gift tax return for the year the affirmative election is made (or after the allocation is made in the case of a late allocation), even where actual allocation is not effective until the end of an ETIP. Treas. Reg. §26.2632-1.

Separate Trusts

In general, portions of a trust are not to be treated as separate trusts. However, portions attributable to different transferors, substantially separate and independent shares of different beneficiaries of a trust, and trusts treated as separate trusts under state law are to be treated as separate trusts for GST tax purposes. IRC Sec. 2654(b). However, treatment of a single trust as separate shares for purposes of the GST tax does not permit treatment as separate trusts for purposes of filing or payment of tax, or for purposes of any other tax. Additions to, or distributions from, such a trust are allocated pro-rata among all shares unless expressly provided otherwise. In general, a separate share is not treated as such unless it exists at all times from and after creation of the trust.

Trusts created from a qualified severance are treated as separate trusts for GST tax purposes, effective for 2001 to 2009. A qualified severance means the division of a single trust into two or more trusts under the trust document or state law if (1) the single trust is divided on a fractional basis, and (2) in the aggregate, the terms of the new trusts provide for the same succession of interests of beneficiaries as are provided in the original trust. In the case of a trust with a GST inclusion ratio of greater than zero and less than one (i.e., the trust is partially protected from the GST by allocations of the GST exemption), a severance is a qualified severance only if the single trust is divided into two trusts, one of which receives a fractional amount equal to the GST applicable fraction multiplied by the single trust's assets. The trust receiving the fractional amount receives an inclusion ratio of zero (i.e., it is not subject to GST tax), and the other trust receives an inclusion ratio of one (i.e., it is fully subject to GST tax). IRC Sec. 2642(a), as added by EGTRRA 2001.

Otherwise, severance of a trust included in the taxable estate (or created in the transferor's will) into single shares will be recognized for GST purposes if (1) the trusts are severed pursuant to the governing instrument or state law, (2) such severance occurs (or a reformation proceeding is begun and is indicated on the estate tax return) prior to the date for filing the estate tax return (including extensions actually granted), and (3) the trusts are funded using (a) fractional interests or (b) pecuniary amounts for which appropriate adjustments are made. Treas. Reg. §26.2654-1.

Proposed regulations provide that a severance must be done on a fractional or percentage basis; a severance based on a specific pecuniary amount is not permitted. The terms of the new trusts must provide in the aggregate for the same succession of beneficiaries. With respect to trusts from which discretionary distributions may be made on a non pro rata basis, this requirement can be satisfied even if each permissible beneficiary might be a beneficiary of only one of the separate trusts, but only if no beneficial interest is shifted to a lower generation and the time for vesting of any beneficial interest is not extended. The separate trusts must be funded with property from the severed trust with either a pro rata portion of each asset or on a non pro rata basis. If funded on a non pro rata basis, the separate trusts must be funded by applying the appropriate severance fraction or percentage to the fair market value of all the property on the date of funding. Prop. Treas. Reg. §26.2642-6.

Planning Point: The advantage of having portions or shares of a trust treated as separate trusts is that the transferor can decide whether or not to allocate a portion of his GST exemption to each separate trust and the trustee can make distributions from the separate trusts in a way which minimizes GST tax.

Nontaxable Gifts

In the case of any direct skip which is a nontaxable gift, the inclusion ratio is zero. For this purpose a nontaxable gift means any transfer of property to the extent the transfer is not treated as a taxable gift by reason of the gift tax annual exclusion (taking into account the split gift provision for married couples–see Q 907) or the "qualified transfer" exclusion (see Q 917). In other words, there is no GST tax imposed on direct skip gifts that come within the gift tax annual exclusion or that are "qualified transfers." However, with respect to transfers after March 31, 1988, a nontaxable gift which is a direct skip to a trust for the benefit of an individual has an inclusion ratio of zero only if (1) during the life of such individual no portion of the trust corpus or income may be distributed to or for the benefit of any other person, and (2) the trust would be included in such individual's estate if the trust did not terminate before such individual died. IRC Sec. 2642(c).

Reverse QTIP Election

A qualified terminable interest property (QTIP) election can be made to qualify property for the estate tax (see Q 864) and gift tax (see Q 920) marital deductions. A reverse QTIP election may be made for such property under the GST tax. The effect of making the reverse QTIP election is to have the decedent or the donor treated as the transferor (see Q 950) for GST tax purposes. However, if a reverse QTIP election is made for property in a trust, the election must be made for all of the property in the trust. However, the Committee Report states that if the executor indicates on the federal estate tax return that separate trusts will be created, such trusts will be treated as separate trusts. In other words, separate trusts can be created so that the QTIP and reverse QTIP election can be made for different amounts, and thus minimize all transfer taxes. IRC Sec. 2652(a)(3). See Let. Ruls. 9133016, 9002014. See "Separate Trusts," above regarding the creation of separate shares from a single trust.

> *Example.* In 2006, decedent (who has made $500,000 of taxable gifts protected by the unified credit) with a $4,000,000 estate leaves $1,500,000 in a credit shelter trust and $2,500,000 to his surviving spouse in a QTIP trust, reducing his estate tax to zero. (Assume each trust would be subject to GST tax to the extent that the $2,000,000 exemption is not allocated to such trust.) The executor allocates $1,500,000 of the decedent's $2,000,000 GST tax exemption to the credit shelter trust and makes a reverse QTIP election as to $500,000 of the QTIP property so that the decedent's full $2,000,000 exemption can be used. The surviving spouse's $2,000,000 exemption amount may then be used to protect the remaining $2,000,000 of property, and the entire $4,000,000 has escaped GST tax (assuming separate QTIP trusts of $2,000,000 and $500,000 are created).

Basis Adjustment

Where the basis of property subject to the GST tax is increased (or decreased) to fair market value because property transferred in a taxable termination occurs at the same time and as a result of the death of an individual, any increase (or decrease) in basis is limited by multiplying such increase (or decrease) by the inclusion ratio used in allocating the GST exemption. IRC Sec. 2654(a)(2).

952. How are individuals assigned to generations for purposes of the GST tax?

An individual (and his spouse or former spouse) who is a lineal descendant of a grandparent of the transferor (or the transferor's spouse) is assigned to that generation which results from comparing the number of generations between the grandparent and such individual with the number of generations between the grandparent and the transferor (or the transferor's spouse). A relationship by legal adoption is treated as a relationship by blood, and a relationship by the half-blood is treated as a relationship of the whole blood. IRC Secs. 2651(a), 2651(b), 2651(c).

A person who could be assigned to more than one generation is assigned to the youngest generation. However, regulations provide that adopted individuals will be treated as one generation younger than the adoptive parent where: (1) a transfer is made to the adopted individual from the adoptive parent, the spouse or former spouse of the adoptive parent, or a lineal descendant of a grandparent of the adoptive parent; (2) the adopted individual is a descendant of the adoptive parent (or the spouse or former spouse of the adoptive parent); (3) the adopted individual is under age 18 at the time of adoption; and (4) the adoption is not primarily for the purpose of avoiding GST tax. Treas. Reg. §26.2651-2.

However, with respect to terminations, distributions, and transfers occurring after 1997, where an individual's parent is dead at the time of a transfer subject to gift or estate tax upon which the individual's interest is established or derived, such individual will be treated as being one generation below the lower of (1) the transferor's generation or (2) the generation of the youngest living ancestor of the individual who is also a descendant of the parents of the transferor or the transferor's spouse. This predeceased parent rule applies to collateral relatives (e.g., nieces and nephews) only if there are no living lineal descendants of the transferor at the time of the transfer. IRC Sec. 2651(e). For a narrower predeceased parent rule that applied to direct skips before 1998, see Q 950.

Regulations make clear that if the generation-skipping property is subject to gift tax or estate tax on more than one occasion, the time for determining application of the predeceased parent rule is on the first of such occasions. In the case of a qualified terminable interest property (QTIP) marital deduction election, the time for determining application of the predeceased parent rule can essentially wait until the surviving spouse dies or makes a gift of the QTIP property. However, where a reverse QTIP election is made, application of the predeceased parent rule is made at the time of the first spouse's death. Also, at times property may be transferred to a trust before the predeceased parent rule is applicable. Later, the predeceased parent rule applies to additional property transferred to the trust. The additional property is treated as being held in a separate trust for GST tax purposes. Each portion has, in effect, a separate transferor. Treas. Reg. §26.2651-1.

An individual who cannot be assigned to a generation under the foregoing rules is assigned to a generation on the basis of his date of birth. An individual born not more than 12½ years after the date of birth of the transferor is assigned to the transferor's generation. An individual born more than 12½ years but not more than 37½ years after the date of birth of the transferor is assigned to the first generation younger than the transferor. There are similar rules for a new generation every 25 years. IRC Sec. 2651(d).

953. Can married couples make a split gift for purposes of the GST tax?

Yes. If a split gift is made for gift tax purposes (see Q 907), such gift will be so treated for purposes of the GST tax. IRC Sec. 2652(a)(2). Split gifts allow spouses to, in effect, utilize each other's annual exclusions and exemptions (see Q 951). A memorandum permitted a taxpayer to elect after his spouse's death to split gifts with his spouse and thus take advantage of his spouse's GST tax exemption where the gifts were made by the taxpayer shortly before the spouse's death. TAM 9404023.

954. What credits are allowed against the GST tax?

For decedents dying before 2005 and after 2010, if a GST (other than a direct skip) occurs at the same time as and as a result of the death of an individual, a credit against the GST tax imposed is allowed in an amount equal to the GST tax actually paid to any state in respect to any property included in the GST, but the amount cannot exceed 5% of the GST tax. IRC Sec. 2604. The credit is eliminated for 2005 to 2010. IRC Secs. 2604(c), 2664, as added by EGTRRA 2001.

955. What are the return requirements with respect to the GST tax?

The person required to file the return is the person liable for paying the tax (see Q 956). In the case of a direct skip (other than from a trust), the return must be filed on or before the due date for the gift or estate tax return with respect to the transfer. In all other cases, the return must be filed on or before the 15th day of the 4th month after the close of the taxable year of the person required to make the return. IRC Sec. 2662.

956. Who is liable for paying the GST tax?

In the case of a taxable distribution, the tax is paid by the transferee. In the case of a taxable termination or a direct skip from a trust, the tax is paid by the trustee. In the case of a direct skip (other than a direct skip from a trust), the tax is paid by the transferor. Unless the governing instrument of transfer otherwise directs, the GST tax is charged to the property constituting the transfer. IRC Sec. 2603. See Q 750 regarding rules for insurance proceeds where a direct skip occurs at death.

APPENDIX A

Actuarial Tables for Taxing Annuities

Gender based Tables I, II, IIA, and III, and Unisex Tables V, VI, VIA and VII for the taxing of annuities, appear on the following pages. (The IRS has provided a simplified method of taxing annuity payments from qualified plans and tax sheltered annuities—see Q 433.)

Gender based Tables I-III are to be used if the investment in the contract does not include a post-June 30, 1986 investment in the contract. Unisex Tables V-VII are to be used if the investment in the contract includes a post-June 30, 1986 investment in the contract.

However, even if there is no investment in the contract after June 30, 1986, an annuitant receiving annuity payments after June 30, 1986 (regardless of when they first began) may elect to treat his entire investment in the contract as post-June 30, 1986 and apply Tables V-VIII. This election may be made for any taxable year in which such amounts are received by the taxpayer; it is irrevocable and applies with respect to all amounts the taxpayer receives as an annuity under the contract in the taxable year for which the election is made or in any subsequent tax year. The election is made by the taxpayer's attaching to his return for that year a statement that he is making the election under Treasury Regulation §1.72-9 to treat the entire investment in the contract as post-June 1986 investment. Treas. Reg. §1.72-9.

If investment in the contract includes both a pre-July 1986 investment and a post-June 1986 investment, an election may be made to make separate computations with respect to each portion of the aggregate investment in the contract using with respect to each portion the tables applicable to it. The amount excludable is the sum of the amounts determined under the separate computations. However, the election is not available (i.e., the entire investment must be treated as post-June 1986 investment) if the annuity starting date is after June 30, 1986 and the contract provides an option (whether or not it is exercised) to receive amounts under the contract other than in the form of a life annuity. Thus, the election is not available if the contract provides: an option to receive a lump sum in full discharge of the obligation under the contract; an option to receive an amount under the contract after June 30, 1986 and before the annuity starting date; an option to receive an annuity for a period certain; an option to receive payments under a refund feature that is substantially equivalent to an annuity for a period certain (i.e., if its value determined under Table VII exceeds 50%); an option to receive a temporary life annuity that is substantially equivalent to an annuity for a period certain (i.e., if the multiple determined under Table VIII exceeds 50% of the maximum duration of the annuity). Treas. Reg. § 1.72-6(d).

Treasury regulations extend some of the Tables to higher and lower ages, but the partial Tables are adequate for all practical purposes. The multiples in Tables I, II, and IIA, or V, VI and VIA need not be adjusted for monthly payments. For quarterly, semi-annual or annual payments, they must be adjusted according to the Frequency of Payment Adjustment Table, below. Table III and Table VII multiples, giving the percentage value of refund features, are never adjusted.

APPENDIX A — ANNUITY TABLES

ALL TABLES ARE ENTERED WITH AGE OF ANNUITANT AT BIRTHDAY NEAREST ANNUITY STARTING DATE.

Frequency of Payment Adjustment Table

If the number of whole months from the annuity starting date to the first payment date is	0-1	2	3	4	5	6	7	8	9	10	11	12
And payments under the contract are to be made:												
Annually	+0.5	+0.4	+0.3	+0.2	+0.1	0	0	-0.1	-0.2	-0.3	-0.4	-0.5
Semiannually	+.2	+.1	0	0	-.1	-.2	....	....	....	....	....	....
Quarterly	+.1	0	-.1	....	....	....	....	....	....	....	....	....

Example. Ed Black bought an annuity contract on January 1 which provides him with an *annual* payment of $4,000 payable on December 31st of each year. His age on birthday nearest the annuity starting date (January 1) is 66. The multiple from Table V for male age 66, is 19.2. This multiple must be adjusted for annual payment by subtracting .5 (19.2 - .5 = 18.7). Thus, his total expected return is $74,800 (18.7 x $4,000). See Treas. Reg. §1.72-5(a)(2).

APPENDIX A — ANNUITY TABLES

Table I — Ordinary Life Annuities — One Life — Expected Return Multiples

Male	Female	Multiples	Male	Female	Multiples
6	11	65.0	59	64	18.9
7	12	64.1	60	65	18.2
8	13	63.2	61	66	17.5
9	14	62.3	62	67	16.9
10	15	61.4	63	68	16.2
11	16	60.4	64	69	15.6
12	17	59.5	65	70	15.0
13	18	58.6	66	71	14.4
14	19	57.7	67	72	13.8
15	20	56.7	68	73	13.2
16	21	55.8	69	74	12.6
17	22	54.9	70	75	12.1
18	23	53.9	71	76	11.6
19	24	53.0	72	77	11.0
20	25	52.1	73	78	10.5
21	26	51.1	74	79	10.1
22	27	50.2	75	80	9.6
23	28	49.3	76	81	9.1
24	29	48.3	77	82	8.7
25	30	47.4	78	83	8.3
26	31	46.5	79	84	7.8
27	32	45.6	80	85	7.5
28	33	44.6	81	86	7.1
29	34	43.7	82	87	6.7
30	35	42.8	83	88	6.3
31	36	41.9	84	89	6.0
32	37	41.0	85	90	5.7
33	38	40.0	86	91	5.4
34	39	39.1	87	92	5.1
35	40	38.2	88	93	4.8
36	41	37.3	89	94	4.5
37	42	36.5	90	95	4.2
38	43	35.6	91	96	4.0
39	44	34.7	92	97	3.7
40	45	33.8	93	98	3.5
41	46	33.0	94	99	3.3
42	47	32.1	95	100	3.1
43	48	31.2	96	101	2.9
44	49	30.4	97	102	2.7
45	50	29.6	98	103	2.5
46	51	28.7	99	104	2.3
47	52	27.9	100	105	2.1
48	53	27.1	101	106	1.9
49	54	26.3	102	107	1.7
50	55	25.5	103	108	1.5
51	56	24.7	104	109	1.3
52	57	24.0	105	110	1.2
53	58	23.2	106	111	1.0
54	59	22.4	107	112	.8
55	60	21.7	108	113	.7
56	61	21.0	109	114	.6
57	62	20.3	110	115	.5
58	63	19.6	111	116	.0

Table II — Ordinary Joint Life and Last Survivor Annuities — Two Lives — Expected Return Multiples

Male\Female	Male 35 / Female 40	35	36	37	38	39	40	41	42	43	44	45	46	47
		40	41	42	43	44	45	46	47	48	49	50	51	52
35	40	46.2	45.7	45.3	44.8	44.4	44.0	43.6	43.3	43.0	42.6	42.3	42.0	41.8
36	41	...	45.2	44.8	44.3	43.9	43.5	43.1	42.7	42.3	42.0	41.7	41.4	41.1
37	42	...	...	44.3	43.8	43.4	42.9	42.5	42.1	41.8	41.4	41.1	40.7	40.4
38	43	...	...	...	43.3	42.9	42.4	42.0	41.6	41.2	40.8	40.5	40.1	39.8
39	44	...	...	...	...	42.4	41.9	41.5	41.0	40.6	40.2	39.9	39.5	39.2
40	45	...	...	...	...	...	41.4	41.0	40.5	40.1	39.7	39.3	38.9	38.6
41	46	...	...	...	...	...	...	40.5	40.0	39.6	39.2	38.8	38.4	38.0
42	47	...	...	...	...	...	...	...	39.6	39.1	38.7	38.2	37.8	37.5
43	48	...	...	...	...	...	...	...	...	38.6	38.2	37.7	37.3	36.9
44	49	...	...	...	...	...	...	...	...	...	37.7	37.2	36.8	36.4
45	50	...	...	...	...	...	...	...	...	...	...	36.8	36.3	35.9
46	51	...	...	...	...	...	...	...	...	...	...	...	35.9	35.4
47	52	...	...	...	...	...	...	...	...	...	...	...	...	35.0

Male\Female		48	49	50	51	52	53	54	55	56	57	58	59	60
		53	54	55	56	57	58	59	60	61	62	63	64	65
35	40	41.5	41.3	41.0	40.8	40.6	40.4	40.3	40.1	40.0	39.8	39.7	39.6	39.5
36	41	40.8	40.6	40.3	40.1	39.9	39.7	39.5	39.3	39.2	39.0	38.9	38.8	38.6
37	42	40.2	39.9	39.6	39.4	39.2	39.0	38.8	38.6	38.4	38.3	38.1	38.0	37.9
38	43	39.5	39.2	39.0	38.7	38.5	38.3	38.1	37.9	37.7	37.5	37.3	37.2	37.1
39	44	38.9	38.6	38.3	38.0	37.8	37.6	37.3	37.1	36.9	36.8	36.6	36.4	36.3
40	45	38.3	38.0	37.7	37.4	37.1	36.9	36.6	36.4	36.2	36.0	35.9	35.7	35.5
41	46	37.7	37.3	37.0	36.7	36.5	36.2	36.0	35.7	35.5	35.3	35.1	35.0	34.8
42	47	37.1	36.8	36.4	36.1	35.8	35.6	35.3	35.1	34.8	34.6	34.4	34.2	34.1
43	48	36.5	36.2	35.8	35.5	35.2	34.9	34.7	34.4	34.2	33.9	33.7	33.5	33.3
44	49	36.0	35.6	35.3	34.9	34.6	34.3	34.0	33.8	33.5	33.3	33.0	32.8	32.6
45	50	35.5	35.1	34.7	34.4	34.0	33.7	33.4	33.1	32.9	32.6	32.4	32.2	31.9
46	51	35.0	34.6	34.2	33.8	33.5	33.1	32.8	32.5	32.2	32.0	31.7	31.5	31.3
47	52	34.5	34.1	33.7	33.3	32.9	32.6	32.2	31.9	31.6	31.4	31.1	30.9	30.6
48	53	34.0	33.6	33.2	32.8	32.4	32.0	31.7	31.4	31.1	30.8	30.5	30.2	30.0
49	54	...	33.1	32.7	32.3	31.9	31.5	31.2	30.8	30.5	30.2	29.9	29.6	29.4
50	55	...	...	32.3	31.8	31.4	31.0	30.6	30.3	29.9	29.6	29.3	29.0	28.8
51	56	...	...	...	31.4	30.9	30.5	30.1	29.8	29.4	29.1	28.8	28.5	28.2
52	57	...	...	...	...	30.5	30.1	29.7	29.3	28.9	28.6	28.2	27.9	27.6
53	58	...	...	...	...	...	29.6	29.2	28.8	28.4	28.1	27.7	27.4	27.1
54	59	...	...	...	...	...	...	28.8	28.3	27.9	27.6	27.2	26.9	26.5
55	60	...	...	...	...	...	...	...	27.9	27.5	27.1	26.7	26.4	26.0
56	61	...	...	...	...	...	...	...	...	27.1	26.7	26.3	25.9	25.5
57	62	...	...	...	...	...	...	...	...	...	26.2	25.8	25.4	25.1
58	63	...	...	...	...	...	...	...	...	...	...	25.4	25.0	24.6
59	64	...	...	...	...	...	...	...	...	...	...	...	24.6	24.2
60	65	...	...	...	...	...	...	...	...	...	...	...	...	23.8

APPENDIX A — ANNUITY TABLES

**Table II — Ordinary Joint Life and Last Survivor Annuities — Two Lives —
Expected Return Multiples — Continued**

Ages Male / Female		61/66	62/67	63/68	64/69	65/70	66/71	67/72	68/73	69/74	70/75	71/76	72/77	73/78
35	40	39.4	39.3	39.2	39.1	39.0	38.9	38.9	38.8	38.8	38.8	38.7	38.7	38.6	38.6
36	41	38.5	38.4	38.3	38.2	38.2	38.1	38.0	38.0	38.0	37.9	37.9	37.8	37.8	37.7
37	42	37.7	37.6	37.5	37.4	37.3	37.3	37.2	37.1	37.1	37.0	37.0	36.9	36.9	36.9
38	43	36.9	36.8	36.7	36.6	36.5	36.4	36.4	36.3	36.3	36.2	36.2	36.1	36.0	36.0
39	44	36.2	36.0	35.9	35.8	35.7	35.6	35.5	35.5	35.4	35.3	35.3	35.3	35.2	35.2
40	45	35.4	35.3	35.1	35.0	34.9	34.8	34.7	34.6	34.6	34.5	34.4	34.4	34.3
41	46	34.6	34.5	34.4	34.2	34.1	34.0	33.9	33.8	33.8	33.7	33.6	33.5	33.5
42	47	33.9	33.7	33.6	33.5	33.4	33.2	33.1	33.0	33.0	32.9	32.8	32.7	32.7
43	48	33.2	33.0	32.9	32.7	32.6	32.5	32.4	32.3	32.2	32.1	32.0	31.9	31.9
44	49	32.5	32.3	32.1	32.0	31.8	31.7	31.6	31.5	31.4	31.3	31.2	31.1	31.1
45	50	31.8	31.6	31.4	31.3	31.1	31.0	30.8	30.7	30.6	30.5	30.4	30.4	30.3
46	51	31.1	30.9	30.7	30.5	30.4	30.2	30.1	30.0	29.9	29.8	29.7	29.6	29.5
47	52	30.4	30.2	30.0	29.8	29.7	29.5	29.4	29.3	29.1	29.0	28.9	28.8	28.7
48	53	29.8	29.5	29.3	29.2	29.0	28.8	28.7	28.5	28.4	28.3	28.2	28.1	28.0
49	54	29.1	28.9	28.7	28.5	28.3	28.1	28.0	27.8	27.7	27.6	27.5	27.4	27.3
50	55	28.5	28.3	28.1	27.8	27.6	27.5	27.3	27.1	27.0	26.9	26.7	26.6	26.5
51	56	27.9	27.7	27.4	27.2	27.0	26.8	26.6	26.5	26.3	26.2	26.0	25.9	25.8
52	57	27.3	27.1	26.8	26.6	26.4	26.2	26.0	25.8	25.7	25.5	25.4	25.2	25.1
53	58	26.8	26.5	26.2	26.0	25.8	25.6	25.4	25.2	25.0	24.8	24.7	24.6	24.4
54	59	26.2	25.9	25.7	25.4	25.2	25.0	24.7	24.6	24.4	24.2	24.0	23.9	23.8
55	60	25.7	25.4	25.1	24.9	24.6	24.4	24.1	23.9	23.8	23.6	23.4	23.3	23.1
56	61	25.2	24.9	24.6	24.3	24.1	23.8	23.6	23.4	23.2	23.0	22.8	22.6	22.5
57	62	24.7	24.4	24.1	23.8	23.5	23.3	23.0	22.8	22.6	22.4	22.2	22.0	21.9
58	63	24.3	23.9	23.6	23.3	23.0	22.7	22.5	22.2	22.0	21.8	21.6	21.4	21.3
59	64	23.8	23.5	23.1	22.8	22.5	22.2	21.9	21.7	21.5	21.2	21.0	20.9	20.7
60	65	23.4	23.0	22.7	22.3	22.0	21.7	21.4	21.2	20.9	20.7	20.5	20.3	20.1
61	66	23.0	22.6	22.2	21.9	21.6	21.3	21.0	20.7	20.4	20.2	20.0	19.8	19.6
62	67	...	22.2	21.8	21.5	21.1	20.8	20.5	20.2	19.9	19.7	19.5	19.2	19.0
63	68	...	...	21.4	21.1	20.7	20.4	20.1	19.8	19.5	19.2	19.0	18.7	18.5
64	69	...	...	...	20.7	20.3	20.0	19.6	19.3	19.0	18.7	18.5	18.2	18.0
65	70	...	...	...	...	19.9	19.6	19.2	18.9	18.6	18.3	18.0	17.8	17.5
66	71	...	...	...	...	...	19.2	18.8	18.5	18.2	17.9	17.6	17.3	17.1
67	72	...	...	...	...	...	...	18.5	18.1	17.8	17.5	17.2	16.9	16.7
68	73	...	...	...	...	...	...	...	17.8	17.4	17.1	16.8	16.5	16.2
69	74	...	...	...	...	...	...	...	...	17.1	16.7	16.4	16.1	15.8
70	75	...	...	...	...	...	...	...	...	...	16.4	16.1	15.8	15.5
71	76	...	...	...	...	...	...	...	...	...	...	15.7	15.4	15.1
72	77	...	...	...	...	...	...	...	...	...	...	...	15.1	14.8
73	78	...	...	...	...	...	...	...	...	...	...	...	...	14.4

Ages Male / Female		74/79	75/80	76/81	77/82	78/83	79/84	80/85	81/86	82/87	83/88	84/89	85/90
35	40	38.6	38.5	38.5	38.5	38.4	38.4	38.4	38.4	38.4	38.4	38.3	38.3
36	41	37.7	37.6	37.6	37.6	37.6	37.5	37.5	37.5	37.5	37.5	37.5	37.4
37	42	36.8	36.8	36.7	36.7	36.7	36.7	36.6	36.6	36.6	36.6	36.6	36.6
38	43	36.0	35.9	35.9	35.8	35.8	35.8	35.8	35.8	35.7	35.7	35.7	35.7
39	44	35.1	35.1	35.0	35.0	35.0	34.9	34.9	34.9	34.9	34.8	34.8	34.8
40	45	34.3	34.2	34.2	34.1	34.1	34.1	34.1	34.0	34.0	34.0	34.0	34.0
41	46	33.4	33.4	33.3	33.3	33.3	33.2	33.2	33.2	33.2	33.1	33.1	33.1
42	47	32.6	32.6	32.5	32.5	32.4	32.4	32.4	32.3	32.3	32.3	32.3	32.3
43	48	31.8	31.8	31.7	31.7	31.6	31.6	31.6	31.5	31.5	31.5	31.4	31.4
44	49	31.0	30.9	30.9	30.8	30.8	30.8	30.7	30.7	30.7	30.7	30.6	30.6
45	50	30.2	30.1	30.1	30.0	30.0	29.9	29.9	29.9	29.9	29.8	29.8	29.8
46	51	29.4	29.4	29.3	29.2	29.2	29.2	29.1	29.1	29.1	29.0	29.0	28.9
47	52	28.7	28.6	28.5	28.5	28.4	28.4	28.3	28.3	28.3	28.2	28.2	28.1
48	53	27.9	27.8	27.8	27.7	27.6	27.6	27.5	27.5	27.5	27.4	27.4	27.4
49	54	27.2	27.1	27.0	26.9	26.9	26.8	26.8	26.7	26.7	26.6	26.6	26.6
50	55	26.4	26.3	26.3	26.2	26.1	26.1	26.0	26.0	25.9	25.9	25.8	25.8
51	56	25.7	25.6	25.5	25.5	25.4	25.3	25.3	25.2	25.2	25.1	25.1	25.0
52	57	25.0	24.9	24.8	24.7	24.7	24.6	24.5	24.5	24.4	24.4	24.3	24.3
53	58	24.3	24.2	24.1	24.0	23.9	23.9	23.8	23.7	23.7	23.6	23.6	23.5
54	59	23.6	23.5	23.4	23.3	23.2	23.2	23.1	23.0	23.0	22.9	22.9	22.8
55	60	23.0	22.9	22.8	22.7	22.6	22.5	22.4	22.3	22.3	22.2	22.2	22.1
56	61	22.3	22.2	22.1	22.0	21.9	21.8	21.7	21.7	21.6	21.5	21.5	21.4
57	62	21.7	21.6	21.5	21.3	21.2	21.1	21.1	21.0	20.9	20.8	20.8	20.7
58	63	21.1	21.0	20.8	20.7	20.6	20.5	20.4	20.3	20.2	20.2	20.1	20.0
59	64	20.5	20.4	20.2	20.1	20.0	19.9	19.8	19.7	19.6	19.5	19.4	19.4
60	65	19.9	19.8	19.6	19.5	19.4	19.3	19.1	19.0	19.0	18.9	18.8	18.7
61	66	19.4	19.2	19.1	18.9	18.8	18.7	18.5	18.4	18.3	18.3	18.2	18.1
62	67	18.8	18.7	18.5	18.3	18.2	18.1	18.0	17.8	17.7	17.7	17.6	17.5
63	68	18.3	18.1	18.0	17.8	17.6	17.5	17.4	17.3	17.2	17.1	17.0	16.9
64	69	17.8	17.6	17.4	17.3	17.1	17.0	16.8	16.7	16.6	16.5	16.4	16.3
65	70	17.3	17.1	16.9	16.7	16.6	16.4	16.3	16.2	16.0	15.9	15.8	15.8
66	71	16.9	16.6	16.4	16.3	16.1	15.9	15.8	15.6	15.5	15.4	15.3	15.2
67	72	16.4	16.2	16.0	15.8	15.6	15.4	15.3	15.1	15.0	14.9	14.8	14.7
68	73	16.0	15.7	15.5	15.3	15.1	15.0	14.8	14.6	14.5	14.4	14.3	14.2
69	74	15.6	15.3	15.1	14.9	14.7	14.5	14.3	14.2	14.0	13.9	13.8	13.7
70	75	15.2	14.9	14.7	14.5	14.3	14.1	13.9	13.7	13.6	13.4	13.3	13.2
71	76	14.8	14.5	14.3	14.1	13.8	13.6	13.5	13.3	13.1	13.0	12.8	12.7
72	77	14.5	14.2	13.9	13.7	13.5	13.2	13.0	12.9	12.7	12.5	12.4	12.3
73	78	14.1	13.8	13.6	13.3	13.1	12.9	12.7	12.5	12.3	12.1	12.0	11.8
74	79	13.8	13.5	13.2	13.0	12.7	12.5	12.3	12.1	11.9	11.7	11.6	11.4
75	80	...	13.2	12.9	12.6	12.4	12.2	11.9	11.7	11.5	11.4	11.2	11.0
76	81	...	...	12.6	12.3	12.1	11.8	11.6	11.4	11.2	11.0	10.8	10.7
77	82	...	...	...	12.1	11.8	11.5	11.3	11.1	10.8	10.7	10.5	10.3
78	83	...	...	...	...	11.5	11.2	11.0	10.7	10.5	10.3	10.1	10.0
79	84	...	...	...	...	...	11.0	10.7	10.5	10.2	10.0	9.8	9.6
80	85	...	...	...	...	...	...	10.4	10.2	10.0	9.7	9.5	9.3
81	86	...	...	...	...	...	...	...	9.9	9.7	9.5	9.3	9.1
82	87	...	...	...	...	...	...	...	...	9.4	9.2	9.0	8.8
83	88	...	...	...	...	...	...	...	...	...	9.0	8.7	8.5
84	89	...	...	...	...	...	...	...	...	...	...	8.5	8.3
85	90	...	...	...	...	...	...	...	...	...	...	...	8.1

2006 Tax Facts on Insurance & Employee Benefits

APPENDIX A — ANNUITY TABLES

Table IIA—Annuities for Joint Life Only — Two Lives — Expected Return Multiples

Male	Male Ages / Female	35/40	36/41	37/42	38/43	39/44	40/45	41/46	42/47	43/48	44/49	45/50	46/51	47/52
35	40	30.3	29.9	29.4	29.0	28.5	28.0	27.5	27.0	26.5	26.0	25.5	24.9	24.4
36	41	...	29.5	29.0	28.6	28.2	27.7	27.2	26.7	26.2	25.7	25.2	24.7	24.2
37	42	...	...	28.6	28.2	27.8	27.3	26.9	26.4	25.9	25.5	25.0	24.4	23.9
38	43	...	...	...	27.8	27.4	27.0	26.5	26.1	25.6	25.2	24.7	24.2	23.7
39	44	...	...	...	...	27.0	26.6	26.2	25.8	25.3	24.8	24.4	23.9	23.4
40	45	...	...	...	...	...	26.2	25.8	25.4	25.0	24.5	24.1	23.6	23.1
41	46	...	...	...	...	...	...	25.4	25.0	24.6	24.2	23.8	23.3	22.9
42	47	...	...	...	...	...	...	...	24.6	24.2	23.8	23.4	23.0	22.6
43	48	...	...	...	...	...	...	...	...	23.9	23.5	23.1	22.7	22.2
44	49	...	...	...	...	...	...	...	...	...	23.1	22.7	22.3	21.9
45	50	...	...	...	...	...	...	...	...	...	...	22.4	22.0	21.6
46	51	...	...	...	...	...	...	...	...	...	...	...	21.6	21.2
47	52	...	...	...	...	...	...	...	...	...	...	...	...	20.9

Male	Male Ages / Female	48/53	49/54	50/55	51/56	52/57	53/58	54/59	55/60	56/61	57/62	58/63	59/64	60/65
35	40	23.8	23.3	22.7	22.1	21.6	21.0	20.4	19.8	19.3	18.7	18.1	17.5	17.0
36	41	23.6	23.1	22.5	22.0	21.4	20.8	20.3	19.7	19.1	18.6	18.0	17.4	16.9
37	42	23.4	22.9	22.3	21.8	21.2	20.7	20.1	19.6	19.0	18.4	17.9	17.3	16.8
38	43	23.2	22.6	22.1	21.6	21.1	20.5	20.0	19.4	18.9	18.3	17.8	17.2	16.7
39	44	22.9	22.4	21.9	21.4	20.9	20.3	19.8	19.3	18.7	18.2	17.7	17.1	16.6
40	45	22.7	22.2	21.7	21.2	20.7	20.1	19.6	19.1	18.6	18.0	17.5	17.0	16.5
41	46	22.4	21.9	21.4	20.9	20.4	19.9	19.4	18.9	18.4	17.9	17.4	16.9	16.3
42	47	22.1	21.6	21.2	20.7	20.2	19.7	19.2	18.7	18.2	17.7	17.2	16.7	16.2
43	48	21.8	21.4	20.9	20.5	20.0	19.5	19.0	18.6	18.1	17.6	17.1	16.6	16.1
44	49	21.5	21.1	20.6	20.2	19.8	19.3	18.8	18.4	17.9	17.4	16.9	16.4	15.9
45	50	21.2	20.8	20.4	19.9	19.5	19.1	18.6	18.1	17.7	17.2	16.7	16.3	15.8
46	51	20.9	20.5	20.1	19.7	19.2	18.8	18.4	17.9	17.5	17.0	16.6	16.1	15.6
47	52	20.5	20.1	19.8	19.4	19.0	18.5	18.1	17.7	17.3	16.8	16.4	15.9	15.5
48	53	20.2	19.8	19.4	19.1	18.7	18.3	17.9	17.5	17.0	16.6	16.2	15.7	15.3
49	54	...	19.5	19.1	18.8	18.4	18.0	17.6	17.2	16.8	16.4	16.0	15.5	15.1
50	55	...	...	18.8	18.4	18.1	17.7	17.3	16.9	16.6	16.2	15.8	15.3	14.9
51	56	...	...	...	18.1	17.8	17.4	17.0	16.7	16.3	15.9	15.5	15.1	14.7
52	57	...	...	...	...	17.4	17.1	16.8	16.4	16.0	15.7	15.3	14.9	14.5
53	58	...	...	...	...	...	16.8	16.4	16.1	15.8	15.4	15.1	14.7	14.3
54	59	...	...	...	...	...	...	16.1	15.8	15.5	15.1	14.8	14.4	14.1
55	60	...	...	...	...	...	...	...	15.5	15.2	14.9	14.5	14.2	13.9
56	61	...	...	...	...	...	...	...	...	14.9	14.6	14.3	13.9	13.6
57	62	...	...	...	...	...	...	...	...	...	14.3	14.0	13.7	13.4
58	63	...	...	...	...	...	...	...	...	...	...	13.7	13.4	13.1
59	64	...	...	...	...	...	...	...	...	...	...	...	13.1	12.8
60	65	...	...	...	...	...	...	...	...	...	...	...	...	12.6

Male	Male Ages / Female	61/66	62/67	63/68	64/69	65/70	66/71	67/72	68/73	69/74	70/75	71/76	72/77	73/78
35	40	16.4	15.8	15.3	14.7	14.2	13.7	13.1	12.6	12.1	11.6	11.1	10.7	10.2
36	41	16.3	15.8	15.2	14.7	14.1	13.6	13.1	12.6	12.1	11.6	11.1	10.6	10.2
37	42	16.2	15.7	15.1	14.6	14.1	13.6	13.0	12.5	12.0	11.5	11.1	10.6	10.1
38	43	16.1	15.6	15.1	14.5	14.0	13.5	13.0	12.5	12.0	11.5	11.0	10.6	10.1
39	44	16.0	15.5	15.0	14.5	13.9	13.4	12.9	12.4	11.9	11.5	11.0	10.5	10.1
40	45	15.9	15.4	14.9	14.4	13.9	13.4	12.9	12.4	11.9	11.4	11.0	10.5	10.0
41	46	15.8	15.3	14.8	14.3	13.8	13.3	12.8	12.3	11.8	11.4	10.9	10.5	10.0
42	47	15.7	15.2	14.7	14.2	13.7	13.2	12.7	12.3	11.8	11.3	10.9	10.4	10.0
43	48	15.6	15.1	14.6	14.1	13.6	13.1	12.7	12.2	11.7	11.3	10.8	10.4	9.9
44	49	15.5	15.0	14.5	14.0	13.5	13.1	12.6	12.1	11.7	11.2	10.8	10.3	9.9
45	50	15.3	14.8	14.4	13.9	13.4	13.0	12.5	12.0	11.6	11.1	10.7	10.3	9.8
46	51	15.2	14.7	14.2	13.8	13.3	12.9	12.4	12.0	11.5	11.1	10.6	10.2	9.8
47	52	15.0	14.6	14.1	13.7	13.2	12.8	12.3	11.9	11.4	11.0	10.6	10.1	9.7
48	53	14.9	14.4	14.0	13.5	13.1	12.6	12.2	11.8	11.3	10.9	10.5	10.1	9.7
49	54	14.7	14.3	13.8	13.4	13.0	12.5	12.1	11.7	11.3	10.8	10.4	10.0	9.6
50	55	14.5	14.1	13.7	13.3	12.8	12.4	12.0	11.6	11.2	10.7	10.3	9.9	9.5
51	56	14.3	13.9	13.5	13.1	12.7	12.3	11.9	11.5	11.1	10.7	10.3	9.9	9.5
52	57	14.1	13.7	13.3	12.9	12.5	12.1	11.7	11.3	10.9	10.6	10.2	9.8	9.4
53	58	13.9	13.6	13.2	12.8	12.4	12.0	11.6	11.2	10.8	10.5	10.1	9.7	9.3
54	59	13.7	13.4	13.0	12.6	12.2	11.9	11.5	11.1	10.7	10.3	10.0	9.6	9.2
55	60	13.5	13.2	12.8	12.4	12.1	11.7	11.3	11.0	10.6	10.2	9.9	9.5	9.1
56	61	13.3	12.9	12.6	12.2	11.9	11.5	11.2	10.8	10.5	10.1	9.8	9.4	9.0
57	62	13.0	12.7	12.4	12.1	11.7	11.4	11.0	10.7	10.3	10.0	9.6	9.3	8.9
58	63	12.8	12.5	12.2	11.8	11.5	11.2	10.9	10.5	10.2	9.8	9.5	9.2	8.8
59	64	12.6	12.3	11.9	11.6	11.3	11.0	10.7	10.4	10.0	9.7	9.4	9.1	8.7
60	65	12.3	12.0	11.7	11.4	11.1	10.8	10.5	10.2	9.9	9.6	9.3	8.9	8.6
61	66	12.0	11.8	11.5	11.2	10.9	10.6	10.3	10.0	9.7	9.4	9.1	8.8	8.5
62	67	...	11.5	11.2	11.0	10.7	10.4	10.1	9.8	9.6	9.3	9.0	8.7	8.4
63	68	...	...	11.0	10.7	10.5	10.2	9.9	9.7	9.4	9.1	8.8	8.5	8.2
64	69	...	...	...	10.5	10.2	10.0	9.7	9.5	9.2	8.9	8.7	8.4	8.1
65	70	...	...	...	...	10.0	9.8	9.5	9.3	9.0	8.8	8.5	8.2	8.0
66	71	...	...	...	...	...	9.5	9.3	9.1	8.8	8.6	8.3	8.1	7.8
67	72	...	...	...	...	...	...	9.1	8.9	8.6	8.4	8.1	7.9	7.7
68	73	...	...	...	...	...	...	...	8.6	8.4	8.2	8.0	7.7	7.5
69	74	...	...	...	...	...	...	...	...	8.2	8.0	7.8	7.6	7.3
70	75	...	...	...	...	...	...	...	...	...	7.8	7.6	7.4	7.2
71	76	...	...	...	...	...	...	...	...	...	...	7.4	7.2	7.0
72	77	...	...	...	...	...	...	...	...	...	...	...	7.0	6.8
73	78	...	...	...	...	...	...	...	...	...	...	...	...	6.7

APPENDIX A — ANNUITY TABLES

Table IIA — Annuities for Joint Life Only — Two Lives — Expected Return Multiples — Continued

Male Ages	Female Ages	74/79	75/80	76/81	77/82	78/83	79/84	80/85	81/86	82/87	83/88	84/89	85/90	86/91
35	40	9.7	9.3	8.9	8.5	8.1	7.7	7.3	6.9	6.6	6.2	5.9	5.6	5.3
36	41	9.7	9.3	8.9	8.4	8.0	7.7	7.3	6.9	6.6	6.2	5.9	5.6	5.3
37	42	9.7	9.3	8.8	8.4	8.0	7.6	7.3	6.9	6.5	6.2	5.9	5.6	5.3
38	43	9.7	9.2	8.8	8.4	8.0	7.6	7.2	6.9	6.5	6.2	5.9	5.6	5.3
39	44	9.6	9.2	8.8	8.4	8.0	7.6	7.2	6.9	6.5	6.2	5.9	5.6	5.3
40	45	9.6	9.2	8.8	8.4	8.0	7.6	7.2	6.9	6.5	6.2	5.9	5.5	5.2
41	46	9.6	9.2	8.7	8.3	7.9	7.6	7.2	6.8	6.5	6.2	5.8	5.5	5.2
42	47	9.5	9.1	8.7	8.3	7.9	7.5	7.2	6.8	6.5	6.2	5.8	5.5	5.2
43	48	9.5	9.1	8.7	8.3	7.9	7.5	7.2	6.8	6.5	6.1	5.8	5.5	5.2
44	49	9.5	9.0	8.6	8.2	7.9	7.5	7.1	6.8	6.4	6.1	5.8	5.5	5.2
45	50	9.4	9.0	8.6	8.2	7.8	7.5	7.1	6.8	6.4	6.1	5.8	5.5	5.2
46	51	9.4	9.0	8.6	8.2	7.8	7.4	7.1	6.7	6.4	6.1	5.8	5.5	5.2
47	52	9.3	8.9	8.5	8.1	7.8	7.4	7.1	6.7	6.4	6.1	5.8	5.5	5.2
48	53	9.3	8.9	8.5	8.1	7.7	7.4	7.0	6.7	6.4	6.0	5.7	5.4	5.1
49	54	9.2	8.8	8.4	8.1	7.7	7.3	7.0	6.7	6.3	6.0	5.7	5.4	5.1
50	55	9.1	8.8	8.4	8.0	7.7	7.3	7.0	6.6	6.3	6.0	5.7	5.4	5.1
51	56	9.1	8.7	8.3	8.0	7.6	7.3	6.9	6.6	6.3	6.0	5.7	5.4	5.1
52	57	9.0	8.6	8.3	7.9	7.6	7.2	6.9	6.6	6.2	5.9	5.6	5.4	5.1
53	58	8.9	8.6	8.2	7.9	7.5	7.2	6.9	6.5	6.2	5.9	5.6	5.3	5.0
54	59	8.9	8.5	8.2	7.8	7.5	7.1	6.8	6.5	6.2	5.9	5.6	5.3	5.0
55	60	8.8	8.4	8.1	7.7	7.4	7.1	6.8	6.4	6.1	5.8	5.6	5.3	5.0
56	61	8.7	8.4	8.0	7.7	7.3	7.0	6.7	6.4	6.1	5.8	5.5	5.2	5.0
57	62	8.6	8.3	7.9	7.6	7.3	7.0	6.7	6.4	6.1	5.8	5.5	5.2	4.9
58	63	8.5	8.2	7.9	7.5	7.2	6.9	6.6	6.3	6.0	5.7	5.5	5.2	4.9
59	64	8.4	8.1	7.8	7.5	7.1	6.8	6.5	6.3	6.0	5.7	5.4	5.2	4.9
60	65	8.3	8.0	7.7	7.4	7.1	6.8	6.5	6.2	5.9	5.6	5.4	5.1	4.9
61	66	8.2	7.9	7.6	7.3	7.0	6.7	6.4	6.1	5.9	5.6	5.3	5.1	4.8
62	67	8.1	7.8	7.5	7.2	6.9	6.6	6.4	6.1	5.8	5.5	5.3	5.0	4.8
63	68	8.0	7.7	7.4	7.1	6.8	6.6	6.3	6.0	5.7	5.5	5.2	5.0	4.7
64	69	7.8	7.6	7.3	7.0	6.7	6.5	6.2	5.9	5.7	5.4	5.2	4.9	4.7
65	70	7.7	7.4	7.2	6.9	6.6	6.4	6.1	5.9	5.6	5.4	5.1	4.9	4.7
66	71	7.6	7.3	7.1	6.8	6.5	6.3	6.0	5.8	5.5	5.3	5.1	4.8	4.6
67	72	7.4	7.2	6.9	6.7	6.4	6.2	6.0	5.7	5.5	5.2	5.0	4.8	4.6
68	73	7.3	7.0	6.8	6.6	6.3	6.1	5.9	5.6	5.4	5.2	4.9	4.7	4.5
69	74	7.1	6.9	6.7	6.4	6.2	6.0	5.8	5.5	5.3	5.1	4.9	4.7	4.5
70	75	7.0	6.8	6.5	6.3	6.1	5.9	5.7	5.4	5.2	5.0	4.8	4.6	4.4
71	76	6.8	6.6	6.4	6.2	6.0	5.8	5.6	5.3	5.1	4.9	4.7	4.5	4.3
72	77	6.6	6.4	6.3	6.1	5.9	5.7	5.5	5.3	5.0	4.9	4.7	4.5	4.3
73	78	6.5	6.3	6.1	5.9	5.7	5.5	5.3	5.1	5.0	4.8	4.6	4.4	4.2
74	79	6.3	6.1	6.0	5.8	5.6	5.4	5.2	5.0	4.9	4.7	4.5	4.3	4.1
75	80	..	6.0	5.8	5.6	5.5	5.3	5.1	4.9	4.8	4.6	4.4	4.2	4.1
76	81	..	..	5.6	5.5	5.3	5.2	5.0	4.8	4.7	4.5	4.3	4.1	4.0
77	82	..	..	..	5.3	5.2	5.0	4.9	4.7	4.5	4.4	4.2	4.1	3.9
78	83	..	..	..	..	5.0	4.9	4.7	4.6	4.4	4.3	4.1	4.0	3.8
79	84	..	..	..	..	..	4.7	4.6	4.5	4.3	4.2	4.0	3.9	3.7
80	85	..	..	..	..	..	..	4.5	4.3	4.2	4.1	3.9	3.8	3.6
81	86	..	..	..	..	..	..	..	4.2	4.1	3.9	3.8	3.7	3.6
82	87	..	..	..	..	..	..	..	..	4.0	3.8	3.7	3.6	3.5
83	88	..	..	..	..	..	..	..	..	..	3.7	3.6	3.5	3.4
84	89	..	..	..	..	..	..	..	..	..	..	3.5	3.4	3.3
85	90	..	..	..	..	..	..	..	..	..	..	..	3.3	3.2
86	91	..	..	..	..	..	..	..	..	..	..	..	..	3.1

APPENDIX A — ANNUITY TABLES

Table III — Percent Value of Refund Feature

Ages Male	Ages Female	1 Yr %	2 Yrs %	3 Yrs %	4 Yrs %	5 Yrs %	6 Yrs %	7 Yrs %	8 Yrs %	9 Yrs %	10 Yrs %	11 Yrs %	12 Yrs %
6	11	..	..	..	..	..	..	..	..	1	1	1	1
7	12	..	..	..	..	..	..	..	..	1	1	1	1
8	13	..	..	..	..	..	..	..	1	1	1	1	1
9	14	..	..	..	..	..	..	..	1	1	1	1	1
10	15	..	..	..	..	..	..	..	1	1	1	1	1
11	16	..	..	..	..	..	..	..	1	1	1	1	1
12	17	..	..	..	..	..	..	..	1	1	1	1	1
13	18	..	..	..	..	..	..	..	1	1	1	1	1
14	19	..	..	..	..	..	..	..	1	1	1	1	1
15	20	..	..	..	..	..	..	..	1	1	1	1	1
16	21	..	..	..	..	..	..	..	1	1	1	1	1
17	22	..	..	..	..	..	..	..	1	1	1	1	1
18	23	..	..	..	..	..	..	..	1	1	1	1	1
19	24	..	..	..	..	..	..	..	1	1	1	1	1
20	25	..	..	..	..	..	..	..	1	1	1	1	1
21	26	..	..	..	..	..	..	..	1	1	1	1	1
22	27	..	..	..	..	..	..	1	1	1	1	1	1
23	28	..	..	..	..	..	..	1	1	1	1	1	1
24	29	..	..	..	..	..	..	1	1	1	1	1	1
25	30	..	..	..	..	..	..	1	1	1	1	1	1
26	31	..	..	..	..	..	1	1	1	1	1	1	1
27	32	..	..	..	..	..	1	1	1	1	1	1	1
28	33	..	..	..	..	..	1	1	1	1	1	1	1
29	34	..	..	..	..	..	1	1	1	1	1	1	1
30	35	..	..	..	..	1	1	1	1	1	1	1	2
31	36	..	..	..	..	1	1	1	1	1	1	1	2
32	37	..	..	..	..	1	1	1	1	1	1	2	2
33	38	..	..	..	1	1	1	1	1	1	1	2	2
34	39	..	..	..	1	1	1	1	1	1	2	2	2
35	40	..	..	..	1	1	1	1	1	2	2	2	2
36	41	..	..	..	1	1	1	1	1	2	2	2	2
37	42	..	..	1	1	1	1	1	2	2	2	2	3
38	43	..	..	1	1	1	1	1	2	2	2	2	3
39	44	..	..	1	1	1	1	1	2	2	2	3	3
40	45	..	..	1	1	1	1	2	2	2	3	3	3
41	46	..	..	1	1	1	1	2	2	2	3	3	3
42	47	..	..	1	1	1	2	2	2	3	3	3	4
43	48	..	1	1	1	1	2	2	2	3	3	4	4
44	49	..	1	1	1	1	2	2	3	3	3	4	4
45	50	..	1	1	1	2	2	2	3	3	4	4	5
46	51	..	1	1	1	2	2	3	3	3	4	4	5
47	52	..	1	1	1	2	2	3	3	4	4	5	5
48	53	..	1	1	2	2	2	3	3	4	5	5	6
49	54	..	1	1	2	2	3	3	4	4	5	5	6
50	55	..	1	1	2	2	3	3	4	5	5	6	7
51	56	..	1	1	2	3	3	4	4	5	6	6	7
52	57	1	1	2	2	3	3	4	5	5	6	7	8
53	58	1	1	2	2	3	4	4	5	6	7	7	8
54	59	1	1	2	2	3	4	5	5	6	7	8	9
55	60	1	1	2	3	3	4	5	6	7	8	8	9
56	61	1	1	2	3	4	4	5	6	7	8	9	10
57	62	1	1	2	3	4	5	6	7	8	9	10	11
58	63	1	2	2	3	4	5	6	7	8	9	10	12
59	64	1	2	3	4	5	6	7	8	9	10	11	12
60	65	1	2	3	4	5	6	7	8	10	11	12	13
61	66	1	2	3	4	5	6	8	9	10	12	13	14
62	67	1	2	3	4	6	7	8	10	11	12	14	15
63	68	1	2	4	5	6	7	9	10	12	13	15	16
64	69	1	3	4	5	7	8	9	11	13	14	16	17
65	70	1	3	4	6	7	9	10	12	13	15	17	19
66	71	1	3	4	6	8	9	11	13	14	16	18	20
67	72	2	3	5	6	8	10	12	14	15	17	19	21
68	73	2	3	5	7	9	11	13	14	16	18	21	23
69	74	2	4	6	7	9	11	13	16	18	20	22	24
70	75	2	4	6	8	10	12	14	17	19	21	23	26
71	76	2	4	6	9	11	13	15	18	20	22	25	27
72	77	2	5	7	9	12	14	16	19	21	24	26	29
73	78	2	5	7	10	12	15	18	20	23	25	28	30
74	79	3	5	8	11	13	16	19	22	24	27	30	32
75	80	3	6	8	11	14	17	20	23	26	29	31	34
76	81	3	6	9	12	15	18	21	24	27	30	33	36
77	82	3	7	10	13	16	20	23	26	29	32	35	38
78	83	4	7	11	14	17	21	24	28	31	34	37	40
79	84	4	8	11	15	19	22	26	29	33	36	39	42
80	85	4	8	12	16	20	24	27	31	34	38	41	44
81	86	4	9	13	17	21	25	29	33	36	40	43	46
82	87	5	9	14	18	23	27	31	35	38	42	45	48
83	88	5	10	15	19	24	28	33	37	40	44	47	50
84	89	5	11	16	21	26	30	34	38	42	46	49	52
85	90	6	11	17	22	27	32	36	41	44	48	51	55

APPENDIX A — ANNUITY TABLES

Table III — Percent Value of Refund Feature — Continued

Ages Male	Ages Female		13 Yrs %	14 Yrs %	15 Yrs %	16 Yrs %	17 Yrs %	18 Yrs %	19 Yrs %	20 Yrs %	21 Yrs %	22 Yrs %	23 Yrs %	24 Yrs %
6	11		1	1	1	1	1	1	1	1	1	1	1	2
7	12		1	1	1	1	1	1	1	1	1	1	1	2
8	13		1	1	1	1	1	1	1	1	1	1	1	2
9	14		1	1	1	1	1	1	1	1	1	1	1	2
10	15		1	1	1	1	1	1	1	1	1	1	2	2
11	16		1	1	1	1	1	1	1	1	1	1	2	2
12	17		1	1	1	1	1	1	1	1	1	2	2	2
13	18		1	1	1	1	1	1	1	1	1	2	2	2
14	19		1	1	1	1	1	1	1	1	1	2	2	2
15	20		1	1	1	1	1	1	1	1	1	2	2	2
16	21		1	1	1	1	1	1	1	1	2	2	2	2
17	22		1	1	1	1	1	1	1	1	2	2	2	2
18	23		1	1	1	1	1	1	1	2	2	2	2	2
19	24		1	1	1	1	1	1	2	2	2	2	2	2
20	25		1	1	1	1	1	1	2	2	2	2	2	2
21	26		1	1	1	1	1	2	2	2	2	2	2	2
22	27		1	1	1	1	1	2	2	2	2	2	2	3
23	28		1	1	1	1	2	2	2	2	2	2	2	3
24	29		1	1	1	2	2	2	2	2	2	2	3	3
25	30		1	1	1	2	2	2	2	2	2	3	3	3
26	31		1	1	2	2	2	2	2	2	3	3	3	3
27	32		1	2	2	2	2	2	2	3	3	3	3	3
28	33		1	2	2	2	2	2	3	3	3	3	3	4
29	34		2	2	2	2	2	2	3	3	3	3	4	4
30	35		2	2	2	2	2	3	3	3	3	4	4	4
31	36		2	2	2	2	3	3	3	3	4	4	4	5
32	37		2	2	2	3	3	3	3	4	4	4	5	5
33	38		2	2	3	3	3	3	4	4	4	5	5	5
34	39		2	3	3	3	3	4	4	4	5	5	5	6
35	40		2	3	3	3	4	4	4	5	5	5	6	6
36	41		3	3	3	4	4	4	5	5	5	6	6	7
37	42		3	3	3	4	4	4	5	5	6	6	7	7
38	43		3	3	4	4	4	5	5	6	6	7	7	8
39	44		3	4	4	4	5	5	6	6	7	7	8	8
40	45		4	4	4	5	5	6	6	7	7	8	8	9
41	46		4	4	4	5	6	6	7	7	8	8	9	9
42	47		4	5	5	5	6	6	7	8	8	9	9	10
43	48		4	5	5	6	6	7	8	8	9	9	10	11
44	49		5	5	6	6	7	7	8	9	9	10	11	12
45	50		5	6	6	7	7	8	9	9	10	11	12	12
46	51		5	6	7	7	8	9	9	10	11	12	12	13
47	52		6	7	7	8	9	9	10	11	12	12	13	14
48	53		6	7	8	8	9	10	11	12	12	13	14	15
49	54		7	8	8	9	10	11	11	12	13	14	15	16
50	55		7	8	9	10	11	11	12	13	14	15	16	17
51	56		8	9	10	10	11	12	13	14	15	16	17	18
52	57		8	9	10	11	12	13	14	15	16	17	18	20
53	58		9	10	11	12	13	14	15	16	17	19	20	21
54	59		10	11	12	13	14	15	16	17	18	20	21	22
55	60		10	11	13	14	15	16	17	18	20	21	22	24
56	61		11	12	13	15	16	17	18	20	21	22	24	25
57	62		12	13	14	16	17	18	20	21	22	24	25	27
58	63		13	14	15	17	18	19	21	22	24	25	27	28
59	64		14	15	16	18	19	21	22	24	25	27	28	30
60	65		15	16	18	19	20	22	24	25	27	28	30	32
61	66		16	17	19	20	22	23	25	27	28	30	32	33
62	67		17	18	20	22	23	25	27	28	30	32	33	35
63	68		18	20	21	23	25	26	28	30	32	33	35	37
64	69		19	21	23	24	26	28	30	32	33	35	37	39
65	70		20	22	24	26	28	30	32	33	35	37	39	41
66	71		22	24	26	28	29	31	33	35	37	39	41	43
67	72		23	25	27	29	31	33	35	37	39	41	43	45
68	73		25	27	29	31	33	35	37	39	41	43	45	47
69	74		26	28	30	33	35	37	39	41	43	45	47	48
70	75		28	30	32	34	37	39	41	43	45	47	49	50
71	76		29	32	34	36	39	41	43	45	47	49	51	52
72	77		31	34	36	38	41	43	45	47	49	51	53	54
73	78		33	35	38	40	43	45	47	49	51	53	55	56
74	79		35	37	40	42	45	47	49	51	53	55	57	58
75	80		37	39	42	44	47	49	51	53	55	57	58	60
76	81		39	41	44	46	49	51	53	55	57	59	60	62
77	82		41	43	46	48	51	53	55	57	59	61	62	64
78	83		43	45	48	50	53	55	57	59	61	62	64	65
79	84		45	48	50	53	55	57	59	61	63	64	66	67
80	85		47	50	52	55	57	59	61	63	64	66	67	69
81	86		49	52	54	57	59	61	63	65	66	68	69	70
82	87		51	54	56	59	61	63	65	66	68	69	71	72
83	88		53	56	58	61	63	65	66	68	70	71	72	73
84	89		55	58	60	63	65	67	68	70	71	73	74	75
85	90		57	60	62	65	67	68	70	71	73	74	75	76

APPENDIX A — ANNUITY TABLES

Table III — Percent Value of Refund Feature — Continued

Ages Male	Ages Female		25 Yrs %	26 Yrs %	27 Yrs %	28 Yrs %	29 Yrs %	30 Yrs %	31 Yrs %	32 Yrs %	33 Yrs %	34 Yrs %	35 Yrs %
6	11		2	2	2	2	2	2	2	2	2	2	2
7	12		2	2	2	2	2	2	2	2	2	2	3
8	13		2	2	2	2	2	2	2	2	2	2	3
9	14		2	2	2	2	2	2	2	2	2	3	3
10	15		2	2	2	2	2	2	2	2	3	3	3
11	16		2	2	2	2	2	2	2	2	3	3	3
12	17		2	2	2	2	2	2	2	3	3	3	3
13	18		2	2	2	2	2	2	2	3	3	3	3
14	19		2	2	2	2	2	2	3	3	3	3	3
15	20		2	2	2	2	2	3	3	3	3	3	3
16	21		2	2	2	2	3	3	3	3	3	3	4
17	22		2	2	2	2	3	3	3	3	3	4	4
18	23		2	2	2	3	3	3	3	3	4	4	4
19	24		2	2	3	3	3	3	3	4	4	4	4
20	25		2	3	3	3	3	3	4	4	4	4	5
21	26		3	3	3	3	3	4	4	4	4	5	5
22	27		3	3	3	3	4	4	4	4	5	5	5
23	28		3	3	3	3	4	4	4	5	5	5	5
24	29		3	3	3	4	4	4	5	5	5	5	6
25	30		3	3	4	4	4	5	5	5	6	6	6
26	31		3	4	4	4	5	5	5	6	6	6	7
27	32		4	4	4	5	5	5	6	6	6	7	7
28	33		4	4	5	5	5	6	6	6	7	7	8
29	34		4	5	5	5	6	6	6	7	7	8	8
30	35		5	5	5	6	6	6	7	7	8	8	9
31	36		5	5	6	6	6	7	7	8	8	9	9
32	37		5	6	6	7	7	7	8	8	9	10	10
33	38		6	6	7	7	7	8	8	9	10	10	11
34	39		6	7	7	8	8	9	9	10	10	11	12
35	40		7	7	8	8	9	9	10	10	11	12	12
36	41		7	8	8	9	9	10	10	11	12	13	13
37	42		8	8	9	9	10	11	11	12	13	13	14
38	43		8	9	9	10	11	11	12	13	13	14	15
39	44		9	9	10	11	11	12	13	14	14	15	16
40	45		9	10	11	11	12	13	14	15	15	16	17
41	46		10	11	11	12	13	14	15	16	16	17	18
42	47		11	11	12	13	14	15	16	17	18	18	19
43	48		11	12	13	14	15	16	17	18	19	20	21
44	49		12	13	14	15	16	17	18	19	20	21	22
45	50		13	14	15	16	17	18	19	20	21	22	23
46	51		14	15	16	17	18	19	20	21	22	24	25
47	52		15	16	17	18	19	20	21	23	24	25	26
48	53		16	17	18	19	20	22	23	24	25	26	28
49	54		17	18	19	21	22	23	24	25	27	28	29
50	55		18	20	21	22	23	24	26	27	28	29	31
51	56		20	21	22	23	25	26	27	28	30	31	32
52	57		21	22	23	25	26	27	29	30	31	33	34
53	58		22	24	25	26	28	29	30	32	33	34	36
54	59		24	25	26	28	29	31	32	33	35	36	38
55	60		25	26	28	29	31	32	34	35	36	38	39
56	61		27	28	29	31	32	34	35	37	38	40	41
57	62		28	30	31	33	34	36	37	39	40	41	43
58	63		30	31	33	34	36	37	39	40	42	43	45
59	64		31	33	35	36	38	39	41	42	44	45	47
60	65		33	35	36	38	40	41	43	44	46	47	48
61	66		35	37	38	40	41	43	44	46	47	49	50
62	67		37	38	40	42	43	45	46	48	49	51	52
63	68		39	40	42	44	45	47	48	50	51	52	54
64	69		41	42	44	46	47	49	50	52	53	54	55
65	70		42	44	46	47	49	50	52	53	55	56	57
66	71		44	46	48	49	51	52	54	55	56	58	59
67	72		46	48	50	51	53	54	56	57	58	59	61
68	73		48	50	52	53	55	56	57	59	60	61	62
69	74		50	52	53	55	56	58	59	60	62	63	64
70	75		52	54	55	57	58	60	61	62	63	64	65
71	76		54	56	57	59	60	61	63	64	65	66	67
72	77		56	58	59	60	62	63	64	65	66	67	68
73	78		58	59	61	62	64	65	66	67	68	68	70
74	79		60	61	63	64	65	66	67	68	69	70	71
75	80		62	63	64	66	67	68	69	70	71	72	72
76	81		63	65	66	67	68	69	70	71	72	73	..
77	82		65	66	68	69	70	71	72	73	74	..	..
78	83		67	68	69	70	71	72	73	74	..	..	..
79	84		68	70	71	72	73	74	75	..	..	..	..
80	85		70	71	72	73	74	75	..	..	..	..	..
81	86		72	73	74	75	75	..	..	..	..	..	..
82	87		73	74	75	76	..	..	..	..	..	..	..
83	88		74	75	76	..	..	..	..	..	..	..	..
84	89		76	77	..	..	..	..	..	..	..	..	..
85	90		77	..	..	..	..	..	..	..	..	..	..

APPENDIX A — ANNUITY TABLES

Table V — Ordinary Life Annuities — One Life — Expected Return Multiples

Age	Multiple	Age	Multiple	Age	Multiple
5	76.6	42	40.6	79	10.0
6	75.6	43	39.6	80	9.5
7	74.7	44	38.7	81	8.9
8	73.7	45	37.7	82	8.4
9	72.7	46	36.8	83	7.9
10	71.7	47	35.9	84	7.4
11	70.7	48	34.9	85	6.9
12	69.7	49	34.0	86	6.5
13	68.8	50	33.1	87	6.1
14	67.8	51	32.2	88	5.7
15	66.8	52	31.3	89	5.3
16	65.8	53	30.4	90	5.0
17	64.8	54	29.5	91	4.7
18	63.9	55	28.6	92	4.4
19	62.9	56	27.7	93	4.1
20	61.9	57	26.8	94	3.9
21	60.9	58	25.9	95	3.7
22	59.9	59	25.0	96	3.4
23	59.0	60	24.2	97	3.2
24	58.0	61	23.3	98	3.0
25	57.0	62	22.5	99	2.8
26	56.0	63	21.6	100	2.7
27	55.1	64	20.8	101	2.5
28	54.1	65	20.0	102	2.3
29	53.1	66	19.2	103	2.1
30	52.2	67	18.4	104	1.9
31	51.2	68	17.6	105	1.8
32	50.2	69	16.8	106	1.6
33	49.3	70	16.0	107	1.4
34	48.3	71	15.3	108	1.3
35	47.3	72	14.6	109	1.1
36	46.4	73	13.9	110	1.0
37	45.4	74	13.2	111	.9
38	44.4	75	12.5	112	.8
39	43.5	76	11.9	113	.7
40	42.5	77	11.2	114	.6
41	41.5	78	10.6	115	.5

Table VI — Ordinary Joint Life and Last Survivor Annuities — Two Lives — Expected Return Multiples

AGES	35	36	37	38	39	40	41	42	43	44	45	46	47	48	49	50
35	54.0	...	...	...	...	...	...	...	...	...	...	...	...	...	...	...
36	53.5	53.0	...	...	...	...	...	...	...	...	...	...	...	...	...	...
37	53.0	52.5	52.0	...	...	...	...	...	...	...	...	...	...	...	...	...
38	52.6	52.0	51.5	51.0	...	...	...	...	...	...	...	...	...	...	...	...
39	52.2	51.6	51.0	50.5	50.0	...	...	...	...	...	...	...	...	...	...	...
40	51.8	51.2	50.6	50.0	49.5	49.0	...	...	...	...	...	...	...	...	...	...
41	51.4	50.8	50.2	49.6	49.1	48.5	48.0	...	...	...	...	...	...	...	...	...
42	51.1	50.4	49.8	49.2	48.6	48.1	47.5	47.0	...	...	...	...	...	...	...	...
43	50.8	50.1	49.5	48.8	48.2	47.6	47.1	46.6	46.0	...	...	...	...	...	...	...
44	50.5	49.8	49.1	48.5	47.8	47.2	46.7	46.1	45.6	45.1	...	...	...	...	...	...
45	50.2	49.5	48.8	48.1	47.5	46.9	46.3	45.7	45.1	44.6	44.1	...	...	...	...	...
46	50.0	49.2	48.5	47.8	47.2	46.5	45.9	45.3	44.7	44.1	43.6	43.1	...	...	...	...
47	49.7	49.0	48.3	47.5	46.8	46.2	45.5	44.9	44.3	43.7	43.2	42.6	42.1	...	...	...
48	49.5	48.8	48.0	47.3	46.6	45.9	45.2	44.5	43.9	43.3	42.7	42.2	41.7	41.2	...	...
49	49.3	48.5	47.8	47.0	46.3	45.6	44.9	44.2	43.6	42.9	42.3	41.8	41.2	40.7	40.2	...
50	49.2	48.4	47.6	46.8	46.0	45.3	44.6	43.9	43.2	42.6	42.0	41.4	40.8	40.2	39.7	39.2
51	49.0	48.2	47.4	46.6	45.8	45.1	44.3	43.6	42.9	42.2	41.6	41.0	40.4	39.8	39.3	38.7
52	48.8	48.0	47.2	46.4	45.6	44.8	44.1	43.3	42.6	41.9	41.3	40.6	40.0	39.4	38.8	38.3
53	48.7	47.9	47.0	46.2	45.4	44.6	43.9	43.1	42.4	41.7	41.0	40.3	39.7	39.0	38.4	37.9
54	48.6	47.7	46.9	46.0	45.2	44.4	43.6	42.9	42.1	41.4	40.7	40.0	39.3	38.7	38.1	37.5
55	48.5	47.6	46.7	45.9	45.1	44.2	43.4	42.7	41.9	41.2	40.4	39.7	39.0	38.4	37.7	37.1
56	48.3	47.5	46.6	45.8	44.9	44.1	43.3	42.5	41.7	40.9	40.2	39.5	38.7	38.1	37.4	36.8
57	48.3	47.4	46.5	45.6	44.8	43.9	43.1	42.3	41.5	40.7	40.0	39.2	38.5	37.8	37.1	36.4
58	48.2	47.3	46.4	45.5	44.7	43.8	43.0	42.1	41.3	40.5	39.7	39.0	38.2	37.5	36.8	36.1
59	48.1	47.2	46.3	45.4	44.5	43.7	42.8	42.0	41.2	40.4	39.6	38.8	38.0	37.3	36.6	35.9
60	48.0	47.1	46.2	45.3	44.4	43.6	42.7	41.9	41.0	40.2	39.4	38.6	37.8	37.1	36.3	35.6
61	47.9	47.0	46.1	45.2	44.3	43.5	42.6	41.7	40.9	40.0	39.2	38.4	37.6	36.9	36.1	35.4
62	47.9	47.0	46.0	45.1	44.2	43.4	42.5	41.6	40.8	39.9	39.1	38.3	37.5	36.7	35.9	35.1
63	47.8	46.9	46.0	45.1	44.2	43.3	42.4	41.5	40.6	39.8	38.9	38.1	37.3	36.5	35.7	34.9
64	47.8	46.8	45.9	45.0	44.1	43.2	42.3	41.4	40.5	39.7	38.8	38.0	37.2	36.3	35.5	34.8
65	47.7	46.8	45.9	44.9	44.0	43.1	42.2	41.3	40.4	39.6	38.7	37.9	37.0	36.2	35.4	34.6
66	47.7	46.7	45.8	44.9	44.0	43.1	42.2	41.3	40.4	39.5	38.6	37.8	36.9	36.1	35.2	34.4
67	47.7	46.7	45.8	44.8	43.9	43.0	42.1	41.2	40.3	39.4	38.5	37.7	36.8	36.0	35.1	34.3
68	47.6	46.7	45.7	44.8	43.9	42.9	42.0	41.1	40.2	39.3	38.4	37.6	36.7	35.8	35.0	34.2
69	47.6	46.6	45.7	44.8	43.8	42.9	42.0	41.1	40.1	39.2	38.3	37.4	36.5	35.7	34.9	34.1
70	47.5	46.6	45.7	44.7	43.8	42.9	41.9	41.0	40.1	39.2	38.3	37.4	36.5	35.7	34.8	34.0
71	47.5	46.6	45.6	44.7	43.8	42.8	41.9	41.0	40.1	39.1	38.2	37.3	36.5	35.6	34.7	33.9
72	47.5	46.6	45.6	44.7	43.7	42.8	41.9	40.9	40.0	39.1	38.2	37.3	36.4	35.5	34.6	33.8
73	47.5	46.5	45.6	44.7	43.7	42.8	41.8	40.9	40.0	39.0	38.1	37.2	36.3	35.4	34.6	33.7
74	47.5	46.5	45.6	44.7	43.7	42.8	41.8	40.9	39.9	39.0	38.1	37.2	36.3	35.4	34.5	33.6
75	47.4	46.5	45.5	44.7	43.6	42.7	41.8	40.8	39.9	39.0	38.1	37.1	36.2	35.3	34.5	33.6
76	47.4	46.5	45.5	44.7	43.6	42.7	41.7	40.8	39.9	38.9	38.0	37.1	36.2	35.3	34.4	33.5
77	47.4	46.5	45.5	44.7	43.6	42.7	41.7	40.8	39.8	38.9	38.0	37.1	36.2	35.3	34.4	33.5
78	47.4	46.4	45.5	44.5	43.6	42.6	41.7	40.7	39.8	38.9	37.9	37.0	36.1	35.2	34.3	33.4
79	47.4	46.4	45.5	44.5	43.6	42.6	41.7	40.7	39.8	38.9	37.9	37.0	36.1	35.2	34.3	33.4
80	47.4	46.4	45.5	44.5	43.6	42.6	41.7	40.7	39.8	38.8	37.9	37.0	36.1	35.1	34.2	33.3
81	47.4	46.4	45.5	44.5	43.5	42.6	41.6	40.7	39.8	38.8	37.9	37.0	36.0	35.1	34.2	33.3
82	47.4	46.4	45.4	44.5	43.5	42.6	41.6	40.7	39.7	38.8	37.9	36.9	36.0	35.1	34.2	33.3
83	47.4	46.4	45.4	44.5	43.5	42.6	41.6	40.7	39.7	38.8	37.9	36.9	36.0	35.1	34.1	33.3
84	47.4	46.4	45.4	44.5	43.5	42.6	41.6	40.7	39.7	38.8	37.8	36.9	36.0	35.0	34.1	33.2
85	47.4	46.4	45.4	44.5	43.5	42.6	41.6	40.7	39.7	38.8	37.8	36.9	36.0	35.0	34.1	33.2
86	47.3	46.4	45.4	44.5	43.5	42.6	41.6	40.6	39.7	38.7	37.8	36.9	35.9	35.0	34.1	33.2
87	47.3	46.4	45.4	44.5	43.5	42.5	41.6	40.6	39.7	38.7	37.8	36.9	35.9	35.0	34.1	33.2
88	47.3	46.4	45.4	44.4	43.5	42.5	41.6	40.6	39.7	38.7	37.8	36.9	35.9	35.0	34.1	33.2
89	47.3	46.4	45.4	44.4	43.5	42.5	41.6	40.6	39.7	38.7	37.8	36.9	35.9	35.0	34.1	33.2
90	47.3	46.4	45.4	44.4	43.5	42.5	41.6	40.6	39.7	38.7	37.8	36.9	35.9	35.0	34.1	33.2

APPENDIX A — ANNUITY TABLES

Table VI — Ordinary Joint Life and Last Survivor Annuities — Two Lives — Expected Return Multiples

AGES	51	52	53	54	55	56	57	58	59	60	61	62	63	64	65	66
51	38.2	...	...	...	...	...	...	...	...	...	...	...	...	...	...	...
52	37.8	37.3	...	...	...	...	...	...	...	...	...	...	...	...	...	...
53	37.3	36.8	36.3	...	...	...	...	...	...	...	...	...	...	...	...	...
54	36.9	36.4	35.8	35.3	...	...	...	...	...	...	...	...	...	...	...	...
55	36.5	35.9	35.4	34.9	34.4	...	...	...	...	...	...	...	...	...	...	...
56	36.1	35.6	35.0	34.4	33.9	33.4	...	...	...	...	...	...	...	...	...	...
57	35.8	35.2	34.6	34.0	33.5	33.0	32.5	...	...	...	...	...	...	...	...	...
58	35.5	34.8	34.2	33.6	33.1	32.5	32.0	31.5	...	...	...	...	...	...	...	...
59	35.2	34.5	33.9	33.3	32.7	32.1	31.6	31.1	30.6	...	...	...	...	...	...	...
60	34.9	34.2	33.6	32.9	32.3	31.7	31.2	30.6	30.1	29.7	...	...	...	...	...	...
61	34.6	33.9	33.3	32.6	32.0	31.4	30.8	30.2	29.7	29.2	28.7	...	...	...	...	...
62	34.4	33.7	33.0	32.3	31.7	31.0	30.4	29.9	29.3	28.8	28.3	27.8	...	...	...	...
63	34.2	33.5	32.7	32.0	31.4	30.7	30.1	29.5	28.9	28.4	27.8	27.3	26.9	...	...	...
64	34.0	33.2	32.5	31.8	31.1	30.4	29.8	29.2	28.6	28.0	27.4	26.9	26.4	25.9	...	...
65	33.8	33.0	32.3	31.6	30.9	30.2	29.5	28.9	28.2	27.6	27.1	26.5	26.0	25.5	25.0	...
66	33.6	32.9	32.1	31.4	30.6	29.9	29.2	28.6	27.9	27.3	26.7	26.1	25.6	25.1	24.6	24.1
67	33.5	32.7	31.9	31.2	30.4	29.7	29.0	28.3	27.6	27.0	26.4	25.8	25.2	24.7	24.2	23.7
68	33.4	32.5	31.8	31.0	30.2	29.5	28.8	28.1	27.4	26.7	26.1	25.5	24.9	24.3	23.8	23.3
69	33.2	32.4	31.6	30.8	30.1	29.3	28.6	27.8	27.1	26.5	25.8	25.2	24.6	24.0	23.4	22.9
70	33.1	32.3	31.5	30.7	29.9	29.1	28.4	27.6	26.9	26.2	25.6	24.9	24.3	23.7	23.1	22.5
71	33.0	32.2	31.4	30.5	29.7	29.0	28.2	27.5	26.7	26.0	25.3	24.7	24.0	23.4	22.8	22.2
72	32.9	32.1	31.2	30.4	29.6	28.8	28.1	27.3	26.5	25.8	25.1	24.4	23.8	23.1	22.5	21.9
73	32.8	32.0	31.1	30.3	29.5	28.7	27.9	27.1	26.4	25.6	24.9	24.2	23.5	22.9	22.2	21.6
74	32.8	31.9	31.1	30.2	29.4	28.6	27.8	27.0	26.2	25.5	24.7	24.0	23.3	22.7	22.0	21.4
75	32.7	31.8	31.0	30.1	29.3	28.5	27.7	26.9	26.1	25.3	24.6	23.8	23.1	22.4	21.8	21.1
76	32.6	31.8	30.9	30.1	29.2	28.4	27.6	26.8	26.0	25.2	24.4	23.7	23.0	22.3	21.6	20.9
77	32.6	31.7	30.8	30.0	29.1	28.3	27.5	26.7	25.9	25.1	24.3	23.6	22.8	22.1	21.4	20.7
78	32.5	31.7	30.8	29.9	29.1	28.2	27.4	26.6	25.8	25.0	24.2	23.4	22.7	21.9	21.2	20.5
79	32.5	31.6	30.7	29.9	29.0	28.2	27.3	26.5	25.7	24.9	24.1	23.3	22.6	21.8	21.1	20.4
80	32.5	31.6	30.7	29.8	29.0	28.1	27.3	26.4	25.6	24.8	24.0	23.2	22.4	21.7	21.0	20.2
81	32.4	31.5	30.7	29.8	28.9	28.1	27.2	26.4	25.5	24.7	23.9	23.1	22.3	21.6	20.8	20.1
82	32.4	31.5	30.6	29.7	28.9	28.0	27.2	26.3	25.5	24.6	23.8	23.0	22.3	21.5	20.7	20.0
83	32.4	31.5	30.6	29.7	28.8	28.0	27.1	26.3	25.4	24.6	23.8	23.0	22.2	21.4	20.6	19.9
84	32.3	31.4	30.6	29.7	28.8	27.9	27.1	26.2	25.4	24.5	23.7	22.9	22.1	21.3	20.5	19.8
85	32.3	31.4	30.5	29.6	28.8	27.9	27.0	26.2	25.3	24.5	23.7	22.8	22.0	21.3	20.5	19.7
86	32.3	31.4	30.5	29.6	28.7	27.9	27.0	26.1	25.3	24.5	23.6	22.8	22.0	21.2	20.4	19.6
87	32.3	31.4	30.5	29.6	28.7	27.8	27.0	26.1	25.3	24.4	23.6	22.8	21.9	21.1	20.4	19.6
88	32.3	31.4	30.5	29.6	28.7	27.8	27.0	26.1	25.2	24.4	23.5	22.7	21.9	21.1	20.3	19.5
89	32.3	31.4	30.5	29.6	28.7	27.8	26.9	26.1	25.2	24.4	23.5	22.7	21.9	21.1	20.3	19.5
90	32.3	31.3	30.5	29.5	28.7	27.8	26.9	26.1	25.2	24.3	23.5	22.7	21.8	21.0	20.2	19.4

Table VI — Ordinary Joint Life and Last Survivor Annuities — Two Lives — Expected Return Multiples

AGES	67	68	69	70	71	72	73	74	75	76	77	78	79	80	81	82
67	23.2	...	...	...	...	...	...	...	...	...	...	...	...	...	...	...
68	22.8	22.3	...	...	...	...	...	...	...	...	...	...	...	...	...	...
69	22.4	21.9	21.5	...	...	...	...	...	...	...	...	...	...	...	...	...
70	22.0	21.5	21.1	20.6	...	...	...	...	...	...	...	...	...	...	...	...
71	21.7	21.2	20.7	20.2	19.8	...	...	...	...	...	...	...	...	...	...	...
72	21.3	20.8	20.3	19.8	19.4	18.9	...	...	...	...	...	...	...	...	...	...
73	21.0	20.5	20.0	19.4	19.0	18.5	18.1	...	...	...	...	...	...	...	...	...
74	20.8	20.2	19.6	19.1	18.6	18.2	17.7	17.3	...	...	...	...	...	...	...	...
75	20.5	19.9	19.3	18.8	18.3	17.8	17.3	16.9	16.5	...	...	...	...	...	...	...
76	20.3	19.7	19.1	18.5	18.0	17.5	17.0	16.5	16.1	15.7	...	...	...	...	...	...
77	20.1	19.4	18.8	18.3	17.7	17.2	16.7	16.2	15.8	15.4	15.0	...	...	...	...	...
78	19.9	19.2	18.6	18.0	17.5	16.9	16.4	15.9	15.4	15.0	14.6	14.2	...	...	...	...
79	19.7	19.0	18.4	17.8	17.2	16.7	16.1	15.6	15.1	14.7	14.3	13.9	13.5	...	...	...
80	19.5	18.9	18.2	17.6	17.0	16.4	15.9	15.4	14.9	14.4	14.0	13.5	13.2	12.8	...	...
81	19.4	18.7	18.1	17.4	16.8	16.2	15.7	15.1	14.6	14.1	13.7	13.2	12.8	12.5	12.1	...
82	19.3	18.6	17.9	17.3	16.6	16.0	15.5	14.9	14.4	13.9	13.4	13.0	12.5	12.2	11.8	11.5
83	19.2	18.5	17.8	17.1	16.5	15.9	15.3	14.7	14.2	13.7	13.2	12.7	12.3	11.9	11.5	11.1
84	19.1	18.4	17.7	17.0	16.3	15.7	15.1	14.5	14.0	13.5	13.0	12.5	12.0	11.6	11.2	10.9
85	19.0	18.3	17.6	16.9	16.2	15.6	15.0	14.4	13.8	13.3	12.8	12.3	11.8	11.4	11.0	10.6
86	18.9	18.2	17.5	16.8	16.1	15.5	14.8	14.2	13.7	13.1	12.6	12.1	11.6	11.2	10.8	10.4
87	18.8	18.1	17.4	16.7	16.0	15.4	14.7	14.1	13.5	13.0	12.4	11.9	11.4	11.0	10.6	10.1
88	18.8	18.0	17.3	16.6	15.9	15.3	14.6	14.0	13.4	12.8	12.3	11.8	11.3	10.8	10.4	10.0
89	18.7	18.0	17.2	16.5	15.8	15.2	14.5	13.9	13.3	12.7	12.2	11.6	11.1	10.7	10.2	9.8
90	18.7	17.9	17.2	16.5	15.8	15.1	14.5	13.8	13.2	12.6	12.1	11.5	11.0	10.5	10.1	9.6

Table VI — Ordinary Joint Life and Last Survivor Annuities — Two Lives — Expected Return Multiples

AGES	83	84	85	86	87	88	89	90
83	10.8	...	...	...	...	...	...	...
84	10.5	10.2	...	...	...	...	...	...
85	10.2	9.9	9.6	...	...	...	...	...
86	10.0	9.7	9.3	9.1	...	...	...	...
87	9.8	9.4	9.1	8.8	8.5	...	...	...
88	9.6	9.2	8.9	8.6	8.3	8.0	...	...
89	9.4	9.0	8.7	8.3	8.1	7.8	7.5	...
90	9.2	8.8	8.5	8.2	7.9	7.6	7.3	7.1

2006 Tax Facts on Insurance & Employee Benefits

APPENDIX A — ANNUITY TABLES

Table VIA — Annuities for Joint Life Only — Two Lives — Expected Return Multiples

AGES	35	36	37	38	39	40	41	42	43	44	45	46	47	48	49	50
35	40.7	...	...	...	...	...	...	...	...	...	...	...	...	...	...	...
36	40.2	39.7	...	...	...	...	...	...	...	...	...	...	...	...	...	...
37	39.7	39.3	38.8	...	...	...	...	...	...	...	...	...	...	...	...	...
38	39.2	38.7	38.3	37.9	...	...	...	...	...	...	...	...	...	...	...	...
39	38.6	38.2	37.8	37.4	36.9	...	...	...	...	...	...	...	...	...	...	...
40	38.0	37.7	37.3	36.9	36.4	36.0	...	...	...	...	...	...	...	...	...	...
41	37.4	37.1	36.7	36.3	35.9	35.5	35.1	...	...	...	...	...	...	...	...	...
42	36.8	36.5	36.2	35.8	35.4	35.0	34.6	34.1	...	...	...	...	...	...	...	...
43	36.2	35.9	35.6	35.2	34.9	34.5	34.1	33.7	33.2	...	...	...	...	...	...	...
44	35.5	35.2	34.9	34.6	34.3	34.0	33.6	33.2	32.8	32.3	...	...	...	...	...	...
45	34.8	34.6	34.3	34.0	33.7	33.4	33.0	32.7	32.3	31.8	31.4	...	...	...	...	...
46	34.1	33.9	33.7	33.4	33.1	32.8	32.5	32.1	31.8	31.4	30.9	30.5	...	...	...	...
47	33.4	33.2	33.0	32.8	32.5	32.2	31.9	31.6	31.2	30.8	30.5	30.0	29.6	...	...	...
48	32.7	32.5	32.3	32.1	31.8	31.6	31.3	31.0	30.7	30.3	30.0	29.6	29.2	28.7	...	...
49	32.0	31.8	31.6	31.4	31.2	30.9	30.7	30.4	30.1	29.8	29.4	29.1	28.7	28.3	27.9	...
50	31.3	31.1	30.9	30.7	30.5	30.3	30.0	29.8	29.5	29.2	28.9	28.5	28.2	27.4	27.4	27.0
51	30.5	30.4	30.2	30.0	29.8	29.6	29.4	29.2	28.9	28.6	28.3	28.0	27.7	27.3	26.9	26.5
52	29.7	29.6	29.5	29.3	29.1	28.9	28.7	28.5	28.3	28.0	27.7	27.4	27.1	26.8	26.5	26.1
53	29.0	28.9	28.7	28.6	28.4	28.2	28.1	27.9	27.6	27.4	27.1	26.9	26.6	26.3	25.9	25.6
54	28.2	28.1	28.0	27.8	27.7	27.5	27.4	27.2	27.0	26.8	26.5	26.3	26.0	25.7	25.4	25.1
55	27.4	27.3	27.2	27.1	27.0	26.8	26.7	26.5	26.3	26.1	25.9	25.7	25.4	25.1	24.9	24.6
56	26.7	26.6	26.5	26.3	26.2	26.1	26.0	25.8	25.6	25.4	25.2	25.0	24.8	24.6	24.3	24.0
57	25.9	25.8	25.7	25.6	25.5	25.4	25.2	25.1	24.9	24.8	24.6	24.4	24.2	24.0	23.7	23.5
58	25.1	25.0	24.9	24.8	24.7	24.6	24.5	24.4	24.2	24.1	23.9	23.7	23.5	23.3	23.1	22.9
59	24.3	24.2	24.1	24.1	24.0	23.9	23.8	23.6	23.5	23.4	23.2	23.1	22.9	22.7	22.5	22.3
60	23.5	23.4	23.4	23.3	23.2	23.1	23.0	22.9	22.8	22.7	22.5	22.4	22.2	22.1	21.9	21.7
61	22.7	22.6	22.6	22.5	22.4	22.4	22.3	22.2	22.1	22.0	21.8	21.7	21.6	21.4	21.2	21.1
62	21.9	21.9	21.8	21.7	21.7	21.6	21.5	21.4	21.3	21.2	21.1	21.0	20.9	20.7	20.6	20.4
63	21.1	21.1	21.0	21.0	20.9	20.8	20.8	20.7	20.6	20.5	20.4	20.3	20.2	20.1	19.9	19.8
64	20.3	20.3	20.2	20.2	20.1	20.1	20.0	20.0	19.9	19.8	19.7	19.6	19.5	19.4	19.3	19.1
65	19.6	19.5	19.5	19.4	19.4	19.3	19.3	19.2	19.1	19.1	19.0	18.9	18.8	18.7	18.6	18.5
66	18.8	18.8	18.7	18.7	18.6	18.6	18.5	18.5	18.4	18.4	18.3	18.2	18.1	18.0	17.9	17.8
67	18.0	18.0	18.0	17.9	17.9	17.9	17.8	17.8	17.7	17.6	17.6	17.5	17.4	17.3	17.3	17.2
68	17.3	17.3	17.2	17.2	17.2	17.1	17.1	17.0	17.0	16.9	16.9	16.8	16.7	16.7	16.6	16.5
69	16.5	16.5	16.5	16.5	16.4	16.4	16.4	16.3	16.3	16.2	16.2	16.1	16.1	16.0	15.9	15.8
70	15.8	15.8	15.8	15.7	15.7	15.7	15.6	15.6	15.6	15.5	15.5	15.4	15.4	15.3	15.3	15.2
71	15.1	15.1	15.1	15.0	15.0	15.0	15.0	14.9	14.9	14.9	14.8	14.8	14.7	14.7	14.6	14.5
72	14.4	14.4	14.4	14.3	14.3	14.3	14.3	14.2	14.2	14.2	14.1	14.1	14.1	14.0	14.0	13.9
73	13.7	13.7	13.7	13.7	13.7	13.6	13.6	13.6	13.6	13.5	13.5	13.5	13.4	13.4	13.3	13.3
74	13.1	13.0	13.0	13.0	13.0	13.0	13.0	12.9	12.9	12.9	12.8	12.8	12.8	12.7	12.7	12.7
75	12.4	12.4	12.4	12.4	12.3	12.3	12.3	12.3	12.3	12.2	12.2	12.2	12.2	12.1	12.1	12.1
76	11.8	11.8	11.7	11.7	11.7	11.7	11.7	11.7	11.6	11.6	11.6	11.6	11.6	11.5	11.5	11.5
77	11.1	11.1	11.1	11.1	11.1	11.1	11.1	11.1	11.0	11.0	11.0	11.0	11.0	10.9	10.9	10.9
78	10.5	10.5	10.5	10.5	10.5	10.5	10.5	10.5	10.5	10.4	10.4	10.4	10.4	10.4	10.3	10.3
79	10.0	10.0	9.9	9.9	9.9	9.9	9.9	9.9	9.9	9.9	9.9	9.9	9.8	9.8	9.8	9.8
80	9.4	9.4	9.4	9.4	9.4	9.4	9.4	9.3	9.3	9.3	9.3	9.3	9.3	9.3	9.2	9.2
81	8.9	8.8	8.8	8.8	8.8	8.8	8.8	8.8	8.8	8.8	8.8	8.8	8.7	8.7	8.7	8.7
82	8.3	8.3	8.3	8.3	8.3	8.3	8.3	8.3	8.3	8.3	8.3	8.3	8.2	8.2	8.2	8.2
83	7.8	7.8	7.8	7.8	7.8	7.8	7.8	7.8	7.8	7.8	7.8	7.8	7.8	7.7	7.7	7.7
84	7.3	7.3	7.3	7.3	7.3	7.3	7.3	7.3	7.3	7.3	7.3	7.3	7.3	7.3	7.3	7.2
85	6.9	6.9	6.9	6.9	6.9	6.9	6.9	6.9	6.9	6.9	6.8	6.8	6.8	6.8	6.8	6.8
86	6.5	6.5	6.5	6.5	6.4	6.4	6.4	6.4	6.4	6.4	6.4	6.4	6.4	6.4	6.4	6.4
87	6.1	6.0	6.0	6.0	6.0	6.0	6.0	6.0	6.0	6.0	6.0	6.0	6.0	6.0	6.0	6.0
88	5.7	5.7	5.7	5.7	5.7	5.7	5.7	5.6	5.6	5.6	5.6	5.6	5.6	5.6	5.6	5.6
89	5.3	5.3	5.3	5.3	5.3	5.3	5.3	5.3	5.3	5.3	5.3	5.3	5.3	5.3	5.3	5.3
90	5.0	5.0	5.0	5.0	5.0	5.0	5.0	5.0	5.0	5.0	5.0	4.9	4.9	4.9	4.9	4.9

(Table VIA continues on the following page.)

APPENDIX A — ANNUITY TABLES

Table VIA — Annuities for Joint Life Only — Two Lives — Expected Return Multiples

AGES	51	52	53	54	55	56	57	58	59	60	61	62	63	64	65	66
51	26.1	...	...	...	...	...	...	...	...	...	...	...	...	...	...	...
52	25.7	25.3	...	...	...	...	...	...	...	...	...	...	...	...	...	...
53	25.2	24.8	24.4	...	...	...	...	...	...	...	...	...	...	...	...	...
54	24.7	24.4	24.0	23.6	...	...	...	...	...	...	...	...	...	...	...	...
55	24.2	23.9	23.5	23.2	22.7	...	...	...	...	...	...	...	...	...	...	...
56	23.7	23.4	23.1	22.7	22.3	21.9	...	...	...	...	...	...	...	...	...	...
57	23.2	22.9	22.6	22.2	21.9	21.5	21.1	...	...	...	...	...	...	...	...	...
58	22.6	22.4	22.1	21.7	21.4	21.1	20.7	20.3	...	...	...	...	...	...	...	...
59	22.1	21.8	21.5	21.2	20.9	20.6	20.3	19.9	19.5	...	...	...	...	...	...	...
60	21.5	21.2	21.0	20.7	20.4	20.1	19.8	19.5	19.1	18.7	...	...	...	...	...	...
61	20.9	20.6	20.4	20.2	19.9	19.6	19.3	19.0	18.7	18.3	17.9	...	...	...	...	...
62	20.2	20.0	19.8	19.6	19.4	19.1	18.8	18.5	18.2	17.9	17.5	17.1	...	...	...	...
63	19.6	19.4	19.2	19.0	18.8	18.6	18.3	18.0	17.7	17.4	17.1	16.8	16.4	...	...	...
64	19.0	18.8	18.6	18.5	18.3	18.0	17.8	17.5	17.3	17.0	16.7	16.3	16.0	15.6	...	...
65	18.3	18.2	18.0	17.9	17.7	17.5	17.3	17.0	16.8	16.5	16.2	15.9	15.6	15.3	14.9	...
66	17.7	17.6	17.4	17.3	17.1	16.9	16.7	16.5	16.3	16.0	15.8	15.5	15.2	14.9	14.5	14.2
67	17.1	16.9	16.8	16.7	16.5	16.3	16.2	16.0	15.8	15.5	15.3	15.0	14.7	14.5	14.1	13.8
68	16.4	16.3	16.2	16.1	15.9	15.8	15.6	15.4	15.2	15.0	14.8	14.6	14.3	14.0	13.7	13.4
69	15.8	15.7	15.6	15.4	15.3	15.2	15.0	14.9	14.7	14.5	14.3	14.1	13.9	13.6	13.3	13.1
70	15.1	15.0	14.9	14.8	14.7	14.6	14.5	14.3	14.2	14.0	13.8	13.6	13.4	13.2	12.9	12.6
71	14.5	14.4	14.3	14.2	14.1	14.0	13.9	13.8	13.6	13.5	13.3	13.1	12.9	12.7	12.5	12.2
72	13.8	13.8	13.7	13.6	13.5	13.4	13.3	13.2	13.1	12.9	12.8	12.6	12.4	12.3	12.0	11.8
73	13.2	13.2	13.1	13.0	13.0	12.9	12.8	12.7	12.5	12.4	12.3	12.1	12.0	11.8	11.6	11.4
74	12.6	12.6	12.5	12.4	12.4	12.3	12.2	12.1	12.0	11.9	11.8	11.6	11.5	11.3	11.2	11.0
75	12.0	12.0	11.9	11.9	11.8	11.7	11.7	11.6	11.5	11.4	11.3	11.1	11.0	10.9	10.7	10.5
76	11.4	11.4	11.3	11.3	11.2	11.1	11.0	10.9	10.9	10.8	10.6	10.5	10.4	10.3	10.1	
77	10.8	10.8	10.8	10.7	10.7	10.6	10.6	10.5	10.4	10.3	10.3	10.2	10.0	9.9	9.8	9.7
78	10.3	10.2	10.2	10.2	10.1	10.1	10.0	10.0	9.9	9.8	9.8	9.7	9.6	9.5	9.4	9.2
79	9.7	9.7	9.7	9.6	9.6	9.6	9.5	9.5	9.4	9.3	9.3	9.2	9.1	9.0	8.9	8.8
80	9.2	9.2	9.1	9.1	9.1	9.0	9.0	9.0	8.9	8.9	8.8	8.7	8.7	8.6	8.5	8.4
81	8.7	8.7	8.6	8.6	8.6	8.5	8.5	8.5	8.4	8.4	8.3	8.3	8.2	8.1	8.0	8.0
82	8.2	8.2	8.1	8.1	8.1	8.1	8.0	8.0	8.0	7.9	7.9	7.8	7.8	7.7	7.6	7.5
83	7.7	7.7	7.7	7.6	7.6	7.6	7.6	7.5	7.5	7.5	7.4	7.4	7.3	7.3	7.2	7.1
84	7.2	7.2	7.2	7.2	7.2	7.1	7.1	7.1	7.1	7.0	7.0	7.0	6.9	6.9	6.8	6.7
85	6.8	6.8	6.8	6.7	6.7	6.7	6.7	6.7	6.6	6.6	6.6	6.5	6.5	6.5	6.4	6.4
86	6.4	6.4	6.3	6.3	6.3	6.3	6.3	6.3	6.2	6.2	6.2	6.2	6.1	6.1	6.0	6.0
87	6.0	6.0	6.0	5.9	5.9	5.9	5.9	5.9	5.9	5.8	5.8	5.8	5.8	5.7	5.7	5.6
88	5.6	5.6	5.6	5.6	5.6	5.5	5.5	5.5	5.5	5.5	5.5	5.4	5.4	5.4	5.3	5.3
89	5.2	5.2	5.2	5.2	5.2	5.2	5.2	5.2	5.2	5.1	5.1	5.1	5.1	5.1	5.0	5.0
90	4.9	4.9	4.9	4.9	4.9	4.9	4.9	4.9	4.9	4.8	4.8	4.8	4.8	4.8	4.7	4.7

Table VIA — Annuities for Joint Life Only — Two Lives — Expected Return Multiples

AGES	67	68	69	70	71	72	73	74	75	76	77	78	79	80	81	82
67	13.5	...	...	...	...	...	...	...	...	...	...	...	...	...	...	...
68	13.1	12.8	...	...	...	...	...	...	...	...	...	...	...	...	...	...
69	12.8	12.5	12.1	...	...	...	...	...	...	...	...	...	...	...	...	...
70	12.4	12.1	11.8	11.5	...	...	...	...	...	...	...	...	...	...	...	...
71	12.0	11.7	11.4	11.2	10.9	...	...	...	...	...	...	...	...	...	...	...
72	11.6	11.4	11.1	10.8	10.5	10.2	...	...	...	...	...	...	...	...	...	...
73	11.2	11.0	10.7	10.5	10.2	9.9	9.7	...	...	...	...	...	...	...	...	...
74	10.8	10.6	10.4	10.1	9.9	9.6	9.4	9.1	...	...	...	...	...	...	...	...
75	10.4	10.2	10.0	9.8	9.5	9.3	9.1	8.8	8.6	...	...	...	...	...	...	...
76	9.9	9.8	9.6	9.4	9.2	9.0	8.8	8.5	8.3	8.0	...	...	...	...	...	...
77	9.5	9.4	9.2	9.0	8.8	8.6	8.4	8.2	8.0	7.8	7.5	...	...	...	...	...
78	9.1	9.0	8.8	8.7	8.5	8.3	8.1	7.9	7.7	7.5	7.3	7.0	...	...	...	...
79	8.7	8.6	8.4	8.3	8.1	8.0	7.8	7.6	7.4	7.2	7.0	6.8	6.6	...	...	...
80	8.3	8.2	8.0	7.9	7.8	7.6	7.5	7.3	7.1	6.9	6.8	6.6	6.3	6.1	...	...
81	7.9	7.9	7.7	7.5	7.4	7.3	7.1	7.0	6.8	6.7	6.5	6.3	6.1	5.9	5.7	...
82	7.5	7.4	7.3	7.2	7.1	6.9	6.8	6.7	6.5	6.4	6.2	6.0	5.9	5.7	5.5	5.3
83	7.1	7.0	6.9	6.8	6.7	6.6	6.5	6.4	6.2	6.1	5.9	5.8	5.6	5.5	5.3	5.1
84	6.7	6.6	6.5	6.4	6.4	6.3	6.2	6.0	5.9	5.8	5.7	5.5	5.4	5.2	5.1	4.9
85	6.3	6.2	6.2	6.1	6.0	5.9	5.8	5.7	5.6	5.5	5.4	5.3	5.2	5.0	4.9	4.7
86	5.9	5.9	5.8	5.8	5.7	5.6	5.5	5.4	5.4	5.3	5.1	5.0	4.9	4.8	4.7	4.5
87	5.6	5.6	5.5	5.4	5.4	5.3	5.2	5.2	5.1	5.0	4.9	4.8	4.7	4.6	4.4	4.3
88	5.3	5.2	5.2	5.1	5.1	5.0	5.0	4.9	4.8	4.7	4.6	4.5	4.4	4.3	4.2	4.1
89	5.0	4.9	4.9	4.8	4.8	4.7	4.7	4.6	4.5	4.5	4.4	4.3	4.2	4.1	4.0	3.9
90	4.7	4.6	4.6	4.6	4.5	4.5	4.4	4.4	4.3	4.2	4.2	4.1	4.0	3.9	3.8	3.8

Table VIA — Annuities for Joint Life Only — Two Lives — Expected Return Multiples

AGES	83	84	85	86	87	88	89	90
83	4.9	...	...	...	...	...	...	...
84	4.7	4.6	...	...	...	...	...	...
85	4.6	4.4	4.2	...	...	...	...	...
86	4.4	4.2	4.1	3.9	...	...	...	...
87	4.2	4.1	3.9	3.8	3.6	...	...	...
88	4.0	3.9	3.8	3.6	3.5	3.4	...	...
89	3.8	3.7	3.6	3.5	3.4	3.2	3.1	...
90	3.7	3.5	3.4	3.3	3.2	3.1	3.0	2.9

2006 Tax Facts on Insurance & Employee Benefits

APPENDIX A — ANNUITY TABLES

Table VII — Percent Value of Refund Feature
Duration of Guaranteed Amount

Age	1 Yr.	2 Yrs.	3 Yrs.	4 Yrs.	5 Yrs.	6 Yrs.	7 Yrs.	8 Yrs.	9 Yrs.	10 Yrs.	11 Yrs.	12 Yrs.	13 Yrs.	14 Yrs.	15 Yrs.	16 Yrs.	17 Yrs.	18 Yrs.	19 Yrs.	20 Yrs.
19	...	...	...	...	...	...	...	...	...	...	...	...	...	...	...	...	...	...	...	...
20	...	...	...	...	...	...	...	...	...	...	...	...	...	...	...	...	...	...	...	1
21	...	...	...	...	...	...	...	...	...	...	...	...	...	...	...	...	...	...	...	1
22	...	...	...	...	...	...	...	...	...	...	...	...	...	...	...	...	...	...	...	1
23	...	...	...	...	...	...	...	...	...	...	...	...	...	...	...	...	...	1	1	1
24	...	...	...	...	...	...	...	...	...	...	...	...	...	...	...	...	...	1	1	1
25	...	...	...	...	...	...	...	...	...	...	...	...	...	...	...	1	1	1	1	1
26	...	...	...	...	...	...	...	...	...	...	...	...	...	...	...	1	1	1	1	1
27	...	...	...	...	...	...	...	...	...	...	...	...	...	...	1	1	1	1	1	1
28	...	...	...	...	...	...	...	...	...	...	...	...	...	...	1	1	1	1	1	1
29	...	...	...	...	...	...	...	...	...	...	...	...	...	...	1	1	1	1	1	1
30	...	...	...	...	...	...	...	...	...	...	...	...	...	1	1	1	1	1	1	1
31	...	...	...	...	...	...	...	...	...	...	...	...	...	1	1	1	1	1	1	1
32	...	...	...	...	...	...	...	...	...	...	...	...	...	1	1	1	1	1	1	1
33	...	...	...	...	...	...	...	...	...	...	...	...	1	1	1	1	1	1	1	1
34	...	...	...	...	...	...	...	...	...	...	...	1	1	1	1	1	1	1	1	1
35	...	...	...	...	...	...	...	...	...	...	...	1	1	1	1	1	1	1	1	1
36	...	...	...	...	...	...	...	...	...	...	1	1	1	1	1	1	1	1	1	1
37	...	...	...	...	...	...	...	...	...	1	1	1	1	1	1	1	1	1	1	1
38	...	...	...	...	...	...	...	...	1	1	1	1	1	1	1	1	1	1	1	2
39	...	...	...	...	...	...	...	1	1	1	1	1	1	1	1	1	1	1	2	2
40	...	...	...	...	...	...	1	1	1	1	1	1	1	1	1	1	1	2	2	2
41	...	...	...	...	...	...	1	1	1	1	1	1	1	1	1	1	2	2	2	2
42	...	...	...	...	...	1	1	1	1	1	1	1	1	1	2	2	2	2	2	2
43	...	...	...	...	...	1	1	1	1	1	1	1	1	2	2	2	2	2	2	3
44	...	...	...	...	1	1	1	1	1	1	1	1	2	2	2	2	2	2	3	3
45	...	...	...	...	1	1	1	1	1	1	1	2	2	2	2	2	2	3	3	3
46	...	...	...	1	1	1	1	1	1	1	2	2	2	2	2	2	3	3	3	3
47	...	...	...	1	1	1	1	1	1	1	2	2	2	2	2	3	3	3	4	4
48	...	...	...	1	1	1	1	1	1	2	2	2	2	2	3	3	3	4	4	4
49	...	...	1	1	1	1	1	1	2	2	2	2	2	3	3	3	4	4	4	4
50	...	...	1	1	1	1	1	2	2	2	2	2	3	3	3	3	4	4	4	5
51	...	...	1	1	1	1	1	2	2	2	2	3	3	3	3	4	4	4	5	5
52	...	...	1	1	1	1	2	2	2	2	3	3	3	4	4	4	5	5	5	5
53	...	1	1	1	1	1	2	2	2	2	3	3	3	4	4	4	5	5	5	6
54	...	...	1	1	1	1	2	2	2	3	3	3	4	4	4	5	5	5	6	7
55	...	1	1	1	1	2	2	2	2	3	3	4	4	4	5	5	6	6	7	7
56	...	1	1	1	1	2	2	2	3	3	3	4	4	5	5	6	6	7	7	8
57	...	1	1	1	2	2	2	3	3	3	4	4	4	5	5	6	6	7	8	9
58	1	1	1	1	2	2	2	3	3	4	4	4	5	5	6	6	7	8	9	9
59	...	1	1	1	2	2	3	3	4	4	5	5	6	6	7	8	9	9	10
60	...	1	1	1	2	2	3	3	4	4	5	6	6	7	8	9	10	10	11
61	...	1	1	1	2	2	3	3	4	4	5	6	6	7	8	9	10	10	11	13
62	...	1	1	2	2	2	3	4	4	5	5	6	7	8	9	10	11	12	13	14
63	...	1	1	2	2	3	3	4	5	5	6	7	8	9	10	11	12	13	14	15
64	...	1	1	2	2	3	4	4	5	6	7	8	8	9	10	12	13	14	15	17
65	...	1	2	2	3	3	4	5	6	6	7	8	9	10	12	13	14	15	17	18
66	1	1	2	2	3	4	5	5	6	7	8	9	10	12	13	14	15	17	18	20
67	1	1	2	3	3	4	5	6	7	8	9	10	11	13	14	15	17	18	20	22
68	1	1	2	3	4	5	6	7	8	9	10	11	13	14	15	17	19	20	22	24
69	1	1	2	3	4	5	6	7	8	10	11	12	14	15	17	19	20	22	24	26
70	1	2	3	4	5	6	7	8	9	11	12	14	15	17	19	20	22	24	26	28
71	1	2	3	4	5	6	8	9	10	12	13	15	17	18	20	22	24	26	28	30
72	1	2	3	4	6	7	8	10	11	13	15	17	18	20	22	24	26	28	30	32
73	1	2	4	5	6	8	9	11	13	14	16	18	20	22	24	26	28	31	33	35
74	1	3	4	5	7	9	10	12	14	16	18	20	22	24	26	28	31	33	35	37
75	1	3	4	6	8	9	11	13	15	17	19	22	24	26	28	31	33	35	38	40
76	2	3	5	7	9	10	12	15	17	19	21	24	26	28	31	33	36	38	40	43
77	2	4	5	7	9	12	14	16	18	21	23	26	28	31	33	36	38	41	43	45
78	2	4	6	8	10	13	15	18	20	23	25	28	31	33	36	38	41	43	46	48
79	2	4	7	9	11	14	17	19	22	25	28	30	33	36	38	41	44	46	48	51
80	2	5	7	10	13	15	18	21	24	27	30	33	36	38	41	44	46	49	51	53
81	3	5	8	11	14	17	20	23	26	29	32	35	38	41	44	47	48	51	54	56
82	3	6	9	12	15	19	22	25	28	32	35	38	41	44	47	49	52	54	56	58
83	3	7	10	13	17	20	24	27	31	34	38	41	44	47	49	52	54	57	59	61
84	4	7	11	15	19	22	26	30	33	37	40	44	47	49	52	55	57	59	61	63
85	4	8	12	16	20	24	28	32	36	40	43	46	49	52	55	57	59	62	63	65
86	4	9	13	18	22	27	31	35	39	42	46	49	52	55	57	60	62	64	66	67
87	5	10	15	20	24	29	33	37	41	45	48	52	55	57	60	62	64	66	68	69
88	5	11	16	21	26	31	36	40	44	48	51	54	57	60	62	64	66	68	70	71
89	6	12	18	23	28	33	38	43	47	50	54	57	60	62	65	67	68	70	72	73
90	7	13	19	25	31	36	41	45	49	53	56	59	62	64	67	69	70	72	74	75

APPENDIX A — ANNUITY TABLES

Table VII — Percent Value of Refund Feature
Duration of Guaranteed Amount

Age	21 Yrs.	22 Yrs.	23 Yrs.	24 Yrs.	25 Yrs.	26 Yrs.	27 Yrs.	28 Yrs.	29 Yrs.	30 Yrs.	31 Yrs.	32 Yrs.	33 Yrs.	34 Yrs.	35 Yrs.	36 Yrs.	37 Yrs.	38 Yrs.	39 Yrs.	40 Yrs.
5	...	...	...	...	...	...	...	...	...	...	...	1	1	1	1	1	1	1	1	1
6	...	...	...	...	...	...	...	...	...	...	...	1	1	1	1	1	1	1	1	1
7	...	...	...	...	...	...	...	...	...	...	1	1	1	1	1	1	1	1	1	1
8	...	...	...	...	...	...	...	...	...	1	1	1	1	1	1	1	1	1	1	1
9	...	...	...	...	...	...	...	...	1	1	1	1	1	1	1	1	1	1	1	1
10	...	...	...	...	...	...	...	1	1	1	1	1	1	1	1	1	1	1	1	1
11	...	...	...	...	...	...	1	1	1	1	1	1	1	1	1	1	1	1	1	1
12	...	...	...	...	...	1	1	1	1	1	1	1	1	1	1	1	1	1	1	1
13	...	...	...	...	1	1	1	1	1	1	1	1	1	1	1	1	1	1	1	1
14	...	...	...	1	1	1	1	1	1	1	1	1	1	1	1	1	1	1	1	1
15	...	...	1	1	1	1	1	1	1	1	1	1	1	1	1	1	1	1	1	1
16	...	...	1	1	1	1	1	1	1	1	1	1	1	1	1	1	1	1	1	1
17	...	1	1	1	1	1	1	1	1	1	1	1	1	1	1	1	1	1	1	1
18	...	1	1	1	1	1	1	1	1	1	1	1	1	1	1	1	1	1	1	2
19	1	1	1	1	1	1	1	1	1	1	1	1	1	1	1	1	1	1	2	2
20	1	1	1	1	1	1	1	1	1	1	1	1	1	1	1	1	2	2	2	2
21	1	1	1	1	1	1	1	1	1	1	1	1	1	1	1	2	2	2	2	2
22	1	1	1	1	1	1	1	1	1	1	1	1	1	1	2	2	2	2	2	2
23	1	1	1	1	1	1	1	1	1	1	1	1	2	2	2	2	2	2	2	2
24	1	1	1	1	1	1	1	1	1	1	1	2	2	2	2	2	2	2	2	2
25	1	1	1	1	1	1	1	1	1	1	2	2	2	2	2	2	2	2	2	3
26	1	1	1	1	1	1	1	1	1	2	2	2	2	2	2	2	2	2	3	3
27	1	1	1	1	1	1	1	1	2	2	2	2	2	2	2	2	2	3	3	3
28	1	1	1	1	1	1	1	2	2	2	2	2	2	2	2	2	3	3	3	3
29	1	1	1	1	1	1	2	2	2	2	2	2	2	2	2	3	3	3	3	4
30	1	1	1	1	1	2	2	2	2	2	2	2	2	3	3	3	3	3	4	4
31	1	1	1	1	2	2	2	2	2	2	2	2	3	3	3	3	3	4	4	4
32	1	1	1	2	2	2	2	2	2	2	2	3	3	3	3	3	4	4	4	5
33	1	1	2	2	2	2	2	2	2	2	3	3	3	3	3	4	4	4	5	5
34	1	2	2	2	2	2	2	2	2	3	3	3	3	3	4	4	4	5	5	5
35	1	2	2	2	2	2	2	2	3	3	3	3	3	4	4	4	5	5	5	6
36	2	2	2	2	2	2	2	3	3	3	3	3	4	4	4	5	5	5	6	6
37	2	2	2	2	2	2	3	3	3	3	3	4	4	4	5	5	6	6	6	7
38	2	2	2	2	2	3	3	3	3	3	4	4	5	5	5	6	6	7	7	8
39	2	2	2	2	3	3	3	3	4	4	4	5	5	5	6	6	7	7	8	9
40	2	2	3	3	3	3	3	4	4	4	5	5	5	6	6	7	7	8	8	9
41	2	3	3	3	3	3	4	4	4	5	5	5	6	6	7	7	8	9	9	10
42	3	3	3	3	3	4	4	4	5	5	6	6	6	7	7	8	9	9	10	11
43	3	3	3	3	4	4	4	5	5	6	6	7	7	8	8	9	9	10	11	12
44	3	3	3	4	4	4	5	5	6	6	7	7	8	8	9	10	10	11	12	13
45	3	4	4	4	5	5	5	6	6	7	7	8	8	9	10	10	11	12	13	14
46	4	4	4	5	5	5	6	6	7	7	8	9	9	10	11	11	12	13	14	15
47	4	4	5	5	5	6	6	7	7	8	9	9	10	11	12	12	13	14	15	16
48	4	5	5	5	6	6	7	7	8	9	9	10	11	12	13	14	15	16	17	18
49	5	5	5	6	6	7	7	8	8	9	10	11	12	13	14	15	16	17	18	19
50	5	5	6	6	7	7	8	9	10	10	11	12	13	14	15	16	17	18	20	21
51	5	6	6	7	8	8	9	10	11	11	12	13	14	15	16	17	19	20	21	22
52	6	7	7	8	8	9	10	11	11	12	13	14	15	17	18	19	20	21	23	24
53	7	7	8	8	9	10	11	12	13	14	15	16	17	18	19	20	22	23	24	26
54	7	8	8	9	10	11	12	13	14	15	16	17	18	19	21	22	23	25	26	28
55	8	9	9	10	11	12	13	14	15	16	17	18	20	21	22	24	25	27	28	30
56	9	9	10	11	12	13	14	15	16	18	19	20	21	23	24	26	27	29	30	32
57	9	10	11	12	13	14	15	17	18	19	20	22	23	25	26	28	29	31	32	34
58	10	11	12	13	14	16	17	18	19	21	22	24	25	27	28	30	31	33	34	36
59	11	12	13	15	16	17	18	20	21	22	24	25	27	28	30	32	33	35	36	38
60	12	14	15	16	17	19	20	21	23	24	26	27	29	31	32	34	35	37	38	40
61	14	15	16	17	19	20	22	23	25	26	28	29	31	33	34	36	37	39	40	42
62	15	16	18	19	20	22	23	25	27	28	30	32	33	35	36	38	40	41	42	44
63	16	18	19	21	22	24	25	27	29	30	32	34	35	37	39	40	42	43	45	46
64	18	19	21	23	24	26	28	29	31	33	34	36	38	39	41	42	44	45	47	48
65	20	21	23	25	26	28	30	31	33	35	37	38	40	42	43	45	46	47	49	50
66	21	23	25	27	28	30	32	34	35	37	39	41	42	44	45	47	48	50	51	52
67	23	25	27	29	31	32	34	36	38	40	41	43	45	46	48	49	50	52	53	54
68	25	27	29	31	33	35	37	38	40	42	44	45	47	48	50	51	52	54	55	56
69	28	29	31	33	35	37	39	41	43	44	46	48	49	51	52	53	54	56	57	58
70	30	32	34	36	38	40	42	43	45	47	48	50	51	53	54	55	57	58	59	60
71	32	34	36	38	40	42	44	46	47	49	51	52	54	55	56	57	59	60	61	62
72	35	37	39	41	43	45	46	48	50	51	53	54	56	57	58	59	60	62	62	63
73	37	39	41	43	45	47	49	51	52	54	55	57	58	59	60	61	62	63	64	65
74	40	42	44	46	48	50	51	53	54	56	57	59	60	61	62	63	64	65	66	67
75	42	44	46	48	50	52	54	55	57	58	59	61	62	63	64	65	66	67	68	69
76	45	47	49	51	53	54	56	58	59	60	62	63	64	65	66	67	68	69	69	70
77	47	50	51	53	55	57	58	60	61	62	64	65	66	67	68	69	70	70	71	72
78	50	52	54	56	57	59	61	62	63	64	66	67	68	69	70	70	71	72	73	73
79	53	55	56	58	60	61	63	64	65	66	67	68	69	70	71	72	73	73	74	75
80	55	57	59	60	62	63	65	66	67	68	69	70	71	72	73	74	74	75	76	76
81	58	59	61	63	64	66	67	68	69	70	71	72	73	74	74	75	76	76	77	78
82	60	62	63	65	66	68	69	70	71	72	73	74	74	75	76	77	77	78	78	79
83	62	64	66	67	68	70	71	72	73	74	74	75	76	77	77	78	79	79	80	80
84	65	66	68	69	70	71	72	73	74	75	76	77	77	78	79	79	80	80	81	81
85	67	68	70	71	72	73	74	75	76	77	78	78	79	79	80	81	81	82	82	83
86	69	70	72	73	74	75	76	77	78	79	80	80	81	81	82	82	83	83	84	84
87	71	72	73	75	76	77	78	79	80	80	81	81	82	83	83	83	84	84	85	85
88	73	74	75	76	77	78	79	80	80	81	82	82	83	83	84	84	85	85	85	86
89	74	76	77	78	79	79	80	81	81	82	83	83	84	84	85	85	85	86	86	87
90	76	77	78	79	80	81	81	82	83	83	84	84	85	85	86	86	86	87	87	87

APPENDIX A — ANNUITY TABLES

Suggested Charitable Gift Annuity Rates—Single Life
(Effective July 1, 2004)

Age	Rate	Age	Rate
0-1	3.7%	54	5.5%
2-5	3.8	55	5.5
6-12	3.9	56	5.6
13-19	4.0	57	5.6
20	4.0	58	5.7
21	4.1	59	5.7
22	4.1	60	5.7
23	4.1	61	5.8
24	4.1	62	5.9
25	4.1	63	5.9
26	4.2	64	6.0
27	4.2	65	6.0
28	4.2	66	6.1
29	4.3	67	6.2
30	4.3	68	6.3
31	4.3	69	6.4
32	4.4	70	6.5
33	4.4	71	6.6
34	4.4	72	6.7
35	4.5	73	6.8
36	4.5	74	6.9
37	4.6	75	7.1
38	4.6	76	7.2
39	4.7	77	7.4
40	4.7	78	7.6
41	4.8	79	7.8
42	4.8	80	8.0
43	4.9	81	8.3
44	5.0	82	8.5
45	5.0	83	8.8
46	5.1	84	9.2
47	5.2	85	9.5
48	5.2	86	9.9
49	5.3	87	10.2
50	5.3	88	10.6
51	5.4	89	11.0
52	5.4	90+	11.3
53	5.5		

WARNING: These annuity rates, for both immediate and deferred annuities and for both single life and two lives, should not be used if the gift portion, based on IRS tables and the applicable discount rate, is not more than 10% of the amount paid for the annuity.

NOTES:
1. The rates are for ages at the nearest birthday.
2. For immediate gift annuities, these rates will result in a charitable deduction of more than 10% if the CMFR [IRC Sec. 7520 interest rate] is 4.0% or higher, whatever the payment frequency. If the CMFR is less than 4.0%, the deduction will be less than 10% when annuitants are below certain ages.
3. For deferred gift annuities with longer deferral periods, the rates may not pass the 10% test when the CMFR is low.
4. To avoid adverse tax consequences, the charity should reduce the gift annuity rate to whatever level is necessary to generate a charitable deduction in excess of 10%.

[See Q 43 regarding charitable gift annuities.]

Source: American Council on Gift Annuities

APPENDIX B

Tax Tables

Income Tax

Individuals, Estates and Trusts
(Tax Years Beginning in 2006)

Col. 1 Taxable Income $	Separate Return Tax on Col. 1 $	Rate on Excess %	Joint Return Tax on Col. 1 $	Rate on Excess %	Single Return Tax on Col. 1 $	Rate on Excess %	Head of Household Tax on Col. 1 $	Rate on Excess %	Trusts and Estates Tax on Col. 1 $	Rate on Excess %
0	0	10.0	0	10.0	0	10.0	0	10.0	0	15.0
2,050	205	10.0	205	10.0	205	10.0	205	10.0	308	25.0
4,850	485	10.0	485	10.0	485	10.0	485	10.0	1,008	28.0
7,400	740	10.0	740	10.0	740	10.0	740	10.0	1,722	33.0
7,550	755	15.0	755	10.0	755	15.0	755	10.0	1,771	33.0
10,050	1,130	15.0	1,005	10.0	1,130	15.0	1,005	10.0	2,596	35.0
10,750	1,235	15.0	1,075	10.0	1,235	15.0	1,075	15.0	2,841	35.0
15,100	1,888	15.0	1,510	15.0	1,888	15.0	1,728	15.0	4,364	35.0
30,650	4,220	25.0	3,843	15.0	4,220	25.0	4,060	15.0	9,806	35.0
41,050	6,820	25.0	5,403	15.0	6,820	25.0	5,620	25.0	13,446	35.0
61,300	11,883	25.0	8,440	25.0	11,883	25.0	10,683	25.0	20,534	35.0
61,850	12,020	28.0	8,578	25.0	12,020	25.0	10,820	25.0	20,726	35.0
74,200	15,478	28.0	11,665	25.0	15,108	28.0	13,908	25.0	25,049	35.0
94,225	21,085	33.0	16,671	25.0	20,715	28.0	18,914	25.0	32,057	35.0
106,000	24,971	33.0	19,615	25.0	24,012	28.0	21,858	28.0	36,179	35.0
123,700	30,812	33.0	24,040	28.0	28,968	28.0	26,814	28.0	42,374	35.0
154,800	41,075	33.0	32,748	28.0	37,676	33.0	35,522	28.0	53,259	35.0
168,275	45,522	35.0	36,521	28.0	42,122	33.0	39,295	28.0	57,975	35.0
171,650	46,703	35.0	37,466	28.0	43,236	33.0	40,240	33.0	59,156	35.0
188,450	52,583	35.0	42,170	33.0	48,780	33.0	45,784	33.0	65,036	35.0
336,550	104,418	35.0	91,043	35.0	97,653	35.0	94,657	35.0	116,871	35.0

Corporations †
(Tax Years Beginning in 2006)

Col. 1 Taxable Income	Tax on Col. 1	Rate on Excess
-0-	-0-	15%
$ 50,000	7,500	25%
$ 75,000	13,750	34%
$ 100,000	22,250	39% *
$ 335,000	113,900	34%
$10,000,000	3,400,000	35%
$15,000,000	5,150,000	38% **
$18,333,333	6,416,667	35%

† Personal Service Corporations are taxed at a flat rate of 35%.

* A 5% surtax is imposed on income above $100,000 until the benefit of the 15 and 25% tax rates has been canceled. Thus, taxable income from $100,001 to $335,000 is taxed at the rate of 39%.

** Corporations with taxable income over $15,000,000 are subject to an additional tax of the lesser of 3% of the excess over $15,000,000 or $100,000. Thus, taxable income exceeding $18,333,333 is taxed at 35%. See Ann. 93-133, 1993-32 IRB 12.

2006 Tax Facts on Insurance & Employee Benefits

APPENDIX B — TAX TABLES

Tax Tables

Income Tax

Individuals, Estates and Trusts
(Tax Years Beginning in 2005)

	Separate Return		Joint Return		Single Return		Head of Household		Trusts and Estates	
Col. 1 Taxable Income $	Tax on Col. 1 $	Rate on Excess %	Tax on Col. 1 $	Rate on Excess %	Tax on Col. 1 $	Rate on Excess %	Tax on Col. 1 $	Rate on Excess %	Tax on Col. 1 $	Rate on Excess %
0	0	10.0	0	10.0	0	10.0	0	10.0	0	15.0
2,000	200	10.0	200	10.0	200	10.0	200	10.0	300	25.0
4,700	470	10.0	470	10.0	470	10.0	470	10.0	975	28.0
7,150	715	10.0	715	10.0	715	10.0	715	10.0	1,661	33.0
7,300	730	15.0	730	10.0	730	15.0	730	10.0	1,711	33.0
9,750	1,098	15.0	975	10.0	1,098	15.0	975	10.0	2,519	35.0
10,450	1,203	15.0	1,045	10.0	1,203	15.0	1,045	15.0	2,764	35.0
14,600	1,825	15.0	1,460	15.0	1,825	15.0	1,668	15.0	4,217	35.0
29,700	4,090	25.0	3,725	15.0	4,090	25.0	3,933	15.0	9,502	35.0
39,800	6,615	25.0	5,240	15.0	6,615	25.0	5,448	25.0	13,037	35.0
59,400	11,515	25.0	8,180	25.0	11,515	25.0	10,348	25.0	19,897	35.0
59,975	11,659	28.0	8,324	25.0	11,659	25.0	10,491	25.0	20,098	35.0
71,950	15,012	28.0	11,318	25.0	14,653	28.0	13,485	25.0	24,289	35.0
91,400	20,458	33.0	16,180	25.0	20,099	28.0	18,348	25.0	31,097	35.0
102,800	24,220	33.0	19,030	25.0	23,291	28.0	21,198	28.0	35,087	35.0
119,950	29,879	33.0	23,318	28.0	28,093	28.0	26,000	28.0	41,089	35.0
150,150	39,845	33.0	31,774	28.0	36,549	33.0	34,456	28.0	51,659	35.0
163,225	44,160	35.0	35,435	28.0	40,863	33.0	38,117	28.0	56,235	35.0
166,450	45,289	35.0	36,338	28.0	41,928	33.0	39,020	33.0	57,364	35.0
182,800	51,011	35.0	40,916	33.0	47,323	33.0	44,415	33.0	63,087	35.0
326,450	101,289	35.0	88,320	35.0	94,728	35.0	91,820	35.0	113,364	35.0

Corporations†
(Tax Years Beginning in 2005)

Col. 1 Taxable Income	Tax on Col. 1	Rate on Excess
$ 50,000	7,500	25%
-0-	-0-	15%
$ 50,000	7,500	25%
$ 75,000	13,750	34%
$ 100,000	22,250	39% *
$ 335,000	113,900	34%
$10,000,000	3,400,000	35%
$15,000,000	5,150,000	38% **
$18,333,333	6,416,667	35%

† Personal Service Corporations are taxed at a flat rate of 35%.

* A 5% surtax is imposed on income above $100,000 until the benefit of the 15 and 25% tax rates has been canceled. Thus, taxable income from $100,001 to $335,000 is taxed at the rate of 39%.

** Corporations with taxable income over $15,000,000 are subject to an additional tax of the lesser of 3% of the excess over $15,000,000 or $100,000. Thus, taxable income exceeding $18,333,333 is taxed at 35%. See Ann. 93-133, 1993-32 IRB 12.

APPENDIX B — TAX TABLES

Transfer Tax Tables

2006 Gift and Estate Tax Table

Taxable Gift/Estate From	Taxable Gift/Estate To	Tax on Col. 1	Rate on Excess
$ 0	$ 10,000	$ 0	18%
10,000	20,000	1,800	20%
20,000	40,000	3,800	22%
40,000	60,000	8,200	24%
60,000	80,000	13,000	26%
80,000	10,0000	18,200	28%
100,000	150,000	23,800	30%
150,000	250,000	38,800	32%
250,000	500,000	70,800	34%
500,000	750,000	155,800	37%
750,000	1,000,000	248,300	39%
1,000,000	1,250,000	345,800	41%
1,250,000	1,500,000	448,300	43%
1,500,000	2,000,000	555,800	45%
2,000,000	....	780,800	46%

2007-2009 Gift and Estate Tax Table

Taxable Gift/Estate From	Taxable Gift/Estate To	Tax on Col. 1	Rate on Excess
$ 0	$ 10,000	$ 0	18%
10,000	20,000	1,800	20%
20,000	40,000	3,800	22%
40,000	60,000	8,200	24%
60,000	80,000	13,000	26%
80,000	10,0000	18,200	28%
100,000	150,000	23,800	30%
150,000	250,000	38,800	32%
250,000	500,000	70,800	34%
500,000	750,000	155,800	37%
750,000	1,000,000	248,300	39%
1,000,000	1,250,000	345,800	41%
1,250,000	1,500,000	448,300	43%
1,500,000	....	555,800	45%

APPENDIX B — TAX TABLES

2010 Gift Tax Only Table

Taxable Gift From	To	Tax on Col. 1	Rate on Excess
$ 0	$ 10,000	$ 0	18%
10,000	20,000	1,800	20%
20,000	40,000	3,800	22%
40,000	60,000	8,200	24%
60,000	80,000	13,000	26%
80,000	10,0000	18,200	28%
100,000	150,000	23,800	30%
150,000	250,000	38,800	32%
250,000	500,000	70,800	34%
500,000	....	155,800	35%

2011- Gift and Estate Tax Table

Taxable Gift/Estate From	To	Tax on Col. 1	Rate on Excess
$ 0	$ 10,000	$ 0	18%
10,000	20,000	1,800	20%
20,000	40,000	3,800	22%
40,000	60,000	8,200	24%
60,000	80,000	13,000	26%
80,000	10,0000	18,200	28%
100,000	150,000	23,800	30%
150,000	250,000	38,800	32%
250,000	500,000	70,800	34%
500,000	750,000	155,800	37%
750,000	1,000,000	248,300	39%
1,000,000	1,250,000	345,800	41%
1,250,000	1,500,000	448,300	43%
1,500,000	2,000,000	555,800	45%
2,000,000	2,500,000	780,800	49%
2,500,000	3,000,000	1,025,800	53%
3,000,000	10,000,000	1,290,800	55%
10,000,000	17,184,000	5,140,800	60%
17,184,000	....	9,451,200	55%

APPENDIX B — TAX TABLES

2005 Gift and Estate Tax Table

Taxable Gift/Estate From	To	Tax on Col. 1	Rate on Excess
$ 0	$ 10,000	$ 0	18%
10,000	20,000	1,800	20%
20,000	40,000	3,800	22%
40,000	60,000	8,200	24%
60,000	80,000	13,000	26%
80,000	10,0000	18,200	28%
100,000	150,000	23,800	30%
150,000	250,000	38,800	32%
250,000	500,000	70,800	34%
500,000	750,000	155,800	37%
750,000	1,000,000	248,300	39%
1,000,000	1,250,000	345,800	41%
1,250,000	1,500,000	448,300	43%
1,500,000	2,000,000	555,800	45%
2,000,000	....	780,800	47%

IRC Secs. 2001(c), 2502(a), 2210, as amended by EGTRRA 2001. See Q 852 and Q 902.

2006 Tax Facts on Insurance & Employee Benefits

APPENDIX B — TAX TABLES

Estate Tax Unified Credit

Year	Exclusion Equivalent	Unified Credit
2000-2001	675,000	220,550
2002-2003	$1,000,000	$345,800
2004-2005	$1,500,000	$555,800
2006-2008	$2,000,000	$780,800
2009	$3,500,000	$1,455,800
2010	NA	NA
2011	$1,000,000	$345,800

IRC Sec. 2010(c), as amended by EGTRRA 2001. See Q 868.

Gift Tax Unified Credit

Year	Exclusion Equivalent	Unified Credit
1977 (1-1 to 6-30)	$ 30,000	$ 6,000
1977 (7-1 to 12-31)	120,667	30,000
1978	134,000	34,000
1979	147,333	38,000
1980	161,563	42,500
1981	175,625	47,000
1982	225,000	62,800
1983	275,000	79,300
1984	325,000	96,300
1985	400,000	121,800
1986	500,000	155,800
1987-1997	600,000	192,800
1998	625,000	202,050
1999	650,000	211,300
2000-2001	675,000	220,550
2002-2009	1,000,000	345,800
2010	1,000,000	330,800
2011-	1,000,000	345,800

IRC Secs. 2505(a), 2010(c), as amended by EGTRRA 2001. See Q 922.

APPENDIX B — TAX TABLES

Maximum State Death Tax Credit (SDTC)

Adjusted Taxable Estate From	To	Credit on Col. 1	Rate on Excess
$ 40,000	$ 90,000	$ 0	.8%
90,000	140,000	400	1.6%
140,000	240,000	1,200	2.4%
240,000	440,000	3,600	3.2%
440,000	640,000	10,000	4.0%
640,000	840,000	18,000	4.8%
840,000	1,040,000	27,600	5.6%
1,040,000	1,540,000	38,800	6.4%
1,540,000	2,040,000	70,800	7.2%
2,040,000	2,540,000	106,800	8.0%
2,540,000	3,040,000	146,800	8.8%
3,040,000	3,540,000	190,800	9.6%
3,540,000	4,040,000	238,800	10.4%
4,040,000	5,040,000	290,800	11.2%
5,040,000	6,040,000	402,800	12.0%
6,040,000	7,040,000	522,800	12.8%
7,040,000	8,040,000	650,800	13.6%
8,040,000	9,040,000	786,800	14.4%
9,040,000	10,040,000	930,800	15.2%
10,040,000		1,082,800	16.0%

For this purpose, the term "adjusted taxable estate" means the taxable estate reduced by $60,000.

Reduction in Maximum SDTC

Year	Multiply Maximum SDTC Above By
2002	75%
2003	50%
2004	25%
2005-2009	0%*
2010	NA
2011-	100%

*deduction for state death taxes paid replaces credit

IRC Secs. 2011(b), 2011(g), 2058, as amended by EGTRRA 2001. See Q 869 and Q 863.

Qualified Family-Owned Business Deduction

Year	Deduction Limitation
1998-2003	$675,000
2004-2010	NA
2011-	$675,000

IRC Secs. 2057(a)(2), 2057(j), as amended by EGTRRA 2001. See Q 866.

2006 Tax Facts on Insurance & Employee Benefits

APPENDIX B — TAX TABLES

Estate Tax Deferral: Closely Held Business

Year	4% Interest Limitation
1997	$153,000

Year	$1,000,000 Indexed
1998	$1,000,000
1999	$1,010,000
2000	$1,030,000
2001	$1,060,000
2002	$1,100,000
2003	$1,120,000
2004	$1,140,000
2005	$1,170,000
2006	$1,200,000

Year	2% Interest Limitation
1998	$410,000
1999	$416,500
2000	$427,500
2001	$441,000
2002	$484,000
2003	$493,800
2004	$532,200
2005	$539,900
2006	$552,000
2007-2009	$540,000*
2010	NA
2011-	$533,000*

*Based upon $1,200,000 as indexed for 2006. May increase.

IRC Secs. 6166, 6601(j). Calculations reflect EGTRRA 2001 changes. See Q 851.

Special Use Valuation Limitation

Year	Limitation
1997-1998	$750,000
1999	$760,000
2000	$770,000
2001	$800,000
2002	$820,000
2003	$840,000
2004	$850,000
2005	$870,000
2006	$900,000

IRC Sec. 2032A(a). See Q 862.

APPENDIX B — TAX TABLES

Qualified Conservation Easement Exclusion

Year	Exclusion Limitation
1998	$100,000
1999	$200,000
2000	$300,000
2001	$400,000
2002-2009	$500,000
2010	NA
2011-	$500,000

IRC Sec. 2031(c)(3). See Q 861.

Gift (and GST) Tax Annual Exclusion

Year	Annual Exclusion
1997-2001	$10,000
2002-2005	$11,000
2006	$12,000

IRC Sec. 2503(b). See Q 751 and Q 917.

Gift Tax Annual Exclusion
(Donee Spouse not U.S. Citizen)

Year	Annual Exclusion
1997-1998	$100,000
1999	$101,000
2000	$103,000
2001	$106,000
2002	$110,000
2003	$112,000
2004	$114,000
2005	$117,000
2006	$120,000

IRC Sec. 2523(i). See Q 917.

APPENDIX B — TAX TABLES

Generation-Skipping Transfer Tax Table

Year	Tax Rate
2001	55%
2002	50%
2003	49%
2004	48%
2005	47%
2006	46%
2007-2009	45%
2010	NA
2011-	55%

IRC Secs. 2641, 2001(c), 2664, as amended by EGTRRA 2001. See Q 951.

Generation-Skipping Transfer Tax Exemption

Year	GST Exemption
1998-2003	$675,000
1997-1998	$1,000,000
1999	$1,010,000
2000	$1,030,000
2001	$1,060,000
2002	$1,100,000
2003	$1,120,000
2004-2005	$1,500,000
2006-2008	$2,000,000
2009	$3,500,000
2010	NA
2011-	$1,120,000*

*Plus increases for indexing for inflation after 2003.

IRC Secs. 2631, 2010(c), as amended by EGTRRA 2001. See Q 752 and Q 951.

Indexed Amounts Source

Year	Rev. Proc.
1999	98-61, 1998-2 CB 811
2000	99-42, 1999-46 IRB 568
2001	2001-13, 2001-3 IRB 337
2002	2001-59, 2001-52 IRB 623
2003	2002-70, 2002-46 IRB 845
2004	2003-85, 2003-49 IRB 1184
2005	2004-71, 2004-50 IRB 970
2006	2005-70, 2005-47 IRB 979

APPENDIX C

One Year Term Rates

The following rates are used in computing the "cost" of pure life insurance protection that is taxable to the employee under: qualified pension and profit sharing plans (Q 423); split-dollar plans (Q 459); and tax-sheltered annuities (Q 481). Notice 2002-8, 2002-1 CB 398; Rev. Rul. 66-110, 1966-1 CB 12.

For these purposes, the rate at insured's attained age is generally applied to the excess of the amount payable at death over the cash value of the policy at the end of the year.

Table 2001 can generally be used starting in 2001. P.S. 58 rates and other rates derived from Table 38 could generally be used in years prior to 2002. However, split dollar arrangements entered into before January 28, 2002, in which the contractual arrangement between the employer and the employee provides that P.S. 58 rates will be used may continue to use P.S. 58 rates.

See Q 142 for Table I, Uniform Premiums for $1,000 of Group-Term Life Insurance Protection and application of the rates.

APPENDIX C — ONE YEAR TERM RATES

Table 2001

One Year Term Premiums for $1,000 of Life Insurance Protection — One Life

Age	Premium	Age	Premium	Age	Premium
0	$0.70	34	$0.98	67	$15.20
1	0.41	35	0.99	68	16.92
2	0.27	36	1.01	69	18.70
3	0.19	37	1.04	70	20.62
4	0.13	38	1.06	71	22.72
5	0.13	39	1.07	72	25.07
6	0.14	40	1.10	73	27.57
7	0.15	41	1.13	74	30.18
8	0.16	42	1.20	75	33.05
9	0.16	43	1.29	76	36.33
10	0.16	44	1.40	77	40.17
11	0.19	45	1.53	78	44.33
12	0.24	46	1.67	79	49.23
13	0.28	47	1.83	80	54.56
14	0.33	48	1.98	81	60.51
15	0.38	49	2.13	82	66.74
16	0.52	50	2.30	83	73.07
17	0.57	51	2.52	84	80.35
18	0.59	52	2.81	85	88.76
19	0.61	53	3.20	86	99.16
20	0.62	54	3.65	87	110.40
21	0.62	55	4.15	88	121.85
22	0.64	56	4.68	89	133.40
23	0.66	57	5.20	90	144.30
24	0.68	58	5.66	91	155.80
25	0.71	59	6.06	92	168.75
26	0.73	60	6.51	93	186.44
27	0.76	61	7.11	94	206.70
28	0.80	62	7.96	95	228.35
29	0.83	63	9.08	96	250.01
30	0.87	64	10.41	97	265.09
31	0.90	65	11.90	98	270.11
32	0.93	66	13.51	99	281.05
33	0.96				

APPENDIX C — ONE YEAR TERM RATES

"P.S. No. 58" Rates

One Year Term Premiums for $1,000 of Life Insurance Protection — One Life

Age	Premium	Age	Premium	Age	Premium
0	$42.10*	35	$ 3.21	70	$ 48.06
1	4.49*	36	3.41	71	52.29
2	2.37*	37	3.63	72	56.89
3	1.72*	38	3.87	73	61.89
4	1.38*	39	4.14	74	67.33
5	1.21*	40	4.42	75	73.23
6	1.07*	41	4.73	76	79.63
7	.98*	42	5.07	77	86.57
8	.90*	43	5.44	78	94.09
9	.85*	44	5.85	79	102.23
10	.83*	45	6.30	80	111.04
11	.91*	46	6.78	81	120.57
12	1.00*	47	7.32	82	130.86*
13	1.08*	48	7.89	83	141.95*
14	1.17*	49	8.53	84	153.91*
15	1.27	50	9.22	85	166.77*
16	1.38	51	9.97	86	180.60*
17	1.48	52	10.79	87	195.43*
18	1.52	53	11.69	88	211.33*
19	1.56	54	12.67	89	228.31*
20	1.61	55	13.74	90	246.45*
21	1.67	56	14.91	91	265.75*
22	1.73	57	16.18	92	286.25*
23	1.79	58	17.56	93	307.98*
24	1.86	59	19.08	94	330.94*
25	1.93	60	20.73	95	355.11*
26	2.02	61	22.53	96	380.50*
27	2.11	62	24.50	97	407.03*
28	2.20	63	26.63	98	434.68*
29	2.31	64	28.98	99	463.35*
30	2.43	65	31.51	100	492.93*
31	2.57	66	34.28	101	523.30*
32	2.70	67	37.31	102	554.30*
33	2.86	68	40.59	103	585.75*
34	3.02	69	44.17	104	617.42*

* Rates are derived by the editor from U.S. Life Table 38, and are based on the underlying actuarial assumptions of the P.S. 58 rates (see following pages).

APPENDIX C — ONE YEAR TERM RATES

P.S. 58 RATES CALCULATIONS

(Net annual premium per $1,000 - 1 year term)

For various tax purposes, P.S. 58 rates can be used for the net annual premium per $1,000 of one year term life insurance where there is only one insured. P.S. 58 equivalent rates (e.g., joint and joint and survivor rates) can also be determined where there is more than one insured (sometimes referred to as Table 38 rates). The derivation of such rates is described below for one and two insureds.

In each instance, the present value of $1,000 is discounted one year at 2.5% to $975.60. $975.60 is then multiplied by the probability of death of the insured(s) during the year. In each of the formulas below, substitute the appropriate q_x from Table 38 for each insured (where two insureds are involved, the second insured is referred to as y rather than x).

required interest rate = i = 2.5%
$1 \div (1 + i) = 1 \div 1.025 = .97560$
$\$1,000 \times .97560 = \$975.60$

q_x - probability of dying in each year of age (from Table 38)
    (e.g., q_x for person age 25 is .00198)

Where two lives are involved q_x and q_y are used
    q_x is probability at first person's age
    q_y is probability at second person's age
    (e.g., q_x for first person, age 35, is .00329
    and q_y for second person, age 45, is .00646)

ONE LIFE
P.S. 58 rate = $975.60 x q_x
    (e.g., rate for person age 50
    = $975.60 x .00945 = $9.22)

TWO LIFE (Joint and Survivor, Second to Die)
P.S. 58 equivalent rate = $975.60 x q_x x q_y
    (e.g., rate for persons age 60 and 70
    = $975.60 x .02125 x .04926 = $1.02)
    after first death use one life rate

TWO LIFE (Joint, First to Die)
P.S. 58 equivalent rate = $975.60 \times [(q_x + q_y) - (q_x \times q_y)]$
    (e.g., rate for persons age 60 and 70
    = $975.60 x [(.02125 + .04926) - (.02125 x .04926)]
    = $67.77)

APPENDIX C — ONE YEAR TERM RATES

Table 38

Age x	q(x)	Age x	q(x)	Age x	q(x)
0	.04315	35	.00329	70	.04926
1	.00460	36	.00350	71	.05360
2	.00243	37	.00372	72	.05831
3	.00176	38	.00397	73	.06344
4	.00141	39	.00424	74	.06901
5	.00124	40	.00453	75	.07506
6	.00110	41	.00485	76	.08162
7	.00100	42	.00520	77	.08873
8	.00092	43	.00558	78	.09644
9	.00087	44	.00600	79	.10479
10	.00085	45	.00646	80	.11382
11	.00093	46	.00695	81	.12358
12	.00102	47	.00750	82	.13413
13	.00111	48	.00809	83	.14550
14	.00120	49	.00874	84	.15776
15	.00130	50	.00945	85	.17094
16	.00141	51	.01022	86	.18511
17	.00152	52	.01106	87	.20032
18	.00156	53	.01198	88	.21661
19	.00160	54	.01299	89	.23402
20	.00165	55	.01408	90	.25261
21	.00171	56	.01528	91	.27239
22	.00177	57	.01658	92	.29341
23	.00183	58	.01800	93	.31568
24	.00191	59	.01956	94	.33921
25	.00198	60	.02125	95	.36399
26	.00207	61	.02309	96	.39001
27	.00216	62	.02511	97	.41721
28	.00226	63	.02730	98	.44555
29	.00237	64	.02970	99	.47493
30	.00249	65	.03230	100	.50525
31	.00263	66	.03514	101	.53638
32	.00277	67	.03824	102	.56816
33	.00293	68	.04160	103	.60039
34	.00310	69	.04527	104	.63286
				105	1.00000

APPENDIX C — ONE YEAR TERM RATES

One Year Term Premiums for $1,000 of Joint and Survivor Life Insurance Protection* (Second-to-Die)

AGE	5	10	15	20	25	30	35	40	45	50
5	.00	.00	.00	.00	.00	.00	.00	.01	.01	.01
10	.00	.00	.00	.00	.00	.00	.00	.00	.01	.01
15	.00	.00	.00	.00	.00	.00	.00	.01	.01	.01
20	.00	.00	.00	.00	.00	.00	.01	.01	.01	.02
25	.00	.00	.00	.00	.00	.00	.01	.01	.01	.02
30	.00	.00	.00	.00	.00	.01	.01	.01	.02	.02
35	.00	.00	.00	.01	.01	.01	.01	.01	.02	.03
40	.01	.00	.01	.01	.01	.01	.01	.02	.03	.04
45	.01	.01	.01	.01	.01	.02	.02	.03	.04	.06
50	.01	.01	.01	.02	.02	.02	.03	.04	.06	.09
55	.02	.01	.02	.02	.03	.03	.05	.06	.09	.13
60	.03	.02	.03	.03	.04	.05	.07	.09	.13	.20
65	.04	.03	.04	.05	.06	.08	.10	.14	.20	.30
70	.06	.04	.06	.08	.10	.12	.16	.22	.31	.45
75	.09	.06	.10	.12	.14	.18	.24	.33	.47	.69
80	.14	.09	.14	.18	.22	.28	.37	.50	.72	1.05
85	.21	.14	.22	.28	.33	.42	.55	.76	1.08	1.58
90	.31	.21	.32	.41	.49	.61	.81	1.12	1.59	2.33
95	.44	.30	.46	.59	.70	.88	1.17	1.61	2.29	3.36
100	.61	.42	.64	.81	.98	1.23	1.62	2.23	3.18	4.66

AGE	55	60	65	70	75	80	85	90	95	100
5	.02	.03	.04	.06	.09	.14	.21	.31	.44	.61
10	.01	.02	.03	.04	.06	.09	.14	.21	.30	.42
15	.02	.03	.04	.06	.10	.14	.22	.32	.46	.64
20	.02	.03	.05	.08	.12	.18	.28	.41	.59	.81
25	.03	.04	.06	.10	.14	.22	.33	.49	.70	.98
30	.03	.05	.08	.12	.18	.28	.42	.61	.88	1.23
35	.05	.07	.10	.16	.24	.37	.55	.81	1.17	1.62
40	.06	.09	.14	.22	.33	.50	.76	1.12	1.61	2.23
45	.09	.13	.20	.31	.47	.72	1.08	1.59	2.29	3.18
50	.13	.20	.30	.45	.69	1.05	1.58	2.33	3.36	4.66
55	.19	.29	.44	.68	1.03	1.56	2.35	3.47	5.00	6.94
60	.29	.44	.67	1.02	1.56	2.36	3.54	5.24	7.55	10.47
65	.44	.67	1.02	1.55	2.37	3.59	5.39	7.96	11.47	15.92
70	.68	1.02	1.55	2.37	3.61	5.47	8.22	12.14	17.49	24.28
75	1.03	1.56	2.37	3.61	5.50	8.33	12.52	18.50	26.65	37.00
80	1.56	2.36	3.59	5.47	8.33	12.64	18.98	28.05	40.42	56.10
85	2.35	3.54	5.39	8.22	12.52	18.98	28.51	42.13	60.70	84.26
90	3.47	5.24	7.96	12.14	18.50	28.05	42.13	62.26	89.70	124.52
95	5.00	7.55	11.47	17.49	26.65	40.42	60.70	89.70	129.26	179.42
100	6.94	10.47	15.92	24.28	37.00	56.10	84.26	124.52	179.42	249.05

*Rates are derived from U.S. Life Table 38. They are based on the underlying actuarial assumptions of the P.S. 58 rates. The method for deriving the rates is also based upon an unofficial informational letter of Norman Greenberg, Chief, Actuarial Branch, Department of the Treasury. The letter indicates that after the first death, the single life regular P.S. 58 rates are to be used. Due to space limitations, the table is presented in 5-year age increments. For planning purposes, it is suggested that each actual age be rounded to the nearest corresponding age in the table, or do the calculation described earlier in this appendix.

APPENDIX D

Valuation Tables

The value of an annuity, an interest for life or term of years, or a remainder or a reversionary interest is valued for most income, estate, gift, and generation-skipping transfer tax purposes using the following valuation tables and the current interest rate for the month in which the valuation date occurs. See Q 910. The Section 7520 interest rate for each month is published in *Tax Facts News*, a National Underwriter publication, as the rate becomes available. It can also be found at www.TaxFactsOnline.com. For purposes of these tables, round the age of any person whose life is used to measure an interest to the age of such person on his birthday nearest the valuation date.

Selected single life and term certain factors are provided here. [See App. C in *Tax Facts on Investments* (Tax Facts 2) for selected unitrust tables. IRS Publications 1457 and 1458 contain extensive valuation tables.] Both the single life and term certain tables provide factors for remainder interests which can be converted into an income factor or an annuity factor. A remainder interest is converted into an income factor by subtracting the remainder factor from 1. An income factor is converted into an annuity factor by dividing the income factor by the appropriate interest rate for the month.

The value of a remainder or income interest is equal to the principal amount multiplied by the appropriate remainder or income factor.

The value of an annuity payable *annually at the end of each year* is equal to the aggregate payment received during the year multiplied by the annuity factor. If the annuity is payable *other than annually at the end of each period*, the value of an annuity payable annually at the end of each year is adjusted to reflect the more frequent payments by multiplying such value by the appropriate Table A annuity adjustment factor. If an annuity is payable at the *beginning of each period during the life of one individual* (or *until the death of the survivor of two persons*), add the amount of one additional payment to the calculation of the value of an annuity payable at the end of each period. If the annuity is payable at the *beginning of each period during a term certain*, the value of an annuity payable annually at the end of each year is adjusted to reflect the more frequent payments by multiplying such value by the appropriate Table B annuity adjustment factor.

Example 1. Jack Jones set up a trust funded with $100,000 to provide income to his mother (age 70) for life with remainder to his son, Tom. Assume the valuation table interest rate for the month is 5.0%. The factor for the present value of the remainder interest which follows a life estate given to a person age 70 at a 5.0% interest rate is .54325 (Single Life Remainder Factors Table). Consequently, Jack has made a gift of $54,325 to Tom ($100,000 x .54325).

The factor for the present value of the income interest given to Jack's mother is .45675 (1 - .54325). Consequently, Jack has made a gift of $45,675 to his mother ($100,000 x .45675). The gift to Jack's mother is a gift of a present interest which may qualify for the annual exclusion (see Q 917).

Example 2. Bob Martin (age 66) transferred property in exchange for a private annuity of $12,000 a year, payable annually at the end of each year for life. Assume the valuation table interest rate for the month is 5.0%. The present value of an annuity payable at the end of each year for the life of a person 66

APPENDIX D — VALUATION TABLES

years of age at an interest rate of 5.0% is calculated as follows. (1) The remainder factor is .48634 (Single Life Factors Table). (2) The income factor is .51366 (1 - .48634). (3) The annuity factor is 10.2732 (.51366 ÷ 5.0%). (4) The present value of the private annuity is $123,278 (10.2732 x $12,000).

If the annuity is payable monthly (i.e., $1,000 per month) at the end of each period, the annuity payable annually at the end of each year as calculated above is adjusted as follows. Multiply the value of the annuity payable annually at the end of each year ($123,278) by an annuity adjustment factor of 1.0227 (Annuity Adjustment Factors Table A). Thus, the value of such an annuity is equal to $126,076 ($123,278 x 1.0227).

If the annuity in either of the two preceding paragraphs is payable at the beginning of the period, add one payment to the value of the annuity calculated above. The value of the $12,000 annual annuity payable at the end of each year is increased to $135,278 ($123,278 + $12,000) if made payable at the beginning of the year. The value of the $1,000 monthly annuity payable at the end of each period is increased to $127,076 ($126,076 + $1,000) if made payable at the beginning of the period.

Example 3. Kim Brown (age 40) transferred property worth $100,000 in exchange for a private annuity payable for her life. Assume the valuation table interest rate for the month is 5.0%. To calculate what quarterly payments payable at the beginning of each period should be, the following steps are taken.

(1) Calculate the annuity factor for an annuity payable annually at the end of each year during the life of a person 40 years of age at a 5.0% interest rate. This factor, 16.0968, is obtained by (a) locating the remainder factor of .19516 in the Single Life Remainder Factors Table, (b) subtracting (a) from 1, and (c) dividing (b) by the interest rate of 5.0%.

(2) Locate the annuity adjustment factor of 1.0186 from the Annuity Adjustment Factors Table A.

(3) Multiply (1) by (2) to obtain a product of 16.3962 (16.0968 x 1.0186).

(4) Divide 1 by the number of periodic payments per year (i.e., 1/4, or .25).

(5) The sum of (3) and (4) is equal to 16.6462 (16.3962 + .25).

(6) Annuity payments should be $6,007 per year ($100,000 ÷ 16.6462).

(7) Quarterly payments should be $1,502 ($6,007 ÷ 4).

APPENDIX D — VALUATION TABLES

ANNUITY ADJUSTMENT FACTORS TABLE A*

FREQUENCY OF PAYMENTS

INTEREST RATE	ANNUALLY	SEMI ANNUALLY	QUARTERLY	MONTHLY	WEEKLY
3.0%	1.0000	1.0074	1.0112	1.0137	1.0146
3.2%	1.0000	1.0079	1.0119	1.0146	1.0156
3.4%	1.0000	1.0084	1.0127	1.0155	1.0166
3.6%	1.0000	1.0089	1.0134	1.0164	1.0175
3.8%	1.0000	1.0094	1.0141	1.0173	1.0185
4.0%	1.0000	1.0099	1.0149	1.0182	1.0195
4.2%	1.0000	1.0104	1.0156	1.0191	1.0205
4.4%	1.0000	1.0109	1.0164	1.0200	1.0214
4.6%	1.0000	1.0114	1.0171	1.0209	1.0224
4.8%	1.0000	1.0119	1.0178	1.0218	1.0234
5.0%	1.0000	1.0123	1.0186	1.0227	1.0243
5.2%	1.0000	1.0128	1.0193	1.0236	1.0253
5.4%	1.0000	1.0133	1.0200	1.0245	1.0262
5.6%	1.0000	1.0138	1.0208	1.0254	1.0272
5.8%	1.0000	1.0143	1.0215	1.0263	1.0282
6.0%	1.0000	1.0148	1.0222	1.0272	1.0291
6.2%	1.0000	1.0153	1.0230	1.0281	1.0301
6.4%	1.0000	1.0158	1.0237	1.0290	1.0311
6.6%	1.0000	1.0162	1.0244	1.0299	1.0320
6.8%	1.0000	1.0167	1.0252	1.0308	1.0330
7.0%	1.0000	1.0172	1.0259	1.0317	1.0339
7.2%	1.0000	1.0177	1.0266	1.0326	1.0349
7.4%	1.0000	1.0182	1.0273	1.0335	1.0358
7.6%	1.0000	1.0187	1.0281	1.0344	1.0368
7.8%	1.0000	1.0191	1.0288	1.0353	1.0378
8.0%	1.0000	1.0196	1.0295	1.0362	1.0387
8.2%	1.0000	1.0201	1.0302	1.0370	1.0397
8.4%	1.0000	1.0206	1.0310	1.0379	1.0406
8.6%	1.0000	1.0211	1.0317	1.0388	1.0416
8.8%	1.0000	1.0215	1.0324	1.0397	1.0425
9.0%	1.0000	1.0220	1.0331	1.0406	1.0435
9.2%	1.0000	1.0225	1.0339	1.0415	1.0444
9.4%	1.0000	1.0230	1.0346	1.0424	1.0454
9.6%	1.0000	1.0235	1.0353	1.0433	1.0463
9.8%	1.0000	1.0239	1.0360	1.0442	1.0473
10.0%	1.0000	1.0244	1.0368	1.0450	1.0482
10.2%	1.0000	1.0249	1.0375	1.0459	1.0492
10.4%	1.0000	1.0254	1.0382	1.0468	1.0501
10.6%	1.0000	1.0258	1.0389	1.0477	1.0511
10.8%	1.0000	1.0263	1.0396	1.0486	1.0520

* For use in calculating the value of an annuity payable at the end of each period or, if the term of the annuity is determined with respect to one or more lives, an annuity payable at the beginning of each period.

APPENDIX D — VALUATION TABLES

ANNUITY ADJUSTMENT FACTORS TABLE B*

FREQUENCY OF PAYMENTS

INTEREST RATE	ANNUALLY	SEMI ANNUALLY	QUARTERLY	MONTHLY	WEEKLY
3.0%	1.0300	1.0224	1.0187	1.0162	1.0152
3.2%	1.0320	1.0239	1.0199	1.0172	1.0162
3.4%	1.0340	1.0254	1.0212	1.0183	1.0172
3.6%	1.0360	1.0269	1.0224	1.0194	1.0182
3.8%	1.0380	1.0284	1.0236	1.0205	1.0192
4.0%	1.0400	1.0299	1.0249	1.0215	1.0203
4.2%	1.0420	1.0314	1.0261	1.0226	1.0213
4.4%	1.0440	1.0329	1.0274	1.0237	1.0223
4.6%	1.0460	1.0344	1.0286	1.0247	1.0233
4.8%	1.0480	1.0359	1.0298	1.0258	1.0243
5.0%	1.0500	1.0373	1.0311	1.0269	1.0253
5.2%	1.0520	1.0388	1.0323	1.0279	1.0263
5.4%	1.0540	1.0403	1.0335	1.0290	1.0273
5.6%	1.0560	1.0418	1.0348	1.0301	1.0283
5.8%	1.0580	1.0433	1.0360	1.0311	1.0293
6.0%	1.0600	1.0448	1.0372	1.0322	1.0303
6.2%	1.0620	1.0463	1.0385	1.0333	1.0313
6.4%	1.0640	1.0478	1.0397	1.0343	1.0323
6.6%	1.0660	1.0492	1.0409	1.0354	1.0333
6.8%	1.0680	1.0507	1.0422	1.0365	1.0343
7.0%	1.0700	1.0522	1.0434	1.0375	1.0353
7.2%	1.0720	1.0537	1.0446	1.0386	1.0363
7.4%	1.0740	1.0552	1.0458	1.0396	1.0373
7.6%	1.0760	1.0567	1.0471	1.0407	1.0383
7.8%	1.0780	1.0581	1.0483	1.0418	1.0393
8.0%	1.0800	1.0596	1.0495	1.0428	1.0403
8.2%	1.0820	1.0611	1.0507	1.0439	1.0413
8.4%	1.0840	1.0626	1.0520	1.0449	1.0422
8.6%	1.0860	1.0641	1.0532	1.0460	1.0432
8.8%	1.0880	1.0655	1.0544	1.0471	1.0442
9.0%	1.0900	1.0670	1.0556	1.0481	1.0452
9.2%	1.0920	1.0685	1.0569	1.0492	1.0462
9.4%	1.0940	1.0700	1.0581	1.0502	1.0472
9.6%	1.0960	1.0715	1.0593	1.0513	1.0482
9.8%	1.0980	1.0729	1.0605	1.0523	1.0492
10.0%	1.1000	1.0744	1.0618	1.0534	1.0502
10.2%	1.1020	1.0759	1.0630	1.0544	1.0512
10.4%	1.1040	1.0774	1.0642	1.0555	1.0521
10.6%	1.1060	1.0788	1.0654	1.0565	1.0531
10.8%	1.1080	1.0803	1.0666	1.0576	1.0541

* For use in calculating the value of a term certain annuity payable at the beginning of each period.

APPENDIX D — VALUATION TABLES

TERM CERTAIN REMAINDER FACTORS

INTEREST RATE

YEARS	3.0%	3.2%	3.4%	3.6%	3.8%	4.0%	4.2%	4.4%	4.6%
1	.970874	.968992	.967118	.965251	.963391	.961538	.959693	.957854	.956023
2	.942596	.938946	.935317	.931709	.928122	.924556	.921010	.917485	.913980
3	.915142	.909831	.904562	.899333	.894145	.888996	.883887	.878817	.873786
4	.888487	.881620	.874818	.868082	.861411	.854804	.848260	.841779	.835359
5	.862609	.854282	.846052	.837917	.829876	.821927	.814069	.806302	.798623
6	.837484	.827793	.818233	.808801	.799495	.790315	.781257	.772320	.763502
7	.813091	.802125	.791327	.780696	.770227	.759918	.749766	.739770	.729925
8	.789409	.777253	.765307	.753567	.742029	.730690	.719545	.708592	.697825
9	.766417	.753152	.740142	.727381	.714865	.702587	.690543	.678728	.667137
10	.744094	.729799	.715805	.702106	.688694	.675564	.662709	.650122	.637798
11	.722421	.707169	.692268	.677708	.663482	.649581	.635997	.622722	.609749
12	.701380	.685241	.669505	.654158	.639193	.624597	.610362	.596477	.582935
13	.680951	.663994	.647490	.631427	.615792	.600574	.585760	.571339	.557299
14	.661118	.643405	.626199	.609486	.593249	.577475	.562150	.547259	.532790
15	.641862	.623454	.605608	.588307	.571531	.555265	.539491	.524195	.509360
16	.623167	.604122	.585695	.567863	.550608	.533908	.517746	.502102	.486960
17	.605016	.585390	.566436	.548131	.530451	.513373	.496877	.480941	.465545
18	.587395	.567238	.547810	.529084	.511031	.493628	.476849	.460671	.445071
19	.570286	.549649	.529797	.510699	.492323	.474642	.457629	.441256	.425498
20	.553676	.532606	.512376	.492952	.474300	.456387	.439183	.422659	.406786
21	.537549	.516091	.495529	.475823	.456936	.438834	.421481	.404846	.388897
22	.521892	.500088	.479235	.459288	.440208	.421955	.404492	.387783	.371794
23	.506692	.484582	.463476	.443329	.424093	.405726	.388188	.371440	.355444
24	.491934	.469556	.448236	.427923	.408567	.390121	.372542	.355785	.339813
25	.477606	.454996	.433497	.413053	.393610	.375117	.357526	.340791	.324869
26	.463695	.440888	.419243	.398700	.379200	.360689	.343115	.326428	.310582
27	.450189	.427217	.405458	.384846	.365318	.346817	.329285	.312670	.296923
28	.437077	.413970	.392125	.371473	.351944	.333477	.316012	.299493	.283866
29	.424346	.401133	.379231	.358564	.339060	.320651	.303275	.286870	.271382
30	.411987	.388695	.366762	.346105	.326648	.308319	.291051	.274780	.259447
31	.399987	.376643	.354702	.334078	.314689	.296460	.279319	.263199	.248038
32	.388337	.364964	.343038	.322469	.303169	.285058	.268061	.252106	.237130
33	.377026	.353647	.331759	.311263	.292070	.274094	.257256	.241481	.226702
34	.366045	.342681	.320850	.300447	.281378	.263552	.246887	.231304	.216732
35	.355383	.332055	.310300	.290007	.271077	.253415	.236935	.221556	.207201
36	.345032	.321759	.300096	.279930	.261153	.243669	.227385	.212218	.198089
37	.334983	.311782	.290228	.270202	.251593	.234297	.218220	.203274	.189377
38	.325226	.302114	.280685	.260813	.242382	.225285	.209424	.194707	.181049
39	.315754	.292747	.271456	.251750	.233509	.216621	.200983	.186501	.173087
40	.306557	.283669	.262530	.243002	.224960	.208289	.192882	.178641	.165475
41	.297628	.274873	.253897	.234558	.216725	.200278	.185107	.171112	.158198
42	.288959	.266350	.245549	.226407	.208791	.192575	.177646	.163900	.151241
43	.280543	.258091	.237474	.218540	.201147	.185168	.170486	.156992	.144590
44	.272372	.250088	.229666	.210946	.193783	.178046	.163614	.150376	.138231
45	.264439	.242334	.222114	.203616	.186689	.171198	.157019	.144038	.132152
46	.256737	.234819	.214810	.196540	.179855	.164614	.150690	.137968	.126340
47	.249259	.227538	.207747	.189711	.173270	.158283	.144616	.132153	.120784
48	.241999	.220483	.200916	.183118	.166927	.152195	.138787	.126583	.115473
49	.234950	.213646	.194309	.176755	.160816	.146341	.133193	.121248	.110395
50	.228107	.207021	.187920	.170613	.154929	.140713	.127824	.116138	.105540

2006 Tax Facts on Insurance & Employee Benefits

APPENDIX D — VALUATION TABLES

TERM CERTAIN REMAINDER FACTORS

INTEREST RATE

YEARS	4.8%	5.0%	5.2%	5.4%	5.6%	5.8%	6.0%	6.2%	6.4%
1	.954199	.952381	.950570	.948767	.946970	.945180	.943396	.941620	.939850
2	.910495	.907029	.903584	.900158	.896752	.893364	.889996	.886648	.883317
3	.868793	.863838	.858920	.854040	.849197	.844390	.839619	.834885	.830185
4	.829001	.822702	.816464	.810285	.804163	.798100	.792094	.786144	.780249
5	.791031	.783526	.776106	.768771	.761518	.754348	.747258	.740248	.733317
6	.754801	.746215	.737744	.729384	.721135	.712994	.704961	.697032	.689208
7	.720230	.710681	.701277	.692015	.682893	.673908	.665057	.656339	.647752
8	.687242	.676839	.666613	.656561	.646679	.636964	.627412	.618022	.608789
9	.655765	.644609	.633663	.622923	.612385	.602045	.591898	.581942	.572170
10	.625730	.613913	.602341	.591009	.579910	.569041	.558395	.547968	.537754
11	.597071	.584679	.572568	.560729	.549157	.537846	.526788	.515977	.505408
12	.569724	.556837	.544266	.532001	.520036	.508361	.496969	.485854	.475007
13	.543630	.530321	.517363	.504745	.492458	.480492	.468839	.457490	.446436
14	.518731	.505068	.491790	.478885	.466343	.454151	.442301	.430781	.419582
15	.494972	.481017	.467481	.454350	.441612	.429255	.417265	.405632	.394344
16	.472302	.458112	.444374	.431072	.418194	.405723	.393646	.381951	.370624
17	.450670	.436297	.422408	.408987	.396017	.383481	.371364	.359653	.348331
18	.430028	.415521	.401529	.388033	.375016	.362458	.350344	.338656	.327379
19	.410332	.395734	.381681	.368153	.355129	.342588	.330513	.318885	.307687
20	.391538	.376889	.362815	.349291	.336296	.323807	.311805	.300268	.289179
21	.373605	.358942	.344881	.331396	.318462	.306056	.294155	.282739	.271785
22	.356494	.341850	.327834	.314417	.301574	.289278	.277505	.266232	.255437
23	.340166	.325571	.311629	.298309	.285581	.273420	.261797	.250689	.240073
24	.324586	.310068	.296225	.283025	.270437	.258431	.246979	.236054	.225632
25	.309719	.295303	.281583	.268525	.256096	.244263	.232999	.222273	.212060
26	.295533	.281241	.267664	.254768	.242515	.230873	.219810	.209297	.199305
27	.281998	.267848	.254434	.241715	.229654	.218216	.207368	.197078	.187316
28	.269082	.255094	.241857	.229331	.217475	.206253	.195630	.185572	.176049
29	.256757	.242946	.229902	.217582	.205943	.194947	.184557	.174739	.165460
30	.244997	.231377	.218538	.206434	.195021	.184260	.174110	.164537	.155507
31	.233776	.220359	.207736	.195858	.184679	.174158	.164255	.154932	.146154
32	.223069	.209866	.197468	.185823	.174886	.164611	.154957	.145887	.137362
33	.212852	.199873	.187707	.176303	.165612	.155587	.146186	.137370	.129100
34	.203103	.190355	.178429	.167270	.156829	.147058	.137912	.129350	.121335
35	.193801	.181290	.169609	.158701	.148512	.138996	.130105	.121798	.114036
36	.184924	.172657	.161225	.150570	.140637	.131376	.122741	.114688	.107177
37	.176454	.164436	.153256	.142856	.133179	.124174	.115793	.107992	.100730
38	.168373	.156605	.145681	.135537	.126116	.117367	.109239	.101688	.094671
39	.160661	.149148	.138480	.128593	.119428	.110933	.103056	.095751	.088977
40	.153302	.142046	.131635	.122004	.113095	.104851	.097222	.090161	.083625
41	.146281	.135282	.125128	.115754	.107098	.099103	.091719	.084897	.078595
42	.139581	.128840	.118943	.109823	.101418	.093670	.086527	.079941	.073867
43	.133188	.122704	.113064	.104197	.096040	.088535	.081630	.075274	.069424
44	.127088	.116861	.107475	.098858	.090947	.083682	.077009	.070880	.065248
45	.121267	.111297	.102163	.093793	.086124	.079094	.072650	.066742	.061323
46	.115713	.105997	.097113	.088988	.081557	.074758	.068538	.062845	.057635
47	.110413	.100949	.092312	.084429	.077232	.070660	.064658	.059176	.054168
48	.105356	.096142	.087749	.080103	.073136	.066786	.060998	.055722	.050910
49	.100530	.091564	.083412	.075999	.069258	.063125	.057546	.052469	.047848
50	.095926	.087204	.079289	.072106	.065585	.059665	.054288	.049405	.044970

APPENDIX D — VALUATION TABLES

TERM CERTAIN REMAINDER FACTORS

INTEREST RATE

YEARS	6.6%	6.8%	7.0%	7.2%	7.4%	7.6%	7.8%	8.0%	8.2%
1	.938086	.936330	.934579	.932836	.931099	.929368	.927644	.925926	.924214
2	.880006	.876713	.873439	.870183	.866945	.863725	.860523	.857339	.854172
3	.825521	.820892	.816298	.811738	.807211	.802718	.798259	.793832	.789438
4	.774410	.768626	.762895	.757218	.751593	.746021	.740500	.735030	.729610
5	.726464	.719687	.712986	.706360	.699808	.693328	.686920	.680583	.674316
6	.681486	.673864	.666342	.658918	.651590	.644357	.637217	.630170	.623213
7	.639292	.630959	.622750	.614662	.606694	.598845	.591110	.583490	.575982
8	.599711	.590786	.582009	.573379	.564892	.556547	.548340	.540269	.532331
9	.562581	.553170	.543934	.534868	.525971	.517237	.508664	.500249	.491988
10	.527750	.517950	.508349	.498944	.489731	.480704	.471859	.463194	.454703
11	.495075	.484971	.475093	.465433	.455987	.446751	.437717	.428883	.420243
12	.464423	.454093	.444012	.434173	.424569	.415196	.406046	.397114	.388394
13	.435669	.425181	.414964	.405012	.395316	.385870	.376666	.367698	.358960
14	.408695	.398109	.387817	.377810	.368078	.358615	.349412	.340461	.331756
15	.383391	.372762	.362446	.352434	.342717	.333285	.324130	.315242	.306613
16	.359654	.349028	.338735	.328763	.319103	.309745	.300677	.291890	.283376
17	.337386	.326805	.316574	.306682	.297117	.287867	.278921	.270269	.261901
18	.316498	.305997	.295864	.286084	.276645	.267534	.258739	.250249	.242052
19	.296902	.286514	.276508	.266870	.257584	.248638	.240018	.231712	.223708
20	.278520	.268272	.258419	.248946	.239836	.231076	.222651	.214548	.206754
21	.261276	.251191	.241513	.232225	.223311	.214755	.206541	.198656	.191085
22	.245099	.235197	.225713	.216628	.207925	.199586	.191596	.183941	.176604
23	.229924	.220222	.210947	.202078	.193598	.185489	.177733	.170315	.163220
24	.215689	.206201	.197147	.188506	.180259	.172387	.164873	.157699	.150850
25	.202334	.193072	.184249	.175845	.167839	.160211	.152943	.146018	.139418
26	.189807	.180779	.172195	.164035	.156275	.148895	.141877	.135202	.128852
27	.178056	.169268	.160930	.153017	.145507	.138379	.131611	.125187	.119087
28	.167031	.158491	.150402	.142740	.135482	.128605	.122088	.115914	.110062
29	.156690	.148400	.140563	.133153	.126147	.119521	.113255	.107328	.101721
30	.146989	.138951	.131367	.124210	.117455	.111079	.105060	.099377	.094012
31	.137888	.130104	.122773	.115868	.109362	.103233	.097458	.092016	.086887
32	.129351	.121820	.114741	.108085	.101827	.095942	.090406	.085200	.080302
33	.121342	.114064	.107235	.100826	.094811	.089165	.083865	.078889	.074216
34	.113830	.106802	.100219	.094054	.088278	.082867	.077797	.073045	.068592
35	.106782	.100001	.093663	.087737	.082196	.077014	.072168	.067635	.063394
36	.100171	.093634	.087535	.081844	.076532	.071574	.066946	.062625	.058589
37	.093969	.087673	.081809	.076347	.071259	.066519	.062102	.057986	.054149
38	.088151	.082090	.076457	.071219	.066349	.061821	.057609	.053690	.050045
39	.082693	.076864	.071455	.066436	.061778	.057454	.053440	.049713	.046253
40	.077573	.071970	.066780	.061974	.057521	.053396	.049573	.046031	.042747
41	.072770	.067387	.062412	.057811	.053558	.049625	.045987	.042621	.039508
42	.068265	.063097	.058329	.053929	.049868	.046120	.042659	.039464	.036514
43	.064038	.059079	.054513	.050307	.046432	.042862	.039572	.036541	.033746
44	.060074	.055318	.050946	.046928	.043233	.039835	.036709	.033834	.031189
45	.056354	.051796	.047613	.043776	.040254	.037021	.034053	.031328	.028825
46	.052865	.048498	.044499	.040836	.037480	.034406	.031589	.029007	.026641
47	.049592	.045410	.041587	.038093	.034898	.031976	.029303	.026859	.024622
48	.046522	.042519	.038867	.035535	.032493	.029717	.027183	.024869	.022756
49	.043641	.039811	.036324	.033148	.030255	.027618	.025216	.023027	.021031
50	.040939	.037277	.033948	.030922	.028170	.025668	.023392	.021321	.019437

2006 Tax Facts on Insurance & Employee Benefits

APPENDIX D — VALUATION TABLES

TERM CERTAIN REMAINDER FACTORS

INTEREST RATE

YEARS	8.4%	8.6%	8.8%	9.0%	9.2%	9.4%	9.6%	9.8%	10.0%
1	.922509	.920810	.919118	.917431	.915751	.914077	.912409	.910747	.909091
2	.851023	.847892	.844777	.841680	.838600	.835536	.832490	.829460	.826446
3	.785077	.780747	.776450	.772184	.767949	.763744	.759571	.755428	.751315
4	.724241	.718920	.713649	.708425	.703250	.698121	.693039	.688004	.683013
5	.668119	.661989	.655927	.649931	.644001	.638136	.632335	.626597	.620921
6	.616346	.609566	.602874	.596267	.589745	.583305	.576948	.570671	.564474
7	.568584	.561295	.554112	.547034	.540059	.533186	.526412	.519737	.513158
8	.524524	.516846	.509294	.501866	.494560	.487373	.480303	.473349	.466507
9	.483879	.475917	.468101	.460428	.452894	.445496	.438233	.431101	.424098
10	.446383	.438230	.430240	.422411	.414738	.407218	.399848	.392624	.385543
11	.411792	.403526	.395441	.387533	.379797	.372228	.364824	.357581	.350494
12	.379882	.371571	.363457	.355535	.347799	.340245	.332869	.325666	.318631
13	.350445	.342147	.334060	.326179	.318497	.311010	.303713	.296599	.289664
14	.323288	.315052	.307040	.299246	.291664	.284287	.277110	.270127	.263331
15	.298236	.290103	.282206	.274538	.267092	.259860	.252838	.246017	.239392
16	.275126	.267130	.259381	.251870	.244589	.237532	.230691	.224059	.217629
17	.253806	.245976	.238401	.231073	.223983	.217123	.210485	.204061	.197845
18	.234139	.226497	.219119	.211994	.205113	.198467	.192048	.185848	.179859
19	.215995	.208561	.201396	.194490	.187832	.181414	.175226	.169260	.163508
20	.199257	.192045	.185107	.178431	.172007	.165826	.159878	.154153	.148644
21	.183817	.176837	.170135	.163698	.157516	.151578	.145874	.140395	.135131
22	.169573	.162834	.156374	.150182	.144245	.138554	.133097	.127864	.122846
23	.156432	.149939	.143726	.137781	.132093	.126649	.121439	.116452	.111678
24	.144310	.138065	.132101	.126405	.120964	.115767	.110802	.106058	.101526
25	.133128	.127132	.121416	.115968	.110773	.105820	.101097	.096592	.092296
26	.122811	.117064	.111596	.106392	.101441	.096727	.092241	.087971	.083905
27	.113295	.107794	.102570	.097608	.092894	.088416	.084162	.080119	.076278
28	.104515	.099258	.094274	.089548	.085068	.080819	.076790	.072968	.069343
29	.096416	.091398	.086649	.082155	.077901	.073875	.070064	.066456	.063039
30	.088945	.084160	.079640	.075371	.071338	.067527	.063927	.060524	.057309
31	.082053	.077495	.073199	.069148	.065328	.061725	.058327	.055122	.052099
32	.075694	.071358	.067278	.063438	.059824	.056422	.053218	.050202	.047362
33	.069829	.065708	.061837	.058200	.054784	.051574	.048557	.045722	.043057
34	.064418	.060504	.056835	.053395	.050168	.047142	.044304	.041641	.039143
35	.059426	.055713	.052238	.048986	.045942	.043092	.040423	.037924	.035584
36	.054821	.051301	.048013	.044941	.042071	.039389	.036882	.034539	.032349
37	.050573	.047239	.044130	.041231	.038527	.036005	.033652	.031457	.029408
38	.046654	.043498	.040560	.037826	.035281	.032911	.030704	.028649	.026735
39	.043039	.040053	.037280	.034703	.032309	.030083	.028015	.026092	.024304
40	.039703	.036881	.034264	.031838	.029587	.027498	.025561	.023763	.022095
41	.036627	.033961	.031493	.029209	.027094	.025136	.023322	.021642	.020086
42	.033789	.031271	.028946	.026797	.024811	.022976	.021279	.019711	.018260
43	.031170	.028795	.026605	.024584	.022721	.021002	.019415	.017951	.016600
44	.028755	.026515	.024453	.022555	.020807	.019197	.017715	.016349	.015091
45	.026527	.024415	.022475	.020692	.019054	.017548	.016163	.014890	.013719
46	.024471	.022482	.020657	.018984	.017449	.016040	.014747	.013561	.012472
47	.022575	.020701	.018986	.017416	.015978	.014662	.013456	.012351	.011338
48	.020825	.019062	.017451	.015978	.014632	.013402	.012277	.011248	.010307
49	.019212	.017552	.016039	.014659	.013400	.012250	.011202	.010244	.009370
50	.017723	.016163	.014742	.013449	.012271	.011198	.010221	.009330	.008519

APPENDIX D — VALUATION TABLES

SINGLE LIFE REMAINDER FACTORS
(For valuation dates occurring after April 30, 1999)

INTEREST RATE

AGE	3.0%	3.2%	3.4%	3.6%	3.8%	4.0%	4.2%	4.4%	4.6%	4.8%
35	.30955	.28849	.26914	.25133	.23494	.21984	.20592	.19307	.18121	.17025
36	.31759	.29644	.27697	.25902	.24248	.22722	.21312	.20010	.18805	.17691
37	.32582	.30458	.28500	.26694	.25025	.23483	.22057	.20737	.19514	.18382
38	.33425	.31295	.29327	.27508	.25826	.24269	.22827	.21490	.20251	.19100
39	.34288	.32152	.30175	.28346	.26651	.25080	.23623	.22270	.21013	.19845
40	.35173	.33031	.31048	.29208	.27502	.25918	.24446	.23078	.21805	.20620
41	.36079	.33935	.31945	.30097	.28380	.26783	.25298	.23915	.22626	.21425
42	.37007	.34860	.32866	.31011	.29284	.27676	.26178	.24782	.23478	.22262
43	.37956	.35809	.33811	.31950	.30215	.28597	.27087	.25678	.24360	.23129
44	.38925	.36780	.34779	.32914	.31172	.29545	.28025	.26603	.25273	.24027
45	.39912	.37769	.35769	.33899	.32152	.30517	.28987	.27555	.26212	.24953
46	.40917	.38778	.36779	.34907	.33155	.31514	.29976	.28533	.27179	.25908
47	.41937	.39804	.37806	.35934	.34179	.32533	.30987	.29535	.28171	.26889
48	.42973	.40847	.38853	.36982	.35225	.33574	.32023	.30563	.29190	.27897
49	.44024	.41907	.39918	.38049	.36292	.34638	.33082	.31615	.30234	.28931
50	.45091	.42985	.41003	.39137	.37381	.35726	.34166	.32694	.31306	.29995
51	.46173	.44079	.42105	.40245	.38491	.36836	.35274	.33798	.32404	.31085
52	.47267	.45186	.43223	.41369	.39619	.37965	.36402	.34924	.33525	.32200
53	.48372	.46306	.44354	.42509	.40764	.39113	.37550	.36070	.34668	.33339
54	.49486	.47437	.45498	.43663	.41925	.40278	.38717	.37237	.35833	.34500
55	.50611	.48580	.46656	.44832	.43102	.41461	.39903	.38424	.37019	.35683
56	.51745	.49734	.47826	.46015	.44295	.42661	.41108	.39631	.38227	.36890
57	.52887	.50897	.49007	.47210	.45502	.43877	.42330	.40857	.39455	.38118
58	.54034	.52067	.50196	.48416	.46720	.45105	.43566	.42098	.40699	.39364
59	.55182	.53240	.51390	.49627	.47945	.46342	.44811	.43351	.41956	.40623
60	.56332	.54415	.52587	.50842	.49177	.47586	.46066	.44613	.43224	.41896
61	.57483	.55594	.53789	.52064	.50415	.48838	.47330	.45887	.44505	.43182
62	.58639	.56777	.54997	.53294	.51664	.50103	.48608	.47175	.45802	.44485
63	.59798	.57967	.56213	.54533	.52923	.51379	.49898	.48478	.47115	.45807
64	.60959	.59160	.57434	.55778	.54189	.52664	.51200	.49793	.48442	.47143
65	.62122	.60355	.58658	.57029	.55463	.53958	.52512	.51121	.49782	.48495
66	.63288	.61555	.59889	.58287	.56746	.55263	.53835	.52461	.51137	.49862
67	.64458	.62761	.61127	.59554	.58040	.56580	.55174	.53818	.52511	.51250
68	.65630	.63971	.62371	.60829	.59342	.57908	.56524	.55188	.53899	.52654
69	.66802	.65181	.63617	.62107	.60649	.59242	.57882	.56568	.55299	.54071
70	.67968	.66387	.64859	.63383	.61956	.60576	.59242	.57951	.56703	.55495
71	.69124	.67583	.66093	.64651	.63256	.61906	.60598	.59332	.58106	.56918
72	.70268	.68768	.67316	.65910	.64547	.63227	.61948	.60707	.59504	.58338
73	.71397	.69939	.68526	.67156	.65827	.64538	.63287	.62073	.60895	.59751
74	.72515	.71100	.69727	.68393	.67099	.65842	.64621	.63435	.62282	.61162
75	.73625	.72253	.70920	.69625	.68367	.67143	.65953	.64796	.63671	.62575
76	.74729	.73402	.72111	.70855	.69633	.68444	.67287	.66160	.65063	.63995
77	.75827	.74545	.73297	.72082	.70898	.69745	.68622	.67526	.66459	.65419
78	.76917	.75681	.74477	.73303	.72159	.71043	.69954	.68892	.67856	.66845
79	.77993	.76804	.75645	.74513	.73408	.72330	.71278	.70250	.69246	.68265
80	.79047	.77906	.76791	.75701	.74637	.73597	.72581	.71588	.70617	.69668
81	.80074	.78979	.77908	.76861	.75838	.74837	.73857	.72899	.71962	.71045
82	.81070	.80021	.78994	.77989	.77006	.76043	.75101	.74178	.73274	.72389
83	.82035	.81031	.80048	.79085	.78141	.77217	.76311	.75423	.74553	.73700
84	.82976	.82017	.81077	.80156	.79252	.78366	.77497	.76645	.75809	.74988

2006 Tax Facts on Insurance & Employee Benefits

APPENDIX D — VALUATION TABLES

SINGLE LIFE REMAINDER FACTORS
(For valuation dates occurring after April 30, 1999)

AGE	5.0%	5.2%	5.4%	5.6%	5.8%	6.0%	6.2%	6.4%	6.6%	6.8%
35	.16011	.15073	.14204	.13399	.12652	.11958	.11314	.10715	.10157	.09638
36	.16658	.15701	.14814	.13990	.13225	.12514	.11852	.11236	.10662	.10127
37	.17331	.16356	.15450	.14608	.13825	.13096	.12416	.11783	.11193	.10641
38	.18031	.17038	.16113	.15253	.14452	.13705	.13009	.12359	.11751	.11183
39	.18759	.17747	.16805	.15927	.15108	.14344	.13629	.12962	.12338	.11753
40	.19516	.18487	.17527	.16631	.15795	.15013	.14281	.13597	.12955	.12355
41	.20305	.19259	.18282	.17368	.16514	.15715	.14966	.14264	.13606	.12989
42	.21125	.20062	.19069	.18138	.17267	.16450	.15685	.14966	.14291	.13657
43	.21977	.20898	.19888	.18941	.18053	.17220	.16437	.15702	.15010	.14360
44	.22860	.21766	.20740	.19777	.18873	.18023	.17224	.16472	.15764	.15098
45	.23772	.22664	.21622	.20644	.19724	.18858	.18042	.17274	.16550	.15867
46	.24714	.23591	.22536	.21542	.20606	.19725	.18893	.18109	.17370	.16671
47	.25682	.24546	.23476	.22468	.21518	.20621	.19775	.18975	.18220	.17505
48	.26678	.25530	.24447	.23425	.22460	.21549	.20688	.19873	.19102	.18373
49	.27702	.26543	.25447	.24412	.23434	.22509	.21633	.20804	.20018	.19274
50	.28756	.27586	.26479	.25432	.24441	.23502	.22612	.21769	.20969	.20210
51	.29838	.28658	.27541	.26482	.25479	.24528	.23625	.22769	.21955	.21182
52	.30946	.29757	.28630	.27561	.26547	.25584	.24669	.23799	.22973	.22186
53	.32078	.30882	.29746	.28667	.27643	.26669	.25742	.24861	.24022	.23222
54	.33234	.32031	.30888	.29801	.28766	.27782	.26845	.25952	.25101	.24290
55	.34413	.33205	.32056	.30961	.29918	.28925	.27978	.27074	.26212	.25389
56	.35617	.34405	.33250	.32149	.31099	.30097	.29140	.28227	.27355	.26522
57	.36844	.35629	.34469	.33363	.32306	.31297	.30333	.29411	.28529	.27686
58	.38089	.36873	.35710	.34600	.33538	.32522	.31551	.30621	.29731	.28878
59	.39350	.38133	.36968	.35855	.34789	.33768	.32790	.31854	.30956	.30095
60	.40624	.39408	.38243	.37127	.36058	.35033	.34050	.33107	.32202	.31334
61	.41914	.40699	.39535	.38418	.37347	.36318	.35331	.34384	.33473	.32598
62	.43223	.42011	.40848	.39732	.38660	.37629	.36639	.35688	.34772	.33892
63	.44550	.43343	.42184	.41069	.39997	.38966	.37974	.37020	.36101	.35216
64	.45895	.44694	.43539	.42427	.41357	.40326	.39334	.38378	.37456	.36568
65	.47255	.46062	.44912	.43805	.42738	.41709	.40718	.39761	.38838	.37947
66	.48634	.47449	.46307	.45206	.44143	.43118	.42128	.41172	.40249	.39357
67	.50034	.48860	.47727	.46633	.45576	.44556	.43569	.42616	.41694	.40803
68	.51452	.50291	.49168	.48083	.47034	.46020	.45038	.44089	.43170	.42281
69	.52885	.51737	.50627	.49552	.48513	.47506	.46531	.45587	.44672	.43786
70	.54325	.53193	.52096	.51034	.50004	.49007	.48040	.47103	.46194	.45312
71	.55767	.54651	.53569	.52520	.51503	.50516	.49558	.48629	.47727	.46851
72	.57206	.56108	.55043	.54009	.53004	.52029	.51082	.50162	.49268	.48399
73	.58640	.57561	.56513	.55495	.54505	.53543	.52607	.51697	.50813	.49952
74	.60073	.59015	.57985	.56984	.56009	.55061	.54139	.53241	.52367	.51515
75	.61510	.60473	.59463	.58480	.57523	.56591	.55683	.54798	.53935	.53095
76	.62954	.61940	.60952	.59989	.59050	.58135	.57243	.56373	.55524	.54696
77	.64404	.63415	.62450	.61509	.60590	.59694	.58819	.57965	.57132	.56318
78	.65858	.64895	.63955	.63036	.62140	.61264	.60408	.59572	.58755	.57957
79	.67308	.66372	.65457	.64563	.63690	.62836	.62001	.61184	.60385	.59604
80	.68740	.67833	.66945	.66077	.65227	.64396	.63582	.62786	.62007	.61244
81	.70147	.69268	.68408	.67566	.66741	.65933	.65142	.64367	.63608	.62864
82	.71522	.70672	.69840	.69024	.68225	.67441	.66673	.65920	.65182	.64458
83	.72864	.72044	.71240	.70451	.69678	.68919	.68175	.67444	.66728	.66024
84	.74183	.73393	.72618	.71857	.71110	.70377	.69657	.68950	.68256	.67574

2006 Tax Facts on Insurance & Employee Benefits

APPENDIX D — VALUATION TABLES

SINGLE LIFE REMAINDER FACTORS
(For valuation dates occurring after April 30, 1999)

INTEREST RATE

AGE	7.0%	7.2%	7.4%	7.6%	7.8%	8.0%	8.2%	8.4%	8.6%	8.8%
35	.09155	.08704	.08283	.07890	.07522	.07179	.06857	.06555	.06273	.06007
36	.09628	.09162	.08726	.08319	.07938	.07581	.07246	.06932	.06638	.06361
37	.10126	.09645	.09194	.08772	.08377	.08006	.07659	.07332	.07025	.06737
38	.10652	.10155	.09689	.09253	.08843	.08459	.08098	.07758	.07439	.07138
39	.11206	.10693	.10212	.09761	.09337	.08938	.08563	.08210	.07878	.07565
40	.11791	.11262	.10766	.10299	.09860	.09447	.09059	.08692	.08347	.08021
41	.12409	.11864	.11352	.10870	.10417	.09989	.09586	.09206	.08848	.08509
42	.13061	.12500	.11972	.11475	.11006	.10564	.10147	.09753	.09381	.09029
43	.13747	.13171	.12627	.12115	.11631	.11174	.10742	.10334	.09948	.09583
44	.14469	.13876	.13317	.12789	.12290	.11819	.11373	.10950	.10551	.10172
45	.15223	.14615	.14040	.13496	.12982	.12496	.12035	.11599	.11185	.10792
46	.16011	.15387	.14796	.14238	.13708	.13207	.12732	.12281	.11853	.11447
47	.16830	.16190	.15584	.15010	.14466	.13950	.13460	.12995	.12553	.12133
48	.17682	.17027	.16406	.15817	.15258	.14727	.14223	.13743	.13287	.12853
49	.18568	.17898	.17262	.16658	.16084	.15539	.15020	.14526	.14056	.13608
50	.19490	.18805	.18155	.17536	.16948	.16388	.15855	.15347	.14862	.14401
51	.20448	.19749	.19084	.18452	.17849	.17275	.16727	.16205	.15707	.15232
52	.21438	.20726	.20047	.19400	.18784	.18196	.17634	.17098	.16587	.16097
53	.22461	.21735	.21043	.20383	.19753	.19151	.18576	.18027	.17501	.16999
54	.23516	.22777	.22072	.21399	.20756	.20140	.19552	.18990	.18451	.17935
55	.24604	.23853	.23136	.22450	.21793	.21166	.20564	.19989	.19437	.18908
56	.25725	.24963	.24233	.23535	.22867	.22227	.21613	.21025	.20461	.19919
57	.26879	.26106	.25365	.24656	.23976	.23324	.22698	.22098	.21522	.20968
58	.28061	.27278	.26528	.25807	.25116	.24453	.23816	.23204	.22616	.22051
59	.29269	.28477	.27716	.26986	.26284	.25610	.24962	.24339	.23740	.23163
60	.30500	.29699	.28929	.28190	.27478	.26794	.26136	.25502	.24892	.24304
61	.31757	.30948	.30170	.29422	.28701	.28007	.27339	.26695	.26075	.25477
62	.33044	.32229	.31443	.30687	.29958	.29255	.28578	.27925	.27295	.26687
63	.34363	.33542	.32750	.31986	.31250	.30539	.29854	.29192	.28553	.27935
64	.35711	.34884	.34087	.33317	.32574	.31857	.31164	.30494	.29847	.29221
65	.37087	.36257	.35455	.34681	.33932	.33208	.32508	.31831	.31177	.30543
66	.38496	.37663	.36858	.36079	.35326	.34597	.33891	.33208	.32547	.31906
67	.39941	.39107	.38299	.37518	.36761	.36028	.35318	.34630	.33963	.33316
68	.41419	.40585	.39777	.38994	.38235	.37499	.36785	.36093	.35422	.34770
69	.42927	.42094	.41286	.40503	.39743	.39006	.38290	.37595	.36920	.36265
70	.44456	.43626	.42820	.42038	.41278	.40540	.39823	.39127	.38450	.37791
71	.46000	.45174	.44371	.43591	.42832	.42095	.41378	.40681	.40003	.39343
72	.47554	.46733	.45934	.45157	.44401	.43666	.42950	.42253	.41575	.40914
73	.49114	.48299	.47506	.46733	.45981	.45249	.44535	.43840	.43162	.42502
74	.50686	.49879	.49092	.48325	.47578	.46849	.46139	.45446	.44771	.44112
75	.52276	.51477	.50698	.49938	.49197	.48474	.47769	.47080	.46408	.45752
76	.53888	.53100	.52330	.51579	.50846	.50130	.49430	.48747	.48079	.47427
77	.55523	.54747	.53988	.53247	.52523	.51815	.51123	.50447	.49786	.49139
78	.57177	.56414	.55668	.54939	.54225	.53528	.52845	.52177	.51523	.50884
79	.58840	.58092	.57360	.56644	.55943	.55256	.54584	.53926	.53282	.52650
80	.60497	.59765	.59048	.58347	.57659	.56985	.56325	.55678	.55044	.54423
81	.62135	.61421	.60721	.60034	.59361	.58701	.58054	.57419	.56797	.56186
82	.63748	.63052	.62368	.61698	.61041	.60395	.59762	.59140	.58530	.57931
83	.65334	.64656	.63991	.63338	.62696	.62066	.61448	.60840	.60243	.59657
84	.66904	.66246	.65599	.64964	.64340	.63727	.63124	.62531	.61949	.61376

2006 Tax Facts on Insurance & Employee Benefits   953

SINGLE LIFE REMAINDER FACTORS
(For valuation dates occurring after April 30, 1999)

INTEREST RATE

AGE	9.0%	9.2%	9.4%	9.6%	9.8%	10.0%	10.2%	10.4%	10.6%	10.8%
35	.05758	.05524	.05304	.05097	.04902	.04718	.04545	.04382	.04227	.04081
36	.06101	.05856	.05626	.05409	.05205	.05012	.04830	.04658	.04495	.04341
37	.06466	.06210	.05969	.05742	.05528	.05325	.05134	.04953	.04782	.04620
38	.06855	.06588	.06336	.06099	.05874	.05662	.05462	.05272	.05092	.04921
39	.07270	.06992	.06729	.06480	.06245	.06023	.05812	.05613	.05424	.05245
40	.07714	.07423	.07149	.06889	.06643	.06411	.06190	.05981	.05782	.05594
41	.08189	.07886	.07600	.07329	.07072	.06828	.06597	.06378	.06170	.05972
42	.08696	.08381	.08083	.07800	.07531	.07277	.07035	.06806	.06587	.06380
43	.09237	.08909	.08598	.08304	.08024	.07758	.07505	.07265	.07036	.06818
44	.09813	.09472	.09148	.08841	.08549	.08272	.08008	.07757	.07518	.07290
45	.10420	.10066	.09730	.09410	.09106	.08817	.08542	.08279	.08029	.07791
46	.11061	.10694	.10345	.10013	.09696	.09395	.09108	.08834	.08573	.08324
47	.11733	.11353	.10991	.10646	.10317	.10004	.09705	.09419	.09147	.08886
48	.12439	.12046	.11671	.11313	.10972	.10646	.10335	.10038	.09754	.09482
49	.13181	.12774	.12385	.12015	.11661	.11322	.10999	.10690	.10394	.10111
50	.13960	.13540	.13138	.12754	.12388	.12037	.11701	.11380	.11073	.10778
51	.14777	.14344	.13929	.13532	.13153	.12789	.12441	.12108	.11789	.11482
52	.15630	.15183	.14755	.14345	.13953	.13577	.13217	.12871	.12540	.12222
53	.16518	.16057	.15616	.15194	.14789	.14400	.14028	.13670	.13327	.12997
54	.17441	.16968	.16514	.16078	.15661	.15260	.14875	.14505	.14150	.13808
55	.18402	.17915	.17449	.17001	.16570	.16157	.15760	.15378	.15011	.14657
56	.19400	.18901	.18422	.17962	.17519	.17093	.16684	.16290	.15911	.15546
57	.20436	.19925	.19434	.18961	.18507	.18069	.17648	.17242	.16851	.16474
58	.21507	.20984	.20481	.19996	.19530	.19080	.18647	.18229	.17827	.17438
59	.22608	.22073	.21558	.21062	.20584	.20123	.19678	.19249	.18835	.18435
60	.23738	.23192	.22666	.22158	.21669	.21196	.20740	.20300	.19875	.19464
61	.24900	.24343	.23806	.23288	.22787	.22304	.21837	.21385	.20949	.20527
62	.26100	.25533	.24985	.24456	.23945	.23451	.22973	.22511	.22064	.21631
63	.27339	.26762	.26205	.25666	.25145	.24641	.24152	.23680	.23222	.22779
64	.28615	.28030	.27463	.26915	.26384	.25870	.25372	.24890	.24422	.23969
65	.29930	.29336	.28761	.28203	.27664	.27140	.26633	.26141	.25664	.25201
66	.31285	.30684	.30101	.29536	.28987	.28456	.27940	.27439	.26953	.26481
67	.32689	.32081	.31491	.30918	.30363	.29823	.29299	.28790	.28296	.27815
68	.34138	.33524	.32928	.32349	.31787	.31240	.30709	.30193	.29691	.29202
69	.35628	.35009	.34408	.33824	.33256	.32703	.32166	.31643	.31134	.30639
70	.37151	.36529	.35924	.35335	.34762	.34204	.33661	.33133	.32618	.32116
71	.38701	.38076	.37467	.36875	.36298	.35736	.35188	.34654	.34134	.33627
72	.40271	.39644	.39034	.38438	.37858	.37293	.36742	.36204	.35679	.35168
73	.41858	.41231	.40619	.40022	.39440	.38872	.38317	.37776	.37248	.36733
74	.43469	.42842	.42230	.41632	.41049	.40479	.39923	.39380	.38849	.38330
75	.45111	.44485	.43874	.43277	.42693	.42123	.41566	.41021	.40489	.39968
76	.46790	.46167	.45558	.44963	.44380	.43811	.43254	.42709	.42176	.41655
77	.48506	.47888	.47282	.46690	.46111	.45543	.44988	.44444	.43912	.43391
78	.50257	.49645	.49044	.48457	.47881	.47317	.46765	.46224	.45694	.45174
79	.52032	.51426	.50833	.50251	.49681	.49122	.48574	.48037	.47510	.46993
80	.53813	.53216	.52630	.52056	.51492	.50939	.50397	.49865	.49343	.48830
81	.55587	.54999	.54422	.53856	.53300	.52754	.52219	.51693	.51176	.50669
82	.57343	.56766	.56198	.55641	.55094	.54557	.54029	.53510	.53000	.52499
83	.59081	.58515	.57958	.57411	.56874	.56346	.55826	.55315	.54813	.54319
84	.60813	.60259	.59715	.59179	.58652	.58134	.57624	.57123	.56629	.56144

APPENDIX E

Employee Benefit Limits: 2001 - 2006

As of 2006, all the preset employee benefit increases mandated by EGTRRA 2001 have taken effect. The employee benefit limits that follow are indexed annually for inflation, rounded to the increment levels set forth below.

Type of Limit	2001 (Notice 2000-66)	2002 (Notice 2001-84)	2003 (Notice 2002-71)	2004 (Notice 2003-73)	2005 (Notice 2004-72)	2006 (Notice 2005-75)	Increment
Defined Benefit Plans	$140,000	$160,000	$160,000	$165,000	$170,000	$175,000	$5,000
Defined Contribution Plans Q 332	$35,000 or 25% of pay	$40,000 or 100% of pay	$40,000 or 100% of pay	$41,000 or 100% of pay	$42,000 or 100% of pay	$44,000 or 100% of pay	$1,000
Elective Deferral Limit for 401(k) Plans and SAR-SEPs Q 241, Q 396	$10,500	$11,000	$12,000	$13,000	$14,000	$15,000	$500
Elective Deferral Limit for SIMPLE IRAs and SIMPLE 401(k) Plans Q 242, Q 396	$6,500	$7,000	$8,000	$9,000	$10,000	$10,000	$500
Elective Deferral Limit for 457 Plans Q 124	$8,500	$11,000	$12,000	$13,000	$14,000	$15,000	$500
Minimum Compensation Amount for SEPs Q 240	$450	$450	$450	$450	$450	$450	$50
Maximum Compensation Amount for VEBAs Q 504; SEPs Q 240; TSAs Q 467; Qualified Plans Q 331, Q 353F	$170,000	$200,000	$200,000	$205,000	$210,000	$220,000	$5,000*
Catch-up for 401(k) Plans Q 397	N/A	$1,000	$2,000	$3,000	$4,000	$5,000	$500
Catch-up for SIMPLE IRAs and SIMPLE 401(k) Plans Q 242, Q 397	N/A	$500	$1,000	$1,500	$2,000	$2,500	$500
Highly Compensated Employee Definition Limit Q 356	$85,000	$90,000	$90,000	$90,000	$95,000	$100,000	$5,000
ESOP Payout Limits Q 412	$155,000 $780,000	$160,000 $800,000	$160,000 $810,000	$165,000 $830,000	$170,000 $850,000	$175,000 $885,000	$5,000
Key Employee Definition Q 357	**	$130,000	$130,000	$130,000	$135,000	$140,000	$5,000

** Prior to 2002, the compensation limit was indexed in increments of $10,000

*** The definition of key employee was different prior to 2002. Indexing of the key employee compensation limit began for years after 2002.

2006 Tax Facts on Insurance & Employee Benefits

APPENDIX E — INDEXED EMPLOYEE BENEFIT LIMITS

Indexed Employee Benefit Limits: 1996-2000

Employee Benefit Limit	2000 (Notice 99-55)	1999 (Notice 98-53)	1998 (Notice 97-58)	1997 (Notice 96-55)	1996 (Notice 95-55)	Incremental
Section 415 Defined Benefit Dollar Limit —see Q 332	$135,000	$130,000	$130,000	$125,000	$120,000	$5,000
Section 415 Defined Contribution Dollar Limit—see Q 332	$30,000	$30,000	$30,000	$30,000	$30,000	$5,000
Elective Deferral Limit For 401(k) Plans and SAR-SEPs— see Qs 241, 405, 397	$10,500	$10,000	$10,000	$9,500	$9,500	$500
Minimum Compensation Amounts for SEPs—see Q 240	$450	$400	$400	$400	$400	$50
Maximum Compensation Limit for VEBAs—see Q 504, SEPs—see Q 240, TSAs—see Q 467, and Qualified Plans—see Qs 337, 404F	$170,000	$160,000	$160,000	$160,000	$150,000*	$10,000
Excess Distributions/ Accumulations	N/A	N/A	N/A	$160,000	$155,000	$5,000
Highly Compensated Employee Definitional Limit**—see Q 356	$85,000	$80,000	$80,000	$80,000	$66,000 $100,000	$5,000
ESOP Payout Limits —see Q 413	$150,000 $755,000	$145,000 $735,000	$145,000 $725,000	$140,000 $710,000	$135,000 $690,000	$5,000
Elective Deferral Limit for SIMPLE IRAs; SIMPLE 401(k) Plans —see Qs 242, 397	$6,000	$6,000	$6,000	6,000	N/A	$500
Elective Deferral Limit for Section 457 Plans —see Q 124	$8,000	$8,000	$8,000	$7,500	$7,500	$500

* The limit for certain collectively bargained plans not yet subject to the OBRA '93 reduced compensation limit is $325,000 in 2006 ($315,000 in 2005).

** The definition of highly compensated employee for years beginning after 1996 was changed; see Q 356.

APPENDIX F

Required Minimum Distribution (RMD) Tables

RMD Uniform Lifetime Table - Distribution Period

Age	Factor	Age	Factor	Age	Factor
10	86.2	45	51.5	80	18.7
11	85.2	46	50.5	81	17.9
12	84.2	47	49.5	82	17.1
13	83.2	48	48.5	83	16.3
14	82.2	49	47.5	84	15.5
15	81.2	50	46.5	85	14.8
16	80.2	51	45.5	86	14.1
17	79.2	52	44.6	87	13.4
18	78.2	53	43.6	88	12.7
19	77.3	54	42.6	89	12.0
20	76.3	55	41.6	90	11.4
21	75.3	56	40.7	91	10.8
22	74.3	57	39.7	92	10.2
23	73.3	58	38.7	93	9.6
24	72.3	59	37.8	94	9.1
25	71.3	60	36.8	95	8.6
26	70.3	61	35.8	96	8.1
27	69.3	62	34.9	97	7.6
28	68.3	63	33.9	98	7.1
29	67.3	64	33.0	99	6.7
30	66.3	65	32.0	100	6.3
31	65.3	66	31.1	101	5.9
32	64.3	67	30.2	102	5.5
33	63.3	68	29.2	103	5.2
34	62.3	69	28.3	104	4.9
35	61.4	70	27.4	105	4.5
36	60.4	71	26.5	106	4.2
37	59.4	72	25.6	107	3.9
38	58.4	73	24.7	108	3.7
39	57.4	74	23.8	109	3.4
40	56.4	75	22.9	110	3.1
41	55.4	76	22.0	111	2.9
42	54.4	77	21.2	112	2.6
43	53.4	78	20.3	113	2.4
44	52.4	79	19.5	114	2.1
				115	1.9

APPENDIX F — RMD TABLES

RMD Tables

RMD Single Life Table - Life Expectancy

Age	Factor	Age	Factor	Age	Factor
0	82.4	37	46.5	74	14.1
1	81.6	38	45.6	75	13.4
2	80.6	39	44.6	76	12.7
3	79.7	40	43.6	77	12.1
4	78.7	41	42.7	78	11.4
5	77.7	42	41.7	79	10.8
6	76.7	43	40.7	80	10.2
7	75.8	44	39.8	81	9.7
8	74.8	45	38.8	82	9.1
9	73.8	46	37.9	83	8.6
10	72.8	47	37.0	84	8.1
11	71.8	48	36.0	85	7.6
12	70.8	49	35.1	86	7.1
13	69.9	50	34.2	87	6.7
14	68.9	51	33.3	88	6.3
15	67.9	52	32.3	89	5.9
16	66.9	53	31.4	90	5.5
17	66.0	54	30.5	91	5.2
18	65.0	55	29.6	92	4.9
19	64.0	56	28.7	93	4.6
20	63.0	57	27.9	94	4.3
21	62.1	58	27.0	95	4.1
22	61.1	59	26.1	96	3.8
23	60.1	60	25.2	97	3.6
24	59.1	61	24.4	98	3.4
25	58.2	62	23.5	99	3.1
26	57.2	63	22.7	100	2.9
27	56.2	64	21.8	101	2.7
28	55.3	65	21.0	102	2.5
29	54.3	66	20.2	103	2.3
30	53.3	67	19.4	104	2.1
31	52.4	68	18.6	105	1.9
32	51.4	69	17.8	106	1.7
33	50.4	70	17.0	107	1.5
34	49.4	71	16.3	108	1.4
35	48.5	72	15.5	109	1.2
36	47.5	73	14.8	110	1.1
				111	1.0

APPENDIX F — RMD TABLES

RMD Joint and Last Survivor Table - Life Expectancy

Ages	35	36	37	38	39	40	41	42	43	44	45	46
35	55.2	54.7	54.3	53.8	53.4	53.0	52.7	52.3	52.0	51.7	51.5	51.2
36	54.7	54.2	53.7	53.3	52.8	52.4	52.0	51.7	51.3	51.0	50.7	50.5
37	54.3	53.7	53.2	52.7	52.3	51.8	51.4	51.1	50.7	50.4	50.0	49.8
38	53.8	53.3	52.7	52.2	51.7	51.3	50.9	50.4	50.1	49.7	49.4	49.1
39	53.4	52.8	52.3	51.7	51.2	50.8	50.3	49.9	49.5	49.1	48.7	48.4
40	53.0	52.4	51.8	51.3	50.8	50.2	49.8	49.3	48.9	48.5	48.1	47.7
41	52.7	52.0	51.4	50.9	50.3	49.8	49.3	48.8	48.3	47.9	47.5	47.1
42	52.3	51.7	51.1	50.4	49.9	49.3	48.8	48.3	47.8	47.3	46.9	46.5
43	52.0	51.3	50.7	50.1	49.5	48.9	48.3	47.8	47.3	46.8	46.3	45.9
44	51.7	51.0	50.4	49.7	49.1	48.5	47.9	47.3	46.8	46.3	45.8	45.4
45	51.5	50.7	50.0	49.4	48.7	48.1	47.5	46.9	46.3	45.8	45.3	44.8
46	51.2	50.5	49.8	49.1	48.4	47.7	47.1	46.5	45.9	45.4	44.8	44.3
47	51.0	50.2	49.5	48.8	48.1	47.4	46.7	46.1	45.5	44.9	44.4	43.9
48	50.8	50.0	49.2	48.5	47.8	47.1	46.4	45.8	45.1	44.5	44.0	43.4
49	50.6	49.8	49.0	48.2	47.5	46.8	46.1	45.4	44.8	44.2	43.6	43.0
50	50.4	49.6	48.8	48.0	47.3	46.5	45.8	45.1	44.4	43.8	43.2	42.6
51	50.2	49.4	48.6	47.8	47.0	46.3	45.5	44.8	44.1	43.5	42.8	42.2
52	50.0	49.2	48.4	47.6	46.8	46.0	45.3	44.6	43.8	43.2	42.5	41.8
53	49.9	49.1	48.2	47.4	46.6	45.8	45.1	44.3	43.6	42.9	42.2	41.5
54	49.8	48.9	48.1	47.2	46.4	45.6	44.8	44.1	43.3	42.6	41.9	41.2
55	49.7	48.8	47.9	47.1	46.3	45.5	44.7	43.9	43.1	42.4	41.6	40.9
56	49.5	48.7	47.8	47.0	46.1	45.3	44.5	43.7	42.9	42.1	41.4	40.7
57	49.4	48.6	47.7	46.8	46.0	45.1	44.3	43.5	42.7	41.9	41.2	40.4
58	49.4	48.5	47.6	46.7	45.8	45.0	44.2	43.3	42.5	41.7	40.9	40.2
59	49.3	48.4	47.5	46.6	45.7	44.9	44.0	43.2	42.4	41.5	40.7	40.0
60	49.2	48.3	47.4	46.5	45.6	44.7	43.9	43.0	42.2	41.4	40.6	39.8
61	49.1	48.2	47.3	46.4	45.5	44.6	43.8	42.9	42.1	41.2	40.4	39.6
62	49.1	48.1	47.2	46.3	45.4	44.5	43.7	42.8	41.9	41.1	40.3	39.4
63	49.0	48.1	47.2	46.3	45.3	44.5	43.6	42.7	41.8	41.0	40.1	39.3
64	48.9	48.0	47.1	46.2	45.3	44.4	43.5	42.6	41.7	40.8	40.0	39.2
65	48.9	48.0	47.0	46.1	45.2	44.3	43.4	42.5	41.6	40.7	39.9	39.0
66	48.9	47.9	47.0	46.1	45.1	44.2	43.3	42.4	41.5	40.6	39.8	38.9
67	48.8	47.9	46.9	46.0	45.1	44.2	43.3	42.3	41.4	40.6	39.7	38.8
68	48.8	47.8	46.9	46.0	45.0	44.1	43.2	42.3	41.4	40.5	39.6	38.7
69	48.7	47.8	46.9	45.9	45.0	44.1	43.1	42.2	41.3	40.4	39.5	38.6
70	48.7	47.8	46.8	45.9	44.9	44.0	43.1	42.2	41.3	40.3	39.4	38.6
71	48.7	47.7	46.8	45.9	44.9	44.0	43.0	42.1	41.2	40.3	39.4	38.5
72	48.7	47.7	46.8	45.8	44.9	43.9	43.0	42.1	41.1	40.2	39.3	38.4
73	48.6	47.7	46.7	45.8	44.8	43.9	43.0	42.0	41.1	40.2	39.3	38.4
74	48.6	47.7	46.7	45.8	44.8	43.9	42.9	42.0	41.1	40.1	39.2	38.3
75	48.6	47.7	46.7	45.7	44.8	43.8	42.9	42.0	41.0	40.1	39.2	38.3
76	48.6	47.6	46.7	45.7	44.8	43.8	42.9	41.9	41.0	40.1	39.1	38.2
77	48.6	47.6	46.7	45.7	44.8	43.8	42.9	41.9	41.0	40.0	39.1	38.2
78	48.6	47.6	46.6	45.7	44.7	43.8	42.8	41.9	40.9	40.0	39.1	38.2
79	48.6	47.6	46.6	45.7	44.7	43.8	42.8	41.9	40.9	40.0	39.1	38.1
80	48.5	47.6	46.6	45.7	44.7	43.7	42.8	41.8	40.9	40.0	39.0	38.1
81	48.5	47.6	46.6	45.7	44.7	43.7	42.8	41.8	40.9	39.9	39.0	38.1
82	48.5	47.6	46.6	45.6	44.7	43.7	42.8	41.8	40.9	39.9	39.0	38.1
83	48.5	47.6	46.6	45.6	44.7	43.7	42.8	41.8	40.9	39.9	39.0	38.0
84	48.5	47.6	46.6	45.6	44.7	43.7	42.7	41.8	40.8	39.9	39.0	38.0
85	48.5	47.5	46.6	45.6	44.7	43.7	42.7	41.8	40.8	39.9	38.9	38.0
86	48.5	47.5	46.6	45.6	44.6	43.7	42.7	41.8	40.8	39.9	38.9	38.0
87	48.5	47.5	46.6	45.6	44.6	43.7	42.7	41.8	40.8	39.9	38.9	38.0
88	48.5	47.5	46.6	45.6	44.6	43.7	42.7	41.8	40.8	39.9	38.9	38.0
89	48.5	47.5	46.6	45.6	44.6	43.7	42.7	41.7	40.8	39.8	38.9	38.0
90	48.5	47.5	46.6	45.6	44.6	43.7	42.7	41.7	40.8	39.8	38.9	38.0

APPENDIX F — RMD TABLES

RMD Joint and Last Survivor Table - Life Expectancy

Ages	47	48	49	50	51	52	53	54	55	56	57	58
47	43.4	42.9	42.4	42.0	41.6	41.2	40.9	40.5	40.2	40.0	39.7	39.4
48	42.9	42.4	41.9	41.5	41.0	40.6	40.3	39.9	39.6	39.3	39.0	38.7
49	42.4	41.9	41.4	40.9	40.5	40.1	39.7	39.3	38.9	38.6	38.3	38.0
50	42.0	41.5	40.9	40.4	40.0	39.5	39.1	38.7	38.3	38.0	37.6	37.3
51	41.6	41.0	40.5	40.0	39.5	39.0	38.5	38.1	37.7	37.4	37.0	36.7
52	41.2	40.6	40.1	39.5	39.0	38.5	38.0	37.6	37.2	36.8	36.4	36.0
53	40.9	40.3	39.7	39.1	38.5	38.0	37.5	37.1	36.6	36.2	35.8	35.4
54	40.5	39.9	39.3	38.7	38.1	37.6	37.1	36.6	36.1	35.7	35.2	34.8
55	40.2	39.6	38.9	38.3	37.7	37.2	36.6	36.1	35.6	35.1	34.7	34.3
56	40.0	39.3	38.6	38.0	37.4	36.8	36.2	35.7	35.1	34.7	34.2	33.7
57	39.7	39.0	38.3	37.6	37.0	36.4	35.8	35.2	34.7	34.2	33.7	33.2
58	39.4	38.7	38.0	37.3	36.7	36.0	35.4	34.8	34.3	33.7	33.2	32.8
59	39.2	38.5	37.8	37.1	36.4	35.7	35.1	34.5	33.9	33.3	32.8	32.3
60	39.0	38.2	37.5	36.8	36.1	35.4	34.8	34.1	33.5	32.9	32.4	31.9
61	38.8	38.0	37.3	36.6	35.8	35.1	34.5	33.8	33.2	32.6	32.0	31.4
62	38.6	37.8	37.1	36.3	35.6	34.9	34.2	33.5	32.9	32.2	31.6	31.1
63	38.5	37.7	36.9	36.1	35.4	34.6	33.9	33.2	32.6	31.9	31.3	30.7
64	38.3	37.5	36.7	35.9	35.2	34.4	33.7	33.0	32.3	31.6	31.0	30.4
65	38.2	37.4	36.6	35.8	35.0	34.2	33.5	32.7	32.0	31.4	30.7	30.0
66	38.1	37.2	36.4	35.6	34.8	34.0	33.3	32.5	31.8	31.1	30.4	29.8
67	38.0	37.1	36.3	35.5	34.7	33.9	33.1	32.3	31.6	30.9	30.2	29.5
68	37.9	37.0	36.2	35.3	34.5	33.7	32.9	32.1	31.4	30.7	29.9	29.2
69	37.8	36.9	36.0	35.2	34.4	33.6	32.8	32.0	31.2	30.5	29.7	29.0
70	37.7	36.8	35.9	35.1	34.3	33.4	32.6	31.8	31.1	30.3	29.5	28.8
71	37.6	36.7	35.9	35.0	34.2	33.3	32.5	31.7	30.9	30.1	29.4	28.6
72	37.5	36.6	35.8	34.9	34.1	33.2	32.4	31.6	30.8	30.0	29.2	28.4
73	37.5	36.6	35.7	34.8	34.0	33.1	32.3	31.5	30.6	29.8	29.1	28.3
74	37.4	36.5	35.6	34.8	33.9	33.0	32.2	31.4	30.5	29.7	28.9	28.1
75	37.4	36.5	35.6	34.7	33.8	33.0	32.1	31.3	30.4	29.6	28.8	28.0
76	37.3	36.4	35.5	34.6	33.8	32.9	32.0	31.2	30.3	29.5	28.7	27.9
77	37.3	36.4	35.5	34.6	33.7	32.8	32.0	31.1	30.3	29.4	28.6	27.8
78	37.2	36.3	35.4	34.5	33.6	32.8	31.9	31.0	30.2	29.3	28.5	27.7
79	37.2	36.3	35.4	34.5	33.6	32.7	31.8	31.0	30.1	29.3	28.4	27.6
80	37.2	36.3	35.4	34.5	33.6	32.7	31.8	30.9	30.1	29.2	28.4	27.5
81	37.2	36.2	35.3	34.4	33.5	32.6	31.8	30.9	30.0	29.2	28.3	27.5
82	37.1	36.2	35.3	34.4	33.5	32.6	31.7	30.8	30.0	29.1	28.3	27.4
83	37.1	36.2	35.3	34.4	33.5	32.6	31.7	30.8	29.9	29.1	28.2	27.4
84	37.1	36.2	35.3	34.3	33.4	32.5	31.7	30.8	29.9	29.0	28.2	27.3
85	37.1	36.2	35.2	34.3	33.4	32.5	31.6	30.7	29.9	29.0	28.1	27.3
86	37.1	36.1	35.2	34.3	33.4	32.5	31.6	30.7	29.8	29.0	28.1	27.2
87	37.0	36.1	35.2	34.3	33.4	32.5	31.6	30.7	29.8	28.9	28.1	27.2
88	37.0	36.1	35.2	34.3	33.4	32.5	31.6	30.7	29.8	28.9	28.0	27.2
89	37.0	36.1	35.2	34.3	33.3	32.4	31.5	30.7	29.8	28.9	28.0	27.2
90	37.0	36.1	35.2	34.2	33.3	32.4	31.5	30.6	29.8	28.9	28.0	27.1

APPENDIX F — RMD TABLES

RMD Joint and Last Survivor Table - Life Expectancy

Ages	59	60	61	62	63	64	65	66	67	68	69	70
59	31.8	31.3	30.9	30.5	30.1	29.8	29.4	29.1	28.8	28.6	28.3	28.1
60	31.3	30.9	30.4	30.0	29.6	29.2	28.8	28.5	28.2	27.9	27.6	27.4
61	30.9	30.4	29.9	29.5	29.0	28.6	28.3	27.9	27.6	27.3	27.0	26.7
62	30.5	30.0	29.5	29.0	28.5	28.1	27.7	27.3	27.0	26.7	26.4	26.1
63	30.1	29.6	29.0	28.5	28.1	27.6	27.2	26.8	26.4	26.1	25.7	25.4
64	29.8	29.2	28.6	28.1	27.6	27.1	26.7	26.3	25.9	25.5	25.2	24.8
65	29.4	28.8	28.3	27.7	27.2	26.7	26.2	25.8	25.4	25.0	24.6	24.3
66	29.1	28.5	27.9	27.3	26.8	26.3	25.8	25.3	24.9	24.5	24.1	23.7
67	28.8	28.2	27.6	27.0	26.4	25.9	25.4	24.9	24.4	24.0	23.6	23.2
68	28.6	27.9	27.3	26.7	26.1	25.5	25.0	24.5	24.0	23.5	23.1	22.7
69	28.3	27.6	27.0	26.4	25.7	25.2	24.6	24.1	23.6	23.1	22.6	22.2
70	28.1	27.4	26.7	26.1	25.4	24.8	24.3	23.7	23.2	22.7	22.2	21.8
71	27.9	27.2	26.5	25.8	25.2	24.5	23.9	23.4	22.8	22.3	21.8	21.3
72	27.7	27.0	26.3	25.6	24.9	24.3	23.7	23.1	22.5	22.0	21.4	20.9
73	27.5	26.8	26.1	25.4	24.7	24.0	23.4	22.8	22.2	21.6	21.1	20.6
74	27.4	26.6	25.9	25.2	24.5	23.8	23.1	22.5	21.9	21.3	20.8	20.2
75	27.2	26.5	25.7	25.0	24.3	23.6	22.9	22.3	21.6	21.0	20.5	19.9
76	27.1	26.3	25.6	24.8	24.1	23.4	22.7	22.0	21.4	20.8	20.2	19.6
77	27.0	26.2	25.4	24.7	23.9	23.2	22.5	21.8	21.2	20.6	19.9	19.4
78	26.9	26.1	25.3	24.6	23.8	23.1	22.4	21.7	21.0	20.3	19.7	19.1
79	26.8	26.0	25.2	24.4	23.7	22.9	22.2	21.5	20.8	20.1	19.5	18.9
80	26.7	25.9	25.1	24.3	23.6	22.8	22.1	21.3	20.6	20.0	19.3	18.7
81	26.6	25.8	25.0	24.2	23.4	22.7	21.9	21.2	20.5	19.8	19.1	18.5
82	26.6	25.8	24.9	24.1	23.4	22.6	21.8	21.1	20.4	19.7	19.0	18.3
83	26.5	25.7	24.9	24.1	23.3	22.5	21.7	21.0	20.2	19.5	18.8	18.2
84	26.5	25.6	24.8	24.0	23.2	22.4	21.6	20.9	20.1	19.4	18.7	18.0
85	26.4	25.6	24.8	23.9	23.1	22.3	21.6	20.8	20.1	19.3	18.6	17.9
86	26.4	25.5	24.7	23.9	23.1	22.3	21.5	20.7	20.0	19.2	18.5	17.8
87	26.4	25.5	24.7	23.8	23.0	22.2	21.4	20.7	19.9	19.2	18.4	17.7
88	26.3	25.5	24.6	23.8	23.0	22.2	21.4	20.6	19.8	19.1	18.3	17.6
89	26.3	25.4	24.6	23.8	22.9	22.1	21.3	20.5	19.8	19.0	18.3	17.6
90	26.3	25.4	24.6	23.7	22.9	22.1	21.3	20.5	19.7	19.0	18.2	17.5

RMD Joint and Last Survivor Table - Life Expectancy

Ages	71	72	73	74	75	76	77	78	79	80	81	82
71	20.9	20.5	20.1	19.7	19.4	19.1	18.8	18.5	18.3	18.1	17.9	17.7
72	20.5	20.0	19.6	19.3	18.9	18.6	18.3	18.0	17.7	17.5	17.3	17.1
73	20.1	19.6	19.2	18.8	18.4	18.1	17.8	17.5	17.2	16.9	16.7	16.5
74	19.7	19.3	18.8	18.4	18.0	17.6	17.3	17.0	16.7	16.4	16.2	15.9
75	19.4	18.9	18.4	18.0	17.6	17.2	16.8	16.5	16.2	15.9	15.6	15.4
76	19.1	18.6	18.1	17.6	17.2	16.8	16.4	16.0	15.7	15.4	15.1	14.9
77	18.8	18.3	17.8	17.3	16.8	16.4	16.0	15.6	15.3	15.0	14.7	14.4
78	18.5	18.0	17.5	17.0	16.5	16.0	15.6	15.2	14.9	14.5	14.2	13.9
79	18.3	17.7	17.2	16.7	16.2	15.7	15.3	14.9	14.5	14.1	13.8	13.5
80	18.1	17.5	16.9	16.4	15.9	15.4	15.0	14.5	14.1	13.8	13.4	13.1
81	17.9	17.3	16.7	16.2	15.6	15.1	14.7	14.2	13.8	13.4	13.1	12.7
82	17.7	17.1	16.5	15.9	15.4	14.9	14.4	13.9	13.5	13.1	12.7	12.4
83	17.5	16.9	16.3	15.7	15.2	14.7	14.2	13.7	13.2	12.8	12.4	12.1
84	17.4	16.7	16.1	15.5	15.0	14.4	13.9	13.4	13.0	12.6	12.2	11.8
85	17.3	16.6	16.0	15.4	14.8	14.3	13.7	13.2	12.8	12.3	11.9	11.5
86	17.1	16.5	15.8	15.2	14.6	14.1	13.5	13.0	12.5	12.1	11.7	11.3
87	17.0	16.4	15.7	15.1	14.5	13.9	13.4	12.9	12.4	11.9	11.4	11.0
88	16.9	16.3	15.6	15.0	14.4	13.8	13.2	12.7	12.2	11.7	11.3	10.8
89	16.9	16.2	15.5	14.9	14.3	13.7	13.1	12.6	12.0	11.5	11.1	10.6
90	16.8	16.1	15.4	14.8	14.2	13.6	13.0	12.4	11.9	11.4	10.9	10.5

RMD Joint and Last Survivor Table - Life Expectancy

Ages	83	84	85	86	87	88	89	90
83	11.7	11.4	11.1	10.9	10.6	10.4	10.2	10.1
84	11.4	11.1	10.8	10.5	10.3	10.1	9.9	9.7
85	11.1	10.8	10.5	10.2	9.9	9.7	9.5	9.3
86	10.9	10.5	10.2	9.9	9.6	9.4	9.2	9.0
87	10.6	10.3	9.9	9.6	9.4	9.1	8.9	8.6
88	10.4	10.1	9.7	9.4	9.1	8.8	8.6	8.3
89	10.2	9.9	9.5	9.2	8.9	8.6	8.3	8.1
90	10.1	9.7	9.3	9.0	8.6	8.3	8.1	7.8

TABLE OF 2005 LEGISLATION, REGULATIONS AND RULINGS

Legislation

Public Law	Q
P.L. 109-8 (BAPCPA)	466, 810, 811
P.L. 109-58 (Energy Tax Incentives Act of 2005)	829
P.L. 109-73 (KETRA 2005)	124, 126, 227, 228, 231, 385, 402, 403, 406, 420, 421, 424, 427, 429, 433, 434, 483, 485, 802, 819, 821, 824, 834

Treasury Regulations

Treas. Reg. Sec.	Q
1.83-3(e)	77, 303
1.401(k)-1	395, 399, 400, 401, 402, 403, 404, 405, 406
1.401(k)-2	395, 404, 406
1.401(k)-3	399
1.401(k)-4	400
1.401(k)-6	395, 404, 406
1.401(m)-1	405
1.401(m)-2	405, 406
1.401(m)-4	405
1.401(m)-5	405, 406
1.411(d)-4	334
25.2702-3(d)(2)	914
25.2702-3(e)	914
26.2651-1	952
26.2651-2	952

Prop. Treas. Reg. Sec.	Q
1.401(a)-20	336
1.401(a)-21	336
1.401(k)-1	401
1.409A-1	115, 129
1.409A-2	115
1.409A-3	115, 119
1.409A-6	115

Treasury Regulations (cont'd)

Prop. Treas. Reg. Sec.	Q
1.415(a)-1	332
1.415(b)-1	372
1.415(b)-2	372
1.415(c)-1	377
1.415(c)-2	377
1.415(d)-1	372, 377
1.417(a)(3)-1	336
54.4980G-1	199
54.4980G-4	199

Revenue Rulings

Rev. Rul.	Q
2005-7	25
2005-30	36, 827
2005-36	236, 344, 908
2005-38	805
2005-55	369

Revenue Procedures

Rev. Proc.	Q
2005-3	71, 458
2005-23	334
2005-24	825
2005-25	303, 407, 408, 431
2005-62	851, 901
2005-70	197, 198, 209, 314, 318, 471, 473, 800, 817, 818, 819, 820, 824, 826, 828, 829, 834, 835, 843, 851, 862, 902, 907, 917, 920

Letter Rulings
(including TAMs)

Let. Rul.	Q
200444033	344
200452033	261
200453015	340

TABLE OF 2005 LEGISLATION, REGULATIONS AND RULINGS

Letter Rulings (cont'd)

Let. Rul.	Q
200510035	338
200521003	826
200528031	236, 344
200536014	808
200537019	827
200537044	236, 344
200543063	464
200544025	464
200544026	464
200544027	464
200544030	464
CCA 200524001	814

Notices

Notice	Q
2005-25	824
2005-42	100, 107
2005-58	123

Notices (cont'd)

Notice	Q
2005-68	802
2005-73	801
2005-81	801
2005-82	801
2005-83	197
2005-84	385
2005-92	227, 228, 232, 402, 406, 420, 421, 424, 427, 429, 433, 434

Miscellaneous

Miscellaneous	Q
Ann. 2005-70	403
AOD 2005-2	498
ILM 200504001	261
INFO 2005-011	826
INFO 2005-0102	826
IR-2005-97	802
TD 9223	407, 408

TABLE OF CASES

Cases added since the previous edition, and cases in which some recent action has been taken, appear in boldface. All references are to question numbers.

A.T. Williams Oil Co. v. Comm.	89
Aaronson, Frank v.	451
Abraham v. Exxon Corp.	355
Abraham, Est. of v. Comm.	613
Ackerman, Est. of v. Comm.	641, 646
Acme Constr. Co., Inc. v. Comm.	120
Acme Pie Co. v. Comm.	365
Adamcewicz v. Comm.	451
Adams v. Comm.	52
Addis v. Comm.	283
Adkins v. United Int'l Investigative Servs, Inc.	176
Aero Indus. Co., Inc. v. Comm.	359
Aetna Life Ins. Co., Tyre v.	677
Aggreko, Inc., Collins v.	176
Al-Murshidi v. Comm.	826
Albertson's, Inc. v. Comm.	120
Albright, Est. of v. Comm.	685
Alderman v. Comm.	423
Alessi v. Raybestos-Manhattan, Inc.	333
Alex v. Comm.	804
Alexander Shokai, Inc. v. Comm.	108
All v. McCobb	672, 684
Allemeier v. Comm.	**814**
Allen v. Comm.	685
Allen, Prudential Ins. Co. v.	296
Allen, Varnedoe v.	135
Allentown Nat'l Bank v. Comm.	631
Allgood, Est. of v. Comm.	868
Allison Engine Co., Grande v.	107
Alpern v. Comm.	227, 238
Altobelli, Est. of v. IBM	337
Amalgamated Sugar Co., Holland v.	323
American Airlines Inc., Wooderson v.	183
American Assn. of Christian Schools v. U.S.	504
American Body & Equipment Co. v. U.S.	245
American Community Mut. Ins. Co., American Trust v.	296
American Design, Inc., Noell v.	333
American Elect. Power Co. v. U.S.	260
American Family Mut. Ins. Co. v. U.S.	162
American Foundry v. Comm.	165
American Nat'l Bank & Trust Co. v. U.S.	688
American Nat'l. Bank v. U.S.	645
American Stores Co. v. Comm.	364
American Stores Employee Benefit Plan, Burke v.	176
American Trust v. American Community Mut. Ins. Co.	296
Anderson v. U.S.	854
Andress v. U.S.	161
Andrews v. Comm.	97, 436
Andrews Distrib. Co., Inc. v. Comm.	120
Anthes v. Comm.	385
Anthony, Est. of v. U.S.	**910**
Arbeitman, National Auto. Dealers and Assoc. Retirement Trust v.	337
Ard, Est. of v. Comm.	642
Ardner v. Comm.	281
Arents, Est. of, Comm. v.	656
Armantrout v. Comm.	132
Armstrong v. Comm.	436
Arnfeld v. U.S.	28
Arnold v. U.S.	270
Aronson v. Comm.	227, 231
Arthur R. Womrath, Inc. v. Comm.	47
Asbestos Workers Local No. 23 Pension Fund v. U.S.	348
Ashcraft v. Comm.	280
Associated Ark. Newspapers Inc. v. Johnson	137
AT&T Global Information Solutions Co., Hopkins v.	349
Atkins, Est. of v. Comm.	609, 612
Atkinson, Early v.	26
Atlantic Oil Co. v. Patterson	74
Atlas Heating & Ventilating Co. v. Comm.	47
Attardo v. Comm.	364
Atwood v. Comm.	259
Auerbach v. Comm.	281
Auner v. U.S.	391
Austell v. Raymond James & Assoc., Inc.	173
Automobile Club of Mich. v. Comm.	361
Auwater v. Donohue Paper Sales Corp. Defined Benefit Pension Plan	334
Avery v. Comm.	264
Avina v. Texas Pig Stands, Inc.	176
Avis Ind. Corp. and Subsidiaries v. Comm.	120
Avis Indus. Corp. v. Comm.	108
Azad v. U.S.	464

2006 Tax Facts on Insurance & Employee Benefits

TABLE OF CASES

Azenaro v. Comm.	808	Berner v. U.S.	436
Baas v. Comm.	231	**Berry v. U.S.**	**117**
Bacon v. Comm.	137	Berzon v. Comm.	918
Baer v. Comm.	716, 717	Bess, U.S. v.	297
Bahen, Est. of v. Comm.	672	Bianchi v. Comm.	365
Bahr, Est. of v. Comm.	863	**Bigelow, Est. of v. Comm.**	**613**
Bailey v. Comm.	803	Billings v. Comm.	631
Bailly, Est. of v. Comm.	863	Bing Management Co., Inc. v. Comm.	323
Baizer v. Comm.	443	Bintliff v. U.S.	623
Baker v. Comm.	803, 826	Bischoff, Est. of v. Comm.	613, 658
Baker v. LaSalle	348	Blaess v. Comm.	97
Baker, Goldin v.	807	Blair v. Comm.	808
Baker, Est. of v. Comm.	857	Blair, Est. of v. Comm.	610
Ballance v. U.S.	863	Blakeley, Herring v.	675
Bank of Boston, Edsen v.	334	Blanche v. Comm.	823
Bank of Cal. (Est. of Manning) v. U.S.	910	Bleichroeder Bing & Co. v. Comm.	136
Baptiste v. Comm.	617	Bloch, Est. of v. Comm.	632
Barbourville Brick Co. v. Comm.	137	Blount, Est. of v. Comm.	610
Bardahl Mfg. Co. v. Comm.	365	Blue v. UAL Corp.	349
Barnes v. U.S.	153	Blue Cross & Blue Shield Miss., Moffitt v.	176
Barr, Est. of v. Comm.	685	Blum v. Higgins	251, 264
Barrett v. Comm.	30	Blumenthal v. Comm.	281, 289, 290, 292
Barrett v. U.S.	808	Board of Trustees of Div. 1181, Mendez-Bellido v.	336
Barrett, Est. of v. Comm.	640	Board of Trustees of N.Y. Hotel Trades Council & Hotel Assoc. of N.Y. City, Inc. Pension Fund v. Comm.	333
Barron v. Comm.	287		
Bartlett, Est. of v. Comm.	645		
Basch Eng'g, Inc. v. Comm.	322		
Basila v. Comm.	115	Boatmen's First Nat'l Bank of Kansas City (Est. of Douthat) v. U.S.	852
Basye, U.S. v.	110		
Bath Assoc., Conery v.	176	Bodine v. Comm.	33, 264
Bausch, Est. of v. Comm.	135	Boecking v. Comm.	47
Beal, Est. of v. Comm.	614, 685	Boeing, Comm. v.	717, 724, 733
Bean v. Comm.	277	Boeing, Nellis v.	337
Beauregard, Est. of v. Comm.	640	Bogene, Inc. v. Comm.	165
Beck, Est. of, Comm. v.	720	Bogley, Est. of v. U.S.	685
Becker v. Comm.	364	Bollinger v. Comm.	322
Behrend v. Comm.	282	Bollotin v. U.S.	466
Beisler v. Comm.	160	Boltinghouse v. Comm.	820
Bel	619	Bolton v. Comm.	717, 806
Bel v. U.S.	646	**Bongard, Est. of v. Comm.**	**613**
Belka v. Rowe Furniture Corp.	117	Bonita House, Inc., Coble v.	173
Bell v. Comm.	42	Bonner, Est. of v. U.S.	862
Bell, Est. of v. Comm.	41, 705	Bonwit, Comm. v.	52
Bell, Est. of v. U.S.	910	Booth v. Comm.	305, 503
Belsky v. First Nat'l Life Ins. Co.	117	Boston Safe Deposit & Trust Co. v. Comm.	611
Bensel, Comm. v.	613		
Benson v. Comm.	41		
Berger v. Xerox Corp.	374	Botany Worsted Mills v. U.S.	108
Berger, Comm. v.	734	Bothun, Est. of v. Comm.	621
Bergman v. Comm.	618	Bouquett v. Comm.	194
Berizzi Bros. Co. v. Comm.	45	Bowers, Wilson v.	613
Berman v. Comm.	436	Bowers, Est. of v. Comm.	631, 640
Bernard McMenamy Contractors, Inc. v. Comm.	391	Bowes v. U.S.	640
		Boyd, Est. of v. Comm.	637

TABLE OF CASES

Bradford-Robinson Printing Co. v. Comm.	89	Carrabba v. Randalls Food Mkts, Inc.	115
Branch v. G. Bernd Co.	182	Carter, Est. of v. U.S.	910
Braun v. Comm.	844	Casale v. Comm.	46, 50, 115, 116, 117
Bright, Est. of v. Comm.	613	Cash v. Comm.	194
Brock v. Comm.	45, 52	Castleberry, Est. of v. Comm.	853
Broderick v. Keefe	631	Castner Garage, Ltd. v. Comm.	96, 155, 299, 301
Broderick, Industrial Trust Co. v.	27	Catalano v. U.S.	618
Brodersen v. Comm.	281	Catawba Indus. Rubber Co. v. Comm.	364
Brodrick v. Gore	613	Caterpillar Tractor Co. v. Comm.	333
Bromley, Est. of v. Comm.	627	Caton v. Comm.	422, 483
Bronk v. Mountain States Tel. & Tel., Inc.	355	Cavenaugh, Est. of v. Comm.	622
Brown v. U.S.	860	Cearley v. Cearley	675
Brown, Re Marriage of	675	Cen-Tex, Inc., Campbell v.	245
Brown Agency, Inc. v. Comm.	45	Central Laborers' Pension Fund v. Heinz	334
Brownell, Lamade v.	634	Centre v. Comm.	116, 117
Bruch, Firestone v.	115	Century Wood Preserving Co. v. Comm.	270
Bruno v. Comm.	108	Cerone v. Comm.	82, 83
Bryant v. Food Lion, Inc.	176	Cervin, Est. of v. Comm.	622
Buczynski v. General Motors Corp.	333	Champion Trophy Mfg. Corp. v. Comm.	47, 52
Buffalo Bills, Inc. v. U.S.	122	Chapin v. McGowan	8
Bunney v. Comm.	87, 214	Chapman, Est. of v. Comm.	642
Burdick, Est. of v. Comm.	865	Charleston Nat'l Bank, Comm. v.	289
Burke v. American Stores Employee Benefit Plan	176	Charlie Sturgill Motor Co. v. Comm.	165
Burnet v. Wells	305	Charlton & Co. v. Comm.	47
Burnet, Colston v.	260	Chas. E. Smith & Sons Co. v. Comm.	365
Burnetta v. Comm.	112, 355	Chase Manhattan Bank, Comm. v.	708, 710, 901
Burr	161	Chase Nat'l Bank v. U.S.	631, 645
Burrey v. Pacific Gas and Elect. Co.	355	Cheeseman v. Comm.	260
Burris, Est. of v. Comm.	618	Chernik v. Comm.	194
Burton v. Comm.	349	Chicago Truck Drivers, Helpers and Warehouse Workers Union, Hickey v.	334
Butler v. Comm.	92, 436	Childs v. Comm.	115, 117, 226
Butler v. U.S.	818	Child's Est., Comm. v.	613
Butts v. Comm.	814	Chism, Est. of	161
Byrd, Est. of v. Comm.	85	Choffin's Est. v. U.S.	604
C. F. Smith Co. v. Comm.	47	Chown v. Comm.	676
Cabral v. Olsten Corp., The	176	Christiernin v. Manning	603
California Trust Co. v. Riddell	622	Christoffersen v. U.S.	25
Campbell v. Cen-Tex, Inc.	245	Church v. U.S.	915
Campbell v. Comm.	226	Citizens Fidelity & Trust Co. v. Comm.	613
Canaday v. Guitteau	52	Citizens Trust Co. v. Comm.	292
Caplan, Est. of v. Comm.	613	Citrus Orthopedic Medical Group, Inc. v. Comm.	132
Caplin v. U.S.	436	City Bank Farmers Trust Co. v. Comm.	613
Cappon v. Comm.	48	Clark v. Comm.	803
Carbine v. Comm.	287	Clark v. Lauren Young Tire Center Profit Sharing Trust	333
Carew, Est. of v. Comm.	610	Cleveland Indians Baseball Co., U.S. v.	836
Carlson v. Carlson	644	Clinton, Dugan v.	349
Carlson v. U.S.	863		
Carlstrom, Est. of v. Comm.	615		
Carlton, Est. of v. Comm.	655		
Carmichael v. Comm.	281		
Carnahan v. Comm.	115		

TABLE OF CASES

CM Holdings, Inc., IRS v.	260	Daubert v. U.S.	619
Cobbs v. Comm.	33, 264	David Metzger Trust v. Comm.	82
Coble v. Bonita House, Inc.	173	Davidson's Est. (Fourth Nat'l Bank	
Cockrill, Est. of v. O'Hara	610	in Wichita) v. Comm.	628
Cohan v. Comm.	26	Davis v. U.S.	153, 613
Cohen v. Comm.	247, 253, 257, 261, 270	Davis, Comm. v.	280
Cohen, In re	348, 421	Davis, Est. of v. Comm.	135, 613, 685
Cole v. U.S.	281	Dawson, Est. of v. Comm.	630
Coleman v. Comm.	808	Dean v. Comm.	260, 483
Collins v. Aggreko, Inc.	176	Degener, Est. of v. Comm.	614
Colston v. Burnet	260	DeLappe v. Comm.	618
Colton v. Comm.	160	Demery v. Extebank	115
Commerce Union Bank v. U.S.	115	Deming v. Comm.	155
Comtec Sys., Inc. v. Comm.	120	Denbigh, Est. of v. Comm.	603
Conery v. Bath Assoc.	176	Dennis v. Comm.	803
Congleton v. Comm.	115	Deobald, Est. of v. U.S.	853
Connelly, Est. of v. U.S.	153, 631, 632, 684	Dependahl v. Falstaff Brewing	
Continental Airlines, Nakisa v.	176	Corp.	111, 117
Conway v. Comm.	30	Detroit Bank & Trust Co.	619
Cook v. Comm.	914	DeVos, Est. of v. Comm.	631, 640
Cook, Est. of v. Comm.	910	Dickman v. Comm.	904
Cooper v. IBM Personal Pension Plan	374	Diedrich v. Comm.	32
Coors v. U.S.	260	Diers v. Comm.	803
Corbin v. U.S.	465	Dill Mfg. Co. v. Comm.	89
Corlett v. Comm.	260	Dillingham, Est. of v. Comm.	903
Corning v. Comm.	305	DiMarco, Est. of v. Comm.	711, 743
Cornwell, Est. of v. Comm.	666	Dimen, Est. of v. Comm.	615
Cotlow v. Comm.	803	Dixon v. U.S.	361
Courtney v. U.S.	685	Dobrzensky v. Comm.	611
Cowles v. U.S.	153	Dodge v. Comm.	155
Cox v. Comm.	803	Doerken, Est. of v. Comm.	610
Crandall v. Comm.	194	Dominion Nat'l Bank v. Comm.	289, 292
Crane, Est. of v. Comm.	619	Don E. Williams Co. v. U.S.	363
Cristofani, Est. of v. Comm.	726	Donaldson, Est. of v. Comm.	676
Crocker, Est. of v. Comm.	261	Donohue Paper Sales Corp. Defined	
Crooks, Wilson v.	612	Benefit Pension Plan, Auwater v.	334
Crosley, Est. of v. Comm.	651	**Donovan, Est. of v. Comm.**	**910**
Crummey v. Comm.	726	Doran v. Comm.	53, 73, 81
Cullison, Est. of v. Comm.	705	Dorroh v. Comm.	436
Cummings v. Comm.	73	Dorson, Est. of v. Comm.	631
Custis v. Comm.	804	Dow Chemical Co. v. U.S.	260
Czepiel v. Comm.	214, 231	Draper, Est. of v. Comm.	628
D.J. Lee, M.D., Inc. v. Comm.	387, 389	du Pont v. Comm.	700
Dallas Dental Labs v. Comm.	392	Duberstein, Comm. v.	137
Dallman, Second Nat'l Bank of		Ducros v. Comm.	73, 74
Danville, Ill. v.	679	Dudderar v. Comm.	245
Dalton, Est. of v. Comm.	603	Dudley, Eggleston v.	667
Danforth v. Comm.	52	Dugan v. Clinton	349
Daniels v. Comm.	716	Dunigan v. U.S.	910
Darcy I. Estes, In re	421	Dunning v. Comm.	305
Darden v. Nationwide Mut. Life		DuPont Est. v. Comm.	676
Ins. Co.	117	Durando v. U.S.	358
Darden, Nationwide Mutual Ins.		D'Ambrosio, Est. of v. Comm.	853
Co. v.	354, 355	D'Angelo Assoc., Inc. v. Comm.	287

968   **2006 Tax Facts on Insurance & Employee Benefits**

TABLE OF CASES

Ealy, Est. of v. Comm.	611, 612	Federated Life Ins. Co. v. Simmons	297
Earl, Lucas v.	31	Fehrs v. U.S.	705, 910
Early v. Atkinson	26	Feingold, Martin v.	505
Earnshaw v. Comm.	483	Felber v. Comm.	224
Eastern Co., Rinard v.	323	Fenton, Est. of v. Comm.	640
Eaton v. Onan Corp.	374	Feroleto Steel Co. v. Comm.	323
Eberl's Claim Serv., Inc. v. Comm.	108	Fidelity Trust Co. (Matthews) v. Comm.	623
Eccles v. Comm.	276	Fidelity-Philadelphia Trust Co. v. Smith	605
Edgar v. Comm.	135	Fiedler, Est. of v. Comm.	665
Edsen v. Bank of Boston	334	Fifth Ave. Coach Lines, Inc. v. Comm.	137
Edwards, Comm. v.	704	Fiorito v. Comm.	613
Edwin's Inc. v. U.S.	365	Firestone v. Bruch	115
Eggleston v. Dudley	667	First Kentucky Trust Co. v. U.S.	628
Eichstedt v. U.S.	856	First Nat'l Bank v. Comm.	289, 294
Elliot Knitwear Profit Sharing Plan v. Comm.	441	First Nat'l Bank & Trust Co. v. Jones First Nat'l Bank of Birmingham v. U.S.	289 611, 633
Ellis Sarasota Bank & Trust Co. v. U.S.	705, 910	First Nat'l Bank of Birmingham (Est. of Sanson) v. Comm.	655
Emeloid Co. v. Comm.	89	First Nat'l Bank of Kansas City v. Comm.	28
Employee Sav. Plan of Amoco Corp., The, Schoonmaker v.	349	First Nat'l Bank of Midland, Texas (Mathers) v. U.S.	619
Engineered Timber Sales, Inc. v. Comm.	322, 364	First Nat'l Bank of Oregon	619
England, Est. of v. Comm.	614	First Nat'l Life Ins. Co., Belsky v.	117
Enright v. Comm.	139	First Trust Co. of St. Paul v. U.S.	115
Epstein v. Comm.	165	Flahertys Arden Bowl, Inc. v. Comm.	443
Ernest Holdeman & Collet, Inc. v. Comm.	167	Flake v. U.S.	297
Essenfeld v. Comm.	73, 135	Flarsheim v. U.S.	135
Estes, In re	348	Fleming v. Comm.	251, 270
Eubank, Helvering v.	31, 803	Fleming, Comm. v.	619
Evans v. Comm.	260, 273, 437	Fleming, Est. of v. Comm.	908
Evanson v. U.S.	852	Fletcher Trust Co. v. Comm.	700
Evers, Est. of v. Comm.	864	Foglesong v. Comm.	838
Everson v. Everson	675	Foil v. Comm.	127, 423
Ewell v. Comm.	808	Fontana, Est. of v. Comm.	862
Exacto Spring Corp. v. Comm.	108	Food Lion, Inc., Bryant v.	176
Exchange Bank & Trust Co. of Fla. v. U.S.	658	Foster v. Comm.	305
Express Oil Change, Inc. v. U.S.	159	Fouke Fur Co. v. Comm.	137
Extebank, Demery v.	115	Fowler, Metropolitan Life Ins. Co. v.	349
Exxon Corp., Abraham v.	355	Fox v. Comm.	260
Exxon Corp., Stahl v.	349	Fox v. Smith	675
Eyefull Inc. v. Comm.	838	Fox, Sanders v.	51, 89
F. Korbel & Bros., Inc., Paris v.	176	Foxman v. Comm.	92
Fabric, Est. of v. Comm.	41, 910	Frackelton v. Comm.	251
Falstaff Brewing Corp., Dependahl v.	111, 117	Francis Jungers, Sole Proprietorship v. Comm.	348
Farnsworth v. Comm.	803	Frane, Est. of v. Comm.	827
Farrell Distributing Corp., Mattson v.	183	Frank v. Aaronson	451
Farwell v. U.S.	651	Frazee v. Comm.	904
Favorite Panama Hat Co. v. Comm.	291	Frazier v. Comm.	161
Fazi v. Comm.	322	Freedman v. U.S.	619
Federal Nat'l Bank v. Comm.	289, 294	Fremont v. McGraw Edison	333
		Freyre v. U.S.	**808**

2006 Tax Facts on Insurance & Employee Benefits 969

TABLE OF CASES

Fried, Est. of v. Comm.	685	Golsen v. U.S.	260
Friedberg, Est. of v. Comm.	627, 642	Goodman v. Comm.	723, 735
Friedman v. Comm.	39	Goodman v. Granger	685
Frost v. Comm.	117	Goodman v. Resolution	
Fruehauf, Est. of v. Comm.	632	Trust Corp.	117, 118
Ft. Orange Paper Co. v. Comm.	137	Goodnow v. U.S.	652
Fuchs, Est. of v. Comm.	611	Goodwyn, Est. of v. Comm.	630, 631
Fuhrman v. Comm.	224	Goos v. Comm.	457
Fujinon Optical, Inc. v. Comm.	359	Gorby, Est. of v. Comm.	645
Funderburg, McGee v.	177	Gordon v. Comm.	436
Funkhouser v. Comm.	424	Gordon, U.S. v.	621
Fusz, Est. of v. Comm.	685	Gore, Brodrick v.	613
G&W Leach Co. v. Comm.	322	GPD, Inc. v. Comm.	838
G. Bernd Co., Branch v.	182	Grace, U.S. v.	658
Gaffney v. U.S.	685	Gradow v. U.S.	853
Gagliardi, Est. of v. Comm.	903	Grande v. Allison Engine Co.	107
Gales v. Comm.	803	Granger, Goodman v.	685
Gallade v. Comm.	348	Grant-Jacoby, Inc. v. Comm.	132
Gallenstein v. U.S.	854	Gravois Planing Mill v. Comm.	303
Gallun v. Comm.	78, 261	Gray v. U.S.	640, 685
Gamble v. Group Hospitalization	128	Gray, Est. of v. Comm.	483
Gann v. Comm.	115	Graybar Elect. Co., Inc. v. Comm.	137
Gannon, Est. of v. Comm.	613	Great West Life Assurance Co.,	
Garber v. Comm.	685	Knox v.	296
Garland v. Comm.	354	Green, Est. of v. Comm.	686
Garratt v. Knowles	115, 128	Green, Est. of v. U.S.	658
Garvey, Inc. v. U.S.	41, 42	Greene v. Comm.	30
Gazette Publishing Co. v. Self	89	Greenlee v. Comm.	443
Geissal v. Moore Med. Corp.	177, 185	Greentree's Inc. v. U.S.	137
General Dynamics Corp., U.S. v.	167	Greenway v. Comm.	281
General Motors Corp., Buczynski v.	333	Gribauskas, Est. of v. Comm.	910
General Signal Corp. v. Comm.	496	Grimes v. Comm.	903
General Smelting Co. v. Comm.	89	Griswold v. Comm.	214
Geo. Blood Enter., Inc. v. Comm.	803	Group Hospitalization, Gamble v.	128
George v. U.S.	427	Guitteau, Canaday v.	52
George Edward Quick Trust v. Comm.	92	Gunther v. U.S.	444, 648
George Pfau's Sons Co. v. Neal	336	Gwinn, Est. of v. Comm.	623, 624
George W. Lasche Basic Profit		H.T. Cushman Mfg. Co. v. Comm.	136
Sharing Plan, Lasche v.	337	Hacker v. Comm.	278
Gesner v. U.S.	632	Hackl v. Comm.	918
Giberson v. Comm.	165	Haderlie v. Comm.	804
Glassner v. Comm.	287	Hagwood v. Newton	337
Glen, Est. of v. Comm.	640	Hahn v. Comm.	854
Godley v. Comm.	613	Haines v. U.S.	92
Golden v. Comm.	73	Hall v. U.S.	803
Goldin v. Baker	807	Hall v. Wheeler	609, 610
Goldman v. U.S.	260	Hall, Est. of v. Comm.	223, 290, 436
Goldsmith v. U.S.	50, 116, 117	Halsted v. Comm.	724
Goldstein v. Johnson & Johnson	115	Hance, Est. of v. Comm.	603
Goldstein, Est. of v. Comm.	803	Hanley v. U.S.	910
Goldstein's Est. v. U.S.	630	Hanna Steel Corp., Wright v.	185
Goldstone, Est. of v. Comm.	676, 735	Hanson v. Comm.	287
Goletto v. W. H. Braum Inc.	180	Harris	161
Golsen v. Comm.	260	Harris v. Comm.	214, 640, 733

970   **2006 Tax Facts on Insurance & Employee Benefits**

TABLE OF CASES

Harris v. U.S.	685
Harrison v. Comm.	293, 911
Harry A. Koch Co. v. Vinal	89
Hart-Wood Lumber Co. v. Comm.	292
Hartford, City of, Sanchez v.	124
Harwood Assoc., Inc. v. Comm.	110
Hass, Est. of v. Comm.	619
Hassett, Liebmann v.	631, 642
Hatboro Nat'l Bank v. Comm.	292
Haugen v. Comm.	464
Haverty Realty & Investment Co. v. Comm.	64
Hawkins v. Comm.	349
Hays v. U.S.	644
Headrick, Est. of v. Comm.	642
Healy v. U.S.	459
Heffelfinger v. Comm.	305
Heffron, U.S. v.	296
Heilbroner, U.S. v.	275
Heiner, Rieck v.	287
Heinz, Central Laborers' Pension Fund v.	334
Heller, Miller v.	117
Hellman v. Comm.	264
Helvering v. Eubank	31, 803
Helvering v. LeGierse	153, 507
Helvering v. Louis	27
Helvering, Jefferson v.	287
Helvering, Meyer's Est. v.	640
Helvering, U.S. Trust Co. of N.Y. v.	644
Hemme, U.S. v.	868
Henderson v. Comm.	826
Hendon, Yates v.	348
Henry, Est. of v. Comm.	645
Hepple v. Roberts & Dybdahl, Inc.	333
Herr v. Comm.	918
Herring v. Blakeley	675
Hetson v. U.S.	685
Hewitt Grain & Provision Co. v. Comm.	291
Hexter v. Comm.	305
Heyen v. U.S.	726
Hickey v. Chicago Truck Drivers, Helpers and Warehouse Workers Union	334
Hickey, Schongalla v.	633
Higgins, Blum v.	251, 264
Hilgren, Est. of v. Comm.	613
Hill v. Comm.	803
Hill, Farrer & Burrill v. Comm.	358
Hinze v. U.S.	685
Hipp v. U.S.	863
Hoelzel, Est. of v. Comm.	603, 910
Hoerl & Assoc., P.C. v. U.S.	122
Hofferbert, Est. of v. Comm.	623
Hoffman v. Comm.	613
Hofford, Est. of v. Comm.	606
Hogan v. Raytheon	349
Holland v. Amalgamated Sugar Co.	323
Holland, Est. of v. Comm.	726
Hollingsworth v. Comm.	918
Holsey v. Comm.	87
Home News Publishing Co. v. Comm.	290
Hooks, Est. of v. Comm.	260
Hooper v. Comm.	628, 654
Hoover v. Comm.	808
Hoover, Est. of v. Comm.	613, 863
Hopkins v. AT&T Global Information Solutions Co.	349
Horne, Est. of v. Comm.	73
Hornstein (Reinhold) v. Comm.	623
Horstmier v. Comm.	41
Howard v. U.S.	618
Howell v. U.S.	423
Howell, State Farm v.	297
Hubert, Est. of, Comm. v.	864, 865
Hubert Transfer & Storage Co. v. Comm.	47
Hull, Est. of v. Comm.	614
Hummell v. S.E. Rykoff & Co.	333
Hunter v. U.S.	632
Hunton v. Comm.	282
Huntsman, Est. of v. Comm.	610, 612
Hunt's Estate v. U.S.	644
Hurwitz v. Sher	337
Hutnik, Est. of v. U.S.	619
Hutson, Est. of v. Comm.	644
Hyde v. Comm.	281
Iannone v. Comm.	348
IBM, Altobelli, Est. of v.	337
IBM Personal Pension Plan, Cooper v.	374
IBM Savings Plan v. Price	**349**
Industrial Trust Co. v. Broderick	27
Infante, Est. of v. Comm.	611, 631
Interstate Drop Forge Co. v. Comm.	137
IRS v. CM Holdings, Inc.	260
Irvine, U.S. v.	908
Isom v. Comm.	803
Iverson v. Comm.	305
Iverson, Est. of	640
Iverson, Est. of v. Comm.	640
J. Aron & Co. v. Comm.	137
J.W. Clause, Est. of	414
Jackson Investment Co. v. Comm.	92
Jacobs v. Reed College TIAA-CREF Retirement Plan	337
Jacoby, Est. of v. Comm.	856
Jacoway, Rousey v.	**216, 348**
James, Est. of v. Comm.	706

2006 Tax Facts on Insurance & Employee Benefits 971

TABLE OF CASES

James F. Waters, Inc. v. Comm.	64	Kinnear v. Comm.	275
Jameson v. Comm.	52	Kinney v. Comm.	281
Jefferson v. Helvering	287	Kitch v. Comm.	808, 827
Jeffrey v. U.S.	437	Kittle v. Comm.	820
Jennings, Est. of v. Comm.	603, 666, 910	Kleemeier, Est. of v. Comm.	686
Jernigan, McAleer v.	636	Klein v. Comm.	287
John B. Canepa Co., The v. Comm.	137	Kline v. Comm.	706
John B. Lambert & Assoc. v. U.S.	89	Knetsch v. U.S.	260
John C. Nordt Co. v. Comm.	137	Knight v. Comm.	916
John Hancock Mut. Life Ins. Co. v. Comm.	617	Knipp, Est. of	612
		Knipp, Est. of v. Comm.	609, 612
John P. Scripps Newspapers v. Comm.	89	Knowles, Garratt v.	115, 128
Johnson v. Comm.	62, 226, 459	Knox v. Great West Life Assurance Co.	296
Johnson v. Johnson	675	Kohlsaat, Est. of	726
Johnson v. Northwest Airlines, Inc.	183	Kolker, Est. of v. Comm.	918
Johnson v. Shawmut Nat'l Corp.	176	Kollipara Rajsheker, M.D., Inc. v. Comm.	322
Johnson, Associated Ark. Newspapers Inc. v.	137	Konner v. Comm.	918
Johnson, Est. of v. Comm.	464, 686	Korbel, Paris v.	185
Johnson & Johnson, Goldstein v.	115	Kramer v. U.S.	685
Jones v. Comm.	60, 214	Krause v. Comm.	806
Jones, First Nat'l Bank & Trust Co. v.	289	Krauss v. U.S.	706
Jordahl, Est. of v. Comm.	632	Kreisberg v. Comm.	804
Jordanos, Inc. v. Comm.	137	Krischer, Est. of v. Comm.	631
Joy Floral Co. v. Comm.	291	Kroloff v. U.S.	619
Kahn v. U.S.	645	Kurz, Est. of v. Comm.	653
Kahn, Est. of	**827**	Kute v. U.S.	428
Kappel v. U.S.	33, 264	Kutz v. Comm.	244
Karan v. Comm.	92	L. Hyman & Co. v. Comm.	47
Kariotis v. Navistar Int'l Transp. Corp.	176	L. Schepp Co.	108
Katz v. Comm.	28	La Fargue v. Comm.	705
Kaufman v. U.S.	710	La Mastro v. Comm.	365
Kaufman, Est. of	161	Labelgraphics, Inc. v. Comm.	108
Kay v. Comm.	260	Lacey v. Comm.	46, 50
Kean v. Comm.	**808**	LaFargue v. Comm.	41
Kearns v. U.S.	610	Lamade v. Brownell	634
Keefe v. Comm.	57	Lambert, Est. of v. Comm.	27
Keefe, Broderick v.	631	Lambeth v. Comm.	64, 69
Kees v. Comm.	194	Lambos v. Comm.	443
Keeter v. U.S.	679	Lancaster, Reich v.	505
Keith v. Comm.	260	Land v. U.S.	613
Kennedy v. Comm.	610, 612, 659	Landfield	293
Kenney v. Comm.	325	Landfield Fin. Co. v. U.S.	294
Kern v. U.S.	619	Landorf v. U.S.	645
Kern County Elec. Pension Fund v. Comm.	441	Lane, Comm. v.	808
Kerr v. Comm.	916	Lang	161
Keystone Consol. Indus., Inc. v. Comm.	363	Lang v. Comm.	618, 620
Keystone Consol. Publishing Co. v. Comm.	270	Lansburgh v. Comm.	617
Kidd v. Patterson	730	Lansing v. Comm.	322
Kiesling v. Comm.	281	Lansons, Inc. v. Comm.	361
Kimbell v. U.S.	613	Larkin v. Comm.	159, 165
King v. Comm.	223, 820	Larotonda v. Comm.	231
		LaSalle, Baker v.	348

972   **2006 Tax Facts on Insurance & Employee Benefits**

TABLE OF CASES

Lasche v. George W. Lasche Basic Profit Sharing Plan	337	Ludden v. Comm.	112
Latendresse v. Comm.	803	Lumpkin v. Comm.	631
Lauren Young Tire Center Profit Sharing Trust, Clark v.	333	Lumpkin, Est. of v. Comm.	153, 631, 645, 684
Laverty v. Comm.	160	Lundy Packing Co. v. U.S.	120
Lawrence, Lynch v.	675	Lutich v. U.S.	619
Lear Eye Clinic, Ltd. v. Comm.	372	Lynch v. Comm.	83, 287
Leavell v. Comm.	840	Lynch v. Lawrence	675
Leder, Est. of v. Comm.	642	M. Buten and Sons, Inc. v. Comm.	136
Lee v. U.S.	52, 260	M.S.D. Inc. v. U.S.	136
Lee Eng'g Supply Co., Inc. v. Comm.	389	MacFarlane & Hays Co. Employees' Profit Sharing Plan & Trust, Nedrow v.	333
Legallet v. Comm.	94	Maddox, Est. of v. Comm.	613
LeGierse, Helvering v.	153, 507	Madsen, Est. of v. Comm.	619
Leidy, Est. of v. Comm.	165	Magnin, Est. of v. Comm.	853
Lemishow v. Comm.	445	Malesa v. Comm.	36
Lengsfield v. Comm.	137	Maller v. Comm.	436
Lennard, Est. of	83	Maltzman v. Comm.	137
Leoni, Est. of v. Comm.	685	Mandel v. Comm.	281
Leslie v. Comm.	290	Mandel v. Sturr	613
Letts, Est. of v. Comm.	864	Manning, Christiernin v.	603
Leuschner, U.S. v.	46, 50	Maresi, Comm. v.	640
Levin v. Comm.	852	Margrave, Est. of v. Comm.	631, 633
Levin, Est. of v. Comm.	685	Marine, Est. of v. Comm.	865
Levine	161	Marprowear Profit Sharing Trust v. Comm.	441
Levine v. Comm.	165	Marten v. Comm.	808
Levine v. U.S.	645	Martin v. Comm.	115, 226, 452
Levine, Est. of v. Comm.	918	Martin v. Feingold	505
Levitt v. U.S.	260	Martin Fireproofing Profit Sharing Plan and Trust v. Comm.	332
Levy, Est. of	615	Mason, Est. of v. Comm.	640
Levy, Est. of v. Comm.	615, 618	Masterson v. U.S.	436
Liebmann v. Hassett	631, 642	Mathews v. U.S.	613
Lima Surgical Assoc., Inc. v. U.S.	504, 505	Mathews, Est. of v. Comm.	613
Lincoln, Est. of v. Comm.	614	Matthews v. Comm.	617
Lingo v. Comm.	911	Mattlage v. Comm.	292
Litman, Est. of v. U.S.	642	Mattson v. Farrell Distributing Corp.	183
Littick, Est. of v. Comm.	612, 613	May v. Comm.	73
Lock Moore & Co., Ltd. v. Comm.	289	May v. McGowan	613
Lockard v. Comm.	720	MBank Dallas, N.A., Profit Sharing Plan for Employees of Republic Fin. Services, Inc. v.	337
Lodder-Beckert v. Comm.	231	McAdams v. Comm.	807
Loewy Drug Co. v. Comm.	137	McAleer v. Jernigan	636
Lofstron v. Comm.	**808**	McAllister v. Resolution Trust Corp.	117, 118
Logan, Est. of v. Comm.	654	McCamant v. Comm.	294
Logsdon v. Comm.	427	McCann, Comm. v.	706
Lomb v. Sugden	613	McClennen v. Comm.	614
London Shoe Co., Inc. v. Comm.	270	McCobb, All v.	672, 684
Looney v. U.S.	685	McCoy v. Comm.	618
Louis, Helvering v.	27	McCoy, Est. of v. Comm.	631
Lovejoy v. Comm.	808		
Lowe, Montgomery v.	333		
Lozon v. Comm.	323		
Lucas v. Earl	31		
Lucas v. Ox Fibre Brush Co.	120		
Lucky Stores, Inc. v. Comm.	364		

2006 Tax Facts on Insurance & Employee Benefits

TABLE OF CASES

Case	Page
McDonald v. Southern Farm Bureau Life Ins. Co.	803
McDonough, Reich v.	505
McDowell, Est. of v. Comm.	910
McGee v. Funderburg	177
McGowan v. Comm.	154
McGowan, Chapin v.	8
McGowan, May v.	613
McGraw Edison, Fremont v.	333
McIngvale v. Comm.	41
McIsaac v. Comm.	803
McKay v. Comm.	56
McKee, Est. of v. Comm.	619, 853
McKelvy v. Comm.	616
McKeon v. Comm.	640
Mearkle, Est. of v. Comm.	602, 603
Medina v. U.S.	420, 443
Mellinger, U.S. v.	290
Mellinger, Est. of v. Comm.	862
Mellon Bank v. U.S.	843
Melman, U.S. v.	617
Meltzer v. Comm.	676
Mendez-Bellido v. Board of Trustees of Div. 1181	336
Mensik v. Comm.	803
Merrimac Hat Corp. v. Comm.	60
Metropolitan Life Ins. Co. v. Fowler	349
Metropolitan Life Ins. Co. v. Person	349
Metropolitan Life Ins. Co. v. Wheaton	349
Mettler v. Comm.	127
Metzger, Est. of v. Comm.	903
Meyer v. Comm.	808
Meyer, Est. of v. Comm.	619
Meyer's Est. v. Helvering	640
Miami Beach First Nat'l Bank v. U.S.	910
Michael K. Berry v. Comm.	808
Michel v. Comm.	226
Michigan Trust Co. v. Comm.	613
Millard v. U.S.	903
Miller v. Comm.	409, 808, 820
Miller v. Heller	117
Miller v. U.S.	862
Miner v. U.S.	619
Minor v. U.S.	116, 117
Minzer, Comm. v.	803
Mitchell, Est. of v. Comm.	611, 613
Mlsna v. Unitel Com., Inc.	176
Modernage Developers, Inc. v. Comm.	120
Moffitt v. Blue Cross & Blue Shield Miss.	176
Molter v. U.S.	685
Monroe v. Patterson	64, 69
Montgomery v. Lowe	333
Montgomery, T.L. James & Co., Inc. v.	618, 675
Montgomery, Est. of v. Comm.	605
Montgomery Eng'g Co. v. Comm.	137
Moody, Est. of v. Comm.	618
Moore v. Comm.	305
Moore, Est. of v. Comm.	863
Moore Med. Corp., Geissal v.	177, 185
Morales-Caban v. Comm.	224
Moreno, Est. of v. Comm.	658
Morgan v. Comm.	910
Morison v. Comm.	291
Morrison v. Comm.	280
Morrissey v. Comm.	443
Morrow v. Comm.	702
Morrow, Est. of v. Comm.	631, 685
Morse v. Comm.	117
Morton v. Comm.	623
Morton v. U.S.	630, 634
Morton, Est. of v. Comm.	683
Moseley v. Comm.	8
Motor Fuel Carriers, Inc. v. Comm.	89
Mott, Comm. v.	305
Mountain State Steel Foundries, Inc. v. Comm.	89
Mountain States Tel. & Tel., Inc., Bronk v.	355
Mudge, Est. of v. Comm.	651
Murillo v. Comm.	231
Murphy, Est. of v. Comm.	613
Mushro v. Comm.	94
N.W.D. Investment Co. v. Comm.	139
Nagy v. Riblet Prod. Corp.	118
Nakisa v. Continental Airlines	176
Nance v. U.S.	618
Napolitano, Est. of v. Comm.	827
National Auto. Dealers and Assoc. Retirement Trust v. Arbeitman	337
National Distributors, Inc., Wilcock v.	183
National Indus. Investors, Inc. v. Comm.	47
National Metropolitan Bank v. U.S.	633
National Presto Indus., Inc. v. Comm.	506
Nationwide Mut. Life Ins. Co., Darden v.	117
Nationwide Mutual Ins. Co. v. Darden	354, 355
Naumoff v. Comm.	726
Navistar Int'l Transp. Corp., Kariotis v.	176
Neal, George Pfau's Sons Co. v.	336
Nedrow v. MacFarlane & Hays Co. Employees' Profit Sharing Plan & Trust	333
Neely v. U.S.	685
Neese v. Comm.	261

TABLE OF CASES

Nellis v. Boeing	337	Owen, Est. of v. Comm.	869
Nelson Bros., Inc. v. Comm.	120	Ox Fibre Brush Co., Lucas v.	120
Neonatology Assoc., P.A., et al. v. Comm.	503	O'Brien v. Comm.	428
Nesbitt v. Comm.	247, 255	O'Connor v. Comm.	428
Neumeister v. Comm.	224	O'Daniel, Est. of v. Comm.	135
New York Post Corp., Spitzler v.	333	O'Donohue v. Comm.	287
Newbold, Est. of v. Comm.	631	O'Hara, Cockrill, Est. of v.	610
Newell v. Comm.	610, 612	O'Malley v. Comm.	443
Newman, Est. of v. Comm.	613	O'Neill Irrev. Trust v. Comm.	843
Newton, Hagwood v.	337	Pacific Gas and Elect. Co., Burrey v.	355
Nichola v. Comm.	210	Pacific Nat'l Bank of Seattle (Morgan Will) v. Comm.	654
Nickerson Lumber Co. v. U.S.	137	Pacific Nat'l Bank of Seattle (Morgan) v. Comm.	628
Nicolai v. Comm.	224	Packard v. Comm.	323, 354
Niekamp v. U.S.	161	Paramount-Richards Theatres, Inc. v. Comm.	81
Noel, Est. of, Comm. v.	630, 633, 641, 646	Paris v. F. Korbel & Bros., Inc.	176
Noell v. American Design, Inc.	333	Paris v. Korbel	185
Northern Nat'l Bank v. Comm.	292	Parker v. Comm.	803
Northwest Airlines, Inc., Johnson v.	183	Parker v. U.S.	853
Northwestern Ind. Tel. Co. v. Comm.	838	Parker-Hannifin Corp. v. Comm.	496
Northwestern Mut. Ins. Co., The v. Resolution Trust Corp.	117	Parson v. U.S.	619
Novelart Mfg. Co. v. Comm.	89	Parsons v. Comm.	30, 79
Nussbaum v. Comm.	57	Patten v. U.S.	854
Oakton Distributors, Inc. v. Comm.	322, 361	Patterson v. Shumate	348
Oates v. Comm.	115	Patterson, Atlantic Oil Co. v.	74
Oates, Comm. v.	115, 803	Patterson, Kidd v.	730
Ocean Cove Corp. Retirement Plan and Trust v. U.S.	441	Patterson, Monroe v.	64, 69
Odom, Ross v.	153	Patton's Will, In re	610
Oetting v. U.S.	865	Paul v. U.S.	436
Okerlund v. U.S.	909	Pearson v. Comm.	194
Okerson v. Comm.	808	Pedro Enter., Inc. v. Perdue	337
Okla. Press Pub. Co. v. U.S.	89	Peerless Pacific Co. v. Comm.	45
Old Colony Trust Co. (Flye's Est.) v. Comm.	654	Peerless Pattern Co. v. Comm.	291
Old Kent Bank & Trust Co. v. U.S.	676	Perdue, Pedro Enter., Inc. v.	337
Old Point Nat'l Bank v. Comm.	631	Perkins v. Comm.	264
Oleander Co., Inc. v. U.S.	165	Perkins v. U.S.	42
Olmo v. Comm.	325	Perl, Est. of v. Comm.	645
Olmsted Inc. Life Agency, Comm. v.	115, 803	Perry, Est. of v. Comm.	642
Olsten Corp., The, Cabral v.	176	Person, Metropolitan Life Ins. Co. v.	349
Omaha Elevator Co. v. Comm.	45	Peters v. U.S.	642
Oman Construction Co. v. Comm.	89	Pettit v. Comm.	52
Omans v. Comm.	**820**	Pettus v. Comm.	918
Onan Corp., Eaton v.	374	Phillies, The v. U.S.	836
Oppenheimer Casting Co. v. Comm.	137	Phillips v. Comm.	92
Orange Securities Corp. v. Comm.	260	Phillips v. Saratoga Harness Racing Inc.	183
Orgera v. Comm.	454	Phillips, Comm. v.	261
Origin Tech. in Business, Inc., Thompson v.	183	Pickett v. Comm.	92
Orzechowski v. Comm.	226, 231	Pickle	161
Ostheimer v. U.S.	803	Piggott, Est. of v. Comm.	609, 610, 634
		Pittman v. U.S.	853
		Pittman Construction v. U.S.	361
		Plastic Binding Corp. v. Comm.	137

2006 Tax Facts on Insurance & Employee Benefits

TABLE OF CASES

Plastic Eng'g & Mfg. Co. v. Comm.	365	Reynard Corp. v. Comm.	89
Plotkin v. Comm.	421	Rhoades, McKee & Boer v. U.S.	383
Porter, Est. of v. Comm.	685	Rhode Island Hosp. Trust Co., U.S. v.	633
Poyda v. Comm.	166	Rhodes' Est., In re	651
Price, IBM Savings Plan v.	**349**	Ribera v. Comm.	808
Prichard v. U.S.	623	Riblet Prod. Corp., Nagy v.	118
Prime v. Comm.	260	Richardson v. Comm.	112, 808
Pritchard, Est. of v. Comm.	642, 744	Richins, Est. of v. Comm.	642
Professional & Executive Leasing, Inc. v. Comm.	355	Riddell, California Trust Co. v.	622
		Rieck v. Comm.	305
Profit Sharing Plan for Employees of Republic Fin. Services, Inc. v. MBank Dallas, N.A.	337	Rieck v. Heiner	287
		Riecker, Est. of v. Comm.	611, 612, 613
		Riefberg, Est. of v. Comm.	631
Propstra v. Comm.	862	Riegelman, Est. of v. Comm.	614
Provident Trust Co., U.S. v.	910	Riley, United Parcel Service, Inc. v.	337
Prudential Ins. Co. v. Allen	296	Rinaldi, Est. of v. U.S.	864
Prudowsky, Est. of v. Comm.	856	Rinard v. Eastern Co.	323
Prunier v. Comm.	51, 89	Rios v. Pulido	820
Pruyn, Est. of v. Comm.	603	Ritchie v. Comm.	808
Pulido, Rios v.	820	Rivera v. Comm.	275
Pulliam v. Comm.	87	Roberts v. Comm.	717
Pulver v. Comm.	358	Roberts & Dybdahl, Inc., Hepple v.	333
Pupin, Comm. v.	616	Robin Haft Trust v. Comm.	82
Pyle, Est. of v. Comm.	683	Robinson v. Comm.	115, 135, 454
Quinlivan, Zenz v.	82	Robinson, Est. of v. Comm.	640, 852
Quinn v. U.S.	365	Robinson, Est. of v. U.S.	660
Rabideau v. Comm.	194	Rockwell, Est. of v. Comm.	631
Rand v. Comm.	305	Rodebaugh v. Comm.	52
Randalls Food Mkts, Inc., Carrabba v.	115	Rodoni v. Comm.	456
Rapco, Inc. v. Comm.	108	Roff v. Comm.	28
Rath, Est. of v. U.S.	66	Rohnert, Est. of v. Comm.	628, 654
Ravel v. Comm.	464	Rollman v. U.S.	918
Raybestos-Manhattan, Inc., Alessi v.	333	Rose v. U.S.	632
Raymond James & Assoc., Inc., Austell v.	173	Rosen v. U.S.	160
		Ross v. Comm.	292
Raytheon, Hogan v.	349	Ross v. Odom	153
Reece v. Comm.	358	Roubik v. Comm.	838
Reed College TIAA-CREF Retirement Plan, Jacobs v.	337	Roundy v. Comm.	428
		Rountree Cotton, Inc. v. Comm.	805
Reed's Est., In re	610	**Rousey v. Jacoway**	**216, 348**
Reich v. Lancaster	505	Rowe Furniture Corp., Belka v.	117
Reich v. McDonough	505	Rubber Assoc., Inc. v. Comm.	137
Reliable Home Health Care Inc. v. Union Central Ins. Co.	117	Rubel v. Rubel	612
		Rudkin Testamentary Trust v. Comm.	**843**
Reliable Steel Fabricators, Inc. v. Comm.	839	Rugby Prod. Ltd. v. Comm.	96, 194, 301
		Rundle v. Welch	683
Remington, Est. of v. Comm.	803	Russell v. Comm.	223
Resch, Est. of v. Comm.	655	Ryerson, U.S. v.	744
Resolution Trust Corp., Goodman v.	117, 118	S.E. Rykoff & Co., Hummell v.	333
		Saia, Est. of v. Comm.	618
Resolution Trust Corp., McAllister v.	117, 118	Salley v. Comm.	260
		Salt, Est. of v. Comm.	612, 613
Resolution Trust Corp., Northwestern Mut. Ins. Co., The v.	117	Samaroo v. Samaroo	349
		Sanchez v. Hartford, City of	124

976   **2006 Tax Facts on Insurance & Employee Benefits**

TABLE OF CASES

Sanders v. Fox	51, 89	Silberman v. U.S.	685
Saratoga Harness Racing Inc., Phillips v.	183	Silverman, Est. of v. Comm.	642
		Simmons, Federated Life Ins. Co. v.	297
Sather v. Comm.	917	Simplot, Est. of v. Comm.	613
Satz, Est. of v. Comm.	640	Simpson v. U.S.	135
Saunders v. Comm.	132	Siskin Memorial Found., Inc. v. U.S.	441
Schelberg, Est. of v. Comm.	684, 685	Skifter, Est. of v. Comm.	632
Scherer, Est. of v. Comm.	610	Skouras v. Comm.	714
Schmidt Baking Co., Inc. v. Comm.	110	Slocum v. U.S.	613
Schner-Block Co., Inc. v. Comm.	137	Smead, Est. of v. Comm.	645, 684
Schongalla v. Hickey	633	Smith v. Comm.	87, 92, 165
Schoonmaker v. Employee Sav. Plan of Amoco Corp., The	349	Smith, Fidelity-Philadelphia Trust Co. v.	605
Schott v. Comm.	914	Smith, Fox v.	675
Schuler v. Comm.	917	Smith, Est. of v. Comm.	631, 852
Schwager v. Comm.	615, 631	Smith, Est. of v. U.S.	648
Schwartz v. Comm.	52	Smithback v. Comm.	165
Scott v. Comm.	622	Snyder v. Comm.	903
Scott v. U.S.	843	Snyder v. U.S.	863
Seavey & Flarsheim Brokerage Co. v. Comm.	136	Southern Farm Bureau Life Ins. Co., McDonald v.	803
Second Nat'l Bank of Danville, Ill. v. Dallman	679	Southern Fruit Distributors v. U.S.	136
		Sperling v. Comm.	281
Security Assoc. Agency Ins. Corp. v. Comm.	803	Spiegel, Est. of v. Comm.	903
		Spillar, Est. of v. Comm.	863
Seda v. Comm.	83	Spitzer v. Comm.	706
Seidel v. Comm.	165	Spitzler v. New York Post Corp.	333
Self, Gazette Publishing Co. v.	89	Spokane Dry Goods Co. v. Comm.	72
Seligmann v. Comm.	729	Springfield Prod., Inc. v. Comm.	120, 363
Selling, Est. of v. Comm.	857	Sproull v. Comm.	116
Seltzer, Est. of v. Comm.	613	Square D Co. v. Comm.	496
Semon Bache & Co. v. Comm.	47	St. Louis County Bank v. U.S.	613
Service Bolt & Nut Co. Profit Sharing Trust v. Comm.	441	St. Louis Refrigerating & Cold Storage Co. v. U.S.	289, 294
Seward, Est. of v. Comm.	651	St. Louis Union Trust Co. (Orthwein) v. U.S.	633, 651
Sewell, Traina v.	348		
Shackelford, Est. of v. U.S.	910	Stahl v. Comm.	808
Shawmut Nat'l Corp., Johnson v.	176	Stahl v. Exxon Corp.	349
Shedco, Inc v. Comm.	323	Stalcup v. U.S.	852
Sheet Metal Workers Local 141 Supplemental Unemployment Benefit Trust Fund v. U.S.	507	Stark v. U.S.	918
		Stark Truss Co., Inc. v. Comm.	322
		State Farm v. Howell	297
Sheet Metal Workers' Nat'l Pension Fund Bd. of Trustees v. Comm.	334	Steel Balls, Inc. v. Comm.	415
		Stefanowski, Est. of v. Comm.	437
Sher, Hurwitz v.	337	Stern v. Comm.	41
Sherman v. Comm.	260	Stern, Comm. v.	297
Sherwin-Williams Co. Employee Health Plan Trust v. Comm.	498	Stevens v. Comm.	281
		Stewart v. Comm.	127
Sherwin-Williams Co. Employee Health Plan Trust v. U.S.	498	Stewart, U.S. v.	622
		Stinson v. U.S.	918
Shimota v. U.S.	428	Stobnicki v. Textron, Inc.	348
Shirar v. Comm.	260	Stockstrom v. Comm.	305
Shumate, Patterson v.	348	Stoddard v. Comm.	8
Siegel, Est. of v. Comm.	685	Stone v. Comm.	844

2006 Tax Facts on Insurance & Employee Benefits

TABLE OF CASES

Stones, In re	348	True, Est. of v. Comm.	**613**
Storey v. U.S.	81	Trujillo v. Comm.	154
Strange, Est. of v. Comm.	613	Trustees of the Directors Guild of	
Strangi, Est. of v. Comm.	**613, 915**	America-Producer Pension	
Strauss v. Comm.	275	Benefits Plans v. Tise	349
Stuit v. Comm.	856	Trustees of the Taxicab Indus.	
Sturgis v. Comm.	52	Pension Fund v. Comm.	333
Sturr, Mandel v.	613	Tuohy, Est. of v. Comm.	683
Sugden, Lomb v.	613	Turner v. Comm.	803
Supplee-Biddle Hardware Co.,		Tuttle v. U.S.	282
U.S. v.	62, 74	212 Corp. v. Comm.	41
Sussman v. U.S.	605	Tyre v. Aetna Life Ins. Co.	677
Swanson v. Comm.	65, 71	U.S. Trust Co. (Chisholm Est.) v. U.S.	865
Sweeney v. Comm.	137	U.S. Trust Co. of N.Y. v. Helvering	644
Swihart v. Comm.	428	UAL Corp., Blue v.	349
T.L. James & Co., Inc.		UB Servs., Inc., Zickafoose v.	176
v. Montgomery	618, 675	Umstead v. U.S.	92
Tallon v. Comm.	226	Union Central Ins. Co., Reliable	
Taylor, U.S. v.	349	Home Health Care Inc. v.	117
Teamsters Local Union No.		United Int'l Investigative Servs,	
727, Williams v.	175	Inc., Adkins v.	176
Teget v. U.S.	110	United Parcel Service, Inc. v. Riley	337
Tennessee Foundry & Mach.		Unitel Com., Inc., Mlsna v.	176
Co. v. Comm.	75	Van Brunt v. Comm.	31
Terre Haute First Nat'l Bank v. U.S.	865	Van Horne, Est. of v. Comm.	910
Terriberry v. U.S.	632	Van Wye, Est. of v. U.S.	684, 685
Texas Pig Stands, Inc., Avina v.	176	Vance v. Comm.	820
Textron, Inc., Stobnicki v.	348	Varnedoe v. Allen	135
Thebaut v. Comm.	918	Veit v. Comm.	115
Third Nat'l Bank v. U.S.	613	Vesuvius Crucible Co. v. Comm.	137
Thomas D. Berry v. Comm.	808	Vinal, Harry A. Koch Co. v.	89
Thomas Kiddie, M.D., Inc.		Vinson & Elkins v. Comm.	383
v. Comm.	323, 354	Vogel Fertilizer Co., U.S. v.	359
Thomason v. Comm.	260	Vorwald v. Comm.	214
Thompson v. Comm.	226	Vreeland v. Comm.	305
Thompson v. Origin Tech. in		Vuono-Lione, Inc. v. Comm.	89
Business, Inc.	183	W. H. Braum Family Partnership	
Thompson, Est. of v. Comm.	613, 615, 633	v. Comm.	903
Thomsen & Sons, Inc. v. U.S.	293	W. H. Braum Inc., Goletto v.	180
Thornley v. Comm.	79	Wachovia Bank & Trust Co. v. U.S.	624
Tidemann v. Comm.	728	Wachtell, Lipton, Rosen & Katz	
Tise, Trustees of the Directors		v. Comm.	383
Guild of America-Producer		Wade v. Comm.	224
Pension Benefits Plans v.	349	Wade, Est. of v. Comm.	654
Todd, Est. of v. Comm.	863	Wadewitz, Est. of v. Comm.	672
Tolley v. Comm.	224	Waite v. U.S.	619
Tolliver v. Comm.	451	Wall, Est. of v. Comm.	632, 653
Tomerlin, Est. of v. Comm.	615, 633	Wallace v. Comm.	136
Tompkins, Est. of v. Comm.	611, 613	Walsh, Est. of v. Comm.	864
Tonkin, U.S. v.	605	Walshire v. Comm.	908
Towne v. Comm.	139	Walton v. Comm.	914
Traina v. Sewell	348	Ward, Marriage of	675
Trammell, Est. of v. Comm.	613	Ware v. U.S.	814
Trantina. v. U.S.	**803**	Wartes v. Comm.	224

TABLE OF CASES

Water Quality Assoc'n Employees' Benefit Corp. v. U.S.	504	Williams v. Teamsters Local Union No. 727	175
Waterman, Est. of v. Comm.	659	Williamson Veneer Co. v. Comm.	291
Waters v. Comm.	135	Willmark Serv. Sys., Inc. v. Comm.	136
Watkins v. Comm.	723	Wilmot, Est. of v. Comm.	619
Watson v. Comm.	633	Wilson v. Bowers	613
Watson, Est. of, Comm. v.	640	Wilson v. Crooks	612
Webber, Est. of v. U.S.	84	Winger's Dept. Store, Inc. v. Comm.	323, 420
Webster v. Comm.	73, 160	Winkle v. U.S.	614
Weeden v. Comm.	32	Winn-Dixie Stores, Inc. v. Comm.	260
Weeks v. Comm.	52	Winokur v. Comm.	824
Weil v. Comm.	305	Wisconsin Nipple and Fabricating Corp. v. Comm.	361
Weil, Est. of v. Comm.	613	Wishard v. U.S.	606
Welch, Rundle v.	683	Wissner v. Wissner	644
Weller v. Comm.	918	Wollenburg v. U.S.	162
Welliver, Est. of v. Comm.	603	Wong Wing Non, Est. of v. Comm.	8, 300
Wellons v. Comm.	110, 503, 505	Wood v. Comm.	454
Wells, Burnet v.	305	Wood v. U.S.	436
Wells Fargo v. Comm.	496	Wood, Est. of v. Comm.	614
Wenger v. Comm.	389	Woodbury v. Comm.	824
Wentz v. Comm.	804	Woodbury v. U.S.	804
West v. Comm.	160	Wooderson v. American Airlines Inc.	183
Westoak Realty and Inv. Co., Inc. v. Comm.	363	Woodhall v. Comm.	92
Weyenberg Shoe Mfg. Co. v. Comm.	137	Woodson-Tenent Labs, Inc. v. U.S.	245
Wheaton, Metropolitan Life Ins. Co. v.	349	Wooley v. U.S.	713, 918
Wheeler v. Comm.	853	Worcester County Trust Co. v. Comm.	613
Wheeler v. U.S.	132	Worden v. Comm.	804
Wheeler, Hall v.	609, 610	Worster, Est. of v. Comm.	47
Wheeling v. Comm.	92	Worthen v. U.S.	685
Whipple Chrysler-Plymouth v. Comm.	139	Wright v. Comm.	281
Whitaker v. Comm.	49, 59, 60, 290	Wright v. Hanna Steel Corp.	185
Whitcomb v. Comm.	139	Wright, Est. of v. Comm.	135, 641
White v. U.S.	27	Wyly, Est. of v. Comm.	620, 853
White, Est. of v. Comm.	665	Xerox Corp., Berger v.	374
Whiteley v. U.S.	621, 677	Yarnall v. Comm.	56
Whitworth, Est. of v. Comm.	685	Yates v. Hendon	348
Wien v. Comm.	676	Yegan v. Comm.	127
Wigutow v. Comm.	110, 165	Yeomans Distrib. Co. v. U.S.	120
Wilcock v. National Distributors, Inc.	183	Young v. Comm.	260, 457, 640
Wilcox Invest. Co. v. Comm.	45	Yuengling v. Comm.	52
Wildenthal, Est. of v. Comm.	620	Zaal v. Comm.	803
Wilder v. Wilder	675	Zabolotny v. Comm.	443
Wilder, Est. of, Comm. v.	602	Zeman, Est. of v. Comm.	665
Wilkin v. Comm.	79	Zenz v. Quinlivan	82
William Bryen Co., Inc. v. Comm.	381	Zickafoose v. UB Servs., Inc.	176
Williams v. Comm.	839	Zipkin v. U.S.	826

TABLE OF IRC SECTIONS CITED

IRC Sec.	Q	IRC Sec.	Q
1(e)	839	22(c)(2)(B)(i)	833
1(f)	828	22(c)(2)(B)(ii)	833
1(f)(8)	828	22(c)(3)	833
1(g)	818, 828	22(d)	833
1(g)(1)	818	22(e)(1)	833
1(g)(4)	818	22(e)(3)	833
1(g)(4)(A)(i)	818	23)	832
1(g)(7)	818	24	832
1(g)(7)(B)	818	24(a)	834
1(h)	806, 815	24(b)(2)	834
1(h)(1)	815	24(b)(3)	834
1(h)(1)(A)	815	24(c)(1)	834
1(h)(1)(B)	815	24(c)(2)	834
1(h)(1)(C)	815	24(d)	834
1(h)(1)(D)	815	24(d)(1)	834
1(h)(1)(E)	815	24(d)(1)(B)(i)	834
1(h)(2)	815	24(d)(3)	834
1(h)(3)	815	24(e)	834
1(h)(4)	815	24(f)	834
1(h)(5)	815	25A	832, 835
1(h)(6)	815	25A(b)(1)	835
1(h)(7)	815	25A(b)(2)	835
1(h)(9)	815	25A(b)(3)	835
1(h)(11)	815	25A(b)(4)	835
1(h)(11)(A)	815	25A(c)	835
1(h)(11)(B)	815	25A(c)(2)(A)	835
1(h)(11)(B)(ii)(III)	415	25A(d)	835
1(h)(11)(B)(iii)	815	25A(e)	835
1(h)(11)(C)	815	25A(e)(2)	810
1(h)(11)(C)(iii)	815	25A(f)(1)	835
1(h)(11)(C)(iv)	815	25A(f)(2)	835
1(h)(11)(D)	815	25A(g)(2)	810, 835
1(h)(11)(D)(i)	823	25A(g)(3)	835
1(i)(1)	828	25A(g)(5)	835
1(i)(1)(B)	828	25A(g)(6)	835
1(i)(2)	828	25A(h)(1)	835
2(a)	830	25A(h)(2)	835
2(b)	831	25B	213, 832
2(b)(1)	831	25B(c)	213
2(c)	831	25B(d)(1)	213
2(d)	831	25B(d)(2)	213
11(a)	61	25B(e)	213
11(b)	838	25B(g)	213
11(b)(2)	840	25C	832
21	133, 832	25D	832
21(b)(2)	133	26(a)	829, 832
21(c)	133	26(b)	829
22	832, 833	30B	832
22(b)	833	30B(g)	832
22(c)	833	32(n)	834

2006 Tax Facts on Insurance & Employee Benefits

TABLE OF IRC SECTIONS CITED

IRC Sec.	Q	IRC Sec.	Q
35	180, 181	68(b)	821
35(c)	181	68(c)	154, 821
38	832	68(d)	821
45E	321	68(e)	821
53	829	68(f)	821
53(b)	838	71	38, 223, 280, 281, 808
53(c)	838	71(a)	38, 808
55	838	71(b)	808
55(a)	829	71(b)(1)(D)	808
55(b)	829	71(b)(2)	808
55(b)(1)(B)	838	71(b)(2)(A)	204
55(b)(2)	829, 838	71(c)	808
55(c)(1)	829	71(c)(1)	808
55(d)	829	71(c)(3)	808
55(d)(2)	838	71(d)	38
55(d)(3)	838	71(f)	808
55(e)	838	72	1, 37, 38, 111, 113, 226,
55(e)(2)	838		227, 246, 249, 259, 267,
55(e)(5)	838		318, 433, 483, 490, 812, 827
56	88, 117, 829	72(a)	1
56(a)	838	72(b)	41, 227, 433, 810
56(b)(1)(F)	821	72(b)(1)	7
56(c)	838	72(b)(2)	7, 11, 13, 15, 22,
56(d)	838		41, 43, 433, 439
56(g)	95, 838	72(b)(2)(A)	434
57(a)	829	72(b)(3)	18, 43, 227, 433, 439
57(a)(7)	815	72(b)(3)(A)	27
58	829	72(b)(3)(B)	27
59(a)(2)	829	72(b)(3)(C)	27
59(j)	818, 829	72(b)(4)	11, 14, 18
61	142, 159, 166	72(c)	8
61(a)	54, 251, 802	72(c)(1)	34, 254
61(a)(1)	435	72(c)(2)	8, 433
61(a)(3)	98	72(c)(3)	9
62	814	72(c)(3)(B)	9, 433
62(a)(1)	814	72(c)(4)	10, 427, 490
62(a)(6)	419	72(d)	433
62(a)(7)	220	72(d)(1)	433
63	817	72(d)(1)(B)	433
63(c)	800, 817	72(d)(1)(B)(i)(II)	433
63(c)(4)	817	72(d)(1)(B)(ii)	433
63(c)(5)	817, 843	72(d)(1)(C)	433
63(c)(6)	817, 843	72(d)(1)(D)	433
63(c)(6)(D)	842	72(d)(1)(E)	433
63(f)	817	72(d)(1)(F)	433
67	814	72(d)(2)	427
67(a)	822, 843	72(e)	3, 5, 33, 95, 247, 259, 264,
67(b)	822		273, 286, 427, 433, 445
67(c)	822	72(e)(1)(B)	250
67(c)(1)	822	72(e)(2)	254
67(e)	843	72(e)(2)(A)	5
68	821	72(e)(2)(B)	427
68(a)	821	72(e)(3)	3

TABLE OF IRC SECTIONS CITED

IRC Sec.	Q	IRC Sec.	Q
72(e)(4)	3, 8	72(t)(2)(A)(ii)	231
72(e)(4)(B)	5	72(t)(2)(A)(iv)	232, 485
72(e)(4)(C)	3, 32, 39	72(t)(2)(A)(v)	485
72(e)(4)(C)(iii)	32	72(t)(2)(B)	231, 485
72(e)(5)	3, 5, 18, 111, 113, 252, 255, 259, 482, 490	72(t)(2)(C)	485
		72(t)(2)(D)	231
72(e)(5)(A)(i)	249	72(t)(2)(E)	231
72(e)(5)(D)	490	72(t)(2)(F)	231
72(e)(5)(E)	18, 36	72(t)(2)(i)	485
72(e)(6)	33, 264	72(t)(2)(ii)	485
72(e)(8)	427, 490	72(t)(2)(iii)	485
72(e)(8)(B)	427	72(t)(3)	485
72(e)(8)(D)	427, 490	72(t)(3)(A)	231
72(e)(9)	812	72(t)(4)	232, 485
72(e)(10)	250, 311	72(t)(6)	231, 242, 243
72(e)(10)(B)	250	72(t)(7)	231
72(e)(11)	3, 250	72(t)(7)(B)	231
72(e)(11)(A)	3	72(t)(8)(A)	228
72(f)	435	72(t)(8)(B)	228
72(h)	34, 35, 36	72(t)(8)(C)	228
72(j)	249, 251	72(t)(8)(D)(i)	228
72(k)	38	72(t)(8)(d)(iii)	228
72(m)(2)	435	72(t)(9)	124, 428, 448
72(m)(3)	142	72(u)	2, 61, 110, 117, 260
72(m)(3)(B)	424, 425	72(u)(1)	2
72(m)(3)(C)	437, 491	72(u)(2)	2
72(m)(7)	202, 228, 428, 466, 810	72(u)(3)	2
72(o)(3)	424	72(u)(4)	4
72(o)(3)(B)	425	72(v)	250, 259, 286
72(p)	124, 402, 420, 422, 451, 466, 483, 484, 490, 823	79	100, 139, 142, 146, 149, 424, 504, 505, 507, 645
72(p)(1)	483	79(a)	139
72(p)(1)(B)	422	79(b)	142
72(p)(2)	420, 421, 422, 483	79(b)(3)	142, 424
72(p)(2)(A)	421, 483	79(d)	143
72(p)(2)(B)	483	79(d)(3)(A)	143
72(p)(2)(b)(i)	421	79(d)(3)(B)	143
72(p)(2)(B)(ii)	421, 422	79(d)(4)	143
72(p)(2)(C)	422, 483	79(d)(5)	143
72(p)(2)(D)	483	79(d)(6)	143
72(p)(2)(D)(i)	421	79(d)(7)	143
72(p)(2)(D)(ii)	421	83	77, 116, 117, 118, 121, 126, 129, 131, 303, 423, 460, 494
72(p)(3)	422, 484		
72(p)(4)(A)	483	83(a)	110, 129, 131
72(q)	4, 111	83(a)(1)	129
72(s)(1)	37	83(b)	129, 131
72(s)(3)	37	83(b)(1)	129
72(s)(5)(D)	37	83(c)(1)	112
72(s)(6)	37	83(e)(3)	126, 129
72(s)(7)	37	83(e)(5)	149
72(t)	231, 427, 428, 429, 473, 483, 493	83(h)	129, 131, 151, 460
72(t)(2)	231	86	220, 221, 222
72(t)(2)(A)(i)	231	86(a)(1)	807

TABLE OF IRC SECTIONS CITED

IRC Sec.	Q
86(a)(2)	807
86(b)(2)	807
86(b)(2)(B)	807
86(c)(1)	807
86(c)(1)(C)(ii)	807
86(c)(2)	807
86(e)	807
86(f)(3)	223
101	1, 95, 152, 249, 310
101(a)	36, 62, 73, 75, 81, 88, 94, 96, 125, 135, 139, 152, 153, 155, 160, 229, 255, 267, 268, 272, 273, 288, 293, 294, 437, 459, 507
101(a)(1)	54, 73, 257, 271, 491
101(a)(2)	63, 70, 277, 280
101(a)(2)(A)	63, 72, 279
101(a)(2)(B)	63, 65, 67, 68, 69, 71, 72, 277, 294
101(b)	134
101(c)	275
101(d)	229, 438
101(d)(1)	276
101(d)(1)(B)	276
101(d)(2)(B)(ii)	276
101(f)	250, 271, 273, 276, 437
101(g)	267, 318, 320
101(g)(1)	267
101(g)(2)(A)	268
101(g)(2)(B)	268
101(g)(2)(B)(i)	268
101(g)(2)(B)(ii)	268
101(g)(2)(B)(iii)	268
101(g)(3)(B)	267, 268
101(g)(3)(D)	267
101(g)(4)(A)	267, 268
101(g)(4)(B)	267, 268
101(g)(4)(C)	267
101(g)(5)	267, 268
101(i)	135, 137
102	257, 802
102(c)	137
103	802
104	155
104(a)	157
104(a)(2)	157
104(a)(3)	96, 98, 155, 164, 193, 194, 299, 300, 301, 318, 436, 507
104(a)(4)	802
104(c)	157
105	107, 159, 162, 165
105(b)	160, 168, 318
105(c)	160, 436
105(e)	161, 165

IRC Sec.	Q
105(g)	161, 436
105(h)	162
105(h)(1)	163
105(h)(3)(A)	162
105(h)(3)(B)	162
105(h)(4)	162
105(h)(5)	162
105(h)(6)	162, 163
105(h)(7)	163
106	100, 107, 139, 159, 166, 168, 507
106(a)	159, 301, 316
106(b)	200
106(b)(1)	209
106(b)(2)	198
106(b)(5)	195
106(c)(1)	107, 311
106(c)(2)	311
106(d)	198, 206, 207, 802
106(d)(1)	195, 198
106(d)(2)	195, 198
108(d)(7)(A)	839
120(e)	494
121	483, 802
121(d)(9)	802
125	101, 104, 105, 107, 168, 195, 199, 202, 377, 471
125(b)(1)	102
125(b)(2)	102
125(d)(1)	99
125(d)(1)(B)	100
125(d)(2)	99, 100
125(d)(2)(C)	100, 139
125(d)(2)(D)	100, 195, 198
125(e)	102
125(f)	100, 311
125(g)(1)	102
125(g)(2)	102
125(g)(3)	102
125(g)(4)	102
127	802
129	103, 107, 133
129(a)	133
129(a)(2)(A)	107
129(b)	133
129(c)	133
129(d)	100, 133
129(d)(1)	133
129(d)(5)	133
129(d)(8)(B)	133
129(d)(9)	133
129(e)(1)	133
129(e)(3)	133
129(e)(4)	133

TABLE OF IRC SECTIONS CITED

IRC Sec.	Q	IRC Sec.	Q
129(e)(8)	133	162(m)(4)(B)	108
129(e)(9)	133	162(m)(4)(C)	108
130	2	162(m)(4)(D)	108
130(d)	2	163	120, 260
132(a)(4)	142	163(a)	225
133	410	163(d)	821, 823
134(b)(3)(C)	802	163(d)(3)	823
135	802	163(d)(4)(B)	815, 823
137	103, 802	163(d)(4)(B)(iii)	815
138	802	163(h)(1)	823
139(a)	802	163(h)(2)	823
139(b)	802	163(h)(2)(F)	823
139(c)	802	163(h)(3)	823
139A	802	163(h)(3)(B)	422, 483
151	164, 198, 800, 819, 820	163(h)(3)(D)	823
151(c)	133	163(h)(4)(A)	823
151(d)(2)	819, 843	163(k)	851
151(d)(3)	819	164(a)	821
151(d)(3)(E)	819	164(b)(5)	821
151(d)(3)(F)	819	164(f)	814, 836, 837
151(d)(4)	819	165	26, 270
151(e)	819	165(a)	62, 821
152	103, 168, 820	165(e)	821
152(a)	820	165(h)	821
152(a)(1)	314	165(h)(2)(A)	821
152(b)(1)	820	165(h)(4)(E)	821
152(b)(2)	820	165(i)(1)	821
152(b)(3)	820	170	43, 821
152(c)	820, 831, 834	170(a)(3)	825
152(d)	812	170(b)	824
152(e)	820	170(b)(1)(A)	824
152(e)(1)	820	170(b)(1)(A)(ii)	100, 464, 686, 917
152(e)(2)	820	170(b)(1)(A)(vii)	824
152(f)(1)	820, 834	170(b)(1)(B)	824
152(f)(1)(B)	820, 834	170(b)(1)(C)	824
152(f)(1)(C)	820, 834	170(b)(1)(C)(ii)	824
162	54, 60, 133, 146, 166, 239, 365, 459, 460, 496, 503, 804, 823	170(b)(1)(C)(iii)	824
		170(b)(1)(D)	824
162(a)	45, 47, 60, 88, 141, 301, 503, 814	170(b)(1)(D)(ii)	824
162(a)(1)	54, 108	170(b)(1)(E)	824
162(c)	814	170(b)(2)	838
162(c)(2)	804	170(c)	802
162(l)	166, 315, 814	170(d)(1)	824
162(l)(1)(B)	315	170(d)(2)	838
162(l)(2)(A)	814	170(e)(1)	824
162(l)(2)(B)	166, 315	170(e)(1)(A)	39, 282, 824
162(l)(2)(C)	166, 315	170(e)(1)(B)	824
162(l)(3)	166	170(e)(5)	824
162(l)(4)	166	170(e)(5)(C)	824
162(m)	108, 120	170(f)(2)(A)	825
162(m)(1)	108	170(f)(2)(B)	825
162(m)(3)	108	170(f)(3)	285
162(m)(4)	108	170(f)(3)(B)(ii)	284

2006 Tax Facts on Insurance & Employee Benefits

TABLE OF IRC SECTIONS CITED

IRC Sec.	Q	IRC Sec.	Q
170(f)(8)	824	219(g)(2)	220
170(f)(10)(A)	283	219(g)(2)(B)	220
170(f)(10)(B)	283	219(g)(2)(C)	220
170(f)(10)(D)	283	219(g)(3)(A)	220
170(f)(10)(E)	283	219(g)(3)(B)(i)	220
170(f)(10)(F)	283	219(g)(3)(B)(ii)	220
170(f)(11)	824	219(g)(3)(B)(iii)	220
170(f)(12)	824	219(g)(5)	224
170(m)	824	219(g)(6)	224
172(d)(4)(D)	419	219(g)(7)	220
179A	832	220(a)	209
199	838	220(b)(2)	209
212	503	220(b)(3)	209
213	154, 157, 166, 428, 821, 826	220(b)(4)	209
213(a)	154, 311, 314	220(c)(2)(A)	209
213(c)	826	220(c)(5)	209
213(d)	107, 202, 315, 826	220(d)(1)	209
213(d)(1)	154, 166, 193, 298, 826	220(d)(3)	209
213(d)(1)(D)	154, 314	220(e)(1)	209
213(d)(2)	826	220(f)(1)	209
213(d)(5)	826	220(f)(2)	209
213(d)(6)	154	220(f)(4)	209
213(d)(7)	154	220(f)(5)(A)	203
213(d)(9)	826	220(f)(5)(B)	203
213(d)(9)(A)	826	220(i)	813
213(d)(10)	202	220(i)(1)	209
213(d)(10)(A)	314	220(i)(2)	209
213(d)(10)(B)	314	221	823
213(d)(11)	314	221(b)	823
213(e)	917	222(c)(2)(A)	835
215	38, 281	223	195, 200
215(a)	808	223(a)	195, 198
215(d)	808	223(b)	198
217	821	223(b)(1)	198, 200
219	217, 220, 648	223(b)(2)	198
219(b)	220	223(b)(3)	198
219(b)(1)	220, 221	223(b)(4)	198
219(b)(2)	240	223(b)(5)	198
219(b)(5)(A)	220, 221	223(b)(6)	198
219(b)(5)(B)	220, 221	223(b)(7)	196
219(b)(5)(C)	220, 221	223(c)(1)(A)	196
219(c)	221	223(c)(1)(B)	196
219(c)(1)	220	223(c)(2)(A)	197
219(c)(2)	218	223(c)(2)(C)	197
219(d)(1)	220	223(c)(3)	196
219(d)(4)	220	223(c)(5)	197
219(f)(1)	223	223(d)(1)	195
219(f)(2)	218	223(d)(2)	202
219(f)(3)	219	223(d)(3)	195
219(f)(5)	239	223(e)(1)	195, 201
219(f)(6)	226	223(e)(2)	201
219(g)	218	223(f)(1)	195, 202, 802
219(g)(1)	224	223(f)(2)	195, 200, 202

TABLE OF IRC SECTIONS CITED

IRC Sec.	Q	IRC Sec.	Q
223(f)(3)(A)	200	280G	109, 120, 377
223(f)(4)	195	280G(b)(2)	109
223(f)(4)(A)	202	280G(b)(2)(C)	109
223(f)(4)(B)	202	280G(b)(4)	109
223(f)(4)(C)	202	280G(b)(5)	109
223(f)(5)	203	291(g)(5)(A)(iii)	224
223(f)(5)(A)	203	301	380
223(f)(5)(B)	203	301(a)	82
223(f)(7)	204	301(c)	52
223(f)(8)(A)	205	302	89
223(f)(8)(B)(i)	205	302(a)	88, 91
223(f)(8)(B)(i)(II)	205	302(b)(3)	82
223(f)(8)(B)(ii)(I)	205	302(c)(2)(A)	83
223(f)(8)(B)(ii)(II)	205	302(c)(2)(B)	83
223(g)	197	302(c)(2)(C)	83
243	838	303	85, 89, 851, 860, 866
262	81, 287	303(a)	85
262(a)	58, 59, 244	303(b)	85
263	166	303(b)(1)	85
264	60	303(b)(2)(A)	85
264(a)	141	303(b)(2)(B)	85
264(a)(1)	45, 47, 56, 57, 60, 88, 94, 96, 117, 287, 288, 291, 459	303(b)(3)	85
		303(b)(4)	85
264(a)(2)	245	303(d)	85
264(a)(3)	245	306	85
264(a)(4)	63, 260, 277	311(b)	839
264(c)	245	312(a)	82
264(d)	245	312(n)(7)	82, 88
264(e)(1)	260	316(a)	82
264(e)(2)(A)	260	318	82, 143, 357
264(e)(2)(B)	260	318(a)	85, 115, 360, 413, 416
264(e)(2)(B)(ii)	260	318(a)(1)	82, 443
264(e)(3)	260	318(a)(3)	82
264(e)(4)	260	318(a)(5)(A)	82, 84
264(e)(5)(A)	260	318(b)	85
264(f)(1)	260	337	110
264(f)(2)	260	351	841
264(f)(3)	260	351(a)	72
264(f)(4)(A)	260	358	72
264(f)(4)(B)	260	368	72
264(f)(4)(E)	260	368(a)(1)(F)	841
264(f)(5)(A)	260	368(c)	72
265	225	381	839
265(a)	194	401	126, 381, 420, 431, 910
265(a)(1)	59, 60, 81, 96, 98, 288, 293, 301	401(a)	210, 250, 322, 323, 370, 378, 442, 466, 467, 478
265(a)(2)	260		
267	355	401(a)(2)	323, 418
267(b)	314, 413, 916	401(a)(3)	324, 325
269A	840	401(a)(4)	326, 327, 329, 330, 351, 352, 404, 405, 408, 467
269A(b)(1)	840		
274(d)	802	401(a)(5)	467
274(n)(1)	814	401(a)(5)(B)	326
275(a)(6)	389	401(a)(5)(C)	330

2006 Tax Facts on Insurance & Employee Benefits

TABLE OF IRC SECTIONS CITED

IRC Sec.	Q	IRC Sec.	Q
401(a)(5)(D)	326	401(a)(26)(H)	373
401(a)(5)(D)(i)	330	401(a)(27)	392, 395
401(a)(5)(D)(ii)	330	401(a)(27)(B)	378
401(a)(5)(F)	326	401(a)(28)	412, 413
401(a)(5)(F)(ii)	327	401(a)(28)(B)(i)	413
401(a)(5)(G)	325, 326	401(a)(28)(B)(ii)	413
401(a)(6)	325	401(a)(28)(C)	413
401(a)(7)	333, 369	401(a)(29)	373
401(a)(8)	384	401(a)(30)	395, 466
401(a)(9)	126, 232, 233, 327, 338, 339, 342, 345, 346, 401, 427, 445, 451, 453, 486, 487, 488, 489	401(a)(31)	447, 466
		401(a)(31)(A)	322
		401(a)(31)(B)	322, 447
401(a)(9)(A)	124, 340, 341, 342, 487	401(a)(31)(B)	333
401(a)(9)(A)(ii)	235, 343, 489	401(c)(1)	179, 354, 418
401(a)(9)(B)(i)	235, 343, 489	401(c)(2)	418
401(a)(9)(B)(ii)	235, 343, 489	401(c)(2)(A)(v)	418
401(a)(9)(B)(iii)	235, 343, 489	401(c)(3)	358
401(a)(9)(B)(iv)	235, 343, 489	401(c)(4)	358
401(a)(9)(B)(iv)(II)	235, 343, 489	401(d)	418
401(a)(9)(C)	124, 340, 487	401(f)	322
401(a)(9)(C)(ii)	342, 384	401(g)	322, 431, 465
401(a)(9)(C)(ii)(I)	124, 340	401(h)	357, 365, 369, 370, 372, 381, 442, 494
401(a)(9)(E)	344, 487		
401(a)(9)(F)	342	401(h)(5)	323
401(a)(9)(G)	339, 346	401(k)	103, 119, 124, 241, 325, 326, 330, 331, 395, 399, 423, 466, 467
401(a)(10)(B)	350		
401(a)(11)	336	401(k)(1)	395
401(a)(11)(B)	335	401(k)(2)	395
401(a)(11)(C)	335	401(k)(2)(B)	402, 403
401(a)(12)	353	401(k)(2)(C)	395
401(a)(13)	348	401(k)(2)(D)	395
401(a)(13)(A)	348	401(k)(3)	404
401(a)(13)(B)	348, 349	401(k)(3)(A)	404
401(a)(13)(C)	348	401(k)(3)(A)(i)	395
401(a)(13)(C)(iii)	348	401(k)(3)(A)(ii)	404
401(a)(13)(D)	348	401(k)(3)(B)	395
401(a)(14)	338, 353	401(k)(3)(C)	404
401(a)(15)	353	401(k)(3)(D)(ii)	404
401(a)(16)	332	401(k)(3)(E)	405
401(a)(17)	128, 240, 242, 330, 331, 334, 352, 467, 504, 505	401(k)(3)(F)	395
		401(k)(3)(G)	404
401(a)(17)(A)	353	401(k)(4)(A)	395
401(a)(17)(B)	353	401(k)(4)(B)	391, 395
401(a)(19)	353	401(k)(4)(C)	325
401(a)(20)	384	401(k)(8)	241, 401, 406
401(a)(22)	378, 412	401(k)(8)(B)	406
401(a)(23)	412	401(k)(8)(C)	406
401(a)(24)	322	401(k)(8)(D)	428
401(a)(25)	384	401(k)(11)	400
401(a)(26)	373, 467	401(k)(11)(A)	400, 404
401(a)(26)(B)(i)	373	401(k)(11)(A)(iii)	400
401(a)(26)(B)(ii)	373	401(k)(11)(B)	400
401(a)(26)(G)	373	401(k)(11)(B)(i)(III)	400

TABLE OF IRC SECTIONS CITED

IRC Sec.	Q	IRC Sec.	Q
401(k)(11)(B)(ii)	400	402(c)(3)(B)	445, 451, 452, 454
401(k)(11)(B)(iii)	400	402(c)(4)	403, 445, 451
401(k)(11)(C)	400	402(c)(6)	445
401(k)(11)(D)(i)	400	402(c)(7)(A)	454
401(k)(11)(D)(ii)	350, 400	402(c)(8)	446
401(k)(12)	399	402(c)(8)(B)	124, 452
401(k)(12)(A)	404	402(c)(8)(B)(v)	452
401(k)(12)(B)(i)	399	402(c)(8)(B)(vi)	452
401(k)(12)(B)(ii)	399	402(c)(9)	452, 453
401(k)(12)(B)(iii)	399	402(c)(10)	446, 452, 453
401(k)(12)(C)	399	402(e)(1)	426, 449
401(k)(12)(D)	399	402(e)(1)(B)	449
401(k)(12)(E)(i)	399	402(e)(3)	119, 243
401(k)(12)(E)(ii)	399	402(e)(4)	432
401(k)(12)(F)	399	402(e)(4)(A)	432
401(l)	330	402(e)(4)(B)	432
401(l)(2)	330	402(e)(4)(D)	430
401(l)(2)(B)	330	402(e)(4)(E)	432
401(l)(4)(A)	330	402(f)	322, 447
401(l)(4)(B)	330	402(g)	119, 124, 242, 396, 397, 401, 405, 418, 466, 473
401(l)(5)(A)	330		
401(l)(5)(C)	330	402(g)(1)	241, 395, 396, 398, 466, 473
401(l)(5)(D)	330	402(g)(1)(C)	397
401(m)	100, 103, 325, 326, 404, 405, 467	402(g)(2)	396, 466, 473
401(m)(1)	405	402(g)(2)(C)	396, 428, 473, 485
401(m)(2)(A)	405	402(g)(2)(D)	396
401(m)(3)	405	402(g)(3)	242, 396, 397, 473, 484
401(m)(4)	405	402(g)(3)(A)	367
401(m)(4)(A)	333, 367, 405	402(g)(3)(D)	242
401(m)(5)	405	402(g)(4)	473
401(m)(5)(C)	405	402(g)(6)	473
401(m)(6)	406, 466	402(g)(7)	473
401(m)(6)(B)	406	402(g)(9)	396, 405, 418
401(m)(6)(C)	406	402(h)(1)	243
401(m)(6)(D)	406	402(h)(2)	240
401(m)(7)	428, 485	402(h)(2)(A)	240, 241
401(m)(10)	405	402(h)(2)(B)	240
401(m)(11)	399, 405	402(h)(3)	243
401(m)(11)(A)(i)	399	402(k)	243
401(m)(11)(A)(ii)	399	402(m)	397
401(m)(11)(B)	399	402A	394
402(a)	423, 428, 431, 433, 441, 448	402A(a)	401
402(A)(c)(3)(B)	401	402A(a)(1)	396
402(b)	110, 111, 118, 126	402A(b)	477
402(b)(1)	110, 111, 423	402A(b)(1)	401
402(b)(2)	113, 325	402A(b)(2)	401
402(b)(4)	110, 111, 423	402A(c)(1)	401
402(c)	431, 450	402A(c)(2)	401
402(c)(1)	445, 449, 451	402A(c)(3)	401, 452
402(c)(1)(C)	445, 451	402A(d)(1)	401
402(c)(2)	445, 447, 451, 452	402A(d)(2)(A)	401
402(c)(3)	451, 452, 454	402A(d)(2)(B)	401
402(c)(3)(A)	445	402A(d)(2)(C)	401

2006 Tax Facts on Insurance & Employee Benefits

TABLE OF IRC SECTIONS CITED

IRC Sec.	Q	IRC Sec.	Q
402A(d)(3)	401	404(a)(1)(C)	383
402A(d)(4)	401	404(a)(1)(D)	383
402A(e)	477	404(a)(1)(E)	383
402A(e)(1)	401	404(a)(2)	365, 383, 466
403	126, 466	404(a)(3)	392
403(a)	250, 423, 433, 441, 446, 451	404(a)(3)(A)	392, 398
403(a)(1)	433	404(a)(3)(A)(ii)	400
403(a)(4)	453	404(a)(3)(A)(iv)	392
403(a)(4)(B)	454	404(a)(3)(A)(v)	383
403(b)	2, 3, 4, 5, 30, 37, 40, 108, 124, 126, 211, 213, 227, 228, 250, 421, 427, 428, 429, 444, 446, 447, 448, 451, 452, 454, 455, 463, 465, 466, 467, 471, 475, 476, 478, 480, 482, 483, 487, 488, 490, 493	404(a)(5)	110, 111, 120, 132, 136, 137, 149
		404(a)(6)	364
		404(a)(7)	240, 392
		404(a)(7)(A)	366
		404(a)(7)(B)	366
		404(a)(7)(C)	366
403(b)(1)	428, 448, 464, 466, 469, 482, 490	404(a)(7)(C)(ii)	366
		404(a)(7)(D)	366
403(b)(1)(A)(i)	464	404(a)(8)(C)	418
403(b)(1)(A)(ii)	464	404(a)(8)(D)	419
403(b)(1)(A)(iii)	464	404(a)(9)	392, 412
403(b)(1)(C)	466	404(a)(9)(A)	415
403(b)(1)(D)	466, 467, 474	404(a)(9)(B)	415
403(b)(1)(E)	466	404(a)(9)(C)	415
403(b)(2)	469, 470	404(a)(10)(B)	474
403(b)(3)	471, 474, 476	404(a)(11)	110
403(b)(4)(B)	471	404(A)(12)	240, 392, 398
403(b)(5)	466	404(d)	110, 120
403(b)(7)	465, 466, 483	404(e)	419, 425
403(b)(7)(A)	465	404(g)	365
403(b)(7)(A)(ii)	466	404(h)(1)(A)	240
403(b)(8)	451, 453	404(h)(1)(B)	240
403(b)(8)(A)(ii)	124, 446, 451	404(h)(1)(C)	240
403(b)(8)(B)	451, 452, 454	404(h)(2)	240, 366
403(b)(9)	474	404(h)(3)	240, 366
403(b)(10)	447, 451, 466, 486, 487, 488, 489	404(j)	366
		404(j)(1)	383, 392
403(b)(11)	451, 466, 478, 483	404(j)(2)	383
403(b)(12)	467	404(k)	428, 445, 815
403(b)(12)(A)	467	404(k)(1)	415
403(b)(12)(A)(i)	467	404(k)(2)	415
403(b)(12)(A)(ii)	467	404(k)(2)(A)	415
403(b)(12)(B)	467, 474	404(k)(5)(A)	415
403(b)(12)(C)	467	404(k)(7)	415
403(b)(13)	451, 480	404(l)	392
403(c)	110, 113, 491	404(m)(1)	243
404	240, 365	404(m)(2)(B)	242, 243
404(a)	364, 365, 400	404(n)	240, 398
404(a)(1)(A)	383	408	211
404(a)(1)(A)(i)	383	408(a)	210
404(a)(1)(A)(ii)	383	408(a)(1)	210, 220
404(a)(1)(A)(iii)	383	408(a)(2)	210
404(a)(1)(B)	383	408(a)(3)	210, 445

990 2006 Tax Facts on Insurance & Employee Benefits

TABLE OF IRC SECTIONS CITED

IRC Sec.	Q	IRC Sec.	Q
408(a)(4)	210	408(m)(2)	815
408(a)(5)	210, 211	408(n)	210
408(a)(6)	210, 233	408(o)	220, 238
408(b)	210, 226	408(p)	242, 400
408(b)(2)(A)	210	408(p)(1)	242
408(b)(2)(B)	210	408(p)(2)	242, 243
408(b)(2)(C)	210	408(p)(2)(A)(ii)	242
408(b)(3)	210, 233	408(p)(2)(A)(iii)	242
408(b)(4)	210	408(p)(2)(B)	242
408(b)(8)(B)	451	408(p)(2)(B)(ii)	242
408(c)	239	408(p)(2)(C)(i)	242, 400
408(d)	444	408(p)(2)(C)(i)(II)	242, 400
408(d)(1)	214, 227	408(p)(2)(C)(ii)	242
408(d)(2)	227	408(p)(2)(D)	242
408(d)(3)	222, 444, 452	408(p)(2)(D)(i)	242
408(d)(3)(A)	446, 452, 456	408(p)(2)(E)	242
408(d)(3)(B)	452	408(p)(3)	242
408(d)(3)(C)	452, 453	408(p)(4)(A)	242
408(d)(3)(C)(ii)	220	408(p)(4)(B)	242
408(d)(3)(D)	222	408(p)(5)(A)	242
408(d)(3)(F)	454	408(p)(5)(B)	242, 400
408(d)(3)(G)	243, 446, 452	408(p)(5)(C)	242, 400
408(d)(3)(H)	227	408(p)(6)(A)	242
408(d)(3)(H)(ii)(III)	227	408(p)(6)(A)(ii)	242
408(d)(4)	214, 226	408(p)(8)	243
408(d)(5)(B)	226	408(p)(9)	242
408(d)(6)	214	408(p)(10)	242, 400
408(d)(7)	241	408(q)	211, 322
408(e)	215	408A	211, 217
408(e)(2)	201, 214	408A(a)	210, 223, 452
408(e)(3)	210, 214	408A(b)	210
408(e)(4)	201, 214	408A(c)(1)	221
408(e)(6)	210	408A(c)(2)	221
408(g)	214	408A(c)(3)	218, 221
408(h)	210	408A(c)(3)(A)	221
408(k)	240	408A(c)(3)(B)	222
408(k)(1)(B)	240	408A(c)(3)(C)(i)	222
408(k)(2)	240	408A(c)(4)	217, 221, 455
408(k)(2)(C)	240	408A(c)(5)	210
408(k)(3)	240	408A(c)(6)	221
408(k)(3)(C)	240	408A(c)(6)(A)	452
408(k)(3)(D)	240	408A(c)(6)(B)	222
408(k)(4)	240, 242	408A(c)(7)	219
408(k)(6)	241	408A(d)(1)	228
408(k)(6)(C)	241	408A(d)(2)	228
408(k)(6)(D)	241	408A(d)(2)(A)(iv)	401
408(k)(6)(E)	241	408A(d)(2)(B)	228
408(k)(6)(F)	241	408A(d)(2)(C)	228
408(k)(6)(H)	241	408A(d)(3)(A)(i)	222
408(k)(7)(B)	240	408A(d)(3)(C)	222
408(k)(8)	240	408A(d)(3)(F)	222, 228
408(l)(2)	242	408A(d)(4)	228
408(m)	214, 426	408A(d)(6)	222

TABLE OF IRC SECTIONS CITED

IRC Sec.	Q	IRC Sec.	Q
408A(e)	222, 452	409A(b)(4)	117, 118, 121
408A(f)	221	409A(d)	505
409	210	410(a)	324
409(A)	496	410(a)(1)	324, 325
409(b)(3)(C)	210	410(a)(2)	324, 373
409(e)	378	410(a)(3)	324, 378
409(e)(2)	412	410(a)(3)(B)	324
409(e)(3)	412	410(a)(3)(D)	324
409(e)(5)	412	410(a)(4)	324
409(h)	335, 412	410(a)(5)	324
409(h)(2)(B)	412, 416	410(b)	324, 325, 326, 329, 395, 467
409(h)(3)	412	410(b)(1)	325
409(h)(4)	412	410(b)(2)	325
409(h)(5)	412	410(b)(2)(A)(i)	325
409(h)(6)	412	410(b)(2)(A)(ii)	325
409(h)(7)	412	410(b)(2)(B)	325
409(l)	410	410(b)(2)(C)	325
409(n)(1)(A)	413	410(b)(2)(C)(i)	325
409(n)(1)(B)	413	410(b)(2)(D)	325
409(n)(2)	413	410(b)(3)	325, 326
409(n)(3)(A)	413	410(b)(4)	325
409(n)(3)(B)	413	410(b)(5)	325
409(n)(3)(C)	413	410(b)(6)(C)	325
409(o)(1)(A)	412	410(b)(6)(E)	325
409(o)(1)(B)	412	410(b)(6)(F)	325
409(o)(1)(C)	412	410(c)(1)(A)	325
409(o)(2)	412	410(c)(1)(B)	325
409(p)	412, 416	410(c)(1)(D)	325
409(p)(2)(A)	416	410(c)(2)	325
409(p)(3)(A)	416	411	333
409(p)(3)(B)	416	411(a)	333
409(p)(4)(A)	416	411(a)(1)	333
409(p)(4)(B)	416	411(a)(2)(A)	333
409(p)(4)(C)	416	411(a)(2)(B)	333
409(p)(4)(D)	416	411(a)(3)(A)	333
409(p)(5)	416	411(a)(3)(B)	333
409(p)(6)(C)	416	411(a)(4)	333
409A	115, 119, 121, 129, 505	411(a)(5)	333
409A(a)	505	411(a)(8)	333, 373
409A(a)(1)	505	411(a)(10)	333, 352
409A(a)(1)(A)(i)	115	411(a)(11)	333
409A(a)(1)(B)	115	411(a)(11)(A)	326, 333
409A(a)(2)(A)	115	411(a)(11)(B)	333
409A(a)(2)(B)(i)	115	411(a)(11)(D)	333
409A(a)(4)	115	411(a)(12)	405
409A(a)(4)(B)(i)	115	411(a)(12)(A)	333
409A(a)(4)(B)(ii)	115	411(a)(12)(B)	333
409A(a)(4)(B)(iii)	115	411(b)(1)(A)	373
409A(a)(4)(C)(i)	115	411(b)(1)(B)	373
409A(a)(4)(C)(ii)	115	411(b)(1)(C)	330, 373
409A(a)(4)(C)(iii)	115	411(b)(1)(F)	373
409A(b)(1)	117, 118	411(b)(1)(H)	333
409A(b)(2)	117, 118	411(b)(2)	333, 373, 378, 382

TABLE OF IRC SECTIONS CITED

IRC Sec.	Q	IRC Sec.	Q
411(d)	352	413(c)(6)	365
411(d)(3)	333	414	351, 357, 496
411(d)(6)	325, 334	414(a)(3)	355
411(d)(6)(A)	334	414(b)	240, 354, 359, 365, 467, 503
411(d)(6)(B)	334	414(c)	240, 354, 359, 467
411(d)(6)(C)	334	414(d)	174, 186, 326, 467
411(d)(6)(D)	334	414(e)	174, 188, 191, 356
411(d)(6)(E)	334	414(e)(4)(C)	191
412	389, 408	414(e)(5)	464, 474
412(a)	385, 389	414(e)(5)(A)	464
412(b)	385	414(e)(5)(C)	467
412(b)(2)	385	414(h)(2)	423
412(b)(2)(E)	385	414(i)	376
412(b)(3)	385	414(j)	371
412(b)(3)(A)	387	414(k)(2)	427
412(b)(5)	375, 389	414(m)	240, 332, 354, 360
412(b)(5)(A)	385	414(m)(1)	360
412(b)(6)	385	414(m)(3)	360
412(c)(3)	388	414(m)(5)	360
412(c)(6)	386	414(m)(6)(B)	360
412(c)(7)	386	414(n)	354
412(c)(7)(E)(i)(I)	388	414(n)(1)	355
412(c)(8)	334	414(n)(1)(A)	355
412(c)(9)	388	414(n)(2)	355
412(c)(9)(B)	388	414(n)(3)(C)	504
412(c)(9)(B)(iv)	388	414(n)(5)	355
412(c)(10)	387	414(n)(5)(C)(ii)	355
412(c)(11)	388	414(n)(6)(A)	355
412(c)(12)	388	414(n)(6)(B)	355
412(d)	390	414(p)	348, 349
412(d)(2)	334	414(p)(1)	349
412(e)	385	414(p)(1)(A)	449
412(g)	385	414(p)(4)(B)	349
412(g)(2)	385	414(p)(5)	349
412(h)	385	414(p)(6)	349
412(i)	373, 408	414(p)(7)	349
412(l)(1)	385	414(p)(10)	124, 466
412(l)(6)	385	414(p)(11)	124, 349
412(l)(7)(C)(i)(IV)	385	414(p)(12)	449
412(l)(8)(B)	375	414(q)	111, 133, 326, 356
412(m)	375	414(q)(1)	356, 467
412(m)(1)	375	414(q)(3)	356
412(m)(4)(B)	375	414(q)(4)	133, 356, 357
412(m)(4)(C)	375	414(q)(5)	356, 357
412(m)(4)(D)	375	414(q)(7)	356
412(m)(5)	375, 389	414(q)(8)	356
412(n)	375	414(q)(9)	356
413	322	414(r)	133, 325
413(b)(5)	388	414(s)	331, 405
413(b)(6)	389	414(s)(1)	331
413(b)(7)	365	414(s)(2)	331
413(c)(4)	388	414(s)(3)	331
413(c)(5)	389	414(t)	143, 504

TABLE OF IRC SECTIONS CITED

IRC Sec.	Q	IRC Sec.	Q
414(u)(2)(C)	397	415(c)(3)(C)	377
414(u)(4)	421, 483	415(c)(3)(D)	331
414(v)	124, 241, 242, 243, 325, 326, 327, 351, 395, 397, 399, 400, 404, 405, 467	415(c)(3)(E)	471
		415(c)(6)	377
		415(c)(7)	474
414(v)(1)	241, 243, 473	415(c)(7)(B)	474
414(v)(2)(A)	242, 397, 399, 400	415(c)(7)(C)	474
414(v)(2)(B)	398	415(d)	372
414(v)(2)(B)(i)	241, 399, 473	415(d)(4)(B)	377, 471
414(v)(2)(B)(ii)	242, 400	415(g)	332
414(v)(2)(D)	124, 397	415(h)	332
414(v)(3)	242	415(k)(2)	372
414(v)(3)(A)	124, 241, 242, 377, 395, 397, 473	415(k)(4)	471
		415(l)	372
414(v)(3)(B)	241, 325, 326, 327, 351, 397, 400, 404, 405, 467	415(m)	126, 128
		415(m)(3)	124
414(v)(4)(A)	397	416	124
414(v)(4)(B)	397	416(b)(1)(A)	352
414(v)(5)	124, 397, 473	416(b)(1)(B)	352
414(v)(5)(B)	397	416(b)(2)	352
414(v)(6)	397	416(c)	352
414(v)(6)(A)(iii)	124	416(c)(1)(C)(iii)	352
414(v)(6)(A)(iv)	241	416(c)(1)(D)(i)	352
414(v)(6)(B)	243	416(c)(1)(D)(ii)	352
414(v)(6)(C)	397	416(c)(1)(D)(iii)	352
415	124, 128, 220, 322, 325, 332, 356, 357, 359, 360, 363, 369, 372, 373, 377, 383, 384, 392, 395, 415, 420, 442, 466, 469, 471, 472, 474, 475, 480, 483, 493, 496, 499	416(c)(1)(E)	352
		416(c)(2)	240, 352
		416(c)(2)(B)(ii)(II)	352
		416(e)	352
		416(f)	352
		416(g)(1)(A)	351
415(a)(2)	471, 472	416(g)(3)(A)	351
415(a)(2)(C)	240	416(g)(3)(B)	351
415(b)	127	416(g)(4)	242
415(b)(1)	332, 372	416(g)(4)(A)	351
415(b)(2)(B)	372	416(g)(4)(C)	351
415(b)(2)(C)	372, 384	416(g)(4)(E)	351
415(b)(2)(D)	372	416(g)(4)(F)	351
415(b)(2)(E)	372	416(g)(4)(G)	350
415(b)(2)(E)(i)	372	416(g)(4)(H)	350, 399
415(b)(2)(E)(ii)	372	416(i)	115, 143, 357, 499
415(b)(3)	372	416(i)(1)	357
415(b)(4)	372	416(i)(1)(A)	351, 357
415(b)(5)(A)	372	416(i)(1)(B)	357
415(b)(5)(B)	372	416(i)(1)(D)	357
415(b)(5)(C)	372	416(i)(4)	352
415(c)	332, 377, 466, 471, 476	416(i)(5)	351, 357
415(c)(1)(A)	240, 241	416(i)(6)	351
415(c)(1)(B)	377	417	337, 338
415(c)(2)	240, 377	417(a)	337
415(c)(3)	124, 329, 331, 357, 377	417(a)(1)	336
415(c)(3)(A)	377	417(a)(2)	337
415(c)(3)(B)	377	417(a)(3)	336, 337

994 **2006 Tax Facts on Insurance & Employee Benefits**

TABLE OF IRC SECTIONS CITED

IRC Sec.	Q
417(a)(4)	336
417(a)(5)	336, 337
417(a)(6)(A)	337
417(a)(6)(B)	337
417(a)(7)	336, 337
417(a)(7)(B)	336
417(b)	336
417(c)	336
417(d)	336
417(e)(1)	336
417(e)(3)	333, 336, 372
417(f)(2)	336
419	132, 496, 503
419(a)	494, 495, 496, 503
419(b)	132, 494, 496
419(c)	496
419(c)(1)	496
419(c)(2)	496
419(c)(3)	496
419(c)(4)	496
419(c)(5)	496
419(d)	495, 496, 497
419(e)(1)	494
419(e)(2)	494
419(e)(3)	494
419(e)(3)(C)	494
419(e)(4)	494
419(g)	494
419A	496, 503
419A(a)	132, 496
419A(b)	496
419A(c)	496
419A(c)(1)	496
419A(c)(2)	496
419A(c)(3)(A)	496
419A(c)(3)(B)	496
419A(c)(4)(A)	496
419A(c)(4)(B)	496
419A(c)(5)(A)	496
419A(c)(5)(B)(i)	496
419A(c)(5)(B)(ii)	496
419A(c)(5)(B)(iii)	496
419A(c)(5)(B)(iv)	496
419A(d)(1)	499
419A(d)(2)	377, 499
419A(d)(3)	499
419A(e)(1)	496, 500
419A(e)(2)	496
419A(f)(5)(A)	496
419A(f)(5)(B)	496
419A(f)(6)	503
419A(f)(6)(A)	503
419A(h)	496

IRC Sec.	Q
419A(h)(1)(A)	496, 499
419A(h)(1)(B)	496
419A(h)(2)	496
420(a)	370
420(b)(1)(C)	370
420(b)(2)	370
420(b)(3)	370
420(b)(5)	370, 494
420(c)(1)	370
420(c)(1)(B)	370, 442
420(c)(2)	370
420(c)(3)	370
420(c)(3)(B)	370
420(d)(1)(A)	365
420(d)(2)	370, 494
420(e)(1)(B)	370, 494
420(e)(1)(D)	370
420(e)(2)	370
421(a)	129
421(a)(1)	129
421(a)(2)	129
421(a)(3)	129
421(b)	129
422	129
422(a)	129
422(a)(1)	129
422(c)(2)	129
424(c)(1)	129
424(c)(4)	129
441(i)	840
444	840
448(c)(3)	838
448(d)(2)	840
453	806
453(a)	806
453(b)	806
453(c)	806
453(d)	806
453(e)	806
453(g)	806
453(i)	806
453A(b)	806
453B(f)	806
453B(g)	816
457	112, 116, 122, 123, 124, 125, 126, 128, 211, 213, 224, 227, 228, 242, 331, 397, 421, 427, 428, 429, 445, 446, 447, 448, 449, 451, 452, 453, 454, 467, 471, 473, 480, 483
457(a)(1)(A)	126, 448
457(a)(1)(B)	126
457(b)	126, 466

2006 Tax Facts on Insurance & Employee Benefits

TABLE OF IRC SECTIONS CITED

IRC Sec.	Q	IRC Sec.	Q
457(b)(2)	124	505(b)(7)	504
457(b)(3)	124	505(c)	502
457(b)(4)	124	511	441, 498, 811, 843
457(b)(6)	124	511(b)	441
457(c)	124, 396, 473	512	441
457(d)	124	512(a)(3)	498
457(d)(1)(A)	124	512(a)(3)(A)	498
457(d)(1)(A)(ii)	124	512(a)(3)(B)	498
457(d)(1)(C)	124, 447	512(a)(3)(B)(ii)	498
457(d)(2)	124	512(a)(3)(E)(i)	498
457(e)(5)	124	512(a)(3)(E)(ii)	498
457(e)(6)	124	512(a)(3)(E)(iii)	498
457(e)(7)	124	512(b)(12)	441
457(e)(9)	124	512(e)(3)	416, 441
457(e)(9)(B)	124	514	44
457(e)(10)	124	514(b)(1)	44
457(e)(11)	123	514(c)(5)	44
457(e)(11)(A)(ii)	123, 124	514(c)(9)	441
457(e)(11)(B)	123	529	811
457(e)(11)(C)	123	529(a)	811
457(e)(12)	123	529(b)	811
457(e)(13)	123	529(b)(1)	811
457(e)(14)	124	529(b)(1)(A)	811
457(e)(15)	124	529(b)(3)	811, 812
457(e)(16)	124, 445, 452	529(c)(2)	905, 906
457(e)(16)(B)	445, 447, 448, 454	529(c)(3)(A)	812
457(e)(17)	124, 480	529(c)(3)(B)	812
457(f)	112, 115, 126	529(c)(3)(B)(v)	811, 835
457(f)(1)(A)	126	529(c)(3)(B)(vi)	811
457(f)(1)(B)	126	529(c)(3)(C)	812
457(f)(2)	126	529(c)(3)(C)(iii)	812
457(f)(3)(B)	126	529(c)(3)(D)	812
457(g)	124, 126	529(c)(4)	858, 859
461(g)	260	529(c)(5)	905
461(h)	260	529(c)(6)	812
469	220, 221, 222	529(d)	811
469(c)	823	529(d)(5)(B)	906
482	838	529(e)(1)	812
483	806, 904	529(e)(2)	812
501	114, 115, 123	529(e)(3)	231, 810
501(a)	110, 124, 250, 324, 441, 686	529(e)(3)(A)	811
501(c)(1)	123	529(e)(3)(B)	811
501(c)(3)	143, 464, 469, 474	529(e)(5)	231, 810, 811
501(c)(8)	325	530(a)	810
501(c)(9)	149, 504, 505	530(b)	810
501(m)	44	530(b)(1)	810
503(a)(1)(B)	441	530(b)(1)(A)(iii)	810
505(a)(1)	504	530(b)(1)(C)	810
505(a)(2)	504	530(b)(1)(D)	810
505(b)	500, 504	530(b)(1)(E)	810
505(b)(1)	504	530(b)(2)	810
505(b)(2)	504	530(b)(4)	810
505(b)(4)	504	530(b)(5)	810

TABLE OF IRC SECTIONS CITED

IRC Sec.	Q	IRC Sec.	Q
530(c)(1)	810	664(d)(2)(D)	825
530(c)(2)	810	665	843
530(d)	810	665(b)	818, 843
530(d)(1)	810	665(c)	843
530(d)(2)(A)	810	666	843
530(d)(2)(B)	810	671	65, 304, 309
530(d)(2)(C)	810, 835	672(a)	844
530(d)(2)(C)(ii)	810	672(c)	844
530(d)(2)(D)	810	673	111, 726, 727, 844
530(d)(3)	858, 905	673(a)	844
530(d)(4)	810, 812	673(b)	304, 844
530(d)(4)(B)	812	674(a)	844
530(d)(4)(C)	810	674(b)	844
530(d)(5)	810	674(b)(7)	844
530(d)(6)	810	674(c)	844
530(d)(7)	810	674(d)	844
530(d)(8)	810	675	844
530(e)	810	676	844
530(g)	810	677	111, 118
531	89, 838	677(a)	305, 844
532(c)	838	677(a)(3)	305, 306
535	838	677(b)	809, 844
535(c)(2)	838	678	307
537	89	682	280, 808
541	838	691(a)	251, 803, 827
542	838	691(c)	92, 205, 437, 438, 439, 827
542(a)(1)	838	691(d)	17
542(a)(2)	838	692(c)(2)	802
543(a)	838, 866	701	842
544	838	703(a)	842
545	838	704(b)	842
581	864	704(e)	842
591	815	705(a)(1)(B)	94
641	308	706(d)	842
641(a)	843	707(c)	166, 913
641(c)	839	708(b)	841
642(b)	843	721	841
642(c)	865	734	92
642(c)(5)	825	736	92, 115
643(g)	843	736(a)	92, 93, 614
645	843	736(b)	92
651	843	736(b)(2)	92
652	308	736(b)(3)	92
652(a)	843	741	92
661(a)(2)	865	742	92
662	308	743	92
664(d)	825	751	92, 824
664(d)(1)(A)	825	751(a)	92
664(d)(1)(B)	825	753	92, 614
664(d)(1)(C)	825	754	92
664(d)(1)(D)	825	761(d)	92
664(d)(2)(A)	825	807(d)(5)	273
664(d)(2)(B)	825	817(h)	21, 25, 247, 273, 465

2006 Tax Facts on Insurance & Employee Benefits

TABLE OF IRC SECTIONS CITED

IRC Sec.	Q	IRC Sec.	Q
854(b)(1)	815	1212(b)(1)(B)	815
854(b)(2)	815	1221	98
854(b)(5)	815	1222	838
857(c)(2)	815	1222(3)	824
904	815	1222(11)	815
904(b)(2)(B)	815	1223(13)	414
911(d)(2)	818	1231	815
936	839	1231(a)(3)(A)	815
1001	98, 263, 815	1231(c)(3)	815
1001(a)	129	1245	92
1011	98	1250	815
1012	94, 816	1250(a)	815
1014	86, 414	1250(b)(1)	815
1014(a)	816	1274(d)	805, 904
1014(b)(6)	816	1274(d)(1)(D)	805
1014(b)(9)	816	1274(d)(2)(B)	806
1014(b)(10)	816	1297	815
1014(c)	816, 827	1361	839, 841
1014(e)	816	1361(b)	109
1014(f)	816	1361(b)(1)(B)	411
1015	816	1361(b)(1)(D)	457
1022	816	1361(b)(3)	839
1031(d)	263	1361(b)(3)(A)	839
1032	118	1361(c)(1)	839
1032(a)	88	1361(c)(2)	839
1033(h)(3)	802	1361(c)(2)(B)(v)	839
1035	3, 30, 36, 249, 250, 259, 263, 286, 302	1361(c)(6)	410, 416
		1361(d)	839
1035(a)	30, 263	1361(d)(2)	839
1035(a)(3)	30	1361(d)(3)	839
1035(b)(2)	30	1361(e)	839
1035(c)	30, 263	1362	839
1041	3, 38, 279, 280, 816	1362(d)(3)	839
		1363	55, 839
1042	413, 414	1363(d)	839
1042(a)	414	1366	55
1042(b)(2)	414	1366(a)	839
1042(b)(3)	414	1366(a)(1)	90, 839
1042(b)(4)	414	1366(a)(1)(A)	76
1042(c)(1)	414	1366(b)	839
1042(c)(3)	414	1366(d)(1)	839
1042(c)(4)(A)	414	1366(d)(2)	839
1042(c)(6)	414	1366(f)(2)	839
1042(d)	414	1366(f)(3)	839
1042(d)(7)	414	1367(a)(1)	839
1042(e)	414	1367(a)(1)(A)	76, 90
1042(e)(3)	414	1367(a)(2)	839
1043	115	1367(a)(2)(A)	839
1059(c)	815	1367(a)(2)(D)	55
1201	838	1367(b)	827
1202	802, 815, 829	1367(b)(2)	839
1202(a)	815	1368	55
1211(b)	815	1368(b)	91

2006 Tax Facts on Insurance & Employee Benefits

TABLE OF IRC SECTIONS CITED

IRC Sec.	Q
1368(b)(2)	839
1368(c)	839
1368(e)(3)	839
1371(c)	839
1371(d)	839
1372	139, 166
1374	839
1375(a)	839
1375(b)(3)	839
1375(b)(4)	839
1377	839
1402(a)	122, 418
1402(b)(1)	122
1402(k)	803
1563	133, 359
1563(d)	359
2001	852
2001(c)	852
2001(e)	860
2001(f)	852
2002	617
2010	868
2011(b)	869
2011(b)(2)	869
2011(g)	869
2012(a)	870
2012(e)	870
2013(a)	871
2013(b)	871
2013(c)(1)	871
2013(d)(3)	871
2014	867
2031	615, 862
2031(c)	861
2031(c)(1)	861
2031(c)(2)	861
2031(c)(3)	861
2031(c)(4)	861
2031(c)(5)	861
2031(c)(6)	861
2031(c)(8)(A)(i)	861
2031(c)(8)(A)(ii)	861
2031(c)(9)	861
2032	862
2032A	613, 862, 864, 951
2032A(a)(3)	862
2032A(b)(1)	862
2032A(b)(4)	862
2032A(e)(1)	862
2032A(e)(2)	862
2032A(e)(7)	862
2032A(e)(8)	862
2032A(h)	862

IRC Sec.	Q
2033	600, 601, 604, 605, 608, 609, 620, 625, 643, 647, 675, 676, 685, 853
2034	617, 853
2035	85, 605, 610, 615, 619, 626, 642, 643, 645, 653, 684, 718, 851, 853, 860, 864, 913, 951
2035(a)	860
2035(b)	860
2035(c)(1)	860
2035(c)(1)(A)	85
2035(c)(2)	851, 860
2035(c)(3)	860
2035(d)	642
2035(e)	860
2036	605, 613, 620, 621, 632, 643, 653, 655, 677, 683, 685, 853, 860
2036(a)	951
2036(a)(1)	652
2036(b)(2)	853
2037	655, 685, 853, 860
2037(a)	606
2037(b)	606
2038	655, 685, 853, 860
2038(a)	650
2039	601, 605, 607, 685, 686
2039(a)	600, 602, 604, 672, 673, 684, 685
2039(b)	600, 648, 672, 673, 686
2039(c)	648, 673, 674, 686
2039(c)(3)	686
2040	854, 908
2040(a)	853
2040(b)	854
2041	633, 653, 677, 853, 865
2041(a)	653, 679
2041(a)(1)	680
2041(a)(2)	680, 682
2041(b)(1)	653
2041(b)(2)	653, 681
2042	611, 612, 615, 620, 625, 632, 633, 634, 638, 642, 643, 644, 645, 652, 656, 673, 684, 686, 853, 860
2042(1)	623, 625, 626, 627
2042(2)	609, 610, 615, 616, 625, 626, 630, 631, 632, 634, 645, 862
2043	626
2043(a)	853
2043(b)	640
2043(b)(2)	640, 863
2044	653, 677, 678, 680, 681, 853, 862, 864, 903

2006 Tax Facts on Insurance & Employee Benefits

TABLE OF IRC SECTIONS CITED

IRC Sec.	Q	IRC Sec.	Q
2053	85, 615, 620, 640, 851, 863, 864, 865, 951	2503(c)	725, 918, 919
		2503(e)	917
2053(a)(3)	640, 866	2503(f)	737, 903
2053(a)(4)	640, 866	2504(c)	852
2053(c)(1)(A)	640	2505	922
2053(c)(1)(D)	851, 863	2505(a)	922
2053(e)	640	2505(b)	922
2054	85, 617, 851	2511	736, 903
2055	604, 616, 865	2511(a)	736
2055(a)	865, 950	2512(a)	909
2055(b)	865	2512(b)	903
2055(c)	865	2513	735, 907, 914
2055(e)(2)	865	2513(a)(1)	852
2055(e)(3)	865	2513(a)(2)	907
2055(f)	861	2514	903
2056	649, 670	2514(e)	727, 740
2056(a)	664, 864	2515	909
2056(b)(1)	864	2517	738
2056(b)(1)(C)	662	2518	903
2056(b)(3)	667, 668, 864	2518(b)	348, 908
2056(b)(4)	864	2518(c)(2)	908
2056(b)(4)(B)	624	2518(c)(3)	908
2056(b)(5)	649, 864	2519	864, 903
2056(b)(6)	665, 666	2522	707, 921
2056(b)(7)	649, 665, 864	2522(a)	43
2056(b)(7)(B)	864	2522(c)	707
2056(b)(7)(B)(ii)	663	2522(c)(2)	921
2056(b)(7)(C)	649, 663, 664, 864	2523	709
2056(b)(8)	649, 864	2523(a)	920
2056(b)(10)	663, 665, 864	2523(e)	920
2056(c)	864	2523(f)(3)	703
2056(d)	649, 854, 864	2523(f)(5)	903
2056A	649, 864	2523(f)(5)(A)(i)	853
2057	866	2523(f)(6)	602, 703, 731, 853
2057(b)(1)(C)	866	2523(i)	917, 920
2057(b)(1)(D)	866	2602	951
2057(b)(3)	866	2603	956
2057(c)	866	2604	954
2057(e)(1)	866	2604(c)	954
2057(e)(2)	866	2611(a)	950
2057(f)	866	2611(b)	950
2057(f)(1)	866	2612(a)	950
2057(j)	866	2612(b)	950
2057(j)(1)	866	2612(c)	950
2058	863	2612(c)(2)	950
2205	617	2613	950
2206	617, 636	2621	951
2210	850, 866	2622	951
2501(a)(1)	900	2623	951
2502(a)	902	2624	951
2502(c)	901	2632	951
2503(a)	43	2632(b)	951
2503(b)	712, 716, 726, 917, 918	2632(c)	951

TABLE OF IRC SECTIONS CITED

IRC Sec.	Q	IRC Sec.	Q
2632(d)	951	2701(e)(5)	913
2632(e)	951	2701(e)(6)	913
2641	951	2701(e)(7)	913
2642	951	2702	727, 914
2642(a)	951	2702(a)	914
2642(a)(1)	951	2702(a)(1)	914
2642(a)(2)	951	2702(a)(2)(B)	914
2642(b)(2)(A)	951	2702(a)(3)(A)(ii)	914
2642(c)	751, 951	2702(b)	914
2642(d)(2)	951	2702(c)(1)	914
2642(e)	951	2702(c)(2)	914
2642(f)	951	2702(c)(4)	914
2642(f)(4)	951	2702(e)	914
2651(a)	952	2703	613, 915, 916
2651(b)	952	2704	853, 916
2651(c)	952	2704(a)	916
2651(d)	952	2704(b)	916
2651(e)	952	2704(b)(1)	916
2652(a)(1)	950	2704(b)(2)	916
2652(a)(2)	953	2704(b)(3)(A)	916
2652(a)(3)	951	2704(b)(3)(B)	916
2652(b)	750	2704(c)(1)	916
2652(c)(2)	950	2704(c)(2)	916
2652(c)(3)	950	2704(c)(3)	916
2653(a)	950	3101(b)	836
2654(a)(1)	816	3102(d)	144
2654(a)(2)	816, 951	3121(a)	206, 243
2654(b)	951	3121(a)(1)	122
2662	955	3121(a)(2)	144
2663(3)	750	3121(a)(4)	170
2664	950, 951, 954	3121(a)(5)	105, 126, 423, 492
2701	853, 913, 916	3121(a)(5)(A)	108
2701(a)(1)	913	3121(a)(5)(C)	240, 241
2701(a)(2)	913	3121(a)(5)(I)	126
2701(a)(3)(A)	913	3121(b)(7)	126
2701(a)(3)(B)	913	3121(u)	836
2701(a)(3)(C)	913	3121(v)(1)	108, 423
2701(a)(4)	913	3121(v)(2)	126
2701(b)	913	3121(v)(2)(A)	122
2701(b)(2)	913, 916	3121(v)(2)(B)	122
2701(b)(2)(C)	913	3121(v)(2)(C)	122
2701(c)(1)	913	3121(w)(3)(A)	123, 464
2701(c)(2)	913	3121(w)(3)(B)	123, 464
2701(c)(3)	913	3306(a)	243
2701(d)	913	3306(b)(1)	122
2701(d)(2)(B)	913	3306(b)(4)	170
2701(d)(3)(A)	913	3306(b)(5)	105, 126
2701(d)(3)(B)	913	3306(b)(5)(C)	240, 241
2701(d)(4)	913	3306(b)(18)	206
2701(d)(5)	913	3306(c)(7)	126
2701(e)(1)	913	3306(r)(2)	122, 126
2701(e)(2)	913, 914	3306(r)(2)(B)	122
2701(e)(3)	913, 916	3401(a)	121

2006 Tax Facts on Insurance & Employee Benefits

TABLE OF IRC SECTIONS CITED

IRC Sec.	Q	IRC Sec.	Q
3401(a)(12)	243	4974(a)	233, 347
3401(a)(12)(C)	239, 240	4974(d)	347
3401(a)(12)(E)	124	4975	443
3401(a)(20)	163	4975(a)	443
3401(a)(22)	207	4975(b)	443
3402(o)	169	4975(c)(1)	443
3405	490, 491	4975(c)(1)(D)	214
3405(a)	40, 269	4975(c)(3)	214, 443
3405(a)(1)	440	4975(d)	420, 443
3405(a)(2)	230, 440	4975(d)(1)	420, 443
3405(b)	40, 269	4975(d)(2)	443
3405(b)(1)	440	4975(d)(3)	410
3405(b)(2)	230, 440	4975(d)(13)	411
3405(c)	322, 412, 420, 440, 466, 490	4975(e)(1)	443
3405(c)(1)	445, 447, 448, 449, 451	4975(e)(2)	443
3405(e)(1)(A)	230	4975(e)(2)(H)	443
3405(e)(1)(B)	230	4975(e)(3)	443
3405(e)(1)(B)(iv)	415	4975(e)(6)	443
3405(e)(8)	412, 440	4975(e)(7)	410, 412, 413, 416
3405(e)(12)	40, 269	4975(e)(8)	410
3508	139, 159, 323	4975(f)(2)	443
4961	389, 443	4975(f)(3)	443
4963(e)	389	4975(f)(6)	416
4971	389	4975(f)(6)(A)	443
4971(a)	389, 390	4975(f)(6)(B)(ii)	443
4971(b)	389	4975(f)(6)(B)(iii)	420, 443
4971(c)(1)	389	4975(f)(6)(C)	443
4971(e)	389	4976	497, 501
4971(f)	389	4976(b)(2)	501
4971(f)(4)	389	4976(b)(4)	501
4972	367, 408	4978	414
4972(a)	367	4979	241, 406, 475, 493
4972(c)	367	4979(f)(2)	241, 406
4972(c)(2)	367	4979A	413, 414
4972(c)(4)	367	4979A(a)	416
4972(c)(6)	367	4979A(c)	416
4972(c)(6)(A)	367	4980	442
4972(c)(7)	367	4980(c)(2)(B)	442
4972(d)(1)(A)(iv)	243	4980(c)(3)(C)	377
4972(d)(1)(B)	367	4980(c)(4)	442
4973	493	4980(d)(2)	442
4973(a)	200, 209, 226	4980(d)(2)(B)(iii)	442
4973(b)	226	4980(d)(3)	442
4973(b)(1)(A)	226	4980(d)(4)	442
4973(b)(2)	226	4980(d)(5)(D)	442
4973(c)	475	4980(d)(5)(E)	442
4973(e)	810, 811	4980B(b)	185
4973(e)(2)	810	4980B(c)	185
4973(f)(1)(A)	226	4980B(c)(5)	185
4973(f)(2)	226	4980B(d)	174
4973(g)	200	4980B(e)	185
4974	124, 233, 339, 346, 347, 486, 488, 493	4980B(f)(1)	173
		4980B(f)(2)	173

TABLE OF IRC SECTIONS CITED

IRC Sec.	Q	IRC Sec.	Q
4980B(f)(2)(B)	177	4980E(b)	199
4980B(f)(2)(B)(i)	177	4980E(d)	199
4980B(f)(2)(B)(i)(I)	177	4980E(d)(3)	199
4980B(f)(2)(B)(i)(II)	177	4980G	199
4980B(f)(2)(B)(i)(III)	177	4999	109
4980B(f)(2)(B)(i)(IV)	177	5000(b)(1)	186
4980B(f)(2)(B)(i)(V)	177	5000(d)	177
4980B(f)(2)(C)	180	5123(a)	122
4980B(f)(2)(D)	180	6011	503
4980B(f)(2)(E)	177	6012(a)	240, 800
4980B(f)(3)	175	6013	218
4980B(f)(3)(B)	176	6013(a)	830
4980B(f)(5)	182	6013(d)(2)	218
4980B(f)(5)(B)	182	6013(d)(3)	297
4980B(f)(5)(C)	182	6017	837
4980B(f)(5)(C)(i)	182	6018(a)	851
4980B(f)(5)(C)(ii)	182	6019	901
4980B(f)(6)(A)	183	6039(a)	129
4980B(f)(6)(B)	183	6039D	106, 133, 145, 171
4980B(f)(6)(C)	183	6041	151
4980B(f)(6)(D)	183	6041A	151
4980B(f)(7)	179	6047(d)	30, 481
4980B(g)	178	6050Q	320
4980B(g)(1)	178	6050Q(a)	320
4980B(g)(1)(A)	178	6050Q(b)	320
4980B(g)(1)(C)	178	6050Q(c)	320
4980B(g)(1)(D)	178	6050S	835
4980B(g)(2)	173, 311	6050T	181
4980B(g)(4)	185	6050T(c)	181
4980C(b)(1)	311	6051(a)	208
4980C(b)(2)	311	6051(f)(2)(B)	170
4980C(c)(2)	311	6052(a)	145
4980C(c)(3)	311	6058(d)	238
4980C(d)	311	6058(e)	238
4980C(f)	267, 268	6072	240
4980D	186	6075	901
4980D(a)	191	6075(a)	851
4980D(b)	191	6075(b)(3)	901
4980D(b)(2)	191	6081(a)	901
4980D(b)(3)(B)	191	6111	503
4980D(b)(3)(C)	191	6112	503
4980D(c)(1)	191	6151(a)	851, 901
4980D(c)(2)	191	6159	851, 901
4980D(c)(3)(A)	191	6161	901
4980D(c)(3)(B)	191	6161(a)(2)	851
4980D(c)(4)	191	6163	851
4980D(d)(1)	191	6166	85, 851, 860, 863
4980D(d)(2)	191	6166(b)(1)	851
4980D(e)	191	6166(b)(2)	851
4980D(f)(2)	191	6166(b)(4)	851
4980D(f)(3)	191	6166(b)(7)	851
4980E	199	6166(b)(8)	851
4980E(a)	199	6166(b)(9)	851

2006 Tax Facts on Insurance & Employee Benefits 1003

TABLE OF IRC SECTIONS CITED

IRC Sec.	Q	IRC Sec.	Q
6166(c)	851	7702(c)(3)(B)(i)	273
6166(g)(1)(A)	851	7702(c)(3)(B)(ii)	273
6166(g)(1)(B)	851	7702(f)(1)	247, 273, 311
6166(g)(3)	851	7702(f)(1)(B)	273
6321	296	7702(f)(2)(A)	311
6323(b)(9)	296	7702(f)(7)(A)	249
6324(a)	617	7702(f)(7)(B)	249
6324(b)	708, 901	7702(f)(7)(B)(iii)	249
6324B	862	7702(f)(7)(C)	249
6331	428	7702(f)(7)(D)	249
6332(b)	296	7702(f)(7)(E)	249
6429	834	7702(f)(8)	273
6501(c)(9)	909, 913, 914	7702(g)	247
6502(c)	503	7702(g)(1)(B)	247
6601(a)	851, 901	7702(g)(1)(C)	247
6601(j)	851	7702(g)(1)(D)	247
6621(a)(2)	801, 851, 901	7702(g)(2)	271
6654	801	7702(j)	273
6654(b)	801	7702A	250, 252, 259, 263
6654(c)	801	7702A(a)(1)	250
6654(d)(1)(A)	801	7702A(a)(2)	250
6654(d)(1)(B)	801	7702A(b)	249, 250, 286, 302, 460
6654(d)(1)(C)	801	7702A(c)(1)	250
6654(d)(2)	801	7702A(c)(1)(B)	250
6654(d)(2)(B)(i)	801	7702A(c)(2)	250
6654(e)	801	7702A(c)(3)(A)	250
6654(l)	843	7702A(c)(3)(B)	250
6654(l)(2)(B)	844	7702A(c)(6)	250
6662	862, 909	7702A(d)	250
6662A	503	7702A(e)(1)	250
6662A(a)	503	7702A(e)(1)(B)	250
6662A(b)	503	7702A(e)(1)(C)	250
6662A(c)	503	7702B	250, 313, 319
6664(c)(1)	862, 909	7702B(a)(1)	318
6693(b)(1)	238	7702B(a)(2)	318
6693(b)(2)	238	7702B(a)(3)	316, 317
6707A	395, 503	7702B(b)	202, 311, 313, 314, 319
6707A(c)(1)	503	7702B(b)(1)(B)	267, 268
6707A(c)(2)	503	7702B(b)(2)(C)	311
6901	617, 708	7702B(c)	314
7282	741	7702B(c)(1)	267, 312
7517	862, 909	7702B(c)(2)	312
7520	347, 862, 910, 913, 914	7702B(c)(2)(A)	267, 268, 312
7520(a)	910	7702B(c)(2)(B)	267, 268, 312
7520(b)	910	7702B(d)	267
7527	180, 181	7702B(d)(1)	267, 318
7701(a)(20)	99, 139, 159, 323, 358	7702B(d)(2)	267, 318
7702	35, 160, 247, 249, 250, 255, 266, 271, 273, 302, 311, 369, 437	7702B(d)(4)	267, 318
		7702B(d)(5)	267, 318
		7702B(e)(1)	311
7702(a)	247, 273	7702B(e)(2)	311
7702(b)	273	7702B(e)(3)	311
7702(c)	273	7702B(g)	267, 268, 311

1004   **2006 Tax Facts on Insurance & Employee Benefits**

TABLE OF IRC SECTIONS CITED

IRC Sec.	Q	IRC Sec.	Q
7702B(g)(4)	311	9801(b)(1)(A)	187
7703(b)	831	9801(c)(1)	187
7704	842	9801(c)(2)(A)	187
7805(b)	361	9801(c)(2)(B)	187
7872	458, 904	9801(d)(1)	187
7872(a)(1)	805	9801(d)(2)	187
7872(b)	805	9801(d)(3)	187
7872(c)(1)(D)	805	9801(f)	103
7872(c)(1)(E)	805	9802(a)(1)	188
7872(c)(2)	805	9802(b)	180
7872(c)(3)	805	9802(b)(1)	188
7872(e)	805	9802(c)	188
7872(f)	805	9803(a)	189
7872(f)(5)	458	9811	191
7872(f)(6)	458	9811(a)(1)	190
7872(f)(10)	805	9811(b)	190
9022(b)	122	9831	186
9801(a)	187	9832(c)	186

GUIDEX

	Federal Income Tax Question Number	Federal Estate Tax Question Number	Federal Gift Tax Question Number
A			
Accelerated Death Benefit	267	......	......
Accident And Health Insurance (see Health Insurance)			
Accident And Health Plans	173-195	......	......
Accidental Death Benefit	155, 159, 160, 167	641, 646	......
Accrued Benefits (see topic under Pension, Profit Sharing, Stock Bonus)			
Accumulated Earnings Tax			
business life insurance, purchase of	89	......	......
credit	89, 838	......	......
deferred compensation	89	......	......
generally	838	......	......
stock redemptions, effect on	89	......	......
Accumulation Distribution	843	......	......
ACP (Actual Contribution Percentage)	405, 406	......	......
Active Participant	224	......	......
Actual Contribution Percentage test	405, 406	......	......
Actual Deferral Percentage test	404, 406	......	......
Additional Indemnity			
generally	271, 272	641	......
group term rider, under	139	641	......
Additional Taxes (see Penalty Taxes)			
Adjusted Basis	816	......	......
Adjusted Current Earnings	95, 838	......	......
Adjusted Gross Estate, Defined	85	851	......
Adjusted Gross Income, Defined	813	......	......
ADP (Actual Deferral Percentage)	404, 406	......	......
Advance Premium Deposits	496	......	......
Affiliated Service Group	360	......	......
Aggregation Rule	3	......	......
Alimony			
annuity contract purchased to pay	38	......	......
general rules	808	......	......
life insurance			
premium payments as alimony	281	......	......
proceeds payable as alimony	280	......	......
transfer pursuant to divorce	280	......	......
Alternate Valuation Date	......	862	......
Alternative Minimum Tax			
corporations			
alternative minimum taxable income	95, 838	......	......
generally	838	......	......
life insurance contracts	95	......	......
small corporation exemption	838	......	......
individuals	829, 832	......	......
Amounts Not Received As An Annuity			
defined	1	......	......
fee, investment advisor	1	......	......
gift of annuity, donee's receipt	3, 32	......	......
gift of endowment contract, donee's receipt	32	......	......
taxation of	3	......	......

2006 Tax Facts on Insurance & Employee Benefits

GUIDEX

	Federal Income Tax Question Number	Federal Estate Tax Question Number	Federal Gift Tax Question Number
Annual Exclusion (see Gift Tax; Generation-Skipping Transfer Tax)			
Annuities, Charitable Gift (see also: Amounts Not Received As An Annuity; Annuities, Commercial; Annuities, Private)			
charity, taxation of	44	......	......
compensation, received as	77	......	......
defined	43	......	......
donor/obligee			
charitable deduction	43	......	921
payments received	43	......	......
Annuities, Nonqualified (see also: Amounts Not Received As An Annuity; Annuities, Private; Annuities, Charitable Gift)			
alimony, in payment of	38	......	......
annuity starting date			
defined	10	......	......
following sale of contract	28	......	......
annuity tables, use of	9	......	......
assets held in separate account	25	......	......
assignments and pledges	3, 31	......	......
basic annuity rule	7	......	......
basis (see "investment in the contract" this entry)			
borrowing to buy	245	......	......
cash withdrawals	3, 20	......	......
charitable gift of			
annuity contract	39	......	921
annuity portion of split life contract	285	......	921
deduction limitations, generally	824	......	921
combination single premium annuity and life insurance	......	605	......
constructive receipt (see Constructive Receipt)			
corporations, contracts held by (see also "nonnatural persons" this entry)			
generally	2, 37, 61	......	......
cost recovery rule	3	......	......
damage settlement, as	157	......	......
death of annuitant			
death benefit	18, 36	600, 607	......
death prior to maturity	36	601	......
death prior to recovery of basis in	27	......	......
distributions requirements	37	......	......
period-certain guarantee (see "refund or period-certain guarantee" this entry)			
refund benefits (see "refund or period-certain guarantee" this entry)			

2006 Tax Facts on Insurance & Employee Benefits

GUIDEX

	Federal Income Tax Question Number	Federal Estate Tax Question Number	Federal Gift Tax Question Number
Annuities, Nonqualified (cont'd)			
death of owner	37	......	......
deduction (see "loss, deduction of" and "premiums" this entry)			
deferred annuity	1-4, 7-24, 30, 35, 36, 40	......	......
defined	1	......	......
deferred compensation, funding with	110, 113, 117	......	......
distributions of annuity contract (see source plan (e.g., Deferred Compensation))			
distributions under			
amounts not received as an annuity	3-6	......	......
amounts received as an annuity	7	......	......
corporation, received by	61	......	......
following sale of contract	29	......	......
premature, excise tax on	4	......	......
requirements	37	......	......
dividends			
general	3	......	......
investment in the contract, effect on	8	......	......
divorce, contract transferred to	38	......	......
employee annuities			
funded deferred compensation	110-113		
public school employer (see Tax Sheltered Annuities)			
tax-exempt employer (see Tax Sheltered Annuities)			
estates, contracts held by (see "nonnatural persons" this entry)			
exchanges			
effective dates, effect on	3, 37	......	......
taxation of	30	......	......
exclusion ratio (fixed annuities)			
calculations			
change of amount or term, effect of	20	......	......
fixed amount annuity	19	......	......
fixed period annuity	19	......	......
joint and survivor annuity (level payment)	13, 14	......	......
joint and survivor annuity (nonlevel payment)	15, 16	......	......
single life annuity	11	......	......
temporary life annuity	12	......	......
following sale of contract	29	......	......
funded deferred compensation	113	......	......
general rule	7	......	......
expected return	9	......	......
fee, investment advisor	1	......	......
fixed amount annuity	......	600, 604	......
calculation of exclusion ratio	19	......	......

2006 Tax Facts on Insurance & Employee Benefits

GUIDEX

	Federal Income Tax Question Number	Federal Estate Tax Question Number	Federal Gift Tax Question Number
Annuities, Nonqualified (cont'd)			
fixed period annuity	......	600, 604	......
calculation of exclusion ratio	19	......	......
general rules for taxing	1	600-608	701-705
gifts of			
donee pays gift tax	32	......	911
donee, taxation of	32	607	......
donor, taxation of	3, 32	......	700-705
interspousal gift, marital deduction	......	......	703
joint and survivor annuity, purchase as gift of	......	......	701
payments, right to receive	31	......	......
refund annuity, naming beneficiary as gift	......	......	702
valuation of annuity	......	......	704
what constitutes gift of contract or consideration	......	......	700
income on the contract			
contracts held by nonnatural persons	2	......	......
individual retirement plan	210	......	......
interest first rule	3	......	......
investment annuity	25	......	......
individual retirement annuity (see Individual Retirement Plans)			
investment in the contract			
death prior to full recovery of	27	......	......
definition	8	......	......
dividends, effect of	6	......	......
exchange, effect of	30	......	......
following sale of contract	29	......	......
funded deferred compensation	113	......	......
joint and survivor annuity			
calculation of exclusion ratio			
level payments	13, 14, 20	......	......
nonlevel payments	15, 16, 20	......	......
purchase of	......	......	701, 731
taxation in estate of first to die	......	602, 603	......
taxation of survivor	17	......	......
valuation of	......	......	704
LIFO rule (see "income on the contract, interest first rule" this entry)			
loans			
exchange, effect on	30	......	......
for purchase	245	......	......
investment in the contract, effect on	3	......	......
treated as withdrawal	3	......	......
loss, deduction of			
death of annuitant	27	......	......
sale or surrender	26	......	......
marital deduction	......	602, 662-665	703
maturity	35	......	......

1010   **2006 Tax Facts on Insurance & Employee Benefits**

GUIDEX

	Federal Income Tax Question Number	Federal Estate Tax Question Number	Federal Gift Tax Question Number
Annuities, Nonqualified (cont'd)			
multiple contracts	3	......	......
nonnatural persons, held by contract funding deferred			
compensation	110	......	......
generally	2, 37, 61	......	......
nonqualified	110, 113	......	......
original issue discount rules, taxed under	1	......	......
partial surrenders	3	......	......
partnerships, contracts held by (see "nonnatural persons" this entry)			
penalty tax	4	......	......
period certain and life annuity	......	600, 604	704
personal injury claim, paid with	157	......	......
post death distributions			
requirements	37	......	......
premature distributions	4	......	......
premiums	244	......	......
primary annuitant	4, 37,	......	......
private annuity (see Annuities, Private)			
qualified funding asset	2, 4	......	......
refund or period-certain guarantee adjustments to investment in the contract			
general	8	......	......
joint and survivor annuity (level payment)	14	......	......
single life annuity	11, 23	......	......
variable annuity	23	......	......
taxation in estate of beneficiary	......	600, 604, 607	......
taxation of beneficiary	18, 27	......	702
retirement income endowment	......	601	......
sale			
deduction of loss	26	......	......
effect on purchaser	29	......	......
taxation of seller	28	......	......
single life annuity			
calculation of exclusion ratio	12, 20	......	......
starting date	10	......	......
straight life	11	600	700, 704, 744
structured settlement	157	......	......
successor owner	37	......	......
supplementary benefits excluded from investment in the contract	8	......	......
surrender	33-34	......	......
survivor's annuity	17	602, 603	701, 704
tables, annuity (App. A)			
tax-free exchanges (see "exchange" this entry)			
tax sheltered (see Tax Sheltered Annuity)			
tax sheltered annuity, funding with	465	......	......

2006 Tax Facts on Insurance & Employee Benefits

GUIDEX

	Federal Income Tax Question Number	Federal Estate Tax Question Number	Federal Gift Tax Question Number
Annuities, Nonqualified (cont'd)			
temporary life annuity			
calculating the exclusion ratio	12, 20	....	....
defined	12	....	....
term riders	8	....	....
third party owned	....	606	....
transfers without adequate consideration (see "gifts" this entry)			
trusts, contracts held by (see "nonnatural persons" this entry)			
unrecovered investment in the contract, defined	7	....	....
value of annuity contract	....	603, 685,	704, 744, 862
variable annuity			
death of annuitant (see "death of annuitant" this entry)			
qualified retirement plan, paid under	434	....	....
taxation generally	21-24	....	....
tax sheltered annuity, funding with	465	....	....
withholding of income tax	40	....	....
wraparound	25	....	....
Annuities, Private (see also: Amounts Not Received As An Annuity; Annuities, Commercial; Annuities, Charitable Gift)			
Chapter 14 valuation rules	....	....	912, 913
death of annuitant	....	608	....
defined	41	....	....
obligor, taxation of	42	....	....
payments received	41	....	....
purchase of as gift	....	....	705
withholding, income tax	41	....	....
Anti-cutback Rules	334	....	....
Applicable Federal Interest Rate			
below market loans	805	....	904
Archer MSA (see Health and Medical Savings Accounts)	195-209	....	....
Asset Reversion (see topic under Pension, Profit Sharing, Stock Bonus)			
Assignments			
annuity	3	....	....
gifts, generally	31	....	....
life insurance			
divorce, pursuant to	38, 281	....	....
viatical settlements	268	....	....
transfer for value rule	64, 277	....	....
Attribution Rules, Family			
generally	82	....	....
waiver of	83	....	....

B

Basis (see also "investment in the contract" under specific topic)			
generally	816	....	....

GUIDEX

	Federal Income Tax Question Number	Federal Estate Tax Question Number	Federal Gift Tax Question Number
Basis (cont'd)			
life insurance policies			
dividends, effect on	252, 255	......	......
transfers pursuant to divorce	280	......	......
partnership interests, sale or liquidation	92	......	......
Roth IRAs	210	......	......
S corporation stock	839	......	......
stock under stock redemption agreements	86, 88	......	......
Below-market Loans			
generally	805	......	904
split dollar plans	458	......	......
Beneficiary (see more specific entry, e.g., Life Insurance, Death Proceeds, etc.)			
Bonus Plan, Section 162	54	......	......
Business Continuation (see Buy-Sell Agreements; Business Life Insurance; Business Health Insurance)			
Business Expenses			
business life insurance	45, 48, 58, 59, 60	......	......
creditor insurance premiums, deduction of	288, 289	......	......
Business Health Insurance			
access requirements	186, 191	......	......
accidental death benefit	155, 159, 160, 167	641, 646	......
benefits			
disability	96, 160, 167	......	......
discrimination	162	......	......
domestic partnership benefits	164	......	......
key person disability	96	......	......
lump-sum payments	160	......	......
mental health	186	......	......
qualified pension plans	192, 369	......	......
qualified profit sharing plans	192	......	......
received by employee	159-161	......	......
sick pay	160	......	......
sight loss and dismemberment	159, 160, 167	......	......
small employers, exemptions	174, 186	......	......
survivors' benefits	159-161	......	......
uninsured benefits	161	......	......
cafeteria plan benefit	100	......	......
COBRA			
asset sale, following	184	......	......
business reorganization, following	184	......	......
buyer, obligation to provide	184	......	......
cost of coverage	180	......	......
cost of pediatric vaccines	173	......	......
coverage	174, 177	......	......
covered employee	179	......	......
definition	173	......	......
duration of coverage	177	......	......
effect of noncompliance	185	......	......
election to receive	182	......	......
exempt employers	174	......	......
Family and Medical Leave Act, effect on	175, 180	......	......

GUIDEX

	Federal Income Tax Question Number	Federal Estate Tax Question Number	Federal Gift Tax Question Number
Business Health Insurance (cont'd)			
COBRA (cont'd)			
gross misconduct	176		
length of coverage	177	......	......
long-term care insurance, exclusions	311	......	......
medical savings accounts, exceptions	202, 209	......	......
notice of, required	183	......	......
pediatric vaccines, cost of	173	......	......
qualified beneficiaries	178	......	......
qualifying events	175	......	......
required notice	183	......	......
requirements	173-185	......	......
sale of assets, following	184	......	......
seller, obligation to provide	184	......	......
stock sales, following	184	......	......
who pays for	180	......	......
coverage			
C corporations, stockholder-employees	165	......	......
COBRA	173-185	......	......
continuation requirements	173-185	......	......
creditable coverage	186, 191	......	......
FICA	170	......	......
FUTA	170	......	......
laid off employees	159	......	......
partners and partnerships	166	......	......
preexisting conditions, exclusion	186, 191	......	......
S corporation stockholder-employees	161, 166	......	......
sole proprietors	166	......	......
terminated employees	159	......	......
value	159	......	......
coverage continuation requirements	173-185	......	......
damages	157	......	......
deduction by employer	167	......	......
disability buy-out	98	......	......
discrimination based on			
health status	186, 188	......	......
discrimination rules, plans			
subject to	162	......	......
employee contributions	159, 160, 162	......	......
employee's tax			
benefits received	159-161	......	......
disability income	160	......	......
domestic partners	164	......	......
highly compensated employees	159	......	......
return of premium rider	159	......	......
sick pay	160	......	......
value of coverage	159	......	......
employer contributions	159	......	......
employer deductions	167	......	......
Family and Medical Leave Act,			
treatment	104, 175, 180	......	......
FUTA taxes	170	......	......
guaranteed renewability	186, 189	......	......
health reimbursement arrangements	159-161	647	......
highly compensated employees, special rules for	162	......	......

1014   **2006 Tax Facts on Insurance & Employee Benefits**

GUIDEX

	Federal Income Tax Question Number	Federal Estate Tax Question Number	Federal Gift Tax Question Number
Business Health Insurance (cont'd)			
information returns	171	......	......
key person insurance	96	646	......
newborns and mothers, standards	190	......	......
nondiscrimination	161, 162	......	......
medical expense reimbursement	159-161	647	......
overhead expense insurance	97	......	......
partners, coverage of	166	......	......
penalty taxes	185, 191	......	......
portability requirements	186, 191	......	......
preexisting condition exclusion, limits on	186, 187	......	......
premiums			
continuation coverage	180	......	......
deductibility of	167	......	......
disability buy-out	98	......	......
key person disability, deductions	96	......	......
overhead expense insurance, deductions	97	......	......
proceeds received by estate	......	647	......
qualified plan, provided by	192	......	......
renewability requirements	186, 189	......	......
reporting requirements	171	......	......
settlements funded by annuities	157	......	......
sick pay			
FICA taxes	170	......	......
FUTA taxes	170	......	......
taxation of	160	......	......
withholding	169	......	......
sight loss and dismemberment benefits	159-161	......	......
Social Security taxes	170	......	......
sole proprietor, coverage of	166	......	......
stockholder-employees, coverage of			
closely held corporations	165	......	......
S corporations	166	......	......
survivors benefits	159-161	......	......
value of coverage	159	......	......
withholding	162, 169	......	......
Business Life Insurance (see also Life Insurance)			
accumulated earnings tax	89	......	......
alternative minimum tax	95	......	......
borrowing to buy	245	......	......
buy-sell agreements, to fund (see Buy-Sell Agreement)			
cash surrender value			
inside buildup	95, 247	......	......
sale of policies	77, 78	......	......
charitable gift of			
cash surrender value	283	......	707
policy or premium	282, 284	......	707
corporations			
premiums, deduction of	47, 52, 54	......	......
creditor insurance (see Creditor Insurance)			
cross purchase agreement (see topic under Buy-Sell Agreement)			

2006 Tax Facts on Insurance & Employee Benefits

GUIDEX

	Federal Income Tax Question Number	Federal Estate Tax Question Number	Federal Gift Tax Question Number
Business Life Insurance (cont'd)			
death proceeds			
compensation, treated as	73	......	......
creditor insurance	288, 293, 294	623, 624	......
distribution by corporate beneficiary	73, 135	......	......
dividends, treated as	73	......	......
employee death benefit exclusion	135	......	......
group life insurance	152	645	......
insurable interest requirement	74	......	......
insured employee, tax liability	52	......	......
partners and partnerships	63, 71	609	......
policy held by trust	73	......	......
receipt of, generally	62, 73	625-635	......
restitution of embezzled funds	75	......	......
S corporation, receipt by	73, 76	......	......
stock redemption agreements, taxation	88	......	......
transfer for value rule	63-72	......	......
deferred compensation, funding with	117, 125	......	......
distributions (see "proceeds" this entry)	52, 55	......	......
employee death benefit exclusion, funding with	135	......	......
employee, on life of			
death benefit (see "death proceeds" this entry)			
policy loan, deduction of interest	260	......	......
premium			
deduction of	45, 47, 55	......	......
income, as	46, 50	......	......
exchange of contract	263	......	......
executive bonus plan	54	......	......
financed insurance	245	......	......
four-out-of-seven rule	245	......	......
group life insurance (see Group Term Life Insurance; Group Permanent Life Insurance)			
insurable interest, requirement of	74	......	......
interest			
policy loans	245, 260	......	......
key person			
corporations	......	610	......
death proceeds, taxation of	......	609-612	......
disability rider	301	......	......
partners	56, 57, 71	609, 612	......
premium			
business expenses	45, 48	......	......
deduction of	45, 47, 56, 57	......	......
income, as	46	......	......
insured employee, tax liability	46, 50	610	......
living proceeds (see also topic under Life Insurance)			
corporation, receipt by	61, 90	......	......
loans, policy			
beneficiary pays interest on	......	......	729
claim against insured's estate, as	......	659	......

GUIDEX

	Federal Income Tax Question Number	Federal Estate Tax Question Number	Federal Gift Tax Question Number
Business Life Insurance (cont'd)			
loans, policy (cont'd)			
exchange, effect on	263	......	......
interest, deduction of	245, 260	......	......
modified endowment contract,			
distribution from	250	......	......
taxability of	259	......	......
transfer subject to	32, 63, 64, 261	......	......
minimum deposit	245	......	......
modified endowment contract	250	......	......
nondeductible expenses			
S corporations, premiums paid by	55	......	......
officer, on life of			
policy loan, deduction of interest	260	......	......
premiums paid by business			
deduction of	45, 47	......	......
income, as	46, 50	......	......
premiums paid by stockholder	48	......	......
partners and partnerships			
death proceeds	62	609-612	......
deduction of premiums	56, 57	......	......
premiums			
creditor insurance (see Creditor Insurance)			
deduction of			
corporation, by	47	......	......
employee, by	59	......	......
executive bonus plan	54	......	......
generally	45, 60	......	......
partners, by	56, 57	......	......
partnership, by	56	......	......
shareholder, by	48, 49	......	......
sole proprietor, by	58	......	......
dividend, as	47	......	......
income, as	46, 51, 52, 53	......	......
insured employee, tax liability	46, 50, 52	610	......
reasonable compensation, as	47	......	......
S corporation, payment by	55	......	......
Section 162 bonus plan	54	......	......
stock redemption agreements, funding for	51	......	......
proceeds			
death (see "death proceeds" this entry)			
living (see "living proceeds" this entry)			
sale of life policy			
employee to corporate employer	78	......	......
employer to employee	77	......	......
grantor trust, to	64, 65	626, 676, 853	700, 903, 914
stockholder to corporation	78	......	......
subject to loan	64, 261	......	......
S corporation	90	......	......
transfer for value rule (see Transfer For Value Rule)			
S corporation			
death proceeds, receipt of	73, 76	......	......

2006 Tax Facts on Insurance & Employee Benefits

GUIDEX

	Federal Income Tax Question Number	Federal Estate Tax Question Number	Federal Gift Tax Question Number
Business Life Insurance (cont'd)			
S corporation (cont'd)			
distributed by..	73	......	......
insurable interest requirement	74	......	......
premiums paid by, effect of.............................	55, 76	......	......
sale or surrender of policy by	90	......	......
Section 457 plan, funding with.............................	125	......	......
sole proprietor..	58, 59	......	......
split dollar arrangement (see Split Dollar Plan)			
stockholder, on life of			
premium paid by another stockholder	49	......	......
premium paid by C corporation			
deduction of..	45, 47, 55	......	......
dividend, as...	47, 52-53, 55	......	......
income, as...	46, 50-53, 55	......	......
reasonable compensation, as	47	......	......
premium paid by S corporation	55	......	......
stock redemptions (see also heading under Buy-Sell Agreement)			
change to cross-purchase plan	69	......	......
generally	51	......	......
transfer of life policy (see also "sale of life policy" this entry)			
transfer for value rule (see Transfer For Value Rule)			
transfer without consideration.........................	79	......	......
transfer for value rule (see Transfer For Value Rule)			
generally	63, 64	......	......
sale or transfer, generally.................................	63	......	......
sale to corporation	67	......	......
sale to insured	65	......	......
sale to non-insured shareholder	68	......	......
tax-free reorganizations	72	......	......
transfers between partners and/or partnerships ..	71	......	......
transfers between shareholders	70	......	......
transfers from corporations to partnerships........	71	......	......
transfers without consideration.........................	79	......	......
Business Purchase Agreement (see Buy-Sell Agreement)			
Buy-Sell Agreement			
Chapter 14 valuation rules....................................	......	912, 915	912, 915
cross purchase agreement (corporation)................	53, 80, 81	610	......
basis of stock purchased.....................................	81	......	......
life insurance funding			
death proceeds, taxation................................	81	611	......
group term life, use of....................................	81	......	......
premiums			
deduction by stockholder.........................	49, 81	......	......
dividend to stockholder	53	......	......
income to stockholder, as.........................	53, 81	......	......
stock redemption, changed to..................	69	......	......
transfer for value, as.................................	64, 70, 81	......	......
sale of stock under	80	......	......

GUIDEX

	Federal Income Tax Question Number	Federal Estate Tax Question Number	Federal Gift Tax Question Number
Buy-Sell Agreement (cont'd)			
cross purchase agreement (partnership)			
deduction by partners	56, 57	......	......
generally	92	611	......
life insurance funding	94	611	......
transfer for value, as	64, 94	......	......
disability buy-out	98	......	......
fixing value for tax purposes	80	613, 915	706, 915
liquidation of partnership interest			
generally	92	......	......
life insurance funding	94	......	......
transfer for value, as	64, 94	......	......
partnership plans	92, 94	611, 612	......
stock redemption agreement	82-88	611	......
accumulated earnings tax	89	......	......
alternative minimum tax	95	......	......
basis after redemption	88	......	......
complete redemptions	82	......	......
constructive ownership of stock			
attribution rules	82	......	......
avoidance through estate			
distributions	84	......	......
waiver of	83	......	......
disability	98	......	......
family attribution rules (see "constructive ownership of stock" this entry)			
life insurance funding			
cross purchase, changed to	69	......	......
death proceeds, taxation of	88	612	......
gain on redemption	86	......	......
premiums			
deduction of	47, 88	......	......
income to insured, as	51	......	......
income to stockholders, as	88	......	......
payments to the estate, taxation of	82	......	......
S corporation, redemption by	91	......	......
Section 302(b) redemption	82	......	......
Section 303 redemption	85	......	......
surviving stockholders, taxation of	87, 88	......	......
transfer for value rule	63-72	......	......
valuation of business interest, effect on	80	613, 915	706, 915

C

C Corporations			
accumulated earnings tax	89, 838	......	......
alternative minimum tax			
generally	838	......	......
life insurance contracts	95	......	......
small corporation exemption	838	......	......
annuities, owned by	2, 37, 61, 110	......	......
attribution rules (see Constructive Ownership Rules)			
charitable contributions, deduction of	838	......	......

GUIDEX

	Federal Income Tax Question Number	Federal Estate Tax Question Number	Federal Gift Tax Question Number
C Corporations (cont'd)			
death benefit, contractual deduction of..................................	136, 137	......	......
income tax, generally	838	......	......
life insurance			
owned by (see Business Life Insurance)			
transfer of policy			
in reorganization...........................	72	......	......
to corporation................................	67, 72	......	......
to stockholders..............................	68-70	......	......
limited liability companies...................	841	......	......
personal service corporation	840	......	......
professional corporation	838	......	......
qualified dividends....................................	815	......	......
stock redemption (see Buy-Sell Agreements)			
tax rates..	838	......	......
Cafeteria Plans..	99-106	......	......
Capital Gains And Losses, Taxation Of			
Individuals...	815	......	......
C corporations..	838	......	......
S corporations..	839	......	......
Carryover Basis	816	......	......
Carve-Out Plan, Group.............................	146	......	......
Cash Balance Plans.....................................	374	......	......
Cash Or Deferred Plans (see "401(k) plan")			
Cash Out of Accrued Benefit....................	333	......	......
Cash Surrender Value (see topic under Life Insurance)			
Cash Value Accumulation Test.................	273	......	......
Cash Value Corridor	273	......	......
Casualty And Theft Losses........................	821	......	......
Catch Up Contributions............................	397	......	......
Chapter 14 Special Valuation Rules (see topic under Valuation)			
Charitable Gifts			
annuity contract			
exchanged for gift...............................	43-44	......	921
gift of...	39	604	......
charitable lead trusts.............................	825	865	914, 921
charitable remainder trusts	825	864, 865	914, 921
deduction limitations...........................	824	......	......
endowment contract.............................	282	......	......
generally	824, 838	865	921
life insurance policy, of	282	616	707
donor retains right to change			
beneficiary...	284	616	......
premium...	282	......	......
split dollar arrangement.......................	283	......	707
split life contract...................................	285	......	......
valuation of income and remainder			
interests...	......	......	910
Charitable Organizations' Employee Annuities (see Tax Sheltered Annuities)			
Charitable Split Dollar	283	......	......

1020   **2006 Tax Facts on Insurance & Employee Benefits**

GUIDEX

	Federal Income Tax Question Number	Federal Estate Tax Question Number	Federal Gift Tax Question Number
Child (Minor)			
gifts to	809	856	716, 725, 918, 919
"Kiddie" tax	818	......	......
unearned income, taxation of	818	......	......
Child Care			
Dependent Care Assistance Program	133	......	......
Child Tax Credit	834	......	......
Church Employees			
group term life insurance for	143	......	......
tax sheltered annuity for	474	......	......
Closely Held Corporations	738, 839, 840	......	......
COBRA			
asset sale, following	184	......	......
business reorganization, following	184	......	......
buyer, obligation to provide	184	......	......
cost of coverage	180	......	......
covered employee	179	......	......
definition	173	......	......
duration of coverage	177	......	......
effect of noncompliance	185	......	......
election to receive	182	......	......
exempt employers	174	......	......
Family and Medical Leave Act, effect on	175, 180	......	......
health coverage tax credit	181	......	......
length of coverage	177	......	......
long-term care insurance, exclusions	311	......	......
notice of, required	183	......	......
required notice	183	......	......
requirements	173-185	......	......
sale of assets, following	184	......	......
seller, obligation to provide	184	......	......
stock sales, following	184	......	......
who pays for	180	......	......
CODA (see "401(k) plan")			
Collateral Assignment (Split Dollar Plans)	457	......	......
Collateral, Policy As (see Creditor Insurance)			
Collectibles, Investment In	214	......	......
Collection Of Taxes			
cash values, from	296	......	708
proceeds, from	297	617	......
College Planning Saving Plans	811	......	......
Combination Single Premium Annuity And Life Insurance	......	605	......
Commissions, Life Insurance Agent	803	......	......
Common Law Employee, Defined	354	......	......
Community Property			
annuity, joint and survivor	......	602	......
generally	......	853(5), 853(12)	......
government insurance	......	644	......
individual retirement plans, applicable to	214, 218	......	......
life insurance, generally	......	618-622	709, 710
marital deduction	......	670, 861	730, 920

2006 Tax Facts on Insurance & Employee Benefits

GUIDEX

	Federal Income Tax Question Number	Federal Estate Tax Question Number	Federal Gift Tax Question Number
Community Property (cont'd)			
pension and profit sharing plans	......	675	738
settlement options, primary beneficiary's estate	......	677	......
Compensation			
deduction for generally	108	......	......
IRA	223	......	......
qualified plan	331	......	......
tax sheltered annuity	471	......	......
Constructive Distributions			
IRA	239	......	......
plan loan as	422	......	......
Constructive Ownership Rules			
family attribution			
generally	82	......	......
waiver of	83	......	......
family hostility	82	......	......
Section 318 rules	82	......	......
Constructive Receipt			
cash surrender values	247, 264, 265	......	......
deferred annuity maturity proceeds	35	......	......
deferred compensation			
funded plans	110, 112	......	......
unfunded plans	117, 118	......	......
dividend accumulations, interest on	253	......	......
endowment maturity proceeds	264, 265, 266	......	......
limited pay policy	248	......	......
retirement income maturity proceeds	35	......	......
Controlled Groups Of Businesses	359	......	......
Corporate Health Plans (see Business Health Insurance)			
Corporations (see C Corporation; S Corporation)			
Cost Basis (see also "investment in the contract" under specific topic)			
generally	816	......	......
S corporation stock	839	......	......
Cost-Of-Living Adjustments (see App. E and App. B)			
Cost Recovery Rule	3	......	......
Coverage Tests (see heading under applicable plan, e.g., Pension, Profit Sharing, Stock Bonus)			
Coverdell Education Savings			
Accounts	810	......	......
CRAT	825	......	914
Credit Union Shares			
tax sheltered annuity, funding with	465	......	......
Creditor Insurance			
bad debt deduction	292	......	......
death proceeds	288, 293, 294	623, 624	......
premium, deduction of	287-291	......	......
Credits			
adoption	832	......	......
child tax	834	......	......

1022 **2006 Tax Facts on Insurance & Employee Benefits**

GUIDEX

	Federal Income Tax Question Number	Federal Estate Tax Question Number	Federal Gift Tax Question Number
Credits (cont'd)			
elderly and disabled taxpayer, for	833	......	......
generally	832	851	922
Hope Scholarship	835	......	......
Lifetime Learning	835	......	......
premature distributions penalties, effect of	4	......	......
Critical Illness Insurance			
employer-provided			
benefits, taxation of	159	......	......
personal			
benefits, taxation of	155	......	......
premium, deductibility of	154	......	......
Cross Purchase Agreement (see under Buy-Sell Agreement)			
Crummey Trusts	307	653, 681	726, 727
CRUT	825	......	914
Custodial Gifts To Minors	809	856	919
D			
Death Benefit, Accelerated	267	......	......
Death-benefit-only Plans	135	685	711
Death Proceeds (see topic under: Life Insurance; Business Life Insurance; Creditor Insurance; Annuities, Commercial; Group Term Life Insurance)			
Debtor, Insurance On The Life Of (see Creditor Insurance)			
Deductible Employee Contributions (see specific plan)			
Deemed IRAs	210	......	......
Deferred Annuity (see Annuities, Commercial; Tax Sheltered Annuities)			
Deferred Compensation (Nonqualified)			
accumulated earnings tax	89	......	......
advance rulings	117, 118	......	......
annuity contract, funded plan			
distribution, employee taxation of	113	......	......
income on the contract, taxation of	110	......	......
assignment of benefits pursuant to divorce	121	......	......
Chapter 14 valuation rules	......	......	913
constructive receipt	117, 118	......	......
contributions under funded plan	110	......	......
controlling shareholder	117, 120	......	......
death benefit			
survivor benefit	121	685	711
death-benefit-only plan	......	685	711
directors' fees	122	......	......
divorce, assignment of benefits pursuant to	121	......	......
economic benefit			
funded plan	110-112	......	......
unfunded plan	117-118	......	......

GUIDEX

	Federal Income Tax Question Number	Federal Estate Tax Question Number	Federal Gift Tax Question Number
Deferred Compensation (Nonqualified) (cont'd)			
educational benefit trust	132	......	......
election to defer	117	......	......
employee's tax			
FICA	110, 122	......	......
funded plan	110, 111, 113, 121, 122	......	......
FUTA	110, 122	......	......
unfunded plan	114, 117, 118, 121, 122	......	......
withholding	121	......	......
employer's deduction			
funded plan	110	......	......
unfunded plan	118, 120	......	......
ERISA requirements			
funded plan	110, 111, 119	......	......
unfunded plan	117, 118, 119	......	......
escrow accounts	117	......	......
excess benefit plan	128	......	......
ex-spouse, assignment of benefits to	121	......	......
falling-net-worth trigger,			
securing the benefit with	117	......	......
FICA taxes	110, 122	......	......
$5,000 death benefit exclusion	121	......	......
forfeitures, funded plans			
consulting services	112	......	......
covenant not to compete	112	......	......
illegal acts	112	......	......
funded plans			
annuities, income on the contract, taxation of	110	......	......
employee taxation	110, 111, 113, 122	......	......
employer deduction	110, 111	......	......
ERISA requirements	110, 111, 128	......	......
secular trusts	111	......	......
substantial risk of forfeiture	112	......	......
FUTA taxes	110, 122	......	......
golden parachute rules,			
effect of on employer's deduction	120	......	......
hardship withdrawals			
advance rulings	117	......	......
constructive receipt	117, 118	......	......
rabbi trusts	118	......	......
hybrid rabbi/secular trusts	117	......	......
incentive stock options	129	......	......
income in respect of decedent, treated as	121	......	......
indemnity insurance, securing the benefit with	117	......	......
independent contractor, coverage for			
deduction by payor	110, 120	......	......
eligibility	117	......	......
"informally" funded	117	......	......
annuities	117	......	......
life insurance	117	......	......
securities	117	......	......
trusts	117, 118	......	......
"interest" on, deductibility	120	......	......

1024   **2006 Tax Facts on Insurance & Employee Benefits**

GUIDEX

	Federal Income Tax Question Number	Federal Estate Tax Question Number	Federal Gift Tax Question Number
Deferred Compensation (Nonqualified) (cont'd)			
irrevocable trusts...	118	......	......
ISOs	129	......	......
judges of state courts	127	......	......
payments received under			
funded plan...	113	......	......
unfunded plan...	121	......	......
rabbi/secular trusts...	117	......	......
rabbi trusts...	118	......	......
rural electric cooperatives (see Section 457 Plans)			
S corporations and single class			
of stock rule	839	......	......
salary continuation, defined..............................	114	......	......
SEC registration, tax implications			
of failure to register plan...............................	117	......	......
Section 401(k) wrap-around plan........................	117, 119	......	......
Section 457 plan (see main entry)			
secular trusts..	111	......	......
securing the promise to pay	117, 118	......	......
self-employment tax			
generally	122	......	......
life insurance agents.......................................	803	......	......
SERP (Supplemental Executive Retirement Plan)	114	......	......
Social Security payroll tax (see			
"FICA taxes" this entry)			
spouse, assignment of benefits to			
pursuant to divorce	121	......	......
state and local deferred compensation			
(see Section 457 Plans)			
statutory stock options..	129	......	......
stock options..	129	......	......
substantial risk of forfeiture	110, 112	......	......
Supplemental Executive Retirement Plan (SERP)	114	......	......
surety bonds, securing the benefit with................	117	......	......
survivor benefit..	121	685	711
tax-exempt employers (see Section 457 Plans)			
third-party guarantees,			
securing the benefit with	117	......	......
"top hat" plans	117	......	......
transfer to qualified plan....................................	117	......	......
"top hat" plan...	124	......	......
unemployment tax, federal (see			
"FUTA taxes" this entry)			
unfunded plans			
advance rulings	117, 118	......	......
constructive receipt	117, 118	......	......
economic benefit...	117-118	......	......
employee's taxation	114, 117, 118, 121, 122	......	......
employer's deduction	118, 120	......	......
ERISA requirements	117, 118, 128	......	......
generally	114, 117	......	......
informal funding..	117, 118	......	......
"securing" the benefits....................................	117, 118	......	......
vesting requirements, funded plans...................	110	......	......

GUIDEX

	Federal Income Tax Question Number	Federal Estate Tax Question Number	Federal Gift Tax Question Number
Deferred Compensation (Nonqualified) (cont'd)			
withholding			
Section 457 plans..................................	126	......	......
unfunded private plans	121	......	......
Defined Benefit Plans (see heading under Pension, Profit Sharing, Stock Bonus)			
Defined Contribution Plans (see heading under Pension, Profit Sharing, Stock Bonus)			
Dependent			
Care Assistance Program........................	133	......	......
defined...	820	......	......
exemption for	820	......	......
Dependent Care Assistance Program........	133	......	......
Direct Skip (GST Tax 950)			
Direct Transfer of Rollover Distribution......	447	......	......
Disability			
disability buy-out plan...........................	98	......	......
disability income...................................	155, 160, 167	......	......
disability provisions in life policy (see Life Insurance)			
income tax credit	833	......	......
premiums			
as medical expense.............................	154, 298	......	......
waived for	300	......	......
qualified plan, payment of	436	......	......
sick pay..	160, 833	......	......
Disclaimers...	......	637, 908	637, 908
Discrimination (see "nondiscrimination" under applicable plan, e.g., Group Life)			
Distribution Requirements			
annuity contracts, nonqualified..............	37	......	......
individual retirement plans	233-237	......	......
pension, profit sharing, stock bonus.......	338-346	......	......
tax sheltered annuities	486-489	......	......
Distributions (see more specific entry (e.g., Individual Retirement Plans; Premature)			
Dividends			
annuity contract.....................................	1, 5	......	......
individual retirement plan, purchased by...........	5	......	......
interest on accumulated dividends.......	253	......	......
investment in the contract, effect on...	6	......	......
premature distribution of, tax on	4	......	......
qualified plan, purchased by...............	5	......	......
tax sheltered annuity..........................	5, 474	......	......
life insurance...	252, 256	......	......
accumulated dividends received by beneficiary...	257	639	......
basis, effect on	252, 254	......	......
excess interest dividends	258	......	......
government life insurance (NSLI).......	295	......	......
group life	148	......	......
interest on accumulated dividends......	253	......	......
paid-up additions, used to purchase....	255	638	......
paid-up policy....................................	256	......	......
post-mortem dividend........................	257	639	......
split dollar plan.................................	458	......	......

GUIDEX

	Federal Income Tax Question Number	Federal Estate Tax Question Number	Federal Gift Tax Question Number
Dividends (cont'd)			
life insurance (cont'd)			
terminal dividends	257	....	....
qualified dividends	815	....	....
Divorce			
alimony			
annuity contract purchased to pay	38	....	....
general rules	808	....	....
life insurance			
premium payments as alimony	281	....	....
proceeds payable as alimony	280	....	....
transfer pursuant to divorce	280	....	....
annuity contract transferred pursuant to	38	....	....
deferred compensation (nonqualified)			
transferred pursuant to	121	....	....
dependency exemptions	820	....	....
individual retirement plan transferred pursuant to	214	....	....
life insurance			
death proceeds payable under decree or agreement	280	640	....
premiums payments pursuant to divorce	281	....	....
transferred pursuant to divorce	280	....	....
trust provisions as incidents of ownership	....	....	631
qualified domestic relations order	349, 426, 466	....	....
Domestic Partnership Benefits	164, 505	....	....
Domestic Relations Order, Qualified	349, 426, 466	....	....
Double Indemnity Proceeds			
generally	271, 272	641	....
group term rider, under	139	641	....

E

Early Distributions (see Premature Distributions)			
Earned Income, defined	418	....	....
Economic Benefit (see also Constructive Receipt)			
cost of insurance protection in			
individual retirement plan	220	....	....
group term life insurance	142, 147	....	....
qualified retirement plan	424, 425	....	....
split dollar plan	458	....	....
deferred compensation			
funded plan	110-112	....	....
unfunded plan	117-118	....	....
Education IRA (see Education Savings Account)			
Education Savings Account	810	858	905
Educational Benefit Trust	132	....	....
Elective Deferrals			
401(k) plans	395, 396	....	....
catch-up contributions as	397	....	....
nonqualified deferred compensation	114, 117	....	....
Roth 401(k)	374, 401	....	....
simplified employee pension	241	....	....

2006 Tax Facts on Insurance & Employee Benefits

GUIDEX

	Federal Income Tax Question Number	Federal Estate Tax Question Number	Federal Gift Tax Question Number
Elective Deferrals (cont'd)			
tax sheltered annuities	473	......	......
Employee Death Benefit Exclusion			
contractual death benefit	135, 136	......	......
deferred compensation, paid under	121, 135	......	......
employer's deduction	136, 137	......	......
generally	134-137	684, 685	......
income in respect of a decedent, as	135	......	......
installments, payment in	135	......	......
life insurance funded	135	......	......
prefunding	136	......	......
qualified plan	437-439	......	......
Section 457 deferred compensation plan, paid under	125, 134	......	......
voluntary death benefit	137	......	......
Employee Plans (see specific plan)			
Employee Retirement Income Security Act of 1974 (see "ERISA")			
Employee Stock Ownership Plan (see Pension, Profit Sharing, Stock Bonus)			
Employer Deduction (see heading under applicable plan)			
Employer Securities			
sale of to ESOP	413, 380	......	......
1042 election	414	......	......
Endorsement (Split Dollar Plans)	457	......	......
Endowment Contracts (see Life Insurance)			
Equity Split Dollar	458	......	......
ERISA			
aggregation of controlled groups	354	......	......
anti-alienation requirements			
exception for criminal acts	348	......	......
IRAs	216	......	......
qualified plans	348	......	......
anti-cutback rule	334	......	......
attachment of plan benefits	348	......	......
church plans	467	......	......
COBRA provisions of	173	......	......
contribution of property to qualified plan	363	......	......
employer securities, investment in by profit sharing plan	391, 410, 411	......	......
employer stock ownership plan (see ESOP)			
ESOP			
defined	410	......	......
requirements	412, 413	......	......
excess benefit plans	128	......	......
401(h) plan, notice of transfer	370	......	......
garnishment of plan benefits	348	......	......
governmental plans	467	......	......
life insurance			
as plan asset in split dollar plan	457	......	......
purchase by VEBA as violation of	505	......	......
multiple employer welfare arrangements	173, 186	......	......

GUIDEX

	Federal Income Tax Question Number	Federal Estate Tax Question Number	Federal Gift Tax Question Number
ERISA (cont'd)			
nonqualified deferred compensation			
funded plans, requirements	110, 111, 128	......	......
unfunded plans, requirements	117, 118, 128	......	......
no reduction of accrued benefit	334	......	......
offset of plan benefits	348	......	......
plan loans	443, 483	......	......
prenuptial agreement, effect of	337	......	......
prohibited transactions	443	......	......
qualified domestic relations order	349	......	......
qualified employer securities	411	......	......
reversions, limitations on	323	......	......
spousal waiver of plan benefits	337	......	......
tax sheltered annuities	466, 467	......	......
unfunded nonqualified deferred			
compensation plans, requirements	117, 118, 128	......	......
vesting requirements	110, 333	......	......
ESOP (see Pension, Profit Sharing, Stock Bonus)			
Estates, Taxation of Generally	843	850-871	......
Estate Tax (Generally)	......	850-871	......
basis, generally	816	......	......
Chapter 14 valuation rules	......	912-916	......
charitable bequests deduction	......	865	......
computation of tax	......	852	......
credits	......	867	......
custodial gifts	......	856	......
deductions	......	865	......
definition	......	850	......
disclaimers	......	908	......
estate taxes previously paid credit	......	871	......
exclusion	......	861	......
extension of time for payment	......	851	......
filing return	......	851	......
gift tax credit	......	870	......
gift within 3 years of death	......	860	......
gross estate	......	853	......
marital deduction	......	864	......
payment of tax	......	851	......
qualified conservation easement	......	861	......
qualified family-owned business interest	......	866	......
renewal commissions	......	857	......
repeal	......	850	......
return	......	851	......
Section 6166 election	......	851	......
spouses, property held jointly by	......	854	......
Social Security benefits	......	855	......
state tax death credit	......	869	......
stepped-up basis	816	......	......
tax rate schedule (App. B)			
taxable estate	......	852	......
unified credit	......	868	......
valuation freeze	......	912	......
valuation of property	......	862	......
Estimated Payments			
contributions to fund qualified plans	396	......	......

2006 Tax Facts on Insurance & Employee Benefits

GUIDEX

	Federal Income Tax Question Number	Federal Estate Tax Question Number	Federal Gift Tax Question Number
Estimated Payments (cont'd)			
income tax			
individuals	801	....	....
S corporation	839	....	....
S corporation shareholders	839	....	....
trusts	843	....	....
Excess Aggregate Contributions			
401(m) plans	405	....	....
tax sheltered annuities	467, 475	....	....
Excess Benefit Plans	128	....	....
Excess Contributions Penalty			
individual retirement plans	226	....	....
qualified plans	404, 367	....	....
SIMPLE IRA plan	243	....	....
simplified employee pensions	240	....	....
tax sheltered annuity	475, 493	....	....
Excess Pension Assets	370	....	....
Exchanges			
annuity contracts (see Annuities, Commercial)			
life insurance (see Life Insurance)			
long-term care insurance contracts			
(see Long-Term Care Insurance)			
tax sheltered annuities (see Tax			
Sheltered Annuities)			
Excise Taxes (see Penalty Taxes)			
Exclusion, Gift Tax Annual	....	....	712-717, 917
Exclusion Allowance	470	....	....
Exclusion Ratio	7	....	....
Executive Bonus Plan	54	....	....
Executives, Limit of Compensation			
deduction for	108	....	....
Exemptions			
dependents	820	....	....
personal	819	....	....
Expected Return	9	....	....

F

Face Amount Certificate			
tax sheltered annuity, as	465	....	....
Family and Medical Leave Act			
effect on cafeteria plans under	104	....	....
effect on COBRA continuation coverage	175, 180	....	....
Family Attribution Rules	82	....	....
FICA (Federal Insurance Contributions)			
accident or health plan	170	....	....
back wages	836	....	....
cafeteria plan benefits	105	....	....
deferred compensation			
funded plan	110, 122	....	....
Section 457 plan	126	....	....
unfunded plan	122	....	....
group life insurance	144	....	....
qualified retirement plans	423	....	....
Section 457 deferred compensation			
plan	126	....	....

GUIDEX

	Federal Income Tax Question Number	Federal Estate Tax Question Number	Federal Gift Tax Question Number
FICA (Federal Insurance Contributions) (cont'd)			
sick pay	170	......	......
tax rates	836, 837	......	......
tax sheltered annuities	492	......	......
Financed Insurance	245	......	......
First-to-Die Life Insurance	302	671	732
5 or 5 Power	......	......	727
$5,000 Employee Death Benefit (see Employee Death Benefit Exclusion)			
501(c)(9) Trusts (VEBAs) (see Voluntary Employees' Beneficiary Associations)			
529 Plans	811	859	906
401(k) Plans			
ACP test	405, 406	......	......
ADP test	404, 406	......	......
contributions			
catch-up	397	......	......
double counting, limitations	404	......	......
excess	406	......	......
excess aggregate	406	......	......
QMACs	404, 405	......	......
QNECs	404, 405	......	......
safe harbor plan	399	......	......
SIMPLE vs. safe harbor	399	......	......
coverage tests	325	......	......
deferred compensation (nonqualified)			
wrap-around plan	117, 119, 395	......	......
definition	394	......	......
distributions			
corrective	406	......	......
hardship	403	......	......
of excess contributions	406	......	......
restrictions on	402	......	......
excess contributions	406	......	......
generally	394	......	......
limit on elective deferrals	396	......	......
nondiscrimination requirement	404, 405, 406	......	......
qualification requirements, generally	322	......	......
Roth 401(k)	394, 401	......	......
safe harbor 401(k) plan	399	......	......
SIMPLE 401(k) requirements	400	......	......
solo 401(k)	398	......	......
special qualification requirements	395-403	......	......
wraparound plans	119, 395	......	......
403(b) Plans (see Tax Sheltered Annuities)			
412(i) Plans			
accrued benefit	373	......	......
funding requirements	408	......	......
generally	407	......	......
Flexible Benefit Plan (Cafeteria Plan)	99-106	......	......
Flexible Spending Arrangement	107	......	......
Four Out of Seven Rule	245	......	......
FSA	107	......	......
FUTA (Federal Unemployment Tax)			
back wages	836	......	......

2006 Tax Facts on Insurance & Employee Benefits

GUIDEX

	Federal Income Tax Question Number	Federal Estate Tax Question Number	Federal Gift Tax Question Number
FUTA (Federal Unemployment Tax) (cont'd)			
cafeteria plan benefits	105	....	....
deferred compensation			
funded plan	110, 122	....	....
Section 457 plan	126	....	....
unfunded plan	122	....	....
Section 457 deferred compensation plan	126	....	....
sick pay	170	....	....
Fully Insured (412(i)) Pension Plan	407, 408	....	....

G

General Power of Appointment	....	853	727
Generation-Skipping Transfer Tax			
allocation of exemption (951)			
annual exclusion (751, 951)			
basis adjustment (951)			
charitable lead annuity trusts (951)			
credit for state GST tax (954)			
direct skip (950)			
estate tax inclusion period (ETIP) (951)			
exemption (752, 951)			
generally (950 - 955)			
generation assignments (952)			
generation-skipping transfers (950)			
inclusion ratio (951)			
life insurance and annuities (750 - 752)			
nontaxable gifts (951)			
payment of (953)			
predeceased parent rule (950, 952)			
returns, filing of (955)			
repeal (950)			
reverse QTIP election (951)			
split gifts (953)			
tax rate schedule (App. B)			
taxable distribution (950)			
taxable termination (950)			
transferor (950)			
Gift Tax (Generally)	....	....	900-922
annual exclusion	....	....	917, 918, 919
below-market loan	....	....	904
Chapter 14 valuation rules (see topic under Valuation)			
charitable contributions deduction	....	....	921
computation of tax	....	....	902
custodianship gifts	....	....	919
definition	....	....	900
disclaimers	....	....	908
donee pays gift tax	32	....	911
exclusions	....	....	917
gifts subject to tax	....	....	903
interest-free loans	....	....	904
joint interests	....	....	903, 909

GUIDEX

	Federal Income Tax Question Number	Federal Estate Tax Question Number	Federal Gift Tax Question Number
Gift Tax (Generally) (cont'd)			
marital deduction	......	......	920
noncitizen spouse (see "marital deduction" and "annual exclusion" this entry)			
payment of tax	......	......	901
return	......	......	901
split-gifts	......	......	907
tax rate schedule (App. B)			
unified credit	......	......	922
valuation (see Valuation)			
Gifts (see also topic under: Annuities, Commercial; Life Insurance)			
charitable (see Charitable Gifts)			
gift tax paid by donee of annuity or endowment contract	32	......	911
minors, to	809	856	716, 725, 918, 919
within 3 years of death			
generally	......	860	......
life insurance	......	642, 718	718
Golden Parachutes (see "parachute payments")			
Government Life Insurance	276, 295	644	......
Government Plans			
401(k), prohibition against	395	......	......
nonqualified deferred compensation	123, 124	......	......
Grantor Trust (see "grantor" under Trusts)			
GRAT	......	......	914
GRIT	......	......	914
Gross Misconduct (see heading under COBRA)			
Group Carve-Out Plan	146	......	......
Group Permanent Life Insurance	150-152	......	......
Group Term Life Insurance			
assignment of	......	645	719, 724, 733, 744
cafeteria plan benefit	100	......	......
charity named as beneficiary	142	......	......
church employees, plan for	143	......	......
contributions, deduction of	141, 496	......	......
cost of excess coverage	142	......	......
death proceeds			
disclaimer of	......	......	908
taxation	152, 271	645	......
deduction of premiums/contributions	141	......	......
deemed death benefit	147	......	......
definition	139, 140	......	......
dependent coverage	142	......	......
discrimination rules	143	......	......
dividends under policy providing permanent benefit	148	......	......
double indemnity rider	139	641	......
evidence of insurability	139, 140	......	......
exemption amount	142	......	......
federal group term	139	......	......
FICA tax, subject to	144	......	......
$50,000 ceiling	142	......	......

2006 Tax Facts on Insurance & Employee Benefits

GUIDEX

	Federal Income Tax Question Number	Federal Estate Tax Question Number	Federal Gift Tax Question Number
Group Term Life Insurance (cont'd)			
generally	138	......	......
groups of fewer than 10	139	......	......
highly compensated employee, coverage of	143, 145	......	......
income to employee, treated as	142-143	......	......
information returns	145	......	......
key employees, coverage of	143	......	......
overview	138	......	......
permanent benefit, policy providing	147, 148	......	......
policy providing permanent benefits	147, 148	......	......
premiums, deduction of	141	......	......
qualified plans, provided under	142	......	......
requirements			
failure to meet	139	......	......
group term life insurance	139, 140	......	......
nondiscrimination	143	......	......
retired lives reserves	149	......	......
rulings from IRS, availability	139	......	......
Social Security tax, subject to	144	......	......
spouse and dependent coverage	142	......	......
supplemental group life	139	......	......
survivor income benefit plan	153	684	743
travel insurance, as	139	......	......
welfare benefit fund, as	494	......	......
withholding	145	......	......
GRUT	......	......	914
Guideline Premium Test	273	......	......

H

Hardship Withdrawals, From			
401(k) plans	403	......	......
nonqualified deferred compensation plans	117, 118	......	......
tax sheltered annuities	466	......	......
Health and Medical Savings Accounts			
Archer MSA	209	......	......
comparable contributions requirement	199	......	......
contributions, HSA	198	......	......
contributions, MSA	209	......	......
cut-off year, MSA	209	......	......
death, of account holder	205	......	......
deduction	813	......	......
definition, HSA	195	......	......
definition, MSA	209	......	......
distributions from, HSA	202	802	......
distributions from, MSA	209	802	......
divorce, transferred due to	204	......	......
eligible individuals	196	......	......
excess contributions	200	......	......
exclusion from income	802	......	......
family coverage	197	......	......
high deductible health plan	197	......	......
penalty tax on distributions	202	......	......
qualified medical expenses	202	......	......
reporting requirements	208	......	......
rollovers	203	......	......

GUIDEX

	Federal Income Tax Question Number	Federal Estate Tax Question Number	Federal Gift Tax Question Number
Health and Medical Savings Accounts (cont'd)			
self-employed individuals	196	......	......
self-only coverage	197	......	......
small employer	209	......	......
Social Security tax, subject to	206	......	......
surviving spouse, acquired by	205	......	......
taxation of, before distribution	201	......	......
taxation of distribution from	202	802	......
withholding, subject to	207	......	......
Health Insurance, Business (see Business Health Insurance)			
Health Insurance, Personal			
accidental death benefit, taxation of	155	646	......
benefits, taxation of	155	......	......
medical expense deduction limitations	826	......	......
medical expense reimbursement proceeds	156	647	......
medicare premiums	154	......	......
no-fault insurance benefits	155	625	......
premium, deductibility of	154	......	......
structured settlement	157	......	......
tax credit of the permanently disabled	833	......	......
Health Reimbursement Arrangements (see also Business Health Insurance)			
C corporation stockholder-employees, for	165	......	......
deduction of expense	166, 167	......	......
general	168	......	......
highly compensated employees, for	162	......	......
nondiscrimination requirements	162	......	......
partners, for	166	......	......
proceeds received by insured's estate	......	647	......
S corporation stockholder-employees, for	166	......	......
sole proprietors, for	166	......	......
stockholder-employees, for	165, 166	......	......
withholding on benefits	162	......	......
Highly Compensated Employee			
cafeteria plan participant	102	......	......
defined, generally	356	......	......
medical expense reimbursement for	162	......	......
Holding Periods (Capital Gains)	816	......	......
Hope Scholarship Credit	835	......	......
HR 10 Plans	358	......	......

I

Incidental Death Benefit Requirement			
individual retirement plans	210	......	......
qualified retirement plans	346, 369	......	......
tax sheltered annuities	488	......	......
Incidental Life Insurance, In			
qualified plans	369	......	......
tax sheltered annuities	481	......	......
Incidents Of Ownership			
business insurance	......	609-612	......
personal insurance	......	630-634	......
Includable Compensation			
qualified plans	331	......	......

GUIDEX

	Federal Income Tax Question Number	Federal Estate Tax Question Number	Federal Gift Tax Question Number
Includable Compensation (cont'd)			
Section 457 plan	123, 124	......	......
tax sheltered annuities	471	......	......
Income In Respect Of A Decedent (IRD)			
deferred compensation, receipt by beneficiary	121	......	......
employee death benefit exclusion	135	......	......
income tax deduction	827	827	......
medical expense reimbursement	155	......	......
sale or liquidation of partnership interest	92	......	......
Income Tax (see also specific subject)			
C corporations	838	......	......
estates	843	......	......
individuals			
adjusted gross income	813	......	......
alimony	808	......	......
alternative minimum tax	829, 832	......	......
basis	816	......	......
below market loans	805	......	904
business expenses	814	......	......
premium rebates	804	......	......
children under age 14	818	......	......
commissions, sales	803	......	......
credits	832-835	......	......
deductions, itemized	821-827	......	......
charitable contributions	824, 825	......	......
interest	823	......	......
itemized, generally	821	......	......
medical expenses	826	......	......
miscellaneous itemized	822	......	......
repeal of phaseout	821	......	......
education savings account	810	858	905
estimated tax	801	......	......
exclusions	802	......	......
exemptions	819, 820	......	......
repeal of phaseout	819	......	......
filing requirements	800, 801, 830, 831	......	......
gross income	802-808	......	......
head-of-household	831	......	......
income in respect of a decedent	827	......	......
installment sales	806	......	......
interest deduction	823	......	......
joint return	830	......	......
minimum tax, alternative	829, 832	......	......
premium rebates	804	......	......
qualified tuition programs	811	......	......
self-employment tax			
commissions, postretirement	803	......	......
deduction	814	......	......
Social Security			
benefits, taxation of	807	......	......
deduction for self-employment taxes	814	......	......
tax rates	836	......	......
who must pay	837	......	......

1036 **2006 Tax Facts on Insurance & Employee Benefits**

GUIDEX

	Federal Income Tax Question Number	Federal Estate Tax Question Number	Federal Gift Tax Question Number

Income Tax (cont'd)
  individuals (cont'd)
    standard deduction 817
      marriage penalty relief 817
    tax rates
      generally 828
      marriage penalty relief 828
      reduced tax rates 828
      Social Security 836
      10% tax bracket 828
      unearned income of minors 818
    taxable income 817, 818
  limited liability companies 841
  marriage penalty relief 817, 828
  partnerships 842
  personal service corporations 840
  professional corporations and associations 838
  qualified tuition programs 811
  S corporations 839
  standard deduction 817
    marriage penalty relief 817
  trusts, generally 843
    grantor trusts 844

Indemnity Insurance
  securing deferred compensation with 117

Indexed Amounts (see App. E or more specific entry under Income Tax)

Individual Retirement Plans (see also Roth IRAs)
  active participant 224
  attachment of plan assets 216
  basis 227
  catch-up contributions 220, 221
  collectibles, investment in 210
  compensation defined 223
  contribution
    employer, made by 239-241
    limits 220, 221
    union, made by 239
  conversion of traditional 222
  custodians, eligibility as 210
  deductions
    borrowing to contribute 225
    eligibility to take 217
    fees and commissions 225
    inherited plan 220
    limitations on 220
    spousal plan 218
    waiver of premium feature 220
    when taken 219
  deemed IRAs 210
  direct rollover transfers 447
  disclosure requirement 212
  distributions
    death proceeds under endowment
      contracts 229

GUIDEX

	Federal Income Tax Question Number	Federal Estate Tax Question Number	Federal Gift Tax Question Number
Individual Retirement Plans (cont'd)			
distributions (cont'd)			
generally	214	......	......
homes, used to buy	228, 231	......	......
minimum required	233-237	......	......
premature	231	......	......
Education IRA (see Education Savings Account)			
Education savings account	810	858	905
eligible individuals	217	......	......
endowment contract			
death proceeds	229	......	......
used to fund	210, 220	......	......
establishment of plan, timing of	219	......	......
estate tax			
inclusion in decedent's estate	......	648	......
income tax deduction for estate tax paid	827	......	......
excess accumulations	233-237	......	......
excess contributions	226	......	......
filing and reporting	238	......	......
flexible premium annuities	210	......	......
group annuity	210	......	......
incidental benefit rule	234	......	......
individual retirement account defined	210	......	......
individual retirement annuity defined	210	......	......
inherited plans deduction, denial of	220	......	......
investment in the contract	227	......	......
life insurance, use of	210	......	......
loss	214	......	......
MDIB rule	234	......	......
minimum distribution incidental benefit rule	234	......	......
minimum required distributions	233-237	......	......
nondeductible contributions limits on	220, 221	......	......
nonrefundable credit	213	......	......
penalty taxes			
excess accumulations	233-237	......	......
excess contributions	226	......	......
plan earnings	215	......	......
prohibited transaction, effect of	214	......	......
requirements	210	......	......
retirement bonds	210	......	......
rollover			
from	222, 452	......	......
to	446, 451	......	......
Roth IRAs (see Roth IRAs)			
saver's credit	213	......	......
SAR-SEPs	241	......	......
72(t) payouts	232	......	......
SIMPLE IRAs	242-243	......	......
simplified employee pensions (SEPs)			
cash or deferred	241	......	......
generally	240	......	......
SAR-SEPs	241	......	......
spouse, contributions to plan for			
deduction limits	220	......	......
eligibility	218	......	......
gift to spouse, as	......	......	739

GUIDEX

	Federal Income Tax Question Number	Federal Estate Tax Question Number	Federal Gift Tax Question Number
Individual Retirement Plans (cont'd)			
substantially equal periodic payments............	232	......	......
survivor benefit, taxation of	......	648	736, 738
trustee-to-trustee transfers	214, 447	......	......
waiver of premium, deduction of	220	......	......
withdrawals of contributions	226	......	......
withholding	230	......	......
wraparound annuity...............................	210	......	......
Installment Payments			
annuities	1	......	......
insurance contracts	1	......	......
life insurance			
cash surrender values	265	600	......
death proceeds	275	626	......
endowment maturity proceeds............	265, 266	600	......
government life insurance...................	295	......	......
qualified retirement plans, under	433, 434	......	......
Installment Sales			
accrual method taxpayer	806	......	......
Chapter 14 valuation rules.....................	......	......	912, 913
generally	806	......	......
Installment Settlements And Options			
(see topic under Life Insurance)			
Insurable Interest, Requirement Of			
business life insurance............................	74	......	......
charitable gifts	......	......	707
personal life insurance	271	......	......
Insurer, Insolvent			
grandfathering of certain dates for annuities and insurance policies...........	3, 245, 249, 250, 260, 263, 274	......	......
Interest (see also Loans)			
death proceeds of life insurance, on	275, 276	......	......
deduction, limitations on generally........	823	......	......
estate tax extended payments................	823	851	......
Interest First Rule.......................................	3	......	......
Interest-Free Loans.....................................	805	......	904
Interest-Only Option			
cash surrender values	251	600	......
death benefit..	275	......	......
endowment maturity proceeds..............	251	600	......
Investment In The Contract (see topic under specific subject (e.g., Annuities, Commercial; Tax Sheltered Annuities)			
IRD (see Income In Respect Of A Decedent)			
Irrevocable Life Insurance Trust...............	......	651-658, 719-728	914

J

Joint And Survivor Annuity (see topic under: Annuities, Commercial; Pension, Profit Sharing, Stock Bonus)

2006 Tax Facts on Insurance & Employee Benefits

GUIDEX

	Federal Income Tax Question Number	Federal Estate Tax Question Number	Federal Gift Tax Question Number
Jointly Owned Property			
generally	......	853(8), 854	903
noncitizen spouse	......	854	......
Judgment, Annuity In Payment Of	157		

K

Keogh Plan	418, 365	674	......
Key Employee, Defined	357	......	......
Key Person, Exception To Deduction Of Policy Loan Interest	260		
Key Person Insurance (see Business Life Insurance, Business Health Insurance)			
Kiddie Tax	818	......	......

L

Leased Employees	355	......	......
Letters Of Credit,			
securing deferred compensation with	117	......	......
Life Insurance			
accelerated death benefit	267		
accidental death benefit	272	641, 646	......
alimony, funding with	280, 281	......	......
alternative minimum tax	95	......	......
basis			
alternative minimum tax, for	95		
dividends, effect of	252, 254	......	......
exchange, effect of	263	......	......
following sale of contract	262	......	......
on surrender	3, 249, 264	......	......
paid-up additions, of	255	......	......
beneficiary			
collection of taxes from	......	617	......
death of	......	677-683	......
taxation of	......	677-683	740
borrowing to buy	245	......	......
business insurance (see Business Life Insurance)			
business owner, on life of (see Business Life Insurance)			
buy-sell agreements (see Business Life Insurance)			
cash surrender values			
alternative minimum tax	95		
annual increases in	247	......	......
constructive receipt	247, 251	......	......
contracts not meeting definition of life insurance	247	......	......
distribution on change of benefits	249	......	......
fixed period or fixed amount option	......	600	......
generally	1	......	......
government life insurance	295	......	......
increases in	247	......	......
inside buildup	247	......	......
installment option	265	600	......
interest-only option	......	600	......
life income option	......	600	......

GUIDEX

	Federal Income Tax Question Number	Federal Estate Tax Question Number	Federal Gift Tax Question Number
Life Insurance (cont'd)			
cash surrender values (cont'd)			
one sum payment...	264		
paid-up additions...	247	....	....
paid-up limited pay policy.............................	248	....	....
variable insurance contract.............................	247	....	....
withdrawal of...	3, 264	....	....
cash value accumulation test.............................	273	....	....
cash value corridor...	273	....	....
cash withdrawals...	1, 3, 250, 264	....	....
Chapter 14 valuation rules.................................	....	....	912, 914
charitable contribution			
death proceeds, taxation of.............................	....	616	....
deduction limitations, generally.....................	824	....	....
donor retaining right to change beneficiary........	284	....	....
policy or premium, of.....................................	282	....	707
split dollar arrangement.................................	283	....	....
split life contract, annuity portion	285	....	....
trusts...	282	....	....
collateral, policy assigned as			
(see Creditor Insurance)			
commissions, taxation of...................................	803	....	....
constructive receipt (see Constructive Receipt)			
conversion of policy			
interest payable on...	263	....	....
creditor insurance (see Creditor Insurance)			
cross purchase agreement (see			
Business Life Insurance)			
death benefit (see "death proceeds" this entry)			
death proceeds...	....	625-635	....
alternative minimum tax.................................	95	....	....
beneficiary liable for tax...................................	....	617, 636	708
benefits includable in term "insurance".............	....	625	....
business life insurance.....................................	62	609-615	....
contract not meeting definition			
of life insurance...	271	....	....
contract owned by other than insured.............	274	633	....
creditor insurance (see Creditor Insurance)			
double indemnity...	271, 272	641	....
estate tax, beneficiary liable			
for payment of...	....	617	....
fixed period or fixed amount option	....	677, 683	....
gift of policy within 3 years of death	....	642, 645	....
government issued policy.................................	276, 295	644	....
group life insurance (see Group			
Term Life Insurance; Group			
Permanent Life Insurance)			
includability in insured's estate.........................	....	626-635	....
assignment of policy by insured.....................	....	634	....
death taxes, proceeds used to pay.....................	....	629	....
incidents of ownership...................................	....	630-632	....
insured's estate, proceeds payable to or for.......	....	627, 628	....
named beneficiary, proceeds payable to............	....	630	....
qualified plan, proceeds payable under.............	....	635	....
third party owned policy.................................	....	633	....

2006 Tax Facts on Insurance & Employee Benefits

GUIDEX

	Federal Income Tax Question Number	Federal Estate Tax Question Number	Federal Gift Tax Question Number
Life Insurance (cont'd)			
death proceeds (cont'd)			
personal life insurance			
double indemnity	271, 272	641	......
excess interest dividends paid under settlement option	258	......	......
fixed amount options	276	600	......
fixed period option	276	600	......
interest earned on	271	......	......
interest-only option	275	600	......
life income option	276	677-683	......
$1,000 interest exclusion	275, 276	......	......
paid up-additions	271	......	......
payment options	275, 276	600	......
settlement options	275, 276	600	......
tax exemption	271, 273	......	......
valuation of	303	687, 688	......
deduction (see "loss, deduction of" and "premiums" this entry)			
deferred compensation, funding with	117, 125	......	......
definition of			
contracts not meeting	247	......	......
generally	273	......	......
disability provisions			
income	299	......	......
premiums as a medical expense	298	......	......
rider on key person policy	301	......	......
waived premiums	300	......	......
distributions (see "proceeds" this entry)			
dividends (see "life insurance" under Dividends)			
divorce, transfers incident to	279, 280, 281	......	......
double indemnity	271, 272	641	......
employee, on life of (see Business Life Insurance)			
endowment contracts			
basis of	254	......	......
charitable gift of	282	......	707
deduction limitations, generally	824	......	......
dividends on	256	......	......
individual retirement plans	97	......	......
maturity proceeds			
constructive receipt	251, 265, 266	......	......
gift of	32	......	......
government life insurance	295	......	......
installment settlement	265, 266	600	......
interest-only option	251	600	......
life income settlement	265, 266	600	......
receipt of	61, 264	......	......
exchanges			
effect on policies date issued	3, 37, 273	......	......
generally	263	......	......
tax sheltered annuities	478	......	......
financed insurance	245	......	......

GUIDEX

	Federal Income Tax Question Number	Federal Estate Tax Question Number	Federal Gift Tax Question Number
Life Insurance (cont'd)			
first-to-die insurance	302	671	732
four-out-of-seven rule	245	......	......
gift of			
beneficiary, lapse of withdrawal right as gift	......	......	740
charitable (see Charitable Gifts)			
community property	......	......	709, 710
donee liable for gift tax	......	......	708, 911
endowment contract	31	......	......
gift tax annual exclusion	......	......	712-717, 724-728
life insurance trusts (see "life insurance" under Trusts)			
minor, to	......	......	716, 725
premiums	......	642, 652	733, 734, 726, 727
proceeds	......	......	735
split gift	......	......	742
spouses, between	279	......	709, 730, 722, 920
spouses, from to third party	......	......	742, 907
third party owner, gift of death proceeds to beneficiary	......	......	735
transfer for value rule, application of	278	......	......
trust, in	......	650-658	719-728
valuation	......	......	744
what constitutes gift of policy or premium	......	......	700
within 3 years of death	......	642, 643, 718	718
government life insurance	276, 295	644	......
group life insurance (see Group Term Life Insurance; Group Permanent Life Insurance)			
guaranteed refunds	1	......	......
guideline premium test	273	......	......
incidents of ownership			
business insurance	......	609-612	......
personal insurance	......	630-634	......
individual retirement plan, used in	210	......	......
installment settlements			
cash surrender values	265	600	......
death proceeds	276	626	......
endowment maturity proceeds	265, 266	600	......
government life insurance	295	......	......
insurable interest, requirement of	271	......	......
interest			
policy loans	260, 245	......	......
prepaid premium	246	......	......
interest-only option			
cash surrender values	251	600	......
death benefit	275	626	......
endowment maturity proceeds	251	600	......
investment in the contract (see "basis" this entry)			
joint and survivor life	302	671	732

2006 Tax Facts on Insurance & Employee Benefits

GUIDEX

	Federal Income Tax Question Number	Federal Estate Tax Question Number	Federal Gift Tax Question Number
Life Insurance (cont'd)			
joint life	302	671	732
key person insurance (see Business Life Insurance)			
levy for delinquent taxes	296, 297	......	......
life income settlement			
cash surrender values	265	600	......
endowment maturity proceeds	265, 266	600	......
limited pay policy	248, 252	......	......
living proceeds	1, 249	......	......
corporation, received by	61	......	......
following sale of contract	262	......	......
loans, modified endowment contracts	250	......	......
loans, policy			
beneficiary pays interest on	......	......	729
claim against insured's estate, as	......	659	......
exchange, effect on	263	......	......
gift of policy subject to	32, 64	......	......
interest, deduction of	245, 260, 309	......	......
sale of policy subject to	64, 78, 79, 261	......	......
taxability of	259	......	......
long-term care coverage, provided under	311	......	......
loss, deduction of			
insolvency of insurer	270	......	......
sale or surrender	270	......	......
minimum premium insurance	245	......	......
modified endowment contract	250	......	......
multiple-life insurance	302	671	732
national service life insurance (NSLI)	276, 295	......	......
paid-up additions			
basis, of	255	......	......
cash surrender values	247	......	......
death proceeds	271	......	......
dividends, used to purchase	254	......	......
government life insurance	295	......	......
partial surrender	3, 250	......	......
partner, on life of (see Business Life Insurance)			
penalty tax, modified endowment contracts	250	......	......
premiums			
business, paid by (see Business Life Insurance)			
creditor insurance (see Creditor Insurance)			
personal insurance			
charitable gift of	282	......	......
deduction	244, 824	......	......
gift of	......	642, 652	726, 727, 733, 734
prepaid premium, interest on	246	......	......
rebates	804	......	......
proceeds			
death (see "death proceeds" this entry)			
living (see "living proceeds" this entry)			
qualified retirement plan, under (see Pension, Profit Sharing, Stock Bonus)			
rebates, premium	804	......	......
retirement income contract			
death of insured before maturity	......	601, 625	......

GUIDEX

	Federal Income Tax Question Number	Federal Estate Tax Question Number	Federal Gift Tax Question Number
Life Insurance (cont'd)			
retirement income contract (cont'd)			
maturity proceeds	35	625	......
sale			
business life insurance (see Business Life Insurance)			
deduction of loss	270	......	......
effect on purchaser	262	......	......
insufficient consideration	......	626, 642	700
participant in qualified plan, to	443	......	......
qualified plan, to	437, 443	......	......
spouses, between	279	......	......
taxation of seller	261	......	......
transfer for value rule, application (see also Transfer For Value Rule)			
second-to-die insurance	302	671	732
Section 457 plan, funding with	125	......	......
settlement options			
death proceeds	275, 276	......	......
seven pay test	250	......	......
single premium	249, 250, 286	......	744
60-day limit			
settlement election	265	......	......
sole proprietor, on life of (see Business Life Insurance)			
split dollar arrangement (see Split Dollar)			
split life contract, charitable gift of	285	......	......
stockholder, on life of (see Business Life Insurance)			
stock redemption agreement (see Business Life Insurance)			
surrender			
deduction of loss	270	......	......
taxation of	3, 249, 264	......	......
survivorship life	302	671	732
taxes, collection from	296, 297	617	708
tax-free exchange (see "exchange" this entry)			
tax sheltered annuity, funding with	465	......	......
1035 exchange	3, 37, 263	......	......
third party owner, death of	......	676	......
transfers (see "gift" and "sale" this entry)			
trust (see "life insurance" under Trusts)			
valuation of policy	303	687, 688	744
withholding of income tax	269	......	......
Life Insurance Agents			
commissions	803	857	......
premium rebates	804	......	......
Life Insurance Trusts (see "life insurance" under Trusts)			
Life Settlements	261	......	......
Lifetime Learning Credit	835	......	......
LIFO Rule	3	......	......
Limited Liability Companies (LLCs)	841	......	......
Limited Partnerships	842	......	914

2006 Tax Facts on Insurance & Employee Benefits

GUIDEX

	Federal Income Tax Question Number	Federal Estate Tax Question Number	Federal Gift Tax Question Number
Living Proceeds, Life Insurance			
corporation, received by	61	......	......
following sale of contract	262	......	......
generally	1, 249	......	......
Loans			
annuity contracts			
exchange, effect on	30	......	......
for purchase	245	......	......
investment in the contract, effect on	3	......	......
treated as withdrawal	3	......	......
applicable federal interest rate	805	......	904
below-market loans	805	......	904
interest deduction limitations	822	......	......
interest-free loans	805	......	904
life insurance (see Life Insurance; Business Life Insurance)			
low interest loans	805	......	904
modified endowment contacts	250	......	......
policy subject to			
gift of	31	......	......
sale of	261	......	......
policy, taxability of	259	......	......
prohibited transaction	443	......	......
qualified retirement plans			
as alienation of benefit	348	......	......
spousal consent rules	336, 337	......	......
tax consequences	420	......	......
tax sheltered annuity	483, 484	......	......
Long-Term Care Insurance			
activities of daily living (ADLs)	312	......	......
benefits, taxation of	318	......	......
cafeteria plan, as part of	311	......	......
chronically ill individual, defined	312	......	......
COBRA, not subject to	311	......	......
disclosure requirements	311	......	......
employees, premiums taxable to	316	......	......
employer, deduction for premiums paid	317	......	......
flexible spending arrangement, offered through	311	......	......
nonforfeiture requirements	311	......	......
nonqualified long-term care contract	319	......	......
per diem limitation on	318	......	......
premiums, deductibility of	314, 315, 317	......	......
qualified long-term care insurance contract, defined	312	......	......
qualified long-term care services	311	......	......
reporting requirements	320	......	......
Loss, Casualty	821	......	......
Low Interest Loans	805	......	904
Lump Sum Distribution (see discussion under Pension, Profit Sharing, Stock Bonus)			

M

Marital Deduction			
annuity	......	602, 662-665	703, 731
nonrefund life annuity	......	662	......

GUIDEX

	Federal Income Tax Question Number	Federal Estate Tax Question Number	Federal Gift Tax Question Number
Marital Deduction (cont'd)			
annuity (cont'd)			
proceeds, qualification for................	......	663-665	......
community property states	......	864	920
deductible limitations	......	864	920
general rules.......................................	......	864	920
life insurance......................................	......	660, 663-670	730
collateral, policy assigned as............	......	624	......
community property states	......	670	730
power of appointment trust	......	660	722
proceeds, qualification for...............	......	663-670	......
settlement options	......	664-666	......
trusts qualifying for deduction........	......	660	722
Uniform Simultaneous Death Act........	......	669	......
noncitizen spouse	......	864	920
Marital Property (see Community Property)			
MDIB Rule	346, 488	......	......
Medical Expense Deduction			
health insurance premiums....................	154, 166, 167	......	......
life insurance premiums........................	298	......	......
limitations generally	826	......	......
long-term care insurance premiums	314, 315	......	......
Medical Expense Reimbursement Plan (see Health Reimbursement Arrangements)			
Medical Savings Accounts (see Health and Medical Savings Accounts)			
Medicare			
deduction of premiums........................	154	......	......
Minimum Coverage Rules...................	324, 325	......	......
Minimum Distribution Incidental Benefit (MDIB) Rule..........................	346, 488	......	......
Minimum Funding Standard................	385	......	......
waiver of	390	......	......
Minimum Participation Rule	373	......	......
Minimum Tax, Alternative			
corporations			
generally	838	......	......
life insurance contracts	95	......	......
individuals	829, 832	......	......
Minority Discount	......	613	......
Minors			
gifts to	809	856	716, 725, 918, 919
"Kiddie" tax			
alternative minimum tax.....................	829	......	......
generally	818	......	......
unearned income, taxation of................	818	......	......
Miscellaneous Itemized Deduction, Limits...	822	......	......
Modified Carryover Basis	816	......	......
Modified Endowment Contract	250	......	......
Money Purchase Plan (see topic under Pension, Profit Sharing, Stock Bonus)			
MRDs			
IRA	233-237	......	......

GUIDEX

	Federal Income Tax Question Number	Federal Estate Tax Question Number	Federal Gift Tax Question Number
MRDs (cont'd)			
pension, profit sharing	338-346	......	......
tax sheltered annuity	486-489	......	......
Multiple-Life Life Insurance	302	671	732
Mutual Funds			
tax sheltered annuity, funding with	465	......	......

N

National Service Life Insurance (NSLI)			
(see also Life Insurance)			
death benefit	295	......	......
spouses $1,000 interest exclusion	276	......	......
Net Earnings From Self-Employment	358	......	......
Net Unrealized Appreciation	430, 432	......	......
Noncitizen Spouse			
annual exclusion	......	......	917
jointly owned property	......	854	......
marital deduction	......	864	920
Nondiscrimination Requirements (see topic under applicable plan)			
Nonqualified Deferred Compensation (see Deferred Compensation (Nonqualified))			
Non-Qualified Stock Options (see Deferred Compensation (Nonqualified))			
Nonstatutory Stock Options (see Deferred Compensation (Nonqualified))			
NQSOs (see Deferred Compensation (Nonqualified))			

O

1035 Exchanges			
annuities	30	......	......
life insurance	263	......	......
Original Issue Discount Rules, Annuity Taxation	1	......	......
Overhead Expense Disability Policy	97	......	......
Owner-Employee	358	......	......

P

Paid-Up Additions	255, 271	638	......
Parachute Payments			
disqualified individual	109	......	......
excess	109	......	......
Partners And Partnerships			
annuity, as owner of	2, 37	......	......
buy-sell agreements	......	611-613, 915	706, 915
life insurance funding	56, 57	......	......
deferred compensation plans funded	110	......	......
employee death benefit exclusion	134	......	......
employee status for qualified plans	358	......	......
health insurance	166	646	......
income continuation	93	614	......
Keogh plans	358	......	......
life insurance			
death proceeds payable to	......	609, 611, 612	......

1048 **2006 Tax Facts on Insurance & Employee Benefits**

GUIDEX

	Federal Income Tax Question Number	Federal Estate Tax Question Number	Federal Gift Tax Question Number
Partners And Partnerships (cont'd)			
life insurance (cont'd)			
funding a sale or liquidation	94	......	......
policy transferred to	71	......	......
premiums	56, 57	......	......
limited liability companies	841	......	......
partnership freeze	......	912, 913	912, 913
partnership income continuation	......	634	......
publicly traded partnerships	842	......	......
sale or liquidation of interest	92, 94	......	912-916
taxation	842	......	......
Pediatric Vaccines (see COBRA)	173	......	......
Penalty Taxes			
disqualified benefits under welfare benefit fund	501	......	......
excessive contributions			
employer, levied against			
excess aggregate contributions	405, 467	......	......
excess contributions	240, 404	......	......
nondeductible employer contributions	367	......	......
participant, levied against			
individual retirement plans	226	......	......
tax sheltered annuities	475	......	......
excessive distributions			
qualified retirement plans	441	......	......
modified endowment contracts, distributions from	250	......	......
nondeductible employer contributions to qualified plans	367	......	......
premature distributions			
individual retirement plans	231	......	......
nonqualified annuities	4	......	......
qualified retirement plans	428	......	......
tax sheltered annuities	485	......	......
prohibited transactions	443	......	......
reversions	442	......	......
underfunding, qualified plans	389, 390	......	......
Pension, Profit Sharing, Stock Bonus			
accident and health benefits received under	388	......	......
accrued benefit			
cash out of	333	......	......
cutbacks prohibited	334	......	......
fully insured plans	373, 407, 408	......	......
tests (3%, 133⅓%, fractional)	373	......	......
vesting requirements	333	......	......
actual contribution percentage (ACP) test	405, 406	......	......
actual deferral percentage (ADP) test	404, 406	......	......
actuarial assumptions, reasonableness of	383	......	......
advantages, generally	321	......	......
affiliated service group, defined	360	......	......
age and service requirement	324	......	......
alienation, prohibition against	348	......	......

2006 Tax Facts on Insurance & Employee Benefits

GUIDEX

	Federal Income Tax Question Number	Federal Estate Tax Question Number	Federal Gift Tax Question Number
Pension, Profit Sharing, Stock Bonus (cont'd)			
allocation of forfeitures	326	......	......
alternate payee	426	......	......
amendments to plans, nondiscriminatory	328	......	......
annual additions	332, 377	......	......
annuity contract			
distribution of	431	......	......
nontransferability requirement	431	......	......
PTE for transfer of	443	......	......
surrender by beneficiary	439	......	......
taxation of benefits	433, 434	......	......
anti-alienation rule	348	......	......
anti-cutback rule	334	......	......
asset reversion	323, 442	......	......
average benefits test	325	......	......
basis	435	......	......
cash balance plans			
defined	374	......	......
defined benefit plan, treatment as	373	......	......
definitely determinable benefit in	384	......	......
generally	374	......	......
permitted disparity in	330	......	......
cash or deferred plan (see "401(k) plan" this entry)			
cash-out, $5,000 limit on involuntary	333	......	......
catch-up contributions	397	......	......
common control, businesses under	359	......	......
community property law	......	675	738
compensation			
defined	331	......	......
limits on	331, 353F	......	......
contributions by employee	405	......	......
contributions by employer			
deduction of			
generally	365	......	......
limitations	383-366	......	......
multiple plans, limitations	366	......	......
when deductible	364	......	......
estimated payments	375	......	......
excludable by employee	423	......	......
415 limits	332, 372, 377	......	......
nondeductible	367	......	......
penalty where nondeductible	367	......	......
property, of	363	......	......
controlled groups	359	......	......
coverage tests	325	......	......
cross testing	329	......	......
current liability	375	......	......
death benefits, taxation of	437-439	673	......
deductible employee contributions			
generally	673, 674	......	......
life insurance, purchased with	424, 425	......	......
loans attributable to	421	......	......
premature distributions of	428	......	......
deduction of employer contributions	365-367	......	......

GUIDEX

	Federal Income Tax Question Number	Federal Estate Tax Question Number	Federal Gift Tax Question Number
Pension, Profit Sharing, Stock Bonus (cont'd)			
deemed distributions	420	....	....
deemed IRAs	210	....	....
deferrals			
elective, limit on	396	....	....
excess	396	....	....
nondiscrimination (ADP) testing	404	....	....
defined benefit (415) limits	332, 372	....	....
defined benefit plans			
qualification, generally (see "qualification requirements" this entry)			
special qualification requirements	373	....	....
defined contribution (415) limits	332, 377	....	....
defined contribution plans			
excess plan	330	....	....
pension	381, 382	....	....
qualification, generally (see "qualification requirements" this entry)			
special qualification requirements	378	....	....
definitely determinable benefits	384	....	....
direct rollover	446, 447	....	....
directed investments	327	....	....
disability benefits, taxation of	436	....	....
discrimination in operation	326	....	....
disqualification, retroactive	361	....	....
disqualified person	443	....	....
distributions			
annuity contract, of	431	....	....
commencement	338, 384-393, 402	....	....
death benefits	437-439	....	....
disability benefits	436	....	....
employer securities	432	....	....
excess aggregate contributions	406	....	....
excess contributions	406	....	....
$5,000 threshold			
consent to distribution not required	333	....	....
457 plans	124	....	....
survivor annuity cashout	336	....	....
25 highest paid employees	328	....	....
401(k) plan restrictions on	402, 403	....	....
incidental benefit rule, required by	346	....	....
investment in the contract	435	....	....
life insurance contract, of	431	....	....
minimum required	338-346	....	....
net unrealized appreciation	430, 432	....	....
premature	428	....	....
required minimum	338-346	....	....
restrictions			
401(k) plans	402, 403	....	....
top 25 employees	326	....	....
rollover of	445	....	....
taxation of			
generally	426	....	....

GUIDEX

	Federal Income Tax Question Number	Federal Estate Tax Question Number	Federal Gift Tax Question Number

Pension, Profit Sharing, Stock Bonus (cont'd)
  distributions (cont'd)
    taxation of (cont'd)

lump sum	426, 430, 673		
periodic	433	673	
preretirement	427		
three-year cost recovery	433, 434		
variable benefits	434	673	
withholding on	322, 440		
diversification requirement (ESOP)	413		
divorce	349, 430		
elective deferrals (see "401(k) plan" this entry)			
employee			
generally	354		
highly compensated, definition	356		
key	357		
leased	355		
taxation of	423-439		
employee contributions	405	673, 674	
employee death benefit exclusion	437-439		
employee stock ownership plan (see ESOP)			
employer securities			
definition of	410		
disposition by ESOP	414		
distributions of	432		
investment in	378, 411		
lump sum distribution	432		
net unrealized appreciation	430, 432		
qualified sales to ESOP	413, 414		
sales to defined contribution plan	380		
ESOP			
annual additions, calculation	332, 377		
deduction for contributions to	415		
definition	410		
disparity, prohibited	330		
distributions of stock, taxation	432		
diversification requirement	413		
dividends	410		
eligibility	410		
eligible individual account plans	410		
employer deductions	415		
employer securities			
disposition of	380		
independent appraisers	413		
investment and disposition	380, 410, 441		
investments	410		
sale to	413, 414, 441		
lender exclusion, repeal	410		
life insurance, incidental rules	369		
loans from plan	410		
multiple employer plans, treatment	30		
net unrealized appreciation	432		
prohibited allocations	416		
prohibited transactions	411, 420, 421, 443		
put option requirement	413		

1052   **2006 Tax Facts on Insurance & Employee Benefits**

GUIDEX

	Federal Income Tax Question Number	Federal Estate Tax Question Number	Federal Gift Tax Question Number
Pension, Profit Sharing, Stock Bonus (cont'd)			
ESOP (cont'd)			
qualification requirements	412, 413	......	......
qualified replacement property	414	......	......
qualified securities, defined	414	......	......
regulations, compliance	412	......	......
repeal of lender exclusion	410	......	......
S corporation	416, 417	......	......
Section 1042 election	414	......	......
special qualification requirements	413	......	......
1042 election	414	......	......
unrelated business taxable income	441	......	......
voting rights, passthrough	413	......	......
excess aggregate contributions	405	......	......
excess benefit plan	128	......	......
excess contributions	367, 404	......	......
excess pension assets	370	......	......
exclusive benefit rule	323	......	......
FICA taxes	423	......	......
$5,000			
benefit from qualified plan	437-439	......	......
consent not required for distribution	333	......	......
death benefit exclusion (see also Employee Death Benefit Exclusion)			
457 plans	124	......	......
survivor annuity cashout	336	......	......
25 highest paid employees	328	......	......
forfeitures, allocation of	326	......	......
401(h) accounts	365, 369, 370	......	......
401(k) plan			
accrued benefits, nonforfeitability	395	......	......
ACP test	405, 406	......	......
actual contribution percentage (ACP)			
calculation and test	405, 406	......	......
actual deferral percentage (ADP)			
calculation and test	404, 406	......	......
ADP test	404, 406	......	......
aggregation, plans and deferrals	395	......	......
alternative safe harbor provisions	399	......	......
cash or deferred election	395	......	......
contributions			
catch-up	397	......	......
double counting, limitations	404	......	......
excess	406	......	......
excess aggregate	406	......	......
QMACs	404, 405	......	......
QNECs	404, 405	......	......
Roth	394, 401	......	......
salary reduction agreements	395, 396	......	......
safe harbor 401(k) plans	399	......	......
SIMPLE 401(k) plans	400	......	......
SIMPLE versus safe harbor plan	399	......	......
solo 401(k) plan	398	......	......
coverage tests	325	......	......

GUIDEX

	Federal Income Tax Question Number	Federal Estate Tax Question Number	Federal Gift Tax Question Number

Pension, Profit Sharing, Stock Bonus (cont'd)
  401(k) plan (cont'd)
    deferrals
      elective .... 394, 395, 396 ....
      excess, treatment .... 396 ....
      wrap-around plan .... 119 ....
    definitions .... 394 ....
    distributions
      corrective .... 406 ....
      generally .... 394 ....
      hardship withdrawals .... 403 ....
      required minimum .... 339-346 ....
      restrictions .... 402 ....
    elective deferrals .... 396, 397 ....
    eligibility .... 395 ....
    employer securities
      investment in .... 411 ....
      net unrealized appreciation .... 432 ....
    failure of nondiscrimination tests .... 406 ....
    FICA, treatment .... 423 ....
    hardship distributions .... 403 ....
    highly compensated employees .... 395, 404 ....
    limit on elective deferrals .... 396 ....
    minimum participation rule, satisfaction .... 373 ....
    negative election .... 395 ....
    nondiscrimination .... 326, 404, 406 ....
    permitted disparity .... 330 ....
    qualification requirements .... 322, 325, 394 ....
                                         395-396
      special requirements .... 395-396 ....
    record keeping requirements .... 404 ....
    restrictions on distributions .... 402 ....
    safe harbor 401(k) plans .... 399 ....
    Roth 401(k) plans .... 394, 401 ....
    SIMPLE 401(k) plans .... 400 ....
    stand-alone plans .... 394 ....
    who may offer .... 394, 395 ....
    withdrawal restrictions .... 402 ....
    wraparound plans .... 119, 395 ....
  412(i) plans
    accrued benefit .... 373 ....
    funding of .... 408 ....
    generally .... 407 ....
  415 limitations .... 332, 372, 377 ....
  full funding limitation .... 386 ....
  fully insured (412(i)) plans .... 373, 407, 408 ....
  funding
    requirements .... 385 ....
    underfunding penalty .... 389, 390 ....
  government pick-up plans .... 423 ....
  health insurance .... 369 ....
  highly compensated employees
    ACP test, aggregation requirements .... 395 ....
    defined .... 356 ....
    excess contributions, distribution .... 406 ....

GUIDEX

	Federal Income Tax Question Number	Federal Estate Tax Question Number	Federal Gift Tax Question Number
Pension, Profit Sharing, Stock Bonus (cont'd)			
highly compensated employees (cont'd)			
nondiscrimination requirements	326-328	......	......
payout restrictions	326	......	......
permitted disparity	330	......	......
simplified employee pensions (SEPs)			
employer contributions, nondiscrimination requirements	240	......	......
top-paid group	353, 356	......	......
HR-10 plans			
distributions and benefits	......	674	736
eligibility	358	......	......
generally	418	......	......
special rules	418	......	......
incidental death benefit			
requirements	346, 369	......	......
incidental life insurance	369	......	......
in-service distributions	427	......	......
insured plans	407, 408	......	......
integration with Social Security	330	......	......
investment in the contract	435	......	......
investment managers' fees, deduction of	365	......	......
joint and survivor annuity			
plans subject to requirement	335	......	......
requirement of	336	......	......
taxation of	433, 439	......	......
waiver of	337	......	......
Keogh plans (see HR-10 plans)			
key employee	357	......	......
leased employees	355	......	......
life insurance			
cost of, taxable	424	......	......
death benefit provided under	437-439	673	......
distribution of policy	431	......	......
incidental rule	369	......	......
included in employee's basis	425	......	......
nontransferability requirement	431	......	......
protection taxable to employee	424	......	......
PTE for transfer of	443	......	......
Table 2001 costs	424	......	......
limitation year	332	......	......
loans from plan			
as alienation of benefit	348	......	......
deemed distributions	422	......	......
defined	422	......	......
interest deduction	422	......	......
Keogh plans, from	420	......	......
multiple loans	422	......	......
prohibited transaction, as	443	......	......
refinancing transactions			
renegotiation, extension, renewal, or revision requirements	421	......	......
spousal consent rules	336, 337	......	......
tax consequences	420	......	......
lump sum distributions	430	......	......

2006 Tax Facts on Insurance & Employee Benefits

GUIDEX

	Federal Income Tax Question Number	Federal Estate Tax Question Number	Federal Gift Tax Question Number

Pension, Profit Sharing, Stock Bonus (cont'd)
  matching contributions
    actual contribution percentage test 405, 406
    correction of excessive... 406
    defined.. 405
    requirements.. 405
    safe harbor 401(k) plan, in..................................... 399
    SIMPLE 401(k) plan, in 400
  MDIB rule 346
  medical expense reimbursement payments 436
  minimum distributions
    failure to make... 338, 347
    MDIB rule 346
    required 339-346
    separate account rules 343
  minimum funding standard....................................... 385
  money purchase plan 381
  net unrealized appreciation.. 430, 432
  new comparability plan.. 329
  nondeductible contributions..................................... 367
  nondiscrimination
    actual contribution percentage (ACP) test 405, 406
    aggregation 326
    amendments, requirements................................... 326, 328
    availability of benefits, rights and features 327
    benefits and contributions 326-328
    cash balance plans.. 374
    contributions and benefits 326
    coverage.. 325
    defined benefit plans... 326
    defined contribution plans.................................. 328, 329, 379, 410
    exceptions and exclusions 326, 330
    highly compensated employees.......................... 328
    insurance contract plans..................................... 408
    multiple plans limitations 366
    new comparability plan....................................... 329
    past service credits 326, 328
    plan amendments 328
    safe harbor provisions 405
    substantiation 326, 327
  nondiscriminatory classification 325
  normal costs, deductibility.. 383
  normal retirement age... 333, 384
  owner-employees (see "HR 10 plans" this entry)
  participant loans (see "plan loans" this entry)
  partners, plans covering (see "HR 10 plans" this entry)
  past service... 324, 328
  penalties (see "Penalty Taxes")
  pension plans
    definition 381
    qualification, generally (see "qualification requirements" this entry)
    special qualification requirements...................... 384

2006 Tax Facts on Insurance & Employee Benefits

GUIDEX

	Federal Income Tax Question Number	Federal Estate Tax Question Number	Federal Gift Tax Question Number
Pension, Profit Sharing, Stock Bonus (cont'd)			
permitted disparity	330	......	......
phased retirement	384	......	......
plan loans			
as alienation of benefit	348	......	......
deemed distributions	422	......	......
defined	422	......	......
interest deduction	422	......	......
Keogh plans, from	420	......	......
multiple loans	422	......	......
prohibited transaction, as	443	......	......
refinancing transactions			
renegotiation, extension, renewal, or revision requirements	421	......	......
spousal consent rules	336, 337	......	......
tax consequences	420	......	......
premature distributions	428	......	......
preretirement survivor annuity	336	......	......
profit sharing plan			
definition	391	......	......
qualification, generally (see "qualification requirements" this entry)			
special qualification requirements	393	......	......
tax-exempt organization, maintained by	391	......	......
prohibited transactions			
exemptions	443	......	......
generally	443	......	......
penalty tax	443	......	......
plan loans	443	......	......
P.S. 58 costs (see "Table 2001 costs")			
QDROs			
defined	349	......	......
effect on required distributions	345	......	......
taxation of payments	426	......	......
QJSAs			
plans subject to requirement	335	......	......
requirement of	336	......	......
taxation of	433, 439	......	......
waiver of	337	......	......
qualification requirements	322, 384, 393	......	......
age requirements and limitations	324	......	......
alienation of benefit prohibited	348, 349	......	......
communication to employees	322	......	......
compensation considered	331, 353	......	......
contributions and benefits,			
elective deferrals to 401(k) plans	395, 396	......	......
employee contributions	405	......	......
employer matching contributions	405	......	......
general rules	326	......	......
integration with Social Security	330	......	......
limitations	332, 352, 377	......	......
nondiscrimination rules	326	......	......
cutbacks in accrued benefits			
prohibited	334	......	......

2006 Tax Facts on Insurance & Employee Benefits

GUIDEX

	Federal Income Tax Question Number	Federal Estate Tax Question Number	Federal Gift Tax Question Number
Pension, Profit Sharing, Stock Bonus (cont'd)			
qualification requirements (cont'd)			
definitely determinable benefits.................	384	......	......
distributions			
commencement	338, 384-393, 402	......	......
minimums required	339-345	......	......
early retirement...................................	353	......	......
economic reality..................................	322	......	......
exclusive benefit rule..........................	323	......	......
generally	322	......	......
incidental death benefit requirement	346	......	......
integration with Social Security...........	330	......	......
joint and survivor annuity....................	335, 336	......	......
minimum coverage	325	......	......
minimum distribution incidental benefit (MDIB)...................................	346	......	......
minimum distributions required.........	339-346	......	......
miscellaneous requirements................	353	......	......
participation	324, 373	......	......
permanent not temporary plan	353	......	......
preretirement survivor annuity	336	......	......
requirements for custodians of funds	322	......	......
reversion to employer prohibited	323	......	......
survivor benefits.................................	336	......	......
TEFRA election	338	......	......
top-heavy plans			
definition	351	......	......
key employee defined.........................	357	......	......
requirements......................................	350, 352	......	......
rollover, effect of	351	......	......
valuation of assets	393	......	......
vesting requirements............................	333, 352	......	......
withholding, mandatory	322, 440	......	......
withdrawals (see "distributions" this entry)			
year of service, definition	333	......	......
qualified domestic relations orders			
defined..	349	......	......
effect on required distributions...........	345	......	......
taxation of distributions......................	426	......	......
qualified replacement plan.......................	442	......	......
qualified transfer to Section 401(h)			
account	370	......	......
ratio percentage test................................	325	......	......
required minimum distributions............	339-345	......	......
restorative payments	332, 377, 392	......	......
retirement age, normal............................	333, 384	......	......
phased retirement	384	......	......
reversion			
employer penalty	442	......	......
prohibited	323	......	......
rollover (see "Rollovers").........................	430	......	......
direct rollover option	447	......	......
withholding on, income tax	448	......	......

GUIDEX

	Federal Income Tax Question Number	Federal Estate Tax Question Number	Federal Gift Tax Question Number
Pension, Profit Sharing, Stock Bonus (cont'd)			
"same desk" rule	402	......	......
savings and thrift plans	379	......	......
Section 415 limitations	332, 372, 377	......	......
self-employeds (see "HR 10 plans" this entry)			
separation from service	402	......	......
separate lines of business	325	......	......
service, year of	325, 333	......	......
severance of employment	402	......	......
SIMPLE plans			
SIMPLE IRAs	242-243	......	......
SIMPLE 401(k) plans	400	......	......
use of to satisfy ADP test	404	......	......
simplified employee pension (see topic under Individual Retirement Plans)			
Social Security integration	330	......	......
special averaging of lump sum distributions	430	......	......
spousal waiver	337	......	......
stock bonus plan			
definition	409	......	......
put option required	412	......	......
special requirements	412	......	......
survivor benefit, taxation of	......	673	736, 738
community property law, effect of	......	675	738
life insurance proceeds	......	673	......
self-employed plan	......	674	......
Table 2001 costs			
generally	424, 425	......	......
replacement of P.S. 58 table	424	......	......
table (App. C)			
target benefit plan	382	......	......
10-year averaging	430	......	......
1042 election	414	......	......
three-year cost recovery	433, 434	......	......
thrift plans	379, 405	......	......
top-heavy plans			
definition	351	......	......
key employee defined	357	......	......
requirements	350, 352	......	......
rollover, effect of	351	......	......
vesting	352	......	......
transfers to, from nonqualified plan	117	......	......
trust earnings	441	......	......
trustee-to-trustee transfers	444	......	......
25 highest paid employees, restrictions	328	......	......
vesting			
generally	333	......	......
top-heavy	352	......	......
voluntary employee contributions	405	......	......
waiver of survivor benefits by			
nonparticipant spouse	337	......	737
withholding	440	......	......
year of service	325, 333	......	......
Personal Exemptions	819	......	......
Personal Holding Companies	838	......	......

2006 Tax Facts on Insurance & Employee Benefits

GUIDEX

	Federal Income Tax Question Number	Federal Estate Tax Question Number	Federal Gift Tax Question Number
Personal Residence Trust.............................	......	......	914
Personal Service Corporations	840	......	......
Policy Loans			
gift of policy subject to	31	......	......
interest deduction limitations	260, 823	......	......
modified endowment contracts.................	250	......	......
sale of policy subject to	261	......	......
taxability of...	259	......	......
Pooled Income Fund	825	865	921
Postretirement Life/Medical Benefits........	152, 323, 369, 494-502	......	......
Powers Of Appointment			
exercise or lapse of power	......	......	903
hanging..	......	......	727
includability in estate of donee	......	853(9)	......
life insurance			
beneficiary elects settlement option	......	683	......
beneficiary has power to appoint to estate	......	682	......
beneficiary has power to withdraw proceeds.......	......	680, 681	740
death proceeds payable to			
beneficiary's estate	......	679	......
income beneficiary's power of appointment........	......	678	......
marital deduction			
general power	......	666	......
power of appointment trust	......	660	......
settlement options	......	665	......
Premature Distributions			
individual retirement plans	231	......	......
nonqualified annuities...............................	4	......	......
qualified retirement plans	428	......	......
tax sheltered annuities	485	......	......
Premiums			
annuities (see Annuities, Commercial)			
business, paid by (see Business Life Insurance; Business Health Insurance)			
creditor insurance (see Creditor Insurance)			
key person insurance (see Business Life Insurance; Business Health Insurance)			
life insurance (see Life Insurance).			
rebates, taxation of....................................	804	......	......
Preretirement Survivor Annuity.................	336	......	......
Private Annuities			
Chapter 14 valuation rules.........................	......	......	912, 913
death of annuitant	......	608	......
defined..	41	......	......
obligor, taxation of....................................	42	......	......
payments received	41	......	......
purchase of as gift	......	......	705
withholding, income tax	41	......	......
Private Split Dollar	462	615	741
Professional Corporations And Associations..	838	......	......
Profit Sharing Plan (see Pension, Profit Sharing, Stock Bonus)			

2006 Tax Facts on Insurance & Employee Benefits

GUIDEX

	Federal Income Tax Question Number	Federal Estate Tax Question Number	Federal Gift Tax Question Number
Prohibited Transactions			
individual retirement plans	214, 215	......	......
qualified retirement plans	443	......	......
P.S. 58 Costs (see "Table 2001 Costs")			

Q

Qualified Conservation Easement	......	861	......
Qualified Domestic Relations Order			
defined	349	......	......
effect on required distributions	345	......	......
tax sheltered annuity, in	466	......	......
taxation of distributions	426	......	......
Qualified Domestic Trust	......	864	......
Qualified Funding Asset			
defined	2, 4	......	......
held by nonnatural person	2	......	......
premature distributions under	4	......	......
Qualified Personal Residence Trust	......	......	914
Qualified Retirement Plans (see Pension, Profit Sharing, Stock Bonus)			
Qualified Tangible Property	......	......	914
Qualified Terminable Interest Property	......	864	920
Qualified Transfers			
for gift tax purposes	......	......	917
Section 401(h), to	370	......	......
Qualified Tuition Program	811	859	906

R

Rabbi Trust	118	......	......
Railroad Retirement, Taxation Of	807	......	......
Reasonable Compensation, Deduction For	108	......	......
Rebates, Premium, Taxation Of	804	......	......
Redemption Of Stock (see "stock redemption agreement" under Buy-Sell Agreements)			
Remainder Interest	......	......	910, 914
Renewal Commissions	803	860	......
Required Minimum Distributions (see Individual Retirement, Pension, Profit Sharing, Stock Bonus, or Tax Sheltered Annuity)			
Restorative Payments	377, 392	......	......
Restricted Stock	130, 131	......	......
Retained Interest	......	853	914
Retired Lives Reserves			
generally	149	......	......
transfers to VEBAs	501	......	......
Retirement Income Contract	35, 431,	......	......
Retirement Income Credit	833	......	......
Reverse Split Dollar	461	615	741
Reversionary Interest Trust	......	657	721
Reversions, Employer			
qualified plans	323, 442	......	......
welfare benefit plan	497, 501	......	......
RMDs			
IRA	233-237	......	......

2006 Tax Facts on Insurance & Employee Benefits

GUIDEX

	Federal Income Tax Question Number	Federal Estate Tax Question Number	Federal Gift Tax Question Number
RMDs (cont'd)			
pension, profit sharing	338-346	......	......
tax sheltered annuity	486-489	......	......
Rollover			
direct transfer of	447	......	......
eligible rollover distribution	446, 451	......	......
estate of decedent dying before 1985	......	648	......
executor, completed by	444	......	......
generally	444, 445	......	......
individual retirement plans			
between IRAs	462	......	......
from	222, 452	......	......
to	446, 451	......	......
qualified domestic relation order			
distributions	449	......	......
qualified retirement plans			
employee contributions, after tax	445	......	......
explanation by plan administrator			
required	447	......	......
rollover from	430, 446	......	......
required distributions, of	444	......	......
Section 402(f) notice	447	......	......
Section 412(i) plans	373, 407, 408	......	......
Section 457 deferred compensation			
plan	444	......	......
60-day limitation	454	......	......
spouse, by			
death of participant, on	453	......	......
qualified domestic relations order	449	......	......
tax sheltered annuities	451, 479	......	......
top-heavy plans, effect on			
determination	351	......	......
withholding, income tax	448	......	......
Roth 401(k) plan	401	......	......
Roth IRAs			
(see also Individual Retirement Plans)			
attachment of plan assets	216	......	......
basis	227	......	......
catch-up contributions	221	......	......
collectibles, investment in	210	......	......
compensation defined	223	......	......
contribution limits	221	......	......
conversion of traditional	222	......	......
custodians, eligibility as	210	......	......
deemed IRAs	210	......	......
direct rollover transfers	447	......	......
disclosure requirement	212	......	......
distributions			
generally	214	......	......
homes, used to buy	214	......	......
minimum required	237	......	......
premature	231	......	......
taxation	228	......	......
eligible individuals	217	......	......
establishment of plan, timing of	219	......	......

GUIDEX

	Federal Income Tax Question Number	Federal Estate Tax Question Number	Federal Gift Tax Question Number
Roth IRAs (cont'd)			
estate tax			
inclusion in decedent's estate............	......	648	......
income tax deduction for estate			
tax paid	827	......	......
excess accumulations............................	233-237	......	......
excess contributions	226	......	......
fees and commissions	225	......	......
filing and reporting................................	238	......	......
individual retirement account defined	210	......	......
individual retirement annuity defined....	210	......	......
investment in the contract	227	......	......
life insurance, use of..............................	210	......	......
minimum required distributions............	237	......	......
penalty taxes			
excess accumulations............................	233-237	......	......
excess contributions	226	......	......
plan earnings	215	......	......
prohibited transaction, effect of............	214	......	......
requirements	210	......	......
rollover			
from..	222, 452	......	......
to	446, 451	......	......
spouse, contributions			
eligibility..	218	......	......
gift to spouse, as	......	......	739
limits..	220	......	......
survivor benefit, taxation of	......	648	736, 738
trustee-to-trustee transfers	214, 447	......	......
withdrawals of contributions	221, 226	......	......
Rural Electric Cooperatives	123	......	......

S

S Corporation			
employee death benefit exclusion	134, 135	......	......
estimated tax..	839	......	......
health insurance....................................	166	......	......
income tax	839	......	......
life insurance			
living proceeds received by..................	90	......	......
premiums paid by S corporation..........	55	......	......
taxation of proceeds received by	76	......	......
transfer of policy to..............................	67	......	......
transfer of policy to stockholders..........	68-70	......	......
nonqualified deferred compensation and			
single class of stock rule......................	839	......	......
professional corporations	838	......	......
qualified retirement plans			
generally..	417	673	736
Keogh plans	358	......	......
prohibited transactions	443	......	......
shareholder's basis in stock	839	......	......
stock redemption	91	......	......
Salary Continuation (see Deferred Compensation (Nonqualified))			

2006 Tax Facts on Insurance & Employee Benefits

GUIDEX

	Federal Income Tax Question Number	Federal Estate Tax Question Number	Federal Gift Tax Question Number

Salary Reduction Agreements
- cafeteria plan 99, 103
- 401(k) plan 395, 396
- SIMPLE 401(k) 400
- SIMPLE IRA 242
- simplified employee pension 241
- tax sheltered annuity (see Tax Sheltered Annuities)

Sale
- annuity contract (see Annuities, Commercial)
- business life insurance contract (see Business Life Insurance)
- personal life insurance contract (see Life Insurance)
- qualified retirement plan, to 414

SAR-SEPs 241

Saver's Credit
- 403(b) plan 473
- 457 plan 124, 213
- individual retirement plan 213
- in general 213

Savings And Thrift Plans 379

School Teachers (see Tax Sheltered Annuities)

Second-to-Die Life Insurance .... 302 ... 671 ... 732

Section 79 (see Group Term Life Insurance)

Section 101(b) Death Benefit Exclusion 134

Section 125 Plan 99-106

Section 162 Bonus Plan 54

Section 302(b) Stock Redemption 82

Section 303 Stock Redemption 85

Section 401(h) Accounts
- generally 365, 369, 370
- welfare benefit fund contributions, impact of and on 370, 494

Section 401(k) Plans (see also "401(k) plans")
- deferred compensation (nonqualified) wrap-around plan 117, 119
- generally 394
- limit on elective deferrals 396
- special qualification requirements 395-402

Section 415 Limitations 332, 372, 377, 471

Section 457 Plan
- annuity contract, distribution of 126
- catch-up contributions 124
- death benefit .... 125 ... 672
- deemed IRAs 210
- distributions under 126
- eligible employers 123
- employee death benefit exclusion 125, 134
- employers subject to requirements 123
- FICA taxes 126
- 403(b) tax sheltered, effect on 457 plan ... 124

1064 **2006 Tax Facts on Insurance & Employee Benefits**

GUIDEX

	Federal Income Tax Question Number	Federal Estate Tax Question Number	Federal Gift Tax Question Number
Section 457 Plan (cont'd)			
FUTA taxes.....................................	126	......	......
judges of state courts	127	......	......
life insurance			
distribution of contract.........................	126	......	......
purchased under...................................	125	......	......
limits on deferrals.................................	124	......	......
plans not meeting requirements			
taxation of deferrals.............................	126	......	......
when treated as ineligible	304	......	......
requirements...	124	......	......
rollover prohibited...................................	444	......	......
rural electric cooperatives	123	......	......
Social Security payroll tax........................	126	......	......
tax-exempt employers...............................	123	......	......
transfers between plans............................	124	......	......
unemployment tax, federal......................	126	......	......
withholding of income tax.......................	126	......	......
Section 501(c)(9)	504	......	......
Section 529 Plans	811	......	......
Section 1035 Exchange	30, 263, 478	......	......
Section 1042 Election	414	......	......
Section 2503(c) Trusts.............................	......	......	918
Section 7520 Interest Rate......................	......	......	910
Section 6166 Election	......	851	......
Secular Trust	111	......	......
Self-Employed Individuals			
employee death benefit exclusion	134	......	......
health insurance for	166, 813	......	......
long-term care insurance for....................	315	......	......
self-employment tax			
commissions, postretirement	803	......	......
deferred compensation (nonqualified)	122	......	......
generally	836, 837	......	......
SEPs (Simplified Employee Pensions)	240, 241	......	......
SERP (Supplemental Executive Retirement Plan)			
(see topic under Deferred Compensation)			
Settlement Options, Death Proceeds........	275, 276	......	......
Seven Pay Test	250	......	......
Sick Pay..	160, 833	......	......
SIMPLE Plans (Savings Incentive Match Plans for Employees)			
SIMPLE IRAs...	242, 243	......	......
SIMPLE 401(k) plans.............................	400	......	......
use of to satisfy ADP test	404	......	......
Simplified Employee Pension	240, 241	......	......
Simultaneous Deaths Of Insured And Policyowner-Beneficiary........................	......	676	......
Single Premium Life Insurance.................	249, 250, 286	......	744
60-day Limit			
election to take annuity	34, 431	......	......
life insurance settlement option...............	265	......	......
rollover...	454	......	......
Social Security			
benefits, taxation of..................................	807	855	......

GUIDEX

	Federal Income Tax Question Number	Federal Estate Tax Question Number	Federal Gift Tax Question Number
Social Security (cont'd)			
FICA tax (see FICA)			
tax	836, 837	......	......
Sole Proprietor			
premiums on life insurance	58, 59	......	......
qualified retirement plans	358	674	......
Special Use Valuation	......	862	......
Split Dollar Plan			
below market loan	459	......	741
charity, arrangement with	283	616	707
death proceeds, taxation of	458	615	......
defined	457	......	......
equity interest owned by employee	460	......	......
income taxation of	458	......	......
private	462	615	741
P.S. 58 rates	458	......	......
reverse	461	615	741
rollout	460	......	......
Table 2001 rates	458	......	......
third party owner	......	676	741
Split Gift	......	......	742, 907
Spousal Assumption			
IRAs	810	......	......
Standard Deduction	817	......	......
Stepped-up Basis	816	......	......
Stock Bonus Plan (see Pension, Profit Sharing, Stock Bonus)			
Stock Purchase Agreement (see Buy-Sell Agreement)			
Stock Redemption (see Buy-Sell Agreement)			
Structured Settlement	157	......	......
Subchapter S Corporation (see S Corporation)			
Substantial Risk of Forfeiture	110, 112, 126	......	......
Supplemental Executive Retirement Plan (SERP) (see topic under Deferred Compensation)			
Surety Bonds			
securing deferred compensation with	117	......	......
Survivor Income Benefit Plan	153	684	743
Survivors' Loss Benefits Under			
No-fault Auto Insurance	......	625	......
Survivorship Life Insurance	302	671	732

T

Tables
  annuity (App. A)
  government's one-year term (P.S. 58 & Table 2001) rates (App. C)
  indexed employee benefit limits (App. E)
  indexed estate, gift, generation-skipping amounts (App. B)
  P.S. 58 (App. C)
  RMD Table (App. F)
  Table 38 (App. C)
  Table 2001 (App. C)

GUIDEX

	Federal Income Tax Question Number	Federal Estate Tax Question Number	Federal Gift Tax Question Number
Tables (cont'd)			
tax rates (App. B)			
uniform gifts annuity rates (App. A)			
uniform group term premium (Table I)	142	......	......
unisex annuity tables (App. A)			
valuation (App. D)			
Table 2001 Costs			
replacement of Table P.S. 58	424, 458	......	......
split dollar plan	458	......	......
value of insurance in qualified plan	424, 425	......	......
Target Benefit Plans	382, 326	......	......
Tax-Exempt Organizations			
deferred compensation plans	123, 124	672	......
employee annuities	463-493	686	736
gifts to	282-285	616, 865	707, 921
Tax-Free Exchange			
annuities, commercial	30	......	......
life insurance policies	263	......	......
tax sheltered annuities	478	......	......
Tax Penalties (see Penalty Taxes)			
Tax Preference Items			
corporations	838	......	......
individuals	829	......	......
Tax Sheltered Annuity			
automatic enrollment	468	......	......
basis (see "investment in the contract" this entry)			
beneficiary designation	......	......	736, 738
changing issuers	478	......	......
church employees			
retirement income account	465, 474	......	......
special rules	474	......	......
commingling with qualified plan assets	466	......	......
contributions			
excess	475	......	......
excludable amount	469	......	......
matching	467	......	......
custodial accounts			
excess contributions	493	......	......
funding with	465	......	......
death benefit	491	686	......
deductible employee contributions		686	736
deduction vs. salary reduction	466	......	......
deemed IRAs	210	477	......
direct rollover	447, 451	......	......
discrimination prohibited	467	......	......
distributions			
commencement, when required	486	......	......
death benefit	491	......	......
loans, when treated as	483	......	......
minimums required	487-489	......	......
premature	466, 485	......	......
prohibited	466	......	......

2006 Tax Facts on Insurance & Employee Benefits

GUIDEX

	Federal Income Tax Question Number	Federal Estate Tax Question Number	Federal Gift Tax Question Number
Tax Sheltered Annuity (cont'd)			
distributions (cont'd)			
taxation, generally	490	......	......
dividends	482	......	......
elective deferrals (see "salary reduction" this entry)			
eligible employers	464	......	......
eligible individuals	464	......	......
employee death benefit exclusion	134	......	......
excess aggregate contributions	467, 475	......	......
exchange of contracts	478	......	......
excise taxes			
excess aggregate contributions	467	......	......
excess contributions	493	......	......
minimum distribution, failure to make	486	......	......
premature distributions	493	......	......
summary	493	......	......
exclusion allowance, repeal of	470	......	......
funding methods	465	......	......
highly compensated employees	467	......	......
incidental death benefit, required distributions	488	......	......
includable compensation	470, 471	......	......
integration with Social Security	467	......	......
investment in the contract			
excess elective deferrals	473	......	......
excess salary reduction	473	......	......
generally	490	......	......
life insurance protection	465, 481	......	......
loans	483, 484	......	......
matching employer contributions	467, 475	......	......
participation requirements	467	......	......
post-retirement employer contributions	476	......	......
purchase of service credits	480	......	......
qualified domestic relations order	466	......	......
qualified plan assets, combining with	465	......	......
requirements, generally	466	......	......
rollover	451, 479	......	......
Roth 401(k)	394, 401	......	......
Roth 403(b)	477	......	......
salary reduction			
calculation of amount	473	......	......
limit on elective deferrals	473	......	......
requirements	466	......	......
Social Security tax, effect on	492	......	......
withholding, effect on	492	......	......
saver's credit	471	......	......
Section 415 limits			
alternative amount	471	......	......
church employees	474	......	......
contributions in excess of	472	......	......
generally	471	......	......
includable compensation	471	......	......

GUIDEX

	Federal Income Tax Question Number	Federal Estate Tax Question Number	Federal Gift Tax Question Number
Tax Sheltered Annuity (cont'd)			
special catchup elections			
catch-up for age 50 and over	471	......	......
increased elective deferral	473	......	......
survivor benefit, taxation of	......	686	736, 738
community property law, effect of	......	......	738
tax benefits, generally	463	......	......
transfers	478	......	......
withholding			
benefits	490, 491	......	......
rollover distributions	448	......	......
salary reduction amounts	492	......	......
Taxable Distribution (GST Tax 950)			
Taxable Income, Definition Of			
C corporations	838	......	......
estates	843	......	......
individuals	817	......	......
partnerships	842	......	......
S corporations	839	......	......
trusts	843	......	......
Taxable Termination (GST Tax 950)			
Taxes, Collection From Insurance	296, 297	617	708
Taxes, Life Insurance Bought To Pay	......	629	......
1035 Exchange			
annuities	30	......	......
life insurance	263	......	......
1042 Election	414	......	......
10 or More Employer Plans	503	......	......
Terminable Interest	......	864	......
Third-Party Guarantees			
securing deferred compensation with	117	......	......
Thrift Plan	379	......	......
Throwback Rule	843	......	......
Top-Heavy Plans			
definition	351	......	......
key employee defined	357	......	......
requirements	350, 352	......	......
rollover, effect of	351	......	......
Transfers			
annuity contract (see Annuities, Commercial)			
business life insurance contract (see Business Life Insurance)			
personal life insurance contract (see Life Insurance)			
Section 457 plans, between	124	......	......
Transfer For Value Rule			
cross purchase changed to stock redemption plan	69	......	......
exceptions	63, 65-72, 278, 279	......	......
generally			
business life insurance	63	......	......
personal life insurance	277	......	......
gift	278	......	......
sale to			
corporation	67, 72	......	......

2006 Tax Facts on Insurance & Employee Benefits

GUIDEX

	Federal Income Tax Question Number	Federal Estate Tax Question Number	Federal Gift Tax Question Number
Transfer For Value Rule (cont'd)			
sale to (cont'd)			
family member...	66	......	......
grantor trust...	64, 65	626, 676, 853	700, 903, 914
insured...	65	......	......
partner...	71	......	......
partnership..	71	......	......
pension plan..	437	......	......
spouse of insured..	66	......	......
stockholder..	68-70	......	......
trust..	65	......	......
stock redemption changed to cross purchase	69	......	......
transfer for value, definition...........................	64, 277	......	......
Trusts			
Chapter 14 valuation rules...............................	......	......	914
charitable gifts in trust			
deduction for...	39, 282, 825	864, 865	921
deferred compensation, funding with	110, 117, 118	......	......
estate...	......	864	......
generally (GST tax, Qs 850-856)	843	853, 854	903, 914, 918
grantor			
generally...	844	853	903, 914
life insurance owned by	304, 309	626, 853	......
transfer for value to....................................	64, 65	626, 676, 853	700, 903, 914
income taxation of...	843-844	......	......
life insurance			
Crummey trust...	......	......	726, 727
death proceeds, taxation of	310	650-658	723
dividends, policy....................................	......	......	728
divorce provisions as incidents of ownership ...	......	......	631
irrevocable trust.....................................	......	651, 914	723
life income beneficiary, estate of	......	652, 653	.....
revocable trust..	......	650	......
trustee has power to apply to			
estate settlement costs	......	654	......
generally...	304	......	......
non-insurance trust assets,			
taxation of...	......	......	720, 726
policy loan	309	......	......
policy, transfer to irrevocable trust............	......	......	719, 722, 724, 725
premium paid by trust	305, 306	......	......
reciprocal trust doctrine............................	......	658	......
reversionary interest trust,			
taxation of...	304	657	721
third party grantor, taxation in			
estate of	......	656	......
trust income			
individuals taxed on.................................	304-308	......	......
premiums paid with..................................	305, 306	......	......
marital deduction..	......	864	920
minors, for (Section 2503(c))...........................	......	......	725
personal residence trust...................................	......	......	914
power of appointment	......	660, 864	......
qualified annuity interest	......	......	914

2006 Tax Facts on Insurance & Employee Benefits

GUIDEX

	Federal Income Tax Question Number	Federal Estate Tax Question Number	Federal Gift Tax Question Number
Trusts (cont'd)			
qualified charitable remainder	......	864	921
qualified domestic trust	......	864	......
qualified personal residence trust	......	......	914
qualified remainder interest	......	......	914
qualified terminable interest property	......	864	920
qualified unitrust interest	......	......	914
rabbi	118	......	......
reciprocal	......	687	......
reversionary interest	304	657	721
secular	111	......	......
valuation of transfer	......	......	910, 914
2503(c) Trust for Minor	......	......	918
U			
Unemployment Taxes (FUTA)			
cafeteria plan benefits	105	......	......
deferred compensation			
funded plan	110, 122	......	......
Section 457 plan	126	......	......
unfunded plan	122	......	......
Section 457 deferred compensation plan	126	......	......
sick pay	170	......	......
Unified Credit	......	868	922
Uniform Gifts (Transfers) To Minors Act	809	856	919
Universal Life Insurance (see also topic under Life Insurance)			
change of options	249	......	......
requirements for death benefit exclusion	273	......	......
Unreasonable Compensation	108	......	......
Unrelated Business Taxable Income			
qualified retirement plan	441	......	......
welfare benefit fund	498	......	......
V			
Valuation			
annuity	......	603, 685, 862	704
business interest subject to purchase agreement	......	613, 915	706, 915
Chapter 14 special valuation rules			
buy-sell sell agreements	......	915	915
corporation or partnership interests			
buy-sell sell agreements	......	915	915
lapse of voting or liquidation rights	......	916	916
restrictions	......	915, 916	915, 916
transfer of	......	913	913
general	......	912	912
joint purchases	......	......	914
partnership (see "corporation or partnership interests" this entry)			
remainder interest transactions	......	......	914
trust, transfer of interest in	......	914	914

GUIDEX

	Federal Income Tax Question Number	Federal Estate Tax Question Number	Federal Gift Tax Question Number
Valuation (cont'd)			
charitable gift annuities	43	......	921
donee pays gift tax	......	......	911
freeze	......	912-916	912-916
generally	......	862	909
joint and survivor annuity	......	603	704
joint interests	......	......	909, 914
life estates	......	862	910, 914
life insurance	......	676, 687	744
penalty for undervaluation	......	862	909
private annuities	......	862	910, 913
remainders	......	862	910, 914
special use valuation	......	862	......
tables (App. D)	......	862	910
Valuation Freeze	......	912-916	912-916
Valuation Of Unmatured Policy	303	......	743
Variable Annuity			
death of annuitant			
death benefit	36	600, 607	......
death prior to maturity	36	601	......
death prior to recovery of basis in	27	......	......
distributions requirements	37	......	......
qualified retirement plan, paid under	434	......	......
taxation generally	21-24	......	......
tax sheltered annuity, funding with	465	......	......
withholding of income tax	40	......	......
wraparound	25	......	......
Variable Life Insurance (see also topic under Life Insurance)			
death proceeds, tax exemption of	271, 273	......	......
diversification requirement	273	......	......
requirements for death benefit exclusion	273	......	......
VEBAs (see Voluntary Employees' Beneficiary Associations)			
Viatical Settlement Provider			
taxation of amount received from	268	......	......
Voluntary Employees' Beneficiary Associations			
application for tax-exempt status	502	......	......
employer's deduction	506	......	......
excise tax on disqualified benefits	501	......	......
participants' taxation	507	......	......
permissible benefits	505	......	......
requirements generally	504	......	......
sale of insurance to by insurance company affiliated with employer	501	......	......
tax-exempt status, application for recognition of	502	......	......
transfers from retired lives reserves	501	......	......
W			
Wage Continuation Plan			
deferred compensation (see Deferred Compensation)			
health insurance	160	......	......

GUIDEX

	Federal Income Tax Question Number	Federal Estate Tax Question Number	Federal Gift Tax Question Number
Waiver of Minimum Funding Standard	390	......	......
Waiver of Premium			
investment in the contract	8	......	......
taxation	300	......	......
Welfare Benefit Funds			
aggregation of funds	496	......	......
deduction limits	494, 496	......	......
deduction timing	494, 495	......	......
definition	494	......	......
educational benefit trust	132	......	......
excessive contributions,			
consequences of	497	......	......
excise tax on disqualified benefits	501	......	......
generally	494-496	......	......
notice to IRS	502	......	......
postretirement death and medical benefits requirements			
failure to meet	501	......	......
key employees	499	......	......
nondiscrimination requirements	500	......	......
reserve for, generally	496	......	......
sale of insurance to by insurance company			
affiliated with employer	501	......	......
Section 401(h) accounts,			
effect of and on qualified transfers to	370, 494	......	......
10 or more employer plans	503	......	......
abusive plans as tax shelters	503	......	......
transfers between	501	......	......
unrelated business taxable income	498	......	......
voluntary employees' beneficiary			
association (VEBA)	504-507	......	......
welfare benefit defined	494	......	......
Withholding, Income Tax			
annuities, commercial	40	......	......
annuities, private	41	......	......
deferred compensation payments			
Section 457 plans	126	......	......
unfunded private plans	121	......	......
individual retirement plans	230	......	......
life insurance	269	......	......
mandatory 20% on rollovers	448	......	......
medical expense reimbursement	162	......	......
qualified retirement plans	440	......	......
rollover distributions	448	......	......
Section 457 deferred compensation plan	126	......	......
sick pay (wage continuation)	160, 169	......	......
tax sheltered annuities	490, 491, 492	......	......
Wraparound Annuity	25	......	......
Wraparound 401(k) plan	119, 395	......	......